A+ Core Hardware Exam

Objectives	Chapters
Domain 1 Installation, Configuration and Upgrading	
1.1 Identify the *names, purpose*, and *characteristics* of system modules. Recognize these modules by sight or definition.	1, 4, 6, 7, 8, 10, 11, 17
1.2 Identify basic procedures for adding and removing field replaceable modules for desktop systems.	4, 5, 6, 7, 8, 10, 11, 17, 18, 22, 23
1.3 Identify basic procedures for adding and removing field replaceable modules for portable systems.	10, 17, 18, 20, 23
1.4 Identify typical IRQs, DMAs, and I/O addresses and procedures for altering these settings when installing and configuring devices.	2, 10, 17, 23
1.5 Identify the *names, purpose*, and *performance characteristics* of standardized/common peripheral ports, associated cabling, and their connectors.	10, 17, 18
1.6 Identify proper procedures for installing and configuring common IDE devices.	8, 11, 23
1.7 Identify proper procedures for installing and configuring common SCSI devices.	11, 22
1.8 Identify proper procedures for installing and configuring common peripheral devices.	4, 10, 11, 17, 18, 19, 20, 21, 23
1.9 Identify procedures to optimize PC operations in specific situations. Predict the effects of specific procedures under given scenarios.	4, 5, 6, 8, 9, 10, 11, 23
1.10 Determine the issues that must be considered when upgrading a PC. In a given scenario determine when and how to upgrade system components.	4, 5, 6, 8, 10, 20, 23
Domain 2 Diagnosing and Troubleshooting	
2.1 Recognize common problems associated with each module and their symptoms, and *identify* steps to isolate and troubleshoot the problems.	3, 4, 5, 6, 7, 8, 9, 10, 17, 20, 22, 23, Appendix A
2.2 Identify basic troubleshooting procedures and tools and how to elicit problem symptoms from customers.	4, 9, 24
Domain 3 PC Preventive Maintenance, Safety and Environmental Issues	
3.1 Identify the various types of preventive maintenance measures, products and procedures and when and how to use them.	9, 11, 24
3.2 Identify various safety measures and procedures and when/how to use them.	4, 24
3.3 Identify environmental protection measures and procedures and when/how to use them.	24
Domain 4 Motherboard/Processors/Memory	
4.1 Distinguish between the popular CPU chips in terms of their basic characteristics.	5
4.2 Identify the types of RAM (Random Access Memory), form factors, and operational characteristics. Determine banking and speed requirements *under given scenarios*.	6, 10
4.3 Identify the most popular types of motherboards, their components, and their architecture (bus structures).	4, 5, 6, 8, 10, 22, 23
4.4 Identify the purpose of CMOS (Complementary Metal-Oxide Semiconductor) memory, what it contains, and how *and when* to change its parameters.	5, 7, 8, 17
5.1 Identify printer technologies, interfaces, and options/upgrades.	18, 21
5.2 Recognize common printer problems and techniques used to resolve them.	21
Domain 6 Basic Networking	
6.1 Identify the common types of network cables, their characteristics and connectors.	18
6.2 Identify basic networking concepts including how a network works.	10, 17, 18
6.3 Identify common technologies available for establishing Internet connectivity and their characteristics.	18, 19

A+ OS Technologies Exam

Objectives	Chapters
Domain 1 Operating System Fundamentals	
1.1 Identify the major desktop components and interfaces, and their functions.	2, 3, 6, 7, 12, 13, 14, 15, 16, 18
1.2 Identify the names, locations, purposes, and contents of major system files.	3, 6, 12, 14, 15
1.3 Demonstrate the ability to use command-line functions and utilities to manage the operating system including the proper syntax and switches.	3, 6, 9, 12, 18, 19
1.4 Identify basic concepts and procedures for creating, viewing and managing disks, directories and files. This includes procedures for changing file attributes and the ramifications of those changes (for example, security issues).	2, 3, 8, 9, 12, 13, 14, 16, 19
1.5 Identify the major Operating System Utilities, their purpose, location, and available switches.	3, 8, 9, 12, 13, 14, 15, 16
Domain 2 Installation, Configuration and Upgrading	
2.1 Identify the procedures for installing Windows 9x, Me, Windows NT 4.0 Workstation, 2000 Professional, and Windows XP and bringing the operating system to a basic operational level.	9, 12, 13, 15
2.2 Identify steps to perform an operating system upgrade from Windows 9x/Me, Windows NT 4.0 Workstation, Windows 2000 Professional, and Windows XP.	12, 13, 14, 15, 16
2.3 Identify the basic system boot sequences and boot methods, including the steps to create an emergency boot disk with utilities installed for Windows 9x/Me, Windows NT 4.0 Workstation, and Windows 2000 Professional, and Windows XP.	12, 13, 14, 15, 16
2.4 Identify procedures for installing/adding a device, including loading/adding/configuring device drivers, and required software.	12, 13, 15, 16, 21
2.5 Identify procedures necessary to optimize the operating system and major operating system subsystems.	3, 6, 9, 12, 14
Domain 3 Diagnosing and Troubleshooting	
3.1 Recognize and interpret the meaning of common error codes and startup messages from the boot sequence, and identify steps to correct the problems.	12, 13, 14, 15, 16, Appendix A
3.2 Recognize when to use common diagnostic utilities and tools. Given a diagnostic scenario involving one of these utilities or tools, select the appropriate steps needed to resolve the problem.	2, 3, 4, 12, 13, 14, 15, 16
3.3 Recognize common operational and usability problems and determine how to resolve them.	3, 9, 11, 12, 14, 15, 16, 18, 21
Domain 4 Networks	
4.1 Identify the networking capabilities of Windows. Given configuration parameters, configure the operating system to connect to a network.	13, 18, 19
4.2 Identify the basic Internet protocols and terminologies. Identify procedures for establishing Internet connectivity. In a given scenario configure the operating system to connect to and use Internet resources.	15, 18, 19

A+ Guide to
Managing and Maintaining Your PC

FIFTH EDITION ENHANCED, COMPREHENSIVE

Jean Andrews, Ph.D.

A+
CompTIA Certified

Center for Systems Security
and Information Assurance
APPROVED COURSEWARE

THOMSON
™
COURSE TECHNOLOGY

Australia • Canada • Mexico • Singapore • Spain • United Kingdom • United States

A+ Guide to Managing and Maintaining Your PC, Fifth Edition Enhanced, Comprehensive

is published by Thomson Course Technology.

Executive Editor:
Bob Woodbury

Managing Editor:
William Pitkin III

Product Manager:
Manya Chylinski

Developmental Editor:
Jill Batistick

Marketing Manager:
Brian Berkeley

Associate Product Manager:
Sarah Santoro

Editorial Assistant:
Jennifer Smith

Copy Editors:
Lori Cavanaugh, Karen Annett

Manufacturing Coordinator:
Melissa Hulse

Production Editor:
Kelly Robinson

Quality Assurance:
Marianne Snow, Christian Kunciw

Cover Design:
Abby Scholz

Internal Design:
Janis Owens, Books by Design

Compositor:
Digital Publishing Solutions

Table of Contents

A+ 2003 Core Hardware Exam

OBJECTIVES	CHAPTERS	PAGE NUMBERS
Domain 1 Installation, Configuration and Upgrading		
1.1 Identify the *names, purpose, and characteristics* of system modules. Recognize these modules by sight or definition. [1.1].		
▪ Motherboard	1, 4	5–21, 168–171
▪ Firmware	1	29–34
▪ Power supply	1, 4	28–29, 117–118
▪ Processor/CPU	1, 11	5–21, 474
▪ Memory	1, 6	5–21, 240–248
▪ Storage devices	1, 7, 8, 11	5–21, 286–292, 308–314, 325–326, 486–488, 492–495
▪ Display devices	1, 10	5–21, 448–453
▪ Adapter cards	1, 10, 17	5–21, 26–28, 411–429, 782
▪ Ports	1, 10, 17	5–21, 26–28, 411–429, 782
▪ Cases	1, 4	5–21, 130–139
▪ Riser cards	4, 17	130–139, 782
1.2 Identify basic procedures for adding and removing field replaceable modules for desktop systems. *Given a replacement scenario, choose the appropriate sequences.* [1.2].		
Desktop components:		
▪ Motherboard	4, 5, 23	141–144, 129–228, 1049–1063
▪ Storage device		
• FDD	7, 23	293–297, 1045–1051
• HDD	8, 23	324–325, 333–350, 1045–1051
• CD/CDRW	11, 23	489–492, 496–500, 1045–1051
• DVD/DVDRW	11	489–492, 496–500
• Tape drive	11	501–509
• Removable storage	11	501–509
▪ Power supply		
• AC adapter	4	117–118
• AT/ATX	4, 23	117–118, 130–149, 1049–1063
▪ Cooling systems		
• Fans	4, 5, 23	141–144, 175–186, 1049–1063
• Heat sinks	5, 23	175–186, 1049–1063 175–186
• Liquid cooling	5	
▪ Processor/CPU	5, 23	219–288, 1049–1063
▪ Memory	6, 23	251–260, 1049–1063
▪ Display device	10, 23	453–455, 1049–1063
▪ Input device		
• Keyboard	10	439–488
• Mouse/pointer devices	10	439–488
• Touch screen	10	439–488
▪ Adapters		

OBJECTIVES	CHAPTERS	PAGE NUMBERS
■ Motherboards		
● CMOS/BIOS settings	5, 23, A	206–216, 229–230, 1063–1065, 1097–1100
● POST audible/visual error codes	3, 5, A	78–81, 229–230, 1097–1100
■ Peripherals	10, 17, 23	410–429, 460–465, 794–800, 1063–1065
■ Computer Case		
● Power Supply	4, 23	126–127, 141–149, 1063–1065
● Slot covers	4, 23	126–127, 1063–1065
● Front cover alingment	23	1063–1066
■ Storage devices and cables		
● FDD	7, 23	297–301, 1045–1051
● HDD	8, 9, 23	350–352, 390–396, 1045–1051
● CD/CDRW	11, 23	488, 514–516, 1045–1051
● DVD/DVDRW	11	488, 514–516
● Tape drive	11	501–505, 514–516
● Removable storage	11	505–509, 514–516
■ Cooling systems		
● Fans	4	141–149, 175–186
● Heat sinks	5	175–186
● Liquid cooling	5	175–186
● Temperature sensors	4	141–149, 175–186
■ Processor /CPU	5, 23	229–230, 1049–1052
■ Memory	6	261–262
■ Display device	10	411–429, 460–465
■ Input device		
● Keyboard	10	439–448
● Mouse/pointer devices	10	439–448
● Touch screen	10	439–448
■ Adapters		
● Network Interface Card (NIC)	10, 18	411–429, 863–865
● Sound Card	10	411–429
● Video Card	10	411–429, 460–465
● Modem	10, 17	411–429, 800–804
● SCSI	22	1023–1024
● IEEE 1394/Firewire	10	411–429
● USB	10	411–429
■ Portable System		
● PCMCIA	20	932–949
● Batteries	20	932–949
● Docking Stations/Port Replicators	20	932–949
● Portable unique storage	20	932–949
2.2 Identify basic troubleshooting procedures and tools and how to elicit problem symptoms from customers. Justify *asking particular questions in a given scenario.* **[2.2]**		
Content may include the following:		
■ Troubleshooting/isolation/problem determiniation procedures	4, 9, 24	141–144, 391–392, 1076–1082
■ Determining whether the hardware or software problem	4, 9, 24	141–144, 391–392, 1076–1082

OBJECTIVES	CHAPTERS	PAGE NUMBERS
• Laser	21	964–973
• Ink Dispersion	21	964–973
• Dot Matrix	21	964–973
• Solid ink	21	964–973
• Thermal	21	964–973
• Dye sublimation	21	964–973
Interfaces include:		
• Parallel	21	964–973
• Network	21	964–973
• SCSI	21	964–973
• USB	21	964–973
• Infrared	21	964–973
• Serial	21	964–973
• IEEE 1394/Firewire	21	964–973
• Wireless	18, 21	819–820, 964–973
Options/Upgrades include:		
• Memory	21	984–995
• Hard drives	21	984–995
• NICs	21	984–995
• Trays and feeders	21	964–973
• Finishers (e.g., stapling, etc.)	21	964–973
• Scanners/fax/copier	21	964–973
5.2 _Recognize_ common printer problems and techniques used to resolve them.		
Printer drivers	21	974–985
Firmware updates	21	983–995
Paper feed and output	21	983–995
Calibrations	21	983–995
Printing test pages	21	983–995
Errors (printed or displayed)	21	983–995
Memory	21	983–995
Configuration	21	983–995
Network connections	21	983–995
Connection	21	983–995
Paper jam	21	983–995
Print quality	21	983–995
Safety precautions	21	983–995
Preventive maintenance	21	983–995
Consumables	21	983–995
Environment	21	983–995
Domain 6 Basic Networking		
6.1 Identify the common types of network cables, their caharacteristics and connectors.		
Cable types include:		
• Coaxial		
• RG6	18	813–818
• RG8	18	813–818
• RG58	18	813–818
• RG59	18	813–818

OBJECTIVES	CHAPTERS	PAGE NUMBERS
▪ Plenum/PVC	18	813–818
▪ UTP		813–818
• CAT3	18	813–818
• CAT5/e	18	813–818
• CAT6	18	
▪ STP	18	813–818
▪ Fiber		
• Single-mode	18	813–818
• Multi-mode	18	813–818
▪ **Connector types include:**		
• BNC	18	813–818
• RJ-45	18	813–818
• AUI	18	813–818
• ST/SC	18	813–818
• IDU/UDC	18	820–821
6.2 Identify basic networking concepts including how a network works. [6.1]		
▪ **Concepts include:**		
▪ Installing and configuring network cards	10, 18	411–439, 842–855
▪ Addressing	18	827–833, 842–855
▪ Bandwidth	18	813–818
▪ Status indicators	18	842–855, 863–865
▪ Protocols		
• TCP/IP	18	827–833, 842–855
• IPX/SPX (NWLINK)	18	827–833
• AppleTalk	18	827–833
• NETBEUI/NETBIOS	18	827–833, 842–855
▪ Full-duplex, half-duplex	17	784
▪ Cabling—Twisted Pair, Coxial, Fiber Optic, RS-232	18	813–818
▪ Networking models		
• Peer-to-peer	18	827–833, 842–855
• Client/server	18	827–833, 842–855
▪ Infrared	10	411–429
▪ Wireless	18	819–823, 842–855
6.3 Identify common technologies available for establishing Internet connectivity and their characteristics. [New]		
▪ **Technologies Include:**		
• LAN	18	812–813
• DSL	18, 19	865–871, 891–903
• Cable	18, 19	865–871, 891–903
• ISDN	18, 19	865–871, 891–903
• Dial-up	18, 19	865–871, 891–903
• Satellite	18, 19	865–871, 891–903
• Wireless	18	819–820, 846–851, 865–871
▪ **Characteristics include:**		
• Definition	18	865–871
• Speed	18	865–871
• Connections	18	865–871

A+ OS Technologies Exam

OBJECTIVES	CHAPTERS	PAGE NUMBERS
Domain 1 Operating System Fundamentals		
1.1 Identify the major desktop components and interfaces, and their functions. Differentiate the characteristics of Windows 9x/Me, Windows NT 4.0 Workstation, Windows 2000 Professional, and Windows XP.		
▪ Contrasts between Windows 9x/Me, Windows NT 4.0 Workstation, Windows 2000 Professional and Windows XP	2, 12, 13, 15	42–43, 523–527, 606, 694–697
▪ Major Operating System components		
• Registry	12, 16	574–578, 749–756
• Virtual Memory	6	264–266
• File System	2, 7, 12	45–48, 289–292, 549–559
▪ Major Operating System Interfaces		
• Windows Explorer	2, 12, 15	45–48, 549–559, 714–718 549–559
• My Computer	12	549–559
• Control Panel	12	668–675, 721–725
• Computer Management Console	14, 15	549–559
• Accessories/System Tools	12	90–95
• Command line	3	855–856
• Network Neighborhood/My Network Places	18	549–559, 714–718
• Task Bar/systray	12, 15	61–62, 90–95, 714–718
• Start Menu	2, 3, 15	61–62, 539–542,
• Device Manager	2, 12, 15	549–559, 721–725
1.2 Identify the names, locations, purposes, and contents of major system files.		
▪ Windows 9x –specific files		
• Io.sys	3	78, 81–87
• MSDOS.sys	3, 12	78, 81–87, 536–538
• Autoexec.bat	3	78, 81–87
• Command.com	3	78, 81–87, 90–95
• Config.sys	3	78, 81–87
• HIMEM.SYS	6	269–273
• EMM386.exe	6	269–273
• win.com	3	78, 81–87
• SYSTEM.INI	12	559–562
• WIN.INI	12	559–562
• Registry data files		
• System.dat	12	574–578
• User.dat	12	574–578
▪ Windows NT–based specific files		
• BOOT.INI	14	648–651
• NTLDR	14	648–651
• NTDETECT.COM	14	648–651
• NTBOOTDD.SYS	14	648–651
• NTUSER.DAT	14	648–651
• Registry data files	15	749–756

OBJECTIVES	CHAPTERS	PAGE NUMBERS
4.2 operating system to connect to and use Internet resources. [4.2]		
▓ Protocols and terminologies		
• ISP	19	891–903
• TCP/IP	18	827–833, 846–851
• Email (POP, SMTP, IMAP)	19	882–888, 908–919
• HTML	19	908–919
• HTTP	19	882–888, 908–919
• HTTPS	19	908–919
• SSL	19	908–919
• Telnet	19	882–888
• FTP	19	882–888, 908–919
• DNS	18	846–851
▓ Connectivity technologies		
• Dial-up networking	19	891–903
• DSL networking	18, 19	827–833, 846–851, 891–903
• ISDN networking	18, 19	827–833, 846–851, 891–903
• Cable	18, 19	827–833, 846–851, 891–903
• Satellite	18, 19	827–833, 846–851, 891–903
• Wireless	18, 19	846–855, 891–903
• LAN	18	827–833, 846–851
▓ Installing and Configuring browsers		
• Enable/disable script support	19	908–919
• Configure Proxy Settings	19	908–919
• Configure security settings	19	908–919
▓ Firewall protection under Windows XP	15, 19	748–749, 903–907

Introduction

A+ Guide to Managing and Maintaining Your PC, FifthEdition Enhanced, Comprehensive was written to be the very best tool on the market today to prepare you to support personal computers. Updated to include the most current technologies with two new appendices on managing and maintaining notebook computers and on Windows XP SP2, this book takes you from the just-a-user level to the I-can-fix-this level for common PC hardware and software concerns. This book achieves its goals with an unusually effective combination of tools that powerfully reinforce both concepts and hands-on real-world experience. It also provides thorough preparation for CompTIA's 2003 A+ Certification exams. Prerequisite to using this book, a student needs to be a competent computer user. No background knowledge of electronics is assumed. An appropriate prerequisite course for this book would be a general course in microcomputer applications.

This book includes:

- **Comprehensive review and practice end-of-chapter material,** including a chapter summary, key terms, review questions, and hands-on projects.
- **Step-by-step instructions** on installation, maintenance, optimizing system performance, and troubleshooting.
- **Video clips** featuring Jean Andrews illustrating key points from the text to aid your understanding of the material.
- **A wide array of photos and screen shots** support the text, displaying in detail the exact hardware and software features you will need to understand to manage and maintain your PC.
- **Several in-depth, hands-on projects** at the end of each chapter designed to make certain that you not only understand the material, but can execute procedures and make decisions on your own.
- **Test preparation on CD-ROM.** Because so many instructors, students and employers are focused on certification, we provide ample opportunity to prepare for the A+ exams. On the CD that accompanies this book, you will find over 400 test preparation questions powered by MeasureUp, a leading test preparation vendor. Additionally, there are over 1000 test preparation questions from Certblaster, which feature A+ testing in 5 different testing modes. In total, there are over 1400 test preparation questions, which means students will have plenty of opportunity to practice, drill, and rehearse for the exam once they have worked through this book. **The unlock code for the A+ CertBlaster questions is: c_a+ (case sensitive).**

In addition, the carefully structured, clearly written text is accompanied by graphics that provide the visual input essential to learning. And for instructors using the book in a classroom, a special CD-ROM is available that includes an Instructor's Manual, an Online Testing system, and a PowerPoint presentation.

Coverage is balanced—while focusing on new hardware and software, the text also covers the real work of PC repair, where some older technology remains in widespread use and still needs support. For example, the book covers all the AGP and PCI expansion slot technologies, but also addresses using ISA expansion slots because many systems with ISA slots are still in use. Also included is thorough coverage of operating system and applications support. While Windows is the primary OS of choice for most PCs, DOS is given comprehensive coverage because it is still used in some troubleshooting situations when Windows will not load. Because Windows XP is currently the preferred Windows OS, two full chapters are devoted to supporting it. In addition, three chapters are dedicated to Windows 9x, Windows NT and Windows 2000, because these operating systems are still present in the workplace. Because occasionally a PC technician sees a Linux installation on the desktop, an appendix covers this OS.

This book provides thorough preparation for CompTIA's A+ 2003 Certification examinations and maps completely to the revised exam objectives. This certification credential's popularity among employers is growing exponentially, and obtaining certification increases your ability to gain employment and improve your salary. To get more information on A+ certification and its sponsoring organization, the Computing Technology Industry Association, see their Web site at *www.comptia.org*.

Features

To ensure a successful learning experience, this book includes the following pedagogical features:

- **Learning Objectives:** Every chapter opens with a list of learning objectives that sets the stage for you to absorb the lessons of the text.
- **Comprehensive Step-by-Step Troubleshooting Guidance:** Troubleshooting guidelines are included in almost every chapter. In addition, Chapter 24 gives insights into general approaches to troubleshooting that help apply the specifics detailed in each chapter for different hardware and software problems.
- **Step-by-Step Procedures:** The book is chock-full of step-by-step procedures covering subjects from hardware installation and maintenance to optimizing system performance.
- **Art Program:** Numerous detailed photographs, three-dimensional art, and screenshots support the text, displaying hardware and software features exactly as you will see them in your work.
- **A+ Table of Contents:** This table of contents indicates every page that relates to each certification objective. This is a valuable tool for quick reference.
- **Applying Concepts:** These sections offer practical applications for the material being discussed. Whether outlining a task, developing a scenario, or providing pointers, the Applying Concepts sections give you a chance to apply what you've learned to a typical PC problem.

Notes: Note icons highlight additional helpful information related to the subject being discussed.

A+ Icons: All of the content that relates to CompTIA's A+ 2003 Certification exams, whether it's a page or a sentence, is highlighted with an A+ icon. The icon notes the exam name and the objective number. This unique feature highlights the relevant content at a glance, so you can pay extra attention to the material.

A+ Exam Tip Boxes: These boxes highlight additional insights and tips to remember if you are planning on taking the A+ Exams.

Caution Icon: This icon highlights critical safety information. Follow these instructions carefully to protect the PC and its data and for your own safety.

Video clips: Short video passages reinforce concepts and techniques discussed in the text, and offer insight into the life of a PC Repair technician.

End-of-Chapter Material: Each chapter closes with the following features, which reinforce the material covered in the chapter and provide real-world, hands-on testing of the chapter's skill set:

CHAPTER SUMMARY

REVIEWING THE BASICS

KEY TERMS

- **Chapter Summary:** This bulleted list of concise statements summarizes all major points of the chapter.
- **Review Questions:** You can test your understanding of each chapter with a comprehensive set of review questions. The "Reviewing the Basics" questions check your understanding of fundamental concepts, while the "Thinking Critically" questions help you synthesize and apply what you've learned.
- **Key Terms:** The content of each chapter is further reinforced by an end-of-chapter key-term list. The definitions of all terms are included at the end of the book in a full-length glossary.

Hands-On Projects: You get to test your real-world understanding with hands-on projects involving a full range of software and hardware problems. Each hands-on activity in this book is preceded by the Hands-On icon and a description of the exercise that follows.

Web Site: For updates to this book and information about our complete line of A+ PC Repair topics, please visit our Web site at *www.course.com/pcrepair*.

Instructor Resources

The following supplemental materials are available when this book is used in a classroom setting. All of the supplements available with this book are provided to the instructor on a single CD-ROM.

Electronic Instructor's Manual: The Instructor's Manual that accompanies this textbook includes additional instructional material to assist in class preparation, including suggestions for classroom activities, discussion topics, and additional projects.

Solutions: Answers to all end-of-chapter material, including the Review Questions, and where applicable, Hands-on Projects, are provided.

ExamView®: This textbook is accompanied by ExamView, a powerful testing software package that allows instructors to create and administer printed, computer (LAN-based), and Internet exams. ExamView includes hundreds of questions that correspond to the topics covered in this text, enabling students to generate detailed study guides that include page references for further review. The computer-based and Internet testing components allow students to take exams at their computers, and also save the instructor time by grading each exam automatically.

PowerPoint presentations: This book comes with Microsoft PowerPoint slides for each chapter. These are included as a teaching aid for classroom presentation, to make available to students on the network for chapter review, or to be printed for classroom distribution. Instructors, please feel at liberty to add your own slides for additional topics you introduce to the class.

Figure Files: All of the figures in the book are reproduced on the Instructor Resource CD, in bit-mapped format. Similar to the PowerPoint presentations, these are included as a teaching aid for classroom presentation, to make available to students for review, or to be printed for classroom distribution.

Daily Lesson Planner: This free teaching tool enables instructors to use our A+ products with even greater ease! It includes detailed lecture notes and teaching instructions that incorporate all of the components of the A+ Total Solutions. A user name and password are required for download. This is available on the Instructor's CD and online at *www.course.com/pcrepair*.

Acknowledgments

Thank you to the wonderful people at Thomson Course Technology who continue to provide support, warm encouragement, patience, and guidance: Kristen Duerr, Kelly Robinson, and Manya Chylinski of CT. You've truly helped make this fifth edition enhanced fun! Thank you, Jill Batistick the Developmental Editor, for your careful attention to detail and your genuine friendship, and to Lori Cavanaugh, our excellent copy editor. Thank you Tony Woodall of Omega Computer Systems for your above-and-beyond research efforts. Thank you, Marianne Snow, for your careful attention to the technical accuracy of the book.

Thank you to all the people who took the time to voluntarily send encouragement and suggestions for improvements to the previous editions. Your input and help is very much appreciated. The reviewers all provided invaluable insights and showed a genuine interest in the book's success. Thank you to:

Wally Beck, Gainesville College

Brian J. Bridson, Baker College of Flint

William L. Congleton, DeVry University

Ryan Shultz, Old Dominion University

Berry Smith, Virginia College at Huntsville

Thank you to Melany Goulding and Joy Dark who were here with me making this book happen. I'm very grateful.

This book is dedicated to the covenant of God with man on earth.

Jean Andrews, Ph.D.

Photo Credits

Figure 1-16	Courtesy of Seagate Technology, LLC
Figure 5-7	Courtesy of Advanced Micro Devices (AMD), Inc.
Figure 5-8	Courtesy of VIA Technologies, Inc.
Figure 5-9	Courtesy of Intel Corporation
Figure 5-10	Courtesy of Advanced Micro Devices (AMD), Inc.
Figure 5-12	Courtesy of Thermaltake Technology Co., Ltd.
Figure 8-6	Courtesy of Maxtor Corporation. © 2003 All rights reserved.
Figure 10-25	Courtesy of Microsoft Corporation
Figure 10-26	© Steve Kahn
Figure 10-29	Mouse and trackball photos courtesy of Microsoft Corporation; touch pad photo courtesy of Acer America, Inc.
Figure 11-5	Courtesy of Panasonic
Figure 11-9	Courtesy of Plextor Corp.
Figure 11-17	Courtesy of Seagate Technology, LLC
Figure 11-23	Photo courtesy of Iomega Corporation. Copyright (c) 2003 Iomega Corporation. All Rights Reserved. Iomega, the stylized "i" logo and product images are property of Iomega Corporation in the United States and/or other countries.
Figure 17-1	Courtesy of Zoom Telephonics, Inc.
Figure 18-8	Wired network card photos and wireless NIC for desktop photo courtesy of 3Com Corporation; wireless NIC for notebook photo courtesy of D-Link Systems, Inc.
Figure 19-16	Courtesy of D-Link Systems, Inc.
Figure 20-24	Courtesy of International Business Machines
Figure 20-25	Courtesy of Microsoft Corporation
Figure 20-26	Courtesy of Acer, Inc.
Figure 20-27	Courtesy of RM plc
Figure 20-28	Courtesy of ASUSTek Computer, Inc. and Microsoft Corporation
Figure 21-6	Courtesy of Epson America, Inc.
Figure 22-6	© 2003 Adaptec, Inc. All Rights Reserved.

Most other photos courtesy of Jennifer Dark and Joy Dark.

Read This Before You Begin

The following hardware, software, and other equipment are needed to do the Hands-on Projects at the end of chapters:

* You need a working PC that can be taken apart and reassembled. Use a Pentium or equivalent computer.
* Troubleshooting skills can better be practiced with an assortment of nonworking expansion cards that can be used to simulate problems.
* Chapters 1–11 and 17–24 use a combination of Microsoft Windows XP, Microsoft Windows 2000 Professional, and Microsoft Windows 9x. Microsoft Windows 9x is needed for Chapter 12. Microsoft Windows NT Workstation 4.0 is needed for Chapter 13, Microsoft Windows 2000 Professional is needed for Chapters 13 and 14, and Microsoft Windows XP Home Edition or Microsoft Windows XP Professional is required for Chapters 15 and 16.
* Equipment required to work on hardware includes a grounding mat and grounding strap and flat-head and Phillips-head screwdrivers. A multimeter is needed for Appendix E projects.
* Before undertaking any of the lab exercises, starting with Chapter 3, please review the safety guidelines below.

CAUTION

This icon highlights critical safety information. Follow these instructions carefully for your own safety.

Protect Yourself, Your Hardware, and Your Software

When you work on a computer it is possible to harm both the computer and yourself. The most common accident that happens when attempting to fix a computer problem is erasing software or data. Experimenting without knowing what you are doing can cause damage. To prevent these sorts of accidents, as well as the physically dangerous ones, take a few safety precautions. The text below describes the potential sources of damage to computers and how to protect against them.

Power to the Computer

To protect both yourself and the equipment when working inside a computer, turn off the power, unplug the computer, and always use a grounding bracelet as described in Chapter 4. Consider the monitor and the power supply to be "black boxes." Never remove the cover or put your hands inside this equipment unless you know about the hazards of charged capacitors. Both the power supply and the monitor can hold a dangerous level of electricity even after they are turned off and disconnected from a power source.

Protect Against ESD

To protect the computer against electrostatic discharge (ESD), commonly known as static electricity, always ground yourself before touching electronic components, including the hard drive, motherboard, expansion cards, processors, and memory modules. Ground yourself and the computer parts, using one or more of the following static control devices or methods:

- **Ground bracelet or static strap:** A ground bracelet is a strap you wear around your wrist. The other end is attached to a grounded conductor such as the computer case or a ground mat, or it can plug into a wall outlet (only the ground prong makes a connection!). The bracelet also contains a current-limiting device called a resistor that prevents electricity from harming you.
- **Ground mats:** Ground mats can come equipped with a cord to plug into a wall outlet to provide a grounded surface on which to work. Remember, if you lift the component off the mat, it is no longer grounded and is susceptible to ESD.
- **Static shielding bags:** New components come shipped in static shielding bags. Save the bags to store other devices that are not currently installed in a PC.

The best solution to protect against ESD is to use a ground bracelet together with a ground mat. Consider a ground bracelet to be essential equipment when working on a computer. However, if you find yourself in a situation without one, touch the computer case before you touch a component. When passing a chip to another person, ground yourself. Leave components inside their protective bags until ready to use. Work on hard floors, not carpet, or use antistatic spray on the carpets. Generally, don't work on a computer if you or the computer have just come inside from the cold.

Besides using a grounding mat, you can also create a ground for the computer case by leaving the power cord to the case plugged into the wall outlet. This is safe enough because the power is turned off when you work inside the case. However, if you happen to touch an exposed area of the power switch inside the case, it is possible to get a shock. Because of this risk, in this book, you are directed to unplug the power cord to the PC before you work inside the case.

There is an exception to the ground-yourself rule. Inside a monitor case, there is substantial danger posed by the electricity stored in capacitors. When working inside a monitor, you *don't* want to be grounded, as you would provide a conduit for the voltage to discharge through your body. In this situation, be careful *not* to ground yourself.

When handling motherboards and expansion cards, don't touch the chips on the boards. Don't stack boards on top of each other, which could accidentally dislodge a chip. Hold cards by the edges, but don't touch the edge connections on the card.

Don't touch a chip with a magnetized screwdriver. When using a multimeter to measure electricity, be careful not to touch a chip with the probes. When changing DIP switches, don't use a graphite pencil, because graphite conducts electricity; a very small screwdriver works very well.

After you unpack a new device or software that has been wrapped in cellophane, remove the cellophane from the work area quickly. Don't allow anyone who is not properly grounded to touch components. Do not store expansion cards within one foot of a monitor, because the monitor can discharge as much as 29,000 volts of ESD onto the screen.

Hold an expansion card by the edges. Don't touch any of the soldered components on a card. If you need to put an electronic device down, place it on a grounded mat or on a static shielding bag. Keep components away from your hair and clothing.

Protect Hard Drives and Disks

Always turn off a computer before moving it, to protect the hard drive, which is always spinning when the computer is turned on (unless the drive has a sleep mode). Never jar a computer while the hard disk is running. Avoid placing a PC on the floor, where the user can accidentally kick it.

Follow the usual precautions to protect disks. Keep them away from magnetic fields, heat, and extreme cold. Don't open the floppy shuttle window or touch the surface of the disk inside the housing. Treat disks with care and they'll generally last for years.

CompTIA Authorized Curriculum Program

The logo of the CompTIA Authorized Curriculum Program and the status of this or other training material as "Authorized" under the CompTIA Authorized Curriculum Program signifies that, in CompTIA's opinion, such training material covers the content of the CompTIA's related certification exam. CompTIA has not reviewed or approved the accuracy of the contents of this training material and specifically disclaims any warranties of merchantability or fitness for a particular purpose. CompTIA makes no guarantee concerning the success of persons using any such "Authorized" or other training material in order to prepare for any CompTIA certification exam.

The contents of this training material were created for the CompTIA A+ Certification exam covering CompTIA certification exam objectives that were current as of November 2003.

State of the Information Technology (IT) Field

Most organizations today depend on computers and information technology to improve business processes, productivity, and efficiency. Opportunities to become global organizations and reach customers, businesses, and suppliers are a direct result of the widespread use of the Internet. Changing technology further changes how companies do business. This fundamental change in business practices has increased the need for skilled and certified IT workers across industries. This transformation has moved many IT workers out of traditional IT businesses and into various IT-dependent industries such as banking, government, insurance, and healthcare.

In the year 2000, the U.S. Department of Labor, Bureau of Labor Statistics, reported that there were 2.1 million computer and data processing services jobs within organizations and an additional 164,000 self-employed workers. This makes the IT industry one of the largest industries in the economy. Even in the recent, more challenging economic times, the job opportunities for skilled and certified IT professionals remain fairly robust.

In any industry, the workforce is important to continuously drive business. Having correctly skilled workers in IT is a struggle with the ever-changing technologies. It has been estimated that technologies change approximately every 2 years. With such a quick product life cycle, IT workers must strive to keep up with these changes to continue to bring value to their employer.

Certifications

Different levels of education are required for the many jobs in the IT industry. Additionally, the level of education and type of training required varies from employer to employer, but the need for qualified technicians remains constant. As technology changes and advances in the industry continue to rapidly evolve, many employers consistently look for employees that possess the skills necessary to implement these new technologies. Traditional degrees and diplomas do not identify the skills that a job applicant has. With the growth of the IT industry, companies increasingly rely on technical certifications to identify the skills a particular job applicant possesses. Technical certifications are a way for employers to ensure the quality and skill qualifications of their computer professionals, and they can offer job seekers a competitive edge over their competition. According to Thomas Regional Industrial Market Trends, one of the 15 trends that will transform the workplace over the next decade is a severe labor and skill shortage, specifically in technical fields, which are struggling to locate skilled and educated workers.

There are two types of certifications, vendor neutral and vendor specific. Vendor neutral certifications are those that test for the skills and knowledge required in specific industry job roles and do not subscribe to a specific vendor's technology solution. Vendor neutral certifications include all of the Computing Technology Industry Association's (CompTIA) certifications, Project Management Institute's certifications, and Security Certified Program certifications. Vendor specific certifications validate the skills and knowledge necessary to be successful by utilizing a specific vendor's technology solution. Some examples of vendor specific certifications include those offered by Microsoft, IBM, Novell, and Cisco.

As employers struggle to fill open IT positions with qualified candidates, certifications are a means of validating the skill sets necessary to be successful within an organization. In most careers, salary and compensation are determined by experience and education, but in IT the number and type of certifications an employee earns also determines salary and wage increases. The Department of Labor, Bureau of Labor Statistics, reported that the computer and data processing industry has grown at a dramatic rate from 1990 to 2000 and is anticipated to grow about 86% in wages and salaries by the year 2010. Robert Half International reported that, in the U.S., starting salaries for help-desk support staff in 2001 ranged from $30,500 to $56,000 and more senior technical support salaries ranged from $48,000 to $61,000.

Certifications provide job applicants with more than just a competitive edge over their non-certified counterparts who apply for the same IT positions. Some institutions of higher education grant college credit to students who successfully pass certification exams, moving them further along in their degree programs. Certifications also give individuals who are interested in careers in the military the ability to move into higher positions more quickly. And many advanced certification programs accept, and sometimes require, entry-level certifications as part of their exams. For example, Cisco and Microsoft accept some CompTIA certifications as prerequisites for their certification programs.

Career Planning

Finding a career that fits a person's personality, skill set, and lifestyle is challenging and fulfilling, but can often be difficult. What are the steps individuals should take to find that dream career? Is IT interesting to you? Chances are that if you are reading this book, this question has been answered. What about IT do you like? The world of work in the IT industry is vast. Some questions to ask yourself: Are you a person who likes to work alone, or do you like to work in a group? Do you like speaking directly with customers or do you prefer to stay behind the scenes? Is your lifestyle conducive to a lot of travel, or do you need to stay in one location? All of these factors influence your decision when faced with choosing the right job. Inventory assessments are a good first step to learning more about your interests, work values, and abilities. There are a variety of Web sites that offer assistance with career planning and assessments.

The Computing Technology Industry Association (CompTIA) hosts an informational Web site called the TechCareer Compass™ (TCC) that defines careers in the IT industry. The TCC is located at *tcc.comptia.org*. This Web site was created by the industry and outlines over 100 industry jobs. Each defined job includes a job description, alternate job titles, critical work functions, activities and performance indicators, and skills and knowledge required by the job. In other words, it shows exactly what the job entails so that you can find one that best fits your interests and abilities. Additionally, the TCC maps over 750 technical certifications to the skills required by each specific job, allowing you to research and plan your certification training. The Web site also includes a resource section, which is updated regularly with articles and links to other career Web sites. The TechCareer Compass is the one-stop location for IT career information.

In addition to CompTIA's TechCareer Compass, there are many other Web sites that cover components of IT careers and career planning. Many of these sites can also be found in the TCC Resources section. Some of these other career planning sites include *YourITFuture.com*, *ITCompass.net*, and *About.com*.

Citation

Bureau of Labor Statistics, U.S. Department of Labor. *Career Guide to Industries, 2002-03 Edition, Computer and Data Processing Services.* On the Internet at http://www.bls.gov/oco/cg/cgs033.htm (visited August 14, 2003).

Bureau of Labor Statistics, U.S. Department of Labor, *Occupational Outlook Handbook, 2002-03 Edition, Computer Support Specialists and System Administrators.* On the internet at http://www.bls.gov/oco/home.htm (visited August 14, 2003).

Thomas Regional Industrial Market Trends. July 8, 2003 Newsletter: *15 Trends that Will Transform the Workforce.* On the Internet at http://www.thomasregional.com/newsarchive2.html?us=3f61ed4162269&to=5&from=0&id=1057266649 (visited September 10, 2003).

How to Become CompTIA Certified

This training material can help you prepare for and pass a related CompTIA certification exam or exams. In order to achieve CompTIA certification, you must register for and pass a CompTIA certification exam or exams. In order to become CompTIA certified, you must:

1. Select a certification exam provider. For more information please visit the following Web site: *www.comptia.org/certification/general_information/test_locations.asp*.

2. Register for and schedule a time to take the CompTIA certification exam(s) at a convenient location.

3. Read and sign the Candidate Agreement, which will be presented at the time of the exam(s). The text of the Candidate Agreement can be found at the following Web site: *www.comptia.org/certification/general_information/candidate_agreement.asp*.

4. Take and pass the CompTIA certification exam(s).

For more information about CompTIA's certifications, such as their industry acceptance, benefits, or program news, please visit *www.comptia.org/certification/default.asp*.

CompTIA is a non-profit information technology (IT) trade association. CompTIA's certifications are designed by subject matter experts from across the IT industry. Each CompTIA certification is vendor-neutral, covers multiple technologies, and requires demonstration of skills and knowledge widely sought after by the IT industry.

To contact CompTIA with any questions or comments: Please call + 1 630 268 1818 or visit *questions@comptia.org*.

Introducing Hardware

In this chapter, you will learn:

- That a computer requires both hardware and software to work

- About the many different hardware components inside and connected to a computer

Like millions of other computer users, you have probably used your microcomputer to play games, explore the Internet, write papers, build spreadsheets, or create a professional-looking proposal or flyer. You can use all these applications without understanding exactly what goes on inside your computer case or monitor. But if you are curious to learn more about microcomputers, and if you want to graduate from simply being the end user of your computer to becoming the master of your machine, then this book is for you. It is written for anyone who wants to understand what is happening inside the machine, in order to install new hardware and software, diagnose both hardware and software problems, and make decisions about purchasing new hardware and operating systems. In addition, this book prepares you to pass the A+ Core Hardware Service Technician exam and the A+ Operating System Technologies exam, the two exams required by CompTIA (*www.comptia.org*) for A+ Certification. The only assumption made here is that you are a computer user—that is, you can turn on your machine, load a software package, and use that software to accomplish a task. No experience in electronics is assumed.

This chapter introduces you to the inside of your computer, a world of electronic and mechanical devices that has evolved over just a few years to become one of the most powerful technical tools of our society.

Hardware Needs Software to Work

In the world of computers, the term **hardware** refers to the computer's physical components, such as the monitor, keyboard, memory chips, and hard drive. The term **software** refers to the set of instructions that directs the hardware to accomplish a task. In order to perform a computing task, software uses hardware for four basic functions: input, processing, storage, and output (see Figure 1-1). Also, hardware components must communicate both data and instructions among themselves, which requires an electrical system to provide power, because these components are electrical. In this chapter, we introduce the hardware components of a computer system and help you see how they work. In Chapter 2, we address how hardware and software work together, with the primary focus on the sophisticated system of communication of data and instructions that includes both hardware and software.

Figure 1-1   Computer activity consists of input, processing, storage, and output

A computer user must interact with a computer in a way that the user and the software understand, such as entries made by way of a keyboard or a mouse (see Figure 1-2). However, software must convert that instruction into a form that hardware can "understand." As incredible as it might sound, every communication between hardware and software, or between software and other software, is reduced to a simple yes or no, which is represented inside the computer by two simple states: on and off.

① User types "LISA"

③ All processing and storage are done in binary form

④ Transmission to printer is in binary form

0110110011001

② Keyboard converts characters to a binary code; bits are transmitted to memory and to CPU for processing

0110110011

⑤ Printer converts binary code to characters before printing

LISA

Figure 1-2   All communication, storage, and processing of data inside a computer are in binary form until presented as output to the user

It was not always so. For almost half a century, people attempted to invent an electronic computational device that could store all 10 digits in our decimal number system and even some of our alphabet. Scientists were attempting to store a charge in a vacuum tube, which is similar to a light bulb. The charge would later be "read" to determine what had been stored there. Each digit in our number system, one through nine, was stored with increasing degrees of charge, similar to a light bulb varying in power from dim all the way up to bright. However, the degree of "dimness" or "brightness" was difficult to measure, and it would change because the voltage in the equipment could not be accurately regulated. For example, an eight would be stored with a partially bright charge, but later it would be read as a seven or nine as the voltage on the vacuum tube fluctuated slightly.

Then, in the 1940s, John Atanasoff came up with the brilliant idea to store and read only two values, on and off. Either there was a charge or there was not a charge, and this was easy to write and read, just as it's easy to determine if a light bulb is on or off. This technology of storing and reading only two states is called binary, and the number system that only uses two digits, 0 and 1, is called the **binary number system**. A 1 or 0 in this system is called a **bit**, or binary digit. Because of the way the number system is organized, grouping is often done in groups of eight bits, each of which is called a **byte**. (Guess what four bits are called? A nibble!)

In a computer, all counting and calculations use the binary number system. Counting in binary goes like this: 0, 1, 10, 11, 100, 101, and so forth. All letters and characters are converted to a binary code before being stored in a computer. For example, the uppercase letter A in binary code is 0100 0001, and the number 25 is 0001 1001 (see Figure 1-3).

To learn more about binary and computer terminology related to the binary and hexadecimal number system, see Appendix C.

The letter A stored as 8 bits:

A =   0 1 0 0 0 0 0 1   =

The number 25 stored as 8 bits:

25 =   0 0 0 1 1 0 0 1   =

Figure 1-3   All letters and numbers are stored in a computer as a series of bits, each represented in the computer as on or off

PC Hardware Components

In this section, we cover the major hardware components of a microcomputer system used for input, output, processing, storage, electrical supply, and communication. Most input and output devices are outside the computer case. Most processing and storage components are contained inside the case. The most important component in the case is the **central processing unit (CPU)**, also called the **microprocessor** or **processor**. As its name implies, this device is central to all processing done by the computer. Data received by input devices is read by the CPU, and output from the CPU is written to output devices. The CPU writes data and instructions in storage devices and performs calculations and other data processing. Whether inside or outside the case, and regardless of the function the device performs, each hardware input, output, or storage device requires these elements to operate:

■ *A method for the CPU to communicate with the device.* The device must send data to and/or receive data from the CPU. The CPU might need to control the device by passing instructions to it, or the device might need to request service from the CPU.

■ *Software to instruct and control the device.* A device is useless without software to control it. The software must know how to communicate with the device at the detailed level of that specific device, and the CPU must have access to this software in order to interact with the device. Each device responds to a specific set of instructions based on the device's functions. The software must have an instruction for each possible action you expect the device to accomplish.

■ *Electricity to power the device.* Electronic devices require electricity to operate. Devices can receive power from the power supply inside the computer case, or they can have their own power supplied by a power cable connected to an electrical outlet.

In the next few pages, we take a sightseeing tour of computer hardware, first looking outside and then inside the case.

Hardware Used for Input and Output

A+
CORE
1.1

✔ A+ EXAM TIP

The A+ Core exam expects you to know many computer terms, and lots of them are found in this chapter. Pay close attention to all key terms.

Most input/output devices reside outside the computer case. These devices communicate with components inside the computer case through a wireless connection or through cables attached to the case at a connection called a **port**. Most computer ports are located on the back of the case (see Figure 1-4), but some models have ports on the front of the case for easy access. For wireless connections, a wireless device communicates with the system using a radio wave or infrared port. The most popular input devices are a keyboard and a mouse, and the most popular output devices are a monitor and a printer.

VIDEO

Examining the
Back of a PC

Figure 1-4   Input/output devices connect to the computer case by ports usually found on the back of the case

The **keyboard** is the primary input device of a computer (see Figure 1-5). The keyboards that are standard today are called enhanced keyboards and hold 104 keys. Ergonomic keyboards are curved to make them more comfortable for the hands and wrists. In addition, some keyboards come equipped with a mouse port used to attach a mouse to the keyboard, although it is more common for the mouse port to be

A+
CORE
1.1

located directly on the computer case. Electricity to run the keyboard comes from inside the computer case and is provided by wires in the keyboard cable.

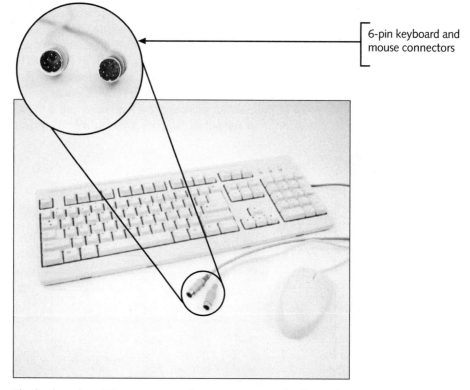

6-pin keyboard and mouse connectors

Figure 1-5   The keyboard and the mouse are the two most popular input devices

A **mouse** is a pointing device used to move a pointer on the screen and to make selections. The bottom of a mouse has a rotating ball or an optical sensor that tracks movement and controls the location of the pointer. The one, two, or three buttons on the top of the mouse serve different purposes for different software. For example, Windows XP uses the left mouse button to execute a command and the right mouse button to display information about the command.

The monitor and the printer are the two most popular output devices (see Figure 1-6). The **monitor** is the visual device that displays the primary output of the computer. Hardware manufacturers typically rate a monitor according to the size of its screen (in inches) and by the monitor's resolution, which is a function of the number of dots on the screen used for display.

15-pin, 3-row analog
video connector

25-pin parallel port
connector for printer

1

Figure 1-6   The two most popular output devices are the monitor and the printer

A very important output device is the **printer**, which produces output on paper, often called **hard copy**. The most popular printers available today are inkjet, laser, thermal, solid ink, and dot matrix printers. The monitor and the printer need separate power supplies. Their electrical power cords connect to electrical outlets. Sometimes the computer case provides an electrical outlet for the monitor's power cord, to eliminate the need for one more power outlet.

In addition to the connectors in Figure 1-6, a digital monitor can use a digital video connector, and a printer sometimes uses a universal serial bus (USB) connector.

Hardware Inside the Computer Case

Most storage and all processing of data and instructions are done inside the computer case, so before we look at components used for storage and processing, let's look at what you see when you first open the computer case. Most computers contain these devices inside the case (see Figure 1-7):

- A motherboard containing the CPU, memory, and other components
- A floppy drive, hard drive, and CD-ROM drive used for permanent storage
- A power supply with power cords supplying electricity to all devices inside the case

- Circuit boards used by the CPU to communicate with devices inside and outside the case
- Cables connecting devices to circuit boards and the motherboard

Pentium II CPU

Power supply

Power cords

CD-ROM drive

Floppy drive is hidden in this bay

Zip drive

Hard drive

Front of case

Data cable

Motherboard

Circuit boards (expansion cards)

Rear of case

Figure 1-7   Inside the computer case

VIDEO

Looking Inside
a PC

Some of the first things you'll notice when you look inside a computer case are circuit boards. A **circuit board** is a board that holds microchips, or integrated circuits (ICs), and the circuitry that connects these chips. Some circuit boards, called **expansion cards**, are installed in long narrow **expansion slots** on the motherboard. All circuit boards contain microchips, which are most often manufactured using **complementary metal-oxide semiconductor (CMOS)** technology. CMOS chips require less electricity and produce less heat than chips manufactured using earlier technologies such as TTL (transistor-transistor logic). The other major components inside the case look like small boxes, including the power supply, hard drive, CD-ROM drive, and floppy drive.

There are two types of cables inside the case: data cables, which connect devices to one another, and power cables or power cords, which supply power. Most often, you can distinguish between the two by the shape of the cable. Data cables are flat and wide, and power cords are round and small. There are some exceptions to this rule, so the best way to identify a cable is to trace its source and destination.

The Motherboard

**A+
CORE
1.1**

The largest and most important circuit board in the computer is the **motherboard,** also called the **main board** or **system board** (see Figure 1-8), which contains the CPU, the component in which most processing takes place. The motherboard is the most complicated piece of equipment inside the case, and Chapter 5 covers it in detail. Because all devices must communicate with the CPU on the motherboard, all devices in a computer are either installed directly on the motherboard, directly linked to it by a cable connected to a port on the motherboard, or indirectly linked to it by expansion cards. A device that is not installed directly on the motherboard is called a **peripheral device.** Some ports on the motherboard stick outside the case to accommodate external devices such as a keyboard, and some ports provide a connection for a device inside the case, such as a floppy disk drive.

VIDEO

Looking at
Motherboards

- PCI slots
- AGP slot for video card
- CPU with fan on top
- Chip set
- Slots for RAM
- Drive connectors
- Power supply connection
- CMOS battery

Figure 1-8   All hardware components are either located on the motherboard or directly or indirectly connected to it because they must all communicate with the CPU

Figure 1-9 shows the ports provided to the outside of the case by a motherboard: a keyboard port, a mouse port, a serial port, a parallel port, four USB ports, a network port, a 1394 port, and three sound ports. A **serial port** is so named because data is transferred serially (one bit follows the next); it is often used for an external modem or a serial mouse (a mouse that uses a serial port). A **parallel port** transmits data in parallel and is most often used by a printer. A **universal serial bus (USB) port** can be used by many different input/output devices such as keyboards, printers, scanners, and digital cameras. A 1394 port (FireWire port) is used for high-speed multimedia devices such as digital camcorders.

1394 port

Parallel port

Network port

Three sound ports

Keyboard and mouse ports

Four USB ports

Serial port

S/PDIF port (digital sound)

Figure 1-9   A motherboard provides ports for common I/O devices

Listed next are the major components found on all motherboards, some of which are labeled in Figure 1-8. The sections that follow discuss these components in detail. Components used primarily for processing:

- Central processing unit (CPU), the computer's most important chip
- Chip set that supports the CPU by controlling many motherboard activities

Components used for temporary storage:

- Random access memory (RAM) used to hold data and instructions as they are processed
- Cache memory to speed up memory access (optional, depending on the type of CPU)

Components that allow the CPU to communicate with other devices:

- Traces, or wires, on the motherboard used for communication
- Expansion slots to connect expansion cards to the motherboard
- The system clock that keeps communication in sync

Electrical system:

- Power supply connections to provide electricity to the motherboard and expansion cards

Programming and setup data stored on the motherboard:

- Flash ROM, a memory chip used to permanently store instructions that control basic hardware functions (explained in more detail later in the chapter)
- CMOS setup chip that holds configuration data

The CPU and the Chip Set

A+
CORE
1.1

The CPU, or microprocessor or processor, is the chip inside the computer that performs most of the actual data processing (see Figure 1-10). The CPU could not do its job without the assistance of the **chip set,** a group of microchips on the motherboard that control the flow of data and instructions to and from the CPU, providing careful timing of activities (see Figure 1-11). While this book will touch on different types of machines, it focuses on the most common personal computers (PCs), referred to as IBM-compatible. These are built around microprocessors and chip sets manufactured by Intel Corporation, AMD, VIA, SiS, Cyrix, and other manufacturers. The Macintosh family of computers, manufactured by Apple Computer, Inc., is built around a family of microprocessors manufactured by Motorola Corporation. You will learn more about the CPU and the chip set in Chapter 5.

CPU fan

Motherboard

Heat sink

Figure 1-10   The CPU is hidden underneath the fan and the heat sink, which keep it cool

Figure 1-11　　This motherboard uses two chips in its chip set (notice the bus lines coming from each chip used for communication)

Storage Devices

In Figure 1-1, you saw two kinds of storage: temporary and permanent. The CPU uses temporary storage, called **primary storage** or **memory**, to temporarily hold both data and instructions while it is processing them. Primary storage is much faster to access than permanent storage. However, when data and instructions are not being used, they must be kept in permanent storage, sometimes called **secondary storage**, such as a floppy disk, CD, or hard drive. Figure 1-12 shows an analogy to help you understand the concept of primary and secondary storage. Suppose you must do some research at the library. You go to the stacks, pull out several books, carry them over to a study table, and sit down with your notepad and pencil to take notes and do some calculations. When you're done, you leave with your notepad full of information and calculations, but you don't take the books with you. In this example, the stacks are permanent storage, and the books (data and instructions) are permanently kept there. The table is temporary storage, a place for you to keep data and instructions as you work with them. The notepad is your output from all that work, and you are the CPU, doing the work of reading the books and writing down information. Reading a book that is lying on the table is much faster than running back and forth to the stacks every time you want to refer to it, which is what the CPU would have to do if it were not for primary storage, or memory. Also, you can see that the table (memory) gives fast but temporary access, while the stacks (secondary storage) give slow but permanent access.

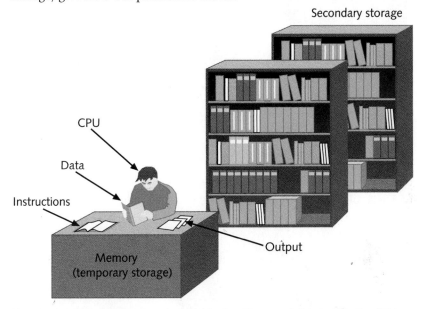

Figure 1-12   Memory is a temporary place to hold instructions and data while the CPU processes both

Primary Storage

Primary storage is provided by devices called memory or **random access memory (RAM)**, located on the motherboard and on other circuit boards. RAM chips can be installed individually directly on the motherboard or in banks of several chips on a small board that plugs into the motherboard (see Figure 1-13). The most common types of boards that hold memory chips are called **single inline memory modules (SIMMs)**, **dual inline memory modules (DIMMs)**, and **RIMMs** (memory modules manufactured by Rambus, Inc.). See Figure 1-14. Most motherboards today use DIMMs. Whatever information is stored in RAM is lost when the computer is turned off, because RAM chips need a continuous supply of electrical power to hold data or software stored in them. This kind of memory is called **volatile** because it is temporary in nature. By contrast, another kind of memory holds its data permanently, even when the power is turned off. This type of memory is **nonvolatile** and is called **read-only memory (ROM)**. You will see examples of ROM chips later in the chapter.

A+
CORE
1.1

DIMM

Two extra slots for
additional DIMMs

Figure 1-13   A SIMM, DIMM, or RIMM holds RAM and is mounted directly on a motherboard

184-pin RIMM

240-pin DDR2 DIMM   184-pin DDR DIMM

168-pin DIMM

72-pin SIMM

30-pin SIM

Figure 1-14   Types of RAM modules

Using Windows XP, you can see what type of CPU you have and how much
memory you have installed. Click Start, right-click My Computer, and then select
Properties on the shortcut menu. Then click the General tab (see Figure 1-15). You

1

can also see which version of Windows you are using. Using Windows 9x or Windows 2000, right-click the My Computer icon on your desktop, select Properties on the shortcut menu, and click the General tab.

System Properties

| System Restore | Automatic Updates | Remote |
| General | Computer Name | Hardware | Advanced |

System:
Microsoft Windows XP
Professional
Version 2002

Registered to:
Jean Andrews
Myrtle Tree Projects, Inc.
55274-0EM-0013541-67353

Computer:
Intel(R)
Pentium(R) 4 CPU 1500MHz
1.50 GHz
256 MB of RAM

[OK] [Cancel] [Apply]

Figure 1-15   System Properties gives useful information about your computer and OS

Secondary Storage

As you remember, the RAM on the motherboard is called primary storage. Primary storage temporarily holds both data and instructions as the CPU processes them. These data and instructions are also permanently stored on devices such as CDs, hard drives, and floppy disks, in locations that are remote from the CPU. Data and instructions cannot be processed by the CPU from this remote storage (called secondary storage), but must first be copied into primary storage (RAM) for processing. The most important difference between primary and secondary storage is that secondary storage is permanent. When you turn off your computer, the information in secondary storage remains intact. The most popular secondary storage devices are hard disks, CDs, DVDs, and floppy disks.

NOTE

Don't forget that primary storage, or RAM, is temporary; as soon as you turn off the computer, any information there is lost. That's why you should always save your work frequently into secondary storage.

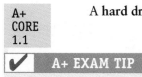

A+
CORE
1.1

A+ EXAM TIP

The A+ Core exam expects you to know that a system can only support four EIDE devices and a motherboard typically provides two EIDE connections: one primary channel and one secondary channel. Each channel can support one or two devices.

A **hard drive** is a sealed case containing platters or disks that rotate at a high speed (see Figure 1-16). As the platters rotate, an arm with a sensitive read/write head reaches across the platters, both writing new data to them and reading existing data from them. Most hard drives today use a technology called Enhanced Integrated Drive Electronics (EIDE), which originated from Integrated Drive Electronics (IDE) technology. IDE provides two connectors on a motherboard for two data cables (see Figure 1-17). Each IDE cable has a connection at the other end for an IDE device and a connection in the middle of the cable for a second IDE device. Therefore, a motherboard can accommodate up to four IDE devices in one system. Hard drives, Zip drives, CD drives, DVD drives, and tape drives, among other devices, can use these four IDE connections, which are controlled by the chip set. A typical system has one hard drive connected to one IDE connector and a CD drive connected to the other (see Figure 1-18).

Figure 1-16   Hard drive with sealed cover removed

NOTE

The industry uses the two terms IDE and EIDE almost interchangeably even though they technically have different meanings. Used correctly, IDE refers to the technology used internally by a hard drive, and EIDE refers to the interface that CD drives, DVD drives, Zip drives, tape drives, and IDE hard drives can use to connect to a motherboard. In this book, we loosely use the term IDE to mean both IDE and EIDE to be consistent with manufacturer documentation. For instance, look closely at Figure 1-17 where the motherboard connectors are labeled Primary IDE and Secondary IDE, when technically they really should be labeled Primary EIDE and Secondary EIDE.

IDE cable going to
CD-ROM drive

Primary IDE connector

Secondary IDE connec

IDE cable going to
hard drive

Figure 1-17   A motherboard usually has two IDE connectors, each of which can accommodate two devices; a hard drive usually connects to the motherboard using the primary IDE connector

40-pin IDE cable

CD-ROM drive

Connection for a secon
device on this cable

Hard drive

Figure 1-18   Two IDE devices connected to a motherboard using both IDE connections and two cables

Figure 1-19 shows the inside of a computer case with three IDE devices. The
CD-ROM drive and the Zip drive share an IDE cable, and the hard drive uses the
other cable. Both cables connect to the motherboard at the two IDE connections.
(You will learn more about IDE and EIDE in Chapter 8.)

CD-ROM drive

Secondary IDE cable

Zip drive

Two IDE connections on the motherboard

Hard drive

Primary IDE cable

Unused connection for fourth IDE device

Both cables connected to motherboard

Figure 1-19   This system has a CD-ROM and a Zip drive sharing the secondary IDE cable and a hard drive using the primary IDE cable

A hard drive receives its power from the power supply by way of a power cord (see Figure 1-20). Looking back at Figure 1-19, you can see the power connections to the right of the cable connections on each drive (the power cords are not connected to make it easier to see the data cable connections). Chapter 8 covers how a hard drive works and how to install one.

Hard drive

Power supply

Power connected

Figure 1-20   A hard drive receives power from the power supply by way of a power cord connected to the drive

Another secondary storage device sometimes found inside the case is a floppy drive that can hold 3½-inch disks, which hold up to 1.44 MB of data. Most motherboards provide a connection for a floppy drive (see Figure 1-21). A floppy drive cable can accommodate two drives. The drive at the end of the cable is drive A. If another drive were connected to the middle of the cable, it would be drive B in a computer system (see Figure 1-22). Electricity to a floppy drive is provided by a power cord from the power supply that connects to a power port at the back of the drive.

Floppy drive connector

Secondary IDE connector

Primary IDE connector

Figure 1-21   A motherboard usually provides a connection for a floppy drive cable

Floppy drive data cable

Two possible connections for another floppy drive

Connection for power cord

Figure 1-22 One floppy drive connection on a motherboard can support one or two floppy drives

VIDEO

Identifying Drives

Floppy drives are not as necessary as they once were, because the industry is moving toward storage media that can hold more data, such as CDs. For years, every PC and notebook computer had a floppy drive, but many newer notebook computers don't, and some manufacturers offer floppy drives on desktop systems as add-on options only.

A CD-ROM (compact disc read-only memory) drive is considered standard equipment on most computer systems today because most software is distributed on CDs. Figure 1-23 shows the rear of a CD-ROM drive with the IDE data cable and power cord connected. Don't let the name of the CD-ROM drive confuse you. It's really not memory but secondary storage, because when you turn off the power, the data stored on a CD remains intact. Chapter 11 discusses different CD technologies and drives, some of which can both read and write data to the disc.

1

CD-ROM drive

IDE cable
Power cord

Figure 1-23 Most CD-ROM drives are EIDE devices and connect to the motherboard by way of an IDE data cable

Motherboard Components Used for Communication Among Devices

When you look carefully at the motherboard, you see many fine lines on both the top and the bottom of the board's surface (see Figure 1-24). These lines, sometimes called **traces**, are circuits, or paths, that enable data, instructions, and power to move from component to component on the board. This system of pathways used for communication and the protocol and methods used for transmission are collectively called the **bus**. (A **protocol** is a set of rules and standards that any two entities use for communication.) The parts of the bus that we are most familiar with are the paths, or lines, of the bus that are used to move data, called the **data bus**.

Binary data is put on a line of a bus by placing voltage on that line. We can visualize that bits are "traveling" down the bus in parallel, but in reality, the voltage placed on each line is not "traveling," but rather is all over the line. When one component at one end of the line wants to write data to another component, the two components get in sync for the write operation. Then the first component places voltage on several lines of the bus, and the other component immediately reads the voltage on these lines.

Bus lines

Bottom of the
CPU socket

Figure 1-24   On the bottom of the motherboard, you can see bus lines terminating at the CPU socket

The CPU or other devices interpret the voltage, or lack of voltage, on each line on the bus as binary digits (0s or 1s). Some buses have data paths that are 8, 16, 32, 64, or 128 bits wide. For example, a bus that has eight wires, or lines, to transmit data is called an 8-bit bus. Figure 1-25 shows an 8-bit bus between the CPU and memory that is transmitting the letter A (binary 0100 0001). All bits of a byte are placed on their lines of the bus at the same time. Remember there are only two states inside a computer: on and off, which represent zero and one. On a bus, these two states are no voltage for a zero and voltage for a one. So the bus in Figure 1-25 has voltage on two lines and no voltage on the other six lines, in order to pass the letter A on the bus. This bus is only 8 bits wide, but most buses today are much wider: 16, 32, 64, or 128 bits wide. Also, most buses today use a ninth bit for error checking. Adding a check bit for each byte allows the component reading the data to verify that it is the same data written to the bus.

Figure 1-25   A data bus has traces or lines that carry voltage interpreted by the CPU and other devices as bits

The width of a data bus is called the **data path size**. A motherboard can have more than one bus, each using a different protocol, speed, data path size, and so on. The main bus on the motherboard that communicates with the CPU, memory, and the chip set goes by several names: **system bus**, memory bus, **host bus**, local bus, front side bus (FSB), or external bus. In our discussions, we'll use the term *system bus* or *memory bus*. The data portion of most system buses on today's motherboards is 64 bits wide with or without additional lines for error checking.

One of the most interesting lines, or circuits, on a bus is the **system clock** or system timer, which is dedicated to timing the activities of the chips on the motherboard. A crystal on the motherboard (Figure 1-26), similar to that found in watches, generates the oscillation that produces the continuous pulses of the system clock. Traces carry these pulses over the motherboard to chips and expansion slots to ensure that all activities are performed in a synchronized fashion. Remember that everything in a computer is binary, and this includes the activities themselves. Instead of continuously working to perform commands or move data, the CPU, bus, and other devices work in a binary fashion. Do something, stop, do something, stop, and so forth. Each device works on a clock cycle or beat of the clock. Some devices, such as the CPU, do two or more operations on one beat of the clock, and others do one operation for each beat. Some devices might even do something on every other beat, but all work according to beats or cycles. You can think of this as similar to children jumping rope. The system clock (child turning the rope) provides the beats or cycles, while devices (children jumping) work in a binary fashion (jump, don't jump). In the analogy, some children jump two or more times for each rope pass.

How fast does the clock beat? The beats, called the **clock speed**, are measured in **hertz (Hz)**, which is one cycle per second; **megahertz (MHz)**, which is one million cycles per second; and **gigahertz (GHz)**, which is one billion cycles per second.

Motherboard crystal
generates the system clock

Figure 1-26   The system clock is a pulsating electrical signal sent out by this component that works much like a crystal in a wristwatch (one line, or circuit, on the motherboard bus is dedicated to carrying this pulse)

Common ratings for motherboard buses today are 1066 MHz, 800 MHz, 533 MHz, or 400 MHz, although you still see some motherboards rated at 200 MHz, 133 MHz, or slower. In other words, data or instructions can be put on the system bus at the rate of 800 million every second. A CPU operates from 166 MHz to almost four GHz. In other words, the CPU can put data or instructions on its internal bus at this much higher rate. Although we often refer to the speed of the CPU and the motherboard bus, talking about the frequency of these devices is more accurate, because the term "speed" implies a continuous flow, while the term "frequency" implies a digital or binary flow: on and off, on and off.

The lines of a bus, including data, instruction, and power lines, often extend to the expansion slots (see Figure 1-27). The size and shape of an expansion slot depend on the kind of bus it uses. Therefore, one way to determine the kind of bus you have is to examine the expansion slots on the motherboard. Figure 1-28 shows three types of expansion slots:

- PCI (Peripheral Component Interconnect) expansion slot used for high-speed input/output devices
- AGP (Accelerated Graphics Port) expansion slot used for a video card
- ISA (Industry Standard Architecture) expansion slot used by older or slower devices

With a little practice, you can identify expansion slots by their length, by the position of the breaks in the slots, and by the distance from the edge of the motherboard to a slot's position. Look for all three of these expansion slots in Figure 1-28. Sometimes a motherboard uses a PCI Express x16 slot instead of an AGP slot for the video card. The newer PCI Express slot is discussed in Chapter 5.

Also, in Chapter 5, you'll learn that each of these types of expansion slots communicates with the CPU by way of its own bus. There is a PCI bus, an AGP bus, and an ISA bus, each running at different speeds and providing different features to accommodate the expansion cards that use these different slots. But all these buses connect to the main bus or system bus, which connects to the CPU.

Pins on connector edge of expansion card

PCI slot

Bus lines

Figure 1-27   The lines of a bus terminate at an expansion slot where they connect to pins that connect to lines on the expansion card inserted in the slot

AGP slot
PCI slots

16-bit ISA slot

Figure 1-28   PCI bus expansion slots are shorter than ISA slots and offset farther; the one AGP slot is set further from the edge of the board

Interface (Expansion) Cards

A+
CORE
1.1

Circuit boards other than the motherboard inside the computer are sometimes called circuit cards, adapter boards, expansion cards, interface cards, or simply **cards**, and are mounted in expansion slots on the motherboard (see Figure 1-29). Figure 1-30 shows the motherboard and expansion cards installed inside a computer case. By studying this figure carefully, you can see the video card installed in the one AGP slot, a sound card and a network card installed in two PCI slots (the other two PCI slots are not used), and a modem card installed in an ISA slot (two ISA slots are not used). Figure 1-30 also shows the ports these cards provide at the rear of the PC case.

VIDEO

Identifying
Expansion
Cards

Modem card

PCI slot

Motherboard
Phone line ports

Figure 1-29   The circuit board is a modem card and is mounted in a PCI slot on the motherboard

You can see a full view of a video card in Figure 1-31. These cards all enable the CPU to connect to an external device or, in the case of the network card, to a network. The **video card** provides a port for the monitor. The sound card provides ports for speakers and microphones. The network card provides a port for a network cable to connect the PC to a network, and the modem card provides ports for phone lines. The technology to access these devices is embedded on the card itself, and the card also has the technology to communicate with the slot it is in, the motherboard, and the CPU.

1

Rear of case

Video port

Sound card ports

Network port

Phone line ports

Modem card

Inside case

Network card

Video card installed in AGP slot

Sound card

PCI slot with sound card installed

PCI slot with network card installed

Empty PCI slots

ISA slot with modem card installed

Modem card

Empty ISA slots

Figure 1-30   Four cards installed on a motherboard, providing ports for several devices

The easiest way to determine the function of a particular expansion card (short of seeing its name written on the card, which doesn't happen very often) is to look at the end of the card that fits against the back of the computer case. A network card, for example, has a port designed to fit the network cable. An internal modem has one, or usually two, telephone jacks as its ports. You'll get lots of practice in this book identifying ports on expansion cards. However, as you examine the ports on the back of your PC, realize that sometimes the motherboard provides ports of its own.

15-pin, 3-row
video port

Figure 1-31   The easiest way to identify this video card is to look at the port on the end of the card

The Electrical System

The most important component of the computer's electrical system is the power supply, which is usually near the rear of the case (see Figure 1-32). This **power supply** does not actually generate electricity but converts and reduces it to a voltage that the computer can handle. A power supply receives 110–120 volts of AC power from a wall outlet and converts it to a much lower DC voltage. Older power supplies had power cables that provided either 5 or 12 volts DC. Newer power supplies provide 3.3, 5, and 12 volts DC. In addition to providing power for the computer, the power supply runs a fan directly from the electrical output voltage to help cool the inside of the computer case. Temperatures over 185 degrees Fahrenheit (85 degrees Celsius) can cause components to fail. When a computer is running, this fan and the spinning of the hard drive and CD-ROM drive are the primary noisemakers.

Every motherboard has one or a pair of connections to receive power from the power supply (see Figure 1-33). This power is used by the motherboard, the CPU, and other components that receive their power from ports and expansion slots coming off the motherboard. In addition, there might be other power connectors on the motherboard to power a small fan that cools the CPU, or to power the CPU itself.

A+
CORE
1.1

Figure 1-32   Power supply with connections

Power connectors
from power supply
to motherboard

Figure 1-33   The motherboard receives its power from the power supply by way of one or two connections located near the edge of the board

Instructions Stored on the Motherboard and Other Boards

Some very basic instructions are stored on the motherboard—just enough to start the computer, use some simple hardware devices such as a floppy disk and keyboard, and search for an operating system stored on a storage device such as a hard drive or

A+
CORE
1.1

CD. These data and instructions are stored on special ROM (read-only memory) chips on the board and are called the **basic input/output system (BIOS)**. Figure 1-34 shows a ROM BIOS chip on an older motherboard. Sometimes other circuit boards, such as a video card, also have ROM BIOS chips.

ROM BIOS chip

Figure 1-34   The ROM BIOS chip on the motherboard contains the programming to start up the PC as well as to perform many other fundamental tasks

In the case of ROM chips, the distinction between hardware and software becomes vague. Most of the time, it's easy to distinguish between hardware and software. For example, a floppy disk is hardware, but a file on the disk containing a set of instructions is software. This software file, sometimes called a **program,** might be stored on the disk today, but you can erase that file tomorrow and write a new one to the disk. In this case, it is clear that a floppy disk is a permanent physical entity, whereas the program is not. Sometimes, however, hardware and software are not so easy to distinguish. For instance, a ROM chip on a circuit board inside your computer has software instructions permanently etched into it during fabrication. This software is actually a part of the hardware and is not easily changed. In this case, hardware and software are closely tied together, and it's difficult to separate the two, either physically or logically. Software embedded into hardware is often referred to as **firmware** because of its hybrid nature.

The motherboard ROM BIOS serves three purposes: The BIOS that is sometimes used to manage simple devices is called **system BIOS,** the BIOS that is used to start the computer is called **startup BIOS,** and the BIOS that is used to change some settings on the motherboard is called **CMOS setup.**

Motherboard manufacturers often publish updates for the ROM BIOS on their motherboards; if a board is giving you problems or you want to use a new feature just released, you might want to upgrade the BIOS. In the past, this meant buying new ROM chips and exchanging them on the motherboard. However, ROM chips on motherboards today can be reprogrammed. Called **flash ROM,** the software stored on these chips can be overwritten by new software that remains on the chip until it is overwritten. (You will learn how to do this in Chapter 5; the process is called flashing ROM.)

The motherboard BIOS might support three technologies, depending on who manufactured the BIOS and when: Advanced Configuration and Power Interface (ACPI), Advanced Power Management (APM), and Plug and Play (PnP).

Advanced Configuration and Power Interface

Some BIOSs on the motherboard and operating systems support a power-saving feature using standards developed by Intel, Microsoft, and Toshiba, called the **Advanced Configuration and Power Interface (ACPI)** standards. Using ACPI, a system can be powered up by an external device such as a keyboard. Windows 2000/XP and Windows 9x support ACPI, as do most newer motherboard BIOSs. Microsoft calls an ACPI-compliant BIOS a "good" BIOS. To see if your BIOS is ACPI-compliant, check this Microsoft URL:

www.microsoft.com/windows2000/professional/howtobuy/upgrading/compat

An older BIOS power management standard is **Advanced Power Management (APM)**, which is also supported by Windows 9x and Windows 2000/XP. APM is used only for power management on legacy notebook computers that can't support ACPI.

Plug and Play

Another feature of both the BIOS and the OS is **Plug and Play (PnP)**, a standard designed to make the installation of new hardware devices easier. If the BIOS is a PnP BIOS, it will begin the process of configuring hardware devices in the system. It gathers information about the devices and then passes that information to the operating system. If the operating system is also PNP-compliant, it will use that information to complete the hardware configuration.

ESCD (extended system configuration data) Plug and Play BIOS is an enhanced version of PnP. It creates a list of all the things you have done manually to the configuration that PnP does not do on its own. This ESCD list is written to the BIOS chip so that the next time you boot, the startup BIOS can faithfully relay that information to Windows. Windows 9x benefits from this information, but it is not important to Windows 2000/XP. The BIOS chip for ESCD BIOS is a special RAM chip called Permanent RAM, or PRAM, that can hold data written to it without the benefit of a battery, which the CMOS setup chip requires.

Motherboard Configuration Settings

Another component on the motherboard, called the **CMOS configuration chip, CMOS setup chip,** or **CMOS RAM chip,** contains a very small amount of memory, or RAM, enough to hold configuration or setup information about the computer (see Figure 1-35). This chip is responsible for remembering the current date and time, which hard drives and floppy drives are present, how the serial and parallel ports are

A+
CORE
1.1

configured, and so forth. When the computer is first turned on, it looks to this CMOS chip to find out what hardware it should expect to find. The CMOS chip is powered by a trickle of electricity from a small battery located on the motherboard or computer case, usually close to the CMOS chip itself, so that when the computer is turned off, the CMOS chip still retains its data.

Coin battery

Firmware chip

Figure 1-35   This firmware chip contains flash ROM and CMOS RAM; CMOS RAM is powered by the coin battery located near the chip

NOTE   On older motherboards, the ROM BIOS chip was clearly labeled and socketed so that technicians could find and replace it easily. On newer motherboards, the chip is not designed to be replaced because the firmware on these chips can be flashed. Therefore, the chip is not clearly labeled, and often the ROM BIOS and CMOS RAM are combined in a single chip, as shown in Figure 1-35.

CMOS setup, stored on the ROM BIOS chip, is a program that can be accessed during startup to change CMOS settings. The keystrokes to enter CMOS setup are displayed somewhere on the screen during startup in a statement such as "Press the Del key to enter setup." Different BIOSs use different keystrokes. The CMOS setup does not normally need to be changed except, for example, when there is a problem with hardware, a new floppy drive is installed, or a power-saving feature needs to be disabled or enabled. The CMOS setup can also hold one or two power-on passwords to help secure a system. Know that these passwords are not the same password that can be required by a Windows OS at startup.

APPLYING CONCEPTS

Reboot your PC and look for the message on the first or second display screen that tells you how to enter CMOS setup. Press that key. What version of BIOS are you using? Exit setup without making any changes. The system should reboot to the Windows desktop.

A motherboard can also retain setup or installation information in different settings of jumpers or DIP switches on the board. **Jumpers** are considered open or

A+
CORE
1.1

closed based on whether a jumper cover is present on two small posts or metal pins that stick up off the motherboard (see Figure 1-36). A group of jumpers is sometimes used to tell the system at what speed the CPU is running, or to turn a power-saving feature on or off. A **dual inline package (DIP) switch** is similar to a light switch and is on or off depending on the direction in which the small switch is set. Many motherboards have at least one, often several, jumpers and perhaps a single bank of DIP switches (see Figure 1-37), although the trend is to include most setup information in CMOS rather than to have a jumper or switch on the board that has to be mechanically set.

NOTE

Even though a computer has many CMOS chips, the term "CMOS chip" has come to mean the one chip on the motherboard that holds the configuration or setup information. If you hear someone ask: "What does CMOS say?" or "Let's change CMOS," the person is talking about the configuration or setup information stored on this one CMOS chip. The program to change CMOS setup is stored in the ROM BIOS chip and can be accessed during startup.

VIDEO

Configuring a
Motherboard

Bank of jumpers

Jumper cover

Figure 1-36   Setup information about the motherboard can be stored by setting a jumper on (closed) or off (open). A jumper is closed if the cover is in place, connecting the two pins that make up the jumper; a jumper is open if the cover is not in place.

Figure 1-37   A motherboard can use a bank of DIP switches for configuration settings

CHAPTER SUMMARY

▶ A computer requires both hardware and software to work.

▶ The four basic functions of the microcomputer are input, output, processing, and storage of data.

▶ Data and instructions are stored in a computer in binary form, which uses only two states for data—on and off, or 1 and 0—which are called bits. Eight bits equal one byte.

▶ The four most popular input/output devices are the printer, monitor, mouse, and keyboard.

▶ The most important component inside the computer case is the motherboard, also called the main board or system board. It contains the most important microchip inside the case, the central processing unit (CPU), a microprocessor or processor, as well as access to other circuit boards and peripheral devices. All communications between the CPU and other devices must pass through the motherboard.

▶ A ROM BIOS microchip is a hybrid of hardware and software containing programming embedded into the chip. These chips are called firmware.

▶ Most microchips are manufactured using CMOS (complementary metal-oxide semiconductor) technology.

▶ Each hardware device needs a method to communicate with the CPU, software to control it, and electricity to power it.

▶ Devices outside the computer case connect to the motherboard through ports on the case. Common ports are serial, parallel, USB, game, keyboard, and mouse ports.

▶ A circuit board inserted in an expansion slot on the motherboard can provide an interface between the motherboard and a peripheral device, or can itself be a peripheral. (An example is an internal modem.)

▶ The chip set on a motherboard controls most activities on the motherboard and includes several device controllers, including the USB controller, memory controller, IDE controller, and so forth.

▶ Primary storage, called memory or RAM, is temporary storage the CPU uses to hold data and instructions while it is processing both.

▶ RAM is stored on single chips, SIMMs, DIMMs, and RIMMs.

▶ Secondary storage is slower than primary storage, but it is permanent storage. Some examples of secondary storage devices are hard drives, CD-ROM drives, DVD drives, Zip drives, and floppy drives.

▶ Most hard drives, CD-ROM drives, and DVD drives use EIDE (Enhanced Integrated Drive Electronics) technology, which can accommodate up to four EIDE devices on one system.

▶ The system clock is used to synchronize activity on the motherboard. The clock sends continuous pulses over the bus that different components use to control the pace of activity.

▶ A motherboard has several buses, including the system bus, the PCI bus, the AGP bus, and the ISA bus.

▶ The frequency of activity on a motherboard is measured in megahertz (MHz), or one million cycles per second. The CPU operates at a much higher frequency than other components in the system, and its activity is measured in gigahertz (GHz), or one billion cycles per second.

▶ The power supply inside the computer case supplies electricity to components both inside and outside the case. Some components external to the case get power from their own electrical cables.

▶ ROM BIOS on a motherboard holds the basic software needed to start a PC and begin the process of loading an operating system. Most ROM chips are flash ROM, meaning that these programs can be updated without exchanging the chip.

▶ The CMOS chip on a PC's motherboard stores setup, or configuration, information. This information can also be set by means of jumpers and DIP switches. When power to the PC is turned off, a battery on the motherboard supplies power to the CMOS chip.

KEY TERMS

For explanations of key terms, see the Glossary near the end of the book.

Advanced Configuration and
    Power Interface (ACPI)
Advanced Power Management
    (APM)
basic input/output system (BIOS)
binary number system
bit
bus
byte
cards
central processing unit (CPU)
chip set
circuit board
clock speed
CMOS configuration chip
CMOS RAM chip
CMOS setup
CMOS setup chip
complementary metal-oxide
    semiconductor (CMOS)
data bus
data path size
dual inline memory module
    (DIMM)
dual inline package (DIP) switch

expansion card
expansion slot
firmware
flash ROM
front side bus (FSB)
gigahertz (GHz)
hard copy
hard drive
hardware
hertz (Hz)
host bus
jumper
keyboard
main board
megahertz (MHz)
memory
microprocessor
monitor
motherboard
mouse
nonvolatile
parallel port
peripheral device
Plug and Play (PnP)
port

processor
power supply
primary storage
printer
processor
program
protocol
random access memory (RAM)
read-only memory (ROM)
RIMM
secondary storage
serial port
single inline memory module
    (SIMM)
software
startup BIOS
system BIOS
system board
system bus
system clock
trace
universal serial bus (USB) port
video card
volatile

REVIEWING THE BASICS

1. Why is all data stored in a computer in binary form?

2. What are the four primary functions of hardware?

3. What three things do electronic hardware devices need in order to function?

4. How many bits are in a byte?

5. What is the purpose of an expansion slot on a motherboard?

6. Which component on the motherboard is used primarily for processing?

7. Name three CPU manufacturers.

8. What technology is most often used today to manufacture microchips?

9. What are two other names for the system bus?

10. What are two other names for the motherboard?

11. List three types of ports that are often found coming directly off the motherboard to be used by external devices.

12. List three kinds of memory modules.

13. What is the difference between volatile and nonvolatile memory?

14. What technology provides for up to four devices on a system, including the hard drive as one of those devices?

15. What is the size of the data path on most system buses today?

16. What is the measurement of frequency of a system bus and CPU? Which is faster, the system bus or the CPU?

17. Name four types of buses that are likely to be on a motherboard today.

18. A power supply receives 120 volts of _____ power from a wall outlet and converts it to 3.3, 5, and 12 volts of _____ power.

19. ROM BIOS chips that can be upgraded without replacing the chips are called _____.

20. List three ways that configuration information can be stored on a motherboard.

THINKING CRITICALLY

1. When selecting secondary storage devices for a new desktop PC, which is more important, a CD-ROM drive or a floppy drive? Why?

2. Based on what you have learned in this chapter, when working on a Word document, why is it important to save your work often? Explain your answer in terms of primary storage and secondary storage.

3. Most buses are 16, 32, 64, or 128 bits wide. Why do you think these bus widths are multiples of eight?

4. Why do you think the trend is to store configuration information on a motherboard in CMOS setup rather than by using jumpers or switches?

5. Why would it be difficult to install four hard drives, one CD-ROM drive, and one DVD drive in a single system?

HANDS-ON PROJECTS

PROJECT 1-1: Identifying Ports on Your Computer

Look at the back of your home or lab computer and make a diagram showing the ports. Label all the ports in the diagram and note which ones are used and which are not used.

PROJECT 1-2: Research on the Internet

The Internet is an incredibly rich source of information about computer hardware and software. Answer these questions, using the Internet as your source:

1. What is the frequency of the fastest CPU for a desktop computer that you can find advertised on the Web? Print the Web page showing the CPU and its frequency.

2. Print a Web page advertising a motherboard. What is the frequency of the system bus?

3. Print a Web page advertising computer memory. How much RAM is on one module?

4. Print the Web page of any hardware device that uses a USB port.

PROJECT 1-3: Identifying Motherboard Components

✔ **A+ EXAM TIP**

The A+ Core exam expects you to be able to recognize components on a mother-board diagram similar to the one in Figure 1-38.

Copy the diagram in Figure 1-38 and label as many of the components on the diagram as you can, using the photograph in Figure 1-8 and other photographs in the chapter. This exercise is very important for visual recognition of motherboard components and for helping you identify these components in motherboard documentation.

Figure 1-38 A motherboard diagram with labels missing

PROJECT 1-4: Examining Your Computer

What type of CPU does your computer have, and how much memory is installed? To answer these questions, using Windows XP, click **Start**, right-click **My Computer**, and select **Properties** on the shortcut menu. The System Properties dialog box appears. Click the **General** tab. (Using Windows 2000 or Windows 98, right-click the **My Computer** icon on your desktop and select **Properties** on the shortcut menu.) The CPU information is listed in this dialog box. Print a screen shot of this dialog box. One quick and easy way to get a hard copy of a screen is to use Paint. Follow these directions to print the screen:

1. Press the **PrintScrn** (print screen) key. This puts the screen capture on your Windows Clipboard.

2. Open Paint. Click **Start, All Programs, Accessories, Paint**.

3. Click **Edit, Paste** to put the contents of the Clipboard into Paint. If necessary, click **Yes** to the dialog box that pops up to confirm the paste.

4. To print the page, click **File, Print**.

Note that you can capture just the active window, instead of the entire screen, by pressing Alt+PrintScrn instead of PrintScrn.

PROJECT 1-5: **Learning to Think in Binary and Hex**

Use Appendices B and C to answer these questions:

1. What is the ASCII code in binary and in decimal for a lowercase z?
2. What is the ASCII code in binary and in decimal for a period?
3. Write the binary numbers from 1 to 20.
4. What is the largest decimal number that can be stored using 8 bits, or 1 byte?
5. Write the hex numbers from 1 to 20.
6. Convert 43 to binary. Convert 43 to hex.
7. What is 1101 1001 in decimal? In hex?

How Hardware and Software Work Together

In this chapter, you will learn:

- About operating systems, what they are, and what they do
- How an OS interfaces with users, applications, and hardware
- How system resources help hardware and software communicate

Computer systems contain both hardware and software, and computer technicians must understand how they work together. Although the physical hardware is the visible part of a computer system, the software is the intelligence of the system that enables the hardware components to work. In the last chapter, you were introduced to the different hardware devices. In this chapter, you'll learn about the different operating systems, what they do, and how they work to control several of the more significant hardware devices. You'll also see how an OS provides the interface that users and applications need to command and use hardware devices.

Introducing Operating Systems

An **operating system (OS)** is software that controls a computer. It manages hardware, runs applications, provides an interface for users, and stores, retrieves, and manipulates files. In general, an operating system acts as the middleman between applications and hardware (see Figure 2-1).

Figure 2-1   Users and applications depend on the OS to relate to all hardware components

Several applications might be installed on a computer to meet various user needs, but it only needs one operating system. The following operating systems are each designed to support different types of hardware systems and user needs:

- *DOS.* DOS, the disk OS, was the first OS among IBM computers and IBM-compatible computers. Today, DOS is outdated as a viable option for a desktop computer operating system. DOS was the OS used by early versions of Windows, including Windows 3.1 and Windows 3.11 collectively referred to as Windows 3.x. Windows 3.x did not perform OS functions, but simply served as a user-friendly intermediate program between DOS, applications, and the user.
- *Windows 9x/Me.* Early OSs that use a DOS core are Windows 95, Windows 98, and Windows Me, collectively called Windows 9x or Windows 9x/Me. These are true operating systems with a DOS core and a user-friendly interface. Of the three OSs, Windows 98 is the most popular.
- *Windows NT, Windows 2000, and Windows XP.* Windows NT came in two versions: Windows NT Workstation for workstations, and Windows NT Server to control a network. Windows 2000 is an upgrade of Windows NT, and Windows XP is an upgrade of Windows 2000. Windows 2000 also came in several versions. Windows 2000 Professional is currently the most popular OS for the corporate desktop. Windows 2000 Server, Advanced Server, and Datacenter

2

Server are network server OSs. Windows XP also currently comes in several versions. The two most popular versions for desktop PCs are Windows XP Home and Windows XP Professional.

- *Windows Server 2003.* Windows Server 2003 is a suite of Microsoft operating systems not intended to be used for a personal computer and not covered in this book.
- *Unix.* Unix is a popular OS used to control networks and to support applications used on the Internet.
- *Linux.* Linux is a scaled-down version of Unix that is provided, in basic form, free of charge; it includes open access to the programming code of the OS. It is often used for server applications.
- *OS/2.* OS/2, developed by IBM and Microsoft, is less common for home desktop PCs, but is used in certain types of networks. Microsoft developed Windows NT using some of the core components of OS/2 and intended it to replace OS/2.
- *Mac OS.* Mac OS is available only for Apple Macintosh computers and is often used for graphics applications and in educational settings.

Every operating system has two main internal components: the shell and the kernel (see Figure 2-2). A **shell** is the portion of the OS that relates to the user and to applications. The shell provides a command, menu, or icon interface to the user using various interface tools such as Windows Explorer, the Control Panel, or My Computer.

Figure 2-2   Inside an operating system, different components perform various functions

An operating system needs a place to keep hardware and software configuration information, user preferences, and application settings that are used when the OS is first loaded and are accessed as needed by hardware, applications, and users. This information can be kept in a database or text files. Windows uses a database called the **registry** for most of this information. In addition, some data is kept in text files called **initialization files**, which often have an .ini or .inf file extension.

What an Operating System Does

Recall that an OS manages hardware, runs applications, provides a user interface, and manages files and folders. We now look at how an OS functions in each of these four major areas.

An OS Provides a User Interface

When a PC is first turned on, the operating system is loaded. After the OS is in control, it either automatically executes a program or turns to the user for its next instruction. If you are working with the OS, you see an interface on the monitor screen. This interface can be command-driven, menu-driven, or icon-driven.

Command-Driven Interfaces

With a command-driven interface, you type commands to tell the OS to perform operations. Computer technicians who are good typists and are very familiar with DOS-like commands often prefer this kind of OS interface. For example, to access a command-driven interface using Windows XP, click the Start button on the Windows taskbar, point to All Programs, point to Accessories, and then click Command Prompt. You will learn to use a Command Prompt window in Chapter 3.

Menu-Driven Interfaces

Some OSs allow you to choose from a list of options displayed on the screen. An example of such a menu-driven interface is Windows Explorer in Windows XP. From the drop-down menus, you can format disks, rename files, copy and delete files, and perform many other operations to manage files and storage devices (see Figure 2-3). Note that Windows Explorer uses icons as well as menus.

Icon-Driven Interfaces

Today's OSs are more likely to use an icon-driven interface than a command-driven one. With an icon-driven interface, sometimes called a **graphical user interface (GUI)**, you perform operations by selecting icons (or pictures) on the screen. When an OS is first executed, the initial screen that appears, together with its menus, commands, and icons, is called the **desktop**. Just about all OSs today offer a combination of menu and icon-driven interfaces such as Windows Explorer, shown in Figure 2-3.

Figure 2-3   A menu-driven interface: Explorer in Windows XP

An OS Manages Files and Folders

A+
OS
1.1
1.4

An operating system is responsible for storing files and folders on a secondary storage device such as a CD, floppy disk, or hard drive, using organizational methods called a **file system**. Windows uses several different file systems; the most popular are FAT and NTFS. The FAT file system is named after the **file allocation table (FAT)**, a table on a hard drive or floppy disk that tracks the locations of files on a disk. The latest version of FAT, FAT32, is a more efficient method of organization for large hard drives than FAT16 (the earlier version). The **New Technology file system (NTFS)** is supported by Windows NT/2000/XP and is designed to be used on hard drives to provide greater security and support more data than the FAT file system.

A floppy disk or hard drive is composed of **tracks**, which are concentric circles on the disk surface, shown in Figure 2-4. Each track is divided into several segments, each called a **sector**. A **cluster**, the smallest unit of space on a disk for storing data, is made up of one or more sectors. A file system, either FAT or NTFS, tracks how these clusters are used for each file stored on the disk.

✔ **A+ EXAM TIP**

The A+ OS exam expects you to know all the key terms in this section.

A+
OS
1.1
1.4

One sector

One track

Figure 2-4   A hard drive or floppy disk is divided into tracks and sectors. Several sectors make one cluster.

Files and Directories

Regardless of the file system used, every OS manages a hard drive by using directories (Windows calls these folders), subdirectories, and files. A **directory table** is a list of files and subdirectories. When a hard drive is first installed and formatted, there is a single directory table on the drive called the **root directory**. For logical drive C, the root directory is written as C:\.

A physical hard drive can be divided into logical drives, sometimes called volumes, such as drive C or drive D.

As shown in Figure 2-5, this root directory can hold files or other directories, which can have names such as C:\Tools. These directories, called **subdirectories, child directories,** or **folders,** can, in turn, have other directories listed in them. Any directory can have files and other directories listed in it, for example, C:\wp\data\myfile.txt in Figure 2-5. The C: identifies the logical drive. If a directory is on a floppy disk, either A: or B: identifies it. If a directory is on a CD or DVD, a letter such as D: or F: identifies it. When you refer to the drive and directories pointing to the location of the file, as in C:\wp\data\myfile.txt, the drive and directories are called the **path** to the file. The first part of the file before the period is called the **filename** (myfile), and the part after the period is called the **file extension** (txt), which, for Windows and DOS, always has three characters or fewer. The file extension identifies the file type, such as .doc for Microsoft Word document files or .xls for Microsoft Excel spreadsheet files.

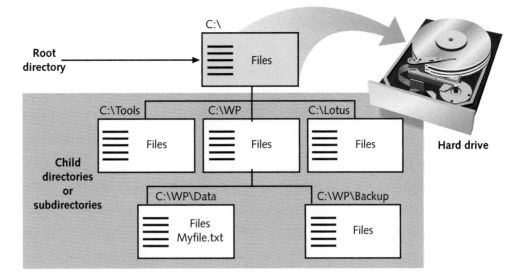

Figure 2-5 A hard drive is organized into groups of files stored in directories. The first directory is called the root directory. All directories can have child directories or subdirectories. Under Windows, a directory is called a folder.

Partitions and Logical Drives on a Hard Drive

A hard drive is organized into one or more **partitions**. A partition can be a primary partition or an extended partition (see Figure 2-6). A primary partition can have one logical drive and an extended partition can have one or more logical drives. For example, a hard drive can have one primary partition with one logical drive in it called drive C:, and one extended partition that can have one or more logical drives such as drive D: and drive E:. Each **logical drive**, sometimes called a **volume**, is formatted using its own file system. For example, if a hard drive is divided into two logical drives, drive C: might be formatted using the FAT32 file system and drive D: might use the NTFS file system. Each logical drive has its own root directory and subdirectories. You will learn more about logical drives and volumes in Chapter 8.

Figure 2-6 A hard drive is divided and organized at several levels

An OS Manages Applications

An operating system is responsible for managing all other software on the PC, including installing and running applications. An application depends on an OS to provide access to hardware resources, manage its data in memory and in secondary storage, and perform many other background tasks. For example, consider a situation in which Windows XP loads and executes an application. The application cannot run or even load itself without Windows XP, much as a document cannot be edited without a word-processing program. Windows XP stays available to the application for the entire time the application is running. The application passes certain functions to Windows XP, such as reading from a CD-ROM or printing.

An application written to work with one OS, such as Windows XP, does not necessarily work with another, such as a Macintosh system, with some exceptions. For instance, Windows 9x/Me is written so that any application designed to work with DOS or Windows 3.x also works with Windows 9x/Me, an early selling point for Windows 9x/Me. However, to take full advantage of an operating system's power and an application's power, buy application software written specifically for your OS.

Application software is downloaded from the Internet or comes written on CD-ROMs or floppy disks; usually it must be installed on a hard drive in order to run. During the installation, the install program creates folders on the hard drive and copies files to them. For Windows, it also makes entries in the Windows registry, and it can place icons on the desktop and add entries to the Start menu. Because the install program does all the work for you, installing a software package usually is very easy. Installing software is covered in later chapters.

Loading Application Software Using the Windows Desktop

Once an application is installed, Windows NT/2000/XP and Windows 9x/Me offer four ways to execute, or load, software:

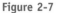
A+ EXAM TIP

The A+ OS exam often expects you to know more than one way to do something. Knowing the four ways to load an application is a good example.

- *Use a shortcut icon.* Place a shortcut icon directly on the desktop for the applications you use often and want to get to quickly. These shortcuts contain the command line used to execute the application. To view this command line, right-click an application icon on the desktop to open a shortcut menu. On the shortcut menu, select Properties. The icon's Properties dialogbox appears (see Figure 2-7). In this dialog box, you can view the complete command line that the icon represents. Chapter 12 explains how to create shortcuts for Windows.
- *Use the Start menu.* Click the Start button, select Programs (or All Programs in Windows XP), and then select the program from the list of installed software.
- *Use the Run command.* Click the Start button, and then click Run to display the Run dialog box (see Figure 2-8). In this dialog box, enter a command line or click Browse to search for a program file to execute.

Figure 2-7   Windows has icons on the desktop that point to program files on the hard drive

Command line

Use Browse to search for
a program file

Figure 2-8 The Windows Run dialog box allows you to enter DOS-like commands

- *Use Windows Explorer or My Computer.* Execute a program or launch an application file by double-clicking the filename in Windows Explorer or My Computer.

APPLYING CONCEPTS

Practice the last three ways listed to load an application. Use Microsoft Paint as your sample application. The program file is Mspaint.exe. Execute the application by using the Start menu, using the Run dialog box, and using Windows Explorer.

Real (16-Bit), Protected (32-Bit), and 64-Bit Operating Modes

Most CPUs operate in two modes: 16-bit or 32-bit, which are sometimes called real mode and protected mode. There are several differences between these two modes, but fundamentally, in 16-bit mode, or **real mode**, the CPU processes 16 bits of data at one time, and in 32-bit mode, or **protected mode**, it processes 32 bits at a time.

NOTE

Three high-end processors that operate in 64-bit mode are the Intel Itanium, the AMD Opteron, and the AMD Athlon 64. Windows XP 64-bit Edition is designed to use this type of processor.

In real mode, an application has complete access to all hardware resources, but in protected mode, the OS controls how an application can access hardware. In protected mode, more than one program can run at the same time, which is a type of **multitasking**. In protected mode, the OS provides to each program a limited and controlled access to hardware resources. Here lies the meaning behind the two terms, real and protected. Real mode means that the software has "real" access to the hardware; protected mode means that more than one program can be running, and each one is "protected" from other programs accessing its hardware resources.

Even after protected mode became available, hardware and software needed to be backward-compatible (able to support older technology), so today's CPUs and operating systems still support real mode. In fact, the CPU starts in real mode and must be told to switch to protected mode. For this reason, an OS starts in real mode and commands the CPU to switch to protected mode before allowing user interaction or loading an application. DOS and the MS-DOS mode of Windows 9x/Me operate in real mode. Windows 9x/Me and Windows NT/2000/XP start in real mode and then switch to protected mode. In protected mode, the OS allots CPU time to an application for a specified period and then preempts the processing to give the CPU to another application, in a process called **preemptive multitasking**. The end result is that the computer appears to be multitasking when it really is not. Windows 95 was the first version of Windows to provide preemptive multitasking.

16-Bit, 32-Bit, and 64-Bit Software   Software written for Windows 3.x are called 16-bit Windows software, and software programs written for Windows XP 64-bit Edition are called 64-bit programs. Data access is 16 bits at a time, and each program is written so that it should not infringe on the resources of other programs that might be running. Software programs written for Windows NT/2000/XP and Windows 9x/Me are called 32-bit programs.

Nearly all software written today is 32-bit or 64-bit (for the Itaniums, Opterons, and Athlon 64) although 16-bit software still exists, and you must know how to support it in a Windows environment. This 16-bit, 32-bit, and 64-bit software can be applications or device drivers. The next section explains what a device driver is, and you will learn more about supporting 16-bit applications and drivers in Chapter 12.

An OS Manages Hardware

An operating system is responsible for communicating with hardware, but the OS does not relate directly to the hardware. Rather, the OS uses device drivers or the BIOS to interface with hardware. Figure 2-9 shows these relationships. Therefore, most PC software falls into three categories:

- Device drivers or the BIOS
- Operating system
- Application software

Device drivers are small programs stored on the hard drive that tell the computer how to communicate with a specific hardware device such as a printer, network card, or modem. These drivers are installed on the hard drive when the device is first installed.

Recall from Chapter 1 that the basic input/output system (BIOS) on the motherboard is hard-coded or permanently coded into a computer chip called the firmware or ROM BIOS chip. BIOS programs fall into three categories: programs to control I/O devices (called **system BIOS**), programs to control the startup of a computer (called **startup BIOS**), and a program to change the setup information stored in CMOS (called **CMOS setup**). Next we look at how an OS uses device drivers and the BIOS to manage hardware.

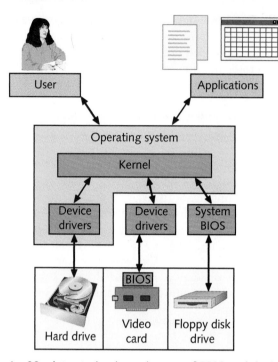

Figure 2-9   An OS relates to hardware by way of BIOS and device drivers

How an OS Uses Device Drivers

Device drivers are software designed to interface with specific hardware devices. They are stored on the hard drive and installed when the OS is first installed or when new hardware is added to a system. The OS provides some device drivers, and the manufacturer of the specific hardware device with which they are designed to interface provides others. In either case, unlike BIOS, device drivers are usually written for a particular OS and might need to be rewritten for use with another.

When you purchase a printer, DVD drive, Zip drive, digital camera, scanner, or other hardware device, bundled with the device is a set of floppy disks or CDs that contain the device drivers (see Figure 2-10). You must install these device drivers under the operating system so it will have the necessary software to control the device. In most cases, you install the device and then install the device drivers. There are a few exceptions, such as a digital camera using a USB port to download pictures. Most often in this case, you install the software to drive the digital camera before you plug in the camera.

2

VIDEO
Device with
Bundled
Software

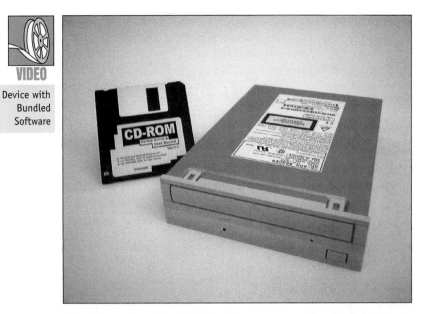

Figure 2-10   A device such as this CD-ROM drive comes packaged with its device drivers stored on a floppy disk or other media. Alternately, you can use device drivers built into the OS.

NOTE   Device drivers come from a number of sources. Some come with and are part of the operating system, some come with hardware devices when they are purchased, and some are provided for downloading over the Internet from a device manufacturer's Web site.

There are three kinds of device drivers: 16-bit real-mode drivers, 32-bit protected-mode drivers, and 64-bit drivers. Windows 95 and Windows 98 support 16-bit and 32-bit drivers. Windows Me, Windows NT/2000, Windows XP Home, and Windows XP Professional use only 32-bit drivers. Windows XP 64-bit Edition only uses 64-bit drivers. Windows 9x/Me and Windows 2000/XP provide hundreds of 32-bit drivers for many different kinds of devices, and device manufacturers also provide their own 16-bit, 32-bit, and 64-bit drivers, which come bundled with the device or can be downloaded from the device manufacturer's Web site.

Device Drivers Under Windows 2000/XP   Before installing a new hardware device on a Windows 2000/XP system, always check the **hardware compatibility list (HCL)** to determine if a driver will work under Windows 2000/XP. Go to this Microsoft Web site and search for your device:
www.microsoft.com/whdc/hcl/search.mspx

Windows 2000/XP and Windows 9x/Me keep information about 32-bit drivers in the Windows registry, a database of hardware and software settings, Windows configuration settings, user parameters, and application settings.

Sometimes, to address bugs, make improvements, or add features, manufacturers release device drivers that are more recent than those included with Windows or bundled with the device. Whenever possible, it is best to use the latest driver available for a device provided by the device manufacturer. You can usually download these updated drivers from the manufacturer's Web site. You will learn how to install, update, and troubleshoot drivers in later chapters.

APPLYING CONCEPTS

Suppose you have just borrowed an HP 995c Deskjet printer from a friend, but you forgot to borrow the CD with the printer drivers on it. You can go to the Hewlett-Packard Web site (*www.hp.com*), download the drivers to a folder on your PC, and install the driver under Windows. Figure 2-11 shows you a Web page from the site listing downloadable drivers for inkjet printers. Search the HP site and find the driver for your HP 995c borrowed printer.

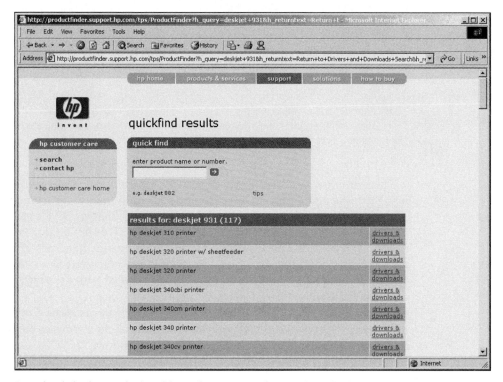

Figure 2-11   Download the latest device drivers from a manufacturer's Web site

Device Drivers Under Windows 9x/Me   Windows 9x/Me comes with 32-bit drivers for hundreds of hardware devices. However, Windows does not provide drivers for all older devices, so a system might sometimes need to use an older 16-bit real-mode device

2

driver. These 16-bit drivers are loaded by entries in the **Config.sys, Autoexec.bat,** and **System.ini** files, text files used to configure DOS and Windows 3.x that Windows 95 and Windows 98 support for backward compatibility. In Chapter 12, you will learn how to install 32-bit and 16-bit drivers under Windows 95/98.

Under DOS, a program such as a device driver that stays in memory until the CPU needs it is called a **terminate-and-stay-resident (TSR)** program. The term is seldom used today, except when talking about real-mode programs.

How an OS Uses System BIOS to Manage Devices

The OS communicates with simple devices, such as floppy drives or keyboards, through system BIOS. In addition, system BIOS can be used to access the hard drive. An OS has a choice of using system BIOS or device drivers to access a device. Most often it uses device drivers because they are faster. The trend today is to use device drivers rather than the BIOS to manage devices.

There is a good way to determine whether the BIOS or a device driver is controlling a device. If the device is configured using CMOS setup, most likely system BIOS controls it. If the device is configured using the OS, most likely a driver controls it. Sometimes you can use the Windows System Information or Device Manager utilities to find out the name of a driver controlling a device.

For example, in Figure 2-12, the setup main menu for an Award BIOS system lets you configure, or set, the system date and time, the Supervisor Password (power-on password), floppy disk drives, the hard drive, and the keyboard. Figure 2-13 shows another setup window for this same BIOS that can configure serial ports, an infrared port, and a parallel port. System BIOS can control all these devices. On the other hand, there is no setup window in this BIOS to control the DVD drive or Zip drive installed on this system. The BIOS is not aware of these devices; this means they are controlled by device drivers.

CMOS setup windows are accessed during startup. A system displays a message at the bottom of the screen saying something like, "Press Del to enter setup." Pressing the indicated key launches a program stored on the ROM BIOS microchip to change the contents of CMOS RAM. This BIOS setup program provides windows like those in Figures 2-12 and 2-13.

```
                        Award BIOS Setup Utility

        Main      Advanced   Power      Boot     Exit

     ┌─────────────────────────────────────────┬─────────────────────────┐
     │ System Time            [11:42:09]        │    Item Specific Help   │
     │ System Date            [04/04/2000]      │                         │
     │ Legacy Diskette A      [1.44M, 3.5 in.]  │ <Enter> to select field;│
     │ Legacy Diskette B      [None]            │ <+>, <Ð> to change value│
     │ Floppy 3 Mode Support  [Disabled]        │                         │
     │                                          │                         │
     │ ▶Primary Master        [Auto]            │                         │
     │ ▶Primary Slave         [Auto]            │                         │
     │ ▶Secondary Master      [Auto]            │                         │
     │ ▶Secondary Slave       [Auto]            │                         │
     │ ▶Keyboard Features                       │                         │
     │                                          │                         │
     │ Language               [English]         │                         │
     │ Supervisor Password    [Disabled]        │                         │
     │ User Password          [Disabled]        │                         │
     │ Halt On                [All Errors]      │                         │
     │ Installed Memory       128MB             │                         │
     └──────────────────────────────────────────────────────────────────┘

    F1   Help  ↑↓ Select Item  Ð/+  Change Values   F5   Setup Defaults
    ESC  Exit  ⇄ Select Menu  Enter  Select Sub Menu  F10  Save and Exit
```

Figure 2-12 Use the BIOS setup main menu for Award BIOS to configure some of the devices controlled by system BIOS

Recall that the system BIOS is stored in ROM. Because access to RAM is faster than access to ROM, at startup a system might copy the system BIOS from ROM to RAM in order to improve performance. This practice is called **shadowing ROM**, or just **shadow RAM**. Because the system BIOS is not used often, if CMOS setup gives you the option, you might want to disable shadow RAM in order to conserve RAM.

NOTE

Sometimes a system becomes unstable (crashes at unexpected times). If your CMOS setup gives you the option, one thing you can try to stabilize the system is to disable shadow RAM.

An OS uses BIOS or device drivers to manage hardware devices. The BIOS or driver communicates with a device by way of system resources on the motherboard. We next look at these resources and how they work.

```
                    Award BIOS Setup Utility
         ┌─────────────┐
         │  Advanced   │
─────────┴─────────────┴─────────────────────────────────────────

┌─────────────────────────────────────────────┬──────────────────────┐
│        I/O Device Configuration              │  Item Specific Help  │
├─────────────────────────────────────────────┼──────────────────────┤
│  Onboard FDC Swap A & B       [No Swap]      │                      │
│  Floppy Disk Access Control   [R/W]          │ <Enter> to select if │
│                                              │ switch drive letter  │
│  Onboard Serial Port 1:       [3F8H/IRQ4]    │ assignments or not.  │
│  Onboard Serial Port 2:       [2F8H/IRQ3]    │                      │
│  UART2 Use Infrared           [Disabled]     │                      │
│                                              │                      │
│  Onboard Parallel Port:       [378H/IRQ7]    │                      │
│  Parallel Port Mode:          [ECP + EPP]    │                      │
│  ECP DMA Select:              [3]            │                      │
│                                              │                      │
│                                              │                      │
│                                              │                      │
│                                              │                      │
│                                              │                      │
└─────────────────────────────────────────────┴──────────────────────┘

  F1   Help  ↑↓  Select Item  Ð/+   Change Values   F5   Setup Defaults
  ESC  Exit  ⇄   Select Menu   Enter Select Sub Menu  F10  Save and Exit
```

Figure 2-13   Use this Award BIOS setup window to configure several I/O devices, including the serial, parallel, and infrared ports

System Resources

A+
CORE
1.4

A **system resource** is a tool used by either hardware or software to communicate with the other. When BIOS or a driver wants to send data to a device (such as when you save a file to the hard drive), or when the device needs attention (such as when you press a key on the keyboard), the device or software uses system resources to communicate. There are four types of system resources: memory addresses, I/O addresses, interrupt request numbers (IRQs), and direct memory access (DMA) channels. Table 2-1 lists these system resources used by software and hardware, and defines each.

As Table 2-1 explains, all four resources are used for communication between hardware and software. Hardware devices signal the CPU for attention using an IRQ. Software addresses a device by one of its I/O addresses. Software looks at memory as a hardware device and addresses it with memory addresses, and DMA channels pass data back and forth between a hardware device and memory.

A+
CORE
1.4

System Resource	Definition
IRQ	A line of a motherboard bus that a hardware device can use to signal the CPU that the device needs attention. Some lines have a higher priority for attention than others. Each IRQ line is assigned a number (0 to 15) to identify it.
I/O addresses	Numbers assigned to hardware devices that software uses to send a command to a device. Each device "listens" for these numbers and responds to the ones assigned to it. I/O addresses are communicated on the address bus.
Memory addresses	Numbers assigned to physical memory located either in RAM or ROM chips. Software can access this memory by using these addresses. Memory addresses are communicated on the address bus.
DMA channel	A number designating a channel on which the device can pass data to memory without involving the CPU. Think of a DMA channel as a shortcut for data moving to and from the device and memory.

Table 2-1   System resources used by software and hardware

All four system resources depend on certain lines on a bus on the motherboard (see Figure 2-14). A bus such as the system bus has three components: the data bus carries data, the address bus communicates addresses (both memory addresses and I/O addresses), and the control bus controls communication (IRQs and DMA channels are controlled by this portion of the bus). Let's turn our attention to a more detailed description of the four resources and how they work.

Figure 2-14   A bus consists of a data bus, an address bus, and a control bus

Interrupt Request Number (IRQ)

When a hardware device needs the CPU to do something—for instance, when the keyboard needs the CPU to process a keystroke after a key has been pressed—the device needs a way to get the CPU's attention, and the CPU must know what to do once it turns its attention to the device. These interruptions to the CPU are called **hardware interrupts,** and the device initiates an interrupt by placing voltage on the designated **interrupt request (IRQ) line** assigned to it. This voltage on the line serves as a signal to the CPU that the device has a request that needs processing. Often, a hardware device that needs attention from the CPU is referred to as "needing servicing." Interrupts initiate many processes that the CPU carries out, and these processes are said to be "interrupt-driven."

Early motherboards had eight IRQ lines. Table 2-2 lists common uses for these eight IRQs. IRQ 2 was reserved in the early days of PCs because it was intended to be used as part of a link to mainframe computers, and IRQs 0 and 1 are always in use by the system clock and keyboard. Thus, only five IRQs were available for devices, and each device had to have its own IRQ. This made it difficult for more than five devices to be connected to a PC at any one time.

IRQ	Device
0	System timer (system clock)
1	Keyboard controller
2	Reserved (not used)
3	COM2
4	COM1
5	LPT2
6	Floppy drive controller
7	LPT1

Table 2-2   Common assignments for the first eight IRQs

✔ **A+ EXAM TIP**

The A+ Core exam expects you to have Table 2-2 memorized.

In Table 2-2, notice the COM and LPT assignments. COM1 and COM2 are preconfigured assignments that can be made to serial devices such as modems, and LPT1 and LPT2 are preconfigured assignments that can be made to parallel devices such as printers. For example, rather than being assigned an IRQ and some I/O addresses, the modem uses the assignments previously made to COM2, which makes it easier to configure the modem and to avoid conflicts with other devices that also need an IRQ and some I/O addresses. You will learn more about COM and LPT assignments in Chapter 10.

A+
CORE
1.4

On motherboards, part of the chip set called the interrupt controller manages the IRQs for the CPU. The CPU actually doesn't know which IRQ is "up" because the interrupt controller manages that. If more than one IRQ is up at the same time, the interrupt controller selects the IRQ that has the lowest value to process first. For example, if a user presses a key on the keyboard at the same time that she moves the mouse configured to use COM1, the keystroke is processed before the mouse action, because the keyboard is using IRQ 1 and the mouse on COM1 is using IRQ 4. Think of the interrupt controller as the "inside man" with the CPU. All devices wait outside the door for the controller to let the CPU know what they need.

The interrupt controller on early motherboards was designed to handle only eight different IRQs. In order to accommodate the need for more devices, a second group of IRQs was later added (IRQs 8 through 15), and a second interrupt controller was added to manage these new IRQs.

This second controller did not have access to the CPU, so it had to communicate with the CPU through the first controller (see Figure 2-15). To signal the first controller, the second controller used one of the first controller's IRQ values (IRQ 2). These last eight IRQs plug into the system using IRQ 2. Because of this, the IRQ priority level became: 0, 1, (8, 9, 10, 11, 12, 13, 14, 15), 3, 4, 5, 6, 7.

Figure 2-15   The second IRQ controller uses IRQ 2 to signal the first IRQ controller

A+
CORE
1.4
OS
1.1
1.5

To see how the IRQs are assigned on your computer, use MSD for DOS and Device Manager for Windows 2000/XP and Windows 9x/Me. (Windows NT does not have Device Manager.) For Windows XP, click Start, right-click My Computer, and select Properties on the shortcut menu. For Windows 2000, right-click My Computer on the desktop and select Properties on the shortcut menu. The System Properties dialog box appears. Click the Hardware tab and then click the Device Manager button. (For Windows XP, see Figure 2-16.) On the menu, click View, and then click Resources by Type, if necessary. Click the plus sign next to Interrupt request (IRQ) to open the list of assigned IRQs. Notice in the figure that IRQs 9 and 11 are each being shared by two devices.

To see current assignments in Windows 9x/Me, click Start, point to Settings, click Control Panel, and double-click System. Click the Device Manager tab, select Computer, and then click Properties. Figure 2-17 shows the Computer Properties dialog box. Notice that IRQ 2 is assigned to the programmable interrupt controller because it is being used to manage IRQs 8 through 15.

Figure 2-16   Use Device Manager to see how your system is using IRQs and other system resources

With interrupts, the hardware device or the software initiates communication by sending a signal to the CPU, but a device can be serviced in another way, called polling. With **polling**, software that is constantly running has the CPU periodically check the hardware device to see if it needs service. Not very many devices use polling as the method of communication; most hardware devices use interrupts. A joystick is one example of a device that does use polling. Software written to manage a joystick has the CPU check the joystick periodically to see if the device has data to communicate, which is why a joystick does not need an IRQ to work.

NOTE

Sharing IRQs is not possible with ISA devices on the ISA bus. However, newer buses are designed to allow more than one device to share an IRQ. In Chapter 5, you will see how the PCI and USB buses do this.

Figure 2-17   Windows 9x/Me Device Manager shows current assignments for system resources

Memory Addresses

A+
CORE
1.4

✔ **A+ EXAM TIP**

Older 16-bit device drivers required a specified range of memory addresses, but newer 32-bit drivers don't care what memory addresses they use. When considering the system resources used by devices, memory addresses are no longer considered. This is why the A+ Core exam covers only three system resources: IRQs, I/O addresses, and DMA channels.

An operating system relates to memory as a long list of cells that it can use to hold data and instructions, somewhat like a one-dimensional spreadsheet. Each memory location or cell is assigned a number beginning with zero. These number assignments are made when the OS is first loaded and are called **memory addresses**. Think of a memory address as a seat number in a theater (see Figure 2-18). Each seat is assigned a number regardless of whether someone is sitting in it. The person sitting in a seat can be data or instructions, and the OS does not refer to the person by name but only by the seat number. For example, the OS might say, "I want to print the data in memory addresses 500 through 650."

Figure 2-18 Memory addresses are assigned to each location in memory, and these locations can store data or instructions

NOTE

Windows offers a calculator that can quickly convert numbers in binary, digital, and hexadecimal. Enter a number in one number system, and then click another number system to make the conversion. To access the calculator in Windows NT/2000/XP or Windows 9x/Me, click Start, Programs, Accessories, and then Calculator.

These addresses are most often displayed on the screen as hexadecimal (base 16 or hex) numbers in segment:offset form (for example, C800:5, which in hex is C8005 and in decimal is 819,205). For more information on the hexadecimal number system and how it applies to memory addresses, see Appendix C.

I/O Addresses

Another system resource made available to hardware devices is input/output addresses, or I/O addresses. **I/O addresses,** or **port addresses,** sometimes simply called ports, are numbers the CPU can use to access hardware devices, in much the same way it uses memory addresses to access physical memory. The address bus on the motherboard sometimes carries memory addresses and sometimes carries I/O addresses. If the address bus has been set to carry I/O addresses, then each device "listens" to this bus (see Figure 2-19). If the address belongs to it, then it responds; otherwise, it ignores the request for information. In short, the CPU "knows" a hardware device as a group of I/O addresses. If it wants to know the status of a printer or a floppy drive, for example, it places a particular I/O address on the address bus on the motherboard.

① CPU turns up signal on bus that says, "I/O addresses are on the address line" ② All I/O device controllers listen for their addresses ③ CPU transmits an I/O address ④ The device that "owns" the address responds

Figure 2-19   I/O address lines on a bus work much like an old telephone party line; all devices "hear" the addresses, but only one responds

A+
CORE
1.4

✔ A+ EXAM TIP

The A+ Core exam expects you to memorize the first I/O address in the I/O address range for the more significant devices.

Table 2-3 lists a few common assignments for I/O addresses. Because these addresses are usually written as hex numbers, you sometimes see them written with 0x first, such as 0x0040, or with the h last, like this: 0040h.

Because IBM made many address assignments when it manufactured the first PC in the late 1970s, common devices such as a hard drive, a floppy drive, or a keyboard use a range of predetermined I/O addresses that never change. Their BIOS is simply programmed to use these standard addresses and standard IRQs. Legacy devices (devices that use older technologies) were designed to use more than one group of addresses and IRQ, depending on how jumpers or DIP switches were set on the device. Newer devices, called Plug and Play devices, can use any I/O addresses or IRQ assigned to them during the boot process. You will learn more about this in Chapter 10.

IRQ	I/O Address	Device
0	0040-005F	System timer
1	0060-006F	Keyboard controller
2	00A0-00AF	Access to IRQs above 7
3	02F8-02FF	COM2 (covered in Chapter 10)
3	02E8-02EF	COM4 (covered in Chapter 10)
4	03F8-03FF	COM1 (covered in Chapter 10)
4	03E8-03EF	COM3 (covered in Chapter 10)
5	0278-027F	Sound card or parallel port LPT2 (covered in Chapter 10)
6	03F0-03F7	Floppy drive controller
7	0378-037F	Printer parallel port LPT1 (covered in Chapter 10)
8	0070-007F	Real-time clock
9-10		Available
11		SCSI or available
12	0238-023F	Motherboard mouse
13	00F8-00FF	Math coprocessor
14	01F0-01F7	IDE hard drive (covered in Chapters 8 and 9)
15	0170-017F	Secondary IDE hard drive or available (covered in Chapters 8 and 9)

Table 2-3   IRQs and I/O addresses for devices

2

DMA Channels

A+
CORE
1.4

Another system resource used by hardware and software is a **direct memory access (DMA) channel**, a shortcut method that lets an I/O device send data directly to memory, bypassing the CPU. A chip on the motherboard contains the DMA logic and manages the process. Earlier computers had four channels numbered 0, 1, 2, and 3. Later, channels 5, 6, and 7 were added. DMA channel 4 is used as IRQ 2 was used, to connect to the higher IRQs. In Figure 2-20, note that DMA channel 4 cascades into the lower DMA channels.

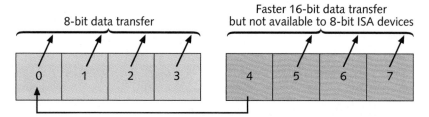

Figure 2-20   DMA channel 4 is not available for I/O use because it is used to cascade into the lower

Some devices, such as a printer, are designed to use DMA channels, and others, such as the mouse, are not. Those that use the channels might be able to use only a certain channel, say channel 3, and no other. Alternately, the BIOS might have the option of changing a DMA channel number to avoid conflicts with other devices. Conflicts occur when more than one device uses the same channel. DMA channels are not as popular as they once were, because their design makes them slower than newer methods. However, slower devices such as floppy drives, sound cards, and tape drives might still use DMA channels.

OS Tools to Examine a System

You have learned about many hardware devices, OS components, and system resources in this chapter. When installing new components or troubleshooting a system, it is important to know how to use OS tools to examine the system. This section discusses several of these tools.

Device Manager

A+
OS
1.5
3.2

Device Manager under Windows 2000/XP and Windows 9x/Me is the primary tool used to manage hardware devices. (Recall that Windows NT does not have a Device Manager.)

✔ A+ EXAM TIP

The A+ OS exam expects you to be familiar with and know how to use all three utilities discussed in this section.

To access Device Manager using Windows XP: Click Start, right-click My Computer, and then select Properties on the shortcut menu. The System Properties dialog box appears. Click the Hardware tab and then click Device Manager, or you can entire Devmgmt.msc in the Run dialog box.

To access Device Manager using Windows 2000: Right-click the My Computer icon on the desktop, select Properties on the shortcut menu, click the Hardware tab, and then click the Device Manager button, or you can entire Devmgmt.msc in the Run dialog box.

To access Device Manager using Windows 9x/Me: Right-click the My Computer icon on the desktop, select Properties on the shortcut menu, and then click the Device Manager tab.

The Device Manager dialog box for Windows XP is shown in Figure 2-21. Click a plus sign to expand the view of an item, and click a minus sign to collapse the view. To find out more information about a device, right-click the device and select Properties on the shortcut menu. You can see the Properties dialog box for the video card in Figure 2-21.

Figure 2-21   Device Manager gives you information about devices

When a device is giving problems, check the Properties dialog box of that device for information. From this window you can also update the driver for a device,

A+
OS
1.5
3.2

Earlier in the chapter you saw how to use Device Manager to view system resources. You can get a printed report of system information using Device Manager, which can be useful to document the status of a system. To print the report using Windows XP, click the printer icon on the Device Manager toolbar. There are three options for the report: System summary, Selected class or device, and All devices and system summary.

System Information

The System Information utility gives information similar to that given by Device Manager plus more. For example, it tells you the BIOS version you are using, the directory where the OS is installed, how system resources are used, information about drivers and their status, and much information about software installed on the system that is not included in Device Manager.

To run System Information using Windows 2000/XP or Windows 9x/Me: Click Start, and then click Run. In the Run dialog box, enter Msinfo32.exe, and then click OK. The System Information dialog box appears (see Figure 2-22).

Figure 2-22 Use the Windows System Information utility to examine your system

2

A+
CORE
1.5
3.2

System Information can be useful when a system is having trouble starting. Use it to get a list of drivers that loaded successfully. If you have saved the System Information report when the system was starting successfully, comparing the two reports can help identify the problem device.

Microsoft Diagnostic Utility (MSD)

DOS and Windows 9x/Me offered the Microsoft Diagnostic Utility (MSD), a utility useful for viewing information about the system, including information about memory, video, ports, device drivers, and system resources.

To load MSD using Windows 9x/Me: Click Start, click Run, enter MSD.EXE in the Run dialog box, and then click OK. The MSD window appears (see Figure 2-23). You will practice using MSD in a project at the end of this chapter.

Figure 2-23   MSD opening screen

CHAPTER SUMMARY

▶ An operating system manages hardware, runs applications, provides an interface for users, and stores, retrieves, and manipulates files.

▶ Operating systems used for desktop computers include DOS, Windows 9x/Me, Windows NT/2000/XP, Unix, a version of Unix called Linux, OS/2, and the Mac OS.

▶ Three types of software are BIOS (firmware) and device drivers, operating systems (OSs), and application software. Sometimes device drivers are considered part of the OS.

▶ Application software relates to the OS, which relates to BIOS and device drivers to control hardware.

▶ A CPU can operate in real or protected mode. In real mode, a CPU processes 16 bits at a time, and in protected mode, it processes 32 bits at a time.

▶ Device drivers are written using either 16-bit or 32-bit code. Most drivers today are 32-bit, protected-mode drivers that Windows loads from the registry.

▶ Windows 95/98 loads older 16-bit device drivers from Autoexec.bat, Config.sys, or System.ini to be backward-compatible with DOS and Windows 3.x.

▶ From the Windows desktop, you can launch programs from the Start menu, a shortcut icon on the desktop, the Run dialog box, Windows Explorer, or My Computer.

▶ Four system resources that aid the communication between hardware and software are I/O addresses, IRQs, DMA channels, and memory addresses.

▶ An IRQ is a line on a bus that a device needing service uses to alert the CPU.

▶ A DMA channel provides a shortcut for a device to send data directly to memory, bypassing the CPU.

▶ Memory addresses are hexadecimal numbers, often written in segment:offset form, assigned to RAM and ROM so that the CPU can access both.

▶ The CPU places a device's I/O address on the address bus when it wants to initiate communication with the device.

▶ Software manages memory by means of memory addresses that point to locations in RAM.

▶ COM and LPT are preconfigured assignments of system resources that a device can use. For example, COM1 is IRQ 4 and I/O addresses 03F8 through 03FF.

▶ Three Windows utilities useful for gathering information about a system are Device Manager, System Information, and Microsoft Diagnostic Utility (MSD).

KEY TERMS

For explanations of key terms, see the Glossary near the end of the book.

Autoexec.bat
child directory
cluster
CMOS setup
Config.sys
desktop
device driver
direct memory access (DMA)
   channel
directory table
file allocation table (FAT)
file extension
file system
filename
folder
graphical user interface (GUI)

hardware compatibility list (HCL)
hardware interrupt
I/O address
initialization files
interrupt request (IRQ) line
logical drive
memory address
multitasking
New Technology file system
   (NTFS)
operating system (OS)
partition
path
polling
port address
preemptive multitasking

protected mode
real mode
registry
root directory
sector
shadow RAM or shadowing ROM
shell
startup BIOS
subdirectory
system BIOS
system resource
System.ini
terminate-and-stay-resident (TSR)
track
volume

REVIEWING THE BASICS

1. List four major functions of an OS.

2. List three well-known OSs.

3. Which operating system is only used on Apple Macintosh computers?

4. What is the latest Microsoft operating system for desktop computers?

5. Which operating system often used for server applications is a scaled-down version of Unix?

6. Which file system is used by floppy disks?

7. What are two file systems used by hard drives?

8. Real mode operates using a(n) _____ -bit data path, and protected mode uses a (n) _____ -bit data path.

9. Which Microsoft operating system(s) support 16-bit device drivers or 32-bit device drivers?

10. Real mode allows programs direct access to _____, but protected mode does not.

11. List three text files that Windows 9x/Me supports for loading device drivers in order to remain backward-compatible with DOS and Windows 3.x.

12. List three types of information that are kept in the Windows registry.

13. Device drivers loaded from Config.sys run in _____ mode.

14. Device drivers loaded from Autoexec.bat run in _____ mode.

15. List four ways to launch an application from the Windows desktop.

16. List four system resources that software uses to manage hardware.

17. What is the IRQ of the system timer?

18. What IRQ does COM2 use?

19. Which DMA channel is used to cascade into the lower four DMA channels?

20. How is a hardware interrupt initiated?

21. If memory addresses are used by the CPU to access memory, then what are I/O addresses used for?

22. What is the I/O address range for the keyboard?

23. Why are DMA channels not as popular as they once were with high-speed devices?

24. Name a device that uses polling in order to be serviced by the CPU.

25. Name one Windows 2000/XP and Windows 9x/Me utility that allows you to see the IRQ assignments made to devices.

THINKING CRITICALLY

1. Name one system resource that a video card most likely will not need.

2. Is a mouse more likely to be controlled by a device driver or by system BIOS?

3. Name one device that is likely to be controlled by system BIOS.

4. If your printer is giving you trouble, what is the best way to obtain an update for the device driver?

HANDS-ON PROJECTS

HANDS-ON PROJECTS

2

PROJECT 2-1: **Using the Windows 2000/XP System Information Utility**

Using Windows 2000/XP, do the following to run the System Information utility and gather information about your system:

1. Click **Start,** click **Run,** and then type **Msinfo32.exe** in the Run dialog box. Click **OK.** The System Information dialog box appears.

2. Browse through the different levels of information in this window and answer the following questions:

   a. What OS and OS version are you using?

   b. What is your CPU speed?

   c. What is your BIOS manufacturer and version?

   d. How much RAM is installed on your video card? Explain how you got this information.

   e. What is the name of the driver file that manages your parallel port? Your serial port?

   f. How is IRQ 10 used on your system? IRQ 4?

   g. Which DMA channels are used on your system and how are they used?

PROJECT 2-2: **Using a Freeware Diagnostic Utility**

You can download many freeware diagnostic utilities from the Internet and use them to examine, troubleshoot, and benchmark a system. Do the following to download and use one utility to examine your system:

1. Go to the CNET Networks Web site at *www.cnet.com* and download the latest version of Fresh Diagnose. Web sites change often, but at the time of this writing, you would click **Downloads,** then **Utilities & Drivers,** and then **Fresh Diagnose 6.0.** Save the utility to a folder on your hard drive named **Downloads.**

2. Double-click the file to execute the program and install the software. When given the opportunity, choose to create a shortcut to the software on your desktop.

3. Click the shortcut to run the Fresh Diagnose program.

4. Browse through the Fresh Diagnose menus and answer the same questions listed in Project 2-1 for the Windows 2000/XP System Information utility.

5. Compare the two programs, Fresh Diagnose and System Information, by answering the following questions:

   a. Which product is easier to use and why?

   b. Which product gives more information about your system?

   c. What is one advantage that System Information has over Fresh Diagnose?

   d. What is one advantage that Fresh Diagnose has over System Information?

   e. Which product do you prefer and why?

PROJECT 2-3: Using Microsoft Diagnostics with Windows 9x/Me

DOS and Windows offer the Microsoft Diagnostics utility. This utility examines your system, displaying useful information about ports, devices, memory, and the like. You can find the MSD.EXE utility in the \TOOLS\OLDMSDOS directory on your Windows 9x/Me installation CD. Using Windows Explorer, copy the utility to your hard drive and store it in a folder named \Tools.

For Windows 9x/Me, boot your PC to an MS-DOS prompt in real mode. To boot into real mode, press **Ctrl** or **F8** as you start the system. The Windows Startup menu appears. Select **Command prompt only**. From the DOS prompt, execute this command: **C:\TOOLS\MSD**. The MSD window appears (shown earlier in Figure 2-23).

Browse carefully through all menu options of this utility and answer the following questions about your system:

1. List the following information or print the appropriate MSD screen that contains it: manufacturer; version number; and date of your system BIOS, video BIOS, and mouse device driver.

2. What kind of video card is installed?

3. How much memory is currently installed on this PC?

4. What version of the OS is the PC running?

5. What CPU is the PC using?

Exit MSD. Save the information you noted to compare with the information that you will obtain from MSD in Windows 2000.

You need Windows 2000 installed on a PC to do the rest of this project:

1. Copy the **MSD.exe** program to a folder on your Windows 2000 PC named \Tools.

2. From within Windows 2000, open a command prompt. (Click **Start**, **Programs**, **Accessories**, and **Command Prompt**.)

2

3. From the command prompt, start MSD using this command: **\Tools\MSD**.

4. Browse through all menu options and answer the same questions about your system as you did for Windows 9x/Me.

PROJECT 2-4: **Using Device Manager**

Using Device Manager under Windows 2000/XP or Windows 9x/Me, answer the following questions about your computer. To access Device Manager using Windows 2000/XP, open the System Properties dialog box, click the **Hardware** tab, and then click **Device Manager**. For Windows 9x/Me, right-click the **My Computer** icon on the desktop, select **Properties** on the shortcut menu, and click the **Device Manager** tab.

1. Does your computer have a network card installed? If so, what is the name of the card?

2. What three settings can you change under Device Manager?

3. What are all the hardware devices that Device Manager recognizes as present?

PROJECT 2-5: **Examining CMOS Setup**

Boot your PC and look for directions on the screen that tell you how to access CMOS setup on your PC, such as "Press Del to enter setup." Access CMOS setup and answer these questions:

1. What keystroke(s) did you use to access CMOS setup?

2. What BIOS does your motherboard use? (Include brand and version.)

3. List the different CMOS setup windows that you can access from the CMOS main menu window.

4. Access the window that gives information about serial ports. What is the name of that window?

5. What I/O addresses and IRQ does the first serial port use?

6. What I/O addresses and IRQ does the first parallel port use?

7. What are the system date and system time reported by CMOS setup?

8. What keys do you press to exit CMOS setup without saving any changes?

Exit CMOS setup without saving any changes you might have accidentally made. Your PC should then boot to the Windows desktop.

Understanding the Boot Process and Command Line

In this chapter, you will learn:

- About the boot process and some tools for troubleshooting a failed boot

- To use many commands at the command prompt

Understanding what happens when you first turn on a PC is essential to knowing what to do when problems arise with booting or when applications or hardware fail after the boot. This chapter focuses on how the hardware boots up to the point an operating system (OS) is loaded, and then spends a little less time on the loading of an OS. In later chapters, you will learn in more detail what happens when each OS is loaded, and how to troubleshoot problems when the OS fails to load correctly.

After a system boots and you are working with an OS, most often you are using the Windows desktop, which is both menu-driven and icon-driven. Using Windows Explorer or My Computer, you can copy files, create folders, and even perform some limited troubleshooting tasks when problems arise. However, if the OS is not functioning well enough to provide a desktop, a PC technician must troubleshoot the system using a command-driven interface. Learning to use the command line is important because it is the tried-and-true tool for the worst operating system problems. Knowing how to use the command prompt is essential to PC troubleshooting.

We begin the chapter by learning how a PC first boots up, and about some troubleshooting tools to use when the boot fails. Then we will look at some essential commands used from a command prompt when troubleshooting a failing system.

Booting Up Your Computer

A+
CORE
1.1
OS
1.2

The term **booting** comes from the phrase "lifting yourself up by your bootstraps" and refers to the computer bringing itself up to an operable state without user intervention. Booting refers to either a "soft boot" or a "hard boot." A **hard boot**, or **cold boot,** involves turning on the power with the on/off switch. A **soft boot,** or **warm boot,** involves using the operating system to reboot. For Windows NT/2000/XP and Windows 9x/Me, one way to soft boot is to click Start, click Shut Down, select Restart from the Shut Down menu, and then click OK. For DOS, pressing the three keys Ctrl, Alt, and Del at the same time performs a soft boot.

✔ A+ EXAM TIP

The A+ OS and Core exams expect you to know the difference between a hard boot and a soft boot.

A hard boot is more stressful on your machine than a soft boot because of the initial power surge through the equipment. Also, a soft boot is faster. Always use the soft boot to restart unless the soft boot method doesn't work. If you must power down, avoid turning off the power switch and immediately turning it back on without a pause, because this can damage the machine. Some PCs have a reset button on the front of the case. Pressing the reset button starts the boot process at an earlier point than does the operating-system method, and is therefore a little slower, but might work when the operating-system method fails. For newer motherboards, pressing the reset button is the same as powering off and on, except that there is no stress to the system caused by the initial power surge.

In the next section, you will learn what happens when the PC is first turned on and the startup BIOS takes control and then begins the process of loading an OS.

Startup BIOS Controls the Beginning of the Boot

A+
CORE
2.1

VIDEO

Beep
Codes

A successful boot depends on the hardware, the BIOS, and the operating system all performing without errors. If errors occur, they might or might not stall or lock up the boot. Errors are communicated as beeps or as messages onscreen. Appendix A, "Error Messages and Their Meanings," lists some examples of these messages. The functions performed during the boot can be divided into four parts, as shown in the following list. Startup BIOS is in control for the first step and the beginning of the second step, when control is turned over to the OS.

Here is a brief overview of all four parts before we look at the first two parts in detail. (The last steps depend on the OS being used and are covered in later chapters.)

3

- *Step 1: Startup BIOS runs the **power-on self test** (POST) and assigns system resources.* The ROM BIOS startup program surveys hardware resources and needs, and assigns system resources to meet those needs (see Figure 3-1). The ROM BIOS startup program begins the startup process by reading configuration information stored in DIP switches, jumpers, and the CMOS chip, and then comparing that information to the hardware—the CPU, video card, disk drive, hard drive, and so on. Some hardware devices have BIOSs of their own that request resources from startup BIOS, which attempts to assign these system resources as needed.
- *Step 2: The ROM BIOS startup program searches for and loads an OS.* Most often the OS is loaded from logical drive C on the hard drive. Configuration information on the CMOS chip tells startup BIOS where to look for the OS. Most new BIOSs support loading the OS from the hard drive, a floppy disk, a CD, or a Zip drive. The BIOS turns to that device, reads the beginning files of the OS, copies them into memory, and then turns control over to the OS. This part of the loading process works the same for any operating system; only the OS files being loaded change.
- *Step 3: The OS configures the system and completes its own loading.* The OS checks some of the same things that startup BIOS checked, such as available memory and whether that memory is reliable. Then the OS loads the software to control a mouse, CD-ROM, scanner, and other peripheral devices. These devices generally have device drivers stored on the hard drive. The Windows desktop is loaded.

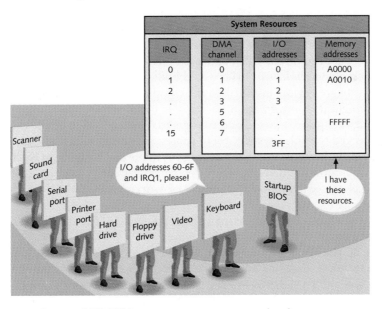

Figure 3-1   Boot Step 1: ROM BIOS startup program surveys hardware resources and needs and assigns system resources to satisfy those needs

A+
CORE
2.1

■ *Step 4: Application software is loaded and executed.* Sometimes an OS is configured to automatically launch application software as part of the boot. When you tell the OS to execute an application, the OS first must find the application software on the hard drive, CD-ROM, or other secondary storage device, copy the software into memory, and then turn control over to it. Finally, you can command the application software, which makes requests to the OS, which, in turn, uses the system resources, system BIOS, and device drivers to interface with and control the hardware. At this point, the user is in control.

Let's look more closely at the first step, beginning with the POST.

POST and Assignment of System Resources

When you turn on the power to a PC, the CPU begins the boot by initializing itself and then turning to the ROM BIOS for instructions. The ROM BIOS then performs POST. Listed below are the key steps in this process.

■ When the power is first turned on, the system clock begins to generate clock pulses.
■ The CPU begins working and initializes itself (resetting its internal values).
■ The CPU turns to memory address FFFF0h, which is the memory address always assigned to the first instruction in the ROM BIOS startup program.
■ This instruction directs the CPU to run POST.
■ POST first checks the BIOS program operating it and then tests CMOS RAM.
■ A test determines that there has been no battery failure.
■ Hardware interrupts are disabled. (This means that pressing a key on the keyboard or using another input device at this point does not affect anything.)
■ Tests are run on the CPU, and it is initialized further.
■ A check determines if this is a cold boot. If so, the first 16 KB of RAM is tested.
■ Hardware devices installed on the computer are inventoried and compared to configuration information.
■ The video card is tested and configured. During POST, before the CPU has checked the video system, beeps sometimes communicate errors. Short and long beeps indicate an error; the coding for the beeps depends on the BIOS. After POST checks and verifies the video controller card (note that POST does not check to see if a monitor is present or working), POST can use the monitor to display its progress.
■ POST checks RAM by writing and reading data. The monitor displays a running count of RAM during this phase.
■ Next, the keyboard is checked, and if you press and hold any keys at this point, an error occurs with some BIOSs. Secondary storage—including floppy disk drives and hard drives—ports, and other hardware devices are tested and configured. The hardware that POST finds is checked against the data stored in the CMOS chip, jumpers, and/or DIP switches to determine if they agree. IRQ, I/O addresses, and DMA assignments are made; the OS completes this process later.
■ Some devices are set up to go into "sleep mode" to conserve electricity.

3

A+
CORE
2.1

- The DMA and interrupt controllers are checked.
- CMOS setup is run if requested.
- BIOS begins its search for an OS.

How the BIOS Finds and Loads the OS

A+
OS
1.2
1.3
2.5
3.2

Once POST and the first pass at assignment of resources are complete, the next step is to load an OS. Startup BIOS looks to CMOS setup to find out which device is set to be the boot device. Most often the OS is loaded from logical drive C on the hard drive. The minimum information required on the hard drive to load an OS is shown in the following list. You can see some of these items labeled in Figure 3-2.

Figure 3-2　A hard drive might contain more than one logical drive; the Master Boot Record at the beginning of the drive contains information about the location of each logical drive, indicates which drive is the boot drive, and holds the master boot program that begins the process of loading an operating system

- A small sector (512 bytes) at the very beginning of the hard drive, called the **Master Boot Record (MBR)**, contains two items. The first item is the master boot program, which is needed to locate the beginning of the OS on the drive.
- The second item in the MBR is a table, called the **partition table,** which contains a map to the logical drives on the hard drive. This table tells BIOS how many partitions the drive has and how each partition is divided into one or more logical drives, which partition contains the drive to be used for booting (called the **active partition**), and where each logical drive begins and ends. Chapter 8 covers all this in more detail.

- At the beginning of the boot drive (usually drive C) is the OS **boot record**, which loads the first program file of the OS. For Windows 9x/Me, that program is **Io.sys**, and for Windows NT/2000/XP, that program is **Ntldr**.
- The boot loader program for the OS (Io.sys or Ntldr) begins the process of loading the OS into memory. For Windows 9x/Me, **Msdos.sys** is needed next, followed by **Command.com**. These two files, plus Io.sys, are the core components of the real-mode portion of Windows 9x/Me. Windows NT/2000/XP has a different set of startup files, which you will learn about in Chapter 14.

NOTE

A **program file** contains a list of instructions for the OS to follow. Program files can be a part of the OS or applications and have a .com, .sys, .bat, or .exe file extension. Ntldr is an exception to that rule because it has no file extension.

APPLYING CONCEPTS

Suppose you turn on your PC and see a black screen with one of these error messages on it:

```
Non-system disk or disk error, press any key
Bad or missing COMMAND.COM
No operating system found
```

Don't panic! You probably have a floppy disk in the drive. Just remove the disk and press any key. Most likely you'll boot normally. Here's what happened:

The BIOS looks to CMOS setup to find out which secondary storage device should have the OS (see Figure 3-3). Setup might instruct the BIOS to look first on drive C, and, if it finds no OS there, then try drive A; or the order might be to search A then C. If BIOS looks first to drive A and finds no disk in the drive, it turns to drive C. If it looks first to drive A and finds a disk in the drive, but the disk does not contain the OS (for Windows 9x/Me, that means the OS boot record, Io.sys, Msdos.sys, and Command.com), then one of the preceding error messages appears.

You must replace the disk with one that contains the OS or simply remove the disk and press any key to force the BIOS to continue to drive C to find the OS.

NOTE

The order of drives that the BIOS follows when looking for an OS is called the boot sequence. You can change the boot sequence on your PC by using CMOS setup.

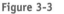

Figure 3-3   Boot Step 2: BIOS searches for and begins to load an operating system (in this example, Windows 9x/Me is the OS)

Loading the MS-DOS Core of Windows 9x/Me

This section describes what first happens during booting when only the MS-DOS core of Windows 9x/Me is loaded, which brings the OS to a real-mode command prompt similar to a DOS command prompt. It's important for a PC technician to

A+
OS
1.2
1.3
2.5
3.2

understand this real-mode DOS core because it is often used as a troubleshooting tool when the hard drive fails. You can boot to a command prompt in several ways, including booting from a Windows startup disk or using the Windows startup menu. You'll learn how to prepare a startup disk later in the chapter. Chapter 12 covers how to use the Windows startup menu in Windows 9x/Me.

In Step 2 of Figure 3-3, the BIOS locates the MBR on the hard drive, which looks to the partition table to determine where the logical boot drive is physically located on the drive. It then turns to the OS boot record of that logical drive.

The OS boot record is a very short program; it loads just one hidden file, which makes up the DOS core, into memory (see Figure 3-3, Step 3; and Figure 3-4). (A **hidden file** is a file that does not appear in the directory list.) The OS boot record program knows the filename, which is Io.sys. The Io.sys file contains the basic I/O software for real mode and requires that the Msdos.sys file be present. Msdos.sys is a text file that contains some parameters and switches you can set to affect the way the OS boots. You will learn about the contents of Msdos.sys and how to change it to affect the boot process in Chapter 12.

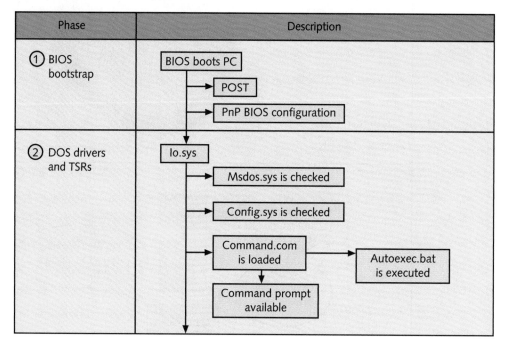

Phase	Description
① BIOS bootstrap	BIOS boots PC → POST → PnP BIOS configuration
② DOS drivers and TSRs	Io.sys → Msdos.sys is checked → Config.sys is checked → Command.com is loaded → Autoexec.bat is executed; Command.com is loaded → Command prompt available

Figure 3-4   Boot Step 3: Operating system completes the boot process; MS-DOS core is loaded and command prompt presented to user

Once Io.sys is loaded into memory, the boot record program is no longer needed, and control is turned over to Io.sys. This program looks for Msdos.sys, reads it, and uses the settings in it. Io.sys then looks on the hard drive for a file named Config.sys. This configuration file contains commands that tell Io.sys how many files it can open at any one time (Files=) and how many file buffers to create (Buffers=). (A buffer is a

3

A+
OS
1.2
1.3
2.5
3.2

temporary holding area for files.) Config.sys also includes the commands to load device drivers (Device=), as well as other information. An example of a typical command in Config.sys follows; it gives real-mode Io.sys access to memory above 1 MB, called extended memory:

```
Device=himem.sys
```

✔ **A+ EXAM TIP**

The A+ OS exam expects you to know that the three OS files necessary to boot to a command prompt in Windows 9x/Me are Io.sys, Msdos.sys, and Command.com. Config.sys and Autoexec.bat are not required but are used if they are present.

Several drivers can be loaded into memory from commands in Config.sys. Io.sys puts these programs in memory wherever it chooses. However, a program can request that it be put in a certain memory location.

Sometimes Config.sys is used to create a RAM drive. A **RAM drive** is an area of memory that looks and acts like a hard drive, but because it is memory, it is much faster. When booting from the Windows 9x/Me startup disk, Windows creates a RAM drive to hold files after they have been uncompressed. This eliminates the need for hard drive access, and there is no room for the files on the floppy disk. An example of a command in Config.sys to create a RAM drive is:

```
device=ramdrive.sys 2048
```

The command tells the OS to create a RAM drive that is 2048K in size.

After Config.sys is executed, Io.sys looks for another OS file, named Command.com. This file has three parts: more code to manage I/O, programs for internal OS commands such as Copy and Dir, and a short program that looks for the Autoexec.bat file.

Some OS commands are **internal commands**, meaning they are embedded in the Command.com file, and others are **external commands**, meaning they have their own program files. An example of an external command is Format, stored in the file Format.com.

Command.com looks for Autoexec.bat and, if found, executes it. The filename **Autoexec.bat** stands for "automatically executed batch file." A **batch file** is a text file that contains a series of commands that are executed in order. Autoexec.bat lists OS commands that execute automatically each time the OS is loaded. The following commands are examples of commands that might be found in the Autoexec.bat file:

- The following Path command lists two paths, separated by semicolons. The OS uses the paths listed in the Path command to locate program files.

```
PATH C:\;C:\Windows;
```

- The Set command is used to create and assign a value to an environmental variable that an application can later read. A software installation program might add a Set command to your Autoexec.bat file. Later, the software uses the environmental variable in the program. An example of a Set command assigning a path to the variable Mypath is:

```
Set Mypath=C:\VERT
```

■ The Restart command causes the system to reboot.

```
Restart.com
```

■ The Temp command lets applications know where to store temporary files. Add the Temp command to Autoexec.bat if applications are putting temporary files in strange locations. An example of a Temp command is:

```
Temp=C:\Temp
```

By default, DOS stores temporary files in C:\Temp, Windows 9x/Me uses C:\Windows\Temp, Windows NT uses C:\Temp, Windows 2000 uses C:\Winnt\Temp, and Windows XP uses C:\Windows\Temp.

■ The Echo command turns on and off the displaying of commands and messages. Use it in a batch file to control output to the screen.

```
Echo off
```

Booting into real mode with a command prompt is completed after Autoexec.bat has finished executing. At this point, Command.com is the program in charge, displaying a command prompt and waiting for a command. On the other hand, if a program or menu was executed from Autoexec.bat, it might ask you for a command.

The command prompt indicates the drive that loaded the OS. If the OS files were loaded from a floppy disk, the command prompt is A:\> (called the A prompt). If the OS was loaded from the hard drive, the command prompt is C:\> (the C prompt). The colon following the letter identifies the letter as the name of a drive, and the backslash identifies the directory on the drive as the root or main directory. The > symbol is the prompt symbol that the OS uses to say, "Enter your command here." This drive and root directory are now the default drive and directory, sometimes called the current or working drive or directory.

Note that commands used at a command prompt are not case sensitive; that is, you can enter WIN, Win, or win.

A+
OS
1.2
1.3
2.5
3.2

If you want to finish loading Windows 9x/Me, use the Win command, which executes the program Win.com. Enter this command at the C prompt:

```
C:\> WIN
```

Emergency Startup Disks

A+
OS
3.2

Although you normally boot from a hard drive, problems with the hard drive sometimes make booting from a floppy disk necessary. A floppy disk with enough software to load an operating system is called a **bootable disk**, or **system disk**. A bootable disk with some utility programs to troubleshoot a failed hard drive is called a **rescue disk, emergency startup disk (ESD)**, or **startup disk**. Having a rescue disk available for an emergency is very important, and a PC technician should always have one or more on hand.

Each OS provides an automated method to create a rescue disk or set of disks. Windows 9x/Me uses a single bootable disk, and Windows 2000 uses a set of four disks. Windows XP uses a different approach to recovering from a failed boot, and does not rely on startup disks. In this section, you will learn how to create a Windows 9x/Me startup disk and use the disk. How to troubleshoot a failed boot using Windows 2000/XP is covered in future chapters.

Windows 9x/Me Startup Disks

A Windows 9x/Me startup disk has everything you need to troubleshoot a failed hard drive or prepare a new hard drive for use. The disk does not need to be created on the same computer that will use it, although in most cases you should use the same version of Windows as used by the computer that will be using the disk. Follow these instructions to create a startup disk for Windows 9x/Me.

1. Click **Start** on the taskbar, point to **Settings**, and then click **Control Panel**.

2. In the Control Panel window, double-click the **Add/Remove Programs** icon.

3. Click the **Startup Disk** tab, and then click the **Create Disk** button (see Figure 3-5).

4. Windows might need the Windows CD to create the disk. Insert the CD if it is requested. Windows then creates the startup disk.

✔ **A+ EXAM TIP**

The A+ OS exam expects you to know each step in creating a Windows 9x/Me startup disk.

Windows places many utility programs on the disk that you will learn to use in the next section. One file is Ebd.cab, a compressed file called a **cabinet file**, that contains several other compressed files. During startup, the contents of the cabinet file are uncompressed and copied to the RAM drive, because there is not enough space for them on the floppy disk, and the startup disk assumes the hard drive might not be accessible. You can also use the Extract command to extract specific files when the RAM drive is not active.

A+
OS
3.2

Figure 3-5   Windows might use the Windows CD to create a startup disk

NOTE

When Windows 9x/Me creates a startup disk, it copies files to the disk from the \Windows \Command\EBD folder. You can also copy these files to a formatted disk to create a startup disk manually.

APPLYING CONCEPTS

If you have access to a Windows 9x/Me computer, create a startup disk and boot from the disk. What messages and questions do you see on the screen when you boot from the disk? If you have access to a Windows 2000 or Windows XP computer, boot it using the Windows 9x/ Me startup disk. What messages or questions do you see? Are there any differences?

Using a Windows 9x/Me Startup Disk with Another OS

In some situations, it is appropriate to use a startup disk created by one OS to boot a failed system that has a different OS installed. For example, suppose Windows NT/2000/XP refuses to boot. Using a different PC, you can create a startup disk under Windows 98 and then use it to boot the Windows NT/2000/XP PC. If you can successfully boot to an A prompt (A:\>), you have demonstrated that the hard drive or files stored on it is the source of the problem. However, it is best to use recovery procedures and disks native to the installed OS.

APPLYING CONCEPTS

Many PC technicians use a Windows 9x/Me startup disk when troubleshooting Windows NT/2000/XP computers, because the Windows 9x/Me startup disk has a useful set of tools and resources that are not as easily available under Windows 2000/XP. Here are three situations in which you might choose to use a Windows 9x/Me startup disk:

- You are helping someone solve a problem with their Windows NT/2000/XP system, which refuses to boot. You have your Windows 98 startup disk handy, so you boot from it and get to an A prompt. In order to get to an A prompt successfully, many subsystems in the computer must be functioning, including the motherboard, CPU, memory, floppy disk drive, power supply, and video system. In fact, you have just proven that the problem is isolated to the hard drive.

  Next, use the Windows 98 Fdisk command stored on the startup disk to examine the partition table of the hard drive. If Fdisk can see the table and describe it correctly, then you know that the partition table is not damaged. You have now isolated the problem to the file system on the hard drive. At that point, you must use tools native to Windows 2000/XP to solve the problem. (Fdisk is covered later in this chapter and in Chapters 8 and 9.)
- A Windows XP computer comes to you for repair with a failed hard drive. You install a new hard drive, but you do not have the Windows installation CD to install Windows XP on the drive. In this situation, you can use a Windows 9x/Me startup disk to boot the system and create a partition table on the drive. This assures you that the drive is functioning properly even without installing an OS.
- Your Windows NT system will not boot, and your term paper is stored on the hard drive! If the hard drive is using the FAT file system, you might be able to use the Windows 98 startup disk to recover the file. There are special considerations for Windows NT/2000/XP. These OSs support more than one file system, and a Windows 9x/Me startup disk supports only FAT16 or FAT32. If a Windows NT/2000/XP hard drive has a different file system installed, such as NTFS (New Technology file system), then the Windows 9x/Me startup disk cannot read that file system. In this situation, you can work from an A prompt, but you will not be able to access the hard drive. The solution is to create rescue disks under these operating systems that can read the file system.

Using the Command Prompt

A+
OS
1.1
1.2
1.3
1.5

In this section, you will first learn how to access a command prompt and how to launch programs from the command prompt. Then you will learn to use several commands to manage files and folders and perform many useful utility tasks when troubleshooting a failing system. Most of the commands in this section work under Windows NT/2000/XP and Windows 9x/Me.

When using Windows 2000/XP, you can get to a command prompt from the Windows desktop and use it to perform many utility tasks. When troubleshooting a failed boot, you can load the Recovery Console, which provides a command prompt but does not provide a Windows desktop. The Recovery Console is sometimes the only tool that is available in the worst-case situations. Many commands in this chapter also work at the Recovery Console command prompt.

Accessing a Command Prompt

There are several ways to get to a command prompt:

✔ **A+ EXAM TIP**

The A+ OS exam expects you to know all these ways to access a command prompt!

- Each Windows OS has a command window that you can access from the Windows desktop. For Windows XP, click Start, All Programs, Accessories, and Command Prompt. The Command Prompt window appears, as shown in Figure 3-6. To access a command prompt window in Windows 2000, click Start, Programs, Accessories, and Command Prompt. To access a command prompt window from a Windows 9x/Me desktop, click Start, Programs, and MS-DOS Prompt. (In Windows 9x/Me, a command prompt window is sometimes called a **DOS box**.) Using a command prompt window, you can enter the DOS-like commands discussed in this chapter. To exit the window, type Exit at the command prompt.
- For all versions of Windows, you can also open a command prompt window using an alternate method: click Start, click Run, and enter Command.com in the Run dialog box. To get a 32-bit version of the 16-bit Command.com program in Windows NT/2000/XP, enter Cmd.exe in the Run dialog box.
- Using Windows 2000/XP, use the four Windows 2000 startup disks or the Windows XP installation CD to boot the PC and load the Recovery Console. You will learn more about loading and using the Recovery Console in Chapter 14.
- Using Windows 9x/Me, when you boot from a bootable disk or a Windows 9x/Me startup disk, you get a command prompt instead of the Windows desktop.

- Using Windows 95 or Windows 98 (not Windows Me), click Start, click Shutdown, and select Restart in MS-DOS mode from the Shutdown dialog box. Using this method, you get a command prompt provided by the DOS real-mode core of Windows 95/98.
- Using Windows 9x/Me, hold down the Ctrl key or the F8 key while booting, which causes the OS to display a startup menu. From the menu, select Command prompt only.

3

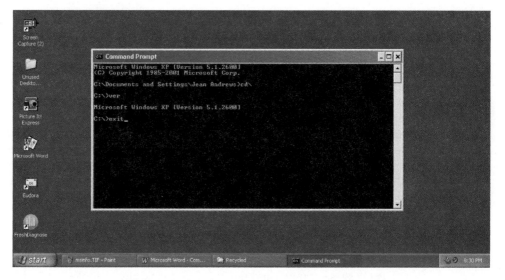

Figure 3-6   A Command Prompt window can be used to practice the commands given in this section

For convenience, you can add a command prompt icon to your Windows desktop for easy access. Locate the program file (Command.com or Cmd.exe) in Windows Explorer and, while holding down the Ctrl key, drag the icon to your desktop. Another way to create the shortcut is to click Start, point to Programs (All Programs in Windows XP), Accessories, and Command Prompt. Right-click Command Prompt and select Create Shortcut on the shortcut menu.

APPLYING CONCEPTS

For practice, try all the preceding methods of accessing a command prompt, except using the Recovery Console. Then create a command prompt icon on your desktop.

A command prompt provides information about the current drive and directory. For example, if you booted a Windows 98 PC from a bootable floppy disk into command prompt mode, you would see the A prompt (A:\>). Recall that the A: indicates the current drive. (A drive letter is always followed by a colon.) The backslash

A+
OS
1.1
1.2
1.3
1.5

indicates the root directory, and the > symbol indicates that you can enter a new command.

To make the hard drive (drive C) the default drive, enter C: at the A prompt.

The prompt now changes to indicate the current directory and drive in the root directory of drive C. It looks like this:

```
C:\>
```

Launching a Program Using the Command Prompt

A+
OS
1.1
1.2
1.3
1.5
3.3

In Chapter 2, you learned how to launch a program from the Windows desktop. You can also launch a program from a command prompt window. At the command prompt, when you type a single group of letters with no spaces, the OS assumes that you typed the filename of a program file you want to execute, which is stored in the current directory. The OS attempts to find the program file by that name, copies the file into RAM, and then executes the program. Let's use as our example the program Mem.exe, a Windows 9x/Me utility that displays how memory is currently allocated. The program file Mem.exe is stored on the hard drive in the C:\Windows\Command folder. Note what happens in Figure 3-7 when you type *mem* at the A: prompt, like this:

```
A:\>mem
```

The OS says it cannot find the program to execute. It looked only on the floppy disk (drive A) for Mem.com, Mem.exe, or Mem.bat, the three file extensions that the OS recognizes for programs. If the OS finds none of these files in the current directory, it stops looking and displays the error message:

```
Bad command or file name
```

To help the OS locate the program file, you must first change the default drive to the hard drive by giving the command:

```
A:\> C:
```

```
A:\>mem
Bad command or file name

A:\>c:

C:\>cd\windows\command

C:\WINDOWS\COMMAND>mem

Memory Type          Total      Used      Free
----------          --------    ----    ------
Conventional          640K      160K      480K
Upper                   0K        0K        0K
Reserved                0K        0K        0K
Extended (XMS)     130,036K    2,112K  127,924K

Total memory       130,676K    2,272K  128,404K

Total under 1 MB      640K      160K      480K

Largest executable program size      479K (490, 816 bytes)
Largest free upper memory block                 (0 bytes)
MS-DOS is resident in the high memory area.

C:\WINDOWS\COMMAND>
```

Figure 3-7   Finding a program file

Notice in Figure 3-7 that the prompt changes to C:\>, indicating that the logical drive C on the hard drive is the default drive. Now you change the default directory on the hard drive to \Windows\Command using the **CD (change directory) command,** like this:

```
C:\>CD\windows\command
```

(Remember that DOS and Windows commands are not case sensitive, so it makes no difference whether you type CD, Cd, or cd.) The prompt now looks like this:

```
C:\WINDOWS\COMMAND>
```

Figure 3-7 shows what happens when you enter the mem command again. The OS locates and executes the program file. In this Chapter 6 you will learn how to interpret the results of the mem command shown in Figure 3-7.

File and Directory Naming Conventions

A+
OS
1.1
1.2
1.3
1.4
1.5
3.3

When working with a command prompt, it is important to understand how to name directories and files, and how to type directory names and filenames in the command line. Under DOS, a filename can contain up to eight characters, a separating period, and a file extension of up to three characters, like this: *filename.ext*. This is called the 8.3 format. Characters can be the letters a through z, the numbers 0 through 9, and the following characters:

```
_ ^ $ ~ ! # % & - { } ( ) @ ' `
```

Be sure to not use a space, period, *, ?, or \ in a filename or file extension. Acceptable file extensions for program files are .com, .sys, .bat, and .exe. For example, the DOS utility program that displays information about the system is Msd.exe.

Under Windows, directory names and filenames can be as long as 255 characters and can contain spaces. When creating subdirectories under directories, know that the maximum depth of directories you can create is dependent on the length of the directory names. When working from a command prompt and using long directory names or filenames, put double quotation marks around the name, like this: "My long filename.doc".

When using long filenames in Windows 9x/Me, remember that the DOS portion of the system can only understand eight-character filenames with three-character extensions. When the DOS part of the system is operating, it truncates long filenames and assigns new eight-character names. For example, under DOS, the filename Mydocument.doc displays with the first few letters and a tilde (~) character:

```
Mydocum~.doc
```

If you have two documents that would have the same name when truncated in this manner, DOS also adds an identifying number. For example, if you have a document named Mydocument.doc and one named Mydocumentnew.doc, DOS truncates these:

```
Mydocu~1.doc
Mydocu~2.doc
```

When you boot using a Windows 9x/Me startup disk or some other MS-DOS disk, be aware of this file-naming convention.

Wildcards

A+
OS
1.1
1.2
1.3
1.4
1.5

As you work at the command prompt, you can use two **wildcards** with filenames to execute a command on a group of files, or in an abbreviated filename if you do not know the entire name. The question mark (?) is a wildcard for one character, and the asterisk (*) is a wildcard for more than one character. For example, if you want to find all files in a directory that start with A and have a three-letter file extension, you would use the following command:

```
dir a*.???
```

Commands to Manage Disks, Hard Drives, Files, and Directories

You can use several OS commands to manage files, directories, floppy disks, and hard drives. This section describes a number of commands with some of their more common options. For more information about these and other OS commands, type the command name at a command prompt, then type /? (slash and question mark). All the commands are available using a Windows 9x/Me startup disk, and some are available using the Windows 2000/XP Recovery Console. Also, some commands have equivalent Windows tools that are available from the Windows 2000/XP or Windows 9x/Me desktop.

Dir

A+
OS
1.3

Use this command to list files and directories. Some examples are:

DIR /P	List one screen at a time.
DIR /W	Use wide format, where details are omitted and files and folders are listed in columns on the screen.
DIR *.txt	Use a wildcard character.
DIR Myfile.txt	Check that a single file is present.

APPLYING CONCEPTS

Your hard drive has failed and you boot your PC using a Windows 98 startup disk. You get to the C prompt and go to the directory containing your term paper: C:\Data\My Term Paper.doc. How will the filename appear on your screen? Find out by using Windows Explorer to create the folder and file on your hard drive. Then boot from a Windows 98 startup disk and use the CD and DIR commands to display the filename.

Rename or Ren

The Rename command renames a file or folder. For example, to change the name of Myfile.txt to Mybackup.txt, use this command:

```
Ren Myfile.txt Mybackup.txt
```

Type

The Type command displays the contents of a text file on your screen. Some examples are:

Type Myfile.txt	Displays file contents.
Type Myfile.txt >PRN	Redirects output to printer.
Type Myfile.txt |More	Displays output one screen at a time.

Del or Erase

The Del or Erase command erases files or groups of files. If the command does not include drive and directory information, like the following examples, the OS uses the default drive and directory when executing the command.

For example, to erase all files in the A:\DOCS directory, use the following command:

```
C:\> ERASE A:\DOCS\*.*
```

To erase all files in the current default directory, use the following command:

```
A:\DOCS> DEL *.*
```

To erase all files in the current directory that have no file extension, use the following command:

```
A:\DOCS> DEL *.
```

To erase the file named Myfile.txt, use the following command:

```
A:\>DEL MYFILE.TXT
```

Copy

The Copy command copies a single file or group of files. The original files are not altered.

To copy a file from one drive to another, use the following command:

```
A:\>COPY drive:\path\filename.ext drive:\path\filename.ext
```

The drive, path, and filename of the source file immediately follow the Copy command; the drive, path, and filename of the destination file follow the source filename. If you do not specify the filename of the copy, the OS assigns the file's original name. If you omit the drive or path of the source or the destination, then the OS uses the current default drive and path.

To copy the file Myfile.txt from the root directory of drive C to drive A, use the following command:

C:\>**COPY MYFILE.TXT A:**

Because the command does not include a drive or path before the filename Myfile.txt, the OS assumes that the file is in the default drive and path.

To copy all files in the C:\DOCS directory to the floppy disk in drive A, use the following command:

C:\>**COPY C:\DOCS*.* A:**

To make a backup file named System.bak of the System.ini file in the \Windows directory of the hard drive, use the following command:

C:\WINDOWS>**COPY SYSTEM.INI SYSTEM.BAK**

If you use the Copy command to duplicate multiple files, the files are assigned the names of the original files. When you duplicate multiple files, the destination portion of the command line cannot include a filename.

NOTE When trying to recover a corrupted file, you can sometimes use the Copy command to copy the file to new media, such as from the hard drive to a floppy disk. During the copying process, if the Copy command reports a bad or missing sector, choose the option to ignore that sector. The copying process then continues to the next sector. The corrupted sector will be lost, but others can likely be recovered.

Xcopy /C /S /Y /D:

The Xcopy command is more powerful than the Copy command. It follows the same general command-source-destination format as the Copy command, but it offers several more options.

For example, use the /S option with the Xcopy command to copy all files in the directory \DOCS, as well as all subdirectories under \DOCS and their files, to the disk in drive A.

C:\>**XCOPY C:\DOCS*.* A: /S**

A+
OS
1.3

To copy all files from the directory C:\DOCS created or modified on March 14, 2004, use the /D switch, as in the following command:

```
XCOPY C:\DOCS\*.* A: /D:03/14/04
```

Use the /Y option to overwrite existing files without prompting, and use the /C option to keep copying even when an error occurs.

Deltree [drive:]path

The Deltree command deletes the directory tree beginning with the subdirectory you specify, including all subdirectories and all files in all subdirectories in that tree. Use it with caution! To delete the C:\DOCS folder and all its contents, use this command:

```
C:\>DELTREE C:\DOCS
```

Mkdir [drive:]path or MD [drive:]path

The Mkdir command (abbreviated MD, for make directory) creates a subdirectory under a directory. To create a directory named \GAME on drive C, use this command:

```
MKDIR C:\GAME
```

The backslash indicates that the directory is under the root directory. To create a directory named CHESS under the \GAME directory, use this command:

```
MKDIR C:\GAME\CHESS
```

The OS requires that the parent directory GAME already exist before it creates the child directory CHESS.

Figure 3-8 shows the result of the Dir command on the directory \GAME. Note the two initial entries in the directory table, the . (dot) and the .. (dot, dot) entries. The Mkdir command creates these two entries when the OS initially sets up the directory. You cannot edit these entries with normal OS commands, and they must remain in the directory for the directory's lifetime. The . entry points to the subdirectory itself, and the .. entry points to the parent directory, in this case, the root directory.

```
C:\>DIR \GAME /P

 Volume in drive C has no label
 Volume Serial Number is 0F52-09FC
 Directory of C:\GAME

 .              <DIR>      02-18-93    4:50a
 ..             <DIR>      02-18-93    4:50a
 CHESS          <DIR>      02-18-93    4:50a
 NUKE           <DIR>      02-18-93    4:51a
 PENTE          <DIR>      02-18-93    4:52a
 NETRIS         <DIR>      02-18-93    4:54a
 BEYOND         <DIR>      02-18-93    4:54a
         7 file(s)              0 bytes
                         9273344 bytes free

 C:\>
```

Figure 3-8　　Dir of the \GAME directory

Chdir [drive:]path or CD [drive:]path or CD..

The Chdir command (abbreviated CD, for change directory) changes the current default directory. Using its easiest form, you simply state the drive and the entire path that you want to be current:

    CD C:\GAME\CHESS

The command prompt now looks like this:

    C:\GAME\CHESS>

To move from a child directory to its parent directory, use the .. variation of the command:

    C:\GAME\CHESS> **CD..**
    C:\GAME>

Remember that .. always means the parent directory. You can move from a parent directory to one of its child directories simply by stating the name of the child directory:

    C:\GAME>**CD CHESS**
    C:\GAME\CHESS>

Do not put a backslash in front of the child directory name; doing so tells the OS to go to a directory named CHESS that is directly under the root directory.

Rmdir [drive:]path or RD [drive:]path

The Rmdir command (abbreviated RD, for remove directory) removes a subdirectory. Before you can use the Rmdir command, three things must be true:

- The directory must contain no files.
- The directory must contain no subdirectories.
- The directory must not be the current directory.

The . and .. entries are present when a directory is ready for removal. For example, to remove the \GAME directory in the preceding example, the CHESS directory must first be removed:

```
C:\>RMDIR C:\GAME\CHESS
```

Or, if the \GAME directory is the current directory, use this command:

```
C:\GAME>RD CHESS
```

Once you remove the CHESS directory, you can remove the \GAME directory. You must first leave the \GAME directory like this:

```
C:\GAME>CD..
C:\>RD \GAME
```

Attrib

The Attrib command displays or changes the read-only, archive, system, and hidden attributes assigned to files. To display the attributes of the file MYFILE.TXT, use this command:

```
ATTRIB MYFILE.TXT
```

To hide the file, use this command:

```
ATTRIB +H MYFILE.TXT
```

To remove the hidden status of the file, use this command:

```
ATTRIB -H MYFILE.TXT
```

To make the file a read-only system file, use this command:

```
ATTRIB +R +S MYFILE.TXT
```

To remove the read-only system status of the file, use this command:

```
ATTRIB -R -S MYFILE.TXT
```

To turn on the archive bit, use this command:

```
ATTRIB +A MYFILE.TXT
```

To turn off the archive bit, use this command:

```
ATTRIB -A MYFILE.TXT
```

The archive bit is used to determine if a file has changed since the last backup.

Sys Drive:

The Sys command copies the system files needed to boot to a disk or hard drive. Use the command if the system files on a drive are corrupt. You can access the drive, but you cannot boot from it. The command to copy system files to the hard drive is:

```
SYS C:
```

Chkdsk [drive:] /F /V

The Chkdsk command reports information about a disk. Use the /F option to have Chkdsk fix errors it finds, including errors in the FAT caused by clusters marked as being used but not belonging to a particular file (called lost allocation units) and clusters marked in the FAT as belonging to more than one file (called cross-linked clusters). To check the hard drive for errors and repair them, use this command:

```
CHKDSK C: /F
```

To redirect the output from the Chkdsk command to a file that you can later print, use this command:

```
CHKDSK C: >Myfile.txt
```

The /V option of the Chkdsk command displays all path and filename information for all files on a disk:

```
CHKDSK C: /V
```

For Windows 2000/XP, Chkdsk is best used in the Recovery Console, and for Windows 9x/Me, Chkdsk is useful when using a startup disk. From the Windows desktop, rather than use Chkdsk, use other error-checking tools such as ScanDisk for Windows 9x/Me or Error-checking for Windows 2000/XP. (These Windows tools are discussed in future chapters.)

Scandisk Drive: /A /N /P

A+
OS
1.3
1.5

The Scandisk command scans a hard drive for errors and repairs them if possible. Scandisk checks the FAT, long filenames, lost and cross-linked clusters, directory tree structure, bad sectors, and compressed structure, if the drive has been compressed using Windows DriveSpace or DoubleSpace. The /A parameter is used to scan all non-removable local drives. Use this command only to display information without fixing the drive:

```
SCANDISK C: /P
```

Use this command to display information and fix errors:

```
SCANDISK C:
```

Use this command to start and stop Scandisk automatically:

```
SCANDISK C: /N
```

If you use the preceding command, Scandisk still stops to report errors.

Windows 9x/Me offers Scandisk from the command prompt and from the desktop. It is not available under Windows NT/2000/XP. For Windows 2000/XP, use Error-checking from the Windows desktop.

Scanreg /Restore /Fix /Backup

The Scanreg command restores or repairs the Windows 98 registry. It uses backups of the registry that Windows 98 Registry Checker automatically makes each day. To restore the registry from a previous backup, use this command:

```
SCANREG /RESTORE
```

A menu appears asking you which backup to use.

To repair a corrupted registry, use this command:

```
SCANREG /FIX
```

To create a new backup of the registry, use this command:

```
SCANREG /BACKUP
```

Don't use this last command if you are having problems with the registry.

3

Defrag Drive: /S

A+
OS
1.3
1.5
2.5

The Defrag command examines a hard drive or disk for **fragmented files** (files written to a disk in noncontiguous clusters) and rewrites these files to the disk or drive in contiguous clusters. Use this command to optimize a hard drive's performance.

Use the /S:N option to sort the files on the disk in alphabetical order by filename.

```
DEFRAG C: /S:N
```

Use the /S:D option to sort the files on the disk by date and time.

```
DEFRAG C: /S:D
```

The Defrag command works under Windows 9x/Me. It is not available from the Windows 2000/XP Recovery Console.

Ver

A+
OS
1.3

Use the Ver command to display the version of the operating system in use. It works under Windows 2000/XP and Windows 9x/Me.

Extract filename.cab file1.ext /D

A+
OS
1.5

The Extract command extracts files from a cabinet file such as the Ebd.cab file on the Windows 98 startup disk. To list the files contained in the cabinet file, use this command:

```
EXTRACT EBD.CAB /D
```

To extract the file Debug.exe from the Ebd.cab file, use this command:

```
EXTRACT EBD.CAB DEBUG.EXE
```

To extract all files from the Ebd.cab cabinet file, use this command:

```
EXTRACT EBD.CAB *.*
```

This command is available under Windows 9x/Me. For Windows 2000/XP, use the Expand command, which is available under the Recovery Console.

Debug

The Debug program is an editor that can view and manipulate the components of a file system on floppy disks and hard drives, including the FAT, directories, and boot records. You can also use Debug to view the contents of memory and hexadecimal memory addresses. To access Debug, enter the command Debug at the command prompt.

Edit [path][filename]

A+
OS
1.3
1.5

The Edit program (Edit.com) is a handy, "quick and dirty" way to edit text files while working at a command prompt. To edit the Autoexec.bat file on a floppy disk, use this command:

```
EDIT A:\AUTOEXEC.BAT
```

If the file does not already exist, Edit creates it. For the Autoexec.bat file on the Windows 98 startup disk, your screen should be similar to the one shown in Figure 3-9. After you have made your changes and want to exit from the editor, press the Alt key to activate the menus, and choose Exit from the File menu. When asked if you want to save your changes, respond Yes to exit the editor and save changes.

The Edit command is available under Windows 9x/Me, but not Windows 2000/XP.

```
  File  Edit  Search  View  Options  Help
                  a:\AUTOEXEC.BAT
@ECHO OFF
set EXPAND=YES
SET DIRCMD=/O:N
set LglDrv=27 * 26 Z 25 Y 24 X 23 W 22 V 21 U 20 T 19 S 18 R 17 Q 16 P 15
set LglDrv=%LglDrv% O 14 N 13 M 12 L 11 K 10 J 9 I 8 H 7 G 6 F 5 E 4 D 3 C
cls
call setramd.bat %LglDrv%
set temp=c:\
set tmp=c:\
path=%RAMD%:\;a:\;%CDROM%:\
copy command.com %RAMD%:\ > NUL
set comspec=%RAMD%:\command.com
copy extract.exe %RAMD%:\ > NUL
copy readme.txt %RAMD%:\ > NUL

:ERROR
IF EXIST ebd.cab GOTO EXT
echo Please insert Windows 98 Startup Disk 2
echo.
pause
GOTO ERROR

F1=Help                                    Line:1    Col:1
```

Figure 3-9   Edit Autoexec.bat

NOTE

In older versions of DOS, Qbasic.exe was required for Edit.com to work correctly.

Editing Autoexec.bat and Config.sys   If you make a mistake when editing Autoexec.bat or Config.sys, you can cause a boot problem. Before editing these files on your hard drive, always make a rescue disk. If you are editing one of these files on a rescue disk, you can make a backup copy of the file before you edit it or have a second rescue disk ready just in case.

A+
OS
1.3
1.5

Do not use word-processing software, such as Word or WordPerfect, to edit Autoexec.bat or Config.sys, unless you save the file as a text (ASCII) file. Word-processing applications place control characters in their document files that prevent the OS from interpreting the file correctly.

NOTE

When working from a command prompt, you can reboot your computer (Ctrl+Alt+Del) to execute the new Autoexec.bat file, or you can type Autoexec.bat at the command prompt. If the computer stalls during the boot, use another startup disk to reboot. You can also press the F5 key to bypass the startup files during the boot.

Fdisk /Status /MBR

A+
OS
1.3

The Fdisk command is used to prepare a hard drive for first use. It creates partitions and logical drives on the hard drive, displays partition information, and restores a damaged Master Boot Record. Table 3-1 shows options for this command.

Fdisk Command Option	Description
/MBR	Repairs a damaged MBR program stored at the beginning of the hard drive just before the partition table
/Status	Displays partition information for all hard drives in the system

Table 3-1   Options for the Fdisk command

Fdisk works under Windows 9x/Me and is useful when booting from a Windows 9x/Me startup disk to examine the partition table on a malfunctioning hard drive, or to prepare a hard drive for first use. You will learn more about the Fdisk command in Chapters 8 and 9. Windows 2000/XP has a different tool, called Disk Management, which works from the Windows desktop to prepare a hard drive for first use. Using the Windows 2000/XP Recovery Console, the command similar to Fdisk /MBR is Fixmbr and the command similar to Fdisk is Diskpart.

Format Drive: /S /V:Volumename /Q /U /Autotest

Recall that the Format command is used to format a disk or a hard drive. For a hard drive using Windows 9x/Me, first run Fdisk to partition the drive and create each logical drive. Then use Format to format each logical drive. Table 3-2 shows options for this command. Chapter 8 covers the details of what happens when you format a hard drive. Format works under Windows 2000/XP Recovery Console and under Windows 9x/Me.

Format Command Option	Description
/V	Allows you to enter a volume label only once when formatting several disks. The same volume label is used for all disks. A volume label appears at the top of the directory list to help you identify the disk.
/S	Stores the system files on the disk after formatting. Writes the two hidden files and Command.com to the disk, making the disk bootable. Not available under Windows 2000/XP or Windows Me.
/Q	Re-creates the root directory and FATs if you want to quickly format a previously formatted disk that is in good condition. /Q does not read or write to any other part of the disk.
/F:size	Specifies the size of a floppy disk. If the size is not specified, the default for that drive is used. The common values for size are: /F:360 is 360K, double-density 5¼-inch disk /F:1.2 is 1.2 MB, high-density 5¼-inch disk /F:720 is 720K, double-density 3½-inch disk /F:1.44 is 1.44 MB, high-density 3½-inch disk
/U	Allows an unconditional format of the disk, which formats the disk more thoroughly by erasing all data. Use this option when you have been getting read/write errors on the disk.
/Autotest	Does not prompt the user before and during the format.

Table 3-2   Options for the Format command

Unformat

The Unformat command might be able to reverse the effect of an accidental format. To unformat a disk, use this command:

```
UNFORMAT C:
```

Using Batch Files

Suppose you have a list of OS commands that you want to execute several times. Perhaps you have some data files to distribute to several PCs in your office, but you have no LAN (local area network), so you must walk from one PC to another, repeatedly doing the same job. A solution is to store the list of commands in a batch file on

3

disk and then execute the batch file at each PC. Windows requires that the batch file have a .bat file extension. For example, store these five OS commands on a disk in a file named MYLOAD.BAT:

```
C:
MD\UTILITY
MD\UTILITY\TOOLS
CD\UTILITY\TOOLS
COPY A:\TOOLS\*.*
```

From the command prompt, you execute the batch file just as you do other program files, by entering the filename, with or without the file extension:

```
A:\>MYLOAD
```

All commands listed in the file will execute, beginning at the top of the list. The preceding batch file creates a subdirectory under the C drive called Utility\Tools, changes that directory to the default directory, and copies all files from the \Tools directory in drive A into that new subdirectory. Any good book on DOS provides examples of the very useful ways you can implement batch files, including adding user menus.

CHAPTER SUMMARY

▶ The boot process can be divided into four parts: POST, loading the OS, the OS initializing itself, and loading and executing an application.

▶ Startup BIOS is in control when the boot process begins. Then the startup BIOS turns control over to the OS.

▶ During the boot, the ROM BIOS startup program performs a power-on self test (POST) and assigns system resources to devices. It then searches secondary storage for an OS.

▶ A hard drive is separated into high-level divisions called partitions; within the partitions, the drive is further divided into logical drives or volumes. Each logical drive has a file system such as NTFS or FAT32.

▶ When the OS loads from a hard drive, the BIOS first executes the Master Boot Record (MBR) program, which turns to the partition table to find the OS boot record. The program in the OS boot record attempts to find a boot loader program for the OS, which for Windows NT/2000/XP is Ntldr. For Windows 9x/Me, the program is Io.sys.

▶ Io.sys, which uses Msdos.sys, and Command.com, form the core of real-mode Windows 9x/Me. These three files are necessary to boot to a command prompt. Config.sys and Autoexec.bat are not required but are used if they are present. Other files are needed to load the GUI desktop and run GUI applications.

▶ Autoexec.bat and Config.sys are two files that contain commands used to customize the 16-bit portion of the Windows 9x/Me load process.

▶ A RAM drive is an area of memory that looks and acts like a hard drive, only it performs much faster. The Windows 9x/Me startup disk uses a RAM drive to hold program files, assuming the hard drive is not accessible.

▶ Typical commands in the Autoexec.bat file include Path, Set, Restart, Temp, and Echo.

▶ A floppy disk with enough software to load an operating system is called a bootable disk, or system disk. A bootable disk with some utility programs to troubleshoot a failed hard drive is called a rescue disk, emergency startup disk (ESD), or startup disk.

▶ Create a startup disk in Windows 9x/Me using the Add/Remove Programs icon in the Control Panel.

▶ Windows 9x/Me uses Command.com to provide a command prompt window. Windows NT/2000/XP uses Command.com and Cmd.exe, a 32–bit version of Command.com, to provide a command prompt window.

▶ The Fdisk command is used to partition a hard drive.

▶ The Format command is used to format floppy disks and logical drives. The /S option with the Format command makes a drive bootable. The Unformat command attempts to reverse the effect of an accidental format.

▶ The Del or Erase command deletes files or groups of files.

▶ The Copy command copies a single file or group of files. More powerful than the Copy command, the Xcopy command supports copying subdirectories.

▶ The Sys command copies the system files needed to boot to a disk or drive.

▶ Mkdir creates a subdirectory, Chdir changes the current directory, and Rmdir removes a subdirectory.

▶ The Attrib command displays or changes the read-only, archive, system, and hidden attributes assigned to files.

▶ Chkdsk and Scandisk both check drives for errors and repair them. Scandisk does a more thorough scan for Windows 9x/Me and basically replaces Chkdsk.

▶ The Defrag command rewrites files on a hard drive in contiguous clusters to improve hard drive performance.

▶ The Scanreg command restores or repairs the Windows 98 registry.

▶ Batch files can be used to execute a group of commands using only a single command.

KEY TERMS

For explanations of key terms, see the Glossary near the end of the book.

active partition	emergency startup disk (ESD)	partition table
Autoexec.bat	external command	power-on self test (POST)
batch file	fragmented file	program file
boot record	hard boot	RAM drive
bootable disk	hidden file	rescue disk
booting	internal command	soft boot
cabinet file	Io.sys	startup disk
CD (change directory) command	Master Boot Record (MBR)	system disk
cold boot	Msdos.sys	warm boot
Command.com	Ntldr	wildcard
DOS box		

REVIEWING THE BASICS

1. What is the difference between a hard boot and a soft boot?

2. What three keys can you press to perform a soft boot when using DOS?

3. What are the four main parts of the boot process?

4. What memory address is always assigned to the first instruction in the ROM BIOS startup program?

5. How does startup BIOS communicate errors during POST if video is not yet available?

6. Name the program that is needed to locate the beginning of the OS on a drive.

7. List three types of information contained in a hard drive's partition table.

8. Give one example of a file system that can be used on a hard drive.

9. What three OS files are necessary to boot to MS-DOS mode? What is the function of each? What additional two files are not required but are used if they are present?

10. Why is it important not to edit Autoexec.bat with word-processing software such as Microsoft Word or WordPerfect?

11. What is the name of the Windows NT/2000/XP boot loader program?

12. What is the purpose of the command Device=himem.sys in the Config.sys file?

13. Give two ways to access a command prompt from Windows 9x/Me.

14. What are two Windows 2000/XP program files that can provide a command prompt window?

15. How many startup disks are needed to boot Windows 2000 from a floppy disk?

16. What are the two wildcard characters that can be used in command lines?

17. What is the /S switch used for with the Format command? The /V switch? The /F:size switch?

18. What is the name of the single directory created when a floppy disk or logical drive is first formatted?

19. Name the Windows 98 command that is used to partition a hard drive.

20. The _____ command erases files or groups of files.

21. What command is used to create a subdirectory? To change the current directory? To remove a subdirectory?

22. The _____ command displays or changes the read-only, archive, system, and hidden characteristics of files.

23. What is a hidden file? Name a Windows 9x/Me file that is hidden.

24. The _____ Console in Windows 2000 can be used to execute commands when troubleshooting a failed boot.

25. What is the purpose of the Ebd.cab file on the Windows 98 startup disk?

26. What icon in the Windows 98 Control Panel is used to create a startup disk?

27. List the steps to add a shortcut to your Windows desktop to access a command prompt window.

28. At a command prompt, how must you type long filenames that contain spaces?

29. When using a real-mode command prompt, how will DOS display the filename Mydocument.doc?

30. What is the batch file used by Windows 98 to control loading 16-bit programs?

THINKING CRITICALLY

1. If a PC boots first to the hard drive before checking the floppy disk for an OS, how do you change this boot sequence so that it first looks on the floppy disk for an OS?

2. A PC continues to reboot. You try to solve the problem by booting from a Windows 98 startup disk. You boot to the A prompt and look on the hard drive. Explain a possible source of the problem and describe how to fix it.

3. Explain the difference between the Copy command and the Xcopy command.

4. Explain the difference between the Chkdsk and Scandisk commands.

5. You need to make 10 duplicates of one floppy disk. Describe how to do this using two different methods. Which method is better and why?

HANDS-ON PROJECTS

HANDS-ON PROJECTS

PROJECT 3-1: **Observing the Boot Process**

1. If your computer has a reset button, press it and then watch what happens. If your computer does not have a reset button, turn it off, wait a few seconds, and then turn it back on. Try to note every beep, every light that goes on or off, and every message you see on the screen. Compare your notes to those of others to verify that you did not overlook something.

2. Answer these questions from observing the boot:

   a. What type of video card are you using?

   b. Who is the BIOS vendor, and what version of the BIOS are you using?

   c. As the computer boots, memory is counted. Observe the memory count and record the amount of memory detected. What number system is used to count this memory?

3. Unplug the keyboard and reboot the computer. What is different about the boot? Write down your observations.

4. Plug in the keyboard again, unplug the monitor, and reboot. After you reboot, plug in the monitor. Did the computer know the monitor was missing?

5. Put a floppy disk that is not bootable in drive A, and reboot. Write down what you observe. If the PC booted to the desktop as usual, why didn't it look to the floppy disk to load the OS?

PROJECT 3-2: Using the Windows 9x/Me Startup Menu

Hard boot your PC. If you are using Windows 95, when you see the message "Starting Windows 95," press **F8**. If you are using Windows 98/Me, press and hold **Ctrl** as the OS loads. Write down what happens when you execute each menu choice by booting several times.

PROJECT 3-3: Creating a Startup Disk Using Windows 9x/Me

Using directions in the chapter, create a startup disk in Windows 9x/Me, and then test it by rebooting the computer with the disk still in the drive. Answer these questions using the Readme.txt file on the startup disk:

1. What command line is recommended to check your hard drive for errors?

2. At what point in the boot process is the RAM drive created?

3. If you reboot your PC after booting from the startup disk, will the RAM drive remain in memory?

4. Using a second disk, create a system disk using Windows Explorer. Compare the contents of the two disks.

PROJECT 3-4: Researching MS-DOS Commands Using Windows 2000/XP

In this chapter you learned about several important MS-DOS commands, but there are more commands. Do the following to find out more about the commands in the chapter and to investigate other commands.

First, access the Help feature of the OS. For Windows XP, do the following:

■ Click **Start,** and then click **Help and Support**. The Help and Support Center window appears. In the Search box, type **Command-line reference A-Z** and then click **Go**.

For Windows 2000, do the following:

■ Click **Start,** and then click **Help**. The Windows 2000 Help window appears. Click the **Search** tab. In the search box, type **Windows 2000 Command Reference**. Click **List Topics**. Click **Windows 2000 Command Reference Main Page,** and then click **Display**.

Use this reference tool to answer the following questions:

1. What are some parameters to the Chkdsk command that you can only use for an NTFS volume?

2. How does Chkdsk handle the situation in which a file is open (that is, currently in use by another program)?

3. Describe the Diskcomp command. What is its purpose? When would you use it?

4. Describe the Find command. What are three parameters you can use with the command? Describe a situation in which it would be useful.

5. What is the purpose of the Assoc command? What is the command to send the output of the Assoc command to a file named MyResults.txt?

PROJECT 3-5: Practicing Commands

Go to a command prompt and do the following. Write down the commands you use.

1. Create a folder on your hard drive named **/testme**.

2. Make that folder the current folder.

3. Select a file in the Program Files folder on your hard drive. What is the name of the file? What is its size in bytes?

4. Copy the file to the /testme folder.

5. Format a floppy disk, making it bootable.

6. Display on the screen the amount of free bytes on the floppy disk. How many bytes are free?

7. Copy the file from the /testme folder to the floppy disk.

8. Make the floppy disk the current drive. What prompt do you now see?

9. Make the file on the floppy disk a hidden file.

10. Display on the screen the amount of free bytes on the floppy disk. How many bytes are free? Calculate how many bytes were used on the floppy disk to hold the file.

11. Unhide the hidden file on the floppy disk.

12. Rename the file **myfile.xxx**. What message appears when you rename the file?

13. Display a list of all files on the floppy disk that begin with the letter M.

PROJECT 3-6: Challenge Project

Using Windows 9x/Me, create your own bootable disk that loads the 16-bit real-mode drivers to use a mouse. Test the mouse by booting from the disk and using the mouse with the EDIT text editor.

Hint: First locate a 16-bit mouse driver file such as Mouse.sys. Load the driver file using a Device= command in Config.sys.

Electricity and Power Supplies

This chapter focuses on the power supply, which provides power to all other components inside the computer case. To troubleshoot problems with the power system of a PC, you need a basic understanding of electricity. This chapter begins by describing the measurements of electricity and the form in which it comes to you as house current. The chapter then addresses the power supply, backup power sources, and how to change a defective power supply. Finally, it introduces you to form factors and explains how Energy Star devices save energy.

Measures and Properties of Electricity

Electrical energy has properties that you can measure in various ways. These measurements are listed in Table 4-1.

NOTE

See Appendix E, "Electricity and Multimeters," for an explanation of how volts, amps, ohms, and watts measure the four properties of electricity.

VIDEO

Using a
Multimeter

Unit	Measures	Computer Example
Volt (for example, 110 V)	Potential difference in a circuit	An AT power supply provides four separate voltages: +12 V, –12 V, +5 V, and –5 V. An ATX power supply provides these voltages and +3.3 V as well.
Amp or **ampere** (for example, 1.5 A)	Electrical current	A 17-inch monitor requires less than 2 A to operate. A small laser printer uses about 2 A. A CD-ROM drive uses about 1 A.
Ohm (for example, 20 Ω)	Resistance	Current can flow in typical computer cables and wires with a resistance of near zero Ω.
Watt (for example, 20 W)	Power (watts are calculated by multiplying volts by amps)	A computer power supply is rated at 200 to 600 W.

Table 4-1   Measures of electricity

NOTE

While volts and amps are measured to determine their value, watts are calculated by multiplying volts by amps.

AC and DC

Electricity can be either AC, alternating current, or DC, direct current. **Alternating current (AC)** cycles, or oscillates, back and forth rather than traveling in only one direction. House current in the United States oscillates 60 times in one second (60 hertz), changing polarity from +110 V to –110 V and causing current to flow in different directions, depending on whether it's positive or negative in the cycle. AC is the most economical way to transmit electricity to our homes and workplaces. By decreasing current and increasing voltage, we can force alternating current to travel great distances. When alternating current reaches its destination, it is made more suitable for driving our electrical devices by decreasing voltage and increasing current.

> **✔ A+ EXAM TIP**
>
> The A+ Core exam expects you to know the difference between a rectifier and a transformer.

Direct current (DC) travels in only one direction and is the type of current that most electronic devices require, including computers. A **rectifier** is a device that converts alternating current to direct current. A **transformer** is a device that changes the ratio of current to voltage. Large transformers reduce the high voltage on power lines coming to your neighborhood to a lower voltage before the current enters your home. The transformer does not change the amount of power in this closed system; if it decreases voltage, then it increases current. The overall power stays constant, but the ratio of voltage to current changes.

A computer power supply changes and conditions the house electrical current in several ways, functioning as both a transformer and a rectifier (see Figure 4-1). It steps down the voltage from the 110-volt house current to 3.3, 5, and 12 volts, or to 5 and 12 volts, and changes incoming alternating current to direct current, which the computer and its peripherals require. The monitor, however, receives the full 110 volts of AC voltage, converting that current to DC.

Label lists voltages for motherboard connector

Vents for cooling fan

External power source

Connectors for hard drives and other drives

P1 power connector to motherboard

Connector for floppy drive

Figure 4-1   Computer power supply with connections

A+
CORE
1.1
1.2

Direct current flows in only one direction, from hot to ground. For a PC, a line may be either +5 or –5 volts in one circuit, or +12 or –12 volts in another circuit, depending on whether the circuit is on the positive side or negative side of the power output. Several circuits coming from the power supply accommodate different devices with different power requirements.

Hot, Neutral, and Ground

When AC comes from the power source at the power station to your house, it travels on a hot line and completes the circuit from your house back to the power source on a neutral line, as shown in Figure 4-2.

Figure 4-2   Normally hot contacts neutral to make a closed circuit in the controlled environment of an electrical device such as a lamp. An out-of-control contact is called a short, and the flow of electricity is then diverted to the ground.

When the two lines reach your house and enter an electrical device, such as a lamp or radio, electricity flows through the device to complete the circuit between the hot line and the neutral line. The device contains resistors and other electrical components that control the flow of electricity between the hot and neutral lines. The hot source seeks and finds ground by returning to the power station on the neutral line.

A short circuit, or a short, occurs when uncontrolled electricity flows from the hot line to the neutral line or from the hot line to ground. Electricity naturally finds the easiest route to ground. Normally that path is through some device that controls the current flow and then back through the neutral line. If an easier path (one with less resistance) is available, the electricity follows that path. This can cause a short, a sudden increase in flow that can also create a sudden increase in temperature—enough to start a fire and injure both people and equipment. Never put yourself in a position where you are the path of least resistance between the hot line and ground!

A fuse is a component included in a circuit and designed to prevent too much current from flowing through the circuit. A fuse is commonly a wire inside a protective case, which is rated in amps. If too much current begins to flow, the wire gets hot and eventually melts, breaking the circuit, as an open switch would, and stopping the current flow. Many devices have fuses, which can be easily replaced when damaged.

To prevent the uncontrolled flow of electricity from continuing indefinitely, which can happen because of a short, the neutral line is grounded. Grounding a line means that the line is connected directly to the earth, so that, in the event of a short, the electricity flows into the earth and not back to the power station. Grounding serves as an escape route for out-of-control electricity. The earth is at no particular state of charge and so is always capable of accepting a flow of current.

The neutral line to your house is grounded many times along its way (in fact, at each electrical pole) and is also grounded at the breaker box where the electricity enters your house. You can look at a three-prong plug and see the three lines: hot, neutral, and ground (see Figure 4-3). Generally, electricians use green or bare wire for the ground wire, white for neutral, and black for hot in home wiring for 110-volt circuits. In a 220-volt circuit, black and red are hot, white is neutral, and green or bare is ground. To verify that a wall outlet is wired correctly, use a simple receptacle tester, as shown in Figure 4-4.

CAUTION

Beware of the different uses of black wire. In PCs, black is used for ground, but in home wiring, black is used for hot!

Even though you might have a three-prong outlet in your home, the ground plug might not be properly grounded. To know for sure, test the outlet with a receptacle tester.

Figure 4-3 A three-prong plug showing hot, neutral, and ground

Figure 4-4 Use a receptacle tester to verify that hot, neutral, and ground are wired correctly

It's very important that PC components be properly grounded. Never connect a PC to an outlet or use an extension cord that doesn't have the third ground plug. The third line can prevent a short from causing extreme damage. In addition, the bond between the neutral and ground helps eliminate electrical noise (stray electrical signals) within the PC sometimes caused by other electrical equipment sitting very close to the computer.

CAUTION

4

Some Common Electronic Components

Understanding what basic electronic components make up a PC and how they work is important. Basic electronic components in a PC include transistors, capacitors, diodes, ground, and resistors. Figure 4-5 shows the symbols for these components.

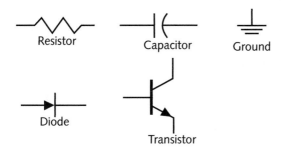

Figure 4-5   Symbols for some electronic components and ground

Materials used to make these and other electronic components can be:

- *Conductors.* Material that easily conducts electricity, such as gold or copper
- *Insulators.* Material that resists the flow of electricity, such as glass or ceramic
- *Semiconductors.* Material such as silicon whose ability to conduct electricity, when a charge is applied, falls between that of a conductor and an insulator

A **transistor** is an electronic device that can serve as a gate or switch for an electrical signal and can amplify the flow of electricity. Invented in 1947, the transistor is made of three layers of semiconductor material. A charge (either positive or negative, depending on the transistor's design) placed on the center layer can cause the two outer layers of the transistor to complete a circuit to create an "on" state. An opposite charge placed on the center layer can make the reverse happen, causing the transistor to create an "off" state. Manipulating these charges to the transistor allows it to hold a logic state, either on or off (translated to binary 0 or 1). When the transistor maintains this state, it requires almost no electrical power. Because the initial charge sent to the transistor is not as great as the resulting current that the transistor creates, sometimes a transistor is used as a small amplifier. The transistor is the basic building block of an integrated circuit (IC), which is used to build a microchip.

A **capacitor** is an electronic device that can hold an electrical charge for a period of time and can smooth the uneven flow of electricity through a circuit. Capacitors inside a PC power supply create the even flow of current the PC needs. Capacitors maintain their charge long after current is no longer present, which is why the inside of a power supply can be dangerous even when it is unplugged.

A **diode** is a semiconductor device that allows electricity to flow in only one direction. (A transistor contains two diodes.) One to four diodes used in various configurations can be used to convert AC to DC. Singularly or collectively, depending on the configuration, these diodes are called a rectifier.

A **resistor** is an electronic device that limits the amount of current that can flow through it.

Protecting Your Computer System

**A+
CORE
3.2**

Now that you have learned some basic information about how electricity is measured and managed, understanding how power is supplied to a computer will be easier. But first, let's look at ways to protect your computer system. As you read the rest of the chapter and when you work on the projects at the end of this chapter, you will begin to look inside a computer and start taking it apart and putting it back together. While working on a computer, it is possible to harm both the computer and yourself. The most common accident when someone attempts to fix a computer problem is erasing software or data. Experimenting without knowing what you are doing can cause damage. You can take many safety precautions to prevent these sorts of accidents, as well as the ones that put you in physical danger. Here are a few general safety precautions to keep in mind:

- Make notes as you work so that you can backtrack later if necessary.
- When unpacking hardware or software, remove the packing tape and cellophane from the work area as soon as possible.
- Keep components away from your hair and clothing.
- Keep screws and spacers orderly and in one place, such as a cup or tray.
- Don't stack boards on top of each other: You could accidentally dislodge a chip this way.
- When handling motherboards and expansion cards, don't touch the chips on the boards. Hold expansion cards by the edges. Don't touch any soldered components on a card, and don't touch chips or edge connectors unless it's absolutely necessary.
- Don't touch a chip with a magnetized screwdriver.
- Don't use a graphite pencil to change DIP switch settings, because graphite is a conductor of electricity, and the graphite can lodge in the switch.
- In a classroom environment, after you have reassembled everything, have your instructor check your work before you put the cover back on and power up.

- Always turn off a computer before moving it. A computer's hard drive always spins while it is on, unless it has a sleep mode. Therefore, it is important not to move, kick, or jar a computer while it is running.
- To protect disks, keep them away from magnetic fields, heat, and extreme cold. Don't open the shuttle window on a floppy disk or touch the disk's surface.

You will learn about additional safety precautions in the remainder of this section.

4

CAUTION

To protect both yourself and the equipment when working inside a computer, turn off the power, unplug the computer, and always use a ground bracelet (which you will learn more about later). Never touch the inside of a computer that is turned on. In addition, consider the monitor and the power supply to be "black boxes." Never remove the cover or put your hands inside this equipment unless you know about the hazards of charged capacitors and have been trained to deal with them. Both the power supply and the monitor can hold a dangerous level of electricity even after you turn them off and disconnect them from a power source. The power supply and monitor contain enough power to kill you, even when they are unplugged.

Static Electricity

Electrostatic discharge (ESD), commonly known as **static electricity,** is an electrical charge at rest. A static charge can build up on the surface of an ungrounded conductor and on nonconductive surfaces such as clothing or plastic. When two objects with dissimilar electrical charges touch, static electricity passes between them until the dissimilar charges become equal. To see how this works, turn off the lights in a room, scuff your feet on the carpet, and touch another person. Occasionally you can see and feel the charge in your fingers. If you can feel the charge, then you discharged at least 3,000 volts of static electricity. If you hear the discharge, then you released at least 6,000 volts. If you see the discharge, then you released at least 8,000 volts of ESD. A charge of much less than 3,000 volts can damage electronic components. You can touch a chip on an expansion card or motherboard, damage the chip with ESD, and never feel, hear, or see the discharge.

ESD can cause two types of damage in an electronic component: catastrophic failure and upset failure. A catastrophic failure destroys the component beyond use. An upset failure damages the component so that it does not perform well, even though it may still function to some degree. Upset failures are more difficult to detect because they are not as easily observed.

✔ **A+ EXAM TIP**

The A+ Core exam emphasizes that you should know how to protect computer equipment as you work on it.

CAUTION

A monitor can also damage components with ESD. Do not place or store expansion cards on top of or next to a monitor, which can discharge as much as 29,000 volts onto the screen.

A+
CORE
3.2

To protect the computer against ESD, always ground yourself before touching electronic components, including the hard drive, motherboard, expansion cards, processors, and memory modules. Ground yourself and the computer parts, using one or more of the following static control devices or methods:

- *Ground bracelet or static strap.* A **ground bracelet** is a strap you wear around your wrist. One end attaches to a grounded conductor such as the computer case or a ground mat or plugs into a wall outlet. (Only the ground prong makes a connection!) The bracelet also contains a resistor that prevents electricity from harming you. Figure 4-6 shows a ground bracelet.

Resistor that prevents
the flow of electricity

Alligator clip connects
ground bracelet to
computer case

Figure 4-6   A ground bracelet, which protects computer components from ESD, can clip to the side of the computer case and eliminates ESD between you and the case

- *Ground mats.* Ground mats can come equipped with a cord to plug into a wall outlet to provide a grounded surface on which to work. If you lift the component off the mat, it is no longer grounded and is susceptible to ESD. Figure 4-7 shows a ground mat.

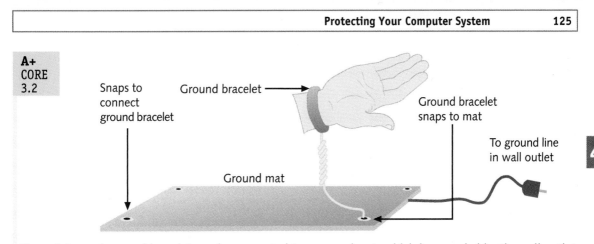

Figure 4-7   A ground bracelet can be connected to a ground mat, which is grounded by the wall outlet

■ *Static shielding bags.* New components come shipped in static shielding bags. These bags are a type of Farady Cage, which is any device that protects against an electromagnetic field. Save the bags to store other devices that are not currently installed in a PC. When working on a PC, you can also lay components on these bags (see Figure 4-8).

Figure 4-8   Static shielding bags help protect components from ESD

The best way to guard against ESD is to use a ground bracelet together with a ground mat. Consider a ground bracelet essential equipment when working on a computer. However, if you are in a situation where you must work without one, touch the computer case or the power supply before you touch a component. When passing a chip to another person, ground yourself and then touch the other person before you pass the chip. Leave components inside their protective bags until you are ready to use them. Work on hard floors, not carpet, or use antistatic spray on the

A+
CORE
3.2

carpets. Generally, don't work on a computer if you or the computer have just come in from the cold, because the potential for ESD is higher.

NOTE

Besides using a ground mat, you can also create a ground for the computer case by leaving the power cord to the case plugged into the wall outlet. This is safe enough because the power is turned off when you work inside the case. However, if you happen to touch an exposed area of the power switch inside the case, you may get a shock. Because of this risk, this book directs you to unplug the power cord to the PC before you work inside the case.

CAUTION

There are exceptions to the rule of always being grounded when you work with PCs. You *don't* want to be grounded when working inside a monitor, with a power supply, or with high-voltage equipment such as a laser printer. These devices maintain high electrical charges, even when the power is turned off. Inside a monitor case, the electricity stored in capacitors poses substantial danger. When working inside a monitor, you don't want to be grounded, because you would provide a conduit for the voltage to discharge through your body. In this situation, be careful not to ground yourself. The situation is similar when working with a power supply. *Don't* wear a ground bracelet when working inside these devices, because you don't want to be the ground for these charges!

EMI (Electromagnetic Interference)

A+
CORE
2.1
3.2

Another phenomenon that can cause electrical problems with computers is **electromagnetic interference (EMI)**. EMI is caused by the magnetic field produced as a side effect when electricity flows. EMI in the radio frequency range, which is called radio frequency interference (RFI), can cause problems with radio and TV reception. Data in data cables that cross an electromagnetic field can become corrupted, causing crosstalk. Using shielded data cables covered with a protective material can partially control crosstalk. Power supplies are also shielded to prevent them from emitting EMI.

NOTE

PCs can emit EMI to other nearby PCs, which is one reason a computer needs to be inside a case. To help cut down on EMI between PCs, always install face plates in empty drive bays or slot covers over empty expansion slots.

VIDEO

Testing for EMI

If mysterious, intermittent errors persist on a PC, one thing to suspect is EMI. Try moving the PC to a new location. If the problem continues, try moving it to a location that uses an entirely different electric circuit. Using an inexpensive AM radio is one simple way to detect the presence of EMI. Turn the tuning dial away from a station into a low-frequency range. With the radio on, you can hear the static that EMI produces. Try putting the radio next to several electronic devices to detect the EMI they emit.

A+
CORE
2.1
3.2

If EMI in the electrical circuits coming to the PC poses a significant problem, you can use a line conditioner to filter the electrical noise causing the EMI. Line conditioners are discussed later in the chapter.

Surge Protection and Battery Backup

4

A+
CORE
1.8

In addition to protecting your PC against ESD and EMI, you need to consider how power coming into a computer is regulated. A wide range of devices on the market filter the AC input to computers and their peripherals (that is, condition the AC input to eliminate highs and lows) and provide backup power when the AC fails. These devices, installed between the house current and the computer, fall into three general categories: surge suppressors, power conditioners, and uninterruptible power supplies (UPSs). All these devices should have the UL (Underwriters Laboratory) logo, which ensures that the laboratory, a provider of product safety certification, has tested the device.

Surge suppressors protect equipment against sudden changes in power level, such as spikes from lightning strikes. Power conditioners and uninterruptible power supplies condition the power passing through them (that is, alter it to provide continuous voltages). Both provide a degree of protection against **swells** or **spikes** (temporary voltage surges) and raise the voltage when it drops during **brownouts** or **sags** (temporary voltage reductions). These devices are measured by the load they support in watts, volt-amperes (VA), or kilovolt-amperes (kVA).

To determine the VA required to support your system, multiply the amperage of each component by 120 volts and then add up the VA for all components. For example, a 17-inch monitor has "1.9 A" written on its back, which means 1.9 amps. Multiply that value by 120 volts, and you see that the monitor requires 228 VA. A Pentium PC with a 17-inch monitor and tape backup system requires about 500 VA or 500 watts of support.

Surge Suppressors

A **surge suppressor**, also called a **surge protector**, provides a row of power outlets and an on/off switch that protects equipment from overvoltages on AC power lines and telephone lines. A surge suppressor might be a shunt type that absorbs the surge, a series type that blocks the surge from flowing, or a combination of the two. A suppressor is measured by **clamping voltage**, a term that describes the let-through voltage, or in joules, a measure of the amount of energy a surge suppressor can absorb. Surge suppressors can come as power strips (note that not all power strips have surge protection), wall-mounted units that plug into AC outlets, or consoles designed to sit beneath the monitor on a desktop. Some provide RJ-11 telephone jacks to protect modems and fax machines from spikes.

A **data line protector** serves the same function for your telephone line to your modem that a surge suppressor does for the electrical lines. Telephone lines carry a small current of electricity and need protection against spikes, just as electrical lines

Whenever a power outage occurs, unless you have a reliable power conditioner or UPS installed, unplug all power cords to the PC, printers, monitors, and the like. Sometimes when the power returns, sudden spikes are accompanied by another brief outage. You don't want to subject your equipment to these surges. When buying a surge suppressor, look for those that guarantee against damage from lightning and that reimburse for equipment destroyed while the surge suppressor is in use.

Surge suppressors are not always reliable, and once the fuse inside the suppressor blows, a surge suppressor no longer protects equipment from a power surge. It might continue to provide power without warning that you have lost protection.

When shopping for a surge protector, consider the let-through voltage rating, joules rating (more than 600 joules), warranty for connected equipment, line noise filtering, and phone line protection. Also, when you plug in a surge protector, know that if the protector is not grounded using a three-prong outlet, the protector cannot do its job.

do. The let-through rating for a data line protector for a phone line should be no more than 260 volts.

Power Conditioners

In addition to providing protection against spikes, **power conditioners** also regulate, or condition, the power, providing continuous voltage during brownouts. These voltage regulators, sometimes called **line conditioners**, can come as small desktop units.

These electricity filters are a good investment if the AC in your community suffers excessive spikes and brownouts. However, a device rated under 1 kVA will probably provide corrections only for brownouts, not for spikes. Line conditioners, like surge suppressors, provide no protection against a total blackout (complete loss of power).

Uninterruptible Power Supply

Unlike a power conditioner, the **uninterruptible power supply (UPS)** provides backup power in the event that the AC fails completely. The UPS also offers some filtering of the AC. The power supplies in most computers can operate over a wide range of electrical voltage input; however, operating the computer under these conditions for extended periods of time can shorten not only the power supply's life, but also the computer's. UPSs offer these benefits:

- Condition the line for both brownouts and spikes
- Provide backup power during a blackout
- Protect against very high spikes that could damage equipment

A UPS device suitably priced for personal computer systems is designed as either a standby device, an inline device, or a **line-interactive** device (which combines features of the first two). Several variations of these three types of UPS devices are on the market at widely varying prices.

A common UPS device is a rather heavy box that plugs into an AC outlet and provides one or more outlets for the computer and its peripherals (see Figure 4-9). It has an on/off switch, requires no maintenance, and is very simple to install.

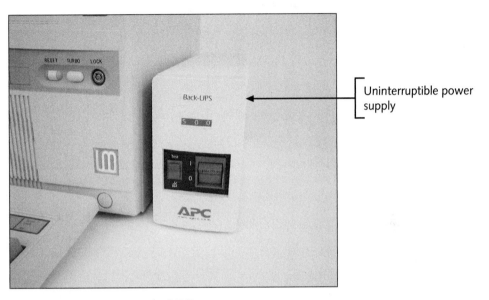

Uninterruptible power supply

Figure 4-9   Uninterruptible power supply (UPS)

The Smart UPS

Some UPSs can be controlled by software from a computer, to allow additional functionality. For example, from the front panel of some UPSs you can check for a weak battery. If the UPS is a **smart UPS** (also called an **intelligent UPS**), you can perform the same function from utility software installed on your computer. To accommodate this feature, a UPS must have a serial port or USB connection to the PC and a microprocessor on board. Some tasks this utility software and a smart UPS can do are:

- Diagnose the UPS
- Check for a weak battery
- Monitor the quality of electricity received
- Monitor the percentage of load the UPS is carrying during a blackout
- Automatically schedule the weak-battery test or UPS diagnostic test
- Send an alarm to workstations on a network to prepare for a shutdown
- Close down all servers protected by the UPS during a blackout
- Provide pager notification to a facilities manager if the power goes out
- After a shutdown, allow for startup from a remote location over phone lines

A+
CORE
1.8

Windows NT, Windows 2000, and Windows XP offer support for smart UPSs. You can monitor and control the devices from the UPS dialog box accessible through the Control Panel. Microsoft and American Power Conversion (APC), a leading manufacturer of UPSs, developed the Windows 2000 controls.

What to Consider When Buying a UPS

When you purchase a UPS, cost often drives the decision about how much and what kind of protection you buy. However, do not buy an inline UPS that runs at full capacity. A battery charger operating at full capacity produces heat, which can reduce the battery's life. The UPS rating should exceed your total VA or wattage output by at least 25 percent. Also, be aware of the degree of line conditioning that the UPS provides. Consider the warranty and service policies as well as the guarantee the UPS manufacturer gives for the equipment that the UPS protects. Table 4-2 lists some UPS manufacturers.

Manufacturer	Web Site
MGE UPS Systems	www.mgeups.com
American Power Conversion Corp. (APC)	www.apcc.com
Tripp Lite	www.tripplite.com
Belkin Components	www.belkin.com
Invensys	www.powerware.com
Liebert Corporation	www.liebert.com
Para Systems, Inc.	www.minuteman-ups.com
Toshiba International Corp.	www.tic.toshiba.com

Table 4-2   UPS manufacturers

The Computer Case and Form Factors

A+
CORE
1.1
1.2
4.3

Power supplies and computer cases are often sold together and must be compatible with each other. Also, the power supply and case must fit the motherboard. For these reasons, you can now turn your attention to the computer case, which is also called the chassis. When you put together a new system, or replace components in an existing system, the form factors of the motherboard, power supply, and case must all match. The **form factor** describes the size, shape, and general makeup of a hardware component.

When you are deciding which form factor to use, the motherboard drives the decision because it determines what the system can do. After you've decided to use a certain form factor for the motherboard, then you must use the same form factor for

4

A+
CORE
1.1
1.2
4.3

the case and power supply. Using a matching form factor for the power supply and case assures you that:

- The motherboard fits in the case.
- The power supply cords to the motherboard provide the correct voltage, and the connectors match the connections on the board.
- The holes in the motherboard align with the holes in the case for anchoring the board to the case.
- Holes in the case align with ports coming off the motherboard.
- For some form factors, wires for switches and lights on the front of the case match up with connections on the motherboard.

Case, Power Supply, and Motherboard Form Factors

✔ **A+ EXAM TIP**

The A+ Core exam expects you to recognize and know the more important features of the AT and ATX boards.

Several form factors apply to power supplies, cases, and motherboards: the AT, ATX, LPX, NLX, BTX, and backplane systems. Each of these form factors has several variations. The four most common form factors used on personal computers today are the AT, Baby AT, ATX, and Mini-ATX. The most popular form factor is the ATX, and the latest is the BTX. These form factors and earlier, less common, and up-and-coming form factors are discussed next.

VIDEO

Identifying
Form Factors

AT Form Factor

The **AT** form factor, sometimes called **full AT**, is used on older motherboards that measure 12" × 13.8". This form factor uses the full-size AT cases that the original IBM AT (Advanced Technology) personal computer used. A smaller, more convenient version of AT called the Baby AT came later. Full AT motherboards cannot be used with smaller AT cases or with newer ATX cases. Their dimensions and configuration make full AT systems difficult to install, service, and upgrade. Another problem with the AT form factor is that the CPU is placed on the motherboard in front of the expansion slots; long cards might not fit in these slots because they will bump into the CPU. You can visualize this problem by looking at the AT motherboard in Figure 4-10.

Recall that power supplies for AT systems supply +5, –5, +12, and –12 volts to the motherboard and other components. The AT board uses two power connections, the **P8 connector** and the **P9 connector** (see Figure 4-11). Most manufacturers no longer produce full AT boards.

CPU and fan

16-bit ISA expansion slots (4)

PCI expansion slots (3)

Keyboard port

Connections to power supply

RAM slots with two SIMMS

Figure 4-10   The CPU on the AT motherboard sits in front of the expansion slots

P1 on an ATX motherboard

(B)

P8 and P9 on an AT motherboard

Figure 4-11   ATX uses a single P1 power connector (A), but AT-type motherboards use P8 and P9 power connectors (B)

Baby AT Form Factor

A+
CORE
1.1
1.2
4.3

Improved flexibility over full AT made **Baby AT** the industry standard form factor from about 1993 to 1997. Power supplies designed for the Baby AT form factor blow air out of the computer case. At 13" × 8.7", Baby AT motherboards are smaller than full AT motherboards and fit in many types of cases, including newer ATX cases designed to provide backward compatibility. The design of Baby AT motherboards did not resolve the problem with the position of the CPU in relation to expansion slots. In addition, because of the motherboard's configuration and orientation within the case, drives and other devices are not positioned close to their connections on the motherboard. This means that cables might have to reach across the motherboard and not be long enough.

ATX Form Factor

ATX is the most commonly used form factor today. It is an open, nonproprietary industry specification originally developed by Intel in 1995. ATX improved upon AT by making adding and removing components easier, providing greater support for I/O devices and processor technology, and lowering costs. Components on the motherboard are arranged so they don't interfere with each other and for better position inside the case. Also, the position of the power supply and drives inside the case makes connecting them to the motherboard easier and makes it possible to reduce cable lengths, which can help reduce the potential for EMI and corrupted data. Connecting the switches and lights on the front of the case to components inside the case requires fewer wires, making installation simpler and reducing the potential for mistakes.

An ATX motherboard measures 12" × 9.6", so it's smaller than a full AT motherboard. On an ATX motherboard, the CPU and memory slots are rotated 90 degrees from the position on the AT motherboard. Instead of sitting in front of the expansion slots, the CPU and memory slots sit beside them, preventing interference with full-length expansion cards (see Figure 4-12).

The ATX power supply and motherboard use a single power connector called the **P1 connector** that includes, in addition to the voltages provided by AT, a +3.3-volt circuit for a low-voltage CPU (refer back to Figure 4-11). In addition to the P1 connector, one or more auxiliary connectors can be used to supply power to the CPU or CPU fan. Cases designed for Baby AT and LPX cannot accommodate ATX motherboards and power supplies, although many ATX cases can accommodate Baby AT motherboards.

P1 power connector

16-bit ISA expansion slot

AGP slot
Five PCI expansion slots

Parallel port
Two serial ports
Two USB ports
Keyboard and
mouse ports

Slot 1 for Pentium III with
supporting braces

Four RAM slots with one
DIMM installed

Figure 4-12   The CPU on an ATX motherboard sits beside the expansion slots and does not block the room needed for long expansion cards

An additional difference between AT and ATX systems is that the power supply fan blows air out of the case rather than into it, which provides better air circulation and cooling for the processor. You'll learn more about case fans later in the chapter.

Another feature of an ATX motherboard not found on AT boards is a **soft switch**, sometimes called the **soft power** feature. Using this feature, an OS, such as Windows 98 or Windows 2000/XP, can turn off the power to a system after the shutdown procedure is done. Also, CMOS can be configured to cause a keystroke or network activity to power up the system (wake on LAN). On older AT systems, when the PC is running and a user presses the power switch on the front of the case, the power turns off abruptly. The operating system has no opportunity to close down gracefully and, on the next power up, the system might have errors. With a soft switch controlling an ATX system and an operating system supporting the feature, if the user presses the power switch on the front of the case while the computer is on, the OS goes through a normal shutdown procedure before powering off.

In addition to regular ATX, there are several other types of ATX boards. **Mini-ATX**, a smaller ATX board (11.2" × 8.2"), can be used with ATX cases and power supplies. **MicroATX** addresses some technologies that have emerged since the original development of ATX. **FlexATX** allows for maximum flexibility in the design of system cases and boards and therefore can be a good choice for custom systems.

NLX Form Factor

**A+
CORE
1.1**

NLX is a form factor for low-end personal computer motherboards and is used with low-profile cases. In NLX systems, the motherboard has only one expansion slot, in which a **riser card**, or **bus riser**, is mounted (see Figure 4-13). Expansion cards are mounted on the riser card, and the card also contains connectors for the floppy and hard drives. The motherboard itself includes a low-end video controller. The NLX form factor is designed to be flexible and to use space efficiently.

Riser card for expansion slots and other connectors

CPU with heat sink attached

FRONT

Memory modules

Two PCI slots

Two ISA slots

REAR

Motherboard

Ports on rear of board for peripheral devices

Figure 4-13   The NLX form factor uses a riser card that connects to the motherboard. The riser card provides expansion slots for the expansion cards.

LPX and Mini-LPX Form Factors

Western Digital originally developed **LPX** and **Mini-LPX**, which each have a riser card similar to NLX systems, and are often used in low-cost systems sold in large electronics stores. Difficult to upgrade, they cannot handle the size and operating temperature of today's faster processors. In addition, a manufacturer often makes proprietary changes to the standard LPX motherboard design, forcing you to use only the manufacturer's power supply. LPX and Mini-LPX use small cases called low-profile cases and slimline cases, which the next section discusses.

Backplane Systems

**A+
CORE
1.1**

Backplane systems do not use a true motherboard. The backplane is a board that normally sits against the back of a proprietary case with slots on it for other cards. **Active backplanes** contain no circuits other than bus connectors and some buffer and driver circuits. **Passive backplanes** contain no circuitry at all; the circuits are all on a mothercard, a circuit board that plugs into the backplane and contains a CPU. These systems are generally not used in personal computers. Passive backplanes are sometimes used for industrial rack-mounted systems and high-end file servers. A rack-mounted system is not designed for personal use, and often several of these systems are mounted in cases stacked on a rack for easy access by technicians.

NOTE

The latest form factor is **BTX (Balanced Technology Extended)**, which is expected to be available by the time this book is in print. BTX is designed for flexibility and for large tower systems to ultra small systems that sit under a monitor. The BTX form factor design focuses on reducing heat with better air flow and improved fans and coolers. It also gives better structural support for the motherboard than does ATX.

Types of Cases

**A+
CORE
1.1
1.2
4.3**

Several types and sizes of cases are on the market for each form factor. The computer case, sometimes called the chassis, houses the power supply, motherboard, expansion cards, and drives. The case has lights and switches on the front panel that can be used to control and monitor the PC. Generally, the larger the case, the larger the power supply and the more amps it carries. These large cases allow for the extra space and power needed for a larger number of devices, such as multiple hard drives needed in a server.

Cases for personal computers and notebooks fall into three major categories: desktop cases, tower cases, and notebook cases.

Desktop Cases

The classic case with four drive bays and around six expansion slots that sits on your desktop doing double duty as a monitor stand is called a desktop case. The motherboard sits on the bottom of a desktop case, and the power supply is near the back. Because of the space a desktop case takes, it has fallen out of favor in recent years and is being replaced by smaller and more space-efficient cases.

For low-end desktop systems, **compact cases**, sometimes called **low-profile** or **slimline cases**, follow either the NLX, LPX, or Mini-LPX form factor. Likely to have fewer drive bays, they generally still provide for some expansion. You can see the rear of a compact case in Figure 4-14. An LPX motherboard that uses this case has a riser card for expansion cards, which is why the expansion card slots in the figure run parallel to the motherboard sitting on the bottom of the case.

Fan

Power cord connectors

Expansion slots

Printer port

Video port

Serial ports
Keyboard port

4

Figure 4-14   Because the expansion slots are running parallel to the motherboard on the bottom of this desktop case, you know a riser card is used

Tower Cases

A **tower case** can be as high as two feet and has room for several drives. Often used for servers, this type of case is also good for PC users who anticipate upgrading, because tower cases provide maximum space for working inside a computer and moving components around. Variations in tower cases include the minitower, midsize tower, and full-size tower.

Midsize towers, also called miditowers, are the most popular. They are midrange in size and generally have around six expansion slots and four drive bays, providing moderate potential for expansion. The minitower, also called a microtower, is the smallest type of tower case and does not provide room for expansion. Figure 4-15 shows a minitower that accommodates a Baby AT or a full ATX system. Full-size towers are used for high-end personal computers and servers. They are usually built to accommodate ATX, Mini-ATX, and Baby AT systems. Figure 4-16 shows examples of each of the three main tower sizes, as well as two desktop cases.

A+
CORE
1.1
1.2
4.3

Figure 4-15   Minitower for Baby AT or full ATX motherboard

Figure 4-16   Tower and desktop cases

Notebook Cases

Notebook cases are used for portable computers that have all the components of a desktop computer. The cost and power of notebook systems varies widely. As with other small systems, notebooks can present difficulties in expansion. The smallest notebook cases are called subnotebooks. Notebook designs are often highly propriet-ary, but are generally designed to conserve space, allow portability, use less power, and produce less heat. The case fan in a notebook usually attaches to a thermometer

A+
CORE
1.1
1.2
4.3

and runs only when temperature needs to be lowered. Additionally, the transformer and rectifier functions of the power supply are often moved to an AC adapter on the power cable.

In summary, when selecting a computer case, remember that the case needs to fit its intended use. Many different manufacturers make cases and power supplies. Some specialize in high-end custom systems, while others make a variety of cases, from rack-mounted servers to low-profile desktops. Table 4-3 lists a few case and power supply vendors.

Manufacturer	Web Site
MGE Company	www.mgecompany.com
Axxion Group Corporation	www.axxion.com
Sunus Suntek	www.suntekgroup.com
Enlight Corporation	www.enlightcorp.com
PC Power and Cooling	www.pcpowerandcooling.com
PCI Case Group	www.pcicase.co.uk
Maxpoint Computers	www.maxpoint.com
Compucase	www.compucasecorp.com

Table 4-3   Manufacturers of cases and power supplies for personal computers

Detecting and Correcting Power Supply Problems

A+
CORE
1.2

If you assemble a PC from parts, most often you purchase a computer case with the power supply already installed. However, you might need to exchange the power supply of an existing PC because it is damaged or you need to upgrade to one with more power. In this section, you will learn how to troubleshoot the power system and power supply in your computer as well as how to upgrade and install power supplies.

Upgrading Your Power Supply

Sometimes a power supply upgrade is necessary when you add new devices. If you are installing a hard drive or DVD drive and are concerned that the power supply is not adequate, test it after you finish the installation. Make as many as possible of the devices in your system work at the same time. For example, you can make both the new drive and the floppy drive work at the same time by copying files from one to the other. If the new drive and the floppy drive each work independently, but data errors occur when both work at the same time, suspect a shortage of electrical power.

If you prefer a more technical approach, you can estimate how much total wattage your system needs by calculating the watts required for each device and adding them together. (Calculate watts by multiplying volts in the circuit by amps required for each device.) However, in most cases, the computer's power supply is more than adequate if you add only one or two new devices.

Most often you purchase a computer case with a power supply already installed, but you can purchase power supplies separately from cases. Power supplies for microcomputers range from 200 watts for a small desktop computer system to 600 watts for a tower floor model that uses many multimedia or other power-hungry devices. Most case vendors also make power supplies (refer back to Table 4-3).

The easiest way to fix a power supply you suspect is faulty is to replace it. You can determine if the power supply really is the problem by turning off the PC, opening the computer case, and setting the new power supply on top of the old one. Disconnect the old power supply's cords and plug the PC devices into the new power supply. Turn on the PC and verify that the new power supply solves your problem before installing it.

Follow this procedure to install a power supply:

1. Turn off the power to the computer.

2. Remove all external power cables from the power supply connections.

3. Remove the computer case cover.

4. Disconnect all power cords from the power supply to other devices.

5. Determine which components must be removed before the power supply can be safely removed from the case. You might need to remove the hard drive, several cards, or the CD-ROM drive. In some cases, you may even need to remove the motherboard.

6. Remove all the components necessary to get to the power supply. Remember to protect the components from static electricity as you work.

7. Unscrew the screws on the back of the computer case that hold the power supply to the case.

8. Look on the bottom or back of the case for slots that hold the power supply in position. Often the power supply must be shifted in one direction to free it from the slots.

9. Remove the power supply.

10. Place the new power supply in position, sliding it into the slots the old power supply used.

11. Replace the power supply screws.

A+
CORE
1.2

12. Replace all other components.

13. Before replacing the case cover, connect the power cords, turn on the PC, and verify that all is working.

14. Turn off the PC and replace the cover.

   In a project at the end of this chapter, you will see additional instructions for taking a computer apart and putting it back together.

4

Introduction to Troubleshooting

A+
CORE
2.1
2.2

Troubleshooting a PC problem begins with isolating it into one of two categories: problems that prevent the PC from booting and problems that occur after a successful boot. Begin by asking the user questions like these to learn as much as you can:

- Please describe the problem. What error messages, unusual displays, or failures did you see?
- When did the problem start?
- What was the situation when the problem occurred?
- What programs or software were you using?
- Did you move your computer system recently?
- Has there been a recent thunderstorm or electrical problem?
- Have you made any hardware, software, or configuration changes?
- Has someone else used your computer recently?
- Can you show me how to reproduce the problem?

Next, ask yourself, "Does the PC boot properly?" Figure 4-17 shows you the direction to take, depending on the answer. If the screen is blank and the entire system is "dead"—no lights, no spinning drive or fan—then proceed to troubleshoot the power system.

   Recall from Chapter 3 that when POST completes successfully, it sounds a single beep indicating that all is well, regardless of whether the monitor is working or even present. If you hear the beep, then the problem is with the video, and the next step is to troubleshoot the video. If you don't hear the beep or you hear more than one, then POST encountered an error. In that case, proceed to troubleshooting the motherboard, a subject Chapter 5 covers.

   If an error message appears on the screen, then the obvious next step is to respond to the message. An example of such an error is "Keyboard not present." If the error message occurs as the OS loads, and you don't understand the message or know how to respond to it, begin by troubleshooting the OS.

   If video works but the boot message is confusing or unreadable, then begin to eliminate the unnecessary. Perform a clean boot. For Windows 9x or Windows 2000/XP, the simplest way is to boot to Safe Mode. If that doesn't work, use your bootable rescue disk or disks.

A+
CORE
2.1
2.2

If the PC boots properly, turn your attention to the system that is not working and begin troubleshooting there. In this chapter, since you are learning about electricity and power supplies, you will look more closely at how to troubleshoot the power system.

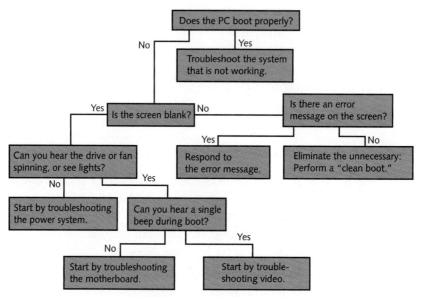

Figure 4-17   Begin PC problem solving by asking the question, "Does the PC boot properly?"

APPLYING CONCEPTS

Your friend Sharon calls to ask your help with a computer problem. Her system has been working fine for over a year, but now strange things are happening. Sometimes the system powers down while she is working for no apparent reason, and sometimes Windows locks up. As you read this section, look for clues as to what the problem might be. Also, as you read, think of questions to ask your friend that will help you.

Troubleshooting the Power System

First, let's look at some general guidelines and some questions to ask when you have power problems:

- Are there any burnt parts or odors? (Definitely not a good sign!)
- Is everything connected and turned on? Are any cable connections loose? Is the computer plugged in?

- Are all the switches turned on? Computer? Monitor? Surge protector? Uninterruptible power supply? Separate circuit breaker? Is the wall outlet (or surge protector) in working condition?
- If the fan is not running, turn off the computer, open the case, and check the connections to the power supply. Are they secure? Are all cards securely seated?

For most of the newer ATX power supplies, a wire runs from the power switch on the front of the ATX case to the motherboard. This wire must be connected to the pins on the motherboard and the switch turned on before power comes up. Check that the wire is connected correctly to the motherboard. Figure 4-18 shows the wire, which is labeled "REMOTE SW," connected to pins on the motherboard labeled "PWR.SW." If you are not sure of the correct connection on the motherboard, see the motherboard documentation.

Remote SW

Figure 4-18   For an ATX power supply, the remote switch wire must be connected to the motherboard before power will come on

Then remove all nonessential expansion cards (modem, sound card, mouse) one at a time. This verifies that they are not drawing too much power and pulling the system down. It is possible that the expansion cards are all good but that the power supply cannot provide enough current for all the add-on boards. Perhaps there are too many cards and the computer is overheating. The temperature inside the case should not exceed 113 degrees F (45 degrees C). You might need to add extra case fans, which is discussed later in the chapter.

**A+
CORE
2.1
2.2**

Vacuum the entire unit, especially the power supply's fan vent, or use compressed air to blow out dust. Excessive dust insulates components and causes them to overheat. Use an ESD-safe service vac that you can purchase from electronic tools suppliers.

NOTE

Remember from earlier in the chapter that strong magnetic or electrical interference can affect how a power system functions. Sometimes an old monitor emits too much static and EMF (electromagnetic force) and brings a whole system down. When you troubleshoot power problems, remember to check for sources of electrical or magnetic interference such as an old monitor or electric fan sitting near the computer case.

Troubleshooting the Power Supply Itself

Problems with the PC's power supply, the house current, or overheating can express themselves in the following ways:

- The PC sometimes halts during booting. After several tries, it boots successfully.
- Error codes or beeps occur during booting, but they come and go.
- The computer stops or hangs for no reason. Sometimes it might even reboot itself.
- Memory errors appear intermittently.
- Data is written incorrectly to the hard drive.
- The keyboard stops working at odd times.
- The motherboard fails or is damaged.
- The power supply overheats and becomes hot to the touch.

✔ **A+ EXAM TIP**

The A+ Core exam expects you to recognize that a given symptom is possibly power or heat related.

An overheated system can cause intermittent problems. Use compressed air or an antistatic vacuum to remove dust from the power supply and the vents over the entire computer. Check that the power supply fan and the fan over the CPU both work.

A brownout (reduced current) of the house current or a faulty power supply might cause symptoms of electrical power problems. If you suspect the house current could be low, check other devices that are using the same circuit. A copy machine, laser printer, or other heavy equipment might be drawing too much power. Remove the other devices from the same house circuit.

A system with a standard power supply of about 250 watts that has multiple hard drives, multiple CD-ROM drives, and several expansion cards is most likely operating above the rated capacity of the power supply, which can cause the system to unexpectedly reboot or give intermittent, otherwise unexplained errors. Upgrade the power supply as needed to accommodate an overloaded power system.

If these suggestions don't correct the problem, check the power supply by exchanging it for one you know is good. For an AT motherboard, be certain to follow the black-to-black rule when attaching the power cords to the motherboard.

You can use a multimeter to measure the voltage output of a power supply and determine if it is supplying correct voltages, but know that a power supply that gives correct voltages when you measure it might still be the source of problems, because power problems can be intermittent. See Appendix E, "Electricity and Multimeters," to learn how to use a multimeter to measure voltage output from a power supply.

An electrical conditioner might solve the problem of intermittent errors caused by noise in the power line to the PC. Try installing an electrical conditioner to monitor and condition voltage to the PC.

Troubleshooting the Power Supply Fan

An improperly working fan sometimes causes power supply problems. Usually just before a fan stops working, it hums or whines, especially when the PC is first turned on. If this has just happened, replace the fan if you are trained to service the power supply. If not, then replace the entire power supply, which is considered a **field replaceable unit (FRU)** for a PC support technician. If you replace the power supply or fan and the fan still does not work, the problem might not be the fan. A short somewhere else in the system drawing too much power might cause the problem. Don't operate the PC if the fan does not work. Computers without cooling fans can quickly overheat and damage chips. To troubleshoot a nonfunctional fan, which might be a symptom of another problem and not a problem of the fan itself, follow these steps:

1. Turn off the power and remove all power cord connections to all components, including the connections to the motherboard, and all power cords to drives. Turn the power back on. If the fan works, the problem is with one of the systems you disconnected, not with the power supply or its fan.

2. Turn off the power and reconnect the power cords to the drives. If the fan comes on, you can eliminate the drives as the problem. If the fan does not come on, try one drive after another until you identify the drive with the short.

3. If the drives are not the problem, suspect the motherboard subsystem. With the power off, reconnect all power cords to the drives.

4. Turn off the power and remove the power to the motherboard by disconnecting P1 or P8 and P9. Turn the power back on.

5. If the fan works, the problem is probably not the power supply but a short in one of the components powered by the power cords to the motherboard. The power to the motherboard also powers interface cards.

6. Remove all interface cards and reconnect plugs to the motherboard.

7. If the fan still works, the problem is one of the interface cards. If the fan does not work, the problem is the motherboard or something still connected to it.

A+
CORE
2.1
2.2

Power Problems with the Motherboard

The motherboard, like all other components inside the computer case, should be grounded to the chassis. Look for a metal screw that grounds the board to the computer case. However, a short might be the problem with the electrical system if some component on the board makes improper contact with the chassis. This short can seriously damage the motherboard. Check for missing standoffs (small plastic or metal spacers that hold the motherboard a short distance away from the chassis), the problem that most often causes these improper connections.

Shorts in the circuits on the motherboard might also cause problems. Look for damage on the bottom of the motherboard. These circuits are coated with plastic, and quite often damage is difficult to spot.

Frayed wires on cable connections can also cause shorts. Disconnect hard drive cables connected directly to the motherboard. Power up with P1 or P8 and P9 connected but all cables disconnected from the motherboard. If the fan works, the problem is with one of the systems you disconnected.

CAUTION

Never replace a damaged motherboard with a good one without first testing or replacing the power supply. You don't want to subject another good board to possible damage.

Overheating

A+
CORE
1.2
2.1
2.2

If your computer hangs after it has been running for a while, you may have an overheating problem. First, check whether there is airflow within the case. Open the case and make sure the CPU and power supply fans are turning and that cables will not fall into the fans and prevent them from turning when you close the case. While you have the case open, use an antistatic vacuum designed to be used around electronic equipment or a can of compressed air (both available at most computer supply stores) to blow dust off the motherboard and the CPU heat sink. Check the vents of the case, and clear any foreign material that may be blocking airflow.

After you close the case, leave your system off for a few hours. When you power up the computer again, let it run for 10 minutes, go into CMOS setup, check the temperature readings, and reboot. Next, let your system run until it shuts down. Power it up again and check the temperature in setup again. A significant difference in this reading and the first one you took after running the computer for 10 minutes indicates an overheating problem.

The problem might be caused by poor air circulation inside the case. The power supply fan in ATX cases blows air out of the case, pulling outside air from the vents in the front of the case across the processor to help keep it cool. Another exhaust fan is usually installed on the back of the case to help the power supply fan pull air through the case (see Figure 4-19). A third fan mounted on the processor is used to keep air circulating near the processor to prevent hot air pockets from forming around the processor. Air circulation problems can be caused by poor placement of

A+
CORE
1.2
1.9
2.1
2.2

vents and fans. Figure 4-20 shows a good arrangement of vents and fans for proper airflow and a poor arrangement.

4

Figure 4-19   Install one exhaust fan on the rear of the case to help pull air through the case

Good arrangement for proper airflow   Poor arrangement for poor airflow

Figure 4-20   Vents and fans need to be arranged for best airflow

A+
CORE
1.2
1.9
2.1
2.2

For better ventilation, use a power supply that has vents on the bottom and front of the power supply. Note in Figure 4-20 airflow is coming into the bottom of the power supply because of these bottom vents. The power supply in Figure 4-19 has vents only on the front and not on the bottom. Compare that to the power supply in Figure 4-21, which has vents on both the front and bottom.

Exhaust fan

Vents on the bottom
of power supply

Figure 4-21   This power supply has vents on the bottom to provide better airflow inside the case

An intake fan on the front of the case might help pull air into the case. Intel recommends you use a front intake fan for high-end systems, but AMD says a front fan is not necessary. Check with the processor manufacturer for specific instructions as to the placement of fans and what type of fan and heat sink to use. You will see some examples of processor fans in the next chapter. Here are some general guidelines to help solve an overheating problem:

- Check your system that vents and at least one exhaust fan are in the right position so that air flows across the processor without expansion cards or ribbon cables obstructing the flow.
- Check with the processor manufacturer Web site that you are using the right size processor fan and heat sink and the right thermal compound recommended for the specific processor.
- Check that your power supply has vents on the bottom.
- Use tie wraps to secure cables and cords so that they don't block airflow across the processor.
- An AGP video card generates a lot of heat. Leave the PCI slot next to the AGP slot open to better ventilate the AGP card.

A+
CORE
1.2
1.9
2.1
2.2

- Install hard drives in large bays using a bay kit to make the small drive fit in the large bay, thus improving airflow around the drive.
- Monitor the temperature inside the case using a temperature sensor that sounds an alarm when a high temperature is reached or uses software to alert you of a problem.

Be careful when trying to solve an overheating problem. Excessive heat itself may damage the CPU and the motherboard, and the hard reboots necessary when your system hangs may damage the hard drive. If you suspect damaged components, try substituting comparable components that you know are good.

4

APPLYING CONCEPTS

Back to Sharon's computer problem. Here are some questions that will help you identify the source of the problem:

- Have you added new devices to your system? (These new devices might be drawing too much power from an overworked power supply.)
- Have you moved your computer recently? (It might be sitting beside a heat vent or electrical equipment.)
- Does the system power down or hang after you have been working for some time?

Intermittent problems like the one Sharon described are often heat related. If the system only hangs but does not power off, the problem might be caused by faulty memory or bad software, but because it actually powers down, you can assume the problem is related to power or heat.

If Sharon tells you that the system powers down after she's been working for several hours, you can probably assume overheating. Check that first. If that's not the problem, the next thing to do is replace the power supply.

Energy Star Systems (The Green Star)

As you build or maintain a computer, one very important power consideration is energy efficiency and conservation. **Energy Star** systems and peripherals have the U.S. Green Star, indicating that they satisfy certain energy-conserving standards of the U.S. Environmental Protection Agency (EPA). Devices that can carry the Green Star are computers, monitors, printers, copiers, and fax machines. Qualifying devices are designed to decrease overall electricity consumption in the United States, to protect and preserve natural resources. These standards, sometimes called the **Green Standards**, generally mean that the computer or the device has a standby program that switches the device to sleep mode when it is not in use. During **sleep mode**, the device must use no more than 30 watts of power.

NOTE   Office equipment is among the fastest growing source of electricity consumption in industrialized nations. Much of this electricity is wasted, because people often leave computers and other equipment on overnight. Because Energy Star devices go into sleep mode when they are unused, they create overall energy savings of about 50 percent.

Power Management Methods and Features

A+
CORE
4.4

Computer systems use several different power management methods to conserve energy. Some are listed below:

- Advanced Power Management (APM), championed by Intel and Microsoft and used on older notebook computers
- AT Attachment (ATA) for IDE drives
- Display Power Management Signaling (DPMS) standards for monitors and video cards
- Advanced Configuration and Power Interface (ACPI), used with Windows 98 and Windows 2000/XP and supported by system BIOS

These energy-saving methods are designed to work incrementally, depending on how long the PC is idle. The following sections discuss several specific features that can sometimes be enabled and adjusted using CMOS setup or using the OS. In CMOS setup, a feature might not be available, setup might include additional features, or a feature might be labeled differently from those described next. (How to change these settings is covered in the next chapter.)

- *Green timer on the motherboard.* This sets the number of minutes of inactivity that must pass before the CPU goes into sleep mode. You can enable or disable the setting and select the number of minutes.
- *Doze time.* **Doze time** is the time that elapses before the system reduces 80 percent of its power consumption. Different systems accomplish this in different ways. For example, when one system enters doze mode, the system BIOS slows down the bus clock speed.
- *Standby time.* **Standby time** is the time that elapses before the system reduces 92 percent of its power consumption. For example, a system might accomplish this by changing the system speed from turbo to slow and suspending the video signal.
- *Suspend time.* **Suspend time** is the time that elapses before the system reduces its power consumption by 99 percent. The way this reduction is accomplished varies. The CPU clock might be stopped and the video signal suspended. After entering suspend mode, the system needs warm-up time so that the CPU, monitor, and other components can reach full activity.
- *Hard drive standby time.* **Hard drive standby time** is the amount of time before a hard drive shuts down.

Figure 4-22 shows the Power Management Setup screen of the CMOS setup for Award BIOS for an ATX Pentium II motherboard.

```
                       ROM PCI/ISA BIOS (<<P2B>>)
                        POWER MANAGEMENT SETUP
                         AWARD SOFTWARE, INC.

 Power Management    : User Define        ** Fan Monitor **
 Video Off Option    : Suspend -> Off   Chasis Fan Speed      : 3300RMP
 Video Off Method    : DPMS OFF         CPU Fan Speed         : 3800RMP
                                        Power Fan Speed       :  Ignore
         ** PM Timers **                     ** Thermal Monitor **
 HDD Power Down      : Disable          CPU Temperature       : 50C/ 112F
 Suspend Mode        : Disable          MB Temperature        : 25C/  77F
                                             ** Voltage Monitor **
       ** Power Up Control **           VCORE Voltage         :   3.3V
 PWR Button < 4 Secs : Soft Off         +3.3V Voltage         :   3.3V
 PWR Up On Modem Act : Enabled          +5V  Voltage          :   5.0V
 AC PWR Loss Restart : Disabled         +12V Voltage          :  12.0V
 Wake On LAN         : Enabled          -12V Voltage          : -12.0V
 Automatic Power Up  : Disabled         -5V  Voltage          :  -5.0V

                                        ESC   : Quit      ↑↓→←: Select Item
                                        F1    : Help    PU/PD/+/- : Modify
                                        F5    : Old Values (Shift)F2 : Color
                                        F6    : Load BIOS  Defaults
                                        F7    : Load Setup Defaults
```

Figure 4-22   A Power Management Setup screen showing power management features

Using the Video options on the left of the screen, you can enable or disable power management of the monitor. With power management enabled, you can control Energy Star features. The PM Timers feature controls doze, standby, and suspend modes for the hard drive. The Power Up Control determines the way the system can be controlled when it starts or when power to the computer is interrupted. The features on the right side of the screen monitor the power supply fan, CPU fan, optional chassis fan, temperatures of the CPU and the motherboard (MB), and voltage output to the CPU and motherboard.

Energy Star Monitors

Most computers and monitors sold today are Energy Star compliant, displaying the green Energy Star logo onscreen when the PC is booting. In order for a monitor's power-saving feature to function, the video card or computer must also support this function. Most monitors that follow the Energy Star standards adhere to the **Display Power Management Signaling (DPMS)** specifications developed by Video Electronics Standards Association (VESA), which allow for the video card and monitor to go into sleep mode simultaneously.

To view and change energy settings of an Energy Star monitor using Windows XP or 2000, right-click the desktop and select Properties. The Display Properties dialog box opens. Click the Screen Saver tab. If your monitor is Energy Star compliant, you will see the Energy Star logo at the bottom. When you click the Power button, the Power Options Properties dialog box opens, and you can change your power options (see Figure 4-23). Your power options might differ depending on the power management features your BIOS supports.

Figure 4-23   Changing power options in Windows 2000

NOTE Problems might occur if system BIOS is turning off the monitor because of power management settings, and Windows 9x/Me is also turning off the monitor. If the system hangs when you try to get the monitor going again, try disabling one or the other setting. It is best to use the OS or BIOS for power management, but not both.

CHAPTER SUMMARY

▶ Electrical voltage is a measure of the potential difference in an electrical system.

▶ Electrical current is measured in amps, and electrical resistance is measured in ohms.

▶ Wattage is a measure of electrical power. Wattage is calculated by multiplying volts by amps in a system.

▶ Microcomputers require direct current (DC), which is converted from alternating current (AC) by the PC's power supply inside the computer case.

▶ A PC power supply is actually a transformer and rectifier, rather than a supplier, of power.

▶ Materials used to make electrical components include conductors, insulators, and semiconductors.

▶ A transistor is a gate or switch for an electrical signal, a capacitor holds an electrical charge, a diode allows electricity to flow in one direction, and a resistor limits electrical current.

▶ To protect a computer system against ESD, use a ground bracelet, ground mat, and static shielding bags.

▶ Protect a computer system against EMI by covering expansion slots (which also reduces dust inside the case), by not placing the system close to or on the same circuit as high-powered electrical equipment, and by using line conditioners.

▶ Devices that control the electricity to a computer include surge suppressors, line conditioners, and UPSs.

▶ A surge suppressor protects a computer against damaging spikes in electrical voltage.

▶ Line conditioners level the AC to reduce brownouts and spikes.

▶ A UPS provides enough power to perform an orderly shutdown during a blackout.

▶ There are two kinds of UPSs: the true UPS (called the inline UPS), and the standby UPS.

▶ The inline UPS is more expensive, because it provides continuous power. The standby UPS must switch from one circuit to another when a blackout begins.

▶ Utility software at a remote computer or a computer connected to the UPS through a USB or serial cable can control and manage a smart UPS.

▶ Data line protectors are small surge suppressors designed to protect modems from spikes on telephone lines.

▶ A form factor is a set of specifications for the size and configuration of hardware components such as cases, power supplies, and motherboards.

▶ The most common form factor today is ATX. There is an ATX variation called Mini-ATX. ATX superseded the earlier AT and Baby AT form factors. BTX is the up-and-coming form factor.

▶ Other form factors include LPX and NLX, in which expansion cards are mounted on a riser card that plugs into the motherboard.

▶ Case types include desktop, low-profile or slimline desktops, minitower, midi-tower, full-size tower, and notebook. The most popular case type in use today is the miditower.

▶ A faulty power supply can cause memory errors, data errors, system hangs, or reboots; it can damage a motherboard or other components.

▶ To reduce energy consumption, the U.S. Environmental Protection Agency has established Energy Star standards for electronic devices.

▶ Devices that are Energy Star compliant go into sleep mode, in which they use less than 30 watts of power.

▶ PCs that are Energy Star compliant often have CMOS settings that affect the Energy Star options available on the PC.

KEY TERMS

For explanations of key terms, see the Glossary near the end of the book.

active backplane
alternating current (AC)
ampere or amp (A)
AT
ATX
Baby AT
backplane system
brownout
BTX (Balanced Technology Extended)
bus riser
capacitor
clamping voltage
compact case
data line protector
diode
direct current (DC)
Display Power Management Signaling (DPMS)
doze time
electromagnetic interference (EMI)
electrostatic discharge (ESD)
Energy Star

field replaceable unit (FRU)
FlexATX
form factor
full AT
Green Standards
ground bracelet
hard drive standby time
intelligent UPS
line conditioner
line-interactive UPS
low-profile case
LPX
MicroATX
Mini-ATX
Mini-LPX
NLX
ohm (Ω)
P1 connector
P8 connector
P9 connector
passive backplane

power conditioner
rectifier
resistor
riser card
sags
sleep mode
slimline case
smart UPS
soft power
soft switch
spike
standby time
static electricity
surge protector
surge suppressor
suspend time
swells
tower case
transformer
transistor
uninterruptible power supply (UPS)
volt (V)
watt (W)

REVIEWING THE BASICS

1. Volts are a measure of what characteristic of electricity?

2. What is the normal voltage of house electricity in the U.S.?

3. Hot wires in home wiring are normally colored ____ and ground wires in computers are normally colored _____.

4. What is the difference between a transformer and a rectifier? Which are found in a PC power supply?

5. What are the five voltages produced by an ATX power supply?

6. What are the four voltages produced by an AT power supply?

7. When working inside a computer, why is it important to not stack boards on top of each other?

8. Describe the purpose of the ground line in a house circuit. Show the electrical symbol for ground.

9. What is the basic electronic building block of an integrated circuit?

10. Why is a power supply dangerous even after the power is disconnected?

11. What is the symbol for a diode?

12. What is a simple way to detect EMI?

13. What is an unintended, high-current, closed connection between two points in a circuit called?

14. Which form factors use a riser card on the edge of the motherboard?

15. List five types of computer case form factors. What is the most popular type of form factor for PCs today?

16. List three advantages an ATX system has over a baby AT system.

17. List four computer symptoms that indicate a faulty power supply.

18. How much power can a device use in sleep mode if it complies with Green Standards?

19. Name one thing that can be set in CMOS that pertains to power management.

20. How can you easily tell if a computer is designed to comply with Green Standards?

21. Name two surge suppressor specifications.

22. What are the two main types of uninterruptible power supplies?

23. How does a smart UPS differ from one that is not smart?

24. If you are asked to identify the form factor of a motherboard, what are two criteria you can use to help you identify the board?

25. What are three motherboard form factors that can be used with a compact case?

THINKING CRITICALLY

1. How much power is consumed by a load drawing 5 A with 120 V across it?

2. You suspect that a power supply is faulty, but you use a multimeter to measure its voltage output and find it to be acceptable. Why is it still possible that the power supply may be faulty?

3. Someone asks you for help with a computer that hangs at odd times. You turn it on and work for about 15 minutes, and then the computer freezes and powers down. What do you do first?

    a. Replace the surge protector.

    b. Replace the power supply.

    c. Turn the PC back on, go into CMOS setup, and check the temperature reading.

    d. Install an additional fan.

4. In Figure 4-24, which motherboard is an AT board? An ATX board?

✔ **A+ EXAM TIP**
The A+ Core exam expects you to identify motherboard form factors, ports, connectors, and other features using rough drawings like the ones in Figure 4-24.

Motherboard A   Motherboard B

Figure 4-24   Motherboard form factor identification

HANDS-ON PROJECTS

4

PROJECT 4-1: Exploring Energy Star Features on a PC

Write down each power management and Energy Star feature that can be set through CMOS on your home or lab computer.

PROJECT 4-2: Making Price and Value Comparisons

At your local computer vendor(s), compare the prices and ratings of two different surge suppressors. Write down your findings.

PROJECT 4-3: Finding PC Power Supply Facts

Remove the cover from your home or lab PC, and answer the following questions:

1. How many watts are supplied by your power supply? (The number is usually printed on the label on the top of the power supply.)

2. How many cables are supplied by your power supply?

3. Where does each cable lead?

4. Does the back of the power supply have a switch that can be set for 220 volts (Europe) or 110 volts (U.S.)?

PROJECT 4-4: Building a Circuit to Turn On a Light

VIDEO

Building a
Circuit

1. From the following components, build a circuit to turn on a light:

   ▶ An AC light bulb or LED (*Note*: An LED has polarity—it must be connected with the negative and positive terminals in the correct positions.)

   ▶ A double-A battery (*Note*: A 9-volt battery can burn out some bulbs.)

   ▶ A switch (A knife switch or even a DIP switch will work.)

   ▶ Three pieces of wire to connect the light, the switch, and the battery

2. Add a second battery to the circuit, and record the results.

3. Add a resistor to the circuit, and record the results.

4. Place an extra wire in the middle of the circuit running from the battery to the switch (thus making a short), and record the results.

PROJECT 4-5: Researching the Market for a UPS for Your Computer System

For a computer system you can access, determine how much wattage output a UPS should have in the event of a total blackout, and estimate how long the UPS should sustain power. Research the market and report on the features and prices of a standby UPS and an inline UPS. Include the following information in your report:

- ▶ Wattage supported
- ▶ Length of time the power is sustained during total blackout
- ▶ Line-conditioning features
- ▶ AC backup present or not present for the inline UPS
- ▶ Surge suppressor present or not present
- ▶ Number of power outlets on the box, and other features
- ▶ Written guarantees
- ▶ Brand name, model, vendor, and price of the device

PROJECT 4-6: Detecting EMI

Use a small, inexpensive AM radio. Turn the dial to a low frequency, away from a station. Put the radio next to several electronic devices. List the devices in order, from the one producing the most static to the one producing the least static. Listen to the devices when they are idle and in use.

PROJECT 4-7: Calculating Wattage Used by Your Drives

Fill in the following table, and then calculate the total wattage requirements of all drives in your system. Look for a wattage rating printed somewhere on the device.

Component	Wattage
Hard drive	
Floppy drive	
CD-ROM drive	
DVD drive	
Zip drive	
Other drive	

Total wattage requirements for all drives:

PROJECT 4-8: Exploring Computer System Form Factors

You will need to open your computer case to answer these questions about your computer system:

1. What type of case do you have?

2. What are the dimensions of your motherboard in inches?

3. What form factor does your motherboard use?

4. What is the power rating of your power supply?

PROJECT 4-9: Taking Apart a Computer and Putting It Back Together

A PC technician needs to be comfortable with taking apart a computer and putting it back together. To learn the most from this project, do it using more than one system. Be sure to use a ground bracelet as you work, and follow the other safety precautions in the chapter. You'll also need a Phillips-head screwdriver, a flat-head screwdriver, paper, and a pencil.

1. Put the computer on a table with plenty of room. Have a plastic bag or cup available to hold screws. When you reassemble the PC, you will need to insert the same screws in the same holes. This is especially important with the hard drive, because screws that are too long can puncture the hard drive housing.

2. Print out all CMOS settings or save them to a floppy disk. Make a bootable disk if you don't already have one. Turn off the PC and unplug it.

3. To remove the cover of your PC:

   ▸ Unplug the monitor, mouse, and keyboard, and move them out of your way.

▶ For a desktop case or tower case, locate and remove the screws on the back of the case. Look for the screws in each corner and one in the top (see Figure 4-25). Be careful not to unscrew any screws besides these. The other screws probably are holding the power supply in place (see Figure 4-26).

▶ After you remove the cover screws, slide the cover forward and up to remove it from the case, as shown in Figure 4-27.

VIDEO

Opening a
Computer Case

▶ For tower cases, the screws are also on the back. Look for screws in all four corners and down the sides (see Figure 4-27). Remove the screws and then slide the cover back slightly before lifting it up to remove it. Some tower cases have panels on either side of the case, held in place with screws on the back of the case. Remove the screws and slide each panel toward the rear, then lift it off the case.

Figure 4-25   Locate the screws that hold the cover in place

Rear view

Power supply
mounting screws

Figure 4-26 Power supply mounting screws

Remove screws

Pull cover back, then up, to remove

Removing a standard case cover

First, remove
the screws
holding the
cover in place

Then carefully
pull the cover
toward the
back

Removing a tower case cover

Figure 4-27 Removing the cover

4. Draw a diagram of all cable connections, DIP switch settings, and jumper set-tings. You might need the cable connection diagram to help you reassemble. You will not change any DIP switch settings or jumper settings in this project, but accidents do happen. Be prepared. If you like, use a felt-tip marker to make a mark across components, to indicate a cable connection, board placement,

motherboard orientation, speaker connection, brackets, and so on, so that you can simply line up the marks when you reassemble.

5. Identify the following major components. (Drawings in this and previous chapters should help.)

   ▶ Power supply

   ▶ Floppy disk drive

   ▶ Hard drive

   ▶ Motherboard

6. Before removing any cables, note that each cable has a color or stripe down one side. This edge color marks this side of the cable as pin 1. Look on the board or drive that the cable is attached to. You should see that pin 1 or pin 2 is clearly marked. (See Figure 4-28.)

Figure 4-28   How to find pin 1 on an expansion card

7. Verify that the edge color is aligned with pin 1. Look at the cable used to connect drive A to the floppy drive controller card. There is a twist in the cable. This twist reverses the leads in the cable, causing the addresses for this cable to be different from the addresses for the cable that doesn't have the twist. The connector with the twist is attached to drive A (see Figure 4-29). Remove the cables to the floppy drives and the hard drives. Remove the power supply cords from the drives.

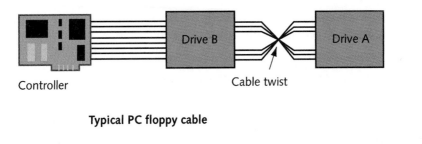

Controller   Cable twist

Typical PC floppy cable

Controller   Reverses original twist

Figure 4-29   Twist in cable identifies drive A

VIDEO

Replacing an
Expansion Card

8. Remove the expansion cards, following these procedures. (If you are working with a tower case, you can lay it on its side so the motherboard is on the bottom.)

   a. Remove the cables from the card. There is no need to remove the other end of the cable from its component (floppy disk drive, hard drive, or CD-ROM drive). Lay the cable over the top of the component or case.

   b. Remove the screw holding the board to the case.

   c. Grasp the board with both hands and remove it by lifting straight up and rocking the board from end to end (not side to side). Rocking the board from side to side might spread the slot opening and weaken the connection.

   d. As you remove cards, don't put your fingers on the edge connectors or touch a chip, and don't stack the cards on top of one another.

9. Examine the board connector for the cable. Can you identify pin 1? Lay the board aside on a flat surface.

10. Remove the floppy drive next. Some drives have one or two screws on each side of the drive attaching the drive to the drive bay. After you remove the screws, the drive usually slides to the front and out of the case. Sometimes there is a catch underneath the drive that you must lift up as you slide the drive forward. Be careful not to remove screws that hold the circuit card on top of the drive to the drive housing. The whole unit should stay intact.

11. Remove the hard drive next. Look for the screws that hold the drive to the bay. Be careful to remove only these screws, not the screws that hold the drive together. Handle the drive with care.

VIDEO

Replacing a
Power Supply

12. You might need to remove the power supply before exposing the motherboard. Unplug the power supply lines to the motherboard. An ATX power supply only has a single power line, but for an AT power supply, carefully note which line is labeled P8 and which is labeled P9. You will want to be certain that you don't switch these two lines when reconnecting them, since this would cause the wrong voltage to flow in the circuits on the motherboard and could destroy the board. Fortunately, most connections today only allow you to place the lines in the correct order, which is always black leads on P8 next to black leads on P9. Remember, "black to black." Look for screws that attach the power supply to the computer case, as shown in Figure 4-30. Be careful not to remove any screws that hold the power supply housing together. You do not want to take the housing apart. After you have removed the screws, the power supply still might not be free. Sometimes it is attached to the case on the underside by recessed slots. Turn the case over and look on the bottom for these slots. If they are present, determine in which direction you need to slide the power supply to free it from the case.

Figure 4-30   Removing the power supply mounting screws

13. The motherboard is the last thing to be removed. It probably has spacers keeping it from resting directly on the bottom of the computer case. Carefully pop off these spacers and/or remove the three or four screws that hold the board to the case.

14. You are now ready to reassemble. Reverse the preceding disassembling activities. Place each card in its slot (it doesn't have to be the same slot, just the same bus) and replace the screw. Don't place the video card near the power supply.

15. Replace the cables, being sure to align the colored edge with pin 1. (In some cases it might work better to connect the cable to the card before you put the card in the expansion slot.)

16. Plug in the keyboard, monitor, and mouse.

17. In a classroom environment, have the instructor check your work before you power up.

18. Turn on the power and check that the PC is working properly before you replace the cover. Don't touch the inside of the case while the power is on.

19. If all is well, turn off the PC and replace the cover and its screws. If the PC does not work, don't panic! Just turn off the power and go back and check each cable connection and each expansion card. You probably have not solidly seated a card in the slot. After you have double-checked, try again.

4

The Motherboard

Chapter 1 introduced the basic hardware components of a computer. In this chapter, we begin to examine in detail how the components of a computer work in harmony and with accuracy. Our starting point is the motherboard, the central site of computer logic circuitry and the location of the most important microchip in the computer, the CPU or processor.

To understand the ideas in this chapter, you should know the definitions of bit, byte, kilobyte, and hexadecimal (hex), and be able to read memory addresses written in hex. (See Appendix C.)

NOTE

Types of Motherboards

A+
CORE
1.1
1.10
4.3
4.4

A motherboard's primary purpose is to house the CPU and allow all devices to communicate with it and with each other. As you learned in the last chapter, the two most popular motherboards are the older AT (see Figure 5-1) and the newer ATX (see Figure 5-2). Each board is available in two sizes. ATX boards include more power-management features, support faster systems, and are easier to install. Table 5-1 summarizes AT and ATX boards and their form factors.

Memory cache slot (COAST)

CPU socket 7

16-bit ISA expansion slots (4)

ROM BIOS

PCI expansion slots (3)

Keyboard port

Connections to power supply

RAM slots with two SIMMS

Figure 5-1　　A typical AT motherboard with memory cache and socket 7 for the Intel Classic Pentium CPU. The CPU with a fan on top is installed as well as two SIMM memory modules.

A+
CORE
1.1
1.10
4.3
4.4

P1 power connector

Two IDE connectors

Floppy drive connector

DIP switches

16-bit ISA expansion slot

5

AGP slot

Five PCI expansion slots

Flash ROM

Parallel port

Two serial ports

Two USB ports

Keyboard and mouse ports

Slot 1 for Pentium III with supporting braces

Four RAM slots with one DIMM installed

Figure 5-2   An ATX motherboard with a Pentium III and one DIMM module installed

Type of Motherboard	Description
AT	• Oldest type of motherboard, still used in some systems • Uses P8 and P9 power connections • Measures 30.5 cm × 33 cm (12 inches × 13 inches)
Baby AT	• Smaller version of AT; small size is possible because motherboard logic is stored on a smaller chip set • Uses P8 and P9 power connections • Measures 33 cm × 22 cm (12 inches × 8.7 inches)

Table 5-1 (continued)

Type of Motherboard	Description
ATX	• Developed by Intel for Pentium systems • Has a more conveniently accessible layout than AT boards • Includes a power-on switch that can be software-enabled and extra power connections for extra fans • Uses a single P1 power connector • Measures 30.5 cm × 24.4 cm (12 inches × 9.6 inches)
Mini ATX	• An ATX board with a more compact design • Measures 28.4 cm × 20.8 cm (11.2 inches × 8.2 inches)
BTX	Recently released new form factors include: • BTX has up to 7 expansion slots and can be up to 325.12 mm wide • MicroBTX has up to 4 expansion slots and can be up to 264.16 mm wide • PicoBTX has none or 1 expansion slot and can be up to 203.20 mm wide

Table 5-1   Types of motherboards

When buying a computer, the two most important components to consider are the CPU and the motherboard. When you buy a motherboard, your selection determines the following components:

- Types, speeds, and how many CPUs (1 or 2) you can use
- Chip set on the board (already installed)
- Memory cache type and size
- Types and number of expansion slots: PCI, PCI Express, AGP, and ISA
- Type of memory, including what kind and how much of SRAM (on-board or inside CPU housing) and DRAM (DIMMs or RIMMs)
- Maximum amount of memory you can install on the board and the incremental amounts by which you can upgrade memory
- Type of case you can use
- ROM BIOS (already installed)
- Presence or absence of IDE, serial ATA, RAID, and SCSI controllers
- Types of ports on the board (serial, parallel, USB, network, modem, and so forth)

Because the motherboard determines so many of your computer's features, selecting the motherboard is a very important decision when you purchase a computer or assemble one from parts. Depending on which applications and peripheral devices you plan to use with the computer, you can take one of three approaches to selecting

**A+
CORE
1.1
1.10
4.3
4.4**

a motherboard. The first option is to select the board that provides the most room for expansion, so you can upgrade and exchange components and add devices easily. A second approach is to select the board that best suits the needs of the computer's current configuration, knowing that when you need to upgrade, you will likely switch to new technology and a new motherboard. The third approach is to select a motherboard that meets your present needs with moderate room for expansion.

Ask the following questions when selecting a motherboard:

- What form factor does the motherboard use?
- Does the motherboard support the number and type of CPU you plan to use? (for example, Socket LGA 775 for the Intel Pentium 4 up to 3.3 GHz)
- What are the supported frequencies of the system bus? (for example, 1066/800/533/400 MHz)
- What type of memory does the board support, and how much memory can the board hold?
- What type and how many expansion slots are on the board?
- What are the embedded devices on the board and what internal slots or connections does the board have? (For example, the board might provide a network port, an internal slot for a wireless network, or both.)
- What type of BIOS does the motherboard use?
- Does the board fit the case you plan to use?
- What is the warranty on the board?
- How extensive and user-friendly is the documentation?
- How much support does the manufacturer supply for the board?

Sometimes a motherboard contains a component more commonly offered as a separate device. A component on the board is called an *embedded component* or an *on-board component*. One example is support for video. The video port might be on the motherboard or might require a video card. The cost of a motherboard with an embedded component is usually less than the combined cost of a motherboard with no embedded component and an expansion card. If you plan to expand, be cautious about choosing a proprietary board that has many embedded components. Often such boards do not easily accept add-on devices from other manufacturers. For example, if you plan to add a more powerful video card, you might not want to choose a motherboard that contains an embedded video controller. Even though you can often set a switch on the motherboard to disable the proprietary video controller, there is little advantage to paying the extra money for it.

If you have an embedded component, make sure you can disable it so you can use another external component if needed.

NOTE

Recall from Chapter 1 that a motherboard is configured through jumpers or DIP switches on the board or through CMOS setup. Embedded components are almost always configured through CMOS setup.

5

Table 5-2 lists some manufacturers of motherboards and their Web addresses.

Manufacturer	Web Address
Abit	www.abit.com.tw
American Megatrends, Inc. (AMI)	www.megatrends.com or www.ami.com
ASUS	www.asus.com
Dell	www.dell.com
First International Computer of America, Inc.	www.fica.com
Gateway	www.gateway.com
Gigabyte Technology Co., Ltd.	us.giga-byte.com
IBM	www.ibm.com
Intel Corporation	www.intel.com
Iwill Corporation	www.iwill.net
MicroStar International	www.msicomputer.com
Motherboards.com	www.motherboards.com
Supermicro Computer, Inc.	www.supermicro.com
Tyan Computer Corporation	www.tyan.com

Table 5-2   Major manufacturers of motherboards

Components on the Motherboard

Now that you have learned about types of motherboards, let's take a look at some components on the motherboard. This section focuses on components that you must know how to use (such as expansion slots), configure (such as the BIOS), and exchange (such as the CPU). Items that can be exchanged without returning the motherboard to the factory are called field replaceable units (FRUs). On older AT motherboards, these FRU components were the CPU, RAM, RAM cache, the ROM BIOS chip, and the CMOS battery. On newer motherboards, FRU components are the CPU, RAM, and the CMOS battery. Also, the motherboard itself is an FRU.

This section looks at the CPU and chip set, ROM BIOS, RAM, buses and expansion slots, and components used to change hardware configuration settings (jumpers, DIP switches, and CMOS). You will learn where these components are on the motherboard and how they function.

The CPU and the Chip Set

Most IBM and IBM-compatible computers manufactured today use microprocessor chips made by Intel (*www.intel.com*) or AMD (*www.amd.com*), or to a lesser degree by Cyrix, which is currently owned by VIA Technologies (*www.via.com.tw*). Early CPUs by Intel were identified by model numbers: 8088, 8086, 80286, 386, and 486. After the 486, Intel introduced the Pentium CPU, and several Intel CPUs that followed included Pentium in their names. The model numbers can be written with or without the 80 prefix and are sometimes preceded with an i, as in 80486, 486, or i486. Pentiums are sometimes identified simply with a P, as in P4 for Pentium 4.

How the CPU Works

The CPU contains three basic components: an input/output (I/O) unit, one or more arithmetic logic units (ALU), and a control unit (see Figure 5-3). The I/O unit manages data and instructions entering and leaving the CPU. The control unit manages all activities inside the CPU itself. The ALU unit does all comparisons and calculations. The CPU also needs places to store data and instructions as it works on them. Registers are small holding areas inside the CPU that work much as RAM does outside the CPU. Registers hold counters, data, instructions, and addresses that the ALU is currently processing. In addition to registers, the CPU has its own internal memory cache that holds data and instructions waiting to be processed by the ALU. Also notice in Figure 5-3 the external bus, where data, instructions, addresses, and control signals are sent into and out of the CPU. The CPU has its own **internal bus** for communication to the internal cache. The CPU's internal bus operates at a much higher frequency than the external, or system, bus. The industry sometimes calls these internal and external buses the **back-side bus (BSB)** and the **front-side bus (FSB)**.

Older CPUs had only a single ALU, but beginning with the Pentium, CPUs contain at least two ALUs so the CPU can process two instructions at once. For the Pentiums, the front-side data bus is 64 bits wide, but the back-side data bus is only 32 bits wide, because of this dual-processing design. This is why the industry calls the Pentium a 32-bit processor; it processes 32 bits at a time internally, even though it uses a 64-bit bus externally. Recall that Intel has 64-bit processors, called Itaniums, that have a 128-bit external data bus, and AMD has the Opteron and the Athlon 64, both of which are 64-bit processors.

Backside bus

Pentium CPU

Registers   Registers

ALU   ALU

Internal memory cache

Control unit

I/O unit

Internal data bus is 32 bits wide

External data bus is 64 bits wide

Figure 5-3   Beginning with the Pentium CPU, a CPU has two arithmetic logic units and can process two instructions at once

How to Rate CPUs

You need to know how to identify a CPU installed in a system and what performance to expect from that CPU. The following attributes are used to rate CPUs:

1. *Processor core speed measured in gigahertz.* The first CPU used in an IBM PC was the 8088, which worked at about 4.77 MHz, or 4,770,000 clock beats per second. An average speed for a new CPU today is about 3.5 GHz, or 3,500,000,000 beats per second. In less than one second, this processor beats more times than a human heart beats in a lifetime!

2. *Word size.* Word size, sometimes called the internal data path size, is the largest number of bits the CPU can process in one operation. Word size ranges from 16 bits (2 bytes) to 64 bits (8 bytes).

3. *Data path.* The data path, sometimes called the external data path size or the front side data bus, is the largest number of bits that can be transported into the CPU. The data path size is the same as the system bus size, or the number of bits that can be on the bus at one time. The data path in Figure 5-3 is 64 bits wide. The word size need not be as large as the data path size; some CPUs can receive more bits than they can process at one time, as in the case of the Pentium in Figure 5-3.

4. *Efficiency and special functionality of programming code.* Permanently built into the CPU chip are programs that accomplish fundamental operations, such as comparing or adding two numbers. Less efficient CPUs require more steps to

perform these simple operations than more efficient CPUs. These groups of instructions are collectively called the **instruction set**. Some instruction sets are tailored for specific functions, such as the Pentiums' Hyper-Threading Technology designed to support multitasking.

5. *The system bus speeds the processor supports.* Today's front side buses run at 1066, 800, 533, or 400 MHz.

6. *The amount of memory included with the CPU.* Most present-day CPUs have a memory cache on the processor chip and also inside the processor housing on a small circuit board. In documentation, the chip is sometimes called a *die*. Memory on the die is called internal cache, primary cache, level 1, or L1 cache. Memory not on the die is called secondary cache, level 2, or L2. In addition, some processors have L3 cache, which is further away from the CPU than L2 cache.

7. *The type of RAM, motherboard, and chip set the processor supports.* RAM comes in a variety of modules, speeds, and features. The processor must fit the motherboard and the chip set embedded in it, and the processor and motherboard determine what type of RAM you can use in the system.

8. *Multiprocessing ability.* Some microchips are really two processors in one and can do more than one thing at a time. Others are designed to work in cooperation with other CPUs installed on the same motherboard.

NOTE Until Intel manufactured the Pentium series of chips, the three most popular ways of measuring CPU power were speed measured in megahertz, word size in bits, and data path size in bits. The criteria for measuring the power of a CPU have changed since the introduction of the Pentium. The word size and path size remained the same for several years, so we became more interested in clock speed, bus speed, internal cache, and especially the intended functionality of the chip, such as its ability to handle graphics well (MMX technology). Now, with Intel's introduction of the Itanium CPU, word size and path size have increased, and once again have become important attributes used to compare processors.

The Pentiums

A+
CORE
1.10
4.1
4.3
4.4

The most popular CPU microchips that Intel manufactures for personal computers are the Pentium series of chips. A Pentium processor has two ALUs, so it can perform two calculations at once; it is therefore a true multiprocessor. Pentiums have a 64-bit external path size and two 32-bit internal paths, one for each ALU. To compare the Pentium family of chips with its competitors, you need to understand bus speed, processor speed, the multiplier, and memory cache. Each is introduced here and discussed in more detail later in the chapter.

Recall that **bus speed** is the frequency or speed at which data moves on a bus. Remember also that a motherboard has several buses; later in the chapter you will learn the details of each. Each bus runs at a certain speed, some faster than others. Only the fastest bus connects directly to the CPU. This bus has many names. It's called the **motherboard bus,** or the **system bus,** because it's the main bus on the motherboard connecting directly to the CPU, or it's called the Pentium bus because it connects directly to the Pentium. It's called the **host bus** because other buses connect to it to get to the CPU, and it's also called the **memory bus** because it connects the CPU to RAM. It's called the external bus or the front side bus because it connects to the front side of the CPU that faces the outside world. Although the name memory bus is the most descriptive, this book most often uses the more popular terms, system bus or front side bus. Common speeds for the system bus are 100 MHz, 133 MHz, 200 MHz, 400 MHz, 533 MHz, 800 MHz, and 1066 MHz, although the bus can operate at several other speeds, depending on the CPU and how the motherboard is configured.

Processor speed is the speed at which the CPU operates internally. If the CPU operates at 3.2 GHz internally but 800 MHz externally, the processor speed is 3.2 GHz, and the system bus speed is 800 MHz. In this case, the CPU operates at four times the speed of the bus. This factor is called the **multiplier.** If you multiply the system bus speed by the multiplier, you get the processor speed, or the speed of the CPU:

System bus speed × multiplier = processor speed

When you read that Intel supports a motherboard speed of 533 MHz or 800 MHz, the speed refers to the system bus speed. Other slower buses connect to the system bus, which serves as the go-between for other buses and the CPU.

Older boards used jumpers on the motherboard or CMOS setup to set the system bus speed and multiplier, which then determine the processor speed. Common multipliers are 1.5, 2, 2.5, 3, 3.5, and 4. You must know the documented CPU speed in order to set the correct motherboard speed and multiplier, so that the CPU runs at the speed for which it is designed.

Newer boards automatically detect the CPU speed and adjust the system bus speed accordingly. Your only responsibility is to make sure you install a CPU that runs at a speed the motherboard can support.

Running a motherboard or CPU at a higher speed than the manufacturer suggests is called overclocking and is not recommended because the speed is not guaranteed to be stable. Also, the actual speed of the CPU might be slightly higher or lower than the advertised speed.

A **memory cache** is a small amount of RAM (referred to as static RAM, or SRAM) that is much faster than the rest of RAM, which is called dynamic RAM (DRAM). DRAM loses data rapidly and must be refreshed often. SRAM is faster than DRAM because SRAM does not need refreshing and can hold its data as long as power is available. The CPU can process instructions and data faster if they are temporarily stored in SRAM cache. The cache size a CPU can support is a measure of its performance, especially during memory-intensive calculations.

5

✔ A+ EXAM TIP

The A+ Core exam expects you to understand the difference between L1, L2, and L3 cache.

Recall that a memory cache can exist on the CPU die or inside the CPU housing on another die. A memory cache on the CPU die is called an **internal cache, primary cache,** or **Level 1 (L1) cache** (see Figure 5-4). A cache outside the CPU microchip is called **external cache,** secondary cache, or **Level 2 (L2) cache.** L2 caches are usually 128K, 256K, 512K, or 1 MB in size. In the past, all L2 cache was contained on the motherboard, but beginning with the Pentium Pro, some L2 cache has been included not on the CPU microchip like the L1 cache, but on a small circuit board with the CPU chip, within the same physical Pentium housing. If there is L2 cache in the processor housing and additional cache on the motherboard, then the cache on the motherboard is called **Level 3 (L3) cache.** Some advanced processors manufactured by AMD have L1, L2, and L3 cache inside the processor housing. In this case, the L3 cache is further removed from the CPU than the L2 cache, even though both are inside the CPU housing.

Figure 5-4   Some Pentiums contain L2 cache on separate dies (discrete L2 cache), and some contain L2 cache on the same die (Advanced Transfer Cache)

Some CPUs use a type of Level 1 cache called **Execution Trace Cache.** For example, the Pentium 4 has 8K of Level 1 cache used for data and an additional 12K of Execution Trace Cache containing a list of operations that have been decoded and are waiting to be executed. Many times a CPU decides to follow one branch of operations in a program of instructions rather than another branch. Only branches of operations that the CPU has determined will be executed are stored in the Execution Trace Cache, making the execution process faster.

Some Pentiums contain L2 cache directly on the same die as the processor core, making it difficult to distinguish between L1 and L2 cache; this is called **Advanced Transfer Cache (ATC).** ATC makes it possible for the Pentium to fit on a smaller and less expensive form factor. The ATC bus is 256 bits wide and runs at the same speed as the processor. Pentium L2 cache stored on a separate microchip within the CPU housing is called **On-Package L2 cache** or **discrete L2 cache** (see Figure 5-4).

A+
CORE
1.10
4.1
4.3
4.4

The back-side bus servicing this cache runs at half the speed of the processor, which is why Intel advertises this cache as "half speed On-Package L2 cache."

Table 5-3 lists the six types of Pentium CPUs: Classic Pentium, Pentium MMX, Pentium Pro, Pentium II, Pentium III, and Pentium 4. Earlier variations of the Pentium II processor included the Celeron and Xeon. Recently, Intel started referring to the Pentium Xeon as simply the Xeon, making it another group of CPUs that are similar to the Pentiums. The Xeon processors are intended to be used in high-end workstations and servers, but are included in the table to make it complete.

NOTE

The Pentium 4 processors use full-speed Advanced Transfer Cache. The Pentium III processors use either ATC or half-speed On-Package cache. The Pentium II processors use half-speed On-Package cache.

Processor	Latest Processor Speeds (MHz or GHz)	Primary L1 Cache	Secondary L2 Cache	System Bus Speeds (MHz)
Classic Pentium	60 to 200 MHz	16K	None	66
Pentium MMX	133 to 266 MHz	32K	None	66
Pentium Pro	150 to 200 MHz	16K	256K, 512K, or 1 MB	60, 66
Pentium II	233 to 450 MHz	32K	256K, 512K	66, 100
Celeron	850 MHz to 2.9 GHz	32K or Execution Trace Cache (ETC)	128K Advanced Transfer Cache or 256K Advanced Transfer Cache	Up to 533
Pentium II Xeon	400 or 450 MHz	32K	512K, 1 MB, or 2 MB	100
Pentium III	450 MHz to 1.33 GHz	32K	512K unified, nonblocking cache or 256K Advanced Transfer Cache	100, 133
Pentium III Xeon	600 MHz to 1 GHz	32K	256K, 1 MB, or 2 MB Advanced Transfer Cache	100 or 133
Xeon MP	1.4 GHz to 3.6 GHz	ETC	L2: 256K, 512K, or 1 MB L3: 512K, 1 MB, 2 MB, or 4 MB	400, 533, 800

Table 5-3 (continued)

Processor	Latest Processor Speeds (MHz or GHz)	Primary L1 Cache	Secondary L2 Cache	System Bus Speeds (MHz)
Xeon	1.8 GHz to 3.2 GHz	ETC	512K or 1 MB Advanced Transfer Cache	400, 533, 800
Pentium 4	1.4 GHz to 2.8 GHz	ETC	256K, 512K, or 1 MB Advanced Transfer Cache	400, 533
Pentium 4 with HT Technology	2.4 GHz to 3.8 GHz	ETC	512K to 1 MB	800
Pentium 4 Extreme Edition with HT	3.2 GHz to 3.46 GHz	ETC	512K L2 and 2 MB L3	800, 1066

Table 5-3   The Intel desktop Pentium and Xeon family of CPUs

You need to be familiar with the older, outdated Pentiums, as they are still in use. The first Pentium to be manufactured by Intel was the Classic Pentium. Occasionally, you see a 166-MHz Classic Pentium system still in use. The Pentium MMX (Multimedia Extension) targeted the home game and multimedia market, and the Pentium Pro and Pentium II targeted the computing-intensive workstation and server market. The Pentium II was the first CPU to use a slot (slot 1) instead of a socket to connect to the motherboard. (CPU sockets and slots are covered later in the chapter.) Intel patented slot 1, thus attempting to force its competitors to stay with the slower socket technology as they developed equivalent processors.

We now turn our attention to the current Intel processors for desktop and notebook systems.

Celeron   The Celeron processor is a low-end Pentium processor that targets the low-end PC multimedia and home market segments. It uses Level 2 cache within the processor housing and works well with the most common Windows applications.

Pentium III   The Pentium III (see Figure 5-5) uses either a slot or a socket and runs with the 100-MHz or 133-MHz system bus with a processor speed up to 1.33 GHz. The Pentium III introduced Intel's performance enhancement called SSE, for Streaming SIMD Extensions. (SIMD stands for single instruction, multiple data, and is a method MMX uses to speed up multimedia processing.) SSE is an instruction set designed to provide better multimedia processing than MMX.

A+
CORE
1.10
4.1
4.3
4.4

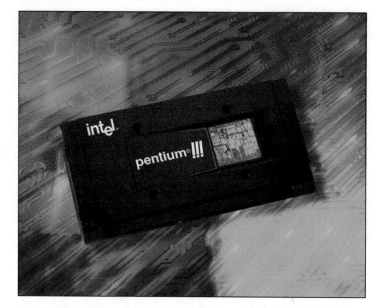

Figure 5-5   This Pentium III is contained in a SECC cartridge that stands on its end in slot 1 on a motherboard

The Pentium III Xeon is a high-end Pentium III processor that runs on the 100-MHz system bus. It is designed for mid-range servers and high-end workstations. It uses a 330-pin slot called the SC330 (slot connector 330), sometimes called slot 2, and is contained within a cartridge called a Single Edge Contact Cartridge (SECC).

Pentium 4   The Pentium 4 processor (see Figure 5-6) currently runs at up to 3.8 GHz and has undergone several improvements since it was first introduced. The first Pentium 4 processors increased performance for multimedia applications such as digital video, as well as for new Web technologies. Intel calls the processor architecture NetBurst.

Later Pentium 4 processors come with Hyper-Threading Technology (executing two threads in parallel to improve multitasking performance). The motherboard and the operating system must both support HT Technology for it to be effective. Windows XP supports HT Technology, but Windows 2000 and Windows 9x/Me do not. The most recent Pentium 4 is the Pentium 4 Extreme Edition with HT Technology, designed for high performance and runs on a 1066 MHz front side bus. Both the Pentium 4 with HT Technology and the Pentium 4 Extreme Edition can use the latest memory module type, DDR2. DDR2 is covered in Chapter 6.

NOTE

When first setting up a system using a Pentium 4 with HT Technology and Windows XP, check CMOS setup to verify that the motherboard support for HT Technology is enabled. If you use a Pentium 4 with HT Technology and an operating system other than Windows XP, use CMOS setup to disable HT Technology to avoid an unstable system.

A+
CORE
1.10
4.1
4.3
4.4

Recently, Intel began using three-digit processor numbers to aid in identifying its processors. The Pentium 4 processors use 5xx (for example, Pentium 4 Processor 530); the Celeron processors use 3xx (for example, Celeron D Processor 340); and the Pentium M processors use 7xx (for example, the Pentium M Processor 735). The numbering system along with the processor family name uniquely identify the processor, making it easier to compare processor benefits and features when making purchasing decisions. Generally, the higher the last two digits of the processor number within the processor family, the better the processor, considering the processor speed, system bus speed, architectural features, and cache size.

5

CPU

Frame to hold cooler

Socket 478

Figure 5-6   The Pentium 4

Mobile Pentiums   Current Intel processors designed for mobility are the Pentium M, Mobile Pentium 4 with Hyper-Threading Technology, Mobile Pentium 4, Mobile Pentium 4 Processor-M, Celeron M, and Mobile Celeron. A Pentium M processor is the processor component of the Intel Centrino technology, which is an integrated component that includes the processor, chipset, and wireless LAN all bundled together for a notebook system. The Pentium M processor runs at up to 2.10 GHz, using a 400 MHz system bus. The Mobile Pentium 4 processor runs at up to 3.46 GHz, using a 533 MHz system bus. Both processors support low voltage technologies designed to produce less heat, run on less power, and be housed in smaller and lighter notebooks.

AMD Processors

A+
CORE
1.10
4.1
4.3
4.4

Table 5-4 lists older and current 32-bit desktop processors made by AMD (*www.amd.com*). Many of these processors are popular in the game and hobbyist markets, and are generally less expensive than comparable Intel processors.

Processor	Latest Clock Speeds (MHz or GHz)	Compares to	System Bus Speed (MHz)	Package Type	Socket or Slot
AMD-K6-2	166 to 475 MHz	Pentium II, Celeron	66, 95, 100	CPGA	Socket 7 or Super Socket 7
AMD-K6-III	350 to 450 MHz	Pentium II	100	CPGA	Super Socket 7
Duron	1 GHz to 1.3 GHz	Celeron	200	CPGA or OPGA	Socket A
Athlon	Up to 1.9 GHz	Pentium III	200	Card	Slot A
Athlon Model 4	Up to 1.4 GHz	Pentium III	266	CPGA	Socket A
Athlon MP	1.4 GHz to 2.1 GHz	Pentium III or Xeon	200 to 400+	OPGA	Socket A
Athlon XP	Up to 2.2 GHz	Pentium 4	266, 333, 400	OPGA	Socket A
Sempron	Up to 2.0 GHz	Celeron	333	754 pins	Socket A

Table 5-4   AMD 32-bit processors

Earlier AMD processors used a special type of 321-pin socket called Super Socket 7, which supports an AGP video slot and 100-MHz system bus. The AMD Athlon can use a proprietary 242-pin slot called Slot A, which looks like the Intel slot 1 and has 242 pins. Also, the AMD Athlon and the AMD Duron use a 462-pin socket called Socket A.

A popular AMD processor for the desktop is the Athlon XP, shown in Figure 5-7. The Athlon MP is designed for multiprocessing (multiple CPUs in the same system). The Sempron is used for low-end systems, similar to the Intel Celeron. The AMD processors for notebook computers include the Mobile AMD Athlon 64, the Mobile AMD Sempron, the Mobile AMD Duron and the Mobile AMD Athlon XP-M.

Figure 5-7   AMD Athlon XP processor

VIA and Cyrix Processors

Table 5-5 shows the performance ratings of the VIA and Cyrix processors. When VIA *(www.via.com.tw)* purchased Cyrix, it introduced a new processor, the VIA C3, which is similar to, but faster than, the Cyrix III processor (see Figure 5-8). The Cyrix and VIA processors use the same sockets as earlier Pentium processors. The VIA C3 also comes in a small EBGA package and even smaller nano BGA package intended for use in personal electronic devices. VIA is now concentrating on developing processors for value PCs and multimedia devices such as home entertainment centers, set top boxes, and other small devices with computer functionality.

Processor	Latest Clock Speeds (MHz)	Compares to	System Bus Speed (MHz)	Socket or Slot
Cyrix M II	300, 333, 350	Pentium II, Celeron	66, 75, 83, 95, 100	Socket 7
Cyrix III	433 to 533	Celeron, Pentium III	66, 100, 133	Socket 370
VIA C3	Up to 1.4 GHz	Celeron	100, 133, 200	Socket 370

Table 5-5   VIA and Cyrix processors

Figure 5-8   VIA C3 processor

64-bit Processors

Recall from Chapter 2 that earlier processors always operated in real mode, using a 16-bit data path. Later, protected mode was introduced, which uses a 32-bit data path. Almost all applications written today use 32-bit protected mode, because most processors for desktop and notebook computers use a 32-bit data path. But this is soon to change because Intel and AMD both have 64-bit processors that are currently used in the server market, and AMD has 64-bit processors for the desktop and notebook market.

To take full advantage of a 64-bit processor, such as the Intel Itanium or the AMD Athlon, software developers must recompile their applications to use 64-bit processing and write operating systems that use 64-bit data transfers. Microsoft provides a 64-bit version of Windows XP that works with the 64-bit processors.

Intel Itaniums   Intel's first 64-bit processors for microcomputers are the Itaniums (see Figure 5-9). Itaniums provide backward compatibility with older 32-bit applications, although the older applications are not able to take full advantage of the Itanium's capabilities.

A+
CORE
1.10
4.1
4.3
4.4

Figure 5-9   The Itanium 2

Earlier CPUs use one of two types of instruction sets: **reduced instruction set computing (RISC)** or **complex instruction set computing (CISC)**. Generally slower than RISC CPUs, CISC CPUs have more instructions that programmers can take advantage of. The Itanium uses a new instruction set called the **explicitly parallel instruction computing (EPIC)** architecture. With EPIC, the CPU receives a bundle of instructions that contains programming commands as well as those for how the CPU can execute two commands at once in parallel, using the CPU's multiprocessing abilities.

Table 5-6 shows the specifications for the two Itanium processors. The Itanium uses an L1 cache on the processor die and L2 and L3 caches on the processor board. The L2 cache is closer to the CPU than the L3 cache.

Processor	Current Processor Speeds	L1 Cache	L2 Cache	L3 Cache	System Bus Speed
Itanium	733 and 800 MHz	32K	96K	2 MB or 4 MB	266 MHz
Itanium 2	900 MHz to 1.6 GHz	32K	256K	1.5 MB to 9 MB	400 or 533 MHz

Table 5-6   The Intel Itanium processors

AMD 64-bit Processors   AMD has concentrated on the 64-bit desktop and mobile processor market since it was first to market with the first 64-bit processor for the desktop, the Athlon 64. Here are the 64-bit processors offered by AMD:

■ The Opteron is a 64-bit processor designed for servers (see Figure 5-10). It runs at up to 2.0 GHz, uses a 244 MHz system bus, and is housed in a 940-pin ceramic micro pin grid array (µPGA) package, which uses Socket 940.

A+
CORE
1.10
4.1
4.3
4.4

- The Athlon 64 runs at up to 2.2 GHz and can use up to a 2000 MHz system bus. It is housed in a 754-pin or 939-pin organic micro PGA (OμPGA) package and uses Socket 754 or Socket 939.
- The Athlon 64 FX runs at up to 2.6 GHz and can use up to a 1.0 GHz system bus. It is housed in a 940-pin or 939-pin organic micro PGA (OμPGA) package.
- The Mobile AMD Athlon 64 is a low voltage processor designed for notebooks. It uses Socket 754 and can run on a 1600 MHz system bus.

Figure 5-10   AMD Opteron, a 64-bit processor (courtesy of Advanced Micro Devices, Inc.)

CPU Heat Sinks and Cooling Fans

A+
CORE
1.2
1.9
2.1

Because a CPU generates so much heat, computer systems use a cooling fan to keep temperatures below the Intel maximum limit of 185 degrees Fahrenheit/85 degrees Celsius (see Figure 5-11). Good CPU cooling fans maintain a temperature of 90–110 degrees F (32–43 degrees C). At one time, CPU cooling fans were optional equipment used to prevent system errors and to prolong the life of the CPU. Today's power-intensive CPUs require one or more cooling fans to maintain a temperature that will not damage the CPU. High-end systems can have as many as seven or eight fans mounted inside the computer case. Ball-bearing cooling fans last longer than other kinds.

The cooling fan usually fits on top of the CPU with a wire or plastic clip. Sometimes a cream-like thermal compound is placed between the fan and the CPU. This compound draws heat from the CPU and passes it to the fan. The thermal compound transmits heat better than air and makes an airtight connection between the fan and the CPU. The fan is equipped with a power connector that connects to one of the power cables coming from the power supply or to a connector on the motherboard.

Older CPUs used a heat sink instead of a cooling fan. A **heat sink** is a clip-on device that mounts on top of the CPU; fingers or fins at its base pull the heat away from the CPU. Today most cooling fans designed to mount on the CPU housing also have a heat sink attached, as shown in Figure 5-11. The combination heat sink and cooling fan is sometimes called a **cooler**. A cooler is made of aluminum or copper. Copper is more expensive, but does a better job. For example, the Volcano 11+ by Thermaltake (*www.thermaltake.com*) is a copper cooler that can be set to run continuously or you can use a temperature-controlled fan speed (see Figure 5-12). The temperature sensor connects to the heat sink.

Cooling fan

Processor

Slot braces

Heat sink

Cooling fan power connectio

Figure 5-11   A CPU cooling fan mounts on the top or side of the CPU housing and is powered by an electrical connection to the motherboard

Figure 5-12   Volcano 11+ by Thermaltake is a copper PC cooler

Heat sinks sometimes mount on top of other chips to keep them cool. For example, in Figure 5-6 you can see a heat sink mounted on top of a chip sitting behind the Pentium 4 CPU. Also notice in Figure 5-6 the frame to hold the cooler for the Pentium 4.

APPLYING CONCEPTS

Before installing a cooling fan, read the directions carefully. Clips that hold the fan and heat sink to the CPU frame or housing are sometimes difficult to install, and you must be very careful to use the right amount of thermal compound. If you use too much compound, it can slide off the housing and damage circuits on the motherboard.

Keeping a system cool is important; if the system overheats, components can be damaged. In addition to using a cooling fan, you can also install an alarm that sounds if a system overheats. Because the fan is a mechanical device, it is more likely to fail than the electronic devices inside the case. To protect the expensive CPU, you can purchase a temperature sensor for a few dollars. The sensor plugs into a power connection coming from the power supply and mounts on the side of the case or the inside of a faceplate. The sensor sounds an alarm when the inside of the case becomes too hot.

In addition to using fans and heat sinks to keep a CPU cool, there are more exotic options such as refrigeration, peltiers, and water coolers. These solutions are described in the following list; for the most part, they are used by hobbyists attempting to overclock a CPU to the max. These cooling systems might include a PCI card that has a power supply, temperature sensor, and processor to control the cooler.

- A peltier is a heat sink carrying an electrical charge that causes it to act as an electrical thermal transfer device. The peltier's top surface can be as hot as 500 degrees F while the bottom surface next to the CPU can be as cool as 45 degrees. The major disadvantage of a peltier is that this drastic difference in temperature can cause condensation inside the case when the PC is turned off.
- Refrigeration can also be used to cool a CPU. These units contain a small refrigerator compressor that sits inside the case and can reduce temperatures to below zero.
- The most popular method of cooling overclocked CPUs is a water cooler unit. A small water pump sits inside the computer case, and tubes move distilled water up and over the CPU to keep it cool.

Some manufacturers of these types of cooling systems are AquaStealth (*www.aquastealth.com*), asetek (*www.vapochill.com*), Thermaltake (*www.thermaltake.com*), and FrozenCPU (*www.frozencpu.com*). Remember, overclocking is not a recommended best practice.

CPU Packages

A+
CORE
1.10
4.1
4.3
4.4

Several package types are used to house Intel and AMD processors in desktop PCs and high-end workstations:

- *SECC (Single Edge Contact Cartridge).* The processor is completely covered with a black plastic housing, and a heat sink and fan are attached to the housing. You can't see the circuit board or edge connector in a SECC package. The Pentium II and Pentium III use a SECC package in slot 1 with 242 contacts. The Pentium II Xeon and Pentium III Xeon use a SECC with 330 contacts. You can see the SECC in Figure 5-5.

- *SECC2 (Single Edge Contact Cartridge, version 2).* This is similar to the SECC, but it does not have the heat sink thermal plate, and the edge connector on the processor circuit board is visible at the bottom of the housing. The Pentium II and Pentium III use the SECC2 package with 242 contacts.

- *SEP (Single Edge Processor).* This package is similar to the SECC package, but the black plastic housing does not completely cover the processor, making the circuit board visible at the bottom of the housing. The first Celeron processors used the SEP package in slot 1. It has 242 contacts.

- *PPGA (Plastic Pin Grid Array).* The processor is housed in a square box designed to fit flat into Socket 370 (see Figure 5-13). Pins are on the underside of the flat housing, and heat sinks or fans can be attached to the top of the housing by using a thermal plate or heat spreader. The early Celeron processors used this package with 370 pins.

Figure 5-13 The Intel Celeron processor is housed in the PPGA form factor, which has pins on the underside that insert into Socket 370

A+
CORE
1.10
4.1
4.3
4.4

- *PGA (Pin Grid Array).* Pins on the bottom of this package are staggered and can be inserted only one way into the socket. The Xeon processors use this package with 603 pins.
- *OOI/OLGA (Organic Land Grid Array).* Used by some Pentium 4s, this 423-pin package is similar to the PGA package, but is designed to dissipate heat faster.
- *FC-PGA (Flip Chip Pin Grid Array).* This package looks like the PPGA package and uses Socket 370. Coolers can be attached directly to the top of the package. Some Pentium III and Celeron processors use this package.
- *FC-PGA2 (Flip Chip Pin Grid Array 2).* This package is similar to the FC-PGA package, but has a heat sink attached directly to the die of the processor. When used by a Pentium III or Celeron processor, it has 370 pins. When used by the Pentium 4, it has 478 pins.
- *PAC (Pin Array Cartridge).* The Itaniums use this flat cartridge, which is about the size of an index card. It uses either the PAC418 socket, which has 418 pins, or the PAC611 socket, which has 611 pins.
- *CPGA (Ceramic Pin Grid Array).* This is a flat package with pins on the underside used by several AMD processors including the Duron, AMD-K6-2, and AMD-K6-III. Number of pins varies among processors.
- *OPGA (Organic Pin Grid Array).* This package is used by the AMD Athlon MP and Athlon XP and some models of the AMD Duron.
- *µPGA (Micro Pin Grid Array).* This package is used by the AMD 64-bit processors, including the AMD Opteron and Athlon 64.
- *FC-LGA, FC-LGA2, FC-LGA4, mPGA478, PPGA INT3,* and *PPGA INT2.* These are the latest Intel packages used by the Pentium 4 and Celeron. The FC-LGA and FC-LGA4 have 775 pins. The FC-PGA2, FC-LGA4, and mPGA478 have 478 pins, and the PPGA INT3 and PPGA INT2 have 423 pins.

URM supporting arms

Figure 5-14   Preparing URM arms to receive the CPU (the arms are in the upright position)

CPU Slots and Sockets

**A+
CORE
1.10
4.4
4.3
4.4**

A processor connects to the motherboard by way of a socket (shown in Figure 5-6 with processor installed) or a slot (shown in Figure 5-14 with no processor installed). The type of socket or slot supplied by the motherboard for the processor must match that required by the processor. Table 5-7 lists several types of sockets and slots that CPUs use. Slots 1 and 2 are proprietary Intel slots, and Socket A and Slot A are proprietary AMD connectors.

5

Connector Name	Used by CPU	Number of Pins	Voltage
Socket 4	Classic Pentium 60/66	273 pins, 21 × 21 PGA grid	5 V
Socket 5	Classic Pentium 75/90/100/120/133	320 pins, 37 × 37 SPGA grid	3.3 V
Socket 7	Pentium MMX, Fast Classic Pentium, AMD KS, AMD KS, Cyrix M	321 pins, 37 × 37 SPGA grid	2.5 V to 3.3 V
Super Socket 7	AMD KS-2, AMD KS-III	321 pins, 37 × 37 SPGA grid	2.5 V to 3.3 V
Socket 8	Pentium Pro	387 pins 24 × 26 SPGA grid	3.3 V
Socket 370 or PGA370 Socket	Pentium III FC-PGA, Celeron PPGA, Cyrix III	370 pins in a 37 × 37 SPGA grid	1.5 V or 2 V
Slot 1 or SC242	Pentium II, Pentium III	242 pins in 2 rows, rectangular shape	2.8 V and 3.3 V
Slot A	AMD Athlon	242 pins in 2 rows, rectangular shape	1.3 V to 2.05 V
Socket A or Socket 462	AMD Athlon and Duron	462 pins, SPGA grid, rectangular shape	1.5 V to 1.85V
Slot 2 or SC330	Pentium II Xeon, Pentium III Xeon	330 pins in 2 rows, rectangular shape	1.5 V to 3.5 V
Socket 423	Pentium 4	423 pins, 39 × 39 SPGA grid	1.7 V and 1.75 V
Socket 478	Pentium 4	478 pins in a dense micro PGA (mPGA)	1.7 V and 1.75 V
Socket PAC418	Itanium	418 pins	3.3 V
PAC611	Itanium 2	611 pins	3.3 V
Socket 603	Xeon DP and MP	603 pins	1.5 and 1.7 V
Socket LGA775	Pentium 4, Celeron	775 lands, not pins	1.5 to 1.6 volts
Sockets 754 and 939	Athlon 64	754 or 939 pins	NA

Table 5-7 CPU sockets and slots

A+
CORE
1.10
4.1
4.3
4.4

Earlier Pentiums used a **pin grid array (PGA)** socket, with pins aligned in uniform rows around the socket. Later sockets use a **staggered pin grid array (SPGA)**, with pins staggered over the socket to squeeze more pins into a small space. PGA and SPGA sockets are all square or nearly square. Earlier CPU sockets, called dual inline package (**DIP**) sockets, were rectangular with two rows of pins down each side. **DIP** and some PGA sockets, called **low insertion force (LIF) sockets**, were somewhat troublesome to install because it was difficult to apply even force when inserting them. Current CPU sockets, called **zero insertion force (ZIF) sockets**, have a small lever on the side that lifts the CPU up and out of the socket. Push the lever down and the CPU moves into its pin connectors with equal force over the entire housing. With this method, you can more easily remove and replace the CPU if necessary.

✔ **A+ EXAM TIP**

The A+Core exam expects you to be familiar with the following slots and sockets: slot 1, slot 2, Slot A, Socket A, Socket 7, Socket 8, Socket 423, Socket 478, and Socket 370.

Most processors today come in more than one package, so it is important to match the processor package to the motherboard that has the right socket or slot. Slot 1, Slot A, and slot 2 are all designed to accommodate processors using SEP or SECC housings that stand on end much like an expansion card. Clips on each side of the slot secure the CPU in the slot. You can attach a heat sink or cooling fan to the side of the CPU case. Some motherboards with a slot 1 can accommodate processors that use flat packages, such as the Celeron housed in a PPGA package, by using a riser CPU card (see Figure 5-15). The riser card inserts into slot 1, and the Celeron processor inserts into Socket 370 on the riser card. This feature, sometimes called a slocket, allows you to upgrade an older Pentium II system to the faster Celeron. Always consult the motherboard documentation to learn which processors the board can support.

VIDEO

Installing a
Processor

Also, be aware of the processor's voltage requirements. For example, the Pentium 4 receives voltage from the +12-volt power line to the motherboard, rather than the lower-voltage lines that previous Pentiums used. For this reason, some motherboards include a new power connector, called the ATX12V (see Figure 5-16). In some setups, a power cord designed to power a drive connects to this small connector. Always read the motherboard and processor documentation to know how to use these auxiliary power connections.

Figure 5-15   A riser card can be used to install a Celeron processor into a motherboard with slot 1

Another variation is the Celeron processor that uses 2.00 volts, and the Pentium III FC-PGA that uses either 1.60 or 1.65 volts. A motherboard built to support only the Celeron may not recognize the need to step down the voltage for a Pentium III FC-PGA processor. This overvoltage can damage the Pentium III. Again, it is always important to use only a processor and processor package that the motherboard documentation claims the board can support.

Figure 5-16   Auxiliary 4-pin power cord from the power supply connects to the ATX12V connector on the motherboard to provide power to the Pentium 4

CPU Voltage Regulator

As you can see from Table 5-7, different CPUs require different levels of voltage on the motherboard. Some CPUs require one voltage for external operations and another for internal operations. Those that require two different voltages are called **dual-voltage CPUs**. Other CPUs are **single-voltage CPUs**. Some older motherboards require that you set their jumpers to set the voltage to the CPU, and others automatically control the voltage without your involvement. A **voltage regulator module (VRM)** controls the amount of voltage to the CPU. A VRM can be embedded in the motherboard or can be added later when you upgrade the processor.

For example, the Classic Pentium used only a single voltage (2.8 volts), but the Pentium MMX uses a core voltage of 2.8 volts and an I/O voltage of 3.3 volts. If you upgrade a system from the Classic Pentium to the Pentium MMX, you can use the motherboard's embedded VRM to regulate the 2.8 volts and install another VRM to regulate the 3.3 volts.

A+
CORE
1.10
4.1
4.3
4.4

APPLYING CONCEPTS

A technician needs to know how to support older technology, and here is an excellent example. Figure 5-17 shows sample documentation of jumper settings to use for various CPU voltage selections on an older motherboard. Notice that the two jumpers called JP16, located near Socket 7 on the board, select the voltage. For single voltage, on a Pentium, Cyrix 6×86, or AMD K5, both jumpers are open. Dual voltage, used by the Pentium MMX, Cyrix M2, and AMD K6, is selected by opening or closing the two jumpers according to the diagram. Follow the recommendations for your CPU when selecting the voltages from documentation.

CPU TYPE	JP16	CPU Voltage	
		Core	I/O
Single Voltage Intel P54C/CQS/CT Cyrix 6x86 AMD K5	2 ◯ ◯ 4 1 ◯ ◯ 3 open	3.5 V	3.5 V
Dual Voltage Intel P55C/MMX Cyrix 6x86L/M2 AMD K6	2 ◯ ◯ 4 1 ◯ ◯ 3 open	2.8 V	3.4 V
	2 ● ◯ 4 1 ● ◯ 3 1-2 closed, 3-4 open	2.9 V	3.4 V
	2 ◯ ● 4 1 ◯ ● 3 1-2 open, 3-4 closed	3.2 V	3.4 V

Figure 5-17   A CPU voltage regulator can be configured using jumpers on the motherboard to apply the correct voltage to the CPU

The Chip Set

A+
CORE
1.10
4.1
4.3
4.4

Recall from Chapter 1 that a chip set is a set of chips on the motherboard that collectively controls the memory cache, external buses, and some peripherals. Intel makes the most popular chip sets; the currently available Intel chip sets are listed in Table 5-8. The types of memory supported are explained in detail in the next chapter.

5

Common Name	Model Number	Processors Supported	System Bus Speed Supported	Memory Supported
"E" chip set family	E8870	Up to four Itanium 2 processors	400 MHz	Up to 128 GB on DDR DIMMs
	E7500, E7501, E7505	Dual Xeon processors	400 MHz or 533 MHzMHz	Up to 16 GB on DDR DIMMs
	E7205	Pentium 4	533 MHz or 400 MHz	Up to 4 GB on DDR DIMMs
i900 Express Series	925XE	Pentium 4	800 MHz, 1066 MHz	Up to 4 GB on DDR2 DIMMs
	925X	Pentium 4, Pentium 4 Extreme Edition	800 MHz	Up to 4 GB on DDR2 DIMMs
	915P, 915G, 915GV	Pentium 4	800 MHz, 533 MHz	Up to 4 GB on DDR2 DIMMs
	910GL	Pentium 4, Celeron, Celeron D	533 MHz	Up to 2 GB on DDR2 DIMMs
i800 Series	875P	Pentium 4	800 MHz or 533 MHz	Up to 4 GB on DDR DIMMs
	865G or 865PE	Pentium 4	800 MHz, 533 MHz or 400 MHz	Up to 4 GB on DDR DIMMs
	865P	Pentium 4	533 MHz or 400 MHz	Up to 4 GB on DDR DIMMs

Table 5-8 (continued)

Common Name	Model Number	Processors Supported	System Bus Speed Supported	Memory Supported
	860	Dual Xeon processors	400 MHz	Up to 4 GB of memory on up to 8 RIMMs
	850, 850E	Pentium 4 or Celeron	400 MHz or 533 MHz	Up to 2 GB of memory on up to 4 RIMMs
	845PE, 845GE, 845E, 845G, 845GV	Pentium 4 or Celeron	400 MHz or 533 MHz	Up to 2 GB on DDR DIMMs or SDR DIMMs
	815, 815E, or 815EP	Celeron or Pentium III	133 MHz, 100 MHz, or 66 MHz	Up to 512 MB of SDRAM DIMMs
Orion	460GX	Up to four Itanium 2 processors	400 MHz	Up to 128 GB of DDR SDRAM DIMMs

Table 5-8 Intel chip sets

Beginning with the Intel i800 series of chip sets, the interconnection between buses is done using a hub interface architecture, in which all I/O buses connect to a hub, which connects to the system bus. This hub is called the hub interface, and the architecture is called Accelerated Hub Architecture (see Figure 5-18). The fast end of the hub, which contains the graphics and memory controller, connects to the system bus and is called the hub's **North Bridge**. The slower end of the hub, called the **South Bridge**, contains the I/O controller hub. All I/O devices, except display and memory, connect to the hub by using the slower South Bridge. On a motherboard, when you see two major chips for the chip set, one is controlling the North Bridge and the other is controlling the South Bridge.

Table 5-9 lists manufacturers of chip sets. Currently, Intel dominates the chip set market for several reasons: it knows more about its own Intel processors than other manufacturers do, and it produces the chip sets most compatible with the Pentium family of CPUs. Intel's investment in research and development also led to the creation of the PCI bus, the universal serial bus, the AGP, and more recently, the Accelerated Hub Architecture.

Company	URL
ALi, Inc.	www.ali.com.tw
AMD	www.amd.com
Intel Corporation	www.intel.com

Table 5-9 (continued)

Company	URL
Philips Semiconductors	www.semiconductors.philips.com
Silicon Integrated Systems Corp. (known as SiS)	www.sis.com
Standard Microsystems Corp.	www.smsc.com
United Microelectronics Corp. (UMC)	www.umc.com
VIA Technologies, Inc. combined with AMD, Inc.	www.via.com.tw

Table 5-9   Chip set manufacturers

5

Figure 5-18   Using Intel 800 series Accelerated Hub Architecture, a hub interface is used to connect slower I/O buses to the system bus

ROM BIOS

A motherboard has ROM BIOS and RAM installed on it. The next chapter discusses RAM, and this section addresses ROM BIOS. Recall from earlier chapters that one ROM chip on the motherboard contains BIOS. BIOS manages the startup process (startup BIOS) and many basic I/O functions of the system (system BIOS). In this section, you will learn to manage BIOS by configuring it and updating it. We first look at updating BIOS.

APPLYING CONCEPTS

When a motherboard becomes unstable or some functions are lost, one solution is to refresh or update the BIOS (called flashing BIOS). When you do, the first step is to accurately identify the BIOS version currently installed. There are several methods to identify your motherboard and BIOS:

- Look on the CMOS setup main screen for the BIOS manufacturer and version number.
- Use third-party software (such as BIOS Agent at *www.unicore.com*) or an OS utility (such as Windows System Information) to determine the BIOS information.
- Stop the boot process and look for the BIOS information reported early in the boot process.

To stop the boot process early so you can read the BIOS information, first try the following:

1. Turn off the system power and then turn it back on.
2. While memory is counting on the screen, hold down the Pause/Break key to stop the startup process.
3. Look for the long string of numbers in the lower-left corner of your screen, which identifies the motherboard.
4. Look for the BIOS manufacturer and version number somewhere near the top of the screen.

If the preceding method does not work, try turning off the PC, unplugging the keyboard, and then turn on the PC. For older systems, the resulting keyboard error will stop the startup process.

To flash ROM, carefully read the motherboard documentation, as different motherboards use different methods. If you can't find the documentation, check the motherboard manufacturer's Web site, and check the directions that came with the upgrade software. Generally, you perform these tasks:

1. Set a jumper on the motherboard, or change a setting in CMOS setup to tell the BIOS to expect an upgrade.
2. Copy the upgraded BIOS software to a bootable disk.
3. Boot from the disk and follow the menu options to upgrade the BIOS. If the menu gives you the option to save the old BIOS to disk, do so in case you need to revert to the old BIOS.
4. Set the jumper back to its original setting, reboot the system, and verify that all is working.

Makers of BIOS code are likely to change BIOS frequently, because providing the upgrade on the Internet is so easy for them. You can get upgraded BIOS code from manufacturers' Web sites or disks, or from third-party BIOS resellers' Web sites or disks. Generally, however, follow the principle that "if it's not broke, don't fix it"; update your BIOS only if you're having a problem with your motherboard or there's a new BIOS feature you want to use.

CAUTION

Be *very careful* that you upgrade the BIOS with the correct upgrade and that you follow the manufacturer's instructions correctly. Upgrading with the wrong file could make your system BIOS useless. If you're not sure that you're using the correct upgrade, *don't guess*. Check with the technical support for your BIOS before moving forward. Before you call technical support, have the information that identifies your BIOS available.

Figure 5-19 shows a sample Web site for flash ROM BIOS upgrades. See the Web site of your BIOS manufacturer or motherboard manufacturer for more information. Table 5-10 lists BIOS manufacturers.

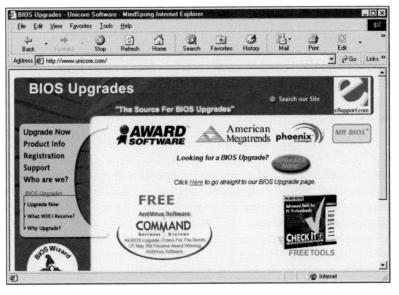

Figure 5-19 Flash ROM BIOS upgrades for most BIOS manufacturers can be downloaded from *www.unicore.com*

Company	URL
American Megatrends, Inc. (AMI)	*www.megatrends.com* or *www.ami.com*
Phoenix Technologies (First BIOS, Phoenix, and Award)	*www.phoenix.com*
Compaq and Hewlett-Packard	*thenew.hp.com*
Dell	*www.dell.com*
IBM	*developer.intel.com*

Table 5-10 (continued)

Company	URL
Wim's BIOS	www.wimsbios.com
Unicore (BIOS upgrades)	www.unicore.com

Table 5-10 BIOS manufacturers

Buses and Expansion Slots

**A+
CORE
1.10
4.3**

As cities grow, so do their transportation systems. Small villages have only simple, two-lane roads, but large cities have one-way streets, four-lane roads, and major freeways, each with their own set of traffic laws, including minimum and maximum speeds, access methods, and protocols. As microcomputer systems have evolved, so have their "transportation" systems. The earliest PC had only a single simple bus. Today's PCs have four or five buses, each with different speeds, access methods, and protocols. As you have seen, backward compatibility dictates that older buses be supported on a motherboard, even when faster, better buses exist. All this makes for a maze of buses on a motherboard.

Bus Evolution

Just as a city's road system improves to increase the speed and number of lanes of traffic, buses have evolved around similar issues, data path and speed. Cars on a freeway generally travel at a continuous or constant speed, but traffic on a computer's CPU or bus is digital (on and off), rather than analog (continuous). The system clock keeps the beat for components. If a component on the motherboard works by the beat, or clock cycle, then it is synchronized, or in sync, with the CPU. For example, as explained earlier in the chapter, the back-side bus of the Pentium works at half the speed of the CPU. This means that the CPU does something on each clock cycle, but the back-side bus is doing something on every other clock cycle.

Some components don't attempt to keep in sync with the CPU, even to work at half or a third of clock cycles. These components work asynchronously with the CPU. They might work at a rate determined by the system clock or by another crystal on or off the motherboard. Either way, the frequency is much slower than the CPU's and not in sync with it. If the CPU requests something from one of these devices and the device is not ready, it issues a **wait state**, a command to the CPU to wait for slower devices to catch up.

The first expansion slots on early PCs were **Industry Standard Architecture (ISA) slots**. These slots had an 8-bit data path and ran at 4.77 MHz. Later, the 16-bit ISA slots were added that ran at 8.33 MHz. The 16-bit slots were backward-compatible with 8-bit cards; an 8-bit card used only a portion of the 16-bit slot. These 16-bit ISA slots are still in use on some older motherboards. In later chapters you will learn how to support these legacy slots and cards.

Buses that work in sync with the CPU and the system clock are called **local buses**. Buses that work asynchronously with the CPU at a much slower rate are called **expansion buses**. The system bus is a local bus, and the ISA bus is an expansion bus. Table 5-11 lists the various buses, in order of throughput speed from fastest to slowest.

Bus	Bus Type	Data Path in Bits	Address Lines	Bus Speed in MHz	Throughput
System bus	Local	64	32	Up to 1600	Up to 3.2 GB/sec
PCI Express	Local	Up to 16 lanes	Up to 16 lanes	2.5 GHz to 40 GHz	312 MB/sec to 6.4 GB/sec
PCI-X	Local I/O	64	32	133	1.06 GB/sec
AGP	Local video	32	NA	66, 75, 100 …	Up to 528 MB/sec
PCI	Local I/O	32	32	33, 66	264 upto MB/sec
VESA or VL Bus	Local video or expansion	32	32	Up to 33	Up to 250 MB/sec
FireWire	Local I/O or expansion	1	Serial	NA	Up to 3.2 Gb/sec (gigabits)
MCA	Expansion	32	32	12	Up to 40 MB/sec
EISA	Expansion	32	32	12	Up to 32 MB/sec
16-bit ISA	Expansion	16	24	8.33	8 MB/sec
USB	Expansion	1	Serial	3	Up to 480 Mbps (megabits)

Table 5-11   Buses listed by throughput

Some motherboard buses in Table 5-11 are outdated, and some are used today. Historically, the 8-bit ISA bus came first and was later revised to the 16-bit ISA bus to meet the demand for wider data path sizes. Then, in 1987, IBM introduced the first 32-bit bus, the MCA (Micro Channel Architecture) bus, and competitors followed with the 32-bit EISA (Extended Industry Standard Architecture) bus. Because these buses are not synchronized with the CPU, they are all expansion buses. Of these buses, the only one still used today is the 16-bit ISA. A relatively new expansion bus is the universal serial bus (USB), which targets slow I/O devices such as the mouse. USB devices are easily installed and configured.

A+
CORE
1.10
4.3

All other buses must connect to the system bus to get to the CPU. A **local I/O bus** is designed to support fast I/O devices such as video and hard drives; it runs synchronized with the system clock, which means that it is also synchronized with the CPU. One type of local I/O bus is the PCI bus, which is standard in Pentium systems. Local I/O buses did not always exist on a PC but were created as the need arose for a bus that was synchronized with the system clock, was not as fast as the system bus, and was faster than an expansion bus. The evolution of local I/O buses includes earlier proprietary designs, the outdated VESA bus, the PCI bus, the AGP bus (for video only), the IEEE 1394 (FireWire) bus, and the newer PCI Express bus. IEEE 1394 is classified as either a local or expansion bus because it can work either synchronously or asynchronously. Figure 5-20 shows various bus connectors. PCI Express currently comes in four different slot sizes called PCI Express x1 (pronounced "by one"), x4, x8, and x16. PCI Express x16 is the fastest and is used for a video card. A motherboard will have either an AGP slot for the video card or a PCI Express x16 slot, but not both. Figure 5-21 shows a motherboard with PCI Express x1 and x16 slots as well as a regular PCI slot.

Figure 5-20   Seven bus connections on expansion cards

What a Bus Does

Look on the bottom of the motherboard, and you see a maze of circuits that make up a bus. These embedded wires carry four kinds of cargo:

- *Electrical power.* Chips on the motherboard require power to function. These chips tap into a bus's power lines and draw what they need.
- *Control signals.* Some wires on a bus carry control signals that coordinate all the activity.
- *Memory addresses.* Components pass memory addresses to one another, telling each other where to access data or instructions. The number of wires that make up the memory address lines of the bus determines how many bits can be used for a memory address. The number of wires thus limits the amount of memory the bus can address.
- *Data.* Data passes over a bus in a group of wires, just as memory addresses do. The number of lines in the bus used to pass data determines how much data can be passed in parallel at one time. The number of lines depends on the type of processor and determines the number of bits in the data path. (Remember that a data path is the part of the bus on which the data is placed; it can be 8, 16, 32, 64, or more bits wide.)

On-Board Ports, Connectors, and Riser Slots

In addition to expansion slots, a motherboard might also have several on-board ports, internal connectors, and riser slots, all of which are discussed next. Ports coming directly off the motherboard are called **on-board ports**. Almost all motherboards have a keyboard port, mouse port, parallel printer port, and one or two serial ports. In addition, the board might have one or more USB ports, a video port, a network port, and a 1394 (FireWire) port.

A motherboard might have several internal connectors including IDE connectors, a floppy drive connector, a Serial ATA connector, a SCSI connector, or a 1394 connector. See Figure 5-21 for examples of PCE and PCI Express slots.

Figure 5-21   Three PCI Express and three PCI slots on a motherboard

To reduce the total cost of a computer system, some motherboards might have a small expansion slot, less than half the length of a PCI slot, called an **audio/modem riser (AMR)** slot (see Figure 5-22) or a **communication and networking riser (CNR)** slot. These small slots accommodate small, inexpensive expansion cards called **riser cards**, such as a modem riser card, audio riser card, or network riser card. Part of a riser card's audio, modem, or networking logic is on the card, and part is on a controller on the motherboard.

> **✔ A+ EXAM TIP**
>
> The A+ Core exam expects you to be familiar with an AMR slot, CNR slot, and riser card.

> **NOTE**
>
> You don't have to replace an entire motherboard if one port fails. Most ports on a motherboard can be disabled through CMOS setup. On older motherboards, look for jumpers or DIP switches to disable a port. Then use an expansion card for the port instead.

Figure 5-22 An audio/modem riser slot can accommodate an inexpensive modem riser card

Hardware Configuration

Recall from Chapter 1 that you can configure the motherboard in three different ways: DIP switches, jumpers, and CMOS. Storing configuration information by physically setting DIP switches or jumpers on the motherboard or peripheral devices is inconvenient, because it often requires you to open the computer case to make a change. A more convenient method is to hold configuration information in CMOS memory. A program in BIOS can then be used to easily make changes to setup. In this section, you will learn more about each method of storing configuration information. You will also see examples of CMOS setup screens.

Setup Data Stored by DIP Switches

Many older computers and a few newer ones store setup data using DIP switches on the motherboard, as shown in Figure 5-23. A DIP (dual inline package) switch has an ON position and an OFF position. ON represents binary 1 and OFF represents binary 0. If you add or remove equipment, you can communicate that to the computer by changing a DIP switch setting. When you change a DIP switch setting, use a pointed instrument such as a ballpoint pen to push the switch. Don't use a graphite pencil, because graphite conducts electricity. Pieces of graphite dropped into the switch can damage it.

Figure 5-23   DIP switches are sometimes used to store setup data on motherboards

Setup Data Stored by Jumpers

Most motherboards use at least one set of jumpers, such as the set in Figure 5-24. If two pins are not connected with a cover, the setting is considered OFF. If the cover is present, the setting is ON. If the cover is hanging on one pin, it is "parked" so you won't lose it. You can see all three situations in Figure 5-24.

a   b   c

Figure 5-24   A 6-pin jumper group on a circuit board (a) has no pins covered, (b) has a cover parked on one pin, and (c) is configured with two jumpers capped or covered

A typical setting that uses jumpers is enabling or disabling keyboard power-up. (With this feature enabled, you can press a key to power up the system.) You change the jumper setting by removing the computer case, finding the correct jumper, and then either placing a metal cover over the jumper or removing the cover already there. Figure 5-25 shows a diagram of a motherboard with the keyboard power-up jumper. For older motherboards, typical uses of jumpers were to indicate the presence of cache memory or to communicate the type and speed of the CPU present.

Figure 5-25   The keyboard power-up jumper allows you to use your keyboard to power up the computer

Setup Data Stored in CMOS Memory

A+
CORE
2.1
4.4

Computers today store most configuration information in CMOS memory, also called the real-time clock/nonvolatile RAM (RTC/NVRAM) chip, which retains the data even when the computer is turned off. (There are actually many CMOS chips on a motherboard, used for various purposes.) On older computers (mostly IBM 286 PCs built in the 1980s), changes are made to the CMOS setup data using a setup program stored on a floppy disk. One major disadvantage of this method, besides the chance that you might lose or misplace the disk, is that the disk drive must be working before you can change the setup. An advantage of this method is that you cannot unintentionally change the setup. If you have an older computer and you do not have the floppy disk with the setup program, check the Web site of the motherboard manufacturer or the BIOS manufacturer for a replacement disk.

Changing CMOS Using the Setup Program   On newer computers, you usually change the data stored in CMOS by accessing the setup program stored in ROM BIOS. You access the program by pressing a key or combination of keys during the boot process. The exact way to enter setup varies from one motherboard manufacturer to another. Table 5-12 lists the keystrokes needed to access CMOS setup for some common BIOS types.

BIOS	Key to Press During POST to Access Setup
AMI BIOS	Del
Award BIOS	Del
Older Phoenix BIOS	Ctrl+Alt+Esc or Ctrl+Alt+s
Newer Phoenix BIOS	F2 or F1
Dell computers using Phoenix BIOS	Ctrl+Alt+Enter
Older Compaq computers such as the Deskpro 286 or 386	Place the diagnostics disk in the disk drive, reboot your system, and choose Computer Setup from the menu
Newer Compaq computers such as the ProLinea, Deskpro, Deskpro XL, Deskpro XE, or Presario	Press the F10 key while the cursor is in the upper-right corner of the screen, which happens just after the two beeps during booting*
All other older computers	Use a setup program on the disk that came with the PC

*For Compaq computers, the CMOS setup program is stored on the hard drive in a small, non-DOS partition of about 3 MB. If this partition becomes corrupted, you must run setup from a bootable CD or floppy disk that comes with the system. If you cannot run setup by pressing F10 at startup, suspect a damaged partition or a virus taking up space in conventional memory.

Table 5-12   How to access CMOS setup

A+
CORE
2.1
4.4

For the exact method you need to use to enter setup, see the documentation for your motherboard. A message such as the following usually appears on the screen near the beginning of the boot:

```
Press DEL to change Setup
```

or

```
Press F8 for Setup
```

When you press the appropriate key or keys, a setup screen appears with menus and Help features that are often very user-friendly. Although the exact menus depend on the maker and version of components you are working with, the sample screens that follow will help you become familiar with the general contents of CMOS setup screens. Figure 5-26 shows a main menu for setup. On this menu, you can change the system date and time, the keyboard language, and other system features.

```
                     AwardBIOS Setup Utility
    Main      Advanced    Power    Boot    Exit

     System Time          [11:42:09]          Item Specific Help
     System Date          [04/04/2000]
     Legacy Diskette A    [1.44M, 3.5 in.]    <Enter> to select field;
     Legacy Diskette B    [None]              <+>, <—> to change value
     Floppy 3 Mode Support [Disabled]

   ▶ Primary Master       [Auto]
   ▶ Primary Slave        [Auto]
   ▶ Secondary Master     [Auto]
   ▶ Secondary Slave      [Auto]
   ▶ Keyboard Features

     Language             [English]
     Supervisor Password  [Disabled]
     User Password        [Disabled]
     Halt On              [All Errors]
     Installed Memory     128MB

  F1   Help  ↑↓ Select Item  —/+   Change Values  F5   Setup Defaults
  ESC  Exit  ←→ Select Menu   Enter Select▶Sub-Menu F10  Save and Exit
```

Figure 5-26   CMOS Setup Main menu

Recall the discussion of power management from Chapter 4. The power menu in CMOS setup allows you to configure automatic power-saving features for your system, such as suspend mode. Figure 5-27 shows a sample power menu.

Figure 5-28 shows a sample Boot menu in CMOS setup. Here, you can set the order in which the system tries to boot from certain devices. Most likely you will want to have the BIOS attempt to boot from the floppy drive first, and if no disk is

A+
CORE
2.1
4.4

present, turn to the hard drive. You will learn more about this in the installation procedures at the end of this chapter, as well as in later chapters.

```
                         AwardBIOS Setup Utility
     ┌──────────────────────────────────────────────────────────────┐
        Main    Advanced   Power    Boot    Exit

        System Time        [11:42:09]           Item Specific Help
        System Date        [04/04/2000]
        Legacy Diskette A  [1.44M, 3.5 in.]   <Enter> to select field;
        Legacy Diskette B  [None]             <+>, <-> to change value
        Floppy 3 Mode Support [Disabled]

      ▶ Primary Master     [Auto]
      ▶ Primary Slave      [Auto]
      ▶ Secondary Master   [Auto]
      ▶ Secondary Slave    [Auto]
      ▶ Keyboard Features

        Language           [English]
        Supervisor Password [Disabled]
        User Password      [Disabled]
        Halt On            [All Errors]
        Installed Memory   128MB

     ─────────────────────────────────────────────────────────────────
     F1   Help  ↑↓ Select Item  -/+   Change Values  F5   Setup~Defaults
     ESC  Exit ←→ Select Menu  Enter  Select▶Sub-Menu F10  Save~and Exit
```

Figure 5-27   CMOS Setup Power menu

```
                         AwardBIOS Setup Utility
     ┌──────────────────────────────────────────────────────────────┐
        Main    Advanced   Power    Boot    Exit

        System Time        [11:42:09]           Item Specific Help
        System Date        [04/04/2000]
        Legacy Diskette A  [1.44M, 3.5 in.]   <Enter> to select field;
        Legacy Diskette B  [None]             <+>, <-> to change value
        Floppy 3 Mode Support [Disabled]

      ▶ Primary Master     [Auto]
      ▶ Primary Slave      [Auto]
      ▶ Secondary Master   [Auto]
      ▶ Secondary Slave    [Auto]
      ▶ Keyboard Features

        Language           [English]
        Supervisor Password [Disabled]
        User Password      [Disabled]
        Halt On            [All Errors]
        Installed Memory   128MB

     ─────────────────────────────────────────────────────────────────
     F1   Help  ↑↓ Select Item  -/+   Change Values  F5   Setup~Defaults
     ESC  Exit ←→ Select Menu  Enter  Select▶Sub-Menu F10  Save~and Exit
```

Figure 5-28   CMOS Setup Boot menu

Depending on the specific BIOS you are working with, an Advanced menu in the setup program or on other menus may contain other configuration options. When you finish, an exit screen such as the one shown in Figure 5-29 gives you various options, such as saving or discarding changes and then exiting the program, restoring default settings, or saving changes and remaining in the program.

```
                    AwardBIOS Setup Utility

    Main      Advanced   Power    Boot    Exit

   System Time            [11:42:09]            ┌─────────────────────┐
   System Date            [04/04/2000]          │  Item Specific Help │
   Legacy Diskette A      [1.44M, 3.5 in.]      ├─────────────────────┤
   Legacy Diskette B      [None]                │ <Enter> to select field;
   Floppy 3 Mode Support  [Disabled]            │ <+>, <−> to change value

  ▶ Primary Master        [Auto]
  ▶ Primary Slave         [Auto]
  ▶ Secondary Master      [Auto]
  ▶ Secondary Slave       [Auto]
  ▶ Keyboard Features

   Language               [English]
   Supervisor Password    [Disabled]
   User Password          [Disabled]
   Halt On                [All Errors]
   Installed Memory       128MB

  F1  Help  ↑↓ Select Item  −/+  Change Values   F5  Setup Defaults
  ESC Exit  ←→ Select Menu  Enter Select▶Sub-Menu F10 Save and Exit
```

Figure 5-29 CMOS Setup Exit menu

Battery Power to CMOS Memory   A small trickle of electricity from a nearby battery enables the CMOS memory to hold configuration data even while the main power to the computer is off. If the battery is disconnected or fails, setup information is lost. An indication that the battery is getting weak is that the system date and time are incorrect after the PC has been turned off.

There are several types of CMOS batteries:

- A 3.6 V lithium battery with a four-pin connector; connects with a Velcro strip
- A 4.5 V alkaline battery with a four-pin connector; connects with a Velcro strip
- A 3.6 V barrel-style battery with a two-pin connector; soldered on
- A 3 V lithium coin-cell battery

A+
CORE
2.1
4.4

Figure 5-30 shows the coin cell, the most common type of CMOS battery.

Coin cell battery

Figure 5-30   The coin cell is the most common type of CMOS battery

✔ **A+ EXAM TIP**

The A+ Core exam expects
you to be familiar with
CMOS settings for these
devices and functions: CPU,
parallel port, serial port,
floppy drive, hard drive,
memory, boot sequence,
date/time, passwords, Plug
& Play BIOS, disabling on-
board devices, disabling
virus protection, power
management, and infrared.
You need to know how and
when it is appropriate to
change these settings.

Setting Startup Passwords in CMOS   Access to a computer can be controlled using a **startup password**, sometimes called a **power-on password**. During booting, or startup, the computer asks for a password. Entering an incorrect password terminates the boot process. The password is stored in CMOS memory and is changed by accessing the setup screen. (This password is not the same as the OS password.) Many computers also provide a jumper near the chip holding CMOS memory; when the jumper is set to on, the computer "forgets" any changes made to default settings stored in CMOS. By jumping these pins, you can disable a password.

Lists of CMOS Settings   Motherboard manuals should contain a list of all CMOS settings, an explanation of their meanings, and their recommended values. When you purchase a motherboard or a computer, be sure the manual is included. If you don't have the manual, you can sometimes go to the motherboard manufacturer's Web site and download the information you need to understand the specific CMOS settings of your computer. Table 5-13 lists some CMOS settings. Several of these will be discussed in future chapters.

Category	Setting	Description
Standard	Date and time	Used to set system date and time (called the CMOS setup real-time clock)
	Keyboard	Used to tell system if keyboard is installed or not; useful if the computer is used as a print or file server and you don't want someone changing settings
	Hard disk type	Used to record size and mapping of the drive or set to automatically detect the HDD (discussed in Chapter 8)
	Floppy disk type	Choices are usually 3½ inch and 5¼ inch
BIOS Features Menu	Quick Boot	Enable/disable. Enable to cause POST to skip some tests and speed up booting
	Above 1 MB Memory test	Used to disable POST check of this memory to speed up booting; the OS checks this memory anyway
	Memory parity error check	For older motherboards, used to enable parity checking to ensure that memory is correct
	System boot Sequence	Used to establish the drive the system turns to first to look for an OS; normally the hard drive (drive C) and then floppy drive (drive A) or CD-ROM
	External cache memory	Enable L2 cache. A frequent error in setup is to have cache but not use it because it's disabled here. Used on older motherboards that have on-board cache memory.
	Password Checking option	Used to establish a startup password. Use this only if you need to prevent someone untrustworthy from using your PC. Sometimes there are two passwords, each with different levels of security.

Table 5-13 (continued)

A+
CORE
2.1
4.4

5

Category	Setting	Description
	Video ROM Shadow C000, 16K	For DOS and Windows 9x, shadowing video ROM is recommended because ROM runs slower than RAM
	System ROM Shadow F000, 64K	Enabling shadow system ROM is recommended
	IDE multiblock Mode	Enables a hard drive to read or write several sectors at a time; depends on the kind of hard drive you have
	Plug and Play (PnP)	Enable/disable. Enable for Windows 9x, which uses PnP data from BIOS. Disable for Windows 2000/XP, which does all the PnP configuration.
	Boot sector virus protection	Gives a warning when something is being written to the boot sector of the hard drive. Can be a nuisance if your software is designed to write to the boot sector regularly. When installing or upgrading an operating system, disable this protection so the OS install process can alter the boot sector without interruption.
Advanced Chip Set Setup	AT cycle wait state	The number of wait states the CPU must endure while it interfaces with a device on the ISA or EISA bus. Increase this if an old and slow ISA card is not working well.
	AGP capability	Switches between AGP 1x, AGP 2x, AGP 4x, and AGP 8x versions to accommodate different video cards
	AGP aperture size	Adjusts the amount of system memory AGP can address
	AGP voltage	AGP operating voltage; set according to video card requirements

Table 5-13 (continued)

**A+
CORE
2.1
4.4**

Category	Setting	Description
	VGA BIOS sequence	Determines order in which PCI/AGP is initialized; important mainly with dual monitors
	Processor serial number	Allows processor ID# to be switched off for privacy (Pentium III only)
	Serial port	Set beginning I/O address and IRQ; sometimes you can enable/disable the port
	Parallel port mode	ECP or EPP (differences are discussed in Chapter 10)
	Infrared	Enable/disable (sometimes enabling infrared disables the second serial port, which uses the same resources)
Power Management Menu	Power management	Disable or enable all power management features; these features are designed to conserve electricity.
	Video off method	Sets which way video to the monitor will be suspended
	HDD power down	Disable or enable the feature to shut down the hard drive after a period of inactivity
	Wake on LAN	Wake on LAN allows your PC to be booted from another computer on the same network; it requires an ATX power supply that supports the feature
	Wake on keyboard	Allows you to power up your PC by pressing a certain key combination
Hard Drive Settings	IDE HDD Autodetect	Detects HDDs installed on either IDE channel; allows you to specify Normal, Large, or LBA mode
	Serial ATA	Configure to IDE or RAID
	SMART monitoring	Monitor HDD for failure
Hardware Device Settings	CPU operating speed	Sets the appropriate speed for your CPU
	External clock	Sets the system bus speed

Table 5-13 (continued)

Category	Setting	Description
	I/O voltage	Sets the appropriate I/O voltage for the CPU
	Core voltage	Sets the appropriate core voltage for the CPU

Note: The titles, locations, and inclusion or exclusion of BIOS categories and settings depend on the manufacturer, BIOS version, or both. For instance, Plug and Play may be a group of settings sharing a category with other settings in one version of BIOS, while Plug and Play may be its own category in another BIOS version.

Table 5-13 CMOS settings and their purpose

5

NOTE

In documentation, a.k.a. stands for "also known as."

Protecting Documentation and Configuration Settings

If the battery goes bad or is disconnected, you can lose the settings saved in CMOS RAM. If you are using default settings, reboot with a good battery and instruct setup to restore the default settings. Setup has to autodetect the hard drive present, and you need to set the date and time, but you can easily recover from the problem. However, if you have customized some CMOS settings, you need to restore them. The most reliable way to restore settings is to keep a written record of all the changes you make to CMOS.

If you are permanently responsible for a computer, you should consider keeping a written record of what you have done to maintain it. Use a small notebook or similar document to record CMOS settings that are not the default settings, hardware and software installed, network settings, and similar information. Suppose someone decides to tinker with a PC for which you are responsible, changes a jumper on the motherboard, and cannot remember which jumper he or she changed. The computer no longer works, and the documentation for the board is now invaluable. Lost or misplaced documentation greatly complicates the otherwise simple job of reading the settings for each jumper and checking them on the board. Keep the documentation well labeled in a safe place. If you have several computers to maintain, you might consider a filing system for each computer. Another method is to tape a cardboard folder to the inside top of the computer case and safely tuck the hardware documentation there. This works well if you are responsible for several computers spread over a wide area.

Regardless of the method you use, it's important that you keep your written record up to date and stored with the hardware documentation in a safe place. Leaving it in

A+
CORE
2.1
4.4

the care of users who might not realize its value is probably not a good idea. The notebook and documentation will be invaluable as you solve future problems with this PC.

APPLYING CONCEPTS

Saving and Restoring CMOS Settings Using Third-Party Utility Software

If you lose CMOS settings, another way to restore them is to use a backup of the settings that you have previously saved on a floppy disk. One third-party utility that allows you to save CMOS settings is Norton Utilities by Symantec (*www.symantec.com*). Sometimes the support CD that comes with a motherboard has a utility on it to save CMOS settings to a floppy disk.

You can also download a shareware utility to record CMOS settings. One example follows, but know that the files might change with new releases of the software.

1. Access the Internet and use a search engine to find a site offering Cmos.zip. Two current locations are: *www.programmersheaven.com/zone24/cat31/4174/htm* and *www.computerhope.com/downlod.htm*
2. Select and download Cmos.zip. You can then exit the Internet.
3. Unzip the compressed file and print the contents of the documentation file.
4. Double-click the Cmos.exe file you unzipped. The program shows the current contents of CMOS memory in a DOS box.
5. Enter **S** (for Save) at the command line. Enter the drive letter of your floppy drive and a filename to save the current CMOS settings to floppy disk, such as **A:MYCMOS**.
6. Enter **Q** to quit the program.

When you want to retrieve the contents of the file from the floppy disk, run the Cmos.exe program again, and enter **L** (for Load) at the command line, specifying the name of the file you saved on the floppy disk.

Building a Computer: An Introduction

Now that you have learned how motherboards work and what components they include, you can begin learning how to build your own computer. A later section of this chapter discusses in detail how a motherboard is installed. First, though, let's look at the overall process for building your own computer. In Chapter 4, you took your first look inside a computer and learned your way around by taking it apart. In this section, you will begin to learn how to put a new one together from separately purchased parts. You will need this information as you learn to install specific components in this chapter and the rest of the book. This chapter focuses on installing the motherboard, but in Chapter 23, you will see the entire process in detail.

Whenever you install or uninstall software or hardware, keep a notebook with details about the components you are working on, configuration settings, manufacturer specifications, and other relevant information. This helps if you need to backtrack later, and can also help you document and troubleshoot your computer system. Keep all hardware documentation for this system together with the notebook in an envelope in a safe place.

The following directions are meant to be a general overview of the process and are not meant to include the details of all possible installation scenarios, which can vary according to the components and OS you are installing. The general process for putting together a computer is as follows:

1. *Verify that you have all parts you plan to install.* Check device manufacturer Web sites for updated BIOS and device drivers for your system.

2. *Prepare the computer case.* Install the case fan, remove the plates that cover the drive bays, and install the spacers that keep the motherboard from touching the case. Because today's CPUs run at high temperatures, it is a good idea to have at least one case fan in addition to the power supply fan, to ensure good case ventilation. Also, preparing the case before actually installing components lessens the risk of damaging components as you install them.

3. *Install drives,* such as the CD-ROM or DVD drive, hard drive, and floppy drive. Have a plan for where to install each drive, to avoid tangling cables or having them interfere with airflow or access to other components. As you install drives, verify jumper settings for Master/Slave or SCSI ID. Some technicians prefer to install the motherboard first, but we are choosing to install the drives first. If the motherboard is already in the case before the drives are installed, there is the risk of dropping a drive on the motherboard and damaging it.

4. *Determine proper configuration settings for the motherboard.* Especially important are any jumpers, DIP switches, or CMOS settings specifically for the CPU, and RAM speeds and timing. Gather as much information as possible from manufacturer documentation. Read the motherboard manual from cover to cover. You can also check manufacturer Web sites for suggestions for optimizing system settings.

5. *Set any jumpers or switches on the motherboard.* This is much easier to do before you put the board in the case.

6. *Install the CPU and CPU cooler.* The CPU comes already installed on some motherboards, in which case you just need to install the cooler. You might need to add thermal grease.

7. *Install RAM* into the appropriate slots on the motherboard.

8. *Install the motherboard and attach cabling* that goes from the case switches to the motherboard, and from the power supply to the drives. Pay attention to

how cables are labeled and to any information in the documentation about where to attach them. (The next section covers details on how to install a motherboard.) Position and tie cables neatly together to make sure they don't obstruct the fans.

9. *Install the video card* (which can also be called the display adapter, video adapter, or graphics accelerator) on the motherboard. Usually this card goes into the AGP slot, as you learned in Chapter 1.

10. *Plug the computer into a power source, and attach the monitor and keyboard.* Note that you do not attach the mouse now, for the initial setup. Although the mouse generally does not cause problems during setup, avoid initially installing anything you don't absolutely need.

11. *Boot the system and enter CMOS setup.* As you learned earlier in the chapter, there are several ways to do this, depending on what type of system you have.

12. *Make sure settings are set to the default.* If components come new from the manufacturer, they are probably already at default settings. If you are salvaging a component from another system, you may need to reset settings to the default. Generally a jumper or switch will set all CMOS settings to default settings. You will need to do the following while you are in CMOS:

   ■ Check the time and date.
   ■ Check the floppy drive type.
   ■ Make sure abbreviated POST is disabled. While you are setting up a system, you generally want it to do as many tests as possible. Once you know the system is working, you can choose to abbreviate POST.
   ■ Set the boot order to drive A, then drive C, if you will be booting the OS from a floppy disk. Set the boot order to CD-ROM, then drive C, if you will be booting the OS from a CD. This determines which drive the system looks to for the OS. You may need to change the boot order later, as explained in Step 19.
   ■ Make sure "autodetect hard disk" is set so that the system automatically looks for drives.
   ■ Leave everything else at their defaults unless you know that particular settings should be otherwise.
   ■ Save and exit.

13. *If you are booting from a floppy disk, insert a bootable setup disk* that contains the files that allow you to format the hard drive. (Refer to Chapter 3 for a list of files that should be on this disk.)

14. *Observe POST* and verify that no errors occur.

15. *Prepare the hard drive for the OS.* You will learn how to do this in Chapter 9.

16. *Reboot the system and run ScanDisk on drive C.* Recall from Chapter 3 that ScanDisk is an OS utility that checks the hard drive for errors and repairs them.

17. *Connect the mouse.*

18. *Install the OS from CD or floppy.* Generally, it is best to install the OS before any expansion cards, such as a sound card or a modem card. Installing multiple cards at once can confuse Plug and Play, especially during OS installation. Unless you are very familiar with all components' resource requirements, it is almost always less trouble to install one device at a time on a new system. If you are setting up multiple systems with the same configuration, build the first system one card at a time. If no major errors occur, then try installing all cards at once on a second system, after the OS has been loaded. If this approach is successful, then you can save a little time by installing all hardware devices before you install the OS. However, you should still reboot whenever you have the option, as the OS detects each device.

19. *Change the boot order in CMOS* so that it does not boot from a CD first. If you set the order as drive A, then drive C, you can boot from a floppy disk later as needed. This is the most common boot order.

20. *Check for conflicts with system resources.* For Windows, use Device Manager to verify that the OS recognizes all devices and that no conflicts are reported. If your motherboard comes with a CD that contains some motherboard drivers, install them now. Remember that the drivers Windows installed for the devices it sensed might not be the latest drivers. Windows makes its best guess at what drivers to use, but if your version of Windows is older than some of your components, it might not have the correct or newest drivers for those devices. Using Device Manager, you can see what drivers are installed for a device. If Windows is not using the newest drivers, update them using the latest drivers from the CD that comes with the device.

21. *Install any other expansion cards and drives*, and install appropriate drivers, one device at a time, rebooting and checking for conflicts after each installation.

22. *Verify that everything is operating properly, and make any final OS and CMOS adjustments*, such as power management settings.

Installing the Motherboard

A+
CORE
1.2
1.9

Now that you have learned the general process of putting together a computer, you will learn how to install a motherboard. The following section explains how to install and configure a motherboard and how to test the installation.

CAUTION

As with any installation, remember the importance of using a ground strap to ground yourself when working inside a computer case, to protect components against ESD.

Preparing the Motherboard to Go into the Case

A+
CORE
1.2
1.9

Before you begin preparing the motherboard, read the manual that comes with it from beginning to end. The steps listed in this section are general, and you will need to know information specific to your motherboard. Visually familiarize yourself with the configuration of the case and the motherboard.

Setting the Jumpers

VIDEO

Preparing a
Motherboard
for Installation

The first step in preparing the motherboard to go in the case is to set the jumpers or DIP switches. When doing an installation, read the motherboard documentation carefully, looking for explanations of how jumpers and DIP switches on the board are used. This information differs from one motherboard to another. For older boards, a jumper group might control the system bus frequency and another group might control the CPU frequency multiple. Set the jumpers and DIP switches according to the hardware you will be installing.

For example, Figure 5-31 shows the documentation for one motherboard that uses three jumpers to configure the BIOS; the jumper group is shown in Figure 5-32. Set the jumper group to the normal setting so that BIOS uses the current configuration for booting. Once set, the jumpers should be changed only if you are trying to recover when the power-up password is lost or flashing BIOS has failed. Figure 5-32 shows the jumper cap in the normal position.

Jumper Position	Mode	Description
1 ... 3	Normal (default)	The current BIOS configuration is used for booting.
1 ... 3	Configure	After POST, the BIOS displays a menu in CMOS setup that can be used to clear the user and supervisor power-on passwords.
1 ... 3	Recovery	Used to recover from a failed BIOS update. Details can be found on the motherboard CD.

Figure 5-31   BIOS configuration jumper settings

A+
CORE
1.2
1.9

Jumpers set for
normal boot

5

Figure 5-32　　BIOS setup configuration jumpers

Adding the CPU, Fan, and Heat Sink

Now that you have set the jumpers on the motherboard, you are ready to add the CPU itself. We'll look at two examples of installing a CPU: a Pentium II installed in slot 1 and a Pentium 4 installed in Socket 478.

Installing a Pentium II in Slot 1　　For slot 1, used by the Pentium II, the motherboard uses a universal retention mechanism (URM), which is preinstalled on the board. Follow these steps to install the fan on the side of the processor first, and then install the processor on the motherboard:

1. *Unfold the URM arms.* Flip both arms up until they lock into position (refer back to Figure 5-14).

2. *Examine the heat sink and fan assembly and processor* to see how the cooling assembly brace lines up with holes in the side of the SECC (see Figure 5-33).

3. *Place the heat sink on the side of the SECC.* The two should fit tightly together, with absolutely no space between them.

4. *After you fit the heat sink and SECC together, place the SECC on a table and push the clamp on the fan down and into place*, to secure the cooling assembly to the SECC (see Figure 5-34).

5. *Insert the cooling assembly and SECC into the supporting arms* (see Figure 5-35). The SECC should fit snugly into slot 1, similar to the way an expansion card settles into an expansion slot. The arms should snap into position when the SECC is fully seated. Be certain you have a good fit.

6. *Lock the SECC into position* by pulling the SECC locks outward until they lock into the supporting arm lock holes.

A+
CORE
1.2
1.9

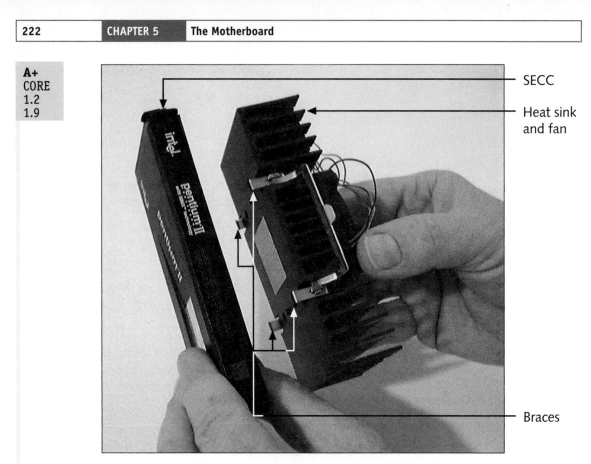

SECC

Heat sink
and fan

Braces

Figure 5-33   The braces on the heat sink and fan assembly align with holes in the side of the SECC

Push clamp
down

Figure 5-34   Push the clamp on the fan down until it locks in place, locking the heat sink and fan to
the SECC

Fan, heat sink and SECC

Supporting arms

Slot 1

5

Figure 5-35 Insert the heat sink, fan, and SECC into the supporting arms and slot 1

7. *Connect the power cord coming from the fan to the power connection on the motherboard* (see Figure 5-36). Look for the power connection near slot 1. If you have trouble locating it, see the motherboard documentation.

Power for CPU fan

Figure 5-36 Connect the fan power cord to the motherboard

A+
CORE
1.2
1.9

Installing a Pentium 4 in Socket 478   If you look back at Figure 5-6, you can see the Pentium 4 installed in Socket 478 on a motherboard. Notice the frame or retention mechanism used to hold the cooler in place. This frame might come separately from the board or be preinstalled. If necessary, follow the directions that come with the motherboard to install the frame.

The next step is to install the CPU. Lift the ZIF socket lever as shown in Figure 5-37. Place the processor on the socket so that the corner marked with a triangle is aligned with the connection of the lever to the socket. After the processor is in place, lower the lever to insert the processor firmly into the socket. As you work, be very careful not to force the processor in at an offset or disoriented position.

Figure 5-37   Install the processor in the mPGA478B socket

Before installing the CPU cooling assembly over the CPU, place a small amount of thermal compound on top of the processor. This grease-like substance helps transfer heat from the processor to the heat sink. Do not use too much; if you do, it may squish out the sides and interfere with other components.

The fan and heat sink are surrounded by a clip assembly. Line up the clip assembly with the retention mechanism already installed on the motherboard, and press lightly on all four corners to attach it. Once the cooling assembly is in place, push down the two clip levers on top of the CPU fan (Figure 5-38). Different coolers use different types of clipping mechanisms, so follow the directions that come with the cooler. Sometimes the clipping mechanism is difficult to clip onto the processor, and the plastic levers and housing are flimsy, so proceed with caution.

The next step is to install RAM in the memory slots. Chapter 6 covers how to buy and install memory for a specific motherboard.

Figure 5-38   The clip levers attach the cooling assembly to the retention mechanism
around the processor

Installing the Motherboard in the Case

Here are the steps for installing the motherboard in the case:

1. Install the faceplate. The **faceplate** or I/O shield is a metal plate that comes with the motherboard and fits over the ports to create a well-fitting enclosure around them. A case might have several faceplates designed for several brands of motherboards. Select the correct one and discard the others (see Figure 5-39). Insert the faceplate in the hole at the back of the case (see Figure 5-40).

VIDEO

Installing a
Motherboard

2. Install the standoffs. **Standoffs**, also called **spacers**, are round plastic or metal pegs that separate the motherboard from the case, so that components on the back of the motherboard do not touch the case. Make sure the locations of the standoffs match the screw holes on the motherboard. If you need to remove a standoff to move it to a new slot, needle-nose pliers work well to unscrew the standoff. The case will have more holes than you need, in order to support several brands of motherboards.

Hole inside case to receive a faceplate

Ports on motherboard will later show through holes in faceplate

Faceplates

Figure 5-39   The computer case comes with several faceplates. Select the faceplate that fits over the ports that come off the motherboard. The other plates can be discarded.

3. Place the motherboard inside the case, and use screws to attach it to the case. Figure 5-41 shows how you must align the standoffs to the holes on the motherboard. The screws fit into the standoffs you installed earlier. There should be at least four standoff/screw sets, and there may be as many as six. Use as many as there are holes in the motherboard.

4. Connect the power cord from the power supply to the P1 power connection on the motherboard. (If you are using an AT motherboard, you have two power connections, P8 and P9, which are connected using the black-to-black rule.)

Faceplate

Figure 5-40   Install the faceplate in the hole at the rear of the computer case

A+
CORE
1.2

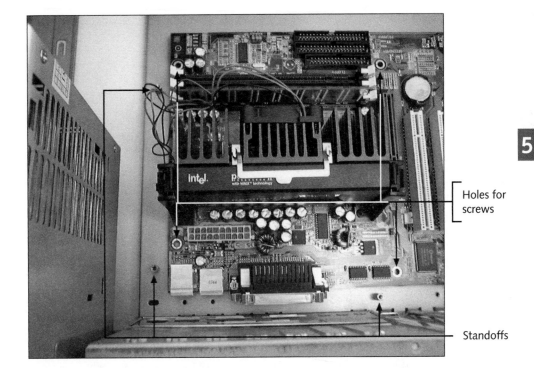

Figure 5-41   Three standoffs and four screw holes are visible

5. Connect the wire leads from the front panel of the case to the motherboard. These are the wires for the switches and lights on the front of the computer. Because your case and your motherboard may not have been made by the same manufacturer, you need to pay close attention to the source of the wires to determine where they connect on the motherboard. For example, Figure 5-42 shows a computer case that has five wires from the front panel that connect to the motherboard.

The five connectors are:

- *Reset switch.* Used to reboot the computer
- *HDD LED.* Controls a light on the front panel that lights up when any IDE device is in use. (LED stands for light-emitting diode; an LED is a light on the front panel.)
- *Speaker.* Controls the speaker
- *Power LED.* Light indicating that power is on
- *Remote switch.* Controls power to the motherboard; must be connected for the PC to power up

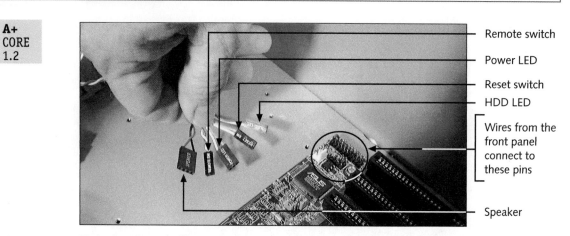

Remote switch

Power LED

Reset switch
HDD LED

Wires from the
front panel
connect to
these pins

Speaker

Figure 5-42   Five wires from the front panel connect to the motherboard

To know which wire connects to which pins, see the motherboard documentation. Sometimes the documentation is not clear, but guessing is okay when connecting a wire to a connection. If it doesn't work, no harm is done.

NOTE

To help orient the connector on the motherboard pins, look for a small triangle embedded on the connector that marks one of the outside wires as pin 1 (see Figure 5-43). Look for pin 1 to be labeled on the motherboard as a small 1 embedded to either the right or the left of the group of pins. Also, sometimes the documentation will mark pin 1 as a square pin in the diagram, rather than round like the other pins.

Figure 5-43   Look for the small triangle embedded on the wire lead connectors to orient the connector correctly to the motherboard connector pins

Completing the Installation

After you install the motherboard, you will install expansion cards and other components. Later chapters cover how to do this. Finally, turn on the system and make sure everything is connected properly. You may need to change the hardware configuration settings discussed in the previous section. As you set configuration data, remember to create a rescue disk of these settings so that you can restore them if something goes wrong.

Troubleshooting the Motherboard and CPU

A+
CORE
2.1

When troubleshooting the motherboard, use whatever clues POST can give you. Recall that, before it checks video, POST reports any error messages as beep codes. When a PC boots, one beep indicates that all is well after POST. If you hear more than one beep, look up the beep code in Appendix A. Error messages on the screen indicate that video is working. If the beep code or error message is not in Appendix A, try the Web site of the ROM BIOS manufacturer for information. Figure 5-44 shows the Web site for AMI with explanations of beep codes produced by its startup BIOS.

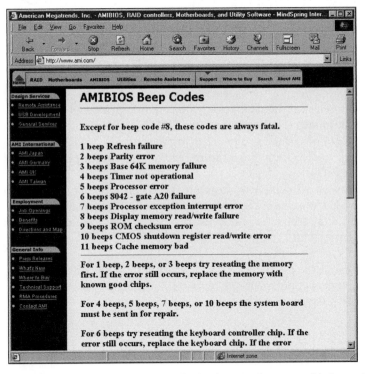

Figure 5-44   The ROM BIOS manufacturer's Web site is a good source of information about beep codes

Remember that you can try substituting good hardware components for those you suspect are bad. Be cautious here. A friend once had a computer that would not boot. He replaced the hard drive, with no change. He replaced the motherboard next. The computer booted up with no problem; he was delighted, until it failed again. Later he discovered that a faulty power supply had damaged his original motherboard. When he traded the bad one for a good one, the new motherboard also got zapped! Check the voltage coming from the power supply before putting in a new motherboard! (Instructions on troubleshooting the power supply are in Chapter 4.)

A+
CORE
2.1

A power-saving feature might be the source of the problem. Ask yourself, "Is the system in a doze or sleep mode?" Many "green," or environmentally friendly, systems can be programmed through CMOS to suspend the monitor or even the drive if the keyboard or CPU has been inactive for a few minutes. Pressing any key usually causes operations to resume exactly where the user left off. If you have just upgraded the CPU and the system will not boot, reinstall the old CPU, flash BIOS, and then try the new CPU again. Verify that you have installed thermal paste between the CPU and the heat sink.

The motherboard might have come bundled with a support CD. Look on it for drivers of board components that are not working. For example, if the USB ports are not working, try updating the USB drivers with those stored on the support CD. Load the CD and follow directions on screen.

If this doesn't resolve the problem, try the following:

- If the fan is running, reseat or replace the CPU, BIOS, or RAM. Try installing a DIMM in a different slot. A POST code diagnostic card is a great help at this point. These cards are discussed in Chapter 24.
- Sometimes a dead computer can be fixed by simply disassembling it and reseating cables, adapter cards, socketed chips, and SIMMs, DIMMs, or RIMMs. Bad connections and corrosion are common problems.
- Check jumpers, DIP switches, and CMOS settings.
- Look for physical damage on the motherboard.
- Check CMOS for a temperature reading that indicates overheating.
- Flash BIOS.
- A dead or dying battery may cause problems. Sometimes, after a long holiday, a weak battery causes the CMOS to forget its configuration.
- Reduce the system to essentials. Remove any unnecessary hardware, such as expansion cards, and then try to boot again.
- Exchange the CPU.
- Exchange the motherboard, but before you do, measure the voltage output of the power supply or simply replace it, in case it is producing too much power and has damaged the board.

CHAPTER SUMMARY

5

▶ The motherboard is the most complicated of all components inside the computer. It contains the CPU and accompanying chip set, the real-time clock, ROM BIOS, CMOS configuration chip, RAM, RAM cache, system bus, expansion slots, jumpers, ports, and power supply connections. The motherboard you select determines both the capabilities and limitations of your system.

▶ The most important component on the motherboard is the CPU, or central processing unit. The CPU is rated according to its speed, efficiency of programming code, word size, data path size, size of internal cache, multiprocessing abilities, and special functions.

▶ Two kinds of static RAM cache for the slower DRAM are internal and external cache, sometimes called Level 1 and Level 2 or Level 3 cache (or L1 and L2 or L3 cache).

▶ L1 cache is contained on the CPU microchip, and L2 and L3 cache are external to this microchip. L2 and L3 can be on the motherboard or in the CPU housing. If a processor has L2 cache, then cache on the motherboard is called L3 cache.

▶ The Itanium, Intel's newest processor family, has L1, L2, and L3 cache.

▶ The Intel Pentium CPU family includes the Classic Pentium, Pentium MMX, Pentium Pro, Pentium II, Celeron, Pentium III, and Pentium 4.

▶ AMD is Intel's chief competitor for the CPU market. AMD produces the AMD Duron, Athlon, Athlon MP, Athlon XP, Opteron, and Athlon 64 processors.

▶ Newer CPUs require extra cooling, which you can accomplish by installing a CPU heat sink and cooling fan on top of or near the CPU.

▶ Some CPU sockets and slots are Socket 7, Socket 370, Socket 423, Socket 478, slot 1, Slot A, slot 2, Socket 603, Socket 775, Socket 754, and Socket 939. A slot looks like an expansion slot.

▶ Because some CPUs require one voltage for internal core operations and another voltage for external I/O operations, when upgrading a CPU, you might have to upgrade or add a voltage regulator module to control these voltages.

▶ Some components can be built into the motherboard, in which case they are called on-board components. Other components can be attached to the system in some other way, such as on an expansion card.

▶ ROM chips contain the programming code to manage POST and system BIOS and to change the CMOS settings. The setup or CMOS chip holds configuration information.

▶ A chip set is a group of chips on the motherboard that supports the CPU. Intel is the most popular manufacturer of chip sets.

▶ A bus is a path on the motherboard that carries electrical power, control signals, memory addresses, and data to different components on the board.

▶ A bus can be 16, 32, 64, or more bits wide. The first ISA bus had an 8-bit data path. The second ISA slot had a 16-bit data path.

▶ Some well-known buses are the 16-bit ISA, 32-bit MCA and EISA buses, and the three local buses: the VESA bus, the PCI bus, the AGP bus, and PCI Express. A local bus is designed to allow fast devices quicker and more direct access to the CPU than other buses.

▶ Jumpers on the motherboard can be used to set the motherboard speed and the CPU multiplier, which determines the CPU speed. Sometimes these settings are autodetected without the use of jumpers.

▶ When building a new system, install the drives, motherboard, and expansion cards. Only install essential components before you install the OS. Then add other components one at a time, verifying that each component works before adding another.

▶ Before installing the motherboard in the case, install the CPU and memory, and set jumpers and DIP switches on the board.

KEY TERMS

For explanations of key terms, see the Glossary near the end of the book.

Advanced Transfer Cache (ATC)
audio/modem riser (AMR)
back-side bus (BSB)
bus speed
communication and networking
   riser (CNR)
complex instruction set
   computing (CISC)
cooler
discrete L2 cache
dual-voltage CPU
Execution Trace Cache
expansion bus
explicitly parallel instruction
   computing (EPIC)
external cache
faceplate
front-side bus (FSB)
heat sink

host bus
Industry Standard Architecture
   (ISA) slot
instruction set
internal bus
internal cache
Level 1 (L1) cache
Level 2 (L2) cache
Level 3 (L3) cache
local bus
local I/O bus
low insertion force (LIF) socket
memory bus
memory cache
motherboard bus
multiplier
North Bridge
on-board ports
On-Package L2 cache

pin grid array (PGA)
power-on password
primary cache
processor speed
reduced instruction set
   computing (RISC)
riser card
single-voltage CPU
South Bridge
spacers
staggered pin grid array (SPGA)
standoffs
startup password
system bus
voltage regulator module (VRM)
wait state
zero insertion force (ZIF) socket

REVIEWING THE BASICS

1. What are the four most popular types of motherboards?

2. How many power cords connect to a Baby AT motherboard?

3. Name 10 components that are contained on a motherboard.

4. If a motherboard has a slot 1, what CPU(s) is it designed to support?

5. Why would you want both ISA and PCI expansion slots on a motherboard?

6. When people speak of bus size, to what are they specifically referring?

7. What characteristics of the motherboard architecture determine the amount of memory that a CPU can address?

8. What was the first Intel CPU to contain external cache?

9. When is it appropriate to use a Celeron rather than a Pentium 4 in a computer system?

10. Which is more powerful, the Celeron or the Xeon processor?

11. Who is the major competitor of Intel in the CPU market?

12. Why did the competitors of the Intel Pentium II choose to stay with Socket 7 rather than use slot 1 for their competing processors?

13. What components inside a computer case keep a CPU cool?

14. Describe the difference between a PGA socket and an SPGA socket.

15. Name a CPU that requires dual voltage. How are the two voltages used?

16. Name a CPU that uses Socket A.

17. What are the three speeds of the most popular motherboards currently available on the market?

18. Name three manufacturers of motherboard chip sets.

19. Name the three most popular manufacturers of system BIOS programs.

20. What is one reason to flash BIOS?

21. What is the easiest way to obtain the latest software to upgrade BIOS?

22. What is the name for the bus that connects L2 cache to the CPU inside the Pentium II processor housing?

23. Why is it best to install drives into a computer case before you install the motherboard?

24. What are the four categories of cargo that are carried over a bus?

25. Describe how you can access the CMOS setup program.

THINKING CRITICALLY

1. Why does a motherboard sometimes support more than one system bus speed?

2. What must software developers do to take advantage of a 64-bit processor such as the Itanium?

3. Why don't all buses on a motherboard operate at the same speed?

4. When you turn off a computer at night, it loses the date, and you must reenter it each morning. What is the problem and how do you solve it?

5. A computer freezes at odd times. At first you suspect the power supply or overheating, but you have eliminated overheating and replaced the power supply without solving the problem. What do you do next?

   a. Replace the CPU

   b. Replace the motherboard

   c. Reinstall Windows

   d. Replace the memory modules

   e. Flash BIOS

HANDS-ON PROJECTS

HANDS-ON
PROJECTS

PROJECT 5-1:   Recognizing Motherboard Components

Obtain the manual for a motherboard. If you don't have a printed manual, use the Internet to search for a motherboard Web site, then download and print a manual. For example, try ASUS at *www.asus.com* or Abit at *www.motherboards.com*. Look for a diagram of the motherboard components. Identify as many components from your diagram as you can. Copy the diagram and circle the components you recognize.

PROJECT 5-2: **Examining the Motherboard in Detail**

1. Look at the back of your computer. Without opening the case, list the ports that you believe come directly from the motherboard.

2. Remove the cover of the case, which you learned to do in Chapter 4. List the different circuit boards in the expansion slots. Was your guess correct about which ports come from the motherboard?

3. To expose the motherboard so you can identify its parts, remove all the expansion boards, as discussed in Chapter 4.

4. Draw a diagram of the motherboard and label these parts:

   ▶ The CPU (include the prominent label on the CPU housing)

   ▶ RAM (SIMMs, DIMMs, or RIMMs)

   ▶ CMOS battery

   ▶ Expansion slots (identify the slots as ISA, EISA, MCA, PCI, AGP, etc.)

   ▶ Each port coming directly from the motherboard

   ▶ Power supply connections

   ▶ Hard drive data connector and floppy drive connector

5. Draw a rectangle on the diagram to represent each bank of jumpers on the board.

6. You can complete the following activity only if you have the documentation for the motherboard: Locate the jumper on the board that erases CMOS and/or the startup password, and label this jumper on your diagram. It is often found near the battery. Some boards might have more than one, and some have none.

7. Reassemble the computer, as you learned to do in Chapter 4.

PROJECT 5-3: **Saving and Restoring CMOS Settings**

Save your CMOS settings on a disk, using either Norton Utilities or the shareware program contained in Cmos.zip. This chapter includes instructions in the section "Saving and Restoring CMOS Settings Using Third-Party Utility Software."

PROJECT 5-4: **Inserting and Removing Motherboards**

Using old or defective expansion cards and motherboards, practice inserting and removing expansion cards and chips.

PROJECT 5-5: **Printing a Summary of Your System Hardware**

1. In Windows XP, click **Start** then right-click **My Computer**.

2. On the shortcut menu, select **Properties**.

3. Click the **Hardware** tab and then click the **Device Manager** button.

4. View devices by type.

5. Expand **Ports (COM & LPT)** if necessary.

6. Click the **Print** button.

7. Print **Selected class or device**.

8. Close all open windows.

PROJECT 5-6: **Understanding Hardware Documentation**

Obtain the manual for the motherboard for your PC. (If you cannot find the manual, try downloading it from the motherboard manufacturer's Web site.) List at least three functions of jumpers on the board as well as the corresponding jumper numbers. List the CPUs that the board supports.

PROJECT 5-7: **Using the Internet for Research**

1. Search the Web sites of Intel and AMD (*www.intel.com* and *www.amd.com*), and print information on the most recent processor for the desktop offered by each company.

2. Using your own or a lab computer, pretend that the motherboard manual is not available and you need to know the settings for the jumpers on the motherboard. Identify the manufacturer of the motherboard, and research the Web site for that manufacturer. Print the jumper settings for the motherboard from on the Web site.

3. Research the Web site for your motherboard and print the instructions for flashing BIOS.

PROJECT 5-8: **Researching the Market**

1. In a current computer magazine, find the speed and price of the fastest PC CPU on the market today.

2. In a current computer magazine, find the speed and price of the fastest PC RAM module on the market today.

PROJECT 5-9: **Researching the Intel Web Site**

5

Research the Intel Web site (*www.intel.com*), and do the following:

1. Print photographs of eight different processor packages used by Intel CPUs.

2. List the processor packages that these processors currently use:

▶ Celeron

▶ Pentium 4 Extreme Edition

▶ Itanium

▶ Itanium 2

PROJECT 5-10: **Labeling the Motherboard**

Figure 5-45 shows a blank diagram of an ATX motherboard. Using what you learned in this chapter and in previous chapters, label as many components as you can.

Figure 5-45 Label the motherboard

Managing Memory

In earlier chapters, you learned how several important hardware components work and how to support them. This chapter looks at another component, memory, and examines how DOS, Windows 9x/Me, and Windows NT/2000/XP manage it. Memory is required in order for a system to work. Memory is stored on microchips, which are often stored on memory modules called SIMMs, DIMMs, or RIMMs. Adding more memory to a system can sometimes greatly improve performance.

RAM on the Motherboard

**A+
CORE
1.1
1.10**

Recall that memory temporarily holds data and instructions as the CPU processes them and that computer memory is divided into two categories: ROM and RAM. ROM retains its data when the PC is turned off, but RAM loses all its data (except for data stored on the CMOS chip). ROM stores its data on chips socketed or soldered to the circuit boards. One or two ROM chips on a motherboard hold system BIOS and startup BIOS programs, and many devices and circuit boards such as video cards have ROM chips on them. In the 1980s, RAM chips were also socketed or soldered directly on motherboards, but today all RAM used as main memory is housed on SIMMs, DIMMs, or RIMMs. This section examines the different RAM technologies. ROM technologies, including how to flash ROM, were covered in the last chapter.

RAM, or random access memory, is divided into two categories: **static RAM (SRAM)** and **dynamic RAM (DRAM)**. DRAM, pronounced "DEE-ram," is memory that needs to be refreshed every few milliseconds. To **refresh** RAM means that the computer must rewrite the data to the chip. RAM is refreshed by the memory controller, which is part of the chip set on the motherboard. Today most DRAM is stored on DIMMs and less commonly on RIMMs (see Figure 6-1).

DIMM

Two extra slots for additional DIMMs

Figure 6-1   DRAM on most motherboards today is stored on DIMMs

Besides serving as main memory, RAM also provides a memory cache. These memory chips hold data as long as the power is on and are therefore called static

A+
CORE
1.1
1.10

RAM (SRAM), pronounced "ESS-ram." A system can have lots of main memory to hold data and instructions as they are processed and a little memory cache to help speed up access time to main memory. Recall from Chapter 5 that cache memory is contained on the motherboard or inside the CPU housing. On the motherboard, it is either on individual chips or on a memory module called a **cache on a stick** (**COAST**). Figure 6-2 shows a motherboard with 256K of SRAM installed on the board in two single chips. A COAST slot is available to hold an additional 256K. At first, the motherboard held all cache memory, and then cache was stored inside the CPU housing. More recently, for Intel processors, all memory cache is stored inside the CPU housing, and for AMD processors, cache is put in both places.

6

SRAM chip manages cache

Jumpers for cache size selection

2 SRAM chips (128 KB each)

Memory cache slot (COAST)

Figure 6-2   SRAM on this older motherboard is stored in individual chips, and the board also has a COAST slot

A+
CORE
1.1
1.10
4.2

DRAM and SRAM use several technologies summarized in Table 6-1. Of all the memory technologies listed, the three current DRAM technologies are DDR, RIMM, and DDR2. Most SRAM is now inside the processor housing. Dual Channel technology applies to the motherboard and allows the memory controller to manage two channels of data between DDR or DDR2 DIMMs and the controller, effectively doubling the data rate. Other technologies are considered obsolete, although you still need to be aware of them in case you see them on older motherboards you support. You will read more about these technologies in the following sections.

A+
CORE
1.1
1.10
4.2

Main Memory (DRAM)	Cache Memory (SRAM)
DRAM needs constant refreshing	SRAM does not need refreshing
Slower than SRAM because of refreshing time	Faster but more expensive
Physically housed on DIMMs, SIMMs, and RIMMs	Physically housed on the motherboard on COAST modules or single chips, or included inside the processor case
Technologies include: • FPM, EDO, and BEDO • SyncLink SDRAM (SLDRAM) • Synchronous DRAM (SDRAM) • Double Data Rate SDRAM (DDR, DDR SDRAM, or SDRAM II) • Direct Rambus DRAM (RIMMs) • Dual channel • DDR2	Technologies include: • Synchronous SRAM • Burst SRAM • Pipelined burst SRAM • Asynchronous SRAM • Housed within the processor case (new trend)
Memory addresses assigned	No memory addresses assigned

Table 6-1   Types of memory (SRAM and DRAM)

Static RAM Technologies

✔ **A+ EXAM TIP**

The A+ Core exam expects you to be familiar with the following technologies that apply to memory on the motherboard: EDO, DRAM, SRAM, SDRAM, DDR, Rambus, SIMM, DIMM, SoDIMM, RIMM, Parity, ECC, single-sided, and double-sided. Look for all these terms in this section.

SRAM provides faster access than DRAM because data does not need to be constantly rewritten to SRAM, saving the CPU time used to refresh data in DRAM. Memory chips are made of transistors, which are switches. An SRAM transistor switch can stay in place as long as it has voltage available because each memory cell comprises several interlinked transistors, but DRAM transistor switches are charged by capacitors, which must be recharged. SRAM chips are more expensive than DRAM chips. Therefore, most computers have a little SRAM and a lot of DRAM. Table 6-2 summarizes how SRAM is used in different memory caches on and off the motherboard. Table 6-2 also summarizes the information about memory caches presented in Chapter 5.

A+
CORE
1.1
1.10
4.2

Memory Cache	Location
L1 cache	On the CPU die. All CPUs today have L1 cache.
L2 cache	Inside the CPU housing. The first CPU to contain L2 was the Intel Pentium Pro.
L2 cache	On the motherboard of older systems.
L3 cache	Inside the CPU housing, farther away from the CPU than the L2 cache. The Intel Itanium housing contains L3 cache.
L3 cache	On the motherboard when there is L2 cache in the CPU housing. L3 is used with some AMD processors.

Table 6-2   The location of memory caches in a system

How Memory Caching Works

Memory caching (see Figure 6-3) is a method used to store data or programs in SRAM for quick retrieval. Memory caching requires some SRAM chips and a cache controller. When memory caching is used, the cache controller anticipates what data or programming code the CPU will request next and copies that data or programming code to SRAM. Then, if the cache guessed correctly, it can satisfy the CPU request from SRAM without accessing the slower DRAM. Under normal conditions, memory caching guesses right more than 90 percent of the time and is an effective way of speeding up memory access.

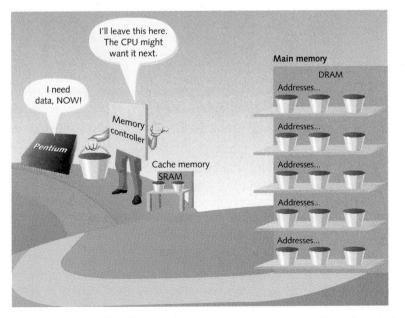

Figure 6-3   A memory cache (SRAM) temporarily holds data in expectation of what the CPU will request next

A+
CORE
1.1
1.10
4.2

Almost all systems today, except for a few AMD processors, have memory caches inside the CPU housing. When making purchasing decisions about processors, look for processors that include as much memory cache as possible for the best performance.

Dynamic RAM Technologies

A+
CORE
1.1
1.10
4.2
4.3

In earlier PCs, main memory was stored on the motherboard as single, socketed chips, but today DRAM is always stored in either DIMM, RIMM, or SIMM modules, which plug directly into the motherboard. The major differences among these modules are the width of the data path that each type of module accommodates and the way data moves from the system bus to the module. Figure 6-4 shows some examples of memory modules.

| 184-pin RIMM | | 168-pin DIMM | 30-pin SIMM |
| 240-pin DDR2 DIMM | 184-pin DDR DIMM | | 72-pin SIMM |

Figure 6-4   Types of RAM modules

Older DRAM and SRAM memory technologies operated asynchronously with the system bus, but newer DRAM and SRAM memory types operate synchronously. To understand the difference between asynchronous and synchronous memory, consider this analogy. Children jump rope with a long rope, and one child on each end turns the rope. A child who cannot keep in step with the turning rope can only run through on a single pass and must come back around to make another pass. A child who can keep in step with the rope can run into the center and jump awhile, until he or she is tired and runs out. Which child performs the most rope-jumping cycles in a given amount of time? The one who keeps in step with the rope. Similarly, synchronous memory retrieves data faster than asynchronous memory, because it keeps time with the system clock.

A+
CORE
1.1
1.10
4.2
4.3

Table 6-3 summarizes DRAM technologies. You will read more details about them in this section.

Technology	Description	Used with
Conventional	Used with earlier PCs but currently not available.	• 30-pin SIMM
Fast page (FPM)	Improved access time over conventional memory. FPM is seldom seen today.	• 30-pin or 72-pin SIMM • 168-pin DIMM
Extended data out (EDO)	Refined version of FPM that speeds up access time. Might still see it on older motherboards.	• 72-pin SIMM • 168-pin DIMM
Burst EDO (BEDO)	Refined version of EDO that significantly improved access time over EDO. Seldom seen today because Intel chose not to support it.	• 72-pin SIMM • 168-pin DIMM
Synchronous DRAM (SDRAM)	SDRAM runs in sync with the system clock and is rated by clock speed, whereas other types of memory run independently of (and slower than) the system clock.	• 66/100/133/150 MHz, 168-pin DIMM • 66/100/133 MHz, 144-pin SO-DIMM
DDR (Double-Data Rate) SDRAM	A faster version of SDRAM and currently the most popular memory type.	• 184-pin DIMM, up to 500 MHz • 200-pin SO-DIMM, up to 400 MHz
Rambus DRAM (RDRAM)	RDRAM is housed on a RIMM, uses a faster system bus (800 MHz or 1066 MHz), and can use a 16- or 32-bit data path.	• 184-pin or 168-pin RIMM with 16-bit single channel • 232-pin RIMM with 32-bit dual channel
DDR2	Faster than DDR and uses less power.	• 240-pin DIMM up to 1 GB size • 214-pin SO-DIMM up to 1 GB size • 244-pin Mini-DIMM

Table 6-3   DRAM memory technologies

A+
CORE
1.1
1.10
4.2
4.3

The goal of each new technology is increasing overall throughput while retaining accuracy. The older the motherboard, the older the memory technology it can use, so as a PC technician, you must be familiar with older technologies even though the boards sold today only use the latest.

NOTE

Smaller versions of DIMMs and RIMMs, called SO-DIMMs and SO-RIMMs, are used in notebook computers. (SO stands for "small outline.") MicroDIMMs are used on subnotebook computers and are smaller than SO-DIMMs.

SIMM Technologies

SIMMs are rated by speed, measured in nanoseconds (ns). Common SIMM speeds are 60, 70, or 80 ns. This speed is a measure of access time, the time the CPU takes to receive a value in response to a request. Access time includes the time it takes to refresh the chips. An access time of 60 ns is faster than an access time of 70 ns. Therefore, the smaller the speed rating is, the faster the chip. **EDO (extended data out)** was used on 72-pin SIMMs on motherboards rated at about 33 to 75 MHz. EDO was also used on earlier DIMMs and video memory and often provides on-board RAM on various expansion boards.

DIMM Technologies

Next came DIMM technologies. DIMMs are also rated by speed and the amount of memory they hold. DIMMs have 168, 184, or 240 pins on the edge connector of the board and hold from 8 MB to 2 GB of RAM. The early DIMMs used EDO (168 pins) or **burst EDO (BEDO)**, which is a refined version of EDO. BEDO was faster than EDO, but never gained a market share because Intel chose not to support it. BEDO and EDO DIMMs have two notches on the edge connector and run at constant speeds independent of the system bus speed.

The first DIMM to run synchronized with the system clock is **synchronous DRAM (SDRAM)** which uses a 64 bit data path, has two notches, and uses 168 pins. An improved version of SDRAM is **Double Data Rate SDRAM (DDR SDRAM)**. DDR runs twice as fast as regular SDRAM, has one notch, and uses 184 pins and a 64-bit data path. Instead of processing data for each beat of the system clock, as regular SDRAM does, it processes data when the beat rises and again when it falls, doubling the data rate of memory. If a motherboard runs at 200 MHz, then DDR memory runs at 400 MHz. A consortium of 20 major computer manufacturers supports DDR. It is an open standard, meaning that its users pay no royalties. After DDR SDRAM was introduced, regular SDRAM became known as Single Data Rate SDRAM (SDR SDRAM). The latest SDRAM is **DDR2 SDRAM**, which is faster than DDR, uses less power, and has a 240-pin DIMM and a 64-bit data path. Another type of SDRAM is **SyncLink DRAM (SLDRAM)**, which was never embraced by the industry and is now obsolete.

168-pin DIMM notch key definitions (3.3 V, unbuffered memory)

DRAM key position

Voltage key position

RFU — Unbuffered
Buffered

5.0 V — Reserved
3.3 V

20 pins   60 pins   88 pins

Figure 6-5   The positions of two notches on a DIMM identify the type of DIMM and the voltage requirement and also prevent the wrong type from being installed on the motherboard

SDRAM modules can use from 1.8 V to 5.0 V of power, so, when buying memory, it is important to match voltage requirements of the module to the voltage supplied by the motherboard. Your motherboard also determines if you can use buffered, unbuffered, registered, or fully buffered DIMMs. Buffers and registers hold data and amplify a signal just before the data is written to the module. Older EDO and FPM modules used buffers, which did not degrade performance. SDRAM modules use registers, which do reduce performance somewhat but make it possible for the motherboard to support a larger number of modules. A fully buffered DIMMs (FB-DIMM) uses an advanced buffering technique that makes it possible for servers to support a large number of DIMMs. If a module doesn't support registers or buffers, it's always referred to as unbuffered.

Notches on memory modules are positioned to identify the technologies that the module supports. In Figure 6-5, the position of the notch on the left identifies the module as registered (RFU), buffered, or unbuffered memory. The notch on the right identifies the voltage used by the module. The position of the notches not only helps identify the type of module but also prevents the wrong kind of module from being used on a motherboard.

To improve overall memory performance, a motherboard can use dual channels with either DDR or DDR2 DIMMs. With **dual channels**, a pair of DIMMs that are equally matched in size, speed, and features can each use a channel to simultaneously feed data to the memory controller. Each channel uses the normal 64-bit data path of the system bus, making an effective data path of 128 bits. In effect, with dual channeling, two system buses feed the memory controller which feeds data to the processor. You'll see an example of a dual channel motherboard later in the chapter.

RIMM Technologies

Direct Rambus DRAM (sometimes called **RDRAM** or **Direct RDRAM** or simply Rambus) is named after Rambus, Inc., the company that developed it. RDRAM data can travel on a 16- or 32-bit data path. RDRAM works like a packeted network, not a traditional system bus, and can run at internal speeds of 800 MHz to 1600 MHz.

RDRAM uses RIMM memory modules. With RIMMs, each socket must be filled to maintain continuity throughout all sockets. If the socket does not hold a RIMM, then it must hold a placeholder module called a **C-RIMM** (**Continuity RIMM**) to ensure continuity throughout all slots. The C-RIMM contains no memory chips (see Figure 6-6). Concurrent RDRAM, an earlier version of Rambus memory, is not as fast as Direct RDRAM. Rambus designed the RDRAM technology but does not actually manufacture RIMMs: It licenses the technology to memory manufacturers. Because these manufacturers must pay licensing fees to use RDRAM, the industry has turned more to SDRAM memory advancements than to Rambus, and particularly to DDR and DDR2 memory because it is faster and cheaper than RIMMs. Future plans by Rambus include a 326-pin, 64-bit RIMM, and a 160-pin, 16-bit SO-RIMM for notebooks.

184-pin RIMM

C-RIMM

Figure 6-6   A C-RIMM or RIMM must be installed in every RIMM slot on a motherboard

Error Checking and Parity

A+
CORE
1.10
4.2
4.3

In older machines, RAM existed as individual chips socketed to the motherboard in banks or rows of nine chips each. Each bank held one byte by storing one bit in each chip, with the ninth chip holding a parity bit (see Figure 6-7). On older PCs the parity chip was separated slightly from the other eight chips. **Parity** refers to an error-checking procedure in which either every byte has an even number of ones or every byte has an odd number of ones. The use of a parity bit means that every byte occupies nine rather than eight bits.

6

Figure 6-7   Eight chips and a parity chip represent the letter A in ASCII with even parity

For a list of 8-bit ASCII codes assigned to letters, see Appendix B, "ASCII Character Set and Ansi.sys," and for more information about the binary number system, see Appendix C, "The Hexadecimal Number System and Memory Addressing."

NOTE

Parity is a method of testing the integrity of the bits stored in RAM or some secondary medium, or testing the integrity of bits sent over a communications device. When data is written to RAM, the computer calculates how many ON bits (binary 1) are in the eight bits of a byte. If the computer uses odd parity, it makes the ninth or parity bit either a 1 or a 0, to make the number of ones in the nine bits odd. If it uses even parity, the computer makes the parity bit a 1 or a 0 to make the number of ones in the nine bits even.

Later, when the byte is read back, the computer checks the odd or even state. If the number of bits is not an odd number for odd parity or an even number for even parity, a **parity error** occurs. A parity error always causes the system to halt. On the screen you see the error message "Parity Error 1" or "Parity Error 2" or a similar error message about parity. Parity Error 1 is a parity error on the motherboard; Parity Error 2 is a parity error on an expansion board. RAM chips that have become undependable and cannot hold data reliably can cause parity errors. Sometimes this happens when chips overheat or power falters.

Older DRAM memory used parity checking, but today's memory uses an altogether new method of error checking called **ECC (error-correcting code)** that can detect and correct an error in a single bit. Memory modules today are either ECC or non-ECC, and there are some improvements in ECC that ECC memory might use. The first ECC method can detect and correct an error in one bit of the byte. Newer ECC methods can detect an error in two bits but cannot correct these double-bit errors.

Some older motherboards support **parity memory**, and some use only **nonparity memory**. If a SIMM has an odd number of chips, it is likely parity memory; an even number of chips usually indicates nonparity memory. Most manufacturers use nonparity memory to save processing time and therefore money.

Some SDRAM, DDR, DDR2, and RIMM memory modules support ECC. DIMMs that support ECC have an odd number of chips on the module (the odd chip is the ECC chip), whereas it normally has only an even number of chips. A DIMM is normally a 64-bit module, but ECC makes it a 71- or 72-bit module; the extra 7 or 8 bits are used to verify the integrity of every 8 bits stored on the module and to correct any error, when possible. ECC memory costs more than regular memory and is slower because of the extra time taken to verify data, but it is more reliable. ECC memory is generally used on servers.

When buying memory to add to a motherboard, know that in most cases you must match the type of memory to the type the board supports. Older boards supported either parity or nonparity memory, and newer boards support either ECC or non-ECC memory. In some cases, you can install parity memory on a nonparity board or ECC memory on a non-ECC board, but error checking will not be enabled. To see if your motherboard supports parity or ECC memory, look for the ability to enable or disable the feature in CMOS setup, or check the motherboard documentation.

CAS Latency and RAS Latency

Two other memory features are **CAS Latency** (CAS stands for "column access strobe") and **RAS Latency** (RAS stands for "row access strobe"). Both features refer to the number of clock cycles it takes to write or read a column or row of data. Values are two or three clock cycles. CAS Latency is used more than RAS Latency. CL2 (CAS Latency 2) is a little faster than CL3 (CAS Latency 3). When selecting memory, use the memory type that the motherboard manufacturer recommends.

Memory Speeds

Several factors contribute to how fast memory runs, and speeds are measured in different ways. Recall that a SIMM's speed is measured in nanoseconds. SDRAM, DDR, and RIMM are measured in MHz or a PC rating. A DDR module is often described with its speed in the name, such as DDR266 for a DDR running at 266 MHz, or DDR333 for a DDR running at 333 MHz.

A PC rating is a measure of the total bandwidth of data moving between the module and the CPU. To understand PC ratings, let's take an example of a DDR DIMM module that runs at 266 MHz (DDR266). The module has a 64-bit (8 bytes) data path. Therefore, the transfer rate is 8 bytes multiplied by 266 MHz, which yields 2128 MB/second. This value equates to the PC rating of PC2100 for a DDR266 DIMM. Current PC ratings are PC1600 (200 MHz), PC2100 (266 MHz), PC2700 (333 MHz), PC3200 (400 MHz), PC 4000 (500 MHz), PC 4200 (533 MHz), and PC 5300 (667 MHz).

A+
CORE
1.10
4.2
4.3

Factors to consider when looking at the overall speed of memory are shown in the following list and in Figure 6-8:

- *The speed of memory in ns, MHz, or PC rating.* Use the fastest memory the motherboard supports.
- *How much memory is installed.* The more memory there is, the faster the system. Generally use as much memory in a system as it can support and you can afford.
- *The memory technology used.* DDR2 is faster than DDR, and DDR is faster than SDR SDRAM. Use what the board supports.
- *CL rating.* The lower the better. Use what the board supports.
- *ECC/parity or non-ECC/nonparity.* Non-ECC or nonparity is faster.

6

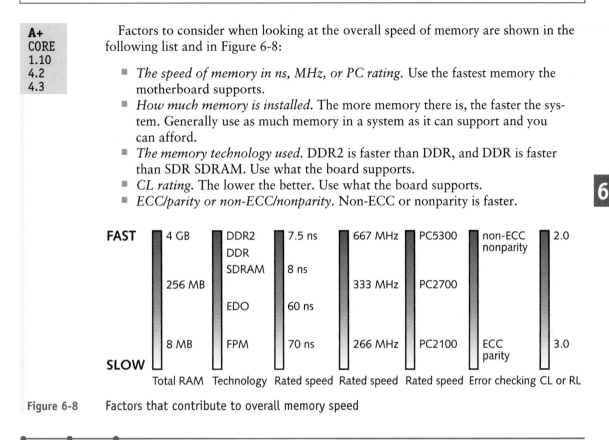

Figure 6-8   Factors that contribute to overall memory speed

Upgrading Memory

A+
CORE
1.2
1.9
1.10

To upgrade memory means to add more RAM to a computer. When first purchased, many computers have empty slots on the motherboard, allowing you to add DIMMs or RIMMs to increase the amount of RAM. This section describes issues you should consider when purchasing and upgrading memory.

What to Look for When Buying Memory Chips and Modules

Memory chips and memory modules come in different sizes, offer different speeds, and use different technologies and features. This section looks at several criteria you should use when buying memory.

Generally, use the fastest memory that your motherboard can support. The documentation for a motherboard states what memory speed to use on the board. Some boards support only one speed and others a variety of speeds. Use the fastest speed supported. Sometimes it is possible, but not recommended, to mix the speed of memory modules on a motherboard, but don't mix the speeds within a single memory bank.

When a computer first boots, the system must detect the type of memory installed. To do so, the system can use two methods: Parallel Presence Detect (PPD), which uses resistors to communicate the type of memory present, or Serial Presence Detect (SPD), which stores information about the memory type in EPROM. When purchasing memory for a system, you must match the method the module uses to what the motherboard expects. See the motherboard documentation to learn which type to buy. If the board does not specify the method used, assume PPD.

Chips can be high-grade, low-grade, remanufactured, or used. Poor-quality memory chips can cause frequent **General Protection Fault (GPF)** errors in Windows, application errors, and errors that hang the system, so it pays to know the quality and type of memory you are buying. The next sections provide some guidelines to ensure that you purchase high-quality memory chips.

Tin or Gold Leads

Memory modules and the banks that hold them can be either tin or gold. On a motherboard, the connectors inside the memory slots are made of tin or gold, as are the edge connectors on the memory modules. Once, all memory sockets were made of gold, but now most are made of tin to reduce cost. You should match tin leads to tin connectors and gold leads to gold connectors to prevent a chemical reaction between the two metals, which can cause corrosion. Corrosion can create intermittent memory errors and even make the PC unable to boot.

Remanufactured and Used Modules

Stamped on each chip of a RAM module is a chip ID that identifies the date the chip was manufactured. Look for the date in the YYWW format, where YY is the year the chip was made, and WW is the week of that year. For example, 0510 indicates a chip made in the tenth week of 2005. Date stamps on a chip that are older than one year indicate that the chip is probably used memory. If some chips are old, but some are new, the module is probably remanufactured. When buying memory modules, look for ones with dates on all chips that are relatively close together and less than a year old.

Re-Marked Chips

New chips have a protective coating that gives them a polished, reflective surface. If the chip's surface is dull or matted, or you can scratch off the markings with a fingernail or knife, suspect that the chip has been re-marked. **Re-marked chips** have been used, returned to the factory, marked again, and then resold.

How Much and What Kind of Memory to Buy

A+
CORE
1.2
1.9
1.10

When you add more memory to your computer, ask yourself these questions:

- How much memory do I have, and how much memory do I need?
- How many memory slots are on my motherboard, and what type and size of memory do these slots support?
- How much memory can I afford?
- What size and type of modules should I buy to be compatible with the memory I already have installed?

This section discusses the answers to these questions in detail.

6

APPLYING CONCEPTS

To determine how much memory your Windows system has, right-click My Computer and select Properties from the menu. In the System Properties dialog box, click the General tab.

How much memory do you need? With the demands today's software places on memory, the answer is probably, "All you can get." Windows 95 and Windows 98 need 16 MB to 32 MB of memory. Windows 2000 and Windows XP require 64 MB of RAM. But for best performance, install 128 MB into a Windows 9x/Me system and 256 MB or more into a Windows 2000/XP system.

To learn what type and size of memory modules your board supports, consult your motherboard documentation. Open the case and look at the memory sockets to determine how many sockets you have and what size and type of modules are already installed. If all slots are full, sometimes you can take out small-capacity modules and replace them with larger-capacity modules, but you can only use the size of modules that the board is designed to support.

Next decide how many and what size and type of modules to buy. To do that you need to understand how some modules are installed in banks and how a motherboard supports only a certain combination of modules.

How Much Memory Can Fit on the Motherboard?

VIDEO

Selecting
Memory

To determine how much memory your computer can physically hold, read the documentation that comes with your computer. Not all sizes of memory modules fit on any one computer. Use the right number of SIMMs, DIMMs, or RIMMs with the right amount of memory on each module to fit the memory banks on your motherboard. Next let's look at several examples.

30-Pin SIMMs   On older motherboards, 30-pin SIMMs are installed in groups of four. SIMMs in each group or bank must be the same type and size. See the motherboard documentation for the exact combination of SIMMs in each bank that the board can support.

A+
CORE
1.2
1.9
1.10

72-Pin SIMMs To accommodate a 64-bit system bus data path, 72-pin SIMMs have a 32-bit data path and are installed in groups or banks of two. Most older motherboards that use these SIMMs have one to three banks that can be filled with two, four, or six SIMMs. The two SIMMs in each bank must match in size and speed. See the motherboard documentation for the sizes and type of SIMMs the board supports.

DIMMs Most DIMMs have a 64-bit data path and can thus be installed as a single module rather than in pairs. Some DIMMs have a 128-bit data path, but they are not widely used now. Pentium motherboards that use DIMM modules use only one socket to a bank, because a DIMM module accommodates a data path of 64 bits. DIMMs come as either single-sided modules (chips on only one side of the module) or double-sided modules (chips on both sides). Single-sided DIMMs come in sizes of 8, 16, 32, 64, and 128 MB, and double-sided DIMMs come in sizes of 32, 64, 128, 256, and 512 MB, 1 GB, and 2 GB.

✔ **A+ EXAM TIP**

The A+ Core exam expects you to know how to upgrade a system using SIMMs, DIMMs, or RIMMs, although SIMMs are for the most part outdated.

For example, a Pentium motherboard might use 168-pin DIMM modules, and the documentation says to use unbuffered, 3.3V, PC100 DIMM SDRAM modules. The PC100 means that the modules should be rated to work with a motherboard that runs at 100 MHz. You can choose to use ECC modules. If you choose not to, then CMOS setup should show the feature disabled. Three DIMM sockets are on the board, and each socket represents one bank. Figure 6-9 shows the possible combinations of DIMMs that can be installed in these sockets.

DIMM Location	168-Pin DIMM		Total Memory
Socket 1 (Rows 0 & 1)	SDRAM 8, 16, 32, 64, 128, 256 MB	×1	
Socket 2 (Rows 2 & 3)	SDRAM 8, 16, 32, 64, 128, 256 MB	×1	
Socket 3 (Rows 4 & 5)	SDRAM 8, 16, 32, 64, 128, 256 MB	×1	
	Total System Memory (Max 768 MB)	=	

Figure 6-9   This table is part of the motherboard documentation and is used to show possible DIMM sizes and calculate total memory on the motherboard

Another more recent Pentium motherboard allows you to use three different speeds of DDR DIMMs in one to four sockets on the board. This board supports up to 4 GB of unbuffered 184-pin non-ECC memory running at PC3200, PC2700, or PC2100. The documentation says the system bus can run at 800 MHz, 533 MHz, or 400 MHz, depending on the speed of the processor installed. Therefore, the speed of the processor determines the system bus speed, which determines the speed of memory modules you can install. Figure 6-10 outlines the possible configurations of these modules, showing that you can install one, two, or four DIMMs and which sockets should hold these DIMMS. In order to take advantage of dual channels on this motherboard, you must populate the sockets according to Figure 6-10, so that identical DIMM pairs are working together in DIMM_A1 and DIMM_B1 sockets, and another pair can work together in DIMM_A2 and DIMM_B2 sockets.

A+
CORE
1.2
1.9
1.10

As you can see, the motherboard documentation is essential when selecting memory. If you can't find the motherboard manual, look on the motherboard manufacturer's Web site.

Mode		Sockets			
		DIMM_A1	DIMM_A2	DIMM_B1	DIMM_B2
Single-channel	(1)	Populated	—	—	—
	(2)	—	Populated	—	—
	(3)	—	—	Populated	—
	(4)	—	—	—	Populated
Dual-channel*	(1)	Populated	—	Populated	—
	(2)	—	Populated	—	Populated
	(3)	Populated	Populated	Populated	Populated

*Use only identical DDR DIMM pairs

Figure 6-10   Motherboard documentation shows that one, two, or four DIMMs can be installed

RIMM Modules

When you purchase a system using RIMMs, all RIMM slots will be filled with either RIMMs or C-RIMMs. When you upgrade, you replace one or more C-RIMMs with RIMMs. Match the new RIMMs with those already on the motherboard, following the recommendations of the motherboard documentation.

Table 6-4 gives one example of the RDRAM memory configuration for a motherboard. In the table, an RDRAM device is one chip on a RIMM module that has a 16- or 18-bit data path (with or without ECC). The board uses two RDRAM channels and has two RIMM banks with two slots in each bank. Memory on a RIMM can be stored in one to four channels. Each bank serves one channel, which is why the motherboard is called a dual-channel board. It uses PC600 or PC800 RDRAM, which for a RIMM refers to the speeds of 600 MHz or 800 MHz.

The board also supports two densities of RIMMs, either 128/144 Mb or 256/288 Mb, which refers to the amount of data each chip (device) on the RIMM can hold. A RIMM that has four chips, each of which holds 128 Mb or 16 MB (8 Mb = 1 MB) of data, yields a RIMM that is 64 MB in size. A chip rated 144 Mb is the ECC version of a non-ECC 128-Mb chip. A 256-Mb RIMM has chips that each hold 32 MB of RAM. Multiply that by the number of devices on the RIMM for the RIMM size. The 288-Mb RIMM is the ECC version of the 256-Mb RIMM.

The motherboard can hold up to four RIMMs. The first bank on this motherboard must contain two RIMMs, and the second bank can contain two RIMMs or two C-RIMMs. The RIMMs in each bank must have the same size and density, meaning that they must hold the same amount of memory and have the same number of DRAM devices or chips. The RIMMs in one bank must run at the same speed as RIMMs in the other bank, although the RIMMs in one bank can have a different size and density than the RIMMs in the other bank.

6

Rambus	4 RDRAM Technology	6 RDRAM Devices per RIMM	8 RDRAM Devices per RIMM	12 RDRAM Devices per RIMM	16 RDRAM Devices per RIMM
128/144 Mb	64 MB	96 MB	128 MB	192 MB	256 MB
256/288 Mb	128 MB	192 MB	256 MB	384 MB	512 MB

Table 6-4   One motherboard's memory configurations using RIMMs

Match Memory Modules to the Motherboard

When you place memory on the motherboard, match the type of memory to the motherboard requirements. For example, if the motherboard supports RIMMs and the documentation says that you must use 600 or 800 speed RIMMs, then 700 speed RIMMs will not work. Also avoid mixing speeds on the same motherboard. For example, if you use a SIMM having one speed in one bank and a SIMM having another speed in the other bank, your computer works only as fast as the slower bank. Always put the slower SIMMs in the first bank. However, to ensure the most reliable results, use the same speed of SIMMs in all banks and buy the same brand of SIMMs.

When purchasing memory from a Web site such as Kingston Technology's site (*www.kingston.com*), look for a search utility that will match memory modules to your motherboard (see Figure 6-11).

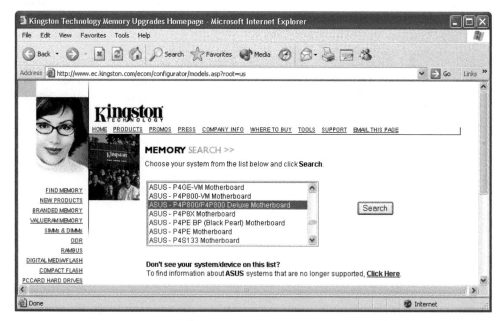

Figure 6-11   Web sites used to purchase memory, such as this Kingston site, often provide excellent support to help you select the right memory modules for your motherboard

Reading Ads About Memory Modules

A+
CORE
1.2
1.9
1.10

Figure 6-12 shows a typical memory module ad listing various types of DIMMs and RIMMs. When you select memory, the speed, size, and type of module are all important. We will now examine the ad to see how it gives all this information to us.

₽ P C   P R O G R E S S
WWW.PCPROGRESS.COM

MEMORY

168-PIN SDRAM PC100/133

128MB	16X64	8NS	$19
128MB PC133	16X64	7.5NS	$16
128MB	16X72	8NS	$24
128MB PC133	16X72	7.5NS	$25
256MB	32X64	8NS	$31
256MB PC133	32X64	7.5NS	$30
256MB	32X72	8NS	$47
256MB PC133	32X72	7.5NS	$43
512MB	64X72	8NS	$79
512MB PC133	64X64	7.5NS	$62
512MB PC133	64X72	7.5NS	$73
1024MB PC133	128X72	7.5NS	$214

DDR RAM PC2100/2700/3200

128MB	16X64	266MHZ	$19
128MB	16X72	266MHZ	$27
256MB	32X64	266MHZ	$32
256MB	32X72	266MHZ	$47
256MB	32X64	333MHZ	$35
256MB	32X64	400MHZ	$56
512MB	64X72	266MHZ	$84
512MB	64X64	333MHZ	$80
512MB	64X64	400MHZ	$102
1024MB	128X72	266MHZ	$299

CORSAIR www.corsairmicro.com
RAMBUS

CMXR128-1066	128MB	RDRAM	1066MHZ	$57
CM616DR256A-800	256MB	RDRAM	800MHZ	$82
CM618DR256A-800	256MB	RDRAM	800MHZ	$105
CMXR256-1066	256MB	RDRAM	1066MHZ	$109
CM616DR512-800	512MB	RDRAM	800MHZ	$252
CM618DR512-800	512MB	RDRAM	800MHZ	$267

VALUE SELECT MEMORY

VS256MB100	256MB PC100	32X64 (SDRAM)	8NS	$48
VS256MB133	256MB PC133	32X64 (SDRAM)	7.5NS	$48
VS256MB133A	256MB PC133	32X64 (SDRAM)	7.5NS	$38
VS256REG133	256MB PC133	32X72 (SDRAM)	7.5NS	$68
VS512MB100	512MB PC100	64X64 (SDRAM)	8NS	$71
VS512MB133	512MB PC133	64X64 (SDRAM)	7.5NS	$72
VS512MB133REG	512MB PC133	64X72 (SDRAM)	7.5NS	$98
VS256MB266	256MB PC2100	32X64 (DDR)	2.5CAS	$36
VS256MB333	256MB PC2700	32X64 (DDR)	2.5CAS	$52
VS256MB400	256MB PC3200	32X64 (DDR)	2.5CAS	$73
VS512MB266	512MB PC2100	64X64 (DDR)	2.5CAS	$85
VS512MB333	512MB PC2700	64X64 (DDR)	2.5CAS	$98
VS512MB400	512MB PC3200	64X64 (DDR)	2.5CAS	$134
VS512MBECC266R	512MB PC2100	64X72 (DDR)	2.5CAS	$126
VS256MB800	256MB PC800	RDRAM		$76
VS256MBECC800	256MB PC800	ECC RDRAM		$99

DDR RAM PC2100/2400/2700/3000/3200/3500

CM72SD256R-2100	256MB (REG)	32X72 ECC DDR	266MHZ	$74
CM72SD512R-2100	512MB (REG)	64X72 ECC DDR	266MHZ	$129
CM73SD512R-2100	512MB (REG)	64X72 ECC DDR	266MHZ	$139
CM73SD512RLP-2100	512MB (REG)	64X72 ECC DDR	266MHZ	$157
CM74SD1024R-2100	1024MB (REG)	128X72 ECC DDR	266MHZ	$319
CM74SD2048R-2100	2048MB (REG)	256X72 ECC DDR	266MHZ	1449
CMX256A-3000C2	256MB (CAS 2)	32X64 DDR	370MHZ	$84
CMX256A-3200C2	256MB (CAS 2)	32X64 DDR	400MHZ	$88
CMX256A-3500C2	256MB (CAS 2)	32X64 DDR	433MHZ	$99
CMX512-2700C2	512MB (CAS 2)	64X64 DDR	333MHZ	$149
CMX512-3000C2	512MB (CAS 2)	64X64 DDR	370MHZ	$157
CMX512-3200C2	512MB (CAS 2)	64X64 DDR	400MHZ	$167
CMX512-3500C2	512MB (CAS 2)	64X64 DDR	433MHZ	$189

XMS LOW LATENCY AND TWIN X DUAL CHANNEL DDR

CMX256A-2700LL	256MB (LL)	32X64 DDR	XMS2700	$89
CMX256A-3200LL	256MB (LL)	32X64 DDR	XMS3200	$99
CMX512-2700LL	512MB (LL)	64X64 DDR	XMS2700	$167
CMX512-3200LL	512MB (LL)	64X64 DDR	XMS3200	$189
TWINX512-2700LL	512MB (LL)	(2)256MB DDR	XMS2700	$179
TWINX512-3200LL	512MB (LL)	(2)256MB DDR	XMS3200	$199
TWINX1024-2700LL	1024MB (LL)	(2)512MB DDR	XMS2700	$334
TWINX1024-3200LL	1024MB (LL)	(2)512MB DDR	XMS3200	$379

6

Figure 6-12 Typical memory ad

VIDEO

Purchasing Memory

For each memory module, the ad lists the amount of memory, density, speed, and price. For DIMMs, the ad lists the density of the module, which tells us the width of the data bus, whether the module supports error checking, and the size of the module. Here's how it works. The density is written as two numbers separated by an ×, such as 16 × 64, and is read "16 by 64." Let's start with the second number, which is 64 or 72. If it's 64, then it's the width of the data bus in bits, grouped as eight bits to a byte. If the number is 72, then it's the width of the data bus plus an extra bit for each byte, used for error checking and correction (for ECC memory).

When calculating the module's size, ignore the ninth bit and use only the value 64 to calculate. Convert this number to bytes by dividing it by 8, and then multiply that value (number of bytes) by the number on the left in the density listing, to determine the size of the module. For example, if the density is 16 × 64, then the size of the module is 16 × (64/8) = 16 × 8 = 128 MB.

There are several choices for DIMMs in the ad. Match the speed of the DIMM to the motherboard speed, and match other features to those specified for your motherboard.

NOTE

When reading memory ads for Rambus memory, 18 in the product code indicates error checking, and 16 indicates no error checking.

Installing Memory

VIDEO

Installing
Memory

When installing RAM modules, remember to protect the chips against static electricity, as you learned in Chapter 4. Always use a ground bracelet as you work. Turn off the power and remove the cover to the case. Handle memory modules with care. Don't stack cards, because you can loosen a chip. Usually modules pop into place easily and are secured by spring catches on both ends. Look for the notches on one side or in the middle of the module that orient the module in the slot. For most SIMMs, the module slides into the slot at an angle, as shown in Figure 6-13. (Check your documentation for any instructions specific to your modules.) Place each module securely in its slot. Turn on the PC and watch POST count the amount of memory during the boot process. If the memory count is not what you expect, power off the system, then carefully remove and reseat each module. To remove a module, release the latches on both sides of the module and gently rotate it out of the socket at a 45-degree angle.

Figure 6-13   Installing a SIMM module

For DIMM modules, small latches on each side of the slot hold the module in place, as shown in Figure 6-14. Pull the supporting arms on the sides of the slot.

outward. Look on the DIMM edge connector for the notches, which help you orient the DIMM correctly over the slot, and insert the DIMM straight down into the slot. When the DIMM is fully inserted, the supporting arms should pop back into place. Figure 6-15 shows a DIMM being inserted into a slot on a motherboard.

For RIMM modules, install the RIMMs beginning with bank 0, followed by bank 1. If a C-RIMM is already in the slot, remove the C-RIMM by pulling the supporting arms on the sides of the socket outward and pulling straight up on the C-RIMM. When installing the RIMM, notches on the edge of the RIMM module will help you orient it correctly in the socket. Insert the module straight down in the socket (see Figure 6-16). When it is fully inserted, the supporting arms should pop back into place.

6

Figure 6-14   Installing a DIMM module

A+
CORE
1.2
1.9
1.10

Figure 6-15   Insert the DIMM into the slot by pressing down until the support arms lock into position

RIMM supporting arms
in outward position

Figure 6-16   Install RIMM modules in banks beginning with bank 0

Most often, placing memory on the motherboard is all that is necessary for installation. When the computer powers up, it counts the memory present without any further instruction and senses the features that the modules support, such as parity or ECC. For some older computers, you must tell CMOS setup the amount of memory present. Read the motherboard documentation to determine what yours requires.

APPLYING CONCEPTS

Troubleshooting Memory

When upgrading memory, if the computer does not recognize new SIMMs, DIMMs, or RIMMs, or if memory error messages appear, do the following:

- Check that you have the right memory modules supported by your motherboard. Verify that CMOS setup recognizes the memory features correctly.
- Check that you have installed the right module size, as stated in the motherboard documentation. Verify each module that was already installed or newly installed.
- Remove and reinstall the module. Make sure it sits in the socket at the same height as other modules.
- Remove the newly installed memory and check whether the error message disappears. Try the memory in different sockets. Try installing the new memory without the old installed. If the new memory works without the old, then the problem is that the modules are not compatible.
- Clean the module edge connectors with a soft cloth or contact cleaner. Blow or vacuum dust from the memory sockets.
- Try flashing your BIOS. Perhaps BIOS has problems with the new memory that a BIOS upgrade can solve.

Recurring errors during normal operations can mean unreliable memory. If the system locks up or you regularly receive error messages about illegal operations and General Protection Faults occur during normal operation, and you have not just upgraded memory, do the following:

- Run a current version of antivirus software to check for viruses.
- Run diagnostic software such as PC Technician (*www.windsortech.com*) to test memory.
- Are the memory modules properly seated? Remove and reinstall each one. For a DIMM module, try a different memory slot.
- Replace memory modules one at a time. For example, if the system only recognizes six out of eight megabytes of RAM, swap the last two SIMM modules. Did the amount of recognized RAM change? You might be able to solve the problem just by reseating the modules.
- Sometimes a problem can result from a bad socket or a broken trace (a fine-printed wire or circuit) on the motherboard. If so, you might have to replace the entire motherboard.
- The problem might be with the OS or applications. Download the latest patch for the software from the manufacturer's Web site.
- If you have just installed new hardware, the hardware device might be causing an error, which the OS interprets as a memory error. Try uninstalling the new hardware.

**A+
CORE
2.1**

- A Windows error that occurs randomly and generates an error message with "exception fault 0E at >>0137:BFF9z5d0" or similar text is probably a memory error. Test, reseat, or replace RAM.

> **NOTE**
> Other than PC Technician, Memtest86 is a utility to test installed memory modules. Check the site *www.memtest86.com* to download this program.

Windows Memory Management

This section discusses how the OS manages memory. You will first learn how DOS and Windows 9x/Me manage memory, and then see how managing memory was greatly improved when Windows NT introduced an entirely different approach. This new approach is used by Windows NT/2000/XP.

OS Memory Management Evolution

Memory management under DOS and Windows 9x/Me can seem complicated because of the way the process has evolved over the past 20 years or so. Like an old house that has been added to and remodeled several times, the present-day design is not as efficient as that of a brand-new house. Decisions made by IBM and Microsoft in the early 1980s still significantly affect, and in some cases limit, the way memory is used under Windows 9x/Me. Because Windows NT, followed by Windows 2000 and Windows XP, have had the luxury of being designed from the ground up, they are free of those limitations.

Early CPUs had only 20 lines on the bus available to handle addresses, so the largest memory address the CPU could use was 11111111111111111111, which is 1,048,575, or 1024K or 1 MB of memory. This 1 MB of memory was used by DOS and divided up according to the scheme shown in Table 6-5.

Range of Memory Addresses	Range Using Hex Terminology	Type of Memory
0 to 640K	0 to A0000	Conventional or base memory
640K to 1024K	A0000 to FFFFF	Upper memory (A through F ranges)
Above 1024K	100000 and up	Extended memory

Table 6-5   Division of memory under DOS and Windows 9x/Me

APPLYING CONCEPTS

Using Windows 9x/Me Device Manager, you can see how the first 1 MB of memory addresses are assigned (see Figure 6-17). To view the list, select Computer and click Properties, then click Memory. Notice in the figure that the system BIOS has been assigned memory addresses in the F range of upper memory. This F range is always reserved for motherboard BIOS and is never requested by other programs. When the CPU is first turned on and needs a program to know how to boot up, it begins with the instructions stored on the ROM BIOS chip that are assigned to these memory addresses.

F range in memory addresses

Figure 6-17   Computer Properties dialog box shows how the first megabyte of memory addresses are assigned

The first 640K of memory was used by DOS and applications, and the addresses from 640K up to 1024K were used by the BIOS and device drivers. Then newer

CPUs and motherboards were developed with 24 address lines and more, so that memory addresses above 1024K became available; they were called **extended memory**. Windows 9x/Me still uses these same divisions of memory, although it makes the most use of extended memory. Memory addresses are expressed using hexadecimal notation. Because the hex numbers in upper memory begin with A through F, the divisions of upper memory are often referred to as the A range, B range, and so on, up to the F range.

How Memory Addresses Are Used

Once memory addresses have been assigned to memory, they can be used for communication with all software layers. Device drivers, the OS, and application software are all working when a computer is running. During output operations, application software must pass information to the OS, which in turn passes that information to a device driver. The device drivers managing input devices must pass information to the OS, which passes it to the application software. These layers of software all identify the data they want to share by referring to the memory address of the data (see Figure 6-18).

Figure 6-18   Applications, the OS, and drivers pass data among them by communicating the address of memory holding the data

A+
OS
1.1

Recall that Windows 95 became the first OS in the evolution of Windows operating systems to support 32-bit, protected-mode application software. However, it still allows 16-bit, real-mode device drivers, and 16-bit software to run in a **virtual DOS machine (VDM)** or to run in real mode. A VDM is an environment that a 32-bit, protected-mode OS provides for a real-mode program to operate in.

If Windows 9x/Me forces all software to run in 32-bit, protected mode or in a VDM, then it can control how that software accesses hardware. For example, in

Figure 6-19, you can see that the 16-bit program running in real mode has direct access to RAM. But in protected mode, more than one program can run, and the programs must depend on the OS to access RAM. This arrangement also allows the OS some latitude in how it uses RAM. If the OS is low on RAM, it can store some data on the hard drive. This method of using the hard drive as though it were RAM is called **virtual memory**, and data stored in virtual memory is stored in a file on the hard drive called a **swap file** or **page file**. The OS manages the entire process, and the applications know nothing about this substitution of hardware resources for RAM.

Real mode: One program has direct access to hardware

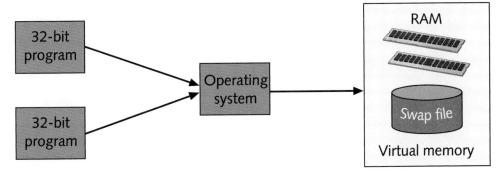

Protected mode: Multiple programs depend on the OS to access hardware

Figure 6-19   Protected mode allows more than one program to run, each protected from the other by the operating system

Windows NT made a break with the past. It requires that all device drivers be 32-bit drivers. It does not allow other software to operate in real mode, but only in a virtual real mode, which it tightly controls. This makes Windows NT a much more stable OS than Windows 9x/Me. (Note that Windows 95 and Windows 98 support 16-bit or 32-bit drivers, but Windows Me only supports 32-bit drivers.)

Table 6-6 summarizes the evolution of operating systems and software as it applies to memory. Notice that Windows NT is the first Microsoft OS to resolve many issues involving real mode, particularly the 1024K limitation imposed by real mode. With DOS, this limitation directly affected memory resource management; in some cases, it can still be significant with Windows 9x/Me.

We now look at how each OS manages memory, beginning with DOS and Windows 9x/Me and then turning our attention to Windows NT/2000/XP.

6

Operating System	Real Mode	Protected Mode
DOS	Operates totally in real mode, but later offered Himem.sys, a device driver that allows programs access to extended memory.	NA
Windows 95/98	Allows real-mode drivers to be loaded during startup; 16-bit DOS applications are allowed a real-mode session.	Switches back and forth between real mode and protected mode as necessary; supports both 16-bit and 32-bit applications in a virtual machine.
Windows NT/2000/XP	NA	All work is done in protected mode. Supports 32-bit applications. 16-bit applications can operate in a virtual machine only.

Table 6-6   Summary of how operating systems have evolved in managing memory

Windows 9x/Me Memory Management

Windows 9x/Me views and manages memory addresses as DOS did. However, because Windows 9x/Me runs in protected mode and uses virtual memory, it can do a better job of managing extended memory than DOS. This section first looks at how Windows 9x/Me manages memory addresses and then at how it manages virtual memory.

How Windows 9x/Me and DOS Manage Memory Addressing

When a PC is first booted, many programs demand memory addresses, including ROM BIOS programs on the motherboard and some circuit boards, device drivers, the OS, and applications. This process of assigning memory addresses to programs is called memory mapping. Sometimes older ROM BIOS programs and device drivers expect to be assigned certain memory addresses and will not work otherwise. Windows 9x/Me is committed to maintain backward compatibility with these old programs. This fact is probably the greatest limitation of Windows 9x/Me today.

There are several types of memory that the OS manages: conventional, upper, and extended memory. To get a clear picture of this memory-addressing schema, consider the memory map shown in Figure 6-20. The first 640K of memory addresses are called **conventional memory**, or base memory. The memory addresses from 640K up to 1024K are called **upper memory**. Memory above 1024K is called extended memory. The first 64K of extended memory is called the **high memory area (HMA)**.

Figure 6-20 Memory address map (not to scale) showing the starting and ending addresses of conventional, upper, and extended memory, including the high memory area

Conventional Memory In the early 1980s, when IBM and Microsoft were designing the original PCs, they decided to make 640K of memory addresses available to the user, thinking that this was plenty for anything the user would ever want to do. This 640K of addresses was intended to hold the OS, the application software, and the data being processed. At that time, 640K of memory addresses was more than enough to handle all the applications available. Today, 640K of memory addresses is grossly inadequate.

The problem caused by restricting the number of memory addresses available to the user to only 640K could have been solved by simply providing more addresses to the user in future versions of DOS. However, another original design decision ruled this out. The next group of memory addresses, the 384K above conventional memory, called upper memory, were assigned to utility operations for the system. The system requires memory addresses to communicate with peripherals. The programs (such as BIOS on a video card or on the motherboard) and data are assigned memory addresses in this upper memory area. For example, the video BIOS and its data are placed in the very first part of upper memory, the area from 640K to 768K. All video ROM written for DOS-based computers assumes that these programs and data are stored in this area. Also, many DOS and Windows applications interact directly with video ROM and RAM in this address range.

Programs almost always expect data to be written into memory directly above the addresses for the program itself, an important fact for understanding memory management. Thus, if a program begins storing its data above its location in conventional memory, eventually it will "hit the ceiling," the beginning of upper memory assigned to video ROM. The major reason that applications have a 640K memory limit is that video ROM begins at 640K. If DOS and Windows 9x/Me allowed applications into these upper memory addresses, all DOS-compatible video ROM would need to be rewritten, and many DOS applications that access these video addresses would not work. The 32-bit device drivers and applications under Windows 9x/Me don't have this problem because they can run from extended memory and turn to the OS to access video.

Upper Memory   The memory map in Figure 6-20 shows that the memory addresses from 640K up to (but not including) 1024K are called upper memory. In the hexadecimal number system (see Appendix C), upper memory begins at A0000 and goes through FFFFF. Video ROM and RAM are stored in the first part of upper memory, hex A0000 through CFFFF (the A, B, and C areas of memory). Sixteen-bit BIOS programs for other legacy expansion boards are assigned memory addresses in the remaining portions of upper memory. BIOS on the motherboard (system BIOS) is assigned the top part of upper memory, from F0000 through FFFFF (the F area of upper memory). Upper memory often has unassigned addresses, depending on which boards are present in the system. Managing memory effectively involves gaining access to these unused addresses in upper memory and using them to store device drivers and TSR (terminate-and-stay-resident) programs.

Extended Memory and the High Memory Area   Memory above 1 MB is called extended memory. The first 64K of extended memory is called the high memory area, which exists because a bug in the programming for the older Intel 286 CPU (the first CPU to use extended memory) produced this small pocket of unused memory addresses. Beginning with DOS 5, the OS capitalized on this bug by storing portions of itself in the high memory area, thus freeing some conventional memory where DOS had been stored. This method of storing part of DOS in the high memory area is called "loading DOS high." You will see how to do this later in the chapter.

Extended memory is actually managed by the OS as a device (the device is memory) that is controlled by a device driver. To access extended memory, you need the device driver (called a memory extender) that controls it, and you must use applications that have been written to use the extended memory. The amount of extended memory you can have on your computer is limited by the amount of RAM that can be installed on your motherboard and the number of memory addresses the CPU and the memory bus can support.

A+
OS
1.2

✔ **A+ EXAM TIP**

The A+ OS exam expects
you to know how and when
to use Himem.sys and
Emm386.exe to manage
upper and extended memory.

Utilities that Manage Memory The two utilities used by Windows 9x/Me to manage memory above 640K are Himem.sys and Emm386.exe. **Himem.sys** is the device driver for all memory above 640K. The program file **Emm386.exe** contains the software that loads device drivers and other programs into upper memory. Himem.sys is automatically loaded by Windows 9x/Me during the boot process, but can also be loaded by an entry in Config.sys. Emm386.exe is not loaded automatically by Windows 9x/Me, but you can load it by an entry in Config.sys.

6

Using Himem.sys Himem.sys is considered a device driver because it manages memory as a device. It can be executed by the Device= command in Config.sys. Figure 6-21 shows an example of a very simple Config.sys file on a floppy disk that loads Himem.sys. The Config.sys file is being edited by the Edit.com text editor utility.

```
 File  Edit  Search  View  Options  Help
                        A:\CONFIG.SYS
device=himem.sys
device=A:\util\mouse.sys
device=A:\util\ansi.sys
files=99
buffers=40




 F1=Help                              Line:6     Col:1
```

Figure 6-21 Config.sys set to use memory above 640K

To create the file on a floppy disk, you can use either of these two methods:

▪ Make drive A the default drive and enter this command:

    A:\> **Edit Config.sys**

▪ Make drive C the default drive and enter this command:

    C:\> **Edit A:Config.sys**

A+
OS
1.2

The second line in the Config.sys file, device=A:\util\mouse.sys, tells DOS to load into memory a device driver from the \Util directory on the floppy disk. This driver allows you to use the mouse while in MS-DOS mode.

The third line in the Config.sys file, device=A:\util\ansi.sys, tells DOS to load the device driver Ansi.sys into memory. Ansi.sys helps control the keyboard and monitor, providing color on the monitor and an additional set of characters to the ASCII character set. For more information about ASCII and ANSI, see Appendix B.

A+
OS
1.2
1.3

Using Emm386.exe   In DOS and Windows 9x/Me, Emm386.exe manages the memory addresses in upper memory. Before we see how to use it, let's begin by examining memory when upper memory addresses are not available. To do that, we use the mem command, which lets us view how memory is currently allocated. Use the /C option to get a complete list and include the |MORE option to page the results on your screen. Figure 6-22 was produced using this command:

MEM/C|MORE

```
Modules using memory below 1 MB:

   Name        Total            Conventional      Upper Memory
   --------   -------------     -------------     ------------
   MSDOS       18,672  (18K)     18,672  (18K)         0   (0K)
   HIMEM        1,168   (1K)      1,168   (1K)         0   (0K)
   DBLBUFF      2,976   (3K)      2,976   (3K)         0   (0K)
   IFSHLP       2,864   (3K)      2,864   (3K)         0   (0K)
   WIN          3,616   (4K)      3,616   (4K)         0   (0K)
   COMMAND      8,416   (8K)      8,416   (8K)         0   (0K)
   SAVE        72,768  (71K)     72,768  (71K)         0   (0K)
   Free       544,720 (532K)    544,720 (532K)        0   (0K)

Memory Summary:

   Type of Memory      Total          Used           Free
   --------------    -----------    -----------    -----------
   Conventional        655,360        110,640        544,720
   Upper                     0              0              0
   Reserved                  0              0              0
   Extended (XMS)    133,156,864         69,632    133,087,232
   --------------    -----------    -----------    -----------
-- More --
```

Figure 6-22   MEM report with /C option on a PC not using upper memory

In Figure 6-22 the first column shows the programs currently loaded in memory. The second column shows the total amount of memory used by each program. The columns labeled Conventional and Upper Memory show the amount of memory being used by each program in each of these categories. This PC is not making use of upper memory for any of its programs. At the bottom of the screen is the total amount of free conventional memory (544,720 bytes) that is available to new programs to be loaded. Making this value as high as possible is the subject of this section.

A+
OS
1.2

Creating and Using Upper Memory Blocks   Figure 6-23 shows an example of a Config.sys file that is set to use upper memory addresses. The first line loads the Himem.sys driver. The second line loads the Emm386.exe file. Emm386.exe assigns addresses in upper memory to memory made available by the Himem.sys driver. The NOEMS switch at the end of the command line says to Windows, "Do not create any simulated expanded memory." Expanded memory is an older type of memory above 1 MB that is no longer used by software. The command to load Emm386.exe must appear after the command to load Himem.sys in the Config.sys file.

```
 File  Edit  Search  View  Options  Help
                    A:\CONFIG.SYS
device=himem.sys
device=emm386.exe noems
dos=high,umb
devicehigh=A:\util\mouse.sys
files=99
buffers=40




 F1=Help                              Line:1     Col:1
```

Figure 6-23   Config.sys set to use upper memory

The command DOS=HIGH,UMB serves two purposes. The one command line can be broken into two commands like this:

```
DOS=HIGH
DOS=UMB
```

The DOS=HIGH portion tells the OS to load part of the DOS core into the high memory area ("loading DOS high"). Remember that the high memory area is the first 64K of extended memory. This memory is usually unused unless we choose to store part of DOS in it with this command line. Including this command in Config.sys frees some conventional memory that would have been used by the OS. The second part of the command, DOS=UMB, creates upper memory blocks. An **upper memory block (UMB)** is a group of consecutive memory addresses in the upper memory area that has had physical memory assigned to it. The OS identifies blocks that are not currently being used by system ROM or expansion boards, and the memory manager makes these blocks available for use.

This command, DOS=UMB, enables the OS to access these upper memory blocks. After the UMBs are created, they can be used in these ways:

- Devicehigh= command in Config.sys
- Loadhigh command in Autoexec.bat
- Loadhigh command at the command prompt (explained in the next section)

The fourth line in the Config.sys file in Figure 6-23 uses a UMB. The command Devicehigh=A:\Util\Mouse.sys tells the OS to load the mouse device driver into one of the upper memory blocks created and made available by the previous three lines. This process of loading a program into upper memory addresses is called loading high.

Loading Device Drivers High   Using the Devicehigh= command in Config.sys, rather than the Device= command, causes the driver to load high. With the Device-high= command, the OS stores these drivers in UMBs using the largest UMB first, then the next largest, and so on until all are loaded. Therefore, to make sure there is enough room to hold them all in upper memory, order the Devicehigh= command lines in Config.sys so that the largest drivers are loaded first.

You can determine the amount of memory a device driver allocates for itself and its data by using the MEM command with the /M filename option:

```
MEM /Mfilename
```

The filename is the name of the device driver without the file extension.

You can also use a UMB from Autoexec.bat using the Loadhigh (LH) command. For example, to load high Mscdex.exe, a utility to access a CD-ROM drive, use either command:

```
LH Mscdex.exe
Loadhigh Mscdex.exe
```

In either case, the program is loaded into the largest UMB available and does not use up more precious conventional memory. Note that before the Loadhigh command will work, the program files Himem.sys and Emm386.exe must be available to the OS, and these three lines must be added to Config.sys and executed by booting the computer:

```
Device=HIMEM.SYS
Device=EMM386.EXENOEMS
DOS=UMB
```

If the Himem.sys and Emm386.exe files are not in the root directory of the boot device, you must include the path to the filename in the Device= line, like this:

```
Device=C:\DOS\HIMEM.SYS
```

NOTE

> When a program is loaded high, two things can go wrong. Either the program might not work from upper memory, causing problems during execution, or there might not be enough room in upper memory for the program and its data. If the program causes the computer to hang when you attempt to run it, or if it simply refuses to work correctly, remove it from upper memory.

Windows 9x/Me, which is mostly a 32-bit OS, "lives" in extended memory together with its device drivers and applications, and uses only base and upper memory for 16-bit components. If you are using all 32-bit drivers and applications in a Windows 9x/Me environment, then you do not need to be concerned about managing base and upper memory. We now turn our attention to how Windows 9x/Me manages virtual memory.

How Windows 9x/Me Manages Virtual Memory

Virtual memory uses hard drive space so that it acts like memory. Windows stores virtual memory in a file called a swap file. The purpose of virtual memory is to increase the amount of memory available. Of course, because a hard drive is much slower than RAM, virtual memory works considerably slower than real memory. For example, a hard drive may have a data access time of 10 milliseconds (10 thousandths of a second, abbreviated 10 ms), whereas RAM speed may be 60 nanoseconds (60 billionths of a second or 60 ns).

Windows 9x/Me automates virtual memory management, and Microsoft recommends that you allow it to do so. To see what virtual memory options Windows 9x/Me offers, click Start, point to Settings, click Control Panel, select System, and then select the Performance tab. Click Virtual Memory and the dialog box in Figure 6-24 appears. These settings are used to tell Windows how to manage the swap file. Unless you have good reason to do otherwise, check "Let Windows manage my virtual memory settings."

One reason you might want to manage virtual memory yourself is to make the file size permanent to prevent Windows from resizing the file, which can slow down performance. To improve performance, first defragment the hard drive so there is plenty of unfragmented space for the file. Then set the maximum and minimum file sizes to the same value, which forces the size not to change. If you have the available hard drive space, set the size to about 2.5 times the amount of RAM.

Notice in Figure 6-24 that you can specify the location of the swap file. The name of the swap file in Windows 9x/Me is **Win386.swp**, and its default location is C:\Windows. You can choose to put the swap file on a compressed drive, but Windows does not compress the swap file itself, to better ensure the file's safety.

6

Figure 6-24 Options for managing virtual memory in Windows 9x/Me

✔ **A+ EXAM TIP**

The A+ OS exam expects
you to know the name of
each OS's swap file.

Memory Paging Windows 9x/Me stores virtual memory in the swap file and manages that memory for application programs. The Windows component called the Virtual Memory Manager (VMM) controls this process, moving 4K segments, called **pages**, in and out of physical RAM, a process called **memory paging**. If RAM is full, the manager takes a page and moves it to the swap file.

If RAM is full much of the time, the VMM might spend excessive time moving pages in and out of RAM. That can cause excessive hard drive use, decrease overall system performance, and even cause the system to lock up or applications to fail. This situation, sometimes called **disk thrashing**, can cause premature hard drive failure. Symptoms of excessive memory paging are:

- Very high CPU use
- Very slow system response
- Constant hard drive use

To avoid excessive memory paging, leave fewer applications open at the same time or install more RAM.

Windows NT/2000/XP Memory Management

As you have seen, managing memory under DOS and Windows 9x/Me can be complicated because of having to deal with conventional, upper, and extended memory for backward compatibility. Windows NT/2000/XP eliminates that complexity, because memory is simply memory; in other words, all memory addresses are used the same way. This approach also causes Windows NT/2000/XP to lose some backward compatibility with legacy software and devices.

The Windows NT/2000/XP memory management model is illustrated in Figure 6-25, which shows the object-oriented approach to memory management. The application or device driver only says, "I want memory." It cannot tell Windows which physical memory or which memory addresses it wants, or even the range of addresses it wants to fall within. Windows uses its virtual memory manager to interface between the application or driver and the physical and virtual memory that it controls. Memory is allocated in 4K segments or pages. Applications and devices written for Windows NT/2000/XP only know how many pages they have. The virtual memory manager takes care of the rest. It is free to store these pages in RAM or on the hard drive in the swap file named **Pagefile.sys** (see Figure 6-25).

Figure 6-25   Windows NT/2000/XP memory management

How Windows 2000/XP Manages Virtual Memory

Under Windows 2000/XP, the default size of the paging file is set to 1.5 times the amount of RAM installed. You might need to change the paging file in order to improve system performance. Here are some guidelines to remember in managing paging files:

- Set the initial and maximum sizes of the file to the same value. This prevents disk fragmentation that might result from setting them to two different values. Windows 2000/XP does not normally need to change the size of the paging file during processing.
- When changing the size of a paging file, remember that you need to balance the file size with disk space usage and that Windows 2000/XP requires at least

5 MB of free space on a disk. In other words, don't make the file too large, especially when the disk it is stored on is active or has limited space. Test performance as you change paging file size, and make changes gradually.

- Moving the paging file to a volume other than the boot volume can help conserve disk space on the boot volume and optimize performance, especially when a system has multiple hard disks.

- When deciding where to put the paging file, know that memory dumps (covered in Chapter 14) cannot be captured if the paging file is on a different physical disk from the operating system.

APPLYING CONCEPTS

To change virtual memory settings and paging file size in Windows 2000/XP, do the following:

1. Right-click My Computer and select Properties on the shortcut menu.
2. The System Properties dialog box opens. Click the Advanced tab.
3. For Windows XP, click Settings under Performance. For Windows 2000, click the Performance Options button.
4. The Performance Options dialog box opens. For Windows XP, click the Advanced tab and then click the Change button. For Windows 2000, click the Change button.
5. The Virtual Memory dialog box opens. In this dialog box, you can change the paging file size and view information about the paging file and the registry. Figure 6-26 shows all three dialog boxes for Windows XP.

Figure 6-26   Use the System Properties dialog box to change paging file settings

NOTE You can also access the Windows 2000/XP Performance Options dialog box from the Computer Management window. Open the Computer Management window, right-click Computer Management (Local), and select Properties on the shortcut menu.

CHAPTER SUMMARY

6

▶ SRAM (static RAM) is fast and is used as a memory cache, which speeds overall computer performance by temporarily holding data and programming that the CPU may use in the near future. SRAM does not require constant refreshing.

▶ DRAM (dynamic RAM) is slower than SRAM because it needs constant refreshing.

▶ DRAM is stored on three kinds of modules: SIMM, DIMM, and RIMM modules.

▶ SIMM memory modules can use either EDO or FPM technology. EDO is faster and only slightly more expensive than FPM, but the motherboard must support this type of memory to make use of its increased speed.

▶ DIMM memory modules can use either BEDO (burst EDO) or synchronous DRAM (SDRAM).

▶ Direct Rambus DRAM, Double Data Rate SDRAM (DDR SDRAM), and DDR2 are the three current memory technologies.

▶ Synchronous DRAM (which moves in sync with the system bus) is a faster kind of memory than the less expensive asynchronous DRAM (which does not move in sync with the system bus) found on SIMMs.

▶ When buying memory, it is best to use only gold edge connectors on memory modules that will be inserted in slots containing gold connections, and to use only tin connectors in tin slots.

▶ When buying memory, beware of remanufactured and re-marked memory chips, because they have been either refurbished or re-marked before resale.

▶ Older motherboards sometimes provided an extra COAST slot to upgrade SRAM, but most systems today come with an optimum amount of SRAM inside the CPU housing and, for some AMD processor systems, on the motherboard.

▶ When upgrading memory, use the type, size, density, and speed of memory that the motherboard supports, and match the memory modules already installed.

▶ Early limitations on the number of memory addresses available to the CPU were rooted in the fact that older motherboards had 20 lines on the bus for memory addresses, yielding a total of 1 MB of memory addresses.

▶ DOS and Windows 9x/Me divide memory into base (conventional), upper, and extended memory.

▶ DOS and Windows 9x/Me use the Himem.sys memory manager extension to allow access to extended memory (memory addresses above 1 MB). Windows 9x/Me and DOS use Himem.sys, along with Emm386.exe, to manage memory above 640K. Emm386.exe contains the software that loads 16-bit device drivers and other programs into upper memory.

▶ You can use a UMB (upper memory block) from Autoexec.bat with the Loadhigh (LH) command.

▶ The MEM command with the appropriate parameters shows exactly where in upper memory the UMBs are located and what software has been assigned addresses in upper memory.

▶ Windows 95/98 uses 16-bit and 32-bit drivers. Windows Me and Windows NT/2000/XP use only 32-bit drivers. Windows 95/98 16-bit drivers use conventional and upper memory, and 32-bit drivers use extended memory. In Windows NT/2000/XP, there are no divisions of memory. All 32-bit drivers just use memory.

▶ Virtual memory uses hard drive space as memory in order to increase the total amount of memory available. In Windows, virtual memory is stored in the swap file. The Windows 9x/Me swap file is Win386.swp, and the Windows 2000/XP swap file is Pagefile.sys.

▶ Virtual memory is managed in Windows 2000/XP from the System Properties dialog box.

KEY TERMS

For explanations of key terms, see the Glossary near the end of the book.

bank
burst EDO (BEDO)
cache on a stick (COAST)
CAS Latency
conventional memory
C-RIMM (Continuity RIMM)
DDR2 SDRAM
Direct Rambus DRAM
Direct RDRAM
disk thrashing
Double Data Rate SDRAM
    (DDR SDRAM)
Dual Channel
dynamic RAM (DRAM)
ECC (error-correcting code)

EDO (extended data out)
Emm386.exe
extended memory
General Protection Fault (GPF)
high memory area (HMA)
Himem.sys
memory paging
nonparity memory
page
page file
Pagefile.sys
parity
parity error
parity memory

RAS Latency
RDRAM
refresh
re-marked chips
SDRAM II
static RAM (SRAM)
swap file
synchronous DRAM (SDRAM)
SyncLink DRAM (SLDRAM)
upper memory
upper memory block (UMB)
virtual DOS machine (VDM)
virtual memory
Win386.swp

6

REVIEWING THE BASICS

1. Name two ways that a SIMM and a DIMM are alike. Name two ways they are different.

2. How many pins are on a SDRAM DIMM? On a DDR DIMM? On a SIMM? On a RIMM?

3. Which is likely to be more expensive, a 512-MB DIMM or a 512-MB RIMM? Why?

4. How many notches are on a DDR SDRAM module?

5. How does a memory cache speed up computer processing?

6. Explain how L1 cache, L2 cache, and L3 cache differ.

7. What types of memory can be used on a 100-MHz motherboard?

8. Looking at an SDRAM DIMM, how can you know for certain the voltage needed by the module?

9. How many 30-pin SIMMs are installed in one bank?

10. How many 72-pin SIMMs are installed in one bank?

11. What are two current speeds of RIMMs?

12. List at least four things you can do if you receive memory errors during a memory upgrade.

13. What might be a symptom in Windows of unreliable memory on a motherboard?

14. List at least four things you can do if you receive memory errors during normal operation when you have not recently upgraded memory.

15. If your motherboard calls for 60-ns memory, can you substitute 70-ns memory? Why or why not?

16. When buying memory, what can you look for that might indicate that the memory is remanufactured?

17. What are the two major categories of static RAM memory?

18. What improvements did DDR make over regular SDRAM?

19. When might there not be any SRAM on a motherboard?

20. List two operating systems that allow 16-bit drivers.

21. List four operating systems that allow only 32-bit drivers.

22. What are the three types of memory addresses that Windows 9x/Me manages? What are the memory address ranges for each?

23. What is the hexadecimal address range for upper memory?

24. Name the two utilities that Windows uses to manage memory above 640K. Give a brief description of each.

25. Define memory paging. What problem can excessive memory paging cause? What are some symptoms of this problem?

26. Give one reason you should make the paging file maximum size the same as the paging file initial size.

27. What is the name of the Windows 9x/Me swap file?

28. What is the name of the Windows 2000/XP swap file?

29. By default, Windows 2000/XP makes the paging file how large compared to the amount of RAM installed?

30. List the steps in Windows 2000 to change the size of the paging file.

THINKING CRITICALLY

1. If your motherboard supports DIMM memory, will RIMM memory still work on the board?

2. If your motherboard supports ECC SDRAM memory, can you substitute SDRAM memory that does not support ECC? If your motherboard supports buffered SDRAM memory, can you substitute unbuffered SDRAM modules?

3. You have just upgraded memory on a computer from 64 MB to 128 MB by adding one DIMM. When you first turn on the PC, the memory count shows only 64 MB. Which of the following is most likely the source of the problem? What can you do to fix it?

    a. Windows is giving an error because it likely became corrupted while the PC was disassembled.

    b. The new DIMM you installed is faulty.

    c. The new DIMM is not properly seated.

    d. The DIMM is installed in the wrong slot.

4. Why is it necessary to understand how to create and use upper memory blocks in Windows 9x/Me?

5. What is the DOS=HIGH,UMB command used for? Explain both parts of the command.

6. Can an application or device driver specify which physical memory or memory addresses it wants in Windows NT/2000/XP? Why or why not?

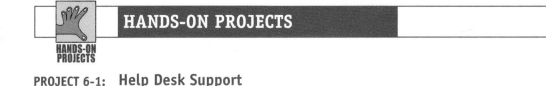

HANDS-ON PROJECTS

PROJECT 6-1: Help Desk Support

1. A friend calls while sitting at his computer and asks you to help him determine how much RAM he has on his motherboard. Step him through the process. List at least two ways to find the answer. He is using Windows 98.

2. Answer Question 1 above, assuming that your friend is using Windows 2000.

3. Your friend has discovered he has 128 MB of RAM and wants to upgrade to 256 MB. He is using DIMMs and his motherboard is running at 133 MHz. Looking at Figure 6-12, what is the estimated cost of the upgrade?

PROJECT 6-2: Planning and Pricing Memory

You need the documentation for your motherboard for this project. If you don't have it, download it from the Web site of the motherboard manufacturer. Use this documentation and the motherboard to answer the following:

1. What is the maximum amount of memory the banks on your motherboard can accommodate?

2. What type of memory does the board support?

3. How many modules are installed, and how much memory does each hold?

4. Look in a computer catalog, such as *Computer Shopper*, or use a retail Web site such as Kingston Technology (*www.kingston.com*) or Crucial Technology (*www.crucial.com*) to determine how much it costs to fill the banks to full capacity. Don't forget to match the speed of the modules already installed, and plan to use only the size modules your computer can accommodate. How much will the upgrade cost?

PROJECT 6-3: Upgrading Memory

To practice installing additional memory in a computer in a classroom environment, remove the SIMMs, DIMMs, or RIMMs from one computer and place them in another computer. Boot the second computer and check that it counts the additional memory. When finished, return the borrowed modules to the original computer.

PROJECT 6-4: Troubleshooting Memory

Follow the rules outlined in Chapter 4 to protect the PC against ESD as you work. Remove the memory module in the first memory slot on a motherboard, and boot the PC. Did you get an error? Why or why not?

PROJECT 6-5: Using Himem.sys and Emm386.exe

Using DOS or Windows 9x/Me, practice using Himem.sys and Emm386.exe:

1. Make a bootable disk that does not contain an Autoexec.bat or Config.sys file, and boot from the disk.

2. Use the **mem** command to display a memory report showing that upper memory is currently not used.

3. Load a mouse driver into upper memory as you saw done in the chapter (see Figure 6-21).

4. Reboot the PC and use the **mem** command to demonstrate that the mouse driver is loaded high.

5. Print the contents of your Config.sys file.

6. List a directory of your floppy disk to the printer. What files on your disk are necessary to make the mouse work when loaded high?

6

Floppy Drives

In the previous chapter, you learned about memory and how to support it. This chapter looks at another important component: floppy drives. Once considered essential devices for file storage and installing software on a computer, floppy drives are now mainly used for trouble-shooting a failed boot and as a quick and easy way to transfer small files from one PC to another when a network is not available. In this chapter, you will learn how data is stored on a floppy disk and how to install a floppy drive on a PC. Even though floppy drives are expected to become obsolete in the next few years, we devote a full chapter to them because much of what you learn about floppy drives is valuable preparation for your study of hard drives in the next chapter.

How Floppy Drives Work

Recall that memory is organized in two ways: physically (pertaining to hardware) and logically (pertaining to software). Similarly, data is stored physically and logically on a secondary storage device. Physical storage involves how data is written to and organized on the storage media, while logical storage involves how the OS and BIOS organize and view the stored data. This section explains first how data is physically stored on a floppy disk and then how the OS logically views the data.

How Data Is Physically Stored on a Floppy Disk

A+
CORE
1.1

Years ago, floppy drives came in two sizes: 5¼ inches and 3½ inches. The 3½-inch disks were formatted as high-density (1.44 MB), extra-high density (2.88 MB), and double density (720K). Today, new computers are equipped with only 3½-inch high-density drives that hold 1.44 MB of data. Figure 7-1 shows the floppy drive subsystem, which consists of the floppy drive, its cable, and its connections. The data cable leaving the floppy drive leads to a controller for the drive on the motherboard. In older computers, the controller board is plugged into an expansion slot. The board communicated with the CPU, passing data to and from the floppy disk. These controller boards were called I/O cards and often served multiple functions, having connections for a hard drive, a floppy drive, and serial and parallel ports. Today, the controller is built into the motherboard so that the data cable goes directly from the drive to the motherboard.

✔ **A+ EXAM TIP**

The A+ Core exam expects you to know that a floppy drive cable has 34 pins.

A floppy drive is connected to either the controller card or motherboard by a 34-pin data cable. The cable has the controller connection at one end and a drive connection at the other. Some older cables have a second drive connection placed in the middle of the cable to accommodate a second floppy drive. Having two drives share the same cable is a common practice for floppy drives as well as hard drives and other drives.

Floppy drives receive power from the power supply by way of a power cord. The power cord plugs into the back of the drive and has a smaller connection than the power cord for other drives in the system.

When floppy disks are first manufactured, the disks have nothing on them; they are blank sheets of magnetically coated plastic. Recall from Chapter 2 that disks are organized in tracks and sectors. Before data can be written to the disk, it must first be mapped in concentric circles called tracks, which are divided into segments called sectors (see Figure 7-2).

Figure 7-1   Floppy drive subsystem: floppy drive, data cable, and power connection

Figure 7-2   3½-inch high-density floppy disk showing tracks and sectors

The process of marking tracks and sectors to prepare the disk to receive data is called **formatting** the disk; you do this using the Windows Explorer shortcut menu or the Format command from a command prompt, as you learned in Chapter 3. Figure 7-2 shows a formatted 3½-inch high-density floppy disk. There are 80 tracks, or circles, on the top side of the disk and 80 more tracks on the bottom. The tracks are numbered 0 through 79. Each side of the disk has 18 sectors, numbered 1 through 18. Although the circles, or tracks, on the outside of the disk are larger than the circles closer to the center, all tracks store the same amount of data. Data is written to the tracks as bits, either 0s or 1s. Each bit is a magnetized, rectangular spot on the disk. Between the tracks and spots are spaces that are not magnetized. This spacing prevents one spot from affecting the magnetism of a nearby spot. The difference between a 0 spot and a 1 spot is the orientation of the spot's magnetization on the disk surface.

Data is written to and read from the disk via a magnetic **read/write head** mechanism in the floppy drive (see Figure 7-3). Two heads are attached at the end of an actuator arm that freely moves over the surface of the disk. The arm has one read/write head above the disk and another below the disk. Moving in unison back and forth across the disk, the two heads lightly touch the surface of the disk, which spins at 360 rpm (revolutions per minute). (Note that the read/write heads of a hard drive never touch the surface. You will learn more about hard drives in the next chapter.) Data is written first to the bottom and then to the top of the disk, beginning at the outermost circle and moving in. Tunnel-erase heads on either side of the read/write head, as shown in Figure 7-4, ensure that the widths of the data tracks do not vary. As the data is written, the erase heads immediately behind and to the sides of the write head clean both sides of the magnetized spot, making a clean track of data with no "bleeding" from the track. The magnetized area does not spread far from the track. All tracks are then the same width, and the distance between tracks is uniform.

Figure 7-3   Inside a floppy disk drive

The disk is actually a piece of Mylar similar to that used for overhead transparencies. The surface of the Mylar is covered with a layer of either cobalt oxide or iron oxide (rust) that can hold a magnetic charge. Some floppy disks use another layer of

**A+
CORE
1.1**

Teflon to protect the oxide layer and to allow the read/write heads to move more smoothly over the surface.

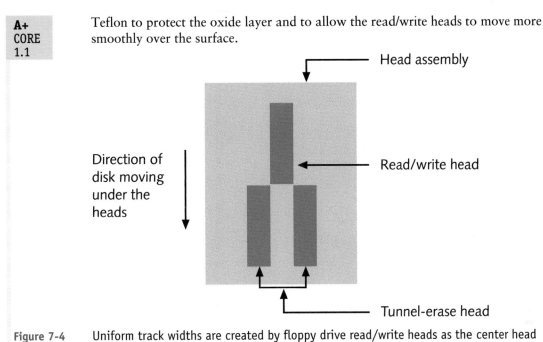

Figure 7-4   Uniform track widths are created by floppy drive read/write heads as the center head writes data while the two tunnel-erase heads clean up from behind

How Data Is Logically Stored on a Floppy Disk

**A+
CORE
1.1
OS
1.1**

A **cluster,** sometimes called a **file allocation unit,** is a group of sectors that is the smallest unit on a disk used to hold a file or a portion of a file. "Sector" refers to the way data is physically stored on a disk, while "cluster" describes how data is logically organized. The BIOS manages the disk as physical sectors, but the OS considers the disk only a long list of clusters that can each hold a fixed amount of data (see Figure 7-5). The OS keeps that list of clusters in the file allocation table (FAT).

The 3½-inch high-density floppy disk has 80 tracks × 18 sectors per track on each side, for a total of 1440 sectors. The disk has only one sector per cluster, making 1440 × 2 sides, or 2880 clusters. Because each cluster holds 512 bytes (one sector) of data, a 3½-inch high-density floppy disk has 2880 × 512 = 1,474,560 bytes of data. Divide this number by 1024 to convert bytes to kilobytes. The storage capacity of this disk is 1440 kilobytes. Divide by 1000 to convert kilobytes to megabytes, and the storage is 1.44 MB.

NOTE

There is a discrepancy in the way the computer industry defines a megabyte. Sometimes 1 megabyte = 1000 kilobytes; at other times, we use the relationship 1 megabyte = 1,024 kilobytes.

A+
CORE
1.1
OS
1.1

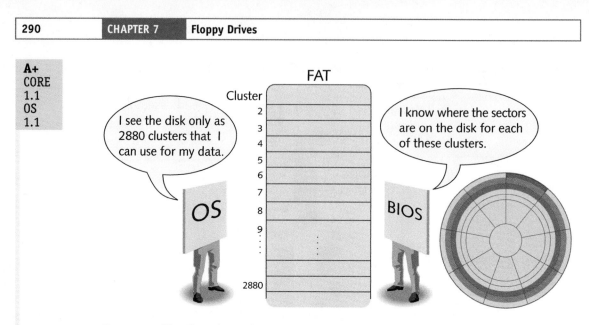

Figure 7-5   Clusters, or file allocation units, are managed by the OS in the file allocation table, but BIOS manages these clusters as one or two physical sectors on the disk

The Formatting Process for a Floppy Disk

Recall that before a floppy disk can be used, it must be formatted. Most floppy disks come already formatted, but occasionally you will need to format one. There are two ways to format a floppy disk:

- Use the Format command from a command prompt. First access a command prompt and then enter this command: Format A:
- To format a disk using Windows Explorer, right-click the 3½ Floppy (A:) icon and select Format on the shortcut menu.

Whether you use the Format command or Windows Explorer to format a floppy disk, the process is similar, regardless of size or density. During formatting, the following are created:

- Tracks and sectors are created by writing tracks as a series of F6s in hex and, as necessary, writing the sector address mark to identify the beginning sector on a track
- The boot record
- Two copies of the file allocation table (FAT)
- The root directory

The next sections describe these basic steps in detail. Chapter 3 described options available with the Format command.

The Boot Record

**A+
CORE
1.1
OS
1.1**

The first sector of each floppy disk contains basic information about how the disk is organized. This information includes the total number of sectors, the number of sectors per cluster, the number of bits in each FAT entry, and other information that an OS or BIOS needs to read the data on the disk. This information is stored in the first sector on the disk, called the **boot sector** or **boot record**. At the end of the boot record is a small program, called the **bootstrap loader,** that can be used to boot from the disk. The boot record indicates the version of DOS or Windows used to format the disk, and is always located at the beginning of the disk at track 0, sector 1 (bottom of the disk, outermost track). This uniform layout and content allows any version of DOS or Windows to read any floppy disk. (You will learn about hard drive boot records in the next chapter.)

✔ **A+ EXAM TIP**

The A+ OS and Core exams expect you to be familiar with the purpose and contents of the boot record, the FAT, and the root directory of a floppy disk.

The boot record includes the name of the program it searches for to load an OS, either Io.sys or Ntldr. If one of these files is on the disk, the file loads the rest of the OS files needed on the disk to boot; then the disk is said to be bootable.

The File Allocation Table

After the boot record is created, the next step in formatting a floppy disk is to write two copies of the FAT to the disk. The FAT lists the location of files on the disk in a one-column table. Because the width of each entry in the column on a floppy disk is 12 bits, the FAT is called a 12-bit FAT, or **FAT12**. The FAT lists how each cluster (or file allocation unit) on the disk is currently used. A file is stored in one or more clusters that do not have to be contiguous on the disk. In the FAT, some clusters might be marked as bad (the 12 bits to mark a bad cluster are FF7h). An extra copy of the FAT immediately follows the first. If the first is damaged, sometimes you can recover your data and files by using the copy.

The Root Directory Table

After creating the file allocation tables, the formatting process sets up the root directory table. Recall that the root directory, or main directory, is a table listing all files and subdirectories assigned to this table. The root directory contains a fixed number of rows to accommodate a predetermined number of files and subdirectories; the number of available rows depends on the disk type. A 3½-inch high-density floppy disk has 224 entries in the root directory. Some important items in a directory are:

- *The filename and extension.* An entry in a directory is only big enough for an eight-character filename. For long filenames, more room in the directory is required. This room is provided by using more than one entry in the directory for a single file, enough to accommodate the length of the filename. Both the long filename and the DOS-version short filename are stored in the directory.

A+
CORE
1.1
OS
1.1

- *Time and date of creation or last update.* The date and time come from the system date and time, which the OS gets from the real-time clock during the boot. At the command prompt, you can change these values with the Date and Time commands. Using the Windows desktop, change the date and time in the Control Panel. The earliest possible date allowed using either method is 1/1/1980.
- *The file attributes.* These are on/off switches indicating the archive, system file, hidden file, and read-only file status of the file or directory. You can use several OS commands or Windows Explorer to change the file attributes.

NOTE

The archive status is a switch used to indicate whether the file has been changed since the last backup and should be backed up next time a backup is made. You will learn more about this process in Chapter 9.

The root directory and all subdirectories contain the same information about each file. Only the root directory has a limitation on the number of entries. Subdirectories can have as many entries as disk space allows. Because long filenames require more room in a directory than short filenames, assigning long filenames reduces the number of files that can be stored in the root directory.

NOTE

See Appendix D, "FAT Details," for tables showing the contents of the floppy disk boot record, the root directory, and the meaning of each bit in the attribute byte.

APPLYING CONCEPTS

If the date and time are wrong in the OS, make the change in CMOS setup. You could make the change in the OS using the Control Panel, but the next time the PC reboots, the OS will pick up the date and time from CMOS. If CMOS loses the correct date and time while the power is off, the CMOS battery might be bad.

NOTE

In Windows, you can use a command prompt or Windows Explorer to manage floppy disks. The easiest way to manage disks, folders, and files in Windows Explorer is to use the shortcut menus. To access a shortcut menu, right-click the item or icon representing what you want to work with. For example, when you right-click the floppy drive item or icon in Explorer, the shortcut menu appears. To format the floppy disk, select Format from the menu.

Exchanging and Supporting Floppy Drives

A+ CORE 1.2

When a floppy drive cannot read a disk or malfunctions in some other way, the problem can have many causes. This section describes problems that can occur with a floppy drive and its support system, how to replace the drive, and how to add another floppy drive to a computer system.

✔ A+ EXAM TIP

The A+ Core exam expects you to know how to install a device such as a floppy disk drive. Given a list of steps for the installation, you should be able to order the steps correctly or identify an error in a step.

Many computers today come with one 3½-inch floppy drive, a hard drive, and a CD-ROM drive. The machine might have one or two empty bays for a second floppy drive or for a Zip drive. If you have no extra bay and want to add another drive, you can attach an external drive that comes in its own case and has its own power supply. Most external drives today connect to the main system using a USB port.

Floppy drives are now so inexpensive that repairing one is impractical. Once you've determined that the drive itself has a problem, open the case, remove the drive, and replace it with a new one. This procedure takes no more than 30 minutes, assuming that you don't damage or loosen something in the process and create a new troubleshooting opportunity.

7

Replacing a Floppy Drive

APPLYING CONCEPTS

Following is a five-step summary of how to replace a floppy drive. Each step is described in more detail in the next sections.

1. Check that the computer and other peripherals are working. Can you boot to the hard drive or another floppy drive? You should know your starting point.
2. Turn off the computer and remove the cover.
3. Unplug the data cable and power cable from the old drive and unscrew and dismount the drive.
4. Slide the new drive into the bay and reconnect the data cable and power cable.
5. Turn on the computer, check the setup and test the drive. Turn off the computer and replace the cover.

Now let's look at each step in detail.

1. Check that the computer and other peripherals are working

Can you boot to the hard drive or another floppy drive? You should know your starting point. Imagine yourself in the following situation. You are asked to install a floppy disk drive in a computer. You remove the cover, install the drive, and turn on

**A+
CORE
1.2**

the PC. Nothing happens. No power, no lights, nothing. Or perhaps the PC does not boot successfully, giving errors during POST that appear to have nothing to do with your newly installed floppy drive. Now you don't know if you created the problem or if it existed before you started. That is why you check the computer before you begin and make sure you know what's working and what's not. The extra time is worthwhile and prevents a situation like this.

Before you start to work, you should do a quick system check of a PC:

- Turn on the computer and verify that it boots to the OS with no errors.
- Using Windows, open a program and perform a task from the program.
- Get a directory listing of files on a floppy disk and a CD.
- If the computer is connected to a printer, print a test page.

2. Turn off the computer and remove the cover

As you learned in Chapter 4, guard the computer against static electricity by using a ground bracelet, working on a hard floor (not on carpet), and grounding yourself before you touch any components inside the case. Never touch anything inside the case while the power is on. Remove the cover and put its screws in a safe place.

Next, prepare to remove the power cable. The power supply cable is a four-pronged cable that attaches to the back of the drive, as shown in Figure 7-6. The cable can be difficult to detach because the connection is very secure. Be careful not to apply so much pressure that you break the corner of the logic board. Steady the board with one hand while you dislodge the power cable with the other hand.

Floppy drive

Power cord

Figure 7-6   Power supply connection on the back of the drive (note how well this drive manufacturer labeled pin 1 on the data connection)

A+
CORE
1.2

3. Unplug the data cable and power cable from the old drive and unscrew and dismount the drive

Before removing the cables and the drive, note carefully how they are assembled, to help you reassemble them later. The data cable might go to an adapter card or directly to the motherboard. Before removing the cable, note that it has a color or stripe down one side. This edge color marks this side of the cable as pin 1. Look on the board to which the cable is attached. Verify that pin 1 or pin 2 is clearly marked, either by a number embossed on the board or by a square solder pad on the bottom of the circuit board, and that the colored edge aligns with pin 1 on both the board and the drive. Sometimes pin 1 on the floppy drive is marked, and sometimes the drive housing is constructed so that the cable built for the drive inserts in only one direction. Note the position of pin 1 on the drive.

Look at the cable connecting drive A to the floppy drive controller card or to the motherboard. There is a twist in the cable. This twist reverses the leads in the cable, causing the addresses for the first connection to be different from the addresses for the second connection that has no twist. The position of the twist on the cable determines which drive will be drive A (see Figure 7-7). The startup BIOS looks to drive A first for a bootable disk, unless a change has been made in CMOS setup, instructing startup BIOS to look to a different drive. By switching the drive to before or after the twist, you exchange drives A and B. Some computers have two drives attached to the same cable. In this case, the drive attached behind the twist is drive A, and the one attached before the twist is drive B. After you are familiar with the cable orientation and connection, remove the cable from the floppy drive.

Now that the cable is detached, you can remove the floppy drive. Some drives have one or two screws on each side that attach the drive to the drive bay. After you remove the screws, the drive usually slides to the front and out of the case. Sometimes you must lift a catch underneath the drive as you slide the drive forward. Be careful not to remove any screws that hold a circuit card on top of the drive to the drive housing; all this should stay intact.

4. Slide the new drive into the bay and reconnect the data cable and power cable

If the new drive is too narrow to fit snugly into the bay, you can buy an adapter kit with extensions for narrow drives that allow them to reach the sides of the bay. Screw the drive down with the same screws used on the old drive. Reaching the screw hole on the back of the drive might be difficult if it is against the side of the case. Make sure the drive is anchored so that it cannot slide forward or backward, or up or down, even if a user turns the case on its side.

Next, reconnect the data cable, making sure that the cable's colored edge is connected to the pin 1 side of the connection, as shown in Figure 7-8. Most connections on floppy drives are oriented the same way, so this one probably has the same orientation as the old drive. The power cable goes into the power connection in only one direction. Be careful not to offset the connection by one pin.

A+
CORE
1.2

Connects to motherboard
or older controller card

Edge color on cable
indicates the pin 1
side of cable

Drive B connections
(2 styles)

Twist in cable

Drive A connector

Figure 7-7   Twist in cable determines which drive will be drive A

Floppy drive

Twist in cable

Colored edge connector

Pin 1 of edge connector

Power connector

Figure 7-8   Connect colored edge of cable to pin 1

5. Turn on the computer, check the setup, and test the drive

A+
CORE
1.2
4.4

Double-check all connections and turn on the computer. If you changed disk types, you must inform CMOS setup by accessing setup and changing the drive type. Test the drive by formatting a disk or doing a Diskcopy. If you determine that all is well, replace the cover and you're done.

Note that you can run the computer with the cover off. If the drive doesn't work, having the cover off makes it easier to turn off the computer, check connections, and try again. Just make certain that you don't touch anything while the computer is on.

**A+
CORE
1.2
4.4**

Leaving the computer on while you disconnect and reconnect a cable is very dangerous for the PC and will probably damage something.

Adding a New Drive

Adding a new drive is no problem if you have an empty bay, an extra power cable,
and an extra connection on the floppy drive data cable. Slide the drive into the bay,
screw it down, connect the cable and power cable, change setup, and you're done. If
you don't have an extra power cable, you can use a "Y" splitter on the power cable
for the existing floppy drive to provide the power connection.

NOTE You can test a floppy drive for accuracy and alignment using a digital diagnostic disk designed
for that purpose and utility software such as TestDrive by MicroSystems Development Technologies, Inc. (*www.msd.com/diags*).

7

When a Floppy Disk Drive Doesn't Work

**A+
CORE
2.1**

✔ A+ EXAM TIP

The A+ Core exam expects
you to be familiar with all
the error messages in this
section, to generally know
the source of the error, and
to select the best next step
to take in solving the problem from a list of steps. To
select the next step, common sense helps. For
example, always check the
simple things first.

Sometimes a problem with the floppy drive arises during POST, and BIOS displays
an error message. Error messages in the 600 range occur when the
floppy drive did not pass the POST test. These problems can be
caused by the power supply, the drive, the controller board (if one is
present), or the motherboard.

Even if POST finds no errors, there may still be a problem. If you
put a disk in a faulty drive and issue a command to access the disk,
an error message such as the following might appear on the screen:

```
General failure reading drive A:, Abort,
Retry, Fail?
```

If nothing happens and the computer simply stops working, the
problem might have several causes, including the following:

- The application you are running points to a different drive.
- Windows just encountered an unrelated error that has locked up the system.
- The system BIOS or CMOS setup is not correctly configured.
- The disk in the drive is not formatted.
- The floppy drive is bad.
- The shuttle window on the floppy disk cannot open fully.
- The cable from the motherboard to the drive is damaged or poorly connected.

- The edge color on the cable is not aligned with pin 1.
- The power supply is bad.
- The power supply cable to the drive is loose or disconnected.
- The command just issued has a mistake or is the wrong command.
- The disk is inserted incorrectly.

You might discover more items to add to this list. I once helped someone with a drive error. We took the 3½-inch floppy disk out of the drive and opened the shuttle window (the spring-loaded metal cover that opens to reveal the disk inside the plastic housing) to find a blade of grass on the disk's surface. We removed the grass, and the disk worked perfectly. She then remembered that she had dropped the disk in the grass. When you have any computer trouble, check simple things first. Here are a few suggestions for solving drive problems:

- Remove the disk. Does the shuttle window move freely? Do you see any dirt, hair, or other foreign material on the disk's Mylar surface? Does the disk spin freely inside the housing cover? Some new disks simply need a little loosening up. Put the disk back in the drive, and try to access it again.
- Does the light on the correct drive go on? Maybe you are trying to access drive B, but the disk is in drive A.
- Does another disk work in the drive? If so, the problem is probably caused by the disk, not the drive. The exception is when the drive is out of alignment. When it is, the drive cannot read a disk that it did not format, although it might read a disk that it formatted with its own alignment. To test this possibility, try several disks and note whether the drive reads only those disks that it has recently formatted. If so, then you might have identified the problem, and you can replace the drive.

A+
CORE
2.1
4.4

- Does the drive light come on? If not, the problem might be with the software or the hardware. Try to access the disk with other software. Can the OS access the drive with a simple Dir A: command? Can Windows Explorer access the disk? How about using the Chkdsk A: command? If the light still doesn't come on, the problem might involve the power to the drive or the hardware connections inside the case. Does the other drive work? If neither light comes on, consider the power supply or the motherboard as the source of your problem.
- Does the light come on at boot and stay on? This is most likely caused by the cable not being attached correctly to pin 1. Check the edge color to see that it aligns with pin 1.
- Has this drive been used recently? Perhaps the system setup has lost CMOS data. The system might think it has a 720K drive when it really has a 1.44-MB drive. Access setup and check the drive specifications. Also check setup to see that drives A and B have not been switched. Some CMOS setups have this option.
- Reboot the machine and try again. Many problems with computers disappear with a simple reboot. If a soft boot doesn't do it, try a hard boot.

A+
CORE
2.1

- Try cleaning the drive's read/write heads. Use a head-cleaning kit that includes a paper disk and a cleaning solution. Follow the directions that come with the kit. You can purchase a kit at any store that sells computer supplies.
- If the drive still does not work with any disk and any software, then you must dig deeper. Inside the case, the hardware that can cause this problem is the drive itself, the data cable from the motherboard to the drive, the power supply, the power cable, or the motherboard. To find the culprit, replace each hardware component with a known good device, one component at a time, until the problem goes away. Having access to another working computer from which you can borrow parts is helpful.

NOTE

When you try to discover which device is causing a problem during a troubleshooting session, you can trade a suspected device for one you know is good (called a known good device). You can also install the device you suspect is bad in a computer system you know is working. If the problem follows the device, then you know the device is bad.

7

- Turn off the computer and open the computer case. Check every connection from the motherboard to the drive. Check the power cable connection.
- Take the power cable from the second working floppy drive and put it on the nonworking one, to eliminate the power cable as the problem.
- Replace the data cable and try the drive again. Make sure to align the cable correctly with pin 1. If that does not work, exchange the drive itself and try again.
- If the drive still does not work, suspect the motherboard or the ROM BIOS on the motherboard. Try flashing ROM.

Some Common Error Messages and Their Meanings

A+
CORE
2.1

Here are some common error messages that might be caused by problems with a floppy drive, followed by what the messages mean.

```
Non-system disk or disk error. Replace and strike any key
when ready.
No operating system found
```

These messages say that you are trying to boot from a disk that is not bootable. Remove the disk from the drive, and press any key. The computer bypasses the floppy drive and loads the OS from the hard drive. If you intended to boot from the floppy drive, the disk should have been formatted and made bootable as described in Chapter 3.

If you had no disk in the floppy drive, you can assume that some critical OS files are missing from the hard drive. In this case, boot from a bootable floppy disk or rescue disk, and check whether the files have been erased accidentally from your hard drive.

```
Bad or missing COMMAND.COM
Error in Config.sys line xx
Himem.sys not loaded
Missing or corrupt Himem.sys
```

These errors appear when the OS loads and the two hidden files are present, but system files such as Command.com, Config.sys, and Himem.sys are not present, are corrupt, or, in the case of Config.sys, have an incorrect entry. Replace the missing or corrupt file. To test for errors in Autoexec.bat and Config.sys, you can hold down the F8 key while DOS loads. That causes lines in these files to execute one at a time as you watch the screen. Also, press F5 to bypass these two files during the boot.

```
Invalid Drive Specification
```

You are trying to access a drive that the OS does not know is available. For example, the error might appear in this situation: During booting, an error message indicates that BIOS cannot access the hard drive. You boot from a floppy disk in drive A and see an A prompt. You then try to access drive C from the A prompt, and you see the preceding error message. DOS or Windows is telling you that it can't find drive C because it failed the test during POST. As far as the OS is concerned, the hard drive does not exist.

```
Not ready reading drive A:, Abort, Retry, Fail?
```

This message means the floppy disk in drive A is not readable. Perhaps the disk is missing or inserted incorrectly. The disk might have a bad boot record, errors in the FAT, or bad sectors.

```
General failure reading drive A:, Abort, Retry, Fail?
```

This message means the floppy disk is badly corrupted or not yet formatted. Sometimes this error means that the floppy drive is bad. Try another disk. If you determine that the problem is the disk and not the drive, the disk is probably unusable. A bad boot record sometimes gives this message.

```
Track 0 bad, disk not usable
```

This message typically occurs when you try to format a disk using the wrong disk type. Check your Format command. Most manufacturers write the disk type on the disk. If you have a 3½-inch floppy disk, you can tell if you are using a high-density or double-density disk by the see-through holes at the corners of the disk. The

**A+
CORE
2.1**

high-density disk has holes on two corners; the double-density has a hole on only one corner. Don't try to format a disk using the wrong density.

```
Write-protect error writing drive A:
```

The disk is write-protected and the application is trying to write to it. To write to a 3½-inch floppy disk, the write-protect window must be closed; that is, the switch must be toward the center of the disk so that you cannot see through the write-protect hole.

CHAPTER SUMMARY

7

▶ Data is stored on floppy disks in concentric circles called tracks or cylinders. Each track is divided into sectors. Each sector holds 512 bytes of data.

▶ Different types of floppy disks vary according to the organization of tracks and sectors, the density at which data can be stored, and the intensity of the magnetic spots on the magnetized plastic surface of the disk.

▶ The smallest logical unit of space allocated to a file is called a cluster. On 3½-inch high-density floppy disks, one cluster is the same as one sector, which is 512 bytes.

▶ When a disk is formatted for use, the formatting process creates tracks and sectors and places a boot record, file allocation table, and root directory on the disk.

▶ The first sector of the disk, called the boot sector or the boot record, stores basic information about how a floppy disk is organized. At the end of a boot record is a small program, called the bootstrap loader, that can be used to boot from the disk.

▶ The file allocation table lists the location of file segments called clusters on a disk in a one-column table.

▶ You can use Windows Explorer to format a floppy disk and to manage files and folders on floppy disks and hard drives.

▶ Before beginning to install hardware such as a floppy drive, check the other peripherals. Then, if you encounter any problems, you know whether they were preexisting or were caused during the installation.

▶ Error messages in the 600 range occur when a floppy drive does not pass the POST test.

▶ When troubleshooting a floppy drive, check the physical condition of the disk as well as error messages, CMOS settings, and cables connected to the drive.

KEY TERMS

For explanations of key terms, see the Glossary near the end of the book.

boot record   cluster   formatting
boot sector   FAT12   read/write head
bootstrap loader   file allocation unit

REVIEWING THE BASICS

1. How many sectors per track are there on a 3½-inch high-density floppy disk?

2. What two cables are connected to a floppy drive inside a computer?

3. Is data written to both sides of a floppy disk?

4. What is the difference between a sector and a cluster?

5. What is another name for a cluster?

6. How does the Format command prepare a disk for use?

7. What is the purpose of the boot record on a disk?

8. If a floppy drive is not working, why is it better to replace the drive than to repair it?

9. What might cause the error, "General failure reading drive A"?

10. What might cause the floppy drive light to remain on during a boot?

11. How can you look at a 3½-inch floppy disk and tell if it is a high-density or double-density disk?

12. How do you format a new floppy disk using an OS command? Using Windows Explorer?

13. What do you check if you get the error, "Write-protect error writing drive A:"?

14. What causes the Invalid Drive Specification error?

15. List the steps that you would follow to install a new floppy drive as drive B.

16. How many pins does a floppy drive data cable have?

17. How does the computer distinguish drive A from drive B?

18. What is the best way to find out whether a device is causing a problem during a troubleshooting session?

19. What do errors during POST in the 600 range indicate?

20. Besides the physical condition of the drive, what should you check when troubleshooting a floppy drive?

21. How many floppy drives can be installed on a single floppy drive cable?

THINKING CRITICALLY

1. Your floppy drive fails, so you replace it with a new one. When you power up and check Windows Explorer, you discover that the system does not recognize the new drive. What should you do first?

   a. Reboot the PC, enter CMOS setup, and verify that CMOS has the drive configured correctly.

   b. Open the case and check that you connected both the data cable and the power cable.

   c. Open the case and verify that the floppy drive cable is not installed backward in the connector.

   d. Return the drive to the store and ask for a replacement.

2. You purchase a new computer system, but it does not have a floppy drive installed. You purchase a floppy drive and open the case, ready to install it, but you don't find a 34-pin connector on the motherboard. Which of the following options would work for you, and which option is the best choice?

   a. Buy a new data cable that uses 40 pins and connect the floppy drive to the 40-pin connector you find on the board.

   b. Buy a special converter that lets you connect the floppy drive to the USB connector on the motherboard.

   c. Return the floppy drive you purchased and buy an external floppy drive that connects to an external USB port on your system.

   d. You cannot install a floppy drive on this system. Just get by without it.

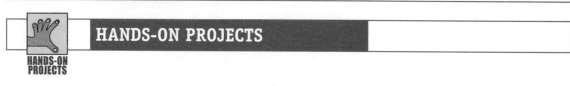

HANDS-ON PROJECTS

PROJECT 7-1: Troubleshooting and Installing Floppy Drives

1. Use a PC with A and B drives. Reverse the drives so that drive A is B and drive B is the new A. Test by booting from the new drive A. When you finish, return the drives to their original assignments to avoid confusing other users.

2. Use a PC with only a drive A. First, verify that you can boot from drive A with a bootable disk. Then turn off the computer, open the case, and examine the data cable to drive A. Look for the twist in the cable. Verify that the cable connects to the drive so that the twist is in line. If the cable has a second drive connector in the center, change the cable so that no twist is between the drive and the controller. Turn on the PC and try to boot from drive A again. Describe what happens. After you finish, turn off the computer and restore the cable to its original position.

3. Reverse the orientation of the floppy drive cable connection to the floppy drive controller so that the edge connector does not align with pin 1. Boot the PC. Describe the problem as a user would describe it. Turn off the computer and restore the cable to the correct orientation.

4. In a lab setting, practice installing a floppy drive in a PC by working with a partner. Turn off the computer, remove a floppy drive from your PC, and replace it with the floppy drive from your partner's PC.

PROJECT 7-2: How Large Is a Cluster?

Remember that each entry in a FAT tracks the use of one cluster. The number of sectors per cluster varies from one file system to another. The Chkdsk command displays the size of one cluster. Another way to determine the size of a cluster with a simple test is to do the following:

1. Open a command prompt window and enter the **Dir** command. How much space is available on your hard drive?

2. Using Edit or Notepad, create a text file containing only a single character.

3. Use the **Dir** command again, note how much disk space is available, and compare the two values, before and after a one-character file is written to the disk. The difference in the two values is the size of one cluster, which is the smallest amount that can be allocated to a file.

4. Verify your calculations using **Chkdsk**.

PROJECT 7-3: **Working with a Floppy Disk**

1. Use Windows Explorer to format a floppy disk.

2. Create some folders and copy several files into the folders on the disk.

3. Delete a few files and then copy a few more onto the disk.

4. If you are using Windows 9x/Me, defragment the disk using the **Defrag** command from the command line.

PROJECT 7-4: **Researching Floppy Drives on the Internet**

7

Use the Internet to answer the following questions:

▶ What is the price of internal floppy drives?

▶ What kind of connections do external floppy disk drives use? What is the price of external drives?

▶ Why do you think external drives cost more than internal drives? What are the advantages of external drives? Internal drives?

Understanding and Installing Hard Drives

This chapter introduces hard drive technology and explains how a hard drive is logically organized. To understand how a hard drive works, it is important to know its physical characteristics as well as how the OS and system BIOS communicate with the hard drive. You will also learn how to install a hard drive and what to do when you experience problems during or immediately after installation.

Hard Drive Technology

A+
CORE
1.1
1.6
1.9
1.10
4.3

Two technologies are important to understanding how hard drives work: the technology used within the hard drive to read and write data to the drive, and the technology used by the hard drive to interface with the system. You will first learn about different hard drive interfaces and then about the way the drive itself works.

NOTE

In documentation, you might see a hard drive abbreviated as HDD (hard disk drive).

Types of Hard Drive Interfaces

VIDEO

Examining
Hard Drive
Systems

The majority of hard drives interface with the motherboard by means of **EIDE** (**Enhanced IDE**), which is an interface standard that applies to other drives besides hard drives, including CD drives, Zip drives, tape drives, and so forth. See Figure 8-1. EIDE is an extension of **IDE** (**Integrated Device Electronics**, formerly **Integrated Drive Electronics**) technology.

IDE connection
on motherboard

Power cord

IDE 40-pin
data cable

Connection for
a second drive

Hard drive

Figure 8-1   A PC's hard drive subsystem

The EIDE and ATA Interface Standards

The EIDE standards that define how hard drives and other drives such as CD, DVD, tape, and Zip drives relate to a system are part of the ATA standards. These ATA storage interface standards control data speeds and methods and are developed by Technical Committee T13 (*www.t13.org*) and published by ANSI (American National Standards Institute, *www.ansi.org*. They are listed in Table 8-1. The ATA standard for EIDE drives allows for up to four IDE devices on the same PC. An EIDE drive such as a CD, DVD, tape, or Zip drive must follow the **ATAPI (Advanced Technology Attachment Packet Interface)** standard in order to connect to a system using an IDE connector. As these standards developed, different drive manufacturers called them different names, which can be confusing. When selecting a drive standard, select the fastest standard your system supports. Keep in mind that the OS, system BIOS on the motherboard, and firmware on the drive must all support this standard. If one of these three does not, the other two will probably revert to a slower standard that all three can use, or the drive will not work. The most popular standard is ATA/ATAPI-6, most often called Ultra ATA/100.

 A+ EXAM TIP

The A+ Core exam expects you to be familiar with EIDE, ATA/ATAPI standards, serial ATA, and PIO, all discussed in this section.

A consortium of manufacturers called the Serial ATA International Organization (SATA-IO, see *www.sata-io.org*) and led by Intel developed the **Serial ATA (SATA)** standards. These standards use a serial data path rather than the traditional IDE parallel data path. The T13 committee is clarifying and further defining it under the latest ATA/ATAPI-7 standard, currently a work in progress. The latest SATA standard allows for external drives and is called **External SATA (eSATA).**

8

Standard (may have more than one name)	Speed	Description
ATA* IDE/ATA	Speeds range from 2.1 MB/ sec to 8.3 MB/sec	The first T13 and ANSI standard for IDE hard drives. Limited to no more than 528 MB. Supports PIO modes 0-2.
ATA-2* Fast ATA	Speeds up to 16.6 MB/sec	Broke the 528-MB barrier. Allows up to four IDE devices, defining the EIDE standard. Supports PIO modes 3-4 and DMA modes 1-2.
ATA-3*	Little speed increase	Improved version of ATA-2 and introduced SMART.
ATA/ATAPI-4*	Speeds up to 33.3 MB/sec	Defined Ultra DMA modes 0-2 and an 80-conductor cable

Table 8-1 (continued)

A+
CORE
1.1
1.6
1.9
1.10
4.3

Standard (may have more than one name)	Speed	Description
Ultra ATA, Fast ATA-2, Ultra DMA Modes 0-2, DMA/33		to improve signal integrity.
ATA/ATAPI-5* Ultra ATA/66, Ultra DMA/66	Speeds up to 66.6 MB/sec	Ultra DMA modes 3-4.
ATA/ATAPI-6* Ultra ATA/100, Ultra DMA/100	Speeds up to 100 MB/sec	Requires the 80-conductor cable. Defined Ultra DMA mode 5, and supports drives larger than 137 GB.
ATA/ATAPI-7* Ultra ATA/133, Serial ATA (SATA), SAS STP	Speeds up to 133 MB/sec	Can use the 80-conductor cable or Serial ATA cable. Defines Ultra DMA mode 6, Serial ATA (SATA), and Serial Attached SCSI (SAS) coexisting with SATA.

* Name assigned by the T13 Committee

Table 8-1 Summary of ATA interface standards for storage devices

DMA or PIO Transfer Modes A hard drive uses one of two methods to transfer data between the hard drive and memory: **DMA (direct memory access) transfer mode** or **PIO (Programmed Input/Output) transfer mode**. Recall from earlier chapters that DMA transfers data directly from the drive to memory without involving the CPU. PIO mode involves the CPU and is slower than DMA. There are several modes for PIO and DMA as both standards have evolved: five PIO modes, from the slowest (PIO mode 0) to the fastest (PIO mode 4), and seven DMA modes from the slowest (DMA mode 0) to the fastest (DMA mode 6).

Most often, when installing a drive, startup BIOS autodetects the drive and selects the fastest mode that the drive and the BIOS support. After installation, verify that CMOS setup recognized the drive correctly.

IDE Cabling Methods Drives currently use two cabling methods: an 80-conductor IDE cable required by ATA/100 and above—called **parallel ATA (PATA)**—or a serial ATA cable. An older 40-conductor cable has 40 wires and 40 pins. The **80-conductor IDE cable** has 40 additional ground wires that reduce crosstalk on the cable. Figure 8-2 shows a comparison between the two parallel cables. The connectors on each cable look the same, and you can use an 80-conductor cable in place of a 40-conductor cable in a system.

A+
CORE
1.1
1.6
1.9
1.10
4.3

40-conductor cable

80-conductor cable

Figure 8-2   In comparing the 80-conductor cable to the 40-conductor cable, note they are about the same width, but the 80-conductor cable has many more and finer wires. Also note the red line down the left side of each cable that indicates Pin 1.

A **serial ATA cable** is much narrower and has fewer pins than a parallel IDE cable (see Figure 8-3). Serial ATA is faster than parallel ATA/100, but is currently more expensive because it is a relatively new technology. Serial ATA cabling has been introduced into the industry not so much to handle the speeds of current drives, but to position the industry for the high-performance large drives expected to soon be inexpensive enough to fit into the desktop hard drive market.

Serial ATA cable

Power cord

Figure 8-3   A hard drive subsystem using the new serial ATA data cable

The IDE controller must use the same type of connector and cabling method as the drive, although you can purchase an adapter to convert an 80-conductor IDE connection on a hard drive to a serial ATA connection. Also, if you want to install an IDE hard drive that uses a newer standard than your motherboard supports, you can install an IDE controller card to support the drive and disable the IDE controller on your motherboard. Some high-end motherboards have both 40-pin IDE connectors

A+
CORE
1.1
1.6
1.9
1.10
4.3

and serial ATA connectors on the same board (see Figure 8-4). (In the figure, the RAID connectors are a third type of IDE connectors that are discussed in Chapter 11).

Two serial
ATA connectors

Two RAID
connectors

Two regular
IDE connectors

Figure 8-4   This motherboard has a variety of IDE drive connectors

Independent Device Timing   As Table 8-1 demonstrates, there are several hard drive standards, each running at different speeds. If two hard drives share the same IDE cable but use different standards, both drives will run at the speed of the slower drive unless the motherboard chip set controlling the IDE connections supports a feature called Independent Device Timing. Most chip sets today support this feature and the two drives can run at different speeds as long as the motherboard supports these speeds.

Drives Larger Than 137GB   Using ATA/100 and earlier standards, system BIOS and the OS address data on a hard drive using 28 bits for the address, making the largest addressable space on a hard drive 137 GB. The newer ATA/ATAPI-6, also called the ATA/133 standard, allows 48 bits for the address, increasing the addressable space on a hard drive up to 144 petabytes (144,000,000,000,000,000 bytes). For your system to support drives larger than 137 GB, the OS, the system BIOS, the IDE controller, and the hard drive must all support the standard. Before investing in a drive larger than 137 GB, verify that your system BIOS, the OS, and the IDE controller support it. If your motherboard does not support these drives, first check with

A+
CORE
1.1
1.6
1.9
1.10
4.3

the BIOS manufacturer for a possible update and flash BIOS. If an updated BIOS is not available, you can purchase an IDE controller that has compliant BIOS on the card. Windows 9x does not support drives larger than 137 GB unless third-party software provided by the hard drive manufacturer is used. Windows 2000/XP support drives larger than 137 GB if service packs are applied.

NOTE

> When making purchasing decisions, a technician needs to match the HDD technologies to the OS, the motherboard BIOS, and the IDE controller of a system. In most cases, when installing a drive, a PC technician does not need to know which IDE standard a hard drive supports, because startup BIOS uses autodetection. With **autodetection**, the BIOS detects the new drive and automatically selects the correct drive capacity and configuration, including the best possible standard supported by both the hard drive and the motherboard. One exception is when you install a new drive that startup BIOS does not recognize, or it detects the drive and reports in CMOS setup that the drive has a smaller capacity than it actually does. In this situation, your older BIOS or IDE controller card does not support the newer IDE standard the drive is using. The solution is to flash BIOS, replace the controller card, or replace the motherboard.

8

Configuring EIDE Drives in a System   Following the EIDE standard, a motherboard can support up to four EIDE devices using parallel ATA cabling. The motherboard offers two IDE connectors, or channels, a primary and secondary channel (see Figure 8-5). Each channel can accommodate an IDE data cable. The cable has two connectors on it: one connector in the middle of the cable and one at the far end for two EIDE devices. An EIDE device can be a hard drive, DVD drive, CD-ROM drive, Zip drive, or other type of drive. One device is configured to act as the master controlling the channel, and the other device on the channel is the slave. There are, therefore, four possible configurations for four IDE devices in a system:

- Primary IDE channel, master device
- Primary IDE channel, slave device
- Secondary IDE channel, master device
- Secondary IDE channel, slave device

These designations are made either by setting jumpers or DIP switches on the devices or by using a special cable-select data cable. Sometimes an IDE 80-conductor cable connector is color-coded as a blue connector for the primary IDE channel, and the motherboards might also be color-coded so that the primary channel connector is blue. This color-coding is intended to ensure that the ATA/66/100/133 hard drive is installed on the primary IDE channel.

A+
CORE
1.1
1.6
1.9
1.10
4.3

Figure 8-5 A motherboard has two IDE channels; each can support a master and slave drive using a single IDE cable

---

A+ EXAM TIP

The A+ Core exam expects you to know how to configure IDE devices in a system.

If a motherboard supports serial ATA, most likely it has two serial ATA connectors. A serial ATA cable can only accommodate a single drive. When installing serial ATA drives using Windows 2000/XP, you can install up to six IDE devices in the system, including up to four parallel ATA devices and up to two serial ATA devices. Using Windows 9x or Windows NT, you can install up to four devices using a combination of parallel ATA and serial ATA devices. You can have up to four parallel ATA devices and up to two serial ATA devices as long as the total number of devices in the Windows 9x or Windows NT system does not exceed four. You will see an example of a parallel ATA installation later in the chapter and an example of a serial ATA installation in Chapter 23.

When installing a hard drive on the same channel with an ATAPI drive such as a CD-ROM drive, always make the hard drive the master and the ATAPI drive the slave. An even better solution is to install the hard drive on the primary channel and the CD drive and any other drive on the secondary channel.

An IDE drive usually connects to the motherboard by way of a data cable from the drive to an IDE connection directly on the motherboard. However, you can use an IDE controller card to provide the two IDE connectors because (1) the motherboard IDE connectors are not functioning, or (2) the motherboard does not support an IDE standard you want to implement (such as a large-capacity drive).

Other Interface Standards

Other than EIDE, the second most popular interface for hard drives as well as other drives is SCSI (small computer system interface), which is discussed in Chapter 22. Some other technologies used by hard drives are USB, IEEE 1394, and Fibre Channel, which can all be used by external hard drives. In addition, external hard drives can use External SATA when shielded serial ATA cables and connectors are used.

USB USB (universal serial bus) is a popular way to connect many external peripheral devices to a system. The first USB standard, USB 1.0, is not fast enough to be used for a hard drive, but the latest standards, USB 1.1 and USB 2.0 (Hi-Speed USB) are fast enough. Most computers today have two or more USB ports, making USB an easy way to add a second external hard drive to a system. For example, Maxtor (*www.maxtor.com*) has a 120-GB external drive for under $200 that works with a USB 2.0 or USB 1.1 interface. Windows 98SE, Windows Me, and Windows 2000/XP support USB 1.1, and Windows XP supports USB 2.0 with a service pack applied. Before buying a USB hard drive, verify your OS and the motherboard USB connection support the same USB standard as the drive. Chapter 10 includes more information about USB.

IEEE 1394 IEEE 1394, also known as FireWire (named by Apple Computers) and i.Link (named by Sony Corporation), uses serial transmission of data and is popular for multimedia and home entertainment applications. For example, Maxtor, Inc. (*www.maxtor.com*), a large hard drive manufacturer, makes a hard drive designed for home entertainment electronics that uses 1394 for the external hard drive interface (see Figure 8-6).

Figure 8-6   Maxtor OneTouch 200 GB FireWire/USB external hard drive

A 1394 device connects to a PC through a 1394 external port or internal connector provided either directly on the motherboard or by way of a 1394 expansion card. Motherboard manufacturers have been slow to support 1394; most favor support for USB instead. Generally, IDE is the slowest, SCSI is midrange, and USB2 and 1394 are the fastest, with some overlaps in their speeds. For a system to use 1394, the operating system must support it. Windows 98, Windows 2000, and Windows XP support 1394, but Windows 95 and Windows NT do not. Chapter 10 includes more information about 1394.

Fibre Channel   Fibre Channel is another type of interface that can support hard drives. Fibre Channel is designed for use in high-end systems that have multiple hard drives. To be precise, Fibre Channel is a type of SCSI technology, but in the industry, it is considered a rival of SCSI for high-end server solutions. As many as 126 devices can be connected to a single Fibre Channel bus, as compared to 16 SCSI devices, including the host adapter. Fibre Channel is faster than SCSI when more than five hard drives are strung together to provide massive secondary storage, but it is too expensive and has too much overhead to be a good solution for the average desktop PC or workstation.

How Hard Drives Work

VIDEO

Inside a Hard
Drive

Hard drives have one, two, or more platters that stack together and spin in unison. Read/write heads are controlled by an actuator and move in unison across the disk surfaces as the disks rotate on a spindle (see Figure 8-7). PCs can use several types of hard drives, all having a magnetic medium on the platters.

Spindle

Platters or disks

Read/write
head

Actuator

Figure 8-7   Inside a hard drive case

Figure 8-8 shows a hard drive with four platters. All eight sides of these four platters are used to store data, although on some hard drives the top side of the first platter just holds information used to track data and manage the disk. Each side, or surface, of one hard drive platter is called a **head**. (Don't confuse this with the read/write mechanism that moves across a platter, which is called a read/write head.) The drive in Figure 8-8 has eight heads. Each head is divided into tracks and sectors. The eight tracks shown in Figure 8-8, all of which are the same distance from the center of the platters, together make up one cylinder. If a disk has 300 tracks per head, it also has the same number of cylinders. As with floppy disks, data is written to a hard drive beginning at the outermost track. The entire first cylinder is filled before the read/write heads move inward and begin filling the second cylinder.

Eight tracks (one
on each head)
make one cylinder

Actuator shaft

Voice coil

Magnet

Magnet housing

8

Figure 8-8   A hard drive with four platters

The drive fits into a bay inside the computer case where it is securely attached with supports or braces and screws. This helps prevent the drive from being jarred while the disk is spinning and the heads are very close to the disk surface.

A hard drive requires a controller board filled with ROM programming to instruct the read/write heads how, where, and when to move across the platters and write and read data. For today's hard drives, the **hard drive controller** mounts on a circuit board on or inside the drive housing and is an integral part of it. The controller and drive are permanently attached to one another. Don't confuse this controller with the IDE controller, which is part of the motherboard chip set and controls the IDE connection on the motherboard.

Tracks and Sectors on the Drive

Before learning how data is written to a hard drive, let's look at how track and sector markings are written to the drive. Older drives used a straightforward method of writing the tracks and sectors on the drive. They had either 17 or 26 sectors per track over the entire drive platter (see Figure 8-9). The larger tracks near the outside of the platter contained the same number of bytes as the smaller tracks near the center of the platter. This arrangement makes formatting a drive and later accessing data simpler but wastes drive space. The centermost track determines the number of bytes that a track can hold and forces all other tracks to follow this restriction.

Figure 8-9   Floppy drives and older hard drives use a constant number of sectors per track

Today's drives eliminate this restriction. The number of sectors per track on a drive is not the same throughout the platter. In this new formatting system, called **zone bit recording** (see Figure 8-10), tracks near the center have the smallest number of sectors per track, and the number of sectors increases as the tracks grow larger. In other words, each track on an IDE drive is designed to have the optimum number of sectors appropriate to the size of the track. What makes this arrangement possible, however, is one fact that seldom changes: every sector on the drive still has 512 bytes. Without this consistency, the OS needs a much more complex interface to the data on the drive.

Figure 8-10   Zone bit recording can have more sectors per track as the tracks get larger

Because each track can have a different number of sectors, the OS cannot communicate with a drive by contacting the hard drive controller (firmware on the hard drive) and using sector and track coordinates, as it does with floppy disks and older hard drives. Newer, more sophisticated methods must be used that are discussed later in the chapter.

Low-Level Formatting

Recall from Chapter 7 that when the OS formats a floppy disk, it writes sector and track markings on the disk. With IDE drives, because the track and sector markings no longer follow a simple pattern, they are written on the hard drive at the factory. This process is called **low-level formatting**. The OS still executes the remainder of the format process (creating a boot sector, file system, and root directory), which is called **high-level formatting** or **operating system formatting.**

With older drives, the system BIOS, OS, or utility software such as Norton Utilities or SpinRite could perform the low-level format; even now a low-level format routine is still part of standard system BIOS. For current drives, however, using system BIOS or standard utility software to do a low-level format would be a catastrophe. Formatting a drive in this way could permanently destroy the drive, unless the drive controller (firmware on the hard drive) were smart enough to ignore the command.

Because IDE drives are low-level formatted by the manufacturer, they are not low-level formatted as part of preventive maintenance, as older drives were. The track and sector markings on the drive created at the factory are normally expected to last for the life of the drive. For this reason, today's drives are considered more disposable than yesterday's drives. When track and sector markings fade, as they eventually do, and the drive gives many "Bad Sector or Sector Not Found" errors or becomes unusable, you just throw the drive away and buy a new one!

NOTE

As computer parts become less expensive and labor becomes more expensive, the trend to replace rather than fix is becoming the acceptable best practice in the PC industry.

On the other hand, options for low-level formatting a drive are becoming more commonplace. Some better-known drive manufacturers offer a low-level format program specific to their drives. If a drive continues to give errors or even totally fails, ask the manufacturer for a program to perform a low-level format of the drive. Sometimes the manufacturer only distributes these programs to dealers, resellers, or certified service centers.

APPLYING CONCEPTS

When purchasing a hard drive, consider the following factors that affect performance, use, and price:

- *The capacity of the drive.* Today's hard drives for desktop systems are in the range of 20 GB to more than 400 GB. The more gigabytes, the higher the price.
- *The spindle speed.* Hard drives for desktop systems run at 5400 RPM or 7200 RPM. 7200 RPM drives are faster, make more noise, put off more heat, and are more expensive than 5400 RPM drives.
- *The technology standard.* Most likely the hard drive standard to select is Ultra ATA/100 or Serial ATA, although you might choose SCSI or 1394. Be sure your motherboard supports the standard you choose.
- *The cache or buffer size.* Look for a 2 MB to 8 MB cache (also called a buffer). The more the better, though the cost goes up as the size increases.

- *The average seek time (time to fetch data).* Look for 12.5 to 8.5 ms (milliseconds). The lower the number, the higher the drive performance and cost.

When selecting a drive, match the drive to what your motherboard supports. Check the motherboard documentation or the CMOS setup screen for options. For example, the CMOS setup screens for one motherboard give these options:

- LBA Mode can be enabled or disabled
- Multi-sector transfers (block mode) can be set to Disabled, 2, 4, 8, or 16 sectors
- PIO Mode can be set to Auto, 0, 1, 2, 3, or 4
- Ultra DMA Mode can be set to Disabled, 0, 1, 2, 3, 4, or 5
- Cable detected displays the type of cable (40-conductor or 80-conductor)

Remember, when you install the drive you won't have to set these values, as autodetection should do that for you. However, reading about the values allows you to know what the board supports and what drive you can purchase.

Then select a drive that is appropriate for the price range and intended use of your system. For example, Seagate has two lines of IDE hard drives: the Barracuda is less expensive and intended for the desktop market, and the Cheetah is more expensive and targets the server market. When purchasing a drive, you can compare price and features by searching the Web sites of the drive manufacturers. Some are listed in Table 8-2. The same manufacturers usually produce IDE drives and SCSI drives.

Manufacturer	Web Site
Fujitsu America, Inc.	*www.fujitsu.com*
IBM PC Company	*www.ibm.com*
Maxell Corporation	*www.maxell.com*
Maxtor Corporation	*www.maxtor.com*
Quantum Corporation	*www.quantum.com*
Seagate Technology	*www.seagate.com*
Western Digital	*www.wdc.com*

Table 8-2   Hard drive manufacturers

Some BIOSs support a method of data transfer that allows multiple data transfers each time software requests data. This method is called **block mode** and should be used if your hard drive and BIOS support it. However, if you are having problems with hard drive errors, you can try disabling block mode. Use CMOS setup to make the change.

It's risky to low-level format a drive using a format program other than one provided by the manufacturer, although some have tried and succeeded. Probably more drives have been permanently destroyed than saved by taking this risk. Drives last several years without a refresher low-level format. By that time, you're probably ready to upgrade to a larger drive anyway.

Communicating with the Hard Drive Controller

8

Now that you have learned about physical characteristics of a hard drive, let's look at how the OS and system BIOS communicate with the hard drive controller (firmware on the HDD), before moving to logical organization of hard drives. Recall from earlier in the chapter that the number of sectors per track varies from one track to another. Therefore, the OS and system BIOS cannot count on using actual hard drive cylinder, head, and sector coordinates when requesting data through the hard drive controller (which is how requests were made with early hard drives; see Figure 8-11). Instead, sophisticated methods have been developed so that system BIOS and the OS can communicate with the hard drive controller, but only the hard drive controller deals with physically locating the data on the drive.

Figure 8-11   With older hard drives, cylinder, track, and sector information was communicated at each level

Calculating Drive Capacity on Older Drives

When hard drives were smaller and used a constant number of sectors per track, measuring drive capacity was straightforward. All sectors in a track held 512 bytes regardless of the track's radius. If you knew the number of tracks, heads, and sectors per track, you could calculate the storage capacity of a drive, because all tracks had the same number of sectors. Software and operating systems were written to interface with system BIOS, which managed a hard drive by assuming that for each hard drive there was a fixed relationship among the number of sectors, tracks, heads, and cylinders.

If you know how many heads, cylinders (tracks), and sectors a drive has, you can calculate the capacity of the drive. This information is usually written on the top of the drive housing. For example, the drive capacity for an older drive that has 855 cylinders, 7 heads, and 17 sectors/track is calculated as 855 cylinders × 7 heads × 17 sectors/track × 512 bytes/sector, which gives 52,093,440 bytes. Divide this value by 1,024 to convert to KB and then divide by 1,024 again to convert to MB, yielding a drive capacity of 49.68 MB.

NOTE When installing a hard drive, it was once necessary to tell CMOS setup the drive capacity by telling it how many heads, cylinders, and sectors the drive had. Today, most startup BIOS offers autodetection, so the BIOS detects the new drive and automatically selects the correct drive capacity and configuration.

Hard Drive Size Limitations

As hard drives have increased in size, other hardware and the OS file system have presented barriers to using the larger drives. File system barriers are discussed later in the chapter and are summarized here:

- For DOS and Windows 9x, the largest volume (logical drive) that FAT16 supports is 2.1 GB. FAT16 cannot be used on hard drives (including all volumes) that exceed 8.4 GB.
- For Windows NT/2000/XP, the largest volume that FAT16 supports is 4 GB.
- Windows 2000/XP does not support a FAT32 volume larger than 32 GB.
- Windows 9x FAT32 does not support hard drives larger than 137 GB.
- Windows 2000 supports hard drives larger than 137 GB if Service Pack 3 or higher is applied, and Windows XP supports these drives if Service Pack 1 or higher is applied.

This section addresses the hard drive size barriers caused by hardware or by hardware interacting with the BIOS or the OS. The barriers discussed in this section occur at 508 MB, 8.4 GB, 33.8 GB, and 137 GB.

As hard drive size and technology improved, it was important for the industry to retain backward-compatibility so that legacy operating systems and other software could work with newer hard drives. As is common in the evolution of computers, clever methods were devised to "trick" older technology into working in newer environments. The older, legacy technology (in this case, software) still sees its world as unchanged because the newer technology (in this case, system BIOS) shelters it from the new methodology. The older technology was deceived at several stages of communication in the following ways.

The first two methods are considered legacy methods and are seldom seen today:

- *CHS mode or normal mode used for drives less than 528 MB.* The hard drive can use a complex cylinder, head, and sector organization that only the hard drive controller knows. However, the controller communicates to system BIOS in terms of the older methodology. When this method is used, the actual organization of the hard drive is called the **physical geometry** of the drive, and the organization communicated to system BIOS is called the **logical geometry** of the drive. This method is called **CHS (cylinder, head, sector) mode**, or **normal mode.** Using CHS mode, a drive can have no more than 1,024 cylinders, 16 heads, 63 sectors per track, and 512 bytes per sector. Therefore, the maximum amount of storage on a hard drive using CHS mode is 528 MB or 504 MB, depending on how the calculations are done (1K = 1,000 or 1K = 1,024).

- *Large mode or ECHS mode used for drives between 504 MB and 8.4 GB.* The hard drive controller sends the logical geometry to system BIOS, but system BIOS communicates a different set of parameters to the OS and other software. This method is called **translation**, and system BIOS is said to be in **large mode**, or **ECHS (extended CHS) mode.** Large mode is not as popular as LBA mode.

- *LBA mode used for drives larger than 504 MB.* The hard drive controller and system BIOS communicate using a method entirely different from cylinder, head, and sector information. System BIOS sends cylinder, head, and sector information to the software, which uses neither logical nor physical geometry. This method of translation is called **LBA (logical block addressing) mode.** System BIOS simply views the drive as a long list of sequential numbers (0, 1, 2, 3, ...) called LBAs or addressable sectors. LBA mode is the most popular way of dealing with drives larger than 504 MB and is the only way of dealing with drives larger than 8.4 GB. Drives larger than 504 MB are called **large-capacity drives**, and the motherboard BIOS that support them is called **enhanced BIOS.**

- *33.8 GB limitation.* The system BIOS on some systems does not recognize a drive larger than 33.8 GB, which can cause the system to lock up during POST, or to boot, but incorrectly report the size of the drive. To deal with the problem, some drives include a jumper setting that tells BIOS at startup that the drive is only 32 GB. Then third-party software is used to access the full capacity of the drive.

- *137 GB limitation.* The system BIOS on some systems does not support the ATA/ATAPI-6 standard, which makes it unable to recognize drives larger than 137 GB.

- *Device drivers.* When reading and writing to the drive, the OS and software can bypass the system BIOS altogether and communicate directly with the hard drive controller by using device drivers. Windows NT/2000/XP uses this method. True to its compromising nature, Windows 9x has its own 32-bit, protected-mode device drivers to access hard drives, bypassing system BIOS. However, to support DOS and other older software, Windows 9x also supports using system BIOS to access drives. However, regardless of the way data is read

8

or written to the drive, the motherboard BIOS must at least recognize the capacity of the drive at startup and record settings correctly in CMOS setup.

To use the operating system to report the capacity of a hard drive, at a command prompt, enter the command Chkdsk. For Windows 9x and Windows NT/2000/XP, using Windows Explorer, right-click the drive letter and select Properties on the shortcut menu. Report the capacity of each logical drive on the hard drive, and then add them together to get the entire hard drive capacity, assuming all space on the hard drive is partitioned and formatted. For Windows 9x, use Fdisk, and for Windows 2000/XP, use Disk Management to report the capacity of an entire hard drive regardless of whether the drive is fully partitioned and formatted.

NOTE

Don't confuse hard drive capacity with the capacity of a logical drive or volume. For example, when using large mode, a hard drive can be up to 8.4 GB, but each logical drive (for example, drive C) on the hard drive using the FAT16 file system can only be 2 GB or 4 GB, depending on the OS used. Therefore, if you are using FAT16 on a large-capacity hard drive, you are forced to use more than one logical drive (drives C, D, and E) on a single hard drive. However, if you use FAT32, your logical volume can be the size of the entire hard drive.

A+
CORE
1.2
1.10

APPLYING CONCEPTS

Installations Using Legacy BIOS

Before installing a new hard drive, know the hard drive standards the BIOS on your motherboard supports. If you want to install a drive in a system whose BIOS does not support it, you have the following choices:

- Let the BIOS see the drive as a smaller drive.
- Upgrade the BIOS.
- Upgrade the entire motherboard.
- Use software that interfaces between the older BIOS and the newer drive.
- Use an adapter card that provides the BIOS to substitute for motherboard BIOS.

This first option may or may not work, depending on your BIOS. Some BIOSs that do not support new drives simply see the larger hard drive as a smaller drive they can support. In this case, the BIOS assigns a drive capacity smaller than the actual capacity. You can use this method, although it wastes drive space. With other BIOSs, the system refuses to boot when it sees a drive it does not support.

Most drive manufacturers provide software that performs the translation between an older BIOS and the newer drive. Examples of such translation or disk overlay software are Disk Manager by Ontrack Data International, Inc. (*www.ontrack.com*), SpeedStor by Storage Dimensions, EZ-Drive by Phoenix (*www.phoenix.com*), and DiscWizard (*www.seagate.com*). You can find the software on a floppy disk with the drive or download it from the drive manufacturer's Web site. Boot from a floppy disk with the software installed, and follow directions on the screen. A small partition or logical drive is created on the hard drive to manage the drive for the older BIOS. It's important to keep this disk in a safe place, in case you need it to access the hard drive because the software on the drive has become corrupted. A disadvantage of using this method is that if you boot from a regular bootable floppy disk, you might not be able to access the hard drive.

Some hard drives come with disk manager software already installed. For example, for some drives manufactured by Maxtor, the disk manager software is found in a directory called \MAX in a 112-MB partition that BIOS recognizes as drive C. The rest of the drive is assigned to other partitions or logical drives, such as drive D or drive E.

Adapter cards are available to provide the BIOS that substitutes for motherboard BIOS. This is the recommended method if your motherboard does not have an upgrade BIOS. One manufacturer of these cards is Promise Technology (*www.promise.com*).

The best solution is to upgrade BIOS. However, remember that the new BIOS must also relate correctly to the chip set on the motherboard. Follow the recommendations of the motherboard manufacturer when selecting a BIOS upgrade.

8

How a Hard Drive is Logically Organized to Hold Data

This section covers how a file system works and how to install one on a hard drive. The goal of this section is to help you understand what must be written on a hard drive so that you can boot from it and get to a command prompt such as C:\> using the hard drive. For this to happen, the drive must have track and sector markings written on the drive, a file system must be installed, and files needed to boot the PC must be copied to the root directory of the drive. Recall that today's hard drives come from the factory already low-level formatted (that is, with track and sector markings already in place). After one of these drives is physically installed and system BIOS has recognized the drive and determined the drive capacity, the next step is to install a file system on the drive. For current Windows operating systems, there are three choices of file systems, FAT16, FAT32, and NTFS. All Windows operating systems support FAT16. Windows 95 Second Edition, Windows 98, Windows 2000, and Windows XP support FAT32. Windows NT, Windows 2000, and Windows XP support NTFS. The NTFS file system is best installed during the Windows setup process or after Windows is installed, so this chapter does not cover it. You can install the FAT16 or FAT32 file system from a command prompt after booting from a startup disk.

Recall from Chapter 3 that for either file system, the high-level divisions are called partitions, and within the partitions, the drive is further divided into logical drives or volumes. Logical drives have letters assigned to them, such as drive C or drive D, and each logical drive has its own file system, such as FAT32 or NTFS, to manage files on the logical drive. This section discusses how partitions and logical drives are

A+
CORE
1.1

organized and used by the OS, and how to use OS commands to partition and format a hard drive for first use.

After physical installation, preparing a hard drive to hold files requires the following three steps:

1. *Low-level format.* This physically formats the hard drive and creates the tracks and sectors. For hard drives today, this has already been done by the time you buy the drive and does not involve an OS.

2. *Partitioning the hard drive.* Even if only one partition is used, this step is still required. The DOS and Windows 9x Fdisk program or the Windows 2000/XP Disk Management utility sets up a partition table at the beginning of the hard drive. This table lists the number of partitions on the drive, their locations, and which partition is the active partition (the partition used to boot). Within each partition, Fdisk or Disk Management creates logical drives, assigning letters to these drives. When using Windows 2000/XP, you can also use the Windows 2000/XP Recovery Console command Diskpart to partition the drive and create logical drives within these partitions. In Windows XP, the Diskpart command is available at a command prompt as well.

3. *High-level format.* This process builds a file system for each logical drive. The OS must do this for each logical drive on the hard drive. As each logical drive is formatted, the OS creates an OS boot record, a root directory, and two copies of FAT for the logical drive, just as it does for a floppy disk. High-level formatting is done using the Format command or, in Windows 2000/XP, using Disk Management.

Hard Drive Partitions and Logical Drives

A+
OS
1.4

Although you might have a 28-GB hard drive that is only a single physical drive, an OS can divide this single physical drive into more than one logical drive. (A logical drive is sometimes called a logical partition; don't let the two uses of the term *partition* confuse you; partitions and logical partitions are divisions at different levels.) Figure 8-12 shows a typical example with the hard drive divided into two partitions. The first partition contains one logical drive (drive C), and the second partition is divided into two logical drives (D and E). The partition table at the very beginning of the drive records all these divisions. The partition table is in the first sector of the hard drive on head 0, track 0, sector 1. This sector is called the master boot sector or the Master Boot Record (MBR). Table 8-3 lists the contents of a partition table. Don't confuse this first physical sector of the hard drive with sector 1 as Windows knows it. The OS's sector 1 comes after the physical sector 1 and is the first sector in the logical drive C.

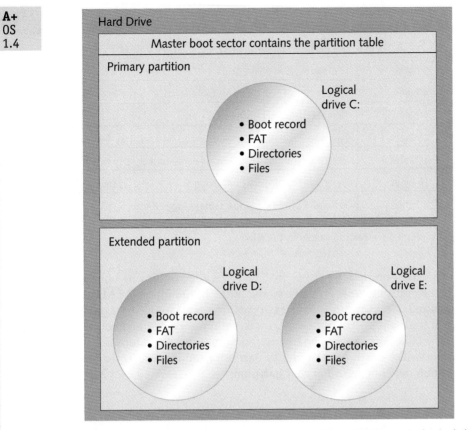

A+
OS
1.4

Figure 8-12 A hard drive is divided into one or more partitions that contain logical drives

Item	Bytes Used	Description
1	446 bytes	Program that calls the boot program on the OS boot record
2	16-byte total	Description of the first partition
	1 byte	Is this the bootable partition? (Yes = 90h, No = 00h)
	3 bytes	Beginning location of the partition
	1 byte	System indicator; possible values are:
		0 = Not a DOS partition
		1 = DOS with a 12-bit FAT
		4 = DOS with a 16-bit FAT
		5 = Not the first partition

Table 8-3 (continued)

8

A+
OS
1.4

Item	Bytes Used	Description
		6 = Partition larger than 32 MB
	3 bytes	Ending location of partition
	4 bytes	First sector of the partition table relative to the beginning of the disk
	4 bytes	Number of sectors in the partition
3	16 bytes	Describes second partition, using same format as first partition
4	16 bytes	Describes third partition, using same format as first partition
5	16 bytes	Describes fourth partition, using same format as first partition
6	2 bytes	Signature of the partition table, always AA55

Table 8-3   Hard drive partition table in the MBR

The Master Boot Record is exactly 512 bytes long, occupying one sector. During POST, the partition table program stored at the beginning of the Master Boot Record executes and checks the integrity of the partition table itself. If the partition table program finds any corruption, it refuses to continue execution, and the disk is unusable. If the table entries are valid, the partition table program looks in the table to determine which partition is the active partition, and it executes the bootstrap loader program in the boot record of that partition.

NOTE   Sometimes the Master Boot Record is the target of a **boot sector virus**, which can cause problems with the boot process and data retrieval. The Windows 2000/XP Fixmbr command or the Windows 9x Fdisk /MBR command is used to repair damage to the program in the MBR.

✔ **A+ EXAM TIP**

The A+ OS exam expects you to know the difference between these terms: active partition, primary partition, extended partition, and logical partition.

The **active partition** is the partition on the hard drive used to boot the OS. It most often contains only a single logical drive (drive C) and is usually the first partition on the drive. Windows 2000/XP calls the active partition the system partition.

Using DOS or Windows 9x, a hard drive can have one or two partitions. Using Windows NT/2000/XP, a drive can have up to four partitions. A partition can be a **primary partition** (having only one logical drive in the partition, such as drive C) or an **extended partition** (having more than one logical drive, such as drive D and drive E). There can be only one extended partition on a drive. Therefore, with DOS and Windows 9x, the drive can have one primary and one extended partition. Under Windows NT/2000/XP, the drive can have four partitions, but only one of them can be an extended partition. The active partition is always a primary partition.

Choice of File Systems

A+
OS
1.4
CORE
1.10

After the hard drive is formatted and ready for use, you are not usually aware that the several logical drives on the hard drive all belong to the same hard drive. For example, Figure 8-13 shows three drives, C, D, and E, that are logical drives on one physical hard drive. If you right-click one drive, such as drive D in the figure, and select Properties on the shortcut menu, you can see the amount of space allotted to this logical drive and how much of it is currently used. Also note in the figure that drive D is formatted using the FAT32 file system. It is possible for one logical drive to be formatted with one file system and other logical drives on the same hard drive to be formatted with a different file system such as FAT16 or NTFS.

File system of drive D

Three logical drives

Size of this logical drive

Figure 8-13   This hard drive contains three logical drives

NOTE

When partitioning a hard drive using the Windows 9x Fdisk utility, you have two choices for a file system, FAT16 or FAT32. Use FAT32 unless the same PC will also be running Windows NT, which does not support FAT32.

FAT16   DOS and all versions of Windows support the FAT16 file system that uses 16 bits for each cluster entry in the FAT. Using FAT16, the smallest cluster size is four sectors. Since each sector is 512 bytes, a cluster that contains four sectors is 2,048 bytes. A one-character file takes up 2,048 bytes of space on a hard drive. For larger drives, the number of sectors in one cluster is even more. When the drive contains many small files, with cluster size so large, these files can create a lot of wasted space called **slack**.

A+
OS
1.4
CORE
1.10

Virtual File Allocation (VFAT)   Windows 95 and Windows for Workgroups offered an improved method of hard drive access, called **VFAT**, or **virtual file allocation table**. VFAT uses 32-bit protected-mode device drivers for hard drive access. In Windows for Workgroups, VFAT is called 32-bit file access. The Windows 95 version of VFAT supports long filenames of up to 255 characters. Using VFAT, the FAT still uses 16 bits per cluster entry. VFAT has been rendered outdated by FAT32.

FAT32   Beginning with Windows 95 OSR2, Microsoft offered a FAT that contains 32 bits per FAT entry instead of the older 12-bit or 16-bit FAT entries. Only 28 bits are used to hold a cluster number; the remaining four bits are not currently used.

FAT32 is efficient for logical drives up to 16 GB. In this range, the cluster size is 8K. After that, the cluster size increases to about 16K for drives in the 16-GB to 32-GB range. You are then reaching a drive size that warrants a more powerful file management system than FAT32, such as NTFS. Windows 2000/XP only supports FAT32 for drives up to 32 GB.

NOTE If you are currently using FAT16 and are considering switching to FAT32, you can use a third-party utility such as PartitionMagic by PowerQuest Corporation (*www.powerquest.com*) to scan your hard drive and tell you how much of the drive is used for slack space. Knowing this can help you decide if the change will yield you more usable drive space.

NTFS   Windows NT/2000/XP supports **NTFS (New Technology file system)**. NTFS is designed to provide more security than does the FAT file system and uses a database called the **master file table (MFT)** to hold information about files and directories and their locations on the hard drive. Whereas the FAT file system writes the FAT and root directory at the beginning of a hard drive, NTFS writes the MFT at the end of a hard drive. Use NTFS under Windows NT/2000/XP when you have a large hard drive, you are not going to install Windows 98 on the drive as a second OS, and security is a concern.

Recall that it is best to install NTFS at the same time you install Windows NT/2000/XP from the setup CD, though you can convert a FAT file system to NTFS after Windows NT/2000/XP is installed.

How Many Logical Drives?   In addition to creating partitions on a hard drive and deciding which type of file system to use, Fdisk, Diskpart, or Disk Management is used to create logical drives within these partitions. The active or primary partition has only one logical drive C. You specify how large this logical drive is when you set the size of the active partition. The extended partition can use all or some of the remaining free space on the drive (some space can go unused). You also decide how large the extended partition is, up to the amount of available free space on the drive.

A+
OS
1.4
CORE
1.10

Within the extended partition, you can put several logical drives. You determine how many logical drives and what portion of the extended partition is allotted to each.

Some people prefer to use more than one logical drive to organize their hard drives, especially if they plan to have more than one OS on the same drive. However, the main reason you need multiple logical drives is to optimize space and access time to the drive. The larger the logical drive, the larger the cluster size, and the more slack or wasted space. When deciding how to allocate space to logical drives, the goal is to use as few logical drives as possible and still keep cluster size to a minimum.

Table 8-4 gives the information you need to determine how to slice your drive. Notice that the largest logical drive possible using DOS or Windows 9x FAT16 is 2 GB. (This limitation is rooted in the largest cluster number that can be stored in a 16-bit FAT entry.) For Windows NT/2000/XP, FAT16 logical drives can be no larger than 4 GB. However, you can see from the table that to make a drive that big, the cluster size must be huge. Also, the largest hard drive that FAT16 can support is 8.4 GB; if the drive is larger than that, you must use FAT32. The sizes for logical drives using NTFS are included to make the table complete.

8

File System	Size of Logical Drive	Sectors Per Cluster	Bytes Per Cluster
FAT16	Up to 128 MB	4	2,048
	128 to 256 MB	8	4,096
	256 to 512 MB	16	8,192
	512 MB to 1 GB	32	16,384
	1 GB to 4 GB*	64	32,768
FAT32	512 MB to 8 GB	8	4,096
	8 GB to 16 GB	16	8,192
	16 GB to 32 GB	32	16,384
	More than 32 GB**	64	32,768
NTFS	Up to 512 MB	1	512
	512 MB to 1 GB	2	1,024
	1 GB to 2 GB	4	2,048
	More than 2 GB	8	4,096

* For DOS and Windows 9x, the largest FAT16 is 2 GB. For Windows NT/2000/XP, the largest FAT16 is 4 GB.

** Windows 2000/XP does not support FAT32 for drives larger than 32 GB.

Table 8-4   Size of some logical drives compared to cluster size for FAT16, FAT32, and NTFS

When you use Fdisk, Diskpart, or Disk Management to create a logical drive, a drive letter is assigned to each logical drive. For a primary partition, drive C is

A+
OS
1.4
CORE
1.10

assigned to the one volume, and drives D, E, and so forth are assigned to volumes in the extended partition. However, if a second hard drive is installed in a system, the program takes this into account when assigning drive letters. If the second hard drive has a primary partition, the program assigns it to drive D, leaving drive letters E, F, G, H, and so forth for the volumes in the extended partitions of both hard drives. For example, in a two-hard-drive system where each hard drive has a primary partition, an extended partition, and three logical drives, the drive letters for the first hard drive are C, E, and F, and the drive letters for the second hard drive are D, G, and H.

If the second hard drive is not going to be the boot device, it does not have to have a primary partition. If you put only a single extended partition on that drive, then the program assigns the drive letters C, D, and E to the first drive and F, G, H, and so forth to the second drive.

When to Partition a Drive

There are several reasons to partition a drive:

- When you first install a new hard drive, you must partition it to prepare it for use.
- If an existing hard drive is giving errors, you can repartition the drive and reformat each logical drive to begin fresh. Repartitioning destroys all data on the drive, so back up important data first.
- If you suspect a virus has attacked the drive, you can back up critical data and repartition to begin with a clean drive.
- If you want to wipe a hard drive clean and install a new OS, you can repartition a drive in preparation for formatting it with a new file system. If you do not want to change the size or number of partitions, you do not have to repartition the drive.

When installing Windows 9x, before you use the Windows 9x CD for Windows 9x upgrades, you can boot from a bootable disk that contains the Fdisk.exe program file. Then use Fdisk to partition the hard drive, and install enough of a previous version of Windows to boot from the hard drive. During a Windows 9x installation, if the drive is not partitioned, the install procedure automatically executes Fdisk to partition the drive.

You can use Fdisk to partition a drive or you can use third-party software such as PartitionMagic. Fdisk is easy to use, but PartitionMagic offers some advantages. A major one is that when Fdisk partitions a drive, it erases all data on the existing partitions that it changes or overwrites, but PartitionMagic protects data when it changes the partitions on the drive. Also, PartitionMagic has a more user-friendly GUI interface.

Sometimes you should not use Fdisk to partition a drive, such as when the drive has been partitioned by third-party software such as Disk Manager or SpeedStor. Recall that these products use drive translation to recognize a large hard drive in a system whose system BIOS does not support large drives. To know if a large hard drive has been partitioned to do disk translation, look for entries in the Config.sys file that point to third-party software to manage the drive. Examples of these

A+
OS
1.4
CORE
1.10

command lines are Dmdrvr.bin, Sstor.sys, Harddrive.sys, and Evdisk.sys. If you find lines with these filenames, use the appropriate third-party software to repartition the drive. Know that if you boot from a floppy disk, you cannot access a hard drive that is using drive translation, unless the floppy disk contains the right drivers provided by the drive translation software. Most drive translation software provides a way to create a floppy disk to be used in emergencies when the hard drive does not boot.

NOTE

> Fdisk under Windows 98 can incorrectly display the size of hard drives larger than 64 GB. The capacity is reported as the true capacity minus 64 GB. For example, Fdisk shows a 120 GB drive to be 56 GB (120 GB – 64 GB). When using Windows 9x, for drives larger than 64 GB, check with the hard drive manufacturer for freeware that you can use to partition and format the drive. For instance, Western Digital has Data Lifeguard Tools and Maxtor has MaxBlast software.

8

Installing a Hard Drive

A+
CORE
1.2
1.6

Now that you know about hard drives, turn your attention to the step-by-step process of installing an IDE hard drive. To install an IDE hard drive, do the following:

VIDEO

Installing a
Hard Drive

1. Set jumpers or DIP switches on the drive, physically install the drive inside the computer case, and attach the power cord and data cable.

2. Inform CMOS setup of the new drive, or verify that autodetect correctly detected the drive.

3. If you are installing an OS on the drive, boot from the OS setup CD. The installation process partitions and formats the drive. Skip Steps 4 and 5.

4. If the drive is not intended to hold an OS (it's a second drive in a two-drive system, for example), use the Fdisk utility or Disk Management to create one or more partitions on the drive, and divide the extended partition (if there is one) into logical drives.

5. For a second drive in a two-drive system, use the Format command or Disk Management to high-level format each logical drive.

To install an IDE drive, you need the drive, an 80-conductor or 40-conductor data cable, and perhaps a kit to make the drive fit into a much larger bay. If the motherboard does not provide an IDE connection, you also need an adapter card.

NOTE

> You will see an example of a Serial ATA drive installation in Chapter 23, which uses a Serial ATA data cable instead of an 80-conductor or 40-conductor.

Prepare for Installation

**A+
CORE
1.2
1.6**

Remember from earlier chapters that keeping notes is a good idea whenever you install new hardware or software or make any other changes to your PC system. As with installing any other devices, before you begin installing your hard drive, make sure you know where your starting point is, and take notes so that you can backtrack later if necessary. How is your system configured? Is everything working properly? Verify which of your system's devices are working before installing a new one. Later, if a resource conflict causes a device to malfunction, the information will help you isolate the problem.

NOTE   When installing hardware and software, don't install too many things at once. If something goes wrong, you won't know what's causing the problem. Install one device, start the system, and confirm that the new device is working before installing another.

Make sure that you have a good bootable disk or Windows 9x rescue disk; test it to make sure it works. As always, just in case you lose setup information in the process, make sure you have a record of your CMOS setup on a disk or, at the least, write down any variations in setup from the default settings. Two good places to record CMOS settings are the notebook you keep about this computer and the manual for the motherboard.

Read Documentation

Before you take anything apart, carefully read all the documentation for the drive and controller card, and the part of your PC documentation that covers hard drive installation. Look for problems you have not considered, such as differing ATAPI standards. Check your motherboard documentation to verify the BIOS accommodates the size and type of hard drive you want to install. If you are not sure which IDE standards your motherboard supports, you can look for different options on the CMOS setup screens.

Plan Drive Configuration

Remember, there are two IDE connectors on a motherboard, the primary and secondary IDE channels. Each channel can support up to two drives, a master and a slave, for a total of up to four IDE drives in a system. When possible, leave the hard drive as the single drive on one channel, so that it does not compete with another drive for access to the channel and possibly slow down performance. Use the primary channel before you use the secondary channel. Put slow devices together on the same channel. For example, suppose you have a Zip drive, CD-ROM drive, and two hard drives. Because the two hard drives are faster than the Zip drive and CD-ROM drive, put the two hard drives on one channel and the Zip drive and CD-ROM drive on the other. Place the fastest devices on the primary channel and the slower devices on the secondary channel. If you have three or fewer devices, allow the fastest hard drive to be your boot device and the only device on the primary channel.

Make sure that you can visualize the entire installation. If you have any questions, find answers before you begin. Either keep reading until you locate the answer, call technical support, or ask a knowledgeable friend. You may discover that what you are installing will not work on your computer, but that is better than coping with hours of frustration and a disabled computer. You cannot always anticipate every problem, but at least you can know that you made your best effort to understand everything in advance. What you learn in thorough preparation pays off every time!

Prepare Your Work Area and Take Precautions

The next step is to prepare a large, well-lit place to work. Set out your tools, documentation, new hardware, and notebook. Remember the basic rules concerning static electricity, which you learned in Chapter 4. Ground yourself and the computer; wear a ground bracelet during the installation. Avoid working on carpet in the winter when there's a lot of static electricity.

8

Some added precautions for working with hard drives are:

- Handle the drive carefully.
- Do not touch any exposed circuitry or chips.
- Prevent other people from touching exposed microchips on the drive.
- When you first take the drive out of the static-protective package, touch the package containing the drive to a screw holding an expansion card or cover, or to a metal part of the computer case, for at least two seconds. This will drain the static electricity from the package and from your body.
- If you must set down the drive outside the static-protective package, place it component-side-up on top of the static-protective package on a flat surface.
- Do not place the drive on the computer case cover or on a metal table.

Turn off the computer and unplug it. Unplug the monitor and move it to one side. Remove the computer case cover. Check that you have an available power cord from the power supply.

NOTE

If there are not enough power cords from a power supply, you can purchase a Y connector that can add an additional power cord.

Examine the locations of the drive bays and the length of the data cables. Decide which bay will hold which drive. Bays designed for hard drives do not have access to the outside of the case, unlike bays for Zip drives and other drives in which disks are inserted. Also, some bays are wider than others to accommodate wide drives such as CD-ROM drives and DVD drives (see Figure 8-14). Will the data cable reach the drives and the motherboard connector? If not, rearrange your plan for locating the drives in the bays, or purchase a custom-length data cable.

**A+
CORE
1.2
1.6**

Motherboard

Stationary wide bay

Removable narrow bay

One interior slot
for a hard drive

Figure 8-14   Plan for the location of drives within bays

Set Jumpers

You normally configure a hard drive by setting jumpers on the drive housing. Often, diagrams of the jumper settings are printed on the top of the hard drive housing (see Figure 8-15). If they are not, see the documentation or visit the Web site of the drive manufacturer. (One hands-on project lets you practice this.) Figure 8-16 shows a typical jumper arrangement. Table 8-5 lists the four choices for jumper settings for this drive. Note that your hard drive might not have the first configuration as an option, but it should have a way of indicating if the drive will be the master device. The factory default setting is usually correct for the drive to be the single drive on a system. Before you change any settings, write down the original ones. If things go wrong, you can revert to the original settings and begin again. If a drive is the only drive on a channel, set it to single. For two drives on a controller, set one to master and the other to slave.

A+
CORE
1.2
1.6

Diagrams of jumper settings

8

Figure 8-15   An IDE drive most likely will have diagrams of jumper settings for master and slave options printed on the drive housing

JB

5 3 1

Single drive configuration

6 4 2

5 3 1

Master drive configuration (dual drives)

6 4 2

5 3 1

Slave drive configuration (dual drives)

6 4 2

Key:

■ Jumper added

▪ Jumper pins

Figure 8-16   Jumper settings on a hard drive and their meanings

A+
CORE
1.2
1.6

Configuration	Description
Single-drive configuration	This is the only hard drive on this IDE channel. (This is the standard setting.)
Master-drive configuration	This is the first of two drives; it most likely is the boot device.
Slave-drive configuration	This is the second drive using this channel or data cable.
Cable-select configuration	The cable-select data cable determines which of the two drives is the master and which is the slave.

Table 8-5   Jumper settings on an IDE hard drive

Some hard drives have a cable-select configuration option. If you choose this configuration, you must use a cable-select data cable. When you use one of these cables, the drive nearest the motherboard is the master, and the drive farthest from the motherboard is the slave. You can recognize a cable-select cable by a small hole somewhere in the data cable.

Mount the Drive in the Bay

Next, look at the drive bay that you will use for the drive. The bay can be stationary or removable. With a removable bay, you first remove the bay from the computer case and mount the drive in the bay. Then you put the bay back into the computer case. In Figure 8-14, you can see a stationary bay for large drives and a removable bay for small drives, including the hard drive. In this example, you will see how the hard drive is installed in a computer case that has three other drives: a DVD drive, a Zip drive, and a floppy drive. Do the following to install the hard drive in the bay:

1. Remove the bay for the hard drive, and insert the hard drive in the bay. You can line up the drive in the bay with the front of the computer case (see Figure 8-17) to see how drives will line up in the bay. Put the hard drive in the bay flush with the front of the bay so it will butt up against the computer case once the bay is in position (see Figure 8-18). Line up other drives in the bay so they are flush with the front of the computer case. In our example, a floppy drive and Zip drive are already in the bay.

2. You must be able to securely mount the drive in the bay; the drive should not move when it is screwed down. Line up the drive and bay screw holes, and make sure everything will fit. After checking the position of the drive and determining how screws are placed, install four screws (two on each side) to mount the drive in the bay.

Do not allow torque to stress the drive. For example, don't force a drive into a space that is too small for it. Also, placing two screws in diagonal positions across the drive can place pressure diagonally on the drive.

**A+
CORE
1.2
1.6**

3. Decide whether to connect the data cable to the drive before or after you insert the bay inside the computer case, depending on how accessible the connections are. In this example, the data cables are connected to the drives first and then the bay is installed inside the computer case. In the photograph in Figure 8-19, the data cables for all the drives in the bay are connected to the drives.

4. The next step is to place the bay back into position and secure the bay with the bay screw or screws (see Figure 8-20).

5. Install a power connection to each drive (Figure 8-21). In Figure 8-21, the floppy drive uses the small power connection, and the other drives use the large ones. It doesn't matter which of the power cords you use, because they all produce the same voltage. Also, the cord only goes into the connection one way.

6. Next, connect the data cable to the IDE connector on the motherboard (see Figure 8-22). Make certain pin 1 and the edge color on the cable align correctly at both ends of the cable. Normally, pin 1 is closest to the power connection.

7. If you are mounting a hard drive in an external bay, install a bay cover in the front of the case. Internal bays do not need this cover (see Figure 8-23).

8. When using a motherboard connection, if the wire connecting the motherboard to the hard drive light on the front of the case was not connected when the motherboard was installed, connect it now. If you reverse the polarity of the LED wire, the light will not work. Your motherboard manual should tell you the location of the LED wires on the motherboard.

8

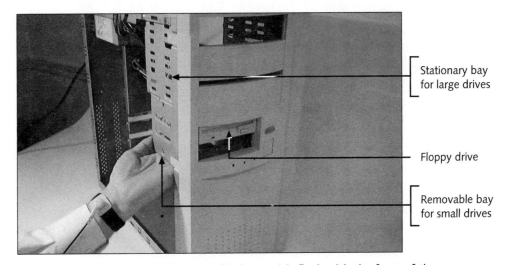

Stationary bay
for large drives

Floppy drive

Removable bay
for small drives

Figure 8-17   Line up the floppy drive in the removable bay so it's flush with the front of the case

A+
CORE
1.2
1.6

Floppy drive

Zip drive

Hard drive

Figure 8-18   Position the hard drive flush with the end of the bay

Connected to Zip drive

Twist in cable for drive A

Hard drive cable

For DVD drive

Figure 8-19   Connect the cables to all three drives

A+
CORE
1.2
1.6

Figure 8-20   Secure the bay with the bay screw

Be sure the screws are not too long. If they are, you can screw too far into the drive housing and damage the drive itself.

CAUTION

If the drive light does not work after you install a new drive, try reversing the LED wire on the motherboard pins.

NOTE

A+
CORE
1.2
1.6

Figure 8-21 Connect a power cord to each drive

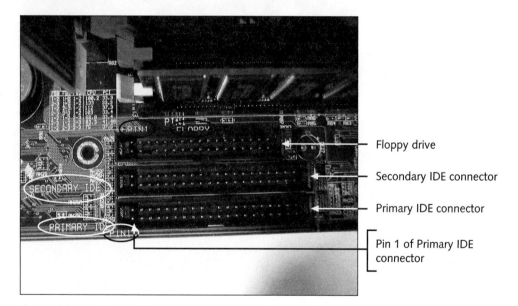

Floppy drive

Secondary IDE connector

Primary IDE connector

Pin 1 of Primary IDE connector

Figure 8-22 Floppy drive and two IDE connectors on the motherboard

A+
CORE
1.2
1.6

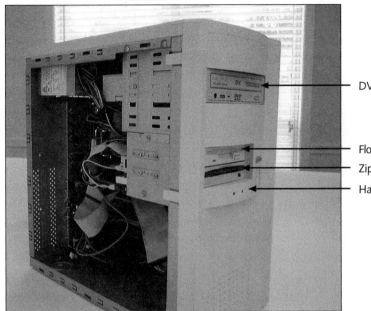

DVD drive in external bay

Floppy drive in external bay
Zip drive in external bay
Hard drive in internal bay

8

Figure 8-23   A tower case may have internal or external bays

9. Before you replace the computer case, plug in the monitor and turn on the computer. Verify that your system BIOS can find the drive before you replace the cover and that it recognizes the correct size of the drive. If you encounter problems, refer to the troubleshooting section at the end of this chapter.

NOTE

The preceding steps to install a hard drive assume that you are using a removable bay. However, some computer cases use small stationary bays like the one in Figure 8-24. For these installations, slide the drive into the bay and secure it with four screws, two on each side of the bay.

A+
CORE
1.2
1.6

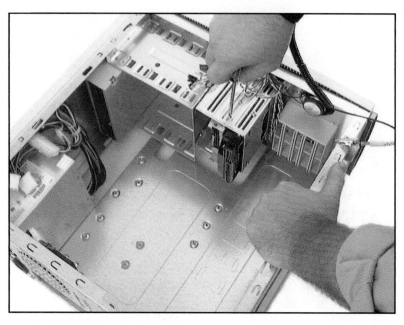

Figure 8-24   To install a drive in a stationary bay, slide the drive in the bay and secure it with four screws

If the Bay Is Too Large

If you are mounting a hard drive into a bay that is too large, a universal bay kit can help you securely fit the drive into the bay. These inexpensive kits should create a tailor-made fit. In Figure 8-25 you can see how the universal bay kit adapter works. The adapter spans the distance between the sides of the drive and the bay.

Drive rails

Bay adapter

Small drive

External bay cover

Figure 8-25   Use the universal bay kit to make the drive fit the bay

Use CMOS Setup to Change Hard Drive Settings

A+
CORE
1.2
1.6
4.4

When you first boot up after installing a hard drive, go to CMOS setup and verify that the drive has been recognized and that the settings are correct. Figures 8-26 through 8-29 show the four typical screens in setup programs, which allow you to change hard drive parameters. In Figure 8-26, you can see the choice for IDE HDD Auto Detection in the third item in the second column. For most hard drive installations, if Auto Detection is not enabled, enable it, and then save and exit setup. Later, after you have rebooted with the new drive detected, you can return to setup, view the selections that it made, and make appropriate changes.

```
                    ROM PCI/ISA BIOS (<<P2B>>)
                       CMOS SETUP UTILITY
                      AWARD SOFTWARE, INC.

    STANDARD CMOS SETUP           SUPERVISOR PASSWORD
    BIOS FEATURES SETUP           USER PASSWORD
    CHIPSET FEATURES SETUP        IDE HDD AUTO DETECTION
    POWER MANAGEMENT SETUP        SAVE & EXIT SETUP
    PNP, AND PCI SETUP            EXIT WITHOUT SAVING
    LOAD BIOS DEFAULTS
    LOAD SETUP DEFAULTS

    Esc : Quit                    ↑↓ → ← : Select Item
    F10 : Save & Exit Setup       (Shift)F2 : Change Color


```

Figure 8-26   CMOS setup utility opening menu

Setup for Large-Capacity Hard Drives

Recall that the two ways BIOS relates to large-capacity drives are LBA and large mode. Notice in Figure 8-27 the column labeled *mode*, referring to how BIOS relates to the drive. Choices are normal, large, LBA, and auto. Most likely, when auto is the choice, setup automatically selects LBA.

8

A+
CORE
1.2
1.6
4.4

```
                    ROM PCI/ISA BIOS (<<P2B>>)
                       STANDARD CMOS SETUP
                       AWARD SOFTWARE, INC.

  Date (mm:dd:yy) : Wed, Mar 25 1998
  Time (hh:mm:ss) :  9 :  5 :  2

  HARD DISKS        TYPE   SIZE   CYLS   HEAD   PRECOMP   LANDZ   SECTOR    MODE
  Primary Master   : Auto     0      0      0         0       0        0   NORMAL
  Primary Slave    : None     0      0      0         0       0        0   ----------
  Secondary Master : Auto     0      0      0         0       0        0   NORMAL
  Secondary Slave  : None     0      0      0         0       0        0   ----------

  Drive A :  2.88M, 3.5 in.
  Drive B :  1.44M, 3.5 in.
  Floppy 3 Mode Support : Disabled       ┌──────────────────────────────────┐
                                         │   Base Memory     :      0K       │
                                         │   Extended Memory :      0K       │
                                         │   Other Memory    :    512K       │
  Video  : EGA/VGA                       │  ─────────────────────────────    │
  Halt On : All Errors                   │   Total Memory    :    512K       │
                                         └──────────────────────────────────┘
  Esc : Quit         ▲▼ ► ◄ : Select Item          PU/PD/+/- : Modify
  F1  : Help         (Shift)F2  : Change Color
```

Figure 8-27   Standard CMOS setup

A+
CORE
1.2
1.6
4.3

In Figure 8-28 (starting with the tenth item in the second column), you can see the hard drive features that the chip set on this motherboard supports. They are Ultra DMA, PIO, and DMA modes. Leave all these settings at Auto, and let BIOS make the choice according to its detection of the features your hard drive supports.

In Figure 8-29, the twelfth item of the first column indicates that BIOS on this motherboard supports block mode. From this screen you can also select the boot sequence (see ninth item in first column). Choices for this BIOS are A, C; A, CD Rom, C; CD Rom, C, A; D, A; F, A; C only; Zip, C; and C, A. Also notice on this screen (eighth item in the first column) that this BIOS supports booting from a SCSI drive even when an IDE drive is present. Booting from the IDE drive is the default setting.

A+
CORE
1.2
1.6
4.3

```
ROM PCI/ISA BIOS (<<P2B>>)
CHIPSET FEATURES
AWARD SOFTWARE, INC.

SDRAM Configuration        : By SPD      Onboard FDC Controller      : Enabled
SDRAM CAS Latency          : 2T          Onboard FDC Swap A & B       : No Swap
SDRAM RAS to CAS Delay     : 3T          Onboard Serial Port          : 3F8H/IRQ4
SDRAM RAS Precharge Time   : 3T          Onboard Serial Port 2        : 2F8H/IRQ3
DRAM Idle Timer            : 16T         Onboard Parallel Port        : 378H/IRQ7
SDRAM MA Wait State        : Normal      Parallel Port Mode           : ECP+EPP
Snoop Ahead                : Enabled     ECP DMA Select               : 3
Host Bus Fast Data Ready   : Enabled     VART2 Use Infrared           : Disabled
16-bit I/O Recovery Time   : 1BUSCLK     Onboard PCI IDE Enable       : Both
8-bit I/O Recovery Time    : 1BUSCLK     IDE Ultra DMA Mode           : Auto
Graphics Aperture Size     : 64MB        IDE0 Master PIO/DMA Mode     : Auto
Video.Memory Cache Mode    : UC          IDE0 Slave  PIO/DMA Mode     : Auto
PCI 2.1 Support            : Enabled     IDE1 Master PIO/DMA Mode     : Auto
Memory Hole At 15M-16M     : Disabled    IDE1 Slave  PIO/DMA Mode     : Auto
DRAM are 64 (Not 72), bits wide
Data Integrity Mode        : Non-ECC     Esc : Quit         ↑↓→← : Select Item
                                         F1  : Help         PU/PD/+/- : Modify
                                         F5  : Old Values    (Shift)F2 : Color
                                         F6  : Load BIOS  Defaults
                                         F7  : Load Setup Defaults
```

Figure 8-28   CMOS setup for chip set features

8

```
ROM PCI/ISA BIOS (<<P2B>>)
BIOS FEATURES SETUP
AWARD SOFTWARE, INC.

CPU Internal Core Speed    : 350Mhz    Video   ROM BIOS   Shadow  : Enabled
                                       C8000  - CBFFF     Shadow  : Disabled
Boot Virus Detection       : Enabled   CC000  - CFFFF     Shadow  : Disabled
CPU Level 1 Cache          : Enabled   D0000  - D3FFF     Shadow  : Disabled
CPU Level 2 Cache          : Enabled   D4000  - D7FFF     Shadow  : Disabled
CPU Level 2 Cache ECC Check : Disabled D8000  - DBFFF     Shadow  : Disabled
BIOS Update                : Enabled   DC000  - DFFFF     Shadow  : Disabled
Quick Power On Self Test   : Enabled
HDD Sequence SCSI/IDE First : IDE      Boot Up NumLock Status       : On
Boot Sequence              : A,C       Typematic Rate Setting       : Disabled
Boot Up Floppy Seek        : Disabled  Typematic Rate (Chars/Sec)   : 6
Floppy Disk Access Control : R/W       Typematic Delay (Msec)       : 250
IDE HDD Block Mode Sectors : HDD MAX
Security Option            : System
PS/2 Mouse Function Control : Auto     Esc : Quit         ↑↓→← : Select Item
PCI/VGA Palette Snoop      : Disabled  F1  : Help         PU/PD/+/- : Modify
OS/2 Onboard Memory > 64M  : Disabled  F5  : Old Values    (Shift)F2 : Color
                                       F6  : Load BIOS  Defaults
                                       F7  : Load Setup Defaults
```

Figure 8-29   CMOS setup for BIOS features

A+
CORE
1.2
1.6
4.3

After you confirm that your drive is recognized and that all its settings are correct, you can use the Fdisk and Format commands to set the logical organization of the drive.

Use Fdisk to Partition a Drive

A+
CORE
1.2
1.7
OS
1.5

To use Fdisk, boot from a startup disk that has the Fdisk.exe utility on it and enter Fdisk at the command prompt. The Fdisk opening menu shown in Figure 8-30 appears. Select option 1 to create the first partition. The menu in Figure 8-31 appears. Use option 1 to create the primary DOS partition. If you plan to install Windows 9x, be sure this partition is at least 150 MB, preferably more. Make this first partition the active partition, which is the partition used to boot the OS. Fdisk automatically makes this partition drive C.

Figure 8-30   Fixed disk setup program (Fdisk) menu

Figure 8-31   Fdisk menu to create partitions and logical drives

A+
CORE
1.2
1.7
OS
1.5

Next, use option 2, shown in Figure 8-31, to create an extended DOS partition using the remainder of the hard drive. Then use option 3 to create logical drives in the extended partition.

When you create logical drives using Fdisk, you decide how large you want each drive to be. If you have at least 512 MB available for the drive, a message appears asking, "Do you wish to enable large disk support (Y/N)?" If you respond Y, then Fdisk assigns the FAT32 file system to the drive. Otherwise, it uses FAT16.

When Fdisk is completed, the hard drive has a partition table, an active and extended partition, and logical drives within these partitions. As shown in Figure 8-30, you can choose option 4 to display partition information (see Figure 8-32). After you exit the Fdisk window, reboot the PC before you format the logical drives.

```
                         Display Partition Information

           Current fixed disk drive: 1

           Partition  Status   Type    Volume Label  Mbytes   System   Usage
             C: 1        A     PRI DOS                 2047     FAT16    84%
                2              EXT DOS                  394              16%


           Total disk space is 2437 Mbytes (1 Mbyte = 1048576 bytes)


           The Extended DOS Partition contains Logical DOS Drives.
           Do you want to display the logical drive information (Y/N)......?[Y]




           Press Esc to return to FDISK Options
```

Figure 8-32   Fdisk displays partition information

Format Each Logical Drive

✔ A+ EXAM TIP

Remember the A+ Core and OS exams often test you on the sequence of steps in installing a device. For example, you should know that after you use Fdisk, you must reboot the PC before you format the drive.

Now that the hard drive is partitioned and logical drives are created and assigned drive letters, the next step is to format each logical drive. The three commands used to format logical drives C, D, and E are:

```
Format C:/S
Format D:
Format E:
```

In the Format command line, the /S option makes the drive bootable, and the drive letter tells the OS which drive to format.

Using Windows to Partition and Format a New Drive

A+
CORE
1.2
1.7
OS
1.5

If you are installing a new hard drive in a system that is to be used for a new Windows installation, it is not necessary to boot from a bootable startup disk. After you have physically installed the drive, boot from the Windows setup CD and follow the directions on the screen to install Windows on the new drive. The setup process partitions and formats the new drive before it begins the Windows installation. If you are installing a second hard drive in a system that already has Windows 2000/XP installed on the first hard drive, use Windows to partition and format the second drive. After physically installing the second hard drive, boot into Windows as usual. Then use Disk Management to partition and format the new drive. This chapter does not cover the details of using Disk Management.

Troubleshooting Hard Drive Installations

A+
CORE
2.1

Sometimes trouble crops up during an installation. Keeping a cool head, thinking things through carefully a second, third, and fourth time, and using all available resources will most likely get you out of any mess. Installing a hard drive is not diffi-cult unless you have an unusually complex situation.

VIDEO

Installing a
Second Hard
Drive

For example, your first hard drive installation should not involve installing a sec-ond SCSI drive in a system that has two SCSI host adapters. Nor should you install a second drive in a system that uses an IDE connection for one drive on the mother-board and an adapter card in an expansion slot for the other drive. If a complicated installation is necessary and you have never installed a hard drive, consider asking for expert help. Know your limitations. Start with the simple and build your way up. Using what you have learned in this chapter, you should be able to install a single IDE drive in a PC or install a second slave IDE drive. After mastering that, tackle something more complicated.

Here are some errors that might occur during a hard drive installation, their causes, and what to do about them. (The next chapter covers troubleshooting hard drives after installation.) This list has been compiled from experience. Everyone makes mistakes when learning something new, and you probably will too. You can then add your own experiences to this list.

- We physically installed an IDE hard drive. We turned on the machine and accessed CMOS setup. The hard drive was not listed as an installed device. We checked and discovered that autodetection was not enabled. We enabled it and rebooted. Setup recognized the drive.

- When first turning on a previously working PC, we received the following error message: "Hard drive not found." We turned off the machine, checked all cables, and discovered that the data cable from the motherboard to the drive was loose. We reseated the cable and rebooted. POST found the drive.

- We physically installed a new hard drive, replaced the cover on the computer case, and booted the PC with a bootable floppy disk in the drive. POST beeped

**A+
CORE
2.1**

■ three times and stopped. Recall that diagnostics during POST are often communicated by beeps if the tests take place before POST has checked video and made it available to display the messages. Three beeps on most computers signal a memory error. We turned off the computer and checked the memory SIMMs on the motherboard. A SIMM positioned at the edge of the motherboard next to the cover had been bumped as we replaced the cover. We reseated the SIMM and booted from a floppy disk again, this time with the cover still off. The error disappeared.

■ We physically installed a new hard drive and turned on the computer. We received the following error: "No boot device available." We forgot to insert a bootable disk. We put the disk in the drive and rebooted the machine successfully.

■ We physically installed the hard drive, inserted a floppy disk in the disk drive, and rebooted. We received the following error message: "Configuration/CMOS error. Run setup." This error message is normal for an older BIOS that does not support autodetection. POST found a hard drive it was not expecting. The next step is to run setup.

■ We physically installed the card and drive and tried to reboot from a floppy disk. Error message 601 appeared on the screen. Any error message in the 600 range refers to the floppy disk. Because the case cover was still off, we looked at the connections and discovered that the power cord to the floppy disk drive was not connected. (It had been disconnected earlier to expose the hard drive bay underneath.) We turned off the machine and plugged in the cable. The error disappeared.

■ The hard drive did not physically fit into the bay. The screw holes did not line up. We got a bay kit, but it just didn't seem to work. We took a break, went to lunch, and came back to make a fresh start. We asked others to help view the brackets, holes, and screws from a fresh perspective. It didn't take long to discover the correct position for the brackets in the bay.

■ We set the jumpers on a hard drive and physically installed the drive. We booted and received the following error message: "Hard drive not present." We rechecked all physical connections and found everything okay. After checking the jumper settings, we realized that we had set them as if this were the second drive of a two-drive system, when it was the only drive. We restored the jumpers to their original state. In this case, as in most cases, the jumpers were set at the factory to be correct when the drive is the only drive.

8

A+
CORE
2.1

If the computer does not recognize a newly installed hard drive, check the following:

▪ Does your system BIOS recognize large drives? Check CMOS setup.

✔ A+ EXAM TIP

The A+ Core exam might give you a symptom and expect you to select a probable source of a problem from a list of sources. These examples of what can go wrong can help you connect problem sources to symptoms.

▪ Has the Fdisk utility been successfully run? Choose Display Partition Information on the Fdisk menu to verify the status.

▪ Format C:/S is the last "format" step. Has this been done?

▪ Has the CMOS setup been correctly configured?

▪ Are there any DIP switches or jumpers that must be set?

▪ Have the power cord and data cable been properly connected? Verify that the data cable stripes are connected to pin 1 on the edge connectors of both the motherboard and the drive.

▪ Check the Web site of the drive manufacturer for suggestions, if the above steps are not productive.

CAUTION

One last warning. When things are not going well, you can tense up and make mistakes more easily. Be certain to turn off the machine before doing anything inside! Not doing so can be a costly error. For example, a friend had been trying and retrying to boot for some time, and got frustrated and careless. He plugged the power cord into the drive without turning the PC off. The machine began to smoke and everything went dead. The next thing he learned was how to replace a power supply!

CHAPTER SUMMARY

◗ Most hard drives today use IDE technology, which has a complex method of organizing tracks and sectors on the disks.

◗ Several ANSI standards pertain to hard drives, including IDE, ATA, Fast ATA, Ultra ATA, Ultra ATA/66, Ultra ATA/100, Ultra ATA/133, and Serial ATA.

◗ An IDE device such as a hard drive can be installed as a master drive, slave drive, or single drive on a system.

◗ The EIDE standards support two IDE connections, a primary and a secondary. Each connection can support up to two IDE devices for a total of four devices on a system.

◗ IDE devices under the EIDE standard can be hard drives, CD-ROM drives, tape drives, Zip drives, and others.

◗ Hard drive capacity for drives less than 8.4 GB is determined by the number of heads, tracks, and sectors on the disk, each sector holding 512 bytes of data.

▶ Large-capacity hard drives must have either LBA mode or large mode set in CMOS in order for system BIOS to support the drive. Without this support, other options can be used, including device driver software or an EIDE controller card.

▶ For the FAT file system, the DOS or Windows operating system views a hard drive through a FAT (file allocation table), which lists clusters, and a directory, which lists files.

▶ A hard drive is divided into partitions, which might also be divided into logical drives, or volumes. A Master Boot Record (MBR) at the beginning of the hard drive contains a table of partition information. Each logical drive contains a boot record, FAT, and root directory for the FAT file system.

▶ Physical geometry is the actual organization of heads, tracks, and sectors on the drive, whereas logical geometry is head, track, and sector information that the hard drive controller presents to system BIOS and the OS. The logical geometry may not be the same as the physical geometry, but, for drives less than 8.4 GB, should yield the same capacity when calculations are made.

▶ Drives larger than 8.4 GB use LBA mode, where the BIOS and OS view the drive as addressable sectors. The capacity of the drive is calculated as the number of addressable sectors multiplied by the number of bytes in one sector, which is almost always 512 bytes.

▶ System BIOS and software can use CHS, large mode, or LBA mode to manage a hard drive. The size of the drive and the drive manufacturer determine the mode used.

▶ The FAT lists all clusters on the hard drive and describes how each is allocated. FAT16 uses 16-bit entries, VFAT enables Windows to use 32-bit, protected-mode device drivers for hard drive access, and FAT32 uses 32-bit entries to hold the cluster numbers.

▶ DOS and the first release of Windows 95 support the FAT16 file system for hard drives. Windows 95 Release 2 and Windows 98 support FAT16 and FAT32 file systems. Windows NT supports FAT16 and the NTFS file systems. Windows 2000 and XP support FAT16, FAT32, and NTFS.

▶ The FAT16 file system can be used for hard drives less than 8.4 GB. DOS and Windows 9x FAT16 logical drives cannot exceed 2 GB. Windows NT/2000/XP FAT16 logical drives cannot exceed 4 GB.

▶ Installing a hard drive includes setting jumpers or DIP switches on the drive; physically installing the adapter card, cable, and drive; changing CMOS setup; and partitioning and formatting the drive.

▶ Protect the drive and the PC against static electricity during installation.

▶ Most BIOSs today can autodetect the presence of a hard drive if the drive is designed to give this information to BIOS.

▶ For DOS or Windows 9x, a drive must have one primary partition and can have one extended partition. The drive boots from the primary partition. The extended partition can be subdivided into several logical drive partitions. Windows NT/2000/XP supports four partitions, one of which can be an extended partition.

▶ Use more than one partition to optimize cluster size, to handle drives greater than 2 GB when using FAT16, or to improve the organization of software and data on the drive.

▶ The OS, or high-level, format for the FAT file system creates the FATs, root directory, and boot record on the drive and marks any bad clusters in the FAT that the low-level format previously identified.

KEY TERMS

For explanations of key terms, see the Glossary near the end of the book.

80-conductor IDE cable
active partition
ANSI (American National Standards Institute)
ATAPI (Advanced Technology Attachment Packet Interface)
autodetection
block mode
boot sector virus
CHS (cylinder, head, sector) mode
DMA (direct memory access) transfer mode
ECHS (extended CHS) mode
EIDE (Enhanced IDE)
enhanced BIOS

extended partition
hard drive controller
External SATA (eSATA)
head
high-level formatting
IDE (Integrated Device Electronics or Integrated Drive Electronics)
large mode
large-capacity drive
LBA (logical block addressing) mode
logical geometry
low-level formatting
master file table (MFT)

normal mode
NTFS (New Technology file system)
operating system formatting
parallel ATA (PATA)
physical geometry
PIO (Programmed Input/Output) transfer mode
primary partition
serial ATA (SATA)
serial ATA cable
slack
translation
VFAT (virtual file allocation table)
zone bit recording

REVIEWING THE BASICS

1. Name four ANSI standards for interfacing with hard drives.

2. What are the two data transfer modes used by hard drives?

3. What are the two types of IDE data cables currently used with hard drives?

4. What is the most popular ATAPI standard currently used for hard drives in desktop systems?

5. If a hard drive has three platters, how many heads does it have?

6. Given that there are 512 bytes per sector, calculate the hard drive storage for the following: heads = 32, tracks (cylinders) = 1,024, sectors/track = 63.

7. For older drives, why does the logical geometry sometimes differ from the physical geometry of a hard drive?

8. What are three modes that system BIOS can use to relate to hard drives?

9. Which mode must be used for a 10 GB hard drive?

10. What is the ATA standard that changes the number of bits used to address data on a hard drive?

11. How does block mode give faster access to a hard drive? How can you disable block mode?

12. What is the purpose of the Master Boot Record (MBR) on a hard drive?

13. When installing a hard drive and a CD-ROM drive on the same IDE channel, which do you configure as the master and which as the slave?

14. Under Windows 98, when would it be appropriate to use FAT16 rather than FAT32 on a new hard drive?

15. What is the largest FAT32 partition allowed by Windows XP?

16. What are three ANSI hard drive interface standards that do not use a traditional hard drive cable?

17. When two drives are connected to the same data cable, how does BIOS know which is the master and which is the slave drive?

18. If a motherboard has two EIDE connections, how many IDE devices can the system support?

19. If a hard drive is too small to physically fit snugly into the drive bay, what can you do?

20. How can you tell which side of a hard drive's data cable connects to pin 1 on the drive?

21. If your BIOS does not support a large-capacity drive that you want to install, what five choices do you have?

22. How can you tell if your motherboard chip set supports Ultra DMA mode?

23. Which Windows 9x and DOS utility is used to partition a hard drive?

24. How can you tell how many partitions a hard drive has been set up to have?

25. What question does the Windows 9x partition utility ask in order to use FAT32 instead of the FAT16 file system?

26. How many sectors are in one cluster for a 1.5-GB partition using FAT16? Using FAT32?

8

THINKING CRITICALLY

1. You install a hard drive and then turn on the PC for the first time. You access CMOS setup and see that the drive is not recognized. Which of the following do you do next?

    a. Turn off the PC, open the case, and verify that memory modules on the motherboard have not become loose.

    b. Turn off the PC, open the case, and verify that the data cable and power cable are connected correctly and jumpers on the drive are set correctly.

    c. Verify that BIOS autodetection is enabled.

    d. Reboot the PC and enter CMOS setup again to see if it now recognizes the drive.

2. You want to set up your desktop system to have a total hard drive space of 150 GB, but your system does not support drives larger than 120 GB. Which of the following do you do?

    a. Buy a new motherboard that will support drives larger than 120 GB.

    b. Use two hard drives in your system that together total 150 GB.

    c. Flash BIOS so that your system will support a 150 GB drive.

    d. Use a special IDE controller card that will support a 150 GB drive.

3. After you use Fdisk to partition your drive, which of the following is the next step?

    a. Use the Format command to format each logical drive.

    b. Access CMOS setup and verify the BIOS recognizes the drive.

    c. Reboot the system.

HANDS-ON PROJECTS

HANDS-ON PROJECTS

PROJECT 8-1: Using Fdisk

Prepare a startup disk (refer to Chapter 3) that contains Fdisk.exe. Boot from the disk and use Fdisk to display information about the partitions on the hard drive. Remove the disk and boot into Windows. Open a command prompt window, and use Fdisk to display partitions on the hard drive. Did Fdisk give the same information using both methods? Why is it very important not to change the partitions during this exercise?

PROJECT 8-2: Examining the CMOS Setting for a Hard Drive

1. From the CMOS setup information on your computer, calculate the capacity of your hard drive. Show your method of calculation.

2. Write down or print out all the CMOS settings that apply to your hard drive. Explain each setting that you can.

PROJECT 8-3: Preparing for Hard Drive Hardware Problems

1. Boot your PC and make certain that it works properly. Make sure you have a bootable disk available in case you need it. Turn off your computer, remove the computer case, and disconnect the data cable to your hard drive. Turn on the computer again. Write down the message that you get.

2. Turn off the computer and reconnect the data cable. Disconnect the power supply cord to the hard drive. Turn on the computer. Write down the error that you get.

3. Boot from the disk and use Fdisk to examine the partition table. Write down the size of each partition and the logical drives in each.

PROJECT 8-4: Researching with the Internet

Suppose you plan to install a Maxtor Quantum Fireball Plus AS 20.5-GB hard drive as a second drive on a PC. You want the drive to be the slave drive, and you know that you must change the current jumper settings. The four jumpers on the drive are labeled *DS*, *CS*, *PK*, and *Rsvd*. The description of the jumpers doesn't tell you how to set the jumpers so the drive is the slave. The documentation is not available. What do you do?

The best solution is to use the Internet to access the drive manufacturer's Web site for this information. In this case, the site is *www.maxtor.com*. Use this example or some other example given by your instructor to determine the correct settings for the jumpers.

PROJECT 8-5: Installing a Hard Drive

In a lab that has one hard drive per computer, you can practice installing a hard drive by removing a drive from one computer and installing it as a second drive in another computer. When you boot up the computer with two drives, verify that both drives are accessible in Windows Explorer. Then remove the second hard drive, and return it to its original computer. Verify that both computers and drives are working.

Optimizing and Protecting Hard Drives

In this chapter, you will learn:

- About supporting hard drives and making backups

- About viruses and other computer infestations, and how to protect against them

- How to troubleshoot hard drives

In the previous chapter you learned about hard drive technology and installation. In this chapter, you will learn about supporting hard drives. You will learn how to optimize hard drive performance through disk compression and caching of hard drives. This chapter also discusses different types of viruses that can infect your hard drive as well as how to remove and prevent them. You will also learn what to do when a hard drive fails or produces errors and how important it is to keep reliable backups of the file system and data. No amount of experience with replacing defective hard drives can substitute for reliable backups. The data itself is often the most valuable thing in your computer case.

Managing Hard Drives

The hard drive is the most important secondary storage device in your computer. In this section, you learn about Windows utilities that protect, optimize, and maintain hard drives. You can access some of these utilities from a command prompt and some from the Windows desktop.

Defrag and Windows Disk Defragmenter

A+
CORE
1.9
3.1
OS
1.3
1.5
2.5

The Defrag command detects and repairs fragmentation. **Fragmentation** occurs when a single file is placed in several cluster locations that are not directly next to each other. The clusters that make up a file are together called a **chain**. When a hard drive is new and freshly formatted, the OS writes files to the drive beginning with cluster 2, placing the data in consecutive clusters. Each new file begins with the next available cluster. Later, after a file has been deleted, the OS writes a new file to the drive, beginning with the first available cluster in the FAT. If the OS encounters used clusters as it writes the file, it simply skips these clusters and uses the next available one. In this way, after many files have been deleted and added to the drive, files become fragmented. On a well-used hard drive, it is possible to have a file stored in clusters at 40 or more locations. Fragmentation is undesirable because when the OS has to access many different locations on the drive to read a file, access time slows down, and if the file becomes corrupted, recovering a fragmented file is more complicated than recovering a file in one continuous chain.

For these reasons, one routine maintenance task is to **defragment** the hard drive periodically. To do this, you can run the Defrag command from a command prompt or use a graphical Disk Defragmenter utility available from the Windows desktop. With Windows NT, you must use third-party software, as Windows NT does not include a defragmenter command. Regardless of the method used, you should defragment your hard drive every month or so as part of a good maintenance plan.

To use Windows XP Disk Defragmenter, first close all open applications. Then choose Start, All Programs, Accessories, and System Tools. Click Disk Defragmenter. From the Disk Defragmenter dialog box (see Figure 9-1) you can select a drive and defragment it. To use Windows 9x/Me or Windows 2000 Disk Defragmenter, choose Start, Programs, Accessories, and then System Tools.

NOTE

Defragmenting a large hard drive may take a long time, so plan for this before you begin. For Windows 9x/Me, if you want to watch the progress as it moves through the FAT, click Show Details in the Disk Defragmenter dialog box.

**A+
CORE
1.9
3.1
OS
1.3
1.5
2.5**

Figure 9-1   Windows XP defragmenting a volume

Using ScanDisk to Correct Cross-Linked and Lost Clusters

As you learned in Chapters 7 and 8, a directory on a floppy disk or hard drive is a table holding information about files in that directory or folder. The directory contains the number of the first cluster in the file. The FAT holds the map to all the other clusters in the file. Occasionally, the mapping in the FAT becomes corrupted, resulting either in lost clusters or cross-linked clusters, as shown in Figure 9-2. Here, File 3 has lost direction and points to a cluster chain that belongs to File 4. Clusters 29 through 31 are called **cross-linked clusters** because more than one file points to them, and clusters 15 through 17 and 28 are called **lost clusters** or **lost allocation units** because no file in the FAT points to them.

In Chapter 3, you learned about the Chkdsk and ScanDisk commands. You can use Chkdsk /F to repair cross-linked and lost clusters. The Chkdsk command is supported by all versions of Windows. For Windows 9x/Me, use it from any command prompt. For Windows 2000/XP, use Chkdsk from a Windows command prompt or from the Recovery Console. The Windows 9x/Me ScanDisk utility is an improvement over Chkdsk and was designed to replace it. ScanDisk can repair cross-linked and lost clusters, check the FAT for other problems with long filenames and the directory tree, scan the disk for bad sectors, and repair problems with the structure of a hard drive that has been compressed using Windows DriveSpace or DoubleSpace.

9

A+
CORE
1.9
3.1
OS
1.3
1.5
2.5

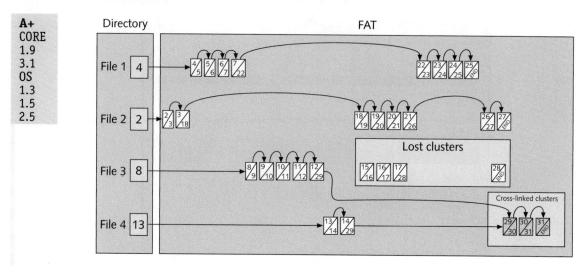

Figure 9-2   Lost and cross-linked clusters

You can use ScanDisk from a command prompt or from the Windows desktop using Windows 9x/Me. For Windows 2000/XP, open Windows Explorer, right-click the drive, and select Properties from the shortcut menu. Click the Tools tab and click Check Now under Error-checking (see Figure 9-3). Check the two boxes, "Automatically fix file system errors" and "Scan for and attempt recovery of bad sectors."

Figure 9-3   Windows XP repairs hard drive errors under the drive's Properties window using Windows Explorer

A+
CORE
1.9
3.1
OS
1.3
1.5
2.5

To use ScanDisk from the Windows 9x/Me desktop, click Start, Programs, Accessories, System Tools, and then ScanDisk. The ScanDisk utility first asks which drive you want to scan and gives you the choice of a Standard or Thorough scan (see Figure 9-4). The Standard scan checks files and folders for errors. The Thorough scan does all that the Standard scan does and also checks the disk surface for bad sectors. Click Start to begin the scan.

In command mode, such as when you've booted from a Windows 9x/Me startup disk, enter the command Scandisk. The screen in Figure 9-5 appears. When the program finishes scanning the disk, it returns you to a command prompt.

✔ A+ EXAM TIP

The A+ OS and Core exams expect you to know how to check a disk for errors using Windows 2000/XP and Windows 9x/Me. Know how and when to use ScanDisk, Chkdsk, and Error-checking.

Use ScanDisk from a Windows 9x/Me startup disk or from the desktop for both troubleshooting and maintenance. Like Defrag, ScanDisk is a good tool to run occasionally to check the health of the drive and possibly avert future problems.

9

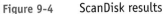
Figure 9-4   ScanDisk results

A+
CORE
1.9
3.1
OS
1.3
1.5
2.5

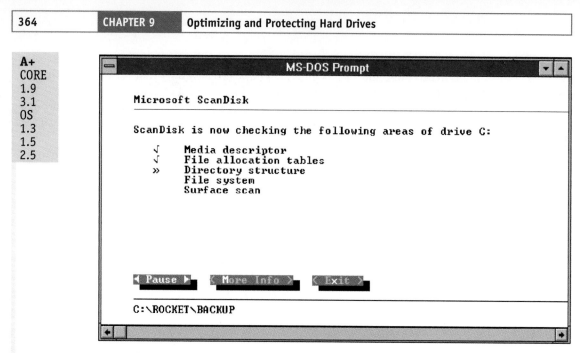

Figure 9-5   ScanDisk in MS-DOS mode

Disk Cleanup

A+
CORE
1.9
OS
1.4
1.5
2.5

Disk Cleanup is a convenient way to delete temporary files on a hard drive, freeing up space and sometimes improving performance. To access Disk Cleanup under Windows 2000/XP and Windows 9x/Me, right-click the drive in Windows Explorer and select Properties from the shortcut menu. The Disk Properties window appears (see Figure 9-6). On the General tab, click Disk Cleanup. From this view, you can se-lect nonessential files to delete in order to save drive space. Disk Cleanup tells you how much total space you can save and how much space each type of removable file is tak-ing; it also describes each type of file. Included in the list are temporary files created by applications that the applications no longer need.

Figure 9-6   The Disk Properties window provides Disk Cleanup, a quick and easy way to delete
temporary files on a hard drive

Disk Compression

**A+
CORE
1.9
OS
1.4**

Disk compression software can help meet the ever-increasing demand for more space
on hard drives to hold software and data. Software packages requiring 200 to 250
MB of hard drive space were unheard of three or four years ago but are now common. Hard drive sizes have increased proportionately. Even so, we often seek ways to
cram more onto nearly full hard drives.

Software to manage disk compression works by (1) storing data on your hard
drive in one big file and managing the writing of data and programs to that file, and
(2) rewriting data in files in a mathematically coded format that uses less space. Most
disk compression programs combine these two methods. This section covers disk
compression methods in several versions of Windows.

NOTE

Disk compression does save hard drive space, but you need to carefully consider the risks
involved as well as performance issues such as longer disk access time. If you do choose to use
disk compression, keep good backups of both the data and the software. If the data and software on your drive are especially valuable, you may want to invest in a larger hard drive instead
of using compression.

Disk Compression in Windows XP and Windows 2000

Using the NTFS file system in Windows 2000/XP, you can compress a single file or
folder or you can compress the entire NTFS volume. When you place a file or folder
on a compressed volume, it will be compressed automatically. When you read a

A+
CORE
1.9
OS
1.4

compressed file from a compressed volume, it will be decompressed automatically and then will be recompressed when you save it back to the compressed volume.

To compress an NTFS volume:

1. Open Windows Explorer.

2. Locate and right-click the root folder for the volume you want to compress. You will find it in the left pane of Windows Explorer.

3. Select **Properties** from the shortcut menu. The Properties dialog box appears.

4. If necessary, click the **General** tab (see Figure 9-7). This window displays the file system used (NTFS), the size of the volume, and the amount of free space. To compress the volume, click the check box labeled **Compress drive to save disk space**. Click **OK**.

5. The Confirm Attribute Changes dialog box appears. Indicate whether you want to compress only the root folder or the entire volume, and then click **OK** to begin compression.

NOTE

The Disk Properties window for a FAT32 volume under Windows 2000/XP will not display the check box to compress the volume.

Figure 9-7   Compressing an NTFS volume

To compress a single folder or file on a Windows 2000/XP NTFS volume, right-click the folder or file and select Properties from the shortcut menu. Click the General tab, and then click Advanced. In the Advanced Attributes window, check

A+
CORE
1.9
OS
1.4

"Compress contents to save disk space." For a FAT32 volume, files and folders cannot be compressed and the General tab does not have an Advanced button.

Disk Compression in Windows 9x/Me

Windows 95 and Windows 98 support drive compression (Windows Me does not) using the **DriveSpace** utility on a FAT16 file system. However, the compressed volume is somewhat unstable and should not be used if important data is on the volume. Use it with caution!

To compress a FAT16 volume in Windows 95/98 using DriveSpace, first back up the data. Then click Start, Programs, Accessories, and System Tools. Select DriveSpace and follow the steps to select and compress the drive. Once the drive is compressed, never trust important data to it.

NOTE

If a Windows 9x/Me utility such as DriveSpace is missing from a menu list, the component might not have been installed when Windows was installed. To install a Windows component after Windows is installed, go to the Control Panel, select Add/Remove Programs, and click the Windows Setup tab.

9

Disk Caching

A+
Core
1.9
OS
2.5

A **disk cache** is a temporary storage area in RAM for data being read from or written to a hard drive, and is used to speed up access time to the drive. The process of disk caching works like this:

1. The CPU asks for data from a hard drive.

2. The hard drive controller sends instructions to the drive to read the data and then sends the data to the CPU.

3. The CPU requests more data, quite often data that immediately follows the previously read data on the hard drive.

4. The controller reads the requested data from the drive and sends it to the CPU. Without a cache, each CPU request requires that data be read from the hard drive, as indicated in the top part of Figure 9-8.

With a hard drive cache, the cache software handles the requests for data, as shown in the lower part of Figure 9-8. The cache program reads ahead of the CPU requests by guessing what data the CPU will request next. Because most data that the CPU requests is in consecutive areas on the drive, the cache program guesses correctly most of the time. The program stores the read-ahead data in memory (RAM). When the CPU requests the next set of data, if the cache program guessed right, the program can send that data to the CPU from memory without having to go back to the hard drive. Some cache software caches entire tracks at a time; other software caches groups of sectors.

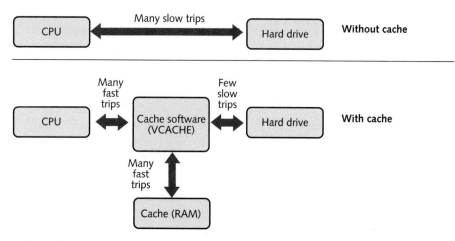

Figure 9-8   A CPU asking a hard drive for data without cache (upper part) and with cache (lower part)

Hardware Cache or Software Cache

There are two kinds of hard drive caches: hardware and software. Some hard drive controllers have a **hardware cache** built right into the controller circuit board. The BIOS on the controller contains the cache program, and RAM chips on the controller hold the cache.

A **software cache** is a cache program stored on the hard drive like other software, and is usually loaded into memory when a computer is booted. The software cache program uses system RAM to hold the cache.

There are advantages and disadvantages to both kinds of hard drive cache. A hardware cache does not use RAM on the system board, but a software cache uses RAM for both the cache program itself and the data being cached. Therefore, a disadvantage of a software cache is that it uses RAM that might otherwise be used for application software and its data.

On the other hand, a software cache is faster because of where the data is stored. Because data is stored in RAM, when the CPU is ready for the data, it only needs to travel from RAM to the CPU on the system bus, the fastest bus on the motherboard. Because the hardware cache is on the controller board, when the CPU is ready for data stored in this cache, the data must travel from the controller board over one or more buses to the CPU.

NOTE

When buying a new hard drive, check whether it includes hardware caches as an option. A controller with its own hardware cache is slightly more expensive than one without a cache. In hard drive ads, the cache is sometimes called a buffer.

Another disadvantage of a hardware cache is that it is a permanent part of the hard drive controller, and today's hard drives have the controller built into the drive housing. Exchanging hard drives to upgrade to a faster hardware cache is impractical, whereas upgrading to a faster software cache is a viable option.

How Disk Caching Methods Have Changed

As operating system technologies have changed, so have software disk caching methods. Here is a summary of how different OSs have accomplished disk caching.

- *DOS.* Before disk caching came along, DOS used buffers to speed disk access. A **buffer** is an area in memory where data waiting to be read or written is temporarily stored. Disk caches do a better job of speeding disk access than buffers, so the only reason to use buffers today is to satisfy the requirements of older software that uses them. Buffers are implemented by putting the Buffers=[*number*] command in Config.sys. This command specifies how many buffers DOS is to make available for use while data is being read.
- *DOS with Windows 3.x.* DOS with Windows 3.x used **SMARTDrive**, a 16-bit, real-mode software cache utility. SMARTDrive caches data both being read from and written to the hard drive, and caches data being read from floppy disks.
- *Windows 9x/Me.* Windows 9x/Me has a built-in 32-bit, protected-mode software cache called **VCACHE**, which is automatically loaded by Windows 9x/Me without entries in Config.sys or Autoexec.bat. VCACHE doesn't take conventional memory or upper memory space the way SMARTDrive does, and it does a much better job of caching.
- *Windows NT/2000/XP.* Versions of Windows after Windows 9x/Me use automated disk caching as an inherited Windows component. When working with caching under these versions of Windows, you can monitor physical disk performance using counters.

To verify that disk caching is enabled for Windows XP, open Windows Explorer, right-click drive C, and select Properties from the shortcut menu. Click the Hardware tab and then click Properties. In the drive's Properties window, click the Policies tab and verify that "Enable write caching on the disk" is checked (see Figure 9-9). For Windows 2000, open the drive's Properties window, click the Disk Properties tab, and verify that Write cache enabled is checked.

9

Figure 9-9   Verify that Windows XP disk caching is enabled

Making Backups

A **backup** is an extra copy of a data or software file that you can use if the original file becomes damaged or destroyed. Losing data due to system failure, a virus, file corruption, or some other problem really makes you appreciate the importance of having backups. This section covers the hardware and software needed to make backups of data and software from a hard drive. Windows 9x/Me and Windows NT/2000/XP offer backup tools, which are also covered in this section.

NOTE

With data and software, here's a good rule of thumb: if you can't get along without it, back it up.

You can use sophisticated methods to create backups in which the backup process is selective, only backing up what's changed, what has not been recently backed up, and so forth. Traditionally, these methods all involve backing up to tapes, because a tape is most likely to be large enough to contain an entire backup of a hard drive and they are inexpensive. In the following discussions of specific backup methods, tape is our medium. These backup methods are designed to reuse tapes and to make the backup process more efficient. On a network, often the backup medium is a device such as another hard drive or a tape drive on a computer somewhere on the network. Full, incremental, and differential backup methods speed up the backup process, and scheduled backups minimize the inconvenience to users. Selective backups only back up data that changes often on the hard drive. By selecting only certain critical folders on the drive to back up, the backup routine goes much faster, and recovery of lost data is much easier.

The Child, Parent, Grandparent Method

Before you perform routine hard drive backups, devise a backup plan or procedure. One common plan, called the **child, parent, grandparent backup method,** makes it easy to reuse tapes. This method is explained in Table 9-1. Put the plan in writing, and keep a log of backups performed.

Name of Backup	How Often Performed	Storage Location	Description
Child backup	Daily	On-site	Keep four daily backup tapes, and rotate them each week. Label the four tapes Monday, Tuesday, Wednesday, and Thursday. A Friday daily (child) backup is not made, because on Friday you make the parent backup.
Parent backup	Weekly	Off-site	Perform the weekly backup on Friday. Keep five weekly backup tapes, one for each Friday of the month, and rotate them each month. Label the tapes Friday 1, Friday 2, Friday 3, Friday 4, and Friday 5.
Grandparent backup	Monthly	Off-site, in a fireproof vault	Perform the monthly backup on the last Friday of the month. Keep 12 tapes, one for each month. Rotate them each year. Label the tapes January, February, and so on.

Table 9-1   The child, parent, grandparent backup method

9

Full, Incremental, and Differential Backups

A+
OS
1.5

Some backup methods are more efficient because they do not always create a complete backup of all data. A **full backup** backs up all data from the hard drive or an area of the hard drive. An **incremental backup** backs up only files that have changed or been created since the last backup, whether that backup is itself an incremental or full backup. **Differential backups** back up files that have changed or been created since the last full backup.

Begin by performing a full backup. The next time you back up, choose the incremental method to back up only files that have changed or been created since the full backup. The second time you perform an incremental backup, you back up only the files that have changed or been created since the last incremental backup.

For example, using the child, parent, grandparent method, you can perform a full backup each Friday. Monday through Thursday, you perform incremental backups. The advantage of this method is that incremental backups are faster and require less storage space than full backups. The disadvantage is that, to recover data, you must begin with the last full backup and work your way forward through each incremental backup until the time that the data was lost. This process can be time-consuming. Plan to make a full backup after at least every sixth or seventh incremental backup. The Windows NT/2000/XP and Windows 9x/Me backup utilities support incremental backups.

If you create differential backups with the child, parent, grandparent method, create a full backup on Fridays. On Monday, do a differential backup to back up all files that have changed since Friday. On Tuesday, a differential backup also backs up all files that have changed since Friday (the full backup). Differential backups don't consider whether other differential backups have been performed. Instead, they compare data only to the last full backup, which is how differential backups and incremental backups differ. Another difference is that incremental backups mark files as having been backed up, but differential backups do not. The advantage of differential backups over incremental ones is that if you need to recover data, you only need to recover from the last full backup and the last differential backup. Differential backups are not supported by Windows 95 but are supported by Windows 98 and Windows NT/2000/XP.

Scheduling Backups

Backups can be performed manually by a user sitting at the computer or can be scheduled to run automatically without user interaction. A scheduled backup is performed automatically by software when the computer is not commonly in use, such as during the middle of the night. Windows 98 and Windows NT/2000/XP support scheduling any program (including backup tasks) to execute at designated dates and times without user intervention.

A+
OS
1.5

Using Windows 98, do the following to create a program called Batch.bat to run a backup and schedule it to run at 11:59 p.m. every Monday night:

1. Using Notepad or WordPad, type the following command line, where the tape drive is E and the /S parameter tells the OS to include subdirectories when copying (hidden files are not copied, but data is not usually hidden):

   ```
   Xcopy C:\Data\*.* E: /S
   ```

2. Save the file as **\Data\Batch.bat**, and exit the text editor.

3. Double-click **My Computer** on the desktop, and then double-click **Scheduled Tasks** to open the Scheduled Tasks window (see Figure 9-10).

4. Double-click **Add Scheduled Task**. The Scheduled Task Wizard appears. Select the program to schedule; click **Browse**, find and click the **Batch.bat** file in the \Data folder, and then click **Open**.

5. Enter a name for the scheduled task, select how often to perform the task, and then click **Next** (see Figure 9-11).

6. Enter the start time and select the day of the week for the task to execute. For example, enter **11:59 PM every Monday**. Click **Next**.

7. The wizard reports the scheduled task parameters. Click **Finish**.

8. To change settings for a scheduled task, double-click **My Computer**, double-click **Scheduled Tasks**, and then right-click the task in the Scheduled Tasks window. Select **Properties** from the shortcut menu. The task Properties dialog box opens (see Figure 9-12).

Figure 9-10   Add a scheduled task under Windows 98

Figure 9-11   Name the scheduled task and select how often it runs

9. Click the **Settings** tab to change the task settings. Notice at the bottom of the Settings sheet that you can direct the scheduler to wake the computer to perform the task. This feature requires a motherboard that supports the option for software to power up the PC. To learn if your motherboard supports the feature, see CMOS setup or the motherboard documentation. If not, then the PC must be turned on for the scheduler to work.

You have just learned how to use a batch file to execute a scheduled backup. Windows offers a more powerful and sophisticated utility called Windows Scripting Host (WSH), which uses Windows commands to execute scripts written in a scripting language such as VBScript or JScript. This utility is also good for making backups. The script is stored in a file that can be placed as an icon on the desktop. To run the script, type *wscript.exe filename* in the Run dialog box, substituting the name of the script file for *filename,* or double-click the desktop icon. You can also make a script file run as a scheduled task.

Figure 9-12   With some computers, the task scheduler can power up the computer to run the task

Backup Software

Most tape drives come with some backup software. You can also purchase third-party backup software or use Windows NT/2000/XP or Windows 9x/Me backup utilities for backing up your hard drive. Because the software only backs up files that are not currently in use, close all files before performing a backup.

APPLYING CONCEPTS

Windows 2000/XP Backup Utility

To perform a backup for Windows 2000/XP (using Ntbackup.exe), follow these steps. The procedure is for Windows XP, but Windows 2000 steps are similar:

1. For Windows XP, click **Start**, point to **All Programs**, **Accessories**, **System Tools**, and click **Backup**. The Backup Wizard appears. Click **Advanced Mode**. For Windows 2000, click **Start**, **Programs**, **Accessories**, **System Tools**, and **Backup**.

2. The Backup utility opens. Click the **Backup** tab (see Figure 9-13). If you want to perform a backup immediately, check the drive and subfolders to back up. Note the box labeled **Backup media or file name** in the lower-left corner, which says where to back up to. Click the **Start Backup** button in the lower-right corner to perform the backup.

3. To perform a scheduled backup, begin by clicking the **Schedule Jobs** tab. Select a date on which you want to schedule a backup, and then click the **Add Job** button.

Figure 9-13 You can perform an immediate backup from the Backup tab

4. The Backup Wizard opens. On the first screen, click **Next**. Select **Backup selected files, drives, or network data** and click **Next**.

5. On the next screen, select what you want to back up, and then click **Next**.

6. Follow the steps through the wizard to choose where you want to save your backup, give a name to the backup, and select the type of backup (Normal, Copy, Incremental, Differential, or Daily). You can also specify how to verify the data, and specify if the data is to be appended to an existing backup or replaces an existing backup.

7. When asked if you want to perform the backup now or later, select **Later** and give the backup a name. Click the **Set Schedule** button.

8. The Schedule Job window appears, as shown in Figure 9-14. Schedule how often the backup is to occur, and then click **OK**.

9. Click **Next** in the wizard, and follow the remaining instructions to complete the backup. At the end of the process, the wizard gives you an onscreen report summarizing information about the backup.

To recover files, folders, or the entire drive from backup using the Windows 2000/XP Backup utility, click the Restore and Manage Media tab on the Backup Utility window (see Figure 9-13). Select the backup job to use for the restore process. The Backup utility displays the folders and files that were backed up with this job. You can select the ones that you want to restore.

NOTE

By default, Windows XP Home Edition does not include the Backup utility. To install it manually, go to the \VALUEADD\MSFT\NTBACKUP folder on your Windows XP setup CD and double-click Ntbackup.msi. The installation wizard will complete the installation.

Figure 9-14   Schedule repeated backups

✔ **A+ EXAM TIP**

The A+ OS exam expects you to know when and how to use the Windows 2000/ XP utility, Ntbackup.exe, and the Windows 9x/Me utility Msbackup.exe.

Windows 9x/Me Backup Utility   Windows 9x/Me offers a Microsoft Backup utility (Msbackup.exe) that can back up to removable disks and tape drives. Windows 98 supports many popular backup devices that Windows 95 did not, including those using parallel ports, IDE/ATAPI devices, and SCSI devices. To use drives and tapes not supported by Windows 9x/Me, use third-party backup software.

To use Windows 98 Microsoft Backup, click Start, point to Programs, Accessories, System Tools, and then click Backup. Follow the Backup Wizard as it steps you through the process of selecting the backup medium and the files, folders, or logical drives you want to back up. To select what to back up, the wizard takes you to a backup window similar to the Windows 2000/XP Backup window.

Disk Cloning Software

You can back up a hard drive by replicating it to a different computer or to another drive on the same computer, such as when you deploy a new operating system with

A+
OS
2.1

application software on multiple computers in a corporate or educational lab. This process, called **disk cloning, disk imaging,** or **drive imaging** is best done with software designed for that purpose. Examples of disk imaging software are Drive Image by PowerQuest (*www.powerquest.com*), ImageCast by Innovative Software (*www.imagecast.com*), and Norton Ghost by Symantec Corp (*www.symantec.com*).

Planning for Disaster Recovery

APPLYING CONCEPTS

Dave was well on his way to building a successful career as a PC repair technician. His PC repair shop was doing well and he was excited about his future. But one bad decision changed everything. He was called to repair a server at a small accounting firm. The call was on the weekend when he was normally off, so he was in a hurry to get the job done. He arrived at the accounting firm and saw that the problem was an easy one to fix, so he decided not to do a backup before working on the system. During his repairs, the hard drive crashed and all data on the drive was lost–four million dollars worth! The firm sued, Dave's business license was stripped, and he was ordered to pay the money the company lost. A little extra time to back up the system would have saved his whole future.

The time to prepare for disaster is before it occurs. If you have not prepared, the damage from a disaster will most likely be greater than if you had made and followed disaster plans. Suppose the hard drive on your PC stopped working and you lost all its data. What would be the impact? Are you prepared for this event? Backups are important, but you should also know how to use them to recover lost data. Also know when the backup was made and what to do to recover information entered since the last backup. Here's where careful recordkeeping pays off.

When you perform a backup for the first time or set up a scheduled backup, verify that you can use the backup tape or disks to successfully recover the data. This is a very important step in preparing to recover lost data. After you create a backup, erase a file on the hard drive, and use the recovery procedures to verify that you can re-create the file from the backup. This verifies that the backup medium works, that the recovery software is effective, and that you know how to use it. After you are convinced that the recovery works, document how to perform it.

NOTE

Verify that your recovery plan works by practicing it before disaster occurs.

Always record your regular backups in a table with the following information:

- Folders or drives backed up
- Date of the backup

- Type of backup
- Label identifying the tape, disk, or other media

If you discover that data has been lost days or weeks ago, you can use this table to help you recover the data. Keep the records in a notebook. You can also store the records in a log file (a file where events are logged or recorded) each time you back up. Store the file on a floppy disk or another PC.

Viruses and Other Computer Infestations

**A+
OS
3.3**

Statistics show that in 2001, one in 10 corporate desktop computers was infected with a computer infestation, and the rate of infestation is increasing 15 percent each year. A computer support person needs to know how to protect computers against computer infestations (including viruses), how to recognize them, and how to get rid of them. Understanding what infestations are, how they work, and where they hide helps technicians deal with them successfully. A computer **infestation** is any unwanted program transmitted to a computer without the knowledge of the user or owner, and is designed to do varying degrees of damage to data and software. Computer infestations do not damage PC hardware. However, when boot sector information is destroyed on a hard drive, the hard drive can appear to be physically damaged. What most people call viruses really fall into four categories of computer infestations: viruses, Trojan horses, worms, and logic bombs. The four types of infestations differ in the way they spread, the damage they do, and the way they hide.

Because viruses are by far the most common kind of computer infestation, one of the most important defenses against them is **antivirus (AV) software**, designed to discover and remove a virus. This section looks at several AV programs and how to use them effectively.

Understanding Computer Infestations

A **virus** is a program that replicates by attaching itself to other programs. The infected program must be executed for a virus to run. The virus might then simply replicate or also do damage by immediately performing some harmful action. A virus might be programmed to perform a negative action in the future, such as on a particular date (for instance, Friday the 13th), or when some logic within the host program is activated.

A virus differs from a **worm**, a program that spreads copies of itself throughout a network or the Internet without a host program. A worm creates problems by overloading the network as it replicates. Worms do damage by their presence rather than by performing a specific damaging act, as a virus does. A worm overloads memory or hard drive space by replicating repeatedly. When a worm (for example,

9

W32.Sobig.F@mm) is loose on the Internet, it can do damage such as sending mass e-mailings.

A **Trojan horse** is a third type of computer infestation that, like a worm, does not need a host program to work; rather it substitutes itself for a legitimate program. Most Trojan horses cannot replicate themselves, although there are some exceptions. One Trojan horse program was disguised as an automatic backup utility downloadable from the Internet. When used, it created backups and replicated itself to the backups. It was programmed to damage several systems on Friday the 13th. In this case, the Trojan horse program is also considered a virus because of its ability to replicate. Because Trojan horse infestations generally cannot replicate and require human intervention to move from one location to another, they are not as common as viruses.

A **logic bomb** is dormant code added to software and triggered at a predetermined time or by a predetermined event. For example, an employee might put code in a program to destroy important files if his or her name is ever removed from the payroll file. Also, viruses, Trojan horses, logic bombs, and worms can occur in combination, such as when a virus gains access to a network by way of a Trojan horse. The virus can plant a logic bomb within application software on the network that sets off a worm when the application executes.

Where Viruses Hide

A program is called a virus for three reasons: (1) it has an incubation period (does not do damage immediately), (2) it is contagious (can replicate itself), and (3) it is destructive. There are several types of viruses and methods that viruses use to avoid detection by antivirus software.

Boot Sector Virus   A **boot sector virus** hides in a boot sector program. It can hide on a hard drive either in the program code of the Master Boot Record or in the boot record program that loads the OS on the active partition of the hard drive. On a floppy disk, a boot sector virus hides in the boot program of the boot sector. One of the most common ways a virus spreads is from a floppy disk used to boot a PC. When the boot program is loaded into memory, so is the virus, which can then spread to other programs.

Many CMOS setups have an option that can protect against some boot sector viruses. It prevents writing to the boot sector of the hard drive. This feature must be turned off before installing Windows 9x/Me or Windows NT/2000/XP, which must write to the boot sector during installation. Windows 9x/Me does not tell you that you must turn the feature off and start the installation over until about halfway through the installation.

File Viruses   A **file virus** hides in an executable (.exe, .com, or .sys) program or in a word-processing document that contains a macro. A **macro** is a small program contained in a document that can be automatically executed when the document is first loaded or later by pressing a key combination. For example, a word-processing macro might automatically read the system date and copy it into a document when you open the document. Viruses that hide in macros of document files are called macro viruses. **Macro viruses** are the most common viruses spread by e-mail, hiding in macros of attached document files.

One well-known example of a macro virus is Melissa, first introduced in 1999 in a Word 97 macro. The virus spread around the world within one working day. The e-mail that initially spread Melissa looked like this:

From: (name of infected user)
Subject: Important Message From (name of infected user)
To: (50 names from alias list)
Here is that document you asked for ... don't show anyone else ;-)
Attachment: LIST.DOC

When the recipient opened the document, a macro executed and immediately e-mailed the List.doc to 50 e-mail addresses listed in the user's address book. The virus infected other Word documents, which, when e-mailed, also spread the virus.

One type of file virus searches a hard drive for files with .exe extensions and then creates another file with the same filename and a .com file extension, and stores itself there. When the user launches a program, the OS first looks for the program name with the .com file extension. It then finds and executes the virus. The virus is loaded into memory and loads the program with the .exe extension. The user appears to have launched the desired program. The virus is then free to do damage or spread itself to other programs.

Multipartite Viruses   A **multipartite virus** is a combination of a boot sector virus and a file virus. It can hide in either type of program.

Cloaking Techniques

NOTE

Antivirus software cannot detect a virus it does not know to look for. Therefore, upgrade your AV software regularly to keep your protection current as new viruses are discovered.

A virus is programmed to attempt to hide from antivirus (AV) software. AV software can only detect viruses identical or similar to those it has been programmed to search for and recognize. AV software detects a known virus by looking for distinguishing characteristics called **virus signatures**, which is why it is important to update your AV software.

A virus attempts to hide from AV software in two ways: by changing its distinguishing characteristics (its signature) and by attempting to mask its presence.

Three types of viruses categorized according to their cloaking techniques are poly-morphic, encrypting, and stealth viruses.

Polymorphic Viruses   A **polymorphic virus** changes its distinguishing characteristics as it replicates. Mutating in this way makes it more difficult for AV software to recognize the presence of the virus.

Encrypting Viruses   One key symptom AV software looks for is a program that can replicate itself. An **encrypting virus** can transform itself into a nonreplicating program to avoid detection. However, it must revert to a replicating program to spread or replicate, and can then be detected by AV software.

Stealth Viruses   A **stealth virus** actively conceals itself, using one or more of the following techniques:

- Because AV software can detect a virus by noting the difference between a program's file size before the virus infects it and after the virus is present, the virus alters OS information to mask the size of the file it hides in.
- The virus monitors when files are opened or closed. When it sees that the file it is hiding in is about to be opened, it temporarily removes itself or substitutes a copy of the file that does not include the virus. The virus keeps a copy of this uninfected file on the hard drive just for this purpose.

The Damage an Infestation Can Cause

Viruses, worms, and Trojan horses have not been known to physically damage a hard drive or other hardware device. The damage they do ranges from minor, such as displaying bugs crawling around on a screen, to major, such as erasing everything written on a hard drive. Infestation damage is called the *payload* and can be accomplished in a variety of ways. A virus can be programmed to drop its payload only in response to a triggering event such as a date, opening a certain file, or pressing a certain key. Figure 9-15 shows the results of a harmless virus that simply displays garbage on the screen.

How Infestations Spread

Understanding how infestations spread is essential to understanding how to protect your computer against them. Some computers are more vulnerable than others, depending on user habits. Here is a list of user activities that make a computer susceptible to infestations.

A+
OS
3.3

- Executing attachments to e-mail messages without first scanning them for viruses
- Trading floppy disks containing program files
- Connecting the computer to an unprotected network
- Buying software from unreliable sources
- Downloading programs from the Internet
- Using floppy disks from unknown sources
- Using shared network programs
- Using used, preformatted floppy disks
- Reading e-mail that automatically executes a word processor to read attached files
- Not write-protecting original program disks

Figure 9-15 The crash virus appears to be destructive, making the screen show only garbage, but does no damage to hard drive data

How a Virus Replicates Once a program containing a virus is copied to your PC, the virus can spread only when the infected program executes. The process is shown in Figure 9-16. Recall from earlier chapters that the first step in executing a program, whether it is stored in a program file or in a boot sector, is to load the program into memory. Viruses hidden in a program can then be executed from memory. A virus can either be a **memory-resident virus** and stay in memory, still working even after the host program terminates, or a **non-memory-resident virus** that is terminated when the host program is closed.

After a virus is loaded into memory, it looks for other programs loaded into memory. When it finds one, it copies itself there and into that same program file on disk. In Figure 9-16, you can see that a virus becomes more dangerous the longer it

A+
OS
3.3

stays loaded into memory and the more programs that are opened while it is there. For this reason, if you want to use a computer that has been used by other people, such as in a computer lab, always reboot before you begin work to clear memory of programs. Use a hard boot, not just a soft boot, to erase all memory-resident programs (including a memory-resident virus) from memory.

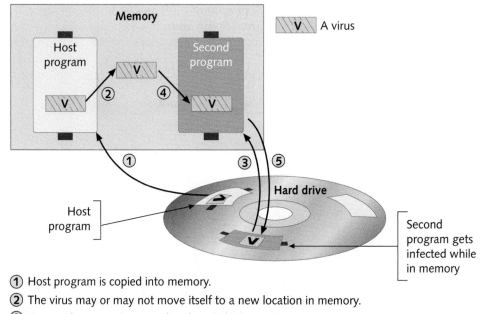

① Host program is copied into memory.
② The virus may or may not move itself to a new location in memory.
③ A second program is opened and copied into memory.
④ The virus copies itself to the second program in memory.
⑤ The newly infected second program is written back to the hard drive.

Figure 9-16   How a virus replicates

How a Trojan Horse Gets into Your Computer   A Trojan horse is an infestation masquerading as a legitimate program. One interesting example of a Trojan horse is the AOL4FREE program. Originally this illegal program could provide unauthorized access to America Online. After AOL blocked the program's usefulness, a new program emerged, also called AOL4FREE. It was not an online access program but a destructive Trojan horse. People passed the program around, thinking that it would provide illegal access to AOL; however, if executed, it actually erased files on their hard drives.

How a Worm Gets into Your Computer   Most worms come to your computer or network through the Internet. A computer communicates with other computers on the Internet by using identifying numbers called ports, which are similar to post office box numbers (see Figure 9-17). When a computer is configured for network or Internet communication, it opens a series of port numbers to send and receive messages. One computer will say to the other, "I have a message for your port 25." If the receiving computer is not protected against worms, it will receive any message from any computer to any port it has opened to service. Worms on the Internet routinely perform "port scanning," meaning that they are constantly looking for open, unprotected ports through which they can invade a system. Once they are in the computer, they are free to move to other computers on the internal network or produce mass e-mailings to bog down the network or Internet.

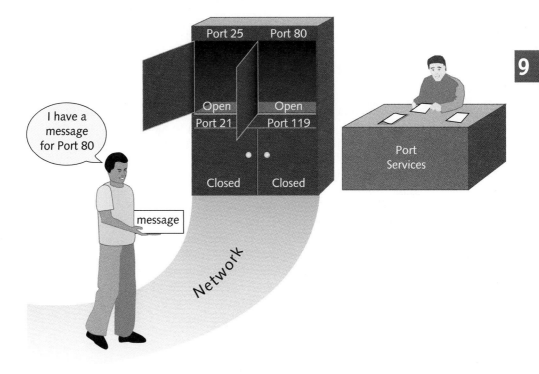

Figure 9-17   A computer receives communication over a network by way of ports or numbers that identify a communication service

The best way to defend against worms is to use a **firewall**, which is software or hardware that prevents worms or hackers from using open ports or services. You will learn more about a Windows XP firewall in Chapter 16 and about Internet communication, ports, and firewalls in Chapter 19.

Virus Hoaxes

A+
OS
3.3

A virus hoax is an e-mail warning about a nonexistent virus. The warning is itself a pest because it overloads network traffic. Here's an example of a virus hoax e-mail message I received:

```
There is a new virus going around in the last couple of
days!! DO NOT open or even look at any mail that you get
that says: "Returned or Unable to Deliver." The virus
will erase your whole hard drive and attach itself to
your computer components and render them useless. Immedi-
ately delete any mail items that say this. AOL has indica-
ted this is a very dangerous virus, and there is NO
remedy for it at this time. Please be careful and forward
to all your online friends ASAP. This is a new email
virus and not a lot of people know about it; just let
everyone know, so they won't be a victim. Please forward
this email to your friends!!!
```

Viruses grow more powerful every day, but it is unlikely that this message is accurate. It is unlikely that a virus can render computer components useless. No virus has been known to do actual physical damage to hardware, although viruses can make a PC useless by destroying programs or data, and a few viruses have been able to attack system BIOS code on the motherboard. However, some can hide in macros in word-processing documents attached to e-mail messages, and a few viruses are able to hide in Web pages transmitted as e-mail messages and interpreted by e-mail software when you first open the messages.

What's most important is not to be gullible and take the bait by forwarding the message to someone else. The potential damage a hoax like this can do is to overload an e-mail system with useless traffic, which is the real intent of the hoax. When I received this e-mail, over a hundred names were on the distribution list.

Before forwarding a virus warning, you can check the Web sites of virus software manufacturers such as the ones listed later in this section. In addition, here are some Web sites that specialize in debunking virus hoaxes:

- *hoaxbusters.ciac.org* by Computer Incident Advisory Capability
- *www.hoaxinfo.com* by Jeff Richards
- *www.hoaxkill.com* by Oxcart Software
- *www.viruslist.com* by Kaspersky Lab
- *www.vmyths.com* by Rhode Island Soft Systems, Inc.

There are many sources for checking for virus hoaxes. Using a search engine, type "virus hoax," a similar phrase, or the name of the virus or virus warning, and you'll find a wealth of information. Always check before sending!

Protecting Against Computer Infestations

A+
OS
3.3

You can do a lot to protect your computer against viruses and other infestations. Your first line of defense is to make backups, use antivirus software regularly, keep Windows current with updates and patches, and implement a firewall. After that, use wisdom when managing programs. Here are some general guidelines:

- Buy antivirus software and set your computer to run the AV program automatically at startup.
- Keep your AV software current by periodically downloading upgrades from the Internet. Many antivirus programs now offer an automatic update feature.
- Set a virus scan program to automatically scan word-processing documents and other e-mail attachments when they are opened. Some Web-based e-mail clients, such as Yahoo! Mail, offer the option to scan attachments before downloading them.
- Implement a firewall. Chapter 19 discusses how to use software or hardware firewalls.
- Keep Windows updated on your computer using the Microsoft Web site *windowsupdate.microsoft.com*. Microsoft is continually solving security problems with patches and service packs for the OS.
- Establish and faithfully execute a plan to make scheduled backups of your hard drive to protect against potential infestation damage.
- Only buy software from reputable vendors.
- Don't trade program files on floppy disks.
- Don't use floppy disks from unknown sources, and always scan floppy disks for viruses, no matter where they came from.
- Download software from the Internet sparingly, and then always scan program files for viruses before executing them.
- Never use pirated software.
- Format floppy disks before first use.
- Write-protect original program floppy disks, or use CDs to install programs.
- In a business environment, adopt strict company policies against using unauthorized software.
- Before using a running computer that others have used, hard-boot the computer.
- Set your computer CMOS settings to boot from drive C, then drive A.
- Turn on antivirus protection for your MBR in the CMOS settings, if available.

Virus Symptoms

Here are some warnings that suggest a virus is at work:

- A message appears that a downloaded document contains macros, or an application asks whether it should run macros in a document. (It is best to disable macros if you cannot verify that they are from a trusted source and that they are free of viruses or worms.)
- A program takes longer than normal to load.

9

- The number and length of disk accesses seem excessive for simple tasks.
- Unusual error messages occur regularly.
- Less memory than usual is available.
- Files mysteriously disappear or appear.
- Strange graphics appear on your computer monitor, or the computer makes strange noises.
- There is a noticeable reduction in disk space.
- The system cannot recognize the hard drive when you boot from a floppy disk.
- The system cannot recognize the CD-ROM drive, although it worked earlier.
- Executable files have changed size.
- Executable files that once worked no longer work and give unexpected error messages.
- The access lights on the hard drive and floppy drive turn on when there should be no activity on that device. (However, sometimes an OS performs routine maintenance on the drive when the system has been inactive for a while.)
- Files constantly become corrupted.
- Strange or bizarre error messages appear.
- Windows error messages about the FAT or partition table appear.
- The hard drive boots but hangs before getting a Windows desktop.
- File extensions or file attributes change without reason.
- The virus scanner software displays a message.
- You receive e-mail messages that you have sent someone an infected message.
- The number of bad sectors on the hard drive continues to increase.
- Task Manager reveals unfamiliar processes running.
- The Sigverif command reveals that uncertified software is installed.

What to Do When You Suspect a Virus Infestation

If you suspect a virus, run a virus scan program to detect and delete the virus. If the antivirus software is not already installed, you can still use it. Consult the documentation for instructions on how to proceed. In many cases, the installation process detects the virus and eliminates it before continuing the installation. However, if the AV software does not recognize the virus or if the virus successfully hides, the AV program cannot detect the virus. If the AV software found nothing, but you still suspect a virus, get the latest upgrade of your AV software and try it or another AV program. Also download recent virus definitions; these are usually part of automatic AV software updates.

If you know the name of the virus or worm, check the Web site of the antivirus software for information about the infestation and how to remove it. The antivirus software vendor might instruct you to download a special program to remove a particular virus or worm. Instructions might tell you to first reboot into Windows Safe Mode or to disable certain services before executing the removal software.

A+
OS
3.3

Table 9-2 lists popular antivirus software and Web sites that provide information about viruses.

Antivirus Software	Web Site
Norton AntiVirus by Symantec, Inc.	www.symantec.com
Dr. Solomon's Software	www.drsolomon.com
McAfee VirusScan by McAfee Associates, Inc.	www.mcafee.com
ESafe by Aladdin Knowledge Systems, Ltd.	www.esafe.com
F-Prot by Frisk Software International	www.f-prot.com
Norman	www.norman.com
PC-cillin by Trend Micro (for home use)	www.antivirus.com
NeaTSuite by Trend Micro (for networks)	www.antivirus.com

Table 9-2   Antivirus software and information

When selecting antivirus software, find out if it can:

- Download new software upgrades and virus definitions from the Internet so that your software knows about new viruses
- Automatically execute at startup
- Detect macros in a word-processing document as it is loaded by the word processor
- Automatically monitor files being downloaded from the Internet, including e-mail attachments and attachments sent during a chat session, such as when using AOL Instant Messenger
- Send virus alerts to your e-mail address to inform you of a dangerous virus and the need to update your antivirus software
- Scan both automatically and manually for viruses

Using Antivirus Software

Antivirus software can work at different times to scan your hard drive or a floppy disk for viruses. Most AV software can be configured to scan memory and the boot sector of your hard drive for viruses each time your PC boots. Often it's not practical to have AV software scan the entire hard drive each time you boot, because that takes too much time. Consider scheduling the AV software to run at the same time every day, such as during lunch hour.

Some AV software can run continuously in the background and scan all programs that execute. However, the software can cause problems with other software, especially during installations. If you have a problem installing a new application, try terminating your AV software.

9

Set your AV software to scan files as they are downloaded from the Internet or a network, and to scan documents for macro viruses each time a document is opened by a word processor.

Troubleshooting Hard Drives

This section contains information you can use to troubleshoot your hard drive. You will learn about error messages, tools that you can use to troubleshoot and maintain your hard drive, how to solve common hard drive problems, and some general troubleshooting guidelines.

An Ounce of Prevention

Taking good care of your hard drive is not difficult, but it does require a little time. Before we begin a discussion of hard drive troubleshooting and data recovery, here are some precautions you can take to protect your data and software as well as the drive itself.

- *Make backups and keep them current.* It's so important that it's worth saying again: keep backups to use if the original data is damaged or deleted. Never trust a computer; it'll let you down. Keep data files in directories separate from the software, to make backing up data easier. Back up the data as often as every four hours of data entry. Rotate the backup disks or tapes by keeping the last two or three most recent backups.
- *Run antivirus software regularly.* If you lose software or data on your hard drive, there's a good chance the source of the problem is a virus. Your best defense against data and software corruption is to install and run antivirus software. Keep the software current because new viruses are constantly turned loose.
- *Defragment files and scan the hard drive occasionally.* A fragmented hard drive increases access time, and reading and writing files wears out the drive. If you are trying to salvage a damaged file, it is much more difficult to recover a fragmented file than one stored in contiguous clusters. Regularly scan your hard drive for lost or cross-linked clusters.
- *Don't smoke around your hard drive.* To a read/write head, a particle of smoke on a hard drive platter is like a 10-foot boulder on the highway. Hard drives are not airtight. One study showed that smoking near a computer reduced the average life span of a hard drive by 25 percent.
- *Don't leave the PC turned off for weeks or months at a time.* Once my daughter left her PC turned off for an entire summer. At the beginning of the new school term, the PC would not boot. We discovered that the Master Boot

A+
CORE
2.1

Record had become corrupted. PCs are like cars in this respect: long spans of inactivity can cause problems.

- *High humidity can be dangerous for hard drives.* I once worked in a basement with PCs, and hard drives failed much too often. After we installed dehumidifiers, the hard drives became more reliable.
- *Be gentle with a hard drive.* Don't bump the PC or move it when the drive is spinning.
- *Take precautions when moving a hard drive or changing CMOS setup.* If you move a hard drive with important data on it from one computer to another, make backups first and verify that both computers use the same translation method (LBA or large mode). Don't change CMOS setup options for the hard drive unless you know what you're doing because changing modes in setup can destroy data, causing the drive to need repartitioning and reformatting.

Resolving Common Hard Drive Problems

9

A+
CORE
2.1
2.2

Although the hard drive itself is a hardware component, problems with hard drives can be caused by software as well. Problems can also be categorized as those that prevent the hard drive from booting and those that prevent data from being accessed. In this section, you will learn about hardware and software problems with hard drives.

When a user brings a problem to you, begin troubleshooting by interviewing the user, being sure to include these questions:

- Can you describe the problem and show me how to reproduce it?
- Was the computer recently moved?
- Was any new hardware or software recently installed?
- Was any software recently reconfigured or upgraded?
- Did someone else use your computer recently?
- Does the computer have a history of similar problems?

Once you gather this basic information, you can begin diagnosing and addressing the hard drive problems.

If a hard drive is not functioning and data is not accessible, setting priorities helps focus your work. For most users, data is the first priority unless they have a recent backup. Software can also be a priority if it is not backed up. Reloading software from the original installation disks or CD can be time-consuming, especially if the configuration is complex or you have written software macros or scripts but did not back them up.

If you have good backups of both data and software, hardware might be your priority. It could be expensive to replace, but downtime can be costly, too. The point is, when trouble arises, determine your main priority and start by focusing on that.

**A+
CORE
2.1
2.2**

Be aware of the resources available to help you resolve a problem:

- Documentation often lists error messages and their meanings.
- The Internet can also help you diagnose hardware and software problems. Go to the Web site of the product manufacturer, and search for the FAQs (frequently asked questions) list or bulletin board. It's likely that others have encountered the same problem and posted the question and answer. If you search and cannot find your answer, then you can post a new question.
- Technical support from the ROM BIOS, hardware, and software manufacturers can help you interpret an error message, or it can provide general support in diagnosing a problem. Most technical support is available during working hours by telephone. Check your documentation for telephone numbers. An experienced computer troubleshooter once said, "The people who solve computer problems do it by trying something and making phone calls, trying something else and making more phone calls, and so on, until the problem is solved."

NOTE Remember one last thing. After making a reasonable and diligent effort to resolve a problem, getting the problem fixed could become more important than resolving it yourself. There comes a time when you might need to turn the problem over to a more experienced technician.

Troubleshooting Hard Drives with Third-Party Software

**A+
CORE
2.1**

To troubleshoot hard drive problems, you might need to use third-party utility software. Three popular utility programs are Norton Utilities, SpinRite, and Partition-Magic. The following descriptions tell you what to expect from this software when a hard drive fails. Note that these are *not* complete listings of the utility software functions, nor of all available software. See specific software documentation for more details.

- *Norton Utilities* by Symantec (*www.symantec.com*) offers several easy-to-use tools to prevent damage to a hard drive, recover data from a damaged hard drive, and improve system performance. Many functions of these tools have been taken over and improved by utilities included with recent versions of Windows. The most commonly used Norton Utilities tools now are the recovery tools. Two examples are Norton Disk Doctor, which automatically repairs many hard drive and floppy disk problems, and UnErase Wizard, which allows you to retrieve accidentally deleted files. When using Norton Utilities, be certain you use the version of the software for the operating system you have installed. Using Norton with the wrong OS can do damage.
- *PartitionMagic* by PowerQuest Corporation (*www.powerquest.com*) lets you manage partitions on a hard drive more quickly and easily than with Fdisk for Windows 9x/Me or Disk Management for Windows NT/2000/XP. You can create new partitions, change the size of partitions, and move partitions without losing data or moving the data to another hard drive while you work. You can

switch between FAT16 and FAT32 without disturbing your data, and you can hide and show partitions to secure your data.

■ *SpinRite* by Gibson Research (*www.grc.com*) is hard drive utility software that has been around for years. Still a DOS application without a sophisticated GUI interface, SpinRite has been updated to adjust to new drive technologies. It supports FAT32, SCSI, Zip drives, and Jaz drives. You can boot your PC from a floppy disk and run SpinRite from a floppy, which means that it doesn't require much system overhead. Because it is written in a language closer to the binary code that the computer understands, it is more likely to detect underlying hard drive problems than software that uses Windows, which can stand as a masking layer between the software and the hard drive. SpinRite analyzes the entire hard drive surface, performing data recovery of corrupted files and file system information. Sometimes, SpinRite can recover data from a failing hard drive when other software fails.

NOTE Always check compatibility between utility software and the operating system with which you plan to use it. One place you can check is the service and support section of the software manufacturer's Web site.

9

Hardware Problems

Hardware problems usually show up at POST, unless there is physical damage to an area of the hard drive that is not accessed during POST. Hardware problems often make the hard drive totally inaccessible.

Sometimes older drives refuse to spin at POST. Drives that have trouble spinning often whine at startup for several months before they finally refuse to spin altogether. If your drive whines loudly when you first turn on the computer, never turn off the computer. One of the worst things you can do for a drive that is having difficulty starting up is to leave the computer turned off for an extended period of time. Some drives, like old cars, refuse to start if they are unused for a long time. Also, data on a hard drive sometimes "fades" off the hard drive over time.

Do not trust valuable data to a drive that has this kind of trouble. Plan to replace the drive soon. In the meantime, make frequent backups and leave the power on.

The read/write heads at the ends of the read/write arms on a hard drive get extremely close to the platters but do not actually touch them. This minute clearance between the heads and platters makes hard drives susceptible to destruction. Should a computer be bumped or moved while the hard drive is operating, a head can easily bump against the platter and scratch the surface. Such an accident causes a "hard drive crash," often making the hard drive unusable.

If the head mechanism is damaged, the drive and its data are probably total losses. If the first tracks that contain the partition table, boot record, FAT, or root directory are damaged, the drive could be inaccessible, although the data might be unharmed.

Here's a trick that might work for a hard drive whose head mechanism is intact but whose first few tracks are damaged. First, find a working hard drive that has the same partition table information as the bad drive. Take the computer case off, place the good drive on top of the bad drive housing, and connect a spare power cord and the IDE data cable to the good drive. Leave a power cord connected to the bad drive. Boot from a disk. No error message should show at POST. Access the good drive by entering C: at the A prompt. The C prompt should show on the monitor screen.

Without turning off the power, gently remove the data cable from the good drive and place it on the bad drive. Do not disturb the power cords on either drive or touch chips on the drive logic boards. Immediately copy the data you need from the bad drive to floppy disks, using the Copy command. If the area of the drive where the data is stored, the FAT, and the directory are not damaged, this method should work.

Here's another trick for an older hard drive having trouble spinning when first turned on. Remove the drive from the case, hold it firmly in both hands, and give the drive a quick and sudden twist that forces the platters to turn inside the drive housing. Reinstall the drive. It might take several tries to get the drive spinning. Once the drive is working, immediately make a backup and plan to replace the drive soon.

Hard Drive Not Found   If your system BIOS cannot find your drive, giving an error message such as "Hard drive not found," the reason is most likely a loose cable or adapter card. Here are some things to do and check:

- Confirm that both the monitor and computer switches are turned on.
- Sometimes startup BIOS displays numeric error codes during POST. Errors in the 1700s or 10400s generally mean fixed disk problems. Check the Web site of the BIOS manufacturer for explanations of these numeric codes.
- Check CMOS setup for errors in the hard drive configuration.
- Turn off the computer and monitor before you do anything inside the case.
- Remove and reattach all drive cables. Check for correct pin 1 orientation.
- If you're using a controller card, remove and reseat it or place it in a different slot.
- Check the jumper or DIP switch settings on the drive.
- Inspect the drive for damage such as bent pins on the connection for the cable.
- Determine if the hard drive is spinning by listening to it or lightly touching the metal drive (with power on).
- Check the cable for frayed edges or other damage.
- Check the installation manual for things you might have overlooked. Look for a section about system setup, and carefully follow all directions that apply.
- Be sure the power cable and disk data cable connections are good.

- If the drive still does not boot, exchange the three field-replaceable units–the data cable, the adapter card (optional), and the hard drive itself–for a hard drive subsystem. Perform the following procedures in order:

  - Reconnect or swap the drive data cable.
  - Reseat or exchange the drive adapter card, if one is present.
  - Exchange the hard drive for a known good unit.

- If the hard drive refuses to work but its light stays on even after the system has fully booted, the problem might be a faulty controller on the hard drive or motherboard. Try replacing the hard drive and then the motherboard.

A bad power supply or a bad motherboard also might cause a disk boot failure. If the problem is solved by exchanging one of the field-replaceable units listed, you still must reinstall the old unit to verify that the problem was not caused by a bad connection.

Invalid Drive or Drive Specification   If you get the error message "Invalid drive or drive specification," the system BIOS cannot read the partition table information. Boot from a floppy disk, and use the Fdisk command to examine the table. If it is corrupt, which might be the result of a boot sector virus, try the Fdisk /MBR command to restore the master boot program. If this does not work, you can repartition the drive, but you will lose all data on the drive. If the data is important and is not backed up, try third-party data recovery software to recover the drive and its data before repartitioning.

NOTE

There is a danger in using the Fdisk/MBR command. Some viruses detect when the MBR is altered or when an attempt is made to alter it, and do further damage at that time. Also, some third-party drive encryption software alters the MBR. If Fdisk/MBR overwrites the data encryption program in the MBR, encrypted data on the hard drive might not be readable. If you have important data on the drive that is not backed up, try to recover the data before using Fdisk/MBR.

Restoring the partition table is impossible if the track is physically damaged. The partition table is written on the very first sector of the hard drive, and this sector must be accessible. If it is accessible, you can create a primary partition that covers the damaged area, which you will never use. Create an extended partition for the remainder of the drive. You will not be able to use this hard drive as your boot device, but it can be used as a secondary hard drive. You can also use third-party partition software that allows you to decide where you want to put a partition on a hard drive.

Don't perform a low-level format on an IDE drive unless the drive is otherwise unusable. Use the low-level format program recommended by the manufacturer, and follow its instructions. Call the drive manufacturer's technical support to find out how to get this program, or check the manufacturer's Web site for details.

9

Damaged Boot Record   If the boot record on a hard drive is damaged, you might get an error message such as "Invalid media type," "Non-DOS disk," or "Unable to read from Drive C." Try third-party data recovery software such as GetDataBack by Runtime Software (*www.runtime.org*) to repair the boot record. If that doesn't work, reformat the volume.

Damaged FAT or Root Directory or Bad Sectors   Error messages that indicate a damaged FAT or root directory or bad sectors somewhere on the hard drive are "Sector not found reading drive C, Abort, Retry, Ignore, Fail?", "Bad Sector," and "Sector Not Found." Try using ScanDisk to repair the damage. If that doesn't work, try third-party recovery software, which might be able to recover the FAT or root directory. If these don't work, reformat the drive. If there is important data on the drive that is not backed up, before you reformat, try using the Copy command from a command prompt to copy these files to another medium.

Cannot Boot from the Hard Drive   Error messages that indicate the hard drive is not bootable are "Non-system disk or disk error...," "Invalid system disk...," and "Command file not found." First verify that the drive can be accessed from a floppy disk. Boot from a rescue disk, and enter C: at the command prompt. If you can access the drive, the problem is missing or corrupted system files on drive C. Do the following:

- For Windows 9x/Me, try the Sys C: command to copy Io.sys, Msdos.sys, and Command.com from the rescue disk to the hard drive.
- Use ScanDisk to scan the drive for errors.
- Run a current version of an antivirus program.

Drive Retrieves and Saves Data Slowly   If the drive retrieves and saves data slowly, run Defrag to rewrite fragmented files to contiguous sectors. Slow data retrieval might be caused by fragmented files that have been updated, modified, and spread over different portions of the drive.

Software Problems with Hard Drives

Here are some general software causes of hard drive problems. The root cause of many of these problems is a virus:

- Corrupted OS files
- Corrupted partition table, boot record, or root directory, making all data on the hard drive inaccessible

- Corrupted area of the FAT that points to the data, the data's directory table, or the sector markings where the data is located
- Corrupted data

Resolving Hard Drive and Data Access Problems   The software problems listed earlier can prevent data or programs on the hard drive from being accessible. For a hard drive and its data to be accessible by DOS or Windows, the following items, listed in the order they are accessed, must be intact for a FAT file system: the partition table, the boot record, the FAT, the root directory, the system files, and data and program files.

- *Partition table.* When the partition table is damaged, BIOS tries to load the OS, first reading the master boot program at the beginning of the partition table information on the hard drive. If the partition table is damaged, this error message appears:

  ```
  Invalid drive or drive specification
  ```

  In this case, you should still be able to boot from a floppy disk. When you get to the A prompt and try to access the hard drive by entering C:, you get the same error. To restore the boot program at the very beginning of the partition table in the Master Boot Record, use this command for Windows 9x/Me or Windows NT:

  ```
  A> Fdisk /Mbr
  ```

  For Windows 2000/XP, use this command from the Recovery Console:

  ```
  Fixmbr
  ```

  Often, these commands solve the problem of a damaged partition table.
- *Boot record.* If the OS boot record on a hard drive is damaged, you cannot boot from the hard drive. After you boot from a floppy disk and try to access the hard drive, you might get one of these error messages:

  ```
  Invalid media type
  Non-DOS disk
  Unable to read from Drive C
  ```

  If the OS boot record is damaged, the best solution is to recover it from the backup copy you made when you first became responsible for the PC. (You can use Norton Utilities to make the backup.) If you don't have a backup, try to repair the boot record using Norton Disk Doctor or SpinRite.
- *FAT and root directory.* The partition table and boot record are easily backed up to disk; they do not change unless the drive is repartitioned or reformatted. Always back them up as soon as you can after you buy a new computer or become responsible for a working one. Unlike the partition table and the boot record, the FAT and the root directory change often and are more difficult to back up. The success of Windows or third-party utilities in repairing a damaged

FAT or root directory depends on the degree of damage to the tables. If these tables are damaged, you may receive this error message:

```
Sector not found reading drive C, Abort, Retry,
Ignore, Fail?
```

Try copying important files on the drive to another medium. If you encounter the error, type I to ignore the bad sector and continue copying. Norton Disk Doctor might be able to repair the FAT or root directory.

■ *System files.* If the two OS hidden files (Io.sys and Msdos.sys) are missing or corrupted, you should see one of these error messages:

```
Non system disk or disk error...
Invalid system disk...
```

Use the following command to copy the two hidden files and the Command.com file from a rescue disk to the hard drive:

```
A:\> Sys C:
```

■ *Data and program files.* Data and program files can become corrupted for many reasons, ranging from power spikes to user error. If the corrupted file is a program file, the simplest solution might be to reinstall the software or recover the file from a previous backup. Restoring a data file that is not backed up is covered in the next section, along with problems that can cause data and program file corruption.

Data and Program File Corruption   To restore a data file that is not backed up, you have three options:

■ Use operating system tools and commands to recover the file.
■ Use third-party software such as Norton Utilities or SpinRite to recover the file.
■ If neither of these approaches works, you can turn to a professional data recovery service. These services can be expensive, but, depending on how valuable the data is, the cost might be justified.

When a data file or program file is damaged, portions of the file may still be intact. The basic approach to recovering data in this situation is to create a new file on another disk or on the hard drive, containing all the sectors from the original file that can be read from the damaged disk or hard drive. Use the Copy command and when you get an error message, try to move on to the next sector. Some of the file might be copied to the new medium. Then edit the newly created file to replace the missing data.

How successfully an OS recovers data depends on how badly damaged the file is. A few examples of how data commonly becomes damaged and what can be done to recover it are discussed in the following list. If a file has been accidentally erased, or the disk or hard drive is otherwise damaged, remember these two things:

- Don't write anything to the disk or hard drive, because you might overwrite data that you could otherwise recover.
- If you are recovering data from a floppy disk, use Diskcopy in DOS or Copy Disk in Windows Explorer to make a copy of the disk before you do anything else. If Copy Disk or Diskcopy doesn't work, try copying the disk with a third-party program such as Norton Utilities.

Here are some problems you may experience with files and the file system:

- *Corrupted file header.* If an application cannot open or read one of its data files, the file header might be corrupted. Many applications place header information (called the file header) at the beginning of the file. This data follows a different format from the rest of the file. The application uses it to identify the file and its contents. If the file header is lost or corrupted and an application needs that header to read the file, you can sometimes recover the contents by treating the file as an ASCII text file.

NOTE Most applications let you import a text file and then convert it to the application's format. Read your application's documentation to learn how to import a text file.

- *Lost clusters.* A disk can develop lost clusters (lost allocation units) if a program cannot properly close a file it has opened. For example, if you boot your computer while an application is running (not a good thing to do for this very reason), the application does not have the opportunity to close a file and may lose clusters. Clusters can also be lost if you remove a floppy disk from a drive while the drive light is still on (also not a good thing to do). Some older applications, such as early versions of MS Access, might not complete writing a file to a floppy disk until the application is closed or another data file is opened. In this case, you must close the application or open a new file before it is safe to remove the floppy disk.

  Lost clusters are clusters that are not incorporated into a file. The Chkdsk and Scandisk commands turn the clusters into a file with the name File0000.chk or a similar filename with a higher number, and store the file in the root directory. To use this utility at a command prompt to access lost clusters, use the command with the /F option, like this:

  ```
  C:\> Chkdsk A:/F
  ```

  Often the file created can be used by the application that it belongs to, although you might have to change the file extension so the application will recognize the file. You can also use Windows 9x/Me ScanDisk to accomplish the same results.

If the drive is compressed, try booting to a command prompt and using ScanDisk to recover the compressed data. Include the name of the compressed volume file on the host drive, like this:

```
Scandisk drvspace.nnn
```

or

```
Scandisk dblspace.nnn
```

Substitute the file extension for the compressed volume file on the host drive (for example, Drvspace.001 or Dblspace.001).
- *Erased file.* A deleted file can sometimes be recovered. First look for the file in the Recycle Bin. If it's not there, try the Unerase or Undelete command at a command prompt, which recovers some erased files.

NOTE Viruses cause many file system problems. When you have a problem with a corrupted system file, program file, or data file, run a current version of antivirus software. The software will probably not help recover the file but might prevent other files from becoming infected.

Getting Technical Support

Sometimes you may not be able to solve a hard drive problem on your own. The first step toward getting more help is to check the Web site of the hard drive manufacturer. Search for the hard drive, and look for problems with solutions. If you still need more help, you might need to call technical support. To make calls to technical support more effective, have as much of the following information as you can available before you call:

- Drive model and description
- Manufacturer and model of your computer
- Exact wording of error message, if any
- Description of the problem
- Hardware and software configuration for your system

CHAPTER SUMMARY

▶ To improve hard drive performance, use Disk Defragmenter regularly. If a drive is giving errors, use Windows 9x/Me ScanDisk or Windows 2000/XP drive properties to check for errors and fix them.

▶ Windows 9x/Me disk compression works by storing data on a drive in one big file, and should not be trusted with valuable data.

▶ Volumes can be compressed under Windows 2000/XP as long as they are using NTFS.

▶ Disk caching uses temporary storage to speed up access to hard drive data and can be controlled either by hardware or software.

▶ DOS uses buffers rather than disk caching. Windows 3.x and 9x use built-in caching programs. Windows NT/2000/XP uses automated caching.

▶ The child, parent, grandparent backup method involves reusing tapes by making daily, weekly, and monthly backups.

▶ A full backup backs up all data from a hard drive. A differential backup backs up files that have changed or been created since the last full backup. An incremental backup backs up only files that have changed or been created since the last backup, whether or not it was a full backup.

▶ You can create backups using utilities included with tape drives or with Windows, or you can purchase third-party software.

▶ Disk cloning replicates a hard drive to a new computer.

▶ For disaster recovery, it is important to create and test a plan that includes keeping records of backups and recovery procedures.

▶ Viruses, which replicate by attaching themselves to other programs, are the most common type of computer infestation. Other types include Trojan horses, worms, and logic bombs.

▶ Viruses can hide in the boot sector, files, macros within files, or in both the boot sector and a file.

▶ Types of viruses that attempt to hide from antivirus software are polymorphic viruses, encrypting viruses, and stealth viruses.

▶ Damage from viruses ranges from an altered monitor display to the erasure of files or even an entire hard drive.

▶ Use antivirus software regularly both to clean out known viruses and to scan for undetected and unmanifested ones.

9

▶ Hard drive problems can be caused by hardware or software problems, and tend to fall into two categories: those that prevent the hard drive from booting and those that prevent data from being accessed.

▶ Three third-party utility software programs used to work with hard drives are Norton Utilities, SpinRite, and PartitionMagic.

▶ Common hard drive problems are corruption in OS files, the partition table, the boot record, the root directory, the FAT, sector markings, or data itself.

▶ For DOS or Windows to access a hard drive using the FAT file system, the following items must be intact, listed in the order in which they are accessed: the partition table, the boot record, the FAT, the root directory, the system files, and data and program files.

▶ High humidity, smoking near the PC, and leaving the PC turned off for long periods can damage a hard drive.

▶ You can use ScanDisk and Chkdsk to recover lost allocation units caused when files are not properly closed by the application creating them.

▶ When data is lost on a hard drive, don't write anything to the drive if you intend to try to recover the data.

▶ Low-level formats should be used only as a last resort to restore an unreliable IDE hard drive. Use only the low-level format program recommended by the drive manufacturer.

KEY TERMS

For explanations of key terms, see the Glossary near the end of the book.

antivirus (AV) software
backup
boot sector virus
buffer
chain
child, parent, grandparent
   backup method
cross-linked clusters
defragment
differential backup
disk cache
disk cloning
disk compression
disk imaging
drive imaging

DriveSpace
encrypting virus
file virus
firewall
fragmentation
full backup
hardware cache
incremental backup
infestation
logic bomb
lost allocation units
lost clusters
macro

macro virus
memory-resident virus
multipartite virus
non-memory-resident virus
polymorphic virus
SMARTDrive
software cache
stealth virus
Trojan horse
VCACHE
virus
virus signature
worm

REVIEWING THE BASICS

1. What is the difference between a cross-linked cluster and a lost cluster? What can cause them?

2. What are two tools that Windows 9x/Me uses to check for cross-linked and lost clusters?

3. What are two tools that Windows 2000/XP uses to check for cross-linked and lost clusters?

4. Of the two tools used by Windows 2000/XP to check for cross-linked and lost clusters, which tool is available from the Recovery Console?

5. Explain two disadvantages of data compression.

6. What file system is necessary to use if a volume is to be compressed under Windows 2000?

7. What is the name of the drive compression utility used by Windows 95/98?

8. How is a hardware cache different from a software cache?

9. Name and define the method DOS used to speed up disk access.

10. How is disk caching accomplished in Windows XP? Windows 9x/Me? Windows 3.x with DOS?

11. What is the difference between an incremental backup and a differential backup?

12. What versions of Windows support incremental backups? Differential backups?

13. What is the Windows Scripting Host utility used for, and what is the command line to execute it?

14. Explain the child, parent, grandparent method of making backups.

15. What must you do before you can use the Windows Backup utility on a Windows XP Home Edition PC?

16. What process is used to replicate a hard drive to a new computer? When might you use this process, and what are some examples of software designed to perform it?

17. Why should you create a disaster recovery plan? What type of information would you include in it?

18. Define and explain the differences between viruses, worms, logic bombs, and Trojan horses.

19. Where can viruses hide?

20. What is the best way to protect a computer or network against worms?

21. What is the best way to determine if an e-mail message warning about a virus is a hoax?

22. Name three ways that a virus can hide from antivirus software.

23. Are boot sector viruses limited to hard drives? Explain.

24. What is the most likely way that a virus will get access to your computer?

25. List three third-party utility programs used to support hard drives.

26. List at least four causes of hard drive problems.

27. List three hardware components to check or examine if a hard drive does not boot.

28. What items must be intact in order for DOS or Windows to be able to access a hard drive using the FAT file system? List them in the order in which they are accessed.

29. What error message might appear if the partition table is damaged? The boot record? The FAT? The system files?

30. If a file header is lost or corrupted and an application needs that header to read the file, how can you recover the contents of the file?

31. Explain how lost clusters are caused and what you can do to recover from them.

32. If an erased file is not found in the Recycle Bin, what command can you use at a command prompt to attempt to recover the file?

33. Before you call the manufacturer's technical support for a hard drive during installation, what should you have in hand?

THINKING CRITICALLY

1. You have an 8-GB hard drive and are using Windows 98. You need to use this system to store a commercial database that will be updated daily. The database will include photographs of products and you expect the data to take up about 10 GB of space. What do you do to solve the problem of too much data and not enough space?

   a. Compress the drive using Windows 98 DriveSpace.

   b. Compress the drive using third-party compression software.

   c. Install a new hard drive to hold the data.

2. You have an important FoxPro database stored on your hard drive. The drive has been giving bad sector errors for several weeks. You kept meaning to back up the data, but have not gotten around to it. Now you attempt to access the database and FoxPro tells you it cannot open the file. What do you try first? Second? Third?

    a. Reenter all the data and promise yourself you'll be more faithful about backups.

    b. Use SpinRite software to attempt to recover the file.

    c. Use ScanDisk to correct the bad sectors.

    d. Change the file extension of the database file to .txt and tell FoxPro to attempt to open the file as an ASCII text file.

3. Your system is very sluggish and takes a long time to boot and to load applications. Applications move very slowly as well. List three possible solutions that were described in this chapter.

9

HANDS-ON PROJECTS

HANDS-ON PROJECTS

PROJECT 9-1: **Using a Windows Command Prompt to Manage a Hard Drive**

On a Windows 2000/XP computer, use a Command window to do the following:

1. Use the Chkdsk command to check the hard drive for errors and correct them. What is the Chkdsk command line that you used?

2. Use the Defrag command to defragment the hard drive. What command line did you use?

On a Windows 9x/Me computer, do the following:

1. Print the contents of Scandisk.ini in the \Windows\Command directory of your hard drive. Scandisk.ini contains settings that ScanDisk reads and uses when it executes.

2. What setting allows ScanDisk to delete the contents of a lost cluster without prompting you first?

3. From the .ini file information, can ScanDisk repair a damaged boot sector of a compressed drive?

4. From a command prompt, type **DEFRAG**. Follow the directions to defragment a disk or hard drive.

5. Reboot using a Windows 9x/Me startup disk. Run **Scandisk** from the command prompt. What errors did it find?

PROJECT 9-2:   Using Windows to Back Up Files and Folders

This exercise lets you practice using Windows Backup and see how the Backup utility manages several situations.

Part I

1. Using Windows Explorer, create a folder called **Backtest** on a hard drive.

2. Use Explorer to find a .txt file, and copy it to the new folder. Copy two other files to the Backtest folder. Make a subfolder called **Subfolder** in Backtest and copy a fourth file to C:\backtest\subfolder.

3. Right-click the **.txt** file and rename it **Overwrite.txt**. Right-click the second file and rename it **Delete.txt**. Rename the third file **NoChange.txt**. Leave the fourth file alone for now. Use Explorer and write down the file sizes before the backup.

4. Click **Start, Programs, Accessories, System Tools,** and **Backup.**

5. Use the directions provided in this chapter to back up the Backtest folder to a floppy disk. Use Explorer and compare the backup file sizes to the original file sizes. How are they different?

6. Delete the file **Delete.txt**. Edit and change the contents of Overwrite.txt. Make no changes to NoChange.txt. Delete **Subfolder**.

7. Using Windows Backup, restore the files from the backup to their original folder.

    a. What did Backup do with the Delete.txt file?

    b. What did Backup do with the Overwrite.txt file?

    c. What did Backup do with the NoChange.txt file?

    d. What did Backup do with the missing subfolder and missing file?

    e. What is the name of the backup file on the floppy disk?

    f. What are the name and path to the error log created by Backup?

    g. Print the error log.

Part II

8. Use Windows Explorer to copy the Backtest folder to a second floppy disk.

9. Delete all files in the Backtest folder on the hard drive.

10. Use Windows Explorer to copy the three files back to the Backtest folder.

11. Delete the files in the Backtest folder on the hard drive.

12. Open the Recycle Bin and restore the three files to the Backtest folder by high-lighting them and using the **File, Restore** option. Did they return to the correct folder?

13. Once again, delete the files in the Backtest folder on the hard drive.

14. Highlight the three files in the Recycle Bin, and click **File, Delete**. Can you still restore the files?

PROJECT 9-3: **Using the Internet to Learn About Viruses**

9

One source of information about viruses on the Web is F-Secure Corporation. Go to the Web site *www.f-secure.com/v-descs* shown in Figure 9-18 for information about viruses; the viruses are listed alphabetically with complete descriptions, including any known sources of the viruses. Print a description of three viruses from this Web site:

Figure 9-18   For complete virus information, see the F-Secure Web site

▶ One virus that destroys data on a hard drive

▶ One harmless virus that only displays garbage on the screen

▶ One virus that hides in a boot sector

The site also lists information about the most recent viruses. Search the Web site at *www.f-secure.com*, list five recent viruses, and describe their payload.

PROJECT 9-4:   **Downloading the Latest Update of AV Software**

If you own antivirus software, download the latest antivirus (AV) definition list from the Internet. For example, for Norton AntiVirus, follow these directions:

1. Log on to the AV site: *www.symantec.com/downloads*.

2. Click **Virus Definition Updates** and then click **Download Virus Definitions**. Select your Norton AntiVirus product and operating system.

3. Follow the directions to download the latest update and signature list for the particular version of your AV software.

4. While online, see if the site offers information on virus hoaxes and create a list of hoaxes if it does.

PROJECT 9-5:   **Troubleshooting a Hard Drive Problem over the Phone**

A friend calls you to say that her hard drive does not work. She is using Windows 98 and has a rescue disk. Over the phone, walk her through the process of booting from the rescue disk and using the utilities on the disk to examine the hard drive. List the utilities on the rescue disk that she should use, in the order that she should use them, and write down what she should do with each utility.

In a lab environment, you can simulate this phone call by sitting with your back to a user sitting at a PC. Talk the user through the process without turning around and looking at the PC screen.

Supporting I/O Devices

This chapter focuses on how to install and support I/O devices. You will first learn about the procedures and guidelines common to most installations, including how to use serial, parallel, USB, and IEEE 1394 ports, as well as expansion slots. Then you will learn about the essential I/O devices for a PC: keyboard, mouse, and video. This chapter builds the foundation for Chapter 11, in which you will learn about multimedia devices.

Basic Principles of Peripheral Installations

When you add a new peripheral to a computer, the device needs a device driver or system BIOS, system resources (which might include an IRQ, DMA channel, I/O addresses, and memory addresses), and application software. Consider these fundamental principles:

- The peripheral is a hardware device controlled by software. You must install both the hardware and the software.
- Software might be of different types. For example, a device could require driver software that interfaces directly with the hardware device and an application software package that interfaces with the driver. You must install all levels of software.
- If the device uses a device driver, it must be written specifically for the OS installed.
- When installing a device, remember from Chapter 2 that more than one peripheral device might attempt to use the same computer resources. This conflict could disable one or both devices. Possible conflicts arise when more than one device or controller attempts to use the same IRQ, DMA channel, I/O addresses, or (for 16-bit drivers) upper memory addresses.
- Device manufacturers often release updates to device drivers or firmware on a device. Update the drivers, the firmware, or both to solve problems with the device or to add new features.

Installation Overview

A+
CORE
1.4
1.5
1.10

You follow three basic steps to install an add-on device:

- Install the device.
- Install the device driver.
- Install the application software.

NOTE

For most installations, you install the device before you install the device driver. However, for some devices such as a digital camera and some modems, you install the device driver first. Check the device documentation to know which to do first.

The device can be either internal (installed inside the computer case) or external (installed outside the case). Devices installed inside the case are drives, such as hard drives, floppy drives, CD-ROM drives, DVD drives, and Zip drives, or devices inserted in expansion slots on the motherboard, such as a modem card, video capture card, and video card. You can install an external device using an existing port

A+
CORE
1.4
1.5
1.10

(serial, parallel, USB, IEEE 1394 port, and so forth), or a port provided by an inter-face card installed in an expansion slot. External devices generally cost more than comparable internal devices because of the added cost of the device case and possibly an AC power adapter. Figure 10-1 shows the back of a PC case with several ports labeled. All ports except the three video ports come directly off the motherboard.

	PS/2 keyboard port
	PS/2 mouse port
	S/PDIF digital sound port
	Parallel port
	Serial port
	IEEE 1394 port
	Four USB ports
	Network port
	Three sound ports
	Three types of video ports

Figure 10-1   Rear of computer case showing ports; only the video ports are not coming directly off the motherboard

We now turn our attention to using standard ports for installing devices on a com-puter system. Then you will learn how to install expansion cards in expansion slots.

Using Ports and Expansion Slots for Add-On Devices

A+
CORE
1.1
1.4
1.5
2.1
4.3
6.2

Devices can be plugged directly into a port (serial, parallel, USB, IEEE 1394, or SCSI), or they can use an expansion card plugged into an expansion slot. This section provides details on both kinds of installations. SCSI installations are covered in Chapter 22.

All computers come with one or two serial ports, and one parallel port. Newer computers have one or more USB ports and possibly an IEEE 1394 FireWire port. Newer motherboards have several on-board ports, but on older motherboards, an **I/O controller card** in an expansion slot supplies the serial and parallel ports. Table 10-1 shows the speeds of various ports, from fastest to slowest.

10

A+
CORE
1.1
1.4
1.5
2.1
4.3
6.2

Port Type	Maximum Speed
1394b (FireWire)*	1.2 Gbps (gigabits per second) or 800 Mbps (megabits per second)
Hi-Speed USB 2.0	480 Mbps
1394a (FireWire)	400 Mbps
Original USB	12 Mbps
Parallel	1.5 Mbps
Serial	115.2 Kbps (kilobits per second)

* IEEE 1394b has been designed to run at 3.2 Gbps, but products using this speed are not yet manufactured.

Table 10-1   Data transmission speeds for various port types

Using Serial Ports

Chapter 1 introduced you to serial ports, which transmit data in single bits, or serially. You can identify these ports on the back of a PC case by (1) counting the pins and (2) determining whether the port is male or female. Figure 10-2 shows serial ports, a parallel port, and a game port for comparison. On the top are one 25-pin female parallel port and one 9-pin male serial port. On the bottom are one 25-pin male serial port and a 15-pin female game port. Serial ports are sometimes called DB-9 and DB-25 connectors. DB stands for data bus and refers to the number of pins on the connector. Serial ports are almost always male ports, and parallel ports are almost always female ports.

To simplify the allocation of system resources, two configurations for serial ports were designated COM1 and COM2, and later two more configurations were designated COM3 and COM4. These COM assignments each represent a designated IRQ and I/O address range, as seen in Table 10-2. Think of the serial ports as physical ports, and think of COM1 and COM2 as logical assignments to these physical ports, much as a phone number is a logical assignment to a physical telephone. In reality, COM1 is just a convenient way of saying IRQ 4 and I/O address 03F8h. Also notice in Table 10-2 that the two parallel port configurations are named LPT1 and LPT2, and each is assigned an IRQ and I/O address range. DOS, all the Windows operating systems, and most applications that use serial devices know about and comply with these assignments. For example, you can tell your communications software to use COM1 to communicate with a modem, and it then knows that the modem is using IRQ 4 to signal the CPU and is "listening" for instructions by way of I/O addresses 03F8h through 03FFh.

A+
CORE
1.1
1.4
1.5
2.1
4.3
6.2

25-pin female parallel port

9-pin male serial port

15-pin female game port

25-pin male serial port

Figure 10-2   Serial, parallel, and game ports

Port	IRQ	I/O Address (in Hex)	Type
COM1	IRQ 4	03F8 – 03FF	Serial
COM2	IRQ 3	02F8 – 02FF	Serial
COM3	IRQ 4	03E8 – 03EF	Serial
COM4	IRQ 3	02E8 – 02EF	Serial
LPT1	IRQ 7	0378 – 037F	Parallel
LPT2	IRQ 5	0278 – 027F	Parallel

Table 10-2   Default port assignments on many computers

Serial ports were originally intended for input and output devices, and parallel ports were intended for printers. Serial ports can be configured for COM1, COM2, COM3, or COM4.

Most serial and parallel ports today connect directly to the motherboard, and the COM and LPT assignments are made in CMOS setup. The ports can also be enabled and disabled in setup. Sometimes the setup screen shows the COM assignments, and sometimes you see the actual IRQ and I/O address assignments (see Figure 10-3). Older I/O controller cards used jumpers and DIP switches to configure the serial and parallel ports on the card.

A+
CORE
1.1
1.4
1.5
2.1
4.3
6.2

```
                    ROM PCI/ISA BIOS (<<P2B>>)
                     CHIPSET FEATURES SETUP
                      AWARD SOFTWARE, INC.

 SDRAM CONFIGURATION       : By SPD    Onboard FDC Controller      : Enabled
 SDRAM CAS Latency         : 2T        Onboard FDC Swap A & B       : No Swap
 SDRAM RAS to CAS Delay    : 3T        Onboard Serial Port 1        : 3F8H/IRQ4
 SDRAM RAS Precharge Time  : 3T        Onboard Serial Port 2        : 2F8H/IRQ3
 DRAM Idle Timer           : 16T       Onboard Parallel Port        : 378H/IRQ7
 SDRAM MA Wait State       : Normal    Parallel Port Mode           : ECP-EPP
 Snoop Ahead               : Enabled   ECP DMA Select               : 3
 Host Bus Fast Data Ready  : Enabled   VART2 Use Infrared           : Disabled
 16-bit I/O Recovery Time  : 1 BUSCLK  Onboard PCI IDE Enable       : Both
 8-bit I/O Recovery Time   : 1 BUSCLK  IDE Ultra DMA Mode           : Auto
 Graphics Aperture Size    : 64MB      IDE0 Master PIO/DMA Mode     : Auto
 Video Memory Cache Mode   : UC        IDE0 Slave  PIO/DMA Mode     : Auto
 PCI 2.1 Support           : Enabled   IDE1 Master PIO/DMA Mode     : Auto
 Memory Hole At 15W-16W    : Disabled  IDE1 Slave  PIO/DMA Mode     : Auto
 DRAM are 64 (Not 72) bits wide
 Data Integrity Mode       : Non-ECC   ESC    : Quit         ↑↓→←: Select Item
                                       F1     : Help      PU/PD/-/- : Modify
                                       F5     : Old Values  (Shift)F2 : Color
                                       F6     : Load BIOS  Defaults
                                       F7     : Load Setup Defaults
```

Serial and parallel port assignments

Figure 10-3　CMOS setup screen for chip set features

To verify that the port is configured correctly for any Windows OS, use Device Manager. Click the + sign beside Ports to reveal the list of ports. Click a communications port, such as COM1, and then click Properties. Click the Port Settings tab. You see the Properties dialog box shown in Figure 10-4 if you are using Windows XP, but other Windows OSs look the same. Note that the drop-down list shows the bits per second, or baud rate, of the port, which is currently set at 128,000 bps.

A serial port conforms to the standard interface called RS-232c (Reference Standard 232 revision c) and is sometimes called the RS-232 port. This interface standard originally called for 25 pins, but because microcomputers only use nine of those pins, manufacturers often installed a modified 9-pin port. Today some computers have a 9-pin serial port, some have a 25-pin serial port, and some have both. Both ports work the same way. The 25-pin port uses only nine pins; the other pins are unused. Serial 25-pin ports are often found on modems. You can buy adapters that convert 9-pin ports to 25-pin ports, and vice versa, to accommodate a cable you already have.

One of the nine pins on a serial port transmits data in a sequence of bits, and a second pin receives data sequentially. The other seven pins are used to establish the communications protocol. Recall from Chapter 1 that a protocol is a set of agreed-upon communication rules established before data actually passes from one device to another. Table 10-3 describes the functions of the pins of a serial port connection to a modem connected to another remote modem and computer. External modems sometimes use lights on the front panel to indicate the state of these pins. The labels on these modem lights are listed in the last column of the table.

Table 10-3 is included not so much to explain the use of each pin as to show that more than just data is included in a serial communication session. Also, when the system is using serial ports, one of the devices is called the **DTE (Data Terminal**

**A+
CORE
1.1
1.4
1.5
2.1
4.3
6.2**

Equipment) and the other device is called the **DCE (Data Communications Equipment)** For example, a modem is called the DCE, and the computer on which it is installed is called the DTE.

Figure 10-4   Properties of the COM1 serial port in Windows XP

The maximum cable length for a serial cable according to RS-232 standards is 50 feet.

Pin Number for 9-Pin	Pin Number for 25-Pin	Pin Use	Description	LED
1	8	Carrier detect	Connection with remote is made.	CD or DCD
2	3	Receive data	Receiving data	RD or TXD
3	2	Transmit data	Sending data	SD or TXD

Table 10-3 (continued)

10

A+
CORE
1.1
1.4
1.5
2.1
4.3
6.2

Pin Number for 9-Pin	Pin Number for 25-Pin	Pin Use	Description	LED
4	20	Data terminal ready	Modem hears its computer.	TR or DTR
5	7	Signal ground	Not used with PCs	
6	6	Data set ready	Modem is able to talk.	MR or DSR
7	4	Request to send	Computer wants to talk.	RTS
8	5	Clear to send to talk.	Modem is ready	CTS
9	22	Ring indicator	Someone is calling.	RI

Table 10-3   9-pin and 25-pin serial port specifications

Null Modem Connection

When two DTE devices, such as two computers, are connected, software can trans-mit data between the devices over a special cable called a **null modem cable,** or a **modem eliminator,** without the need for modems. The cable is not a standard serial cable but has several wires cross-connected in order to simulate modem communica-tion. For example, two computers can be connected by a null modem cable using their serial ports. Based on the 9-pin specifications in Table 10-3, each computer expects to send data on pin 2 and receive data on pin 3. A 9-pin null modem cable would connect pin 2 on one end of the cable to pin 3 on the other end of the cable with a single wire. Similarly, pin 3 would connect to pin 2 on the other end of the cable, so that the received data on one end is the sent data on the other end. Crossing pins 2 and 3 allows data to be sent from one computer and received by the other on the serial port pins that each computer expects to use. Standard modem software can often be used to transmit data, but because there are no actual modems in the connec-tion, very fast, accurate transfer is possible.

Table 10-4 describes the pins connected and crossed for a 25-pin null modem cable. Figure 10-5 shows the same information in a graphic.

Pin on one end is	Connected to the pin on the other end	So that
2	3	Data sent by one computer is received by the other.
3	2	Data received by one computer is sent by the other.

Table 10-4 (continued)

A+
CORE
1.1
1.4
1.5
2.1
4.3
6.2

Pin on one end is	Connected to the pin on the other end	So that
6	20	One end says to the other end, "I'm able to talk."
20	6	One end hears the other end say, "I'm able to talk."
4	5	One end says to the other, "I'm ready to talk."
5	4	One end hears the other say, "I'm ready to talk."
7	7	Both ends are grounded.

Table 10-4   Pin connections for a 25-pin null modem cable

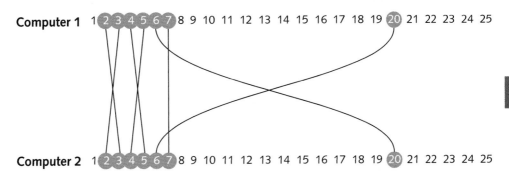

Figure 10-5   Wire connections on a 25-pin null modem cable used to transmit data

10

Infrared Transceivers

An **infrared transceiver**, sometimes called an **IrDA (Infrared Data Association) transceiver** or an infrared port, supports infrared devices such as wireless keyboards, mice, and printers, and often connects to a USB or serial port. In addition, a PC might use an infrared device to connect to a network. If the transceiver is Plug and Play, connect the device and turn on the PC. Windows automatically detects and installs the infrared driver, using the Add New Hardware Wizard. For legacy transceivers, install the transceiver using the Add New Hardware icon in the Control Panel, or run the device driver setup program. The transceiver uses the resources of the serial port for communication and creates a virtual infrared serial port and virtual infrared parallel port for infrared devices. During the installation, you are told what these virtual ports are and given the opportunity to change them. For example, if you physically connect the transceiver to COM2, the virtual ports will be COM4 for infrared serial devices and LPT3 for an infrared printer. The IRQ and I/O addresses for the infrared system are those assigned to COM2. To activate the transceiver, double-click the Infrared icon in the Control Panel. If the icon is not visible, press F5 to refresh the Control Panel.

A+
CORE
1.1
1.4
1.5
2.1
4.3
6.2

In addition, sometimes a motherboard provides a 5-pin connection for its own proprietary IrDA-compliant infrared transceiver. In this case, the transceiver mounts on the outside of the case, and a wire goes through a small hole in the case to connect to the 5-pin connection. The motherboard manual instructs you to use CMOS setup to enable "UART2 Use Infrared." **UART (universal asynchronous receiver-transmitter)** refers to the logic on the motherboard that controls the serial ports on the board.

When you enable COM2 to use infrared, the COM2 serial port is disabled because the infrared transceiver is using the resources for that port. The transceiver drivers are then installed and used the same way as described earlier.

A common problem with infrared devices is the line-of-sight issue: there must be an unobstructed "view" between the infrared device and the receiver. This is the main reason the industry is moving away from infrared and toward other wireless technologies. Short-range radio technology such as Bluetooth is becoming the most popular way to connect a wireless I/O device to a nearby computer, because with radio waves there is no line-of-sight issue.

NOTE

Infrared standards are defined by the Infrared Data Association (IrDA). Their Web site is *www.irda.org*.

Using Parallel Ports

Parallel ports, commonly used by printers, transmit data in parallel, eight bits at a time. If the data is transmitted in parallel over a very long cable, the data integrity is sometimes lost because bits may separate from the byte they belong to. Most parallel cables are only six feet (1.8 meters) long, though no established standard sets maximum cable length. However, avoid using a parallel cable longer than 15 feet (4.5 meters) to ensure data integrity. Hewlett-Packard recommends that cables be no longer than 10 feet (3 meters).

Parallel ports were originally intended to be used only for printers. However, some parallel ports are now used for input devices. These bidirectional parallel ports are often used for fast transmission of data over short distances. One common use is to download and upload data from a PC to a laptop. Some external CD-ROM drives use a bidirectional parallel port to transmit and receive data. If you use an existing parallel port to install a peripheral device, installation is very simple. Just plug the device into the port and load the software. To accommodate a second parallel port, configure the port as LPT2. An example of this is described in the next section.

A+
CORE
1.1
1.4
1.5
2.1
4.3
6.2

The uses of the pin connections for a 25-pin parallel port are listed in Table 10-5.

Pin	Input or Output from PC	Description
1	Output	Strobe
2	Output	Data bit 0
3	Output	Data bit 1
4	Output	Data bit 2
5	Output	Data bit 3
6	Output	Data bit 4
7	Output	Data bit 5
8	Output	Data bit 6
9	Output	Data bit 7
10	Input	Acknowledge
11	Input	Busy
12	Input	Out of paper
13	Input	Select
14	Output	Auto feed
15	Input	Printer error
16	Output	Initialize paper
17	Output	Select input
18	Input	Ground for bit 0
19	Input	Ground for bit 1
20	Input	Ground for bit 2
21	Input	Ground for bit 3
22	Input	Ground for bit 4
23	Input	Ground for bit 5
24	Input	Ground for bit 6
25	Input	Ground for bit 7

Table 10-5   25-pin parallel port pin connections

10

A+
CORE
1.1
1.4
1.5
2.1
4.3
6.2

Types of Parallel Ports

Parallel ports fall into three categories: standard parallel port (SPP), **Enhanced Parallel Port (EPP)**, and **Extended Capabilities Port (ECP)**. The standard parallel port is sometimes called a normal parallel port or a Centronics port, named after the 36-pin Centronics connection used by printers (see Figure 10-6). A standard port allows data to flow in only one direction and is the slowest of the three types of parallel ports. EPP and ECP are both bidirectional. ECP was designed to increase speed over EPP by using a DMA channel; therefore, when using ECP mode you are using a DMA channel. Over the years both hardware and software manufacturers have implemented several parallel port designs, all attempting to increase speed and performance. To help establish industry standards, a committee supported by the Institute of Electrical and Electronics Engineers (IEEE) was formed in the early 1990s and created the **IEEE 1284** standards for parallel ports. These standards require backward compatibility with previous parallel port technology. Both EPP and ECP are covered under the IEEE 1284 specifications.

NOTE

When using EPP or ECP printers and parallel ports, be sure to use a printer cable that is IEEE 1284 compliant. Look for the label somewhere on the cable. Older, noncompliant cables will not work properly with these printers. Also, note that a printer using a parallel port can use a 36-pin Centronics connector, or some newer printers use the smaller 36-pin Micro-Centronics or mini-Centronics connector.

DB 25-pin connection (PC end)

36-pin Centronics connection (printer end)

Figure 10-6 A parallel cable has a DB-25 connection at the PC end of the cable and a 36-pin Centronics connection at the printer end of the cable

Configuring Parallel Ports

A+
CORE
1.1
1.4
1.5
2.1
4.3
6.2

When configuring a parallel port, if the port is on an I/O card, look to the card documentation to learn how to assign system resources to the port. If the parallel port is coming directly off the motherboard, then look to CMOS setup to configure the port (look back at Figure 10-3). Setup can have up to four different settings for parallel ports. For the BIOS in Figure 10-3, choices for parallel port mode are Normal, EPP, ECP, and EPP + ECP. If you select ECP or EPP + ECP, you must also make an ECP DMA selection. Choices are DMA Channel 1 or 3.

NOTE

If you have trouble using a serial or parallel port, check CMOS setup to make sure the port is enabled. If you have problems with resource conflicts, try disabling ECP mode for the parallel port. EPP mode gives good results and does not tie up a DMA channel.

Using USB Ports

A relatively new I/O bus is the USB, originally created by a seven-member consortium including Compaq, Digital Equipment, IBM, Intel, Microsoft, NEC, and Northern Telecom. USB is designed to make the installation of slow peripheral devices as effortless as possible. USB is much faster than regular serial ports and uses higher-quality cabling. USB is also much easier to manage because it eliminates the need to resolve resource conflicts manually. USB is expected to ultimately replace both serial and parallel ports as the technology matures and more devices are built to use USB.

10

USB allows for **hot-swapping** and is **hot-pluggable**, meaning that a device can be plugged into a USB port while the computer is running, and the host controller will sense the device and configure it without your having to reboot the computer. Some I/O devices that use a USB connection are mice, joysticks, keyboards, printers, scanners, monitors, modems, digital cameras, fax machines, and digital telephones. One to four USB ports are found on most new motherboards (see Figure 10-7), and older motherboards that have no USB ports can be upgraded by adding a PCI-to-USB controller card in a PCI slot to provide a USB port. Sometimes a motherboard will have a USB port on the front of the case for easy access (see Figure 10-8).

USB Version 1 (sometimes called Basic Speed USB or Original USB) allows for two speeds, 1.5 Mbps (megabits per second) and 12 Mbps, and works well for slow I/O devices. USB Version 2 (sometimes called Hi-Speed USB or USB2) allows for up to 480 Mbps, which is 40 times faster than Original USB. Hi-Speed USB is backward-compatible with slower USB devices. The USB Implementers Forum, Inc. (*www.usb.org*), the organization responsible for developing USB, has adopted the symbols shown in Figure 10-9 to indicate if the product is certified by the organization as compliant with Original USB or Hi-Speed USB.

A+
CORE
1.1
1.4
1.5
2.1
4.3
6.2

Two USB ports

A-Male connector to computer

B-Male connector to device

Figure 10-7   A motherboard with two USB ports and a USB cable; note the rectangular shape of the connection as compared to the nearby serial and parallel D-shaped ports

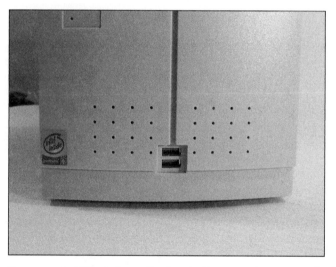

Figure 10-8   One or more USB ports on the front of a computer case make for easy access

Figure 10-9   Hi-Speed and Original USB logos appear on products certified by the USB forum

A+
CORE
1.1
1.4
1.5
2.1
4.3
6.2

A **USB host controller**, which for most motherboards is included in the chip set, manages the USB bus. Sometimes a motherboard has two USB controllers; each is enabled and disabled in CMOS setup. As many as 127 USB devices can be daisy chained together using USB cables, so one device provides a USB port for the next device. Figure 10-10 shows a keyboard and a mouse daisy chained together and connecting to a single USB port on an iMac computer. There can also be a standalone **hub** into which several devices can be plugged.

Figure 10-10   A keyboard and a mouse using a USB port daisy-chained together

For full-speed devices, use Hi-Speed USB cables, which can be up to 16.4 feet (5 meters) long, to connect devices or a device and a hub. The USB cable has four wires, two for power and two for communication. The two power wires (one carries voltage and the other is a ground) allow the host controller to provide power to a device. The connector on the host computer or hub end is called the A-Male connector, and the connector on the device end of the cable is called the B-Male connector. The A-Male connector is flat and wide, and the B-Male connector is square.

In USB technology, the host controller polls each device, asking if data is ready to be sent or requesting to send data to the device. The host controller manages communication to the CPU for all devices, using only a single IRQ (see Figure 10-11), I/O address range, and DMA channel. The OS and the USB host controller automatically assign system resources at startup.

10

A+
CORE
1.1
1.4
1.5
2.1
4.3
6.2

Figure 10-11   The USB controller has a single IRQ line that it raises when any USB device needs attention

Windows 95 OSR 2.1 was the first Microsoft OS to support USB, although Windows 98 offers much improved USB support. Besides Windows 95 with the USB update and Windows 98, Windows 2000 and Windows XP support Original USB, but Windows NT does not. Using Windows XP, you can download a patch for the OS that supports Hi-Speed USB.

Preparing to Install a USB Device

To install a USB device, you need:

- A motherboard or expansion card that provides a USB port
- An OS that supports USB
- A USB device
- A USB device driver

Windows provides many USB device drivers. If you are installing a USB device, don't use a device driver from the manufacturer that claims to work only for Windows 95. Windows 98 and later OSs made several improvements in USB support that you should take advantage of.

Installing a USB Device

Some USB devices such as printers require that you plug in the device before installing the drivers, and some USB devices such as scanners require you to install the drivers before plugging in the device. For some devices, it doesn't matter which is installed first. On the other hand, the documentation for one digital camera says that if you install the camera before installing the driver, the drivers will not install properly. Therefore, carefully read and follow the device documentation.

A+
CORE
1.1
1.4
1.5
2.1
4.3
6.2

Follow these steps to install a USB device where the device is plugged in before installing the drivers:

1. Using Device Manager, verify that the USB host controller driver is installed under Windows. See Figure 10-12 for an example of Windows XP Device Manager displaying the Properties dialog box for a USB controller. Note in the figure the symbol for USB. If the controller is not installed, install it from the Control Panel by double-clicking the **Add New Hardware** icon. If you have a problem installing the controller, verify that support for USB is enabled in setup.

10

Figure 10-12 Using Device Manager, verify that the USB controller is installed and working properly

If USB devices do not work, use CMOS setup to make sure USB support is enabled on the motherboard.

NOTE

**A+
CORE
1.1
1.4
1.5
2.1
4.3
6.2**

2. Turn off the PC and plug in the USB device. When you reboot, Windows should launch the Found New Hardware Wizard to install the device drivers. If the wizard does not launch, go to the Control Panel and use the Add New Hardware icon. If that fails to install the drivers, look for and run the setup program on the CD or floppy disk that came with the device. After the drivers are installed, you should see the device listed in Device Manager. Verify that Windows sees the device with no conflicts and no errors.

3. Install the application software to use the device. For example, most scanners come with some software to scan and edit images. After you install the software, use it to scan an image.

Using IEEE 1394 Ports

FireWire and **i.Link** are common names for another peripheral bus officially named **IEEE 1394** (or sometimes simply called 1394) after the group that designed the bus. IEEE was primarily led by Apple Computer and Texas Instruments in the initial design. FireWire is similar in design to USB, using serial transmission of data, but faster. FireWire supports data speeds as high as 3.2 Gbps (gigabits per second), much faster than USB. Whereas USB is targeted to replace slow serial and parallel ports, FireWire is likely to replace SCSI as a solution for high-volume, multimedia external devices such as digital camcorders, DVDs, and hard drives. SCSI is a very fast, but difficult to configure, peripheral bus.

For interesting information about 1394, surf the 1394 Trade Association's Web site at *www.1394ta.org.*

FireWire devices are hot-pluggable and can be daisy chained together and managed by a host controller using a single set of system resources (an IRQ, an I/O address range, and a DMA channel). One host controller can support up to 63 FireWire devices. Just as with USB, FireWire must be supported by the operating system. Windows XP, Windows 2000, and Windows 98 all support FireWire. (Windows 95 and Windows NT do not.)

A variation of 1394 is **IEEE 1394.3**, which is designed for peer-to-peer data transmission. Using this standard, imaging devices such as scanners and digital cameras can send images and photos directly to printers without involving a computer.

IEEE 1394 ports are sometimes found on newer high-end motherboards and are expected to become standard ports on all new motherboards, as commonplace as USB ports are now. These ports have two types of connectors: a 4-pin port that does

A+
CORE
1.1
1.4
1.5
2.1
4.3
6.2

not provide voltage to a device and a 6-pin port that does (see Figure 10-13). The two extra pins in the 6-pin port are used for voltage and ground. The cable for a 6-pin port is wider than the 4-pin cable.

4-pin cable   (Device requires AC adapter.)

6-pin cable   (Two pins are used for voltage and ground.)

Figure 10-13   Two types of IEEE 1394 cable connectors; the 6-pin cable provides voltage to the device from the PC

10

The four wires used for data in a 1394 cable are two pairs of shielded twisted-pair cable wrapped in a common cord. *Shielding* refers to enclosing wires in a protective covering to reduce interference, and *twisted-pair* refers to two wires being twisted to reduce interference. Some network cabling is also shielded and uses twisted-pair wires. In fact, IEEE 1394 uses a design similar to Ethernet, the most popular network design. Just as with Ethernet, data is broken into small packets before it is sent over 1394 cable. Each device on the IEEE 1394 network can communicate with any other device on the network without involving the computer's CPU.

IEEE 1394 uses **isochronous data transfer,** meaning that data is transferred continuously without breaks. This works well when transferring real-time data such as that received by television transmission. Because of the real-time data transfer and the fact that data can be transferred from one device to another without involving the CPU, IEEE 1394 is an ideal medium for data transfers between consumer electronics products such as camcorders, VCRs, TVs, and digital cameras.

Figure 10-14 shows an example of how this might work. A person can record a home movie using a digital camcorder and download the data through a digital VCR to a 1394-compliant external hard drive. The 1394-compliant digital VCR can connect to and send data to the hard drive without involving the PC. The PC can later read the data off the hard drive and use it as input to video-editing application software. A user can edit the data and design a professional video presentation complete with captioning and special effects. Furthermore, if the digital camcorder is also 1394-compliant, it can download the data directly to the PC by way of a 1394 port on the PC. The PC can then save the data to a regular internal hard drive.

A+
CORE
1.1
1.4
1.5
2.1
4.3
6.2

Personal computer   IEEE 1394 hard disk   Digital VCR

Digital camcorder

Figure 10-14 IEEE 1394 can be used as the interface technology to connect consumer audio/visual equipment to a PC

The two standards for IEEE 1394 are IEEE 1394A and 1394B. 1394A supports speeds up to 1.2 Gbps, and allows for cable lengths up to 4.5 meters (15 feet). A newer standard, 1394B, supports speeds up to 3.2 Gbps and extends the maximum cable length to 100 meters (328 feet).

Windows 98, Windows 2000, and Windows XP support IEEE 1394. Windows 98 Second Edition supports IEEE 1394 storage devices but not IEEE 1394 printers and scanners. Windows 2000/XP supports all these devices. For Windows 98 Second Edition, you can download an update from the Microsoft Web site (*windowsupdate.microsoft.com*). The update solves previous problems that occurred when devices were removed while the PC was still running.

To use a 1394 port with Windows, follow these steps:

1. Verify that Windows recognizes that an IEEE 1394 controller is present on the motherboard. Using Device Manager, look for the 1394 Bus Controller listed as an installed device. Click the + sign beside the controller in Device Manager to see the specific brand of 1394 controller that the board contains. If the controller is not installed or is not working, reinstall the driver. In the Control Panel, double-click the **Add New Hardware** icon. If you have problems installing the driver, verify that 1394 support is enabled in setup.

2. Plug the device into the 1394 port. Install the device drivers for the 1394-compliant device. Without rebooting, you should be able to use the Add New Hardware icon in the Control Panel. For example, after you have installed the drivers for a camcorder, you should see the device listed in Device Manager under Sound, video, and game controllers. If you don't see the device listed, turn the device off and then on.

3. Install the application software to use the device. A 1394-compliant camcorder is likely to come bundled with video-editing software, for example. Run the software to use the device.

A+
CORE
1.1
1.4
1.5
2.1
4.3
6.2

For motherboards that don't support IEEE 1394, you can install an IEEE 1394 host adapter to provide the support. For example, FireBoard 800 is an expansion card by Unibrain, Inc. that uses a PCI expansion slot and follows the IEEE 1394B standard. See *www.unibrain.com*.

When installing a 1394 device, just as with USB, you might install the device first or the drivers first. Read the device documentation to know how to proceed.

Next we look at general directions for installing an expansion card in an expansion slot. Then we turn our attention to the specifics of using PCI slots and ISA slots. Later in the chapter, you will learn about using AGP slots.

Installing an Expansion Card in an Expansion Slot

A+
CORE
1.4
1.10
4.3

To install a Plug and Play (PnP) expansion card such as a video card, modem card, network card, IEEE 1394 controller, USB controller, floppy drive controller, hard drive controller, wireless NIC, sound card, or some other specialized device, follow these general directions:

- Protect the PC from ESD by using an antistatic bracelet and ground mat.
- Shut down the PC and unplug it. Move things out of the way, and remove the case cover. Figure 10-15 shows a computer case with panels on the side. Remove the screws on the rear of the case that hold the panel in place, and slide the panel to the rear.
- Locate the slot you plan to use, and remove the faceplate from the slot. In Figure 10-16, you can see two PCI slots that have their faceplates removed, and two more PCI slots with faceplates in place. Sometimes a faceplate punches out, and sometimes you remove a faceplate screw to remove the faceplate.

VIDEO

Disabling
Onboard Ports

- Insert the expansion card in the expansion slot. Be careful to push the card directly into the slot, without rocking it from side to side. Rocking it from side to side can widen the expansion slot, making it more difficult to keep a good contact. If you have a problem getting the card into the slot, you can insert the end away from the side of the case in the slot first and gently rock the card from front to rear into the slot. The card should feel snug in the slot. You can almost feel it drop into place. Later, if the card does not work, most likely it is not seated securely in the slot. Check that first and then, if possible, try a different slot.
- Insert the screw that connects the card to the case (see Figure 10-16). Be sure to use this screw; if it's not present, the card can creep out of the slot over time.
- Replace the case cover, power cord, and other peripherals. (If you like, you can leave the case cover off until you've tested the device, in case it doesn't work and you need to reseat it.)

A+
CORE
1.4
1.10
4.3

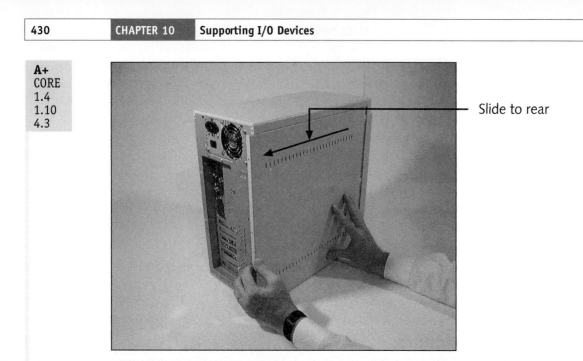

Slide to rear

Figure 10-15   Some cases have panels on each side; slide the panel to the rear to remove it

Figure 10-16   Secure an expansion card in the slot with a screw

■ Plug in whatever device is intended to use the port on the rear of the card. For example, for a video card, plug in the monitor; for a sound card, plug in the speakers; or for a modem card, plug in the phone line.

A+
CORE
1.4
1.10
4.3

- Reboot the PC. The Found New Hardware Wizard launches, prompting you to install the device drivers. Install the drivers and finish the wizard.
- Test the device.

Using Specialized Devices and Extra Ports

VIDEO

Firewire Ports

Sometimes an external specialized device, such as a CAD/CAM device or security reader, comes bundled with an expansion card that provides a port for the device. When installing such devices, always read the documentation carefully before you begin. Also, motherboards sometimes offer special slots or connectors to be used for such things as IDE controllers, RAID controllers, USB controllers, temperature sensors, and internal audio input. Follow the motherboard documentation and the device documentation to install these devices.

Some motherboards provide extra ports that can be installed in expansion slot openings off the back of the case. For example, the motherboard diagrammed in Figure 10-17 has a 1394 port coming directly off the board to the outside of the case. The board also has a connector that can be used to support an extra 1394 port, or the connector can be used for an internal 1394 hard drive. When used to provide an extra port, a cable connects to the connector at one end and to a module that looks like a faceplate that provides the extra port. To install this extra port, connect the cable to the motherboard connector and install the module in the place of a faceplate in an empty expansion slot.

10

P4P800 IEEE-1394 connector

TPAO- GND TPBO- +12V GND

1

TPAO+ GND TPBO+ +12V +12V

Figure 10-17   This motherboard has a 10-pin 1394 connector that can be used for an internal 1394 hard drive or to provide an extra 1394 port

Using PCI Expansion Slots

A+
CORE
1.4
1.10
4.3

The **PCI (Peripheral Component Interconnect) bus** is now the standard local I/O bus. The original PCI standard has a 32-bit data path and runs at 33 MHz or 66 MHz, depending on the speed of the motherboard (the system bus speed).

There have been several revisions of the PCI standards. The PCI-X standard allows for 64-bit data transfers using speeds of 133 MHz, 266 MHz, and higher. Conventional PCI Revision 2.3 changed the voltage requirement of PCI from 5.0-volt signaling to 3.3-volt signaling. The latest PCI standards is PCI Express, which allows for data transfer speeds up to 5 GHz. For a complete list of all the PCI standards, see the Web site of the PCI Special Interest Group (*www.pcisig.org*).

Most motherboards today have three or more regular PCI slots and one slot designed for a video card. The slot intended for the video card is an AGP slot or a PCI Express x16 (pronounced "by sixteen") slot. For example, the motherboard in Figure 10-18 has three regular PCI slots, one PCI Express x16 slot with a video card installed, and two PCI Express x1 slots. (See Figure 5-21 for a close-up of this same motherboard.) Figure 10-19 shows the pinouts (position and meaning of each pin) for the regular PCI slot.

Figure 10-18   Asus P5AD2 motherboard with the MSI GeForce FX5750 video card installed in a PCI Express x16 slot

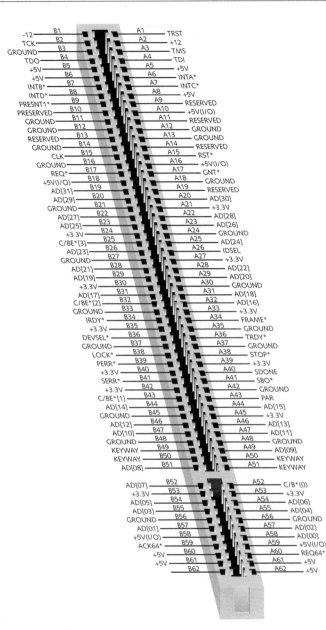

Figure 10-19 Standard PCI slot pinouts

The PCI bus controller, which is part of the motherboard chip set, manages the PCI bus and the expansion slots. The PCI bus controller assigns IRQ and I/O addresses to PCI expansion cards, which is why you don't see jumpers or DIP switches on these cards. To be more accurate, the PCI bus assigns resources to a PCI slot; move the card to a different slot to assign a new set of resources to it.

A+
CORE
1.4
1.10
4.3

10

**A+
CORE
1.4
1.10
4.3**

The PCI bus uses an interim interrupt between the PCI card and the IRQ line to the CPU. PCI documentation calls these interrupts A, B, C, D, and so forth. One interrupt is assigned to each PCI expansion slot. The PCI bus controller then maps each of these internal PCI bus interrupts to IRQs, using the IRQs available after legacy ISA bus devices claim their IRQs. The startup BIOS records which IRQs have been used by ISA devices and then assigns the unused ones to the PCI bus controller during the boot process.

When installing a PCI card, most likely you do not need to configure the IRQ or I/O address for the card, because the startup BIOS and PCI bus controller do this for you.

Use Device Manager to see which IRQ has been assigned to a PCI device. For example, Figure 10-20 displays the resources assigned to a PCI network card for Windows 2000. Notice that the IRQ assigned to the card is IRQ 9.

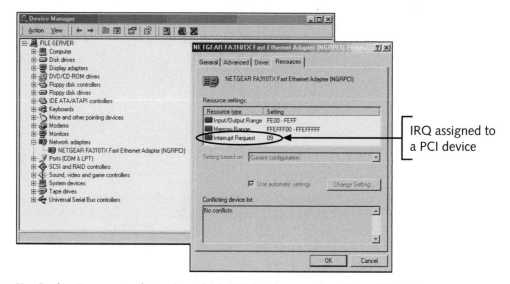

Figure 10-20   Use Device Manager to determine which IRQ has been assigned to a PCI device

APPLYING CONCEPTS

Sometimes BIOS gives the PCI bus controller an IRQ that a legacy ISA device needs, which can prevent either device from working. In CMOS setup, you can specify which IRQ to assign to a PCI slot, or you can tell setup that a particular IRQ is reserved for a legacy device, and thereby prevent the PCI bus from using it. See Figure 10-21.

A+
CORE
1.4
1.10
4.3

IRQ assignment for PCI slots: choices are Auto, 5, 7, 9, 10, 11, 12, 14, or 15 for each slot

Reserve an IRQ for an ISA legacy device

```
                    ROM PCI/ISA BIOS (<<P2B>>)
                       PNP AND PCI SETUP
                       AWARD SOFTWARE, INC.

   PNP OS Installed       : No        DMA  1 Used By ISA      : No/ICU
   Slot 1 (RIGHT) IRQ     : Auto      DMA  3 Used By ISA      : No/ICU
   Slot 2 IRQ             : Auto      DMA  5 Used By ISA      : No/ICU
   Slot 3 IRQ             : Auto
   Slot 4 (LEFT) IRQ      : Auto      ISA MEM Block BASE      : No/ICU
   PCI Latency Timer      : 32 PCI Clock

                                      SVMBIOS SCSI BIOS       : Auto
   IRQ  3 Used By ISA     : No/ICU    USB IRQ                 : Enabled
   IRQ  4 Used By ISA     : No/ICU
   IRQ  5 Used By ISA     : No/ICU
   IRQ  7 Used By ISA     : No/ICU
   IRQ  9 Used By ISA     : No/ICU
   IRQ 10 Used By ISA     : No/ICU
   IRQ 11 Used By ISA     : No/ICU
   IRQ 12 Used By ISA     : No/ICU
   IRQ 14 Used By ISA     : No/ICU    ESC  : Quit      ↑↓ → ←: Select Item
   IRQ 15 Used By ISA     : No/ICU    F1   : Help      PU/PD/-/- : Modify
                                      F5   : Old Values  (Shift)F2 : Color
                                      F6   : Load BIOS  Defaults
                                      F7   : Load Setup Defaults
```

Figure 10-21   CMOS setup screen for Plug and Play and PCI options

10

If two heavy-demand PCI devices end up sharing an IRQ, they might not work properly. If you suspect this is the case, try moving one of the devices to a different PCI slot, so that a device with a heavy demand (such as a 1394 adapter) is matched with a low-demand device (such as a modem).

Using ISA Expansion Slots

Using legacy ISA expansion slots is a little more difficult than using either USB or PCI, because the configuration is not as automated. The ISA bus itself does not manage system resources, as do USB and PCI bus controllers. It is up to the ISA device to request system resources at startup. If the ISA device does not support Plug and Play (PnP), then you select the I/O address, DMA channel, and IRQ by setting jumpers or DIP switches on the card. If the ISA device is PnP-compliant, then at startup PnP allocates the required resources to the device. Once the device and its drivers are installed, look at Device Manager to find out what resources it is using. To discover if a device is PnP-compliant, look for "Ready for Windows" on the box or read the documentation.

When adding a legacy ISA expansion card to a system, the most difficult problems you are likely to encounter are resource conflicts between two legacy devices or problems using legacy device drivers. We next turn our attention to solving these problems.

Solving Problems with Legacy ISA Cards

A+
CORE
1.4
1.10
4.3

Suppose you install a legacy network card in a system, and the card does not work and the modem card has stopped working. Most likely you have a resource conflict. The tool to use for help in resolving hardware conflicts in Windows is Device Manager. This tool is not infallible, because it depends on what the OS knows about resources being used, and sometimes a device does not tell the OS what it is using. Also, recall that Windows 95 and 98 allow legacy 16-bit drivers, but Windows Me and Windows NT/2000/XP do not. Follow this general approach when installing a legacy device:

✔ **A+ EXAM TIP**

The A+ Core exam expects you to know how to solve problems when installing legacy devices and legacy drivers. On the job, these problems can often be solved simply by purchasing a new PCI PnP card, or at least downloading a 32-bit driver for the legacy card.

1. Know the system resources already in use. See the documentation for devices already installed, use Device Manager, or try both. As you learned in earlier chapters, you should keep a notebook dedicated to your PC, in which you keep records of each device and its present settings, as well as any changes you make to your system.

2. Know what resources the device will need (see the documentation). Install the device using resources that are not already used by your system. If the device is set to use a resource already in use, read the documentation to see if you can set a jumper or DIP switch to use an alternate resource. For example, Figures 10-22 and 10-23 show modems that have a bank of DIP switches on the back of the card and a bank of jumpers on the card itself. By using combinations of these DIP switches and jumpers, you can configure this modem to use a specific set of IRQ and I/O addresses.

Figure 10-22   Diagram of a modem card

A+
CORE
1.4
1.10
4.3

Two RJ-11
phone
connections

Speaker port
Microphone port

Bank of DIP
switches

Figure 10-23   Ports and DIP switches on the back of an internal legacy modem

NOTE

Don't change a DIP switch or jumper on a device without writing down the original settings so
you can backtrack, or without carefully reading the documentation.

10

3. If a card does not work after you install it, try reseating the card in the slot or using a different slot.

4. If the device still does not work or another device stops working, suspect a resource conflict. If you do have a conflict, use Device Manager, CMOS setup, and documentation for the motherboard and devices to first identify and then resolve the conflict. To find out what resources your system is using for Windows 9x/Me, follow Step 5.

5. Click **Start**, point to **Settings**, click **Control Panel**, **System**, and then **Device Manager**. Click **Computer** and then **Properties**. Select the **View Resources** tab. The window in Figure 10-24 is displayed. From it, you can view current assignments for IRQs, I/O addresses, DMA channels, and upper memory addresses.

6. Once you have found the conflicting resource, try the following to resolve the conflict:

   ▪ If the device is a legacy ISA device, physically set the device's jumpers or DIP switches to use a different resource.
   ▪ If a legacy device can only use one IRQ, then use CMOS setup to reserve that IRQ for the device.
   ▪ If your BIOS supports PCI bus IRQ steering, enable the feature. That alone might solve the problem. In Device Manager, go to the device's Properties dialog box, click the **IRQ Steering** tab, and check **Use IRQ Steering**. Windows 9x/Me is then allowed to assign the IRQ based on what it knows about IRQs currently being used.

- Using PCI bus IRQ steering, tell Windows 98 to use a different IRQ for a PCI device. To do that, use the Properties dialog box for the device in Device Manager.
- Move the device to a different slot. Use the slot closest to the CPU, if you can.
- Disable PCI bus IRQ steering.
- Suspect that the documentation for the device is wrong, that the device is faulty, or that there is a problem with the motherboard or the OS. Try a new device in this system, or try this device in another working system.

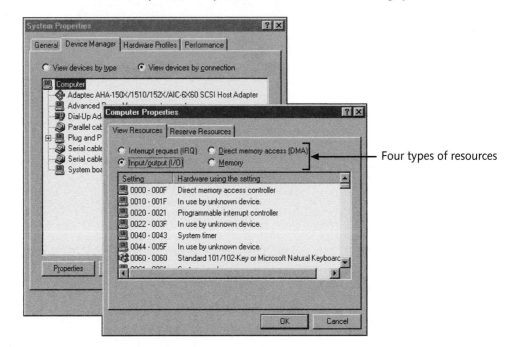

Four types of resources

Figure 10-24　Use Device Manager to see I/O addresses currently in use

Solving Problems with Legacy Drivers

Windows 9x/Me contains 32-bit drivers for hundreds of hardware devices, and even more are provided by the device manufacturers. However, some older legacy devices do not have 32-bit drivers, so you are forced to use a 16-bit, real-mode device driver. These 16-bit drivers are loaded by entries in the Config.sys, Autoexec.bat, or System.ini file and probably use upper memory addresses. Back up these files before you begin the installation. Then run a setup program on the floppy disk or CD provided with the device. Use the Run dialog box or double-click the program filename in Explorer. The setup program copies the driver files to the hard drive and adds the DEVICE= command to Config.sys. In addition, it might make entries in Autoexec.bat, or, for drivers written for Windows 3.x, it might make entries in System.ini. After you have verified that the device is working, note the changes made to Autoexec.bat, Config.sys, and System.ini. You might want to keep a record of the

**A+
CORE
1.4
1.10
4.3**

commands the setup program put in these files, in case you need it for future troubleshooting.

If you have problems with installing or running a legacy driver, do the following:

- Make every effort to locate a 32-bit driver for the device. Check the Microsoft Web site at *support.microsoft.com*, and check the device manufacturer's Web site. Use a search engine to search the Web for shareware drivers.
- Create an empty copy of Autoexec.bat and Config.sys on your hard drive. Boot up into MS-DOS mode and run the setup program from the command prompt. Look at the entries it puts into Autoexec.bat and Config.sys and copy these command lines into your original versions of Autoexec.bat and Config.sys.

In the rest of the chapter, we will look at the essential I/O devices for a PC: the keyboard, pointing devices, and video display.

Keyboards

**A+
CORE
1.2
1.5
2.1**

Keyboards have either a traditional straight design or a newer ergonomic design, as shown in Figure 10-25. The word ergonomic means "designed for safe and comfortable interaction between human beings and machines." The ergonomically safer keyboard is designed to keep your wrists high and straight. Some users find it comfortable, and others do not. Figure 10-26 demonstrates the correct position of hands and arms at the keyboard. Keyboards also differ in the feel of the keys as you type. Some people prefer more resistance than others, and some like more sound as the keys make contact. A keyboard might have a raised bar or circle on the F and J keys to help your fingers find the home keys as you type. Another feature is the depth of the ledge at the top of the keyboard that holds pencils, etc. Some keyboards have a mouse port on the back, and specialized keyboards have trackballs or magnetic scanners for scanning credit cards in retail stores.

Figure 10-25   An ergonomic keyboard

Figure 10-26   Keep wrists level, straight, and supported while at the keyboard

Computer keyboards have been criticized by users who work with them for hours at a time because they can cause a type of repetitive stress injury (RSI) known as carpal tunnel syndrome (CTS). CTS is caused by keeping the wrists in an unnatural position and having to execute the same motions (such as pressing keys on a keyboard) over prolonged periods.

You can help prevent CTS by keeping your elbows at the same level as the keyboard and keeping your wrists straight and higher than your fingers. I've found that a keyboard drawer that slides out from under a desk surface is much more comfortable, because the keyboard is low enough for me to keep the correct position. If I'm working at a desk with no keyboard drawer, I sometimes type with the keyboard in my lap to relieve the pressure on my arms and shoulders.

Keyboards use one of two common technologies in the way the keys make contact: foil contact or metal contact. When you press a key on a foil-contact keyboard, two layers of foil make contact and close a circuit. A small spring just under the keycap raises the key again after it is released.

The more expensive and heavier metal-contact keyboards generally provide a different touch to the fingers than foil-contact keyboards. Made by IBM and AT&T, as well as other companies, the metal-contact keyboards add an extra feel of solid construction that is noticeable to most users, giving the keystroke a clear, definitive contact. When a key is pressed, two metal plates make contact, and again a spring raises the key when it is released.

Keyboard Connectors

Keyboards connect to a PC by one of four methods: a PS/2 connector (sometimes called a mini-DIN), a DIN connector, a USB port, or the more recently available wireless connection. The DIN connector (DIN is an acronym of the German words meaning "German industry standard") is round and has five pins. The smaller round PS/2 connector has six pins (see Figure 10-27). Table 10-6 shows the pinouts for both connector types. If the keyboard you use has a different connector from the keyboard port of your computer, use a keyboard connector adapter, like the one shown in Figure 10-28, to convert DIN to PS/2 or PS/2 to DIN. Also, some keyboards are cordless, using radio transmission (or, for older cordless devices, infrared) to communicate with a sensor connected to the keyboard port. For example, a cordless keyboard made by Logitech (*www.logitech.com*) uses a receiver that plugs into a normal keyboard port.

6-pin PS/2 connector
(mini-DIN)

5-pin DIN connector

Figure 10-27   Two common keyboard connectors are a PS/2 connector and a DIN connector

Description	6-Pin Connector (PS/2)	5-Pin Connector (DIN)
Keyboard data	1	2
Not used	2	3
Ground	3	4
Current (+5 volts)	4	5
Keyboard clock	5	1
Not used	6	—

Table 10-6   Pinouts for keyboard connectors

10

**A+
CORE
1.2
1.5
2.1**

DIN connection

PS/2 connection

Figure 10-28   A keyboard adapter

Installing Keyboards

Most often, installing a keyboard simply means plugging it in and turning on the PC. Because the system BIOS manages the keyboard, no keyboard drivers are necessary. The exception to this is a wireless keyboard that needs a driver to work. In this case, you must use a regular keyboard to install the software to use the wireless keyboard. Plug in the receiver, insert the CD or floppy disk, and run the setup program on the disk. You can then use the wireless keyboard.

Troubleshooting Keyboards

**A+
CORE
1.2
1.5
2.1**

Often dirt, food, or drink in the keyboard causes one or more keys to stick or not work properly. Because of its low cost, the solution for a malfunctioning keyboard is most often to replace it. However, you can try a few simple things to repair one.

A Few Keys Don't Work

If a few keys don't work, remove the caps on the bad keys with a chip extractor. Spray contact cleaner into the key well. Repeatedly depress the contact in order to clean it. Don't use rubbing alcohol to clean the key well, because it can leave a residue on the contact. If this method of cleaning solves the problem, then clean the adjacent keys as well.

Turning the keyboard upside down and lightly bumping multiple keys with your flat palm will help loosen and remove debris.

A+
CORE
1.2
1.5
2.1

The Keyboard Does Not Work at All

If the keyboard does not work at all, first determine that the cable is plugged in. PC keyboard cables may become loose or disconnected. If the cable connection is good and the keyboard still does not work, swap it with another keyboard of the same type that you know is in good condition, to verify that the problem is in the keyboard, not the computer.

CAUTION Always power down a PC before plugging in a keyboard. Plugging in a keyboard while the power is on might damage the motherboard.

If the problem is in the keyboard, check the cable. If possible, swap the cable with a known good one, perhaps from an old discarded keyboard. Sometimes a wire in a PC keyboard cable becomes pinched or broken. Most cables can be easily detached from the keyboard by removing the few screws that hold the keyboard case together, then simply unplugging the cable. Be careful as you work; don't allow the keycaps to fall out! In Appendix E you can learn how to use a multimeter to test a cable for continuity. You can use this method to verify that the cable is good.

On the motherboard, the chip set and the ROM BIOS chip both affect keyboard functions. You might choose to flash BIOS to verify that system BIOS is not the source of the problem. Otherwise, the entire motherboard might have to be replaced, or you can try substituting a USB keyboard for the PS/2 keyboard.

10

Key Continues to Repeat After Being Released

This problem can be caused by a dirty contact. Some debris may have conductive properties, short the gap between the contacts, and cause the key to repeat. Try cleaning the key switch with contact cleaner.

Very high humidity and excess moisture sometimes short key switch contacts and cause keys to repeat, because water is an electrical conductor. The problem usually resolves itself after the humidity level returns to normal. You can hasten the drying process by using a fan (not a hot hair dryer) to blow air at the keyboard.

Keys Produce the Wrong Characters

This problem is usually caused by a bad chip. PC keyboards actually have a processor mounted on the logic board inside the keyboard. Try swapping the keyboard for one you know is good. If the problem goes away, replace the keyboard.

Major Spills on the Keyboard

When coffee or sugary drinks spill on the keyboard, they create a sticky mess. The best solution to stay up and running is to simply replace the keyboard. You can try to save the keyboard by thoroughly rinsing it in running water, perhaps from a

A+
CORE
1.2
1.5
2.1

bathroom shower. Make sure the keyboard dries thoroughly before you use it. Let it dry for two days on its own, or less if you set it out in the sun or in front of a fan. In some situations, such as a factory setting where dust and dirt are everywhere, consider using a clear, plastic keyboard cover.

NOTE

For a list of keyboard manufacturers, see Table 10-7 near the end of the next section, "Pointing Devices."

Pointing Devices

A+
CORE
1.2
1.3
2.1

A pointing device allows you to move a pointer on the screen and perform tasks such as executing (clicking) a command button. Common pointing devices are the mouse, the trackball, and the touch pad (see Figure 10-29). IBM ThinkPad notebooks use a unique and popular pointing device embedded in the keyboard (see Figure 10-30).

Figure 10-29   The most common pointing devices: a mouse, a trackball, and a touch pad

Figure 10-30   An IBM ThinkPad pointing device

A+
CORE
1.2
1.3
2.1

Mouse technologies include the wheel mouse and the optical mouse. Inside a wheel mouse is a ball that moves freely as you drag the mouse on a surface. As shown in Figure 10-31, two or more rollers on the sides of the ball housing turn as the ball rolls against them. Each roller turns a wheel. The turning of the wheel is sensed by a small light beam as the wheel "chops" the light beam when it turns. The chops in the light beams are interpreted as mouse movement and sent to the CPU. One of two rollers tracks the x-axis (horizontal) movement of the mouse, and a second roller tracks the y-axis (vertical) movement.

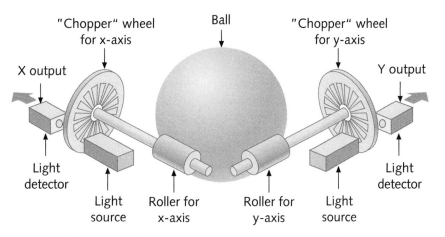

Figure 10-31 How a wheel mouse works

An optical mouse replaces the ball in a standard mouse with a microchip, miniature red light, and camera. The light illuminates the work surface, the camera takes 1500 snapshots every second, and the microchip reports the tiniest changes to the PC. An optical mouse works on most opaque surfaces and doesn't require a mouse pad. The bottom of an optical mouse has a tiny hole for the camera rather than a ball, and the light glows as you work.

A mouse can have two or three buttons. Software must be programmed to use these buttons. Almost all applications use the left button, and Windows uses the right button to display shortcut menus. The center button has recently been converted into a scroll wheel that you can use to move through large documents on screen. Many applications allow you to customize mouse button functions.

A mouse can connect to the computer by several methods:

- By using a dedicated round mouse port coming directly from the motherboard (**motherboard mouse** or **PS/2-compatible mouse**). Be aware that the keyboard uses a port that looks just like the mouse port. These ports are not interchangeable.
- By using a mouse bus card that provides the same round mouse port (**bus mouse**) as discussed earlier
- By using the serial port (the mouse is then called a **serial mouse**)

10

- By using a USB port
- By using a Y-connection with the keyboard so that both the keyboard and the mouse can share the same port
- By using a cordless technology whereby the mouse sends signals to a sensor on the PC or to an access point connected to the PC

Except for the cordless mouse, all of the above methods produce the same results (that is, the mouse port type is transparent to the user). Therefore, the advantages and disadvantages of each connection type are based mainly on the resources they require. The motherboard mouse is most users' first choice because the port on the motherboard does not take any resources that other devices might need. If you are buying a new mouse that you plan to plug into the motherboard port, don't buy a bus mouse unless the motherboard documentation states that you can use a bus mouse. The motherboard port and the bus port are identical, but a bus mouse might not work on the motherboard port.

If you have a motherboard mouse port, use it. If it becomes damaged, you can switch to a serial port or USB port. The motherboard mouse port most likely uses IRQ 12. If you are not using a mouse on this port, the motherboard might release IRQ 12 so that other devices can use it. Check the documentation for your motherboard to determine how the unused IRQ is managed.

The serial mouse requires a serial port and an IRQ for that port. Most people prefer a USB or bus mouse to a serial port mouse because they can assign the serial ports to other peripheral devices. A bus mouse can use a bus card if the motherboard does not have a mouse port.

Cleaning the Mouse

The rollers inside the wheel mouse housing collect dirt and dust and occasionally need cleaning. Remove the cover of the mouse ball from the bottom of the mouse. The cover usually comes off with a simple press and shift or turn motion. Clean the rollers with a cotton swab dipped in a very small amount of liquid soap.

Touch Screens

A **touch screen** is an input device that uses a monitor or LCD panel as the backdrop for input options. The monitor displays user options and the touch screen receives those options as input. A touch screen can be embedded inside a monitor for a desktop system or an LCD panel in a notebook, or the touch screen can be installed on top of the monitor screen or LCD panel as an add-on device. As an add-on device, the touch screen has its own AC adapter to power it. The touch screen is a grid that senses clicks and drags (similar to those created by a mouse) and sends these events to the computer by way of a serial or USB connection.

A+
CORE
1.2
1.5
2.1

When installing a touch screen add-on device, follow the manufacturer's directions to attach the touch screen to the monitor or LCD panel, connect the USB or serial cable and the power cable, and then install the touch screen device drivers and management software. Reboot the PC. The touch screen must then be calibrated to account for the monitor's resolution using the management software. If the resolution is later changed, the touch screen must be recalibrated. The screen can be cleaned with a damp cloth using a solution of alcohol and water.

Other Pointing Devices

Other pointing devices are trackballs and touch pads. A trackball is really an upside-down wheel mouse. You move the ball on top to turn rollers that turn a wheel sensed by a light beam. A touch pad allows you to duplicate the mouse function, moving the pointer by applying light pressure with one finger somewhere on a pad that senses the x, y movement. Some touch pads let you double-click by tapping their surfaces. Buttons on the touch pad serve the same function as mouse buttons. Use touch pads or trackballs where surface space is limited, because they remain stationary when you use them. Touch pads are popular on notebook computers.

Table 10-7 lists manufacturers of keyboards and pointing devices.

Manufacturer	Web Site
Mitsumi	*www.mitsumi.com*
Logitech	*www.logitech.com*
Microsoft	*www.microsoft.com*
Intel	*www.intel.com*
Belkin	*www.belkin.com*
Keytec, Inc.	*www.magictouch.com*

Table 10-7 Manufacturers of keyboards and pointing devices

Troubleshooting a Mouse

If the mouse does not work or the pointer moves like crazy over the screen, do the following to troubleshoot the mouse:

- Check the mouse port connection. Is it secure? Is the mouse plugged into the keyboard port?
- Check for dust or dirt inside the mouse. Reboot the PC.

10

A+
CORE
1.2
1.5
2.1

- Try a new mouse.
- Using Device Manager and the Add New Hardware icon in the Control Panel, first uninstall and then reinstall the mouse driver. Reboot the PC.
- Reboot the PC and select the logged option from the startup menu to create the Bootlog.txt file. Continue to boot and check the log for errors.

Computer Video

A+
CORE
1.1

The primary output device of a computer is the monitor. The two necessary components for video output are the video controller and the monitor itself.

Monitors

The common types of monitors today are rated by screen size, resolution, refresh rate, and interlace features. Many older VGA (Video Graphics Adapter) monitors are still in use, but most sold today meet the standards for Super VGA. Monitors use either the older CRT (cathode-ray tube) technology used in television sets or the newer LCD (liquid crystal display) technology used in notebook PCs and in **flat panel monitors** for the desktop.

How a CRT Monitor Works

Most monitors use CRT technology, in which the filaments at the back of the cathode tube shoot a beam of electrons to the screen at the front of the tube, as illustrated in Figure 10-32. Plates on the top, bottom, and sides of the tube control the direction of the beam. The beam is directed by these plates to start at the top of the screen, move from left to right to make one line, and then move down to the next line, again moving from left to right. As the beam moves vertically down the screen, it builds the image. By turning the beam on and off and selecting the correct color combination, the grid in front of the filaments controls what goes on the screen when the beam hits that portion of the line or a single dot on the screen. When hit, special phosphors on the back of the monitor screen light up and produce colors. The grid controls which one of three electron guns fires, each gun targeting a different color (red, green, or blue) positioned on the back of the screen.

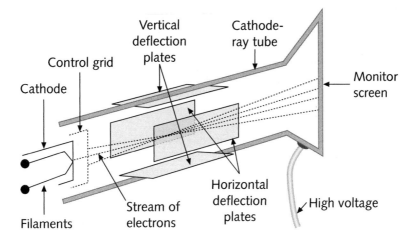

Figure 10-32   How a CRT monitor works

Choosing the Right Monitor   The features available on monitors are summarized in Table 10-8 and discussed next.

Monitor Characteristic	Description
Screen size	Diagonal length of the screen surface
Refresh rate	The number of times an electronic beam fills a video screen with lines from top to bottom in one second
Interlaced	The electronic beam draws every other line with each pass, which lessens the overall effect of a lower refresh rate.
Dot pitch or pixel pitch	The distance between adjacent dots on the screen
Resolution	The number of spots, or pixels, on a screen that can be addressed by software
Multiscan	Monitors that offer a variety of refresh rates so they can support several video cards
Connectors	15-pin analog video (RGB video) or digital video (DVI)

Table 10-8   Some features of a monitor

Screen Size   The screen size of a monitor is the one feature that most affects price. The larger the screen size is, the more expensive the monitor. Common screen sizes are 14 inches, 15 inches, 17 inches, and 21 inches. Macintosh computers can use special monitors designed for page layouts on legal-sized paper. The 15-inch monitor is most popular, while the small 14-inch monitor is losing popularity.

A+
CORE
1.1

When you match a monitor to a video card, a good rule of thumb is to match a low-end video card to a small, 14-inch monitor, a midrange video card to a 15-inch monitor, and a high-end video card to a 17-inch or larger monitor, to get the best performance from both devices. However, you can compare the different features of the video card to those of the monitor, such as the resolutions supported, the refresh rate, and the bandwidth. **Bandwidth** as it applies to analog communication is the difference between the highest and lowest frequencies that an analog communications device such as a video cable can carry.

Monitor sizes are measured on the diagonal. The monitor I'm now using is advertised as having a 17-inch screen. The actual dimensions of the lighted screen are 9½ inches by 11½ inches. The diagonal measurement of the lighted area is 15 inches, and the diagonal measurement of the screen surface is 17 inches.

Refresh Rate   The **refresh rate**, or vertical scan rate, is the number of times in one second an electronic beam can fill the screen with lines from top to bottom. Refresh rates differ among monitors. The Video Electronics Standards Association (VESA) set a minimum refresh rate standard of 70 Hz, or 70 complete vertical refreshes per second, as one requirement of Super VGA monitors. Slower refresh rates make the image appear to flicker, while faster refresh rates make the image appear solid and stable. The refresh rate is set by using the Display icon in the Control Panel.

CAUTION

If you spend many hours in front of a computer, use a good monitor with a high refresh rate. The lower refresh rates that cause monitor flicker can tire and damage your eyes.

Interlaced or Noninterlaced   **Interlaced** monitors draw a screen by making two passes. On the first pass, the electronic beam strikes only the even lines, and on the second pass, the beam strikes only the odd lines. The result is that a monitor can have a slow refresh rate with a less noticeable overall effect than there would be if the beam hit all lines for each pass. Interlaced monitors generally have slightly less flicker than **noninterlaced** monitors, which always draw the entire screen on each pass. Buy an interlaced monitor if you plan to spend long hours staring at the monitor. Your eyes will benefit.

Dot Pitch   **Dot pitch** is the distance between the spots, or dots, on the screen that the electronic beam hits. Remember that three beams build the screen, one for each of three colors (red, green, and blue). Each composite location on the screen is really made up of three dots and is called a triad. The distance between a color dot in one triad and the same color dot in the next triad is the dot pitch. The smaller the pitch is, the sharper the image. Dot pitches of .28 mm or .25 mm give the best results and

**A+
CORE
1.1**

cost more. Although less expensive monitors can have a dot pitch of .35 mm or .38 mm, they can still create a fuzzy image, even with the best video cards.

Resolution   **Resolution** is a measure of how many spots on the screen are addressable by software. Each addressable location is called a **pixel** (for picture element), which is composed of several triads. Because resolution depends on software, the video controller card must support the resolution, and the software you are using must make use of the monitor's resolution capabilities. The standard for most software packages is 800 x 600 pixels, although many monitors offer a resolution of 1024 x 768 pixels or higher. The resolution is set in Windows from the Display icon in the Control Panel, and requires a driver specific for that resolution. Higher resolution usually requires more video RAM.

Multiscan Monitors   **Multiscan monitors** offer a variety of vertical and horizontal refresh rates so they can support a variety of video cards. They cost more but are much more versatile than other monitors.

Green Monitors   A Green monitor saves electricity, making a contribution to conserving natural resources. A Green monitor meets the requirements of the EPA Energy Star program and uses 100 to 150 watts of electricity. When the screen saver is on, the monitor should use no more than 30 watts of electricity.

10

Monitors and ELF Emissions

There is some debate about the danger of monitors giving off ELF (extremely low frequency) emissions of electromagnetic fields. Standards to control ELF emissions are Sweden's MPR II standard and the TCO '95 standards. The TCO '95 standards also include guidelines for energy consumption, screen flicker, and luminance. Most monitors manufactured today comply with the MPR II standard, but very few comply with the more stringent TCO '95 standards.

Flat Panel Monitors

**A+
CORE
1.1
1.3**

Flat panel monitors are increasing in popularity, although they still cost much more than comparable CRT monitors. Flat panel monitors take up much less desk space than CRT monitors, are lighter, and require less electricity to operate. An LCD panel produces an image using a liquid crystal material made of large, easily polarized molecules. Figure 10-33 shows the layers of the LCD panel that together create the image. At the center of the layers is the liquid crystal material. Next to it is the layer responsible for providing color to the image. These two layers are sandwiched between two grids of electrodes. One grid of electrodes is aligned in columns, and the

A+
CORE
1.1
1.3

other electrodes are aligned in rows. The two layers of electrodes make up the electrode matrix. Each intersection of a row electrode and a column electrode forms one pixel on the LCD panel. Software can manipulate each pixel by activating the electrodes that form it. The image is formed by scanning the column and row electrodes, much as the electronic beam scans a CRT monitor screen.

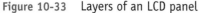

Figure 10-33   Layers of an LCD panel

The polarizer layers outside the glass layers in Figure 10-33 are responsible for preventing light from passing through the pixels when the electrodes are not activated. When the electrodes are activated, light on the back side of the LCD panel can pass through one pixel on the screen, picking up color from the color layer as it passes through.

Two kinds of LCD panels are on the market today: **active-matrix** and **dual-scan passive matrix** displays. A dual-scan display is less expensive than an active-matrix display and provides a lower-quality image. With dual-scan display, two columns of electrodes are activated at the same time. With active-matrix display, a transistor that amplifies the signal is placed at every intersection in the grid, which further enhances the pixel quality.

Flat panel monitors are built to receive either an analog signal or a digital signal from the video card and have two ports to accommodate either signal. If the signal is analog, it must be converted to digital before the monitor can process it. Flat panel monitors are designed to receive an analog signal so that you can use a regular video card that works with a CRT monitor, thus reducing the price of upgrading from a CRT to an LCD monitor. As you will see in the upcoming discussion of video cards,

A+
CORE
1.1
1.3

video cards convert digital data from the CPU to analog before sending it to the monitor. Therefore, with analog flat panel monitors, the data is converted from digital to analog and back to digital before being used by the flat panel monitor. These conversions reduce the quality of the resulting image. For the best output, use a digital flat panel monitor along with a digital video card designed to support the monitor. You will see an example of a video card that supports digital flat panel monitors in the next section.

NOTE

When shopping for a flat panel monitor, know that these monitors are measured in pixel pitch rather than dot pitch. Also consider optimum resolution (1280x1024 is good), brightness, contrast ratio (1000:1 is excellent), type of connector, and color intensity.

A+
CORE
1.2

APPLYING CONCEPTS

Installing Dual Monitors

To increase the size of your Windows desktop, you can install more than one monitor for a single computer. The following dual-monitor installation procedure assumes that you use Windows XP and that you already have a monitor installed. Setting up dual monitors gives you more space for your Windows desktop as well as some redundancy if one goes down. To install dual monitors, you can use two video cards, one for each monitor, or you can use a video card that provides two video ports.

To install a second monitor and a dual-monitor setup using two video cards:

1. Verify that the original video card works properly, determine whether it is PCI or AGP, and decide whether it is to be the primary monitor.
2. Verify that the new PCI video card is compatible with Windows XP.
3. Boot the PC and enter CMOS setup. If CMOS has the option to select the order that video cards are initialized, verify that the currently installed card is configured to initialize first. If it does not initialize first, then, when you install the second card, video might not work at all when you first boot with two cards.
4. Install a second video card in the PCI slot nearest to the AGP slot if the original monitor has an AGP adapter, or in the PCI slot immediately next to the original PCI adapter if the original monitor has a PCI adapter, and attach the second monitor.
5. Boot the system. Windows recognizes the new hardware and may prompt you for the location of the drivers. If Windows does not recognize you have new hardware to install, go to the Control Panel and select **Add Hardware** to manually install the drivers.
6. Now you are ready to configure the new monitor. Right-click the desktop and select **Display Properties** from the shortcut menu. The Display Properties dialog box shown in Figure 10-34 appears. Select the **Settings** tab.

10

A+
CORE
1.2

Using Dual
Monitors

Display Properties   ? ✕

| Themes | Desktop | Screen Saver | Appearance | Settings |

Drag the monitor icons to match the physical arrangement of your monitors.

1   **2**

Display:
2. Plug and Play Monitor on NVIDIA RIVA TNT2 Model 64 ▾

Screen resolution
Less ─────╫───── More
1024 by 768 pixels

Color quality
Highest (32 bit) ▾

☐ Use this device as the primary monitor.
☑ Extend my Windows desktop onto this monitor.

Identify   Troubleshoot...   Advanced

OK   Cancel   Apply

Figure 10-34   You must choose to activate a second monitor before it will be used by Windows

7. Notice that there are two numbered blue boxes that represent your two monitors. If necessary, arrange the boxes so that they represent the physical arrangement of your monitors.

8. Notice that when you click a box, the Display drop-down menu changes to show the selected monitor, and the Screen resolution and the Color quality display settings also follow the selected monitor. This lets you customize the settings for each monitor.

9. On the Settings tab of the Display Properties dialog box, adjust your Screen resolution and the Color quality settings according to your preferences. Check **Extend my Windows desktop onto this monitor**. To save the settings, click **Apply**. Depending on the Advanced display settings in effect, you might be asked to restart your computer. The second monitor should initialize and show the extended desktop.

NOTE

Settings for each video adapter that you add to your system must be saved and applied individually. Windows 2000/XP supports up to 10 separate monitors on a single system, and Windows 9x/Me supports up to nine monitors.

A+
CORE
1.2

10. Close the **Display Properties** dialog box. From the **Start** menu, open an application and verify that you can use the second monitor by dragging the application over to the second monitor's desktop.

Once you add a second monitor to your system, you can move from one monitor to another simply by moving your mouse. Switching from one monitor to the other does not require any special keystroke or menu option.

Video Cards

A+
CORE
4.3

Installing a
Video Card

Recall that the video controller card is the interface between the monitor and the computer. These cards are sometimes called graphic adapters, video boards, graphics cards, or display cards. Sometimes the video controller with a video port is integrated into the motherboard. If you are buying a motherboard with an integrated video controller, make sure that you can disable the controller on the motherboard if it needs replacement or gives you trouble. You can then install a video card and bypass the controller and port on the motherboard.

There are four ways that a video card can pass data to a monitor or other display device, which determines the type of port on the back of the video card that connects to the monitor or television cable. Figure 10-35 shows a video card that has three of the four ports.

Figure 10-35   This ATI Radeon video card has three ports for video out: DVI, S-Video, and regular RGB video

The four methods of data transfer are:

- *RGB video port.* This is the standard method of passing three separate signals for red, green, and blue, which most video cards and CRT monitors use. This method uses a regular 15-pin Super-VGA port (commonly called a VGA port).

- *DVI (Digital Visual Interface) port.* This method is the digital interface standard used by digital monitors such as a digital flat panel monitor, and digital TVs (HDTV). For a video card that only has a DVI port, you can purchase a VGA converter so you can connect a standard VGA video cable to use a regular analog monitor.

- *Composite video.* Using this method, the red, green, and blue (RGB) are mixed together in the same signal. This is the method used by television, and can be used by a video card that is designed to send output to a TV. This method uses a Composite Out port, which is round and is the same size as the S-Video Out port showing in Figure 10-35, but has only a single pin in the center of the port. Composite video does not produce as sharp an image as RGB video or S-Video.

- *S-Video (Super-Video).* This method sends two signals over the cable, one for color and the other for brightness, and is used by some high-end TVs and video equipment. It uses a 4-pin round port. The television and the video card must support this method and you must use a special S-Video cable like the one in Figure 10-36. This standard is not as good as RGB for monitors, but is better than Composite video when output to a television.

Figure 10-36   An S-Video cable used to connect a video card to an S-Video port on a television

The quality of a video subsystem is rated according to how it affects overall system performance, video quality (including resolution and color), power-saving features, and ease of use and installation. Because the video controller on the video card is separate from the core system functions, manufacturers can use a variety of techniques to improve performance without being overly concerned about compatibility with functions on the motherboard. An example of this flexibility is the many ways memory is managed on a video controller. Two main features to look for in a video card are the bus it uses and the amount and type of video RAM it has or can support. Also know that a motherboard might have its own on-board video controller and video port, but that this video subsystem is probably very basic and lacks many of the features you'll read about in this section.

The Buses Used by Video Cards

Four buses have been used for video cards in the past 10 years or so: the VESA bus, the regular PCI bus, the AGP bus, and the newer PCE Express bus. The VESA and AGP buses were developed specifically for video cards, and the PCI buses are used for many types of cards, including a video card.

Video cards currently use the AGP bus or the PCI Express x16 bus. If a second video card is installed for dual monitors, it uses a regular PCI slot. A motherboard will have a PCI Express x16 slot or an AGP slot, but not both. PCI Express x16 is much faster than AGP, but currently AGP is still the most popular slot for a video card (see Figure 10-37).

10

— AGP slot

Figure 10-37   A motherboard will have only one AGP slot, which is used to support a video/graphics card

AGP can share system memory with the CPU to do its calculations, and therefore does not always have to first copy data from system memory to video memory on the graphics card. This feature, known as direct memory execute (DIME), is probably the

A+
CORE
4.3

most powerful feature of AGP. The first AGP specification defined AGP 2X, which allowed AGP to transfer two cycles of data during a single AGP clock beat. The AGP 2.0 specification defined AGP 4X, which can transfer four cycles of data during a single AGP clock beat, yielding an overall data throughput of more than 1 GB/sec (gigabytes per second). The latest AGP standard is AGP 8X that runs at eight cycles of data per clock cycle (2.1 GB/sec).

Figure 10-37 shows a 132-pin AGP slot on a motherboard. Another AGP standard, called the AGP Pro, has provisions for a longer slot. This 180-pin slot has extensions on both ends that contain an additional 20 pins on one end and 28 pins on the other end, to provide extra voltage to the AGP video card in the slot. AGP Pro is used for video cards that consume more than 25 watts of power. The first AGP Pro standard ran at the same speed as AGP 4X.

APPLYING CONCEPTS

When matching video cards to AGP slots, be aware of the several variations in AGP slots. All AGP speeds support a 3.3-V slot identified by a notch or key near the right end of the slot and a 1.5-V slot identified by a notch or key near the left end of the slot. In addition, there is an AGP universal slot that has no notch and can accommodate either 1.5-V or 3.3-V cards. The AGP Pro slot might be a 1.5-V, 3.3-V, or universal slot. AGP slots on a motherboard are backward-compatible with older AGP standards, but you should not use a faster AGP video card in a slower AGP slot. Also, when using an AGP Pro video card, leave the PCI slot next to it empty in order to improve ventilation and prevent overheating. Chapter 23 shows an example of a video card installation.

In order for AGP to work at its full potential, the motherboard must run at a minimum of 100 MHz, and the operating system must support AGP. Windows 98, Windows 2000, and Windows XP support AGP.

Graphics Accelerators

A+
CORE
1.9
4.2

One of the more important advances made in video cards in recent years is the introduction of graphics accelerators. A **graphics accelerator** is a type of video card that has its own processor to boost performance. With the demands that graphics applications make in the multimedia environment, graphics accelerators have become not just enhancements, but common necessities.

The processor on a graphics accelerator card is similar to a CPU but specifically designed to manage video and graphics. Some features included on a graphics accelerator are MPEG decoding, 3-D graphics, dual porting, color space conversion, interpolated scaling, EPA Green PC support, digital output to flat panel display monitors, and application support for popular high-intensity graphics software such as Auto-CAD and Quark. All these features are designed to reduce the burden on the motherboard CPU and perform the video and graphics functions much faster than the motherboard CPU.

Video Memory

Older video cards had no memory, but today they need memory to handle the large volume of data generated by increased resolution and color. Video memory is stored on video cards as memory chips.

The amount of data a video card receives from the CPU for each frame (or screen) of data is determined by the screen resolution (measured in pixels), the number of colors (called color depth and measured in bits), and enhancements to color information (called alpha blending). The more data required to generate a single screen of data, the more memory is required to hold that data. Memory on the video card that holds one frame of data before it is sent to the monitor is called a frame buffer.

Several factors affect the amount of memory required for the frame buffer, which can be as much as 8 MB. However, in addition to needing memory to hold each frame buffer, a graphics accelerator card might also need memory for other purposes. Software that builds 3-D graphics on screen often uses textures and backgrounds, and sometimes a graphics card holds these backgrounds in memory to build future screens. Large amounts of video RAM keep the card from having to retrieve this data from the hard drive or system RAM multiple times. In addition, to improve performance, the graphics card might use buffering, in which the card holds not just the frame being built, but the next few frames. Because of backgrounds and buffering, a high-end card might need as much as 512 MB of RAM. See the graphics card documentation for information about memory recommendations for maximum performance.

10

Listed below are several types of video memory:

- **Video RAM (VRAM)** is a type of dual-ported memory, which means that video memory can be accessed by both the input and output processes at the same time.
- **SGRAM (synchronous graphics RAM)** is similar to SDRAM, discussed in Chapter 6. It is not dual-ported memory, but is faster than VRAM because it can synchronize itself with the CPU bus clock and uses other methods to increase overall performance for graphics-intensive processing.
- **WRAM (window RAM)** is dual ported and less expensive than VRAM. WRAM was named more for its ability to manage full-motion video than for its ability to speed up Microsoft Windows video processing. WRAM's increased speed is primarily due to its own internal bus on the chip, which has a data path that is 256 bits wide.
- **MultiBank DRAM (MDRAM)** is not dual ported, but is faster than VRAM or WRAM. It uses relatively small 32K blocks of memory that can be independently accessed.

A+
CORE
1.9
4.2

- **3-D RAM** was designed specifically to improve performance when simulating 3-D graphics. This chip can calculate which pixel of a 3-D graphic to display, depending on whether or not the pixel is behind other pixels, and therefore out of sight in a 3-D graphic. If the pixel is not to be visible, the chip writes it back to memory for use later.
- **Direct RDRAM (DRDRAM)**, also discussed in Chapter 6, is used on video cards and game systems and is designed to work well with video streaming.
- **Graphics DDR (GDDR), Graphics DDR2 (GDDR2), and Graphics DDR3 (GDDR3)** are types of SDRAM specifically designed for video cards. Recall that DDR and DDR2 SDRAM are discussed in Chapter 6. DDR3 is an advanced version of DDR2. GDDR3 is considered the up and coming video memory that is expected to replace other types.

When upgrading memory on a video card, you must match the memory to the card. Remove the card from the system and then install the new memory chip. When you turn on the system, video memory counts up on screen before system memory is counted. Verify that the correct amount of video memory is installed. For more information about video cards, including graphics accelerators, see the Web sites of the manufacturers listed in Table 10-9.

Manufacturer	Web Site
ASUSTeK Computer, Inc.	www.asus.com
ATI Technologies, Inc.	www.ati.com
Creative Technology, Ltd.	www.creative.com
Gainward Co., Ltd.	www.gainward.com
Hercules Computer Technology	www.hercules.com
Matrox Graphics, Inc.	www.matrox.com
MSI Computer Corporation	www.msicomputer.com
nVidia	www.nvidia.com
VisionTek	www.visiontek.com

Table 10-9   Video card manufacturers

Troubleshooting Video Problems

A+
CORE
2.1

For monitors as well as other devices, do the easy things first. Make simple hardware and software adjustments. Many monitor problems are caused by poor cable connections or bad contrast/brightness adjustments. When servicing a monitor, take the time to clean the screen with a soft dry cloth.

**A+
CORE
2.1**

Typical monitor problems and how to troubleshoot them are described next.

Power Light (LED) Does Not Go On; No Picture

- Is the monitor plugged in? Verify that the wall outlet works by plugging in a lamp, radio, etc.
- If the monitor power cord is plugged into a power strip or surge protector, verify that the power strip is turned on and working and that the monitor is also turned on. Look for an on/off switch on the front and back of the monitor. Some monitors have both.
- If the monitor power cord is plugged into the back of the computer, verify that the connection is tight and the computer is turned on.
- A blown fuse could be the problem. Some monitors have a fuse that is visible from the back of the monitor. It looks like a black knob that you can remove (no need to go inside the monitor cover). Remove the fuse and look for the broken wire indicating a bad fuse.
- The monitor may have a switch on the back for choosing between 110 volts and 220 volts. Check that the switch is in the right position.

If none of these solutions solves the problem, the next step is to take the monitor to a service center.

10

NOTE

When you turn on your PC, the first thing you see on the screen is the firmware on the video card identifying itself. You can use this information to search the Web, especially the manufacturer's Web site, for troubleshooting information about the card.

Power LED Is On, No Picture on Power-up

- Check the contrast adjustment. If there's no change, then leave it at a middle setting.
- Check the brightness adjustment. If there's no change, then leave it at a middle setting.
- Make sure the cable is connected securely to the computer.
- If the monitor-to-computer cable detaches from the monitor, exchange it for a cable you know is good, or check the cable for continuity.
- If this solves the problem, reattach the old cable to verify that the problem was not simply a bad connection.
- Confirm that the proper system configuration has been set up. Some older motherboards have a jumper or DIP switch you can use to select the monitor type.
- Test a monitor you know is good on the computer you suspect to be bad. Do this and the previous step to identify the problem. If you think the monitor is bad, make sure that it also fails to work on a good computer.
- Check the CMOS settings or software configuration on the computer. When using Windows 2000/XP or Windows 9x/Me, boot into Safe Mode. For

Windows 2000/XP, press F8 and then choose Safe Mode from the menu, and for Windows 9x/Me press F5 during the boot. This allows the OS to select a generic display driver and low resolution. If this works, change the driver and resolution.

- Reseat the video card. For a PCI card, move the card to a different expansion slot. Clean the card's edge connectors, using a contact cleaner purchased from a computer supply store.
- If there are socketed chips on the video card, remove the card from the expansion slot and then use a screwdriver to press down firmly on each corner of each socketed chip on the card. Chips sometimes loosen because of thermal changes; this condition is called **chip creep**.
- Trade a good video card for the video card you suspect is bad. Test the video card you think is bad on a computer that works. Test a video card you know is good on the computer that you suspect may be bad. Whenever possible, do both.
- If the video card has socketed chips that appear dirty or corroded, consider removing them and trying to clean the pins with contact cleaner. Normally, however, if the problem is a bad video card, the most cost-effective measure is to replace the card.
- Go into CMOS setup and disable the shadowing of video ROM.
- Test the RAM on the motherboard with diagnostic software.
- For a motherboard that is using an AGP or a PCI-Express video card, try using a PCI video card in a PCI slot.
- Trade the motherboard for one you know is good. Sometimes, though rarely, a peripheral chip on the motherboard of the computer can cause the problem.

Power Is On, but Monitor Displays the Wrong Characters

- Wrong characters are usually not the result of a bad monitor but of a problem with the video card. Trade the video card for one you know is good.
- Exchange the motherboard. Sometimes a bad ROM or RAM chip on the motherboard displays the wrong characters on the monitor.

Monitor Flickers, Has Wavy Lines, or Both

- Monitor flicker can be caused by poor cable connections. Check that the cable connections are snug.
- Does the monitor have a degauss button to eliminate accumulated or stray magnetic fields? If so, press it.
- Check if something in the office is causing a high amount of electrical noise. For example, you might be able to stop a flicker by moving the office fan to a different outlet. Bad fluorescent lights or large speakers can also produce interference. Two monitors placed very close together can also cause problems.
- If the vertical scan frequency (the refresh rate at which the screen is drawn) is below 60 Hz, a screen flicker may appear. Use the Display icon in the Control Panel to make the adjustment. Use the highest refresh rate offered.

▪ For older monitors that do not support a high enough refresh rate, your only cure may be to purchase a new monitor.

▪ Before making a purchase, verify that the new monitor will solve the problem.

▪ Open the Control Panel, click Display, and then click Settings to see if a high resolution (greater than 800 x 600 with more than 256 colors) is selected. Consider these issues:

1. The video card might not support this resolution/color setting.

2. There might not be enough video RAM; see the video card documentation for the recommended amount.

3. The added (socketed) video RAM might be a different speed than the soldered memory.

No Graphics Display or the Screen Goes Blank when Loading Certain Programs

This problem may be caused by the following:

▪ A special graphics or video accelerator card is not present or is defective.

▪ Software is not configured to do graphics, or the software does not recognize the installed graphics card.

▪ The video card does not support the resolution and/or color setting.

▪ There might not be enough video RAM; see the video card for the recommended amount.

▪ The added (socketed) video RAM might be a different speed than the soldered memory.

▪ The wrong adapter/display type is selected. Start Windows from Safe Mode to reset the display.

Screen Goes Blank 30 Seconds or One Minute After the Keyboard Is Left Untouched

A Green motherboard (one that follows energy-saving standards) used with an Energy Saver monitor can be configured to go into standby or doze mode after a period of inactivity. This might be the case if the monitor resumes after you press a key or move the mouse. Doze times can be set for periods from as short as 20 seconds to as long as one hour. The power LED normally changes from green to orange to indicate doze mode. Monitors and video cards using these energy-saving features are addressed in Chapter 4.

You might be able to change the doze features by entering the CMOS menu and looking for an option such as Power Management; in Windows, open the Control Panel, select Display, and then select Screen Saver.

10

A+
CORE
2.1

Some monitors have a Power Save switch on the back. Make sure this is set as you want.

Problems might occur if the motherboard power-saving features are turning off the monitor, and Windows screen saver is also turning off the monitor. If the system hangs when you try to get the monitor going again, try disabling one or the other. If this doesn't work, then disable both.

Poor Color Display

For this problem, try the following:

* Read the monitor documentation to learn how to use the color-adjusting buttons to fine-tune the color.
* Exchange video cards.
* Add more video RAM; see the video card for the recommended amount.
* Check if a fan, a large speaker (speakers have large magnets), or a nearby monitor could be causing interference.

Picture Out of Focus or Out of Adjustment

For this problem, try the following:

* Check the adjustment knobs on the control panel on the outside of the monitor.
* Change the refresh rate. Sometimes this can make the picture appear more focused.
* You can also make adjustments inside the monitor that might solve the problem. If you have not been trained to work inside the monitor, take it to a service center.

Crackling Sound

Dirt or dust inside the unit might be the cause. Someone trained to work on the inside of the monitor can vacuum inside it.

Configuring or Changing Monitor Settings and Drivers in Windows

If the video card is supported by Windows, you can change the driver and settings by double-clicking the Display icon in the Control Panel. For drivers not supported by Windows, you can reinstall the drivers by using the CD or floppy disks that come with the video card. The settings for this type of driver can most likely be changed through the Control Panel's Display icon.

A+
CORE
2.1

Changing the Video Driver Configuration

Double-click the Display icon in the Control Panel or right-click the desktop and select Properties from the shortcut menu. Select the Settings tab to change the color palette, the resolution (for example, from 800 x 600 to 1600 x 1200), or the driver for the video card or monitor type. Click Advanced on the Settings tab to show the Change Display Type window. From this window, you can change the video card or the monitor type. For Windows XP, click Advanced, the Adapter tab, Properties, and the Driver tab (see Figure 10-38).

Figure 10-38   Updating the video card drivers in Windows XP

If you increase the resolution, the Windows icons and desktop text become smaller. Select Large Fonts on the Appearance tab.

Returning to Standard VGA Settings

When the display settings don't work, return to standard VGA settings as follows:

- For Windows 2000/XP or Windows 9x/Me, reboot the system and press the F8 key after the first beep.
- When the Windows 2000/XP Advanced Options menu or the Windows 9x/Me startup menu appears, select Safe Mode to boot up with minimal configurations and standard VGA display mode. For Windows 2000/XP you can also try Enable VGA Mode from the Advanced Options menu.
- Double-click the Display icon in the Control Panel, and reset to the correct video configuration.

CHAPTER SUMMARY

▶ Adding new devices to a computer requires installing hardware and software and resolving possible resource conflicts.

▶ All hardware devices require some resources from a computer, which might include an IRQ, DMA channel, I/O addresses, and for legacy devices, some upper memory addresses to contain their device drivers.

▶ Use Device Manager under Windows to determine what resources currently installed devices use.

▶ Most computers provide one or two serial ports and one parallel port to be used for a variety of devices. Newer motherboards also provide one or more USB ports and an IEEE 1394 port.

▶ The PCI bus is presently the most popular local bus. The VESA local bus is an outdated standard designed by the Video Electronics Standards Association for video cards. For video cards, the VESA bus was replaced by PCI, which was then replaced by the AGP bus and more recently by the PCI Express bus.

▶ Generally, expansion cards use PCI Express or PCI slots rather than older and slower ISA slots.

▶ UART logic on a motherboard chip set controls serial ports.

▶ Because data might become corrupted, parallel cables should not exceed 15 feet (4.5 meters) in length. HP recommends that the cables not exceed 10 feet (3 meters).

▶ Three types of parallel ports are standard, EPP, and ECP. The ECP type uses a DMA channel.

▶ Serial ports are sometimes configured as COM1, COM2, COM3, or COM4, and parallel ports can be configured as LPT1, LPT2, or LPT3.

▶ The USB bus only uses one set of system resources for all USB devices connected to it, and USB devices are hot-pluggable.

▶ The IEEE 1394 bus provides either a 4-pin or 6-pin connector, uses only one set of system resources, and is hot-pluggable.

▶ The PCI bus runs in sync with the CPU, and the PCI controller manages system resources for all PCI cards. Resources are assigned to PCI slots during startup.

▶ A keyboard can use a DIN, PS/2, USB, or wireless connection.

▶ Two types of monitors are CRT and LCD. CRT costs less but LCD requires less desktop space.

▶ Features to consider when purchasing a monitor are screen size, refresh rate, interlacing, dot pitch or pixel pitch, resolution, multiscan ability, and type of connector (analog or digital) used by the monitor.

▶ A video card is rated by the bus that it uses and the amount of video RAM on the card. Both features affect the overall speed and performance of the card.

▶ Some types of video memory are VRAM, SGRAM, WRAM, 3-D RAM, MDRAM, G-DDR, G-DDR2, G-DDR3, and DRDRAM.

KEY TERMS

For explanations of key terms, see the Glossary near the end of the book.

3-D RAM
active matrix
bandwidth
bus mouse
chip creep
DCE (Data Communications
   Equipment)
dot pitch
DTE (Data Terminal Equipment)
dual-scan passive matrix
ECP (Extended Capabilities Port)
EPP (Enhanced Parallel Port)
FireWire
flat panel monitor
graphics accelerator
Graphics DDR (G-DDR)
Graphics DDR2 (G-DDR2)
Graphics DDR3 (G-DDR3)

hot-pluggable
hot-swapping
hub
i.Link
I/O controller card
IEEE 1284
IEEE 1394
IEEE 1394.3
infrared transceiver
interlaced
IrDA (Infrared Data
   Association) transceiver
isochronous data transfer
modem eliminator
motherboard mouse
MultiBank DRAM (MDRAM)
multiscan monitor

noninterlaced
null modem cable
PCI (Peripheral Component
   Interconnect) bus
pixel
PS/2-compatible mouse
refresh rate
resolution
serial mouse
SGRAM (synchronous graphics
   RAM)
touch screen
UART (universal asynchronous
   receiver-transmitter)
USB host controller
VRAM (video RAM)
WRAM (window RAM)

10

REVIEWING THE BASICS

1. Identify three things that may cause monitor flicker.

2. What is the value of installing additional video RAM?

3. Describe what to do if you've just spilled soda pop on your keyboard.

4. Explain how to check that chips on a video card are properly seated in their sockets.

5. When troubleshooting problems with a monitor in Windows 2000, why would you enter Safe Mode?

6. Describe how to boot Windows 98 into Safe Mode.

7. Why would an external modem cost more than an internal modem?

8. Name three possible ways a scanner might interface with a motherboard.

9. By definition, what system resources does COM1 use? COM2? COM3? COM4?

10. To what does RS-232 refer?

11. How many pins are on a typical serial port?

12. Why is AGP technology described as being more like a port than a bus?

13. What is a null modem cable, and what is it often used for?

14. What is the name of the technology within the chip set that controls the speed of serial ports?

15. Why might you choose to use ECP mode for your parallel port rather than EPP mode?

16. When might you need to disable ECP mode for a parallel port?

17. How would you disable a serial port on a motherboard?

18. What Windows OSs support USB? Include the OS version numbers where that information is important.

19. What is the maximum speed of Original USB? Of Hi-Speed USB?

20. What is the maximum length of a USB Hi-Speed cable?

21. What are two other names for FireWire? What is the highest data throughput approved for FireWire?

22. List the steps in Windows 9x/Me to display the list of I/O addresses currently in use.

23. When installing a device, why would you prefer to use a PCI expansion slot rather than an ISA expansion slot?

24. If PCI is attempting to use an IRQ that is used by a legacy ISA device, how can you force PCI to not use the IRQ?

25. What criteria affect how much video RAM is needed for a video card to hold one frame buffer?

26. Give three examples of monitor screen sizes. How are monitor screen sizes measured?

27. Which provides better quality, an interlaced monitor or a noninterlaced monitor? Why?

28. What type of monitor can offer a variety of refresh rates?

29. What makes a device an ergonomic device?

30. How many pins are there on a DIN connector and a PS/2 connector for a keyboard?

31. What three colors are used to build all colors on a color monitor screen?

32. Which gives better image quality, a .25-mm dot pitch monitor or a .28-mm dot pitch monitor? Why?

33. If a mouse begins to be difficult to operate, what simple thing can you do to help?

THINKING CRITICALLY

1. You plug a new scanner into a USB port on your Windows XP system. When you first turn on the scanner, what should you expect to see?

    a. A message displayed by the scanner software telling you to reboot your system.

    b. The Found New Hardware Wizard launches.

    c. Your system automatically reboots.

2. You install the software bundled with your digital camera to download pictures from your camera to your system using a serial port. Next you plug the camera into the port using a serial cable and turn on your camera. You attempt to use the software to download pictures, but the software does not recognize the camera is present. What do you do next?

    a. Return the camera and purchase one that uses a USB port for downloading.

    b. Reinstall the bundled software.

    c. Access CMOS setup and verify that the serial port is enabled.

    d. Use Device Manager to verify that the OS recognizes the serial port.

    e. Replace the serial cable.

3. You turn on your Windows 2000 computer and see the system display POST messages. Then the screen turns blue with no text. Which of the following items could be the source of the problem, and which items could *not* be the source?

    a. The video card

    b. The monitor

    c. Windows

    d. WordPerfect software installed on the system

10

HANDS-ON PROJECTS

HANDS-ON PROJECTS

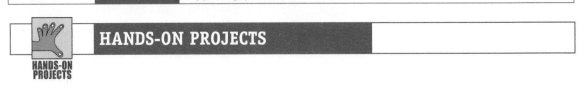

CAUTION

Unless you follow proper procedures, working inside your computer can damage it seriously. To ensure safety in your work setting, follow every precaution listed in Chapter 4.

PROJECT 10-1: Installing a Device

Install a device on a computer. If you are working in a classroom environment, you can simulate an installation by moving a device from one computer to another.

PROJECT 10-2: Researching a Computer Ad

Pick a current magazine ad for a complete, working computer system, including computer, monitor, keyboard, and software, together with extra devices such as a mouse or printer. Write a four- to eight-page report describing and explaining the details in this ad. This exercise will give you a good opportunity to learn about the latest offerings on the market as well as current pricing.

PROJECT 10-3: Comparing Two Computer Ads

Find two ads for computer systems containing the same processor. Compare the two ads. Include in your comparison the different features offered and the weaknesses and strengths of each system.

PROJECT 10-4: Planning the Design of a 9-Pin Null Modem Cable

Draw a chart similar to Table 10-4, showing the pinouts (functions of each pin) for a 9-pin null modem cable.

PROJECT 10-5: Searching the Internet for a Video Driver

You are about to upgrade your PC from Windows 98 to Windows XP. Before performing the upgrade, search the Internet for a new video controller for your Matrox G200 MMS graphics card. What is the name of the file you need to download from the Matrox Web site for the upgrade?

PROJECT 10-6: Exploring Parallel Port Modes

Examine CMOS setup on your PC, and answer the following questions about your parallel port:

1. Is a parallel port coming directly off the motherboard?

2. What modes are available for the parallel port?

3. What is the currently selected mode?

4. If the parallel port supports ECP, what DMA channels can you select for this mode?

Disable the parallel port using CMOS setup. Reboot the PC and attempt to use the port by executing a print command. What error message do you get?

PROJECT 10-7: Working with a Monitor

1. Using a Windows OS, list the steps to change the monitor resolution.

2. Using the Display icon in the Windows Control Panel, practice changing the background, screen saver, and appearance. If you are not using your own computer, make sure to restore each setting after making changes.

3. Pretend you have made a mistake and selected a combination of foreground and background colors that makes reading the screen impossible. Solve the problem by booting Windows into Safe Mode. Correct the problem and then reboot. (Windows 9x/Me, Windows 2000, and Windows XP all have Safe Mode. Windows NT does not.)

4. From the Display Properties dialog box, change the resolution using the sliding bar under Display area. Make a change and then make the change permanent. You can go back and adjust it later if you like.

5. Work with a partner who is using a different computer. Unplug the monitor in the computer lab or classroom, loosen or disconnect the computer monitor cable, or turn the contrast and brightness all the way down, while your partner does something similar to the other PC. Trade PCs and troubleshoot the problems.

6. Turn off the PC, remove the case, and loosen the video card. Turn on the PC and write down the problem as a user would describe it. Turn off the PC, reseat the card, and verify that everything works.

7. Insert into a system a defective video card provided by your instructor. Describe the problem in writing, as a user would.

10

Multimedia Devices and Mass Storage

In this chapter, you will learn:

- About multimedia devices such as sound cards, digital cameras, and MP3 players

- About optical storage technologies such as CD and DVD

- How certain hardware devices are used for backups and fault tolerance

- How to troubleshoot multimedia and mass storage devices

The ability to create output in a vast array of media—audio, video, and animation, as well as text and graphics—has turned PCs into multimedia machines. The multimedia computer has much to offer, from video conferencing for executives to tools for teaching the alphabet to four-year-olds. This chapter examines multimedia devices, what they can do, how they work, and how to support them. You will also learn about storage devices such as CDs, DVDs, removable drives, and tape drives, including installation and troubleshooting. These mass storage devices are used to hold multimedia data and, in some cases, to store backups.

Multimedia on a PC

The goal of multimedia technology is to create or reproduce lifelike representations for audio, video, and animation. Remember that computers store data digitally and ultimately as a stream of only two numbers: 0 and 1. In contrast, sights and sounds have an infinite number of variations and are analog in nature. The challenge for multimedia technology is to bridge these two worlds.

CPU Technologies for Multimedia

**A+
CORE
1.1**

Three enhancements by Intel to CPU technology designed with multimedia applications in mind are **MMX (Multimedia Extensions)**, used by the Pentium MMX and Pentium II; **SSE (Streaming SIMD Extension)**, used by the Pentium III; and SSE2, SSE3, and Hyper-Threading for the Pentium 4. **SIMD**, which stands for **single instruction, multiple data**, is a process that allows the CPU to receive a single instruction and then execute it on multiple pieces of data rather than receiving the same instruction each time the data is received. SSE2 has a larger instruction set than SSE, and SSE3 improves on SSE2. The Pentium 4 can use MMX, SSE, SSE2, SSE3, and Hyper-Threading.

> ✔ **A+ EXAM TIP**
>
> The A+ Core exam expects you to be familiar with the characteristics of the different processors. Know which Pentium processors use MMX, SSE, and SSE2.

Multimedia software tends to use input/output operations more than it performs complex computations. Both MMX and SSE were designed to speed up the repetitive looping of multimedia software and manage the high-volume input/output of graphics, motion video, animation, and sound. MMX technology added new instructions designed for repetitive processing, more efficient ways to pass those instructions to the CPU, and increased CPU cache. SSE added improvements to 3D graphics and speech recognition, and Hyper-Threading enhances multitasking. For its processors, AMD uses 3DNow!, a CPU instruction set designed to improve performance with 3D graphics and other multimedia data. In addition, HyperTransport! increases bandwidth and PowerNow! improves the processor's performance and lowers power requirements.

NOTE

To know if software or hardware is taking advantage of a CPU enhancement for multimedia, look on the product package for the Intel MMX, Intel SSE, Intel SSE2, Intel SSE3, or AMD 3DNow!, HyperTransport!, or PowerNow! symbols.

Now let's look at some specific devices used for multimedia support. Many multimedia capabilities are added to a system using sound cards and other adapter cards. There are also externally attached devices such as digital cameras or MP3 players. In this section, you will learn about these and other devices.

Sound Cards

A sound card is an expansion card that records sound, saves it in a file on your hard drive, and plays it back. Some cards give you the ability to mix and edit sound, and even to edit the sound using standard music score notation. Sound cards have ports for external stereo speakers and microphone input. Also, sound cards may be Sound Blaster-compatible, meaning that they understand the commands sent to them that have been written for a Sound Blaster card, which is generally considered the standard for PC sound cards. Some cards play CD audio by way of a cable connecting the CD drive to the sound card. For good sound you definitely need external speakers, and perhaps an amplifier.

Sound passes through three stages when it is computerized: first, the sound is digitized—that is, converted from analog to digital; next, the digital data is stored in a compressed data file; and later the sound is reproduced or synthesized (digital to analog or digital out). Digitizing sound is discussed next, followed by a discussion of sound card installation. Table 11-1 lists some sound card manufacturers.

Manufacturer	Web Site
Abit	www.abit.com.tw
Aopen	www.aopen.com
Creative	www.creative.com
Elements	www.elements-pc.com
Guillemot Corporation	www.hercules.com
SIIG	www.siig.com
SoundBlaster	www.soundblaster.com
Syba	www.syba.com
Turtle Beach	www.tbeach.com

11

Table 11-1   Sound card manufacturers

NOTE

A good source for information about hardware devices (and software) is a site that offers product reviews and technical specifications and compares product prices and features. Check out these sites: CNET Networks *(www.cnet.com)*, Price Watch *(www.pricewatch.com)*, Tom's Hardware Guide *(www.tomshardware.com)*, and Epinions, Inc. *(www.epinions.com)*.

Sampling and Digitizing the Sound

Sound is converted from analog to digital storage by first sampling the sound and then digitizing it. When you record sound, the analog sound is converted to analog voltage by a microphone and passed to the sound card, where it is digitized. The critical factor in the performance of a sound card is the accuracy of the samples (determined by the sample size, which can be either 8 or 16 bits). The **sampling rate** of a sound card, the number of samples taken of the analog signal over a period of time, is usually expressed as samples (cycles) per second, or **hertz (Hz)**. One thousand hertz (one kilohertz) is written as kHz. A low sampling rate provides a less accurate representation of the sound than a high sampling rate. Our ears detect up to about 22,000 samples per second, or hertz. Studies show that in order to preserve the original sound, a digital sampling rate must be twice the frequency of the analog signal. Therefore, the sampling rate of music CDs is 44,100 Hz, or 44.1 kHz. When you record sound on a PC, the sampling rate is controlled by the recording software.

The larger the sample size is, the more accurate the sampling. If 8 bits are used to hold one number, then the sample range can be from -128 to +127. This is because 1111 1111 in binary (FF in hex) equals 255 in decimal, which, combined with zero, equals 256 values. Sound samples are considered both positive and negative numbers, so the range is -128 to +127 rather than 0 to 255. However, if 16 bits are used to hold the range of numbers, then the sample range increases dramatically, because 1111 1111 1111 1111 in binary (FFFF in hex) is 65,535 in decimal, meaning that the sample size can be -32,768 to +32,767, or a total of 65,536 values. High-fidelity music CDs use this 16-bit sample size.

Thus, an 8-bit sound card has a sample size of 256. A 16-bit sound card has a sample size of 65,536. Sound cards typically use 8- or 16-bit sample sizes, with a sampling rate from 4,000 to 44,000 samples per second. For high-quality sound, use a 16-bit sound card. Samples may also be recorded on a single channel (mono) or on two channels (stereo).

NOTE Don't confuse the sample size of 8 bits or 16 bits with the ISA bus size that a legacy sound card might use to attach to the motherboard. A sound card may use an 8-bit sample size but a 16-bit ISA bus or 32-bit PCI bus. When you hear people talk about an 8-bit sound card, they are speaking of the sample size, not the bus size.

Installing a Sound Card

A+
CORE
1.2

Most sound cards come with a device driver as well as all the software needed for normal use, such as application software to play music CDs. The installation of a sample sound card is described in the following procedure. The card used is a PnP Creative Labs Sound Blaster card that uses a PCI slot and supports a 128-voice wave table (a table of stored sample sounds that is used to reconstruct and reproduce recorded sound). It works under DOS 6+, Windows 9x/Me, and Windows NT/2000/ XP. The card comes with drivers and software on a CD and a user's guide.

**A+
CORE
1.2**

The three main steps in the following example are to install the card itself in an empty PCI slot on the motherboard, install the driver, and then install the applications stored on the CD that comes with the sound card.

The Sound Blaster card shown in Figure 11-1 has several ports that are labeled in the figure. Typical color codes for these ports are:

- Blue–Line in
- Red or pink–Microphone in
- Green–Line out (Front speakers out, usually center port on the card)
- Black–Rear out (Powered speakers or amplifier)
- Yellow–Center out (Subwoofer speaker)

11

Speaker Out jack
Connects external devices such as a cassette, DAT, or minidisc player for playback and recording

TAD/Modem connector
Connects internal audio sources such as TAD (telephone answering device) or modem

CD audio connector
Connects a CD drive using a CD audio cable

TV/IDE connector
Connects video card or IDE CD drive for audio input

Microphone In jack
Connects an external microphone for voice input

Line Out (Front) jack
Connects powered front speakers or an external amplifier; also supports headphones or passive speakers

Auxiliary In/Line Out (Rear) jack
Connects powered rear speakers or an external amplifier

Joystick/MIDI connector
Connects a joystick or a MIDI device (an optional MIDI adapter allows you to connect the joystick and MIDI device simultaneously)

Amplifier
enabled

Amplifier
disabled

Figure 11-1 The Sound Blaster sound card has three internal connections and one jumper group that controls amplifier support

The sound card has three internal connections (connections to something inside the case) and one jumper group that enables or disables a speaker amplifier. If you are using a speaker system with an external amplifier, disable the amplifier on the card by setting the jumper on the sound card to "disable amplifier."

NOTE The trend for today's motherboards is to embed sound capability on the board. For example, the motherboard shown in Figure 1-9 of Chapter 1 has three regular sound ports (Line in, Line out, and Microphone) and an S/P DIF port (Sony/Philips Digital Interface port) for digital sound output). If this onboard sound is giving problems or you simply want to upgrade to a better sound, you can use CMOS setup to disable the onboard sound and then install a sound card.

APPLYING CONCEPTS

Follow these steps to install a sound card:

1. Make sure that you are properly grounded. Wear a ground bracelet and follow other procedures to guard against ESD, as described in Chapter 4.
2. Turn off the PC, remove the cover, and locate an empty expansion slot for the card. Because this installation uses the connecting wire from the sound card to the CD drive (the wire comes with the sound card), place the sound card near enough to the CD drive so that the wire can reach between them.
3. Attach the wire to the sound card (see Figure 11-2) and to the CD drive.
4. Remove the cover from the slot opening at the rear of the PC case, and place the card into the PCI slot, making sure that the card is seated firmly. Use the screw taken from the slot cover to secure the card to the back of the PC case.
5. Check again that both ends of the wire are still securely connected and that the wire is not hampering the CPU fan, and then replace the case cover.

NOTE Some high-end sound cards have a power connector to provide extra power to the card. For this type of card, connect a power cable with a miniature 4-pin connector to the card.

6. Plug in the speakers to the ports at the back of the sound card, and turn on the PC. The speakers may or may not require their own power source. Check the product documentation or manufacturer's Web site for more information.

**A+
CORE
1.2**

Notice that the installation in the example was in a system using a CD drive. Later in the chapter, you'll see an example of a sound card installed in a system with a DVD drive.

Figure 11-2   Connect the wire to the sound card that will make the direct audio connection from the CD drive

NOTE

If you are using a speaker system with an amplifier, disable the amplifier on your sound card, as mentioned earlier. For this sound card, you do that by setting a jumper on the card to disable amplifier support (see Figure 11-1).

Installing the Sound Card Driver

After the card is installed, the device drivers must be installed. The next example uses a driver installation under Windows 98, but a Windows 2000/XP installation works about the same way and differences are noted. When Windows 9x/Me and Windows 2000/XP start, they detect that new hardware is present. The New Hardware Wizard opens, indicating that the OS discovered the Sound Blaster PCI128.

Follow these steps for Windows 98 to install the sound card driver:

1. In the New Hardware Wizard, select **Search for the Best Driver for Your Device (Recommended)** and click the **Next** button.
2. Clear all check boxes and check only the **Specify a Location** check box.

3. Click the **Browse** button and point to the driver path, such as **D:\Audio\English \Win98drv** for Windows 98 or D:\Audio\English\Win2k for Windows 2000.

In this example, the CD drive is drive D, and the sound card's user guide listed the location of the driver on the CD. Substitute your CD drive letter, if necessary; for other sound card installations, see the documentation for the location of the driver on the CD.

4. Click **Next** to continue the driver installation.

5. Click **Finish** when the installation is complete, and reboot your PC.

With most sound cards, the CD containing the sound card driver has application software for the special features offered by the card. Sometimes, as with the previous example, the software is installed at the same time as the drivers, so you can use the software at this point in the installation. For other sound cards, you can install the additional software after the driver is installed and the sound card is working. See the documentation that comes with the sound card to learn if application software is present, and how and when to install it.

After you install the driver, reboot, and enter Windows 98, verify that the card and the driver are correctly installed by using Device Manager.

1. Click **Start**, point to **Settings**, click **Control Panel**, and then double-click **System**.

2. Select the **Device Manager** tab. Figure 11-3 shows the sound card installed.

Figure 11-3   Device Manager shows the sound card installed and the resources it is using

**A+
CORE
1.2**

3. To see the resources used by the card, select the card and then click **Properties**. The Properties dialog box appears. Click the **Resources** tab.

Notes on Windows 2000/XP Installations   For Windows 2000/XP, the Found New Hardware Wizard steps you through the installation process. To use manufacturer-provided drivers rather than Microsoft drivers, click the Have Disk button in a wizard dialog box. Then locate the drivers on the manufacturer's CD that came bundled with the card. Windows 2000/XP is looking for a driver information file that has an .inf extension.

Also, Windows XP might proceed with the installation using Microsoft drivers without displaying a dialog box that contains the Have Disk button. To prevent this from happening, run the setup program on the manufacturer's CD that is bundled with the card *before* installing the card. Later, after the card is installed, Windows will use the manufacturer's installed drivers for the card.

When installing a device, Windows XP verifies that Microsoft has digitally signed the drivers. Depending on how the OS is configured, you might or might not be allowed to proceed if the drivers are not digitally signed. If the drivers have been written for Windows XP, even though they are not certified by Microsoft, they should still work in a Windows XP system.

After the installation, use Device Manager to verify there are no errors. To access Device Manager using Windows 2000/XP, right-click My Computer and select Properties on the shortcut menu. In the System Properties dialog box, click the Hardware tab, and then click the Device Manager button. To see the properties for a device, right-click the device and select Properties on the shortcut menu.

Troubleshooting problems with sound cards is covered later in the chapter.

11

Digital Cameras

**A+
CORE
1.8**

Digital cameras are becoming more popular as quality improves and prices decrease. Digital camera technology works much like scanner technology, except it is much faster. It essentially scans the field of image set by the picture taker and translates the light signals into digital values, which can be stored as a file and viewed, manipulated, and printed with software that interprets the stored values appropriately.

TWAIN is a standard format used by digital cameras and scanners for transferring images. You can transfer images from the camera to your computer's hard drive using a cable supplied with the camera. The cable might attach directly to the camera or connect to a cradle the camera sits in to recharge or upload images. The cable can use a serial, parallel, USB, or FireWire (IEEE 1394) connection. The camera can also use a wireless or infrared connection, or it can use a removable storage medium such as a flash RAM card to upload images.

A+ CORE 1.8

Technologies used by digital cameras to hold images include embedded memory that cannot be removed or exchanged and removable flash memory. Both these types of memory retain data without a battery. Types of flash memory on the market today include CompactFlash (CF), CompactFlash II (slightly thicker than CompactFlash), SmartMedia, SanDisk MultiMediaCard, Secure Digital (SD) card, several Memory Sticks, and the newer xD-Picture Card. Another storage option is IBM Microdrive, which uses the CompactFlash II form factor together with hard disk drive (HDD) technology, meaning the data is stored on a magnetic disk. A third option is a Mini CD-R/RW which is installed in the digital camera and can also be moved to a computer and read by a regular CD-ROM drive. Figure 11-4 shows a digital camera that uses a CF Type I card and a USB cable for uploading images.

You can use a Web site such as *www.cdnet.com* or *www.compusa.com* to find and compare other digital cameras, storage media, and flash card readers. Select the camera first and then purchase the card storage device the camera supports. Some cameras might come bundled with the storage device.

A+ EXAM TIP

The A+ Core exam expects you to know how to install the software bundled with your digital camera before attaching the camera to your PC.

To transfer images to your PC, first install the software bundled with your camera or other device that contains the images. After the images are on the PC, use the camera's image-editing software, or another program such as Adobe PhotoShop, to view, touch up, and print the picture. The picture file, which is usually in **JPEG (Joint Photographic Experts Group)** format, can then be imported into documents. JPEG is a common compression standard for storing photos. Most JPEG files have a .jpg file extension. In addition, a high-end camera might support the uncompressed TIFF format. **TIFF (Tagged Image File Format)** files are larger, but retain more image information and give better results when printing photographs.

USB port on PC

Slot to install flash memory

SD flash memory

Figure 11-4 This digital camera uses a Secure Digital flash card and uploads images by way of a USB cable

A+
CORE
1.8

Most digital cameras have a video-out port that allows you to attach the camera to any TV, using a cable provided with the camera. You can then display pictures on TV or copy them to videotape. Table 11-2 lists manufacturers of digital cameras.

VIDEO

Types of
Memory Cards

Manufacturer	Web Site
Canon	www.usa.canon.com
Casio	www.casio.com
Epson	www.epson.com
Fujifilm	www.fujifilm.com
Hewlett-Packard	www.photosmart.com
Kodak	www.kodak.com
Minolta	www.minolta.com
Nikon	www.nikonusa.com
Olympus	www.olympusamerica.com
Sony	www.sony.com/di
Toshiba	www.toshiba.com

Table 11-2   Digital camera manufacturers

11

MP3 Players

A popular audio compression method is **MP3**, a method that can reduce the size of a sound file as much as 1:24 without much loss of quality. An MP3 player is a device or software that plays MP3 files. MP3 players are small but can store a lot of information. Figure 11-5 shows a typical MP3 player.

Compression Methods Used with MP3 Players

One of the better-known multimedia data compression standards is MPEG, an international standard for data compression for motion pictures, video, and audio. Developed by the **Moving Pictures Experts Group (MPEG)**, it tracks movement from one frame to the next and stores only what changes, rather than compressing individual frames. MPEG compression can yield a compression ratio of 100:1 for full-motion video (30 frames per second, or 30 fps).

There are currently several MPEG standards: MPEG-1, MPEG-2, and MPEG-4. MPEG-1 is used to compress audio on CD and is the basis for MP3. MPEG-2 is used to compress video films on DVD. MPEG-3 was never fully developed or used. MPEG-4 is used for video transmissions over the Internet.

Figure 11-5 This MP3 player by Panasonic is about 3 inches × 2 inches, has no moving parts, and includes a USB cable for downloading MP3 files

MPEG compression is possible because it cuts out or drastically reduces sound that is not normally heard by the human ear. In the regular audio CD format (uncompressed), one minute of music takes up about 10 MB of storage. The same minute of music in MP3 format takes only about 1 MB of memory. This makes it possible to download music in minutes rather than hours. Sound files downloaded from the Internet are most often MP3 files. MP3 files have an .mp3 file extension. For more information about MPEG and MP3, see *www.mpeg.org*.

How MP3 Players Work

Most portable MP3 players today store MP3 files in onboard memory or hard drives, which can be expanded using an add-on flash RAM card such as SmartMedia, CompactFlash, or Memory Stick. MP3 files are downloaded from the PC to the MP3 player, in contrast to a digital camera, which transfers or uploads data to the PC.

You can download and purchase MP3 music files from Web sites such as EMusic (*www.emusic.com*) and MP3.com (*www.mp3.com*). Once the files are downloaded to your PC, you can play them on your PC using MP3 player software such as Windows Media Player or MusicMatch Jukebox (see *www.musicmatch.com*), transfer them to a portable MP3 player, or convert them into an audio CD if your computer has a writable CD drive. There are also CD/MP3 players that can play CDs in either standard audio format or MP3 format. A CD can store 10 hours or more of music in MP3 format. You can also play the MP3 files directly from the Internet without first downloading them, which is called **streaming audio**. MP3 files are generally transferred to portable devices using a USB or serial cable.

Also, you can convert files from your regular music CDs into MP3 files (a process called ripping), and play them on your computer or download them to an MP3 player. "Ripper" software copies the music file from the CD, and encoder software compresses the file into MP3 format. CD rippers, MP3 encoders, and MP3 player software can be downloaded from the Internet. For example, see the MusicMatch site at *www.musicmatch.com*.

Table 11-3 lists some manufacturers of MP3 players.

Manufacturer	Web Site
Creative Labs	www.creative.com
Apple Computers	www.apple.com
Imation	www.imation.com
Intel	www.intel.com
Panasonic	www.panasonic.com
Pine Technology	www.xfxforce.com
Rio (was SONICblue)	www.rioaudio.com
Samsung	www.samsungusa.com
Sensory Science (owned by SONICblue)	www.sensoryscience.com
Sony	www.sonystyle.com

Table 11-3   MP3 player manufacturers

Video Capture Card

A video capture card following the NTSC (National Television Standards Committee) standards for the USA is another multimedia option. With this card, you can capture input from a camcorder or directly from TV. Video can be saved as motion clips or stills, edited, and, with the right card, copied back to video tape for viewing with a VCR and television. Look for these features on a video capture card:

- An IEEE 1394 (FireWire) port to interface with a digital camcorder
- Data transfer rates, which affect price
- Capture resolution and color-depth capabilities
- Ability to transfer data back to the digital camcorder or VCR

- Stereo audio jacks
- Video-editing software bundled with the card

Other options include a TV tuner that makes it possible to turn your PC into a television, complete with instant replay and program scheduling. Ports on a video capture card might include an antenna or cable TV port for input and a TV or VCR port for output. Other ports are a PC monitor video port and possibly an IEEE 1394 port for a camcorder. Expect the card to fit into an AGP slot and take the place of your regular video card. For an excellent example of a video capture card, see the All-in-Wonder 9800 Pro card from ATI Technologies at *www.ati.com*.

Table 11-4 lists some manufacturers of video capture cards.

Manufacturer	Web Site
ASUS	*www.asus.com*
ATI	*www.ati.com*
Creative Labs	*www.creative.com*
Matrox	*www.matrox.com*
Pinnacle Systems	*www.pinnaclesys.com*

Table 11-4   Video capture card manufacturers

Optical Storage Technology

**A+
CORE
1.1**

CDs and DVDs are popular storage media for multimedia data, and CDs are the most popular way of distributing software. Both DVD and CD technologies use patterns of tiny pits on the surface of a disc to represent bits, which a laser beam can then read. This is why they are called optical storage technologies. CD drives use the **CDFS (Compact Disc File System)** or the **UDF (Universal Disk Format) file system,** and DVD drives use the newer UDF. Windows supports both file systems, which include several standards used for audio, photographs, video, and other data. Most CD drives support several CDFS formats, and most DVD drives support several UDF formats and the CDFS format for backward compatibility. In this section, you will learn about the major optical storage technologies, including their similarities and differences, their storage capacities, and variations within each type.

CD

A+
CORE
1.1

Of the multimedia components discussed in this chapter, the most popular is the CD drive. CDs are used to distribute software and sound files. CD drives are read-only devices. Read/writable CDs and drives are discussed later in the chapter.

During the manufacturing process, data can be written to a CD disc only once, because the data is actually embedded in the surface of the disc. Figure 11-6 shows a CD surface laid out as one continuous spiral of sectors of equal length that hold equal amounts of data. If laid out in a straight line, this spiral would be 3.5 miles long. The surface of a CD stores data as pits and lands. **Lands** are raised areas and **pits** are recessed areas on the surface; each represents either a 1 or a 0, respectively. The bits are read by the drive with a laser beam that distinguishes between a pit and a land by the amount of deflection or scattering that occurs when the light beam hits the surface.

Figure 11-6   The spiral layout of sectors on a CD surface

11

A small motor with an actuator arm moves the laser beam to the sector on the track it needs to read. If the disc were spinning at a constant speed, the speed near the center of the disc would be greater than the speed at the outer edge. To create the effect of **constant linear velocity (CLV)**, the CD drive uses a mechanism that speeds up the disc when the laser beam is near the center of the disc, and slows down the disc when the laser beam is near the outer edge. Thus, the beam is over a sector for the same amount of time, no matter where the sector is. (Because the outer edge has more sectors than the inner edge, the light beam needs more time to read near the outer edge than it does near the inner edge.) The transfer rate of the first CD drives was about 150 kilobytes per second of data (150 KBps), with the rpm (revolutions per minute) set to 200 when the laser was near the center of the disc. This transfer rate was about right for audio CDs. To show video and motion without a choppy effect, the speed of the drives was increased to double speed (150KBps × 2), quad speed (150KBps × 4), and so on. CD drives with speeds at 52x and 56x (52 and 56 times the audio speed) are not uncommon now. Audio CDs must still drop to the original speed of 200 rpm and a transfer rate of 150 KBps.

A+
CORE
2.1
3.1

Because of the problems of changing speeds using CLV, newer, faster CD drives use a combination of CLV and **constant angular velocity (CAV)**, the same technology used by hard drives, whereby the disc rotates at a constant speed.

When you choose a CD drive, look for the multisession feature, which means that the drive can read a disc that has been created in multiple sessions. To say a disc was created in **multisessions** means that data was written to the disc at different times rather than in a single long session.

Some CD drives have power-saving features controlled by the device driver. For example, when the drive waits for a command for more than five minutes, it enters Power Save Mode, causing the spindle motor to stop. The restart is automatic when the drive receives a command.

Table 11-5 lists manufacturers of CD drives.

A+
CORE
2.1
3.1

APPLYING CONCEPTS

Caring for CD Drives and Discs

Most problems with CDs are caused by dust, fingerprints, scratches, surface defects, or random electrical noise. Don't use a CD drive if it is standing vertically, such as when someone turns a desktop PC case on its side to save desk space. Use these precautions when handling CDs or DVDs:

- Hold the CD by the edge; do not touch the bright side of the disc where data is stored.
- To remove dust or fingerprints, use a clean, soft, dry cloth.
- Do not write or paste paper on the surface of the CD. Don't paste any labels on the top of the CD, because this can imbalance the CD and cause the drive to vibrate.
- Do not subject the CD to heat or leave it in direct sunlight.
- Do not use cleaners, alcohol, and the like on the CD.
- Do not make the center hole larger.
- Do not bend the CD.
- Do not drop the CD or subject it to shock.
- If a CD gets stuck in the drive, use the emergency eject hole to remove it. Turn off the power to the PC first. Then insert an instrument such as a straightened paper clip into the hole to eject the tray manually.
- When closing a CD tray, don't push on the tray. Press the close button on the front of the drive.

NOTE

A CD, CD-R, CD-RW, or DVD is expected to hold its data for many years; however, you can prolong the life of a disc by protecting it from exposure to light.

Manufacturer	Web Site
Acer Peripherals	*global.acer.com*
ASUS	*www.asus.com*
Addonics Technologies	*www.addonics.com*
Axonix	*www.axonix.com*
BenQ	*www.benq.com*
Circo Technology	*www.circotech.com*
Creative Labs	*www.creativelabs.com* or *www.creative.com*
Hewlett-Packard	*www.hpcdwriter.com*
Panasonic	*www.panasonic.com*
Samsung	*www.samsung.com*
Sanyo	*www.sanyo.com*
Sony	*www.sony.com*
TDK	*www.tdk.com/multimedia*

Table 11-5 CD drive manufacturers

How a CD Drive Can Interface with the Motherboard

**A+
CORE
1.2**

CD drives can interface with the motherboard in several ways:

- Using an EIDE interface; the drive can share an EIDE connection and cable with a hard drive. EIDE is the most popular interface method for CD drives. These drives follow the ATAPI (Advanced Technology Attachment Packet Interface) standard, an extension of the IDE/ATA standard that allows tape drives, CD drives, and other drives to be treated just like another hard drive on the system.
- Using a SCSI interface with a SCSI host adapter
- Using a portable drive and plugging into an external port on your PC, such as a USB port, 1394 port, or SCSI port

Installing a CD Drive

✔ A+ EXAM TIP

The A+ Core exam expects you to know how to install an optical drive, such as a CD drive.

Once installed, the CD or CD-RW drive becomes another drive on your system, such as drive D or E. After it is installed, you access it just like any other drive by typing D: or E: at the command prompt, or by accessing the drive through Windows Explorer.

The most popular interface for a CD drive is EIDE, although you will occasionally see a SCSI CD drive. Figure 11-7 shows the rear of an EIDE CD drive. Note the jumper bank that can be set to cable

A+ CORE 1.2

select, slave, or master. Recall from Chapter 8 that, for Enhanced IDE (EIDE), there are four choices for drive installations: primary master, primary slave, secondary master, and secondary slave. If the drive will be the second drive installed on the cable, then set the drive to slave. If the drive is the only drive on the cable, choose master, because single is not a choice. The cable select setting is used if a special EIDE cable-select cable determines which drive is master or slave. If the CD drive shares an IDE channel with a hard drive, make the hard drive the master and the CD drive the slave.

> **NOTE** The computer industry often uses the term IDE when it really means EIDE. Technically, for today's computers, EIDE refers to the interface standard, and IDE refers to how hard drive firmware stores data on the drive. For the most part, this chapter uses EIDE to refer to the interface standard. One exception is the labeling shown in Figure 11-7 where the manufacturer labeled its CD drive's interface as an IDE connection when it really meant an EIDE connection. You should also know that most motherboard manufacturers label their EIDE connections as IDE connections.

Figure 11-7   Rear view of an IDE CD drive

When given the choice of putting the CD drive on the same cable with a hard drive or on its own cable, choose to use its own cable. A CD drive that shares a cable with a hard drive can slow down the hard drive's performance. Most systems today have two EIDE connections on the motherboard, probably labeled IDE1 and IDE2, so most likely you will be able to use IDE2 for the CD drive.

> **NOTE** For ATA/100 hard drives and above, you use an 80-conductor IDE cable for the hard drive on one channel and a regular 40-conductor cable for the CD drive on the other channel.

APPLYING CONCEPTS

Follow these general steps to install a CD drive, using safety precautions to protect the system against ESD:

1. Open the case and slide the drive into an empty bay. If the bay uses rails, screw the rails in place. If you have no rails, then put two screws on each side of the drive, tightening the screws so the drive can't shift, but avoiding overtightening them. Use the screws that come with the drive; screws that are too long can damage the drive. If necessary, buy a mounting kit to extend the sides of the drive so that it fits into the bay and attaches securely.

2. Connect a power cord to the drive.

3. For EIDE drives, connect the 40-pin cable to the IDE motherboard connector and the drive, being careful to follow the pin 1 rule: match the edge color on the cable to pin 1 on both the adapter card and the drive. Generally, the colored edge is closest to the power connector.

4. Attach the audio cord if you have a sound card. Don't make the mistake of attaching a miniature power cord designed for a 3½-inch disk drive coming from the power supply to the audio input connector on the sound card. The connections appear to fit, but you'll probably destroy the drive by making this connection.

5. Some drives have a ground connection, with one end of the ground cable attaching to the computer case. Follow the directions included with the drive.

6. Check all connections and turn on the power. Press the eject button on the front of the drive. If it works, then you know power is getting to the drive. Put the case cover back on.

7. Turn on the PC. If the drive is Plug and Play, Windows launches the Found New Hardware Wizard. Windows supports EIDE CD drives using its own internal 32-bit drivers without add-on drivers, so the installation of drivers requires little intervention on your part. If the Found New Hardware Wizard does not launch, go to the Control Panel and launch the **Add New Hardware** Wizard. Click **Next** when you are prompted to begin installing the software for the new device. Complete the installation by following the directions of the Add New Hardware Wizard.

8. The drive is now ready to use. Press the eject button to open the drive shelf, and place a CD in the drive. Data on CDs is written only on the bottom, so be careful to protect it. Now access the CD using Windows Explorer.

If you have a problem reading the CD, verify that you placed the CD in the tray label-side-up and that the format is compatible with your drive. If one CD doesn't work, try another—the first CD may be defective or scratched. When installing a CD-R or CD-RW drive, after you have verified the drive can read a CD, install the burning software that came bundled with the drive.

11

A+
CORE
1.2

NOTE

A CD drive can be set so that when you insert a CD, software on the CD automatically executes, a feature called Autorun or Autoplay. To turn the feature on using Windows 9x/Me, open Device Manager, right-click the CD drive, and select Properties. In the Properties dialog box, select the Settings tab and then select Auto insert notification. For Windows XP, many options for various content on CDs are available. To customize how Windows XP handles a CD, open My Computer and right-click the drive. The CD drive Properties dialog box appears; click the Autoplay tab (see Figure 11-8). To prevent a CD from automatically playing when Autoplay is enabled, hold down the Shift key when inserting the CD.

Figure 11-8   For Windows XP, use My Computer to tell the OS how to handle the Autoplay feature for your CD drive.

CD-R and CD-RW

A+
CORE
1.1

A CD is a read-only medium, meaning that CD drives can only read, not write. In the past, writing to a CD required expensive equipment and was not practical for personal computer use. Now, **CD-R (CD-recordable)** drives and discs are much more affordable, making burning your own CDs a viable option. These CD-R discs can be read by regular CD drives and are excellent ways to distribute software or large amounts of data. Besides allowing for a lot of data storage space on a relatively inexpensive medium, another advantage of distributing software and data on a CD-R disc is that you can be assured no one will edit or overwrite what's written on the disc.

You can tell the difference between a CD and a CD-R disc by the color of the bottom of the disc. CD-R discs are blue, black, or some other color, and CDs are silver. When you purchase and install a CD-R drive, good software to manage the writing process is important, because some less robust software can make burning a disc difficult. Also, some CD-R drives are multisession drives, and some are not.

Also available at a slightly higher cost is a **CD-RW (CD-rewritable)** drive, which allows you to overwrite old data with new data. The process of creating a CD-RW disc is similar to that used for CD-R discs. The chemicals on the surface of the CD-RW disc are different, allowing the process of writing a less reflective spot to the disc surface to be reversed so that data can be erased. One drawback to CD-RW discs is that the medium cannot always be read successfully by older CD drives or by some audio CD players.

CD-RW discs are useful in developing CDs for distribution. A developer can create a disc, test for errors, and rewrite to the disc without wasting many discs during development. After the disc is fully tested, CD-R discs can be burned for distribution. The advantage of distributing on CD-R discs rather than CD-RW discs is that CD-R discs are less expensive and can be read by all CD drives.

Combo CD and DVD drives are becoming popular as the prices of optical drives continue to drop. An example is the External USB 2.0 DVD/CD-RW Combo Drive by Addonics.

11

DVD

With multimedia, the ability to store massive amounts of data is paramount to the technology's success. The goal of storing a full-length movie on a single unit of a computerized, inexpensive storage medium has been met by more than one technology, but the technology that has clearly taken the lead in popularity is **DVD (digital video disc or digital versatile disc)** (see Figure 11-9). It takes up to seven CDs to store a full-length movie, but it only requires one DVD. A DVD can hold 8.5 GB of data, and if both the top and bottom surfaces are used, it can hold 17 GB of data, which is enough for more than eight hours of video storage. DVD uses the Universal Disk Format (UDF) file system.

The discrepancy in the computer industry between one billion bytes (1,000,000,000 bytes) and 1 GB (1,073,741,824 bytes) exists because 1 KB equals 1,024 bytes. Even though documentation might say that a DVD holds 17 GB, in fact it holds 17 billion bytes, which is only 15.90 GB.

When you look at the surface of a CD and a DVD, it is difficult to distinguish between the two. They both have the same 5-inch diameter and 1.2-mm thickness, and the same shiny surface. However, a DVD can use both the top and bottom surface for data. If the top of the disc has no label, data is probably written on it, and it is most likely a DVD. Because DVD uses a shorter wavelength laser, it can read smaller, more densely packed pits, which increases the disc's capacity. In addition, a second layer is added to DVD, an opaque layer that also holds data and almost doubles the capacity of the disc. (One layer on one side of a DVD can hold 4.7 GB of data. If two layers are used, one side can hold 8.5 GB of data.)

Figure 11-9   This external DVD drive by Plextor can use an IEEE 1394 or Hi-Speed USB connection and supports several speeds and read/write standards including 4X DVD+R, 2.4X DVD+R/RW, 12X DVD-ROM, 16X CD-R write, 10X CD-RW rewrite, and 40X CD read

DVD uses MPEG-2 video compression and requires an MPEG-2 controller to decode the compressed data. This decoder can be firmware on a controller card that comes bundled with the DVD drive, software that comes bundled with the DVD drive and is installed at the time the DVD drive is installed, or the decoder is contained on a video capture card. Audio is stored on DVD in Dolby AC-3 compression. This audio compression method is also the standard used by HDTV (high-definition TV). Dolby AC-3 compression is also known as Dolby Digital Surround or Dolby Surround Sound. It supports six separate sound channels of sound information for six different speakers, each producing a different sound. These speakers are known as Front Left and Right, Front Center, Rear Left and Right, and Subwoofer. Because each channel is digital, there is no background noise on the channel, and a sound engineer can place sound on any one of these speakers. The sound effects can be awesome!

Besides DVD-ROM, new DVD devices have recently come on the market that are read-writable. Table 11-6 describes these devices. The last three items in Table 11-6 compete with one another. All have similar but not identical features, so compatibility and standards are issues. It's yet to be seen which of these three media will prevail in the marketplace, although DVD-RAM appears to be moving ahead. When purchasing one, pay close attention to compatibility with other media, such as CD, and to the availability and price of discs.

Two new and competing DVD formats are HD-DVD (high-density DVD) and Blu-ray Disc, both using blue laser formats. HD-DVD can hold up to 30 GB of data, and Blu-ray can hold up to 50 GB of data. Each standard is backed by a strong consortium of industry leaders, and both groups claim to be the solution for the confusing and complex DVD standards that plague the current market. For more information about HD-DVD, see *www.dvdsite.org* and for information about Blu-ray, see *www.blu-raydisc.com*.

DVD Device	Description
DVD-ROM	Read-only device. A DVD-ROM drive can also read CDs.
DVD-R	DVD recordable. Uses a similar technology to CD-R drives. Holds about 4.7 GB of data. Can read DVD-ROM discs.
DVD-RAM	Recordable and erasable. Multifunctional DVD device that can read DVD-RAM, DVD-R, DVD-ROM, and CD-R discs.
DVD-R/RW or DVD-ER	Rewritable DVD device, also known as erasable, recordable device. Media can be read by most DVD-ROM drives.
DVD+R/RW	A technology similar to and currently competing with DVD-RW. Can read DVD-ROM and CD-ROM discs but is not compatible with DVD-RAM discs.

Table 11-6   DVD devices

Table 11-7 lists manufacturers of optical drives.

Manufacturer	Web Site
Addonics	*www.addonics.com*
BenQ	*www.benq.com*
Creative Labs	*www.creative.com*
Hewlett-Packard	*www.hp.com*
IBM	*www.ibm.com*
Intel	*www.intel.com*
Pioneer	*www.pioneerelectronics.com*
Plextor	*www.plextor.com*
Sony Electronics	*www.songstyle.com*
Toshiba	*www.toshiba.com*

Table 11-7   Optical drive manufacturers

11

NOTE

A DVD combo drive such as the Combo DVD + RW/+R and DVD-RW/-R drive by Sony gives you optional recordable and rewritable standards.

APPLYING CONCEPTS

Installing a DVD Drive

As an example of installing a DVD drive, this section uses the Creative PC-DVD Encore by Creative Labs, Inc. (*www.americas.creative.com*), because it uses a hardware decoder. This installation is more complicated than that of a software decoder. Except for the documentation and sample DVD game disc, the parts included in the kit are shown in Figure 11-10. The data coming from the DVD drive is split into video data and sound data. Recall that video data must be decoded before being sent to the monitor, and sound data must be decoded before being sent to a regular sound card (one that does not process Dolby sound). This is accomplished by the DVD decoder card. Figure 11-11 shows the flow of data in the completed system.

Installing a
DVD Drive

Decoder card-to-sound
card cable
DVD drive-to-decoder card
cable (audio)
IDE data cable
DVD drive

TV out cable

DVD application software
VGA loopback cable

Driver files
DVD decoder card

Figure 11-10　Parts included in the DVD drive kit

> **NOTE**
> A good example of a DVD drive that uses a software decoder is the Creative Lab's Ovation 16x. This EIDE drive comes with an audio cable, EIDE cable, and CD that contains the drivers and decoder software. Installation is much simpler than in the following example, because there is no decoder card to install.

To help make the final installation of parts easier to visualize and understand, we set up the installation outside the case and took the photo shown in Figure 11-12. No power was on while the components were in this position!

The DVD decoder card (see Figure 11-13) has connections for audio in, audio out, video in, and video out. In addition, there are two other external ports, one for TV out and one for Dolby digital sound out. Use the TV out port to play DVD movies from your PC, and use the Dolby port if you have a Dolby speaker system.

The rear of the DVD drive is shown in Figure 11-14, and a diagram of the rear panel is shown in Figure 11-15. Looking closely at Figure 11-14, note that the jumper is set so that the drive will be a slave on the IDE connection.

Figure 11-11   Data flow in the DVD subsystem

Looking at the location of the bay for the DVD drive, we decide to connect the audio cable first, slide the drive into the bay, and then connect the remaining cable and cord. Survey your own situation for the best approach. Follow these steps to install the DVD components:

1. Turn off the PC and remove the case cover. Confirm that the jumper on the DVD drive is set to slave (the default setting).
2. Connect the DVD drive audio cord to the analog audio connection on the rear of the drive.
3. Remove the faceplate covering the bay opening on the front of the computer case.
4. Slide the drive into the bay from the front of the bay.
5. Secure the drive in the bay with two screws on each side of the drive.
6. Attach the IDE data cable to the drive, carefully aligning the edge color of the cable with pin 1 on the drive.

A+
CORE
1.2

7. Connect a power cord to the power connection on the drive.

8. Connect the audio cord coming from the DVD drive to the audio-in connection on the DVD decoder card.

9. Connect the second audio cord first to the audio-out connection on the DVD decoder card and then to the audio-in connection on the sound card (see Figure 11-12). The cord has two plugs at the sound-card end. Select the plug that fits the sound-card connection.

Video data "loops back" to DVD decoder

Decoded audio data to sound card

Video card

Sound card

DVD decoder card

IDE data cable carries video data

DVD drive

Audio data to decoder

VGA output to monitor

Audio output to speakers

Figure 11-12   The complete DVD subsystem, including the drive (right) and various components installed on the motherboard (left)

- Output to a Dolby digital sound device
- Audio out (to sound card)
- Audio in (from DVD drive)
- PCI connection
- VGA in (from video card using loopback cable)
- VGA out (to monitor)
- TV out (using TV cable provided)

Figure 11-13   DVD decoder card

10. Insert the DVD decoder card in a PCI expansion slot, and secure it with a screw.

- IDE connection
- Power
- Jumper in slave position
- Audio out

Figure 11-14   Rear of DVD drive (see Figure 11-15 for an explanation of each connection)

- 40-pin IDE connection

MASTER
SLAVE
CABLE SELECT
DIGITAL   ANALOG
AUDIO   AUDIO
DG   RGGL

39   HOST INTERFACE   1   POWER
40   2   +5V G G +12V

Digital audio connector for professional digital recording (not used)

Audio connector to sound card by way of decoder card

MASTER
SLAVE
CABLE SELECT
Master

MASTER
SLAVE
CABLE SELECT
Slave (default)

Master/Slave setting for IDE configuration

Power in

Figure 11-15   Rear panel of the DVD drive

11

11. Replace the case cover. Install the video loopback cable (see Figure 11-16), which presents video data to the DVD decoder for decoding before the video data is sent on to the monitor.

Video out—
from DVD decoder
to monitor

Video out—
from video card

Video in—to
DVD decoder

Figure 11-16   The video loopback cable installed in the DVD subsystem

12. Turn on the PC. Windows recognizes and uses the drive as a CD drive without additional device drivers. To use the drive as a DVD drive, you must install the device drivers that come bundled with the drive. Insert the installation disk in the floppy disk drive, and enter **A:Setup** in the Run dialog box to start the installation.

In the next sections, we look at two more types of drives used for storage and backups: tape drives and removable drives, and we also look at using a second hard drive in a system for backing up data.

Hardware Used for Backups and Fault Tolerance

How valuable is your data? How valuable is your software? In many cases, the most valuable component on the desktop is not the hardware or the software, but the data. Think about each computer you support. What would happen if the hard drive failed? You should create backups to prepare for that situation. Whether your hard drive contains a large database or just a few word-processing files, make backups. Never keep an important file on only one medium. Make a copy to a disk, to a file server, or to tape backup. Consider keeping some of your backups in an off-site location.

Your backup policy depends on what you are backing up and your organization's policies. If you use your PC to interface with a server, for example, and all data is stored on the server and not on the PC, then you will only back up software. (The person responsible for the server usually backs up the data. You may want to check with the responsible party in your organiation to make sure this is being done.) If you keep original application disks and CDs in a safe place, and if you have multiple copies of them, you might decide not to back up the applications. In this case, if a hard drive fails, your chore is to reload several software packages.

However, if you maintain a large database on the hard drive of your PC, you need to seriously consider a sophisticated backup method. Suppose this database is quite large and is edited several times a day. If this database is lost, so are thousands of labor hours. Plan for the worst case! A good tape backup system is probably in order. Maintain five or 10 tapes, on which a complete backup of the database is made each night.

Popular hardware devices used for making hard drive backups on standalone personal computers or small servers include tapes or removable drives. However, if a PC is connected to a file server in a business environment, the most practical backup approach is to back up data from the PC's hard drive to the file server. Data on both the PC and the file server can become corrupted. However, the file server most likely uses its own automated backup utility to back up to either tape or a larger mainframe computer. Before you back up to the server, check with the server administrator to ensure that space is available and company policy allows you to do this.

This section first discusses using tape drives and then using removable drives for backups.

NOTE

For backing up large amounts of data to a file server or other media, invest in backup software such as Ghost by Symantec (*www.symantec.com*) or WinZip by WinZip Computing (*www.winzip.com*), which compresses the data to conserve space.

Tape Drives

A+ CORE 1.2

Tape drives (see Figure 11-17) are an inexpensive way of backing up an entire hard drive or portions of it. Tape drives are more convenient for backups than floppy disks or other types of removable disks. Tapes currently have capacities of up to 40 GB compressed and come in several types and formats. Although tape drives don't require that you use special backup software to manage them, you might want to invest in specialied backup software to make backups as efficient and effortless as possible. Many tape drives come with bundled software, and Windows offers a Backup utility that can use tape drives. Several of the more common standards and types of tape drives and tapes are described in this section.

11

A+
CORE
1.2

Figure 11-17   The Certance TapeStor Travan 20-GB external tape drive by Seagate is shown with a USB cable, tape cassette, power adapter, user guide and drivers on CD

The biggest disadvantage of using tape drives is that data is stored on tape by **sequential access;**to read data from anywhere on the tape, you must start at the beginning of the tape and read until you come to the sought-after data. Sequential access makes recovering files slow and inconvenient, which is why tapes are not used for general-purpose data storage.

Table 11-8 lists some manufacturers of tape drives.

Manufacturer	Web Site
DLT	*www.dlttape.com*
Exabyte	*www.exabyte.com*
Hewlett Packard	*www.hp.com*
Imation	*www.imation.com*
Iomega	*www.iomega.com*
Quantum Corporation	*www.quantum.com*
Seagate	*www.seagate.com*
Sony	*www.sony.com*

Table 11-8   Tape drive manufacturers

How a Tape Drive Interfaces with a Computer

A+
CORE
1.2

A tape drive can be external or internal. An external tape drive costs more but can be used by more than one computer. A tape drive can interface with a computer in these ways:

- An external tape drive can use the parallel port (see Figure 11-18) with an optional pass-through to the printer (so that the drive and the printer can use the same parallel port).
- An external or internal drive can use a SCSI bus. This method works well if the tape drive and the hard drive are on the same SCSI bus, which contains a data pass-through just to the SCSI system.
- An external or internal drive can use a USB connection, its own proprietary controller card, or the floppy drive interface.
- An internal drive can use the IDE ATAPI interface.

11

Figure 11-18   An external tape drive can use the parallel port for input/output, with an optional pass-through to the printer

Currently, the most popular tape drive interfaces for internal drives are SCSI and IDE ATAPI; for external drives, USB is the most popular. Figure 11-19 shows the rear of an ATAPI tape drive. You can see the connections for a power supply and a 40-pin IDE cable as well as jumpers to set the drive to master, slave, or cable select. This setup is similar for any EIDE device. When installing an ATAPI tape drive, avoid putting the drive on the same IDE data cable as the hard drive, or it might hinder the hard drive's performance. A typical configuration is to install the hard drive as the sole device on the primary IDE channel and let a CD drive and tape drive share the second channel. Set the CD drive to master and the tape drive to slave on that channel.

Jumper bank to set master, slave, or cable select

40-pin connection for IDE cable

Power supply connection

Figure 11-19   The rear of an ATAPI IDE tape drive

The Tapes Used by a Tape Drive

Tape drives accommodate one of two kinds of tapes: full-sized **data cartridges** are 4 × 6 × ⅝ inches, and the smaller **minicartridges,** like the one in Figure 11-20, are 3¼ × 2½ × ⅗ inches. Minicartridges are more popular because their drives can fit into a standard 3½-inch drive bay of a PC case.

The technology used by tape drives to write to tapes is similar to that used by floppy drives (see Chapter 7). A FAT at the beginning of the tape tracks the location of data and bad sectors on the tape. The tape must be formatted before data can be written to it. Purchase factory-formatted tapes to save time.

When purchasing tapes, carefully match tapes to tape drives because several standards and sizes exist. One standard developed by 3M is Travan, which is backed by many leaders in the tape drive industry. There are different levels of Travan standards, called TR-1 through TR-8. Other tape standards include DAT, VXA-1, VXA-2, AIT-2, AIT-3, DLT (Digital Linear Tape), LTO, SDLT (Super DLT), SLR and MLR QIC cartridges. Quarter-Inch Cartridge Drive Standards, Inc. (QIC at *www.qic.org*) is a trade association responsible for shaping many of these standards. For an interesting photo gallery of tape media see *www.BackupWorks.com*. Note that tape drives are likely to be able to read other formats than the formats they use for writing. For example, the Seagate Certance 40-GB tape drive writes to and reads 40-GB TR-6 tapes, and can read from 20-GB TR-5 tapes. Read the tape drive documentation to know what tapes the drive supports.

A+
CORE
1.2

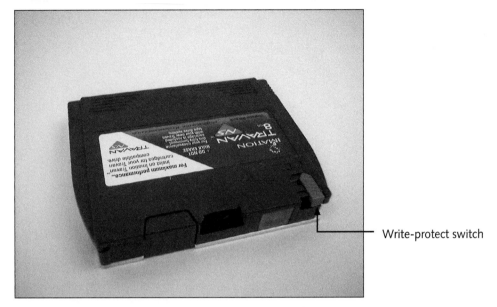

Write-protect switch

Figure 11-20   Minicartridge for a tape drive has a write-protect switch

11

Removable Drives

A+
CORE
1.2
1.8
2.1

A removable drive can be either an external or internal drive. Using a removable drive provides several advantages:

- Increases the overall storage capacity of a system
- Makes it easy to move large files from one computer to another
- Serves as a convenient medium for making backups of hard drive data
- Makes it easy to secure important files (To keep important files secure, keep the removable drive locked in a safe when it is not being used.)

When purchasing a removable drive, consider how susceptible the drive is when dropped. The **drop height** is the height from which the manufacturer says you can drop the drive without making it unusable. Also consider how long the data will last on the drive. The **half-life** (sometimes called life expectancy or shelf life) of the disk is the time it takes for the magnetic strength of the medium to weaken by half. Magnetic media, including traditional hard drives and floppy disks, have a half-life of five to seven years, but writable optical media such as CD-Rs have a half-life of 30 years.

Types of Removable Drives

This section covers several of the newer and older removable drives on the market. One newer drive is the IBM Microdrive introduced earlier in the chapter. The drive comes in several sizes up to 4 GB. It uses the CompactFlash II form factor, and you can purchase a PC Card adapter to make it convenient to use in a laptop computer (see Figure 11-21).

Figure 11-21 The IBM Microdrive inserts into a PC Card adapter, which fits into a notebook PC Card slot

A less expensive and more convenient type of drive, ranging in size from 1 GB to 32 GB, is the flash pen drive. One popular example of a flash pen drive is the Jump-Drive by Lexar Media (*www.lexarmediashop.com*). The drive (see Figure 11-22) offers 64 MB or 4 GB of storage, conveniently fits on a keychain, and snaps into a USB port.

Another removable drive is the Iomega HDD drive by Iomega (*www.iomega.com*). The drive (see Figure 11-23) is small enough to fit into your shirt pocket and uses a USB or 1394 connection. It comes bundled with Iomega Automatic Backup and Symantec Norton Ghost software, holds from 20 GB to 250 GB of data, and is a great backup solution for a PC hard drive. Iomega says it's rugged enough that you don't have to worry about dropping it.

Figure 11-22 This JumpDrive holds 128 MB of data and snaps into a USB port

A+
CORE
1.2
1.8
2.1

Figure 11-23   This 60-GB HDD portable hard drive by Iomega has a USB 2.0 and FireWire connection and is small enough to fit in your pocket. It comes with drivers that let you run applications from the drive as well as Symantec Norton Ghost for using the drive as a backup medium.

11

One type of older removable drive is the Iomega 3½-inch Zip drive, which stores 100 MB, 250 MB, or 750 MB of data on each of its disks, and has a drop height of 8 feet (see Figure 11-24). An internal Zip drive uses an EIDE interface. The external Zip drive plugs into the parallel port, a USB port, a SCSI port, or a 1394 port. The drive and disk look like a traditional 3½-inch floppy disk drive and disk, but the disk is slightly larger. If you include a Zip drive on a new PC, consider it an add-on, not a replacement for the standard 3½-inch floppy disk drive. Zip drives can't read standard 3½-inch floppy disks.

Another removable drive is SuperDisk, originally developed by Imation, which stores 120 MB or 240 MB of data. The drives are currently made by other manufacturers, but Imation still makes the removable disks. SuperDisk 120-MB drives are backward-compatible with double-density (720K) and high-density (1.44 MB) floppy disks, and SuperDisk 240-MB drives are backward-compatible with SuperDisk 120-MB drives and both sizes of floppy disks. The SuperDisk is really two disk drives in one. It can use the old technology to read from and write to regular floppy disks, and it can use laser technology to read and write 120-MB or 240-MB disks. SuperDisk is up to 27 times faster than regular floppy drives. One advantage SuperDisk has over Zip drives is its backward compatibility with regular floppy disks. A disadvantage of SuperDisk is that the medium is not as popular as Zip drives, so if you plan to exchange the disks with other users, most likely you need to use another medium. SuperDisk drives can be purchased as external (parallel port and USB) or internal drives.

A+
CORE
1.2
1.8
2.1

Figure 11-24 An internal Zip drive kit includes the IDE Zip drive, documentation, drivers on floppy disk, and one Zip disk

Installing a Removable Drive

Installing an internal removable drive such as a Zip drive is similar to installing a hard drive. For an EIDE drive, set the drive to master or slave on an IDE channel. If the external or internal drive is a SCSI drive, the SCSI host adapter must already be installed and configured. How to install a SCSI host adapter is covered in Chapter 22. Do the following to install a removable drive:

1. Read the documentation about how to install the drive. Some USB or 1394 devices require you to install the software before plugging up the device. Other installations plug up the device and then install the software. The documentation will tell you the correct order to use.

2. If you install the software before you install the device, install the software now.

3. Identify the connectors. Many removable drives use either the parallel port, a USB port, a 1394 port, or a SCSI port for connection.

4. For a parallel device, turn off your PC and connect the parallel cable from the drive to the parallel port on the PC. If you have a printer, connect the printer cable to the printer port on the drive. Go to Step 9.

5. For a USB or 1394 device, connect the USB or 1394 cable to the USB or 1394 port. Go to Step 9.

6. For a SCSI device, with the SCSI host adapter installed, connect the SCSI cable to the drive and to the SCSI port on the host adapter.

**A+
CORE
1.2
1.8
2.1**

7. For a SCSI drive, set the drive's SCSI ID. If the device is the last one on a SCSI chain, install a terminator on the device.

8. You might also need to set the host adapter to recognize an external device. See the documentation for the host adapter. (SCSI is covered in Chapter 22.)

9. Check all your connections and plug the AC power cord for the drive into a wall socket.

10. Turn on your PC. If you have not yet installed the software, do that now.

11. If you have problems, turn everything off and check all connections. Power up and try again. You can use Device Manager to uninstall the device drivers and get a fresh start.

Fault Tolerance, Dynamic Volumes, and RAID

Fault tolerance is a computer's ability to respond to a fault or catastrophe, such as a hardware failure or power outage, so that data is not lost. If data is important enough to justify the cost, you can protect the data by continuously writing two copies of it, each to a different hard drive. This method is most often used on high-end, expensive file servers, but it is occasionally appropriate for a single-user workstation. In addition, sometimes you can improve performance by writing data to two or more hard drives so that a single drive is not excessively used.

Collectively, the methods used to improve performance and automatically recover from a failure are called **RAID (redundant array of independent disks)**. There are several levels of RAID, but this section discusses only the most commonly used levels. We first look at how an operating system supports fault tolerance and improves hard drive performance, and then at how these methods are implemented with RAID hardware.

Dynamic Volumes under Windows

Windows implements fault tolerance and writing data across multiple hard drives to improve performance by using a type of hard drive configuration first introduced by Windows 2000 called dynamic volumes or dynamic disks. We first explain what a dynamic volume is and then look at different ways to implement fault tolerance under each OS.

Basic Disks and Dynamic Disks   Windows 2000/XP offers two ways to configure a hard drive: as a basic disk or a dynamic disk. A **basic disk** is the same as the configuration used with DOS, Windows 9x/Me, and Windows NT. By default, Windows 2000/XP uses basic disk configuration. With basic disk configuration, you generally create partitions of a set size and then do not change them. If you want to change the size of a partition, you either have to reinstall Windows

11

(if Windows is installed on that partition) or use special third-party software that allows you to change the size of a partition without losing your data. Within partitions, you create logical drives (sometimes called basic volumes) of set size.

Dynamic disks don't use partitions or logical drives; instead, they use **dynamic volumes,** which are called dynamic because you can change their size. Data to configure the disk is stored in a disk management database that resides in the last 1 MB of storage space at the end of a hard drive. DOS, Windows 9x/Me, and Windows NT cannot read dynamic disks. Dynamic disks are compatible only with Windows 2000 and Windows XP.

NOTE   Because a dynamic disk requires 1 MB of storage for the disk management database, if you are partitioning a basic disk and expect that one day you might want to convert it to a dynamic disk, leave 1 MB of space on the drive unpartitioned, to be used later for the disk management database.

**A+
CORE
1.6
1.7
1.9**

Types of Dynamic Volumes   A dynamic volume is contained within a dynamic disk and is a logical volume similar to a logical drive in a basic disk. There are five types of dynamic volumes:

- A **simple volume** corresponds to a primary partition on a basic disk and consists of disk space on a single physical disk.
- A **spanned volume** appears as a simple volume but can use space from two or more physical disks. It fills the space allotted on one physical disk before moving on to the next. This increases the amount of disk space available for a volume. However, if one physical disk on which data that is part of a spanned volume fails, all data in the volume is lost. Spanned volumes are sometimes called JBOD (just a bunch of drives).
- A **striped volume** (also called **RAID 0**) also can use space from two or more physical disks and increases the disk space available for a single volume. The difference between a spanned volume and a striped volume is that a striped volume writes to the physical disks evenly rather than filling allotted space on one and then moving on to the next. This increases disk performance as compared to access time with a spanned volume.
- A **mirrored volume** (also called **RAID 1**) duplicates data on another drive and is used for fault tolerance. Each drive has its own volume, and the two volumes are called mirrors. If one drive fails, the other continues to operate and data is not lost. A variation of mirroring is disk duplexing, which uses two controllers, one for each drive, thus providing more fault tolerance than mirroring. Mirrored volumes are only supported by server OSs (such as Windows 2000 Server and Windows 2003 Server).
- A **RAID-5 volume** is striped across three or more drives and uses parity checking, so that if one drive fails, the other drives can recreate the data stored on the

failed drive. RAID-5 volumes increase performance and volume capacity and provide fault tolerance. RAID-5 volumes are only supported by server OSs (such as Windows 2000 Server and Windows 2003 Server).

Figure 11-25 illustrates the difference between basic disk and dynamic disk organization. A basic disk or a dynamic disk can use any file system supported by Windows 2000/XP (FAT16, FAT32, and NTFS). Note that Windows 2000 Professional and Windows XP do not support the types of dynamic disks that provide fault tolerance (mirrored volume and RAID-5), so the only reasons to use dynamic disks under these OSs are to improve disk performance and to increase the size of a single volume. Dynamic drives offer little advantage for a system with only a single hard drive, and they are not supported at all on laptop computers.

Figure 11-25 Basic disks use partitions and logical drives to organize a hard drive, and dynamic disks use dynamic volumes to organize multiple hard drives

After Windows 2000/XP is installed, you can use the Windows 2000/XP Disk Management utility to switch from basic to dynamic or dynamic to basic, and change the file system on either type of disk. For a striped volume using Windows 2000/XP, each hard drive in the array must have the same amount of free space available to the volume and must use the same file system (FAT16, FAT32, or NTFS). Table 11-9 summarizes which methods are used by the various OSs. The table uses the prevalent terms in the documentation for each OS to describe the methods supported.

Windows Version	Volume and RAID Types Supported
Windows 9x/Me	—
Windows NT Workstation	RAID 0 (striped)
Windows 2000 Professional	Simple, spanned, and striped (RAID 0)
Windows XP Professional	Simple, spanned, and striped (RAID 0)
Windows NT Server, Windows 2000 Server, and Windows 2003 Server	Simple, spanned, striped (RAID 0), mirrored (RAID 1), and RAID 5

Table 11-9 Types of volumes and RAID used in different versions of Windows

Hardware RAID

A+
CORE
1.6
1.7
1.9

Another way to implement RAID is to use hardware. In order to use hardware RAID, your hard drive controller or motherboard must support RAID. (The OS is not aware of a hardware RAID implementation.) A group of hard drives implementing RAID is called an **array**. Here are the different ways your motherboard or adapter can support a RAID array:

- *The motherboard IDE controller supports RAID.* Figure 11-26 shows a motherboard that has two regular IDE connectors, two serial ATA connectors that can be configured for RAID, and two parallel RAID connectors. This board supports spanning, RAID 0, RAID 1, and a combination of RAID 0 and RAID 1. First you install the drives and then use CMOS setup to configure the RAID array.
- *Install a RAID-compliant IDE controller card and disable the IDE controller on your motherboard.* Use this option if your motherboard does not support RAID. Install the controller card and drives and then use the software bundled with the controller card to configure the RAID array.
- *The motherboard SCSI controller supports RAID or you install a SCSI host adapter that supports RAID.* How to install and use SCSI devices is discussed in Chapter 22.

When installing a hardware RAID system, install the hard drives, connecting the data cables to the RAID connectors on the motherboard or controller. Next enter CMOS setup and verify that the RAID drives were autodetected correctly and the correct RAID type is selected, or use the controller card's software to configure your RAID array. The OS and applications see the RAID array as a single volume such as drive D:. Later, if errors occur on one of the drives in the RAID array, the RAID drivers notify the OS and thereafter direct all data to the good drives.

For file servers using RAID 5 that must work continuously and hold important data, it might be practical to use hardware that allows for hard drive hot-swapping, which means you can remove one hard drive and insert another without powering down the computer. However, hard drives that can be hot-swapped cost significantly more than regular hard drives.

Regular IDE connectors

Serial ATA connectors

RAID IDE connectors

Figure 11-26   This motherboard supports RAID 0 and RAID 1

11

NOTE

For best performance and reliability, use a hardware RAID implementation instead of software RAID. Using hardware RAID, the RAID controller duplicates the data so the OS is not involved. Also, for an OS implementation of RAID, the OS active partition cannot be part of the RAID array, so you must have a non-RAID drive in your system as well as the RAID array. If this drive fails, then the system goes down regardless of the health of the RAID array. Therefore, for the best fault tolerance, use hardware RAID.

Troubleshooting Guidelines

✔ A+ EXAM TIP

The A+ Core exam expects you to be a good PC troubleshooter and presents different troubleshooting scenarios for you to solve. This section is good preparation for that skill.

This section covers some troubleshooting guidelines for CD, CD-RW, DVD, DVD-RW, tape drives, and sound cards. As with other components you have learned about, remember not to touch chips on circuit boards or disk surfaces where data is stored, stack components on top of one another, or subject them to magnetic fields or ESD.

Problems with CD, CD-RW, DVD, or DVD-RW Installation

A+
CORE
2.1
OS
3.3

Use the following general guidelines when a CD, CD-RW, DVD, or DVD-RW drive installation causes problems. These guidelines are useful if your computer does not recognize the drive (e.g., no drive D is listed in Windows Explorer):

- Check the data cable and power cord connections to the drive. Is the stripe on the data cable correctly aligned to pin 1? (Look for an arrow or small 1 printed on the drive. For a best guess, pin 1 is usually next to the power connector.)
- For an EIDE drive, is the correct master/slave jumper set? For example, if both the hard drive and the CD or DVD drive are hooked to the same ribbon cable, one must be set to master and the other to slave. If the CD or DVD drive is the only drive connected to the cable, then it should be set to single or master.
- For an EIDE drive, is the IDE connection on the motherboard disabled in CMOS setup?
- If you are using a SCSI drive, are the proper IDs set? Is the device terminated if it is the last item in the SCSI chain? Are the correct SCSI drivers installed?
- If you are booting from a Windows 9x/Me startup disk, check drivers, including entries in Config.sys and Autoexec.bat, and verify that Mscdex.exe is in the correct directory.
- Is another device using the same port settings? Check system resources listed in Device Manager. Is there an IRQ conflict with the IDE primary or secondary channel or the SCSI host the drive is using?
- Suspect a boot virus. This is a common problem. Run a virus scan program.

Troubleshooting Sound Problems

Problems with sound can be caused by a problem with the sound card itself, but they can also be a result of system settings, bad connections, or a number of other factors. Here are some questions you can try to answer to diagnose the problem.

- Is the sound cable attached between the drive and the analog audio connector on the sound card?
- Are the speakers turned on?
- Is the speaker volume turned down?
- Are the speakers plugged into the line "Out" or the "Spkr" port of the sound card (the middle port)?
- Is the transformer for the speaker plugged into an electrical outlet on one end and into the speakers on the other end?
- Is the volume control for Windows turned down? (To check for Windows 98, click Start, Programs, Accessories, Multimedia, and Volume Control.)
- Does the sound card have a "diagnose" file on the install disk?

A+
CORE
2.1
OS
3.3

- Does Device Manager report a problem with the card? Is another device using the same I/O addresses or IRQ number?
- Is this a new installation? If so, you might have the wrong drivers installed. Try downloading new or updated drivers.
- Using Device Manager, uninstall the sound card and then reinstall it using the Add New Hardware applet in the Control Panel.
- To check for a bad connection, turn off the computer, and then remove and reinstall the sound card.
- Replace the sound card with one you know is good.

Troubleshooting Tape Drives

The following list describes tape drive problems you might encounter and suggestions for dealing with them.

A Minicartridge Does Not Work

- If you are trying to write data, verify that the minicartridge is write-enabled.
- Are you inserting the minicartridge correctly? Check the user guide.
- Check that you are using the correct type of minicartridge. See the user guide.
- Is the minicartridge formatted? The software performs the format, which can take an hour or more.
- Use the backup software to retension the tape. Some tape drives require this, and others do not. Retensioning fast-forwards and rewinds the tape to eliminate loose spots.
- Take the minicartridge out and reboot. Try the minicartridge again.
- Try using a new minicartridge. The old one may have worn out.
- The tape might be unspooled, a problem usually caused by dust inside the drive. Blow all dust out of the drive and use a new tape.
- As with floppy disks, if the tape was removed from the drive while the drive light was on, the data being written at that time may not be readable.

Data Transfer Is Slow

- Change tape software settings for speed and data compression.
- If supported by the tape drive, try an accelerator card to improve speed.
- Try a new minicartridge.
- If the tape drive can do so, completely erase the tape and reformat it. Be sure that the tape drive can perform this procedure before you tell the software to do it.

11

**A+
CORE
2.1
OS
3.3**

- If you have installed an accelerator card, verify that the card is connected to the tape drive.
- Check that there is enough memory for the software to run.

The Drive Does Not Work After the Installation

- Check that pin 1 is oriented correctly to the data cable at both ends.
- Check for a resource conflict. The tape drive normally requires an IRQ, DMA channel, and I/O address.

The Drive Fails Intermittently or Gives Errors

- The tape might be worn out. Try a new tape.
- Clean the read/write head of the tape drive. See the tape drive user guide for directions.
- For an external tape drive, move the drive as far as you can from the monitor and computer case.
- Reformat the tape.
- Retension the tape.
- Verify that you are using the correct tape type and tape format.

CHAPTER SUMMARY

▶ Multimedia PCs and devices are designed to create and reproduce lifelike presentations of sight and sound.

▶ MMX, SSE, SSE2, SSE3, and Hyper-Threading by Intel and 3DNow!, HyperTransport!, and PowerNow! by AMD improve the speed of processing graphics, video, and sound, using improved methods of handling high-volume repetition during I/O operations.

▶ To take full advantage of MMX, SSE, or 3DNow! technology, software must be written to use its specific capabilities.

▶ All computer communication is digital. To be converted to digital from analog, sound and images are sampled, which means their data is measured at a series of representative points. More accurate sampling requires more space for data storage.

▶ Installing a sound card includes physically installing the card, then installing the sound card driver and sound application software.

▶ The middle plug on the sound card is used for the speaker out, or sound out, function.

▶ Digital cameras use light sensors to detect light and convert it to a digital signal stored in an image file (usually JPEG format).

▶ MP3 is a version of MPEG compression used for audio files. Portable MP3 players store and play MP3 files downloaded from a PC, using internal memory and flash storage devices.

▶ A video capture card allows you to capture input from a camcorder or directly from TV.

▶ CDs are optical read-only devices with data physically embedded into the surface of the disc.

▶ The speed of some CD drives slows down as the laser beam moves from the inside to the outside of the disc.

▶ Internal CD drives can have an EIDE or SCSI interface, and external CD drives can use a USB port, 1394 port, or SCSI port.

▶ The most common interface for internal CD drives is EIDE, which uses the ATAPI standard, an extension of the IDE/ATA standard developed so that tape drives, CD drives, and other drives can be treated just like another drive on the system.

▶ Data is only written to the shiny underside of a CD, which should be protected from damage.

▶ A DVD can store a full-length movie and uses an accompanying decoder card to decode the MPEG-compressed video data and Dolby AC-3 compressed audio.

11

▶ Tape drives are an inexpensive way to back up an entire hard drive or portions of it. Tape drives are more convenient for backups than floppy disks or other types of removable disks.

▶ Some popular removable drives are Microdrive, JumpDrive, Iomega HDD, Zip drive, and SuperDisk.

▶ Five types of dynamic volumes used by Windows 2000 Server are simple volume, spanned volume, striped volume (RAID 0), mirrored volume (RAID 1), and RAID 5.

▶ Windows XP supports spanned and striped (RAID 0) volumes.

▶ Hardware RAID is considered a better solution for fault tolerance than software RAID.

KEY TERMS

For explanations of key terms, see the Glossary near the end of the book.

array
basic disk
CDFS (Compact Disc File System)
CD-R (CD-recordable)
CD-RW (CD-rewritable)
constant angular velocity (CAV)
constant linear velocity (CLV)
data cartridge
drop height
DVD (digital video disc or
   digital versatile disc)
dynamic disk
dynamic volume
fault tolerance
half-life

hertz (Hz)
JPEG (Joint Photographic Experts
   Group)
lands
minicartridge
mirrored volume
MMX (Multimedia Extensions)
Moving Pictures Experts Group
   (MPEG)
MP3
multisession
pits
RAID (redundant array of
   inexpensive disks or redundant
   array of independent disks)

RAID 0, RAID 1, and RAID-5
   volume
sampling rate
sequential access
SIMD (single instruction,
   multiple data)
simple volume
spanned volume
SSE (Streaming SIMD Extension)
streaming audio
striped volume
TIFF (Tagged Image File Format)
UDF (Universal Disk Format)
   file system

REVIEWING THE BASICS

1. What must be true before MMX, SSE, SSE2, and 3DNow! technology can improve multimedia performance on a PC?

2. What is the significance of the multisession feature on a CD drive?

3. Name three ways a CD drive can interface with a motherboard.

4. Which side of a CD contains data?

5. If a CD drive and a hard drive are sharing the same data cable in a computer system, what type of connection is the CD drive using? Which of the two drives should be set to master? Which to slave?

6. What unit of measure is used to express the sampling rate of a sound card?

7. Why must sound and video input into a PC be converted from analog to digital?

8. What is the sampling rate (in Hz) of music CDs?

9. How many samples can be stored in 8 bits?

10. What would be a quick, short test to see if a sound card was successfully installed?

11. In a system that uses a CD drive instead of a DVD drive, the audio wire connects the _____ to the _____.

12. Why would you want to retension a backup tape?

13. Which holds more data, a Microdrive or a Zip drive?

14. How is the direction of data flow different for data transfers for MP3 players and digital cameras?

15. Name three advantages that MMX technology added to the Pentium processor family.

16. With which Pentium processor was SSE introduced?

17. What is the significance of Sound Blaster compatibility for a sound card?

18. Which port(s) on a sound card is used to send sound out?

19. What is the difference between MPEG, JPEG, and MP3? Explain what each one is used for.

20. Name at least four features you should look for when buying a video capture card.

21. What are the three ways that data on a DVD can be decoded?

22. What is the most popular way an internal DVD drive interfaces with a motherboard?

23. What is the difference between CD, CD-R, and CD-RW drives?

24. Rank these storage methods in order of their storage capacity: DVD, floppy disk, CD, tape.

25. Which version of RAID is supported by Windows XP? Does this RAID version provide fault tolerance?

11

THINKING CRITICALLY

1. You have just installed a new sound card and its drivers and connected the speakers and amplifier. You insert a music CD into the drive to test the drive. Windows Media Player launches and says it is playing the CD, but you don't hear music. What do you do first?

   a. Check the volume controls on the speaker amplifier.

   b. Check the connections of the amplifier and speakers to the card.

c. Check Device Manager for errors with the sound card.

d. Verify that the amplifier has power.

2. You have just upgraded your computer from Windows 98 to Windows XP. Now your system has no sound. What are the first two things you do?

a. Check Device Manager to see if the sound card is recognized and has no errors.

b. Reinstall Windows 98.

c. Use Device Manager to uninstall the sound card.

d. Identify your sound card by opening the case and looking on the card for manufacturer and model.

e. Identify your sound card by finding the documentation and driver CD that came with the card.

f. Download Windows XP drivers for the sound card from the sound card manufacturer's Web site.

3. You have just installed a new DVD drive and its drivers, but the drive does not work. You check the power and data cables and feel comfortable that the hardware installation is correct. You then decide to reload the device drivers. What is the first thing you do?

a. Open the Control Panel and launch the Add New Hardware Wizard.

b. Open Device Manager and choose Update Driver.

c. Remove the data cable from the DVD drive so Windows will no longer recognize the drive and allow you to reinstall the drivers.

d. Open Device Manager and uninstall the drive.

4. Which method of fault tolerance is the least expensive per MB of storage, disk duplexing or disk striping with parity? Explain your answer.

5. Does RAID 0 provide fault tolerance? Explain your answer.

HANDS-ON PROJECTS

PROJECT 11-1: Practicing Troubleshooting Skills

1. A friend calls to say that he just purchased a new sound card and speakers to install in his PC. He wants some help from you over the phone. The PC already has a CD drive installed. Your friend installed the sound card in an expansion slot and connected the audio wire to the sound card and the CD drive. List the steps you would guide him through to complete the installation.

2. Suppose that the audio wire connection in Step 1 does not fit the connection on the CD drive. You think that if the problem is a wrong fit, perhaps you can improvise to connect audio from the CD drive directly to the sound card. Your friend tells you that the CD drive has a port for a headphone connection and the sound card has a port for audio in. How might you improvise to provide this direct connection? Check your theory using the appropriate audio wire.

3. Work with a partner. Each of you should set up a problem with sound on a PC and have the other troubleshoot it. Suggestions for a problem to set up include:

   ▶ Speaker cables disconnected

   ▶ Speaker turned off

   ▶ Speaker cable plugged into the wrong jack

   ▶ Volume turned down all the way

As you troubleshoot the problem, write down its initial symptoms as a user would describe them, and the steps you take toward the solution.

PROJECT 11-2: Installing a Sound Card

Install a sound card in your lab computer. Verify that the card works by playing a music CD or playing music from the Internet.

PROJECT 11-3: Using the Internet for Research

Make a presentation or write a paper about digital cameras. Cover what features to look for when buying one and how to compare quality from one camera to another. Use the following Web sites, and include citations from three other useful Web sites in the results of your research.

▷ *www.imaging-resource.com*

▷ *www.pcphotoreview.com*

▷ *www.steves-digicams.com*

PROJECT 11-4: Exploring Multimedia on the Web

Do the following to investigate how to experience multimedia on the Web:

1. Go to the Macromedia Web site *(www.macromedia.com)* and download the latest version of Flash Player, software used to add animation, video, and sound to Web sites.

2. Using a search engine, find at least two Flash-enabled Web sites, and then use Flash to explore these sites.

3. Go to the Microsoft Web site *(www.microsoft.com)* and download the latest version of Windows Media Player, software used to play music and video stored locally or online.

4. Use Media Player to play a music CD, a radio station on the Web, and a video clip on the Web.

5. Answer these questions:

   a. What are the two sites you found that use Macromedia Flash?

   b. What music CD did you play?

   c. What radio station did you play? What was the station's Web site?

   d. What video clip did you play? At which Web site did you locate the clip?

Supporting Windows 9x/Me

As a PC support technician, you need to know how to install, use, and troubleshoot the Windows OSs commonly used today. You need a general knowledge of how hardware, Windows, and applications work. In Chapter 2, you learned how hardware and software work together, and in Chapter 3 you were introduced to the DOS portion of Windows 9x/Me. This chapter covers how Windows 9x/Me is structured, how it is used, how it works with various software programs and hardware devices, and how to troubleshoot it. Although Windows 9x/Me is gradually being replaced by Windows XP, it is still in use, and you need to know how to work with it.

Windows 9x/Me has had several releases, including Windows 95, Windows 95 Service Release 2 (also known as Windows 95 SR2, Windows 95 Rev B, Windows 95B, and Windows 95 OSR2), Windows 98, Windows 98 Second Edition (SE), and Windows Me (Millennium Edition). Each of these OSs uses the same basic architecture, and each release improves on previous versions and adds new features.

To learn which version of Windows is installed, right-click the My Computer icon and select Properties from the shortcut menu. The System Properties window opens. Click the General tab.

Windows 9x/Me Architecture

Like other OSs, Windows 9x/Me has a shell and a kernel. A **shell** is the portion of the OS that relates to the user and to applications. The shell provides a command, menu, or icon interface to the user using various interface tools such as Windows Explorer, the Control Panel, or My Computer.

The core, or **kernel**, of the OS is responsible for interacting with hardware. It has more power to communicate with hardware devices than the shell, so that applications operating under the OS cannot get to hardware devices without the shell passing those requests to the kernel. This structure provides a more stable system.

The two most important parts of the shell are the user component and the GDI. The **user component** manages input from the keyboard and other user devices, output from the user interface, and the **GDI (Graphics Device Interface)**. The GDI is a component of the OS responsible for presenting the graphical interface to the user and providing graphics support to output devices. The purposes of each component are listed in Table 12-1.

Component Name	Main Files Holding the Component	Functions
Kernel	Kernel32.dll, Krnl386.exe	Handles the basic OS functions such as managing memory, file I/O, and loading and executing programs
User	User32.dll, User.exe	Controls the mouse, keyboard, ports, and desktop, including the position of windows, icons, and dialog boxes
GDI	GDI32.dll, GDI.exe	Draws screens, graphics, and lines, and manages printing

Table 12-1   Core components of Windows 9x/Me

As you learned in Chapter 1, Windows 9x/Me is a compromise OS that bridges two worlds. In Figure 12-1, you can see that DOS was a 16-bit OS, used only 16-bit device drivers, and managed base, upper, and extended memory. Windows NT/2000/XP is a true 32-bit OS. In compromise, the core components of Windows 9x/Me (kernel, user, and GDI) are compiled as a combination of 16-bit and 32-bit code, and Windows 9x/Me accepts both 16-bit and 32-bit drivers. From

Chapter 6, you learned that it manages memory the same way that DOS does, and uses memory paging and virtual memory as does Windows NT/2000/XP.

- 16-bit and 32-bit core
- Virtual machine
- Memory paging
- Base and upper memory
- Extended memory
- 16-bit drivers
- 32-bit drivers

- 16-bit core
- Base and upper memory
- Extended memory
- 16-bit drivers

Windows 3.x + DOS

- 32-bit core
- Virtual machine
- Memory paging
- 32-bit drivers

Windows NT

Windows 9x/Me

Figure 12-1　　Windows 9x/Me is the bridge from DOS to Windows NT/2000/XP

The Windows 9x/Me core relates to users, software, and hardware by way of several modules, as seen in Figure 12-2. Configuration data is primarily stored in the Windows 9x/Me registry, a database that also contains the initialization information for applications, a database of hardware and software settings, Windows configuration settings, user parameters, and application settings. In addition, some data is kept in text files called initialization files, which often have an .ini or .inf file extension.

Figure 12-2　　The Windows 9x/Me architecture as it relates to the user, software, and hardware

Virtual Machines

Before we look at the different components in Figure 12-2, you need to understand how these components relate to applications and hardware. Applications call on the OS to access hardware or other software by using an **application programming interface (API) call**. When applications are first loaded by Windows 9x/Me, the methods to access hardware and software are made available to the software through an interface called a **virtual machine (VM)**. An application sees a virtual machine as a set of resources made available to it through these predefined APIs. An OS can provide a virtual machine to a single application that commands all the resources of that virtual machine, or the OS can assign a virtual machine to be shared by two or more applications. Think of virtual machines as multiple logical machines within one physical machine, similar in concept to several logical drives within one physical drive.

Figure 12-3 shows several virtual machines that Windows 9x/Me can provide. In the figure, the system virtual machine (system VM) is the most important VM under Windows 9x/Me, and is where all OS processes run. It can also support 32-bit and 16-bit Windows applications, but DOS programs run in their own virtual machines.

Figure 12-3   Windows 9x/Me uses the virtual machine concept

A DOS program expects to directly control the hardware of the entire PC, memory included. If a DOS program begins to use memory addresses not assigned to it, errors occur in a multitasking environment. Windows 9x/Me solves this problem by providing the DOS program with its own virtual machine. In effect, the application says, "I want all of memory and all of this and all of that." Windows 9x/Me says, "OK, here they are," and gives the program its own PC, including all the virtual memory addresses it wants from 0 to 4 GB as well as its own virtual hardware! As far as the DOS program is concerned, it can go anywhere and do anything within its own PC. The DOS program does not try to communicate with any other application or to access the data of another program, because it thinks there are no other programs; it controls its entire world, and is the only program in it. That's a virtual machine.

NOTE

One important result of running DOS programs in individual virtual machines is that when a DOS program makes an error, the virtual machine it is using hangs, but other programs and the OS are isolated from the problem and thus are not affected.

Windows 16-bit applications offer a slightly different challenge to Windows 9x/Me. These programs make some of the same mistakes that DOS programs do and can cause the system to hang. However, they also sometimes expect to access other programs and their data. The 16-bit Windows programs don't expect to control the hardware directly and are content to route their reqests to Windows. Windows 9x/Me places these programs within the system virtual machine because they communicate with hardware through the OS, but Windows 9x/Me puts these programs together in their own memory space so they can share memory addresses.

The result of this arrangement is that when a 16-bit Windows program causes an error called a Windows Protection Error or a General Protection Fault, it can disturb other 16-bit programs, causing them to fail. However, it does not disturb DOS programs in their own virtual machines or 32-bit programs that don't share their virtual memory addresses.

12

Installing Windows 9x/Me, Hardware, and Software

In this section, you learn how to install Windows 9x/Me and how to install hardware and applications with Windows 9x/Me.

Installing Windows 9x/Me

Remember as you proceed with Windows 9x/Me installation that there are separate CDs for installing Windows 9x/Me on a PC without Windows (Microsoft labels the OS as Windows 9x/Me for a New PC) and for installing Windows 9x/Me on a PC with an earlier version of Windows (Microsoft labels the OS as Windows 9x/Me Upgrade). The CDs for installing Windows on a new PC are significantly more expensive than the upgrade CDs. To use the upgrade CDs, a previous version of Windows must be installed on your hard drive.

A problem arises if you have just replaced a failed hard drive with a new hard drive and you want to do a fresh installation using a Windows 9x/Me Upgrade CD. During the OS installation, the upgrade CD asks you to provide a Microsoft floppy disk or CD from an earlier version of Windows. If you cannot provide the CD or floppy, the upgrade installation terminates and you must use the more expensive version, Windows 9x/Me for a New PC.

First, let's look at how to prepare your hard drive for installation.

Preparing for Installation

A+
OS
2.1
2.2

Before installing Windows 9x/Me, verify that your system meets requirements for the OS. Check the following:

- Verify that the minimum and recommended hardware requirements for Windows 9x/Me are met. Table 12-2 lists these requirements. In order for Windows 9x/Me to perform satisfactorily, the PC should meet the recommended requirements.
- Windows 95/98 claims that it supports legacy hardware devices, but Windows Me does not. To check whether a particular hardware product has been tested for use with Windows Me, go to *www.microsoft.com/whdc/hcl/search.mspx*.
- You also need to check software packages and programs for compatibility. You can do this by checking the documentation or the manufacturer's Web site for each program.

Description	Windows 95	Windows 98	Windows Me
Processor	486 — 25 MHz or higher	486DX — 66 MHz (Pentium is recommended)	Pentium 150 MHz
RAM	4 MB (8 MB is recommended)	16 MB (24 MB is recommended)	32 MB
Free hard drive space	50 MB	195 MB (315 MB is recommended)	320 MB

Table 12-2   Minimum and recommended hardware requirements for Windows 9x/Me

Windows Me does not support 16-bit legacy drivers that work under Windows 95/98, so it's important to verify that your hardware devices are compatible with Windows Me.

Windows 9x/Me is most likely to be installed as an upgrade from Windows 95 to Windows 98 or to Windows Me, or on a clean hard drive. If you are having problems with your current operating system and applications, consider doing a clean install rather than an upgrade. A **clean install** ignores any settings in the currently installed OS, including information about installed hardware or software. Therefore, after the clean install, you must reinstall all hardware and applications.

NOTE

Before deciding to do a clean install, verify that you have all the application software installation CDs or floppy disks and then back up all data on the drive. Also take time to verify that the backups are good and that you have all device driver software. Before installing Windows Me, verify that all your hardware devices qualify for Windows Me.

You do not need to format the hard drive before you begin the installation, although you should delete all folders on the hard drive used for the OS or applications, including the \Windows folder, files, and subfolders. This forces Setup to perform a clean install and make certain that no corrupted system files or applications remain, but still retain any data files that might be on the drive. If you like, you can also format the hard drive. Do this if you suspect a virus is present. If you suspect a boot sector virus is present, use the Fdisk/MBR command (discussed in Chapters 3 and 8) to rewrite the master boot sector program. Then do the clean install.

After Windows 9x/Me is installed, reinstall all the application software. Then, if you formatted the hard drive, restore the data from backups. This method takes longer than an upgrade, but gives you the advantage of a fresh start. Any problems with corrupted applications or system settings will not cause you problems in the new installation.

An **upgrade install** carries forward as much information as it can about what the current OS knows concerning installed hardware and software, user preferences, and other settings. An upgrade is faster than a clean install because you don't need to reinstall software and hardware. However, problems with an old installation sometimes carry forward into the upgrade.

You can perform an upgrade or a clean install with either the Windows 9x/Me for a New PC CD or the Windows 9x/Me Upgrade CD. If you are doing an upgrade, the old operating system must be in good enough shape to boot up, because you must begin an upgrade from within the currently installed OS.

Installing Windows 9x/Me as a Clean Installation

Recall that you can change CMOS settings to specify the order in which system BIOS looks for an OS on the drives on your PC. You might need to change the boot order in CMOS, depending on how you plan to load the OS. Older PCs could only boot from a hard drive or floppy disk. This meant that to use a CD-ROM drive, you first had to boot these PCs from floppy disks and then install the CD-ROM drivers. There are more choices with newer PCs, some of which can boot from a hard drive, floppy drive, Zip drive, CD-ROM drive, or other type of drive. These newer PCs have

12

A+
OS
2.1

drivers for drive types other than hard drives and floppy drives written into their BIOS, allowing you to boot from a different medium.

> **NOTE** If the PC is on a network, it is possible to install the OS from another computer on the network. However, if you want to do an upgrade, you must begin the upgrade from within the current OS. Therefore, if you are performing an installation across a network, you are forced to do a clean install.

After you have verified that the system qualifies and decided to perform a clean installation, do the following to prepare your system:

- If you have important data on your hard drive, back it up to another medium. How to perform a backup is covered in Chapter 9.
- If your system BIOS runs a program to protect the boot sector of your hard drive from viruses, enter CMOS setup and disable the program because it might interfere with the installation. After the installation you can turn the program back on. While you're in CMOS setup, verify that the boot sequence is first the floppy disk or CD-ROM, depending on the media that you have for the Windows 9x/Me setup.
- For a new hard drive, recall from Chapter 8 that the drive is partitioned using Fdisk and formatted using the Format command before an OS is installed. The Windows 9x/Me installation will do this for you, or you can do it prior to the installation.

You are now ready to perform the installation. Do the following to begin.

Windows 9x/Me comes on a set of floppy disks or on a CD. If you are installing the OS from floppy disks, you can boot from the hard drive or floppy disk. To boot from the floppy disk, insert the Windows 9x/Me Disk 1, which is bootable, and boot the PC. At the A prompt, enter the command *Setup.exe*. You can also boot from a hard drive; go to a C prompt, and insert the Windows 9x/Me Disk 1 in the floppy disk drive. Enter the command *A:\Setup* to execute the Setup program on the floppy disk. Either way, the Windows 9x/Me setup screen appears. Follow the directions on the screen.

> **NOTE** Your CD-ROM drive might be configured to run a CD automatically when it is first inserted. This Autoplay feature causes the Setup opening menu to appear without your entering the Setup command (see Figure 12-4). To disable the feature, hold down the Shift key while inserting the CD.

A+
OS
2.1

Figure 12-4   The opening screen of the Windows 98 CD provides links you can use to navigate the CD

If you are installing Windows 98 or Windows Me from a CD (and your PC can boot from a CD-ROM drive), insert the CD in the drive and reboot. If your PC cannot boot from a CD, boot from a floppy disk or hard drive, then insert the CD in the CD-ROM drive, and enter the command *D:\Setup.exe*, substituting the drive letter of your CD-ROM drive for *D* if necessary. The Windows 95 setup CD is not bootable, so you will need a bootable floppy disk to begin the Windows 95 installation.

12

NOTE

To speed up the installation, you can copy the files and folders on the Windows 9x/Me CD to a folder on your hard drive and run the Setup program from that folder. Also, having the Windows 9x/Me CD files on your hard drive makes it easier to access the files later when adding Windows components or updating drivers.

Installing Windows 9x/Me as an Upgrade

If you are doing an upgrade, do the following to prepare your system before you begin the installation, in addition to the items listed previously:

- Verify that you have enough space on the hard drive. Delete files in the Recycle Bin and temporary directories.
- Run ScanDisk to check and repair errors on the hard drive. From Windows 9x/Me, click Start, Programs, Accessories, System Tools, and ScanDisk, and then scan each logical drive in the system. From a Windows startup disk, enter the command *Scandisk* at the command prompt.
- Run a current version of antivirus software to check for viruses.

- Check Config.sys and Autoexec.bat for potential problems. Verify that any hardware devices using device drivers loaded from these files work under the old OS, so you know your starting point if problems occur under the new OS.

- The Windows 9x/Me upgrade process moves commands in Autoexec.bat that are used to load terminate-and-stay resident programs (TSRs) required for 16-bit Windows drivers and applications to Winstart.bat. Look for the Winstart.bat file in the root directory after the installation is done. If setup does not find any TSRs to put in the file, it will not be created.

- If TSRs such as QEMM386 (a memory manager by Quarterdeck) are loaded from Config.sys or Autoexec.bat, and problems arise because they run during the installation, disable them by converting these lines to remarks or comments—type *REM* at the beginning of the command lines. Later, after the installation, you can activate these lines again by removing the REMs.

- If you are connected to a network, verify that the connection works. If it does, Windows setup should be able to reestablish the connection correctly at the end of the installation.

- Create a Windows 9x/Me rescue disk for use in the event that the installation fails.

- Decide if you want to use FAT16 or FAT32 for your file system. If you choose FAT16, you can later convert to FAT32 using the Windows Drive Converter. To access the Converter after Windows 98 is installed, click Start, Programs, Accessories, System Tools, and Drive Converter (FAT32). As an alternative, you can use the Run dialog box. For the 16-bit version, enter *cvt.exe*, and for the 32-bit version, enter *cvt1.exe*, and then click OK. The Drive Converter Wizard steps you through the process.

- If you are installing Windows 98 on a compressed drive, be aware that the registry can reside on any compressed drive, but the swap file can reside on a compressed drive only if the drive is compressed using protected-mode software such as DriveSpace. (Compressed drives, discussed in Chapter 9, are hard drives that have a portion of their data compressed in order to save space on the drive.) DriveSpace marks the area for the swap file as uncompressible. If your drive is compressed with real-mode compression software, such as Double-Space, then know that you cannot put the swap file on this compressed drive. The best practice is to back up the data and then uncompress the drive. You can later compress it using Windows 98 DriveSpace.

- Windows Me will not install on a compressed drive, so you must uncompress any portions of your hard drive that are compressed. If you are not sure whether your hard drive is compressed, run ScanDisk, which will tell you.

- Uninstall power management tools and disk management tools.

A+
OS
2.1

Sometimes Microsoft releases last-minute documentation on the setup CD. Check the Readme.txt file for any setup information provided. Now that everything is ready for the installation, do the following to get to the setup screen:

1. Start the PC, loading the current operating system.

2. Close all open applications, including any antivirus software that is running. Close any icons that are open in the System Tray.

3. Insert the CD in the CD-ROM drive or the floppy disk in the floppy drive. Open the Run dialog box and enter the command **D:\Setup.exe**, substituting the drive letter for your CD-ROM drive or floppy drive for D if necessary. Click **OK**.

4. Follow the instructions on the setup screen. When you have the opportunity to select the folder to install Windows, select the folder that the current OS is installed in; most likely that is \Windows. If you use the same folder, Setup uses whatever settings it finds there.

Installation Process from the Setup Screen

A+
OS
2.1
2.2

After you get to the setup screen, the installation process is the same, no matter whether you are doing an upgrade or a clean install. When installing Windows 9x/Me, you have the option of creating the Startup disk, as discussed earlier. Be sure to do so to help prepare for emergencies. During the installation, you are also asked to choose from four setup options:

12

- *Typical.* This option installs all components that are usually installed with Windows 9x/Me. Most often, this is the option to choose.
- *Portable.* Use this option when installing Windows 9x/Me on a notebook computer.
- *Compact.* Use this option if you are short on hard drive space and want the smallest possible installation. No optional components are installed. After the installation, if you need a component, you can install it by double-clicking the Add/Remove Programs applet in the Control Panel.
- *Custom.* Use this option if you know you need components not normally installed under the Typical installation. You have the opportunity to select any group of components to include in the installation.

✔ **A+ EXAM TIP**

The A+ OS exam expects you to know about all four setup options.

During the installation, Setup records information in log files. The primary log file is Setuplog.txt, a text file that Windows uses when recovering from a crash to determine how far it got in the installation. Figure 12-5 shows a portion of Setuplog.txt in which the system ran a virus check on CMOS and began checking drives. The Detection Log (Detlog.txt) keeps a record of hardware detected, as shown in Figure 12-6.

If the system fails to respond during the hardware detection phase, an entry is recorded in Detcrash.log, a binary file Windows uses to help recover from a crash caused by a hardware problem. Windows does not use the contents of Detlog.txt; it is created only for the benefit of the user.

For example, if Setup suspects that a network card is present, because it sees a network driver installed in Config.sys, it records in Setuplog.txt and Detlog.txt that it is about to look for the card. If it finds the card, it records the success in Detlog.txt. However, if an error occurs while Setup searches for the card, an entry is made in the Detcrash.log file.

Figure 12-5 Windows records information about the setup process in Setuplog.txt

Figure 12-6 The Detlog.txt file shows what hardware has been detected

If the system crashes while trying to detect the network card and Setup is then restarted, it looks at Detcrash.log and Setuplog.txt to determine what it was trying to do at the time of the crash. It skips that step and goes to the next step, so it doesn't make the same mistake twice.

Although Setup might crash several times during the installation, progress is still being made. By reading the content of the log files, Setup is able to skip steps that cause a problem and move forward.

NOTE Be careful not to delete the log files during the installation, especially if you've just experienced a crash. Also, restart by using the power on/power off method so that the ISA bus is fully initialized, which does not always happen during a warm boot.

In certain situations you might want to force Setup to begin installation at the beginning instead of looking to Setuplog.txt for the entry point–for example, when you think you might have resolved a problem with hardware and want Setup to attempt to find the hardware again. To do this, delete Setuplog.txt to force a full restart.

Once the installation is complete, do the following:

- Go to the Control Panel and verify that the system date and time are correct. If they are not correct, make the change in CMOS setup.
- Using the Control Panel, open the Add/Remove Programs applet, click the Windows Setup tab, and install any additional Windows components.
- Access the Internet and go to the Microsoft Web site (*support.microsoft.com*). Download and install any available **service packs** or **patches**, which are updates and fixes to the OS released by Microsoft.
- If this is an upgrade installation, open and test the applications you already had installed under Windows 9x/Me. Any problem you have with a particular application may be solved by uninstalling and then reinstalling it, or installing any patches necessary to make it work with the new OS. Check the application manufacturer's Web site for available updates.

Downloading and Installing Updates for Windows 9x/Me

Between releases of OS versions, Microsoft often produces OS updates in the form of patches or service packs that add features, fix bugs, or address security issues. The Microsoft Web site, *windowsupdate.microsoft.com*, provides a list of updates available for your OS. In Windows 98 and Windows Me, you can access this page by clicking Windows Update on the Start menu. The update process examines your system and recommends available updates for you to select, download, and install following directions on the screen.

12

Configuring the Windows 9x/Me Startup with Msdos.sys

In Windows 9x/Me, the text file Msdos.sys contains several parameters that affect how the OS boots. You can change some entries in this file to customize the boot process. The file is a hidden, read-only, system file, so before you can edit it, you must first use the Attrib command at the command prompt to make the file available for editing. (Note that you can change the hidden and read-only attributes using Windows Explorer, but not the system attribute.) Also, make a backup copy of the file in case you want to revert to the form it was in before changes were made.

Follow these steps to change the options in Msdos.sys:

1. Go to an OS command prompt.

2. Go to the root directory of your hard drive by entering:

   `CD\`

3. Make the file available for editing by entering:

   `ATTRIB -R -H -S MSDOS.SYS`

4. Make a backup copy of the file by entering:

   `COPY MSDOS.SYS MSDOS.BK`

5. Use Edit.com to edit the file by entering:

   `EDIT MSDOS.SYS`

6. Save the file and return it to a hidden, read-only, system file by entering:

   `ATTRIB +R +H +S MSDOS.SYS`

Table 12-3 lists each entry in the Msdos.sys file and its purpose. You can refer to this table as you read about the different options available when installing and configuring Windows 9x/Me.

Command Line Variable Name	Purpose of the Values Assigned to the Variable
AutoScan	0 = computer does not scan hard drive.
	1 = default. Prompts the user before running ScanDisk on the hard drive when booting up after the computer was not shut down properly.
	2 = automatically scans without prompting the user.
BootMulti	0 = default. Boot only to Windows 9x/Me.
	1 = allows for a dual boot.

Table 12-3 (continued)

A+
OS
1.2
2.1

Command Line Variable Name	Purpose of the Values Assigned to the Variable
BootWin	1 = default. Boot to Windows 9x/Me.
	0 = boot to previous version of DOS.
BootGUI	1 = default. Boot to Windows 9x/Me with the graphic user interface.
	0 = boot only to the command prompt for DOS 7.0 (the DOS core of Windows 95) or 7.1 (the DOS core of Windows 98). Autoexec.bat and Config.sys will be executed, and you will be in real-mode DOS.
BootMenu	0 = default. Don't display the startup menu.
	1 = display the startup menu.
BootMenuDefault	1 through 8 = the value selected from the startup menu by default. (Normally this value should be 1.)
BootMenuDelay	n = number of seconds delay before the default value in the startup menu is automatically selected.
BootKeys	1 = default. The function keys work during the boot process (F4, F5, F6, F8, Shift+F5, Ctrl+F5, Shift+F8).
	0 = disable the function keys during the boot process. (This option can be used to help secure a workstation.)
BootDelay	n = number of seconds the boot process waits (when it displays the message "Starting Windows 95" or "Starting Windows 98") for the user to press F8 to get the startup menu (default is 2 seconds).
Logo	1 = default. Display the Windows 9x/Me logo screen.
	0 = leave the screen in text mode.
Drvspace	1 = default. Load Drvspace.bin, used for disk compression, if it is present.
	0 = don't load Drvspace.bin.
DoubleBuffer	1 = default. When you have a SCSI drive, enables double buffering for the drive. (See the drive documentation.)
	0 = don't use double buffering for the SCSI drive.
Network	1 = if network components are installed, include the option "Safe Mode with network support" in the startup menu.
	0 = don't include the option on the startup menu. (This is normally set to 0 if the PC has no network components installed. The startup menu is renumbered from this point forward in the menu.)

12

Table 12-3 (continued)

A+
OS
1.2
2.1

Command Line Variable Name	Purpose of the Values Assigned to the Variable
BootFailSafe	1 = default. Include Safe Mode in the startup menu.
	0 = don't include Safe Mode in the startup menu.
BootWarn	1 = default. Display the warning message when Windows 9x/Me boots into Safe Mode.
	0 = don't display the warning message.
LoadTop	1 = default. Load Command.com at the top of conventional memory.
	0 = don't load Command.com at the top of conventional memory. (Use this option when there is a memory conflict with this area of memory.)

Table 12-3 Contents of the Msdos.sys file options section

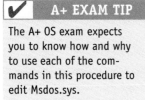

A+ EXAM TIP

The A+ OS exam expects you to know how and why to use each of the commands in this procedure to edit Msdos.sys.

Figure 12-7 shows a sample Msdos.sys file. The lines containing Xs at the bottom of the file are used to ensure that the file size is compatible with other programs.

```
[Paths]
WinDir=C:\WIN95
WinBootDir=C:\WIN95
HostWinBootDrv=C

[Options]
BootMulti=1
BootGUI=1
BootMenu=1
Network=0
;
;The following lines are required for compatibility with other programs.
;Do not remove them (MSDOS.SYS needs to be >1024 bytes).
;xxxxxxxxxxxxxxxxxxxxxxxxxxxxxxxxxxxxxxxxxxxxxxxxxxxxxxxxxxxxxxxxxxa
;xxxxxxxxxxxxxxxxxxxxxxxxxxxxxxxxxxxxxxxxxxxxxxxxxxxxxxxxxxxxxxxxxxb
;xxxxxxxxxxxxxxxxxxxxxxxxxxxxxxxxxxxxxxxxxxxxxxxxxxxxxxxxxxxxxxxxxxc
;xxxxxxxxxxxxxxxxxxxxxxxxxxxxxxxxxxxxxxxxxxxxxxxxxxxxxxxxxxxxxxxxxxd
;xxxxxxxxxxxxxxxxxxxxxxxxxxxxxxxxxxxxxxxxxxxxxxxxxxxxxxxxxxxxxxxxxxe
;xxxxxxxxxxxxxxxxxxxxxxxxxxxxxxxxxxxxxxxxxxxxxxxxxxxxxxxxxxxxxxxxxxf
;xxxxxxxxxxxxxxxxxxxxxxxxxxxxxxxxxxxxxxxxxxxxxxxxxxxxxxxxxxxxxxxxxxg
;xxxxxxxxxxxxxxxxxxxxxxxxxxxxxxxxxxxxxxxxxxxxxxxxxxxxxxxxxxxxxxxxxxh
;xxxxxxxxxxxxxxxxxxxxxxxxxxxxxxxxxxxxxxxxxxxxxxxxxxxxxxxxxxxxxxxxxxi
;xxxxxxxxxxxxxxxxxxxxxxxxxxxxxxxxxxxxxxxxxxxxxxxxxxxxxxxxxxxxxxxxxxj
;xxxxxxxxxxxxxxxxxxxxxxxxxxxxxxxxxxxxxxxxxxxxxxxxxxxxxxxxxxxxxxxxxxk
;xxxxxxxxxxxxxxxxxxxxxxxxxxxxxxxxxxxxxxxxxxxxxxxxxxxxxxxxxxxxxxxxxxl
;xxxxxxxxxxxxxxxxxxxxxxxxxxxxxxxxxxxxxxxxxxxxxxxxxxxxxxxxxxxxxxxxxxm
;xxxxxxxxxxxxxxxxxxxxxxxxxxxxxxxxxxxxxxxxxxxxxxxxxxxxxxxxxxxxxxxxxxn
;xxxxxxxxxxxxxxxxxxxxxxxxxxxxxxxxxxxxxxxxxxxxxxxxxxxxxxxxxxxxxxxxxxo
;xxxxxxxxxxxxxxxxxxxxxxxxxxxxxxxxxxxxxxxxxxxxxxxxxxxxxxxxxxxxxxxxxxp
;xxxxxxxxxxxxxxxxxxxxxxxxxxxxxxxxxxxxxxxxxxxxxxxxxxxxxxxxxxxxxxxxxxq
;xxxxxxxxxxxxxxxxxxxxxxxxxxxxxxxxxxxxxxxxxxxxxxxxxxxxxxxxxxxxxxxxxxr
;xxxxxxxxxxxxxxxxxxxxxxxxxxxxxxxxxxxxxxxxxxxxxxxxxxxxxxxxxxxxxxxxxxs
```

Figure 12-7 A sample Msdos.sys file

Installing Hardware with Windows 9x/Me

A+
OS
1.1
2.4

After a hardware device is physically installed in a system, the next step is to install the software necessary to interface with it. This software, called a device driver, is written to interface with a specific device and operating system. Knowing how to install and troubleshoot device drivers is an essential skill of a PC support technician.

When a new device is installed and you power up the PC, Windows recognizes it and immediately launches the Found New Hardware Wizard. If the wizard does not launch automatically, you can start it manually. Go to the Control Panel and double-click the Add New Hardware icon, which launches the wizard. Alternately, you can run an installation setup program on the floppy disk or CD that came bundled with the device. Look for and run a setup program named Setup.exe or Install.exe. Also, if you downloaded a driver file from the Internet, double-click on the file to launch the setup program.

NOTE The Control Panel contains several applets, or small programs, that are used to manage Windows. You can view these applets in a list or as icons. Use the View menu in the Control Panel to change their appearance.

One step in the Found New Hardware wizard is to select the hardware device from a list of devices. If you click OK, Windows uses a Windows driver for the device, or you can click Have Disk to use your own drivers (see Figure 12-8). If you have a driver on a floppy disk or CD or you downloaded a driver from the Internet to a folder on your hard drive, click Have Disk and point the wizard to the disk, CD, or folder that contains the driver. Sometimes you must select a folder on the disk or CD for the operating system to use, such as \Win98 to locate the drivers to install under Windows 98 (or \Win2k for Windows 2000 or \WinXP for Windows XP).

12

Click here to use device drivers other than Windows default drivers

Figure 12-8   To use device drivers supplied by the device manufacturer, click Have Disk

Viewing and Changing Current Device Drivers

You can view and change current device drivers from the Control Panel. For example, to view the current video driver in Windows 98, click Start, Settings, Control Panel, and then double-click Display. Click the Settings tab to view the currently installed display driver, as shown in Figure 12-9.

Figure 12-9   Use the Settings tab of the Display Properties window to view the currently installed display driver

To change the video card driver, click Advanced, click the Adapter tab, and then click the Change button. You see the Windows 98 Update Device Driver Wizard. Click Next to see the dialog box in Figure 12-10, which includes options to let Windows 98 search for a new driver from its list of Windows drivers or to display a list of all the drivers in a specific location, so you can select the driver you want. To provide your own driver, click the second option and then click Next. Then click Have Disk to provide the new driver from a floppy disk, a CD, or a file downloaded from the Internet.

If the new driver fails, try uninstalling and then reinstalling the device. To uninstall a device, access Device Manager. (Click Start, Settings, Control Panel, double-click System, and then click Device Manager.) Select the device and then click Remove (see Figure 12-11). Then reboot the PC and allow the Found New Hardware Wizard to launch.

Figure 12-10   The Windows 98 Update Device Driver Wizard enables you to install a new device driver for a previously installed device

12

Figure 12-11   Use Device Manager to uninstall a device

A+
OS
1.1
2.4

Plug and Play and Hardware Installations

Remember that Plug and Play (PnP) is a set of design specifications for both hardware and software that works to make hardware installations effortless. For a system to be truly Plug and Play, it must meet these criteria:

- The system BIOS must be PnP. (To know if your BIOS is PnP, you can use MSD, a 16-bit command-line diagnostic utility.)
- All hardware devices and expansion cards must be PnP-compliant.
- The OS must be Windows 9x/Me or another OS that supports PnP.
- A 32-bit device driver must be available (from the device manufacturer or Windows).

If all these things are true, hardware installation should be just a matter of installing the new hardware device, turning on the PC, and perhaps providing the 32-bit driver, if it is not included with Windows 9x/Me. During the boot process, Windows 9x/Me surveys the devices and their needs for resources and allocates resources to each device. Windows 9x/Me is free to assign these resources to the devices and avoids assigning the same resource to two devices. For PnP to work, each device in the system must be able to use whatever resources the OS assigns to it.

NOTE

Keep in mind that Windows 9x/Me is a compromise OS, attempting to bridge the 16-bit world and the 32-bit world. It makes many compromises between these two worlds.

Although it supports 16-bit device drivers and applications, Windows 9x/Me works better using 32-bit drivers and 32-bit applications. If you are using older 16-bit drivers under Windows 9x/Me, search for 32-bit drivers to replace them. Look on the device manufacturer's Web site or the Microsoft Web site.

NOTE

To learn whether a driver is 16-bit or 32-bit, look at how Windows loads it. If the driver is a 32-bit driver written for Windows 9x/Me, it is loaded from the registry. System.ini can contain both 16-bit and 32-bit drivers. If the driver is loaded from Autoexec.bat or Config.sys, it is a 16-bit driver written for DOS. Also look in Device Manager for an exclamation point beside the device, which indicates that the driver has a problem. This might indicate that the driver is a 16-bit driver.

During the Windows 95/98 installation, Windows setup tries to substitute 32-bit drivers for all 16-bit drivers it finds in use, and, if it can, eliminates the Autoexec.bat and Config.sys files altogether. However, if it can't substitute a 32-bit driver for an older 16-bit driver, it puts (or keeps) the proper lines in the Config.sys file and sets itself up to use the older driver. Windows Me does not support 16-bit drivers, and therefore does not allow them to be loaded from Autoexec.bat or Config.sys.

Installing Applications in Windows 9x/Me

As the bridge between earlier and later versions of Windows, Windows 9x/Me can use both 16-bit and 32-bit software. This section shows you how to install both.

Preparing for Software Installation

As with installing hardware, you can do several things to prepare your system and to increase the likelihood that installing software on Windows 9x/Me will be successful:

- *Check available resources.* Check your computer resources to make sure you have (1) enough space on your hard drive, (2) the minimum requirements for memory, and (3) the proper CPU and video monitor. Read the documentation to make sure your system meets the minimum requirements. Remember that you should not completely fill your hard drive with software and data, because the operating system needs extra space for temporary files and for the swap file, which changes size depending on how much space is needed.

NOTE

For best performance with Windows 9x/Me, allow a minimum of 100 MB of unused hard drive space for working with temporary files used by applications.

- *Protect the original software.* After the installation is complete, put the original floppy disks or CDs from which you installed the software in a safe place. If you have the original software handy, reinstalling it will be easier should something go wrong with the installed software.
- *Back up the registry and system configuration files.* Many older software packages edit Config.sys, Autoexec.bat, Win.ini, and System.ini files during the installation. Newer software might add its own entries to the Windows registry. Before you begin the installation, make backup copies of all these files so that you can backtrack if you want to. (You will learn more about backing up the registry later in the chapter.)

Installing Software

To install software designed for Windows 9x/Me, access the Control Panel and double-click the Add/Remove Programs icon. Insert the software CD in the CD-ROM drive or the floppy disk in the floppy disk drive, and then click the Install button. Follow directions on the setup screen. If the CD-ROM drive is set to Autorun, a setup screen might appear automatically as soon as you insert the software installation CD in the drive. For older software, click Start and Run to display the Run dialog box. Enter the drive and name of the installation program, for example, *A:Install* or *D:Setup*. Either way, the installation program loads and begins executing. If the installation

12

program asks you a question you cannot answer, you can always abandon the installation and try again later.

Most software asks you for a serial number unique to your copy of the software. The number is probably written on the CD or on the first floppy disk, or it might be stamped on the documentation. If necessary, write the serial number on the floppy disk, on the label side of the CD, or on the CD case, so that you have it if you lose the documentation later. Copyright agreements often allow you to install the software on only one computer at a time. This serial number identifies the copy of the software that you have installed on this machine.

After the installation is complete and the software is working, update your backup copies of Autoexec.bat, Config.sys, System.ini, Win.ini, and the registry so that they reflect the changes the application software made to these configuration files.

Troubleshooting Software Installations

If you have difficulty installing software in Windows 9x/Me, try the following:

- If an application locks up when you first open it, try deleting all files and folders under \Windows\Temp. A software installation sometimes leaves files and folders in the Windows temporary directories. To conserve space on the hard drive, delete all files and folders under \Windows\Temp.
- Look at the Readme.htm hypertext file in the \Windows directory, which will point you to the Programs.txt file, also in the \Windows directory. If there is a software problem that was known when Windows shipped, information about the problem and what to do about it might be in these text files. You can also check the Web site of the software manufacturer or the Microsoft Web site for additional insight.

NOTE

A **hypertext** file is a text file that contains hypertext tags to format the file and create hyperlinks to different points in the file or to other files. Hypertext files are used on the World Wide Web and are read and displayed using a Web browser such as Microsoft Internet Explorer or Netscape Navigator. To read a hypertext file using Windows Explorer, double-click the filename; your default browser will open the file.

Supporting DOS Applications Under Windows 9x/Me

Windows 3.x used **PIF (program information file)** files to manage the virtual machine environment for DOS applications and provided a PIF editor to alter these files. Each application had its own PIF file that was used to specify the DOS environment that Windows 3.x created for it. If an application had no PIF file, Windows 3.x used the settings in the _Default.pif file in the \Windows\System folder.

Windows 9x/Me manages the environment for DOS applications in a slightly different fashion. The Apps.inf file has a section named [PIF95] that contains a master list of settings to be used for all DOS applications listed in the file.

To customize the settings for a DOS application, use the Properties feature of the DOS program file, which creates an individual PIF for the program file and serves as the PIF editor. Right-click the program filename, and select Properties from the shortcut menu. Windows searches for the program's PIF file and, if none is found, creates one using default values. If Windows 9x/Me was installed over Windows 3.x, then _Default.pif still exists in the \Windows\System directory and default values are read from it. Regardless of where the default values come from, any changes are stored in the PIF for the application. To make changes, from the Properties window of the program file, click the Program tab (see Figure 12-12). (Note that the Program tab will not be present for Windows applications.)

Figure 12-12   Properties sheets for a DOS application affect the way Windows 9x/Me provides an environment for the application

If you select "Use current MS-DOS configuration", Windows executes the contents of Dosstart.bat, stored in the Windows folder. **Dosstart.bat** is a type of Autoexec.bat file that executes in two situations: when you select "Restart the computer in MS-DOS mode" from the shutdown menu, or when you run a program in MS-DOS mode. This file can be used to load real-mode device drivers, but Set commands are not executed.

A+ EXAM TIP

The A+ OS exam expects you to know how to support legacy software. Know the purpose of Dosstart.bat.

If you select "Specify a new MS-DOS configuration", you can change the Autoexec.bat and Config.sys files used for this MS-DOS mode only. For example, if the application runs slowly in DOS mode and does a lot of disk accessing, you can add entries to run real-mode SmartDrive here. SmartDrive is a 16-bit driver used to manage disk caching. It is not normally run under Windows 9x/Me, having been replaced by the faster 32-bit Vcache, which is built into Windows 9x/Me.

In this situation, because Windows 9x/Me does not manage disk access in MS-DOS mode, loading SmartDrive from the Advanced Program Settings window is appropriate, because Vcache will not be running.

Using Windows 9x/Me

Windows 9x/Me offers a variety of methods and tools to manage the OS. This section shows you how to use keystroke shortcuts, how to manage the desktop, and how to use Windows Explorer and Device Manager.

Keystroke Shortcuts in Windows

Table 12-4 lists a few handy keystrokes to use when working with Windows, including the function keys you can use during startup. You can also use the mouse to accomplish some of these tasks, but keystrokes are faster for experienced typists. Also, in some troubleshooting situations, the mouse is not usable. At those times, knowing these keystrokes is very valuable.

General Action	Keystrokes	Description
While loading Windows	F4	Load previous version of DOS.
	F5	Start in Safe Mode.
	F8 or Ctrl	Display startup menu.
	Shift + F8	Step-by-step confirmation.
Working with text anywhere in Windows	Ctrl + C Ctrl + Ins	Shortcuts for Copy.
	Ctrl + A	Shortcut for selecting all text.
	Ctrl + X	Shortcut for Cut.
	Ctrl + V	Shortcut for Paste.
	Shift + Ins	
	Shift + arrow keys	Hold down the Shift key, and use the arrow keys to select text, character by character.
Managing programs	Alt + Tab	Hold down the Alt key and press Tab to move from one loaded application to another.
	Ctrl + Esc	Display Start menu.

Table 12-4 (continued)

General Action	Keystrokes	Description
	Alt + F4	Close a program window, or, if no window is open, shut down Windows.
	Double-click	Double-click an icon or program name to execute the program.
	Ctrl + Alt + Del	Display the Task List, which you can use to switch to another application, end a task, or shut down Windows.
Managing files, folders, icons, and shortcuts	Ctrl + Shift while dragging a file	Create a shortcut.
	Ctrl while dragging a file	Copy a file.
	Shift + Delete	Delete a file without placing it in the Recycle Bin.
	F2	Rename an item.
	Alt + Enter	Display an item's Properties window.
Selecting items	Shift + click	To select multiple entries in a list (such as filenames in Explorer), click the first item, hold down the Shift key, and click the last item you want to select in the list. All items between the first and last are selected.
	Ctrl + click	To select several nonsequential items in a list, click the first item to select it. Hold down the Ctrl key and click other items anywhere in the list. All items you click are selected.
Using menus	Alt	Press the Alt key to activate the menu bar.
	Alt, letter	After the menu bar is activated, press a letter to select a menu option. The letter must be underlined in the menu.

12

Table 12-4 (continued)

General Action	Keystrokes	Description
	Alt, arrow keys	After the menu bar is activated, use the arrow keys to move over the menu tree.
	Alt, arrow keys, Enter	After the menu bar is activated and the correct option is highlighted, press Enter to select the option.
	Esc	Press Escape to exit a menu without making a selection.
Managing the desktop	Print Screen	Copy the desktop into the Clipboard.
	Ctrl + Esc	Display the Start menu and move the focus to the menu. (Use the arrow keys to move over the menu.)
	Alt + M	After the focus is on the Start menu, minimizes all windows and moves the focus to the desktop.
Working with windows	Ctrl + Tab and Ctrl + Shift + Tab	Move through tabbed pages in a dialog box.
	Shift + Close (X) button on a window	Close current folder and its parent folders.
	F5	Refresh the contents of a window.
Using the Windows key (key labeled with the Windows flag icon)	Win	Display the Start menu.
	Win + E	Start Windows Explorer.
	Win + M	Minimize all windows.
	Win + Tab	Move through items on taskbar.
	Win + R	Display the Run dialog box.
	Win + Break	Display the System Properties window.
Using the Applications shortcut menu key (key labeled with a box and arrow icon).	Application key	When an item is selected, display its shortcut menu

Table 12-4 Keystrokes that make working with Windows easier

Managing the Windows 9x/Me Desktop

A+
OS
1.1

From the Windows 9x/Me desktop you can make applications automatically load at startup, create shortcuts to files and applications, and make the environment more user-friendly. In this section, you will learn some ways to manage the Windows 9x/Me desktop.

To control display settings, right-click anywhere on the desktop and select Properties from the shortcut menu. The Display Properties window appears as shown in Figure 12-13.

Some of the more common things you can do from each tab on the window are:

- *Background.* Select desktop wallpaper or a pattern.
- *Screen Saver.* Select a screen saver and change its settings; change power settings for the monitor.
- *Appearance.* Pick and customize a color scheme for the desktop.
- *Effects.* Specify icon settings.
- *Web.* Set Active Desktop properties.
- *Settings.* Change the color range and display size.

✔ A+ EXAM TIP

Because you can't always depend on the mouse working, the A+ OS exam expects you to know how to troubleshoot using keystrokes. It's a good idea to practice using these keystrokes before taking the exam. A project at the end of this chapter will help you practice.

12

Figure 12-13   The Display Properties window lets you change settings for your desktop

You can also hide and unhide the taskbar at the bottom of the desktop. Click Start, Settings, Taskbar, and Start Menu. The Taskbar Properties window appears. (You can also reach this window by right-clicking the taskbar and selecting

A+
OS
1.1

Properties from the shortcut menu.) Then click the Taskbar Options tab, and select Auto hide (see Figure 12-14).

Figure 12-14   Use the Taskbar Properties window to change taskbar settings

Working with Shortcuts

A **shortcut** on the desktop is an icon that points to a program you can execute, or to a file or folder. The user double-clicks the icon to load the software. You can create a shortcut in several ways; one way is through the Start Menu Programs tab on the Taskbar Properties window you saw in Figure 12-14.

From here, click the Add button. The Create Shortcut Wizard appears, as shown in Figure 12-15. Enter the name of the program to which you want to create a shortcut, or browse for the file on your computer. In this example, we are creating a desktop shortcut to the Notepad application.

Once you enter or select the name of the program for which you want to create a shortcut, click Next. You then have the option to select where to place the shortcut. Select Desktop at the top of the folder list to create a desktop shortcut, and then click Next. Follow the directions in the wizard to complete the process.
Remember that you can create a shortcut for a program or a data file, name it, and select where to place it (either on the desktop or on the Start menu). If you want a program to load whenever Windows 9x/Me starts, create a shortcut and put it in the StartUp folder of the Start menu. All items in the StartUp folder execute automatically when Windows 9x/Me starts.

A+
OS
1.1

Taskbar Properties

Taskbar Options   Start Menu Programs

Customize Start menu

You can customize your Start menu by adding or removing items from it.

Add...   Remove...   Advanced...

Create Shortcut

Type the location and name of the item you want to create a shortcut to. Or, search for the item by clicking Browse.

Command line:

notepad.exe

Browse...

< Back   Next >   Cancel

Apply

Figure 12-15   Select the item to which you want to point the shortcut

Here are some other ways to create a shortcut:

- Select the file, folder, or program in Explorer or in a My Computer window. From the File menu, select Create Shortcut.
- From the File menu in Explorer, click New and then click Create Shortcut.
- Right-click the file, folder, or program to which you want to create a shortcut, and select Create Shortcut from the menu.
- Drag the file, folder, or program to the desktop.
- Right-click the file, folder, or program and hold down the mouse button while dragging the item to the desktop. When you release it, a dialog box appears. Choose Create Shortcut(s) Here.

NOTE

To edit a shortcut, right-click it and select Properties from the menu. To delete a shortcut, select Delete from this same menu.

A+
OS
1.1

Managing Icons

An icon on the desktop can be a shortcut to an application, or it can represent a file that belongs to an application. The telltale sign of the difference is the small, bent-arrow shortcut symbol on the icon, as seen in Figure 12-16. The icon on the right represents the document file MyLetter1.doc stored in the \Windows\Desktop folder, and the icon on the left is a shortcut to the file MyLetter2.doc, which can be stored anywhere on the drive. Also shown in Figure 12-16 are the contents of the \Windows\Desktop folder as seen by Explorer. You can add an icon to the desktop by putting a file in this folder. One way to delete an icon on the desktop is to delete the corresponding file in this folder; however, as you will see, this method can cause problems.

Figure 12-16   One icon is a shortcut, and the other icon represents a file stored in the Desktop folder

If you delete a shortcut icon from the desktop or the \Windows\Desktop folder, such as Shortcut to MyLetter2.doc, the shortcut is gone, but the actual file that the shortcut points to is not deleted. If you delete a document icon, such as MyLetter1.doc, the document itself is deleted. An error can occur if the actual document file, MyLetter2.doc, is deleted, but the shortcut to the deleted document remains on the desktop. Figure 12-17 shows a sample error message that occurs when this shortcut is used.

A+
OS
1.1

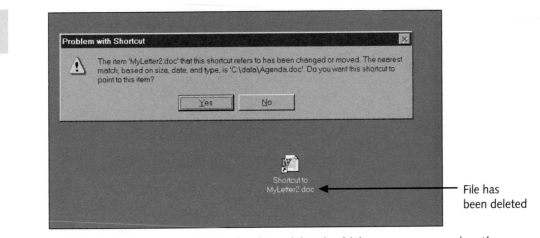

Figure 12-17   The file that the shortcut points to has been deleted, which causes an error when the shortcut is used

Windows Explorer

A+
OS
1.1
1.3
1.4
1.5

In this section, you learn how to use Windows Explorer to manage floppy disks and hard drives in Windows 9x/Me. You can open Windows Explorer using several methods:

- Click Start, Programs, and Windows Explorer.
- Right-click My Computer and select Explore from the menu.
- Right-click Start and select Explore from the menu.
- Open My Computer and then click the View menu, Explorer Bar, and Folders.

Figure 12-18 shows computer resources in the My Computer folder as seen when using Windows Explorer. (You can also access My Computer by double-clicking the desktop icon in Windows 9x/Me.)

12

A+
OS
1.1
1.3
1.4
1.5

Figure 12-18   The My Computer view in Windows Explorer

Shortcut Menu Options

A+
OS
1.1
1.3
1.4
1.5

The easiest way to manage drives, disks, folders, and files in Windows Explorer is to use the shortcut menus. To access a shortcut menu, right-click the icon representing the item you want to work with. Figure 12-19 shows the shortcut menu for the floppy drive as an example.

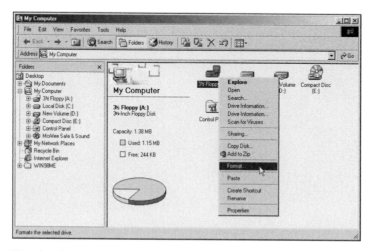

Figure 12-19   Use the shortcut menu to manage items in Explorer

Here are some tasks you can perform from a shortcut menu:

- If you select Explore, you can see the contents of the selected disk or folder in the current Explorer window. If you select Open, the contents of the disk or folder appear in a separate window.
- The Create Shortcut option creates a shortcut icon for the selected item.
- Selecting the Properties option brings up a dialog box showing information about the selected item and allows you to change settings for the item.
- If you selected a disk or drive, the shortcut menu contains a Format option. Recall that you can use Explorer to format a floppy disk by selecting Format from the shortcut menu.
- The Backup option enables you to make a backup of a disk, and the Sharing option enables you to share a drive, folders, or files with other users on your network.
- For floppy drives, if you select Copy Disk, the dialog box shown in Figure 12-20 opens, where the disk listed under "Copy from" is the source disk and the disk listed under "Copy to" is the target disk. Click Start to copy the disk.

12

Figure 12-20   Copying a disk using Windows

- The shortcut menu for files gives you additional options such as printing and e-mailing the file.
- The shortcut menu for a folder allows you to create a file. The menu lists applications you can use to create the file.

As you can see, some options on shortcut menus are the same for files, folders, drives, and disks; others are specific to particular items. The additional shortcut menu options may differ, depending on what programs you have installed to work with a particular item.

Now let's look in more detail at ways to use Windows 9x/Me Explorer to work with files and folders on your floppy disk or hard drive.

Creating a Folder

To create a folder, first select the folder you want to be the parent folder by clicking the folder's name. For example, to create a folder named Games under the folder named Download, first click the Download folder. Then click the File menu, select

New, and select Folder from the submenu that appears. The new folder will be created under Download, but its name will be New Folder. The name New Folder is automatically selected and highlighted for the user to type a new name. Type Games to change the folder name, as shown in Figure 12-21. The maximum depth of folders under folders depends on the length of the folder names. Recall from Chapter 3 that you can also create a folder using the MD command from a command prompt.

Figure 12-21   Edit the new folder's name

Deleting a Folder

To delete a folder from Explorer, right-click the folder and select Delete from the shortcut menu. A confirmation dialog box asks if you are sure you want to delete the folder. If you click Yes, you send the folder and all its contents, including subfolders, to the Recycle Bin. Empty the Recycle Bin to free your disk space. Files and folders sent to the Recycle Bin are not deleted until you empty it. Recall from Chapter 3 that you can also delete a folder using the RD command from a command prompt.

File Attributes

Using Explorer, you can view and change the file attributes. From Explorer, right-click a file and select Properties from the shortcut menu. The Properties window shown in Figure 12-22 appears. From the Properties window, you can change the read-only, hidden, and archive attributes (but not the system attribute) of the file. Recall from Chapter 3 that you can change all the attributes of a file or folder using the Attrib command from a command prompt.

4EMY3.TIF Properties

General | Summary | Preview |

4EMY3.TIF

Type of file: TIF Image Document

Opens with: Imaging Preview   Change...

Location: C:\Captures

Size: 769 KB (788,466 bytes)

Size on disk: 776 KB (794,624 bytes)

Created: Today, September 18, 2002, 12:40:51 PM

Modified: Today, September 18, 2002, 12:40:52 PM

Accessed: Today, September 18, 2002

Attributes: ☐ Read-only   ☐ Hidden   ☑ Archive

[OK]   [Cancel]   [Apply]

Figure 12-22   Properties of a file in Windows

Folder Properties

You can also view and change the properties assigned to folders. Select the folder, and then click the Explorer menu, click Tools, Folder Options, and click the View tab. From this window you can change how and when files appear in the folder.

Windows identifies file types primarily by the file extension. In Windows Explorer, by default, Windows 9x/Me hides the extensions of files if it knows which application to use to open or execute the file. For example, just after installation, it hides .exe, .com, .sys, and .txt file extensions but does not hide .doc, .ppt, or .xls files until the software to open these files has been installed. To display all file extensions, open the View tab in the Folder Options window, and uncheck "Hide file extensions for known file types".

Device Manager

Device Manager gives a graphical view of hardware devices configured under Windows and the resources and drivers they use. Using Device Manager, you can make changes, update drivers, and uninstall device drivers. You can also use Device Manager to print a report of system configuration. When a device driver is being installed, Windows 9x/Me might inform you of a resource conflict, or the device simply might not work. Use Device Manager as a useful fact-finding tool for resolving the problem.

Device Manager is one tab on the System Properties window. To access System Properties, right-click the My Computer icon on the desktop and select Properties

12

A+
OS
1.1
1.5
3.2

from the shortcut menu, or double-click the System icon in the Control Panel. From the System Properties window, click the Device Manager tab. The list of devices appears, as seen in Figure 12-23.

A + sign next to the device name indicates that you can click the sign for a list of manufacturers and models installed. The open diamond symbol indicates a SCSI device, and the three-forked symbol is used for USB. Symbols that indicate a device's status are:

- A red X through the device name indicates a disabled device.
- An exclamation point on a yellow background indicates a problem with the device. (The device might still be functioning.)
- A blue I on a white field indicates that automatic settings were not used and resources have been manually assigned. It does not indicate a problem with the device.
- For Windows Me, a green question mark indicates a compatible driver is installed (not the driver designed for the device), which means the device might not be fully functional.

For a better explanation of a problem, click the device and select Properties. The Device Properties dialog box that opens can give you helpful information about solving problems with I/O addresses, DMA channels, and IRQs used by the device, as well as the names of devices that are also attempting to use the same resources.

In fact, before you start hardware installation, you might want to use Device Manager to print a summary of all hardware installed on the PC and resources being used. This printout can be a record of your starting point before the installation, as well as a tool to help resolve conflicts during the installation. To print this summary, access Device Manager and click Print. From the Print dialog box, select All Devices and System Summary for a complete listing.

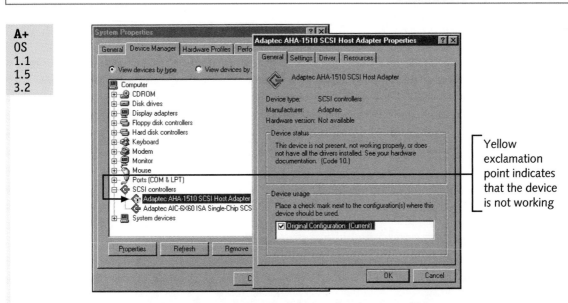

Figure 12-23 The Properties window of an installed device that is not working

Yellow exclamation point indicates that the device is not working

NOTE

If you have a problem with an installed device, use Device Manager to uninstall the device. Select the device and click the Uninstall button. Then reboot and reinstall the device, looking for problems during the installation that point to the source of the problem. Sometimes reinstalling a device is all that is needed to solve the problem.

12

Booting Windows 9x/Me

A+
OS
1.2
1.5

In Chapter 3, you learned how to boot to a command prompt. In this section, you will learn about the startup process in Windows 9x/Me, including the differences between booting Windows 95 and booting Windows 98/Me. Finally, you will learn how to cause an application to load at startup. First, however, you'll learn more about important files that Windows 9x/Me uses when booting.

Files Used to Customize the Startup Process

Windows 9x/Me uses several files to control the startup process. Recall that DOS requires Io.sys, Msdos.sys, and Command.com in the root directory of the boot device in order to load. In addition, Autoexec.bat and Config.sys are text files that can contain settings for environmental variables and commands to load drivers and TSRs. Windows 9x/Me supports Autoexec.bat and Config.sys for backward compatibility with DOS.

If Autoexec.bat or Config.sys files are present in the root directory, the command lines in them are executed during the boot. They are used to customize the loading process. Just as DOS uses text files to hold information about what is loaded, Windows 3.x also uses text files to hold custom settings that help control the loading process. These files are called **initialization files,** and some entries in them are read and used by Windows 9x/Me. However, most Windows 9x/Me settings are stored in the Windows registry rather than in text files.

You can edit these text files with the Edit.com program from the command prompt or any text editor from within Windows. The Windows System Configuration Editor (**Sysedit**) is a handy Windows text editor designed to be used with these files. To use Sysedit, type *sysedit* in the Run dialog box. These files automatically appear for editing: Autoexec.bat, Config.sys, **Win.ini, System.ini,** and **Protocol.ini** (see Figure 12-24).

Figure 12-24   Sysedit can be used to edit Windows system files

Recall that an initialization file, which has an .ini file extension, is used by Windows and application software to store configuration information needed when they are first loaded. An application can have its own .ini files and registry, and can also store its information in the Windows .ini files and the Windows registry. Table 12-5 shows Windows .ini files, which Windows 9x/Me supports for backward compatibility with Windows 3.x.

System.ini and Win.ini are used by both Windows 3.x and Windows 9x/Me. A sample Windows 9x/Me System.ini file is shown in Figure 12-25. The two sections required for the boot process are [boot] and [386Enh]. Windows 3.x kept many more entries in these sections than does Windows 9x/Me, which really only uses these files for backward compatibility with older applications.

A+
OS
1.2
1.5

Windows Initialization File	General Purpose of the File
System.ini	Contains hardware settings and multitasking options. Older protected mode (32-bit) drivers loaded from the [386Enh] section can cause problems.
Progman.ini	Contains information about Program Manager groups
Win.ini	Contains information about user settings, including printer, fonts, file associations, and settings made by applications
Control.ini	Contains information about the user's desktop, including color selections, wallpaper, and screen saver options
Mouse.ini	Contains settings for the mouse
Protocol.ini	Contains information about the configuration of the network

Table 12-5 Windows .ini files

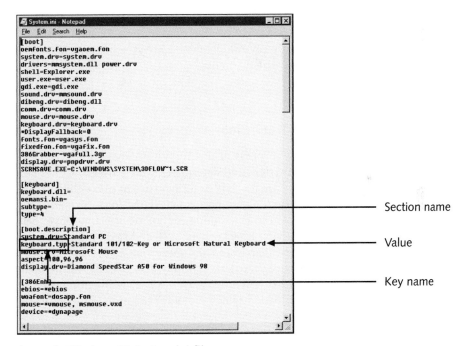

Figure 12-25 A sample Windows 98 System.ini file

12

Initialization files are only read when Windows or an application using .ini files starts up. If you change the .ini file for an application, you must restart the software for the change to take effect. If you want the application to ignore a line in the .ini file, you can turn the line into a **comment** line by putting a semicolon or the letters REM at the beginning of the line.

A+
OS
1.2
1.5

We now turn our attention to the Windows 9x/Me startup process, in which these and other files are used.

CAUTION

Sometimes it is necessary to manually edit an .ini file that belongs to an application, but you should normally not edit System.ini or other Windows 9x/Me initialization files. Incorrect changes to these files might result in Windows not running correctly, and Windows sometimes overwrites these files when changes are made to it through the Control Panel.

The Windows 9x/Me Startup Process

A+
OS
2.3
2.5

Windows 9x/Me first loads in real mode and then switches to protected mode. With DOS, the two core real-mode system files responsible for starting up the OS, Io.sys and Msdos.sys, remain in memory, running even after the OS is loaded. With Windows 9x/Me, Io.sys is responsible only for the initial startup process performed in real mode. Then control is turned over to Vmm32.vxd, which works in protected mode, and Io.sys is terminated. Recall that Windows 9x/Me includes a file named Msdos.sys, but it is only a text file that contains some parameters and switches you can set to affect the way the OS boots.

Startup in Windows 9x/Me is a five-phase process, as shown in Figure 12-26. We will look at each phase.

Phase 1: BIOS POST and Bootstrap

Startup BIOS begins the process. If the BIOS is a Plug and Play (PnP) BIOS, it examines the devices on the system and determines which are PnP-compliant. BIOS first enables the devices that are not PnP and then tries to make the PnP devices use the leftover resources. It also looks to permanent RAM for information about hardware, and uses that information to help configure PnP devices that have their configuration information recorded there. It performs POST and saves information that Windows uses later to complete the hardware configuration.

BIOS looks for a device (hard drive, floppy disk, CD-ROM drive, and so forth) containing the OS and loads Windows 9x/Me. The MBR program on the boot device executes the bootstrap loader, which looks for the initial hidden file of Windows 9x/Me (Io.sys).

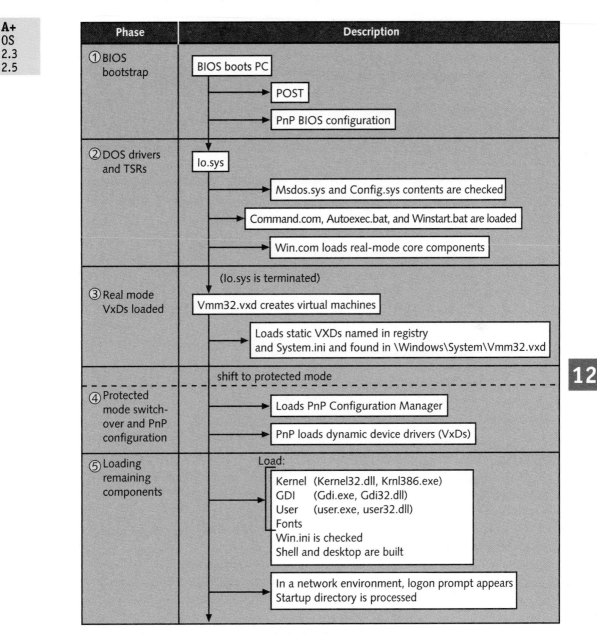

Phase	Description
① BIOS bootstrap	BIOS boots PC POST PnP BIOS configuration
② DOS drivers and TSRs	Io.sys Msdos.sys and Config.sys contents are checked Command.com, Autoexec.bat, and Winstart.bat are loaded Win.com loads real-mode core components
③ Real mode VxDs loaded	(Io.sys is terminated) Vmm32.vxd creates virtual machines Loads static VXDs named in registry and System.ini and found in \Windows\System\Vmm32.vxd
④ Protected mode switch-over and PnP configuration	shift to protected mode Loads PnP Configuration Manager PnP loads dynamic device drivers (VxDs)
⑤ Loading remaining components	Load: Kernel (Kernel32.dll, Krnl386.exe) GDI (Gdi.exe, Gdi32.dll) User (user.exe, user32.dll) Fonts Win.ini is checked Shell and desktop are built In a network environment, logon prompt appears Startup directory is processed

12

Figure 12-26   Windows 9x/Me core components and the loading process

Phase 2: The OS Is Loaded

In Phase 2, BIOS turns control over to Io.sys, which creates a real-mode operating system environment. Next, Io.sys checks the text file Msdos.sys for boot parameters.

Then Io.sys automatically loads the following drivers if they are present: Himem.sys, Ifshlp.sys, Setver.exe, and Drvspace.bin (or Dblspace.bin).

- Himem.sys provides access to extended memory.
- 16-bit programs use Ifshlp.sys to access the file system.
- Setver.exe is included for backward compatibility with DOS applications that expect all DOS components to be from the same version. Setver.exe "asks" the DOS application what version of DOS it expects to use and presents DOS components to that application as if they were all from that version, even if they are actually from different versions.
- Drvspace.bin and Dblspace.bin provide disk compression. One of these two files is loaded only if Io.sys finds Dlbspace.ini or Drvspace.ini in the root directory of the boot drive.

Io.sys also sets several environmental variables to default settings. In DOS, these default settings were loaded from Config.sys. Entries in Io.sys cannot be edited, but an entry in Config.sys overrides the default entry in Io.sys. Therefore, if you want to use settings different from the default, put the command in Config.sys, which is executed at this point in the load. The default Io.sys entries are listed in Table 12-6.

Entry	Description
Buffers=30	The number of file buffers to create.
DOS=HIGH	The DOS core of Windows 9x/Me is loaded into the high memory area (HMA).
Files=60	The number of files that can be open at one time under 16-bit applications.
Lastdrive=Z	The last letter that can be assigned to a logical drive.
Shell=Command.com /P	Loads Command.com and executes Autoexec.bat.
Stacks=9,256	The number of frames of instructions that can be held in memory in a queue at one time. Used for backward compatibility with older applications.

Table 12-6   Entries in Io.sys that once were in Config.sys

Next, Io.sys loads Command.com and follows instructions stored in Autoexec.bat and Winstart.bat. The default assignments made to environmental variables that were stored in Autoexec.bat in DOS are shown in the following list:

- Tmp=c:\windows\temp
- Temp=c:\windows\temp
- Prompt=pg
- Path=c:\windows;c:\windows\command

The Tmp and Temp variables are used by some software to locate where to put their temporary files. You can change any of these variables by making an entry in Autoexec.bat. Next, Io.sys loads Win.com. Then Win.com loads other real-mode core components.

Phase 3: Static VxDs

In Phase 3, Io.sys relinquishes control to the virtual machine manager (VMM) component housed in Vmm32.vxd along with some virtual device drivers. A **virtual device driver (VxD)** works with a virtual machine to provide access to hardware for software running in the VM. Under Windows 3.x, these VxDs were loaded from System.ini and had a .386 file extension. Under Windows 9x/Me, if stored in individual files, they have a .vxd file extension. They are called **static VxDs** because once they are loaded into memory, they remain there. (Conversely, **dynamic VxDs** are loaded into and unloaded from memory as needed.)

Vmm32.vxd is built specifically for a particular computer when Windows 9x/Me is installed and contains some VxDs critical for a successful boot; each installation of Windows will have a different build of this file. (The VxD drivers now included in Vmm32.vxd were listed in the [386Enh] section of System.ini under Windows 3.x.) Vmm32.vxd terminates Io.sys and, while still in real mode, loads static VxD device drivers as identified in four different locations. They can be embedded in Vmm32.vxd, named in the registry or System.ini, or stored in the .vxd files in the \Windows\System\Vmm32 directory.

If you suspect a problem with a VxD that is part of the Vmm32.vxd file, then store a new version of the .vxd file in the \Windows\System\Vmm32 directory. If Windows finds a VxD driver there, it uses that driver instead of the one embedded in Vmm32.vxd. Also, VxD drivers are listed in the registry and in System.ini. Normally, the entries are the same, and entries are only listed in System.ini for backward compatibility. However, if an entry in System.ini differs from an entry in the registry, the value in System.ini is used.

Phase 4: Protected-Mode Switchover and PnP Configuration

At the beginning of Phase 4, Vmm32.vxd switches to protected mode and loads Configuration Manager. Configuration Manager is responsible for configuring legacy and PnP devices. It uses any information that PnP BIOS might have left for it and loads the 32-bit VxDs for the PnP devices.

Phase 5: Loading the Remaining Components

In Phase 5, with Vmm32.vxd still in control, the three core components are loaded, then fonts and other associated resources are loaded. Win.ini is checked and commands stored there are executed to allow backward compatibility. The shell and user desktop are loaded. If the computer is working in a networked environment, a logon dialog box is displayed, and the user can log on to Windows 9x/Me and the network. Finally, any processes stored in the Startup directory are performed.

12

A+
OS
2.3
2.5

Differences Between the Windows 95 and Windows 98/Me Boot Process

Windows 98 made some minor changes in what happens during startup to speed up the boot process. For instance, Windows 95 waits two seconds, displaying "Starting Windows 95" so that you can press a key to alter the boot process. Windows 98 eliminated this two-second wait and, in its place, allows you to press and hold the Ctrl key as it loads. If you do, you see the startup menu that is also available with Windows 95.

APPLYING CONCEPTS

Loading an Application at Startup

If you want an application to load automatically at startup, you can:

- Place a shortcut in the folder C:\Windows\All Users\Startup Menu\Programs\StartUp.
- Put the name of the program file in the Load= or Run= line in Win.ini.
- Manually edit the registry key HKEY_LOCAL_MACHINE\SOFTWARE\ Microsoft\Windows\CurrentVersion\Run.

Try one of these methods yourself.

Troubleshooting Tools for Windows 9x/Me

A+
OS
1.5
3.1
3.2

Now let's look at some support tools that are useful for troubleshooting problems with the OS during or after the boot. Table 12-7 lists several tools that monitor and improve system performance, control the OS, and help with troubleshooting. Several major tools are covered in this section; in the next section, you will see how to use these tools in troubleshooting situations.

NOTE

Tools new with Windows Me are System Restore and System File Protection. System Restore automatically backs up the registry and other system files when the system is idle. System File Protection is similar to Windows 2000 System File Protection; it prevents system files from being accidentally deleted and prevents application installations from overwriting newer DLL files with older or nonstandard versions.

A+
OS
1.5
3.1
3.2

Tool	Win 95	Win 98/ME	Description
Automatic Skip Driver Agent Filename: Asd.exe Location: \Windows		X	Automatically skips drivers that prevent Windows from loading and records problems encountered in the log file Asd.log. To run, select Automatic Skip Driver Agent from the Tools menu of the System Information window.
Microsoft System Information Filename: MSInfo32.exe Location: \Program Files\ Common files\Microsoft shared\Msinfo	X	X	Displays system information, including installed hardware and device drivers. To run, click Start, Programs, Accessories, System Tools, and System Information, or type Msinfo32.exe in the Run dialog box.
Hardware Diagnostic tool (Hwinfo.exe)		X	Displays the same information as System Information, but in text form. Enter hwinfo/ui in the Run dialog box.
Registry Checker Filename: Scanreg.exe Location: \Windows\Command		X	Backs up, verifies, and recovers the Registry. To run, select Registry Checker from the Tools menu of the System Information window.
Windows Update Filename: Iexplore.exe Location: *www.microsoft.com/ windowsupdate*	X	X	Downloads service packs (fixes) for Windows from the Microsoft Web site.
System options in Control Panel (example: System Properties)	X	X	Several applets in the Control Panel can be used to monitor and tweak system performance.
System Configuration Utility Filename: MsConfig.exe Location: \Windows\System		X	Allows you to temporarily modify the system configuration to help with troubleshooting. To run, select System Configuration Utility from the Tools menu of the System Information window or type Msconfig in the Run dialog box.

12

Table 12-7 (continued)

Tool	Win 95	Win 98/ME	Description
System File Checker Filename: Sfc.exe Location: \Windows\System		X	Verifies system files. This tool scans for changed, deleted, or corrupted system files and restores them from the originals on the Windows CD. To run, select System File Checker from the Tools menu of the System Information window.
System Monitor Filename: Sysmon.exe Location: \Windows		X	System Monitor tracks the performance of some important system components. To run, click Start, Programs, Accessories, System Tools, and System Monitor.
Microsoft Backup Filename: Msbackup.exe Location: \Program Files\ Accessories\Backup	X	X	Backs up files and folders to prevent loss when your hard drive fails. To run, click Start, Programs, Accessories, System Tools, and Backup. The utility is covered in Chapter 9.
System Recovery Filename: pcrestor.bat Location: On the Windows 98/Me CD in \Tools\Sysrec		X	Uses a full system backup created by Microsoft Backup to reinstall Windows and restore the system to its state as of the last backup.
Dr. Watson Filename: Drwatson.exe Location: \Windows		X	Traps errors in log files created by applications and takes a snapshot of the system to use for troubleshooting.
Scheduled Task Wizard Filename: Mstask.exe Location: \Windows\System	X	X	Schedules tasks such as MS Backup to run at predetermined times.
Version Conflict Manager Filename: Vcmui.exe Location: \Windows		X	Replaces an older Windows file with a newer file that was saved when Windows or an application was installed.
System Configuration Editor Filename: Sysedit.exe Location: \Windows\System	X	X	Text editor to edit files that configure how Windows loads. To run it, enter Sysedit.exe in

Table 12-7 (continued)

A+
OS
1.5
3.1
3.2

Tool	Win 95	Win 98/ME	Description
			the Run dialog box. Sysedit automatically opens Protocol.ini, System.ini, Win.ini, Config.sys, and Autoexec.bat for editing.
Task Manager Filename: Taskman.exe Location: \Windows	X	X	Run, switch, and end applications, and access the Shutdown menu. To run it, type Taskman in the Run dialog box.
Signature Verification Tool Filename: sigverif.exe Location: \Windows		X	Checks system drivers for digital signatures given to them by Microsoft, which ensures they have been tested by Microsoft. To run it, use the System Information window.
Digital Signature Check		X	Identifies drivers that have been digitally signed by Microsoft to verify their integrity. To use it, enable this key in the registry: HKEY_LOCAL_ MACHINE\Software \Microsoft\Driver Signing.

Table 12-7   Windows 9x/Me system performance and troubleshooting tools

12

✔ **A+ EXAM TIP**

To prepare for the A+ OS exam, know the purpose of all the utilities in Table 12-7 and the program filename of the utility.

System Applet in the Control Panel

One useful applet in troubleshooting a system is the System Properties window. To access the System applet, right-click My Computer and select Properties from the shortcut menu, or click the System icon in the Control Panel. The applet offers several tools for performance monitoring and troubleshooting. For example, the Performance tab in Figure 12-27 shows a performance report from two computers, one in need of performance tuning and one running at optimal performance. Key messages to look for on this screen (see Figure 12-27a) are "Some drives are using MS-DOS compatibility" under File System, and "MS-DOS compatibility mode" under Virtual Memory. These messages mean that real-mode drivers are being used, which can slow down performance, especially when used with hard drive access. Figure 12-27b indicates that both these components are using 32-bit protected-mode drivers.

Whenever you see MS-DOS mode (real mode) drivers being used, do whatever you can to see that these drivers are replaced with 32-bit protected-mode drivers. One important tool to use for this process is the text file Ios.ini, which contains the Windows 9x/Me Safe Driver List. Windows 9x/Me uses this list to determine if it can safely substitute a protected-mode driver for a real-mode one. Also, if it attempts to make the substitution but fails, it often records the problem in another file, Ios.log. Check this file for information about the problem.

If a real-mode driver is being used, and you believe that a protected-mode driver should be used in its place, first check Ios.log for any error messages. If you don't find an error message, add the real-mode driver name to the safe driver list in the Ios.ini file. Anything following the semicolon on the line is a comment. You can also use REM to comment out a line.

a. Adjustments are needed in order to use 32-bit protected-mode resource

b. System running at optimal performance

Figure 12-27   The Performance tab under System Properties in the Control Panel can tell you if your file system and virtual memory are running at optimal performance

Sample lines in the Ios.ini file are:

```
[SafeList]
386max.sys ; Qualitas
extrados.pro; Qualitas Memory Manager
extrados.max; Qualitas Memory Manager
4dos.com ; 4DOS shell program
ad-dos.com ; Afterdark
ad-wrap.com ; Afterdark
adi2.com ; Afterdark
aspi3x70.sys; DTC SCSI driver
```

System Monitor

System Monitor allows you to monitor how system resources are being used by applications. It can monitor the file system, memory, the kernel, printer sharing services, and network performance data.

APPLYING CONCEPTS

System Monitor is not automatically installed in a typical installation. To install it, go to the Control Panel, and select Add/Remove Programs. Click Windows Setup, and then select Accessories. To run System Monitor, click Start, point to Programs, Accessories, System Tools, and then click System Monitor.

Figure 12-28 shows System Monitor tracking the kernel and disk cache hits and misses. Under the File menu, you can add and delete items the monitor is tracking. Use System Monitor to help determine if an application is using an inordinate amount of resources or has a memory leak. A memory leak occurs when you exit software and it unloads from memory, but it does not release the memory addresses that it was using for its data back to the OS. Memory leaks can occur when software is corrupted, poorly written, or plagued with a virus. You notice memory leaks when your system gets sluggish after you have launched and exited an application several times before rebooting the system. A reboot releases all memory addresses.

Figure 12-28   System Monitor can track the performance of several system resources

System Configuration Utility

A+
OS
1.5

Like loading Windows in Safe Mode, the System Configuration Utility (Msconfig.exe) reduces the startup process to its essentials. If starting Windows in this condition eliminates the problem you are troubleshooting, you can use this utility to add items back one at a time until the problem occurs; the source of the problem is related to the last item you added. To use the utility, do the following:

1. To access the utility, click **Start**, point to **Programs, Accessories, System Tools**, and then click **System Information**. The Microsoft System Information window opens.

2. From the **Tools** menu, select **System Configuration Utility** (see Figure 12-29). The System Configuration Utility dialog box opens, as shown in Figure 12-30. Another way to access the utility is to type Msconfig in the Run dialog box.

Figure 12-29   The System Information window provides access to many Windows support tools

3. To diagnose a problem, select **Diagnostic startup – interactively load device drivers and software**, and then click **OK** to restart your computer.

4. If this solves the problem, then the clean start was successful. Next, select **Selective startup** from the dialog box shown in Figure 12-30 and methodically select first one item and then another to restore, until the problem reappears. Begin by restoring all entries in Autoexec.bat and Config.sys, to determine if real-mode drivers and programs loaded from these files are the source of the problem.

5. If the problem still occurs, even with the clean boot, then try the following:

   ▪ If you have not already done so, scan for a virus, using a current version of antivirus software.
   ▪ Use Registry Checker to check for corrupted system files.

A+
OS
1.5

- Use System File Checker to check for corrupted system files.
- Check the CMOS setup screen for wrong settings.

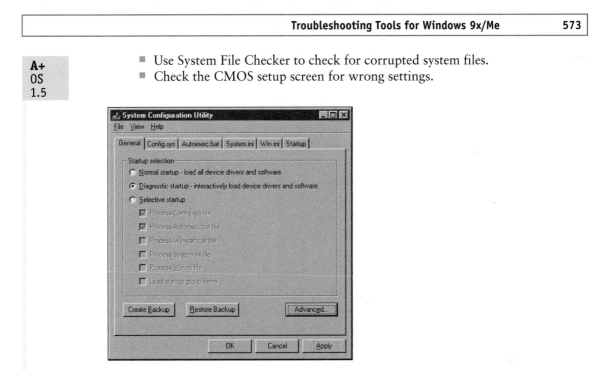

Figure 12-30   The Windows 98 System Configuration Utility helps troubleshoot Windows configuration problems

12

Dr. Watson

A+
OS
3.1
3.2

A troubleshooting tool you can use when you have problems running an application is Dr. Watson. **Dr. Watson** is a Windows utility that can record detailed information about the system, errors that occur, and the programs that caused them in a log file named \Windows\Drwatson\WatsonXX.wlg, where XX is an incrementing number. Start Dr. Watson (see Figure 12-31), and then reproduce the application error.

Next, look at the events logged in the Dr. Watson window under the Diagnosis tab. Use this information to check the Microsoft Web site, *support.microsoft.com*, for the problem and solution. For errors that you cannot reproduce at will, you can load Dr. Watson each time Windows starts by creating a shortcut to Drwatson.exe in the StartUp folder.

A+
OS
3.1
3.2

Figure 12-31   The Dr. Watson opening window

The Windows 9x/Me Registry

A+
OS
1.1
1.2
1.3
1.5
3.1

In supporting and troubleshooting Windows 9x/Me, you need to understand the role of the registry and .ini files. The registry is a database of configuration information and settings for users, hardware, applications, and the OS. Starting with Windows 9x/Me, the registry takes over the essential functions of .ini files. However, Windows 9x/Me still supports .ini files for compatibility with Windows 3.x and legacy software and hardware devices. Entries that 16-bit Windows applications make in Win.ini and System.ini are not added to the registry because these applications cannot access the registry. Entries made in .ini files by applications that can access the registry are copied into the registry. In this section, you will examine how the registry is organized, what kinds of information are in the registry, how and why you might edit the registry, and how to recover from a corrupted registry.

How the Registry Is Organized

The registry organizes information in a hierarchical database with a treelike, top-to-bottom design. The Windows 9x/Me System.ini file contains setup parameters. Figure 12-25 shows a portion of the System.ini file. Notice that section names appear in square brackets, key names to the left of the equal signs, and values assigned to these key names to the right of the equal signs. The Windows 9x/Me registry takes on a similar but enhanced design that allows for keys to cascade to several levels on the tree. Figure 12-32 shows a portion of a Windows 9x/Me registry. Consider names on the left of the window as similar to section names in System.ini; these names are called

A+
OS
1.1
1.2
1.3
1.5
3.1

keys by Windows 9x/Me. On the right of the window are value names, such as ScreenSaveTime, and to the right of each name is the **value data** assigned to that name, such as "60." The value names, called values by Windows 9x/Me, are similar to the key names in System.ini, and the value data is similar to the values assigned to key names in System.ini.

The registry is organized into the six major keys, or branches listed in Table 12-8. The registry is contained in two files, System.dat and User.dat, located in the Windows directory as hidden, read-only, system files, although the information forms only a single database.

Figure 12-32   Structure of the Windows 9x/Me registry

Key	Description
HKEY_CLASSES_ROOT	Contains information about file associations and OLE data. (This branch of the tree is a mirror of HKEY_LOCAL_MACHINE\ Software\Classes.)
HKEY_USERS	Includes user preferences, including desktop configuration and network connections.
HKEY_CURRENT_USER	If there is only one user of the system, this is a duplicate of HKEY_USERS. For a multiuser system, this key contains information about the current user preferences.
HKEY_LOCAL_MACHINE	Contains information about hardware and installed software.
HKEY_CURRENT_CONFIG	Contains the same information in HKEY_LOCAL_MACHINE\ Config and has information about printers and display fonts.
HKEY_DYN_DATA	Keeps information about Windows performance and Plug-and-Play information.

Table 12-8   Six major branches, or keys, of the Windows 9x/Me registry

12

Recovering from a Corrupted Registry

Windows 95 has a way to recover from a corrupted registry that is different from the method used by Windows 98/Me. These methods are discussed next.

Windows 95 Backup of the Registry   Windows 95 maintains a backup copy of the two registry files and names the backup files System.da0 and User.da0. Each time Windows 95 boots successfully, it makes a new backup of the two registry files. If Windows 95 has trouble loading and must start in Safe Mode, it does not back up the registry.

If Windows 95 does not find a System.dat file when it starts, it automatically replaces it with the backup System.da0. If both System.dat and User.dat are missing, or if the WinDir= command is missing in Msdos.sys, Windows 9x/Me tells you that the registry files are missing and starts in Safe Mode. It then displays the Registry Problem dialog box. Click the Restore From Backup and Restart buttons to restore the registry files from System.da0 and User.da0. If these files are also missing, the registry cannot easily be restored. You can either restore the files from your own backups or run Windows 9x/Me Setup. There is another option. Look for the file System.1st in the root directory of the hard drive. This is the System.dat file created when Windows 9x/Me was first installed. In an emergency, you can revert to this file.

Windows 98/Me Registry Checker   Windows 98/Me offers a utility called the Registry Checker, which is not available with Windows 95. It automatically backs up the registry each day, and by default, it keeps the last five days of backups. In an emergency, you can recover the registry from one of these backups. You can also tell Registry Checker to make an additional backup on demand, for example, when you make changes to the registry and want to back them up before you make new changes.

To access Registry Checker, select Start, point to Programs, Accessories, System Tools, and then click System Information. The Microsoft System Information window opens (see Figure 12-33). From the menu bar, select Tools and then Registry Checker. Registry Checker tells you if the registry is corrupted and fixes it, if allowed. You can also create a new backup at this time.

A+
OS
1.1
1.2
1.3
1.5
3.1

Figure 12-33   The Registry Checker is available under Programs, Accessories, System Tools, System Information; it is used to back up, restore, and repair the Windows 98 registry

Backups are kept in cabinet files in the \Windows\Sysbckup folder as rb001.cab, rb002.cab, and so on. To revert to one of these backups, you must first be in MS-DOS mode. For Windows Me, boot from a bootable disk. For Windows 98, boot from a bootable disk or boot to an MS-DOS prompt from the Windows 98 startup menu. (Windows Me does not have this option on the startup menu.) From the MS-DOS prompt (not a DOS box within a Windows session), use the commands in Table 12-9 to repair or recover the registry.

Command	Purpose
Scanreg /Restore	Restores the registry from a previous backup. A screen appears asking you which backup to use.
Scanreg /Fix	Repairs the corrupted registry. If the problem is inherent to the registry itself, this might work. If you want to undo a successful change to the registry, then use the Restore option instead.
Scanreg /Backup	Creates a new backup of the registry at the DOS prompt. Don't do this if the registry is giving you problems.
Scanreg /Opt	Optimizes the registry. ScanReg looks for and deletes information in the registry that is no longer used. This reduces the size of the registry, which might speed up booting.
Scanreg /?	Help feature of ScanReg.

Table 12-9   Commands used to repair or recover the Windows 98 or Windows Me registry

12

A+
OS
2.1

Modifying the Registry

When you make a change in the Control Panel, Device Manager, or many other places in Windows 9x/Me, the registry is modified automatically. This is the only way most users will ever change the registry. However, on rare occasions you might need to edit the registry manually. For example, if a virus infected your registry, an antivirus technical staff person or directions downloaded from an antivirus Web site might direct you to edit the registry and delete any entries added by the virus. The first step in editing the registry is to back up the two registry files System.dat and User.dat. The next step is to use Regedit.exe, located in the Windows folder. You can use Explorer to locate the file, then double-click it, or you can click Start, then Run, and type Regedit in the Run dialog box. When you do, the window in Figure 12-34 opens. Open one branch of the tree by clicking the + sign to the left of the key, and close the branch by clicking the – sign. To search for an entry in the registry, click the Edit menu and then click Find.

Figure 12-34   The six major keys, or branches, of the registry seen in the Registry Editor

Troubleshooting Windows 9x/Me

A+
OS
2.1

This section covers Windows 9x/Me troubleshooting. It is important for you to know how to troubleshoot problems that occur during a Windows installation, problems that occur during the boot process, and problems that occur during normal Windows operations.

NOTE

For specific error messages that occur during installation and what to do about them, go to the Microsoft Web site *support.microsoft.com* and search for the error message.

Troubleshooting Windows 9x/Me Installations

A+
OS
2.1

Table 12-10 lists some problems that might occur while installing Windows 9x/Me and what to do about them.

Symptom	Description and Solution
An error message about BIOS appears during installation.	This is most likely caused by BIOS not allowing changes to the boot sector to protect it from viruses. Disable the feature in CMOS setup.
Windows 9x/Me stalls during the first restart after installation.	This is probably caused by legacy hardware that is not configured correctly. Try the following: ▪ Remark (REM) out all entries in Config.sys and Autoexec.bat. ▪ Disable the ISA enumerator by commenting out this line in System.ini: Device=ISAPNP.386.
During the first restart after installation, an error message appears with information about a bad or missing file.	This is probably caused by an error in Config.sys or Autoexec.bat. Try renaming both files so they are not executed. If this solves the problem, then comment out each line in the file, one at a time, until you know which line caused the problem.
During the first restart after the installation, you get an error message about a missing or damaged VxD file.	Run Windows setup again and select the option to Verify or replace the missing VxD (virtual device driver).
After upgrading from Windows 95 to Windows 98, the startup screen still says Windows 95.	This can be caused by one of two problems. First, the Io.sys file might not have been updated. If so, use the Sys C: command to replace it. Or, the file Logo.sys is in the root directory, which overrides the logo screen embedded in Io.sys. Delete or rename the file.
"Invalid system disk" error appears during setup.	▪ Suspect a boot sector virus. Run a current version of antivirus software. ▪ If this error occurs while installing Windows when disk management software such as DiskPro is running, Windows might have damaged the hard drive MBR. To recover from this problem, see the documentation for the disk management software.

Table 12-10   Some problems and solutions when installing Windows 9x/Me

12

Troubleshooting the Windows 9x/Me Boot Process

A+
OS
2.3
3.1

When the boot process does not complete correctly, you can go through these basic steps to troubleshoot it:

1. Check and address any error messages that occur during a normal boot.

2. If you cannot boot to a normal desktop, boot in Safe Mode and begin troubleshooting there. If you can boot to Safe Mode but cannot boot normally, you probably have a driver problem of some kind, because the main difference between Safe Mode and normal booting is the drivers that are loaded.

3. If you cannot boot using Safe Mode, the GUI portion of the OS is not functioning. Boot to the command prompt using the startup menu. Use commands at the C prompt for troubleshooting.

4. If the startup menu is not accessible, the MS-DOS core of the OS is not functioning. Boot from an emergency startup disk, and try to access drive C.

5. If you cannot access drive C, then the hard drive is not accessible. Try Fdisk. If Fdisk does not work, treat the problem as a hardware problem.

Error Messages Received While Loading Windows 9x/Me

Error messages are your first indications that something is going wrong with the Windows 9x/Me boot process. You can use these messages to figure out how to solve some Windows 9x/Me boot problems. Table 12-11 shows error messages that Windows 9x/Me might produce and gives advice about what to do when you see them. Specific errors are covered later in this section.

Error Message or Problem	What to Do
MS-DOS compatibility mode	■ Windows is using real-mode drivers to access the hard drive rather than the preferred 32-bit drivers. After backing up the Config.sys and System.ini files, remove any references to real-mode drivers for the hard drive in these files. ■ The problem might be due to an outdated motherboard BIOS. Consider updating the BIOS.
Bad or missing file Real-mode driver missing or damaged Error in config.sys line xx	■ Verify that Config.sys, Autoexec.bat (root directory of the hard drive), and System.ini (Windows folder) are present and in the right location.

Table 12-11 (continued)

Error Message or Problem	What to Do
	■ Check Config.sys and Autoexec.bat for errors using the step-by-step confirmation option from the Windows 9x/Me startup menu. To check System.ini, rename the file so that it will not be used and boot with a bare-bones version of the file. ■ Look in the Win.ini file for applications that are attempting to load at startup but have been deleted or uninstalled. Check the Load= or Run= lines.
Cannot open file *.inf	■ This error is caused by insufficient memory. Disable any TSRs running in Autoexec.bat. ■ Close any applications that are running or remove them from the Start folder.
Insufficient disk space	Run ScanDisk and Defragmenter. Check free space on the hard drive.
Invalid system disk	Suspect a boot sector virus. Run a current version of antivirus software.
Bad or missing command.com	Io.sys could be missing or corrupted. Restore the file from a backup or an emergency startup disk. To restore all real-mode files needed to begin loading Windows 9x/Me, do the following: (1) boot from a Windows 9x/Me emergency startup disk, (2) restore Io.sys, Msdos.sys, Drvspace.bin, and Command.com by executing the command SYS C:, and (3) remove the floppy disk and reboot.
Invalid VxD dynamic link call from IFSMGR	This error is caused by a missing or corrupted Msdos.sys file. Restore the file from a backup or from an emergency startup disk.
Missing system files	Run the SYS C: command.
System Registry file missing	Either System.dat or User.dat is corrupted or missing. For Windows 95, restore them by using either System.da0 or User.da0. For Windows 98/Me, run ScanReg.

Table 12-11 (continued)

12

Error Message or Problem	What to Do
VxD error returns to command prompt	A VxD file is missing or corrupted. Run Windows Setup from the Windows 9x/Me CD, and choose Verify installed components.
Error containing the text "Kernel32.dll"	An error that contains this text probably indicates a corrupted kernel. Try restoring system files. If that doesn't work, reinstall Windows. Note that this error may appear at other times, not just during the boot process.

Table 12-11   Error messages received while loading Windows 9x/Me

Windows has several tools you can use to help troubleshoot problems with booting:

- Use the System Configuration Utility (Msconfig.exe) to limit what loads during the boot in order to attain the cleanest possible boot.
- Use Device Manager to disable a device that you think is causing a problem.
- Use Automatic Skip Driver Agent (ASDA) to keep Windows from installing a driver that might be corrupted, including built-in Windows drivers.
- The Windows 9x/Me startup menu includes Safe Mode, the command prompt, and other troubleshooting options.

Windows 9x/Me Startup Menu Options

Normally, when you load Windows, the message "Starting Windows" appears and then the OS loads. However, you can force the startup menu to appear rather than the "Starting Windows" message by pressing the F8 key or holding down the Ctrl key during the boot.

The Windows 9x/Me startup menu options are:

1. Normal

2. Logged (\Bootlog.txt)

3. Safe Mode

4. Safe Mode with network support

5. Step-by-step confirmation

6. Command prompt only

7. Safe Mode command prompt only

8. Previous version of MS-DOS

What to expect when you select each menu option is described next. Option 4 appears if the OS is configured for a network, and Option 8 appears if a previous

A+
OS
2.3
3.1

version of DOS was retained during the Windows 9x/Me installation. Option 6 is not available with Windows Me.

Normal   In Msdos.sys, if BootGUI=1, then this option starts Windows 9x/Me. If BootGUI=0, then this option boots to the DOS 7.0 or DOS 7.1 prompt (the DOS core of Windows 9x/Me). Either way, the commands in Autoexec.bat and Config.sys are executed.

If a problem appears when you boot in normal mode but does not appear when you boot in Safe Mode, then suspect that Config.sys, Autoexec.bat, System.ini, and Win.ini are the sources of your problem. To eliminate Config.sys or Autoexec.bat as the source of the problem, boot using the Step-by-step confirmation option on the startup menu. To eliminate Win.ini or System.ini as the source of the problem, use the following procedure:

1. Change the name of the System.ini file in the Windows folder to System.sav.

2. Find the System.cb file in the Windows folder, and make a copy of it. Rename the copy System.ini. Do not rename the original System.cb file because you may need it at another time.

3. In the [boot] section of the System.ini file, add this line and then save the file:

   ```
   drivers=mmsystem.dll
   ```

4. Change the name of the Win.ini file in the Windows folder to Win.sav.

5. Restart your computer.

If this works, the problem was in the Win.ini or System.ini files, and you can reexamine these files in detail to determine the exact source of the problem.

NOTE

If your mouse stops working when you copy the System.cb file and rename it System.ini, add the following lines in the specified sections of the new System.ini file:

```
[boot]
mouse.drv=mouse.drv
[386Enh]
mouse=*vmouse,imsmouse.vxd
```

Logged (\Bootlog.txt)   This option is the same as Normal, except that Windows 9x/Me tracks the load and startup activities and logs them to the Bootlog.txt file. A portion of a sample Bootlog.txt file is shown in Figure 12-35. Notice that this file contains information about which components loaded successfully and which did not. This file can be a helpful tool when troubleshooting.

12

A+
OS
2.3
3.1

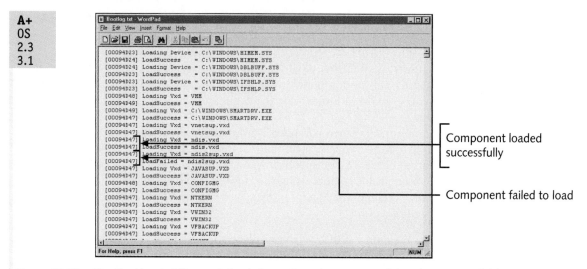

Component loaded successfully

Component failed to load

Figure 12-35 The Bootlog.txt file contains information about successful and unsuccessful boot activities

Safe Mode (Press F5 While Loading) When you have problems with the Windows 9x/Me boot process but no error message appears during the boot, you can use Safe Mode to troubleshoot the problems. You can reach Safe Mode either from the startup menu or by pressing F5 while Windows is loading. Figure 12-36 shows Windows 98 booted into Safe Mode. Safe Mode does not execute entries in the registry, Config.sys, Autoexec.bat, and the [boot] and [386Enh] sections of System.ini. Also, when you enter Safe Mode, Windows 98/Me includes support for networks, but Windows 95 does not.

Figure 12-36 Windows 98 Safe Mode

A+
OS
2.3
3.1

Safe Mode starts Windows 9x/Me with a minimum default configuration to give you an opportunity to correct an error in the configuration. For example, if you selected a video driver that is incompatible with your system, Windows 9x/Me detects the problem when it starts and enters Safe Mode with a standard VGA driver selected. You can then go to Device Manager, select the correct driver, and restart Windows.

From the startup menu, you can choose to enter Safe Mode if you know of a problem you want to correct. For example, if you selected a group of background and foreground colors that makes reading the screens impossible, you can reboot and choose Safe Mode. Safe Mode gives you the standard color scheme along with the VGA mode. Go to Display Properties, make the necessary corrections, and reboot.

Sometimes you will use Safe Mode for troubleshooting when you don't know exactly what the problem is. In that situation, once you are in Safe Mode, use the following checklist:

- Use a current version of antivirus software to scan for a virus.
- Sometimes loading in Safe Mode is all that is needed. Try to reboot the PC in normal mode.
- If the Safe Recovery dialog box appears, select the option of Use Safe Recovery. Windows 9x/Me then attempts to recover from previous boot problems. Try to boot again.
- If you had problems with a device installation before the Windows failure, disable or remove the device in Device Manager. Reboot after disabling each device that you suspect to be a problem.
- If you have just made configuration changes, undo the changes and reboot.
- Look for real-mode drivers or TSRs (programs loaded in Config.sys, Autoexec.bat, or System.ini) that might be causing a problem, and disable them by inserting a semicolon or a REM at the beginning of the command line.
- Try to boot again. If the problem is still not solved, restore the registry. For Windows 95, make backups of System.dat and User.dat. Then overwrite them with System.da0 and User.da0. For Windows 98/Me, use ScanReg to restore the registry from backups. (ScanReg was covered earlier in the chapter.)
- Run ScanDisk to repair errors on the hard drive and optimize it. While in Safe Mode, select Start, Programs, Accessories, System Tools, and ScanDisk. Under Type of Test, select Thorough. (See Figure 12-37.)

12

A+
OS
2.3
3.1

Figure 12-37 Use ScanDisk to check the hard drive for errors

- Run the Defragmenter utility to optimize the drive (covered in Chapter 9).
- For Windows 98, run System File Checker to verify system files.
- For Windows 98/Me, run Automatic Skip Driver Agent to skip loading any driver that causes a problem. Reboot and examine the Asd.log file for recorded errors.
- For Windows 98/Me, use the System Configuration Utility to reduce the system to essentials and reboot. If the problem goes away, restore one item at a time until the problem returns. Then you can identify the item that is the source of the problem.
- Using Explorer, search for files in system folders that have changed recently. To sort file and folder names by date last modified using Explorer, click the Modified column heading. To reverse the sort order, hold down the Ctrl key while clicking the Modified column heading. If software or drivers have been installed recently, suspect that they might be the source of the problem.

Safe Mode with Network Support　　This option allows you access to the network when booting into Safe Mode. It is useful if Windows 95 is stored on a network server and you need to download changes to your PC in Safe Mode. This option is not available on the startup menu in Windows 98/Me, which automatically includes network support.

To eliminate the network connection as a source of a boot problem you are troubleshooting, first boot in Safe Mode without network support and then boot in Safe Mode with network support. If the boot without network support succeeds but the boot with network support gives errors, then suspect that the network drivers might be the source of the problem. For Windows 98/Me, disable the network card in Device Manager to eliminate the network drivers as the source of the problem.

A+
OS
2.3
3.1

Step-by-Step Confirmation   This option asks for confirmation before executing each command in Io.sys, Config.sys, and Autoexec.bat. You can accomplish the same thing by pressing Shift+F8 when the message "Starting Windows 95/98" appears.

Command Prompt Only   This option is not available with Windows Me. Under Windows 95/98, it executes the contents of Autoexec.bat and Config.sys but doesn't start Windows 95/98. You get a DOS prompt instead. Type WIN to load Windows 95/98. This command executes the file Win.com. You can use several switches with the WIN command when troubleshooting the OS. Table 12-12 lists these switches.

Command/Switch	Purpose
WIN /D:M	Starts Windows in Safe Mode
WIN /D:F	Turns off 32-bit disk access; use this option if there appears to be a problem with hard drive access
WIN /D:S	Instructs Windows not to use memory address F000:0, which is used by BIOS
WIN /D:V	Instructs Windows that the system BIOS should be used to access the hard drive rather than the OS
WIN /D:X	Excludes all upper memory addresses from real-mode drivers

Table 12-12   Switches used with the WIN command

12

✔ **A+ EXAM TIP**

The A+ OS exam expects you to know how Win.com is used.

In a troubleshooting situation, try each switch until you find one that works. You can then identify the source of the problem, and can sometimes put entries in the System.ini file to make the switch a permanent part of the load.

Safe Mode Command Prompt Only   This option does not execute the commands in Autoexec.bat or Config.sys. You get a DOS prompt.

Previous Version of MS-DOS   This option loads a previous version of DOS if one is present. You can get the same results by pressing F4 when the message "Starting Windows 95/98" appears. This option is not available in Windows 98 SE or Windows Me.

Troubleshooting with the Startup Menu

If you tried using the tools recommended in the previous sections, but have not yet identified the source of the problem, use the following checklist to troubleshoot using the startup menu:

- Try a hard boot. A soft boot might not do the trick, because TSRs are not always "kicked out" of RAM with a soft boot.
- If you have not already done so, try Safe Mode next.

- Try the Step-by-step confirmation option next. Look for error messages caused by a missing or corrupted driver file. Try not allowing real-mode drivers to load. After the problem command within Autoexec.bat or Config.sys is identified, you can eliminate the command or troubleshoot it. Specific commands in these files and their purposes were covered in Chapter 3.

- Use the Logged option next, and examine the Bootlog.txt file that is created to see if it identifies the problem.

- Try booting using the Command prompt only option. From the command prompt, run the real-mode version of ScanDisk, which you can find in the \Windows\Command folder, to scan the hard drive for errors. From a command prompt, enter this command: C:\Windows\Command\Scandisk. If the Scandisk.exe program on the hard drive is corrupted, use the one on the emergency startup disk.

- From the command prompt in Windows 98/Me, type Scanreg/Fix and try to reboot.

- Next, type Scanreg/Restore and select the latest known good backup of the Windows 9x/Me registry. Try to reboot.

- From the command prompt, you can use the WIN command with the switches listed in Table 12-12. If one of these commands solves the problem, look for real-mode drivers that might be in conflict, eliminating those that you can. Examine Bootlog.txt for errors and try booting from Safe Mode again.

- Try booting with the Safe Mode command prompt only. Remember that when you are in Safe Mode, the registry is not executed. If you suspect a corrupted registry, restore it to its last saved version as you learned to do earlier. Then try the WIN command with or without the switches, as necessary.

Using the Startup Disk for Troubleshooting

If you cannot solve the boot problems by using the troubleshooting utilities within Windows or on the startup menu, use an emergency startup disk to recover from the failed boot. If you do not have an emergency startup disk, create one on another computer and use it to work with the computer that has the problem. Before using the startup disk, it is a good idea to check it for viruses on a working computer by scanning it with antivirus software. If you find a virus on the emergency startup disk, destroy the disk and use a working computer to create a new one.

To use the emergency startup disk, place it in the floppy disk drive and turn on the PC. It will boot to a startup menu or to an A prompt, depending on the version of Windows 9x/Me you are using. Figure 12-38 shows the startup menu.

**A+
OS
2.3
3.1**

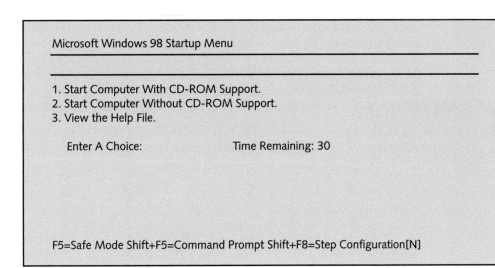

Microsoft Windows 98 Startup Menu

1. Start Computer With CD-ROM Support.
2. Start Computer Without CD-ROM Support.
3. View the Help File.

    Enter A Choice: Time Remaining: 30

F5=Safe Mode Shift+F5=Command Prompt Shift+F8=Step Configuration[N]

Figure 12-38   Windows 98 rescue disk startup menu

If you are using a version for which the startup disk boots to a menu, select the first option, which is to start the PC with CD-ROM support. The OS then examines the system for problems and provides an A prompt where you can enter commands.

If the system failed to boot from the hard drive, the first step in troubleshooting at this point is to see if you can access the hard drive. Enter DIR C: at the A prompt. If this step works, then the problem lies in the software used on the hard drive to boot, including the OS boot record, OS hidden files, and command interface files. If you cannot access the hard drive, the problem is with the partition table, the Master Boot Record, the hard drive, its cabling, or its power source. In this case, you need to examine the hard drive for errors.

Use Fdisk to examine the partition table. If the table is corrupted, most likely you have lost everything on your hard drive. Try using the Fdisk /MBR command to restore the Master Boot Record on the drive. If this does not work, try creating new partitions on the drive and formatting the drive. All data and software on the drive will be lost. If you cannot use Fdisk on the drive, treat the problem as a hardware problem.

After you complete troubleshooting the hard drive, eliminating physical problems with the hard drive subsystem, CMOS, and the partition table, the next step is to run the Windows 9x/Me Setup program. When given the opportunity, select Verify installed components. Setup then restores damaged or missing system files.

**A+
OS
3.2**

Accessing the CD-ROM Drive when Booting from a Floppy Disk   Because Windows is normally loaded from a CD, your emergency startup disk should include the drivers necessary to access the CD-ROM drive. When you are recovering from a failed hard drive, you will not have access to the 32-bit Windows CD-ROM drivers on the hard drive. Windows 98 and later versions of Windows automatically add the real-mode CD-ROM device drivers to their rescue disks, but Windows 95 does not. This section explains how to add this function to a Windows 95 rescue disk.

12

A+
OS
3.2

Two files are required to access a CD-ROM drive while in real mode: the 16-bit device driver provided by the manufacturer of the CD-ROM drive (or a generic real-mode driver that works with the drive), and the 16-bit real-mode OS interface to the driver, Mscdex.exe. The device driver is loaded from Config.sys, and Mscdex.exe is loaded from Autoexec.bat.

✔ **A+ EXAM TIP**

The A+ OS exam expects you to know how to add CD-ROM support to a Windows 95 startup disk.

For example, let's say your CD-ROM drive comes with a floppy disk that includes the following files:

- *Install.exe.* CD-ROM installation program
- *Cdtech.sys.* CD-ROM device driver
- Instruction files and documentation

To make your Windows 95 rescue disk capable of accessing the CD-ROM drive when you boot from this disk, first you need to copy two files to the root directory of the rescue disk: Mscdex.exe from the C:\Windows\Command folder and Cdtech.sys from the floppy disk bundled with your CD-ROM drive. Then add the following command or a similar one to the Config.sys file (the parameters in the command lines are explained in the following list):

```
DEVICE = A:\CDTECH.SYS /D:MSCD001
```

Put the following command or a similar one in your Autoexec.bat file on the floppy disk:

```
MSCDEX.EXE /D:MSCD001 /L:E /M:10
```

The explanations of these command lines are as follows:

- When the program Mscdex.exe executes, it uses the MSCD001 entry as a tag back to the Config.sys file to learn which device driver is being used to interface with the drive. In this case it is Cdtech.sys.
- To Mscdex.exe, the drive is named MSCD001 and is being managed by the driver Cdtech.sys.
- Mscdex.exe will use Cdtech.sys as its "go-between" to access the drive.
- Mscdex.exe also assigns a drive letter to the drive. If you want to specify a drive letter, use the /L: option in the command line. In our example, the CD-ROM drive will be drive E. If you don't use the /L: option, then the next available drive letter is used.
- The /M: option controls the number of memory buffers.
- If the files referenced in these two commands are stored on the floppy disk in a different directory from the root directory, then include the path to the file in front of the filename.

Troubleshooting Windows 9x/Me Hardware and Software

A+
OS
3.3

Now that you know about some of the tools used for troubleshooting, you can learn about the general approaches you should take to troubleshooting problems.

Troubleshooting a PC problem begins with isolating it into one of two categories: problems that prevent the PC from booting and problems that occur after a successful boot. Begin by asking the user questions like the following to learn as much as you can:

- When did the problem start?
- Were there any error messages or unusual displays on the screen?
- What programs or software were you using?
- Did you move your computer system recently?
- Has there been a recent thunderstorm or electrical problem?
- Have you made any hardware, software, or configuration changes?
- Has someone else been using your computer recently?
- Can you show me exactly what you did when this problem occurred? (Have the user reproduce the problem and watch each step.)
- Next, ask whether the PC boots properly. If not, then begin troubleshooting the failed boot.

Here are some general tips for troubleshooting hardware:

- Try rebooting the computer. The problem with the device may disappear when Windows redetects it.
- Frequent system lockups and General Protection Faults might indicate corrupted memory modules. Try using memory-testing software to check for intermittent memory errors, which indicate the module needs replacing. An example of memory-testing software is DocMemory by CST, Inc. (*www.docmemory.com*).
- For external devices such as monitors, printers, and scanners, try turning on the device before turning on the computer. If your computer is on and you are rebooting, leave the device on and online.
- If a device doesn't work with one application, try it with another. If the problem only occurs with one application, the problem is probably not with the hardware device but with that application.
- Check Device Manager for errors it reports about the device. If it reports errors, use the Hardware Troubleshooter in Device Manager to help resolve the problem or go to the Microsoft Web site and search for the error message.
- The driver might be corrupted or need updating. Look on the Web for updated device drivers. Search the device manufacturer's Web site or the Microsoft Web site for information about problems with the device and solutions.

12

▪ Use Device Manager to uninstall the device and then reinstall it. If you uninstall the device and then reboot, Windows should recognize an uninstalled device and automatically launch the Found New Hardware Wizard. If it doesn't launch, then chances are the device is not working or is not PnP.

▪ For PnP devices on expansion cards such as sound cards, modems, and network cards, if you uninstall the device in Device Manager and Windows does not recognize the device when you reboot, the device might not be working. The expansion card needs to be reseated or moved to a different expansion slot. If that doesn't work, the card needs replacing.

▪ If none of these things work, ask yourself what changed since the device last worked. For example, maybe you added another hardware device that conflicts with the one you are using, or maybe you have added software that conflicts with the software that the problem device is using. Try disabling other devices or try uninstalling software that you suspect is causing the problem. Use Automatic Skip Driver Agent to eliminate other devices that might prevent the problem driver from working.

For application software problems, try the following:

▪ Address any error messages that appear when using the software.

▪ If you don't understand the error message, write it down or print it, and then look it up on the Microsoft support Web site or the product manufacturer's Web site. Follow the directions given on the Web sites to resolve the problem.

▪ Read the documentation that came with the application and documents on the manufacturer Web site. Perhaps you are using a function incorrectly.

▪ A virus might be the source of the problem. Run current antivirus software.

▪ Consider that data files might be corrupted. Try creating new data files used by the software.

▪ Consider that the hardware the software is using might have a problem. For the hard drive, run ScanDisk and Defrag and check for free disk space. Delete files in the \Windows\Temp folder. For a device other than the hard drive, try using another application to access the device.

▪ Try uninstalling and reinstalling the software. Back up the data first.

▪ Launch Dr. Watson and then try to reproduce the error with the application. Look in the Dr. Watson log files for clues and search the Microsoft Web site.

▪ Perhaps the application depends on OS files that are corrupted. Try restoring Windows system files. Check the Microsoft Web site for Windows 9x/Me service packs that might resolve the problem. Install all Windows service packs. You might have to reinstall Windows.

- Ask yourself, "When was the last time the software worked?" What happened differently then? Did you get an error message that seemed insignificant at the time? What has happened to your computer since the software last worked? Have you added more software or changed the hardware configuration?
- A configuration file, which contains software settings, might be corrupted. Look for a file with a file extension of .ini, .inf, or .cfg.

If the system is performing slowly, try the following:

- The problem might be caused by lack of resources. If your system is running low on memory or has too many applications open, it might not be able to support a device. A corrupted Windows system file or registry can also cause problems with hardware devices. Try verifying system files or restoring the registry from backup.
- Check the hard drive. Run ScanDisk and Defrag. Delete unneeded files and empty the Recycle Bin. Generally clean up the hard drive, making plenty of room for the swap file and temporary files used by applications.
- Suspect a virus. Run a current version of antivirus software. Clean or delete all files that contain viruses. Restore system files.
- Check for applications loaded at startup that use system resources. Close applications not currently in use.
- Look for icons in the **System Tray**, the small area on the right side of the taskbar at the bottom of the screen. These icons represent small applets that are loaded at startup and take system resources. Keep these icons to a minimum.
- Clean up the registry using the Scanreg /opt command.
- Remove extraneous software such as fancy screen savers and desktop wallpaper and photos.
- Verify that Windows is using optimum caching on the hard drive and CD-ROM drive. Go to the System Properties window and click the Performance tab. Click File System. The File System Properties window appears (see Figure 12-39). On the Hard Disk tab, select Full Read-ahead optimization, and on the CD-ROM tab, select Large cache size.

12

If an application locks up, press Ctrl+Alt+Del and select the program in the Close Program dialog box. Click End Task.

A+
OS
3.3

Figure 12-39   Verify that the hard drive is set for optimal caching

Windows Help and the Microsoft Web Site

A+
OS
3.2

Windows Help might provide useful information when you try to resolve a problem. To access the Troubleshooting tool of Windows Help, click Start, click Help, and then click Troubleshooting. The Help information includes suggestions that can lead you to a solution. For example, in Figure 12-40, the Hardware Troubleshooter suggests that you check to see that the device is not listed twice in Device Manager. If this is the case, you should remove the second occurrence of the device.

Also, the Microsoft Web site (*support.microsoft.com*) (see Figure 12-41), has lots of information on troubleshooting. Search for the device, an error message, a Windows utility, a symptom, a software application, an update version number, or key words that lead you to articles about problem and solutions. You can also go to *www.microsoft.com* to browse for links on hardware and software compatibility. Other sources of help are application and device user and installation manuals, training materials, and the Web sites of application and device manufacturers.

NOTE

For those who are serious about learning to provide professional support for Windows 95 or Windows 98, two good books are *Microsoft Windows 95 Resource Kit* and *Microsoft Windows 98 Resource Kit*, both by Microsoft Press.

A+
OS
3.2

Figure 12-40   Troubleshooter making a suggestion to resolve a hardware conflict

12

Figure 12-41   Microsoft Technical Support Web site

CHAPTER SUMMARY

▶ Windows 9x/Me has a shell and kernel; the Windows 9x/Me core consists of the kernel, the user, and the GDI.

▶ Virtual machines (VMs) are multiple logical machines within one physical machine. If an application crashes or produces another type of error within a VM, only that VM is affected, instead of the entire system.

▶ Although Windows 95/98 supports 16-bit drivers, using 32-bit drivers whenever possible is better.

▶ Before installing Windows 9x/Me as an upgrade, verify that you have enough hard drive space, run ScanDisk or Chkdsk, run antivirus software, back up critical system files, disable TSRs that might cause problems if they run during installation, verify that any network connections work, make sure that the swap file is on a drive compressed with protected-mode software, and decide whether you want to use FAT16 or FAT32.

▶ If Windows is already installed and you want to do a clean install, use the setup screen to install the new OS in a different folder than the one used by the currently installed OS, which is probably \Windows.

▶ Before performing a Windows 98/Me upgrade, check hardware and software compatibility, run antivirus software, and back up your system. The Setup Wizard on the Windows 98 CD will guide you through the setup process. After setup is complete, test installed applications and back up your system again.

▶ When adding new hardware to Windows 9x/Me, use the Add New Hardware Wizard. Select the hardware from a list of devices to use a Windows driver, or click Have Disk to use your own drivers (from a manufacturer's disk or downloaded from the Internet to a folder on your hard drive). Alternately, you can run the setup program provided by the device manufacturer.

▶ For a Windows 9x/Me system to be truly Plug and Play (PnP), the system BIOS must be PnP, all hardware devices and expansion cards must be PnP-compliant, and a 32-bit device driver must be available for any installed hardware device.

▶ Dosstart.bat is a type of Autoexec.bat file that executes when you restart the computer in MS-DOS mode or when you run a program in MS-DOS mode.

▶ An OS that supports protected mode can create a virtual real mode for a 16-bit application so that the application thinks it is the only program running, has all memory available to it, and accesses data using a 16-bit data path. Windows 9x/Me ordinarily runs a 16-bit DOS application in a virtual DOS machine.

▶ Windows keystroke shortcuts are useful for experienced typists who may find them faster than the mouse; they are also useful in troubleshooting situations when the mouse does not work.

▶ In the Display Properties window, you can change the background, screen saver, appearance, icon effects, Active Desktop settings, color range, and display size for the desktop.

▶ Starting with Windows 9x/Me, the Windows registry takes over the essential functions of .ini files. However, Windows 9x/Me still supports System.ini and Win.ini for backward compatibility with legacy hardware devices and legacy software applications.

▶ The registry is contained in two files, System.dat and User.dat. Windows 95 maintains backups of these files, called System.da0 and User.da0, that you can use when troubleshooting. Windows 98/Me keeps compressed backups of the registry and system files in cabinet files named rb000.cab, rb001.cab, and so forth.

▶ Changes in the Control Panel, Device Manager, and other locations in Windows 9x/Me can change the registry automatically. The Regedit utility is used to edit the registry manually.

▶ The Registry Checker (Scanreg.exe) backs up, verifies, and recovers the registry. It automatically backs up the registry every day and keeps the last five days of backups.

▶ The System Configuration Utility (Msconfig.exe) allows you to modify the system configuration temporarily to help with troubleshooting. It reduces the startup process to essentials.

▶ The Dr. Watson utility (Drwatson.exe) helps you troubleshoot applications by trapping errors in log files and taking a snapshot of the system.

▶ The System Configuration Editor (Sysedit.exe) is a text editor used to edit system files. When you run Sysedit, it automatically opens Protocol.ini, System.ini, Win.ini, Config.sys, and Autoexec.bat.

▶ Device Manager lists hardware devices installed on a system. For more information about a specific device in Device Manager, click the device and select Properties.

▶ The five phases of the Windows 9x/Me boot process are BIOS POST and bootstrap, loading the OS, the loading of real-mode VxDs, protected-mode switchover and PnP configuration, and loading remaining components.

▶ Applications are loaded at startup by a shortcut in the StartUp folder, the name of the program file in the Load= or Run= line in Win.ini, or an entry in the registry.

▶ When troubleshooting Windows 9x/Me boot problems, first check error messages, then boot in Safe Mode, then boot to the command prompt using the startup menu, and finally try booting from an emergency startup disk.

▶ To force the Windows 9x/Me startup menu to appear, hold down either the Ctrl key or the F8 key during the boot.

▶ In Logged mode, Windows tracks startup activities and logs them to the Bootlog.txt file.

12

▶ You can reach Safe Mode either from the Windows startup menu or by pressing F5 while Windows is loading.

▶ Safe Mode starts Windows 9x/Me with a minimum default configuration to give you an opportunity to correct an error in the configuration.

▶ Choosing Command Prompt Only from the startup menu executes the contents of Autoexec.bat and Config.sys but does not start Windows. Instead it brings you to a DOS prompt. Use the WIN command to load Windows 9x/Me.

▶ Use the startup disk to recover from a failed boot when you cannot solve the problem using the startup menu or cannot boot from the hard drive. If you do not have a startup disk or the one you have has a virus, use a working computer to create a new disk.

KEY TERMS

For explanations of key terms, see the Glossary near the end of the book.

application programming interface (API) call	kernel	Sysedit
clean install	keys	System.ini
comment	patch	System Tray
Dosstart.bat	PIF (program information file)	upgrade install
Dr. Watson	Protocol.ini	user component
dynamic VxD	service pack	value data
GDI (Graphics Device Interface)	shell	virtual device driver (VxD)
hypertext	shortcut	virtual machine (VM)
initialization files	static VxD	Win.ini

REVIEWING THE BASICS

1. What are the three core components of Windows 9x/Me?

2. Which are preferable to use: 32-bit drivers or 16-bit drivers?

3. What is the function of the Autorun.inf file included on the Windows 9x/Me installation CD? The Setup.exe file? The Readme.txt file?

4. List at least five things you need to do to prepare your hard drive for an upgrade installation of Windows 9x/Me.

5. What are the four types of installations that you can choose during setup of Windows 9x/Me?

6. What are the log files Setuplog.txt, Detlog.txt, and Detcrash.log used for?

7. What type of disk should you always create when prompted to do so during Windows 9x/Me setup? Why is this such an important step?

8. Give two situations in which Windows keyboard shortcuts might be useful.

9. What is the Windows keyboard shortcut to display the startup menu while Windows is loading? To go through step-by-step confirmation of startup? To move from one loaded application to another?

10. How do you access the Display Properties window? What are two settings you can change from this window?

11. When adding hardware to Windows 9x/Me, how do you indicate that you want to use a Windows driver? A manufacturer-provided or downloaded driver?

12. Use the _____ applet in the Control Panel when installing 32-bit software designed for Windows 9x/Me. Use the _____ option on the Start menu when installing older 16-bit software.

13. What is a comment line? How is a comment line noted within a file?

14. Explain the purpose of the System Configuration Utility. How would you use it in troubleshooting?

15. Name four configuration files that Windows 9x/Me includes for backward compatibility with legacy software and hardware.

16. The Windows registry is contained in two files, _____ and _____. The Windows 95 backups of these files are called _____ and _____.

17. Which version of Windows includes the Registry Checker? How often does this utility back up the registry?

18. Explain the difference between the Regedit and Scanreg utilities.

19. Name the files that Sysedit automatically displays for editing. Give a short description of each.

20. List the five phases of the Windows 9x/Me boot process and give a short description of each.

21. Explain how the file Setver.exe is used in Windows 9x/Me.

22. What Msdos.sys entry can be used to backtrack from a Windows 9x/Me installation to the underlying version of DOS? What happens when this entry is set to =0? To =1?

23. List the options on the Windows 9x/Me startup menu and give a short description of each. Which option appears for Windows 95 but not for Windows 98, and why? Which option appears for Windows 95/98, but not for Windows Me?

24. Which startup menu options execute Autoexec.bat and Config.sys? Which do not?

12

25. What Windows utility allows you to control what drivers are loaded during Windows startup?

26. _____ is a Windows utility that can record detailed information about the system, errors that occur, and the programs that caused them in a log file.

27. What parts of the Windows load does Safe Mode not execute?

28. Name two ways to end an application that is hung without rebooting the PC.

29. After using the Windows 98 startup menu to boot the system to a command prompt, what command can you use to load the Windows desktop?

30. What function key do you press during bootup to start Windows 98 in Safe Mode?

THINKING CRITICALLY

1. An application loads at startup. List the steps you would take to stop an application from loading at this time.

2. Place these tools in the order you would use them when troubleshooting the Windows 9x/Me boot process: emergency startup disk, Safe Mode, error messages, and the command prompt.

3. You attempt to install a new hardware device, but Windows 98 locks up during the boot. You remove the device and try to reboot, but Windows 98 still locks up. Which tools do you use to solve the problem and what do you do with them? (Note you might use more than one of these tools.)

    a. Device Manager

    b. System Information utility

    c. Windows 98 startup disk

    d. Scanreg

    e. Registry Checker

HANDS-ON PROJECTS

PROJECT 12-1: Practicing Keystrokes

Disconnect your mouse and reboot your PC, then practice using the keyboard in case you must troubleshoot a system when the mouse does not work.

1. Open Explorer and select the file Io.sys in the root directory of the hard drive. The file will be hidden, so you must unhide it. From the View menu, select Folder Options, click the View tab, and then select Show all files. List the keys you needed to do this step.

2. What is the exact size of the file in bytes, and the date and time the file was last modified?

3. Which key do you press to move down through the logical drives listed in Explorer?

4. Which key do you press to move down through files listed in a folder in Explorer?

PROJECT 12-2: Installing a Windows Component

12

Using the Add/Remove Programs applet in the Control Panel, look for Windows components that are not installed and install one. You need access to the Windows 98 CD, or the files on the CD must be copied to the hard drive or a network drive.

PROJECT 12-3: Using Shortcuts

Create a shortcut on your desktop to Notepad (Notepad.exe), a text editor. Using a second method for creating shortcuts, add a shortcut to the Windows command prompt (Command.com). First, locate the two program files on your hard drive by clicking Start, Find, and using the Find dialog box. Then create the shortcuts. List the steps you took to create each shortcut.

PROJECT 12-4: Using the Windows 9x/Me Startup Menu

As soon as your computer displays the message "Starting Windows 95/98" during the boot process, press the **F8** function key. Select **Logged(\Bootlog.txt)**. After the boot is complete, open the file **Bootlog.txt** and print its contents. Shut down Windows, reboot the computer, and then press **F8** again. Select the **Safe Mode** option, and note the differences in the screen's appearance. Shut down Windows, reboot the computer, and then press **F8** again. This time choose the **Step-by-step confirmation** option. Write down each command that executes.

PROJECT 12-5: Using Windows Utilities and Files

1. Place a shortcut to Task Manager on your desktop. Print a screen shot of the Properties window of the shortcut. Test the shortcut.

2. Cause Sysedit to launch automatically at startup. Print the screen showing how you did this.

3. Edit Msdos.sys so that it automatically displays the startup menu when loading Windows. Print the contents of the file.

PROJECT 12-6: Troubleshooting a Boot Problem

Edit the Config.sys file on your PC. If you are using an installation of Windows 9x/Me that does not use a Config.sys file, then create one. Enter a command line in the file that you know will cause an error. Boot the PC. Press **F8** during the boot, and walk through the boot process to demonstrate how this procedure can help you diagnose a problem with startup files.

Correct the command line in Config.sys, reboot, and walk through each command in the boot process.

PROJECT 12-7: Tools for Troubleshooting a Device Driver

Using Automatic Skip Driver Agent (ASDA), disable one or more devices at startup. Print a screen shot of ASDA showing the disabled devices. Reboot and verify that the devices are not available. Using ASDA, enable the devices, reboot, and verify that the devices work.

Be sure you have the drivers for the devices available on the hard drive, floppy disk, or CD. Using Device Manager, uninstall a device. Print a screen shot of Device Manager showing that the device is not installed. Reinstall the device and verify that it is working.

PROJECT 12-8: Preparing a Hard Drive for the Installation of Windows 9x/Me

Do the following to prepare a hard drive for a new installation of Windows 9x/Me:

1. Boot from a Windows 9x/Me startup disk, and then use Fdisk to create primary and extended partitions on the drive. The primary partition will contain drive C. If there is room on the drive, create two logical drives in the extended partition.

2. Format all three logical drives, placing system files on drive C.

3. Verify that you can boot to drive C, get a C prompt, and access all three drives.

4. Use the DIR command to print a directory of each drive to a local printer. Use these or similar commands: DIR C:>PRN, DIR D:>PRN, and DIR E:>PRN.

5. Using ScanDisk, scan each logical drive disk surface for errors.

This project requires that you completely erase everything on your hard drive. If you have important data on the drive, don't do this project!

CAUTION

PROJECT 12-9: Installing Windows 9x/Me

Follow the instructions in this chapter to install Windows 9x/Me using a Typical installation. Create the rescue disk when prompted to do so. Write down each decision you have to make as you perform the installation. If you get any error messages during the installation, write them down and list the steps you took to recover from the error. How long did the installation take?

12

Understanding and Installing Windows 2000 and Windows NT

Windows NT, Windows 2000, and Windows XP share the same basic Windows architecture and have similar characteristics. Windows NT introduced a new file system, NTFS, that represents a break with past Windows operating systems; Windows 2000 and Windows XP use it as well. Windows 2000 is the culmination of the evolution of Microsoft operating systems from the 16-bit DOS operating system to a true 32-bit, module-oriented operating system, complete with desktop functionality, user-friendly Plug and Play installations, and other easy-to-use features. Windows XP includes additional support for multimedia, Plug and Play, and legacy software, making the final step for Microsoft to announce the merging of Windows 9x/Me and Windows NT operating systems into a single OS. (There will be no future updates to Windows 9x/Me, as Microsoft considers this OS a legacy technology.) This chapter lays the foundation for understanding the architecture of Windows NT/2000/XP and then shows you how to install Windows 2000 Professional. You will also learn how to install hardware and software under Windows 2000. Because a PC support technician occasionally sees Windows NT still used, the last part of the chapter covers Windows NT installation and support.

Windows NT/2000/XP Architecture

A+
OS
1.1

For the corporate desktop or home PC, in most cases you would choose Windows XP rather than Windows 2000. However, if you must select between Windows 98 and Windows 2000, Windows 2000 is the better choice for the corporate desktop. Because of its improved power management, Windows 2000 is also a better choice for notebook computers. For the business environment, Windows 2000 is more secure and reliable and offers better support for very large hard drives. Windows 98 is the better choice for the home PC. Windows 98 works better than Windows 2000 with games, music, and video, and supports the widest variety of hardware and software products.

Windows 2000 includes four operating systems:

> ✔ **A+ EXAM TIP**
>
> Microsoft offers several operating systems designed to run on servers, including Windows NT Server, Windows 2000 Server, and Windows 2003 Server. None of the server operating systems is covered on the A+ exams.

- *Windows 2000 Professional* was designed to replace both Windows 9x and Windows NT Workstation as a personal computer desktop or notebook OS. It is an improved version of Windows NT Workstation, using the same new technological approach to hardware and software, and has all the popular features of Windows 9x, including Plug and Play.
- *Windows 2000 Server* is the improved version of Windows NT Server and is designed as a network operating system for low-end servers.
- *Windows 2000 Advanced Server* is a network operating system that has the same features as Windows 2000 Server but is designed to run on more powerful servers.
- *Windows 2000 Datacenter Server* is a network operating system that is a step up from Windows 2000 Advanced Server. It is intended for use in large enterprise operations centers.

Now let's look at the architecture of Windows NT/2000/XP in more detail, including how the OS relates to applications, networking features, and the management of hard drives and memory.

Windows NT/2000/XP Modes

Windows NT/2000/XP operates in two modes, user mode and kernel mode, which each take advantage of different CPU functions and abilities (see Figure 13-1). This section explains both modes.

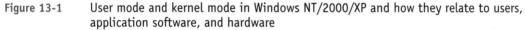

Figure 13-1   User mode and kernel mode in Windows NT/2000/XP and how they relate to users, application software, and hardware

User Mode

User mode is a processor mode in which programs have only limited access to system information and can access hardware only through other OS services. The OS has several **subsystems**, or OS modules, that use this mode and interface with the user and with applications. The Windows tools you use, such as Windows Explorer, run primarily in user mode. In Figure 13-1, note the Win32 subsystem, which is probably the most important user mode subsystem because it manages and provides an environment for all 32-bit programs, including the user interface (such as the one for Explorer). The Win32 security subsystem provides logon to the system and other security functions, including privileges for file access.

All applications relate to Windows NT/2000/XP by way of the Win32 subsystem, either directly or indirectly. Figure 13-2 shows how various programs that run under Windows NT/2000/XP interact with subsystems. For instance, each legacy DOS application resides in its own NTVDM. An **NTVDM (NT virtual DOS machine)** is a carefully controlled environment that Windows NT/2000/XP provides. In it a DOS application can interface with only one subsystem and cannot relate to anything outside the system, so it is similar to the Windows 9x virtual DOS machine introduced in Chapter 12. All 16-bit Windows 3.x applications reside in a **Win16 on Win32 (WOW)** environment. Within the WOW, these 16-bit applications can communicate with one another and the WOW, but that's as far as their world goes. Figure 13-2 shows three 16-bit Windows 3.x applications residing in a WOW that resides in one NTVDM. Because each DOS application expects to run as the only application on a PC, each has its own NTVDM.

13

Figure 13-2 Environment subsystems in Windows NT/2000/XP user mode include NTVDMs for DOS and Windows 3.x applications and optional multithreading for 32-bit applications

You can see in Figure 13-2 that 32-bit applications do not require an NTVDM and can relate to the Win32 subsystem directly, because they are written to run in protected mode. They can also use a single line of communication (called single-threading) with the Win32 subsystem or multiple lines for interfacing (called **multi-threading**) with the Win32 subsystem, depending on what the process requests. A **thread** is a single task that the process requests from the kernel, such as the task of printing a file. A **process** is a program or group of programs that is running, together with the system resources assigned to it, such as memory addresses, environmental variables, and other resources. Sometimes a process is called an instance, such as when you say, "Open two instances of Internet Explorer." Technically, you are saying to open two Internet Explorer processes. An example of multithreading is Microsoft Word requesting that the subsystem read a large file from the hard drive and print a job at the same time. Single-threading happens when the application does not expect both processes to be performed at the same time but simply passes one request followed by another.

Kernel Mode

Kernel mode is a processor mode in which programs have extensive access to system information and hardware. Kernel mode is used by two main components: the HAL and a group of components collectively called executive services. The **HAL (hardware abstraction layer)** is the layer between the OS and the hardware. The HAL is available in different versions, each designed to address the specifics of a particular

CPU technology. **Executive services** interface between the subsystems in user mode and the HAL. Executive services components manage hardware resources by way of the HAL and device drivers. Windows NT/2000/XP was designed to port easily to different hardware platforms. Because only the components operating in kernel mode actually interact with hardware, they are the only parts that need to be changed when Windows NT/2000/XP moves from one hardware platform to another.

Applications in user mode have no access to hardware resources. In kernel mode, executive services have limited access to hardware resources, but the HAL primarily interacts with hardware. Limiting access to hardware mainly to the HAL increases OS integrity because more control is possible. With this isolation, an application cannot cause a system to hang by making illegal demands on hardware. Overall performance is increased because the HAL and executive services can operate independently of the slower, less efficient applications using them.

Networking Features

A+
OS
4.1

✔ **A+ EXAM TIP**

The A+ OS exam expects you to know all the key terms in this section.

A workstation running Windows NT/2000/XP can be configured to work as one node in a workgroup or one node on a domain. A **workgroup** is a logical group of computers and users that share resources (Figure 13-3), where administration, resources, and security on a workstation are controlled by that workstation. Each computer maintains a list of users and their rights on that particular PC. A Windows **domain** is a group of networked computers that share a centralized directory database of user account information and security for the entire set of computers (Figure 13-4). A workgroup uses a **peer-to-peer** networking model, and a domain uses a **client/server** networking model. Using the client/server model, the directory database is controlled by a Network Operating System (NOS). Popular NOSs are Windows Server 2003, Windows 2000 Server, Novell NetWare, Unix, Linux, and Mac OS. Windows for the desktop has network client software built in for Windows (Microsoft Client), Mac (AppleTalk Client), and Novell NetWare (Client for NetWare). Alternately, for Novell NetWare, you can install Novell's version of its client software. You should also know that Windows XP does not include AppleTalk Client.

In a Windows NT Server, Windows 2000 Server, or Windows Server 2003 domain, a network administrator manages access to the network through a centralized database. In Figure 13-4, you see the possible different components of a Windows domain. Every domain has a **domain controller**, which stores and controls a database of (1) user accounts, (2) group accounts, and (3) computer accounts. This database is called the directory database or the **security accounts manager (SAM)** database.

Because the domain controller database is so important, Windows allows backup copies of the database to exist on more than one computer in the domain. Under Windows NT, a network can have a primary domain controller and one or more backup domain controllers. The **primary domain controller (PDC)** holds the original

13

A+
OS
4.1

directory database, and read-only copies are stored on **backup domain controllers (BDCs)**. An administrator can update the database on the PDC from any computer on the network, and the BDCs later get a copy of the updated database.

With Windows 2000, a network can have any number of domain controllers, each keeping a copy of the directory that can be edited. An administrator can update the directory on any one of these domain controllers, which will then communicate the change to the other domain controllers.

Figure 13-3   A Windows workgroup is a peer-to-peer network where no single computer controls the network and each computer controls its own resources

When Windows NT and Windows 2000 domain controllers are on the same network, conflicts can result because of the differences in the way the domain controllers work in each OS. For this reason, Windows 2000 runs in two modes: native mode and mixed mode. **Native mode** is used when no Windows NT domain controllers are present, and **mixed mode** is used when there is at least one Windows NT domain controller on the network. Mixed mode is necessary when a large network is being upgraded from Windows NT to Windows 2000, and some servers have been upgraded but others have not. When you install Windows 2000 Server, the default mode is mixed mode. After the installation, an administrator can choose to migrate to native mode by using the Computer Management console, which you will learn about in the next chapter. Once you change a domain to native mode, you cannot change it back to mixed mode.

A+
OS
4.1

Figure 13-4   A Windows domain is a client/server network where security on each PC or other device is controlled by a centralized database on a domain controller

In addition to native mode and mixed mode, another networking feature new to Windows 2000 is **Active Directory**, a directory database and service that allows for a single administration point for all shared resources on a network. In Windows 2000, the security accounts manager (SAM) database is part of Active Directory. Active Directory can track file locations, databases, Web sites, users, services, and peripheral devices, including printers, scanners, and other hardware. It uses a locating method similar to that used by the Internet. Windows 2000 Server versions provide Active Directory, and Windows 2000 Professional acts as an Active Directory client, or user, of the directory.

Windows NT/2000/XP Logon

Regardless of whether Windows NT/2000/XP computers are networked or not, every Windows NT/2000/XP workstation has an **administrator account** by default. An administrator has rights and permissions to all computer software and ha dware resources and is responsible for setting up other user accounts and assigning them privileges. During the Windows NT/2000/XP installation, you enter a password to the default administrator account. When the workstation is part of a Windows workgroup, you can log on as an administrator after the OS is installed and create local user accounts. If the workstation is part of a domain, a network administrator sets up global user accounts that apply to the entire domain, including giving access

13

A+
OS
4.1

to the local workstations. Local user accounts, as well as other ways to secure a workstation, are covered in Chapter 16.

When Windows NT/2000/XP starts up, you must log on before you can use the OS. For Windows NT/2000, you see the logon screen when you press Ctrl+Alt+Del. Windows XP displays a logon screen by default. To log on, enter a user name and password, and click OK. Windows NT/2000/XP tracks which user is logged on to the system and grants rights and permissions according to the user's group or to specific permissions granted this user by the administrator. If you do not enter a valid account name and password, Windows NT/2000/XP does not allow you access to the system.

How Windows NT/2000/XP Manages Hard Drives

A+
OS
1.4
2.1

Windows NT incorporated new ways of managing hard drives that are also used in Windows 2000 and Windows XP. Windows NT/2000/XP assigns two different functions to hard drive partitions holding the OS (see Figure 13-5). The **system partition,** normally drive C, is the active partition of the hard drive. This is the partition that contains the OS boot record. Remember that the MBR program looks to this OS boot record for the boot program as the first step in turning the PC over to an OS. The other partition, called the **boot partition,** is the partition where the Windows NT/2000/XP operating system is stored.

System partition
(Active partition)

Boot partition

Startup BIOS
looks here for
the boot record
(usually in C:).

Windows NT/
2000/XP OS
is installed here
(usually in \WINNT
or \Windows).

Figure 13-5   Two types of Windows NT/2000/XP hard drive partitions

NOTE

Don't be confused by the terminology here. It is really true that, according to Windows NT/2000/XP terminology, the Windows OS is on the boot partition, and the boot record is on the system partition, although that might seem backward. The PC boots from the system partition and loads the Windows NT/2000/XP operating system from the boot partition.

The system partition and the boot partition can be the same partition or separate partitions. Windows NT/2000/XP is designed to use two partitions in this way so that the Windows system files do not have to be stored on the same partition used to boot the OS. For Windows NT, both partitions can be formatted with either FAT16 or NTFS. Windows 2000/XP uses NTFS, FAT16, or FAT32, although NTFS under

A+
OS
1.4
2.1

Windows NT is not compatible with an NTFS volume under Windows 2000/XP. Know that Windows 9x and DOS cannot read files stored on an NTFS volume. If you want these OSs to access the volume, use the FAT32 file system.

Recall that Windows 9x can use Fdisk to create two partitions: a primary partition and an extended partition. The primary partition contains drive C, and the extended partition can contain several volumes or logical drives. Also recall that each FAT16 volume can be no larger than 2 GB. Using Windows NT/2000/XP, you can have up to four partitions. The first partition must be a primary partition and, if it is the boot device, can have only a single drive C. There can be up to four primary partitions on the drive, each containing a single logical drive. However, one of the four partitions can be an extended partition, which means it can have several volumes or logical drives. Because of the way Windows NT/2000/XP uses the FAT, each FAT16 volume can be up to 4 GB. However, to make the volume compatible with Windows 9x, limit the size to 2 GB.

Now that you've seen how partitions work in Windows NT/2000/XP, let's look at how file systems work.

A Choice of File Systems

Table 13-1 summarizes which file systems are supported by which operating systems. You need this information to plan your Windows NT/2000/XP installation. Windows versions not discussed in this chapter are included for comparison. Windows NT/2000/XP does not support the High Performance File System (HPFS) used by OS/2. If a hard drive is using HPFS, use the Windows NT/2000/XP Convert.exe utility to convert an HPFS partition to an NTFS partition. This program can also convert a FAT16 partition to NTFS.

13

	DOS	Windows 95	Windows 98	Windows NT	Windows 2000	Windows XP
FAT16	X	X	X	X	X	X
FAT32		X (for OSR2)	X		X	X
NTFS				X	X	X

Table 13-1   Operating system support for file systems

Although Windows NT 4.0 does not support FAT32, you can use third-party utility software packages such as FAT32 for Windows NT 4.0 by Winternals (*www.winternals.com*) to manage the interface, making it possible for Windows NT to read from and write to FAT32.

When a hard drive is formatted for NTFS, each cluster can range from 512 bytes on smaller disks to 4K on larger disks. Clusters are numbered sequentially by logical cluster numbers (LCN) from the beginning to the end of the disk. Each cluster number is stored in a 64-bit entry, compared to either 16 bits for FAT16 or 32 bits for FAT32.

The FAT file system uses three components to manage data on a logical drive: the FAT, directories, and data files. In contrast, the NTFS file system uses a database called the **master file table (MFT)** as its core component. The MFT tracks the contents of a logical drive using one or more rows in the table for each file or directory on the drive. As shown in Figure 13-6, the MFT contains information about each file in one record, or row, including header information (abbreviated H in Microsoft documentation); standard information (SI) about the file, including date and time; filename (FN); security information about the file, called the security descriptor (SD); and data about the location of the file. Entries in the MFT are ordered alphabetically by filename to speed up a search for a file listed in the table.

Figure 13-6   The Windows NT/2000/XP file system Master File Table uses three methods to store files, depending on the file size

Referring again to Figure 13-6, note that the data area in the MFT record is 2K for small hard drives but can be larger for larger hard drives. For small files, if the data can fit into the 2K area, the file description and the file's data are fully contained within the MFT.

If the file is moderately large and the data does not fit into the MFT, the data area in the MFT becomes an extended attribute (EA) of the file, which points to the location of the data. The data itself is moved outside the table to clusters called runs. The

A+
OS
1.4
2.1

record in the MFT for this moderately large file contains pointers to these runs. Each data run, or cluster, assigned to the file is given a 64-bit virtual cluster number (VCN). The MFT maps the VCNs for the file onto the LCNs for the drive. This mapping is stored in the area of the MFT record that would have contained the data if the file had been small enough. If the file is so large that the pointers to all the VCNs cannot be contained in one MFT record, then additional MFT records are used. The first MFT record is called the base file record and holds the location of the other MFT records for this file.

Advantages of ÑTFS and FAT

When choosing between the NTFS file system and the FAT16 or FAT32 file system, consider the advantages that NTFS offers over FAT:

- NTFS is a recoverable file system. NTFS retains copies of its critical file system data and automatically recovers a failed file system, using this information the first time the disk is accessed after a file system failure.
- NTFS under Windows 2000/XP supports encryption (encoding files so they can't be deciphered by others) and disk quotas (limiting the hard drive space available to a user). Windows NT NTFS does not support these features.
- NTFS supports compression (reducing the size of files and folders). Windows 9x supports compression of an entire logical drive but not compression of individual files or folders.
- NTFS provides added security in the event you boot from floppy disks:

    - If you boot a PC using a DOS or Windows 9x boot disk, you can access the hard drive of a Windows NT/2000/XP system that uses the FAT file system, but you cannot access an NTFS file system.
    - If you boot a PC using the Windows 2000/XP Recovery Console or the three Windows NT startup disks, you can only access the NTFS file system if you provide an administrator account and password. In fact, if the administrator forgets his or her password to the OS, the hard drive is not accessible; when using Windows tools, the only recourse is to reload the OS.

NOTE Third-party utility software can sometimes help you recover a forgotten administrator password. For example, ERD Commander 2003 by Winternals (*www.winternals.com*) is a bootable operating system on CD that contains Locksmith, a utility that lets you reset a forgotten administrator password. Boot a Windows NT/2000/XP system from the ERD Commander 2003 CD to launch a Windows-like desktop from which you can use several recovery tools.

- NTFS supports mirroring drives, meaning that two copies of data can be kept on two different drives to protect against permanent data loss in case of a hard drive crash. This feature makes the NTFS an important alternative for file servers.

A+
OS
1.4
2.1

- NTFS uses smaller cluster sizes than FAT16 or FAT32, making more efficient use of hard drive space when small files are stored.
- NTFS supports large-volume drives. NTFS uses 64-bit cluster numbers, whereas FAT16 uses 16-bit cluster numbers and FAT32 uses 32-bit cluster numbers. Because the number of bits assigned to hold each cluster number is so large, the cluster number itself can be large, and the table can accommodate very large drives with many clusters. Overall, NTFS is a more effective file system for drives over 1 GB and offers more robust drive compression, allowing compression of individual folders and files.

The advantages of the FAT file system over NTFS include:

- The FAT file system has less overhead than the NTFS file system, and therefore works best for hard drives that are less than 500 MB.
- The FAT file system is compatible with Windows 9x and DOS operating systems. If you plan to use either DOS or Windows 9x on the same hard drive as Windows NT/2000/XP, use the FAT file system so that DOS and Windows 9x can access files used by Windows NT/2000/XP.
- In the event of a serious problem with Windows NT/2000/XP, if you are using FAT on the active partition of the drive, you can boot the PC from a DOS or Windows 9x startup disk and access the drive.

You can choose to have Windows NT/2000/XP use NTFS by directing it to convert the hard drive from FAT to NTFS, or by having Windows NT/2000/XP partition a drive so that one partition of the drive uses the FAT format and the other uses the NTFS format. Windows NT/2000/XP allows you to format logical drives with either FAT or NTFS on the same extended partition.

Installing Windows 2000 Professional

A+
OS
2.1
2.2
2.3

This section explains how to install Windows 2000 on a system with a newly installed hard drive, called a clean install, and how to install Windows 2000 as an upgrade from Windows 9x or Windows NT, called an upgrade installation. Just as with Windows NT and Windows XP, Windows 2000 can be installed to be dual-booted with another OS. Before any type of installation, verify that your system meets the minimum requirements for Windows 2000. You must have at least 650 MB of free space on your hard drive, at least 64 MB of RAM, and a 133-MHz Pentium-compatible CPU or higher.

Planning the Installation

Before you install Windows 2000, you need to select a file system (NTFS, FAT16, or FAT32) and verify that your computer, your peripheral hardware devices, and your

A+
OS
2.1
2.2
2.3

software qualify for Windows 2000. The best way to verify compatibility in these three areas is to visit the Microsoft Web site at *www.microsoft.com/windows2000/professional/howtobuy/upgrading/compat* (see Figure 13-7).

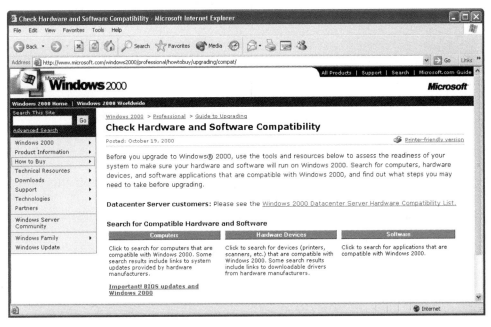

Figure 13-7   Use the Microsoft Web site to verify that your computer, peripheral devices, and applications all qualify for Windows 2000

Here is a brief explanation of why you must verify all three components:

- Windows NT/2000/XP does not use system BIOS to interface with hardware devices. For that reason, a hardware device must be specifically designed to interact with Windows NT/2000/XP. Don't assume that because a device is compatible with Windows NT, it works with Windows 2000. In some instances this is not the case, so check the HCL for Windows 2000 to be sure.
- Software applications must also qualify for Windows 2000. If an application is not listed on the Microsoft Web site, it might still work with Windows 2000. You can verify compatibility by checking with the application manufacturer's Web site or technical support, or you can just install the application under Windows 2000 and test it yourself.
- Your motherboard BIOS must meet the **Advanced Configuration and Power Interface (ACPI)** standards developed by Intel, Microsoft, and Toshiba, which apply to system BIOS, the OS, and certain hardware devices and software to control when a device goes into an inactive state in order to conserve power. To take full advantage of Windows 2000 power management abilities, your system

13

A+
OS
2.1
2.2
2.3

BIOS must be ACPI-compliant. If your BIOS is not ACPI-compliant and you install Windows, Windows does not install ACPI support but installs an older HAL that does not support ACPI. If you later flash your BIOS to make it ACPI-compliant, you have to reinstall Windows to include ACPI support.

NOTE If you have problems with Windows 2000 or NT detecting your hard drive, the problem might be out-of-date system BIOS. Try flashing BIOS and then try the Windows installation again. Chapter 5 gives more information about flashing BIOS.

Microsoft calls a BIOS that is ACPI-compliant a "good BIOS" and puts it on the Good BIOS list. The Microsoft site allows you to search for ACPI-compliant computers by model and manufacturer. The Microsoft Web site tells you if a system is compatible with Windows 2000 and sometimes provides a link to the BIOS Web site where you can download an upgrade to the BIOS. If you are upgrading BIOS, do that before you begin the Windows 2000 installation. You can install Windows 2000 on a system that is not ACPI-compliant, but you cannot use some of its power management features.

Installing Windows 2000 on Networked Computers

✔ A+ EXAM TIP

The A+ OS exam expects you to know about unattended installations and about the convenience of putting the Windows setup files in the \i386 directory on a file server. A server used in this way is called a **distribution server**.

If you are installing Windows 2000 on a networked PC, consider where the Windows 2000 installation files are stored. You can install the OS from a CD in the computer's CD-ROM drive, or you can store the files on a file server on the network and perform the installation from the file server. If you will be doing multiple installations on the network, consider using a file server. Copy all the files from the \i386 folder on the Windows 2000 CD to a folder on the file server and then share that folder on the network. During the installation, when you are ready for the CD, point the setup program to the file server folder instead.

Windows 2000 offers a number of options for installation that can be automated so you don't need to sit at the computer responding to the questions that setup asks during installation. One method, called an **unattended installation**, is performed by storing the answers to installation questions in a text file or script that Windows 2000 calls an **answer file**. A sample answer file is stored on the Windows 2000 CD. If you must perform many installations on computers that have the same Windows 2000 setup, it might be worth your time to develop an answer file to perform unattended installations. How to set up unattended installations is beyond the scope of this chapter.

NOTE To learn how to create an unattended installation of Windows 2000, go to the Microsoft Support Web site (*support.microsoft.com*) and search for the Microsoft Knowledge Base article 216258. You can also search the Web site for other articles on this subject.

A+
OS
2.1
2.2
2.3

Another option is **drive imaging**, sometimes called **disk cloning** or disk imaging, which replicates the drive to a new computer or to another drive on the same computer. All contents of the drive, including the OS, applications, and data, get duplicated to the new drive. To clone a drive after the installation, use the Sysprep.exe utility to remove configuration settings such as the computer name that uniquely identifies the PC. Then clone the entire hard drive to a new PC using third-party drive-imaging software. Examples of drive-imaging software are Drive Image by PowerQuest (*www.powerquest.com*), ImageCast by Innovative Software (*www.imagecast.com*), and Norton Ghost by Symantec Corp. (*www.symantec.com*).

✔ **A+ EXAM TIP**

The A+ OS exam expects you to know about drive imaging.

When installing Windows 2000 on a network, just as with other operating systems, you need to know how to configure the computer to access the network. You should know these things before you begin the installation:

- The computer name and workgroup name for a peer-to-peer network
- The username, user password, computer name, and domain name for a domain network
- For TCP/IP networks, how the IP address is assigned, either dynamically (gets its IP address from a DHCP server when it first connects to the network) or statically (IP address is permanently assigned to the workstation). If the IP address is statically assigned, you need the IP address for the workstation. (DHCP servers, which are used to assign IP addresses when a computer connects to a network, are covered in Chapters 18 and 19.)

Upgrade or Clean Install?

If you are installing Windows 2000 on a new hard drive, then you are doing a clean install. If Windows 9x or Windows NT is already installed on the hard drive, then you have three choices:

- You can perform a clean install, overwriting the existing operating system and applications.
- You can perform an upgrade installation.
- You can install Windows 2000 in a second partition on the hard drive and create a dual-boot situation.

Each of these options has advantages and disadvantages.

Clean Install, Erasing Existing Installations

A clean install that overwrites the existing installation has some advantages; one advantage is that you get a fresh start. With an upgrade, problems with applications or the OS might follow you into the Windows 2000 load. If you erase everything (format the hard drive), then you are assured that the registry as well as all applications are as clean as possible. The disadvantage is that, after Windows 2000 is installed, you must reinstall application software on the hard drive and restore the data from backups. If you do a clean

13

A+
OS
2.1
2.2
2.3

install, you can choose to format the hard drive first, or simply do a clean install on top of the existing installation. If you don't format the drive, the data will still be on the drive, but the previous operating system settings and applications will be lost.

If you decide to do a clean install, verify that you have all the application software CDs or floppy disks and software documentation. Back up all the data, and verify that the backups are good. Then, and only then, format the hard drive or begin the clean install without formatting the drive. If you don't format the hard drive, be sure to run a current version of antivirus software before you begin the installation.

Upgrading the Existing Operating System   All versions of Windows 9x and Windows NT Workstation 3.51 and higher can be upgraded to Windows 2000. The advantages of upgrading are that all applications and data and most OS settings are carried forward into the new Windows 2000 environment, and the installation is faster. If you perform an upgrade, you must begin the installation while you are in the current OS. If you are working from a remote location on the network, you cannot do an upgrade.

You cannot upgrade a compressed Windows 9x drive. You must uncompress it before you can upgrade to Windows 2000 Professional.

Creating a Dual Boot   The ability to boot from both Windows NT/2000 and another OS, such as DOS or Windows 9x, is called a **dual boot**. Don't create a dual boot unless you need two operating systems, such as when you need to verify that applications and hardware work under Windows NT/2000 before you delete the old OS. Windows NT/2000 does not support a second operating system on the same partition, so you must have at least two partitions on the hard drive. All applications must be installed on each partition to be used by each OS.

Recall that Windows NT/2000/XP can support up to four partitions on a hard drive. All four can be primary partitions (which can have only one logical drive), or one of the partitions can be an extended partition (which can have several logical drives). For the first primary partition, the active partition, that drive is drive C. For a dual boot with Windows 2000, one OS is installed in the active partition on drive C, and the other OS is installed on another partition's logical drive.

You must decide what file system to use for the Windows 2000 partition: FAT16, FAT32, or NTFS. If you choose to use a dual boot with DOS, use FAT16 for the Windows 2000 partition so that DOS can read the partition. For Windows 9x, use either the FAT16 or FAT32 file system, not NTFS, so that Windows 9x can read the Windows 2000 partition.

Windows 2000 uses the latest version of NTFS, the one introduced by Windows NT Server 4.0, NTFS Version 5.0 (NTFS5). NTFS4 is used by Windows NT Workstation 4.0. The NTFS5 version includes numerous enhancements over previous versions but cannot be read by Windows NT Workstation 4.0 unless Windows NT 4.0 Service Pack 4 is applied. For this reason, if you create a dual boot between Windows 2000 and Windows NT using NTFS for both operating systems, you can encounter the following problems:

- The file system data structures might not be the same.
- Disk utilities, such as Chkdsk under Windows NT, might not work on the drive.
- Windows NT cannot read encrypted files and folders.
- You cannot use Windows 2000 to repair a damaged Windows NT 4.0 NTFS partition. Windows NT 4.0 only allows access to an NTFS drive from within Windows NT 4.0 and not from any other OS.

For these reasons, using a dual boot between Windows 2000 and Windows NT is not recommended.

Planning an Upgrade from Windows 9x to Windows 2000

Because the Windows 9x registry and the Windows 2000 registry are not compatible, transfer of information from one to the other will not be as complete as with an upgrade from Windows NT to Windows 2000, where information in the registry is easily ported into the new OS. Until you perform the upgrade, you cannot know exactly what Windows 2000 was able to import from Windows 9x, although Setup might inform you or ask for additional help in some cases.

To test your system and be alerted to potential problems, running the Check Upgrade Only mode of Windows 2000 Setup is a good idea. This does not actually install Windows 2000 but instead just checks for compatibility and reports any upgrade issues with hardware or software. Run the utility to produce the report, Upgrade.txt, which is stored in the C:\Windows directory.

13

Hardware Compatibility   One issue to consider in upgrading from Windows 9x to Windows 2000 is that Windows 2000 does not import drivers from Windows 9x, because they are generally not compatible. As you learned earlier, a hardware device must be designed to be compatible with Windows 2000. If you want to install a device but its driver is not included in Windows 2000, you might have to download a driver from either the Microsoft site or the manufacturer's Web site. Check for compatibility and make sure you have all the required device drivers before you begin your Windows 9x-to-Windows 2000 upgrade. Windows 2000 attempts to carry over installed hardware devices that are compatible with Windows 2000, asking for new drivers where necessary; it ignores and does not install incompatible devices.

If Setup cannot find a critical driver such as the driver to control a hard drive, it cancels the upgrade.

Another thing you need to know is that Windows 2000 deletes all the Windows 9x system files and replaces them with Windows 2000 system files in the same directory.

Software Compatibility   Basically, the main advantage of performing an upgrade from Windows 9x to Windows 2000 rather than doing a clean install of Windows 2000 is that you do not have to reinstall software that is compatible with Windows 2000. If an application was written for Windows 9x, it might or might not be compatible with Windows 2000. Windows 9x applications store registry data differently from Windows 2000 applications and may rely on APIs specific to Windows 9x. If an application doesn't work after you upgrade to Windows 2000, try reinstalling it. If that doesn't work, check the software manufacturer's Web site for a patch or upgrade.

Planning an Upgrade from Windows NT to Windows 2000

Upgrading to Windows 2000 from Windows NT is much easier than upgrading from Windows 9x. However, you need to be aware of some considerations before performing the upgrade:

- If you are upgrading from Windows NT using NTFS, Setup automatically upgrades to the Windows 2000 version of NTFS.
- If you are upgrading from Windows NT using FAT16 or Windows NT with third-party software installed that allows Windows NT to use FAT32, Setup asks you whether you want to upgrade to NTFS.

Hardware Compatibility   Generally, most hardware devices and their corresponding drivers that worked under Windows NT work under Windows 2000 as well, although some third-party drivers might need to be updated for Windows 2000. As always, it is a good idea to check the HCL on the Microsoft Web site or run the Check Upgrade Only mode of Windows 2000 Setup.

Software Compatibility   Nearly all applications that run with Windows NT Workstation 3.51 and later will run with Windows 2000 without modification. Here are some exceptions:

- Antivirus software and third-party network software, both of which must be removed before upgrading to Windows 2000
- Some disk management tools

A+
OS
2.1
2.2
2.3

- Custom tools for power management, which are replaced in Windows 2000 by ACPI. Windows 2000 also provides minimal support for APM (Advanced Power Management), which must be removed before the upgrade. Windows 2000 considers APM a legacy tool, uses it only on notebook computers, and uses only enough APM features to support a notebook computer's battery. With ACPI-compliant BIOS, the BIOS senses information about the system and turns that information over to the OS to make decisions about the system's power management functions.
- Custom solutions that are workarounds for Windows NT not supporting Plug and Play, which are unnecessary in Windows 2000 because it provides complete support for Plug and Play
- Software to monitor and control a UPS (uninterruptible power supply)

Now that you know about advantages and disadvantages of installing Windows 2000 as a clean install and as an upgrade, including issues to consider with specific upgrades, let's look at step-by-step procedures for how to do both.

Steps to Install Windows 2000

✔ **A+ EXAM TIP**

The A+ OS exam expects you to know when Winnt.exe and Winnt32.exe are used for the setup process, and to know the upgrade paths for Windows 2000.

You can use two programs to install Windows 2000: Winnt.exe and Winnt32.exe. Winnt.exe is the 16-bit version of the setup program and Winnt32.exe is the 32-bit version. Both are located in the \i386 directory. You can use Winnt.exe for a clean install on a computer running MS-DOS, but not to perform an upgrade. Use Winnt32.exe for a clean install or an upgrade on a computer running Windows. Regardless of whether you use Winnt.exe or Winnt32.exe, the program executed is called Setup in Windows documentation. Here are the situations in which you can perform a clean install or upgrade:

- To perform a clean install when working at the local computer, you can boot from the Windows CD or run Winnt32.exe or Winnt.exe from a command prompt. Run Winnt.exe only if you have booted into MS-DOS.
- If you want to perform an upgrade, you must be working at the local PC. You can boot from the Windows CD or run the Winnt32.exe program from within Windows 9x or Windows NT Version 4.0. You cannot perform an upgrade for earlier versions of Windows NT.
- When installing Windows from across the network to a remote PC, you can only do a clean install. In this situation, run Winnt32.exe on the local Windows computer to perform a clean install on the remote PC.

13

A+
OS
2.1
2.2
2.3

Also, before you begin any OS installation, access CMOS setup and verify these settings:

- If you want to begin the installation by booting from the Windows CD, verify that the boot sequence is first the CD-ROM, then the hard drive.
- Disable any virus protection setting that prevents the boot sector from being altered.
- Also, because Windows 2000 prefers to handle its own Plug and Play hardware installations without the help of BIOS, Microsoft recommends that you disable the Plug and Play feature of your motherboard BIOS.

Next we look at the step-by-step procedures for clean installations and upgrades.

If you are having problems with Windows Setup detecting your hard drive, the problem might be out-of-date BIOS. Try flashing BIOS and then attempting the Windows installation again. Chapter 5 gives more information about flashing BIOS.

Clean Installation

The Windows 2000 package comes with documentation and a CD. For United States distributions, the package includes a floppy disk to provide 128-bit data encryption. (This disk is not included in distributions to other countries because of laws that prohibit 128-bit data encryption software from leaving the United States.)

If your PC is capable of booting from a CD, then insert the CD and turn on the PC. The Welcome to the Windows 2000 Setup Wizard appears (see Figure 13-8). Select "Install a new copy of Windows 2000," click Next, and proceed to Step 6 in the following procedure. However, if your PC does not boot from a CD and you have a clean, empty hard drive, first create a set of Windows 2000 setup disks to boot the PC and to begin the installation. The remaining installation is done from the CD.

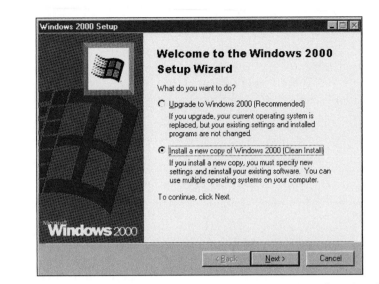

Figure 13-8   Using the Setup Wizard, you can do an upgrade, do a clean install, or create a dual boot

To make the four setup disks, follow these directions:

1. Using a working PC, format four floppy disks.

2. Place the Windows 2000 CD in the CD-ROM drive and a formatted floppy disk in the floppy disk drive. For Windows 9x, click **Start**, then **Run**, and enter this command in the Run dialog box:

```
D:\bootdisk\makeboot.exe A:
```

Substitute the letter of the CD-ROM drive for D: and the letter of the floppy drive for A:, if necessary.

3. Insert new disks in the drive as requested. Label the disks Windows 2000 Setup Disks 1, 2, 3, and 4.

4. Now begin the Windows 2000 installation. Boot the PC from the first setup disk created earlier. You will be asked to insert each of the four disks in turn and then asked to insert the Windows 2000 CD.

5. The Windows 2000 license agreement appears. Accept the agreement and the Welcome screen appears, as shown in Figure 13-8. The setup process is now identical to that of booting directly from the CD. Save the four setup floppy disks in case you have future problems with Windows 2000.

6. Windows 2000 searches the hard drive for partitions and asks which partition to use. If the partitions are not created, it creates them for you. You are asked to decide which file system to use. If the hard drive has already been formatted with the FAT16 or FAT32 file system, you are asked if you want to upgrade to

13

A+
OS
2.1
2.2
2.3

the NTFS file system. Be aware that if you convert the file system to NTFS, you cannot revert to FAT16 or FAT32. You can also convert from FAT16 or FAT32 to NTFS after the installation is complete. If the hard drive is already partitioned and contains a partition larger than 2 GB, and you select the FAT file system, then Windows 2000 automatically formats the drive using the FAT32 file system. It puts the entire partition in one logical FAT32 drive.

7. During installation, you are given the opportunity to change your keyboard settings for different languages, enter your name and company name, and enter the product key found on the CD case. You are also given the opportunity to enter date and time settings and an administrator password. Be sure to remember the password. It is required when you log on to the system later to set up new users and perform other administrative tasks. If you forget it and no one else has administrator privileges, you might have to reinstall Windows 2000.

8. If Setup recognizes that you are connected to a network, it provides the Networking Settings window to configure the computer to access the network. If you select Typical settings, then Setup automatically configures the OS for your network. If the configuration is not correct after the installation, you can make changes.

9. At this point in the installation, you are asked to remove the Windows 2000 CD and click **Finish**. The computer then restarts. After Windows 2000 loads, it completes the process of connecting to the network. You are asked questions about the type of network. (For example, does the network use a domain or workgroup?) When the configuration is complete, verify that you have access to the network if there is one.

Clean Install When the Hard Drive Has an Operating System Installed

If you use Windows 9x and your PC automatically detects a CD in the CD-ROM drive, follow these directions to do a clean install when another OS is already installed:

1. Using antivirus software, scan memory and your hard drive for viruses.

2. Insert the Windows 2000 CD in the CD-ROM drive. If your PC detects the CD, a window opens with the message "This CD-ROM contains a newer version of Windows than the one you are presently using. Would you like to upgrade to Windows 2000?" Answer **No**. The Install Windows 2000 window appears (see Figure 13-9).

A+
OS
2.1
2.2
2.3

Figure 13-9   Windows 2000 Setup window

3. Click **Install Windows 2000**. The Windows Setup Wizard opens, as shown in Figure 13-8. Select **Install a new copy of Windows 2000 (Clean Install)**. Windows displays the license agreement and asks you to accept it. Enter the product key from the back of the CD case, and you will be given the opportunity to select special options.

4. After a reboot, the installation continues as described earlier.

If your PC does not automatically recognize a CD, then insert the CD in the CD-ROM drive and do the following:

1. Click **Start** and then click **Run**. In the Run dialog box, enter the command **D:\i386\ winnt32.exe**. Substitute the drive letter of the CD-ROM drive for D:, if necessary.

2. The Windows 2000 Setup Wizard appears, as shown earlier in Figure 13-8. Select **Install a new copy of Windows 2000 (Clean Install)**. The installation continues as described earlier.

13

Upgrade Installation

To upgrade your operating system from Windows 9x or Windows NT using the Windows 2000 CD, first prepare for the installation:

1. Verify that all devices and applications are Windows 2000-compatible. Download and install any patches or upgrades from hardware or software manufacturers.

2. Using antivirus software, scan memory and your hard drive for viruses.

3. Back up all critical system files and data files. Back up the registry in case you need to backtrack to the current installation. If you have important data on your hard drive, back up the data.

4. Close all applications and disable any virus-scanning software. If the hard drive is compressed, decompress the drive.

You are now ready to perform the upgrade. Do the following:

1. Insert the Windows 2000 CD in the CD-ROM drive. If your system is set to detect the CD automatically, it runs the setup program and shows a message asking if you want to upgrade your computer to Windows 2000. Answer **Yes** and the installation begins. If Windows does not detect the CD, click **Start**, then **Run**, enter **D:\i386\winnt32.exe** in the Run dialog box, and then click **OK**. Substitute the drive letter of the CD-ROM drive for D:, if necessary. On the Welcome to Windows 2000 Setup Wizard window, select **Upgrade to Windows 2000 (Recommended)**. Follow the directions on the screen.

2. Windows 2000 Setup performs the upgrade in two major stages: the Report phase and the Setup phase. During the Report phase, Windows 2000 Setup scans the hardware, device drivers, current operating system, and applications for compatibility. In this phase, you are given the opportunity to provide third-party DLL files that make a device driver or application Windows 2000-compatible, if Setup recognizes that the device driver or application will not work without the fix. Next, Setup generates a report of its findings. If its findings indicate that an unsuccessful installation is likely, you can abandon the installation and perhaps check with hardware and software manufacturers for fixes. In the Report phase, Setup also creates an answer file that it uses during the Setup phase, installs the Windows 2000 boot loader, and copies Windows 2000 installation files to the hard drive.

A+
CORE
2.1
2.2
2.3

3. The PC reboots and the Setup phase begins, which has two parts: the Text mode and the GUI mode. In the Text mode, Setup installs a Windows 2000 base in the same folder that the old OS is in, usually C:\Windows for Windows 9x and C:\WINNT for Windows NT. The target folder cannot be changed at this point. Setup then moves the Windows registry and profile information to %windir%\setup\temp, where %windir% is the path to the Windows folder, most likely C:\Windows\setup\temp.

4. The PC reboots again and the GUI mode of Setup begins. Setup reads information that it saved about the old Windows system and makes appropriate changes to the Windows 2000 registry. It then migrates application DLLs to Windows 2000 and reboots for the last time. The upgrade is complete.

NOTE   During installation, Windows 2000 records information about the installation to a file called Setuplog.txt. This file is useful when troubleshooting any problems that occur during installation.

After the Installation: Backing Up the System State

A+
OS
1.5
2.1
2.2
2.3
2.4

After you have completed installing Windows 2000, do the following:

1. Access the Internet and download and install all OS service packs, updates, and patches.

2. Verify that all hardware works and install additional devices, such as printers, as needed.

3. Create user accounts for Windows 2000. (Chapter 16 covers creating user accounts.)

4. Install additional Windows components and install applications. (Don't attempt to install applications and components before you first download and install service packs and patches.)

5. Verify that the system functions properly, and back up the system state. This backup of the system can later help you recover the OS in the event of system failure. (You will learn more about recovering from system failure in the next chapter.)

13

APPLYING CONCEPTS

Windows 2000 calls the files critical to a successful operating system load the **system state data**. This includes all files necessary to boot the OS, the Windows 2000 registry, and all system files in the %SystemRoot% folder, the folder in which Windows 2000 is installed. For an upgrade, the folder will most likely be C:\Windows, the original Windows folder before the upgrade. For a clean install, the default folder is C:\WINNT. When you back up the system state data, you cannot select which files you want to back up because Windows 2000 always backs up all of them. Here is the process:

1. Click **Start**, point to **Programs**, **Accessories**, **System Tools**, and then click **Backup**. The Backup dialog box opens. Click the **Backup** tab (see Figure 13-10).
2. Check the **System State** box in the list of items you can back up. Notice in Figure 13-10 that the system state includes the boot files and the registry. It also includes the COM+ (Component Object Model) Registration Database, which contains information about applications and includes files in the Windows folders.
3. Select the destination for the backup. You can back up to any media, including a folder on the hard drive, Zip drive, tape drive, or network drive. Click **Start Backup** to begin the process.

   Later, if you have problems with a corrupted Windows 2000 installation, you can click the Restore tab in the Backup dialog box illustrated in Figure 13-10. Use this Restore window to restore the system to its state at the last backup.

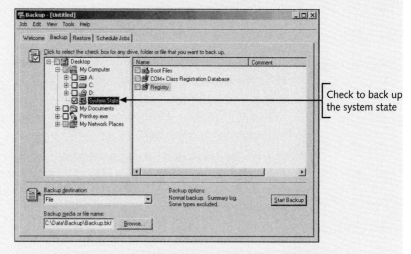

Figure 13-10   Back up the Windows 2000 registry and all critical system files

A+
OS
1.5
2.1
2.2
2.3
2.4

NOTE When you back up the system state, the registry is also backed up to the folder %SystemRoot%\repair\RegBack. If you later have a corrupted registry, you can copy files from this folder to the registry folder, which is %SystemRoot%\System32\Config.

Installing Hardware and Applications Under Windows 2000

A+
OS
2.1
2.4

This section discusses how to install hardware and software with Windows 2000 and includes special considerations for legacy hardware. As with Windows 98, Windows 2000 has an Add New Hardware Wizard that automatically launches when new hardware is detected. Software is best installed from the Add/Remove Programs icon of the Control Panel.

Installing Hardware

Windows 2000 can automatically detect and install Plug and Play (PnP) devices, as long as you also have PnP-compliant drivers. If a device is PnP, Windows 2000 automatically does the following:

- Identifies the device you are installing
- Determines what system resources the device needs and assigns them so that there are no conflicts with other devices
- Configures the device as necessary
- Loads any device drivers needed to run the device
- Informs the system of any configuration changes

For PnP devices, the Add New Hardware Wizard automatically launches at startup. Any user can complete the installation if the following are true: the device drivers can be installed without user input, all files necessary for a complete installation are present, the drivers have been digitally signed (**digital signatures** are digital codes used to authenticate the source of files), and there are no errors during installation. If one of these conditions is not met, the installation is abandoned until someone with administrator privileges logs on.

Most devices designed to work with Windows 2000 are PnP-compatible. If a device is not PnP and you are logged on with administrator privileges, you can use the Add/Remove Hardware applet in the Control Panel to install the device.

If you are using the Add/Remove Hardware Wizard, you have to provide information such as where the driver for the device is located. Some devices that don't work with Windows 2000 may be completely incompatible and will not work at all. If you

13

A+
OS
2.1
2.4

install a device and have a problem with it, you can attempt to update the device driver as follows:

1. In the Control Panel, double-click the **System** icon. The System Properties dialog box opens. Select the **Hardware** tab (see Figure 13-11).

2. Click the **Device Manager** button. The Device Manager opens, as shown in Figure 13-11. Expand the device class tree by clicking the plus sign, and locate the device for which you want to update a driver. For this example, we are using the floppy disk drive.

3. Right-click the floppy drive and select **Properties** from the shortcut menu (see Figure 13-11).

Figure 13-11 Use Device Manager to access a device's properties

4. The Floppy disk drive Properties dialog box opens (see Figure 13-12). On the **Driver** tab, click **Update Driver**. The Update Device Driver Wizard appears. If an update exists, follow directions on the screen to update the driver.

NOTE

You must be logged on with administrator privileges to make changes from Device Manager.

A+
OS
2.1
2.4

Floppy disk drive Properties   ? ×

General   Driver

Floppy disk drive

Driver Provider: Microsoft
Driver Date: 11/14/1999
Driver Version: 5.0.2183.1
Digital Signer: Microsoft Windows 2000 Publisher

To view details about the driver files loaded for this device, click Driver
Details. To uninstall the driver files for this device, click Uninstall. To update
the driver files for this device, click Update Driver.

[Driver Details...]   [Uninstall]   [Update Driver...]

[OK]   [Cancel]

Figure 13-12   A device's Properties dialog box provides a way to update its drivers

Installing Applications

The process of installing applications in Windows 2000 is not much different than
that of earlier versions of Windows. If you are familiar with the installation wizards
and setup programs used with Windows 9x, you should recognize all but a few
minor details of these same components in Windows 2000.

The Windows 2000 Add/Remove Programs utility looks significantly different
than in Windows 9x, and it provides more options. From the Windows 2000
Add/Remove Programs window, you can change or remove presently installed programs (see Figure 13-13); add new programs from a CD, a floppy disk, or from
Microsoft over the Internet; and add or remove Windows components. In Figure
13-13, note the expanded drop-down menu in the upper-right corner, which shows
how you can sort the view of presently installed programs.

13

Figure 13-13   Making changes to currently installed programs

Supporting Windows NT

A+
OS
2.1
2.3
3.1
3.2

Though Windows 2000 and Windows XP are gradually replacing Windows NT, Windows NT is still around; therefore, knowing how to support it is important. Much of what you learn in this section carries over to later Windows OSs. First we will look at different ways to install Windows NT, and then we'll look at how to troubleshoot the Windows NT boot process.

Installing Windows NT as the Only OS

✔ **A+ EXAM TIP**

The A+ OS exam does not have extensive coverage of Windows NT, but you should know about installing it and supporting the boot process.

Windows NT comes with three disks that contain a simplified version of Windows NT, enough to boot a PC. If the hard drive does not contain an OS, the installation begins by booting from these three disks. After Windows NT is loaded from these three disks, it can access the CD-ROM drive, and installation continues from the CD. The program on the CD executed at that point is Winnt.exe, a 16-bit program. A faster version of Winnt.exe on the CD named Winnt32.exe, a 32-bit program, can be used instead of Winnt.exe in certain situations. Winnt32.exe can be run only after Windows NT has already been installed for the first time; it is used to upgrade from an older NT version to a newer version or to reinstall a corrupted version. It must be executed from within Windows NT.

The three startup disks can later be used to boot the PC if files on the hard drive become corrupted. You can also create a new set of bootable disks.

A+
OS
2.1
2.3
3.1
3.2

The Windows NT installation files are stored in the \i386 directory on the CD-ROM drive. If hard drive space is plentiful, you can copy the contents of the \i386 directory and its subdirectories to the hard drive and install from there, which is faster because access to the hard drive is faster than access to the CD-ROM drive. If the computer is connected to a network, the contents of the \i386 directory can be copied to a network server, and the Winnt.exe program can be executed from the server to install Windows NT on the PC, if certain conditions exist. (Installations from servers are not covered in this chapter.) To perform an upgrade to Windows NT, boot the OS and execute the Winnt.exe program on the Windows NT CD.

Troubleshooting the Windows NT Boot Process

In this section, you will learn how to troubleshoot the Windows NT boot process and about some diagnostic tools that you can use for maintenance and troubleshooting. Many general troubleshooting tips you learned in earlier chapters apply to Windows NT as well. Troubleshooting the Windows 2000 boot process is covered in Chapter 14.

The following list includes things you can do and the order in which you should do them to troubleshoot a failed Windows NT boot. You will learn more about these tools and processes later in this section. Windows NT does not have a Safe Mode as does Windows 9x, nor does it have several of the useful troubleshooting utilities of Windows 9x that you learned about in the last chapter.

NOTE

As Windows NT/2000/XP is booting, if it thinks there is a problem you should know about or the system is set for a dual boot, a **boot loader menu** appears and gives you options such as which OS you want to load or how you want to handle a problem.

13

APPLYING CONCEPTS

To recover from a failed Windows NT boot:

- If the Windows NT boot loader menu appears, use the Last Known Good configuration to return to the last registry values that allowed for a successful boot. Any configuration changes since the last good boot will be lost.
- If you cannot boot from the hard drive, boot using the three boot disks that came with the OS. If you don't have these three disks, you can create them on a working PC. Check for corrupted boot and system files that you can replace. (How to create the three boot disks is covered later in this section.)
- Boot from the three disks, and select the option "To repair a damaged Windows NT version 4.0 installation."

A+
OS
2.1
2.3
3.1
3.2

- Try reinstalling Windows NT in the same folder it currently uses. Tell the Setup program this is an upgrade.
- As a last resort, if you are using the NTFS file system and you must recover data on the hard drive, move the hard drive to another system that runs Windows NT and install the drive as a secondary drive. You might then be able to recover the data.

Last Known Good Configuration

Each time Windows NT boots and the first logon is made with no errors, the OS saves a copy of the hardware configuration from the registry, which is called the **Last Known Good configuration**. (All hardware configuration sets stored in the registry, including the Last Known Good, are called control sets.) If an error occurs the next time the PC boots, it can use the Last Known Good configuration.

The key in the registry that contains the Last Known Good configuration is HKEY_LOCAL_MACHINE\HARDWARE.

If Windows NT detects the possibility of a problem, it adds the Last Known Good option to the Windows NT boot loader menu. You can select this Last Known Good option to revert to the control set used for the last good boot. For example, if you install a new device driver, restart Windows NT, and find that the system hangs, you can use the Last Known Good option to revert to the previous configuration.

Because the configuration information is not saved to the Last Known Good control set until after the logon, don't attempt to log on if you have trouble with the boot. Doing so causes the Last Known Good to be replaced by the current control set, which might have errors.

For example, if you install a new video driver, restart Windows, and find the screen very difficult to read, don't log on. Instead, press the reset button to reboot the PC. When given the choice, select Last Known Good from the boot loader menu.

To prevent hard drive corruption, if you have problems booting Windows NT, wait for all disk activity to stop before pressing the reset button or turning off the PC, especially if you are using the FAT file system.

If you accidentally disable a critical device, Windows NT decides to revert to the Last Known Good for you. You are not provided with a menu choice.

Reverting to the Last Known Good causes the loss of any changes made to the hardware configuration since the Last Known Good was saved. Therefore, it is wise to make one hardware configuration change at a time and reboot after each change. That way, if problems during booting are encountered, only the most recent change is lost. When installing several hardware devices, install them one at a time, rebooting each time.

NOTE

If you have problems booting in Windows NT, don't log on. If you do, you will overwrite your previous Last Known Good.

Windows NT Boot Disks

With Windows 9x and DOS, any single floppy disk could be formatted as a boot disk or system disk. Windows NT is different. It requires three disks to hold enough of Windows NT to boot. However, just as with Windows 9x, you can use Explorer to format a single disk just to hold data or software, but you cannot make the disk a startup disk, as is the case with Windows 9x.

If you try to boot from a disk that has been formatted by Windows NT, this error message appears:

```
BOOT: Couldn't find NTLDR
Please insert another disk
```

If the original three disks to boot Windows NT become corrupted or are lost, you can make extra copies using Winnt32.exe if you are running Windows NT, or using Winnt.exe if you are running another OS, such as DOS or Windows 9x. You do not have to be working on the PC where you intend to use the disks in order to make them, because the disks don't contain unique information for a specific PC.

Creating Windows NT Boot Disks   Do the following to create boot disks using Windows NT:

1. Click **Start**, click **Run**, and then enter one of the following commands in the Run dialog box. Substitute the letter of your CD drive for E in the command line, if necessary:

   ```
   E:\i386\winnt32.exe /ox
   E:\i386\winnt.exe /ox
   ```

The /OX parameters cause the program to create only the set of three disks, without performing a complete installation. In Figure 13-14, you can see the command line from within Windows NT used to create the disks when drive E contains the Windows NT installation CD.

2. The program asks for the location of the installation files. In this example, you would enter E:\i386. You are then prompted to insert three disks. The program creates the disks beginning with disk 3, then 2, then 1.

Windows NT does not have a Safe Mode as does Windows 9x, so if the PC later cannot boot Windows NT from the hard drive, these three disks can be used to load Windows NT, which loads using a generic VGA mode. After Windows NT is loaded, use a fourth disk—the Emergency Repair Disk (ERD)—to restore critical system files to their state at the time the last update was made to the ERD.

13

Figure 13-14   Using Winnt32.exe to create a set of boot disks

The Windows NT Emergency Repair Disk

The **Emergency Repair Disk (ERD)** contains information unique to your OS and hard drive. You are given the opportunity to create the disk during installation. Always create this disk, because it is your record of critical information about your system that can be used to fix a problem with the OS.

The ERD enables restoration on your hard drive of the Windows registry, which contains all the configuration information for Windows. In addition, the disk includes information used to build a command window to run DOS-like commands. The files on the ERD are listed in Table 13-2. Files stored on the ERD are also written to the hard drive during the installation. Using Explorer, you can see the files listed in the *winnt_root*\repair folder.

NOTE

In Microsoft documentation, *winnt_root*\ is the folder that Windows NT is installed in, which most likely is C:\Winnt\.

File	Description
Setup.log	A read-only, hidden system file used to verify the files installed on a system
System._	A compressed file containing part of the registry
Sam._	A compressed file containing some of the security part of the registry
Security._	A compressed file containing some of the security part of the registry
Software._	A compressed file containing software information in the registry
Default._	A compressed file containing part of the registry
Config.nt	The Windows NT version of Config.sys used in creating a command window
Autoexec.nt	The Windows NT version of Autoexec.bat
Ntuser.da_	A compressed file containing information about authorized users of the system

Table 13-2   Files on the Windows NT Emergency Repair Disk

A+
OS
2.1
2.3
3.1
3.2

After the installation, you can create a new ERD or update the current one by using the Rdisk.exe utility in the *winnt_root*\system32 folder. You should update the disk any time you make any major changes to the system, for example, when you install hardware or software. To use the Rdisk.exe utility, click Start, then Run, and then either click Browse or enter the path to the utility. Add the /S option so that the utility also updates the registry.

If Windows NT is stored on drive D, the command line is:

```
D:\Winnt\System32\rdisk.exe /s
```

First, files are updated in the D:\Winnt\Repair directory; then you are given the opportunity to create a new ERD.

Using the Boot Disks and the ERD to Recover from a Failed Boot

In case of problems with the OS, you can do several things to attempt to load Windows NT from the hard drive, which are beyond the scope of this book. However, in the case of a hard drive failure, you can boot from the three boot disks that come with the Windows NT CD or that you made using either Winnt.exe or Winnt32.exe. The Windows NT programs on these disks may also request that you provide the ERD. Insert the first boot disk, and reboot. You will be prompted to insert disk 2, followed by disk 3. The Setup menu in Figure 13-15 then appears. Select the option to repair a damaged installation by pressing R, and follow directions on the screen.

13

```
Windows NT Workstation Setup

Welcome to Setup.
The Setup program for the Microsoft(R) Windows NT(TM) OS version 4.0
prepares Windows NT to run on your computer.

        *To learn more about Windows NT Setup before continuing, press F1
        *To set up Windows NT now, press ENTER
        *To repair a damaged Windows NT version 4.0 installation, press R
        *To quit Setup without installing Windows NT, press F3
```

Figure 13-15   Windows NT Workstation Setup menu

NOTE

Windows NT does not have a Device Manager. When installing and troubleshooting hardware, look for individual icons in the Control Panel to manage hardware devices. For a detailed report of the system configuration, use the WinMSD command. At a command prompt enter `Winmsd /a /f`. The command creates the report in the current directory.

CHAPTER SUMMARY

▶ Windows 2000 is actually a suite of operating systems: Windows 2000 Professional, Windows 2000 Server, Windows 2000 Advanced Server, and Windows 2000 Datacenter Server.

▶ The two architectural modes of Windows NT/2000/XP are user mode and kernel mode. Kernel mode is further divided into two components: executive services and the hardware abstraction layer (HAL).

▶ A process is a unique instance of a program running together with the program resources and other programs it may use. A thread is one task that the process requests from the kernel, such as the task of printing a file.

▶ An NTVDM provides a DOS-like environment for DOS and Windows 3.x applications.

▶ Windows 3.x 16-bit applications run in a WOW.

▶ A workgroup is a group of computers and users sharing resources. Each computer maintains a list of users and their rights on that particular PC. A domain is a group of networked computers that share a centralized directory database of user account information and security.

▶ Of all Windows NT/2000/XP accounts, the administrator account has the most privileges and rights. It can create user accounts and assign them rights.

▶ Windows 2000 can run in native mode and mixed mode. Native mode is used when all domain servers are Windows 2000 servers. Mixed mode is used when a domain has both Windows 2000 and Windows NT servers controlling the domain.

▶ Windows NT can operate using two different file systems: FAT16 and NTFS. NTFS offers more security and power than FAT16, but FAT16 is backward-compatible with older OSs. Windows 2000/XP supports FAT16, FAT32, and NTFS. NTFS under Windows 2000/XP is not compatible with NTFS under Windows NT.

▶ Windows NT/2000/XP offers a clean install and an upgrade installation. A clean install overwrites all information from previous operating system installations on the hard drive.

▶ System BIOS, hardware, and software must be compatible with Windows 2000. Check the HCL and the Compatible Software Applications list on the Microsoft Web site before beginning an installation. If you need to flash BIOS, do it before you begin the installation.

▶ A PC can be configured to dual boot between Windows NT or 2000 and another OS, such as Windows 9x or DOS.

▶ Windows 2000/NT supports a dual boot, but each operating system must be installed in its own partition, and an application must be installed twice, once for each OS.

▶ A Windows 2000 upgrade installation is done in two phases, the Report phase and the Setup phase.

▶ Windows 2000 supports Plug and Play and automatically launches the Add New Hardware Wizard when it senses a new device has been installed on the system. Windows NT does not support Plug and Play.

▶ Windows 2000 has a Device Manager to view, uninstall, and update devices, but Windows NT does not have a Device Manager. In Windows NT, hardware devices are managed from applets in the Control Panel.

▶ Applications can be installed in Windows 2000 using the Add/Remove Programs applet in the Control Panel.

▶ Four disks are important in recovering from a failed Windows NT boot. Three disks are required to boot Windows NT, and an Emergency Repair Disk (ERD) can be prepared to recover critical system files on the hard drive.

KEY TERMS

13

For explanations of key terms, see the Glossary near the end of the book.

ACPI (Advanced Configuration and Power Interface)
Active Directory
administrator account
answer file
backup domain controller (BDC)
boot loader menu
boot partition
client/server
digital signature
disk cloning
distribution server
domain
domain controller

drive imaging
dual boot
Emergency Repair Disk (ERD)
executive services
HAL (hardware abstraction layer)
kernel mode
Last Known Good configuration
master file table (MFT)
mixed mode
multithreading
native mode
NTVDM (NT virtual DOS machine)
peer-to-peer

primary domain controller (PDC)
process
security accounts manager (SAM)
subsystem
system partition
system state data
thread
unattended installation
user mode
Win16 on Win32 (WOW)
workgroup

REVIEWING THE BASICS

1. What layer of Windows NT/2000/XP is most responsible for interacting with hardware?

2. What is one reason that interaction with hardware is limited to only one or two components of Windows NT/2000/XP?

3. What are the two modes of the Windows NT/2000/XP architecture?

4. Which of these two modes contains the NTVDM?

5. What is the name of the folder on the Windows NT/2000 CD where the installation files are stored?

6. Before you install Windows 2000, how can you determine if the OS supports all the hardware on your PC?

7. What is one reason not to upgrade from Windows 98 to Windows NT?

8. What file systems does Windows NT support? Windows 2000?

9. If you have Windows 98 installed on a PC using FAT32 and you are creating a dual boot with Windows NT, what must you do first so that Windows NT can access the entire hard drive?

10. How many bits are used to store a cluster number in the Windows NT NTFS file system?

11. What is the file system that is common to DOS, Windows 9x, and Windows NT?

12. Which of the two Windows 2000 setup programs is a 32-bit program? A 16-bit program?

13. What must you know in order to log on to the Windows 2000 Recovery Console?

14. Windows NT/2000/XP is installed using a system partition and a boot partition. Which of these partitions must be the active partition of the hard drive?

15. In a Windows NT/2000/XP workgroup, where is access to an individual workstation on the network controlled?

16. In a Windows NT/2000/XP domain, where is access to an individual workstation on the network controlled?

17. What is the first Windows NT/2000/XP program that is loaded and run when Windows NT is booted?

18. What is required before Windows 2000 can provide full power management functionality?

19. Name three manufacturers responsible for the initial development of ACPI.

20. Explain the difference between Windows 2000 native mode and mixed mode.

21. If you are installing Windows 2000 on a new hard drive and your system cannot boot from a CD, how do you begin the installation?

22. If you install Windows 2000 on an 8-GB hard drive, use a single partition for the drive, and choose not to use the NTFS file system, what file system will Windows 2000 automatically use?

23. What is the command to create a set of Windows 2000 boot disks?

24. If your BIOS is not ACPI-compliant, what should you do before you install Windows 2000?

25. If an administrator is concerned about security on a system, which file system is appropriate?

26. Can you perform an upgrade of Windows 2000 from a remote computer on the network? Explain your answer.

27. For a person to be able to install hardware, what privileges or permissions must be assigned to their user account?

28. How many floppy disks are needed in order to boot Windows NT from disk?

29. When there is a problem booting to Windows NT and the Last Known Good configuration is used, what is lost?

30. What Windows NT utility program is used to create the Windows NT ERD?

13

THINKING CRITICALLY

1. You are planning an upgrade from Windows 98 to Windows 2000 Professional. Your system uses a modem card that you don't find listed on the Microsoft Windows 2000 list of compatible devices. What do you do next?

   a. Abandon the upgrade and continue to use Windows 98.

   b. Check the Web site of the modem manufacturer for a Windows 2000 driver.

   c. Buy a new modem card.

   d. Install a dual boot for Windows 98 and Windows 2000 and only use the modem when you have Windows 98 loaded.

2. You have just installed Windows 2000 and now attempt to install your favorite game that worked fine under Windows 98. When you attempt the installation, you get an error. What is your best next step?

   a. Purchase a new version of your game, one that is compatible with Windows 2000.

   b. Download any service packs or patches to Windows 2000.

   c. Reinstall Windows 98.

3. You have a critically important, irreplaceable data file stored on your Windows NT hard drive, which uses the NTFS file system, and you have not made a backup of the file. When you boot up the system, you see a blue screen with a strange error message that you have never seen and don't understand. You have another Windows NT system that is working that might be of help to you. What is your next step?

   a. Step back from the problem, take a deep breath, and carefully consider your options.

   b. Use your three boot disks to boot the non-working system and attempt to repair the Windows NT installation.

   c. Format the hard drive and perform a fresh installation of Windows NT.

   d. Remove the hard drive from the non-working system, install it as a second drive in the working system, and attempt to rescue the critical data file.

HANDS-ON PROJECTS

HANDS-ON PROJECTS

PROJECT 13-1: Preparing for Windows 2000

Use the Microsoft Web site *www.microsoft.com/windows2000/professional/ howtobuy/upgrading/compat* to research whether your home or lab PC qualifies for Windows 2000. Fill in the following table and print the Web pages showing whether each hardware device and application installed on your PC qualifies for Windows 2000.

Hardware Device or Application	Specific Device Name or Application Name and Version	Does It Qualify for Windows 2000?
Motherboard BIOS		
Video card		
Modem card (if present)		
Sound card (if present)		
Printer (if present)		
Network card (if present)		
CD-ROM drive (if present)		
DVD drive (if present)		
SCSI hard drive (if present)		
Other device		
Application 1		
Application 2		
Application 3		

PROJECT 13-2: Listing Windows Components

13

After installing Windows 2000, list the Windows components included under the Add/Remove Programs applet in the Control Panel that Windows 2000 Setup did not install on your PC.

PROJECT 13-3: Backing Up the System State

Back up the Windows 2000 system state to a folder named C:\MyBackup. You will use this backup in the next chapter in a recovery process. Print a screen shot of Explorer showing the size of the backup file in the MyBackup folder.

PROJECT 13-4: Using the Internet for Problem Solving

Access the *support.microsoft.com* Web site for Windows NT Workstation support. Print one example of an article from the Knowledge Base that addresses a problem with booting Windows NT.

PROJECT 13-5: **Using the Internet for Research**

You want to install Windows NT on a PC using a dual boot with Windows 98. The Windows 98 logical drive is using FAT32, and you want Windows NT to be able to access the data files on this logical drive. Use the Internet to answer these questions:

1. What third-party software allows Windows NT to read from FAT32 volumes? How much does it cost? What URL did you use to answer the question?

2. What third-party software allows Windows NT to write to FAT32 volumes? How much does it cost? What URL did you use to answer the question?

Managing and Troubleshooting Windows 2000

I n the last chapter, you learned about the Windows NT/2000/XP architecture and how to install Windows 2000 and Windows NT. You also learned how to troubleshoot the Windows NT boot process. Recall that Windows NT does not provide many support tools to aid in troubleshooting when the OS does not boot correctly. Windows 2000 and Windows XP have more troubleshooting tools and options. Some of these tools and options work with both Windows 2000 and Windows XP, and some work with only one OS or the other. In this chapter, you learn about the details of the Windows NT/2000/XP boot process, and specifically how to troubleshoot the Windows 2000 boot process. In addition, this chapter covers supporting and troubleshooting Windows 2000 after it boots, including problems you might have with system errors and performance. In the next two chapters, you will learn about Windows XP.

Understanding the Windows NT/2000/XP Boot Process

A+
OS
1.2
2.3

Understanding the boot process and making changes to it are critical when supporting Windows NT/2000/XP. In this section you learn what happens during the boot process, as well as how to solve boot problems. The following is a look behind the scenes, with a description of each step in the boot process. As you read, refer to Table 14-1 for an outline of the boot sequence for Intel-based computers.

1. *BIOS executes POST.* First, startup BIOS performs POST, which executes regardless of which OS is present. After POST, BIOS turns to the hard drive to load an OS. Remember from earlier chapters that BIOS looks for the partition information at the beginning of the hard drive.

2. *BIOS executes the MBR program.* The first thing on the hard drive that BIOS needs is the master boot program. Remember that the master boot program is the very first thing written in the first sector of a hard drive. The master boot program is followed by the partition table itself, and both are stored in the Master Boot Record. BIOS executes this master boot program, which examines the partition table, looking for the location of the active partition on the drive, and then turns to the first sector of the active partition to find and load the program in the boot sector of that active partition. So far in the boot process, nothing is different between Windows NT/2000/XP and other OSs.

Step Performed by	Description
1. Startup BIOS	POST (power-on self test) is executed.
2. Startup BIOS	MBR (Master Boot Record) is loaded, and the master boot program within the MBR is run. (The master boot program is at the very beginning of the hard drive, before the partition table information. The program searches for and loads the OS boot record of the active partition.)
3. MBR program	The boot sector from the active partition is loaded, and the program in this boot sector is run.
4. Boot sector program	Ntldr (NT Loader) file is loaded and run.
5. Windows NT/2000/XP loader	The processor is changed from real mode to flat memory mode, in which 32-bit code can be executed.

Table 14-1 (continued)

Step Performed by	Description
6. Windows NT/2000/XP loader	Minifile system drivers (described below) are started so files can be read.
7. Windows NT/2000/XP loader	Reads Boot.ini file and builds the boot loader menu described in the file. (This menu is discussed in Chapter 13.)
8. Windows NT/2000/XP loader	If the user chooses Windows NT/2000/XP, then the loader runs Ntdetect.com to detect hardware present; otherwise, it runs Bootsect.dos.
9. Windows NT/2000/XP loader	Ntldr reads information from the registry about device drivers and loads them. Also loads the Hal.dll and Ntoskrnl.exe.
10. Windows NT/2000/XP loader (the last step performed by the loader)	Ntldr passes control to Ntoskrnl.exe; load is complete.

Table 14-1   Steps in the Intel-based CPU boot process

3. *The MBR program executes the OS boot program.* Remember that when DOS or Windows 9x/Me boots, the OS boot sector contains the name of the initial OS load program, Io.sys. When Windows NT/2000/XP is installed, it edits this boot sector of the active partition, instructing it to load the Windows NT/2000/XP program Ntldr at startup, instead of Io.sys. (It does this even when the PC is configured for a dual boot.)

4. *The boot program executes Ntldr.* With the execution of Ntldr, Windows NT/2000/XP then starts its boot sequence. This program is responsible for loading Windows NT/2000/XP and performing several chores to complete the loading process. It then passes control to the OS.

5. *Ntldr changes the processor mode and loads a file system.* Up to this point, the CPU has been processing in real mode. Windows NT/2000/XP does not process in real mode. Ntldr is a 32-bit program that begins by changing the CPU mode from real mode to a 32-bit mode called **32-bit flat memory mode** in order to run its 32-bit code. Next a temporary, simplified file system called the **minifile system** is started so that Ntldr can read files from either a FAT or an NTFS file system.

6. *Ntldr reads and loads the boot loader menu.* Ntldr then is able to read the **Boot.ini** file, a hidden text file that contains information needed to build the boot loader menu. The user can make a selection from this menu or accept the default selection by waiting for the preset time to expire.

14

7. *Ntldr uses Ntdetect.com.* If Ntldr is to load Windows NT/2000/XP as the OS, Ntldr runs the program Ntdetect.com, which checks the hardware devices present and passes the information back to Ntldr. This information is used later to update the Windows NT/2000/XP registry concerning the Last Known Good hardware profile used.

8. *Ntldr loads the OS and device drivers.* Ntldr then loads Ntoskrnl.exe, Hal.dll, and the System hive. The System hive is a portion of the Windows NT/2000/XP registry that includes hardware information used to load the proper device drivers for the hardware present. You will learn more about the System hive in Chapter 16.

9. *Ntldr passes control to Ntoskrnl.exe.* Ntldr then passes control to Ntoskrnl.exe, and the boot sequence is complete.

10. *An operating system other than Windows NT/2000/XP is chosen.* If a selection was made from the boot loader menu to load an OS other than Windows NT/2000/XP, such as DOS or Windows 9x/Me, Ntldr does not load Ntdetect.com or complete the remaining chores to load Windows NT/2000/XP. Instead, Ntldr loads and passes control to the program Bootsect.dos, which is responsible for loading the other OS.

The files needed to boot Windows NT/2000/XP successfully are listed in Table 14-2. (In the table, references to *winnt_root* follow Microsoft documentation conventions and mean the name of the directory where Windows NT/2000/XP is stored, which is \\Winnt by default. Also, Microsoft sometimes refers to this root folder as %SystemRoot%.)

NOTE When repairing a corrupted hard drive, a support person often copies files from one PC to another. However, the Bootsect.dos file contains information from the partition table for a particular hard drive and cannot be copied from another PC.

File	Location
Ntldr	Root folder of the system partition (usually C:\\)
Boot.ini	Root folder of the system partition (usually C:\\)
Bootsect.dos	Root folder of the system partition (usually C:\\)
Ntdetect.com	Root folder of the system partition (usually C:\\)
Ntbootdd.sys*	Root folder of the system partition (usually C:\\)
Ntoskrnl.exe	*winnt_root*\\system32 folder of the boot partition
Hal.dll	*winnt_root*\\system32 folder of the boot partition

Table 14-2 (continued)

File	Location
System	*winnt_root*\system32\config folder of the boot partition
Device drivers	*winnt_root*\system32\drivers folder of the boot partition

*Ntbootdd.sys is used only with a SCSI boot device.

Table 14-2   Files needed to boot Windows NT/2000/XP successfully

Customizing the Windows NT/2000/XP Boot Process

The Boot.ini file contains information about how the Windows NT/2000/XP boot is configured and can be used to customize the boot process. As you learned earlier in this chapter, Ntldr reads this file and uses it to see what operating systems are available and how to set up the boot. Figure 14-1 shows an example of a Boot.ini file for Windows 2000.

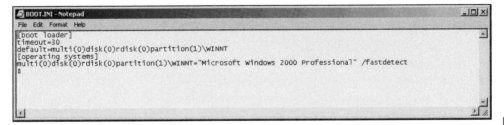

Figure 14-1   A sample Boot.ini file

There are two main sections in Boot.ini: the [boot loader] section and the [operating systems] section. The [boot loader] section contains the number of seconds the system gives the user to select an operating system before it loads the default operating system; this is called a timeout. In Figure 14-1, the timeout is set to 30 seconds. If the system is set for a dual boot, the path to the default operating system is also listed in the [boot loader] section.

The [operating systems] section of the Boot.ini file provides a list of operating systems that can be loaded, including the path to the boot partition of each operating system. Here is the meaning of each entry in Figure 14-1 that points to the location of the OS:

- *Multi(0)*. Use the first hard drive controller.
- *Disk(0)*. Used only when booting from a SCSI hard drive.
- *Rdisk(0)*. Use the first hard drive.
- *Partition(1)*. Use the first partition on the drive.

You can add switches to the [operating systems] section of the Boot.ini file, either by editing the file manually or through the System Properties dialog box. In

14

A+
OS
2.3

Figure 14-1, the only switch used in this Boot.ini file is /fastdetect, which causes the OS not to attempt to inspect any peripherals connected to a COM port at startup.

The recommended way to change Boot.ini settings is through the System Properties dialog box, which is easier and safer than editing the file manually. For Windows 2000, do the following:

1. On the Start menu, point to **Settings** and then click **Control Panel**.

2. Double-click the **System** icon.

3. The System Properties dialog box opens. Click the **Advanced** tab (see Figure 14-2).

System Properties

General | Network Identification | Hardware | User Profiles | **Advanced**

Performance
Performance options control how applications use memory, which affects the speed of your computer.

Performance Options...

Environment Variables
Environment variables tell your computer where to find certain types of information.

Environment Variables...

Startup and Recovery
Startup and recovery options tell your computer how to start and what to do if an error causes your computer to stop.

Startup and Recovery...

OK | Cancel | Apply

Figure 14-2 You can access startup and recovery options from the System Properties dialog box

 NOTE

To view or edit the Boot.ini file using a text editor such as Notepad, you must first change the folder options to view hidden system files. Open Windows Explorer, select the root directory, click Tools on the menu bar, click Folder Options, and then select the View tab. Uncheck the option to "Hide protected operating system files."

4. Click the **Startup and Recovery** button.

5. The Startup and Recovery dialog box opens (see Figure 14-3). Change settings as desired and then click **OK** to save them (or click Cancel if you do not want to save them).

A+
OS
2.3

Figure 14-3   Changing the default operating system and timeout value in the Startup and Recovery dialog box changes the Boot.ini settings

Troubleshooting the Windows 2000 Boot Process

A+
OS
2.3
3.1
3.2
3.3

When problems arise with booting, as with all PC problems, try the simple things first. Turn off the power and restart the system. Check for loose cables, switches that are not on, stuck keys on the keyboard, a wall outlet switch that has been turned off, and similar easy-to-solve problems. The next step is to determine at what point in the boot the system fails. Ask what has happened since the last successful boot. Has new hardware or software been installed? Has there been a power surge or electrical storm? Has a user tinkered with the system? If you cannot pinpoint the source of the problem, then several tools can help you troubleshoot the boot. Windows 2000 offers an Advanced Options menu, which includes starting the computer in Safe Mode. Use this option to prevent many device drivers and system services that normally load during the boot from loading. You can then fix or disable these devices or services once the OS loads. The second utility, called the Recovery Console, is new in Windows 2000. Its command-line interface lets you perform maintenance and repairs to the hard drive. Another tool is the emergency repair disk, which is used to recover from problems with corrupted or missing operating system files or a corrupted hard drive boot sector. These three tools are discussed next.

14

Advanced Options Menu

A+
OS
2.3
3.1
3.2
3.3

As a PC boots and the "Starting Windows" message appears at the bottom of the screen, press the F8 key to display the Windows 2000 **Advanced Options menu,** shown in Figure 14-4. As with the Windows 9x/Me startup menu, this menu can be used to diagnose and fix problems when booting Windows 2000. The purpose of each menu option is outlined in the following sections.

```
Windows 2000 Advanced Options Menu
Please select an option:

        Safe Mode
        Safe Mode with Networking
        Safe Mode with Command Prompt

        Enable Boot Logging
        Enable VGA Mode
        Last Known Good Configuration
        Directory Services Restore Mode (Windows 2000 domain controllers only)
        Debugging Mode

        Boot Normally

Use ↑ and ↓ to move the highlight to your choice.
Press Enter to choose.
```

Figure 14-4 Press the F8 key at startup to display the Windows 2000 Advanced Options menu

Safe Mode

✔ **A+ EXAM TIP**

The A+ OS exam expects you to be able to select the appropriate next step in troubleshooting a failed boot when given a specific scenario. As you study the tools in this section, pay attention to how a tool affects the installed OS, applications, and data. The idea is to fix the problem by using the tool that least affects the OS, applications, and data.

Safe Mode boots the OS with a minimum configuration and can be used to solve problems with a new hardware installation or problems caused by user settings. Safe Mode boots with the mouse, monitor (with basic video), keyboard, and mass storage drivers loaded. It uses the default system services (it does not load any extra services) and does not provide network access. When you boot in Safe Mode, you see "Safe Mode" in all four corners of your screen. You have a GUI interface in Safe Mode. The screen resolution is 600 x 800 and the desktop wallpaper (background) is black. After the OS loads in Safe Mode, you can disable the problem device, scan for viruses, run diagnostic software, or take other appropriate action to diagnose and solve problems. When you load Windows 2000 in Safe Mode, all files used for the load are recorded in the Ntbtlog.txt file.

Safe Mode with Networking

A+
OS
2.3
3.1
3.2
3.3

Use this option when you are solving a problem with booting and need access to the network to solve the problem. For example, if you have just attempted to install a printer, which causes the OS to hang when it boots, and the printer drivers are downloaded from the network, boot into Safe Mode with Networking. Uninstall the printer and then install it again from the network. Also use this mode when the Windows 2000 installation files are available on the network, rather than the Windows 2000 installation CD, and you need to access these files.

Safe Mode with Command Prompt

This Safe Mode option does not load a GUI desktop automatically. Use it to get a command prompt. If the first Safe Mode option does not load the OS, then try this option.

Enable Boot Logging

When you boot with this option, Windows 2000 loads normally and you access the regular desktop. However, all files used during the load process are recorded in a file, Ntbtlog.txt. Use this option to see what did and did not load during the boot. If you have a problem getting a device to work, check Ntbtlog.txt to see what driver files loaded. Boot logging is much more effective if you have a copy of Ntbtlog.txt that was made when everything worked as it should. Then you can compare the good load to the bad load, looking for differences.

Enable VGA Mode

Use this option when the video setting does not allow you to see the screen well enough to fix a bad setting. This can happen because of a corrupted video driver or when a user creates a desktop with black fonts on a black background, or something similar. Booting in this mode gives you a very plain VGA video. Go to the Display settings, correct the problem, and reboot normally.

14

Last Known Good Configuration

NOTE

Each time the system boots completely and the user logs on, the Last Known Good configuration is saved. If you have booted several times since a problem started, the Last Known Good will not help you recover from the problem, because all saved versions of the Last Known Good reflect the problem.

Just as with Windows NT, Windows 2000 keeps the Last Known Good configuration in the registry. Use this option if you suspect the system was configured incorrectly. It restores Windows 2000 to the settings of the last successful boot, and all system setting changes made after this last successful boot are lost.

A+
OS
2.3
3.1
3.2
3.3

Directory Services Restore Mode (Windows 2000 Domain Controllers Only)

This option applies only to domain controllers and is used as one step in the process of recovering from a corrupted Active Directory. Recall that Active Directory is the domain database managed by a domain controller that tracks users and resources on the domain. The details of how all this works are beyond the scope of this chapter.

Debugging Mode

This mode gives you the opportunity to move system boot logs from the failing computer to another computer for evaluation. Connect another computer to the failing computer by way of the serial port. In this mode, Windows 2000 sends all the boot information to the serial port. For more details, see the *Windows 2000 Professional Resource Kit* (Microsoft Press).

Recovery Console

The Advanced Options menu can help if the problem is a faulty device driver or system service. However, if the problem goes deeper than that, the next tool to use is the **Recovery Console**. Use it when Windows 2000/XP does not start properly or hangs during the load. The Recovery Console is a command-driven operating system that does not use a GUI. With it you can access the FAT16, FAT32, and NTFS file systems.

The purpose of the Recovery Console is to allow you to repair a damaged registry, system files, or file system on the hard drive. You must enter the Administrator password in order to use the Console and access an NTFS volume. You are not allowed into all folders, and you cannot copy files from the hard drive to a floppy disk without setting certain parameters. If the registry is so corrupted that the Recovery Console cannot read the password in order to validate it, you are not asked for the password, but you are limited in what you can do at the Console.

APPLYING CONCEPTS

The Recovery Console software is on the Windows 2000 CD and the four Windows 2000 setup disks. You can launch the Recovery Console from the CD or four disks, or manually install the Recovery Console on the hard drive and launch it from there. If you have not already created the Windows 2000 setup disks, you can go to a working Windows 2000 PC and create the disks by following the directions given in Chapter 13. Follow these steps to load Windows 2000 from the disks and access the Recovery Console:

1. Insert the first of the four setup disks, and restart the PC. You are directed to insert each of the four disks in turn, and then the Setup screen appears as shown in Figure 14-5.

A+
OS
2.3
3.1
3.2
3.3

Windows 2000 Professional Setup

Welcome to Setup

This portion of the Setup program prepares Microsoft®
Windows 2000 (TM) to run on your computer.

- To set up Windows 2000 now, press ENTER.
- To repair a Windows 2000 installation, press R.
- To quit Setup without installing Windows 2000, press F3.

ENTER=Continue   R=Repair   F3=Quit

Figure 14-5   Use this Windows Setup screen to access the Recovery Console

2. Type **R** to select the "To repair a Windows 2000 installation" option. The Windows 2000 Repair Options window opens (see Figure 14-6). Type **C** to select the Recovery Console.

Windows 2000 Professional Setup

Windows 2000 Repair Options:

- To repair a Windows 2000 installation by using
  the recovery console, press C.

- To repair a Windows 2000 installation by using
  the emergency repair process, press R.

If the repair options do not successfully repair your system,
run Windows 2000 Setup again.

C=Console   R=Repair   F3=Quit

14

Figure 14-6   Windows 2000 offers two repair options

3. The Windows 2000 Recovery Console window opens (see Figure 14-7). The Recovery Console looked at the hard drive and determined that only a single Windows 2000 installation was on the drive installed in the C:\Winnt folder. (The Winnt folder might be on a different drive on your machine.) Press **1** and then press **Enter** to select that installation.

4. Enter the Administrator password, and press **Enter**. If you don't know the password, you cannot use the console.

5. You now have a command prompt. You can use a limited group of DOS-like commands at this point to recover a failed system. These commands are listed and described in

Table 14-3. To leave the Recovery Console and start Windows 2000, type **Exit** at the command prompt.

Microsoft Windows 2000 (TM) Recovery Console.

The Recovery Console provides system repair and recovery functionality.

Type EXIT to quit the Recovery Console and restart the computer.

1: C:\WINNT

Which Windows 2000 installation would you like to log onto
(To cancel, press ENTER)? 1
Type the Administrator password:
C:\WINNT>

Figure 14-7   The Windows 2000 Recovery Console command prompt

NOTE

To retrieve the last command, press F3 at the command prompt. To retrieve the command one character at a time, press the F1 key.

Command	Description
Attrib	Changes the attributes of a file or folder, and works the same as the DOS version, as in the following example: `Attrib -r -h -s filename` Removes the read, hidden, and system attributes from the file.
Batch	Carries out commands stored in a batch file: `Batchfile1file2`. The commands stored in file1 are executed, and the results written to file2. If no file2 is specified, results are written to the screen.
Cd	Displays or changes the current directory.
Chkdsk	Checks a disk and repairs or recovers the data.
Cls	Clears the screen.

Table 14-3 (continued)

A+
OS
2.3
3.1
3.2
3.3

Command	Description
Copy	Copies a single uncompressed file. For example, `Copy A:\File1 C:\Winnt\File2` copies the file named File1 on the floppy disk to the hard drive's Winnt folder, naming the file File2. Use the command to replace corrupted files.
Del	Deletes a file: `Del File1`.
Dir	Lists files and folders.
Disable	Used when a service or driver starts and prevents the system from booting properly: `Disable servicename` Disables a Windows 2000 system service or driver, restarts the computer without it, and helps you determine the problem.
Diskpart	Creates and deletes partitions on the hard drive. Enter the command with no arguments to display a user interface.
Enable	Enables a Windows 2000 system service or driver: `Enable servicename`.
Exit	Quits the Recovery Console and restarts the computer.
Expand	Expands a compressed file and copies it from a floppy disk or a CD to the destination folder; for example: `Expand A:\File1 C:\Winnt` Expands the file on the floppy disk and copies it to the hard drive.
Fixboot	Rewrites the OS boot sector on the hard drive. If a drive letter is not specified, the system drive is assumed. Type the `Fixboot C:` command when the boot sector is damaged.
Fixmbr	Rewrites the Master Boot Record boot program. This command is the same as `Fdisk/MBR`. Use this command when the Master Boot Record is damaged.
Format	Formats a logical drive. If no file system is specified, NTFS is assumed. Type `FormatC:/fs:FAT32` to use the FAT32 file system. Type `FormatC:/fs:FAT` to use the FAT16 file system.
Help	Help utility appears for the given command: `Help Fixboot`.
Listsvc	Lists all available services.
Logon	Allows you to log on to an installation with the Administrator password.
Map	Lists all drive letters and file system types.
Md or Mkdir	Creates a directory: `MDC:\TEMP`.
More or Type	Displays a text file on screen: `TYPE filename.txt`.
Rd or Rmdir	Deletes a directory: `RD C:\TEMP`.
Rename or Ren	Renames a file: `Rename File1.txtFile2.txt`.

Table 14-3 (continued)

14

Command	Description
Set	Displays or sets Recovery Console environmental variables.
Systemroot	Sets the current directory to the directory where Windows 2000 is installed.
Type	Displays contents of a text file: `Type File1.txt`.

Table 14-3 Commands available from the Recovery Console

Using the Recovery Console to Restore the Registry

If you suspect that the Windows 2000 registry is damaged, you can use the Recovery Console commands to restore the registry from the last backup that you created. (This process also works for the Windows XP registry.) The registry consists of five files–Default, Sam, Security, Software, and System–which are stored in the %SystemRoot%\System32\Config folder. A backup of the registry is stored in the %SystemRoot%\repair\RegBack folder every time you back up the system state (see Figure 14-8).

Five files make up the registry

Figure 14-8 Windows puts a backup of the registry in the C:\WINNT\repair\RegBack folder

To restore the registry from this backup using the Recovery Console, first rename the registry files so that you can backtrack if necessary. From the Recovery Console command prompt, perform the steps outlined in Table 14-4. These actions restore the registry to its state at the time of the last backup.

Command	Description
1. `Systemroot`	Makes the Windows folder the current folder.
2. `CD System32\Config`	Makes the Windows registry folder the current folder.

Table 14-4 (continued)

A+
OS
2.3
3.1
3.2
3.3

Command	Description
3. Ren Default Default.save Ren Sam Sam.save Ren Security Security.save Ren Software Software.save Ren System System.save	Renames the five registry files.
4. Systemroot	Returns to the Windows folder.
5. CD repair\RegBack	Makes the registry backup folder the current folder.
6. Copy default C:\Winnt\system32\config Copy Sam C:\Winnt\system32\config Copy Security C:\Winnt\system32\config Copy Software C:\Winnt\system32\config Copy System C:\Winnt\system32\config	Copies the five registry files from the backup folder to the registry folder. For hardware problems, first try copying just the System hive and reboot. For software problems, first try copying just the Software hive and then reboot. Then try copying all five hives.

Table 14-4   Steps to restore the Windows 2000/XP registry

Installing the Recovery Console

Although the Recovery Console is often launched from the Windows CD to recover from system failure, you can also install it on your working system so it appears on the OS boot loader menu. Use it to address less drastic problems that occur when you can boot from the hard drive. To install the Recovery Console:

1. Open a command window in Windows 2000.

2. Change from the current directory to the \i386 folder on the Windows 2000 CD.

3. Enter the command **winnt32 /cmdcons**. The Recovery Console is installed.

4. Restart your computer. Recovery Console should now be shown with the list of available operating systems on the OS boot loader menu.

14

Emergency Repair Process

If options on the Advanced Options menu fail to recover the system and the Recovery Console fails as well, your next option is the **Emergency Repair Process**. Use this option only as a last resort because it restores the system to the state it was in immediately after the Windows 2000 installation. All changes since the installation are

A+
OS
2.3
3.1
3.2
3.3

lost. The process uses an Emergency Repair Disk (ERD), but the disk does not contain the same information as the Windows NT ERD (Windows NT Emergency Repair Disk).

Recall that the Windows NT ERD contains a copy of the registry and that you should update the disk any time you make significant changes to the registry. You can then use the disk to repair a corrupted registry, restoring it to its state when you last updated the ERD.

The Windows 2000 ERD contains information about your current installation but does not contain a copy of the registry because it is too large to fit on a single floppy disk. The Windows 2000 ERD points to a folder on the hard drive where the registry was backed up when Windows 2000 was installed. This folder is %SystemRoot%\repair, which most likely is C:\Winnt\repair.

APPLYING CONCEPTS

Using the Windows 2000 ERD to recover from a corrupted registry returns you to the installation version of the registry, and you lose all changes to the registry since that time. Because of the way the ERD works, you do not need to update the disk once you've created it. Before a problem occurs, follow these directions to create the disk:

1. Click **Start**, point to **Programs**, **Accessories**, and **System Tools**, and then click **Backup**. The Backup window appears with the Welcome tab selected (see Figure 14-9). Select **Emergency Repair Disk**.
2. The Backup tab and the Emergency Repair Diskette dialog box open. If you check the box shown in Figure 14-10, the system backs up your registry to a folder under the Repair folder, %SystemRoot%\repair\RegBack.
3. Click **OK** to create the disk. Label the disk "Windows 2000 Emergency Repair Disk," and keep it in a safe place.

If your hard drive fails, you can use the ERD to restore the system, including system files, boot files, and the registry, to its state at the end of the Windows 2000 installation. Follow these steps:

1. Boot the PC from the four Windows 2000 setup disks. The Setup menu appears (refer back to Figure 14-5). Select option **R**.
2. When the Windows 2000 Repair Options window opens (refer back to Figure 14-6), select option **R**.
3. You are instructed to insert the Emergency Repair Disk. Follow the instructions on the screen to repair the installation.

If this process does not work, then your next option is to reinstall Windows 2000. If you have access to a Windows 98 startup disk, it is a good idea to use Windows 98 ScanDisk to scan the hard disk surface for errors before you do the installation. If you suspect that a virus damaged the file system, also use the Fixmbr command or the Fdisk /MBR command discussed in earlier chapters to replace the master boot program in case it has been corrupted by the virus. Windows 2000 also offers a utility called InoculateIT Antivirus AVBoot, a command-line tool that can scan memory, the MBR sector, and OS boot sectors for viruses. You will learn to use the utility in a project at the end of the chapter.

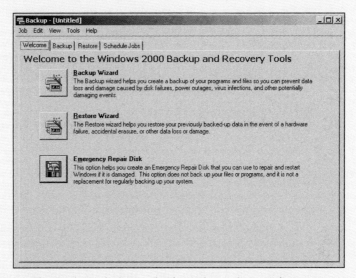

Figure 14-9 Use the Backup window to back up the registry and create an emergency repair disk

Figure 14-10 Create an ERD and back up the registry to the hard drive

14

Tools For Maintenance and Troubleshooting

A+
OS
1.5

In this section, you will learn about many tools you can use for maintenance and troubleshooting in Windows 2000. You learned about some tools earlier in this chapter, as well as in previous chapters on other versions of Windows. All tools discussed in this section work under Windows XP, although in some cases, the menus have changed slightly. Of the tools discussed in this section, all except Windows File Protection, Microsoft Management Console, and automated Windows Update are available under Windows NT. In this section, you will learn how to use tools to manage hard disks, applications, system processes, and other Windows components.

Using the Backup Tool to Restore the System State

In Chapter 13, you learned how to back up the system state after installing Windows 2000 and verifying that the system is working. To use the backup (Ntbackup.exe) to restore the system state after the system fails or the registry becomes corrupted, begin the same way you did to make the backup by clicking Start, pointing to Programs, Accessories, and System Tools, and then clicking Backup. The Backup dialog box opens showing the Backup tab. Click the Restore tab, which is shown in Figure 14-11.

Figure 14-11   Restore the system state from the Restore tab of the Backup dialog box

A+
OS
1.5

From the Restore tab, first select the backup you want to restore. Then, in the list box in the lower-left corner, select the location to which the backup is to be restored. Click the Start Restore button in the lower-right corner to start the process. Remember that you can restore the system state as a way of restoring the registry. If you need to restore the registry and cannot boot to the Windows desktop, try the procedure to restore the registry using the Recovery Console given earlier in the chapter.

Windows 2000 Support Tools

A+
OS
3.3

Windows 2000 offers several support tools that you can install. They are located in the \Support\Tools folder on the Windows 2000 CD. To install them, run the Setup program located in that folder. Enter this command in the Run dialog box:

```
D:\Support\Tools\Setup.exe
```

Substitute the drive letter of your CD-ROM drive for D in the command line, if necessary. The list of tools installed is shown in Figure 14-12.

One of these utilities is Dependency Walker (Depends.exe), which lists all the files used by an application. It can be useful when troubleshooting a failed application installation if you have a report of files used by the application on a computer where the installation is good, or to help resolve General Protection Faults. Compare the reports, looking for DLL files that are missing on the bad installation, are not the correct size, or are incorrectly date-stamped. Software applications often use DLL files for added functionality and to relate to the operating system. To use the utility, click Start, point to Programs, Windows 2000 Support Tools, and Tools, and then click Dependency Walker. Figure 14-13 shows a Dependency Walker window. Click File on the menu bar, click Open, and then select the main executable file for an application. In the figure, Apache.exe is selected. Apache is a popular Web server application. The window lists all supporting files that Apache.exe uses and how they depend on one another.

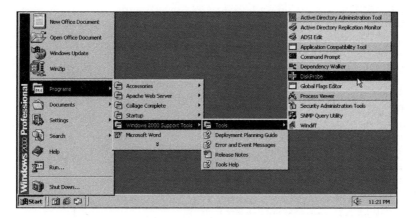

Figure 14-12   Windows 2000 support tools

14

A+
OS
3.3

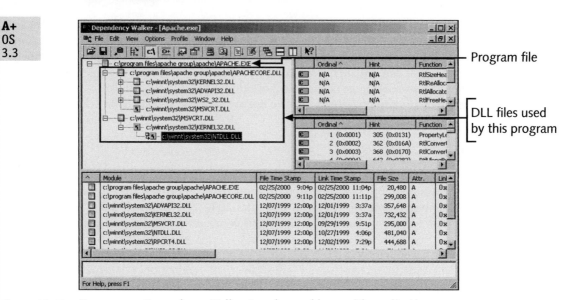

— Program file

DLL files used
by this program

Figure 14-13   You can use Dependency Walker to solve problems with applications

Windows File Protection

A+
OS
2.4
3.3

Windows 2000 provides a feature called **WFP (Windows File Protection)** to protect system files from modification. Files protected have a .sys, .dll, .ttf, .fon, .ocs, or .exe file extension. Earlier versions of Windows sometimes allowed these files to be overwritten by unsigned, non-Microsoft versions during program installations. Changes to shared system files can cause errors within a program, incompatibility between two or more programs, mismatches between file versions, or even system instability.

WFP prevents these problems and protects files from modification through two tools. One is a background process that notifies WFP when a protected file is modified. WFP then checks the file signature to see whether it is the correct Microsoft version of the file. If the file version is not correct, WFP looks in the Dllcache folder, which contains cached copies of system files, or asks that the Windows 2000 CD be inserted so that WFP can find the file and restore it from the CD. Replacing incorrect system files with correct ones from the Windows 2000 CD requires administrative permissions. If a non-administrator user is logged on when WFP activates, WFP does not prompt that user to insert the Windows 2000 CD, but waits until an administrator logs on to request the CD and replace the file.

NOTE

If a file has been modified, is correctly signed as a Microsoft-approved version, and is not present in the Dllcache folder, WFP adds it to that folder to be used as the correct version on future scans.

A+
OS
2.4
3.3

When WFP restores a file, it shows the following message by default, replacing *file_name* with the name of the system file it restored:

```
A file replacement was attempted on the protected system
file file_name. To maintain system stability, the file
has been restored to the correct Microsoft version. If
problems occur with your application, please contact the
application vendor for support.
```

If you see this message, carefully note what application was working at the time and what happened just before the message. In addition to software installations, viruses, and software applications, errors can cause attempted modifications to system files. It is important to have as much information as possible to figure out which applications might need to be scanned for viruses or replaced altogether.

The other tool that WFP provides is the **SFC (System File Checker)**. (The program filename is Sfc.exe.) The system or an administrator might use this tool in several situations. If the administrator set the system to perform an unattended installation, the SFC checks all protected system files after Setup is completed to see whether they were modified by programs added during the installation, as well as the catalog files that contain the file signatures. If any incorrect modifications have been made or if any important system files are unsigned, WFP retrieves a copy of the file from the Dllcache folder or requests it from the Windows 2000 CD.

An administrator can also activate the SFC manually from a command prompt and use it to verify that the system is using correct versions of all protected system files, either as a preventative maintenance measure or when it is suspected that system files have become corrupted or deleted. To use System File Checker, the administrator types Sfc.exe from the command prompt with one of the switches listed in Table 14-5. You can also access the Run dialog box from the Start menu and type C:\Winnt\system32\sfc.exe /scannow (or another switch).

14

Switch	Function
/cachesize=x	Sets the size of the file cache, in megabytes
/cancel	Discontinues scans of protected system files
/enable	Enables normal operation of WFP
/purgecache	Empties the file cache and immediately scans all protected system files, populating the Dllcache folder with confirmed correct versions of system files (may require insertion of the Windows 2000 CD as source for correct versions)
/quiet	Replaces incorrect versions of system files with correct ones without prompting the user
/scanboot	Performs a scan of protected system files every time the system boots

Table 14-5 (continued)

A+
OS
2.4
3.3

Switch	Function
/scannow	Performs an immediate scan of protected system files
/scanonce	Performs a scan of protected system files the next time the system boots
/?	Displays a list of available switches for the sfc command

Table 14-5   Switches for the Sfc.exe utility

Computer Management

A+
OS
1.1
1.4
1.5
2.5

Computer Management is a window that consolidates several Windows 2000 administrative tools that you can use to manage the local PC or other computers on the network. To use most of these tools, you must be logged on as an administrator, although you can view certain settings and configurations in Computer Management if you are logged on with lesser privileges. To access Computer Management, open the Control Panel, open the Administrative Tools window, and then double-click the Computer Management icon. The Computer Management window appears (see Figure 14-14). Some tasks you can perform from this window include monitoring problems with hardware, software, and security. You can share folders, view device configurations, add new device drivers, start and stop services, and manage server applications.

NOTE

By default, the Administrative Tools group is located in the Control Panel. In addition, you can add the Administrative Tools group to appear in the Start menu when you click Start, Programs, and Administrative Tools. To do that, right-click the taskbar and select Properties. On the Taskbar and Start Menu Properties dialog box, select the Advanced tab. Check Display Administrative Tools, and click OK.

A+
OS
1.1
1.4
1.5
2.5

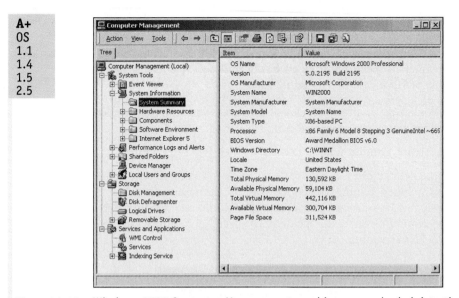

Figure 14-14 Windows 2000 Computer Management combines several administrative tools into a single easy-to-access window

Disk Management

✔ **A+ EXAM TIP**

The A+ OS exam expects you to be able to use the Computer Management window. Disk Management is one of the more important tools in this window.

The Computer Management console contains a tool called **Disk Management** that you can use to create partitions on basic disks or volumes on dynamic disks, and to convert a basic disk to a dynamic disk. This graphical, user-friendly utility replaces the Fdisk utility of earlier Windows OSs. To access the utility, select Disk Management in the Computer Management console or enter Diskmgmt.msc in the Run dialog box.

14

When Disk Management first loads, it examines the drive configuration for the system and displays all drives in a graphical format so you can see how each drive is allocated.

The Disk Management window shown in Figure 14-15 displays three drives. Disk 0 is a basic hard drive using the NTFS file system. Disk 1 is a dynamic hard drive that has not yet been allocated into volumes. The third drive is a CD-ROM drive shown with a CD in the drive.

A+
OS
1.1
1.4
1.5
2.5

After you install a new second hard drive in the system, and then first access Disk Management, it asks if you want to create a basic disk or dynamic disk using the new drive. Disk Management displays the new disk with unallocated space, as shown in Figure 14-15. This second hard drive has been designated as a dynamic disk.

To create a volume on this dynamic disk:

1. Right-click an unallocated area of the drive, and select **Create Volume** on the shortcut menu (see Figure 14-15).

2. The Create Volume Wizard launches. Click **Next** to continue.

3. On the next screen (see Figure 14-16), select a volume type, either Simple volume, Spanned volume, or Striped volume. In our example, only Simple volume is available, because we are working with only one dynamic drive. You need to have more than one dynamic drive to specify a volume as striped or spanned. Click **Next** to continue.

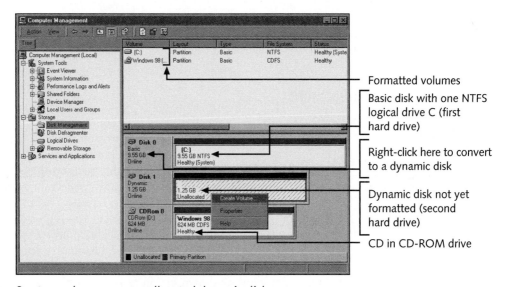

Formatted volumes

Basic disk with one NTFS logical drive C (first hard drive)

Right-click here to convert to a dynamic disk

Dynamic disk not yet formatted (second hard drive)

CD in CD-ROM drive

Figure 14-15 Create a volume on an unallocated dynamic disk

4. Follow the wizard through the process of specifying the volume size, a drive letter, file system (NTFS, FAT, or FAT32), and allocation unit size (default is 512 bytes). The wizard then creates the dynamic volume.

The process for creating a partition on a basic disk is similar; the main difference is that the wizard is called the Create Partition Wizard. Access it by right-clicking the unallocated portion of the basic disk, selecting Create Partition, and following the directions in the wizard.

A+
OS
1.1
1.4
1.5
2.5

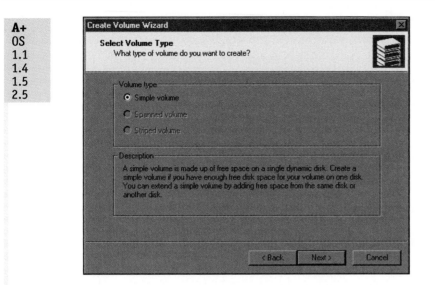

Figure 14-16   Disk Management provides the Create Volume Wizard to help you create volumes

Microsoft Management Console

A+
OS
1.1
1.5

When Windows combines several administrative tools in a single window, the window is called a **console**. Individual tools within the console are called **snap-ins**. An example of a console is Computer Management. Event Viewer and System Information are two snap-ins in that console. Another example of a console is Recovery Console, introduced earlier in the chapter. Windows 2000/XP offers a way for you to create your own customized consoles using the console-building utility **Microsoft Management Console (MMC)**. Table 14-6 lists some available snap-ins for MMC.

14

Snap-in	Description
Active X Control	Enables you to add ActiveX controls to your system
Certificates	Provides certificate management at the user, service, or computer level
Component Services	Links to the Component Services management tool, which is located on the Control Panel
Computer Management	Links to the Computer Management tools on the Control Panel
Device Manager	Lets you see what hardware devices you have on your system and configure device properties
Disk Defragmenter	Links to the Disk Defragmenter utility (Defrag.exe)

Table 14-6 (continued)

Snap-in	Description
Disk Management	Links to the Disk Management tool
Event Viewer	Links to the Event Viewer tool, which displays event logs for the system
Fax Service Management	Enables you to manage fax settings and devices
Folder	Enables you to add a folder to manage from MMC
Group Policy	Provides a tool to manage group policy settings
Indexing Service	Searches files and folders using specified parameters
IP Security Policy Management	Manages Internet communication security
Link to Web Address	Enables you to link to a specified Web site
Local Users and Groups	Provides a tool to manage settings for local users and groups
Performance Logs and Alerts	Gives you an interface from which to set up and manage logs of performance information and alerts about system performance
Removable Storage Management	Enables you to manage settings and configuration information for removable storage devices such as Zip drives and tape backup drives
Security Configuration and Analysis	Enables you to manage configuration of security settings for computers that use security template files
Services	Provides a centralized interface for starting, stopping, and configuring system services
Shared Folders	Provides information about shared folders, open files, and current sessions
System Information	Contains information about the system that you can use when troubleshooting

Table 14-6   Some MMC snap-ins

Creating a Customized Console

✔ A+ EXAM TIP

The A+ OS exam expects you to be able to use Microsoft Management Console to create a customized console.

As with the Computer Management console, you must have administrative privileges to perform most tasks from the MMC. You can use MMC to create your own customized consoles. You can also save a console in a file, which is assigned an .msc file extension. Store the file in the C:\Documents and Settings*user*\Start Menu\Programs \Administrative Tools folder to make it appear as a program when you click Start, Programs, and Administrative Tools. In the

A+
OS
1.1
1.5

path, substitute the name of the user. For example, for the Administrator, the path to the .msc file is C:\Documents and Settings\Administrator\Start Menu\Programs \Administrative Tools.

Follow these directions to open MMC and create a console that contains some popular utility tools:

1. Click **Start,** click **Run,** enter **MMC** in the Run dialog box, and then click **OK.** An empty console window appears, as shown in Figure 14-17.

2. Click **Console** on the menu bar, and then click **Add/Remove Snap-in.** The Add/Remove Snap-in window opens. The window illustrated in Figure 14-18 is empty because no snap-ins have been added to the console.

Figure 14-17   An empty console

14

3. Click **Add.** You see a list of snap-ins that can be added to a console, as shown in Figure 14-18. Select a snap-in and then click **Add.**

4. A dialog box opens that allows you to set the parameters for the snap-in. The dialog box offers different selections, depending on the snap-in being added. When you have made your selections, click **Finish.** The new snap-in appears in the Add/Remove Snap-in window.

5. Repeat Steps 3 and 4 to add all the snap-ins that you want to the console. When you finish, click **Close** from the Add Standalone Snap-in window illustrated in Figure 14-18, then click **OK.**

6. Figure 14-19 shows a console with four snap-ins added. To save the console, click **Console** on the menu bar, and then click **Save As.** The Save As dialog box opens.

7. The default location for the console file is shown in Figure 14-19. This is the location that ensures the console appears as an option under Administrative Tools on the Start menu. Select this location for the file, name the file, and click **Save.**

A+
OS
1.1
1.5

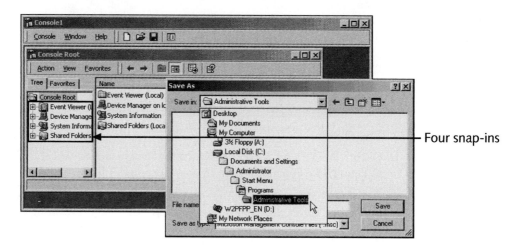

Figure 14-18   List of snap-ins available to be added to a console

Four snap-ins

Figure 14-19   Saving a console with four snap-ins

NOTE

After you create a console, you can copy the .msc file to any computer or place a shortcut to it on the desktop.

A+
OS
1.1
1.5

8. Close the console window by clicking **Console** on the menu bar, and then clicking **Exit**.

To use the console, click Start, Programs, and Administrative Tools, and then select the console.

Event Viewer

A+
OS
1.5
3.1
3.2
3.3

The Event Viewer MMC snap-in connects to the Event Viewer tool, which displays logs about significant system events that occur in Windows NT/2000/XP or in applications running under these OSs, such as a hardware or network failure, OS error messages, a device or service that has failed to start, or General Protection Faults. Three different logs are shown in Event Viewer, and are displayed in Windows 2000, as shown in Figure 14-20:

- *The application log* records application events that the developer of the program sets to trigger a log entry. One type of event recorded in this log is an error recorded by the Dr. Watson utility, which you will learn about later in the chapter.
- *The security log* records events based on audit policies, which an administrator sets to monitor user activity such as successful or unsuccessful attempts to access a file or log on to the system. Only an administrator can view this log.
- *The system log* records events triggered by Windows components, such as a device driver failing to load during the boot process. Windows NT/2000/XP sets which events are recorded in this log. All users can access this log file.

Three types of events are recorded in the system and application logs:

- *Information* events are recorded when a driver, service, or application functions successfully.
- *Warning* events are recorded when something happens that may indicate a future problem but does not necessarily indicate that something is presently wrong with the system. For example, low disk space might trigger a warning event.
- *Error* events are recorded when something goes wrong with the system, such as a necessary component failing to load, data getting lost or becoming corrupted, or a system or application function ceasing to operate.

You can open Event Viewer from the Computer Management console, or you can locate it by double-clicking the Administrative Tools icon in the Control Panel. To view a log within Event Viewer, click the log that you want to view in the left pane. This generates a summary of events that appears in the right pane. Double-click a specific event to see details about it (see Figure 14-20).

Notice in the figure that 878 events are listed in the system log. You may only want to view certain events and not the entire list to find what you're looking for. To filter events, right-click a log in the left pane, and select Filter on the shortcut menu. To filter events, you can use several criteria, which are listed in Table 14-7.

14

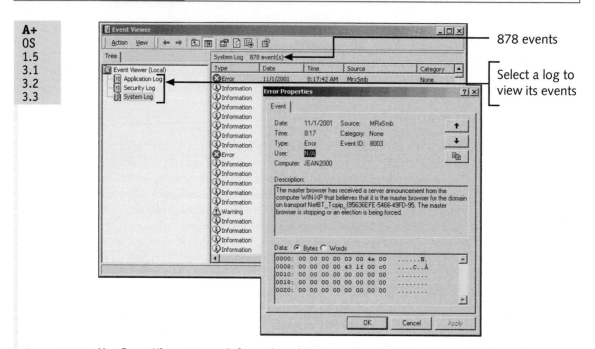

878 events

Select a log to
view its events

Figure 14-20 Use Event Viewer to see information about security audits in the security log and error,
warning, or information events for the system and application logs

Property	Description
Category	The category that the event falls under, such as an attempt to log on to the system or access a program
Computer	The name of a computer on the system
Event ID	A number that identifies the event and makes tracking events easier for support personnel
Event source	The application, driver, or service that triggered the event
Event type	The type of event, such as information, error, or warning
From: To:	The range of events that you want to view. You can view the events from first to last event, or you can view all events that occurred on a specific date and in a specific time range.
User	The logon name for a user

Table 14-7 Log properties that can be used to filter events

Another way you can avoid a ballooning log file is to set a size limit and specify
what happens when the log reaches this limit. If you right-click a log, select
Properties on the shortcut menu, and click the General tab, you can set the maximum

A+
OS
1.5
3.1
3.2
3.3

size of the log in megabytes (as well as view general information about the log). You can set the log to overwrite events as needed, overwrite events that are more than a specified number of days old, or not overwrite events at all. Select this last option when system security is high and you do not want to lose any event information. If you select this option, the system simply stops recording events when the log file reaches the maximum size (see Figure 14-21).

Figure 14-21   View information about a log, including maximum size of the log file, in the System Log Properties dialog box

14

To allow the system to record events in the log after a log reaches maximum size, you have to review the events and clear the log manually, either by clicking the Clear Log button in the Properties dialog box or selecting Clear All Events from the Action menu. Before clearing the log, Event Viewer gives you a chance to save it.

Performance Monitoring and Optimization

Maintaining optimal performance, or addressing performance problems when they develop, involves a three-part process in which you analyze data provided by monitoring tools such as Task Manager and System Monitor, determine areas in which performance is below the baseline, and identify and take the steps necessary to correct the problem.

Principles for Optimizing Performance

Here are some principles to remember when trying to optimize performance on your Windows NT/2000/XP system:

- One of the most important things you can do is establish a **baseline** of acceptable performance for your system, defining what you consider normal performance under a typical workload. Baselines can be created when the OS is first installed, when major changes are made, and on a periodic basis such as once a month. Figure out what resources the system uses when you are running all required programs and services. That will help you decide whether you need to add more resources (such as more RAM) to the system. Heavily used Windows 2000 computers may benefit from having as much as 512 MB of RAM, whereas machines used more moderately may only need 128 MB of RAM.
- If you add RAM, remember that you also need to increase the size of the paging file. You might also increase paging file size if the peak usage of the paging file is too close to the limit.
- Replacing one component may not help much if other components have not been upgraded. For example, if you install a faster CPU, you need to look at the amount of RAM and the size of the hard drive as well.
- Each application is assigned a priority level, which determines its position in the queue for CPU resources. This priority level can be changed for applications that are already loaded by using Task Manager. If an application performs slowly, increase its priority. You should only do this with very important applications, because giving an application higher priority than certain background system processes can sometimes interfere with the operating system.
- In general, upgrading an existing PC is recommended as long as the cost of the upgrade stays below half the cost of buying a new machine. Even if you just keep the case, power supply, and an expansion card or two, buying a new motherboard and hard drive can be almost like having a whole new system at a lower cost.

The rest of this section discusses two tools that you can use to monitor system performance: Task Manager and System Monitor.

Task Manager

A+
OS
1.5
3.2

Task Manager (Taskman.exe) allows you to view the applications and processes running on your computer as well as performance information for the processor and the memory. There are three ways that you can access Task Manager:

- Press Ctrl+Alt+Delete. The Windows Security window opens. Click the Task Manager button.
- Right-click a blank area on the taskbar, and then select Task Manager on the shortcut menu.
- Press Ctrl+Shift+Esc.

A+
OS
1.5
3.2

Task Manager has three tabs: Applications, Processes, and Performance. On the Applications tab (see Figure 14-22), each application loaded can have one of two states: Running or Not Responding. If an application is listed as Not Responding, you can end it by selecting it and clicking the End Task button at the bottom of the window. You will lose any unsaved information in the application.

Figure 14-22   The Applications tab in Task Manager shows the status of active applications

The Processes tab lists system services and other processes associated with applications, together with how much CPU time and memory the process uses. This information can help you determine which applications are slowing down your system. The Performance tab, shown in Figure 14-23, provides more detail about how a program uses system resources. You can use these views to identify which applications and processes use the most CPU time.

On the Performance tab, note the four frames at the bottom of the window. These frames give the following information:

- The *Totals* frame indicates how much the system is currently being used by counting handles (indicates a device or file is being accessed), threads (unit of activity within a process), and processes (programs running). Use these entries to know how heavily the system is used.
- The *Physical Memory* frame lists Total (amount of RAM), Available (RAM not used), and System Cache (RAM in use). Use these entries to know if you must upgrade RAM.

Figure 14-23   The Performance tab shows more detail about how system resources are being used

■ The *Commit Charge* frame lists Total (current size of virtual memory, also called the page file or swap file), Limit (how much of the paging file can be allocated to applications before the size of the paging file must be increased), and Peak (maximum amount of virtual memory used in this session). Use these entries to learn if you must increase the size of the paging file.

■ The *Kernel Memory* frame indicates how much RAM and virtual memory the OS uses. This frame lists Total (sum of RAM and virtual memory), Paged (how much of the paging file the OS uses), and Nonpaged (how much RAM the OS uses). Use this frame to learn how much memory the OS is using. If usage is high, look for OS processes you can eliminate.

By reading the information in the frames in Figure 14-23, you can see that the OS is using about 28 MB of memory. The system contains about 130 MB of RAM, and the maximum paging file size is set to about 311 MB. How to change the maximum and initial size of the paging file is covered in Chapter 6.

NOTE

If your desktop locks up, you can use Task Manager to refresh it. Press Ctrl+Alt+Del and then click Task Manager. Click the Processes tab. Select Explorer.exe (the process that provides the desktop) and then click End Process. Click Yes. Then click the Applications tab. Click New Task. Enter Explorer.exe in the Create New Task dialog box and click OK. Your desktop will be refreshed and any running programs will still be open.

System Monitor

In most cases, you can find the information you need from Task Manager to determine if the system needs performance tuning or upgrading. If this information is not detailed enough, use System Monitor, which provides more system performance detail than Task Manager. There are three components of System Monitor: objects, instances, and counters. Objects are hardware or software system components, and instances are multiples of objects. For example, Microsoft Word is an object, but if you have Word open in two separate windows on the desktop, then two instances of this one object are running. Counters show information on specific characteristics of an object and constantly gather data and update the counter display. You can specify which counters to show for an object.

Important objects to monitor using System Monitor include Memory, Paging File, Processor, and Physical Disk (the hard drive). In the following example, you will access System Monitor and then add and view counters for the Memory object.

1. In the Control Panel, double-click the **Administrative Tools** icon.

2. In the Administrative Tools window, double-click the **Performance** icon.

3. The Performance window opens (see Figure 14-24). System Monitor is highlighted and the System Monitor details pane appears on the right. The pane is blank because no objects are being monitored. Right-click the pane and select **Add Counters** on the shortcut menu (see Figure 14-24).

4. The Add Counters window opens (see Figure 14-25). From the Performance object drop-down list, select the **Memory** object.

5. You have the option to view all counters, but that makes a messy, hard-to-read display. By default, the "Select counters from list" option is selected. Locate and click the **Available Bytes** counter, which tells you how much physical memory remains. Click **Add**.

6. Scroll down the list until you see the **Page Faults/sec** counter. This tells you how many pages were requested but not immediately available in memory. Click **Add**.

7. Click **Close** to close the Add Counters window.

Figure 14-26 shows System Monitor in the process of monitoring the two counters you selected. The lines tracking the counters are color-coded to match the counters listed at the bottom of the graph. Look at the left side of the graph. The line representing Page Faults/sec begins at 0 and spikes when an application is opened. The line representing Available Bytes begins at 30 and dips lower, showing fewer bytes are available when applications are active. The vertical line on the right moves to the right as monitoring continues.

14

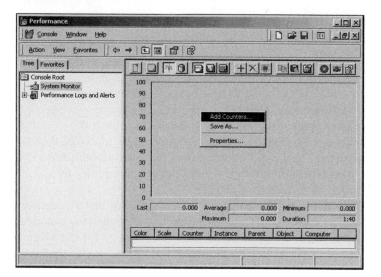

Figure 14-24 Access System Monitor through the Performance window

Figure 14-25 In the Add Counters window, select a performance object and counters to monitor

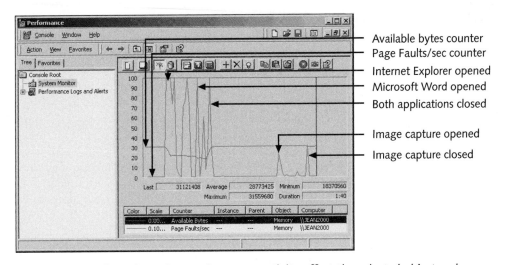

Figure 14-26 System Monitor shows how changes in system activity affect the selected object and counters

Dr. Watson and Memory Dumps

A+
OS
3.1
3.2
3.3

Two tools that can produce text output useful in diagnosing problems with the OS and applications are Dr. Watson and memory dumps. Recall from Chapter 12 that Dr. Watson is used to debug errors in applications by recording error events to a log file. It can help solve problems such as when an application fails to install or load, when the system locks, or when error messages appear. In Windows 2000, these events are recorded in the Drwtsn32.log file. Dr. Watson automatically launches when an application error occurs, or you can launch it manually by entering Drwtsn32.exe in the Run dialog box or at a command prompt. The log file is written to the \Documents and Settings*user*\Documents\DrWatson folder.

Another tool that helps you understand what happened when an error occurs is a **memory dump**. It saves the contents of memory at the time a stop error halts the system in a file called a **dump file**. A **stop error** is an error so severe that the operating system stops all processes. How to capture and interpret memory dumps is beyond the scope of this book.

Windows Update

A+
OS
2.2
3.2
3.3

In the process of maintaining and troubleshooting Windows 2000, remember that the Microsoft Web site offers patches, fixes, and updates for known problems and has an extensive knowledge base documenting problems and their solutions. You learned how to download a Windows update in Chapter 12; the process is basically the same for Windows 2000 as it is for Windows 9x/Me. You can access Windows

14

A+
OS
2.2
3.2
3.3

Update by going to the Microsoft site *windowsupdate.microsoft.com*, or you can click Windows Update on your Start menu, which takes you directly to the site.

If you think you might later want to uninstall a critical update or service pack, select the option to Save uninstall information. Later, to uninstall the fix, again execute the downloaded file. When given the option, select "Uninstall a previously installed service pack."

A+ EXAM TIP

The A+ OS exam expects you to know that applying the latest OS service packs, patches, and updates is always done as one of the last steps after installing or upgrading an OS.

In addition to critical updates and service packs that Microsoft creates to address known problems with Windows, the Windows Update tool also uses ActiveX controls to scan your system, find your device drivers and system files, and compare these files to the ones on the Windows Update server. If you do not already have Active Setup and the ActiveX controls installed on your computer, a prompt to install them appears when you access the site. After Windows Update scans your system and locates update packages and new versions of drivers and system files, it offers you the option of selecting files for download.

NOTE

Because ActiveX controls have open access to the Windows operating system, there is some risk of an ActiveX control causing damage to data or software on your computer. Some system administrators require that ActiveX controls be disabled when they are not specifically needed for tasks such as Windows Update downloads.

In addition to the information in this chapter, other important sources of information about Windows 2000 are the Microsoft Web site at *support.microsoft.com* and the *Windows 2000 Professional Resource Kit* by Microsoft Press. The *Resource Kit* includes a CD that contains additional Windows 2000 utilities. These resources can further help you understand Windows 2000 and solve problems with the OS. Also remember that user manuals are an excellent source of information, as well as the Web, training manuals, and product installation documentation.

NOTE

In addition to the support tools described here, third-party diagnostic software can be of help. For example, ConfigSafe by imagineLAN, Inc. (*www.imaginelan.com*) is a utility that tracks configuration changes to Windows 9x/Me or Windows NT/2000/XP and can restore the system to a previously saved configuration. It comes preinstalled with some Windows 2000 installations. To use ConfigSafe to make a backup of the registry before installing a new device or application, click Start, Programs, and ConfigSafe. The ConfigSafe window appears; select the Camera icon. Type a name for the snapshot of the registry and click OK. Later if you need to restore the registry, open the CongfigSafe window and follow directions on screen.

CHAPTER SUMMARY

▶ The boot process for Windows NT, Windows 2000, and Windows XP works the same under each OS, although the tools to troubleshoot a failed boot are slightly different for each OS.

▶ The boot process can be customized with entries in Boot.ini. The Boot.ini file can be edited with a text editor, but it is best to change the file using the System Properties dialog box.

▶ Tools to use to troubleshoot problems with loading Windows 2000 are the Advanced Options menu, the Recovery Console, and the Emergency Repair Process.

▶ To access the Advanced Options menu, press F8 when starting Windows 2000.

▶ The Advanced Options menu includes Safe Mode, Safe Mode with networking, Safe Mode with command prompt, enable boot logging, enable VGA mode, Last Known Good configuration, directory services restore mode, and debugging mode.

▶ The Recovery Console is a command interface with a limited number of commands available to troubleshoot a failing Windows 2000 load. The console requires that you enter the Administrator password.

▶ Access the Recovery Console by first booting from the Windows 2000 CD or from the four setup disks, or install the console under the boot loader menu and access it from there.

▶ Using the Recovery Console, you can restore the registry to the state it was in at the time of the last backup of the registry.

14

▶ The Emergency Repair Process lets you restore the system to its state at the end of the Windows 2000 installation. Don't use it unless all other methods fail, because you will lose all changes made to the system since the installation. The Emergency Repair Process requires the emergency repair disk.

▶ Back up the Windows 2000 system state on a regular basis using the Backup utility. This backup includes system files, files to load the OS, and the registry. Back up the system state before editing the registry.

▶ Windows 2000 Support Tools can be installed from the Windows 2000 CD and include several utilities to support hardware and applications.

▶ Windows File Protection (WFP) protects the system files against an application, a virus, or a user changing or deleting them. System File Checker is part of the WFP system.

▶ Disk Management is a tool found in the Computer Management console. Disk Management replaces Fdisk in older Windows OSs, and is used to partition and format a hard drive and to convert a basic disk to a dynamic disk.

▶ Microsoft Management Console (MMC) can be used to create customized consoles to manage the OS.

▶ Event Viewer is used to view system, application, and security events.

▶ When monitoring performance, begin by establishing a baseline that helps determine what performance should be expected of a system.

▶ Task Manager is used to measure performance, giving information about the processor, memory, the hard drive, and virtual memory.

▶ System Monitor gives more detail than Task Manager, and can be used to monitor object and instance performance over time by using counters that you select for monitoring.

▶ Information about application errors and stop errors can be recorded by Dr. Watson and memory dumps.

▶ Windows Update uses the Microsoft Web site to download patches and fixes to Microsoft OSs and applications.

▶ Additional sources of support for Windows 2000 include the Microsoft support Web site at *support.microsoft.com* and the *Windows 2000 Professional Resource Kit* by Microsoft Press.

KEY TERMS

For explanations of key terms, see the Glossary near the end of the book.

32-bit flat memory mode	dump file	Recovery Console
Advanced Options menu	Emergency Repair Process	SFC (System File Checker)
baseline	memory dump	snap-ins
Boot.ini	Microsoft Management Console (MMC)	stop error
console	minifile system	WFP (Windows File Protection)
Disk Management		

REVIEWING THE BASICS

1. In the Windows NT/2000/XP boot process, what file reads and loads the boot menu?

2. Where is the Boot.ini file stored?

3. What does %SystemRoot% mean?

4. List the steps to restore the Windows 2000 system state from the backup made with the Backup utility.

5. In what folder does Windows 2000 store a backup of the registry when backing up the system state?

6. Under what circumstances would you use the Enable VGA Mode option on the Advanced Options menu?

7. What key do you press to display the Advanced Options menu during startup?

8. When you look at a Windows desktop, how can you tell if the system has been booted into Safe Mode?

9. What is the purpose of Safe Mode with networking under the Advanced Options menu?

10. What is the name of the log file that Windows 2000 uses when booting in Safe Mode?

11. List the steps to load the Recovery Console when using the four Windows 2000 rescue disks.

12. Why is the Administrator password required in order to use the Recovery Console?

13. In Question 12, under what circumstances is the password not required?

14. What is the purpose of the Systemroot command under the Recovery Console?

15. Under the Recovery Console, what is the command that gives the same results as Fdisk/MBR?

16. What is the command to install the Recovery Console on the boot loader menu?

17. Before you can perform the Windows 2000 Emergency Repair Process, what disk must you have? What is contained on the disk?

18. When would you use System File Checker? What is the command to execute it?

19. What is the command to install the Windows 2000 Support Tools?

20. What is the name of the log file created by Dr. Watson?

21. Name two Windows utilities that can be used to monitor OS performance.

22. What tool can you use to create a console containing Device Manager and Event Viewer?

23. What is the file extension assigned to a console file?

24. Name one snap-in contained in a Computer Management console.

25. What is the program filename for System File Checker?

14

26. List three ways to access the Task Manager.

27. List the steps used to end an application when it refuses to respond to keystrokes or the mouse action.

28. What are the three logs kept by Event Viewer?

29. In what folder do you put a console file that you want displayed when you are logged on as an administrator and then click Start, Programs, and Administrative Tools?

30. Before clearing the Event Viewer log, explain how you can save the log for later viewing.

THINKING CRITICALLY

1. Your Windows 2000 system boots to a blue screen and no desktop. What do you do first?

   a. Reinstall Windows 2000.

   b. Attempt to boot into the Advanced Options menu.

   c. Attempt to boot into the Recovery Console.

   d. Attempt to use the Emergency Repair Process.

2. You were unable to use the Emergency Repair Process to restore a failed Windows 2000 system, but there is a very important data file on the hard drive that you need to recover. The hard drive is using the NTFS file system. What do you do?

   a. Boot using a Windows 98 startup disk and use the Copy command to attempt to recover the file.

   b. Boot to the Recovery Console using the Windows 2000 setup CD and attempt to recover the file.

   c. Reinstall Windows 2000 and then recover the file.

   d. Boot to the Advanced Options menu and use Safe Mode to recover the file.

3. You need to install a customized console on 10 computers. What is the best way to do that?

   a. When installing the console on the first computer, write down each step to make it easier to do the same chore on the other nine.

b. Create the console on one computer and copy the .mmc file to the other nine.

c. Create the console on one computer and copy the .msc file to the other nine.

HANDS-ON PROJECTS

HANDS-ON
PROJECTS

PROJECT 14-1: Using the Microsoft Knowledge Base

Using the Microsoft support Web site (*support.microsoft.com*), print information about the following:

▶ Troubleshooting IEEE 1394 devices running under Windows 2000 Professional

▶ How to set up Windows 2000 to support multiple CPUs

▶ How to set up and troubleshoot multiple monitors with Windows 2000 Professional

PROJECT 14-2: Using DiskProbe to Back Up the MBR

Windows 2000 DiskProbe edits individual sectors on a hard drive and can edit the MBR, boot sectors, and the FAT16, FAT32, and NTFS file system tables, as well as data files. Research DiskProbe and find directions that show you how to back up the MBR, which contains the partition table. Follow these directions and answer these questions:

1. In the C:\ProgramFiles\Support Tools folder, find the document Dskprtrb.doc, which describes how to use DiskProbe. Print the page from the document that describes how to save the MBR record on a floppy disk.

2. If the Windows 2000 Support Tools are not installed, install them now.

3. Run DiskProbe (click **Start,** point to **Programs, Windows 2000 Support Tools,** and **Tools,** and then click **DiskProbe**).

4. Follow the directions to save the MBR, including the partition table, to a floppy disk.

5. How many bytes of data are included in the MBR? What is the file size?

6. What is the disadvantage of using DiskProbe to restore the MBR in the event it becomes corrupted?

14

PROJECT 14-3: Creating a Windows 2000 Antivirus Boot Disk

Windows 2000 offers an antivirus program that can scan memory, the MBR sector, and OS boot sectors for viruses. Follow these directions to create the boot disk and scan your system for viruses. Use the disk when you suspect that a virus has attacked your Windows 2000 hard drive.

1. Insert the Windows 2000 CD in the CD-ROM drive, and insert an empty floppy disk in the floppy disk drive.

2. Click **Start** and then click **Run**. In the Run dialog box, enter the following command, substituting the drive letter of your CD-ROM drive for D, if necessary: **D:\VALUEADD\3RDPARTY\CA_ANTIV\Makedisk.bat**

3. Label the disk Windows 2000 AVBoot.

4. Boot from the floppy disk. When the scan finishes, Windows 2000 automatically loads.

Note: If your PC is not set to boot from a floppy disk before booting from the hard drive, change the boot sequence in CMOS setup.

PROJECT 14-4: Using Dependency Walker

Follow these steps to use Dependency Walker to list the files used by Internet Explorer:

1. If the Windows 2000 Support Tools are not installed, install them now.

2. Run Dependency Walker (click **Start**, point to **Programs, Windows 2000 Support Tools,** and **Tools,** and then click **Dependency Walker**).

3. Set Dependency Walker to show all supporting files used by Internet Explorer.

4. List the files or print the screen showing them.

PROJECT 14-5: Creating Baselines for Your System

> ✔ **A+ EXAM TIP**
>
> The A+ OS exam expects you to know filenames of Windows utility programs so that you can run the utility from a command prompt.

In this chapter, you learned about several tools you can use to establish baselines for a system before a problem occurs. One tool to help establish a baseline is the boot log. Using the Windows 2000 Advanced Options menu, boot with Enable Boot Logging. Print the Ntbtlog.txt file created. Then boot with Safe Mode. Again print the Ntbtlog.txt file. Compare the two files and mark the differences. Keep these two reports in case you ever have problems booting this system, because they can provide a picture of what a normal boot should be.

PROJECT 14-6: **Finding Windows 2000 Utilities**

The following table lists some important Windows utilities covered in this chapter. Fill in the right side of the table with the filename and path of each utility. (*Hint*: You can use Windows Explorer or Search to locate files.)

Utility	Filename and Path
System File Checker	
Disk Defragmenter	
Command window	
Chkdsk	
System Information	
Task Manager	

14

Installing and Using Windows XP Professional

In this chapter, you will learn:

- About the features and architecture of Windows XP

- How to install Windows XP

- How to use Windows XP

- How to install hardware and applications with Windows XP

Windows XP is the latest generation of Microsoft operating systems. Windows XP currently comes in several varieties: Windows XP Professional, Windows XP Home Edition, Windows XP Media Center Edition, Windows XP Tablet PC Edition, and Windows XP 64-Bit Edition. This chapter focuses on Windows XP Professional, which is the upgrade from Windows 2000 Professional. Features of Windows XP that you already learned about in chapters on earlier versions of Windows are not covered in detail, where they have not changed in Windows XP; more discussion is given to new features or changes to existing ones. This chapter builds the foundation you will need to manage and provide technical support for Windows XP, the focus of the next chapter.

Features and Architecture of Windows XP

A+
OS
1.1

Windows XP integrates features of Windows 9x/Me and Windows 2000, while providing added support for multimedia and networking technologies. The look and feel of Windows XP differs slightly from its predecessors, and utilities and functions are organized differently under menus and windows. You'll learn about many of these differences in this chapter.

NOTE

Windows XP is replacing all previous versions of Windows in the home market and for the corporate desktop. If your hardware and applications qualify, select Windows XP Home Edition for a home PC over Windows 98/Me. For a corporate environment, choose Windows XP Professional over Windows NT/2000. The only exception is compatibility issues with older hardware and software.

Windows XP Features

Windows XP Home Edition and Windows XP Professional have these features, among others:

- A new user interface, shown in Figure 15-1. Notice how different it looks from the desktops of earlier Windows versions such as Windows 98 and Windows 2000.
- The ability for two or more users to be logged on simultaneously. Each user has a separate profile, and Windows XP can switch between users, keeping a separate set of applications open for each user.
- Windows Media Player for Windows XP, a centralized application for working with digital media
- Windows Messenger for instant messaging, conferencing, and application sharing
- The ability to burn a CD simply by dragging and dropping a folder or file onto the CD-R device icon
- An expanded Help feature
- Advanced security features

In addition to these features of Windows XP Home Edition, Windows XP Professional offers:

- A way for someone to remotely control your computer, called Remote Desktop
- A way for an administrator to manage user profiles from a server (roaming profiles)
- Additional security features
- Multilingual capabilities
- Support for new higher-performance processors

A+
OS
1.1

Figure 15-1   The Windows XP desktop and Start menu

Windows XP Media Center Edition is an enhanced version of Windows XP Professional, and includes additional support for digital entertainment hardware such as video recording integrated with TV input. It's designed for the high-end PC home market and is only available when preinstalled on a high-end PC manufactured by a Microsoft partner. Windows XP Tablet PC Edition is also built on Windows XP Professional with additional support for tablet PCs. For more information about tablet PCs, see Chapter 20.

There is also Windows XP 64-Bit Edition, designed to be used with a high-end 64-bit CPU such as the Intel Itanium or AMD Opteron. This Windows XP version is designed mostly for servers or heavily technical workstations that run scientific and engineering applications and need greater amounts of memory and higher performance than standard desktop PCs. For example, an aircraft designer who uses software to simulate how various conditions affect aircraft materials might use Windows XP 64-Bit Edition on a system that supports resource-intensive simulation and animation applications.

Windows Internet Explorer, Windows Media Player, a firewall, and other Microsoft products are tightly integrated with the Windows XP operating system. Some users see this as a disadvantage, and others see it as an advantage. Tight integration allows applications to interact easily with other applications and the OS,

15

A+
OS
1.1

but makes it more difficult for third-party software to compete with Microsoft applications.

Windows XP provides several enhancements over Windows 2000 and other earlier versions. Table 15-1 summarizes the advantages and disadvantages of Windows XP.

Advantages	Disadvantages
Provides better integration of Windows 9x/Me and NT than Windows 2000 did	Requires nearly a gigabyte of hard drive space for the operating system itself, and at least a 233-MHz processor with 64 MB of RAM
Offers significant GUI enhancements over earlier versions of Windows	Programs used with Windows XP may need more than the minimum system requirements for the operating system
Adds features but uses only slightly more total memory for the OS than Windows 2000	Nearly eliminates support for device drivers not approved by Microsoft
Adds advanced file sorting options, such as sorting pictures by resolution or sound files by artist	Security concerns with centralized storage of online information in Microsoft Passport, a repository of the user IDs and passwords you use on the Internet
Includes built-in support for compressed files	
Has improved troubleshooting tools and is generally more stable than previous Windows OSs	

Table 15-1   Advantages and disadvantages of Windows XP

Windows XP Architecture

Windows XP uses the same kernel architecture as Windows NT and Windows 2000, with components operating in either user mode or kernel mode. Figure 15-2 shows how the different OS components relate. Notice in the figure that some low-level device drivers such as those that access the hard drive have direct access to hardware, just as they do with Windows NT and Windows 2000. All 16-bit and 32-bit applications relate to the kernel by way of the Win32 subsystem operating in user mode. As you will learn in the next chapter, the boot process is also the same, and the files needed for a successful boot are the same as those for Windows NT/2000.

Windows XP is generally more stable than Windows NT and Windows 2000. It was designed to avoid situations that occurred with Windows NT/2000, which caused drivers and applications to bring these systems down. Installing Windows XP should also be easier than installing Windows NT or Windows 2000. In addition, Windows XP has increased security, including a built-in Internet firewall designed to protect a home PC connected directly to the Internet by way of an always-on

A+
OS
1.1

connection such as a cable modem or DSL. Firewalls, cable modems, and DSL are covered in Chapters 18 and 19.

Figure 15-2   The Windows XP architecture uses the same basic structure and components as Windows NT and Windows 2000

15

Installing Windows XP

A+
OS
2.1
2.2

Installing Windows XP involves many of the same considerations and decisions that you learned about when installing Windows 2000. In this section, you learn how to install Windows XP as a clean install and as an upgrade, including how to set up a dual boot.

Planning the Installation

A+
OS
2.1
2.2

Before installing Windows XP, do the following:

- Verify that the system meets the minimum and recommended requirements shown in Table 15-2.
- Verify that all installed hardware components and software are compatible with Windows XP.
- Decide how you will partition your hard drive and what file system you will use.
- For a PC on a network, decide whether the PC will be configured as a workstation in a workgroup or as part of a domain. (Workgroups and domains were covered in Chapter 13.)
- Make a final checklist to verify that you have done all of the above and are ready to begin the installation.

NOTE

Remember that the requirements of an OS vary depending on which version you have installed and what applications and hardware you have installed with it.

Component or Device	Minimum Requirement	Recommended Requirement
One or two CPUs	Pentium II 233 MHz or better	Pentium II 300 MHz or better
RAM	64 MB	128 MB up to 4 GB
Hard drive partition	2 GB	2 GB or more
Free space on the hard drive partition	640 MB (bare bones)	2 GB or more
CD-ROM drive	12x	12x or faster
Accessories	Keyboard and mouse or other pointing device	Keyboard and mouse or other pointing device

Table 15-2   Minimum and recommended requirements for Windows XP Professional

APPLYING CONCEPTS

Minimum Requirements and Hardware Compatibility

Recall from earlier chapters that you can use the My Computer icon on the Windows desktop to determine the current CPU and available RAM. To see how much hard drive space is available, open Windows Explorer, right-click the drive letter, and select Properties from the shortcut menu. Part of the installation process for an upgrade is to clean up the hard drive, which might free some hard drive space. Even though Windows XP requires only 640 MB to

A+
OS
2.1
2.2

install, you cannot achieve acceptable results unless you have at least 1.5 GB of free hard drive space on the volume that holds Windows XP.

There are several ways you can verify that software and hardware qualify for Windows XP. One way is to run the Readiness Analyzer. Use the following command from the Windows XP CD, substituting the drive letter of your CD-ROM drive for D in the command line, if necessary:

```
D:\I386\Winnt32 /checkupgradeonly
```

Depending on the release of Windows XP, your path might be different. The process takes about 10 minutes to run and displays a report that you can save and later print. The default name and path of the report is C:\Windows\compat.txt. The report is important if you have software you are not sure will work under Windows XP. If the analyzer reports that your software will not work under Windows XP, you might choose to upgrade the software or set up a dual boot with your old OS and Windows XP. (Dual-boot setup is covered later in the chapter.)

Readiness Analyzer also checks hardware compatibility. Another way to verify your hardware is to go to the Microsoft Web site and search on each hardware device by type. The process is different from that of Windows 2000. Begin at the Windows Catalog page (*www.microsoft.com/windows/catalog*). Click the Hardware tab. A list of hardware device categories appears on the left side of the screen. Select a category or use the search utility on the page. Figure 15-3 shows the beginning of the list of qualifying modem cards. There might be a copy of the Windows XP Professional HCL in the hcl.txt file on the Windows XP CD in the support folder. But for the most up-to-date information, use the Microsoft Web site.

If your hardware does not qualify for Windows XP, check the hardware manufacturer's Web site for an upgrade and download the upgraded drivers before you begin the installation. If you plan to erase the hard drive as part of the installation, store these drivers on floppy disks or on a network drive until you're ready to install them under Windows XP. If you cannot find an upgrade, sometimes a device will work if you substitute a Windows driver written for a similar device. Check the documentation for your device, looking for information about other devices it can emulate. It is especially important to know that your network card or modem card qualifies for Windows XP before you install the OS, because you need the card to access the Internet to get upgrades. If you are not sure an important hardware component qualifies, then install Windows XP as a dual boot with your current OS. Later, when you get the component working under Windows XP, you can uninstall the other OS.

15

Figure 15-3   To see if your hardware device qualifies for Windows XP, search by hardware category, manufacturer name, or product name

Hard Drive Partitions and File Systems

Windows XP needs at least a 2-GB partition for the installation and should have about 1.5 GB of free space on that partition. You can install Windows XP on the same partition as another OS, but Windows XP overwrites the existing OS on that partition. If you do not have a free 2-GB partition for the installation, you must delete smaller partitions and repartition the drive. Deleting a partition erases all data on it, so be sure to create backups first. Follow these general directions to ensure that partitions on the hard drive are adequate to install Windows XP:

- For Windows 9x/Me, use Fdisk at the command prompt, and for Windows 2000, use Disk Management to determine what partitions are on the drive, how large they are, what logical drives are assigned to them, and how much free space on the drive is not yet partitioned.
- If existing partitions are too small, look at the free space on the drive. If there is enough free space that is not yet partitioned, use that free space to create a new partition that is at least 2 GB.

A+
OS
2.1
2.2

- If you cannot create a 2-GB or larger partition, back up your data, delete the smaller partitions, and create a 2-GB or larger active partition on the drive.
- If you have free space on the drive for other partitions, don't partition them at this time. First install Windows XP and then use Disk Management under Windows XP to partition the remaining free space on the drive.

The same concerns about selecting a file system for Windows 2000 apply to Windows XP. The file systems supported by Windows XP are the same as those supported by Windows 2000: FAT16, FAT32, and NTFS. Recall that the NTFS file system used by Windows 2000 is incompatible with the Windows NT NTFS file system, causing a potential problem when installing Windows 2000 and Windows NT on the same PC as a dual boot. Because the Windows XP NTFS file system is the same as the Windows 2000 NTFS file system, a dual boot between these two OSs should be no problem. Here are the general directions for selecting a file system:

- Use the NTFS file system if you are interested in file and folder security, file compression, control over how much disk space a user is allowed, or file encryption.
- Use the FAT32 file system if you are setting up a dual boot with Windows 9x/Me and each OS must access all partitions.
- Use the FAT16 file system if you are setting up a dual boot with MS-DOS or Windows NT and each OS must access all partitions.

Joining a Workgroup or a Domain

If you are installing Windows XP on a network, you must decide how you will access the network. If you have fewer than 10 computers networked together, Microsoft recommends that you join these computers in a workgroup, in which each computer controls its own resources. In this case, each user account is set up on the local computer, independently from user accounts on other PCs. There is no centralized control of resources. For more than 10 computers, Microsoft recommends that you use a domain controller running a network operating system such as Windows 2003 Server to control network resources. (Windows XP Professional installed on a workstation can then be a client on this Windows network.) You will also want to use a domain controller if you want to administer and secure the network from a centralized location, or if several centralized resources on the network are shared by many users. How to manage workgroups is covered in Chapter 18, but managing a domain controller is beyond the scope of this book.

15

NOTE

Windows XP Home Edition does not support joining a domain. If you plan to use a domain controller on your network, install Windows XP Professional.

A+
OS
1.1
2.2

Upgrade or Clean Install?

If you plan to set up a dual boot, then you will perform a clean install for Windows XP. If you already have an OS installed and you do not plan a dual boot, then you have a choice between an upgrade and a clean install. Things to consider when making this decision are:

✔ **A+ EXAM TIP**

The A+ OS exam expects you to know the upgrade paths available to Windows XP.

- You can use the less expensive upgrade version of Windows XP Professional to upgrade from Windows 98, Windows Me, Windows NT 4.0, and Windows 2000 to Windows XP Professional.
- You can use the less expensive upgrade version of Windows XP Home Edition to upgrade from Windows 98 or Windows Me to Windows XP Home Edition.
- If you currently have Windows 95 installed, you must do a clean install using the more expensive "For a New PC" version of Windows XP Professional or Windows XP Home Edition.
- Regardless of whether you have an OS currently installed, you can still choose to do a clean install if you want a fresh start. Unless you erase your hard drive, reformat it, or delete partitions before the upgrade, data on the hard drive is not erased even if you convert to a new file system during the installation. However, OS settings and installed software do not carry forward into the new installation.

Final Checklist

Before you begin the installation, complete the final checklist shown in Table 15-3 to verify that you are ready.

Things to Do	Further Information
Does the PC meet the minimum or recommended hardware requirement?	CPU: RAM: Hard drive size: Free space on the hard drive:
Have you run the Readiness Analyzer or checked the Microsoft Web site to verify that all your hardware and software qualify?	List hardware and software that need to be upgraded:
Do you have the product key available?	Product key:
Have you decided how you will join a network?	Workgroup name: Domain name: Computer name:

Table 15-3 (continued)

Things to Do	Further Information
Will you do an upgrade or clean install?	Current operating system:
	Does the old OS qualify for an upgrade?
Is your hard drive ready?	Size of the hard drive partition:
	Free space on the partition:
	File system you plan to use:
For a clean install, will you set up a dual boot?	List reasons for a dual boot:
	For a dual boot
	Size of the second partition:
	Free space on the second partition:
	File system you plan to use:
Have you backed up important data on your hard drive?	Location of backup:

Table 15-3   Checklist to complete before installing Windows XP

Installation Process

Follow these general directions to perform a clean install of Windows XP on a PC that does not already have an OS installed:

1. Boot from the Windows XP CD, which displays the menu shown in Figure 15-4. This menu might change slightly from one Windows XP release to another. Select the first option and press Enter. If your PC does not boot from a CD, go to a command prompt and enter the command **D:\i386\Winnt.exe**, substituting the drive letter of your CD-ROM drive for D, if necessary. (The path might vary depending on the release of Windows XP.) The End-User License agreement appears. Accept the agreement.

2. Setup lists all partitions that it finds on the hard drive, the file system of each partition, and the size of the partition. It also lists any unpartitioned free space on the drive. From this screen, you can create and delete partitions and select the partition on which you want to install Windows XP. If you plan to have more than one partition on the drive, create only one partition at this time. The partition must be at least 2 GB in size and have 1.5 GB free. After the installation, you can use Disk Management to create the other partitions. Figure 15-5 shows an example of the list provided by Setup when the entire hard drive has not yet been partitioned.

15

3. If you created a partition in Step 2, Setup asks which file system you want to use to format the partition, NTFS or FAT. If the partition is at least 2 GB in size, the FAT file system will be FAT32. Select a file system for the partition. The Setup program formats the drive, completes the text-based portion of setup, and loads the graphical interface for the rest of the installation. The PC then restarts.

4. Select your geographical location from the list provided. Windows XP will use it to decide how to display dates, times, numbers, and currency. Select your keyboard layout. Different keyboards can be used to accommodate special characters for other languages.

5. Enter your name, the name of your organization, and your product key.

6. Enter the computer name and the password for the Administrator account. This password is stored in the security database on this PC. If you are joining a domain, the computer name is the name assigned to this computer by the network administrator managing the domain controller.

7. Select the date, time, and time zone. The PC might reboot.

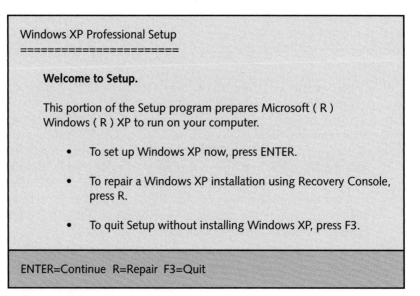

Windows XP Professional Setup
========================

Welcome to Setup.

This portion of the Setup program prepares Microsoft (R)
Windows (R) XP to run on your computer.

- To set up Windows XP now, press ENTER.

- To repair a Windows XP installation using Recovery Console, press R.

- To quit Setup without installing Windows XP, press F3.

ENTER=Continue R=Repair F3=Quit

Figure 15-4   Windows XP Setup opening menu

It is *very* important that you remember the Administrator password. You cannot log on to the system without it.

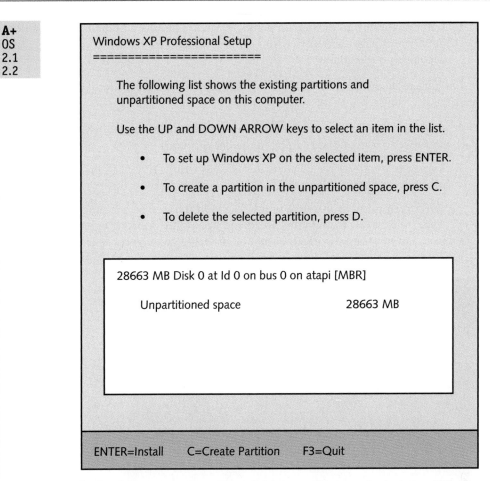

A+
OS
2.1
2.2

Windows XP Professional Setup
==========================

    The following list shows the existing partitions and
unpartitioned space on this computer.

    Use the UP and DOWN ARROW keys to select an item in the list.

       •   To set up Windows XP on the selected item, press ENTER.

       •   To create a partition in the unpartitioned space, press C.

       •   To delete the selected partition, press D.

    28663 MB Disk 0 at Id 0 on bus 0 on atapi [MBR]

        Unpartitioned space   28663 MB

    ENTER=Install   C=Create Partition   F3=Quit

Figure 15-5   During Setup, you can create and delete partitions and select a partition on which to install Windows XP

8. If you are connected to a network, you will be asked to choose how to config-ure your network settings. The Typical setting installs Client for Microsoft Networks, File and Printer Sharing, and TCP/IP using dynamically assigned IP addresses. The Custom setting allows you to configure the network differently. If you are not sure which to use, choose the Typical settings. You can change them later. How networks are configured is covered in Chapter 18.

NOTE

During a normal Windows XP installation, setup causes the system to reboot three times.

9. Enter a workgroup or domain name. If you are joining a domain, the network administrator will have given you specific directions on how to configure user accounts on the domain.

For a clean install on a PC that already has an OS installed, follow these general directions:

1. Close any open applications. Close any boot management software or antivirus software that might be running in the background.

2. Insert the Windows XP CD in the CD-ROM drive. Autorun launches the opening window shown in Figure 15-6.

3. Select the option to **Install Windows XP**. On the next screen, under Installation Type, select **New Installation**. Read and accept the licensing agreement. The installation process works the same as in the preceding procedure, resuming at Step 3.

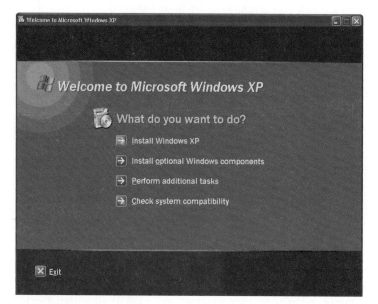

Figure 15-6   Windows XP Setup menu

When performing an upgrade to Windows XP, follow these general directions:

- Clean up the hard drive: erase unneeded or temporary files, empty the Recycle Bin, run Disk Defragmenter, and do a ScanDisk of the drive.
- If you have determined that you must upgrade hardware or software and that these upgrades are compatible with your old OS, perform the upgrades and verify that the hardware or software is working.
- If you do not have the latest BIOS for your motherboard, flash your BIOS.
- Back up important files.

A+
OS
2.1
2.2

- Scan the hard drive for viruses using a current version of antivirus software.
- If you have a compressed hard drive, uncompress the drive. The only exception is that if you are using Windows NT file compression on an NTFS drive, you do not need to uncompress it.
- Uninstall any hardware or software that you know is not compatible with Windows XP and for which you have no available upgrade.

2. Insert the Windows XP Upgrade CD in the CD-ROM drive. The Autorun feature should launch the Setup program, with the menu shown in Figure 15-6. Select the option to **Install Windows XP**.

3. If the Setup menu does not appear, you can enter the Setup command in the Run dialog box. Recall that the command is D:\i386\Winnt.exe, where you substitute the drive letter of your CD-ROM drive for D, if necessary.

4. On the next screen, under Installation Type, select **Upgrade**. The menu gives you two options:

   - *Express Upgrade.* This upgrade uses existing Windows folders and all the existing settings it can.
   - *Custom Upgrade.* This upgrade allows you to change the installation folder and the language options. Using this option, you can also change the file system to NTFS.

5. Select the type of upgrade, and accept the licensing agreement.

6. Select the partition on which to install Windows XP. If the drive is configured as FAT and you want to convert to NTFS, specify that now. Note that Windows XP has an uninstall utility that allows you to revert to Windows 98 if necessary. This uninstall tool does not work if you convert FAT to NTFS.

7. Setup performs an analysis of the system and reports any compatibility problems. Stop the installation if the problems indicate that you will not be able to operate the system after the installation.

8. For an upgrade from Windows 98 or Windows Me to Windows XP, the Setup program converts whatever information it can in the registry to Windows XP. At the end of the installation process, you are given the opportunity to join a domain. For Windows NT and Windows 2000 upgrades, almost all registry entries are carried forward into the new OS; the information about a domain is not requested because it is copied from the old OS into Windows XP.

15

NOTE

Antivirus software designed to be used with the Windows NT NTFS file system might not run under the Windows XP NTFS file system because of the way some antivirus programs filter software as it accesses the file system. You might have to upgrade your antivirus software after Windows XP is installed.

A+
OS
2.1
2.2

Upgrading from Windows NT or Windows 2000 to Windows XP is the easiest type of upgrade because these operating systems all have similar registries and support applications and devices in the same way. Nearly all applications that run on Windows NT or Windows 2000 will run on Windows XP. When you upgrade from Windows NT to Windows XP, the NTFS file system is automatically converted to the Windows XP version.

Setting Up a Dual Boot

✔ **A+ EXAM TIP**

The A+ OS exam expects you to be familiar with a dual boot and how to set one up.

You can configure Windows XP to set up a dual boot with another operating system. Start the installation as you would for a clean install on a PC with another operating system already installed. When given the opportunity, choose to install Windows XP on a different partition than the other OS. Windows XP recognizes that another OS is installed and sets up the startup menu to offer it as an option for booting. After the installation, when you boot with a dual boot, the **boot loader menu** automatically appears and asks you to select an operating system, as shown in Figure 15-7.

Please select the operating system to start:

    Microsoft Windows XP Professional
    Microsoft Windows 98

Use the up and down arrow keys to move the highlight to your choice.
Seconds until highlighted choice will be started automatically: xx
Press ENTER to choose.

For troubleshooting and advanced startup options for Windows, press F8.

Figure 15-7   Menu displayed for a dual boot

The first active partition (drive C) must be set up with a file system that both operating systems understand. For example, for a dual boot with Windows 98, use the FAT32 file system. For a dual boot with Windows 2000, use either the FAT32 or the NTFS file system. You should install the other operating system first, and then you can install Windows XP in a different partition. When you install Windows XP on another active partition or an extended partition, it places only the files necessary to

A+
OS
2.1
2.2

boot in the first active partition, which it calls the system partition. This causes Windows XP to initiate the boot rather than the other OS. The rest of Windows XP is installed on a second partition, which Windows XP calls the boot partition. This is the same way that Windows NT and Windows 2000 manage a dual boot with an older OS.

> When setting up a dual boot, always install the older operating system first.

Earlier Windows operating systems were not aware of applications installed under the other OS in a dual boot. For example, in a dual boot with Windows 98 and Windows 2000, an application had to be installed twice, once under Windows 98 and once under Windows 2000. However, Windows XP is able to use an application installed under the other OS in a dual boot. For example, if you set up a dual boot with Windows XP and Windows 98, an application installed under Windows 98 can be executed from Windows XP. This application might be listed under the Start menu of Windows XP. If it is not, you can use Windows XP Explorer to locate the program file. Double-click the application to run it from Windows XP. This makes implementing a dual boot easier because you don't have to install an application under both OSs.

After the Installation

Immediately after you have installed Windows XP, there are several things to do to activate the OS, prepare it for use, and back up the hard drive in preparation for a disaster. These steps are discussed next.

15

Product Activation

Product activation is a method used by Microsoft to prevent unlicensed use of its software so that you must purchase a Windows XP license for each installation of Windows XP. The license was introduced with Microsoft Office XP, and Microsoft says it will continue using product activation in all future Microsoft products. The first time you log on to the system after the installation, the Activate Windows dialog box appears with these three options (see Figure 15-8):

▪ Yes, let's activate Windows over the Internet now
▪ Yes, I want to telephone a customer service representative to activate Windows
▪ No, remind me to activate Windows every few days

If you choose to activate Windows over the Internet and are connected to the Internet at the time, the process is almost instant. Windows XP sends a numeric identifier to a Microsoft server, which sends a certificate activating the product on your PC.

You have up to 30 days after installation to activate Windows XP; after that the system will not boot. If you install Windows XP from the same CD on a different computer and you attempt to activate Windows from the new PC, a dialog box appears telling you of the suspected violation of the license agreement. You can call a Microsoft operator and explain what caused the discrepancy. If your explanation is reasonable (for example, you uninstalled Windows XP from one PC and installed it on another), the operator can issue you a valid certificate. You can then type the certificate value into a dialog box to complete the boot process.

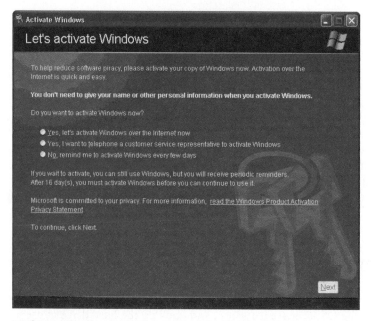

Figure 15-8 Product activation is a strategy used by Microsoft to prevent software piracy

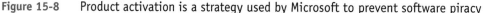

Now access the Internet and download any service packs, updates, or patches for the OS from the Microsoft Web site. You can also install any additional Windows components at this time.

Transferring User Files and Preferences to a New PC

Windows XP offers a utility that helps you transfer user files and preferences from one computer to another that has just had Windows XP installed. The **User State Migration Tool (USMT)** transfers user files and folders, display properties, taskbar options, and browser and e-mail settings from a Windows 9x/Me or Windows NT/2000/XP computer. This utility can help make a smooth transition because a user who is moving from one PC to another does not have to copy files and reconfigure OS settings. The process involves three steps:

A+
OS
2.1
2.2

1. Use a Windows XP computer to create a disk that contains the Files and Settings Transfer Wizard. This PC does not need to be the same PC that will later receive the transfer.

2. Use the disk on the source computer (the user's old computer) to run the wizard and copy the user state to a server hard drive or removable media such as a Zip drive.

3. On the destination computer (the user's new computer), use the wizard to transfer the user state to this computer.

To begin the process, use the Files and Settings Transfer Wizard to create the disk. To access the wizard, click Start, All Programs, Accessories, System Tools, and Files and Settings Transfer Wizard. The wizard's Welcome window opens. When you click Next, the wizard asks if this is the New computer or Old computer. Select New computer and then click Next. Figure 15-9 shows the next screen, with which you can choose to create the disk or declare that you are ready to put the information on the new computer. On the screen, note that you can also use the Windows XP CD to launch the wizard on the old computer rather than creating the disk.

Files and Settings Transfer Wizard

Do you have a Windows XP CD?

You will also need to run this wizard on your old computer. You can either create a wizard disk to use on your old computer, or use the wizard from the Windows XP CD.

To create a Wizard Disk, insert a blank, formatted disk into this computer's disk drive. Make sure the old computer has the same type of drive.

- ○ I want to create a Wizard Disk in the following drive:
  - 3½ Floppy (A:)
- ○ I already have a Wizard Disk
- ○ I will use the wizard from the Windows XP CD
- ○ I don't need the Wizard Disk. I have already collected my files and settings from my old computer.

< Back   Next >   Cancel

15

Figure 15-9   The first step in using the Files and Settings Transfer Wizard is to create the wizard disk

After you have created the disk or chosen to use the Windows XP CD, go to the old computer, launch the wizard, and retrieve the files and settings. Then return to this screen on the new computer, and choose to put the information on the new computer.

Instead of using the wizard, you can also use two commands at the command prompt. Scanstate copies the information to a server or removable media, and Loadstate copies the information to the destination computer. These utilities can be included in batch files and executed automatically when implementing Windows XP

A+
OS
2.1
2.2

over a large number of computers in an enterprise. For details on how to use the command lines in a batch file, see the *Windows XP Resource Kit* by Microsoft Press.

Preparing for Later Problems with the OS

A+
OS
3.2

After the installation is complete, hardware and software are installed, and user preferences are set, it is a good idea to guard against later problems with the OS by creating a backup of the hard drive. Windows XP offers a utility called **Automated System Recovery (ASR)** that allows you to restore an entire hard drive volume or logical drive to its state at the time the backup of the volume was made. This process creates the backup and creates an ASR floppy disk that allows you to use the backup to recover the system later. You will learn how to recover a failed system using a backup in the next chapter. In this section, you learn how to create the backup.

The backup file created will be just as large as the contents of the hard drive volume, so you will need a massive backup medium such as another partition on the same hard drive, on another local hard drive or file server, a tape drive, or a writeable CD-R or CD-RW drive.

Do not back up the logical drive or volume to a folder on the same volume. The ASR backup process allows you to do this, but restoring later from this backup does not work. Also, to better protect your installation, back up to a different hard drive or other media.

By default, Windows XP Home Edition does not include the Backup utility. To install it manually, go to the \VALUEADD\MSFT\NTBACKUP folder on your Windows XP setup CD and double-click Ntbackup.msi. The installation wizard will complete the installation.

Follow these directions to create the backup and the ASR floppy disk:

1. Click **Start, All Programs, Accessories, System Tools,** and **Backup.** The Backup or Restore Wizard appears (see Figure 15-10).

2. Click the **Advanced Mode** link. The Backup Utility window appears. Click **Automated System Recovery Wizard.** On the following screen, click **Next.**

3. The Backup Destination window appears. Select the location of the medium to receive the backup and insert a disk into the drive. This disk will become the ASR disk. Click **Next.**

Just as with Windows 2000, you can back up the system state as discussed in Chapter 13. If you back up the system state when you complete an installation and a failure occurs in the future, you can restore the system state without overwriting user data on the hard drive. This is less drastic than the Automated System Recovery process that restores the entire volume.

A+
OS
3.2

Figure 15-10   Use the Backup or Restore Wizard to back up the hard drive partition after the Windows
XP installation is complete

4. Click **Finish.** The backup process shows its progress, as seen in Figure 15-11.

5. When the backup is finished, label the ASR disk with the name of the disk, the
date it was created, and the computer's name, and put the disk in a safe place.

15

Figure 15-11   The Backup utility can create a backup of drive C and an ASR disk to be used later for the
Automated System Recovery utility

Using Windows XP

**A+
OS
1.1**

Now that you have learned how to install Windows XP successfully and guard the system against potential failure, let's take a closer look at how it works and what it can do. One difference you will note immediately when using Windows XP for the first time is the desktop shown in Figure 15-12. When the OS is first installed, the Recycle Bin is the only shortcut on the desktop. Also note that the Start menu is organized with a more graphical look. Notice in Figure 15-12 that the user name for the person currently logged on shows at the top of the Start menu. Applications at the top of the Start menu are said to be "pinned" to the menu and are permanently listed there until you change them in a Start menu setting. Applications that are used often are listed below the pinned applications and can change from time to time. The programs in the white column on the left side of the Start menu are user-oriented, and the programs in the dark column on the right side of the menu are OS-oriented.

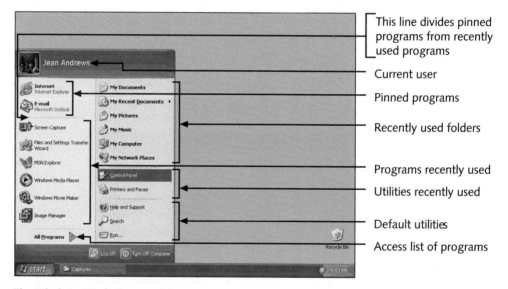

Figure 15-12   The Windows XP desktop and Start menu

When you click All Programs, the list of currently installed software appears. Figure 15-13 shows the default entries that appear when you click Accessories and then System Tools. You have already seen two of these tools: Backup, and Files and Settings Transfer Wizard. Also, after Windows is installed, you can use the Activate Windows option on this menu to activate Windows XP. You will learn about other options on this menu later in this chapter and in the next chapter.

When you drill down to windows and menus on these windows, you will notice you have more control over how and where things appear. Overall, if you are familiar with earlier versions of Windows, learning to use Windows XP is easy and

**A+
OS
1.1**

intuitive. One example of how you can change the way a window appears is the Control Panel. To access the Control Panel, click Start and then click Control Panel. Figure 15-14 shows the Control Panel in Category View. Select a category to see the applets in that category, or click Switch to Classic View to see the applets when you first open the Control Panel, as you did with earlier versions of Windows.

Figure 15-13   Click Start, All Programs to view the list of currently installed software

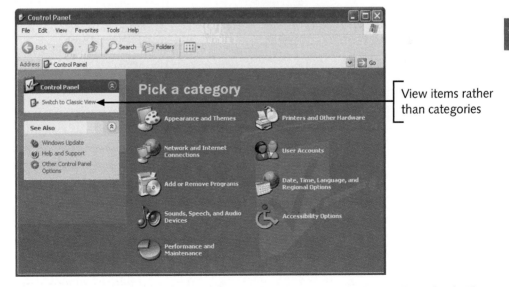

View items rather than categories

Figure 15-14   The Control Panel is organized by category, although you can easily switch to Classic View

15

Customizing the Windows XP Desktop

A+
OS
1.1

You can do several things to customize the Windows XP desktop. For example, you can change the background on the desktop (called the wallpaper), create shortcuts, and control what goes in the system tray. This section looks at each of these ways to make the desktop look and work the way you want it to.

NOTE

Each user account has a different desktop configuration, so if you want to create a customized desktop for a user, you must first log on to the system under that user account.

Managing Shortcuts

When you first install Windows XP, only the Recycle Bin shows on the desktop by default. To add other shortcuts that normally were on the Windows 2000 desktop, right-click anywhere on the desktop and select Properties from the shortcut menu. (You can also select the Display icon in the Control Panel.) The Display Properties dialog box appears (see Figure 15-15). Click the Desktop tab.

Figure 15-15   Managing the Windows XP desktop

Click Customize Desktop to display the Desktop Items window, also shown in Figure 15-15. You can check My Documents, My Computer, My Network

A+
OS
1.1

Places, and Internet Explorer to add these icons to the desktop. Also notice on this window the option to have Windows clean up your desktop by moving any shortcuts that you have not used in the last 60 days to a separate folder.

You can add a program shortcut to the desktop by clicking Start, clicking All Programs, right-clicking a program name in the list that appears, and then selecting Copy from the shortcut menu. Then right-click anywhere on the desktop, and select Paste from the shortcut menu. A shortcut is created and placed on the desktop. You can also use Windows Explorer to create a shortcut. From Explorer, right-click a program filename or the filename of a document or data file, and then select Create Shortcut from the shortcut menu (see Figure 15-16). Then, drag the shortcut created to the desktop. Chapter 12 listed several other ways to create shortcuts in Windows 9x/Me, which also work for Windows XP.

Figure 15-16   Create a shortcut to a file using the file's shortcut menu in Explorer

15

NOTE

Changing the wallpaper (desktop background) is easy in Windows XP. Right-click the desktop and select Properties. In the Display Properties dialog box, click the Desktop tab. Select the wallpaper and click Apply. Any photographs you have stored in C:\Documents and Settings\%username%\My Documents\My Pictures appear in the list for you to use as wallpaper. You can also use photographs you have stored in other folders as your wallpaper. Using Explorer, right-click the photograph and select Set as Desktop Background from the shortcut menu.

Windows XP Taskbar and System Tray

You can control the taskbar from the Taskbar and Start Menu windows. Access these windows by using the Taskbar and Start menu icon in the Control Panel or by right-clicking the taskbar and selecting Properties. Either way, the window in Figure 15-17 appears. From it you can add items to and remove items from the Start menu, control how the taskbar manages items in the system tray, and specify how the taskbar is displayed.

Figure 15-17 Use the Taskbar and Start Menu Properties window to control what appears in the Start menu and taskbar

You might want to display frequently used programs as icons in the taskbar. To do that, right-click the taskbar, select Toolbars, and then click Quick Launch. Also, the system tray can sometimes become cluttered with several icons for running services such as the volume control and network connectivity. Windows XP automatically hides these icons. To display them, click the left arrow on the right side of the taskbar. In addition, by using the options on the taskbar shortcut menu, you can add programs to the Quick Launch toolbar, customize taskbar properties, and add new toolbars to the taskbar.

Windows Messenger

When Windows XP starts, it loads Windows Messenger by default, which consumes system resources even if you are not using it. To stop Windows Messenger from loading at startup, click Start, All Programs, and Windows Messenger. Click Tools on the menu bar, and then click Options. The Options window opens, as shown in

Figure 15-18. Click the Preferences tab and uncheck "Run this program when Windows starts." Click OK.

Figure 15-18   Disable Windows Messenger at startup

Managing Audio and Video

15

Windows XP has several built-in features to manage audio and video, including support for inputting images from digital cameras and scanners, a Windows Movie Maker for editing video, and Windows Media Player, Version 8. (Windows Me has Media Player, Version 7.) With Media Player you can play DVDs, CDs, and Internet radio. There's a jukebox for organizing audio files, including MP3 files used on music CDs. You can also burn your own music CDs using Media Player with a CD-R or CD-RW drive. To access the Media Player, click Start, All Programs, and Windows Media Player. Figure 15-19 shows the Media Player window.

As with older versions of Windows, you can record and manage sound from the Entertainment group of Windows and manage sounds for Windows events from the Sounds applet in the Control Panel. If you have a microphone connected to a sound card, you can record sound by clicking Start, All Programs, Accessories, Entertainment, and Sound Recorder. The Sound Recorder appears, as shown in Figure 15-20. Click the Record button (the red dot in the lower-right corner) to record and save a sound, such as your own voice, in a sound file. There are several types of sound files, including MP3 files (with the .mp3 file extension), which can be used on audio

CDs, and Wave files (with the .wav file extension). Windows uses .wav files to record sound. Later, you can substitute this .wav file for one of the Windows sounds that plays when you open or close applications, shut down Windows, or perform many other Windows activities that can be accompanied by sound. To change the sounds for various Windows events, go to the Control Panel, open the Sounds and Audio Devices applet, and select the Sounds tab.

Figure 15-19 Windows Media Player

Figure 15-20 Record sounds using Windows Sound Recorder

Media Player has its own volume control, but there is another way to adjust sound. From the Control Panel, open the Sounds and Audio Devices applet and select the Volume tab. If you check "Place volume icon in the taskbar," you can easily adjust the sound from the taskbar.

NOTE   Two ways to control sound volume are to use the Windows controls or use the manual controls on an amplifier or speaker. In addition, notebooks often have manual volume controls.

Multiple Logins and Remote Assistance

Windows XP allows more than one user to be logged in at the same time. To switch from one account to another, click Start and then click Log Off. The Log Off Windows dialog box opens, giving you two choices: Switch User and Log Off. Click Switch User and then select a new account from the list of user accounts. After you enter a password, the screen goes blank and then the desktop configured for the new user appears. Each user can have his or her own set of applications open at the same time. When users switch back and forth, Windows keeps separate instances of applications open for each user.

Windows XP also offers a new feature called **Remote Assistance**. Using this utility, a user sitting at the PC can give a support technician at a remote location full access to the desktop. The technician can use the desktop just as she would if sitting in front of the PC. This is useful when an inexperienced user has trouble following the technician's directions as the technician investigates and troubleshoots problems with Windows XP.

Installing Hardware and Applications

A+
OS
2.4

In this section, you will learn how to install hardware and applications under Windows XP, and you will also learn several ways to solve problems with both. Later in this chapter and the next chapter, you will learn about more tools and procedures you can use to troubleshoot a failed system, program, or hardware device. We will first look at how to install hardware.

15

Installing Hardware

If your hardware device comes bundled with drivers for Windows XP on CD or floppy disk, use those drivers. If the drivers are not written for Windows XP, go to the manufacturer's Web site to download Windows XP drivers or visit the Microsoft Web site *(www.microsoft.com/technet)* and search on the driver or device. Have the drivers compatible with Windows XP available and then install the device.

After the device is installed and Windows XP first starts, it automatically launches the Found New Hardware Wizard, as with earlier Windows operating systems. The wizard gives you two options:

A+
OS
2.4

- Install the software automatically (Recommended)
- Install from a list or specific location (Advanced)

Select the option to install the software automatically, and then click Next. During the installation process, you can click Have Disk to provide a driver supplied by the manufacturer, rather than selecting the device from a list, which results in using a Windows driver. Also, Windows XP might proceed with the installation using Microsoft drivers without displaying a dialog box that contains the Have Disk button. To prevent this from happening, run the setup program on the manufacturer's CD that is bundled with the device before installing the device. Later, after the device is installed, Windows will use the manufacturer's installed drivers for the device.

When installing a device, Windows XP verifies that Microsoft has digitally signed the drivers. If the drivers have been written for Windows XP, even though they are not certified by Microsoft, they should still work in a Windows XP system.

Windows XP offers three processes that help solve problems with devices:

- Providing a way to automatically find an update for a driver
- Rolling back a driver in case an updated driver fails
- Verifying that the driver is certified by Microsoft

These processes are all available from Device Manager.

Using Device Manager

A+
OS
1.1
2.4
3.2
3.3

After a device is installed, you can use Device Manager to verify that Windows XP sees no problems with the device. There is more than one way to access Device Manager:

- Click Start, right-click My Computer, and then select Manage from the shortcut menu. The Computer Management window appears (see Figure 15-21). Under System Tools, click Device Manager.
- Open the System applet in the Control Panel, select the Hardware tab, and click Device Manager.
- Enter Devmgmt.msc in the Run dialog box.

NOTE

If you do not have an always-on connection to the Internet, connect to the Internet before you launch the Update Device Driver Wizard.

Using Device Manager, you can verify that there are no resource conflicts with the device and that it works properly as viewed by Windows XP. From Device Manager, Windows XP offers a way to update a driver using the Update Device Driver Wizard. Right-click a device and select Properties from the shortcut menu. The Properties window for that device appears (see Figure 15-22). Select the Driver tab, click Update Driver to launch the wizard, and follow directions on the screen. The wizard goes to the Microsoft Web site, searches for updates to the driver, informs you if there is an

A+
OS
1.1
2.4
3.2
3.3

update, and asks permission to install the update. Windows XP only suggests an update if the hardware ID of the device exactly matches the hardware ID of the update. A hardware ID is a number assigned to a device by the manufacturer that uniquely identifies the product.

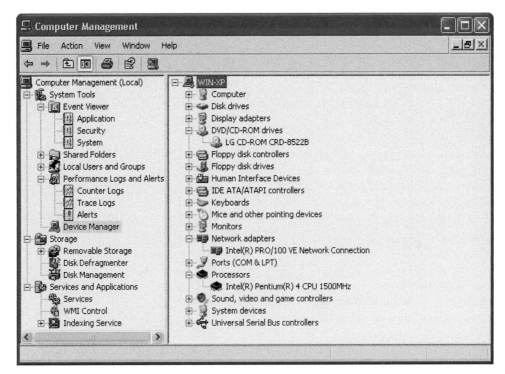

Figure 15-21   Device Manager is one tool available in the Computer Management window

15

If you update a driver and the new driver does not perform as expected, you can revert to the old driver by using the Driver Rollback feature. To revert to a previous driver, open the Properties window for the device (see Figure 15-22), and click Roll Back Driver. If a previous driver is available, it will be installed. In many cases, when a driver is updated, Windows saves the old driver in case you want to revert to it. Note that Windows does not save printer drivers when they are updated and does not save drivers that are not functioning properly at the time of an update.

By default, Device Manager hides legacy devices that are not Plug and Play. To view installed legacy devices, click the View menu of Device Manager, and check Show hidden devices (see Figure 15-23).

You can also copy an older driver from another PC or a backup medium to this PC for a rollback. Two files are needed: a .sys file and an .inf file. The .sys file is the actual driver, and the .inf file contains information about the driver. Put these files in the %systemroot%\system32\reinstallbackups\ folder, and then perform the rollback.

Figure 15-22   Use the Properties window for a device to obtain an updated driver from the Microsoft Web site

Figure 15-23   By default, Windows XP does not display legacy devices in Device Manager. Show these hidden devices by using the View menu.

A+
OS
1.1
2.4
3.2
3.3

Verify that Drivers Are Certified by Microsoft

Windows 2000 and Windows XP support the verification of digital signatures assigned to device drivers and application files, which certifies that the driver or other software has been tested and approved by Microsoft's Windows Hardware Quality Labs (WHQL) for Windows 2000 or Windows XP. If you suspect a problem with a driver, do one of the following to verify that it is digitally signed by Microsoft:

- *Use the File Signature Verification tool.* Enter the command Sig-verif.exe in the Run dialog box. This command displays information about digitally signed files, including device driver files and application files, and logs information to *systemroot*\Sigverif.txt.
- *Use the Driver Query tool.* To direct output to a file, including information about digital signatures, enter this command in the Run dialog box:

```
Driverquery /si > myfile.txt
```

- *Use Device Manager.* In a device's Properties dialog box, click the Driver tab and then click Driver Details. In the Driver File Details window under Digital Signer, look for Microsoft Windows XP Publisher (for Microsoft drivers) or Microsoft WHQL (for manufacturer drivers).

If a driver is not digitally signed, you can control how Windows handles it during the hardware device installation by using the Hardware tab of the System Properties window.

NOTE   Use the Driver Query tool to save information about your system to a file when the system is healthy. Later, if you have a problem with drivers, you can compare a report to one created then to help identify the problem driver.

15

Installing Applications

A+
OS
3.3

Applications are installed under Windows XP as they are under other Windows OSs. You can use the Add or Remove Programs icon in the Control Panel, or you can run the application's setup program from the Run dialog box. You can only install software if you have Administrator privileges. An installed program is normally made available to all users when they log on. If a program is not available to all users, try installing the program files in the C:\Documents and Settings\All Users folder.

Software is uninstalled using the Add or Remove Programs applet in the Control Panel. Open the applet and select the software to uninstall (see Figure 15-24). Then click the Change/Remove icon. If other users are logged on to the system, the Warning message in Figure 15-24 appears. Log everyone off and then uninstall the software.

A+
OS
3.3

Figure 15-24 To uninstall software using the Add or Remove Programs applet, only one user, an administrator, should be logged on to the system

NOTE

You can cause a program to launch automatically each time you start Windows by putting a shortcut to the program in the Startup menu folder for the user. For each user, this folder is C:\Documents and Settings*Username*\Start Menu\Programs\Startup. If you want the software to start up automatically for all users, put the shortcut in this folder: C:\Documents and Settings \All Users\Start Menu\Programs\Startup.

Installing Legacy Software

DOS and Windows 9x/Me applications that would not work under Windows NT and Windows 2000 are more likely to work under Windows XP. Some legacy applications that you should not attempt to run under Windows XP are older versions of antivirus software, and maintenance and cleanup utilities. In these cases, it is best to upgrade your software to versions designed to work under Windows XP.

If a legacy application does not start up and run successfully after you have installed it, try the following:

- Check the Microsoft Web site for updates to Windows XP or the Microsoft application (*windowsupdate.microsoft.com*). How to perform Windows XP updates is covered in the next chapter.
- Check the software manufacturer's Web site for updates or suggestions on how to run the software under Windows XP.
- Consider upgrading the software to a later version.
- Use the Windows XP Compatibility Mode utility.

The **Compatibility Mode utility** provides an application with the environment it expects from the operating system it was designed for, including Windows 95,

A+
OS
3.3

Windows 98, Windows Me, Windows NT, and Windows 2000. (Compatibility mode does not apply to DOS applications.) There is more than one way to use the utility, but the easiest way is to create a shortcut on the desktop to an installed application and then set the properties of the shortcut to use compatibility mode. After you create the shortcut to the application, right-click it and select Properties from the shortcut menu. The Properties window appears (see Figure 15-25). Select the Compatibility tab, check "Run this program in compatibility mode for," and then select the operating system that you want Windows XP to emulate. Click Apply to apply the change. Run the software to find out whether the problem is solved.

Figure 15-25 Setting Windows XP to run a legacy program in compatibility mode

15

If it is not solved, you can provide Microsoft with information that might help it fix the problem in some future Windows XP update. To provide the information, run the Program Compatibility Wizard. Click Start, All Programs, Accessories, and Program Compatibility Wizard. Follow directions on the wizard screen to locate the program file. After you locate the program file, you are asked to test the application and then respond to the questions shown in Figure 15-26.

A+
OS
3.3

Figure 15-26 Using the Program Compatibility Wizard

If you answer, "No, I am finished trying compatibility settings," then the screen in Figure 15-27 appears. If you respond Yes to the question, "Would you like to send this information to Microsoft?", then the information needed to help Microsoft solve problems with the application is transmitted to the Microsoft Web site over the Internet.

Figure 15-27 If running a legacy program in compatibility mode does not solve the problem, you can send helpful information to Microsoft

CHAPTER SUMMARY

▶ There are presently five versions of Windows XP: Windows XP Home Edition, Windows XP Professional, Windows XP Media Center Edition, Windows XP Tablet PC Edition, and Windows XP 64-Bit Edition.

▶ Windows XP integrates features of Windows 9x/Me and Windows 2000, while providing added support for multimedia and networking technologies.

▶ Although the Windows XP interface looks different from that of earlier versions of Windows and the OS organizes some utilities and functions differently, Windows XP is built on the same basic architecture as Windows NT and Windows 2000 and has the same basic kernel structure.

▶ Windows XP requires only 640 MB of free hard drive space for installation; however, acceptable performance cannot be achieved without 1.5 GB of free space on the Windows XP partition.

▶ Windows XP supports the same file systems as Windows 2000: FAT16, FAT32, and NTFS.

▶ You can install Windows XP as a dual boot with Windows 2000, because they both use the same version of NTFS. To dual boot Windows XP with Windows 9x/Me or Windows NT, you must use FAT32 or FAT16. Always install the other OS first, and install Windows XP on a different partition than another OS.

▶ A clean install is required if you plan to dual boot Windows XP with another OS. Perform an upgrade if you have another version of Windows installed and you do not plan to dual boot.

▶ Before upgrading to Windows XP, clean up the hard drive by deleting unnecessary files and running Disk Defragmenter and ScanDisk, uncompress the drive, and delete known incompatible software.

15

▶ An Express Upgrade uses existing folders and settings as much as possible. A Custom Upgrade allows you to change folders, language, and the file system.

▶ Unlike earlier versions of Windows, Windows XP is aware of applications installed under another OS when it is installed as a dual boot.

▶ Microsoft uses product activation to prevent the use of its software products, including Windows XP, on more than one computer.

▶ The User State Migration Tool (USMT) enables a user to make a smooth transition from one computer to another by transferring user files and settings. The Scanstate and Loadstate commands accomplish the same thing from the command prompt.

- Differences in the Windows XP desktop from earlier versions include the absence (by default) of any shortcuts other than the Recycle Bin and the more graphical organization of the Start menu.

- Windows XP allows more than one user to be logged on at the same time, each with their own instances of open applications.

- Windows XP offers processes to help find updates for a driver, roll back a driver if an update fails, and verify that a driver is certified by Microsoft.

- The Computer Management, Disk Management, and Device Manager tools work much the same way in Windows XP as they did in Windows 2000.

- Windows XP Device Manager hides legacy devices (non-Plug and Play devices) by default.

- You can only install software in Windows XP if you have Administrator privileges.

- DOS applications and older Windows applications that did not work under earlier versions of Windows are more likely to work under Windows XP.

- Compatibility mode in Windows XP provides an application written for Windows 9x/Me or later with the environment for which it was designed.

KEY TERMS

For explanations of key terms, see the Glossary near the end of the book.

Automated System Recovery (ASR)	Compatibility Mode utility	Remote Assistance
boot loader menu	product activation	User State Migration Tool (USMT)

REVIEWING THE BASICS

1. Name the five versions of Windows XP.

2. What are at least three similarities between Windows XP and Windows 2000? At least three differences?

3. How much free space on a partition does Windows XP require for installation? How much does it require for acceptable operation?

4. How much memory is required to install Windows XP? How much is recommended to run applications under Windows XP?

5. When you are trying to determine if your computer can support Windows XP, list the steps to know how much RAM is currently installed.

6. Which version of Windows XP must be installed on a system that is using the Intel Itanium processor? Why?

7. How many processors in a system can Windows XP support?

8. List two ways to check hardware and software compatibility for Windows XP.

9. What file system do you use if you are installing Windows XP as a dual boot with Windows 9x/Me? Windows NT? Windows 2000?

10. Name at least four things you should do before performing an upgrade to Windows XP.

11. What are the two upgrade options for Windows XP? Explain the difference between them.

12. How long do you have to activate Windows XP? What happens if you don't?

13. What is the first Microsoft product to use product activation?

14. Explain the purpose of the USMT utility and list the three steps needed to use it.

15. What two commands can you use from the command prompt to perform the same functions as the Files and Settings Transfer Wizard?

16. How are the Windows XP desktop and Start menu different from those in Windows 2000?

17. Give two ways to create shortcuts in Windows XP.

18. What are two ways you can access the Windows XP Device Manager?

19. Name the two files that are needed to copy an older driver from another PC or a backup medium to your Windows XP PC for a device driver rollback.

20. What is the path for the report file created when you run Readiness Analyzer?

21. Which OS are DOS applications more likely to work under: Windows 2000 or Windows XP?

22. List at least three things you can do if a legacy application does not start up and run correctly after you install it under Windows XP.

23. What legacy applications should you not attempt to run under Windows XP?

24. Where should you place a shortcut if you want the associated application to start automatically on startup for all users? Give the entire path.

25. What command launches the Driver Query tool?

15

THINKING CRITICALLY

1. If you find out that one of your applications is not supported by Windows XP and you still want to use XP, what can you do to solve this incompatibility problem?

2. Is it possible to install Windows XP on a system that does not have a CD-ROM drive or other optical drive? Explain your answer.

3. You connect to the Internet using a telephone line and modem and you want to upgrade your system from Windows 98 to Windows XP. You search the Microsoft Web site for your modem, but don't find it. What is your best next step?

   a. Install Windows XP as a dual boot with Windows 98.

   b. Buy and install a new modem.

   c. Install Windows XP and then buy a new modem.

   d. Check the modem's Web site for Windows XP drivers.

4. You have upgraded from Windows 98 to Windows XP. You want to install a Web camera on your PC, but the drivers that came bundled with your camera are written for Windows 98 and Windows 2000. What is your best next step?

   a. Buy a new Web camera.

   b. Reinstall Windows 98.

   c. Check the camera manufacturer's Web site for Windows XP drivers.

   d. Check the Microsoft Web site for your Web camera drivers.

HANDS-ON PROJECTS

HANDS-ON PROJECTS

PROJECT 15-1: **Using Shortcuts**

Create a shortcut on your desktop to Notepad (Notepad.exe), a text editor. Using a second method for creating shortcuts, add a shortcut to the Windows command prompt (Cmd.exe). First, locate the two program files on your hard drive by clicking Start, clicking Search, and using the Search dialog box. Then create the shortcuts. List the steps you took to create each shortcut.

PROJECT 15-2: Preparing for an Upgrade

On a PC with Windows 2000 or an earlier version of Windows installed, run the Readiness Analyzer from the Windows XP CD to determine whether the PC is ready for Windows XP installation. Make a list of any hardware or software components found incompatible with Windows XP, and draw up a plan for getting the system ready for an XP upgrade.

PROJECT 15-3: Updating Windows

On a Windows XP system connected to the Internet, click **Start, All Programs,** and **Windows Update.** This takes you to the Microsoft Web site, which searches your system and recommends Windows XP updates. Print the Web page showing a list of recommended updates. For a lab PC, don't perform the updates unless you have your instructor's permission.

PROJECT 15-4: Installing Windows XP

CAUTION

This project will erase everything on your hard drive. Do not do it if you have important data on the hard drive.

Prepare your hard drive for a clean installation of Windows XP by formatting the hard drive. Follow the instructions in the chapter to install Windows XP. Put Windows XP in a 2-GB partition. Write down each decision you had to make as you performed the installation. If you get any error messages during the installation, write them down and list the steps you took to recover from the error. How long did the installation take?

Once you have installed Windows XP, use Disk Management to partition and format the remainder of the hard drive. Print a screen shot of Disk Management showing the two partitions. Create an ASR backup of the system partition in the second partition. Print a screen shot showing the files on the ASR floppy disk, using Windows Explorer to view the files.

15

Managing and Supporting Windows XP

In this chapter, you will learn:

- How to use Windows XP features to secure the PC and protect users and their data

- About the Windows NT/2000/XP registry

- About tools for troubleshooting and maintaining Windows XP

- How to troubleshoot the Windows XP boot process

You were introduced to Windows XP in the last chapter and learned how to install and use it. This chapter takes you further in learning to support this OS. You will learn about security features that protect the Windows XP system, its users, and their data. You'll also learn how the Windows NT/2000/XP registry is organized and how to edit it, and about many troubleshooting tools available under Windows XP. Finally, you will learn how to troubleshoot the Windows XP boot process. In later chapters, you will learn more about how Windows XP is used on networks and about additional security features it has when networked.

Security Using Windows NT/2000/XP

A+
OS
1.4
2.4

Security under Windows NT/2000/XP is much improved over Windows 9x/Me and has two goals: to secure the system resources including hardware and software from improper use, and to secure users' data from improper access. In this section you will learn about some features of Windows NT/2000/XP that support these goals. At the heart of Windows NT/2000/XP security is the concept of user accounts.

User Accounts and Profiles

A **user account** defines a user to Windows and records information about the user including the user name, password used to access the account, groups that the account belongs to, and the rights and permissions assigned to the account. Permissions assigned to a user account control what the user can and cannot do and access in Windows. There are three types of user accounts in Windows NT/2000/XP:

- **Global user accounts,** sometimes called domain user accounts, are used at the domain level, created by an administrator, and stored in the SAM (security accounts manager) database on a domain controller. A user can log on to any computer on the networked domain using a global user account, and the information about a global user account's rights and permissions apply to each workstation in the domain. The centralized SAM database is part of Active Directory, a repository of information used to manage a Windows network that is itself managed by Windows 2000 Server or Windows 2003 Server.

- A **local user account** is created on a local computer and allows a user access to only that one computer. An administrator creates a local user account, assigns a user name and password to the account, and gives the account rights and permissions. As a general rule, a user account should have no more rights than a user needs to do his or her job. For example, an administrator, responsible for setting up and maintaining user accounts in an office workgroup, can set the permissions on a user account to deny the user the right to install a printer, install software, or do any other chores that change the PC software or hardware environment.

- Every Windows XP workstation has two **built-in user accounts** that are set up when the OS is first installed: an administrator account and a guest account. An administrator has rights and permissions to all computer software, data, and hardware resources. Under Windows NT/2000/XP, the administrator can create other user accounts and assign corresponding rights and permissions to individual accounts, to groups of selected accounts, or to all accounts that use the computer. A guest account has very limited privileges and gives someone who does not have a user account access to a computer. The guest account is useful in a business environment where many people use a single computer for limited purposes and it is not practical for all of them to have unique user accounts.

How user accounts are set up depends on whether the computer is a standalone workstation (not networked), belongs to a workgroup, or belongs to a domain. Recall from Chapter 13 that in a workgroup, each computer manages the security for its own resources. Each local user account is set up on the local computer independent of other accounts on other PCs, and there is no centralized control of resources. If a user on one computer needs access to resources on another computer in the workgroup, the other computer must have the same user account and password that the first computer does. This chapter focuses on setting up security for standalone workstations and for workstations in a workgroup. It does not cover managing user accounts at the domain level.

After an administrator creates a local user account and the user logs on for the first time, the system creates a **user profile** for that user. When the user changes settings to customize his or her computer and then logs off, the user profile is updated so that settings can be restored the next time the user logs on.

If the computer is networked to other computers in a Windows workgroup, the administrator must create a user account on each computer in the workgroup that this user needs to access. When the user logs on to each computer in the workgroup, he or she would have to reestablish the user profile at each computer, re-creating desktop settings and application settings for each computer unless the administrator implements a feature called roaming user profiles. With **roaming user profiles**, settings established by a user at one computer are stored in a file on a file server on the network and shared with all computers in the workgroup. When a user moves from one computer to another computer in the workgroup, the roaming profile follows the user so that he or she does not have to redo settings at each computer.

Another type of profile used with workgroups is a **mandatory user profile**. This profile is a roaming user profile that applies to all users in a user group, and individual users cannot change that profile. It is used in situations where users only perform specific job-related tasks. A profile that applies to a group of users is called a **group profile**. An administrator creates roaming and mandatory profiles using the Computer Management console under the Administrative Tools applet in the Control Panel.

To view all profiles stored on a Windows XP computer, use the System Properties window. Click Start and then right-click My Computer. Select Properties and then click the Advanced tab. Under User Profiles, click the Settings button (see Figure 16-1).

16

Figure 16-1 View all user profiles stored on this PC using the System Properties window

Next, we turn our attention to how to create and manage local user accounts.

Administering Local User Accounts

When setting up accounts for users where security is a concern, you should follow a few guidelines about passwords for both users and administrators:

- User names for Windows NT/2000/XP logon can consist of up to 15 characters.
- Passwords can be up to 127 characters.
- Do not use a password that is easy to guess, such as one consisting of real words, your telephone number, or the name of your pet.
- The most secure type of password is a combination of letters, numbers, and even non-alphanumeric characters.
- User accounts can be set up with or without passwords. Passwords provide greater security. Where security is a concern, always set a password for the Administrator account.
- Passwords can be controlled by the administrator, but generally, users should be allowed to change their own passwords.

APPLYING CONCEPTS

As an administrator, you can create a user account using the Computer Management console or the User Accounts applet in the Control Panel. If the account is created in Computer Management it will have Limited privileges. If it is created using the Control Panel, it will have Administrator privileges. To create a local user account using Computer Management, follow these steps:

1. Log on to the computer as the administrator.
2. Click **Start** and then right-click **My Computer**. Select **Manage** on the shortcut menu. The Computer Management console window opens. (Note that you can also access Computer Management by way of the Control Panel, Administrative Tools applet.)
3. Expand **Local Users and Groups** by clicking the plus sign to its left. Right-click **Users** and then select **New User** on the shortcut menu. The New User window opens (see Figure 16-2). Enter the User name, enter the password twice, and check the boxes to decide how and when the password can be changed. You can also enter values for the Full name and Description to help identify the user. Click **Create**.

Figure 16-2   Create a user account using either Computer Management or the User Account applets in Control Panel

4. The account is created with the default type Limited, which means the account cannot create, delete, or change other accounts; make system-wide changes; or install software. If you want to give the account Administrator privileges, then open the **Control Panel** and double-click the **User Accounts** applet.

16

A+
OS
1.4
2.4

5. The User Accounts window opens listing all accounts. To make changes to an account, click **Change an account**, and then click the account you want to change.
6. In the next window, you can choose to change the name of the account, change the password, remove a password, change the picture icon associated with the account, change the account type, or delete the account. Click **Change the account type**.
7. In the next window, select **Computer administrator** and click **Change Account Type**. Click **Back** twice on the menu bar to return to the opening window.

Sometimes a user forgets his or her password or the password is compromised. If this happens and you have Administrator privileges, you can access the account through the Control Panel or the Computer Management Console to provide the user with a new password. This action is called resetting the password. However, resetting a password under Windows XP causes the OS to lock the user out from using encrypted email or files or using Internet passwords stored on the computer.

For this reason, each new user should create a **forgotten password floppy disk** for use in the event the user forgets the password. To create the disk, open the User Accounts applet in the Control Panel, click your account, and select "Prevent a forgotten password" under Related Tasks in the left pane of this window. Follow the wizard to create the disk. If a user enters a wrong password at logon, he or she has the opportunity to use the forgotten password floppy disk to log on.

NOTE

The forgotten password floppy disk should be kept in a protected place so that others cannot use it to gain unauthorized access to the computer.

Controlling How a User Logs On

With Windows NT/2000, there was only one way to log on to the system: pressing the Ctrl+Alt+Del keys to open the logon window. In a Windows XP workgroup, you have some options as to how logging on works:

- *Welcome screen.* The default option is a Welcome screen that appears when the PC is first booted or comes back from a sleep state. All users are listed on the Welcome screen along with a picture (which can be the user's photograph); a user clicks his or her user name and enters the password.
- *Logon window.* Instead of the Welcome screen, the user must press Ctrl+Alt+Del to get to a logon window similar to Windows NT/2000.
- *Fast User Switching.* Fast User Switching enables more than one user to be logged on to the system. If this option is disabled, only one user can log on at a time. If the option is enabled, when a user clicks Start, Log Off, then the Log Off Windows dialog box offers three options: Switch User, Log Off, and Cancel. When Fast User Switching is disabled, the Switch User option does not

A+
OS
1.4
2.4

appear. Disable Fast User Switching when you want to conserve resources because performance is poor when several users leave applications open.

To change the way a user logs on, from Control Panel, open the User Accounts applet. Click "Change the way users log on or off" (see Figure 16-3). Make your selections and then click Apply Options to close the dialog box.

Figure 16-3   Options to change the way users log on or off

User Groups

User groups are an efficient way for an administrator to manage multiple user accounts that require the same privileges and similar profiles. When installed, Windows XP sets up several user groups including:

- Administrators, who have access to all parts of the system, can install or uninstall devices and applications, and can perform all administrative tasks.
- **Backup Operators** can back up and restore any files on the system regardless of their access privileges to these files.
- **Power Users** can read from and write to parts of the system other than their own local drive, install applications, and perform limited administrative tasks.
- **Limited Users** (known as Users in Windows NT/2000) have read-write access only on their own folders, read-only access to most system folders, and no access to other users' data. They cannot install applications or carry out any administrative responsibilities.
- **Guests** use a workstation once or occasionally and have limited access to files and resources. A guest account has permission to shut down a computer.

16

Creating a New User Group

A+
OS
1.4
2.4

You can also create your own user group and customize the permissions and profiles for this group of users. To create a new group:

1. Click **Start**, right-click **My Computer**, and select **Manage** on the shortcut menu.

2. The Computer Management console opens. Expand **Local Users and Groups** by clicking the plus sign.

3. To create a new group, right-click the **Groups** folder and select **New Group** on the shortcut menu.

4. The New Group window opens, as shown in Figure 16-4. In this window, enter a name and description of the new group and click the **Add** button to find and select users to add to this group. When finished, click **Create** to finish creating the group.

Figure 16-4 Create a new user group

You can also change the profile settings assigned to users in a group. For example, to control what a user or a user group can do, including the ability to change the system date and time, go to the Control Panel and access the Administrative Tools applet. Double-click the Local Security Policy icon. The Local Security Settings window appears (see Figure 16-5). Under Local Policies, the User Rights Assignment group lists several activities, which can be managed by changing the user groups that have the right to do these activities. Right-click "Change the system time," and then select Properties on the shortcut menu. The Change the system time Properties dialog box appears, as shown in Figure 16-5. From this dialog box, you can add and remove the user groups that have the right to change the system time.

A+
OS
1.4
2.4

Figure 16-5   Local policies can be assigned to a user group, affecting all users in the group

Group Policy

Another way to control how the system can be used is by applying settings called a **Group Policy**. Group Policy is normally intended to be used on a domain where group polices are managed by Active Directory, although you can use it on a stand-alone computer or a computer in a workgroup. Group Policy can be applied to your computer, regardless of the currently logged-on user (called Computer Configuration) or can be applied to each user who logs on (called User Configuration). Computer-based policies are applied just before the logon window is displayed, and user-based policies are applied after a user logs on. The Group Policy console is a Microsoft Management Console (MMC) snap-in that can be accessed by typing gpedit.msc in the Run dialog box. From the console you can control such things as how Media Player, Internet Explorer, and NetMeeting work, as well as many Windows settings and components. For a standalone computer or a computer in a workgroup, use Computer Configuration instead of User Configuration to implement Group Policy settings.

16

Disk Quotas

An administrator can set **disk quotas**, which limit how much disk space a user can access. This is important when two or more users are using a single computer and need to share its storage capacity. A disk quota does not specify where a user's files must be located; it just specifies how much total space the user can take up on a volume. The disk quota set applies to all users. You can only set disk quotas if you are using NTFS.

APPLYING CONCEPTS

To set disk quotas:

1. Log on as an administrator, and open **My Computer**.
2. Find the partition that you want to set a disk quota on. Right-click it and select **Properties** on the shortcut menu.
3. Click the **Quota** tab and the **Enable quota management** check box. See Figure 16-6.

Figure 16-6   Setting disk quotas

In this view, you can specify that users have unlimited access to disk space, you can specify the amount of space for users, and you can set a level of disk space used that will trigger a warning message to a user. For this example, all users are restricted to 500 MB of storage space and warned when they have used 400 MB.

4. Click the **Limit disk space to** radio button, enter **500** in the box next to it, and select **MB** from the drop-down menu to the right of the box.
5. In the box next to **Set warning level to**, enter **400**, and then select **MB** from the drop-down menu. This warns users when they have used 400 MB of their allotted 500 MB of storage space.

6. Click **Deny disk space to users exceeding quota limit** so that no user can use more than the specified amount of disk space.

7. Click **OK**. You are prompted to enable disk quotas. Click **OK** to respond to the prompt (see Figure 16-7).

Disk Quota

⚠ You should enable the quota system only if you intend to use quotas on this disk volume. When you enable the quota system, the volume will be rescanned to update disk usage statistics. This might take several minutes.

Press OK to enable the quota system now.

[OK]   [Cancel]

Figure 16-7   The prompt at the end of the quota-setting process gives you information about enabling quotas

EFS (Encrypted File System)

A+
OS
1.4

Another Windows 2000/XP security feature is the **Encrypted File System (EFS)**. EFS applies only to the Windows 2000/XP NTFS file system. In the past, it was possible to bypass an existing operating system's security measures by installing a new operating system or booting from a startup disk. In Windows 98, a password could be put on a file using a FAT file system, but you could boot from a startup disk, get to the file at the command prompt, copy it to a floppy disk, and access the file without using the password. That method does not work with EFS, which protects encrypted data even when someone who is not authorized to view those files or folders has full access to a computer's data storage. When an unauthorized user attempts to access a file encrypted using EFS, he receives the error "Access Denied."

16

✔ **A+ EXAM TIP**

The A+ OS exam expects you to know how to use file encryption under Windows XP.

Encryption is the process of putting readable data into code that must be translated before it can be accessed, usually by using a **key** that encrypts the data and also provides a way to "unlock" the code and translate it back into readable data.

To ensure that a file can be accessed if a user is not available or forgets the password to log on to the system, an administrator for the OS can decrypt a file. In this case, the administrator is called a data recovery agent (DRA).

NOTE

Do not confuse the term *key* as it is used in encryption with the term *registry key* which applies to information placed in the registry.

How to Use Encryption

A+
OS
1.4

A user does not have to go through a complex process of encryption to use EFS; from a user's perspective, it's just a matter of placing a file in a folder marked for encryption. Encryption can be implemented at either the folder or file level. If a folder is marked for encryption, every file created in the folder or copied to the folder will be encrypted. At the file level, each file must be encrypted individually. Encrypting with EFS at the folder level is encouraged and considered a best practice because it provides greater security: Any file placed in an encrypted folder is automatically encrypted so the user doesn't have to remember to encrypt it. An encrypted file remains encrypted if you move it from an encrypted folder to an unencrypted folder on the same or another NTFS logical drive.

In the following example, you encrypt the My Documents folder for an existing user named User2, create a file in that folder that automatically becomes encrypted because the folder is encrypted, and decrypt the folder so that others can access it.

1. In Windows Explorer, locate the My Documents folder for User2. In this example, the correct path is C:\Documents and Settings\User2\My Documents.

2. Right-click the **My Documents** folder, and choose **Properties** on the shortcut menu. The My Documents Properties dialog box appears (see Figure 16-8).

3. On the **General** tab, click the **Advanced** button. The Advanced Attributes dialog box appears.

Figure 16-8   Encrypt folder contents

4. Check the box labeled **Encrypt contents to secure data,** and click **OK** (see Figure 16-8).

5. Click **Apply.** This causes the Confirm Attribute Changes dialog box to open if any files or folders exist in the selected folder (see Figure 16-9).

My Documents Properties   ? X

General | Sharing

My Documents

Type: File Folder

Location: C:\Documents and Settings\Jean Andrews

Size: 393 KB (403,049 bytes)

Size on disk: 428 KB (438,272 bytes)

Contains: 10 Files, 12 Folders

Created: Thursday, November 01, 2001, 1:13:31 PM

Attributes: ☐ Read-only   [Advanced...]
               ☐ Hidden

Confirm Attribute Changes   X

You have chosen to make the following attribute changes:

   encrypt

Do you want to apply this change to this folder only, or do you want to apply it to all subfolders and files as well?

○ Apply changes to this folder only

◉ Apply changes to this folder, subfolders and files

[OK]   [Cancel]

[OK]   [Cancel]   [Apply]

Figure 16-9   Apply changes to all folder contents

6. In this example, the subfolder My Pictures exists within the My Documents folder. If necessary, click the **Apply changes to this folder, subfolders and files** radio button to encrypt any objects in this folder and its subfolders. (If you do not want to apply the changes to all subfolders and files, you select "Apply changes to this folder only.") Click **OK.**

7. Open Microsoft Word, type some text in a file, and save the file in User2's My Documents folder. This file is automatically encrypted, because the My Documents folder is encrypted. If an unauthorized user attempts to access the encrypted document, the user receives an error message.

Here are three ways to decrypt a file or folder to allow others to view it:

▪ From the file's Properties dialog box, click the Advanced button. In the Advanced Attributes dialog box, uncheck "Encrypt contents to secure data."

▪ Encryption is removed automatically when a file or folder is moved to a FAT logical drive (volume) because the FAT file system does not support encryption.

▪ Use the Cipher command discussed next.

16

The Cipher Command

**A+
OS
1.4**

If you are encrypting a large number of files or folders from a command prompt or using a batch file, you can use the Cipher command:

```
CIPHER [/E, /D] [/S:dir] [pathname[...]]
```

- /E encrypts the specified files or folders.
- /D decrypts the specified files or folders.
- /S:dir applies the action to the specified folder (directory) and all its subfolders.
- Pathname is the path to and the name of the file or folder that is to be encrypted or decrypted.

For example, at the command prompt, to decrypt all files in the C:\Public folder, use this command:

```
CIPHER /D C:\Public\*.*
```

Internet Connection Firewall

**A+
OS
4.2**

Windows 2000/XP offers several security features that protect the system from unauthorized access over a network or over the Internet, which you will learn about in later chapters. One feature new to Windows XP is Internet Connection Firewall. Recall from Chapter 9 that a firewall is hardware or software that protects a computer or network from unauthorized access. **Internet Connection Firewall (ICF)** is Windows XP software designed to protect a PC from unauthorized access from the Internet when the PC is connected directly to the Internet.

NOTE

You should not use ICF on a PC that has Internet access from a LAN (local area network) because it can prevent others on the LAN from accessing resources on the PC.

ICF works by examining every communication that comes to the PC to determine if the communication has been initiated by the PC or is being initiated by an outside device or computer. If the communication is initiated by some source other than the PC, it is refused. With ICF, you can browse the Web, but those on the Web cannot initiate a communication with your PC in order to gain unauthorized access to data stored there.

To enable ICF, open the Network Connections applet in Control Panel, right-click the network connection icon that you use to connect to the Internet, and then select Properties on the shortcut menu. This might be a connection to the Internet by way of a dial-up modem, a cable modem, or a DSL connection. (All these connection types are covered in later chapters.) The connection Properties dialog box opens as shown in Figure 16-10 for a modem connection. Click the Advanced tab and select

**A+
OS
4.2**

"Protect my computer and network by limiting or preventing access to this computer from the Internet." If you would like the firewall to record dropped packets in a log file, click Log Dropped Packets. Click OK. Remember, don't do this for a regular network connection if you want others on the network to have access to resources on your PC.

Figure 16-10   Enable Internet Connection Firewall and log dropped packets

> Windows XP Service Pack 2 made significant changes to the Windows Firewall. For more informa-tion about this service pack, see Appendix H.
>
> **NOTE**

We now turn our attention to several utilities that allow you to customize and troubleshoot Windows XP. We begin by looking at the Windows NT/2000/XP registry and learning how to edit it.

16

The Windows NT/2000/XP Registry

**A+
OS
1.1
1.2
1.5**

The Windows NT/2000/XP registry is a hierarchical database containing information about all the hardware, software, device drivers, network protocols, and user configu-ration needed by the OS and applications. Many components depend on this informa-tion, and the registry provides a secure and stable location for it. Table 16-1 lists ways in which some components use the registry Information in this section about the registry applies to Windows NT, Windows 2000, and Windows XP.

Component	Description
Setup programs for devices and applications	Setup programs can record configuration information in the registry and query the registry for information needed to install drivers and applications.
User profiles maintained and used by the OS	Windows maintains a profile for each user that determines the user's environment. User profiles are kept in files, but, when a user logs on, the profile information is written to the registry, where changes are recorded, and then later written back to the user profile file. The OS uses this profile to control user settings and other configuration information specific to this user.
Files active when Ntldr is loading the OS	During the boot process, NTDetect.com surveys present hardware devices and records that information in the registry. Ntldr loads and initializes device drivers using information from the registry, including the order in which to load them.
Device drivers	Device drivers read and write configuration information from and to the registry each time they load. The drivers write hardware configuration information to the registry and read it to determine the proper way to load.
Hardware profiles	Windows can maintain more than one set of hardware configuration information (called a **hardware profile**) for one PC. The data is kept in the registry. An example of a computer that has more than one hardware profile is a notebook that has a docking station. Two hardware profiles describe the notebook, one docked and the other undocked. This information is kept in the registry.
Application programs	Many application programs read the registry for information about the location of files the program uses and various other parameters that were stored in .ini files under Windows 9x/Me.

Table 16-1 Components that use the Windows NT/2000/XP registry

The next section looks at how the registry is organized, how to view the contents of the registry, how to back up and recover the registry, and how Windows makes changes to the registry.

How the Registry Is Organized

A+
OS
1.1
1.2
1.5

When studying how the registry is organized, keep in mind that there are two ways to look at this organization: physical and logical.

Logical Organization of the Registry

Logically, the organization of the registry looks like an upside-down tree with five branches, called keys or subtrees (see Figure 16-11), which are categories of information stored in the registry. Each key is made up of several subkeys that may also have subkeys, and subkeys hold, or contain, values. Each value has a name and data assigned to it. Data in the registry is always stored in values, the lowest level of the tree.

Figure 16-11   The Windows NT/2000/XP registry is logically organized in an upside-down tree structure of keys, subkeys, and values

16

Figure 16-12 shows the Windows Registry Editor, the window you see when you first open the editor: There are five high levels, one for each key or subtree. Notice in the figure that the HKEY_CURRENT_USER subtree has been opened to show subkeys under it; several subkeys have their own subkeys. If you click a subkey that has a value assigned to it, that value appears on the right side of the window. Later in this section, you will see how to edit values in the registry.

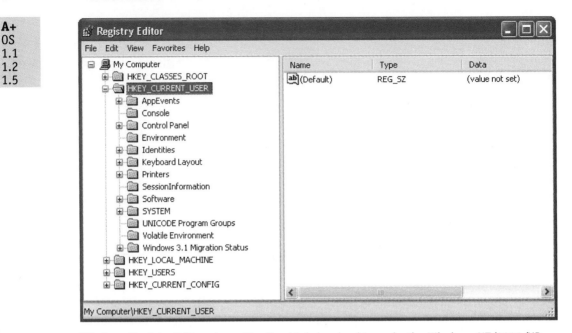

Figure 16-12 Windows Registry Editor shows the five high-level subtrees in the Windows NT/2000/XP registry

The five subtrees of the registry, shown in Figure 16-12, are listed in Table 16-2 together with their primary functions. As the table shows, the HKEY_LOCAL_MACHINE subtree is the mainstay key of the registry.

Subtree (Main Keys)	Primary Function
HKEY_CURRENT_USER	Contains information about the currently logged-on user
HKEY_CLASSES_ROOT	Contains information about software and the way software is configured. This key points to data stored in HKEY_LOCAL_MACHINE.
HKEY_CURRENT_CONFIG	Contains information about the active hardware configuration, which is extracted from the data stored in the HKEY_LOCAL_ MACHINE subkeys called SOFTWARE and SYSTEM
HKEY_USERS	Contains information used to build the logon screen and the ID of the currently logged-on user
HKEY_LOCAL_MACHINE	Contains all configuration data about the computer, including information about device drivers and devices used at startup. The information in this key does not change when different users log on.

Table 16-2   The five subtrees of the Windows NT/2000/XP registry

Physical Organization of the Registry

A+
OS
1.1
1.2
1.5

The physical organization of the registry is quite different from the logical organization. Physically, the registry is stored in five files called **hives**. There is no one-to-one relationship between the subtrees and these five files, even though there are five of each. Figure 16-13 shows the way the subtrees are stored in hives as follows:

- HKEY_LOCAL_MACHINE consists of four hives: the SAM hive, the Security hive, the Software hive, and the System hive.
- HKEY_CURRENT_CONFIG data is kept in portions of two hives: the Software hive and the System hive.
- HKEY_CLASSES_ROOT data is kept in a portion of the Software hive.
- HKEY_USERS data is kept in the Default hive.
- HKEY_CURRENT_USER data is kept in a portion of the Default hive.

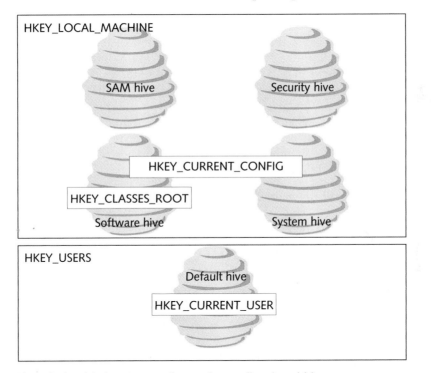

Figure 16-13 The relationship between registry subtrees (keys) and hives

16

From Figure 16-13, you can also see that some subtrees use data contained in other subtrees. For instance, the HKEY_CURRENT_USER data is a subset of the data in the HKEY_USERS subtree. HKEY_CURRENT_CONFIG and HKEY_CLASSES_ROOT subtrees use data contained in the HKEY_LOCAL_MACHINE subtree. However, don't let this physical relationship cloud your view of the logical relationship among these subtrees. Although data is shared among the different subtrees, logically speaking, none of the five subtrees is subordinate to any other.

The registry hives are stored in the \%SystemRoot%\system32\config folder as a group of files. In a physical sense, each hive is a file. Each hive is backed up with a log file and a backup file, which are also stored in the \%SystemRoot%\system32 \config folder.

Editing the Registry

When you make a change in the Control Panel, Device Manager, or many other places in Windows NT/2000/XP, the registry is modified automatically. This is the only way most users will ever change the registry. However, on rare occasions you might need to edit the registry manually, for example, when you are following the directions of Microsoft technical support staff to delete references in the registry to viruses or worms. Changes to the registry take effect immediately and are permanent.

Before you edit the registry, you should back it up so that you can restore it if something goes wrong. Backing up the system state, which you learned to do in Chapter 13, is one way to back up the registry. In Chapter 13, you backed up the system state after a Windows 2000 installation, but you can also back up the system state at any time. When the system state is backed up, the Backup utility also puts a copy of the registry files in the %SystemRoot%\repair folder.

Windows NT/2000 offers two registry editors, each with a slightly different look and feel, and with some slight differences:

- Regedt32.exe located in the \%SystemRoot%\system32 folder, which shows each key in a separate window. Use it to edit the registry.
- Regedit.exe located in the \%SystemRoot% folder, which shows all keys in the same window and has a look and feel similar to Explorer. Use it to search and view the registry.
- Regedt32.exe has a Security menu that allows you to apply permissions to keys and subkeys to control which user accounts have access to these keys. Under the Options menu, you have the option to work in read-only mode. Regedit.exe has the advantages that you can export the registry to a text file and use a more powerful search tool than the one in Regedt32.exe, but has the disadvantage that it cannot display registry values longer than 256 characters.

To access a registry editor, type the program name in the Run dialog box. With Windows XP, typing either Regedt32 or Regedit in the Run dialog box launches the Regedit.exe program.

The following example uses Regedit.exe under Windows XP to view the registry and look at registry values. To access Regedit.exe, double-click the filename in Windows Explorer or enter the filename in the Run dialog box. Figure 16-14 shows a detailed view of the registry.

A+
OS
1.1
1.2
1.5

Nothing listed under
Data indicates the
default value is used

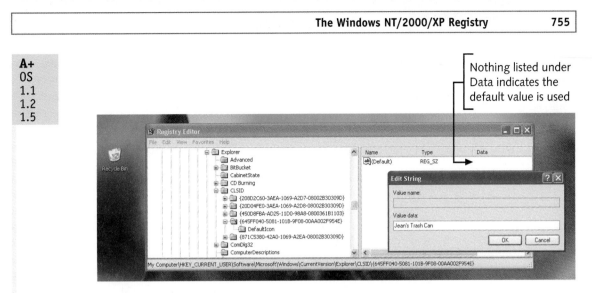

Figure 16-14   Editing a registry subkey value

Let's look at one example of editing the registry. Follow these directions to first back up the system state before editing the registry:

1. Click **Start, All Programs, Accessories, System Tools, Backup.** The Backup or Restore Wizard appears.

2. Click **Advanced Mode.** The Backup Utility window appears. Click the **Backup** tab.

3. Check the **System State** box, and under **Backup media or file name**, select the location to store the backup.

4. Click **Start Backup.** In the dialog box that appears, click **Start Backup** again to confirm the action. After the backup is done, click **Close** to close the Backup utility.

To change the name of the Recycle Bin on the Windows XP desktop for the currently logged on user, do the following:

1. To open Registry Editor, click **Start, Run**, and then type **Regedit** in the Run dialog box. Click **OK.** The Registry Editor window appears.

2. Locate the following subkey, which is the name of the Recycle Bin on the Windows desktop, by double-clicking the yellow folder icon of each subkey, moving down through the tree to the lowest subkey value. As you move down the tree, if the currently selected subkey has a value, that value appears in the right pane of the window.

HKEY_CURRENT_USER\Software\Microsoft\Windows\CurrentVersion\
Explorer\CLSID\645FF040-5081-101B-9F08-00AA002F954E

16

A+
OS
1.1
1.2
1.5

3. Figure 16-14 shows the subkey. The right pane shows nothing listed under Data, so the default value is used, which is the value for Recycle Bin. Position the window on the screen so that you can see the Recycle Bin icon.

4. Double-click the name of the value in the right pane. The Edit String dialog box appears. The Value data should be empty in the dialog box. If a value is present, you selected the wrong value. Check your work and try again.

5. Enter a new name for the Recycle Bin. For example, in Figure 16-14, the new name is "Jean's Trash Can." Click **OK**.

6. To see your change, right-click the desktop and select **Refresh** on the shortcut menu. The name of the Recycle Bin changes.

7. To restore the name to the default value, in the Registry Editor window, again double-click the name of the value. The Edit String dialog box appears. Delete your entry and click **OK**.

8. To verify the change is made, right-click the desktop and select **Refresh** on the shortcut menu. The Recycle Bin name should return to its default value.

From these directions, you can see that changes made to the registry take effect immediately. Therefore, take extra care when editing the registry. If you make a mistake and don't know how to correct a problem you create, then you can restore the system state to recover.

Other Maintenance and Troubleshooting Tools

A+
OS
3.1
3.2

This section discusses other commonly used tools that Windows XP provides for maintenance and troubleshooting. Some tools are new or changed in Windows XP, and some operate just as they do in Windows 2000. Table 16-3 lists several tools and their functions. Some tools are executed from a command line (have an .exe file

✔ **A+ EXAM TIP**

The A+ OS exam expects you to know the program filename of important Windows utilities.

extension), others are Microsoft Management Console snap-ins (have an .msc file extension), and others are tools built into Windows XP (such as Safe Mode). MMC was discussed in Chapter 14. MMC snap-ins are executed from the Run dialog box or can sometimes be accessed using Windows menus. Some command-line programs can be executed from the Run dialog box, and all can be executed from a command prompt window. Several tools listed in the table are dis-

cussed later in the chapter. For more extensive information about any of these tools, search Help and Support on your Windows XP computer, search the Microsoft Knowledge Base at *support.microsoft.com*, or see the book, *Microsoft Windows XP Professional Resource Kit Documentation* by Microsoft Press. In addition, to get help about a command-line tool, from a command prompt, enter the tool name followed by /?. For example, to get help about Defrag, enter Defrag /?.

Tool	Description
Add or Remove Programs	From the Control Panel, uninstalls software that is causing a problem
Automated System Recovery (ASR)	Drastically recovers a failed system. Use only as a last resort, because the logical drive on which Windows is installed is formatted and restored from the most recent backup. All data and applications written to the drive since the last backup are lost.
Backup (Ntbackup.exe)	Backs up and restores data and software
Boot logging	An option on the Advanced Options startup menu to log events to the Ntbtlog.txt file
Bootcfg (Bootcfg.exe)	Views and edits the contents of the Boot.ini file used to hold startup settings
Cacls.exe	Changes access control lists (ACLs) assigned to a file or group of files to control which users have access to a file and the type of access they have (read, write, change, or full). For more information on Cacls, type Help Cacls at a command prompt.
Chkdsk (Chkdsk.exe)	Checks and repairs errors on a logical drive
Cipher.exe	Displays and changes the encryptions applied to files and folders using the NTFS file system
Compact.exe	Displays and changes the compressions applied to files and folders using the NTFS file system
Computer Management (Compmgmt.msc)	Console provides access to several snap-ins used to manage and troubleshoot a system
Convert.exe	Converts a FAT16 or a FAT32 logical drive to NTFS
Defrag.exe	A command-line tool to defragment a logical drive or floppy disk, it is similar to the graphic tool, Disk Defragmenter.
Dependency Walker (Depends.exe)	Provides a list of files needed for an application to load
Device Driver Roll Back	Replaces a driver with the one that worked before the current driver was installed

Table 16-3 (continued)

16

Tool	Description
Device Manager (Devmgmt.msc)	Displays and changes device drivers and other hardware settings
DirectX Diagnostic Tool (Dxdiag.exe)	Used to troubleshoot problems with the DirectX application programming interface (API) used by Microsoft
Disk Cleanup (Cleanmgr.exe)	Deletes unused files to make more disk space available
Disk Defragmenter (Dfrg.msc)	Defragments a logical drive or floppy disk
Disk Management (Diskmgmt.msc)	Displays and changes partitions on hard drives and formats drives
DiskPart (Diskpart.exe)	A command-line tool to manage partitions and volumes of a hard drive similar to the graphic tool, Disk Management. Use DiskPart to write scripts to automate disk management tasks. It's also a handy way to assign drive letters to IDE devices.
Dr. Watson (Drwtsn32.exe)	Records errors and information about those errors when applications fail. Errors are recorded in a log file named **Drwatson.log.** Note this is a different name from the log filename in Windows 2000, which is Drwtsn32.log.
Driver Signing and Digital Signatures (Sigverif.exe)	Verifies that drivers, system files, and software have been approved by Microsoft
Error Reporting	Produces an error report and sends it to Microsoft when the error occurs and the PC is connected to the Internet
Event Viewer (Eventvwr.msc)	Records and displays system problems
Expand.exe	Extracts a file from a cabinet file or compressed file
Fsutil (Fsutil.exe)	Displays information about drives and file systems and does advanced management tasks on those drives
Getmac (Getmac.exe)	Displays the MAC address for the installed network adapter (discussed in Chapter 18)
Group Policy (Gpedit.msc)	Displays and changes policies controlling users and the computer

Table 16-3 (continued)

A+
OS
3.1
3.2

Tool	Description
Group Policy Result (Gpresult.exe)	Displays currently applied group policies (also know as Resultant Set of Policies, or RSoP), which helps to determine which of several policies are active for computers and users.
Group Policy Update (Gpupdate.exe)	Immediately puts into effect changes you have just made to local group policies
Help and Support	Provides helpful information, connects to Windows newsgroups, enables Remote Assistance, and steps you though many other troubleshooting tasks
Last Known Good Configuration	A startup option used when normal or Safe Mode does not work. Using this tool, you can revert the system back to before a driver or application that is causing problems was installed.
Performance Monitor (Perfmon.msc)	Reports information about performance problems
Program Compatibility Wizard	Looks at legacy software and attempts to resolve issues that prevent the software from working in Windows XP
Recovery Console	Provides a command line to perform troubleshooting tasks when the desktop will not load
Registry Editor (Regedit.exe)	Displays and changes entries in the registry
Remote Assistance	Allows a user to share his computer with a support technician at a remote location so that the technician can control the computer
Remote Desktop	Allows a support technician to control a Windows XP computer remotely
Runas.exe	Runs a program using different permissions than those assigned to the currently logged-on user
Safe Mode	Loads the Windows desktop with a minimum configuration and then used to troubleshoot problems with device drivers, display settings, and other startup options that are causing problems

16

Table 16-3 (continued)

Tool	Description
SC (Sc.exe)	Communicates commands to the Service Controller, which starts, stops, and manages programs that run in the background such as device drivers or Internet Connection Firewall
Services (Services.msc)	Graphical version of SC
System Configuration Utility (Msconfig.exe)	Controls settings used to troubleshoot a failing system
System File Checker (Sfc.exe)	Verifies the version of all system files when Windows loads
System Information (Msinfo32.exe)	Displays information about hardware, applications, and Windows that is useful when troubleshooting. Figure 16-15 shows a view of the System Information window.
System Information (Systeminfo.exe)	A version of System Information to be used from a command-prompt window. Information is listed on screen as text only. To direct that information to a file, use the command Systeminfo.exe >Myfile.txt. Later the file can be printed and used to document information about the system.
System Restore	Used to restore the system to a previously working condition, it restores the registry, some system files, and some application files.
Task Killing Utility (Tskill.exe)	Stops a process or program currently running. Useful when managing background services such as an e-mail server or Web server.
Task Lister (Tasklist.exe)	Lists currently running processes similar to the list provided by Task Manager
Task Manager (Taskman.exe)	Lists and stops currently running processes. Use Task Manager to stop a locked-up application.
Uninstall Windows XP Professional	Used to uninstall Windows XP and revert back to a previously installed OS
Windows File Protection	Protects system files and restores overwritten system files as needed

Table 16-3 (continued)

Tool	Description
Windows Update (Wupdmgr.exe)	Updates Windows by examining the system, comparing it to available updates on the Microsoft Web site, and recommending appropriate updates

Table 16-3   Windows XP maintenance and troubleshooting tools

Figure 16-15   The System Information window displays important information about the system's hardware, software, and environment

Help on the Web

Microsoft offers help and updates on the Web. In earlier chapters, you learned to use the Microsoft Knowledge Base at *support.microsoft.com*. This section shows you how to access the Windows Update feature and Windows XP newsgroups.

Windows Update

Windows XP has an automated way to update the OS, applications, and device drivers made available on the Microsoft Web site. If no user interaction is required, anyone can perform the update, but if decisions must be made during the update, only someone with administrator privileges can perform the update.

To do an update including updating the OS, software and drivers, click Start, All Programs, and Windows Update. The Update Wizard takes you to the Microsoft Windows Update Web site (see Figure 16-16). Click "Scan for updates" and follow the directions on screen. This update process includes updating drivers, a process that

16

can also be started from Device Manager (Devmgmt.msc), as you learned in the last chapter.

Figure 16-16   The Windows Update utility manages the process of downloading updates from the Microsoft Web site

If an update is available for your computer, a window similar to the one shown in Figure 16-17 appears. Note in the figure that the update process found one critical update, nine updates to Windows XP that it does not consider critical, and no updates for drivers. To view information about these updates, click them. In this example, the critical update was designed to solve a problem with security, and the nine noncritical updates were about running Java applets, connecting to a UPS (uninterruptible power supply) service, using a CD burner, running legacy applications using compatibility mode, problems with the Files and Settings Transfer Wizard, problems using Remote Assistance across a firewall, and problems with Windows Messenger and Movie Maker. By default, only the critical update is selected for installing. To install noncritical updates, select the updates you want and then click Add. After you have selected what to update, click "Review and install updates" and follow directions on the screen.

Sometimes errors occur during the update process or a later patch will corrupt an earlier patch. Microsoft offers a tool, Qfecheck.exe, that can be downloaded from the Microsoft Web site. You use Qfecheck.exe to scan a system for patches and report whether these patches or hotfixes are installed correctly. The tool examines

A+
OS
2.2

the registry for patches that it thinks are installed and then verifies that these patches are installed and working correctly. To learn more about Qfecheck.exe and to download it, go to the Microsoft support site at *support.microsoft.com* and search for Knowledge Base Article 282784.

> **NOTE** Windows XP does not ship with support for USB 2.0 (USB Hi-Speed). If you have a USB 2.0 port on your PC, the Update Wizard will recommend that you update the USB driver to support USB 2.0 unless you have already installed a third-party USB 2.0 driver. If you want to download the Microsoft USB 2.0 driver, first uninstall the third-party driver and then perform Windows Update.

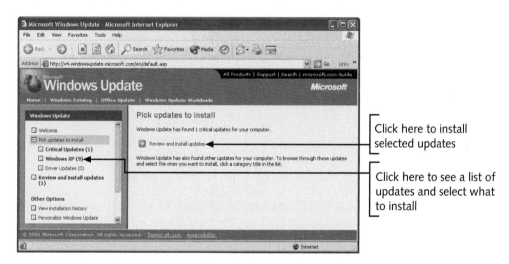

Figure 16-17 Windows Update process found updates appropriate to this computer

Windows Newsgroups

If you have exhausted your sources of information and still have not resolved a problem, sometimes you can get help from a Windows newsgroup.

To access a newsgroup, click Start, and then Help and Support. On the Help and Support window, click "Get support, or find information in Windows XP newsgroups." Then click "Go to a Windows Web site forum." Click "Go to Windows Newsgroups." In the forum, you can post a question or read questions and answers posted by other users. Microsoft does not support this forum, so be careful about following the advice of users posting answers to questions on the forum. In addition to newsgroups and the Microsoft Web site, many good Windows support Web sites exist. To get a very long list of these sites, go to a search engine on the Web such as *www.google.com* and enter Windows Help in the search box.

16

Troubleshooting the Boot Process

A+
OS
2.3
3.1
3.2
3.3

The Windows XP boot process works the same way as the Windows NT and Windows 2000 boot process. Refer to Chapter 14 for a review of the process and the files required for a successful boot. Many tools you learned about in Chapter 14 to recover from a failed Windows 2000 boot also work under Windows XP. They are briefly mentioned in this section to make the troubleshooting process complete. In addition, Windows XP has added two tools for solving problems with the boot process: System Restore and Automated System Recovery. The tools to use when troubleshooting a failed boot are listed below in the order you should use them. Each tool discussed is more drastic than the one before it, affecting more of the system, installed hardware and software, and user data.

- Last Known Good Configuration and, in certain situations, Driver Rollback
- Safe Mode on the Advanced Options menu
- System Restore
- Windows 2000/XP Boot Disk
- Recovery Console
- Automated System Recovery
- Reinstall Windows XP using the Windows XP CD

You learned how to use the Last Known Good Configuration for Windows NT and Windows 2000 in Chapter 14. In addition, you can use Driver Rollback discussed in Chapter 15 if you suspect that a single device driver is the source of the problem. The Windows XP Advanced Options menu, shown in Figure 16-18, is also similar to that of Windows 2000. Refer to Chapter 14 for a discussion of each of the options on the menu and how to use them. Try Safe Mode with Networking first. If that doesn't work, try Safe Mode.

NOTE

To access the Advanced Options menu, press F8 while Windows is loading.

The next tool to use if these don't work is System Restore, a tool new to Windows XP, which is discussed next. If that doesn't work, then try a Windows XP boot disk that you must manually create. If this disk doesn't work, the next tool to use is the Recovery Console. Commands for the Recovery Console for Windows XP are the same as for Windows 2000 and were covered in Chapter 14. If the Recovery Console fails, then use the Automated System Recovery process to restore the hard drive to its state as of the last ASR backup. If you don't have an ASR backup, then your only recourse is to reinstall Windows XP following directions given in Chapter 15. Be sure to scan for viruses before you reinstall.

A+
OS
2.3
3.1
3.2
3.3

Windows Advanced Options Menu
Please select an option:

     Safe Mode
     Safe Mode with Networking
     Safe Mode with Command Prompt

     Enable Boot Logging
     Enable VGA Mode
     Last Known Good Configuration (your most recent settings that worked)
     Directory Services Restore Mode (Windows domain controllers only)
     Debugging Mode

     Start Windows Normally
     Reboot
     Return to OS Choices Menu

Use the up and down arrow keys to move the highlight to your choice.

Figure 16-18   Windows XP Advanced Options menu

System Restore

The **System Restore** utility is new to Windows XP. It is similar to ScanReg used on previous versions of Windows; however, System Restore cannot be executed from a command prompt. ScanReg is not included in Windows XP. If you can load Windows XP, then you can use System Restore to restore the system state to its condition at the time a snapshot was taken of the system settings and configuration. The restore process does not affect user data on the hard drive but can affect installed software and hardware, user settings, and OS configuration settings. Also, the restore process cannot help you recover from a virus or worm infection unless the infection is launched at startup. The restoration is taken from a snapshot of the system state, called a **restore point,** that was created earlier. The system automatically creates a restore point before you install new software or hardware or make other changes to the system. You can also manually create a restore point at any time.

16

NOTE

The main difference between System Restore and Automated System Recovery is that System Restore does not affect user data on the hard drive, but Automated System Recovery does. To recover a failed system without destroying data, make it a habit to always create a restore point every time you make a change to the system.

APPLYING CONCEPTS

To manually create a restore point:

1. Click **Start**, **All Programs**, **Accessories**, **System Tools**, and **System Restore**. The System Restore window appears.
2. The System Restore window gives you two choices: Restore my computer to an earlier time and Create a restore point. Select **Create a restore point**, and then click **Next**.

3. Type a description of the restore point such as "Just before I updated the video driver." The system automatically assigns the current date and time to the restore point.
4. Click **Create** and then **Close**. The restore point is saved.

Before using System Restore to undo a change, if the change was made to a hardware device, first try Driver Rollback so that as few changes as possible to the system are lost. If Driver Rollback does not work or is not appropriate, do the following to revert the system back to the restore point:

1. Click **Start**, **All Programs**, **Accessories**, **System Tools**, and **System Restore**.
2. If necessary, click **Restore my computer to an earlier time**, and then click **Next**. A window appears as shown in Figure 16-19. Notice the two restore points in the figure, one created by the system and one created manually.

Figure 16-19   Restore points are automatically created daily and every time software or hardware is installed

A+
OS
2.3
3.1
3.2
3.3

3. Select the date and time and the specific restore point. Click **Next** twice.

Windows XP reboots and restores the system state to the settings saved in the restore point. Changes to user data are not affected but any installation or configuration changes made after the restore point are lost.

✔ **A+ EXAM TIP**

The A+ OS exam expects you to know how to boot to a system restore point.

When selecting a restore point, select a point as close to the present as you can so that as few changes to the system as possible are lost. Accessing System Restore using the previous process assumes you can boot to a Windows desktop. If you can't do that, first try booting into Safe Mode and then use the previous procedure from the Safe Mode desktop. If that doesn't work, try booting to the Advanced Options menu. From the Advanced Options menu, select Safe Mode. When you do that, Windows XP asks if you want to go directly to System Restore rather than to Safe Mode. Choose to go directly to System Restore.

NOTE

To roll back the system to a Windows XP restore point using Windows XP requires that you can boot from the hard drive. However, there are other options using third-party utility software. For example, ERD Commander 2003 by Winternals (*www.winternals.com*) is an operating system that can be loaded from CD. Boot from the ERD Commander 2003 CD, which loads a GUI interface that looks like Windows XP. Using this Winternals desktop, you can access the registry, event logs, and Disk Management Console and reset a forgotten administrator password. You can also roll back the Windows XP system to a restore point.

MS-DOS Startup Disk

Using Windows Explorer, you can create an MS-DOS startup disk that can be used to boot into MS-DOS mode, giving you an A prompt. This bootable disk is sometimes needed when following a BIOS manufacturer's procedure to flash BIOS. Also, the disk can be useful if the system will not boot, the hard drive is not using the NTFS file system, and you need to access the drive to recover data files. You cannot launch Windows XP using the startup disk or use it to recover from a failed installation.

To create a startup disk, using Windows Explorer, right-click drive A and select Format on the shortcut menu. The Format dialog box opens, as shown in Figure 16-20. Check "Create an MS-DOS startup disk," and then click Start. The unhidden files that Windows puts on the startup disk are shown in Figure 16-21. In addition to these files, Autoexec.bat, Config.sys, and the Windows 98 versions of Io.sys and Msdos.sys are also placed on the disk as hidden files.

16

Figure 16-20   Windows XP gives you the ability to create an MS-DOS startup disk

Figure 16-21   Files on the MS-DOS startup disk created by Windows XP

Windows XP Boot Disk

A+
OS
2.3
3.1
3.2
3.3

When troubleshooting a failed boot, if System Restore does not work, the next tool to try is the Windows XP boot disk. (You can also create and use a Windows 2000 boot disk to troubleshoot a failed Windows 2000 system.) If you boot from the disk and the Windows 2000/XP desktop loads successfully, then the problem is associated with a missing or damaged boot sector, master boot record, partition table, Ntldr file, Ntdetect.com file, Ntbootdd.sys (if it exists), boot.ini file, or a virus infection. However, a boot disk cannot be used to troubleshoot problems associated with unstable device drivers or those that occur after the Windows 2000 or Windows XP logon screen is displayed.

You first create the boot disk by formatting the disk using a working Windows 2000/XP computer and then copying files to the disk. These files can be copied from a Windows 2000/XP setup CD, or a Windows 2000/XP computer that is using the same version of Windows 2000 or Windows XP as the problem PC. Do the following to create the disk:

1. Obtain a floppy disk and format it on a Windows 2000/XP computer

2. Using Explorer, copy Ntldr and Ntdetect.com from the \i386 folder on the Windows 2000 or Windows XP setup CD or a Windows 2000/XP computer to the root of the floppy disk.

3. If your computer boots from a SCSI hard drive, then obtain a device driver (*.sys) for your SCSI hard drive, rename it Ntbootdd.sys, and copy it to the root of the floppy disk. (If you used an incorrect device driver, then you will receive an error after booting from the floppy disk. The error will mention a "computer disk hardware configuration problem" and that it "could not read from the selected boot disk." If this occurs, contact your computer manufacturer for the correct version of the SCSI hard drive device driver for your computer.) Chapter 22 gives more information about SCSI.

4. After viewing Boot.ini on the problem computer, obtain an identical copy from another known good computer (or create your own) and copy it to the root of the floppy disk.

If the problem computer is booting from an IDE hard drive then its Boot.ini should be similar to:

```
[boot loader]
timeout=30
default=multi(0)disk(0)rdisk(0)partition(1)\WINDOWS
[operating systems]
multi(0)disk(0)rdisk(0)partition(1)\WINDOWS="Microsoft Windows XP
Professional" /fastdetect
```

16

A+
OS
2.3
3.1
3.2
3.3

Note that there is a carriage return after the /fastdetect switch.

5. Write-protect the floppy disk so it cannot become infected with a virus.

You have now created the Windows XP boot disk. Check CMOS setup to make sure the first boot device is set to the floppy disk, and then insert the boot disk and reboot your computer. If you did not enter Windows XP successfully by using the boot disk, then the next tool to try is the Recovery Console.

NOTE

To learn more about the Windows XP boot disk, see the Microsoft Knowledge Base Articles 305595 and 314503 at the Microsoft Web site *support.microsoft.com*. To learn more about the Windows NT/2000 boot disk, see the Microsoft Knowledge Base Article 301680.

If you loaded Windows XP successfully, but with error messages, then do the following to attempt to repair the Windows XP installation:

- Load the Recovery Console and use the Fixmbr and Fixboot commands to repair the MBR and the boot sector.
- Run anti-virus software.
- Use Disk Management to verify that the hard drive partition table is correct.
- Defragment your hard drive.
- Copy Ntldr, Ntdetect.com, and Boot.ini from your floppy disk to the root of the hard drive.
- If you're using a SCSI hard drive, copy Ntbootdd.sys from your floppy disk to the root of the hard drive.

Automated System Recovery

After you finish a Windows XP installation, if you create the Automated System Recovery disk set, you can use this or a later set of the recovery disks to restore the system partition to its state when the backup was made. You will lose any changes made to the volume or logical drive holding Windows XP since the backup. Everything on the volume since the ASR backup and disk were made is lost, including software and device drivers installed, user data, and any changes to the system configuration. For this reason, it's a good idea to make fresh copies of the ASR disk set periodically. You learned how to make this backup and disk in the previous chapter.

If you use the Automated System Recovery process, know that you will lose all data stored on the Windows XP volume since the last backup was made.

A+
OS
2.3
3.1
3.2
3.3

To restore the hard drive to its state when the last ASR disk set was made, do the following:

1. Insert the Windows XP CD in the CD-ROM drive, and hard boot the PC.

2. A message says "Press any key to boot from CD." Press any key.

3. A blue screen appears with the message, "Press F6 to load RAID or SCSI drivers." If your system uses RAID or SCSI, press **F6**.

4. At the bottom of the blue screen, a message says, "Press F2 to run the Automated System Recovery process." Press **F2**.

5. The screen shown in Figure 16-22 appears, instructing you to insert the ASR floppy disk. Insert the disk and then press **Enter**.

```
Windows Setup
===========



          Please insert the disk labeled:

   Windows Automated System Recovery Disk

             Into the floppy drive.



          Press any key when ready.
```

Figure 16-22   Automatic System Recovery process must have the ASR floppy disk

16

Windows XP Setup does the following:

- Loads files it needs to run
- Repartitions and reformats the drive
- Installs Windows from the Windows XP CD
- Launches the Automatic System Recovery Wizard to restore the Windows system state, applications, and data to what they were at the time of the last ASR backup.

The ASR recovery process erases everything on the volume being restored. Figure 16-23 shows one of the previous steps in the recovery process, in which you reformat the logical drive just before the Windows XP installation process begins.

```
Windows XP Professional Setup
==========================




          Please wait while Setup formats the partition

                 \Device\Harddisk0\Partition1

      on  28663  MB  Disk  0  at  Id 0  on  bus  0  on  atapi  [MBR].


    ┌────────────────────────────────────────────────────┐
    │  Setup is formatting...          45%               │
    │  ┌──────────────────────────────────────────────┐ │
    │  │████████████████                              │ │
    │  └──────────────────────────────────────────────┘ │
    └────────────────────────────────────────────────────┘
```

Figure 16-23   As part of the Automatic System Recovery process, Windows XP Setup repartitions and reformats the volume holding Windows XP

Error Messages and Their Meanings

Table 16-4 lists some Windows XP error messages and what they mean. Most of these errors occur when booting.

Error Message	What It Means and What to Do About It
Invalid partition table Error loading operating system Missing operating system	The program in the MBR displays these messages when it cannot find the active partition on the hard drive or the boot sector on that partition. Use Fdisk or Diskpart from a command prompt to check the hard drive partition table for errors. Sometimes Fdisk/mbr solves the problem. Third-party recovery software such as PartitionMagic might help. If a setup program came bundled with the hard drive (such as Data Lifeguard from Western Digital or MaxBlast from Maxtor), use it to

Table 16-4 (continued)

A+
OS
2.3
3.1
3.2
3.3

Error Message	What It Means and What to Do About It
	examine the drive. Check the hard drive manufacturer's Web site for other diagnostic software.
A disk read error occurred NTLDR is missing NTLDR is compressed	A disk is probably in the floppy disk drive. Remove the disk and reboot. When booting from the hard drive, these errors occur if Ntldr has been moved, renamed, or deleted, or is corrupted, if the boot sector on the active partition is corrupted, or you have just tried to install an older version of Windows such as Windows 98 on the hard drive. First try replacing Ntldr. Then check Boot.ini settings.
A text error message appears on a blue screen and then the system halts. These Windows NT/2000/XP errors are called **stop errors** or **blue screens (BSOD)**. Some stop errors follow.	Stop errors are usually caused by viruses, errors in the file system, a corrupted hard drive, or a hardware problem.
Stop 0x00000024 or NTFS_File_System	The NTFS file system is corrupt. Immediately boot into the Recovery Console, and copy important data files that have not been backed up to another media before attempting to recover the system.
Stop 0x00000050 or Page_Fault_in_Nonpaged_Area	Most likely RAM is defective.
Stop 0x00000077 or Kernel_Stack_Inpage_Error	Bad sectors are on the hard drive, there is a hard drive hardware problem, or RAM is defective. Try running Chkdsk or, for the FAT file system, run Scandisk using a Windows 98 startup disk.
Stop 0x0000007A or Kernel_Data_Inpage_Error	There is a bad sector on the hard drive where the paging file is stored; there is a virus or defective RAM. Try running Chkdsk or Scandisk.

Table 16-4 (continued)

16

A+
OS
2.3
3.1
3.2
3.3

Error Message	What It Means and What to Do About It
Stop 0x0000007B or Inaccessible_Boot_Device	There is a boot sector virus or failing hardware. Try Fdisk/mbr or fixmbr.
Black screen with no error messages	This is likely to be a corrupted MBR, partition table, boot sector, or Ntldr file. Boot the PC using a Windows XP boot disk and then try the fixmbr and fixboot commands from the Recovery Console. You might have to reinstall Windows.

Table 16-4   Windows XP error messages and their meanings

CHAPTER SUMMARY

▸ Windows NT/2000/XP requires a valid user account before you can use Windows. The user account identifies the user to Windows. Permissions assigned to a user account control what the user can and cannot do and access in Windows.

▸ Local user accounts apply to a single standalone computer or a single computer in a workgroup, and global user accounts are managed from a domain controller and apply to every computer in the domain.

▸ When using Windows in a domain, global user account information is stored in the SAM, which is part of Active Directory in Windows 2000 Server and Windows .2003 Server.

▸ When a user makes changes to the system, the changes are often recorded in the user profile so the next time the user logs on, these changes automatically take effect.

▸ Methods that administrators can use to manage and secure multiple computers and users include roaming user profiles, mandatory user profiles, and group profiles.

▸ Passwords on user accounts are needed to secure computers and their resources. Passwords should not be easy to guess and should be a combination of letters, numbers, and non-alphanumeric characters.

▸ An administrator can create a user account using the Computer Management console or the User Accounts applet in Control Panel.

▶ Resetting a password under Windows XP causes the OS to lock out the user from using encrypted e-mail or files or using Internet passwords stored on the computer. For that reason, it is a good idea for a user to create a Windows XP forgotten password floppy disk.

▶ In Windows NT/2000, you can only log on to the system by pressing Ctrl+Alt+Del to open the logon window. In a Windows XP workgroup, you can use the logon window, Welcome screen, or Fast User Switching.

▶ Windows XP user groups include Administrators, Backup Operators, Power Users, Limited Users, and Guests. In this list, each group has fewer permissions and rights than the previous group.

▶ Using disk quotas, an administrator can limit the amount of hard drive space a user can use.

▶ File and folder encryption and disk quotas in Windows 2000/XP require using the NTFS file system.

▶ Internet Connection Firewall (ICF) prevents communication from the Internet from accessing the system if the communication has not been initiated by the local computer.

▶ The Windows NT/2000/XP registry is organized logically into five subtrees or keys and organized physically into five files called hives. There is no one-to-one correspondence between the subtrees and the hives.

▶ The registry is edited using a registry editor, which is accessed by entering Regedit in the Run dialog box. Changes to the registry are immediate, so always make a backup of the system state before editing the registry.

▶ Windows XP offers many troubleshooting and maintenance tools. Some are available from the command line. Others are Microsoft Management Console (MMC) snap-ins, and still others are built into Windows XP.

▶ You can get help on the Web for Windows XP. Microsoft offers Windows Update and Microsoft Knowledge Base. There are also Windows newsgroups and other Web sites where you can get help.

▶ Two recovery tools new to Windows XP are Automated System Recovery and System Restore.

▶ The Automated System Recovery (ASR) process creates a backup and an ASR floppy disk that can be used to restore the backup of the volume or logical drive holding Windows XP.

▶ The Windows XP System Restore utility is similar to ScanReg in earlier versions of Windows but cannot be executed at a command prompt. System Restore restores the system state using restore points, which are snapshots of the system state.

16

KEY TERMS

For explanations of key terms, see the Glossary near the end of the book.

Backup Operator	Group Policy	mandatory user profile
blue screen (BSOD)	group profile	Power User
built-in user account	Guest	restore point
disk quota	hardware profile	roaming user profile
Drwatson.log	hive	stop error
Encrypted File System (EFS)	Internet Connection Firewall (ICF)	System Restore
encryption	key	user account
forgotten password floppy disk	Limited User	user profile
global user account	local user account	

REVIEWING THE BASICS

1. Which operating system has the most security: Windows 9x/Me or Windows XP?

2. What is the difference between joining a workgroup and joining a domain?

3. Where is user account information stored on a Windows 2000/2003 domain?

4. When is the local user profile created?

5. How are a roaming profile and a mandatory profile the same? How are they different?

6. What is the difference between the tools ASR and System Restore?

7. What are two important criteria that make for a good password?

8. What can a user do to keep from having the administrator reset a forgotten password?

9. Which user group has more rights, Power Users or Administrators?

10. When using Group Policy on a computer in a workgroup, which type of configuration do you use?

11. What do you implement to control how much disk space a user can take up?

12. Explain how to decrypt a file using My Computer.

13. What command can you use at the command prompt to encrypt a file?

14. Which applet in Control Panel is used to enable and disable Internet Connection Firewall?

15. Which Windows registry subtree contains information about the currently logged-on user?

16. Which Windows registry subtree gets all its information from the HKEY_LOCAL_MACHINE subtree?

17. In Windows NT/2000/XP, a file that contains part of the Windows registry is called a(n) _____.

18. What is the Windows XP command to access the registry editor?

19. What is the name of the utility program that allows you to view and edit Boot.ini?

20. How is Dr. Watson different in Windows XP from how it was in Windows 2000?

21. How is the registry editor different in Windows XP from how it was in Windows 2000?

22. What is the name of the snap-in file for Disk Defragmenter?

23. Looking at a program filename and file extension, how can you tell if the program is an MMC snap-in or a command-line program?

24. What is the name of the log file created when boot logging is enabled from the Advanced Options startup menu?

25. What is a restore point, and what is it used for?

26. ScanReg has been replaced by System Restore in Windows XP. What is the main advantage that ScanReg has over System Restore?

27. Can you use an MS-DOS startup disk to launch Windows XP? To recover data files? To recover from a failed installation of Windows XP?

28. What are two recovery tools new to Windows XP that are used to recover from a failed boot?

29. When trying to restore a failed system, what should you do next if Recovery Console does not work?

30. Place these tools in the order in which you should try them when troubleshooting the boot process: Recovery Console, Advanced Options Menu, System Restore.

16

THINKING CRITICALLY

1. Suppose a user has encrypted important data files and now is no longer working for your company. How do you decrypt these files so they can be read?

2. If your computer at home is connected to the Internet by way of your spouse's computer, which is connected to the Internet using cable modem, which computer should have Internet Connection Firewall enabled?

3. Your Windows XP system locks up occasionally. What are some probable causes and solutions? *Note:* This question combines skills learned in this and other chapters.

   a. The hard drive has errors. Run _____ to correct file system errors.

   b. An application might not be compatible with Windows XP. To find out if you have applications installed that are not certified by Microsoft for Windows XP, run the _____ utility.

   c. The hard drive might be full. To find out use _____.

   d. The system might have a virus. To eliminate that possibility, use _____.

4. You are attempting to upload images from your digital camera to your Windows XP system using a USB connection, but you get errors. Select the appropriate task or tasks to solve the problem. List the selected tasks in the order you should perform them.

   a. Update Windows XP with service packs or patches

   b. Reinstall the digital camera software

   c. Reboot your system

   d. Verify the camera is turned on

HANDS-ON PROJECTS

PROJECT 16-1: Problem-Solving Using the Microsoft Knowledge Base

Your hard drive has been attacked by a malicious virus, and you have decided to restore it from the last backup made by the ASR backup process. You cannot find the ASR floppy disk required for the restore process. Search the Microsoft Knowledge Base for the steps to re-create the ASR floppy disk when the ASR backup is available. Print the Knowledge Base article.

PROJECT 16-2: Using the Microsoft Management Console

Microsoft Management Console under Windows XP works the same as it does under Windows 2000. Follow the step-by-step directions in Chapter 14 to create a customized console in Windows XP. Put two snap-ins in the console: Device Manager and Event Viewer.

PROJECT 16-3: Using System Restore

Create a restore point. Make a change to the display settings. Restore the system using System Restore. Are the changes still in effect? Why or why not?

PROJECT 16-4: Using the ASR Process

Create an ASR backup following directions in the chapter. Add a few data files to the hard drive. Restore the system using the ASR process. Do the data files still exist on the hard drive? Why or why not?

PROJECT 16-5: Exploring the Internet Connection Firewall

Using the Windows XP Help and Support Center, answer these questions about Internet Connection Firewall:

1. List the steps to view the contents of the log file that ICF uses to record dropped packets.

2. What is the filename of this log file?

3. What applet in Control Panel can you use to change the location of this file?

4. Which version of Windows XP does not include ICF? Why do you think this is so?

5. Explain how you could use ICF to record when others on your local network access your Windows XP computer.

16

Supporting Modems

Most home computers and some corporate desktop computers have modems. Also, when travelling, notebook users typically use modems to connect to the Internet and corporate networks. This chapter focuses on how modems work as well as how to install and troubleshoot them. In Chapters 18 and 19, you will learn how to connect a PC to a network and how to connect a PC to the Internet using a modem, cable modem, DSL, or other hardware for the connection.

All About Modems

**A+
CORE
1.1**

A **modem** is a device used by a PC to communicate over a phone line. A modem can be an external device (see Figure 17-1) connected to a USB or serial port, a modem card (see Figure 17-2) using either an ISA, PCI, or PCI Express slot, or a smaller and less expensive modem riser card, discussed in Chapter 5. On notebook computers, a modem is an embedded component on the motherboard or is a PC Card installed in a PC Card slot.

Figure 17-1   Zoom V.92 Mini Fax External Modem uses a USB connection

Figure 17-2   3Com U.S. Robotics 56K Winmodem modem card

Table 17-1 lists some modem manufacturers.

Manufacturer	Web Site
3 Com U.S. Robotics	www.usr.com
AOpen	www.aopen.com
Apache Micro Peripherals	www.apache-micro.com
Askey	www.askey.com
Aztech	www.aztech.com
Best Data	www.bestdata.com
Creative Labs	www.creative.com
ESS Technology	www.esstech.com
Global Village	www.globalvillage.com
Motorola	www.motorola.com
Zoom	www.zoom.com

Table 17-1　Modem manufacturers

Regardless of the type of modem card, whether an embedded or external device, a modem is both hardware and firmware. Firmware stored in ROM chips on the device contains the protocol and instructions needed to format and convert data so that it can be transported over phone lines to a receiving modem on the other end. In general, modems are considered hardware, but it is fundamental to understanding communications that you also consider them to be firmware.

Computers are digital; regular phone lines are analog. Earlier chapters discussed the difference between digital data and analog data, and Figure 17-3 shows how this concept applies to phone lines. Data stored inside a PC is communicated to a modem as binary, or digital, data (0s and 1s). A modem converts this data into an analog signal (in a process called **modulation**) that can travel over a phone line. Then the modem at the receiving end converts the signal back to digital data (in a process called **demodulation**) before passing it on to the receiving PC. The two processes of MOdulation/DEModulation lead to the name of the device: modem.

Sound traveling over regular phone lines is transmitted as analog signals, meaning that there are an infinite number of sound frequencies, just as there are an infinite number of sound frequencies in the human voice. Even though the data from a PC is inherently digital, it too must be converted to an analog signal in order to be transmitted over phone lines. PC data must be converted from two simple states or measurements (0 and 1, or off and on) to waves (like sound waves) that have a potentially infinite number of states or measurements. Modems use different characteristics of waves to correspond to the 0s and 1s of digital communication.

17

Figure 17-3   Modems convert a digital signal to analog and then back to digital

A+
CORE
1.5
6.2

On a PC, the modem provides a connection for a regular phone line called an **RJ-11** connection, which is the same type of connection that you see for a regular phone wall outlet (Figure 17-4). In addition to a line-in connection from the wall outlet, a modem also has an extra RJ-11 connection for a telephone.

Figure 17-4   An RJ-11 connection on a modem is the same as that used for a regular phone connection

✓   A+ EXAM TIP

The A+ Core exam expects you to be familiar with these terms: RJ-11, half-duplex, and full-duplex.

A modem must be able to both receive and transmit data. Communication in which transmission can be in only one direction at a time is called **half-duplex**; an example of this type of communication is a CB radio. A modem that can only communicate in one direction at a time is called a half-duplex modem. Communication that allows transmission in both directions at the same time is called **full-duplex**; a regular voice phone conversation is an example of full-duplex communication. If a modem can communicate in both directions at the same time, it is a full-duplex modem; most modems today are full-duplex.

How Modems Are Rated

Using Windows, you can view the properties of an installed modem on a PC. Many people install their modems by simply choosing settings supplied by others, or by allowing the installation program to use default options. This section explains what each modem property means and how it affects the modem's performance and compatibility with other modems.

Getting Started

When you first use a modem to make a dial-up call to another PC, you hear the modem making noises as the dial-up is completed. What you hear are the sounds of the two modems establishing the rules of communication between them. The process is called **handshaking, or training**. In this handshaking phase, the calling modem and the receiving modem communicate the protocols and determine speeds they can support, decide how to handle data compression and error checking, and agree on what methods of data transfer to use. The protocols agreed on must be supported by both modems, and they attempt to use the faster and more reliable protocols first.

Modem Speeds

The speed at which a modem passes data over phone lines is partly determined by the transmission standard the modem is using. Modem speed is usually measured in **bits per second (bps)**. On older, slower modems, you might find the speed expressed as **baud rate**, which is the number of times a signal changes in one second. On older modems, the baud rate is equal to the bps, because one signal represents one bit. On more modern modems, one signal can represent more than one bit, so faster modems are measured in bps (and baud rates may differ from the bps). When modem speed is measured using baud rate, the number of bits per second is always equal to or a multiple of the baud rate. The most common rated modem speed in use today is 56.6 Kbps, although a few modems are still rated at 28.8 Kbps or 33.6 Kbps.

The maximum speed of a modem is often written into the manufacturer's name for the modem.

To see what your modem's rating is when using Windows 2000/XP, from Control Panel, click the Printers and Other Hardware category, double-click Phone and Modem Options, and then click the Modems tab. You see the Phone and Modem Options dialog box shown in Figure 17-5. In this figure, the installed modem is labeled as a Generic SoftK56 modem using COM3 resources. The 56K portion of the name indicates the maximum speed of the modem: 56 Kbps.

For Windows 9x/Me, to see similar information, from Control Panel, double-click Modems and then click the General tab.

17

Figure 17-5   The maximum modem speed is often included in the modem name (in this case, 56 Kbps)

The Ceiling on Modem Speeds

Many factors limit modem speeds. Analog phone lines were designed to provide only sufficient audio signal quality to support the transmission of the human voice, affecting the ability to attain high transmission speeds for data. Newer digital phone lines have limitations as well. Older phone lines (installed before 1940) were analog from beginning to end, with no digital components. This is not true today. Regular (analog) telephone lines are always analog as they leave a house or office building; however, the analog signals are almost always converted to digital signals at some point in the transmission. These digital signals are then transmitted and converted back to analog signals at some point before they travel the last step between the local central telephone company office and the phone of the person receiving the call.

Because of the sampling rate (8,000 samples every second) used by phone companies when converting an analog signal to digital, and taking into account the overhead of data transmission (bits and bytes sent with the data that are used to control and define transmissions), the maximum transmission rate that a modem can attain over a regular phone line is about 56,000 bps or 56 Kbps.

Other factors further limit modem speed. The line often has some disturbance, called **noise**, which can be caused by lines bumping against one another in the wind, bad wiring, lightning, or interference from nearby fluorescent lighting, radios, or TVs. This reduction in line quality is called a dirty or noisy line. A line that consistently produces high-quality results is called a clean line.

Modem Standards

The telecommunications industry sets standards to determine modem speed and protocols. The industry-approved standards for international communication were written by the **CCITT** (**Comité Consultatif International Télégraphique et Téléphonique**). In 1992, the CCITT was incorporated into the **ITU** (**International Telecommunication Union**), an intergovernmental organization approved by the United Nations to be responsible for adopting standards governing telecommunications. You might see the standards used by modems referred to as the CCITT standards (more commonly) or as the ITU standards. The CCITT standards are listed in Table 17-2. Look for a modem that supports the most standards including the latest standard, **V.92**. The more standards a modem supports, the better it can communicate with a variety of other modems.

NOTE Avoid purchasing a modem using only a proprietary standard, because it may be able to communicate only with another modem produced by the same manufacturer.

Standard	Applies Mainly to	Description
Bell 212A	Speed (up to 1,200 bps)	This older standard supports 1,200 bps.
CCITT V.32	Speed (up to 9,600 bps)	This standard runs at 9,600 bps, includes error checking, and can negotiate standards with other modems. This standard was used for quite some time.
HST	Speed (up to 14.4 Kbps)	This older proprietary standard, created by U.S. Robotics, supports 9,600 or 14,400 bps. (U.S. Robotics also supports the CCITT standards.)
CCITT V.32bis	Speed (up to 14.4 Kbps)	This standard is an improvement over V.32 (up to 14.4 Kbps); *bis* means "second" in Latin and has a speed of 14,400 bps.
CCITT V.34	Speed (up to 33.6 Kbps)	This standard transmits at 28,800 bps, or 28.8 Kbps. Optional higher speeds are 31.2 Kbps and 33.6 Kbps.
MNP Class 4	Error correction	Developed by Microcom, Inc. and called the Microcom Networking Protocol (MNP), this standard provides error detection and correction and also automatically adjusts the speed of transmission according to the quality of the phone line. Earlier classes of MNP standards for error correction are Class 2 and Class 3.

Table 17-2 (continued)

17

Standard	Applies Mainly to	Description
CCITT V.42	Error correction	This error-correcting standard adopted the methods used by MNP Class 4. Data corrupted during transmission is automatically retransmitted using this standard. A modem can use this standard for error correction and one of the standards listed above for speed.
MNP Class 5	Data compression	The MNP Class 5 standard provides data compression, which can double normal transmission speeds between modems. It is common to see both MNP Class 4 and MNP Class 5 supported by a modem. They are sometimes called MNP-4 and MNP-5.
CCITT V.42bis	Data compression	An improved version of V.42 that also uses data compression. Many modems use the V.42bis standard for data compression and error checking and, at the same time, use the V.34 standard for data transmission protocols.
V.44	Data compression	An improved version of V.42bis.
K56flex	Speed (up to 56 Kbps)	One of two earlier standards used to attain a speed of up to 56 Kbps. This standard was backed by Lucent Technologies and Rockwell International Corp.
x2	Speed (up to 56 Kbps)	One of two earlier standards that supports a speed of 56 Kbps. This standard was supported by U.S. Robotics.
V.90	Speed (up to 56 Kbps)	The standard that replaced both K56flex and x2.
V.92	Speed (up to 56 Kbps)	Improves on V.90 adding three new features: quick connect (reduces handshake time), modem on hold (allows call waiting without breaking the connection to the ISP), and improved upload speeds for large files.

Table 17-2   Modem transmission standards

NOTE

Although most modems today are rated and advertised to transmit at 56 Kbps, they seldom accomplish this speed. When one PC communicates with another, even if both PCs are equipped with 56K modems and using clean phones lines, the actual speed attained will most likely not exceed 34 Kbps. When you connect to your ISP (Internet service provider) using a 56 Kbps modem, if the ISP uses a digital connection to the phone company, you can achieve higher transmission speeds.

Data Compression

A modem includes firmware housed on the modem that can perform error correction and data compression. These and other functions of data communication can be performed by either hardware (firmware on the modem) or software (programs on the PC).

When data compression is performed by a modem, it applies to all data transmitted by the modem. If data compression is performed by the software on the PC, it applies to single-file transfer operations. Data compression done by the modem follows either the MNP-5, CCITT V.42, or V.42bis protocol. All three protocols also perform error correction.

Error Correction

As shown in Table 17-2, several standards include error correction; one modem often supports more than one standard. During the handshaking process, the answering modem tries to establish an error-correction protocol with the other modem by first suggesting the fastest, best standard. If the calling modem responds by accepting that standard, then both use it. If the calling modem does not support the suggested protocol, then the two modems negotiate to find the best protocol they both can use or they simply decide not to use error correction.

Error correction works by breaking up data into small packets called **frames**. The sending modem performs some calculations on a frame of data and sums these calculations into a checksum. A **checksum** is a summary calculation of data and is used later to check or verify the accuracy of the data when received. A checksum works somewhat like a parity bit, except it is a little more complicated and applies to more data. The checksum is attached to the data frame, and they are transmitted together. The receiving modem performs the same calculations and compares its answer to the checksum value received. If the values do not agree, then the receiving modem requests a new transmission of the packet. This process does slow down data transmission, especially on dirty or noisy phone lines, but accuracy is almost 100 percent guaranteed.

More About Handshaking

17

Now that you understand several different protocols that must be established between two modems before they can communicate data, you can better understand what happens when two modems perform a handshake. Here are some key points about the process:

- When a modem answers an incoming call, this answering modem sends a modem tone, sometimes called a **guard tone**, which the calling modem recognizes as another modem and not a human voice, and so it does not break the connection.
- The answering modem sends a signal called the **carrier.** This is an unmodulated (unchanging) or continuous tone at a set frequency (also called pitch), that depends on the speed of communication the answering modem attempts to

establish with the calling modem. This process, called "establishing carrier," sounds like static, which you hear during handshaking.

■ After carrier is established, the two modems enter the equalization stage, which sounds like hissing or buzzing on the line. Both modems are testing the line quality and compensating for poor quality by changing the way they transmit. When this process completes, the speed of transmission, called the **modem speed** or the **line speed**, is set between them.

■ The speakers on the modems are now turned off. Next the modems begin to talk about how they will transmit data. The answering modem asks if the other modem can support MNP-4, MNP-5, V.42, V.42bis, and so on. After some interchange, the methods of data transmission are agreed on, and handshaking is complete. The two modems can now communicate.

External modems show you what is happening by turning lights on and off on the front of the modem and displaying messages on an LCD panel (called a display read-out). Internal modems, of course, don't have these lights available for you to see, so communications software sometimes displays a pseudo-modem panel on your computer screen.

When a modem is first activated (turned on), it initializes itself and then raises (turns on) its Clear to Send (CTS) signal and, for an external modem, the CTS light also goes on. When the PC receives the CTS signal from its modem, it raises its Request to Send (RTS) signal in order to begin a call. For external modems, the RTS or RS light goes on.

Communications technicians use the terms *raising* and *dropping* signals to mean that the signal has either started or stopped, respectively.

NOTE

Serial Port (UART) Settings

✔ **A+ EXAM TIP**

The A+ Core exam expects you to be able to distinguish between modem settings and port settings when configuring a modem.

Recall from Chapter 10 that the chip responsible for any communication over a serial port is called the UART (universal asynchronous receiver-transmitter). An external modem is likely to use a serial port, and an internal modem has serial port (UART) logic on the modem card. Therefore, in addition to modem-to-modem communication, we must consider UART-to-UART (serial port to serial port) communication. The settings that control serial-port communication are called **port settings**. These port settings are described in Table 17-3. The speed of the transmission between the serial port and a device it is connected to, such as a modem, is measured in bps and is called the **port speed**.

Don't confuse modem settings with port settings. Modem settings control modem-to-modem communication, and port settings control UART-to-modem communication.

NOTE

Port Setting	Description	Common Values
	transmission in bps? The port speed should usually be about four times the modem speed.	57,600; 115,200; 230,400; 460,800; 921,600 bps
Data bits	How many bits are to be used to send a single character of data? Only 7 bits are required for standard ASCII characters, but in most cases, you should use 8 bits.	7 or 8 bits
Parity	Will there be error checking, and if so, what will be its format? In most cases, let the modem do error checking and use no parity checking on the serial port.	Odd, even, or none
Stop bits	What will be the code to indicate that a character (its string of bits) is starting or ending? In most cases, use 1 bit.	1, 1.5, or 2 bits
Flow control	How will the flow of data be controlled? **Flow control** stops the flow of data if the receiving port is being overloaded. Flow control is controlled by software (Xon/Xoff) or hardware (RTS/CTS). Always use RTS/CTS.	Software (Xon/Xoff) or hardware (RTS/CTS)

Table 17-3   Port settings control how a serial port communicates

To understand how port settings and modem settings affect communication, look at Figure 17-6. Communication between the DTE and the DCE (computer and modem) is controlled by the port settings (RS-232, digital, port speed), and communication between two DCE devices (two modems) is controlled by the modem settings (phone line, analog, line speed).

To see the modem and port settings using Windows 2000/XP, open Device Manager and right-click the modem. Select Properties on the shortcut menu. The modem's Properties dialog box opens. Click the Modem tab to view the maximum port speed. If the modem is an internal modem, you cannot view or change the other port settings. To view the port setting for an external modem using a serial port, in Device Manager, right-click the serial port and select Properties. The serial port's Properties dialog box opens as shown in Figure 17-7.

17

Figure 17-6 A computer communicates with a modem differently from the way a modem communicates with another modem

Figure 17-7 Port settings for a Windows 2000 serial port

To see the modem and port settings using Windows 98, open Device Manager and select the modem. Then click Properties. The modem Properties dialog box opens. Click the Connection tab (see Figure 17-8). In this dialog box, click the Advanced button and the Advanced Connection Settings dialog box opens, also shown in Figure 17-8. From these two dialog boxes, you can see all the port settings listed in Table 17-3, except the port speed, which is on the Modem tab of the modem's Properties dialog box.

Figure 17-8   Port and modem settings under Windows 98

A+
CORE
4.4

Regardless of the expansion slot an internal modem uses, it has its own UART on the modem card and provides its own serial port logic to the computer system. This is why an internal modem must be assigned its own COM port that its UART controls. A typical configuration for a PC is to assign COM1 to the serial mouse and COM2 to the internal modem. (An external modem does not need a COM port assigned to it, because it uses the port assignments already configured on the system.) The UART on the motherboard is not used by the internal modem, because the modem is not using the COM ports on the motherboard.

NOTE   Sometimes a COM port on a motherboard can compete for resources with the COM port on an internal modem, causing a conflict. In this case, use CMOS setup to disable the conflicting COM port on the motherboard.

17

Modem Features

In addition to the UART logic, speed, protocols, data compression, and error correction used to rate a modem, modems have other features. Some additional abilities you might want to look for in a modem are:

- *Caller ID* (provided that you subscribe to that service from the phone company) is supported.
- *Call waiting (sometimes called Netwaiting or modem on hold)* allows you to receive an incoming call while connected to your ISP if your phone company service includes call waiting.
- *Display readout* on external modems provides information about the status of the modem. (See Chapter 10, Table 10-3, for a list of modem lights and their meanings. The modem can also have an LCD panel for messages such as Training or Idle.)
- *Fax capabilities* allow you to use your PC as an incoming and outgoing fax machine. Look for easy-to-use fax software bundled with the modem.
- *Flash ROM* allows you to upgrade your modem to support future standards.
- *Plug and Play for Windows* makes modem installation more automatic.
- *Voice/data capability* allows the modem to also serve as a telephone, complete with a built-in speaker and microphone.
- *Auto-answer* makes it possible for the modem to receive incoming calls while you are away from the PC.
- *Expansion slot or port type*; the type of expansion slot (PCI or ISA) an internal modem uses or the port (USB port or serial port) an external modem uses affects ease of installation and the performance of the modem.

VIDEO

Installing a
Modem

Installing and Configuring a Modem

**A+
CORE
1.2
1.3
1.4
1.8**

APPLYING CONCEPTS

Bill was hurriedly setting up a computer for a friend. When he got to the modem, he installed it as he had installed many modems in the past. He put the modem in the PCI slot and turned on the PC for Plug and Play to do its job. When the Found New Hardware Wizard launched, he installed the drivers, but the modem wouldn't work. He tried again and again to reinstall the modem, but still it didn't work. After four hours of trying to get the modem to work, he concluded the modem was bad. Then it hit him to read the instructions that came with the modem. He opened the booklet and in very large letters on the very first page it said, "The modem WILL NOT WORK if you install the card first and the software second." Bill took the card out and followed instructions and within five minutes he was surfing the net. Bill says that from that day forward he *always* reads *all* instructions first and leaves his ego at the door!

A+
CORE
1.2
1.3
1.4
1.8

Follow these general steps to install an internal modem:

1. Read the modem documentation. The manufacturer's instructions to install the modem might be different from those listed here.

2. Determine which serial port is available on your system.

3. Set any jumpers or DIP switches on the modem card. (See your documentation for details about your card. An example is shown in Figure 17-9. Common jumper and DIP switch settings are for COM ports, IRQ, and I/O addresses, and to indicate whether the card will use Plug and Play.) Most modern PnP modems have no jumpers or DIP switches.

Two jumper banks used for COM port selection

Figure 17-9   A modem might have jumpers to set IRQ and COM values; the default jumper settings should be set to use Plug and Play rather than dictate these values

4. Turn off your computer and remove the case. Find an empty slot, remove the faceplate, and save the screw. Mount the card firmly in the slot, and replace the screw to anchor the card.

5. Replace the cover. (You can test the modem before replacing the cover.)

6. Plug the telephone line from the house into the line jack on the modem. The second RJ-11 jack on the modem is for an optional telephone. It connects a phone so that you can more easily use this same phone jack for voice communication.

For an external modem, follow these general steps:

1. If the modem does not come with a cable, buy a high-quality cable. Don't skimp on price. Connect the cable to the modem and to the serial or USB port.

2. Plug the electrical cord from the modem into an 110V AC outlet.

3. Plug the telephone line from the house into the line jack on the modem. The second jack on the modem is for an optional telephone.

17

**A+
CORE**
1.2
1.3
1.4
1.8

Turn on your computer and follow these steps to configure the modem using Windows XP:

1. When you turn on the PC, Windows Plug and Play detects a new hardware device. In most cases, Windows XP will install its own drivers without giving you the opportunity to use manufacturer's drivers on CD. You might have to boot twice: once to allow Plug and Play to detect the UART and again to detect the modem. Also, if your modem has add-on features such as a Fax service, you might have to reboot again as this feature is installed. Follow onscreen directions until you reach the Windows desktop.

NOTE

Sometimes an installation disk has several directories, one for each operating system it supports. For example, for Windows XP, look for a directory named \WINXP. The OS is looking for a directory that has a file with an .inf extension.

2. After the modem drivers are installed, verify the OS configured the modem correctly. From the **Control Panel**, double-click the **Phone and Modem Options** icon. When the Phone and Modem Options dialog box opens, click the **Modems** tab. Select the modem and click **Properties**. The modem's Properties dialog box opens.

3. Verify that the modem speed is set to the highest value in the Maximum Port Speed text box, which is the highest value supported by this modem.

4. If you want to use Windows to make calls without using other software, create a dial-up Networking Connection. Right-click **My Network Places** and select **Properties** on the shortcut menu. The Network Connections window opens (see Figure 17-10).

5. Click **Create a new connection**. The New Connection Wizard launches. Click **Next**. The Network Connection Type dialog box opens (also shown in Figure 17-10). Select the type of connection and click **Next**. For example, if you want to connect to the Internet through your ISP, click **Connect to the Internet**. Complete the wizard. You need to know the phone number of your ISP, your user name, and password. Chapter 19 gives more information about connecting to an ISP.

6. For easy access, you can copy the Network Connection you just created from the Network Connections window to your desktop as a shortcut.

A+
CORE
1.2
1.3
1.4
1.8

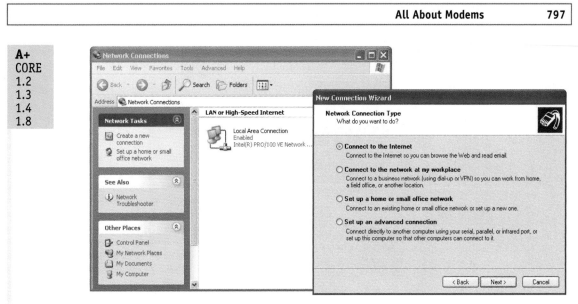

Figure 17-10   Create a Windows XP dial-up Network Connection

For Windows 98, installing and configuring the modem is the same as Windows XP except it will be easier to use manufacturer's drivers on CD. Also, when you are verifying the modem properties, you are faced with more choices in Windows 98 than you are in Windows XP. Use the properties listed below unless you have a specific reason to do otherwise (such as to compensate for a noisy phone line).

- Set the modem speed at the highest value in the drop-down list, which is the highest value supported by this modem.
- Set the port protocol at "8, No, and 1," which is computer jargon for 8 bits, no parity, and 1 stop bit.
- Use hardware flow control.

Creating a dial-up connection in Windows 98 is done differently than in Windows XP.

To create a Dial-Up Networking connection for Windows 98, double-click the My Computer icon, and then double-click Dial-Up Networking. The Dial-Up Networking window opens. Double-click the Make New Connection icon to start the Make New Connection Wizard, shown in Figure 17-11. Follow the wizard to create the connection. Later, you can copy the connection to your Windows desktop as a shortcut.

Problems during modem installation and ways to detect and resolve conflicts are covered in the Troubleshooting section later in this chapter. The last step after the modem installation is complete is to test the modem using communications software.

17

Figure 17-11   Create a Windows 98 Dial-Up Networking connection

Testing a Modem

An excellent utility you can use to test a modem is HyperTerminal, a quick and easy way to make a phone call from a Windows PC. For Windows 2000/XP and Windows 98, click Start, point to Programs (for Windows XP, point to All Programs), Accessories, Communications, and then click HyperTerminal. Follow instructions on screen to make a call. Even if you dial an out-of-service number, you can still hear your modem make the call. This confirms that your modem is installed and configured to make an outgoing call.

NOTE

If you don't see HyperTerminal in the Accessories group of Windows, it might not be installed. To install a Windows utility, use the Add/Remove Programs icon in Control Panel.

The OS can also perform a diagnostic test on the modem. For Windows 2000/XP, open Device Manager, right-click the modem, and select Properties on the shortcut menu. The modem's Properties dialog box opens. Click the Diagnostics tab and then click the Query Modem button. See Figure 17-12.

Figure 17-12 Windows XP uses AT commands to perform a diagnostic test of a modem

If the OS cannot communicate with the modem, nothing appears in the Command and Response box. However, if the OS receives responses from the modem, the dialog appears.

Notice in Figure 17-12 that each command begins with "AT". These commands are called AT commands, which stand for "Attention". The **AT command set** was developed by Hayes Microcomputer Products, a pioneer of modem communication. The command set is a de facto standard. (A de facto standard is one that has no official backing but is considered a standard because of widespread use and industry acceptance.) When a modem is in command mode and bits and bytes are sent to it from a PC, the modem interprets the bytes as commands to be followed, rather than as data to be sent over a phone line. It leaves command mode when it either receives an incoming call or dials out, and returns to command mode when a call is completed or a special escape sequence is sent to it by its computer. In command mode, the OS can use AT commands to query the modem. In the troubleshooting section that follows, you will learn how you can use an AT command to tell the modem to initialize itself.

17

A+
CORE
1.2
1.3
1.4
1.8

APPLYING CONCEPTS

Larry is setting up his home office to telecommute to his workplace using a dial-up connection to his office building. A friend has given him a modem card, which he has installed in a PCI slot. When he turns on his Windows 2000 PC, the Found New Hardware Wizard launches. The wizard does not recognize the modem and asks Larry to select the device from a list of devices. Larry does not know the manufacturer or model of the modem because there was nothing written on the card to identify it. Larry calls you asking for help. What do you tell him?

Troubleshooting Guidelines for Modems

A+
CORE
2.1

This section provides a guide to solving problems with modems and communicating over phone lines. Some keys to troubleshooting are to determine what works and what doesn't work, find out what worked in the past but doesn't work now, and discover what has changed since things last worked. Much of this can be determined by asking the user and yourself questions and by trying the simple things first. Below is a list of problems you may encounter with your modem and suggestions on how you can proceed.

The modem does not respond

- Make sure the modem is plugged into the phone wall jack.
- If you are using an external modem, make sure it is plugged in to the computer and that the connection is solid.
- There are two RJ-11 ports on a modem. Check that the phone line from the wall outlet is connected to the line-in port. (However, on most modems, either port will work for line-in.)
- Plug a phone directly into the wall jack you are using, and make sure that there is a dial tone.
- If necessary, make sure to instruct the modem to dial an extra character to get an outside line, such as 9 or 8.

If this is a new installation that has never been used, check these things:

- Read the modem's documentation for tips and ideas to help solve problems with an installation.
- Make sure the modem and the software are set to the same COM port and IRQ.
- Make sure no other device is configured to the same COM port or IRQ as the modem. Consider removing any PCI or ISA cards that you don't need and that might conflict with the modem.

**A+
CORE
2.1**

- For an internal modem, using CMOS setup, disable the serial port on the motherboard that uses the COM port settings that the modem is set to use, so there will be no conflicts for these port settings. For an external modem using a serial port, verify that the COM port the modem is using is enabled. Check Device Manager for reported errors on the modem and the port the modem is using.

- If you are using an internal modem, verify the modem is securely seated in the expansion slot.

- Try installing an internal modem in a different expansion slot. First, use Device Manager to uninstall the modem. Then move it to a new slot and restart your computer to launch the Found New Hardware Wizard.

- If you are using an external modem, substitute a known-good cable. For a USB modem, verify that USB is enabled in CMOS setup.

- Using Device Manager, uninstall the modem and then reboot. Try installing the drivers again.

- Using Device Manager, uninstall the modem. Then check the CD that came with the modem for a setup program such as Setup.exe. Run the program to have it install the drivers manually.

- For a notebook computer where the modem is an embedded component, look on the CD that came with the notebook motherboard for a setup program to install the modem. First uninstall the modem in Device Manager before running the setup program.

- Check that the software correctly initialized the modem. If you did not give the correct modem type to the software, it may be trying to send the wrong initialization command. Try AT&F. (For Windows 2000/XP, from Control Panel, double-click Phone and Modem Options. Click the Modems tab and then click Properties. In the modem's Properties dialog box, click the Advanced tab. The dialog box in Figure 17-13 opens. Enter the AT&F command under Extra initialization commands.) Retry the modem. (Under Windows 9x/Me, click Start, point to Settings, and click Control Panel. Double-click Modems. Select the modem and click Modem Properties, Connection, Advanced. Enter the AT&F command under Extra settings.)

- Make sure you have enough RAM and hard drive space. Then close all other applications currently running, reboot the PC, and try the modem again.

- For a Windows 2000/XP system, verify the drivers are certified by Microsoft. Non-certified drivers should work, but if they don't, then uninstall the modem and reinstall it using Microsoft generic drivers.

- Replace the modem with one you know works.

17

Figure 17-13　The Extra initialization commands text box allows you to send extra AT commands to the modem on any call

The modem says there is no dial tone, even though you can hear it

- Make sure the phone cord from the wall outlet is plugged in to the line jack on the modem.
- The modem might not be able to detect the dial tone, even if you can hear it. Try unplugging any other equipment plugged into this same phone line, such as a fax machine.
- Try giving the ATX0 command before you dial. Enter the command under Extra initialization commands, as in Figure 17-13. If that doesn't help, then remove the ATX0 command.
- Straighten your phone lines! Don't let them get all twisted and crossed with other heavy electrical lines.
- If there has been a recent lightning storm, the modem may be damaged. Replace the modem with one you know works.

The modem dials and then says that the other end is busy, even when you know that it is not

- This can happen with international calls if the modem does not recognize the signal as a ring. Try giving the ATX0 command first.
- Straighten the phone lines and remove extra equipment, as described earlier.

The sending modem and the receiving modem take a very long time to negotiate the connection

A+
CORE
2.1

- This is probably because of a noisy phone line. Try calling again or use a different number. If you verify the problem is with the phone line, ask the phone company to test your phone line.
- Remove other equipment from your line. A likely suspect is a credit card machine.
- Turn off data compression and try again.
- Turn off error correction and try again.
- Try forcing your modem to use a slower speed.

During a connection, it sounds as if the handshaking starts all over again

Modems normally do this if the phone line is noisy and would cause a lot of data to become corrupted; it's called retraining and can sometimes solve the problem as the modems renegotiate, compensating for the noisy line. Follow the steps listed previously to clear your line of equipment and twisted phone lines.

File transfers are too slow

Make sure your modem is configured to use data compression, if possible.

The modem loses connection at odd times or is slow

- Check the communications software for the speed assigned to it. People often set the communications software speed to the modem speed instead of the port speed, which is what the software asks for and which should be about four times the modem speed.
- You may have a noisy phone line. Try the connection using the same brand and model of modem on both lines. If performance is better, the problem is most likely the phone line.
- Is the phone line from the modem to the jack too long? About four feet is the limit; otherwise, electromagnetic interference may be the problem.
- Straighten the phone lines and clear the line of any extra equipment.
- Disable call waiting. To do this, enter *70 before the dialing number. Some communications software has a setting to disable call waiting. If not, you can enter these three characters in the Extra initialization commands box in the modem Properties dialog box (see Figure 17-13).
- Reinstall the modem. Allow Windows to detect the modem for you and install its own drivers.

17

The modem drops the connection and gives the NO CARRIER message

A+
CORE
2.1

- Most likely the connection was first dropped by the remote modem. Is someone trying to use a phone extension on this line?
- Disable call waiting.
- Remove extra equipment from the line, and straighten the phone lines.
- Check the modem settings and make sure "Error control required to connect" is not checked.
- For Windows 9x/Me, try using a different modulation type under Advanced Connection Settings of your modem's Properties dialog box.
- The remote modem may not support the high speeds used. Try reducing the port speed to 9600 or lower.

When the weather is bad, the connection disconnects often

This is caused by a dirty phone line. Remove any extra equipment and straighten the lines. (This can help your connection regardless of weather conditions.)

When large files are downloaded, some data is lost

Make sure that hardware flow control is on and that software flow control is off for the software, the COM port, and the modem. (Use software settings options, the COM port Properties dialog box, and the modem Properties dialog box.)

The connection fails when large files are uploaded or downloaded

There may be a buffer overflow. Try these things to gain better control of data flow:

- Make sure that hardware flow control is on and that software flow control is off for the software, the COM port, and the modem.
- Is the serial port speed set too high for your UART chip? Lower the port speed.
- For an external modem, try a different cable.

You get nothing but garbage across the connection

- Check the port settings. Try 8 data bits, no parity, and one stop bit (8, No, and 1).
- Slow down the port speed.
- Slow down the modem speed.
- Try a different modulation type.

CHAPTER SUMMARY

▌ A modem is an external or internal device used by a PC to communicate over a phone line.

▌ Modem cards use either a PCI or ISA slot, although the motherboard on some systems has a shortened slot that supports a modem riser card.

▌ External modems use a USB or serial port.

▌ Modems are both hardware and firmware.

▌ Modems convert digital computer signals to analog signals (through modulation) for transmission over phone lines, and then back into digital signals on the receiving end (through demodulation).

▌ A modem can be either half-duplex (like a CB radio, with which communication can travel in only one direction at a time) or full duplex (like a regular voice phone conversation, in which communication can travel in two directions at once).

▌ Modems are classified according to how they set communication rules (handshaking), and how fast they pass data over phone lines (measured in bits per second).

▌ The most commonly used modem speed rating today is 56.6 Kbps. The current standard for 56 Kbps transmission is the V.92 standard.

▌ Modem standards were written by the CCITT, now called the ITU. The more standards a modem supports, the more easily it can communicate with other modems.

▌ The firmware housed on a modem can perform error correction and data compression. These data communication functions can also be performed by software on the PC.

▌ Features to look for in a modem include caller ID, call waiting, display readout, Flash ROM, Plug and Play, auto-answer, and the ability to serve as a telephone or fax machine.

▌ Computers are classified as DTE, and modems are classified as DCE. Communication between DTEs through DCEs is affected by the port speed on either end and by the communication speed between the two DCEs.

▌ Port settings include the port speed, data bits required to send a single character, parity for error checking, stop bits to communicate when a character ends, and flow control to stop data flow when necessary.

▌ HyperTerminal is a Windows utility used to test a modem connection and troubleshoot a modem.

17

◗ As with other devices, when troubleshooting a modem, determine what does and does not work, what worked in the past but doesn't work now, and what has changed since things last worked.

◗ Common causes of modem problems include line noise, bad connections, interference from other devices, and speed mismatches.

KEY TERMS

For explanations of key terms, see the Glossary near the end of the book.

AT command set
baud rate
bits per second (bps)
carrier
CCITT (Comité Consultatif International Télégraphique et Téléphonique)
checksum
demodulation
error correction
flow control

frame
full-duplex
guard tone
half-duplex
handshaking
ITU (International Telecommunication Union)
line speed
modem

modem speed
modulation
noise
port settings
port speed
RJ-11
training
V.92

REVIEWING THE BASICS

1. Explain why a modem is considered both hardware and firmware.

2. Converting a digital signal to analog is called _____. Converting analog back to digital is called _____.

3. Communication in only one direction at a time is _____ communication. Communication in both directions at the same time is _____ communication.

4. Why is the maximum transmission rate of today's modems limited to 56.6 Kbps? Why might a modem not transmit at this speed?

5. What organization is responsible for setting telecommunications standards?

6. Name two standards that pertain to data compression.

7. Why is a modem required to support more than one standard for transmission speed?

8. What happens when the receiving modem finds that the checksum is incorrect during data transmission with error checking?

9. Using Windows XP, how do you control the port settings for an external modem connected to a serial port?

10. What two ports are most often used to connect an external modem to a PC?

11. Describe the difference between port speed and modem speed.

12. What type of connection does a telephone jack use?

13. Why is it best to not have the serial port UART perform parity checking?

14. What company invented the AT command set for a PC to communicate with a modem?

15. List three hardware reasons why a modem might not respond.

16. What is the tool you can use in Windows under the Accessories group to make a phone call to test a modem?

17. What is the complete AT command to cause a modem to reconfigure itself to factory default settings?

18. List the steps in Windows 98 to have Windows run a diagnostic test on the modem.

19. List the steps in Windows 2000 to have Windows run a diagnostic test on the modem.

20. When Windows performs these diagnostic tests, what command set is it using?

THINKING CRITICALLY

1. You have purchased a modem bundled with a CD that includes drivers for Windows 98, Windows Me, Windows NT, Windows 2000, and Windows XP. You install the modem in a PCI slot and begin to install the modem drivers under Windows XP when you receive the message that the drivers that came bundled with the modem are not digitally signed by Microsoft. What should you do?

   a. Remove the modem and install one that is certified as Windows XP compatible

   b. Continue the installation using the bundled drivers

17

    c. Stop the installation and use generic Microsoft drivers for your modem

    d. Check with the modem manufacturer for certified Windows XP drivers

2. A friend has just moved to a new apartment and set up his computer. He calls saying he cannot dial up to his ISP and asks you for help. List the first three things you should have him check.

HANDS-ON PROJECTS

PROJECT 17-1: Performing a Quick Modem Test

Perform a quick test of your modem using these two methods:

1. Use Windows HyperTerminal to make a call from your computer to any phone number. Describe what happens. What does this test confirm and not confirm about your modem and its setup?

2. Following instructions in the text, perform a diagnostic test using the Windows 2000/XP Device Manager or the Windows 98 Control Panel. What AT commands were used in the test, and what information can you gather from the output of the commands?

PROJECT 17-2: Researching Modems

Use the Internet to do the following:

1. Print a Web page of a modem manufacturer describing the specifications for a USB external modem.

2. Print a Web page of a different modem manufacturer describing the specifications of a serial-port external modem.

3. Print a Web page of a third modem manufacturer describing the specifications of an internal modem.

PROJECT 17-3: **Finding Out About Your Modem**

Using the tools you learned about in this chapter, answer these questions about your modem:

1. What port does the modem use?

2. What interrupt does the modem use?

3. What port address does the modem use?

4. What UART chip is used?

5. What is the highest possible port speed?

6. What model of modem is installed?

PROJECT 17-4: **Changing Your Modem's Connection Settings**

Following the directions in the troubleshooting guidelines, change your modem's connection settings so that the modem speaker remains on for the entire time that the modem is connected. Use the ATM2 command under the Windows 2000/XP Extra initialization commands or Windows 98 Extra settings box.

Make a call with this setting and then describe what happens. After you finish the call, remove the extra setting.

PROJECT 17-5: **Troubleshooting a Modem**

View and print a log file of a modem session using either Windows 2000/XP or Windows 98:

▶ For Windows 2000/XP, logging is always turned on. To view and print the log file, click the Diagnostics tab on the modem's Properties dialog box. Then click View log. The log file opens in Notepad. The filename is ModemLog_*modemname*.txt, and it is stored in the Windows root folder.

▶ For Windows 98, in the Advanced Connections Settings dialog box, check the box **Append to Log**. This action causes Windows 98 to create a log file named Modemlog.txt in the folder where Windows is installed. Make a phone call using the modem, and then disconnect. Print the log file that is created.

17

PCs on a Network

This chapter discusses how to connect PCs in networks and how to connect those networks to each other. You'll learn how local networks are built, how bridges and switches can segment large local networks, and how routers connect networks. You'll also learn about the different technologies used to connect PCs and networks to the Internet, the largest network of all. You'll learn how to support PCs connected to a network, how computers are identified on a network, how to share computer resources over a network, and how to troubleshoot a network connection. In the next chapter, you'll learn how to connect to the Internet and how to use the resources on it.

Physical Network Architectures

A+
CORE
6.3
OS
4.1

Connecting devices on a **LAN (local area network)** provides a way for workstations, servers, printers, and other devices to communicate and share resources. There are several LAN architectures, or ways of connecting nodes on a network. (A **node**, or **host**, is one device on the network such as a workstation, server, or printer.) The four most popular physical network architectures (sometimes called hardware protocols) for local networks are Ethernet, wireless LAN, Token Ring, and FDDI. An older type of network technology is Attached Resource Computer network (ARCnet), which is seldom seen today. This section discusses the most popular architectures, including the network problems they were designed to solve as well as their advantages and disadvantages.

NOTE

The **Institute of Electrical and Electronics Engineers (IEEE)** creates standards for computer and electronics industries. The networking standard IEEE 802 consists of a series of specifications for networking. For example, IEEE 802.2 describes the standard for Logical Link Control, which defines how networks that use different protocols communicate with each other. For more information on the IEEE 802 standards, see the IEEE Web site, *www.ieee.org*.

Before we get into the details of network architecture, you need to know a few terms and what they mean:

- A PC makes a direct connection to a network by way of a **network adapter**, which is most often an expansion card called a **network interface card (NIC)**, using a PCI slot. However, the adapter can also be an external device providing a network port or wireless connection. The device can connect to the PC using a USB port, SCSI external port, or serial port. In addition, the adapter can be embedded on the motherboard, which provides the network port. In any case, the adapter must match the type and speed of the physical network being used, and the network port must match the type of connectors used on the network. Laptops can make connections to a network through a PC Card NIC, a built-in network port, a wireless connection, or an external device that connects to the laptop by way of a USB port. (You will learn about PC Cards in Chapter 20.)
- Communication on a network follows rules of communication called network protocols. Communication over a network happens in layers. The OS on one PC communicates with the OS on another PC using one set of protocols, and the NIC communicates with other hardware devices on the network using another set of networking protocols. Examples of OS protocols are TCP/IP and NetBEUI, and examples of hardware protocols are Ethernet and Token Ring. You'll learn more about these protocols later in the chapter.

A+
CORE
6.3
OS
4.1

▪ Data is transmitted on a network in pieces called **packets, datagrams,** or **frames.** Information about the packet that identifies the type of data, where it came from, and where it's going is placed at the beginning and end of the data. Information at the beginning of the data is called a header, and information at the end of the data is called a trailer. If the data to be sent is large, it will be divided into several packets small enough to travel on the network.

Ethernet

A+
CORE
6.1
6.2

Ethernet is the most popular network architecture used today. The three variations of Ethernet are primarily distinguished from one another by speed: 10-Mbps Ethernet, 100-Mbps or Fast Ethernet, and Gigabit Ethernet. These three types are described in the following list. Figure 18-1 shows several types of cables used with Ethernet, and Table 18-1 compares cable types and Ethernet versions.

▪ *10-Mbps Ethernet.* The first Ethernet specification was invented by Xerox Corporation in the 1970s, and in 1980 it was enhanced and became known as Ethernet IEEE 802.3. This type of Ethernet operates at 10 Mbps (megabits per second) and uses either **shielded twisted-pair (STP) cable, unshielded twisted-pair (UTP) cable,** or **coaxial cable.** STP uses a covering around the pairs of wires inside the cable that protects it from electromagnetic interference caused by electrical motors, transmitters, or high-tension lines. It costs more than unshielded cable, so it's only used when the situation demands it. Twisted-pair cable uses a connector called an **RJ-45 connector** that looks like a large phone jack, and thin coaxial cable uses a **BNC connector.** There are several variations of this speed of Ethernet. **10BaseT** Ethernet uses UTP cable that is rated by category. CAT-3 (category 3) is less expensive than the more popular CAT-5 cable. **10Base5** Ethernet (sometimes called **ThickNet**) uses thick coaxial cable such as RG8. **10Base2** Ethernet (sometimes called **ThinNet**) uses a less expensive, smaller coaxial cable such as RG58.

▪ *100-Mbps Ethernet or Fast Ethernet.* This improved and most popular version of Ethernet (sometimes called **100BaseT** or **Fast Ethernet**) operates at 100 Mbps and uses UTP or STP cable. 100BaseT networks can support slower speeds of 10 Mbps so that devices that run at either 10 Mbps or 100 Mbps can coexist on the same LAN. Two variations of 100BaseT are 100BaseTX and 100BaseFX. The most popular variation is 100BaseTX. Fast Ethernet uses CAT-5 twisted-pair cable, enhanced CAT-5 (CAT-5e), or CAT-6 that has less crosstalk than CAT-5 or CAT-5e. 100BaseFX uses fiber-optic cable, shown in Figure 18-1. Fiber cable comes in three types: single-mode (thin, difficult to connect, expensive, and best performing), multimode (most popular), and plastic fiber (thick, easy to connect, short cable lengths required).

18

A+
CORE
6.1
6.2

- *1000-Mbps Ethernet or Gigabit Ethernet.* Another version of Ethernet operates at 1000 Mbps and uses twisted-pair cable and fiber-optic cable. **Gigabit Ethernet** is currently replacing 100BaseT Ethernet as the choice for LAN technology. Because it can use the same cabling and connectors as 100BaseT, a company can upgrade from 100BaseT to Gigabit without great expense.
- *10-Gigabit Ethernet.* This version, which is currently under development, will operate at 10 billion bits per second (10 Gbps). It will use fiber cable and is expected to be used for major backbones and large metropolitan area networks (MANs).

a. Coaxial cable

b. Unshielded twisted-pair (UTP)

c. Fiber-optic cables with tight and loose sheaths

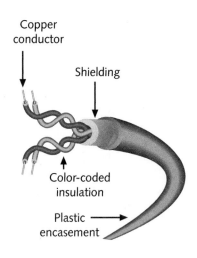

d. Shielded twisted-pair (STP)

Figure 18-1   Networking cables

A+
CORE
6.1
6.2

Cable System	Speed	Cables and Connectors	Maximum Cable Length
10Base2 (ThinNet)	10 Mbps	Coaxial uses a BNC connector	185 meters or 607 feet
10Base5 (ThickNet)	10 Mbps	Coaxial uses an AUI 15-pin D-shaped connector	500 meters or 1,640 feet
10BaseT and 100BaseT (Twisted-pair)	10 or 100 Mbps	UTP or STP uses an RJ-45 connector	100 meters or 328 feet
10BaseF, 10BaseFL, 100BaseFL, 100BaseFX, 1000BaseFX, or 1000BaseX (fiber-optic)	10 Mbps, 100 Mbps, or 1 Gbps	Fiber-optic cable uses an ST or SC fiber-optic connector	500 meters up to 2 kilometers (6,562 feet)
1000BaseT (Gigabit Ethernet)	1 Gbps	Twisted-pair cable with RJ-45 connectors or Fiber-optic	100 meters or 328 feet

Table 18-1   Variations of Ethernet and Ethernet cabling

✔ A+ EXAM TIP

The A+ Core exam expects you to know the details of Table 18-1.

Important coaxial cables you should be aware of are RG59, which is used for cable TV and VCR transmission; RG6, which is used for satellite dish signals and video applications requiring greater shielding than RG59; RG8, used by ThickNet Ethernet; and RG58, used by ThinNet Ethernet. Also, the outside jacket of coaxial cable is normally made of extruded PVC (polyvinyl chloride), which is not safe when used inside plenums (areas between the floors of buildings). In these situations, more expensive plenum cable covered with Teflon is used, because it does not give off toxic fumes when burned.

Ethernet Topology

✔ A+ EXAM TIP

The A+ Core exam expects you to know about these cable types: RG6, RG8, RG58, RG59, plenum/PVC, UTP, CAT3, CAT5/e, CAT6, STP, fiber, single-mode fiber, and multimode fiber. You should also know about the following connector types: BNC, RJ-45, AUI, ST/SC, and IDC/UDC.

Ethernet networks can be configured as either a bus topology or a star topology. Topology is the arrangement or shape used to physically connect devices on a network to one another. Figure 18-2 shows examples of bus and star topologies. A **bus topology** connects each node in a line and has no central connection point. Cables just go from one computer to the next, and then the next. A **star topology** connects all nodes to a centralized hub. PCs on the LAN are like points of a star around the hub in the middle, which connects the nodes on the LAN.

The star arrangement is more popular because it is easier to maintain than the bus arrangement. In a star topology, a hub passes all data that flows to it to every device connected to it. An Ethernet hub **broadcasts** the data packet to every device, as shown in Figure 18-3.

18

**A+
CORE
6.1
6.2**

Think of a **hub** as just a pass-through and distribution point for every device connected to it, without regard for what kind of data is passing through and where the data might be going. See Figure 18-4.

Bus design

Terminator   Terminator

Star design

Hub

Figure 18-2   Ethernet is a simple and popular network technology

Figure 18-3   Any data received by a hub is replicated and passed on to every device connected to it

In Figure 18-3, when computer A sends data to the hub, the hub replicates the data and sends it to every device connected to it. Computers B, C, and D each get a copy of the data. It's up to these computers to decide if the data is intended for them. For this reason, a hub can generate a lot of unnecessary traffic on a LAN, which can result in slow performance when several nodes are connected to the hub.

A+
CORE
6.1
6.2

RJ-45 port

Twisted-pair cable

RJ-45 connector

BNC terminator

BNC port

Figure 18-4   A hub is a pass-through device to connect nodes on a network

 A+ EXAM TIP

The A+ Core exam expects you to know the difference between a patch cable and a crossover cable.

As networks grow, more hubs can be added. Figure 18-5 shows an example of a network that uses three hubs in sequence. The hubs themselves form a bus network, but the computers connected to each hub form a star. This combination network configuration, which uses a logical bus for data delivery but is wired as a physical star, is an example of a **star bus topology**.

18

Figure 18-5   A star bus network uses more than one hub

A+
CORE
6.1
6.2

APPLYING CONCEPTS

When connecting a PC to a hub, use a network cable called a **patch cable** or a straight-through cable. When connecting two hubs, use a crossover cable. A **crossover cable** is a network cable in which the read wire and the write wire on one hub exchange functions when they are connected to the second hub. On the other hand, a hub might provide a special port that allows a normal patch cable to be used to connect the hub to another hub, bridge, or switch.

A crossover cable can also be used to connect two PCs when a hub is not used to make the simplest network of all. To identify a cable, look for the cable type and the cable rating printed on the cable, such as "CAT-5e patch cable."

Repeaters

VIDEO

Ethernet Cables

Because signals transmitted over long distances on a network can weaken (in a process called **attenuation**), devices are added to amplify signals in large LANs (see Figure 18-6). For example, if a 10Base2 (ThinNet) Ethernet cable exceeds 185 meters (607 feet), amplification is required. A **repeater** is a device that amplifies signals on a network. There are two kinds of repeaters. An **amplifier repeater** simply amplifies the incoming signal, noise and all. A **signal-regenerating repeater** reads the signal and then creates an exact duplicate of the original signal before sending it on. Ethernet uses a signal-regenerating repeater.

Signal weakens

Signal regenerated

Repeater

Figure 18-6   A repeater on a network restores the clarity of the signal, which degrades over a distance because of attenuation

Repeaters help overcome limitations on the length of cables that can be used, because with a repeater, signals can travel farther. But there are still limitations, because Ethernet networks limit the maximum amount of time a signal can take to reach the network, and because repeaters can slow down travel time, too many repeaters can cause problems on a network. For the typical Ethernet network, a hub acts as a signal-regenerating repeater.

Wireless LANs

A+
CORE
1.3
1.8
5.1
6.2
6.3

Wireless LAN (WLAN) technology, as the name implies, uses radio waves or infrared light instead of cables or wires to connect computers or other devices. Connections are made using a wireless NIC, which includes an antenna to send and receive signals. Wireless LANs are popular in places where networking cables are difficult to install, such as outdoors or in a historic building with wiring restrictions, or where there are many mobile users, such as on a college campus. Wireless devices can communicate directly (such as a handheld device communicating with a PC via an infrared connection), or they can connect to a LAN by way of a wireless **access point** (**AP**), as shown in Figure 18-7. Access points are placed so that nodes can access at least one access point from anywhere in the covered area. When devices use an access point, they communicate through the access point instead of communicating directly.

VIDEO

Using a
Multifunction
Router

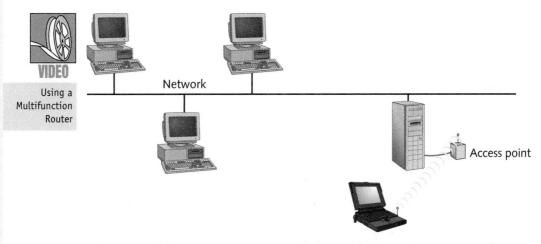

Figure 18-7   Nodes on a wireless LAN connect to a cabled network by way of an access point

NOTE

A LAN using a bus formation is often depicted in a logic diagram as a straight line with devices connecting to it, and a LAN using a ring formation is sometimes depicted as a circle. This method merely shows that devices are connected and is a nondescriptive way of drawing a LAN that might use a bus, ring, or star topology. Because most LANs are Ethernet, the most common way of drawing a LAN is to use a straight line.

18

The first IEEE standard that outlined wireless LAN specifications was IEEE 802.11, published in 1990. Most current wireless LAN devices operate under the 1999 IEEE 802.11b standard. This standard is also called **Wi-Fi (Wireless Fidelity)**, and called **AirPort** by Apple Computers. It supports 11Mbps. 802.11b uses a frequency range of 2.4 GHz in the radio band and has a distance range of about 100 meters. 802.11b is a popular and inexpensive network solution for home and office. It has the

A+
CORE
1.3
1.8
5.1
6.2
6.3

disadvantage that many cordless phones use the 2.4-GHz frequency range and cause network interference.

The next up-and-coming Wi-Fi standard is 802.11g, which uses the 2.4 GHz band and is therefore compatible with 802.11b, but faster, supporting up to 54 Mbps. Apple Computers calls 802.11g AirPort Extreme. Although 802.11b is currently more popular, most new wireless devices use 802.11g. Another IEEE standard is 802.11a, which works in the 5.0-GHz frequency range and is therefore not compatible with 802.11b/g. It has a shorter range from a wireless device to an access point (50 meters compared with 100 meters for 802.11b/g), supports 54 Mbps, and does not encounter interference from cordless phones, microwave ovens, and Bluetooth devices, as does 802.11b/g. Most wireless devices today support all three IEEE standards; look for **802.11a/b/g** on the packages. Another standard is 802.11d, which is designed to run in countries outside the United States where other 802.11 versions do not meet the legal requirements for radio band technologies. A newer IEEE wireless standard is WiMAX, which is defined under IEEE 802.16d and 802.16e. WiMAX supports up to 75 Mbps with a range up to 6 miles and uses 2 to 11 GHz frequency. It is expected to first be deployed for use in public hotspots and eventually compete with DSL and cable modem as a wireless broadband solution for business and residential use.

Bluetooth is a standard for short-range wireless communication and data synchronization between devices. This standard was developed by a group of electronics manufacturers, including Ericsson, IBM, Intel, Nokia, and Toshiba, and it is overseen by the Bluetooth Special Interest Group. Bluetooth, which has a range of only 10 meters, also works in the 2.4-GHz frequency range, is easy to configure, and is considered a viable option for short-range connections such as connecting a PDA to a cell phone so that the PDA can connect to a remote network.

Although wireless LANs have some obvious advantages in places where running cables would be difficult or overly expensive, wireless LANs tend to be slower than wired networks, especially when they are busy. Another problem with wireless LANs is security. Companies are reluctant to use them when it is possible for an unauthorized person with a receiving device to intercept wireless LAN transmissions. Security on a wireless LAN is accomplished by filtering the MAC addresses of wireless NICs that are allowed to use the access point, and by encrypting data sent over the wireless LAN. For more information on Wi-Fi, see *www.wi-fi.org*, and for more information on AirPort, see *www.apple.com*. For information on Bluetooth, see *www.bluetooth.com*. For information on WiMAX, see *www.wimaxforum.org*.

Token Ring and FDDI

A+
CORE
6.1

Token Ring is an older, mostly outdated LAN technology developed by IBM that transmits data at 4 Mbps or 16 Mbps. Physically, a Token Ring network is arranged in a star topology, because each node connects to a centralized device and not to other nodes in the network. However, a token actually travels in a ring on the network. The token is either free or busy, and a node must have the token to communicate. Because it is

A+
CORE
6.1

physically a star and logically a ring, it is sometimes called a **star ring topology**. The centralized device to which the network nodes connect is called a Controlled-Access Unit (CAU), a Multistation Access Unit (MSAU or sometimes just MAU), or a Smart Multistation Access Unit (SMAU).

Each workstation contains a Token Ring LAN card that connects each workstation to an MSAU. Token Ring cables can be either UTP or STP cables that have two twisted pairs, for a total of four wires in the cable. Token Ring connectors can be RJ-45 connectors, but the connector pins are not the same as RJ-45 connectors used on Ethernet. Token Ring can also use another type of connector that has no "male" or "female" version, known as a **Universal Data Connector (UDC)** or an **IBM Data Connector (IDC)**. Because there is no "male" or "female" connector, any connector can connect to any other connector.

Fiber Distributed Data Interface (FDDI, pronounced fiddy) uses a token that travels in a ring like Token Ring. But with FDDI, data frames travel on the ring without the token, and multiple nodes can have data on the ring at the same time. Nodes on a FDDI network can be connected in a ring using a **ring topology**, meaning that each node is connected to two other nodes, although most FDDI networks use hubs in a physical star topology. FDDI provides data transfer at 100 Mbps, which is much faster than Token Ring or regular Ethernet and a little faster than Fast Ethernet, which also runs at about 100 Mbps. It is often used as the network technology for a large LAN in a large company. FDDI can also be used as a backbone network to connect several LANs in a large building.

How NICs Work

A+
CORE
1.5
6.3
OS
4.1

An internal NIC plugs into a motherboard expansion slot, provides a port or ports (or antenna in the case of a wireless NIC) for connection to a network, and manages the communication and hardware network protocol for the PC. An external NIC provides the same functions and can use a PC Card slot or USB port. An individual NIC can be designed to support Ethernet, Token Ring, FDDI, or wireless architectures, but only one architecture. However, it might be designed to handle more than one cabling system. See Figure 18-8 for some examples of network cards. The network card and the device drivers controlling it are the only components in the PC that are aware of the type of physical network being used. In other words, the type of network in use is transparent to the applications using it.

A network card sends and receives data to and from the system bus in parallel, and sends and receives data to and from the network in series. In addition, the network card must convert the data it is transmitting into a signal that is in a form appropriate to the network. For example, a fiber-optic FDDI card contains a laser diode that converts data to light pulses before transmission, and a twisted-pair Ethernet card converts data from the 5-volt signal used on the motherboard to the voltage used by twisted-pair cables. The component on the card responsible for this signal conversion is called the **transceiver** (transmitter-receiver). It is common for an Ethernet card to contain more than one transceiver, each with a different port on the back of the card,

VIDEO

Wireless
Network Cards

18

A+
CORE
1.5
6.3
OS
4.1

in order to accommodate different cabling media. This type of Ethernet card is called a **combo card** (see Figure 18-9).

a. FDDI

b. Token ring

Wired network cards

c. Ethernet

d. Wireless

Wireless network cards

Figure 18-8 Four different types of network cards: (a) FDDI, (b) Token Ring, (c) Ethernet, and (d) wireless

A+
CORE
1.5
6.3
OS
4.1

Combo card

BNC port

RJ-45 port

RJ-45 connector

Twisted-pair (UTP) cable

ThinNet coaxial cable attaches here

Terminator

BNC T-connector

Figure 18-9   This Ethernet combo card can use either a BNC or RJ-45 connection, depending on the cabling system used

Different networks have different ways of identifying network nodes. Ethernet, WLAN, and Token Ring cards have MAC addresses hard-coded on the card by their manufacturers. Called **MAC (Media Access Control) addresses, hardware addresses, physical addresses, adapter addresses,** or Ethernet addresses, they are 6-byte (48-bit) hex addresses unique to each card. Part of the MAC address refers to the manufacturer; therefore, no two adapters should have the same MAC address.

Network cards require an IRQ and an I/O address range. If the network card is on the PCI bus, then the PCI bus controller manages the IRQ and I/O address requirements. Network cards may be Plug and Play, or legacy cards can use jumpers or DIP switches on the card to determine which resources to request. When selecting a network card, three things are important:

- The speed and type of network to which you are attaching (for example, 100BaseT Ethernet, Token Ring, FDDI, type of WLAN, or a proprietary network standard)
- Except for wireless connections, the type of cable you are using (for example, shielded twisted-pair, coaxial, or fiber-optic cable)
- The type of slot you are using (PCI Express, PCI, or ISA). ISA is outdated and rarely seen today.

18

Segmenting a Network

As you have learned, when two or more computers are connected, they form a network and are sometimes connected by hubs. For small networks, hubs are sufficient, but in larger networks, more intelligent devices are needed that can help reduce the traffic on the network. Bridges and switches are used to divide networks into segments, which decrease the amount of traffic on the overall network. This section describes how bridges and switches work and explains how they differ from each other.

Before we discuss these devices, you need to understand the following terms and concepts:

- All communication on a local network uses the MAC address of the NIC to identify the destination computer. Other computers on the network receive the packet, but because it is not addressed to them, they discard it.
- Bridges and switches are more intelligent than hubs and make decisions about whether to allow traffic to pass or where to forward that traffic, reducing traffic on each segment and improving network performance.

A network engineer will add a bridge or switch at a strategic place on the network, such as between two floors or between two buildings, to contain heavy traffic within each of two segments created by the bridge. Bridges and switches use MAC addresses, which they store in routing tables, to determine where to send packets.

To help you understand how bridges work, suppose your town has a river running through it, as shown in Figure 18-10. Traffic on the West Side must pass over the bridge to reach the East Side. At the bridge stands an attendant who looks at the source and destination addresses of each traveler (packet). Suppose a traveler from the West Side is searching for her destination and approaches the bridge attendant. The attendant looks at the address where the traveler wants to go (the destination address). The attendant then searches for the destination address in his routing table. If he finds the address in the table, the table tells which side the address is on. He then grants or refuses the traveler permission to pass, based on that knowledge. If the attendant does not find the destination address in the routing table, he allows the traveler to cross. Also, the attendant updates his routing table by adding information he has just learned. By knowing that the traveler came from the West Side and knowing the source address of the traveler, he can enter this source address into his routing table as one address on the West Side. At first, the attendant doesn't know much about addresses on each side, but as many travelers come from both sides of the bridge, his table becomes more complete, and he becomes more efficient at his job.

A **bridge** on a network works in a similar way to our hypothetical bridge separating two sides of town with an attendant. A network bridge keeps a routing table for each network segment to which it connects. The tables start out empty, and all data packets that reach the bridge from one segment are passed on to the other segment connected to the bridge. As packets appear at the bridge, the bridge records the source MAC address in its routing table for that segment. The next time a packet appears at the bridge, the bridge looks at the packet's destination and routes it across only if the destination is on a different network segment or the bridge does not recognize the destination. Figure 18-11 shows a bridge device.

Figure 18-10   A bridge is an intelligent device making decisions concerning network traffic

Figure 18-11   A bridge

To understand the difference between a bridge and a switch, we must look at a more complicated situation that involves three or more network segments, as shown in Figure 18-12When a packet arrives at a bridge, the bridge searches the routing table of only that segment. The bridge makes only a single decision: "Is this packet destined for a node on its own network segment?" If the answer is "Yes," then the packet is refused. It will reach its destination without using the bridge. If the answer is "No," then the bridge simply broadcasts the packet to all other network segments connected to it, except the network segment that the packet came from. In Figure 18-12, if a packet arrives from network segment A, the bridge searches its routing table for network segment A. If it doesn't find the MAC address of the packet in that table, it broadcasts the packet to network segments B and C.

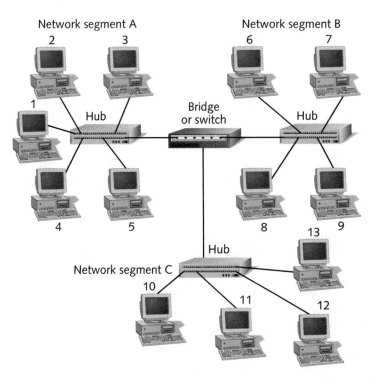

Figure 18-12   A bridge or switch connects two or more segments and decides whether to allow the packet to pass through, depending on its destination MAC address

You can now clearly see why bridging does not work well with large networks (such as the Internet). Broadcasting messages over several large networks would produce much unnecessary traffic on those networks. Bridging is effective at separating high-volume areas on a LAN and works best when used to connect LANs that usually do not communicate outside their immediate network.

A **switch**, on the other hand, does not work by sending broadcast messages. Just like a bridge, a switch keeps a table of the MAC addresses of all the devices connected to it. It uses this table to determine which path to use when sending packets. Recall the discussion of Figure 18-10 for a moment. Like a bridge, a switch does not let a packet pass to other networks if it is addressed to a location on its own network segment. However, unlike a bridge, a switch passes a packet only to its destination network segment, instead of to all segments other than the one it came from (the source). Figure 18-13 compares how a bridge works with how a switch works.

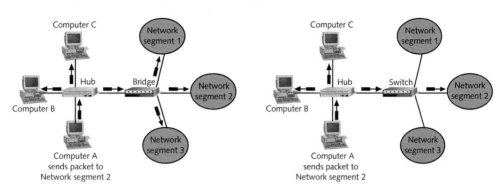

Figure 18-13   A switch is more intelligent than a bridge and can determine which network segment a packet needs to be sent to

For example, in Figure 18-12, if Computer 10 on Network segment C sends a packet to Computer 7 on Network segment B, the switch receives the packet because the hub on Computer 10's network segment is broadcasting. Using the destination address in the header of the packet, the switch searches all tables for all network segments connected to it to determine the segment to which the packet is addressed. The switch then forwards the packet to Network segment B, rather than broadcasting the packet to all network segments connected to it.

Network cards, hubs, bridges, and switches are all part of the physical infrastructure of a network. As you've learned, that physical infrastructure uses a hardware protocol to control communication between devices. For most LANs, that protocol is Ethernet. However, in addition to the hardware protocol, there is a layer of network communication at the operating system level. The OS can use one of several communication protocols such as TCP/IP or AppleTalk. For example, a Windows network might use TCP/IP to communicate at the OS level, and the devices on the LAN (hubs, NICs, and bridges) might use Ethernet. The next section looks at the different OS networking protocols, how they work, and how to configure a computer to use them.

18

Windows on a Network

A+
CORE
6.2
OS
4.1

As a system of interlinked computers, a network needs both software and hardware to work. Software includes an operating system installed on each computer on the network, and perhaps an **NOS (network operating system)** to control the entire network and its resources. If the network is small (fewer than 10 computers), it can be a **peer-to-peer network**, in which each computer on the network has the same authority as the other computers. Recall from Chapter 13 that a Windows peer-to-peer network is called a workgroup. Larger networks use the **client/server** model, in which access to a network is controlled by an NOS using a centralized database. A

A+
CORE
6.2
OS
4.1

client computer provides a user ID and password to a **server** that validates the data against the security database. In a Windows network, this server is called the domain controller, and the network model is called a domain. Popular network operating systems are Windows NT/2000, Windows 2003 Server, Novell NetWare, Unix, and Linux. Windows has client software built in for Windows and Novell NetWare servers. Alternately, for Novell NetWare, you can install Novell client software.

A network can have more than one workgroup or domain in operation, and some computers might not belong to any workgroup or domain. A computer joins a workgroup or domain in order to share resources with other computers and devices in the group or domain. Company policy controls how many workgroups or domains can exist within the company network based on user needs, security concerns, and administrative overhead required to manage the groups.

At the physical network level, Windows supports Ethernet, ATM, Token Ring, and other networking protocols. At the operating system level, Windows supports the three suites of protocols shown in Figure 18-14 and described in the following list. AppleTalk, which is shown in the figure but not listed here, is a networking protocol for Macintosh computers. The figure also shows the different ways a computer or other device on the network can be addressed. Use this figure as a reference point throughout this section to understand the way the protocols and addresses relate on the network.

Figure 18-14 An operating system can use more than one method to address a computer on the network, but at the network level, a MAC address is always used to address a device on the network

- **TCP/IP (Transmission Control Protocol/Internet Protocol)** is the protocol suite used on the Internet and so should be your choice if you want to connect your network to the Internet, with each workstation having Internet access. Novell NetWare, Linux, Unix, and Mac OS also support TCP/IP.
- **IPX/SPX (Internetwork Packet Exchange/Sequenced Packet Exchange)** is an NWLink protocol suite designed for use with the Novell NetWare operating system. Novell NetWare is an OS designed to control access to resources on a network, similar to Windows 2003 Server. An OS designed to manage a network is called an NOS. IPX/SPX is similar to TCP/IP but is not supported on the Internet.
- **NetBEUI (NetBIOS Extended User Interface)** is a proprietary Windows protocol suite used only by Windows computers. NetBEUI is faster than TCP/IP and easier to configure but does not support routing to other networks, and therefore is not supported on the Internet. It should only be used on an isolated network. Windows XP does not automatically install NetBEUI, as Microsoft considers it a legacy protocol.

✔ **A+ EXAM TIP**

The A+ Core and OS exams expect you to be familiar with the protocols listed and described here.

To use one of these protocols on a network, the first step is to physically connect the computer to the network by installing the NIC in the computer and connecting the network cable to the hub or other network device. (For wireless LANs, after installing the NIC, you put the computer within range of an access point.) The next step is to install the protocol in the operating system. Once the protocol is installed, it automatically associates itself with any NICs it finds, in a process called binding. **Binding** occurs when an operating system-level protocol such as TCP/IP associates itself with a lower-level hardware protocol such as Ethernet. When the two protocols are bound, communication continues between them until they are unbound, or released.

You can determine which protocols are installed in Windows by looking at the properties of a network connection. For example, in Windows 2000 you can open the Control Panel and double-click the Network and Dial-up Connections icon. Then right-click the Local Area Connection icon (see Figure 18-15). The Local Area Connection Properties dialog box opens, as shown in the figure. You can see that two of the three protocols provided with Windows 2000 are installed because they are checked. In this situation, the PC is using a TCP/IP network, but one network printer uses IPX/SPX and does not support TCP/IP. Because the PC uses that printer, it must have IPX/SPX installed. (A **network printer** is a printer that any user on the network can access, through its own network card and connection to the network, through a connection to a standalone print server, or through a connection to a computer as a local printer, which is shared on the network.) There is no problem with more than one operating system protocol operating on the network at the same time.

18

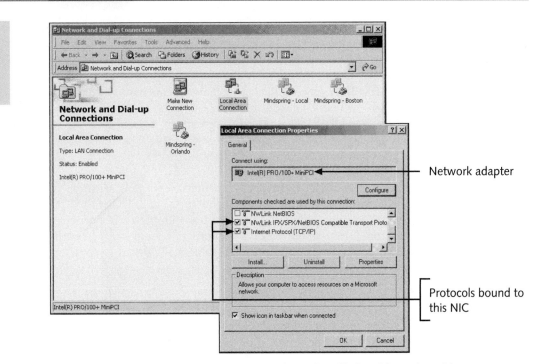

Figure 18-15   Two of three Windows 2000 network protocols are installed and bound to this network adapter

Addressing on a Network

Every device on a network has a unique address. Part of learning about a network is learning how a device (such as a computer or a printer) or a program (such as a Web server) is identified on the network. On a network, four methods are used to identify devices and programs:

- *Using a MAC address.* As you learned earlier, a MAC address is a unique address permanently embedded in a NIC and identifying a device on a LAN. A MAC address is a value expressed as six pairs of hexadecimal numbers and letters, often separated by hyphens. The MAC address is used only by devices inside the local network, and is not used outside the LAN.
- *Using an IP address.* An **IP address** is a 32-bit address consisting of a series of four 8-bit numbers separated by periods. An IP address identifies a computer, printer, or other device on a TCP/IP network such as the Internet or an intranet. (An **intranet** is a company network that uses TCP/IP.) Because the largest possible 8-bit number is 255, each of the four numbers can be no larger than 255. An example of an IP address is 109.168.0.104. Consider a MAC address a local address and an IP address a long-distance address.

A+
CORE
6.2
OS
4.1
4.2

- *Using character-based names.* Character-based names include domain names, **host names,** and **NetBIOS (Network Basic Input/Output System)** names used to identify a PC on a network with easy-to-remember letters rather than numbers. (Host names and NetBIOS names are often just called **computer names.**)
- *Using a port address.* Recall from Chapter 9 that a port address is a number that identifies a program or service running on a computer to communicate over the network. These port addresses are not the same as the port addresses, also called I/O addresses, discussed in previous chapters. Port addresses will be covered in the next chapter.

✔ **A+ EXAM TIP**

The A+ Core and OS exams expect you to know each of the methods of identifying devices and programs on a network.

Figure 18-14 shows examples of each of these addresses and at what layer of the network they are used. The sections that follow explain the different address types in more detail.

MAC Addresses

MAC addresses are used at the lowest (physical) networking level for NICs and other networking devices on the same network to communicate. If a host does not know the MAC address of another host on the same network, it uses the operating system to discover the MAC address. Because the hardware protocol (for example, Ethernet) controls traffic only on its own network, computers on different networks cannot use their MAC addresses for communication. In order for the host to communicate with a host on another LAN across the corporate intranet or Internet, it must know the address of the host used by the TCP/IP protocols. These addresses are IP addresses (see Figure 18-16).

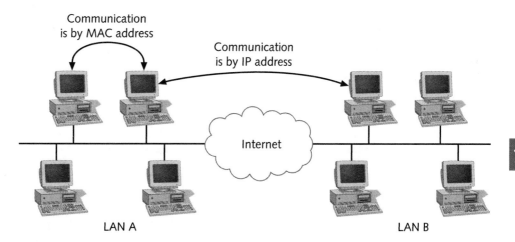

Figure 18-16   Computers on the same LAN use MAC addresses to communicate, but computers on different LANs use IP addresses to communicate over the Internet

A+
CORE
6.2
OS
4.1
4.2

If your PC is connected to the Internet or any other TCP/IP network, follow these directions to display the IP address and the NIC's MAC address in Windows NT/2000/XP:

1. Click **Start, Programs** (for Windows XP, **All Programs**), **Accessories,** and then **Command Prompt.** A command prompt window appears.

2. At the command prompt, type **ipconfig/all |more.** The screen shown in Figure 18-17 appears.

3. The |more option causes the results to appear one screen at a time instead of scrolling by so fast you cannot read them. Press **Enter** to see each screen.

4. To exit the command prompt window, type **Exit** at the command prompt.

```
Windows 2000 IP Configuration

Host Name ...............................: JEAN2000
Primary DNS Suffix ....................:
Node Type.................................: Hybrid
IP Routing Enabled ....................: No
WINS Proxy Enabled..................: No
DNS Suffix Search List ...............: prestige.net


Ethernet adapter Local Area Connection:

Connection-specific DNS Suffix .: prestige.net
Description ...............................: Intel(R) PRO/100+ MiniPCI
Physical Address........................: 00-10-A4-90-1B-AA
DHCP Enabled...........................: Yes
Autoconfiguration Enabled ........: Yes
IP Address .................................: 192.168.1.101
Subnet Mask .............................: 255.255.255.0
Default Gateway .......................: 192.168.1.1
DHCP Server .............................: 192.168.1.1
DNS Servers...............................: 208.220.88.13
                                             64.8.16.13
Lease Obtained .........................: Wednesday, August 01, 2006 2:14:06 AM
Lease Expires .............................: Tuesday, August 07, 2006 2:14:06 AM
```

Figure 18-17   Results of Windows 2000 ipconfig/all |more command shows the current IP configuration for this network

A+
CORE
6.2
OS
4.1
4.2

Windows 9x/Me uses Winipcfg instead of Ipconfig. If you are using Windows 9x/Me, follow these instructions to see your MAC address and IP address:

1. Click **Start** and then click **Run**. In the Run dialog box, type **winipcfg** and then press **Enter**. The IP Configuration window opens (see Figure 18-18).

Figure 18-18   Use the Windows 9x/Me Winipcfg utility to display a PC's IP address and MAC address

2. Click the NIC in the drop-down list of network devices. The Adapter Address that appears is the MAC address; in this case, it is 00-20-78-EF-0C-5A.

3. Click **OK**.

IP Addresses

All protocols of the TCP/IP suite identify a device on the Internet or an intranet by its IP address. An IP address is 32 bits long, made up of 4 bytes separated by periods, as in this address: 190.180.40.120. The largest possible 8-bit number is 11111111, which is equal to 255 in decimal, so the largest possible IP address in decimal is 255.255.255.255, which in binary is 11111111.11111111.11111111.11111111. Each of the four numbers separated by periods is called an **octet** (for 8 bits) and can be any number from 0 to 255, making a total of 4.3 billion potential IP addresses (256 × 256 × 256 × 256). Because of the allocation scheme used to assign these addresses, not all of them are available for use.

The first part of an IP address identifies the network, and the last part identifies the host. It's important to understand how the bits of an IP address are used in order to understand how routing happens over interconnected networks such as the Internet, and how TCP/IP can locate an IP address anywhere on the globe. When data is routed over interconnected networks, the network portion of the IP address is used to locate the right network. Once the data arrives at the local network, the host portion of the IP address is used to identify the one computer on the network that is to receive the data. Finally, the IP address of the host must be used to identify its MAC address so the data can travel on the host's LAN to that host. The next section explains this in detail.

18

Classes of IP Addresses

When a business, college, or some other organization applies for IP addresses, a range of addresses appropriate to the number of hosts on the organization's networks is assigned. IP addresses that can be used by companies and individuals are divided into three classes: Class A, Class B, and Class C, based on the number of possible IP addresses in each network within each class. IP addresses are assigned to these classes according to the scheme outlined in Table 18-2.

You can determine the class of an IP address and the size or type of company to which an address is licensed by looking at the address. More importantly, you also can determine what portion of an IP address is dedicated to identifying the network and what portion is used to identify the host on that network.

Class	Network Octets (Blanks in the IP address stand for octets used to identify hosts.)	Total Number of Possible Networks or Licenses	Host Octets (Blanks in the IP address stand for octets used to identify networks.)	Total Number of Possible IP Addresses in Each Network
A	0.__.__.__ to 126.__.__.__	127	__.0.0.1 to __.255.255.254	16 million
B	128.0.__.__ to 191.255.__.__	16,000	__.__.0.1 to __.__.255.254	65,000
C	192.0.0.__ to 223.255.255.__	2 million	__.__.__.1 to __.__.__.254	254

Table 18-2   Classes of IP addresses

Figure 18-19 shows how each class of IP address is divided into the network and host portions. A Class A address uses the first (leftmost) octet for the network address and the remaining octets for host addresses. A Class A license assigns a single number that is used in the first octet of the address, which is the network address. The remaining three octets of the IP address can be used for host addresses that uniquely identify each host on this network. The first octet of a Class A license is a number between 0 and 126. For example, if a company is assigned 87 as its Class A network address, then 87 is used as the first octet for every host on this one network. Examples of IP addresses for hosts on this network are 87.0.0.1, 87.0.0.2, and 87.0.0.3. (The last octet does not use 0 or 255 as a value, so 87.0.0.0 would not be valid.) In the example address 87.0.0.1, the 87 is the network portion of the IP address, and 0.0.1 is the host portion. Because three octets can be used for Class A host addresses, one Class A license can have approximately $256 \times 256 \times 254$ host addresses, or about 16 million IP addresses. Only very large corporations with heavy communication needs can get Class A licenses.

A Class B address uses the first two octets for the network portion and the last two for the host portion. A Class B license assigns a number for each of the two leftmost octets, leaving the third and fourth octets for host addresses. How many host addresses are there in one Class B license? The number of possible values for two octets is about 256 × 254, or about 65,000 host addresses in a single Class B license. (Some IP addresses are reserved, so these numbers are approximations.) The first octet of a Class B license is a number between 128 and 191, which gives about 63 different values for a Class B first octet. The second number can be between 0 and 255, so there are approximately 63 × 256, or about 16,000, Class B networks. For example, suppose a company is assigned 135.18 as the network address for its Class B license. The first two octets for all hosts on this network are 135.18, and the company uses the last two octets for host addresses. Examples of IP addresses on this company's Class B network are 135.18.0.1, 135.18.0.2, and 135.18.0.3. In the first example listed, 135.18 is the network portion of the IP address, and 0.1 is the host portion.

Figure 18-19   The network portion and host portion for each class of IP addresses

A Class C license assigns three octets as the network address. With only one octet used for the host addresses, there can be only 254 host addresses on a Class C network. The first number of a Class C license is between 192 and 223. For example, if a company is assigned a Class C license for its network with a network address of 200.80.15, some IP addresses on the network would be 200.80.15.1, 200.80.15.2, and 200.80.15.3.

Class D and Class E IP addresses are not available for general use. Class D addresses begin with octets 224 through 239 and are used for **multicasting**, in which one host sends messages to multiple hosts, such as when the host transmits a video conference over the Internet. Class E addresses begin with 240 through 254 and are reserved for research.

18

Different Ways of Assigning IP Addresses

A+
OS
4.1

When a small company is assigned a Class C license, it obtains 254 IP addresses for its use. If it has only a few hosts (say, less than 25 on a network), many IP addresses go unused, which is one reason there is a shortage of IP addresses. But suppose that the company grew, now has 300 workstations on the network, and is running out of

A+
OS
4.1

IP addresses. There are two approaches to solving this problem: use private IP addresses and use dynamic IP addressing. Many companies combine both methods. An explanation of each of these solutions follows.

Public, Private, and Reserved IP Addresses

When a company applies for a Class A, B, or C license, it is assigned a group of IP addresses that are different from all other IP addresses and are available for use on the Internet. The IP addresses available to the Internet are called **public IP addresses.**

One thing to consider, however, is that not all of a company's workstations need to have Internet access, even though they may be on the network. So, while each workstation may need an IP address to be part of the TCP/IP network, those not connected to the Internet don't need addresses that are unique and available to the Internet; these workstations can use private IP addresses. **Private IP addresses** are IP addresses used on private intranets that are isolated from the Internet. Because the hosts are isolated from the Internet, no conflicts arise.

In fact, a small company most likely will not apply for a license of public IP addresses at all, but instead rely solely on private IP addresses for its internal network. A company using TCP/IP can make up its own private IP addresses to use on its intranet. IEEE recommends that the following IP addresses be used for private networks:

- 10.0.0.0 through 10.255.255.255
- 172.16.0.0 through 172.31.255.255
- 192.168.0.0 through 192.168.255.255

NOTE IEEE, a nonprofit organization, is responsible for many Internet standards. Standards are proposed to the networking community in the form of an RFC (Request for Comment). RFC 1918 outlines recommendations for private IP addresses. To view an RFC, visit the Web site *www.rfc-editor.org.*

When assigning isolated IP addresses, also keep in mind that a few IP addresses are reserved for special use by TCP/IP and should not be used. They are listed in Table 18-3.

IP address	How it is used
255.255.255.255	Broadcast messages
0.0.0.0	Currently unassigned IP address
127.0.0.1	Indicates your own workstation

Table 18-3 Reserved IP addresses

A+
OS
4.1

All IP addresses on a network must be unique for that network. A network administrator may assign an IP address to a standalone computer (for example, if someone is testing networking software on a PC that is not connected to the network). As long as the network is a private network, the administrator can assign any IP address, although a good administrator avoids using the reserved addresses.

Dynamically Assigned IP Addresses   If an administrator must configure each host on a network manually, assigning it a unique IP address, the task of going from PC to PC to make these assignments and keeping up with which address is assigned to which PC can be an administrative nightmare. The solution is to have a server automatically assign an IP address to a workstation each time it comes onto the network. Instead of permanently assigning IP addresses (called **static IP addresses**) to workstations, an IP address (called a **dynamic IP address**) is assigned for the current session only. When the session terminates, the IP address is returned to the list of available addresses. Because not all workstations are online at all times, fewer IP addresses than the total number of workstations can satisfy the needs of the network. Also, you can use private IP addresses for the range of IP addresses that can be assigned to workstations. When a workstation has an IP address assigned to it, it is said that the workstation is leasing the IP address. **Internet service providers (ISPs)**, organizations through which individuals and businesses connect to the Internet, use dynamic IP addressing for their subscribers.

The server that manages these dynamically assigned IP addresses is called a **DHCP (Dynamic Host Configuration Protocol)** server. In this arrangement, workstations are called DHCP clients. DHCP software resides on both the client and the server to manage the dynamic assignments of IP addresses. DHCP client software is built into Windows NT/2000/XP and Windows 9x/Me.

✔ **A+ EXAM TIP**

The A+ OS exam expects you to know what a DHCP server is and understand when APIPA addressing is used.

When you configure a DHCP server, you specify the range of IP addresses that can be assigned to clients on the network. Figure 18-20 shows the configuration window for a DHCP server embedded as firmware on a router. (Routers are used to connect networks and are discussed later in the chapter.) Access the configuration window using a Web browser on the network and then enter the IP address of the router in the Web browser address box. In the figure, you can see that the router's IP address is 192.168.1.1, and the starting IP address to be assigned to clients is 192.168.1.100. Because the administrator specified that the server can have up to 50 clients, the range of IP addresses is therefore 192.168.1.100 to 192.168.1.149. Also shown in the figure is a list of currently assigned IP addresses and the MAC address of the computer that currently leases that IP address.

When a PC first connects to the network, it attempts to lease an address from the DHCP server. If the attempt fails, it uses an **Automatic Private IP Address (APIPA)** in the address range 169.254.x.x.

18

Beginning IP address

IP addresses currently assigned to MAC addresses

Number of addresses that can be assigned

Figure 18-20 A DHCP server has a range of IP addresses it can assign to clients on the network

Network Address Translation If hosts on a network using private IP addresses need to access the Internet, a problem arises because the private IP addresses are not allowed on the Internet. The solution is to use **NAT** (**Network Address Translation**), which uses a single public IP address to access the Internet on behalf of all hosts on the network using other IP addresses. Using NAT, a networked computer trying to access the Internet must go through a server, router, or other device that substitutes its own IP address for that of the computer requesting the information. Because the device is standing in proxy for other hosts that want Internet access, it is called a **proxy server.** Figure 18-21 shows how a proxy server stands between the network and the Internet. This proxy server has two network cards installed. One card connects to the LAN, and the other connects to a cable modem and then to the ISP and the Internet.

NOTE

Windows 98 SE, Windows Me, Windows 2000, and Windows XP offer a NAT service called Microsoft Internet Connection Sharing (ICS). With it, two or more PCs on a home network can share the same IP address when accessing the Internet. Under ICS, one PC acts as the proxy server for other PCs on the home network.

Figure 18-21   A proxy server stands between a private network and the Internet

Because a proxy server stands between a LAN and the Internet, it often does double duty as a firewall. Recall from Chapter 9 that a firewall is software or hardware that protects a network from illegal entry. Because networks are so often attacked by worms and hackers from the Internet, even a small LAN often has a router or other device between the LAN and the Internet that serves as a proxy server, DHCP server, and firewall. As a firewall, it filters out any unsolicited traffic coming from the Internet. Chapter 19 gives more information about firewalls.

Host Names and NetBIOS Names

Each computer on a TCP/IP network is assigned an IP address, but these numbers are hard to remember. Host names and NetBIOS names use characters rather than numbers to identify computers on a network and are easier to remember and use than IP addresses. In addition, a company might have a **domain name** that can be used to identify the network. An example of a domain name is *amazon.com*. Domain names are covered in the next chapter.

Recall that NetBEUI is a proprietary, legacy Windows network protocol used for Windows LANs that are not connected to the Internet. NetBEUI supports NetBIOS, a protocol that applications use to communicate with each other. Before TCP/IP became such a popular protocol, Windows assumed that the protocol of choice would be NetBEUI and that all computers on a network would be assigned a NetBIOS name such as *joesmith* or *Workstation12*. These names usually are assigned when the operating system is installed. In contrast, TCP/IP identifies computers by IP addresses, but TCP/IP also allows a computer to be assigned a character-based host name such as *joesmith*. The host name can also have a domain name attached that

18

**A+
OS
4.1**

identifies the network: *joesmith.mycompany.com*. On a TCP/IP network, the NetBIOS name or host name must be associated with an IP address before one computer can find another on the network. This process of associating a character-based name with an IP address is called **name resolution**.

Two name resolution services track relationships between character-based names and IP addresses: **DNS (Domain Name System,** also called **Domain Name Service)** and Microsoft **WINS (Windows Internet Naming Service)**. DNS tracks host names and WINS tracks NetBIOS names. A **DNS server** and a WINS server are computers that can find an IP address for another computer when only the host name and domain name are known, using either the DNS or WINS system. Windows networks sometimes use a combination of DNS and WINS; DNS is the more popular method.

Windows 98 assumes that a computer name is a NetBIOS name, which can have only 15 characters, but Windows 2000 and Windows XP assume that the computer name is a host name that uses the TCP/IP convention for host names. If the name is 15 characters or fewer, it works as a NetBIOS name or a TCP/IP name. If a host name is used, it can be up to 63 characters including letters, numbers, and hyphens, as long as the computer is not part of a workgroup. If the computer is part of a workgroup, the host name should not exceed 15 characters. Microsoft now considers the default naming convention to be TCP/IP host names rather than NetBIOS names.

Now that you know about the operating system protocols used on a network and how various types of addresses identify computers and devices on the network, let's turn our attention to how to install and configure a NIC and how to configure the OS to access and use resources on a network.

How Computers Find Each Other on a LAN

When an application wants to communicate with another computer on the same TCP/IP LAN, the requesting computer knows the name of the remote computer. Before TCP/IP communication can happen between the two computers, the first computer must discover the IP address of the remote PC. For Windows 98 using NetBIOS names, the computer runs through the following checklist in the order shown to discover the IP address. (A Windows 2000/XP computer using just TCP/IP and not NetBEUI uses DNS to resolve the name, not WINS, and begins at Step 5. If NetBEUI is running on this Windows 2000/XP computer, it tries DNS first, beginning at Step 5, and then turns to NetBEUI in Steps 1 through 4 to resolve the name.)

1. The computer checks the NetBIOS name cache. This cache is information retained in memory from name resolutions made since the last reboot.

2. If the computer has the IP address of a WINS server, it queries the server. A WINS server is a Windows NT/2000 server on the network that maintains a database of NetBIOS names and IP addresses.

3. The computer sends a broadcast message to all computers on the LAN asking for the IP address of the computer with the broadcasted NetBIOS name.

4. The computer checks a file named **LMHosts**, which is stored on the local computer. This file, called a host table, contains the NetBIOS names and associated IP addresses of computers on the LAN if someone has taken the time to manually make the entries in the file.

5. If the IP address is still not discovered, the computer assumes that the network is using DNS instead of WINS, so it checks the file named **Hosts** stored on the local computer. The Hosts file is another host table that contains host names and associated IP addresses, and is similar to the information kept by DNS servers.

6. If the computer has the IP address of a DNS server, it queries the DNS server.

Both the LMHosts and Hosts host tables are stored in the \Windows \System32\drivers\etc folder of a Windows 2000/XP computer or in the \Windows folder of a Windows 9x/Me computer. LMHosts serves as a local table of information similar to that maintained by a WINS server for NetBIOS names, and Hosts serves as a local table of information similar to that kept by a DNS server.

If you look in the \Windows\System32\drivers\etc folder of a Windows 2000/XP computer or in the \Windows folder of a Windows 9x/Me computer, you will see a sample of each file named LMHosts.SAM and Hosts.SAM, where the SAM stands for sample. Open each file with Notepad to examine it. Entries in a host table file beginning with the # symbol are comments and are not read by the name resolution process. The sample files contain many commented lines. You can add your entries to the bottom of the file without the # symbol. Then save the file in the same folder as the sample file, naming it Hosts or LMHosts with no file extension. An example of a Hosts file is shown in Figure 18-22. It tells this computer the IP address of the domain name *apache.test.com*. Recall that a domain name is a name of a network. In the example, apache is the host name, and the domain name is test.com. The **fully qualified domain name (FQDN)** is *apache.test.com*, which is often loosely called the domain name.

In this example, the computer named *apache.test.com* is used as a Web server for a private network. In order for people on the network to use this domain name, the Hosts file on each PC must have the entry shown in Figure 18-22, and the Web server must have the same IP address at all times. One way to accomplish this is to assign a static IP address to the server. Alternately, if your DHCP server supports this feature, you can configure it to assign the same IP address to your Web server each time if you tell the DHCP server your Web server's MAC address.

18

A+
OS
4.1

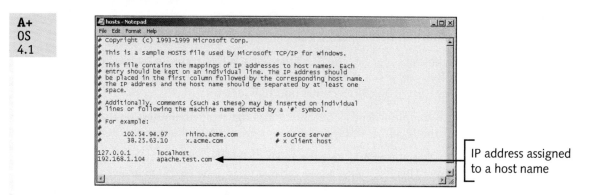

IP address assigned
to a host name

Figure 18-22   An entry in your client Hosts file will tell the client the IP address of an intranet Web site
when no DNS service is running in Windows 98

Installing a Network Card and Connecting to a Network

A+
CORE
1.2
1.9
6.2

VIDEO

Setting up a
Network with
Crossover
Cables

Connecting a PC to a network requires a NIC, a patch cable, and a device for the PC
to connect to, such as a hub. (Wireless PCs require a wireless NIC and require the PC
to be within range of an access point.)

Installing a network card and connecting the PC to a network involves three general steps: (1) Put the NIC in the PC, and install the NIC's drivers, (2) configure the
NIC using Windows, so that it has the appropriate addresses on the network and the
correct network protocols, and (3) test the NIC to verify that the PC can access
resources on the network. This section discusses these steps using Windows 2000/XP
and Windows 9x/Me. In the following sections you will also learn how to manage
resources on the network and how to troubleshoot a failed network connection.

Installing a NIC Using Windows 2000/XP

✔ **A+ EXAM TIP**

The A+ Core and OS exams
expect you to know how to
configure a network
connection.

To install a NIC using Windows 2000/XP, do the following:

1. Physically install the network card in the PC. (If the card is Plug
   and Play, it most likely has no jumpers or DIP switches to set.)

2. Turn on the PC. The Found New Hardware Wizard launches to
   begin the process of loading the necessary drivers to use the new
   device. It is better to use the manufacturer's drivers, not the
   Windows drivers. When given the opportunity, click **Have Disk**
   and insert the floppy disk or CD that came bundled with
   the NIC.

A+
CORE
1.2
1.9
6.2

3. After the Windows desktop loads, verify that the drivers installed successfully. Open **Device Manager**, right-click the card from the list of devices, and click **Properties**. The card's Properties window appears (see Figure 18-23). Look for any conflicts or other errors reported by Device Manager. If errors are reported, try downloading updated drivers from the Web site of the network card's manufacturer. You'll find other troubleshooting tips for installing NICs later in this chapter.

NOTE

Sometimes Windows XP will install its own drivers without asking if you want to use manufacturer-provided drivers. To prevent this from happening, you can run the setup program on the CD that comes bundled with the network adapter card before you install the card. Then, after you boot with the new card installed, Windows will find the already-installed manufacturer drivers and use those drivers.

VIDEO

Setting up a
Network with
Hub and Patch
Cables

18

Figure 18-23   A network adapter's resources show in the Properties window of the Device Manager window

4. Connect a network patch cable to the NIC port and to the network hub or a wall jack connected to a hub. You are now ready to configure the NIC to access the network.

A+
CORE
1.2
1.9
6.2

Incidentally, there are three ways to access the network adapter Properties window:

- As described earlier, open Device Manager, right-click the network adapter, and select Properties from the shortcut menu.
- From the Control Panel, launch the Windows XP Network Connections applet or the Windows 2000 Network and Dial-up Connections applet. Right-click the Local Area Connection icon and select Properties from the shortcut menu. Click Configure.
- Right-click My Network Places and select Properties from the shortcut menu. The Windows XP Network Connections applet or Windows 2000 Network and Dial-up Connections applet launches. Right-click the Local Area Connection icon and select Properties from the shortcut menu. Click Configure.

The first step to configure the OS for the network is to give the computer a name. Remember that if you plan to use NetBEUI as a networking protocol instead of TCP/IP, limit the computer name to 15 characters. For Windows 2000/XP, the protocol is TCP/IP by default. Follow these directions to name a computer:

1. Right-click **My Computer** and select **Properties** from the shortcut menu. The System Properties window appears.

2. For Windows XP, click the **Computer Name** tab, then click the **Change** button. The Computer Name Changes dialog box appears (see Figure 18-24). For Windows 2000, click the **Network Identification** tab, and then click the **Properties** button. The Identification Changes window appears.

3. Enter the Computer name (**win-xp** in the example shown in Figure 18-24). Each computer name must be unique within a workgroup or domain.

4. Select **Workgroup** and enter the name of the workgroup (**GOLDEN** in this example). Recall that a workgroup is a group of computers on a network that share files, folders, and printers. All users in the workgroup must have the same workgroup name entered in this window. If the PC is to join a domain (a network where logging on is controlled by a server), enter the name of the domain here, such as *mycompany.com*. When configuring a PC on a network, always follow the specific directions of the network administrator responsible for the network.

5. Click **OK** to exit the Windows XP Computer Name Changes dialog box or the Windows 2000 Identification Changes window, and click **OK** to exit the System Properties window. You will be asked to reboot the computer for changes to take effect.

6. After rebooting a Windows XP system, click **Start, My Network Places,** and then click **View workgroup computers** to view this computer and others on the network. On the Windows 2000 desktop, open **My Network Places,** and double-click **Computers Near Me.** Figure 18-25 shows an example of My Network Places.

A+
CORE
1.2
1.9
6.2

Figure 18-24   Windows XP uses the Computer Name Changes dialog box to assign a host name to a computer on a network

Figure 18-25   Windows XP My Network Places shows all computers on the LAN in a common workgroup

My Network Places for Windows 2000/XP and Network Neighborhood for Windows 9x/Me can be viewed on the desktop and in Windows Explorer. By default, Windows XP puts My Network Places only in Windows Explorer, Windows 2000 puts My Network Places in both places, and Windows 98 puts Network Neighborhood in both places.

18

A+
CORE
1.2
1.9
6.2
OS
4.1
4.2

Installing and Configuring TCP/IP Using Windows 2000/XP

When a network card is installed in Windows 2000/XP, TCP/IP is installed by default. However, if TCP/IP has been uninstalled or gives you problems, you can install it again. Also, Windows makes some assumptions about how TCP/IP is configured, and these settings might not be appropriate for your network. This section addresses all these concerns.

Before you install and configure TCP/IP, you might need to ask the network administrator the following questions:

1. Will the PC use dynamic or static IP addressing?

2. If static IP addressing is used, what are the IP address, subnet mask, and default gateway for this computer?

3. Do you use DNS? If so, what are the IP addresses of your DNS servers?

4. Is a proxy server used to connect to other networks (including the Internet)? If so, what is the IP address of the proxy server?

In dynamic addressing the computer asks a DHCP server for its IP address each time it connects to the network. The server also gives the PC its subnet mask and default gateway so that the computer knows how to communicate with other hosts that are not on its own network. A **gateway** is a computer or other device that allows a computer on one network to communicate with a computer on another network. A **default gateway** is the gateway a computer uses to access another network if it does not have a better option. A **subnet mask** is a group of four dotted decimal numbers that tells TCP/IP if a remote computer's IP address is on the same or a different network.

Most likely, you will be using dynamic IP addressing, and you will obtain the DNS server address automatically. The DHCP server might also act as the proxy server so that computers inside the network can make connections to computers outside the network using the proxy server's public IP address.

To set the TCP/IP properties for a connection, follow these steps:

1. For Windows XP, open the **Network Connections** applet, and for Windows 2000 open the **Network and Dial-up Connections** applet. Right-click the **Local Area Connection** icon, and then select **Properties** from the shortcut menu. See Figure 18-26.

2. Select **Internet Protocol (TCP/IP)** from the list of installed components, and then click the **Properties** button. The Internet Protocol (TCP/IP) Properties dialog box opens, which is also shown in Figure 18-26.

3. For dynamic IP addressing, select **Obtain an IP address automatically**. (This is the most likely choice.) For static IP addressing, select **Use the following IP address**, and enter the IP address, Subnet mask, and Default gateway.

A+
CORE
1.2
1.9
6.2
OS
4.1
4.2

Figure 18-26 To configure TCP/IP under Windows XP, use the Internet Protocol (TCP/IP) Properties dialog box

4. To disable DNS until the DHCP server gives the computer the DNS server address, select **Obtain DNS server address automatically**. (This is the most likely choice.) If you have the IP addresses of the DNS servers, click **Use the following DNS server addresses,** and enter the IP addresses. Click **OK** twice to close both windows.

5. Open **My Network Places** and verify that your computer and other computers on the network are visible. If you don't see other computers on the network, reboot the PC.

NOTE

To connect a Windows 2000 computer to a network using NetBEUI, use the Properties window of the local area connection to install the NetBEUI Protocol, which automatically binds itself to the NIC providing this local network connection. Then assign a name to the computer. Remember to limit the name to 15 characters. Windows XP does not support NetBEUI. However, you can manually install it using the Windows XP Setup CD. For directions, see the Microsoft Knowledge Base Article 301041 at *support.microsoft.com*.

18

Installing a NIC Using Windows 9x/Me

After a NIC is physically installed and the PC is turned on, Windows 9x/Me automatically detects the card and guides you through the process of installing drivers. After the installation, verify that the card is installed with no errors by using Device Manager. In Device Manager, the network card should be listed under Network adapters. Right-click the card and select Properties to view the card's properties.

Connect a network patch cable to the NIC port and to the network hub or a wall jack connected to a hub. You are now ready to configure the NIC to access the network.

A+
CORE
1.2
1.9
6.2
OS
4.1
4.2

Assigning a Computer Name

To assign a name to a Windows 9x/Me computer, follow these directions:

1. Access the **Control Panel** and double-click the **Network** icon.

2. Click the **Identification** tab (see Figure 18-27).

3. Enter the name of the workgroup (Golden in this example). Enter the computer name (Patricia in this example). Each computer name must be unique within the workgroup.

4. Click **OK** to exit the window. You will be asked to reboot the system.

After you have rebooted, open Network Neighborhood on the Windows desktop. You should be able to see this computer and others on the network. Figure 18-28 shows an example of Network Neighborhood. If you cannot see other computers, you might have to install and configure TCP/IP, as described next.

Figure 18-27   Each computer in a workgroup in Windows 98 must be assigned a name that other users on the network will see in their Network Neighborhood window

A+
CORE
1.2
1.9
6.2
OS
4.1
4.2

Figure 18-28   Windows 98 Network Neighborhood shows all computers on the LAN in a common workgroup

Installing and Configuring TCP/IP Using Windows 98

If TCP/IP is not already installed, you must install it. For Windows 98, do the following:

1. Access the **Control Panel** and double-click the **Network** icon. The Network window opens.

2. Click **Add** to display the Select Network Component Type window, as shown in Figure 18-29.

Figure 18-29   To install TCP/IP in Windows 98, use the Select Network Protocol window

18

A+
CORE
1.2
1.9
6.2
OS
4.1
4.2

3. Select **Protocol** and click **Add**. The Select Network Protocol window opens. Select **Microsoft** on the left and **TCP/IP** on the right (see Figure 18-29). Click **OK**. The system asks for the Microsoft Windows 98 CD and requests that you reboot the system.

4. When you return to the Network window, notice that TCP/IP is automatically bound to any network cards or modems that it finds installed.

The next step is to configure TCP/IP. Most likely, you will be using dynamic IP addressing, and the DNS service is initially disabled (later the DHCP server will tell the PC to enable it). In Windows 98, do the following to configure TCP/IP bound to a NIC to communicate over a local network:

1. In the Network window, select the item where TCP/IP is bound to the NIC. (In Figure 18-30, that item is TCP/IP->NETGEAR FA311 Fast Ethernet PCI Adapter.) Then, click **Properties**. The TCP/IP Properties window appears.

Figure 18-30   To configure TCP/IP in Windows 98, select the binding and click Properties to view the TCP/IP Properties window

2. If static IP addressing is used, click **Specify an IP address**, and then enter the IP address and subnet mask supplied by your administrator. If dynamic IP addressing is used, click **Obtain an IP address automatically**. Most likely this will be your selection.

3. Click the **DNS Configuration** tab, and choose to enable or disable DNS (see Figure 18-31). If you enable DNS, enter the IP addresses of your DNS servers. If your network administrator gave you other specific values for the TCP/IP configuration, you will find the tabs for these settings on this window. But in most cases, the preceding steps are sufficient to configure TCP/IP.

A+
CORE
1.2
1.9
6.2
OS
4.1
4.2

Figure 18-31   Configure DNS service under TCP/IP for Windows 98

4. When finished, click **OK** to exit the Properties window, and then click **OK** to exit the Network window.

5. On the desktop, verify that you can see your computer and others on the network in Network Neighborhood. If you don't see others on the network, reboot the PC.

NOTE   To use NetBEUI on a Windows 9x/Me network, first verify that NetBEUI is installed or install it as you do TCP/IP. It should automatically bind itself to any network adapters installed. NetBEUI needs no other configuration.

Installing a Wireless NIC

18

A+
CORE
1.2
1.3
1.8
1.9
6.2
6.3
OS
4.2

Installing a wireless NIC works the same way as installing a regular NIC, except you must use the NIC's configuration software to specify wireless network parameters. A wireless connection requires the computer to be within an acceptable range of an access point or another wireless device that it will communicate with directly. This distance is determined by the type of wireless technology used, which most likely will be 802.11b/g. These wireless standards support ranges from 100 meters to more than 500 meters, depending on the speed at which the access point or other computer is configured to run. Generally, the higher the speed, the shorter the range is between devices.

A+
CORE
1.2
1.3
1.8
1.9
6.2
6.3
OS
4.2

Do the following to install and configure a wireless NIC in a PC or notebook:

1. A wireless NIC uses an internal or external antenna. If it uses an external antenna, remove the antenna from the NIC. Turn off the computer, open the case, and install the NIC. For an external antenna, screw the antenna on the NIC and raise it to an upright position. Turn on the computer. The computer immediately detects the device and launches the Found New Hardware Wizard. Follow the wizard to load the device drivers using the CD that came bundled with the NIC. If Windows prompts you to restart the computer, do so.

2. Configure the NIC to use the same wireless parameters as the access point or other computer. Run a setup program on the CD that came with the NIC to install the NIC configuration software, and then launch the software.

3. Consult the documentation to find out how to use the software. Figure 18-32 shows an example of the configuration window for a wireless NIC, but yours might look different. Using the configuration software, you can view the status of the wireless connection and change the wireless parameters.

✔ **A+ EXAM TIP**

The A+ Core exam expects you to know how to install and configure a wireless NIC. The A+ OS exam expects you to know how to configure a wireless NIC.

VIDEO

Installing a Wireless NIC

Figure 18-32 Wireless NIC configuration software reports the status of the current connection

A+
CORE
1.2
1.3
1.8
1.9
6.2
6.3
OS
4.2

Figure 18-32 shows an example of wireless configuration software reporting the following information about the connection:

- *State*. The state is the status of the current connection and reports the BSS ID (basic service set identifier), which is the MAC address of the access point device that the NIC is currently using.
- *Current Channel*. 802.11b uses 14 different channels. The United States can use channels 1 through 11. The access point device is configured to use one of these 11 channels, which is reported by the NIC software.
- *Current Tx Rate*. Current transmission rate, which is 11 Mbps in the figure.
- *Throughput, Link Quality,* and *Signal Strength*. These values indicate throughput rate and how strong the signal is.

Figure 18-32 also shows a Rescan button. You can click this button to tell the NIC to scan for a new access point.

4. Click the **Configuration** tab to change how the NIC functions (see Figure 18-33). Most likely, you will not need to change any defaults.

Figure 18-33 Configure how a wireless NIC will connect to a wireless LAN

18

A+
CORE
1.2
1.3
1.8
1.9
6.2
6.3
OS
4.2

Changes you can make on this screen include:

- *Mode.* The mode indicates if the computer is to communicate through an access point (Infrastructure mode) or if the computer is to communicate directly with another wireless device (Ad Hoc mode).
- *SSID.* The SSID (service set identifier) is currently set to ANY, which means the NIC is free to connect to any access point it finds. You can enter the name of an access point to specify that this NIC should connect only to a specific access point. If you don't know the name assigned to a particular access point, ask the network administrator responsible for managing the wireless network.
- *Tx Rate.* You can specify the transmission rate or leave it at fully automatic so that the NIC is free to use the best transmission rate possible.
- *PS Mode.* When this setting is disabled, the PC is not allowed to enter sleep mode; network communication continues uninterrupted. Enable PS Mode to allow the PC to go into sleep mode.

5. This NIC supports encrypted wireless transmission. To enable encryption, click the **Encryption** tab (see Figure 18-34). Select 64-bit or 128-bit encryption, and enter a secret passphrase. This passphrase is a word, such as "ourpassphrase," which generates a digital key used for encryption. Every computer user on this wireless network must enter the same passphrase, which can be changed at any time. Click **OK** to close the configuration software.

6. The next step is to configure the NIC to use TCP/IP or NetBEUI. This step is covered earlier in the chapter; it works the same way for wireless NICs as it does for regular NICs.

After the NIC is configured to use the OS network protocol, you should immediately see network resources in My Network Places or Network Neighborhood. If you don't, then try rebooting the PC. Also, try moving the computer to a better hot spot. Using the wireless NIC's utility window, try reconnecting to the wireless network. To do this for the utility window showing in Figure 18-32, click Rescan.

Also, it is possible that the access point has been configured for MAC address filtering in order to control which wireless NICs can use the access point. Check with the network administrator to determine if this is the case; if necessary, give the administrator the NIC's MAC address to be entered into a table of acceptable MAC addresses.

A+
CORE
1.2
1.3
1.8
1.9
6.2
6.3
OS
4.2

Figure 18-34   Enter a passphrase that generates a key to be used for 128-bit encryption to secure a wireless LAN

Using Resources on the Network

A+
OS
1.1
4.1

Now you have learned how networks are structured, how to install NICs, and how to set up Windows networking. Let's look next at how to use resources on a network once it's been set up. This section covers how to share folders, files, applications, and even entire hard drives. In Chapter 21 you will learn how to share printers on a network.

Sharing Files, Folders, and Applications

If users on a LAN working on a common project need to share applications, files, or printers, then all these users must be assigned to the same workgroup or domain on the LAN. Recall that Windows 2000/XP makes shared resources available by way of My Network Places, and Windows 9x/Me uses Network Neighborhood. Open either applet to see the names of all computers on the network. Figure 18-35 shows Windows 2000 My Network Places. Drill down to see shared files, folders, and printers in your workgroup. Using Network Neighborhood or My Network Places, you can copy files from one computer to another, use shared applications installed on one computer from another computer, and share printers.

18

A+
OS
1.1
4.1

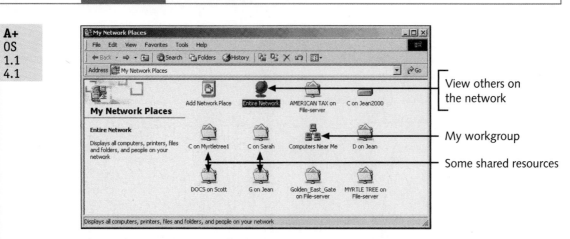

Figure 18-35   View and access shared resources on the network using My Network Places in Windows 2000

Workgroups can be effective when several people work on a common project. For example, if a group of people is building a Web site, sharing resources on the LAN is an effective method of passing Web pages around as they are built. Or one computer on the LAN can be designated as the file server. The user of this computer makes a portion of hard drive space available for the Web site files. All users have access to this one resource, and the Web site files are kept neatly in a single location. When using workgroups, each user is responsible for protecting shared resources by using password protection for read and write privileges to files and folders.

To share resources over a peer-to-peer network, you must first install Client for Microsoft Networks and File and Printer Sharing. Client for Microsoft Networks is the Windows component that allows you to use resources on the network made available by other computers, and File and Printer Sharing allows you to share resources on your computer with others in your workgroup. After these components are installed, the last thing to do is to share the folders, files, or printers that you want others to be able to access. All these steps are covered in this section.

Installing Windows 2000/XP Components Needed to Share Resources

A+
OS
4.1

Client for Microsoft Networks and File and Printer Sharing are installed by default during a Windows 2000/XP installation. However, if you have a problem sharing resources on a LAN, you can try to uninstall and reinstall them. Do the following to install these components:

 A+ EXAM TIP

The A+ OS exam expects you to know how to share resources on a LAN and control who has access to these resources.

1. Open the Windows XP **Network Connections** applet or the Windows 2000 **Network and Dial-up Connections** applet. Right-click the **Local Area Connection** icon and select **Proper-ties** from the shortcut menu. The Local Area Connection Proper-ties dialog box appears (see Figure 18-36).

2. Click **Install** on the **General** tab. The Select Network Compo-nent Type window appears, which is also shown in

A+
OS
4.1

Figure 18-36.Select **Client** and then click **Add.** The Select Network Client window opens. Select **Client for Microsoft Networks.** You will need the Windows 2000 or Windows XP CD or other access to the installation files.

Figure 18-36 Use the Network Connections applet to install a network client, service, or protocol using Windows XP

> 3. Also install the service for sharing files and printers with others on the Microsoft network. In the Select Network Component Type window, select **Service** and click **Add.** The Select Network Service dialog box opens. Select **File and printer sharing for Microsoft Networks,** and then click **OK.** You might need the Windows XP CD.

NOTE When trying to secure a PC, you can take some preventive measures to ensure that other network users will not be allowed access. Windows 2000/XP installs File and Printer Sharing by default. To help secure the PC, you can disable this feature; open the Local Area Connection Properties dialog box, uncheck "File and printer sharing for Microsoft Networks," and click OK.

NOTE To further secure a Windows 2000/XP PC, you can prevent it from showing in the My Network Places windows of other network users. From the Control Panel, open the Administrative Tools applet and double-click Service. Right-click the Computer Browser service and select Properties from the shortcut menu. Under Startup type, select Disabled and click Apply. When you restart the PC, it will not be visible in My Network Places over the network.

Installing Windows 98 Components Needed to Share Resources

To install Client for Microsoft Networks and File and Print Sharing in Windows 98, open the Network applet in the Control Panel and click Add. Select Client and then

18

click Add. The Select Network Client window opens. Select Microsoft on the left and Client for Microsoft Networks on the right. You might need the Windows 9x/Me CD. Using the same method, install File and Print Sharing for Microsoft Networks.

Once these two components are installed, you must choose to enable File and Print Sharing. On the Network window, click the File and Print Sharing button (see Figure 18-37). The File and Print Sharing window opens. Check both options to share both files and printers, and then click OK.

Figure 18-37 Turn on Windows 98 File and Print Sharing so others on the LAN can access resources on this PC

When they are installed, Client for Microsoft Networks and File and Print Sharing should automatically bind themselves to the TCP/IP protocol. You can verify this by accessing the TCP/IP Properties window and clicking the Bindings tab. Verify that Client for Microsoft Networks and File and Print Sharing are checked.

A+
OS
4.1

Sharing Files and Folders with the Workgroup

After the computer is configured for File and Print Sharing, use Windows 2000/XP
or Windows 9x/Me to make a folder or file available to others on the LAN:

1. Using Windows Explorer, select the folder or file. In this example, we are using
   a folder named **C:\data**. Right-click the folder name. If the Windows 98 or Windows 2000 system is configured for file and printer sharing, the shortcut menu
   lists **Sharing**. For Windows XP, select **Sharing and Security** (see Figure 18-38).
   The data Properties dialog box opens, as shown in Figure 18-39.

Figure 18-38 In Windows XP, use Windows Explorer to share a file or folder with others on a network

18

2. For Windows 2000 or Windows 98, click the **Shared As** option button, and for
   Windows XP, check **Share this folder on the network**. Enter a name for the
   shared folder. In the figure, the name is JEAN'S DATA.This action makes the
   folder available to others on the network. They can see the folder when they
   open My Network Places or Network Neighborhood on their desktop.

3. For Windows 98 or Windows 2000, click the **Depends on Password** option button in the Access Type section.

A+
OS
4.1

Figure 18-39   Using Windows 98, a user on a network can share a folder with others on the network

4. To allow others the right to make changes to the folder, enter a password under **Full Access Password**. For read-only access, enter a different password. Click **OK** to exit the window.

   For Windows XP, you can allow others the right to change your files by checking **Allow network users to change my files**. Click **OK** to exit the window.

5. For added security when using Windows 2000/XP, set up a user account and password for each user who will have access to shared resources. This added security requires that a user give a valid password before accessing shared files, folders, or printers on the Windows 2000/XP PC.

NOTE   Applications can also be shared with others in the workgroup. If you share a folder that has a program file in it, a user on another PC can double-click the program file in My Network Places or Network Neighborhood and execute it remotely on their desktop. This is a handy way for several users to share an application that is installed on a single PC.

A+
OS
4.1

When using the Depends on Password option, be sure to enter a password in both the Read-Only Password and Full Access Password fields. If you leave a password field empty, then no password is required for a user to have the corresponding read-only or full access to the folder. Distribute the two passwords to people who need to access the folder. You control the access rights (permissions) by selecting which password(s) you give.

Network Drive Maps

A **network drive map** is one of the most powerful and versatile methods of communicating over a network. By using network file service (NFS) client/server software, the network drive map makes one PC (the client) appear to have a new hard drive, such as drive E, that is really hard drive space on another host computer (the server). Even if the host computer uses a different OS, such as Unix, the drive map still functions. Using a network drive map, files and folders on a host computer are available even to network-unaware DOS applications. The path to a file simply uses the remote drive letter instead of a local drive such as drive A or drive C. To set up a network drive under Windows 2000/XP or Windows 9x/Me, follow these steps:

1. On the host computer, using directions given earlier in the chapter, share the drive or folder on a drive to which you want others to have access.

2. On the remote computer that will use the network drive, connect to the network and access **Windows Explorer**. Click the **Tools** menu shown in Figure 18-40. Select **Map Network Drive**.

Figure 18-40 Mapping a network drive to a host computer in Windows 98, using Windows Explorer

18

3. The Map Network Drive dialog box appears, as shown in Figure 18-41. Select a drive letter from the drop-down list.

Figure 18-41 To map a network drive in Windows 98, enter a drive letter to use on your PC and the path to the host computer

4. Enter a path to the host computer. Use two backslashes, followed by the name of the host computer, followed by a backslash and the drive or folder to access on the host computer. For example, to access the Public folder on the computer named Scott, enter **\\Scott\Public** and then click **OK**.

NOTE

If a network drive does not work, go to My Network Places or Network Neighborhood, and verify that the network connection is good.

Figure 18-42 shows the results of the drive mapping. Windows Explorer displays a new drive K. Folders listed on the right side of the figure are on the host PC.

A+
OS
4.1

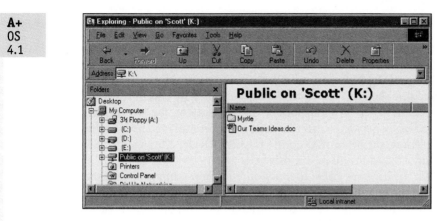

Figure 18-42   Content on the right side of Windows Explorer belongs to the host computer. This computer sees the content as belonging to its drive K.

Troubleshooting a Network Connection

A+
CORE
2.1
6.2
OS
3.3
4.1

APPLYING CONCEPTS

T.J. has just used a crossover cable to connect his two computers together. My Network Places on both computers refuse to display the other computer. What should T.J. check?

If you have problems connecting to the network, follow the guidelines in this section. First, here are some symptoms of NIC problems:

- You cannot make a connection to the network.
- My Network Places or Network Neighborhood does not show any other computers on the network.
- You receive an error message while you are installing the NIC drivers.
- Device Manager shows a yellow exclamation point or a red X beside the name of the NIC.
- There are two lights on a NIC: one stays on steadily to let you know there is a physical connection, and another blinks to let you know there is activity. If you see no lights, you know there is no physical connection between the NIC and the network. This means there is a problem with the network cable, the card, or the hub.

18

A+
CORE
2.1
6.2
OS
3.3
4.1

VIDEO

Troubleshooting
a Network

Here are some ways you can try to solve networking problems:

- Determine whether other computers on the network are having trouble with their connections. If the entire network is down, the problem is not isolated to the PC and the NIC you are working on.
- Make sure the NIC and its drivers are installed by checking for the NIC in Device Manager. Try uninstalling and reinstalling the NIC drivers.
- For a legacy network card that cannot successfully connect to the network, the problem might be an IRQ conflict. Check Device Manager for conflicts. Try to download and install 32-bit drivers.
- Check the network cable to make sure it is not damaged and that it does not exceed the recommended length for the type of network you are using.
- Connect the network cable to a different port on the hub. If that doesn't help, you may have a problem with the cable or the NIC itself. Uninstall the NIC drivers, replace the NIC, and then install new drivers.
- Check to see whether you have the most current version of your motherboard BIOS. The motherboard manufacturer should have information on its Web site about whether an upgrade is available.
- When a network drive map is not working, first check My Network Places or Network Neighborhood, and verify that you can access other resources on the remote computer. You might need to log on to the remote computer with a valid user ID and password.

 A+ EXAM TIP

The A+ OS exam expects you to know how to use Ping, Ipconfig, and Winipcfg.

Sometimes you might have trouble with a network connection due to a TCP/IP problem. Windows TCP/IP includes several diagnostic tools that are useful in troubleshooting problems with TCP/IP. You will learn about several of these in the next chapter. The most useful is **Ping (Packet Internet Groper)**, which tests connectivity and is discussed here. Ping sends a signal to a remote computer. If the remote computer is online and hears the signal, it responds. Ipconfig under Windows NT/2000/XP and Winipcfg under Windows 9x/Me test the TCP/IP configuration. Try these things to test TCP/IP configuration and connectivity:

- For Windows NT/2000/XP, enter *Ipconfig /all* at the command prompt. For Windows 9x/Me, click Start, click Run, enter *Winipcfg* in the Run dialog box, and then click OK. If the TCP/IP configuration is correct and an IP address is assigned, the IP address, subnet mask, and default gateway appear along with the adapter address. For dynamic IP addressing, if the PC cannot reach the DHCP server, then it assigns itself an IP address. This is called IP autoconfiguration and the IP address is called an Automatic Private IP Address (APIPA). The Winipcfg window and the results of the Ipconfig command both show the IP address as the IP Autoconfiguration Address, and the address begins with 169.254. In this case, suspect that the PC is not able to reach the network or the DHCP server is down.

A+
CORE
2.1
6.2
OS
3.3
4.1

- Try to release the current IP address and lease a new address. To do this with Winipcfg, select the network card, click the Release button, and then click the Renew button. For Ipconfig, first use the *Ipconfig /release* command, and then use the *Ipconfig /renew* command.
- Next, try the loopback address test. At a command prompt, enter the command *Ping 127.0.0.1* (with no period after the final 1). This IP address always refers to your local computer. It should respond with a reply message from your computer. If this works, TCP/IP is likely to be configured correctly. If you get any errors up to this point, then assume that the problem is on your PC. Check the installation and configuration of each component such as the network card and the TCP/IP protocol suite. Remove and reinstall each component, and watch for error messages, writing them down so that you can recognize or research them later as necessary. Compare the configuration to that of a working PC on the same network.
- Next, Ping the IP address of your default gateway. If it does not respond, then the problem may be with the gateway or with the network to the gateway.
- Now try to Ping the host computer you are trying to reach. If it does not respond, then the problem may be with the host computer or with the network to the computer.
- If you have Internet access and substitute a domain name for the IP address in the Ping command, and Ping works, then you can conclude that DNS works. If an IP address works, but the domain name does not work, the problem lies with DNS. Try this command: *ping www.course.com.*

APPLYING CONCEPTS

Back to T.J.'s problem connecting his two computers. The problem might be the hardware or software. Begin with the hardware. Do the lights display correctly on the NICs? If so, T.J. can assume the hardware is functioning. Next check the driver installation. Does Device Manager on both computers show no errors or conflicts with each network adapter? Next, check the configuration. In this situation, T.J. should have used static IP addressing. What is the IP address of each PC? Open a command window and try to Ping the local computer, and then try to Ping the remote computer. Does each computer have a computer name? Try rebooting each computer.

18

Connecting Networks

A+
CORE
6.3

So far you have learned how LANs can be structured and how to set them up, including how to divide large ones into segments using bridges and switches. Other devices and technologies are used to connect networks, allowing them to communicate with each other within a building or over a large geographical area as a **WAN (wide area**

**A+
CORE
6.3**

network). This section discusses routers, which are used to connect networks, as well as bandwidth technologies that networks use to communicate with each other.

Routers

Routers (see Figure 18-43) are responsible for data traveling across interconnected networks. A router can route data to the correct network in a way that is similar to a switch's method. However, a router can also forward a message to its correct destination over the most efficient available route, to destinations far removed from the LANs to which it is connected. Switches and bridges use MAC addresses to make decisions, but for TCP/IP, routers use IP addresses to determine the path by which to send a packet.

Figure 18-43 A typical router for a large enterprise network

Figure 18-44 shows a simplified view of the way networks work together to send data over the maze of networks called the Internet. A user in California must pass through many networks to gain access to a server in New York. Each network operates independently of all other networks but can receive a packet from another network and send it on to a third network–while it also manages its own internal traffic. A router is a **stateless** device, meaning that it is unconcerned about the data it is routing but is concerned about the destination address of that data.

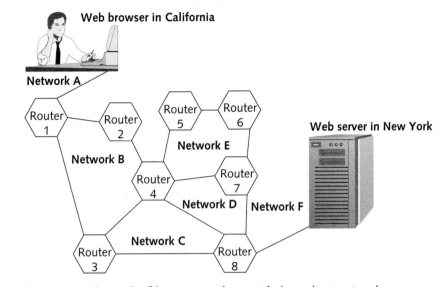

Figure 18-44   The Internet is a web of interconnecting, yet independent, networks

Routers that connect networks belong to more than one network. In Figure 18-44, Network B contains four routers: Routers 1, 2, 3, and 4. But Routers 3 and 4 also belong to Network C. Network C contains Router 8, which also belongs to the same network as the server in New York that the user wants to access.

How many paths are there on the Internet by which the user in California can access the server in New York? One path is through Router 1, then 3, then 8, and finally to the server. Data going from the server to the user may travel a different path than data traveling from the user to the server. In fact, if a lot of data is divided into several packets, each packet may take a different route. The packets may not arrive at the user's PC in the same order in which they were sent and may have to be reassembled before they are presented to the application that will use them.

In Figure 18-44, a router that belongs to a network has an IP address for that network. However, if a router belongs to more than one network, it has a unique IP address for each network. Physically, this is accomplished by having one NIC for each network a router belongs to, with each NIC having a unique IP address. Router 4 in the diagram belongs to four networks (B, C, D, and E) and would therefore have four network cards and four IP addresses, one for each network.

A router can transmit a data packet to a remote network (a network it is not directly connected to) only if the protocol used to produce the data packet is a **routable protocol**. Recall that Windows supports several networking protocols: TCP/IP, NWLink, IPX/SPX, NetBEUI, and AppleTalk. TCP/IP is routable, as is IPX/SPX. AppleTalk is by the MAC OS. NetBEUI is not routable.

A **brouter** functions as both a bridge and a router. The device can route packets that are using routable protocols, including TCP/IP and IPX/SPX packets, and in these cases works as a router. It forwards packets that are not routable, such as

18

NetBEUI packets, to other local network segments in the manner that a bridge forwards packets.

Like switches, routers use tables to determine the best route by which to send the data to its destination. When the router receives a packet, it first looks at the packet's destination IP address. When it has the address, the router can use the tables and current network conditions to decide which path would be best for the packet. If there is no good route directly to the destination, the router may forward the packet to another router. When a packet is sent across a network, it may go through several routers.

NOTE

A router "learns" about new routes and best routes as it attempts to send packets. You can see the effects of what routers learn when you first attempt to access a new Web site with your browser. If the browser is slow to respond, click Stop and Refresh to cause the browser to resend the request. The new attempt often receives a quicker response because the routers along the way learned about routes that did or did not work.

Bandwidth Technologies

When you study the infrastructure of networks and how they connect to each other, much attention is given to how much data can travel over a given communication system in a given amount of time. This measure of data capacity is called **bandwidth** (or **data throughput** or **line speed**). The greater the bandwidth is, the faster the communication. In analog systems, bandwidth is the difference between the highest and lowest frequency that a device can transmit. Frequencies are measured in cycles per second, or hertz (Hz). In digital systems such as computers and computer networks, bandwidth is a measure of data transmission in bits per second (bps), thousands of bits per second (Kbps), or millions of bits per second (Mbps). The Internet depends on technologies that provide varying degrees of bandwidth, each serving a different purpose and following a different set of standards. A list of bandwidth technologies, their speeds, and their uses is shown in Table 18-4. Different bandwidth technologies are used for LANs and larger networks, because the larger the network, the more bandwidth it requires. In this section, you will learn about some common bandwidth technologies.

A+
CORE
6.3

Technology	Maximum Throughput Speeds	Common Uses
GSM mobile telephone service	9.6 to 14.4 Kbps	Wireless technology used for personal and business mobile telephones
Regular telephone (POTS, for Plain Old Telephone Service)	Up to 56 Kbps	Home and small business access to an ISP using a modem
X.25	56 Kbps	Provides communication between mainframes and terminals
ISDN	64 Kbps to 128 Kbps	Small to medium-size business access to an ISP
IDSL (ISDN Digital Subscriber Line)	128 Kbps	Home and small business access to an ISP
DSL Lite or G.Lite	Up to 384 Kbps upstream and up to 6 Mbps downstream	Less expensive version of DSL
ADSL (Asymmetric Digital Subscriber Line)	640 Kbps upstream and up to 6.1 Mbps downstream	Most bandwidth is from ISP to user
SDSL (Symmetric DSL)	1.544 Mbps	Equal bandwidths in both directions
HDSL (High-bit-rate DSL)	Up to 3 Mbps	Equal bandwidths in both directions
Cable modem	512 Kbps to 5 Mbps	Home or small business to ISP
VDSL (Very-high-rate DSL)	Up to 55 Mbps over short distances	Future technology of DSL under development
802.11b wireless	Up to 11 Mbps	Currently most popular wireless
802.11a wireless	Up to 54 Mbps	Shorter range than 802.11b, but faster
802.11g	Up to 54 Mbps	Compatible with and replacing 802.11b
Frame Relay	56 Kbps to 45 Mbps	Businesses that need to communicate internationally or across the country
Fractional T1	n times 64 Kbps (where n = number of channels or portions of a T1 leased)	Companies expecting to grow into a T1 line, but not yet ready for a T1

Table 18-4 (continued)

18

Technology	Maximum Throughput Speeds	Common Uses
T1	1.544 Mbps	To connect large companies to branch offices or an ISP
Token Ring	4 or 16 Mbps	Used for local network
Ethernet	10 or 100 Mbps	Most popular technology for a local network
T3	45 Mbps	Large companies that require a lot of bandwidth and transmit extensive amounts of data
OC-1	52 Mbps	Base rate of transmission used by SONET and ATM. Multiples are called Optical Carrier levels (OCx).
FDDI	100 Mbps	Older network backbones
ATM	25, 45, 155, or 622 Mbps	Large business networks and LAN backbones
OC-3, OC-24, OC-256	155 Mbps, 1.23 Gbps, 13 Gbps	Internet backbones: use optical fiber
Gigabit Ethernet	1 Gbps	Latest Ethernet standard
OC-768	40 Gbps	Currently fastest OC level
SONET (Synchronous Optical Network)	52 Mbps to 20 Gbps	Major backbones make use of different OC levels

Table 18-4   Bandwidth technologies

Here is a summary of some of the more common bandwidth technologies:

- *Regular telephone lines.* Regular telephone lines, the most common way to connect to an ISP, require an internal or external modem. As you learned in Chapter 17, a modem converts a PC's digital data (data made up of zeros and ones) to analog data (continuous variations of frequencies) that can be communicated over telephone lines.

- *Cable modem.* **Cable modem** communication uses cable lines that already exist in millions of households. Just as with cable TV, cable modems are always connected (always up). Cable modem is an example of broadband media. **Broadband** refers to any type of networking medium that carries more than one type of transmission. With a cable modem, the TV signal to your television and the data signals to your PC share the same cable. Just like a regular modem, a cable modem converts a PC's digital signals to analog when sending them and converts incoming analog data to digital.

- *ISDN.* **ISDN (Integrated Services Digital Network)** is a technology developed in the 1980s that uses regular phone lines, and is accessed by a dial-up connection. For home use, an ISDN line is fully digital and consists of two channels, or phone circuits, on a single pair of wires called B channels, and a slower channel used for control signals, called a D channel. Each B channel can support speeds up to 64,000 bps. The two lines can be combined so that data effectively travels at 128,000 bps, about three to five times the speed of regular phone lines.

- *DSL.* **DSL (Digital Subscriber Line)** is a broadband technology that uses ordinary copper phone lines and a range of frequencies on the copper wire that are not used by voice, making it possible for you to use the same phone line for voice and DSL at the same time. The voice portion of the phone line requires a dial-up as normal, but the DSL part of the line is always connected.

- *Satellite access.* People who live in remote areas and want high-speed Internet connections often are limited in their choices. DSL and cable modems may not work where they live, but satellite access is available from pretty much anywhere. Technology is even being developed to use satellites to offer Internet access on commercial airlines. Customers can use their own laptops to connect to the Internet through a connection at their seats to a satellite dish in the airplane. A satellite dish mounted on top of your house or office building communicates with a satellite used by an ISP offering the satellite service.

- *Wireless access.* Wireless refers to several technologies and systems that don't use cables for communication, including public radio, cellular phones, one-way paging, satellite, infrared, and private, proprietary radio. Because of its expense and the concern that increasing use of wireless might affect our health, as well as airplane control systems, pacemakers, and other sensitive electronic devices, wireless is not as popular as wired data transmission. Wireless is an important technology for mobile devices and for Internet access in remote locations where other methods are not an option.

18

CHAPTER SUMMARY

◗ The most popular physical network architecture for LANs is Ethernet.

◗ Before data is sent over a network, it is divided into packets small enough for the network on which they will be traveling. Before they are transmitted on the network, headers and trailers are added to the packets to tell where data came from and where it is going.

◗ Ethernet uses a logical bus and can be configured as a star topology, in which all nodes connect to a centralized hub, or a bus topology, which connects nodes in a line and has no central connection point. An Ethernet hub broadcasts all data that flows through it to every node connected to it. It does not make decisions about where to send packets.

◗ Token Ring networks are physically configured in a star topology but are logically rings because of how data packets travel on them. A data packet is preceded by a token, which travels in one direction around the ring, up and down the connection from the PC to the hub.

◗ A FDDI network uses tokens and is structured as a ring but does not require a centralized hub as a Token Ring network does. It is faster than Token Ring.

◗ Wireless LANs make connections using radio or infrared technology. A wireless LAN can be used in combination with a wired LAN.

◗ A PC connects to a network using a NIC (network interface card) or network adapter, which communicates with NICs on other PCs using a set of hardware protocols (such as Ethernet or Token Ring). The OSs on the two computers use a different set of protocols (such as TCP/IP or NetBEUI) to communicate.

◗ NICs and the device drivers that control them are designed to work with a particular network architecture and are the only PC components that are aware of the type of physical network being used. A NIC can be designed to use more than one type of cabling.

◗ A NIC is identified by a MAC address, a physical address unique to the device that is assigned at the factory and generally does not change.

◗ Bridges and switches are used to segment large networks, decreasing the overall amount of traffic on the network and making it easier to manage.

◗ A bridge that connects several network segments only decides whether a packet is destined for a computer on its own segment; if it is not, the bridge sends the packet to all other network segments. A switch sends a packet only to the network segment for which it is destined. Both keep source and destination MAC addresses in routing tables and learn new addresses as packets are sent.

- The three protocols that Windows supports for network communications are TCP/IP (the protocol suite for the Internet), IPX/SPX (designed for use with Novell NetWare), and NetBEUI (a proprietary Windows protocol for use on networks isolated from the Internet). Only TCP/IP is supported on the Internet.

- When an OS protocol is installed on a computer, it automatically binds itself to any NICs it finds. More than one OS networking protocol can be associated with a single NIC.

- The four types of addresses on a Windows network are MAC addresses, IP addresses, character-based names (such as NetBIOS names, host names, domain names), and port addresses.

- MAC addresses are used only for communication within a network.

- IP addresses identify devices on the Internet and other TCP/IP networks. They consist of four numbers separated by periods. The first part of an IP address identifies the network, and the last identifies the host. The class of an IP address determines how much of the address is used as the network identifier and how much is used for the host identifier.

- IP addresses can either be public or private. For private IP addresses to be able to access the Internet, they must go through NAT (Network Address Translation) so that their requests all appear to be coming from a single public IP address for that network.

- Character-based names, such as fully qualified domain names, are used as an easy way to remember IP addresses.

- The IP address associated with a host name can change. DNS (Domain Name Service) and WINS (Windows Internet Naming Service) track the relationships between host names and IP addresses. DNS is more popular because it works on all platforms.

- Windows 98 assumes that a computer name is a NetBIOS name, which can have up to 15 characters. Windows 2000 and Windows XP assume that a computer name is a host name, which follows the TCP/IP convention and can have up to 63 characters.

- When installing a NIC, physically install the card, install the device drivers, install the OS networking protocol you intend to use (might already be installed by default), configure the OS protocol, and give the computer a name.

18

▶ NetBEUI is a fast network protocol that can be used on an isolated network. For Internet access, use TCP/IP. TCP/IP requires that the PC be assigned an IP address.

▶ When configuring TCP/IP, you must know if IP addresses are statically or dynamically assigned.

▶ Two files on a PC track IP addresses and related NetBIOS or host names. LMHosts tracks NetBIOS names on a NetBEUI network, and Hosts tracks host names on a TCP/IP network.

▶ Before users on a network can view or access resources on a PC, Client for Microsoft Networks and File and Print Sharing must be installed, and the resources must be shared.

▶ Network drive mapping makes one PC appear to have a new hard drive when that hard drive space is actually on another host computer. Use Windows Explorer to map a network drive.

▶ When troubleshooting a NIC on a PC, check connections in the rest of the network, cabling and ports for the PC, the NIC itself (substituting one known to be working, if necessary), BIOS, and device drivers.

▶ Ping is a useful TCP/IP utility to check network connectivity.

▶ Two other useful troubleshooting tools are Ipconfig (Windows NT, Windows 2000, and Windows XP) and Winipcfg (Windows 9x/Me), which test TCP/IP configuration.

▶ Routers are used to connect networks. If a router belongs to more than one TCP/IP network, it has a unique IP address for each network and routes packets according to IP addresses.

▶ Routers are more efficient than switches in choosing routes for packets over long distances.

▶ TCP/IP and IPX/SPX are routable networking protocols. NetBEUI, a Microsoft proprietary protocol, is not.

▶ Bandwidth measures how much data can travel over a given communications system in a given amount of time. Common bandwidth technologies include regular telephone lines, cable modem, ISDN, DSL, satellite access, and wireless access.

KEY TERMS

For explanations of key terms, see the Glossary near the end of the book.

10Base2
10Base5
10BaseT
100BaseT
802.11a/b/g
access point (AP)
adapter address
AirPort
amplifier repeater
attenuation
Automatic Private IP Address
 (APIPA)
bandwidth
binding
Bluetooth
BNC connector
bridge
broadband
broadcast
brouter
bus topology
cable modem
client
client/server
coaxial cable
combo card
computer name
crossover cable
data throughput
datagram
default gateway
DHCP (Dynamic Host
 Configuration Protocol)
DNS (Domain Name System, or
 Domain Name Service)
DNS server
domain name
DSL (Digital Subscriber Line)
dynamic IP address
Ethernet

Fast Ethernet
Fiber Distributed Data Interface
 (FDDI)
frame
fully qualified domain name
 (FQDN)
gateway
Gigabit Ethernet
hardware address
host
host name
Hosts (file)
hub
IBM Data Connector (IDC)
Institute of Electrical and
 Electronics Engineers (IEEE)
Internet service provider (ISP)
intranet
IP address
IPX/SPX (Internetwork Packet
 Exchange/Sequenced Packet
 Exchange)
ISDN (Integrated Services Digital
 Network)
LAN (local area network)
line speed
LMHosts
MAC (Media Access Control)
 address
multicasting
name resolution
NAT (Network Address
 Translation)
NetBEUI (NetBIOS Extended
 User Interface)
NetBIOS (Network Basic Input/
 Output System)
network adapter
network drive map
network interface card (NIC)
network operating system (NOS)

network printer
node
octet
packet
patch cable
peer-to-peer network
physical address
Ping (Packet Internet Groper)
private IP address
proxy server
public IP address
repeater
ring topology
RJ-45 connector
routable protocol
router
server
shielded twisted-pair (STP) cable
signal-regenerating repeater
star bus topology
star ring topology
star topology
stateless
static IP address
subnet mask
switch
TCP/IP (Transmission Control
 Protocol/Internet Protocol)
ThickNet
ThinNet
Token Ring
transceiver
Universal Data Connector (UDC)
unshielded twisted-pair (UTP)
 cable
WAN (wide area network)
Wi-Fi
WINS (Windows Internet
 Naming Service)
wireless LAN (WLAN)

18

REVIEWING THE BASICS

1. Name three types of Ethernet currently in use. What transmission speed does each support?

2. What is the maximum length of a cable on a 100BaseT network?

3. What does the 100 in the name 100BaseT indicate?

4. What is broadcasting? Name a network connection device that uses it and one that does not.

5. What is one advantage of using repeaters? What is a disadvantage?

6. What topology does a Token Ring network use?

7. How is a FDDI network like a Token Ring network? How is it different?

8. What IEEE standards describe Ethernet? What IEEE standards describe wireless LAN?

9. Can a NIC be designed to use more than one network architecture? More than one type of cabling? Explain.

10. What connecting device do you use for a small LAN? For two network segments? Two or more connected networks? Give reasons for your answers.

11. How do switches route packets differently from bridges?

12. Describe the structure of an IP address. How is it different from a MAC address?

13. Name two networking devices that transmit packets based on MAC addresses.

14. How many potential IP addresses are there?

15. How many networks and addresses are available for Class A IP addresses? Class B? Class C?

16. Why are Class D and E addresses not available to individuals and companies?

17. Which octets are used for the network address and for host addresses in Class A? Class B? Class C?

18. In what class is the IP address 185.75.255.10?

19. In what class is the IP address 193.200.30.5?

20. Describe the difference between public and private IP addresses. If a network is using private IP addresses, how can the computers on that network access the Internet?

21. Why is it unlikely that you will find the IP address 192.168.250.10 on the Internet?

22. Which operating system does not automatically include the NetBEUI protocol?

23. What are the two ways an IP address can be assigned to a PC? What is one advantage of each?

24. What are the Ping, Ipconfig, and Winipcfg utilities used for?

25. What two Windows components are required to share resources on a network and access those shared resources?

26. How is a router a more intelligent device than a switch?

27. Why is a router called a stateless device?

28. Of IPX/SPX, TCP/IP, and NetBEUI, which is routable and which is not?

29. Place the following bandwidth technologies in the order of their highest speed, from slowest to fastest: DSL, ISDN, regular telephone lines, cable modem, T1, Ethernet.

30. Give two examples of broadband technology.

THINKING CRITICALLY

1. You have just installed a network adapter and have booted up the system. You open the Windows 2000 My Network Places and only see your local computer. What is the first thing you check?

   a. Is File and Printer Sharing installed?

   b. Is the NetBEUI protocol installed?

   c. Are the lights on the adapter functioning correctly?

   d. Has the computer been assigned a computer name?

2. You work in the Accounting Department and have been using a network drive to post Excel spreadsheets to your workgroup as you complete them. When you attempt to save a spreadsheet to the drive, you see the error message, "You do not have access to the folder 'J:\'. See your administrator for access to this folder." What should you do first? Second?

   a. Ask your network administrator to give you permission to access the folder.

   b. Check My Network Places to verify that you can connect to the network.

   c. Save the spreadsheet to your hard drive.

18

  d. Using Windows Explorer, remap the network drive.

  e. Reboot your PC.

3. Your job is to support the desktop computers in a small company of 32 employees. A consulting firm is setting up a private Web server to be used internally by company employees. The static IP address of the server is 192.168.45.200. Employees will open their Web browser and enter *personnel.mycompany.com* in the URL address box to browse this Web site. What steps do you take so that each computer in the company can browse the site using this URL?

4. Linda has been assigned the job of connecting five computers to a network. The room holding the five computers has three network ports that connect to a hub in an electrical closet down the hallway. Linda decides to install a second hub in the room. The new hub has four network ports. She uses a crossover cable to connect one of the four ports on the hub to a wall port. Now she has five ports available (two wall ports and three hub ports). While installing and configuring the NICs in the five computers, she discovers that the PCs connected to the two wall ports work fine, but the three connected to the hub refuse to communicate with the network. What could be wrong and what should she try next?

HANDS-ON PROJECTS

HANDS-ON PROJECTS

PROJECT 18-1: Investigating Your PC

If you are connected to the Internet or a network, answer these questions:

1. What is the hardware device used to make this connection (modem or network card)? List the device's name as Windows sees it.

2. If you are connected to a LAN, what is the MAC address of the NIC? Print the screen that shows the address.

3. What is the IP address of your PC?

4. What Windows utilities did you use to answer the first three questions?

5. Print the screen that shows which network protocols are installed on your PC.

PROJECT 18-2: Researching IP Address Classes

Use the Web site *www.flumps.org/ip/* by Paul Rogers to answer these questions:

1. List three companies that have a Class A IP address.

2. List three companies that have a Class B IP address.

3. Who owns IP address class license 9.x.x.x?

4. Find another Web site on the Internet that gives similar information. How does the information on the new site compare with the information on the *www.flumps.org/ip/* site?

PROJECT 18-3: Researching a Wireless LAN

Suppose you want to connect two computers to your company LAN using a wireless connection. Use the Internet to research the equipment needed to create the wireless LAN, and answer the following:

1. Print a Web page showing an access point device that can connect to an Ethernet LAN.

2. How much does the device cost? How many wireless devices can the access point support at one time? How is the device powered?

3. Print three Web pages showing three different network adapters a computer can use to connect to the access point. Include one external device that uses a USB port and one internal device. How much does each device cost?

4. What is the total cost of implementing a wireless LAN with two computers using the wireless connection?

PROJECT 18-4: Showing How Bridges, Switches, and Routers Work

Use Figure 18-45 to complete the following activities:

18

1. If a packet is sent from Computer 2 to Computer 7, show where the packet will be sent if:

   ▪ Device A is a router, Device E is a switch, and all other connecting devices are hubs.
   ▪ Device A is a router, Device E is a bridge, and all other connecting devices are hubs.

2. If a packet is sent from Computer 11 to Computer 9, show where the packet will be sent if:

- Device A is a router, Device E is a switch, and all other connecting devices are hubs.
- Device A is a router, Device E is a bridge, and all other connecting devices are hubs.

3. Create two scenarios of your own, deciding which computer is sending the packet, which computer is to receive it, and what types of devices are used. Have another student try to figure out what devices are used based on which computers receive a packet in your scenario.

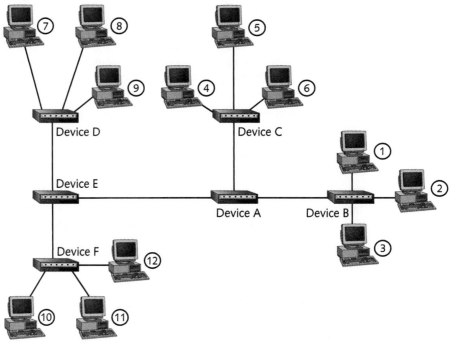

Figure 18-45   How will packets travel?

CHAPTER 19

PCs on the Internet

In this chapter, you will learn:

- About the TCP/IP suite of protocols

- How to connect to the Internet using dial-up, DSL, and cable modem connections

- About supporting common Internet clients such as Web browsers, email clients, and file transfer software

In earlier chapters, you learned how different versions of Windows work on a single PC. In Chapter 18, you learned about connecting PCs to a network. This chapter takes the next logical step in effectively using PCs by discussing connections to the Internet using Windows. You will learn how the TCP/IP suite of protocols is used, how to create and troubleshoot dial-up and broadband connections to the Internet, and how to support popular applications that use the Internet, such as Web browsers, email clients, and FTP software.

The TCP/IP Suite of Protocols

A+
OS
4.2

In Chapter 18, you learned how the operating system uses TCP/IP to make resources on a network available to the user, and how to install and configure the hardware and software necessary for networking. This chapter focuses on the applications on a desktop computer that use TCP/IP to access resources on a local network and on the Internet.

Most applications that use the Internet are **client/server applications**, which means the application has two components. The application (client) software makes a request for data from server software running on another computer. The World Wide Web itself is probably the most popular client/server application: The client is a Web browser, and the server is a Web host. The requested data is called a Web page, which can have graphics, sound, and video embedded as part of the requested data (see Figure 19-1).

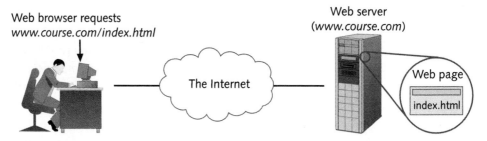

Web browser requests
www.course.com/index.html

Web server
(*www.course.com*)

The Internet

Web page

index.html

Figure 19-1   A Web browser (client software) requests a Web page from a Web server (server software); the Web server returns the requested file or files to the client

A PC support technician must know how to connect PCs to the Internet and support common client/server applications used on the Internet. Before we turn our attention to these applications, you will learn more about how the protocols in the TCP/IP suite are used on intranets and the Internet to support these applications. First, we look at how a client addresses a server application on another computer.

Using IP and Port Addresses to Identify Services

A server on the Internet or an intranet might be running a Web server application, an email server application, and an FTP server application, all at the same time. (**FTP**, the **File Transfer Protocol**, is a quick and easy way to move files over a TCP/IP network.) Each service is an executable program running under the OS on that server. For example, one Web server is Apache HTTP Server by the Apache Software Foundation (*www.apache.org*), and an email server is Ntmail by Gordano LTD (*www.ntmail.co.uk*). The Apache and Ntmail programs can both be running as

A+
OS
4.2

background services on a computer. How does a Web browser on a client PC say, "I want to speak with the Web server" and an email program say, "I want to speak with the email server," if both programs are running on the same computer using the same IP address? The answer is by using an identifying number, called a **port, port address**, or **port number**, that has been assigned to each service when it is started. (Don't confuse these port numbers or addresses with I/O addresses assigned to hardware devices, which were discussed in previous chapters.)

Each service "listens" at its assigned port. A network administrator can assign any port number to a server, but there are established port numbers for common services and protocols. A Web server is normally assigned port 80, and an email server receiving mail is normally assigned port 25, as shown in Figure 19-2. Port assignments are shown at the end of an IP address, following a colon. Using these default port assignments, the Web server would communicate at 138.60.30.5:80, and the email server would communicate at 138.60.30.5:25. Another example of a port number assigned to a common service is the use of port 119 for **NNTP (Network News Transfer Protocol)**, the protocol used for newsgroups.

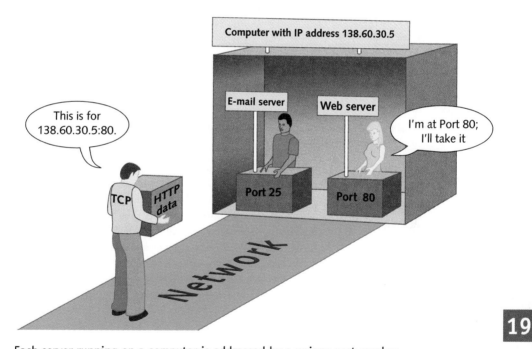

Figure 19-2   Each server running on a computer is addressed by a unique port number

19

Unless the administrator has a good reason to do otherwise, he or she uses the common port assignments listed in Table 19-1. (One reason not to use the default port assignments is concern about security. Some malicious software targets systems using default port assignments.) If a Web server is assigned a different port number, it can be accessed by entering the server's IP address in the address box of the Web

A+
OS
4.2

browser, followed by a colon and the port number of the Web server, like this: 138.60.30.5:8080.

Port	Protocol	Service	Description
20	FTP	FTP	File transfer data
21	FTP	FTP	File transfer control information
23	Telnet	Telnet	Telnet, an application used by Unix computers to control a computer remotely
25	SMTP	Email	Simple Mail Transfer Protocol; used by client to send email
80	HTTP or HTTPS	Web browser	World Wide Web protocol
109	POP2	Email	Post Office Protocol, version 2; used by client to receive email
110	POP3	Email	Post Office Protocol, version 3; used by client to receive Email
119	NNTP	News server	News servers
143	IMAP	Email	Internet Message Access Protocol, a newer protocol used by clients to receive email

Table 19-1   Common TCP/IP port assignments for well-known services

✔ **A+ EXAM TIP**

The A+ OS exam expects you to know about the different protocols used on the Internet, which are listed in Table 19-1.

The Web browser initiates a request using an IP address and port number but is unaware of all that happens in order for the request to reach the Web server. Also notice in Table 19-1 that each service has one or more designated protocols. These protocols are the rules of communication between the client and server components of the applications. We now have yet another layer of communication protocols used in networking. Recall from the last chapter that at the lowest networking level, the network or hardware protocol controls communication among physical networking devices such as Ethernet NICs and hubs. The next layer up is the OS protocol used on the network, such as TCP/IP, AppleTalk, or NetBEUI. Now, on top of the hardware and OS protocols, we add a third level of protocols that control how applications such as those listed in Table 19-1 communicate using the network. These applications protocols are all supported by TCP/IP and are discussed in the next section, together with other protocols that are part of the TCP/IP suite. Figure 19-3 shows all these different layers of protocols and how they relate to one another. Note in the figure that each protocol can be classified as a TCP/IP protocol, including the OS and applications protocols, or it is classified as a network (hardware) protocol used by networking hardware such as a phone line, NIC, or hub. As you read this section, this figure can serve as your roadmap to the different protocols.

Figure 19-3   How software, protocols, and technology on a TCP/IP network relate to each other

TCP/IP Protocol Layers

Within the TCP/IP suite, several protocols operate; the more significant ones are introduced in this section, from the top layer down. However, you should know that the TCP/IP protocol suite includes more protocols than just these.

Applications Protocols

Four of the most common applications that use the Internet are Web browsers, email, chat rooms, and FTP. When one of these applications wants to send data to a counterpart application on another host, it makes an API (application programming interface) call to the operating system, which handles the request. (An API call is a common way for an application to ask an operating system to do something.) The API call causes the OS to generate a request. For Web browsers, the request will be an HTTP request. **HTTP (Hypertext Transfer Protocol)** is the protocol used for the World Wide Web and used by Web browsers and Web servers to communicate. In other words, HTTP formats the request, and encrypts and compresses it as necessary. It adds an HTTP header to the beginning of the data that includes the HTTP version being used and how the data is compressed and encrypted, if that was done.

19

A+
OS
4.2

Later, when the response is received from the server, it decrypts and decompresses the data as necessary before passing it on to the browser.

Once the response is passed to the browser, a session is established. **Sessions** (established communication links between two software programs), sometimes called **sockets,** are managed by the browser and Web server using HTTP. However, TCP/IP at the OS level can also create a limited type of session.

Later in the chapter, you will learn more about Web and email protocols and how they work.

TCP/IP Protocols Used by the OS for Network Communication

Looking back at Figure 19-3, you can see three layers of protocols between the applications protocols and the physical network protocols. These three layers make up the heart of TCP/IP communication. In the figure, TCP or UDP manages communication with the applications protocols above them as well as the protocols shown underneath TCP and UDP, which control communication on the network.

Remember from the last chapter that all communication on a network happens by way of packets delivered from one location on the network to another. When a Web browser makes a request for data from a Web server, a packet is created and an attempt is made to deliver that packet to the server. In TCP/IP, the protocol that guarantees packet delivery is **TCP (Transmission Control Protocol).** TCP makes a connection, checks whether the data is received, and resends it if it is not. TCP is therefore called a **connection-oriented protocol.** TCP is used by applications such as Web browsers and email.

On the other hand, **UDP (User Datagram Protocol)** does not guarantee delivery by first connecting and checking whether data is received; thus UDP is called a **connectionless protocol** or a **best-effort protocol.** Guaranteed delivery takes longer and is used when it is important that data reach its destination accurately. UDP is primarily used for broadcasting and other types of transmissions, such as streaming video or sound over the Web, where guaranteed delivery is not as important as fast transmission.

Moving down the protocol layers, TCP and UDP pass a request to **IP (Internet Protocol),** which is responsible for breaking up and reassembling data into packets and routing them to their destination (see Figure 19-4).

Up to this point, the data with its header information is one long stream of bytes, sometimes too much data for transmission over a network. IP looks at the size of the data and breaks it into individual packets, which can be up to 4K in size. IP adds its own IP header, which includes the IP address of its host (source IP address) and that of the server (destination IP address), and then passes the packet off to the hardware.

A+
OS
4.2

Figure 19-4   TCP turns to IP to prepare the data for networking

If TCP is used to guarantee delivery, TCP uses IP to establish a session between client and server to verify that communication has taken place. When a TCP packet reaches its destination, an acknowledgment is sent back to the source (see Figure 19-5). If the source TCP does not receive the acknowledgment, it resends the data or passes an error message back to the higher-level application protocol.

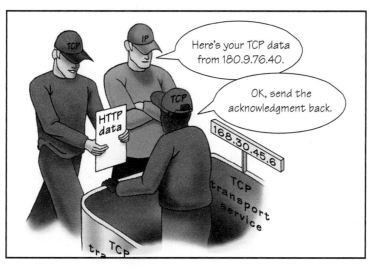

19

Figure 19-5   TCP guarantees delivery by requesting an acknowledgment

A+
OS
4.2

Other protocols that operate in this part of the transmission process include the following:

- **ARP (Address Resolution Protocol)** is responsible for locating a host on a local network.
- **RARP (Reverse Address Resolution Protocol)** is responsible for discovering the Internet address of a host on a local network.
- **ICMP (Internet Control Message Protocol)** is responsible for communicating problems with transmission. For example, if a packet exceeds the number of routers it can pass through on its way to its destination, called a **time to live** (TTL) or a **hop count,** a router kills the packet and returns an ICMP message to the source, saying that the packet has been killed.

Network Protocols Used by Hardware

As you learned in earlier chapters, network protocols used by PC hardware to communicate on a network are included in the firmware and drivers on a single NIC; for phone-line connections, these protocols are included on a modem and its drivers. The protocol used depends on the type of physical network that the data is traveling on. For example, for a regular phone line, the most popular protocol today is **PPP (Point-to-Point Protocol)**, and the device managing that protocol is a modem. PPP is sometimes called a **line protocol** or, less commonly, a **bridging protocol.** You will learn more about PPP later in the chapter. An earlier version of a line protocol is **Serial Line Internet Protocol (SLIP)**, which does not support encrypted passwords and is seldom used today. As you learned in the last chapter, Ethernet is the most popular network technology used for LANs, and its network or hardware protocol is also called Ethernet.

TCP/IP Utilities

A+
OS
4.1

When TCP/IP is installed as a Windows 9x/Me or Windows NT/2000/XP component, a group of utility tools is also installed that can be used to troubleshoot problems with TCP/IP. The most commonly used TCP/IP utilities are Ping, Winipcfg, and Ipconfig, which you learned about in the last chapter. Table 19-2 lists these and other TCP/IP utilities, and lists the purpose for each. The program files are found in the \Windows or \Winnt folder.

NOTE   To cause a network connection to release and renew its IP address in Windows XP, right-click My Network Places and select Properties from the shortcut menu. The Network Connections window appears. Select the network connection you want to repair and click "Repair this connection." You can also right-click the network connection you want to repair and select Repair from the shortcut menu.

Utility	Description
ARP (Arp.exe)	Manages the IP-to-Ethernet address translation tables used to find the MAC address of a host on the network when the IP address is known
Getmac (Getmac.exe)	Windows utility (new in Windows XP) that displays the NIC's MAC address
Ipconfig (Ipconfig.exe)	Displays the IP address of the host and other configuration information (A command used by Unix similar to Ipconfig is config) Some parameters are: Ipconfig /all Displays all information about the connection Ipconfig /release Releases the current IP address Ipconfig /renew Requests a new IP address Ipconfig /? Displays information about Ipconfig
FTP (Ftp.exe)	Transfers files over a network
Nbtstat (Nbtstat.exe)	Displays current information about TCP/IP and NetBEUI when both are being used on the same network
Netstat (Netstat.exe)	Displays information about current TCP/IP connections
NSLookup (Nslookup.exe)	Displays information about domain names and their IP addresses
Ping (Ping.exe)	Verifies that there is a connection on a network between two hosts
Route (Route.exe)	Allows you to manually control network routing tables
Telnet (Telnet.exe)	Allows you to communicate with another computer on the network remotely, entering commands to control the remote computer
Tracert (Tracert.exe)	Traces and displays the route taken from the host to a remote destination; Tracert is one example of a trace-routing utility
Winipcfg (Winipcfg.exe)	Displays IP address and other configuration information in a user-friendly window (not available under Windows NT/2000/XP). In the Winipcfg window, use Release and Renew to cause the system to release the current IP address and request a new one, which can sometimes solve TCP/IP connectivity problems when using a DHCP server.

Table 19-2   Utilities installed with TCP/IP on Windows

19

Microsoft SNMP Agent

In addition to the utilities that are automatically installed with TCP/IP, another useful utility is Microsoft SNMP Agent. This utility can be installed after you install TCP/IP; use the Add or Remove Programs applet in the Control Panel. **SNMP (Simple Network Management Protocol)** provides system management tools for networks. A system administrator can monitor remote connections to computers running Windows clients with SNMP Agent. The administrator will most likely use the utility sparingly because it can be a security risk. For more information about SNMP, see RFC 1156 (*www.rfc-editor.org*).

APPLYING CONCEPTS

Using NSLookup

An interesting tool that lets you read information from the Internet name space is NSLookup, which requests information about domain name resolutions from the DNS server's zone data. Zone data is information about domain names and their corresponding IP addresses kept by a DNS server. The NSLookup utility program is included in Windows 2000/XP. For example, to use Windows 2000 to retrieve what the DNS server knows about the domain name *www.microsoft.com*, follow these directions:

1. Click **Start**, **Programs**, **Accessories**, and **Command Prompt**. A command window appears.
2. Enter the command **Nslookup www.microsoft.com**. Figure 19-6 shows the results. Notice in the figure that the DNS server knows about three IP addresses assigned to *www.microsoft.com*. It also reports that this information is nonauthoritative, meaning that it is not the authoritative, or final, name server for the *www.microsoft.com* computer name.

A+
OS
4.1

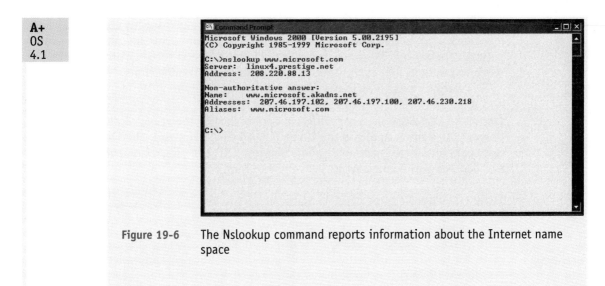

Command Prompt

```
Microsoft Windows 2000 [Version 5.00.2195]
(C) Copyright 1985-1999 Microsoft Corp.

C:\>nslookup www.microsoft.com
Server:  linux4.prestige.net
Address:  208.220.88.13

Non-authoritative answer:
Name:    www.microsoft.akadns.net
Addresses:  207.46.197.102, 207.46.197.100, 207.46.230.218
Aliases:  www.microsoft.com


C:\>
```

Figure 19-6   The Nslookup command reports information about the Internet name space

Connecting to the Internet

A+
CORE
1.8
6.3
OS
4.2

This section covers three ways to connect to the Internet: via a standard dial-up connection, DSL, and cable modem. You will learn how each type of connection is made as well as some advantages and disadvantages of each.

Dial-up Networking

✔ **A+ EXAM TIP**

The A+ Core and OS exams expect you to know how to connect to the Internet using a dial-up, cable modem, DSL, LAN, ISDN, satellite, and wireless connection. All these connections have many things in common. Skills learned in making one type of connection can be used when making another type.

To connect to the Internet over a phone line using a dial-up connection, you need to have a modem installed on your PC, as well as drivers to control the modem. In Chapter 17 you learned how to install and use a modem. In Chapter 18, you learned how to install TCP/IP and bind it to your NIC; the same procedure is used for binding TCP/IP to a modem. This section assumes that TCP/IP is installed and bound to the modem. It covers how to connect to the Internet, beginning with how to install and configure the Dial-up Networking feature in Windows, and continuing with how to create and test the connection to your Internet service provider (ISP).

When a Windows PC connects to a network using a modem and regular phone line, the process is called **dial-up networking**. In effect, the modem on the PC acts like a network card, providing the physical connection to the network and the firmware at the lowest level of communication. After the dial-up connection is made, the PC's

19

A+
CORE
1.8
6.3
OS
4.2

application software relates to the network as though it were directly connected using a network card, but a network card is not needed. The modems and phone lines in between are transparent to the user, although transmission speeds with direct network connections are much faster than those of dial-up connections.

This section covers how to use dial-up networking utilities in Windows 2000/XP and Windows 9x/Me. Note that in Windows 9x/Me, Dial-up Networking and Network Connections are two different applets located under My Computer. In Windows 2000, a single applet in the Control Panel called Network and Dial-up Connections combines both functions, and in Windows XP, this single Control Panel applet is called Network Connections.

How Dial-up Networking Works

Dial-up networking works by using PPP to send packets of data over phone lines. The network protocol (TCP/IP, NetBEUI, or IPX/SPX) packages the data, making it ready for network traffic, and then PPP adds its own header and trailer to these packets. Figure 19-7a shows how this works. The data is presented to the network protocol, which adds its header information. Then the packet is presented to the line protocol, PPP, which adds its own header and trailer to the packet and presents it to the modem for delivery over phone lines to a modem on the receiving end.

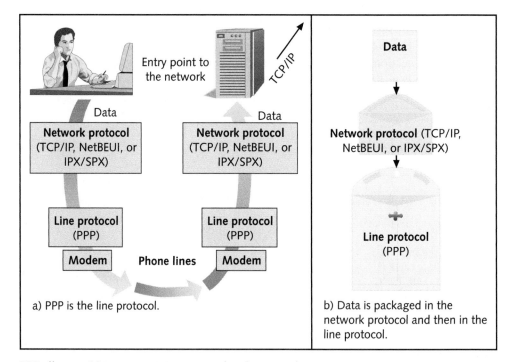

a) PPP is the line protocol.

b) Data is packaged in the network protocol and then in the line protocol.

Figure 19-7   PPP allows a PC to connect to a network using a modem

A+
CORE
1.8
6.3
OS
4.2

The modem is connected to a PC or server. The receiving computer strips off the PPP header and trailer information and sends the packet to the network still packaged in the TCP/IP protocols, or other network protocols. In Figure 19-7b, these two protocols act like envelopes. Data is put in a TCP/IP envelope for travel over the network. This envelope is put in a PPP envelope for travel over phone lines. When the phone line segment of the trip is completed, the PPP envelope is discarded.

APPLYING CONCEPTS

Creating a Dial-up Connection in Windows 2000/XP

For your PC to connect to your ISP and use the Internet, you need answers to these questions:

- What is the phone number of the ISP?
- What is your user ID and password for the ISP?
- Will DNS servers be assigned at connection (most likely, yes)? If not, what is the IP address of one or two DNS servers?
- How will your IP address be assigned (most likely dynamically)?

Creating a dial-up connection in Windows 2000/XP is easy. A wizard steps you through. For Windows XP:

1. To launch the New Connection Wizard in Windows XP, right-click **My Network Places** and select **Properties** from the shortcut menu. (Alternately, you can open **My Computer** and double-click **Dial-up Networking**.) The Network Connections window appears (see Figure 19-8). Click **Create a new connection**.

Figure 19-8　　Using Windows XP, launch the New Connection Wizard

19

2. The New Connection Wizard opens. Click **Next** to skip the welcome screen. On the next screen, select **Connect to the Internet** and click **Next**.

3. On the next screen, select **Set up my connection manually** and click **Next**. On the following screen, select **Connect using a dial-up modem**. Click **Next**.

4. Enter a name to identify the connection, such as the name and city of your ISP. Click **Next**. In the following screen, enter the access phone number of your ISP. Click **Next**.

5. On the next screen (see Figure 19-9), enter your user name and password at the ISP. This screen gives options to make the logon automatic, make this the default connection to the Internet, and turn on Internet Connection Firewall. Make your choices and click **Next**.

Figure 19-9   The New Connection Wizard asks how to configure the connection

6. On the next screen, you can add a shortcut to the connection on the desktop. Make your choice and click **Finish**. A connection icon is added to the Network Connections window; if you selected the option, a shortcut is added to the desktop.

To use the connection, double-click the connection icon. The Connect dialog box appears. Click Dial. You will hear the modem dial up the ISP and make the connection.

Windows XP makes assumptions about your connection. To view or change the configuration:

1. Open the Connect dialog box. Click **Properties**. The connection Properties window appears, as shown in Figure 19-10. Click the **Networking** tab.

A+
CORE
1.8
6.3
OS
4.2

Figure 19-10 Configure an Internet connection using the Properties windows of the connection icon

2. Select **Internet Protocol (TCP/IP)** and click **Properties**. The Internet Protocol (TCP/IP) Properties window appears, also shown in Figure 19-10.

3. Windows XP assumes you are using dynamic IP addressing ("Obtain an IP address automatically") and the ISP will give DNS information when you log on ("Obtain DNS server address automatically"). Most likely these are the correct options, but if necessary, you can change them and click **OK**. From this Properties window, you can change the ISP's access phone number and how the phone call is made.

NOTE

To launch the connection wizard in Windows 2000, right-click My Network Places and select Properties from the shortcut menu. The Network and Dial-up Connections window appears. Click Make New Connection. The wizard launches and steps you through the process to create a connection. The process is similar to that of Windows XP.

Creating a Dial-up Connection in Windows 98

To use Windows 98 or Windows NT to communicate with a network over phone lines, Dial-up Networking must be installed as an OS component on your PC using the Add/Remove Programs applet in the Control Panel. (Network and Dial-up Connections in Windows 2000 and Network Connections in Windows XP are installed by default.)

When Windows 98 installs Dial-up Networking, it also "installs" a dial-up adapter. In terms of function, think of this dial-up adapter as a virtual network card. Remember that in the last chapter, you learned how TCP/IP is bound to a network interface card. A dial-up adapter is a modem playing the role of a network card for

19

dial-up networking. After Dial-up Networking is installed, open the Device Manager to see your "new" dial-up adapter listed under Network adapters, as shown in Figure 19-11. You can also see it listed as an installed network component in the Network window of the Control Panel.

Figure 19-11　After Dial-up Networking is installed, a new virtual network device, a dial-up adapter, is listed as an installed hardware device

You are now ready to create a Dial-up Networking connection. To create the connection in Windows 98:

1. After Dial-up Networking is installed, click **Start**, point to **Programs, Accessories,** and **Communications,** and then click **Dial-up Networking.** The Dial-Up Networking window appears, as shown in Figure 19-12.

2. Double-click **Make New Connection.** The Make New Connection Wizard appears, also shown in Figure 19-12. Click **Next** to move past the first screen.

3. Enter a name for the connection. If your modem is already installed, it appears in the modem list.

4. In the next dialog box, type the phone number to dial, and then click **Next** to continue.

5. Click **Finish** to build the icon. The icon appears in the Dial-Up Networking window.

A+
CORE
1.8
6.3
OS
4.2

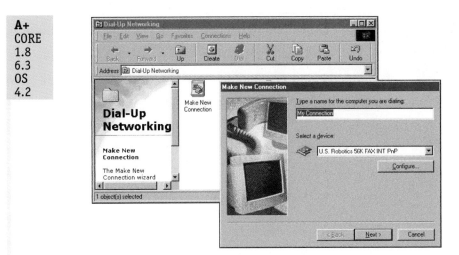

Figure 19-12   Creating a Windows 98 Dial-up Networking Connection icon

Next you will configure the connection. In Windows 98, do the following:

1. Right-click the icon you created for the connection, and select **Properties** from the shortcut menu.

2. Click the **General** tab. Verify that the correct phone number is entered for your ISP.

3. Click the **Server Types** tab. Figure 19-13 shows the resulting dialog box. Verify that these selections are made:

▪ Type of Dial-up Server: **PPP: Internet, Windows NT Server, Windows 98**
▪ Advanced Options: Select **Enable software compression** (software compression is most likely enabled, but this option really depends on what the ISP is doing). Also, click **Log on to network**.
▪ Allowed Network Protocols: **TCP/IP**

4. Click **TCP/IP Settings** to open the TCP/IP Settings dialog box, as shown in Figure 19-14. Most likely you will specify:

▪ **Server assigned IP address**
▪ **Server assigned name server addresses**
▪ **Use IP header compression**
▪ **Use default gateway on remote network**

19

Figure 19-13 Configuring the server type for a connection to the Internet in Windows 9x/Me

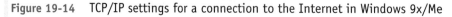

Figure 19-14 TCP/IP settings for a connection to the Internet in Windows 9x/Me

A+
CORE
1.8
6.3
OS
4.2

5. Click **OK** twice to complete the Dial-up Networking connection.
6. To connect to your ISP, double-click the icon you created for it, which is now correctly configured. The first time you use the icon, enter the user ID and password to connect to your ISP. Check the option to remember the user name and password if you don't want to have to enter them every time, but remember that this selection might not be wise if others who cannot be trusted have access to your PC.
7. Click **Connect**. You should hear the modem making the connection.

Dial-up Networking Problems

In this section, you learn about some of the most common problems and errors that you may encounter with dial-up networking and what to do about them. As always, check the simple things first before trying more difficult solutions.

NOTE

In Chapter 17, you learned how to create a modem log file to help troubleshoot problems with modems. In Windows 9x/Me, this file is called Modemlog.txt; in Windows 2000/XP, it is called ModemLog *modemname*.txt). In addition to these log files, you can create a log file to help troubleshoot problems with a Windows 9x/Me dial-up adapter. To create the log file, open the Network applet in the Control Panel, select Dial-Up Adapter, and then click Properties. In the Properties window, click the Advanced tab. In the Property box, select "Record A Log File," and in the Value box, select Yes. Click OK. The file, Ppplog.txt, is created in the Windows folder; the file can get very large, so turn off logging when you don't need it. For tips on how to interpret the file, see the Microsoft Knowledge Base Article 156435, at *support.microsoft.com*.

You cannot make a connection If you have a problem connecting to the Internet using a dial-up connection, first find out what works and what doesn't work. Try the following:

- Find out the answers to these questions: At what point does the connecting process fail? Do you hear the modem hissing? If so, the problem is probably with the user ID and password. If not, then the problem might be the phone number, phone line, or modem. Is the phone line plugged in? Does the phone line work? Can you hear a dial tone?
- Check the Dial-up Networking connection icon for errors. Is the phone number correct? Does the number need to include a 9 to get an outside line? Has a 1 been added in front of the number by mistake?
- Try dialing the number manually from a phone. Do you hear beeps on the other end?
- Try another phone number.
- Does the modem work? Check Device Manager for reported errors about the modem.
- Print the Modemlog or Ppplog text file from a successful connection on another computer and the same file from the unsuccessful connection on the problem

19

A+
CORE
1.8
6.3
OS
4.2

computer. Compare the two printouts to identify the point in the connection at which an error occurs. (See Chapter 17 for directions to log modem events to a text file.)

- Are all components installed? Check for the dial-up adapter and TCP/IP, and check the configuration of each.
- Reboot your PC and try again.
- Try removing and reinstalling each network component. Begin with TCP/IP.

You can connect, but you get the message "Unable to resolve hostname"
This error message means that TCP/IP cannot determine how to route a request to a host. Right-click the Dial-up Networking connection icon, select Properties, and check for the following:

- Under Server Types, try making TCP/IP the only network protocol allowed.
- If your ISP provides the IP addresses of the DNS servers, enter them in the TCP/IP Settings dialog box (see Figure 19-14).
- Make sure "Use default gateway on remote network" is selected in the TCP/IP Settings dialog box.
- Try *not* selecting "Use IP header compression."

After connecting, you get the error message "Unable to establish a compatible set of network protocols" This error is most likely caused by a problem with the installation and configuration of Dial-up Networking or TCP/IP. Try the following:

- Verify that the dial-up adapter and TCP/IP are installed and configured correctly.
- Remove and reinstall TCP/IP. Be sure to reboot after the installation.
- For Windows 9x/Me, try putting the PC in a different workgroup.
- Compare the modem log file (Modemlog *modemname*.txt or Ppplog.txt) with one created during a successful connection.

When you double-click the Web browser, the modem does not dial automatically When this error occurs, go to the Control Panel and open the Internet Connections applet or Internet Options applet. Click the Connections tab and check "Dial whenever a network connection is not present."

DSL and Cable Modem Connections

Recall that DSL and cable modem are called broadband technologies because they support the transmission of more than one kind of data at once. These connections can carry voice, data, sound, and video simultaneously. When using cable modem or DSL (as well as ISDN or satellite), if you are connecting a single PC to the Internet using an ISP, then the TCP/IP settings are no different from those used by a modem-to-phone line connection. In most cases, cable modem and DSL, like LANs, use a

A+
CORE
1.8
6.3
OS
4.2

network card in the PC for the physical connection to the network, which in this case is the Internet. The network card provides a network port for a network cable. (Some newer cable modems use USB to connect to a PC.) For cable modem service to the Internet, the network or USB cable connects to a cable modem. For DSL, the phone line connects to a DSL box, which might also be a small router. The connection between the NIC and the broadband device most likely uses **PPPoE (Point-to-Point Protocol over Ethernet)**, a protocol specifically designed to support broadband connections. PPPoE is included in Windows XP.

For cable modem and DSL Internet connections, generally the installation goes like this:

1. Install the network card and the drivers to control the card.

2. Use a network cable to connect the PC to a cable modem or DSL box.

3. Install TCP/IP and bind TCP/IP to the card.

4. Configure TCP/IP to connect to the Internet or LAN.

5. Install the application software (for example, a browser) to use the connection.

In the following section, you'll learn about the different ways to connect to the Internet using these faster-than-phone-line connections and the details of installing these services.

Cable Modem

A cable modem uses a regular TV cable to connect to a TV cable wall outlet. Figure 19-15 illustrates what the arrangement looks like. The cable modem also has an electrical connection to provide power to the box. A cable modem connects to a network card or USB port in your PC. Your cable modem company will provide you with the TCP/IP settings to use to configure TCP/IP. For a home installation, some cable modem companies will do the entire installation for you. You might need to purchase the cable modem and NIC, or they might be included in the installation fee. A service technician comes to your home, installs the network card if necessary, and configures your PC to use the service.

19

A+
CORE
1.8
6.3
OS
4.2

If you don't have on-site service from the cable modem company, follow these instructions to install the cable modem:

1. Install the network card and drivers. For most cable modem companies, the MAC address of the network card in the PC or the MAC address of the NIC in the cable modem must be entered in an online list of valid addresses that identify your PC or cable modem as a subscriber to the cable modem service. When the PC first connects to the service, the system recognizes the PC and assigns it a valid IP address, subnet mask, IP address of the default gateway, and IP address of a domain name server. If the cable company help desk technician needs the MAC address of the PC, use Winipcfg or Ipconfig to display it. If the technician needs the MAC address of the cable modem, look for it printed somewhere on the back of the cable modem.

2. Configure TCP/IP to use the network card, using the TCP/IP configuration information provided by the cable modem company.

3. Shut down the PC and connect one end of the network or USB cable to the network or USB port on the back of the PC. Connect the other end of the cable to the cable modem. Be sure the cable modem is plugged in and turned on. There is usually a switch on the back of the box. Connect the TV cable from the TV cable outlet to the cable modem. (Refer back to Figure 19-15.) Turn on the PC.

Figure 19-15   Cable modem connecting to a PC through a network card installed on the PC

4. When the PC starts, you should immediately be connected to the Internet. Test the connection using your Web browser or email client. If you are not connected, try the following:

■ For Windows 2000/XP, use Ipconfig /release and Ipconfig /renew to lease a new IP address, and then check for connectivity again. (Alternately, for Windows XP, you open the Network Connections window, select the connection, and then click "Repair this connection" under Network Tasks to release and renew

A+
CORE
1.8
6.3
OS
4.2

the IP address.) For Windows 9x/Me, use Winipcfg to access the IP Configuration window. Select the network card and click **Release All.** Wait a moment, click **Renew,** and check for Internet connectivity again.

- If this doesn't work, turn off the PC and the cable modem. Wait a full five minutes until all connections have timed out at the cable modem company. Turn on the cable modem, and then turn on the PC. After the PC boots up, again check for connectivity.
- Try another cable TV jack in your home.
- If this doesn't work, call the cable modem help desk. The technician there can release and restore the connection at that end, which should restore service.

DSL and ISDN

DSL/ISDN service is provided by the local telephone company. The telephone company's responsibility for the phone system ends at your house. Inside your house, you are responsible for your home phone network. A DSL/ISDN connection uses a DSL/ISDN converter box that is sometimes combined with a router as a single device so that more than one PC can use the DSL/ISDN line. A DSL connection most likely will use a DSL router and an ISDN connection will use a device called a Terminal Adapter (TA) or an ISDN router. The device connects to the PC by way of a network cable and card.

As with a cable modem, a technician from the phone company most likely will install DSL/ISDN for you. The installation process on the PC works the same as that of a cable modem.

Sharing Internet Connections

A+
OS
4.2

VIDEO

Securing a
Wireless LAN

There are several ways that computers on a LAN or WLAN can share an Internet connection. Here are a few options:

- If one computer on the LAN has a direct connection to the Internet by way of a phone line, cable modem, or DSL, it can serve as a host computer for others on the LAN. Windows XP and Windows 98 **Internet Connection Sharing (ICS)** is designed to manage this type of connection. Using ICS, the host computer uses NAT and acts as the proxy server for the LAN. Windows XP ICS also includes a firewall. However, enabling this firewall will prevent others on the LAN from accessing resources on this PC.
- For broadband connections (cable modem and DSL), the broadband converter box can connect to a network device such as a router that manages the connection for the entire network. The router has a network connection to the converter box and one or more network ports for devices on the network. In this situation, the router is also likely to have firewall software embedded in it and is controlled by way of a Web browser. A user on any computer on the network can enter the IP address of the router in a Web browser and bring up the

19

A+
OS
4.2

software on the router to configure it. The router can serve as a DHCP server, a NAT proxy server, and a firewall.

▪ The router can also serve as a wireless access point for computers to connect wirelessly to the Internet. An example of a router that is also a wireless access point is the AirPlus D1-714P+ by D-Link (*www.dlink.com*) shown in Figure 19-16. It has one port for the converter box, four ports for computers on the network, and a parallel printer port designed to manage a network printer. The router can also support several computers with wireless adapters.

Figure 19-16   This D-Link router allows computers on a LAN to share a broadband Internet connection and is an access point for computers with wireless adapters

APPLYING CONCEPTS

Windows Internet Connection Sharing

To use Internet Connection Sharing in Windows XP or Windows 98, the computer that has a direct connection to the Internet by way of a phone line, cable modem, or DSL is the host computer. Follow these general directions to configure the LAN for Internet Connection Sharing using Windows XP:

1. Following directions earlier in the chapter, install and configure the hardware (modem, cable modem, or DSL) to connect to the Internet, and verify that the connection is working.

2. Open the Network Connections window in the Windows XP Control Panel, and click the link to **Set up a home or small office network**. The Network Setup Wizard opens. Click **Next** in this window and the next.

3. Select the connection method for your host computer, which is **This computer connects directly to the Internet. The other computers on my network connect to the Internet through this computer.** Click **Next**.

A+
OS
4.2

4. The wizard looks at your hardware connections (NIC or modem) and selects the one that it sees as a "live" connection. Verify that the wizard selected correctly and then follow the wizard to enter a description for your computer, your computer name, and your workgroup name.

5. The next screen of the wizard offers you the option of creating a Network Setup Disk that you can use to quickly configure every other computer on the LAN that is to use the Internet connection (see Figure 19-17). Select the option to **Create a Network Setup Disk**, insert a blank floppy disk in the drive, and click **Next**.

Figure 19-17   Create a Network Setup Disk to configure other computers on the LAN

6. The next screen gives you the option to format the disk. If it needs formatting, click **Format Disk**. Otherwise, click **Next**.

7. The wizard tells you that to use the disk, you must insert it into the next computer on the network, and run the program named Netsetup.exe from the disk. Click **Next** and then click **Finish**.

8. Use the Network Setup Disk on each computer on the LAN that is to use the shared connection.

19

A+
OS
4.2

Implementing a Firewall

Recall from previous chapters that one of the more important things to do when setting up access to the Internet is to install a good firewall. A firewall can function in several ways:

- Firewalls can filter data packets, examining the destination IP address or source IP address or the type of protocol used (for example, TCP or UDP).
- Firewalls can filter ports so that outside clients cannot communicate with inside services listening at these ports.
- Firewalls can filter applications such as FTP so that users inside the firewall cannot use this service over the Internet.
- Some firewalls can filter information such as inappropriate Web content for children or employees.

There are several variations of firewalls, from personal firewalls to protect a single PC to expensive firewall solutions for large corporations. A firewall is implemented either as software installed on a computer or as embedded firmware on a hardware device, as explained in the following sections.

Hardware Firewall   The best firewall solution is a hardware firewall that stands between a LAN and the Internet (see Figure 19-18). A hardware firewall is better than software on each PC because it protects the entire network. For most home and small-office LANs, a router is used as a hardware firewall. You can buy a router with enough ports to connect several computers and perhaps a network printer to it. Some routers also serve double duty as a wireless access point to the network, DHCP server, and proxy server. The router connects directly to the cable modem or DSL converter. Note that some DSL devices are also routers and include embedded firewall firmware. Three companies that make routers suitable for small networks are D-Link (*www.dlink.com*), Linksys (*www.linksys.com*), and NetGear (*www.netgear.com*). You saw an example of a router in Figure 19-16.

VIDEO

Using a
Hardware
Firewall

Software Firewalls   Firewall software can be installed on a PC that is connected directly to the Internet or, for a network, you can install firewall software on each PC on the LAN. Some examples of firewall software are ZoneAlarm (see Figure 19-19) by Zone Labs (*www.zonelabs.com*), Norton Personal Firewall by Symantec (*www.symantec.com*), Check Point Software by Check Point Software Technologies (*www.checkpoint.com*), McAfee Personal Firewall by McAfee (*www.mcafee.com*), Personal Firewall Pro by Sygate (*www.sygate.com*), and Internet Connection Firewall, which is part of Windows XP. When evaluating firewall software, look for its ability to control traffic coming from both outside and inside the network. Also, you should know that some software firewalls, such as Windows XP Internet Connection Firewall (ICF), can prevent others on a LAN from accessing resources on the Windows XP PC, which is one reason that a hardware firewall is the best solution to protect a LAN.

A+
OS
4.2

Figure 19-18   A hardware firewall stands between the Internet and a local network

Figure 19-19   ZoneAlarm allows you to determine the amount of security the firewall provides

Always use firewall software on a single computer that connects to the Internet by a dial-up connection and on a notebook computer used for travel. But know that a firewall does not substitute for antivirus software, which should also be installed and running.

19

Supporting Internet Clients

A+
OS
4.2
Now that you've learned how to connect to the Internet, let's look at some ways of using it. Earlier in the chapter in Table 19-1, you saw a list of application services that use the Internet. In this section, you will learn how to support some of the most common Internet clients: Web browsers, email, and FTP.

Supporting Web Browsers

A Web browser is a software application on a user's PC that is used to request Web pages from a Web server on the Internet or an intranet. A Web page is a text file with an .htm or .html file extension. It can include text coded in **HTML (Hypertext Markup Language)** that can be interpreted by a Web browser to display formatted text and graphics, as well as play sounds. If the HTML code on the Web page points to other files used to build the page, such as a sound file or a photograph file, these files are also downloaded to the browser. In this section, you will learn about the addresses that Web browsers use to locate resources on a Web server and how to troubleshoot common problems that occur with Web browsers.

How a URL Is Structured

Earlier in the chapter you saw that a Web browser requests a Web page by sending an IP address followed by an optional port number. This works well on an intranet, but on the Internet, a more user-friendly address is preferred. A **URL (Uniform Resource Locator)** is an address for a Web page or other resource on the Internet. Figure 19-20 shows the structure of a URL.

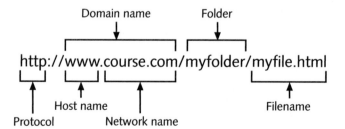

Figure 19-20 A URL contains the protocol used, the host name of the Web server, the network name, and the path and filename of the requested file

The first part of the URL shown in Figure 19-20 indicates the protocol, which in this case is HTTP. The protocol part of the URL specifies the rules, or protocol, the Web server should use when transmitting the page to the browser. A Web server is sometimes called an HTTP server.

Recall from Chapter 18 that a host name identifies a server or another computer within a network. In this example, the host name is *www* (a Web server), and *course.com* is the name of the Course Technology network, sometimes called the domain name. A name that contains not only the network name (in this case, *course.com*) but also the host on that network is called a fully qualified domain name (FQDN), as you learned in Chapter 18. In this case, the FQDN is *www.course.com*. The Web page requested is located in the folder *myfolder* on the *www* server, and the file within that folder is named *myfile.html*. The FQDN must be resolved to an IP address before the request can happen.

The last segment, or suffix, of a domain name is called the **top-level domain** (*.com* in our example) and tells you something about the organization or individual that owns the name. Some domain names in the United States end in the suffixes listed in Table 19-3. There are other endings as well, including codes for countries, such as .uk for the United Kingdom. With the growth of the Internet, there has been a shortage of available domain names; because of this shortage, additional suffixes are being created.

Domain Suffix	Description
.air	Aviation industry
.biz	Businesses
.com	Commercial institutions
.coop	Business cooperatives
.edu	Educational institutions
.gov	Government institutions
.info	General use
.int	Organizations established by international treaties between governments
.mil	U.S. military
.museum	Museums
.name	Individuals
.net	Internet providers or networks
.org	Nonprofit organizations
.pro	Professionals

Table 19-3   Suffixes used to identify top-level domain names

19

Domain names stand for IP addresses and provide an easy way to remember them, but domain names and IP addresses are not necessarily permanently related. A host computer can have a certain domain name, can be connected to one network and

A+
OS
4.2

assigned a certain IP address, and then can be moved to another network and assigned a different IP address. The domain name can stay with the host while it connects to either network. It is up to a name resolution service, such as DNS or WINS, to track the relationship between a domain name and the current IP address of the host computer.

When banking or doing some other private business on the Web, you might have noticed HTTPS in the address box of your browser. To ensure privacy between the Web server and the browser, the data can be encrypted before transmission. In this case, the browser address box shows the protocol to be **HTTPS (HTTP secure)**. The secure protocol being used is SSL or TLS. **SSL (secure socket layer)** is the de facto standard developed by Netscape and used by Microsoft and Netscape browsers; it uses an encryption system that uses a digital certificate. Public keys are secret codes used to encrypt and later decrypt the data, and are exchanged before data is sent (see Figure 19-21). A **digital certificate**, also called a **digital ID** or **digital signature**, is a code assigned to you by a certificate authority such as VeriSign (*www.verisign.com*) that uniquely identifies you on the Internet and includes a public key. Recall from Chapter 15 that Microsoft uses digital certificates to validate or digitally sign device drivers certified by Microsoft. **TLS (Transport Layer Security)** is an improved version of SSL.

Figure 19-21   Using secure HTTP, a Web server and browser encrypt data using a public key before the data is transmitted

A+
OS
4.2

✔ **A+ EXAM TIP**

The A+ OS exam expects you to know how to install and configure a browser, including how to enable and disable script support and configure proxy and security settings. You will get the practice of installing a browser in a project at the end of this chapter.

Configuring a Browser

The two most popular browsers are Internet Explorer and Netscape Navigator. Using Internet Explorer, you can control support options using the Internet Options window. Using Netscape Navigator, you control the browser options by clicking Edit on the menu bar and then clicking Preferences. There are three ways to access the Internet Options window to control Internet Explorer:

- Open the Internet Options applet in the Control Panel.
- From Internet Explorer, click Tools on the menu bar and then click Internet Options.
- Right-click the Internet Explorer icon and select Properties from the shortcut menu.

To control how and if scripts are executed, click the Advanced tab. Scripts are small programs embedded inside a Web page that control how the Web page functions. Under the Security tab, you can also click the Custom Level button (see Figure 19-22) to control how scripts are run as well as other security settings. Under the Connections tab of the Internet Options window, you can control proxy settings for an Internet Connection, giving the browser the IP address of the proxy server to use. However, if you only have one proxy server on your LAN, the browser should find the server without your having to give it an IP address.

Solving Browser Performance Problems

If you notice poor browser performance, use the tools you have seen in earlier chapters, such as Defrag, ScanDisk, and System Information, to make sure that you have enough free hard drive space, that the hard drive is clean, and that the virtual memory settings are optimized. If you perform these tasks and the browser is still slow, try the following procedure using the most popular browser, Internet Explorer (IE), as an example:

1. Use the instructions from the previous section to open the Internet Properties window, as shown in Figure 19-23 for Windows 2000. (In Windows XP, this window is called Internet Options.)

2. Click **Delete Files** under the Temporary Internet files heading to clean out the IE cache. The Delete Files dialog box appears, asking you to confirm the deletion. Click **OK**. IE must search the entire cache each time it accesses a Web page. If the cache is too big, performance is affected.

19

Figure 19-22   Security settings, Web content, Internet connections, and other browser functions are controlled from the Internet Options window

Figure 19-23   Use the Internet Properties window to control the Internet Explorer environment

A+
OS
4.2

3. Click **Clear History** under the History heading to clean out the shortcuts cache. The Internet Options dialog box appears, asking you to confirm the deletions. Click **OK**. If this cache gets too big, performance slows down. Also, if you reduce the number of days that Internet Explorer keeps pages in the history folder, performance might improve because there will be less material for Internet Explorer to search. For example, change the number of days to keep pages in history from the default value of 20 to 7.

4. Click **OK** to close the window.

Suppress Image Downloading   Slow browser performance can be caused by a slow Internet connection. In this case, one thing you can do is to suppress the downloading of images. Image files can be large and account for most of the downloaded data from Web sites. For Internet Explorer 5.x, you can download and install Web Accessories for Internet Explorer 5.x, which can be used to suppress the downloading of images from Web sites. (IE version 6 includes the ability to suppress downloading images without added software.) If the Microsoft site has been updated since the writing of this book, you may need to search for the Web Accessories for Internet Explorer. Follow these directions:

1. Go to this Microsoft Web site: *www.microsoft.com/windows/ie/downloads/archive/default.asp*

2. Scroll down and click the **Web Accessories** heading, and then scroll down, find Web Accessories from Microsoft, and click the **Download it now** link.

3. Another page opens, with more information about the Internet Explorer 5.x Web Accessories. On the right side of the page, locate the box labeled Download, and click the link to the file **ie5wa.exe**.

4. Click **Save** to save the file on disk. When the download window opens, choose to download the file to a location on your hard drive, and then click **Save**. Remember where you saved the file.

5. After you download the file ie5wa.exe, double-click it, then click **Yes** to install accessories.

6. Close the IE browser, and reopen it.

7. To use the IE Web Accessories to suppress downloading images, right-click the IE menu bar. If Favorites is already checked and on your menu bar, you can move on to Step 8. If it is not, click **Links** on the shortcut menu. This action adds the Links menu to the menu bar items.

19

A+
OS
4.2

8. Click **Favorites** on the menu bar, click **Links**, and then click **Toggle Images**. Web pages should now download without their images. You may have to click the **Refresh** button on your toolbar for the changes to take effect on an open page.

9. To reset the browser to download images, click **Favorites**, click **Links**, and then click **Toggle Images** again.

IE version 6 includes the option to suppress images, sound, animation, and video. Use the following procedure:

1. Open the **Tools** menu and then click **Internet Options**.

2. The Internet Options window opens. Click the **Advanced** tab.

3. Scroll down to the multimedia section of the check box list, and clear the check box or boxes for the feature or features that you do not want to display (**Show pictures, Play animations, Play videos**, or **Play sounds**).

NOTE

To display an individual video or picture when you have cleared the related check boxes, right-click the icon with which it has been replaced on the Web page.

Browser Updates and Patches

Browser manufacturers are continually improving their products, and generally speaking, you should use the most current version of the browser to take advantage of the latest features and fixes to known problems. However, if you have an older computer or operating system, you might not want to update a browser that requires a lot of system resources, because your older PC might not be able to support it. In this case, it's better to keep an older version on your PC unless you are having problems with your version.

If you are using Internet Explorer, check the Windows support Web site at *support.microsoft.com* to find information about specific problems with Internet Explorer. Search for the product and the error message for articles that describe the problem and possible solutions. Also check the Windows update Web site at *windowsupdate.microsoft.com* for updates or patches for known Internet Explorer problems. Download the patch and install it following the same general instructions you have seen in earlier chapters.

If you are not using the latest version of your Web browser, try downloading the latest version. If you use your browser for banking on the Internet, be sure to download a version that supports 128-bit encryption for better security features. If the new version creates problems on your system, you can revert to your original version by uninstalling the new version.

Supporting Email

A+
OS
4.2

Email is a client/server application used to send text messages to individuals and groups. When you send an email message, it travels from your computer to your email server. Your email server sends the message to the recipient's email server. The recipient's email server sends it to the recipient's PC, but not until the recipient asks that it be sent by logging in and downloading email. Different parts of the process are controlled by different protocols.

Figure 19-24 shows the journey made by an email message as well as the protocols that control the different parts of the journey. The sender's PC and email server both use **SMTP (Simple Mail Transfer Protocol)** to send an email message to its destination. Once the message arrives at the destination email server, it remains there until the recipient requests delivery. The recipient's email server uses one of two protocols to deliver the message: either **POP (Post Office Protocol)** or **IMAP4 (Internet Message Access Protocol, version 4)**, a newer email protocol. The current version of POP is version 3, often abbreviated as POP3. IMAP is slowly replacing POP for receiving email.

Figure 19-24   The SMTP protocol is used to send email to a recipient's mail server, and the POP3 or IMAP4 protocol is used to download email to the client

NOTE   SMTP is defined in RFC 821 and RFC 822 (see *www.rfc-editor.org*). When Email experts speak of error messages created during email transactions, they sometimes call these messages 822 messages.

Email client software communicates with an email server when it sends and receives email. Two common email clients are Eudora and Microsoft Outlook Express. Figure 19-24 shows a user with one email server. In fact, it's possible to

19

A+
OS
4.2

have two email servers, one for sending email and the other for receiving email. Figure 19-25 shows this arrangement.

Figure 19-25   An email client can use one server to send email and another to receive email

The email server that takes care of sending email messages (using the SMTP protocol) is often referred to as the SMTP server. The email server from which you collect messages sent to you is often referred to as the POP server, because it uses the POP protocol.

When you configure your email client software for the first time, you need to enter the addresses of your email servers. If you are connecting to email via an Internet service provider, the ISP can tell you these addresses. For example, if your ISP is *MyISP.net*, you might have an outgoing mail server address of *smtp.myISP.net* and an incoming mail server address of *pop3.myISP.net*.

In most email client software, you enter the addresses of your POP or IMAP server and your SMTP server in a dialog box when setting up the program, along with your email address you will use when sending email. Look for menus or icons labeled Options, Preferences, Configuration, Setup, or similar names. After you enter the addresses, the software saves this and other configuration information in an initialization file, the Windows registry, or some other location. When you first log on to the email server, you will be asked for your user ID and password, which are used to validate your right to access the account.

Supporting FTP

A+
OS
1.4
4.2

A common task of communications software is file transfer, the passing of files from one computer to another. For file transfer to work, the software on both ends must use the same protocol. The most popular way to transfer files over the Internet is with FTP, which can transfer files between two computers using the same or different operating systems. For example, when upgrades for software become available, software vendors often provide files for customers to download to their PCs via FTP.

A+
OS
1.4
4.2

This service is commonly provided by Windows NT/2000/2003, or Unix servers that offer access to files using FTP, and are called FTP servers or FTP sites. These commercial FTP sites only provide the ability to download a file to your PC. However, the FTP utility itself offers remote users the ability to copy, delete, and rename files, make directories, remove directories, and view details about files and directories, provided the user has the appropriate permissions on the FTP site.

Most communications applications provide an FTP utility that has a unique look and feel, but the basics of file transfer are the same from one utility to another. If you don't have graphical FTP software installed on your PC, you can use FTP commands from a command prompt.

FTP from a Command Prompt

FTP can be initiated at a Windows NT/2000/XP, Windows 9x/Me, or DOS command prompt, if a connection to a network or the Internet is established. A sample set of FTP commands entered at the command prompt is shown in Table 19-4.

Command Entered at the Command Prompt	Description
FTP	Execute the FTP program, ftp.exe.
OPEN 110.87.170.34	Open a session with a remote computer having the given IP address.
LOGIN: XXXXXX	The host computer provides a prompt to enter a user ID for the computer being accessed.
PASSWORD: XXXXXX	The host computer requests the password for that ID. Logon is then completed by the host computer.
CD /DATA	Change directory to the /DATA directory.
GET YOURFILE.DAT	Copy the file YOURFILE.DAT (or whatever file you want) from the remote computer to your computer.
PUT MYFILE.DAT	Copy the file MYFILE.DAT (or whatever file you want) from your computer to the remote computer.
BYE	Disconnect the FTP session.

Table 19-4   A sample FTP session from a command prompt

19

A+
OS
1.4
4.2

File Transfer Using FTP Software

FTP client software can be downloaded from the Internet or directly from your ISP. This example looks at how to use FTP using such software:

1. Start the FTP utility software. In this example we are using WS_FTP Pro by Ipswitch (*www.ipswitch.com*). The FTP utility screen that appears is similar to the one in Figure 19-26. Note that more recent versions of WS_FTP Pro might look and work slightly differently.

Figure 19-26   A typical FTP utility provided by an Internet service provider

2. Click **Connect** to log on to an FTP site. A Session Profile dialog box appears, similar to the one in Figure 19-26.

3. Enter the Host Name, for example *ftp.course.com*. Enter the User ID and Password for this host computer, and then click **OK**.

4. The connection is made and your ID and password are passed to the host. After you have been authenticated by the host computer, a screen similar to that in Figure 19-27 appears.

5. The files on the left belong to you, and the files on the right belong to the remote host computer. You can drag and drop files either to or from the other computer, or you can use the commands at the bottom of the window. Notice in Figure 19-27 the choices near the bottom of the window: ASCII, Binary, or Auto. These choices refer to the format to be used to transfer the files. Text files are written in ASCII code; therefore, use ASCII for text files, and use Binary for all others. If you are not sure which to use, choose **Auto**.

A+
OS
1.4
4.2

6. When the transfer of files is complete, click **Exit** to leave the utility.

Figure 19-27   An FTP utility screen showing local and remote files

A+ EXAM TIP

The A+ OS exam expects
you to know the difference
between a binary file and a
text file.

Many Web pages provide a link on the page offering you the ability
to download a file. Click the link to download the file. This file is
probably not being downloaded from the Web server, but from an
FTP server. When you click the filename on the Web page, the program controlling the page executes FTP commands to the FTP server
to download the file to you. If you receive an error, you can sometimes solve the problem by going directly to the company's FTP
server and using an FTP utility (such as the one in the previous procedure) to download the file, or even see a list of other files that you might also like to
download.

NOTE

A Web browser can also serve as an FTP client. Enter the URL of the FTP server in the address box
(for example, *ftp.course.com*). The browser changes menu options to become an FTP client. For
example, the Login As command is added to the File menu. To log on to the FTP server in Internet Explorer, click File on the menu bar, and then click Login As. The Log On As dialog box
appears for you to enter a user ID and password. Files and folders on the FTP server then display
in the browser.

19

CHAPTER SUMMARY

▶ Ports are used to address particular software or services running on a computer. Common port assignments are port 80 for HTTP (Web browser requests), port 25 for SMTP (sending email), port 110 for POP3 (receiving email), and port 20 for FTP.

▶ Generally, an API call is a way for an application to ask an operating system to do something. A browser uses an API call to access a Web server and make its request for information.

▶ TCP guarantees that a packet reaches its destination and so is called a connection-oriented protocol. UDP does not guarantee delivery and so is called a connection-less or best-effort protocol.

▶ IP is responsible for breaking data into packets and passing them from TCP or UDP to the hardware.

▶ PPP is used in dial-up networking to send packets of data over phone lines. It manages network transmission from one modem to another.

▶ Winipcfg and Ipconfig report configuration information about the current TCP/IP connection for a device and can release and renew the IP address. Winipcfg is supported in Windows 9x/Me, and Windows NT/2000/XP supports Ipconfig.

▶ Other TCP/IP utilities useful in solving networking problems are Tracert, Ping, and Nbtstat.

▶ Before you can create a dial-up connection to the Internet, you need to have a modem installed along with the drivers to run it, as well as TCP/IP installed and bound to the modem.

▶ The Windows Dial-up Networking utility is used to connect to a network using a modem and a phone line. When a dial-up connection is made, a PC's application software relates to the network as though the computer were directly connected to the network using a network card.

▶ You can create a dial-up networking connection through the Network Connections applet in the Control Panel of Windows XP, through the Network and Dial-up Connections applet in the Control Panel of Windows 2000, and in Windows 9x/Me and Windows NT through the Dial-up Networking applet in My Computer.

▶ When experiencing problems with dial-up networking, make sure the modem is working, all necessary components are installed, and the phone number to dial and other settings are configured correctly.

▶ DSL and cable modem are broadband Internet connections that use a converter box connected to a NIC in a PC by way of a network cable. The connection can use the PPPoE protocol.

◗ Computers can share an Internet connection. Windows XP and Windows 98 use Internet Connection Sharing (ICS) to manage the connection on the host computer, or you can use a router that stands between the converter box and the network.

◗ Use a firewall on the host computer or router to protect the network from unsolicited activity from the Internet.

◗ A URL consists of a protocol, a host name, a network or domain name, and a top-level domain extension. Common top-level domains include .com for commercial institutions, .gov for divisions of government, and .org for nonprofit organizations.

◗ When you experience poor browser performance, try cleaning up your hard drive and making sure your system settings are optimized. If that doesn't work, try clearing your browser cache, clearing the Web page history, suppressing image downloads, or downloading updates.

◗ Email uses SMTP to send messages and POP3 to receive messages. POP3 is being replaced by IMAP. Your ISP will provide you with information on the server types and addresses that it uses to send and receive email.

◗ FTP is used to transfer files from one computer to another, whether or not the computers are using the same operating system. Both computers must have an FTP utility installed. It can be executed from user-friendly GUI software or from a command prompt.

KEY TERMS

For explanations of key terms, see the Glossary near the end of the book.

ARP (Address Resolution
    Protocol)
best-effort protocol
bridging protocol
client/server application
connectionless protocol
connection-oriented protocol
dial-up networking
digital certificate
digital ID
digital signature
FTP (File Transfer Protocol)
hop count
HTML (Hypertext Markup
    Language)
HTTP (Hypertext Transfer
    Protocol)

HTTPS (HTTP secure)
ICMP (Internet Control Message
    Protocol)
IMAP4 (Internet Message Access
    Protocol, version 4)
Internet Connection Sharing (ICS)
IP (Internet Protocol)
line protocol
NNTP (Network News Transfer
    Protocol)
POP (Post Office Protocol)
port
port address
port number
PPP (Point-to-Point Protocol)
PPPoE (Point-to-Point Protocol
    over Ethernet)

RARP (Reverse Address Resolution
    Protocol)
session
SLIP (Serial Line Internet Protocol)
SMTP (Simple Mail Transfer
    Protocol)
SNMP (Simple Network
    Management Protocol)
socket
SSL (secure socket layer)
TCP (Transmission Control
    Protocol)
time to live (TTL)
TLS (Transport Layer Security)
top-level domain
UDP (User Datagram Protocol)
URL (Uniform Resource Locator)

19

REVIEWING THE BASICS

1. Explain how a single physical computer can be a Web server and an email server at the same time.

2. Give the service and protocol for the following ports: port 21, port 25, port 80, and port 110.

3. What are API calls used for? Why are they necessary?

4. Which protocol used by Web browsers and Web servers is responsible for guaranteeing delivery? For breaking data into packets? For decrypting and decompressing data as necessary?

5. Explain the difference between a connection-oriented protocol and a connectionless protocol, and give an example of each.

6. What TCP/IP utility would you use to display the route taken over the Internet by a communication between a Web browser and Web server?

7. What utility would you use to display information about the name space kept by a DNS server for a particular domain name?

8. Explain the functions of the following TCP/IP utilities: NSLookup, Winipcfg, Ipconfig, and Microsoft SNMP Agent.

9. What is the full command line to use Ipconfig to release the current IP address?

10. What utility new to Windows XP can be used to display a NIC's MAC address?

11. What must you do to get your system ready for creating a dial-up networking connection?

12. If TCP/IP is bound to a modem on your system, does it also need to be bound to a network card? Why or why not?

13. Explain how PPP is used by dial-up networking.

14. Place these stages of creating a dial-up networking connection in Windows 9x/Me in the correct order: creating a connection, verifying installation of the dial-up adapter, installing the Dial-up Networking feature, entering configuration information for your ISP.

15. How is the process for creating a dial-up connection in Windows XP different from the process for Windows 9x/Me?

16. Explain at least four things you can try if you cannot make a connection to the Internet using a dial-up networking connection.

17. What should you try if you can connect but you get the error message "Unable to resolve hostname"? If you get the error message "Unable to establish a compatible set of network protocols"?

18. What protocol is commonly used to manage the connection between a broadband converter box and a PC?

19. What Windows XP and Windows 98 component can be used to share an Internet connection with other computers on the LAN?

20. Label the component parts of this URL: *http://www.companyabc.com/Reports/december2004.doc*

21. Give the type of organization that would use the following top-level domains: .mil, .net, .air, .com, .org, .gov.

22. What are three things you can do to improve slow browser performance?

23. What protocol is used for sending email? For receiving it?

24. Explain what FTP is used for.

25. What is defined in RFC 1156? RFC 822?

THINKING CRITICALLY

1. You are trying to connect to the Internet using a Windows XP dial-up connection. You installed a modem card and tested it, so you know it works. Next you create a dial-up connection icon in the Network Connections window. Then you double-click the icon and the Connect dialog box opens. You click Dial to make the connection. An error message displays saying, "There was no dial tone." What is the first thing you do?

   a. Check Device Manager for errors with the modem.

   b. Check with the ISP to verify that you have the correct phone number, user name, and password.

   c. Check the phone line to see if it's connected.

   d. Check the properties of the dial-up connection icon for errors.

2. You connect to the Internet using a cable modem. When you open your browser and try to access a Web site, you get the error, "The Web page you requested is not available offline. To view this page, click Connect." What might be the problem(s) and what do you do?

   a. The browser has been set to work offline. On the File menu, verify that Work Offline is not checked.

   b. The cable modem service is down. In the Network Connections window, right-click the LAN connection and select Repair on the shortcut menu.

19

      c. Internet Connection Firewall is enabled on your PC. Disable it.

      d. The cable modem is down. Go to Device Manager and check for errors with the cable modem.

3. This question combines skills learned in this and previous chapters. You have set up a small LAN in your home with two Windows XP PCs connected to the Internet using a DSL connection. You have a DSL router box connected to the DSL line and to a small hub. Your two PCs connect to the hub. You have enabled Internet Connection Firewall on the LAN connection on both PCs, and you can browse the Internet from either PC. However, you discover that each PC cannot use the resources on the other PC. What is the problem and what do you do?

      a. The network hub is not working. Try replacing the hub.

      b. The NICs in each PC are not working. Try replacing one NIC and then the next.

      c. The LAN connections in the Network Connections window are not working. Delete the connections and recreate them.

      d. Internet Connection Firewall on each PC is preventing the PC from providing resources to others on the LAN. Disable Internet Connection Firewall.

HANDS-ON PROJECTS

HANDS-ON
PROJECTS

PROJECT 19-1: Practicing TCP/IP Networking Skills

While connected to the Internet or another TCP/IP network, answer these questions:

1. What is your current IP address?

2. Release and renew your IP address. Now what is your IP address?

3. Are you using dynamic or static IP addressing? How do you know?

4. What is your adapter address for this connection?

5. What is your default gateway IP address?

6. What response do you get when you ping the default gateway?

PROJECT 19-2: **Practicing Dial-up Networking Skills with Windows 9x/Me**

This project requires you to have a modem installed and working.

1. Open **My Computer** and open the **Dial-up Networking** folder.

2. Double-click the **Make New Connection** option.

3. Enter the name **TEST** for the name of the computer that you are dialing. Click **Next**.

4. Enter your home phone number. Click **Next**.

5. Click the **Finish** button to create the Test dial-up.

6. Double-click the newly created **Test dial-up** icon, and confirm that it dials correctly. Describe what happens.

PROJECT 19-3: **Using a Browser Help Utility**

Using your browser's help utility, print instructions for changing the size of the browser cache and cleaning out the cache.

PROJECT 19-4: **Solving Browser Problems**

Follow these instructions to solve problems with Netscape Navigator:

1. List the steps to access the Netscape Web site and search for information about a problem. Search the site for information about Error 403.6, IP Restriction error. Print any information you find about the error.

2. Print the Netscape Web site page that allows you to use SmartUpdate to download the latest fixes for Netscape Navigator. Download the update and apply it to your browser.

3. Perform the procedures to clean out the browser cache.

Now do the same three steps for Microsoft Internet Explorer:

1. List the steps to access the Microsoft Web site and search for information about a problem. Search the site for information about Error 403.6, IP Restriction error. Print any information you find about the error.

2. Print the Microsoft Web site page that allows you to use the Update wizard to download the latest fixes for Internet Explorer. Download the update and apply it to your browser.

3. Perform the procedures discussed in the chapter to clean out the browser cache.

19

PROJECT 19-5: Using Web Accessories for Internet Explorer

Using the instructions in the chapter, download and install Web Accessories for Internet Explorer. Use the tool to display and print the links on the Web page *www.foxnews.com*.

PROJECT 19-6: Using FTP

Practice using FTP by downloading the latest version of Netscape, a Web browser. Do the following:

1. Using your current browser as an FTP client, locate the latest version of Netscape at the Netscape FTP site (*ftp.netscape.com*) and download it to your PC.

2. Repeat the process to download Netscape, this time using FTP commands from a command prompt window.

20

Notebooks, Tablet PCs, and PDAs

In this chapter, you will learn:

- How to support, upgrade, and add peripheral devices to notebooks
- About technologies relating to personal digital assistants (PDAs)

So far in this book, you've learned how computers work, explored some of the devices used to work with them, examined operating systems, and discovered how to connect a PC to a network. Most devices and software you've learned about relate to desktop computers, which are stationary and cannot be moved easily. This chapter covers three types of devices that are more portable: notebook computers, tablet PCs, and personal digital assistants (PDAs). As a PC technician, you must be familiar with these devices and aware of specific concerns when supporting them.

NOTE For more information about supporting notebooks than is presented in this chapter, see Appendix H.

VIDEO

Trouble-shooting Notebooks

Notebook Computers

A **notebook** or **laptop computer** is a computer designed to be portable (see Figure 20-1). Notebooks use the same technology as PCs but with modifications to use less power, consume less space, and operate on the move. This section discusses the special needs of supporting notebooks and shows how to add memory to a notebook, add peripheral devices, and find online resources for notebook support.

Figure 20-1 A notebook is a computer designed for portability

Notebooks and their replacement parts cost more than desktop PCs with similar features, because their components are designed to be more compact. They use thin LCD panels instead of CRT monitors for display, compact hard drives, and small memory modules and CPUs that require less power than regular components. Recall that LCD monitors, including notebook LCD panels, use several different technologies and that active matrix (sometimes called thin film transistor or TFT) technology generally gives better quality than does passive matrix (sometimes called dual-scan twisted nematic or DSTN) technology.

The types and features of notebooks vary widely, as they do for PCs. However, notebooks are generally purchased as a whole unit that includes both hardware and software, and you are not as likely to upgrade the hardware and OS on a notebook as you might for a desktop PC. In fact, some notebook manufacturers refuse to support a notebook that has had the OS upgraded or new hardware components added. When supporting any notebook, pay careful attention to the stipulations on the warranty that accompanies it. Some warranties are voided if you open the notebook case or install memory, batteries, or a hard drive that was not made by, or at least authorized by, the notebook's manufacturer.

In contrast, most desktop PCs are designed to be highly modular, letting you easily interchange, upgrade, and enhance components. In fact, PCs are often assembled from components purchased from various vendors and manufacturers. Notebook computers' design, on the other hand, can be very proprietary, which means that many of the skills needed to support them are brand-specific. In this section, we'll look at a few universal support issues, but remember that procedures can vary from one notebook brand to another.

Windows Notebook Features

Windows 2000/XP and Windows 98 include several features that can be useful when supporting notebooks:

- *Multilink Channel Aggregation,* a feature that allows you to use two modem connections at the same time to speed up data throughput when connected over phone lines. It works on both regular analog phone lines and ISDN. To use the feature, you must have two phone lines and two modem cards that are physically designed to connect two phone lines at the same time.
- *ACPI (Advanced Configuration and Power Interface),* developed by Intel, Microsoft, and Toshiba to control power on notebooks and other devices. ACPI allows a device to turn on a notebook or allows a notebook to turn on a device. For example, if you connect an external CD-ROM drive to the notebook, it can turn on the notebook, or the notebook can cycle up and turn on an external CD-ROM drive. The BIOS of the notebook and the device must support ACPI for it to work.
- *Power management,* including automatically powering down a PC Card when it is not in use, support for multiple battery packs, and individual power profiles. Power profiles are described in the next section.
- *Support for PC Cards,* including many Windows drivers for PC Card devices.
- *Windows 9x/Me Briefcase.* When returning from a trip with a notebook, you might want to update your desktop PC with all e-mail documents and other files created or updated during the trip. To do this, use Windows 9x/Me **Briefcase,** a system folder used to synchronize files between two computers. Briefcase automatically updates files on the original computer to the most recent version. You can use a null modem cable, disk, or network for the file transfer.
- *Windows 2000/XP Offline Files and Folders,* which replaces Windows 9x/Me Briefcase, stores shared network files and folders in a cache on the notebook hard drive so you can use them offline. When you reconnect to the network, Offline Files and Folders synchronizes the files in the cache with those on the network.
- *Folder redirection under Windows 2000/XP* lets you point to an alternate location on a network for a folder. This feature can make the location of a folder transparent to the user. For example, a user's My Documents folder is normally located on the local computer's logical drive C. Using folder redirection, an

20

administrator can put this My Documents folder on a file server. Having this folder on a shared file server has two important benefits:

- Regardless of which computer a user logs on, her My Documents folder is available.
- A company routinely backs up data on a shared file server so backing up the user's data happens without her having to do anything.

When using folder redirection with Offline Files and Folders, a user can access her My Documents folder even when the notebook is not attached to the company network.

- *Hardware profiles under Windows 2000/XP* let you specify which devices are to be loaded on startup for a particular user or set of circumstances. For example, you might set two different hardware profiles for a notebook computer, one for when it is on the road and one for when it is at home connected to a home network.

To create a hardware profile in Windows 2000/XP for a mobile user:

1. From the **Start** menu, open the **Control Panel.**

2. Double-click the **System** icon. (In Category View, click **Performance and Maintenance** and then click **System.**)

3. The System Properties dialog box opens. Click the **Hardware** tab.

4. Click the **Hardware Profiles** button at the bottom of the Hardware tab. The Hardware Profiles dialog box opens (Figure 20-2).

5. Select a profile from the list of available hardware profiles and then click the **Copy** button.

6. Type a new name for the profile, and then click **OK.**

7. Under *When Windows starts*, select either the option for Windows 2000/XP to wait for you to select a hardware profile or the option for Windows 2000/XP to start with the first profile listed if you don't select one in the specified number of seconds. Close all open windows.

8. Restart the computer and, when prompted, select the new hardware profile.

9. Open the **System Properties** dialog box. Click the **Hardware** tab, click **Device Manager,** and then double-click the icon for a device that you want enabled or disabled in the new profile.

10. Click the **General** tab in the Properties dialog box for the device and in the area for Device usage, select the option to enable the device, and disable it for the current profile or for all hardware profiles. Close all open dialog boxes.

Figure 20-2 Windows XP allows you to set a hardware profile for different hardware configurations

Caring for Notebooks

A notebook's user manual gives specific instructions on how to care for the notebook. Generally, however, observe the following guidelines:

- LCD panels on notebooks are fragile and can be damaged fairly easily. Take precautions against damaging a notebook's LCD panel.
- Don't connect the notebook to a phone line during an electrical storm.
- Run antivirus software and always keep the software current.
- When connected directly to the Internet, for Windows XP or Windows Me, turn on Internet Connection Firewall.
- Only use battery packs recommended by the notebook manufacturer. Keep the battery pack away from moisture or heat, and don't attempt to take the pack apart. When it no longer works, dispose of it correctly. Chapter 24 covers how to dispose of batteries. Things to do to prolong the life of your battery are discussed in the following section.
- Use an administrator password to protect the system from unauthorized entry, especially if you are connected to a network.
- Don't tightly pack the notebook in a suitcase because the LCD panel might get damaged. Use a good-quality carrying case.
- Don't pick up or hold the notebook by the display panel. Pick it up and hold it by the bottom.
- Don't move the notebook while the hard drive is being accessed (the drive indicator light is on). Wait until the light goes off.

20

■ Don't put the notebook close to an appliance such as a TV, large audio speakers, or refrigerator that generates a strong magnetic field.

■ Don't place your cell phone on a notebook while the phone is in use.

■ As with any computer, keep the OS current with the latest Windows updates.

Power Management

**A+
CORE
1.3**

A notebook can be powered in several ways including an AC adapter (to use regular house current to power the notebook), a DC adapter (to use DC power such as that provided by automobile cigarette lighters), and a battery pack. Types of batteries include the older and mostly outdated Ni-Cad (nickel-cadmium) battery, the longer-life NiMH (nickel-metal-hydride) battery, and the current Lithium Ion battery that is more efficient than earlier batteries. A future battery solution is a fuel cell battery, technically called a Direct Methanol Fuel Cell (DMFC) battery. A DMFC initially provides up to five hours of battery life, and future versions will provide up to 10 hours of battery life. A notebook user might need one or more batteries and a DC adapter for travel and an AC adapter at home and for recharging the batteries.

✔ **A+ EXAM TIP**

The A+ Core exam expects you to know the three ways a notebook can be powered: battery, DC adapter, and AC adapter. Also be familiar with these types of batteries: Lithium ion, NiMH, and fuel cell.

Here are some general do's and don'ts for switching power sources and protecting the battery, which apply to most notebooks. See a notebook's user manual for specific instructions.

■ Don't recharge the battery pack until all the power is used. Recharging too soon can shorten the battery life.

■ When you're recharging it, don't use the battery until it's fully recharged.

■ If you're not using the notebook for a long time, remove the battery from the notebook.

■ Use power management features of your OS, which are covered next. While working with your notebook, you can dim the LCD panel to conserve battery power.

■ While working with your notebook and using the battery, if you get a message that the battery is low, you can immediately plug in the AC or DC adapter without first powering down your notebook.

■ To extend the life of your battery, some manufacturers recommend that you don't leave the battery in the notebook while the notebook is turned on and connected to an electrical outlet.

■ To recharge the battery, leave the notebook turned off while it is connected to an electrical outlet with the battery inserted.

Windows 2000/XP and Windows 9x/Me have features to help manage power consumption. The goal is to minimize power consumption to increase the time before a battery pack needs recharging. Instructions are given for Windows 2000/XP, but Windows 9x/Me works about the same way.

To access the Power Management dialog box using Windows 2000/XP, open the Control Panel, and double-click the Power Options applet (in Windows 9x/Me, the

**A+
CORE
1.3**

applet is named Power Management). Figure 20-3 shows the Power Options Properties dialog box for one Windows 2000 notebook. (A different brand of notebook might have different tabs in its Properties dialog box.) Use this dialog box to create, delete, and modify multiple power management schemes to customize how Windows 2000/XP manages power consumption.

Figure 20-3 The Power Options Properties dialog box of Windows 2000/XP allows you to create and manage multiple power schemes

For example, one power-saving feature of Windows 2000/XP and Windows 9x puts a notebook into **hibernation**. When a computer hibernates, it stores whatever is currently in memory and then shuts down. When it returns from hibernating, it restores everything to the way it was before the shutdown. When hibernating, the notebook uses a very small amount of power. When you step away from the notebook for a few minutes, you can save power by directing the notebook to hibernate. Before you direct a notebook to hibernate, make sure you know the keystrokes or buttons required to restore the system to an active state without turning off the computer.

20

If the notebook supports hibernating, to configure Windows 2000/XP to cause the notebook to hibernate when you close the lid of the notebook, do the following:

1. In the Power Options Properties dialog box, click the **Hibernate** tab (see Figure 20-4), and verify that hibernate support is enabled. If there is no Hibernate tab, your notebook does not support hibernating.

2. Click the **Advanced** tab. Figure 20-5 shows the Advanced page, which you use to control what happens when you press the shutdown button or close the lid of the notebook.

Figure 20-4   Verify that hibernate support is enabled

3. Click the **When I close the lid of my portable computer** list arrow and select **Hibernate** (see Figure 20-6).

4. Click **Apply** and then click **OK** to close the Power Options dialog box and save your changes.

If you need to use the notebook for extended periods away from an electrical outlet, you can use extra battery packs. When the notebook signals that power is low, remove the old battery and replace it with a charged one. See the notebook's user

A+
CORE
1.3

guide for directions. Here is an example of directions for exchanging the battery pack for one notebook:

1. Save your work and turn off the notebook.

2. Remove all cables connected to the notebook.

3. Set the notebook on its back.

4. Slide the battery release panel to the left to expose the battery, as shown in Figure 20-7.

5. Lift the battery out of the computer.

6. Before placing a new battery in the slot, clean the edge connectors of the battery with a clean cloth.

Figure 20-5 The Advanced tab of the Power Options Properties dialog box allows you to control the behavior of the power button and what happens when you close the lid of your notebook

20

A+
CORE
1.3

Figure 20-6   Choices of action when you close the lid of your notebook

Figure 20-7   Slide the battery release panel to the left to expose the battery pack

A+
CORE
1.3

VIDEO

Notebook
Battery Packs

Using Windows 2000/XP, you can monitor and manage batteries on notebooks that are ACPI- and APM-enabled. You can access the battery meter directly by adding the battery status icon to the taskbar. Follow these steps:

1. From the **Start** menu, open the **Control Panel**.

2. Double-click **Power Options** to open the Power Options Properties dialog box.

3. Click the **Advanced** tab.

4. Click the **Always show icon on the taskbar** check box (refer back to Figure 20-6), and then click **OK**.

Note that the Power Options Properties dialog box also offers tabs on which you can set alarms to alert you when battery power is low or critical.

Connecting Peripheral Devices to Notebooks

A notebook provides ports on its back or sides (see Figure 20-8), which are used for connecting peripherals. In addition to the ports labeled in Figure 20-8, a notebook might have these slots, switches, and ports, several of which are discussed next:

Power jack for AC adapter

RJ-11 port for phone line

PS/2 port

VGA port

Security keyhole

Parallel port

Two USB ports

RJ-45 port for network

Figure 20-8   Ports on the back of a notebook

20

- PC Card slot with lock switch and eject button
- Headphone jack
- Microphone jack
- Infrared port
- Secure Digital (SD) card slot

**A+
CORE
1.3**

- CompactFlash Card slot
- Wireless antenna on/off switch
- Serial port

Port Replicator

Some notebooks have a connector on the bottom of the notebook to connect to a port replicator, such as the one shown in Figure 20-9, or a docking station, shown in Figure 20-10. A **port replicator** provides a means to connect a notebook to a power outlet and provides additional ports to allow a notebook to easily connect to a full-sized monitor, keyboard, and other peripheral devices. A **docking station** provides the same functions as a port replicator, but also adds secondary storage, such as a Zip drive or floppy disk drive.

IBM ThinkPad notebook computer

Port replicator

Figure 20-9 A port replicator makes it convenient to connect a notebook computer to resources and peripherals at your office

Figure 20-10 An IBM ThinkPad dock, an example of a docking station

USB ports have become a popular way of adding devices to notebooks. For example, if the notebook does not have an RJ-45 port for an Ethernet connection, you can buy a device that plugs into the USB port and provides the Ethernet port. Another example shown in Figure 20-11 involves a wireless keyboard and mouse that use a

**A+
CORE
1.3**

receiver connected to a USB or PS/2 port. Installing this keyboard and mouse on a Windows 2000/XP notebook is very simple. You plug the receiver into the port. Windows displays a message that it has located the device, and the mouse and keyboard are ready to use. This ease of installation is quickly making USB the preferred method of connecting peripheral devices.

Keyboard PS/2 connector

USB connector

Figure 20-11 This wireless keyboard and mouse by Logitech use a receiver that connects to either a USB or keyboard port

PC Card Slots and Other Proprietary Slots

Another popular way to add peripheral devices to a notebook is to use **PC Cards**, also called **PCMCIA (Personal Computer Memory Card International Association) Cards** in **PC Card slots** (see Figure 20-12), formally called **PCMCIA slots**. A PC Card is about the size of a credit card, but thicker, and inserts into a PC Card slot. Once intended only for memory cards, PC Card slots can now be used by many devices, including modems, network cards for wired or wireless networks, CD-ROMs, sound cards, SCSI host adapters, IEEE 1394 controllers, USB controllers, and hard disks. Unlike PCs, notebooks don't have the traditional expansion slots that connect to an I/O bus to add peripheral devices to a system. In notebooks, PC Card slots connect to the 16-bit PCMCIA I/O bus on the notebook motherboard. Some docking station PCs also have a PC Card slot, so that the device you use with your notebook can also be attached to the docking station.

 A+ EXAM TIP

The A+ Core exam expects you to know about matching Type I, II, and III PCMCIA cards to the appropriate PCMCIA slot.

The PCMCIA organization has developed four standards for these slots. The latest PCMCIA specification, **CardBus**, improves I/O speed, increases the bus width to 32 bits, and supports lower-voltage PC Cards while maintaining backward compatibility with earlier standards. Three standards for PCMCIA slots pertain to size and are named Type I, Type II, and Type III. Generally, the thicker the PC Card, the higher the standard. A thick hard drive card might need a Type III slot, but a thin modem card might only need a Type II slot.

20

Type I cards can be up to 3.3-mm thick and are primarily used for adding RAM to a notebook PC. Type II cards can be up to 5.5-mm thick and are often used as modem cards. Type III cards can be up to 10.5-mm thick, large enough to accommodate a portable disk drive. When buying a notebook PC, look for both Type II and Type III PC Card slots. Often, one of each is included. For improved performance, look for 32-bit CardBus slots.

Figure 20-12 Many peripheral devices are added to a notebook using a PC Card slot; here, a modem PC Card is inserted in a PC Card slot

A PC Card might contain a data cable to an external device, or it might be self-contained. For example, in Figure 20-13, the PC Card on the left is the interface between the notebook PC and an external CD-ROM drive. The card is inserted in the PC Card slot, and the data cable from the PC Card connects to the external CD-ROM drive, which requires its own power supply connected to a wall outlet. The PC Card on the right in Figure 20-13 is a modem card; when inserted in the PC Card slot, it provides a direct connection for the telephone line to the modem (see Figure 20-14).

Another use of a PC Card is to interface with a network. Figure 20-15 shows a PC Card that serves as the NIC to an Ethernet 100BaseT network. The RJ-45 connection is at the end of a small cord connected to the PC Card. This small cord is called a dongle or pigtail and is used so that the thick RJ-45 connection does not have to fit flat against the PC Card.

Some proprietary slots used on notebooks include a slot for a Secure Digital (SD) Card and a slot for a CompactFlash Card. Both cards are not much larger than a postage stamp. These slots are used primarily for flash memory but can also be used for other devices. For example, in Chapter 11, you saw the IBM Microdrive, a miniature 1-GB hard drive that is useful for storing multimedia files, which uses a CompactFlash Type II slot.

Figure 20-13 Two examples of PC Cards, one self-contained (the modem), the other connected to an external device (the CD-ROM drive)

Figure 20-14 Connect the phone line to the modem PC Card

There are several flash memory products on the market, including CompactFlash Type I and II, SmartMedia (introduced in Chapter 11), Secure Digital (SD), Memory Stick, and MagicGate. These flash cards can be used in sockets designed specifically for them or you can purchase adapter sleeves that enable the cards to use a PC Card slot. The card must be PCMCIA compliant.

Flash cards and PC Cards can also be read by desktop computers when the card is inserted in a card reader that can handle the specific format. For example, one card reader is the SwapBox PC Card Reader by SCM Microsystems (*www.scmmicro.com*). The card reader interfaces with a desktop computer by way of an ISA or PCI slot. PC Cards, such as a modem card or Ethernet card, can be inserted in the reader, which can handle Type I, II, and III PC Cards. In addition, when used with adapter

20

sleeves, the SwapBox can accept other PCMCIA-compliant cards, such as Smart-Media and CompactFlash cards.

Dongle or pigtail

RJ-45 connection

PC Card

Figure 20-15   This PC Card serves as a NIC for an Ethernet 100BaseT network

Using PC Card Slots and Other Slots

The operating system must provide two services for a PC Card or another type proprietary card: a socket service, and a card service. The socket service establishes communication between the card and the notebook when the card is first inserted, and then disconnects communication when the card is removed. The card service provides the device driver to interface with the card once the socket is created.

PC Cards and some other proprietary cards can be hot-swapped, but you must stop, or unplug, one card before inserting another. Hot-swapping allows you to remove one card and insert another without powering down the PC. For example, if you currently use a wireless network card in the PC Card slot of a Windows 2000 notebook and want to switch to a CD-ROM card, first turn off the network card, remove the network card, and then insert the CD-ROM card with the attached external CD-ROM drive. For Windows 2000, to stop the card, use the Add/Remove Hardware icon in the Control Panel. The Add/Remove Hardware Wizard starts; click Next, and select Uninstall/Unplug a device in the next dialog box. Click Next, and then select Unplug/Eject a device in the next dialog box. A list of devices appears (see Figure 20-16). Select the device and click Next. The final window tells you that you can safely unplug the device and gives you the option to display an Unplug/Eject icon in the taskbar when the device is used again.

NOTE

A bug in Windows XP causes the system to hang if you remove a PC Card while the system is in sleep mode or is hibernating. To solve the problem, download the latest service pack for Windows XP.

In Windows XP, use the Safely Remove Hardware icon in the system tray to stop a card, and for Windows 9x/Me, use the PC Card icon in the Control Panel.

**A+
CORE
1.3**

Figure 20-16 Before removing a PC Card from the notebook, stop the card (open the socket)

The first time you insert a PC Card in a notebook, the Found New Hardware Wizard starts and guides you through the installation steps in which you can use the drivers provided by the hardware manufacturer or use Windows drivers. The next time you insert the card in the notebook, the card is detected and starts without help.

If you are having problems getting a notebook to recognize a PC Card, try the following:

- Make sure the system is on and not in hibernation or standby mode when you insert the card.
- When you first insert a card and the notebook does not recognize it, the slot might be disabled in CMOS setup. Reboot the notebook and enter the CMOS setup program. Look for the feature to enable or disable a PC Card slot or other slot on the Power Management screen or an Advanced Settings screen.
- In Device Manager, verify the PCMCIA or PC Card controller is functioning correctly with no errors. You can update the controller drivers; be sure to use drivers provided by the notebook manufacturer. Check the driver CD that came bundled with the notebook.
- A program, such as antivirus software, might be interfering with the Card Services program. Try disabling any software not certified for your OS by Microsoft.
- Try installing the card's drivers before you insert the card. Look for a setup program on the manufacturer's CD bundled with the card.

20

Upgrading Memory

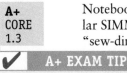

A+
CORE
1.3

Notebooks use four types of memory (see Figure 20-17) that are all smaller than regular SIMMs, DIMMs, or RIMMs. **SO-DIMMs** (**small outline DIMMs,** pronounced "sew-dims") come in three types. 72-pin SO-DIMMs, which support 32-bit data transfers, use FPM or EDO (which you learned about in Chapter 6), and could be used as single modules in 386 or 486 machines but must be used in pairs in Pentium machines. 144-pin SO-DIMMs, which support 64-bit data transfers, use EDO and SDRAM and can be used as single modules in Pentium machines. 200-pin SO-DIMMs are 2.625 inches wide and contain DDR SDRAM. They have a single notch offset from the middle of the module. Another type of memory for notebooks is the 160-pin **SO-RIMM** (**small outline RIMM**), which uses a 64-bit data path and the Rambus technology discussed in Chapter 6. Also, before notebooks used memory modules, some notebooks used memory stored on a small card the size of a credit card. This **credit card memory** was installed in a special memory slot. Sub-notebooks sometimes use 144-pin **MicroDIMMs** that are smaller than SO-DIMMs and have a 64-bit data path.

VIDEO

Upgrading
Memory on a
Notebook

2.35" 72–pin SO–DIMM   2.66" 144–pin SO–DIMM

160–pin SO–RIMM

Credit card memory

Figure 20-17   Four types of memory used on notebook computers

CAUTION

Before upgrading memory, make sure you are not voiding your warranty. Search for the best buy, but make sure you use memory modules made by or authorized by your notebook's manufacturer and designed for the exact model of your notebook. Installing generic memory might save money but might also void the notebook's warranty.

A+ EXAM TIP

The A+ Core exam expects you to be familiar with SO-DIMM and MicroDIMM modules used on laptops.

A+
CORE
1.3

APPLYING CONCEPTS

To install memory, most often all you do is remove a small cover on the bottom of the notebook to expose the memory module to replace it. The following example of installing memory on a notebook is more complicated. Always check the notebook user guide for specific directions.

1. Turn off the notebook and remove all cables.
2. Lift the keyboard brace, as shown in Figure 20-18. (Your notebook might have a different way to enter the system, such as from the bottom of the case.)

Figure 20-18 Lift the keyboard brace

3. Turn the keyboard over and toward the front of the notebook (see Figure 20-19). The keyboard is still connected to the notebook by the ribbon cable.
4. Lift the plastic sheet covering the memory module socket.
5. Insert the SO-DIMM module into the socket. See Figure 20-20. The socket braces should snap into place on each side of the module when the module is in position.
6. Replace the keyboard and keyboard brace. (If you entered from the bottom, you might be replacing a cover on the bottom of the case in this step.)
7. Power up the notebook so that it can detect the new memory.

20

Ribbon cable connecting
keyboard to notebook

Figure 20-19   Turn the keyboard over toward the front of the notebook to expose the
memory module socket

Figure 20-20   Install the SO-DIMM into the memory socket

Other Field Replaceable Units for Notebooks

Be cautious about working inside a notebook. If the notebook is under warranty,
sometimes only an authorized technician can open the notebook case without voiding
the warranty. Also, many notebooks require specialized tools to open the case (case
crackers) or odd-sized torx screwdrivers. Internal cables and connectors are much
smaller than those of desktop PCs and more easily bent or broken. Notebook

A+
CORE
1.3

cables and parts are proprietary and very few models are alike. Other than a simple memory upgrade, a PC technician needs extra patience and training to work inside a notebook.

Besides memory, other field replaceable units (FRUs) for notebooks might be the hard drive, the LCD panel, the motherboard, the CPU, the keyboard, the PC Card socket assembly, the optical drive (CD or DVD drive), the floppy drive, a sound card, a pointing device, the AC adapter, the battery pack, and the DC controller. Parts either made or approved by the notebook manufacturer must be used to replace all these parts. The **DC controller** is a card inside the notebook that converts voltage to CPU core voltage. The DC controller can support battery mode, AC adapter mode, and various sleep modes, and must be specifically rated for the notebook's processor.

A hard drive for a notebook computer can be an external or internal drive. External devices, including hard drives, connect to ports on the notebook or to a port provided by a PC Card. Internal notebook drives are much smaller than desktop drives; for a comparison, see Figure 20-21. When installing an internal hard drive, floppy drive, CD/CD-RW drive, DVD/DVD-RW drive, or removable drive, follow specific directions given by the notebook's manufacturer. For example, to replace the hard drive for the notebook shown in Figure 20-22, first remove the floppy disk drive to reveal the hard drive under it. Remove the screws holding the hard drive in place, remove the drive, and replace it with a drive designed to fit this particular cavity.

Hard drive for a desktop computer

Hard drive for a notebook

Figure 20-21   Hard drives for notebooks are smaller than hard drives for desktop computers

A notebook does not contain the normal PCI Express, PCI, and ISA expansion slots found in desktop systems. Most internal cards such as modems, SCSI host adapters, IEEE 1394 controllers, USB controllers, and network adapters use proprietary slots designed and supported by the notebook manufacturer. It is expected that the notebook industry will soon embrace a more standard method of connecting an internal card to a notebook using the **Mini PCI** specifications, which is the PCI industry standard for desktop computer expansion cards, but applied to a much smaller form

20

factor for notebook expansion cards. It is expected that when the standard gains widespread acceptance, internal cards for notebooks no longer will be so proprietary, thus reducing their cost.

The standards include three types of cards—Type I, II, and III—that specify how the internal card provides a port on the notebook and how the card connects to the motherboard. Type I and II cards connect to the motherboard using a 100-pin stacking connector, and Type III cards use a 124-pin stacking connector and are smaller than the Type I and II cards and are expected to be the most popular. Figure 20-23 shows an example of a Mini-PCI card that you install inside a notebook to provide wireless connectivity.

Bottom of notebook

Floppy drive

Hard drive

Figure 20-22   First remove the floppy drive to reveal the hard drive cavity

Figure 20-23   This Cisco 802.11b wireless internal adapter is a Type III Mini-PCI card made by IBM

Online Resources for Troubleshooting Notebooks

**A+
CORE
1.3**

Except for the differences discussed in this section, notebooks work identically to desktop PCs, and the troubleshooting guidelines in previous chapters also apply to notebooks. When troubleshooting notebooks, be especially conscious of warranty issues; know what you can do within the guidelines of the warranty. The documentation that comes with a notebook is much more comprehensive than what comes with a PC and most often contains troubleshooting guidelines for the notebook. Remember that the loaded OS and the hardware configuration are specific to the notebook, so you can rely on the notebook's manufacturer for support more than you can for a desktop PC. Support CDs that come bundled with a notebook include device drivers for all embedded devices. You can also download additional or updated drivers from the notebook manufacturer's Web site.

Sometimes a notebook is designed so that the hard drive can be replaced or upgraded without violating warranties. See the notebook documentation for details. For questions about supporting a notebook that are not answered in the documentation, see the notebook manufacturer's Web site. Some popular manufacturers of notebooks and their Web sites are listed at the end of this section.

Tablet PCs

A tablet PC is a type of notebook computer that is designed for users who require a more graphical, user-friendly interface and need more portability than a full-size notebook allows. A tablet PC is a cross between a notebook computer and a pad and pencil. It costs about the same or more than a notebook, but is smaller, more portable, and provides many of the same features of a notebook plus lets you use a digital pen or stylus to write handwritten text on the LCD panel, which also serves as a touch screen. See Figure 20-24.

There are three tablet PC form factors:

- A convertible tablet PC looks like a regular clamshell notebook with LCD monitor and keyboard. To convert to a slate-top tablet PC, rotate the LCD panel 180 degrees and lay the back of the LCD panel flat against the bottom of the notebook. See Figure 20-25.
- A slate model tablet PC such as the one shown in Figure 20-24 is slimmer and lighter than a notebook. It can easily dock to a desktop so you can use a regular monitor, mouse, and keyboard.
- A tablet PC with a docking station offers some interesting variations such as a grab-and-go docking station that lets you dock or undock your tablet PC without having to power down. (Microsoft calls this feature Surprise Hot Docking.) Another type of docking station has dual-monitor support, which uses a regular monitor for some open applications while others are shown on the tablet PC's LCD panel.

20

Figure 20-24   Tablet PC

Figure 20-25   Acer TMC 110 tablet PC

Using a digital pen, a user can write on the LCD panel/touch screen pad, comfortably resting her hand on it because the pad only picks up data written by the digital pen. Handwriting-recognition software interprets handwriting and can import it into Word documents, Excel spreadsheets, PowerPoint presentations, and other application files. Tablet PCs use Microsoft Windows XP Tablet PC Edition, which is

Windows XP Professional with additional features included, such as voice recognition and handwriting-recognition software. Features of a tablet PC include:

- A functioning Windows XP computer with the power of a full-sized notebook
- On-screen writing ability for handwritten notes and drawings
- Voice recognition and handwriting-recognition software that can import interpreted text into Word documents, Excel spreadsheets, and other application files
- Ability to record handwritten notes on top of other files such as a handwritten note written on a PowerPoint presentation or photograph (see Figure 20-26)

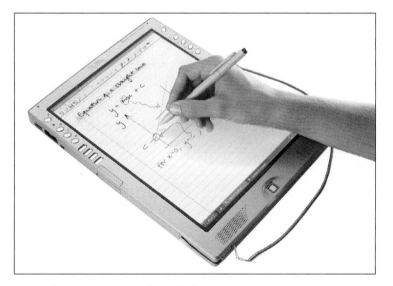

Figure 20-26   Handwritten note on a tablet PC document

- Built-in support for wireless, wired, and dial-up networking
- AC power adapter and rechargeable battery
- Windows XP Tablet PC Edition
- PC Card, USB ports, and VGA port for peripheral devices
- Hardware keyboard or onscreen software keyboard
- Accessories might include extra batteries, portfolio-style case, additional flash memory, screen protector, extra digital pens, or wireless keyboard

Because a tablet PC uses Windows XP Tablet PC Edition operating system, which is an extension of Windows XP Professional, an application written for Windows XP Professional should have no problem working on a tablet PC. Also, many industries have software written specifically for the tablet PC, including real estate, legal, architecture, and medicine. An example of an application written specifically for a tablet PC is OmniForm Filler Solution for the Tablet PC by ScanSoft (*www.scansoft.com*) that uses the handwriting-recognition abilities built into Windows XP Tablet PC

20

Edition to provide the ability to check boxes and radio buttons, select from drop-down lists, and add digital photographs or drawings to forms.

Table 20-1 lists manufacturers of notebooks and tablet PCs.

Manufacturer	Web Site
Acer America	*global.acer.com*
Apple Computer	*www.apple.com*
Compaq Computer	*www.hp.com*
Dell Computer	*www.dell.com*
Gateway	*www.gateway.com*
Hewlett-Packard	*www.hp.com*
IBM	*www.ibm.com*
Micron PC	*www.micronpc.com*
NEC	*www.nec.com*
PC Notebook	*www.pcnotebook.com*
Sony	*www.sonystyle.com*
Toshiba America	*www.csd.toshiba.com*
VIA Technologies	*www.via.com.tw*
ViewSonic	*www.viewsonic.com*
WinBook	*www.winbook.com*

Table 20-1 Notebook and tablet PC manufacturers

APPLYING CONCEPTS

As a PC support technician, many times you are called on to help people make good purchasing decisions. Choosing among a notebook, tablet PC, and PDA is most often a function of a user's lifestyle and job description. Here is a good example of a user finding just the right product to fit her needs.

Lacey is a successful real estate agent in a resort town on the Atlantic coast. She has many clients who live in distant cities and often works with these clients in long-distance relationships. Lacey tried to use a notebook computer, but found it awkward to carry a notebook when viewing real estate and working out of her car. She got frustrated with her notebook and sold it at an online auction Web site. Next, she tried using a PDA to track her clients and real estate listings, but the small screen also frustrated her. Then she came across an ad for a tablet PC and bought one. During the first week she owned the tablet PC, she was looking for a beach house for a client who lived in Oklahoma. She found just the right property, but it needed a lot of renovation. She took pictures with her digital camera and uploaded these to her tablet PC. Then she wrote several handwritten notes across each photograph pointing out problems that needed correcting and her ideas for renovation. She e-mailed the entire proposal to her client and made the sale!

Now Lacey has imported into her tablet PC all the forms necessary for a client to list or make an offer on a property. Clients can fill out these forms by hand on her tablet PC while on site, and Lacey can later convert them to typed text before printing the forms for the client's signature. Lacey also says she can informally take notes at a client meeting on her tablet PC without the raised LCD panel of her old notebook computer standing stiffly between her and her client. She likes being able to appear professional, yet casual and friendly at the same time.

PDAs

Notebooks and tablet PCs provide portability or flexibility, but even the smallest can be cumbersome in some situations, especially for simple tasks such as checking addresses, viewing stock prices, or recording and receiving short messages. **PDAs (personal digital assistants)**, sometimes called personal PCs or handheld PCs, provide greater ease of use for such situations (see Figure 20-27). A PDA, such as a Palm Pilot or a Pocket PC, is a small, handheld computer with its own operating system and applications. A PDA connects to your desktop computer by way of a USB or serial connection and is powered using an AC adapter or battery.

Like a notebook, a PDA uses either a grayscale or color active matrix or dual-scan passive matrix display, and can sometimes benefit from additional memory. Other PDA hardware includes a stylus used to operate the PDA by touching the screen. You tap the screen with the stylus to open applications or make menu selections. You can also hold down the stylus to scroll through menu options. For quick access to commonly used applications such as a calendar or an address book, most PDAs provide application buttons below the screen that you can press to open the application. A PDA might use an AC/DC adapter that can plug into the PDA itself or into the universal cradle. Some PDAs have optional accessories such as the fold-out keyboard shown in Figure 20-27.

When purchasing a PDA, first decide how you will use it, and then match the features of the PDA to its intended purpose. Following are the main factors to consider when purchasing a PDA. The next sections cover several of these items.

20

- What applications come with the PDA, and what applications can be added later?
- How easy is the PDA to use, and how thorough is its documentation?
- How easy is it to keep the PDA synchronized with your desktop computer or notebook, and will your organization approve the type of PDA synchronization?

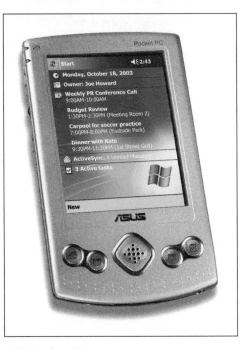

Figure 20-27   ASUS Pocket PC

Figure 20-28   This fold-out keyboard attaches to a PDA

- What support is available on the manufacturer's Web site? What software for the PDA can be downloaded from this site? What is the cost of that software?
- What type of batteries does the PDA use, and what is the battery life?
- Can the PDA use e-mail and the Web, and what extra hardware and software is required to do that?
- What additional devices can be purchased to make the PDA more versatile and easier to use?

- What operating system does the PDA use? How easy is the OS to use?
- What is the warranty? Does the warranty cover such things as dropping the PDA or damaging the LCD panel by pressing too hard on it?
- What is the price of the PDA, and what is the price of additional years of warranty?

Battery Life on a PDA

Battery life on a PDA varies by model, and short battery life is one of the largest complaints made about PDAs. Some PDAs use rechargeable batteries, and others do not. If your PDA's battery runs down all the way and discharges, you lose all the data and applications on the PDA! Many manufacturers suggest that you get in the habit of setting your PDA in its cradle whenever you are not carrying it, and that you never trust it with data or downloaded software for more than a few hours. It is a good idea to have a cradle and adapter wherever you use your PDA; you may want to keep one at your home, another at your office, and another in your briefcase.

Applications on a PDA

You can use a PDA to store addresses and phone numbers, manage a calendar, run word-processing software, send and receive e-mail, access Web sites, play music, and exchange information with a desktop computer. Some PDAs come with all application software preinstalled, and others require the user to download applications at additional cost. Other PDAs support only the preinstalled applications and cannot download others. Some PDAs allow you to download e-mail or Web site content from a desktop computer or a notebook, and others can access the Internet directly by way of a modem or wireless connection. Not all Web sites are designed to be accessed by a PDA, and the Web content a PDA can read is more limited than the content a desktop or notebook computer can read.

Connecting a PDA to a PC

Typically, a PDA comes with a universal cradle that has an attached cable to connect to a desktop computer or notebook by way of a serial or USB port, or a PDA might use an infrared connection. The process by which the PDA and the PC "talk" to each other through the universal cradle, cable, and USB or serial connection is called **synchronization**. This process enables you to back up information on your PDA to the PC, work with PDA files on the PC, and download applications to the PDA that you downloaded from the Web using the PC. Special software, such as ActiveSync by Microsoft, might be needed to synchronize a PDA and the other computer attached via the cable. You need to install this software before connecting the PDA to the PC.

20

Follow the instructions in the PDA documentation and on the CD included with it to install the software.

Some PDAs can also synchronize with a desktop or notebook computer through wireless technology. The ASUS PDA shown in Figure 20-27 supports the Bluetooth standard introduced in Chapter 18. For wireless synchronization to occur, both the PDA and the PC must be set up to use the same wireless standard (for example, Bluetooth, Wi-Fi, or 802.11a). The PC and the PDA must each have a wireless transmitter/receiver (transceiver) and software installed to use it. Some PDAs have an embedded transceiver, and others require an add-on device. Again, study the PDA documentation to learn if a PDA supports wireless technology.

To set up communication between a PDA and a PC, do the following:

- Read the PDA documentation about how to synchronize it with the PC and install on the PC the synchronization software that came bundled with the PDA. If the synchronization software must first be launched, launch it.
- Connect the PDA to the PC by way of a USB cable or serial cable that most likely also came bundled with the PDA.
- The PDA and PC should immediately synchronize. Data entered on one device should be reflected on the other.

If you have problems, check these things:

- Is the USB or serial cable plugged in at both ends?
- For a USB connection, verify the USB controller is working in Device Manager with no conflicts.
- Is the USB or serial port enabled in CMOS setup?
- Is the PDA turned on?
- Check the PDA documentation for other things to do and try.
- Uninstall and reinstall the PDA software on the PC.
- Check the Web site of the PDA manufacturer for problems and solutions.

PDA Manufacturers and Operating Systems

There are two main operating systems for PDAs: Windows Mobile by Microsoft (*www.microsoft.com*) and Palm OS by PalmSource (*www.palmsource.com*). Windows Mobile supports smart phones and PDAs. Earlier handheld OSs by Microsoft are Pocket PC and Windows CE. Given the prominence of Microsoft Windows in most markets it has entered, it is interesting to note that Palm OS and Windows Mobile have basically equal shares of the market for PDA OSs. The principal difference between the two OSs is in the applications they support. Windows Mobile 2003 for Pocket PC is considered a more versatile OS that can better be used to download and run applications similar to those supported by Windows, such as Microsoft Word or Excel. Palm OS is less complex, easier to use, and considered the better choice if the PDA is to be used only for simple tasks such as using email, an address book, or a calendar. Table 20-2 lists some manufacturers of PDAs running

Palm OS, and Table 20-3 lists some manufacturers of PDAs running
Windows Mobile.

Manufacturer	Web Site
Garmin	www.garmin.com
HandEra	www.handera.com
Handspring	web.palmone.com
IBM	www.ibm.com
Palm One	www.palmone.com
Samsung	www.samsung.com
Sony	www.sonystyle.com

Table 20-2   Manufacturers of Palm OS PDAs

Manufacturer	Web Site
ASUS	www.asus.com
Casio	www.casio.com
Compaq	www.hp.com
Hewlett-Packard	www.hp.com
Toshiba	www.toshiba.com

Table 20-3   Manufacturers of Windows Mobile PDAs

Hewlett-Packard sponsors a forum to promote open source software (programming code is made
public and no royalties are paid) to use the Linux operating system on handheld computers. For
more information, see www.handhelds.org.

20

CHAPTER SUMMARY

- Notebook computers are designed for travel. They use the same technology as PCs, with modifications for space, portability, and power conservation. A notebook generally costs more than a PC with the same specifications.

- When supporting notebooks, pay careful attention to what the warranty allows you to change on the computer.

- Windows supports Multilink Channel Aggregation so that a computer can use two phone lines to connect to the Internet to yield a faster connection.

- Other Windows support for notebooks includes support for ACPI power management, PC Card support, Windows 9x/Me Briefcase, and Windows 2000/XP Offline Files and folder redirection.

- Windows XP notebook support includes the ability to create hardware profiles and power schemes that manage the computer's attached devices and power settings differently, depending on whether the computer is connected to a port replicator or not.

- A notebook can be powered by its battery pack or by an AC or DC adapter connected to a power source.

- Notebooks use credit card memory, SO-DIMMs, and SO-RIMMs for upgrading memory.

- Upgrading memory on a notebook varies from one notebook to another; see the notebook's user guide for specific instructions.

- When upgrading components on a notebook, including memory, use components that are the same brand as the notebook, or use only components recommended by the notebook's manufacturer.

- PC Cards are a popular way to add peripheral devices to notebooks. The latest PC Card specification is CardBus. There are three types of PC Cards, which vary in thickness: Types I, II, and III.

- Notebook settings and procedures vary more widely from model to model than those of desktop computers. Check the manufacturer's documentation and Web site for information specific to your notebook model.

- A tablet PC is a notebook computer with a touch screen that can input handwritten notes, interpreting them as text.

- A tablet PC can be a convertible model or a slate model and can come with a docking station that supports surprise hot docking.

- Input on a tablet PC can be by handwriting, voice, keyboard, or an on-screen keyboard.

▶ A PDA provides even more portability than a notebook computer or tablet PC for applications such as address books and calendars. PDAs are designed to provide handheld computing power and can interface with a desktop or notebook computer to transfer files and applications.

▶ PDAs synchronize with PCs through a USB, serial, or wireless port. For wireless, check that the PC and PDA support the same wireless standard.

KEY TERMS

For explanations of key terms, see the Glossary near the end of the book.

Briefcase	laptop computer	PCMCIA slot
CardBus	MicroDIMM	PDA (Personal Digital Assistant)
credit card memory	Mini PCI	port replicator
DC controller	notebook	SO-DIMM (small outline DIMM)
docking station	PC Card	SO-RIMM (small outline RIMM)
folder redirection	PC Card slot	synchronization
hardware profiles	PCMCIA (Personal Computer Memory Card	
hibernation	International Association) Card	

REVIEWING THE BASICS

1. How are notebooks different from desktop PCs?

2. Why are notebooks usually more expensive than PCs with comparable power and features?

3. What Windows 98 feature allows a notebook user to synchronize files on a notebook and desktop computer?

4. What are four types of memory devices or modules used in a notebook?

5. What type of monitor does a notebook use?

6. What is the thickness of a Type I PC Card? Of a Type III PC Card?

7. What term refers to a PC Card you can remove and replace without powering off?

8. What two services must an OS provide for a PC Card to work?

9. What is the small cord sometimes found on the end of a PC Card called?

10. What applet in the Windows 2000 Control Panel do you use to stop a PC Card before removing it? In Windows 98?

20

11. How do you solve the problem when a Windows XP notebook hangs after a PC Card has been removed while the notebook was in sleep mode?

12. What type of SO-DIMM has 72 pins? 144 pins? 160 pins?

13. List 10 devices that a notebook manufacturer might consider to be field replaceable units.

14. Why is understanding the warranty on notebooks so important?

15. What is the purpose of a DC controller on a notebook?

16. What happens if the battery on your PDA discharges?

17. What are the two most popular operating systems currently used by PDAs?

18. What are the advantages of Palm OS over Windows Mobile?

19. What are the advantages of Windows Mobile over Palm OS?

20. List the ways that a PDA can synchronize with a PC.

THINKING CRITICALLY

1. Your friend has a Windows 98 notebook computer and has purchased Windows 2000 and installed it as an upgrade on his notebook. He calls to tell you about the upgrade and says that he cannot connect to the Internet. His notebook has an embedded modem that he uses for communication. What do you tell him to do?

   a. Reinstall Windows 98.

   b. Using another computer, download and install the Windows 2000 modem drivers from the notebook manufacturer's Web site.

   c. Search the CDs that come with the notebook for Windows 2000 modem drivers and install them.

   d. Perform a clean install of Windows 2000.

2. A friend asks you for help in determining the best product to buy: a notebook, tablet PC, or PDA. She is a paralegal and spends a lot of time at the courthouse researching real estate titles. She wants a device to take notes with as she works. List three questions you would ask her to help her make her decision.

HANDS-ON PROJECTS

PROJECT 20-1: Observing Notebook Features

Examine a notebook, its documentation, and the manufacturer's Web site, and then answer these questions:

1. How do you exchange the battery pack on the notebook?

2. What type of SO-DIMM or SO-RIMM does the notebook use?

3. How much memory is currently installed?

4. What is the capacity of the hard drive?

5. What OS is installed?

6. What processor is installed?

7. What ports are on the notebook?

8. How many PC Card slots does the notebook have?

9. How much does the notebook weigh?

10. What is the cost of a new battery pack?

11. Can you buy memory from the Web site? How much does it cost to upgrade the notebook's memory to full capacity?

PROJECT 20-2: Researching Wireless Notebook Systems

Use the Web for the following research:

1. Find a notebook that has integrated wireless technology. Print the Web page advertising the notebook.

2. Drill down to the detailed specifications for the notebook, and answer these questions:

    a. What type of wireless technology does the notebook support?

    b. Does the notebook have a built-in wireless access point, or is the wireless adapter an optional add-on? If the access point is built in, where is the antenna LED located on the notebook? If the adapter is optional, where is it installed?

    c. If the notebook requires you to buy additional devices in order to connect to a wireless network, what devices must you buy?

20

3. Suppose you have a PC with a USB port. Find a device that uses this USB port and provides a wireless access point for your notebook to connect to the PC. Make sure that the device is compatible with the notebook's wireless technology. Print a Web page about this device.

PROJECT 20-3: Researching PC Card Modems

Some employees in your company spend a lot of time on the road and, while traveling, need easy Internet access. Research how they can use a cellular phone to connect a notebook computer to the Internet. Using the Motorola Web site (*www.motorola.com*) or a similar site, do the following:

1. Print the Web page of a modem card or a USB device for a notebook computer that can accommodate a cellular phone connection.

2. Print the Web page of a cellular phone that can accommodate a modem card connection to a notebook.

3. Is the connection between the cellular phone and the notebook wireless or does it use a cable? If a cable is used, print the page that shows or describes the cable that connects the notebook to the cellular phone.

PROJECT 20-4: Researching PDAs

Select two different PDAs, one using Windows Mobile and one using Palm OS. (See Tables 20-2 and 20-3 for suggested manufacturers.) Using information from the Web site of the manufacturer of each PDA, write the following:

1. Short description of the features of the PDA including its model number

2. Price

3. Manufacturer

4. Type of battery and battery life

5. Ability for Web and e-mail access

6. Additional devices that can be purchased

7. Operating system

8. Built-in or bundled applications

9. Warranty

Supporting Printers

In this chapter, you will learn:

- How printers work
- How to install printers and share them over a local area network
- How to troubleshoot printer problems

This chapter discusses the three main types of printers, how they work, and how to support them. Printers connect to a PC by way of a parallel port, serial port, USB port, SCSI port, IEEE 1394 port, wireless connection (radio or infrared), or network connection. You'll also learn how to install a printer, how to share a printer with others on a network, and how to troubleshoot printer problems.

How Printers Work

**A+
CORE
5.1**

This section discusses how printers work, the various types of printers, and how to support them. Local printers connect directly to a computer by way of a parallel port, serial port, USB port, infrared connection, wireless connection, IEEE 1394 port, SCSI port, or PC Card connection, or a computer can access a network printer by way of the network. Printers can have a variety of options, including extra paper trays to hold different sizes of paper, special paper feeders, staplers, collators, and sorters. Printers can also be combined with fax machines, copiers, and scanners in the same machine. Most often, printers are powered by AC power, but some printers use batteries. Let's begin by looking at several types of printers for desktop computing.

NOTE

If you can afford it, the best practice is to purchase one machine for one purpose instead of bundling many functions into a single machine. For example, if you need a scanner and a printer, purchase a good printer and a good scanner rather than a combo machine. Routine maintenance and troubleshooting are easier and less expensive on single-purpose machines, although the initial cost is higher.

✔ **A+ EXAM TIP**

The A+ Core exam expects you to know that printers can connect using these interfaces: parallel, network, SCSI, USB, infrared, serial, IEEE 1394 (FireWire), and wireless.

There are two major categories of printers: impact printers and non-impact printers. An impact printer creates a printed page by using some mechanism that touches or hits the paper. An example of an impact printer is a dot-matrix printer. A non-impact printer does not use a mechanism to touch the page. Examples of non-impact printers are laser, inkjet (ink dispersion), solid ink, dye-sublimation, and thermal printers.

Laser Printers

✔ **A+ EXAM TIP**

The A+ Core exam expects you to be familiar with these types of printers: laser, ink dispersion, dot-matrix, solid ink, thermal, and dye-sublimation.

Laser printers are a type of electrophotographic printer that range from small, personal desktop models to large network printers capable of handling and printing large volumes continuously. Figure 21-1 shows an example of a typical laser printer for a desktop computer system.

Laser printers require the interaction of mechanical, electrical, and optical technologies to work. Understanding how they work will help you support and service them. This section also explains why the safety precautions stated in laser printer user manuals are necessary.

A+
CORE
5.1

Figure 21-1   A desktop laser printer

How a Laser Printer Works

Laser printers work by placing toner on an electrically charged rotating drum and then depositing the toner on paper as the paper moves through the system at the same speed the drum is turning. Figure 21-2 shows the six steps of laser printing. The first four use the printer components that undergo the most wear. These components are contained within the removable cartridge to increase the printer's life. The last two steps are performed outside the cartridge.

The six steps of laser printing are:

1. *Cleaning.* The drum is cleaned of any residual toner and electrical charge.

2. *Conditioning.* The drum is conditioned to contain a high electrical charge.

3. *Writing.* A laser beam discharges a lower charge only to places where toner should go.

4. *Developing.* Toner is placed on the drum where the charge has been reduced.

5. *Transferring.* A strong electrical charge draws the toner off the drum onto the paper. This is the first step that takes place outside the cartridge.

6. *Fusing.* Heat and pressure fuse the toner to the paper.

Note that Figure 21-2 shows only a cross-section of the drum, mechanisms, and paper. Remember that the drum is as wide as a sheet of paper. The mirror, blades, and rollers in the drawing are also as wide as paper. Also know that toner responds to a charge and moves from one surface to another if the second surface has a more positive charge than the first. As you visualize the process, first note the location of the removable cartridge in the drawing, the photosensitive drum inside the cartridge turning in a clockwise direction, and the path of the paper, which moves from right to left.

21

Figure 21-2   The six progressive steps of laser printing

Step 1: Cleaning. Figure 21-3 shows a clear view of the cleaning step. First a sweeper strip cleans the drum of any residual toner, which is swept away by a sweeping blade. A cleaning blade completes the physical cleaning of the drum. Next the drum is cleaned of any electrical charge by erase lamps in the hinged top cover of the printer. The lamps light the surface of the drum to neutralize any electrical charge left on it.

Figure 21-3   The cleaning step cleans the drum of toner and electrical charge

Step 2: Conditioning. The conditioning step puts a uniform electrical charge of –600 V on the surface of the drum. The charge is put there by a primary charging roller or primary corona, which is charged by a high-voltage power supply assembly. The primary charging roller in Figure 21-2 is inside the toner cartridge and regulates the charge on the drum, ensuring that it is a uniform −600 V.

Step 3: Writing. In the writing step, the uniform charge applied in Step 2 is discharged only where you want the printer to print. This is done by controlling mirrors to reflect laser beams onto the drum in a pattern that re-creates the image desired. This is the first step in which data from the computer must be transmitted to the printer. Figure 21-4 shows the process. Data from the PC is received by the formatter (1) and passed on to the DC controller (2), which controls the laser unit (3). The laser beam is initiated and directed toward the octagonal mirror called the **scanning mirror**. The scanning mirror (4) is turned by the scanning motor in a clockwise direction. There are eight mirrors on the eight sides of the scanning mirror. As the mirror turns, the laser beam is directed in a sweeping motion that can cover the entire length of the drum. The laser beam is reflected off the scanning mirror, focused by the focusing lens (5), and sent on to the mirror (6), which is also shown in Figure 21-2. The mirror deflects the laser beam to a slit in the removable cartridge and onto the drum (7).

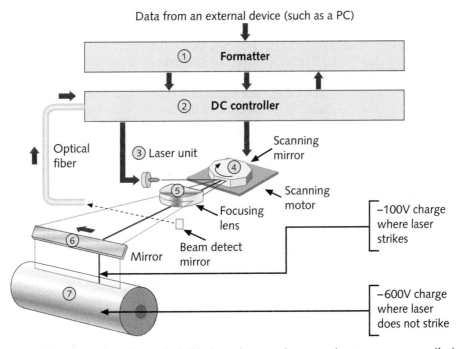

Figure 21-4 The writing step, done by an invisible laser beam, mirrors, and motors, causes a discharge on the drum where the images will be

21

The speed of the motor turning the drum and the speed of the scanning motor turning the scanning mirror are synchronized so that the laser beam completes one pass, or scanline, across the drum and returns to the beginning of the drum (right side of the drum in Figure 21-4) to begin a new pass, until it completes the correct number of passes for each inch of the drum circumference. For example, for a 1200 dots per inch (dpi) printer, the beam makes 1200 passes for every one inch of the drum circumference. The laser beam is turned on and off continually as it makes a single pass down the length of the drum, so that dots are written along the drum on every pass. For a 1200-dpi printer, 1200 dots are written along the drum for every inch of linear pass. The 1200 dots per inch down this single pass, combined with 1200 passes per inch of drum circumference, accomplish the resolution of 1200×1200 dots per square inch of many desktop laser printers.

NOTE A laser printer can produce better-quality printouts than a dot-matrix printer, even when printing at the same dpi, because it can vary the size of the dots it prints, creating a sharp, clear image. Hewlett-Packard (HP) calls this technology of varying the size of dots **REt (Resolution Enhancement technology)**.

In a laser printer, where the laser beam strikes the surface of the drum, the drum discharges from its conditioned charge of –600 V down to –100 V where toner will be placed on the drum. Toner does not stick to the highly charged areas of the drum.

Just as the scanning laser beam is synchronized to the rotating drum, the data output is synchronized to the scanning beam. Before the beam begins moving across the scanline of the drum, the **beam detect mirror** detects the laser beam by reflecting it to an optical fiber. The light travels along the optical fiber to the DC controller, where it is converted to an electrical signal that synchronizes the data output. The signal is also used to diagnose problems with the laser or scanning motor.

The laser beam has written an image to the drum surface as a –100 V charge. The –100 V charge on this image area will be used in the developing stage to transmit toner to the drum surface.

Step 4: Developing. Figure 21-5 shows the developing step, in which toner is applied by the developing cylinder to the discharged (-100 V) areas of the drum. Toner transfers from the cylinder to the drum as the two rotate very close together. The cylinder is coated with a layer of toner, made of black resin bonded to iron, which is similar to the toner used in photocopy machines. The toner is held on the cylinder surface by its attraction to a magnet inside the cylinder. (A toner cavity keeps the cylinder supplied with toner.) A **control blade** prevents too much toner from sticking to the cylinder surface. The toner on the cylinder surface takes on a negative charge (between –200 V and –500 V) because the surface is connected to a DC power supply, called the DC bias.

The negatively charged toner is more negative than the -100 V on the drum surface but less negative than the -600 V surface. This means that the toner is attracted to the -100 V area of the drum surface (the -100 V area is positive relative to the toner). The toner is repelled from the -600 V part of the drum surface, which is negative relative to the toner. The result is that toner sticks to the drum where the laser beam has hit and is repelled from the area where the laser beam has not hit.

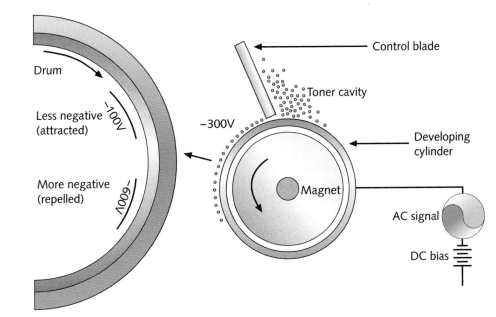

Figure 21-5   In the developing step, charged toner is deposited onto the drum surface

You can adjust printer density manually at the printer or through software controlling the printer. When you adjust print density with laser printers, you are adjusting the DC bias charge on the developing cylinder, which controls the amount of toner attracted to the cylinder; this in turn results in a change in print density.

Step 5: Transferring. In the transferring step, the transfer charging roller, or transfer corona (shown in Figure 21-2), produces a positive charge on the paper that pulls the toner from the drum onto the paper when it passes between the transfer charging roller and the drum. The static charge eliminator (refer again to Figure 21-2) weakens the positive charge on the paper and the negative charge on the drum so that the paper does not adhere to the drum, which it would otherwise do because of the difference in charge between the two. The stiffness of the paper and the small radius of the drum also help the paper move away from the drum and toward the fusing assembly. Very thin paper can wrap around the drum, which is why printer manuals usually instruct you to use only paper designated for laser printers.

Step 6: Fusing. The fusing step causes the toner to bond with the paper. Up to this point, the toner is merely sitting on the paper. The fusing rollers apply both pressure and heat to the paper. The toner melts and the rollers press the toner into the paper. The temperature of the rollers is monitored by the printer. If the temperature exceeds an allowed maximum value (410 degrees F for some printers), the printer shuts down.

The previous steps describe how a black-and-white printer works. Color laser printers work in a similar way, but the writing process repeats four times, one for each toner color of cyan, magenta, yellow, and black. Then the paper passes to the fusing stage, when the fuser bonds all toner to the paper and aids in blending the four tones to form specific colors.

21

Inkjet Printers

A+
CORE
5.1

Inkjet printers use a type of ink dispersion printing and don't normally provide the high-quality resolution of laser printers, but are popular because they are small and can print color inexpensively. Most inkjet printers today give photo-quality results, especially when used with photo-quality paper. Until this new technology was developed, increasing the quality of an inkjet printer meant increasing the dpi (dots per inch). Earlier inkjet printers used 300 x 300 dpi, but inkjet printers today can use up to 4800 x 1200 dpi. Increasing the dpi has drawbacks. It increases the amount of data sent to the printer for a single page, and all those dots of ink can produce a wet page. An improved technology that gives photo-quality results mixes different colors of ink to produce a new color that then makes a single dot. Hewlett-Packard calls this PhotoREt II color technology. HP mixes as many as 16 drops of ink to produce a single dot of color on the page.

Inkjet printers tend to smudge on inexpensive paper, and they are slower than laser printers. The quality of the paper used with inkjet printers significantly affects the quality of printed output. Only use paper designed for an inkjet printer, and use a high-grade paper to get the best results. Figure 21-6 shows one example of an inkjet printer.

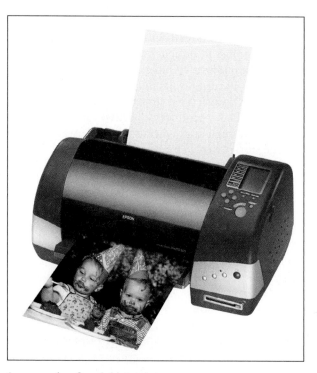

Figure 21-6   An example of an inkjet printer

How an Inkjet Printer Works

A+
CORE
5.1

An inkjet printer uses a print head that moves across the paper, creating one line of text with each pass. The printer puts ink on the paper using a matrix of small dots. Different types of inkjet printers form their droplets of ink in different ways. Printer manufacturers use several technologies, but the most popular is the bubble-jet. Bubble-jet printers use tubes of ink that have tiny resistors near the end of each tube. These resistors heat up and cause the ink to boil. Then, a tiny air bubble of ionized ink (ink with an electrical charge) is ejected onto the paper. A typical bubble-jet print head has 64 or 128 tiny nozzles, all of which can fire a droplet simultaneously. (High-end printers can have as many as 3000 nozzles.) Plates carrying a magnetic charge direct the path of ink onto the paper to form shapes.

Inkjet printers include one or more ink cartridges. When purchasing an inkjet printer, look for the kind that uses two separate cartridges, one for black ink and one for three-color printing. If an inkjet printer does not have a black ink cartridge, then it combines all colors of ink to produce a dull black. Having a separate cartridge for black ink means that it prints true black and, more importantly, does not use the more expensive colored ink. You can replace the black cartridge without also replacing the colored ink cartridge.

Figure 21-7 shows two ink cartridges. The cartridge on the left contains red, blue, and yellow ink (officially named magenta, cyan, and yellow), and the cartridge on the right contains black ink. (Some inkjet printers use more than three colors and more than two cartridges.) The print head assemblage in the figure is in the center position because the top cover has been lifted. Normally when the printer is not in use, the head assemblage sits to the far right of the printing area. This is called the home position, and helps protect the ink in the cartridges from drying out.

Print head assemblage

Black ink cartridge

Color ink cartridge

21

Top cover

Figure 21-7   The ink cartridges of an inkjet printer

Dot-Matrix Printers

**A+
CORE
5.1**

Dot-matrix printers are less expensive than other types of printers, but they don't give nearly the print quality. Many desktop PC users have replaced them with inkjet or laser printers. The one reason you still see so many around is that they are impact printers and can print multicopy documents, which some businesses still find useful. A dot-matrix printer has a print head that moves across the width of the paper, using pins to print a matrix of dots on the page. The pins shoot against a cloth ribbon, which hits the paper, depositing the ink. The ribbon provides both the ink for printing and the lubrication for the pinheads.

Occasionally, you should replace the ribbon of a dot-matrix printer. Although the print head can wear out, replacing it is probably not cost-effective, because it costs almost as much as a low-end dot-matrix printer itself. If the print head fails, check on the cost of replacing the head versus the cost of buying a new printer. Overheating can damage a print head (see Figure 21-8), so keep it as cool as possible to make it last longer. Keep the printer in a cool, well-ventilated area, and don't use it to print more than 50 to 75 pages without allowing the head to cool down.

— Print head

Figure 21-8   Keep the print head of a dot-matrix printer as cool as possible so it will last longer

Thermal Printers and Solid Ink Printers

Two similar and relatively new technologies are thermal printers and solid ink printers. Both are non-impact printers that use heat to produce printed output. **Thermal printers** use wax-based ink that is heated by heat pins that melt the ink onto paper.

**A+
CORE
5.1**

The print head containing these heat pins is as wide as the paper. The internal logic of the printer determines which pins get heated to produce the printed image. Thermal printers are popular in retail applications for printing bar codes and price tags. A thermal printer can burn dots onto special paper, as done by older fax machines (called direct thermal printing), or the printer can use a ribbon that contains the wax-based ink (called thermal wax transfer printing).

One variation of thermal printing uses thermal dye sublimation technology to print identification cards and access cards. A **dye-sublimation printer** uses solid dyes embedded on different transparent films. As the print head passes over each color film, it heats up, causing the dye to vaporize onto the glossy surface of the paper. Because the dye is vaporized onto the paper rather than jetted at it, the results are more photo-lab quality than with inkjet printing.

Solid ink printers such as the Xerox Phaser 8200 store ink in solid blocks, which Xerox calls ColourStixs. The sticks or blocks are easy to handle and several can be inserted in the printer to be used as needed, avoiding the problem of running out of ink in the middle of a large print job. The solid ink is melted into the print head, which spans the width of the paper. The head jets the liquid ink onto the paper as it passes by on a drum. The design is simple, print quality is excellent, and solid ink printers are easy to set up and maintain. The greatest disadvantage to solid ink printing is the time it takes for the print head to heat up to begin a print job, which is about 15 minutes. For this reason, some solid ink printers anticipate that a print job might be coming based on previous use of the printer, and automatically heat up.

Table 21-1 lists some printer manufacturers. After the table, turn our attention to how to install a printer on a computer and share it with others on the network.

Printer Manufacturer	Web Site
Brother	www.brother.com
Canon	usa.canon.com
Hewlett-Packard	www.hp.com
IBM	www.ibm.com
Lexmark	www.lexmark.com
Okidata	www.okidata.com
SATO	www.satoamerica.com
Seiko Epson	www.epson.com
Tally	www.tally.com
Xerox	www.xerox.com

21

Table 21-1   Printer manufacturers

Installing and Sharing a Printer

A+
CORE
1.8
5.2
OS
2.4

A printer can be connected to a port on a computer, and then the computer can share the printer with others on the network. There are also network printers with Ethernet ports that can connect the printer directly to the network. Each computer on the network that uses the printer must have printer drivers installed so the OS on each computer can communicate with the printer and provide the interface between applications it supports and the printer. This section covers how to install a local printer, how to share that printer with others on the network, and how a remote computer on the network can use a shared printer. A printer connected to a computer by way of a port on the computer is called a **local printer**, and a printer accessed by way of a network is called a **network printer**. A computer can have several printers installed. Windows designates one printer to be the **default printer**, which is the one Windows prints to unless another is selected.

Installing a Local Printer

✔ **A+ EXAM TIP**

The A+ Core and OS exams expect you to know how to install a local and network printer.

Follow these steps to install a local printer:

1. Physically attach the printer to the computer by way of a parallel port, serial port, 1394 port, USB port, SCSI port, IEEE 1394 port, PC Card connection, infrared connection, or wireless access point. Recall from Chapter 10 that you should use an IEEE 1284-compliant printer cable for a parallel port connection. For wireless printers, verify that the software for the wireless port on your PC is installed and the port is enabled. For infrared wireless printers, place the printer in line of sight of the infrared port on the PC. (Most wireless printers have a status light that stays lit when a wireless connection is active.)

2. Install the printer drivers using one of two approaches. You can have Windows install the driver, or you can use the printer manufacturer's installation program. In most cases, it is best to use the printer manufacturer's method. The exception is if you have several similar printers installed. Windows does a better job of preventing files used by one printer installation from being overwritten by files from another installation.

   a. To use the manufacturer's installation process, insert the printer driver CD that comes bundled with the printer in the CD-ROM drive, and follow directions onscreen to install the printer.

   b. Alternately, you can use the Windows printer windows to install the printer drivers. For Windows XP, open the Printers and Faxes window by

A+
CORE
1.8
5.2
OS
2.4

clicking **Start, Control Panel,** and **Printers and Faxes** (in Classic view) or **Printers and Other Hardware** (in Category view). For Windows 2000 and Windows 98, click **Start, Settings,** and **Printers** to open the Printers window. Click **Add a Printer** and follow the Add Printer Wizard to install the printer drivers.

3. After you install the printer drivers, test the printer. Open the Printers and Faxes window or Printers window and right-click the printer. Select **Properties** from the shortcut menu. Click the **General** tab and then click the **Print Test Page** button.

From the Printers window (called the Printers and Faxes window for Windows XP), you can also delete printers, change the Windows default printer, purge print jobs to troubleshoot failed printing, and perform other printer maintenance tasks. If a printer is giving you problems or you want to upgrade the printer drivers to add new functionality, search the printer manufacturer's Web site for the latest drivers for your printer and operating system. Download the drivers to a folder on the hard drive such as C:\Downloads\Printer, and then double-click the driver file to extract files and launch the installation program to update the printer drivers.

Sharing a Printer with Others in a Workgroup

To share a local printer using Windows, File and Printer Sharing must be installed, and to use a shared printer on a remote PC, Client for Microsoft Networks must be installed. In most cases, it is easiest to simply install both components on all computers on the network. How to install the components under Windows 2000/XP and Windows 98 was covered in Chapter 18.

To share a local printer connected to a Windows 2000/XP workstation, do the following:

1. Open the Printers window or Printers and Faxes window by clicking **Start, Control Panel,** and **Printers and Faxes**. Right-click the printer you want to share, and select **Sharing** from the shortcut menu. The printer's Properties dialog box opens, as shown in Figure 21-9 for Windows XP; the dialog box in Windows 2000 is similar. Select **Share this printer** and enter a name for the printer.

2. If you want to make drivers for the printer available to remote users who are using an operating system other than the OS being used, then click **Additional Drivers**.

21

A+
CORE
1.8
5.2
OS
2.4

3. The Additional Drivers window appears, as shown in Figure 21-9. Select the OS. In the figure, Windows 2000, XP, 95, 98, and Me are selected so that users of these OSs will have the printer drivers they need. Click **OK** twice to close both windows. You might be asked for the Windows installation CD or other access to the installation files. A shared printer shows a hand icon under it in the Printers window, and the printer is listed in My Network Places or Network Neighborhood of other PCs on the network.

Figure 21-9   Sharing a printer on a Windows XP PC

To share a local printer with others in the workgroup connected to a Windows 98 computer, do the following:

1. Open the Printers window by clicking **Start**, **Settings**, and **Printers**.

2. Right-click the printer you want to share. From the shortcut menu, select **Sharing**. (This Sharing option is grayed out if File and Printer Sharing is not available.)

3. The Properties dialog box opens with the Sharing tab selected (see Figure 21-10).

4. Select **Shared As** and give the printer a **Share Name**. Click **OK** to exit.

The printer is listed in Network Neighborhood or My Network Places.

A+
CORE
1.8
5.2
OS
2.4

Figure 21-10   When using Windows 98, use the printer Properties dialog box to share a connected printer with other computers on the network

Using a Shared Printer

Recall that for a remote PC to use a shared network printer, the drivers for that printer must be installed on the remote PC. There are two approaches to installing shared network printer drivers on a remote PC. You can perform the installation using the drivers on CD (either the Windows CD or printer manufacturer's CD), or you can perform the installation using the printer drivers on the host PC. The installations work about the same way for Windows 2000/XP and Windows 98. The Windows XP installation is shown here, but differences for Windows 2000 and Windows 98 are noted.

To use a shared printer on the network by installing the manufacturer's printer drivers from CD, do the following using Windows XP:

1. Open the Printers and Faxes window and double-click **Add a printer**. The Add Printer Wizard opens. Click **Next**.

2. In response to the question, "Select the option that describes the printer you want to use:", select **A network printer, or a printer attached to another computer**. Click **Next**. The wizard window in Figure 21-11 opens.

3. Enter the host computer name and printer name. Begin with two backslashes and separate the computer name from the printer name with a backslash. Or, you can click **Browse**, search the list of shared printers on the network, and select the printer to install. (If your network is using static IP addressing and

21

A+
CORE
1.8
5.2
OS
2.4

you know the IP address of the host PC, you can enter the IP address instead of the host name in this step.) Click **Next**.

Figure 21-11   To use a network printer under Windows XP, enter the host computer name followed by the printer name, or have Windows XP browse the network for shared printers

4. Windows XP searches for Windows XP drivers on the host computer for this printer. If it finds them (meaning that the host computer is a Windows XP machine), then the wizard skips to Step 6. If it doesn't find the drivers (the host computer is not a Windows XP machine), a message asks if you want to search for the proper driver. Click **OK**.

5. Click **Have Disk** to use the manufacturer's drivers, or to use Windows drivers, select the printer manufacturer and then the printer model from the list of supported printers. Click **OK** when you finish.

6. In response to the question, "Do you want to use this printer as the default printer?", answer **Yes** if you want Windows to send documents to this printer until you select a different one. Click **Next**. Click **Finish** to complete the wizard.

7. The printer icon appears in the Printers and Faxes window. To test the printer installation, right-click the icon and select **Properties** from the shortcut menu. Click the **General** tab and then click **Print Test Page**.

A+
CORE
1.8
5.2
OS
2.4

Here are some additional things to know about installing a network printer using the Windows 98 Add Printer Wizard:

- When the wizard asks, "Do you print from MS-DOS-based programs?", answer Yes if you have any intention of ever doing so.
- The wizard gives you the opportunity to name the printer. You might include the location of the printer, such as 3rd Floor Laser or John's Laser.
- Sometimes a DOS-based program has problems printing to a network printer. You can choose to associate the network printer with a printer port such as LPT1 to satisfy the DOS application. Click Capture Printer Port, and then select the port from the drop-down menu in the Capture Printer Port dialog box (see Figure 21-12).

Figure 21-12   Associate a network printer with a printer port to help DOS applications in Windows 98

- The Windows 98 Add Printer Wizard gives you the opportunity to print a test page on the last window of the wizard. It's always a good idea to print this test page to verify that the printer is accessible.
- Know that the Windows 98 Add Printer Wizard does not attempt to use the printer drivers on the host PC, but always installs local Windows 9x/Me drivers or uses the manufacturer's CD.

Another way to install a shared printer is to first use My Network Places or Network Neighborhood to locate the printer on the network. This method is faster when one Windows 9x/Me PC is providing a shared printer to be installed on other

21

A+
CORE
1.8
5.2
OS
2.4

Windows 9x/Me PCs, because the remote PCs can use the printer drivers on the host PC. Do the following:

1. On a remote PC that uses Windows 2000/XP, open **My Network Places** and find the printer. Right-click the printer and select **Connect** from the shortcut menu. See Figure 21-13. (For Windows 9x/Me, open **Network Neighborhood** and find the printer. Right-click the printer and select **Install** from the shortcut menu.)

Figure 21-13   Install a shared printer in Windows 2000 using My Network Places

2. If the host computer is using the same OS as you are, or if you have a Windows NT/2000/XP host computer and the additional drivers for your OS have been installed, you can use those drivers for the installation. If Windows cannot find the right drivers, it sends you an error message and gives you the opportunity to install the drivers from your Windows CD or the printer manufacturer's CD.

NOTE   When installing a shared printer on a Windows 9x/Me PC where the host computer is also a Windows 9x/Me PC, you must first share the \Windows folder on the host PC so the remote PC can access the printer drivers. This is a security risk, so remove the share status on this important folder as soon as all remote PCs have the printer installed.

Other Methods of Sharing Printers over a Network

You have just seen how a printer can be installed as a local printer on one PC and then shared with others in a workgroup. The three ways to make a printer available on a network are summarized here:

- A regular printer can be attached to a PC using a port on the PC, and then that PC can share the printer with the network. (This method was described in the previous section.)
- A network printer with embedded logic to manage network communication can be connected directly to a network with its own NIC.
- A dedicated device or computer called a print server can control several printers connected to a network. For example, HP has software called HP JetDirect, designed to support HP printers in this manner. For more information, see the HP Web site, *www.hp.com.*

If printers are available on the network using one of the last two methods, follow the printer manufacturer's directions to install the printer on each PC. If you don't have these directions, do the following:

1. Download the printer drivers from the printer manufacturer's Web site and decompress the downloaded file, if necessary.

2. Open the Printers window and start the wizard to add a new printer. Select the option to install a local printer but do not ask Windows to automatically detect the printer.

3. When given the opportunity, choose to create a new port rather than use an existing port (such as LPT1: or LPT2:). Choose to create a standard TCP/IP port. To create the port, you will need the IP address of the printer or the name of the printer on the network.

4. When given the opportunity, click **Have Disk** so you can point to and use the downloaded driver files that will then be used to complete the printer installation.

NOTE Because a network printer has no OS installed, the printer's NIC contains all the firmware needed to communicate over the network. For a PC, some of this software is part of Windows, including the network protocols, TCP/IP and IPX/SPX. A network printer's NIC firmware usually supports TCP/IP and IPX/SPX. The network printer documentation will tell you which protocols are supported. One of these protocols must be installed on a PC using the printer.

One shortcut you might take to speed up the process of installing a printer connected directly to the network is to install the printer on one PC and then share it on the network. Then, you can install the printer on the other PCs by using My Network Places for Windows 2000/XP or Network Neighborhood for Windows 98, following the directions given earlier. Find the printer, right-click it, and then select

21

A+
CORE
1.8
5.2
OS
2.4

Connect (for Windows 2000/XP) or Install (for Windows 9x/Me) from the shortcut menu. The disadvantage of using this method is that the computer sharing the printer must be turned on when other computers on the network want to use the printer.

Troubleshooting Guidelines for Printers

A+
CORE
5.2

This section first discusses general printer troubleshooting and then explains how to troubleshoot problems specific to each of the three major types of printers. To help prevent problems with printers, follow the manufacturer's directions when using the printer and perform routine printer maintenance. When supporting printers using Windows, it is helpful to understand how Windows manages print jobs, so we will begin there.

How Windows Handles Print Jobs

A+
OS
3.3

Windows manages print jobs using one of these methods:

- For Windows NT/2000/XP or Windows 9x/Me using a PostScript printer, the print job data is converted to the PostScript language. PostScript, a language used to communicate how a page is to print, was developed by Adobe Systems. PostScript is popular with desktop publishing, the typesetting industry, and the Macintosh OS.
- For Windows 2000/XP, a printer language that competes with PostScript is PCL (Printer Control Language). PCL was developed by Hewlett-Packard but is considered a de facto standard in the printing industry. Many printer manufacturers use PCL.
- For Windows 9x/Me applications using a non-PostScript printer, the print job data is converted to Enhanced Metafile Format (EMF). This format embeds print commands in the data to help speed printing.
- Text data that contains no embedded control characters is sent to the printer as is. When DOS applications use this type of printing, the data is called raw data and the print job is sent directly to the printer, bypassing the printer queue.

Normally, when Windows receives a print job from an application, it places the job in a queue and prints from the queue, so that the application is released from the printing process as soon as possible. Several print jobs can accumulate in the queue, which you can view in the Printers window. This process is called **spooling**. (The word spool is an acronym for *s*imultaneous *p*eripheral *o*perations *on-l*ine.) Most printing from Windows uses spooling.

If the printer port, printer cable, and printer all support bidirectional communication, the printer can communicate with Windows. For example, Windows 2000 can ask the printer how much printer memory is available and what fonts are installed.

A+
OS
3.3

The printer can send messages to the OS, such as an out-of-paper or paper-jam message.

Printer Maintenance

A+
CORE
5.2

Routine printer maintenance procedures vary widely from manufacturer to manufacturer and printer to printer. First, make sure consumables for the printer are on hand, such as paper, ink ribbons, color stixs, toner cartridges, and ink cartridges. For each printer you support, research the printer documentation or the manufacturer's Web site for specific maintenance procedures and how often you should perform them. For example, the maintenance plan for the HP Color LaserJet 4600 printer says to replace the transfer roller assembly after printing 120,000 pages and replace the fusing assembly after 150,000 pages. The plan also says the black ink cartridge should last for about 9000 pages and the color ink cartridge for about 8000 pages. HP sells the image transfer kit, the image fuser kit, and the ink cartridges designed for this printer. The kits, called **printer maintenance kits**, include specific printer components, step-by-step instructions for performing maintenance, and any special tools or equipment you need to do maintenance. The Web site and printer documentation include instructions to command the printer to report how many pages have printed since each maintenance task was performed.

✔ **A+ EXAM TIP**

The A+ Core exam expects you to know that printers use certain consumables and require routine preventive maintenance.

When you perform routine maintenance on a printer, clean inside and outside the printer. Clean the outside of the printer with a damp cloth. Don't use ammonia-based cleaners. Clean the inside of the printer with a dry cloth and remove dust, bits of paper, and stray toner. Don't use an antistatic vacuum cleaner. For a laser printer, wipe the rollers from side to side with a dry cloth to remove loose dirt. Don't touch the soft black roller (the transfer roller), or you might affect the print quality.

If you get toner on your clothes, dust it off and clean your clothes with cold water. Hot water will set the toner.

The printer manufacturer's Web site is an important resource when supporting printers. Here are some things to look for:

- *Online documentation.* Expect the printer manufacturer's Web site to include documentation on installing, configuring, troubleshooting, using, upgrading, and maintaining the printer. Also look for information on printer parts and warranty, compatibility information, specifications and features of your printer, a way to register your printer, and how to recycle or dispose of a printer. You might also be able to download your printer manual in PDF format.

21

**A+
CORE
5.2**

- *A knowledge base of common problems and what to do about them.* Some Web sites also offer a newsgroup service or discussion group where you can communicate with others responsible for supporting a particular printer. Also look for a way to e-mail for technical support.
- *Updated device drivers.* Sometimes you can solve printer problems by downloading and installing the latest drivers. Also, a manufacturer makes new features and options available through these drivers. Be sure you download files for the correct printer and OS.
- *Flash BIOS updates.* Some high-end printers have firmware that can be flashed to solve problems and add features. Be careful to verify that you download the correct update for your printer.
- *Catalog of options and upgrades for purchase.* Look for memory upgrades, optional trays, feeders, sorters, staplers, printer stands, and other equipment to upgrade your printer.
- *Replacement parts.* When a printer part breaks, buy only parts made by or approved by the printer manufacturer. Manufacturers also sell consumable supplies such as toner and ink cartridges.
- *Printer maintenance kits.* The best practice is to buy everything you need for routine maintenance either from the printer manufacturer or an approved vendor.
- *Additional software.* Look for software to use with your printer, such as software to produce greeting cards or edit photographs.

Following is a guide for general and specific printer troubleshooting. If you exhaust this list and still have a problem, turn to the manufacturer's Web site for additional information and support.

APPLYING CONCEPTS

Jill is the PC support technician responsible for supporting 10 users, their peer-to-peer network, printers, and computers. Everything was working fine when Jill left work one evening, but the next morning three users meet her at the door, complaining that they cannot print to the network printer and that important work must be printed by noon. What do you think are the first three things Jill should check?

General Printer Troubleshooting

**A+
CORE
5.2
OS
3.3**

Printing problems can be caused by the printer, the PC hardware or OS, the application using the printer, the printer cable, or the network. Follow the steps in Figure 21-14 to isolate the problem to one of the following areas:

- The application attempting to use the printer
- The OS and printer drivers

A+
CORE
5.2
OS
3.3

- Connectivity between the PC and the printer
- The printer itself

The sections that follow address printer problems caused by all of these categories, starting with hardware.

Figure 21-14 How to isolate a printer problem

21

Verify That a Printer Self-Test Page Can Print

To eliminate the printer as the problem, first check that the printer is on, and then print a self-test page. For directions to print a self-test page, see the printer's user guide. For example, you might need to hold down a button or buttons on the printer's front panel. If this test page prints correctly, then the printer works correctly. A printer test page generally prints some text, some graphics, and some information about the printer, such as the printer resolution and how much memory is installed. Verify that the information on the test page is correct. For example, if you know that the printer should have 2 MB of on-board printer memory, but the test only reports 1 MB, then there is a problem with memory. Also, some printers allow you to flash BIOS on the printer.

If the self-test page does not print or prints incorrectly (for example, it has missing dots or smudged streaks through the page), then troubleshoot the printer until it prints correctly. Does the printer have paper? Is the paper installed correctly? Is there a paper jam? Is the paper damp or wrinkled, causing it to refuse to feed? Are the printer cover and rear access doors properly closed and locked? Try resetting the printer. For a laser printer, check that a toner cartridge is installed. For an inkjet printer, check that ink cartridges are installed. Has the protective tape been removed from the print cartridge? Check that power is getting to the printer. Try another power source. Check the user guide for the printer and the printer Web site for troubleshooting suggestions. For a laser printer, replace the toner cartridge. For inkjet printers, replace the ink cartridge.

If none of these steps works, you may need to take the printer to a certified repair shop. Before you do, though, try contacting the manufacturer. The printer documentation can be very helpful and most often contains a phone number for technical support.

Problem with the printer cable If the printer self-test worked, but the OS printer test did not work, the problem might be with the printer cable.

- Check that the cable is firmly connected at both ends.
- A business might use an older switch box (sometimes called a T-switch) to share one printer between two computers. A printer cable connects to the printer port of each computer. The two cables connect to the switch box. A third cable connects from the switch box to the printer. A switch on the front of the box controls which computer has access to the printer. Switch boxes were built with older dot-matrix printers in mind. Some switch boxes are not recommended for inkjet or laser printers that use a bidirectional parallel cable, and can even damage a printer. For these printers, remove the switch box.
- Try a different cable. Use a shorter cable. (Cables longer than 10 feet can sometimes cause problems.) Verify that the cable is IEEE 1284-compliant.

- Try printing using the same printer and printer cable but a different PC.
- Enter CMOS setup of the PC and check how the parallel port is configured. Is it disabled? Set to ECP or bidirectional? Recall that an ECP parallel port requires the use of a DMA channel. Try setting the port to bidirectional.

Problems with Laser Printers

This section covers some problems that can occur with laser printers. For more specific guidelines for your printer model, refer to the printer documentation or the manufacturer's Web site.

Poor print quality or a Toner Low message is displayed   Poor print quality, including faded, smeared, wavy, speckled, or streaked printouts, often indicates that the toner is low. All major mechanical printer components that normally create problems are conveniently contained within the replaceable toner cartridge. In most cases, the solution to poor-quality printing is to replace this cartridge. Follow these general guidelines:

- If you suspect the printer is overheated, unplug it and allow it to cool.
- Remove the toner cartridge and gently rock it from side to side to redistribute the toner. Replace the cartridge. If this solves the problem, plan to replace the toner cartridge soon. To avoid flying toner, don't shake the cartridge too hard.
- If this doesn't solve the problem, try replacing the toner cartridge immediately.
- EconoMode (a mode that uses less toner) may be on; turn it off.
- On some laser printers, you can clean the mirror. Check the user guide for directions.
- A single sheet of paper may be defective. Try new paper.
- The paper quality may not be high enough. Try a different brand of paper. Only use paper recommended for use with a laser printer.
- Clean the inside of the printer with a dry, lint-free cloth. Don't touch the transfer roller.
- If the transfer roller is dirty, the problem will probably correct itself after several sheets print. If not, then take the printer to an authorized service center.
- Does the printer require routine maintenance? Check the Web site of the printer manufacturer for how often to perform the maintenance and to purchase the required printer maintenance kit.

NOTE   Extreme humidity may cause the toner to clump in the cartridge and give a Toner Low message. If this is a consistent problem in your location, you might want to invest in a dehumidifier for the room where your printer is located.

21

**A+
CORE
5.2
OS
3.3**

Printer stays in warm-up mode   The "warming up" message on the front panel of the printer should turn off as soon as the printer establishes communication with the PC. If this doesn't happen, try the following:

- Turn off the printer and disconnect the cable to the computer.
- Turn on the printer. If it now displays a Ready message, the problem is communication between the printer and computer.
- Verify that the cable is connected to the correct printer port, not to a serial port.
- Verify that data to the installed printer is being sent to the parallel port. For example, open the Properties dialog box of the installed printer. Verify that the print job is being sent to LPT1, as shown in Figure 21-15.

Figure 21-15   Verify that print data is being sent to the correct parallel port

- Check that the parallel port is enabled in CMOS setup and set to the correct mode.
- Replace the cable.

VIDEO

Clearing a
Paper Jam

A paper jam occurs or Paper Out message appears   If paper is jammed inside the printer, follow the directions in the printer documentation to remove the paper. Don't jerk the paper from the printer mechanism, but pull evenly on the paper, with care.

A+
CORE
5.2
OS
3.3

- Check for jammed paper from both the input tray and the output bin. Check both sides.
- If there is no jammed paper, then remove the tray and check the metal plate at the bottom of the tray. Can it move up and down freely? If not, replace the tray.
- When you insert the tray in the printer, does the printer lift the plate as the tray is inserted? If not, the lift mechanism might need repair.
- Damp paper can cause paper jams. Be sure to only use dry paper in a printer.

One or more white streaks appear in the print   Remove the toner cartridge, shake it from side to side to redistribute the toner supply, and replace the cartridge.

- Streaking is usually caused by a dirty developer unit or corona wire. The developer unit is contained in the toner cartridge. Replace the cartridge or check the printer documentation for directions on how to remove and clean the developer unit. Allow the corona wire to cool and clean it with a lint-free swab.

Print appears speckled   Try replacing the cartridge. If the problem persists, the power supply assembly may be damaged.

- Replace the laser drum.

NOTE

If loose toner comes out with your printout, the fuser is not reaching the proper temperature. Professional service is required.

Printed images are distorted   If printed images are distorted and there is no paper jam, foreign material inside the printer might be interfering with the mechanical components. Check for debris that might be interfering with the printer operation. If the page has a gray background or gray print, the photoreceptor drum is worn out and needs to be replaced.

Printing is slow   Laser printers are rated by two speed properties: the time it takes to print the first page (measured in seconds) and the print speed (measured in pages per minute). Try the following if the printer is slow:

- Space is needed on the hard drive to manage print jobs. Clean up the drive. Install a larger drive if necessary.
- Add more memory to the printer. See the printer manual for directions.
- Lower the printer resolution and the print quality (which lowers the REt settings).
- Verify that the hard drive has enough space.
- Upgrade the computer's memory or the CPU.

A portion of the page does not print   For some laser printers, an error occurs if the printer does not have enough memory to hold the entire page. For other printers,

21

only a part of the page prints. Some may signal this problem by flashing a light or displaying an error message on their display panels. (Some HP LaserJet printers have a control panel and send an error message for low memory, "20 Mem Overflow.") The solution is to install more memory or to print only simple pages with few graphics. Print a self-test page to verify how much memory is installed. Check the user guide to determine how much memory the printer can support and what kind of memory to buy.

Problems with Inkjet Printers

This section covers some problems that can occur with inkjet printers. For more specific guidelines for your printer, refer to the printer documentation or the manufacturer's Web site.

Print quality is poor   Is the correct paper for inkjet printers being used? The quality of paper determines the final print quality, especially with inkjet printers. In general, the better the quality of the paper used with an inkjet printer, the better the print quality. Do not use less than 20-lb. paper in any type of printer, unless the printer documentation specifically says that a lower weight is satisfactory.

- Is the ink supply low, or is there a partially clogged nozzle?
- Remove and reinstall the cartridge.
- Follow the printer's documentation to clean each nozzle.
- In the Printer Setup dialog box, click the Media/Quality tab, then change the Print Quality selection. Try different settings with sample prints.
- Is the print head too close to or too far from the paper?
- There is a little sponge in some printers near the carriage rest that can become clogged with ink. It should be removed and cleaned.
- If you are printing transparencies, try changing the fill pattern in your application.

Printing is intermittent or absent   Make sure the correct printer driver is installed.

- Is the ink supply low?
- Are nozzles clogged?
- Replace the ink cartridges or replenish the ink supply.
- Sometimes, leaving the printer on for a while will heat up the ink nozzles and unclog them.

VIDEO

Replacing Ink
Cartridges

Lines or dots are missing from the printed page   The ink nozzles on an inkjet cartridge occasionally dry out, especially when the printer sits unused for a long time. Symptoms are missing lines or dots on the printed page. You had to clean the inkjet nozzles of older inkjet printers manually, but newer printers often let you clean the nozzles automatically, using software or buttons on the front panel of the printer. Using the printer software or buttons, you can also calibrate or align the ink cartridges on inkjet printers.

A+
CORE
5.2
OS
3.3

When the printer software is installed, it places a printer toolbox icon on the desktop and adds one or more tabs to the printer Properties dialog box. Use the printer Properties dialog box to clean the inkjet nozzles or align the cartridges:

1. For Windows 2000 or Windows 9x/Me, open the Printers window. (For Windows XP, open the Printers and Faxes window.) Right-click the inkjet printer icon, and select **Properties** from the shortcut menu.

2. Click the **Services** tab. Figure 21-16 shows the two services available for this printer.

3. Click **Clean the print cartridges** to clean the inkjet nozzles automatically.

4. A test page prints. If the page prints sharply with no missing dots or lines, then you are finished. If the page does not print correctly, perform the auto-clean again.

Figure 21-16   Use the Services tab in the printer's Properties dialog box to auto-clean the inkjet nozzles

5. You might need to perform the auto-clean procedure six or seven times to clean the nozzles completely. If the problem persists, don't attempt to clean the nozzles manually; contact the manufacturer or vendor for service.

Ink streaks appear on the printed page   Sometimes dust or dirt gets down into the print head assemblage, causing streaks or lines on the printed page. Follow the manufacturer's directions to clean the print cartridge assemblage. Use clean distilled water and cotton swabs to clean the cartridge cradle and the face and edges of the print cartridge, being careful not to touch the nozzle plate. To prevent the inkjet nozzles from drying out, don't leave the print cartridges out of their cradle for longer than 30 minutes.

21

Problems with Dot-Matrix Printers

**A+
CORE
5.2
OS
3.3**

This section covers some problems that can occur with dot-matrix printers. Again, for more specific guidelines for your printer, see the printer documentation or the manufacturer's Web site.

Print quality is poor Begin with the ribbon. Does it advance normally while the carriage moves back and forth? If not, replace the ribbon.

- If the new ribbon still does not advance properly, check the printer's advance mechanism.
- Adjust the print head spacing. Look for a lever adjustment you can use to change the distance between the print head and plate.
- Check the print head for dirt. Make sure it's not hot before you touch it. If debris has built up, wipe each wire with a cotton swab dipped in alcohol or contact cleaner.

Print head moves back and forth but nothing prints Check the ribbon. Is it installed correctly between the plate and print head?

- Does the ribbon advance properly? Is it jammed? If the ribbon is dried out, it needs to be replaced.

Problems Printing from Windows

**A+
OS
3.3**

If a self-test page works, but you still cannot print to a local printer from Windows, try the following:

- The print spool might be stalled. Try deleting all print jobs in the printer's queue. Double-click the printer icon in the Printers window. Select Printer on the menu bar, and then select Purge Print Documents. (It may take a moment for the print jobs to disappear.)
- Try to print a test page using the Printers window. Right-click the printer you want to test, and choose Properties from the shortcut menu. Click the Print Test Page button to send a test page to the printer.
- Verify that the correct default printer is selected.
- Verify that the printer is online. See the printer documentation for information on how to determine the status from the control panel of the printer.
- If you still cannot print, reboot the PC. Verify that the printer cable or cable connections are solid.
- Verify that the printer is configured for the correct parallel port.
- Try removing and reinstalling the printer driver. To uninstall the printer driver, right-click the printer icon in the Printers window, and select Delete. Then reinstall the printer.

A+
OS
3.3

- In CMOS setup, check the configuration of the USB, serial, or parallel port that the printer is using.
- Check the parallel port mode in CMOS setup. If ECP mode is selected, verify that a DMA channel is available and not conflicting with another device. Try setting the port to bidirectional.
- Check the Web site of the printer manufacturer for an updated printer driver. Download and install the correct driver.
- In the printer's Properties dialog box, click "Disable bidirectional support for this printer." The PC and printer might have a problem with bidirectional communication.
- Check the resources assigned to the printer port. Open Device Manager, select LPT1, and click Properties. Verify that the resources are assigned correctly for LPT1 (I/O addresses are 0378 to 037B) and that Device Manager reports "No conflicts."
- In the printer's Properties dialog box, try disabling "Check Port State Before Printing."
- Try a different cable.
- Verify printer properties. Try lowering the resolution.
- If you can print from DOS, but not from Windows, try disabling printer spooling. Go to the printer's Properties dialog box, and select Print Directly to the Printer. Spooling holds print jobs in a queue for printing, so if spooling is disabled, printing from an application can be slower.
- If you have trouble printing from an application, you can also bypass spooling by selecting Print from the File menu in the application, selecting the option to print to a file, and then dragging that file to the icon representing your printer.
- If you have trouble printing from an application in Windows 9x/Me, the application may be incompatible with Windows. One way to try to solve this problem is to click Start, click Run, and type mkcompat.exe. This utility enables you to troubleshoot and solve problems that may make an application incompatible with a certain version of Windows.
- Verify that enough hard drive space is available for the OS to create temporary print files.
- Use Chkdsk, Error-checking (Windows 2000/XP), or ScanDisk (Windows 9x/Me) to verify that the hard drive does not have errors. Use Defragmenter to optimize the hard drive.
- Boot Windows into Safe Mode and attempt to print. If this step works, then there might be a conflict between the printer driver and another driver or application.
- If you have access to a port tester device, test the parallel port.
- Check the printer documentation for troubleshooting steps to solve printer problems.
- Try the printer on another PC. Try another power cable and another printer cable.

21

A+
OS
3.3

Troubleshooting Printing from Applications

If you can print a Windows test page, but you cannot print from an application, try the following:

- Verify that the correct printer is selected in the Print Setup dialog box.
- Try printing a different application file.
- Delete any files in the print spool. From the Printers window, double-click the printer icon. Click Printer on the menu bar of the window that appears, and then click Purge Print Documents.
- Reboot the PC. Immediately enter Notepad or WordPad, type some text, and print.
- Reopen the application giving the print error and attempt to print again.
- Try creating data in a new file and printing it. Keep the data simple.
- Try printing from another application.
- If you can print from other applications, consider reinstalling the problem application.
- Close any applications that are not being used.
- Add more memory to the printer.
- Remove and reinstall the printer drivers.
- For DOS applications, you may need to exit the application before printing will work. Verify that the printer is configured to handle DOS printing.

Troubleshooting Networked Printers

A+
OS
3.3
CORE
5.2

When troubleshooting problems with connectivity between a PC on the network and a network printer, try the following:

- Is the printer online?
- Check that you can print a test page from the computer that has the printer attached to it locally. Right-click the printer you want to test, and choose Properties from the shortcut menu. Click the Print Test Page button to send a test page to the printer.
- Verify that the correct default printer is selected.
- If you cannot print from the local printer, solve the problem there before attempting to print over the network.
- Return to the remote computer, and verify that you can access the computer to which the printer is attached. Go to Network Neighborhood or My Network Places, and attempt to open shared folders on the printer's computer. Perhaps you have not entered a correct user ID and password to access this computer; if so, you will be unable to use the computer's resources.
- Using the Printers window, delete the printer, and then use Windows 2000/XP My Network Places or Windows 9x/Me Network Neighborhood to reconnect 6the printer.

A+
OS
3.3
CORE
5.2

- Is the correct network printer selected on the remote PC?
- Can you print to another network printer? If so, there may be a problem with the printer. Look at the printer's configuration.
- Is enough hard drive space available on the remote PC?
- For DOS applications, you may need to exit the application before printing will work. Verify that the printer is configured to handle DOS printing over the network.
- If a PC cannot communicate with a network printer connected directly to the network, try installing a second network protocol that the network printer supports, such as IPX/SPX. If this works, then suspect that the firmware on the NIC is having a problem with TCP/IP. Try flashing the network printer's BIOS. Go to the printer manufacturer's Web site to read directions for flashing BIOS and to download the latest BIOS updates.

A+
CORE
5.2

APPLYING CONCEPTS

Now back to Jill and her company's network printer problem. Generally, Jill should focus on finding out what works and what doesn't work, always remembering to check the simple things first. Jill should first go to the printer and check that the printer is online and has no error messages, such as a Paper Out message. Then Jill should ask, "Can anyone print to this printer?" To find out, she should go to the closest PC and try to print a Windows test page. If the test page prints, she should next go to one of the three PCs that do not print and begin troubleshooting that PC's connection to the network. If the test page did not print at the closest PC, the problem is still not necessarily the printer. To eliminate the printer as the problem, the next step is to print a self-test page at the printer. If that self-test page prints, then Jill should check other PCs on the network. Is the entire network down? Can one PC see another PC on the network? Perhaps part of the network is down (maybe because of a hub serving one part of the network).

CHAPTER SUMMARY

- The three most popular types of printers are laser, inkjet, and dot-matrix. Laser printers produce the highest quality, followed by inkjet printers. Dot-matrix printers have the advantage of being able to print multicopy documents. Other printer types are solid ink, thermal, and dye-sublimation printers.

- The six steps that a laser printer performs to print are cleaning, conditioning, writing, developing, transferring, and fusing. The first four steps take place inside the removable toner cartridge.

21

▶ Inkjet printers print by shooting ionized ink at a sheet of paper.

▶ The nozzles of an inkjet printer tend to clog or dry out, especially when the printer remains unused. The nozzles can be cleaned automatically by means of printer software or buttons on the front panel of the printer.

▶ Dot-matrix printers print by projecting pins from the print head against an inked ribbon that deposits ink on the paper.

▶ Before users on a network can view or access resources on a PC, Client for Microsoft Networks and File and Printer Sharing must be installed, and these resources must be shared.

▶ When troubleshooting printers, first isolate the problem. Narrow the source to the printer, cable, PC hardware, operating system including the device driver, application software, or network.

KEY TERMS

For explanations of key terms, see the Glossary near the end of the book.

beam detect mirror	laser printer	scanning mirror
control blade	local printer	solid ink printer
default printer	network printer	spooling
dye-sublimation printer	printer maintenance kit	thermal printer
inkjet printer	REt (Resolution Enhancement technology)	

REVIEWING THE BASICS

1. List the six steps used by a laser printer to print a page.

2. Which document exhibits better quality, one printed with 600 dpi or one printed with 1200 dpi? Why?

3. What are two possible settings in CMOS for parallel port mode?

4. During the laser printing process, what determines when the toner sticks to the drum and when it does not stick to the drum?

5. Why is it less expensive to maintain an inkjet printer that has a black ink cartridge than one that does not?

6. What technology makes an inkjet printer a photo-quality printer?

7. What should you do if an inkjet printer prints with missing dots or lines on the page?

8. What can you do to help a dot-matrix printer last longer?

9. List two possible ways to improve printing speed.

10. When a laser printer is short on memory, what is a possible symptom of this problem?

11. What two Windows components are used to share resources on a network and access those shared resources?

12. How do you share a local printer with others in the workgroup?

13. What are two ways to install a printer that is being shared by another computer on the network?

14. When would you want to enable Capture Printer Port while installing a network printer?

15. What company developed PostScript? PCL?

16. When you are isolating a printer problem, what are the four major possible sources of the problem?

17. In Windows 98, what is the mkcompat.exe utility used for?

18. How can you eliminate the printer as the source of a printing problem?

19. How can you be sure that a printer cable is not the source of a printer problem?

20. Why is it important not to remove ink cartridges from an inkjet printer and leave the cartridges outside the printer for an extended period of time?

THINKING CRITICALLY

1. A Windows 98 computer has a locally installed printer that you must make available to eight other Windows 98 computers on the network. What is the best way to do this?

   a. Use the Add Printer icon in the Printers window for each of the eight PCs.

   b. Use Network Neighborhood to install the printer on each of the eight PCs.

   c. Use the printer manufacturer's setup program from the printer's CD on each of the eight PCs.

   d. Install the printer on each of the eight PCs while sitting at the host PC. Use Network Neighborhood on the host PC.

21

2. You are not able to print a Word document on a Windows XP computer to a network printer. The network printer is connected directly to the network, but when you look at the Printers and Faxes window, you see the name of the printer as \\SMITHWIN2K\HP LaserJet 8100. In the following list, select the possible sources of the problem.

    a. The SMITHWIN2K computer is not turned on.

    b. The HP LaserJet 8100 printer is not online.

    c. The SMITHWIN2K printer is not online.

    d. The Windows XP computer has a stalled printer spool.

    e. The HP LaserJet 8100 computer is not logged on to the workgroup.

3. You are not able to print a test page from your Windows 2000 PC to your local HP DeskJet printer. Which of the following are possible causes of the problem?

    a. The network is down.

    b. The printer cable is not connected properly.

    c. The Windows print spool is stalled.

    d. You have the wrong printer drivers installed.

    e. File and Printer Sharing is not enabled.

HANDS-ON PROJECTS

HANDS-ON PROJECTS

PROJECT 21-1: **Practicing Printer Maintenance**

For an inkjet printer, follow the procedures in the printer's user guide to clean the printer nozzles and ink cartridges. For a laser printer, follow the procedures in its user guide to clean the inside of the printer where the toner cartridge is installed.

PROJECT 21-2: **Sharing a Local Printer**

Practice networking skills using Windows 2000/XP or Windows 9x/Me:

1. Share a local printer with others on the network.

2. Install a shared printer on a remote PC. Verify that you can print to the printer.

PROJECT 21-3: **Researching Printer Web Sites**

Your company plans to purchase a new printer, and you want to evaluate the printer manufacturers' Web sites to determine which site offers the best support. Research three Web sites listed in Table 21-1 and answer these questions, supporting your answers with printed pages from the Web site:

1. Which Web site made it easiest for you to select a new printer based on your criteria for its use?

2. Which Web site made it easiest for you to find help for troubleshooting printer problems?

3. Which Web site gave you information about routine maintenance for its printers?

PROJECT 21-4: **Researching a Printer Maintenance Plan**

You have been asked to recommend a maintenance plan for a laser printer. Search the manufacturer's Web site for information, and then write a maintenance plan. Include in the plan the tasks that need to be done, how often they need doing, and what tools and components are needed to perform the tasks. Use the Hewlett-Packard LaserJet 8100 DN printer unless your instructor tells you to use a different printer, perhaps one that is available in your lab.

21

All About SCSI

In this chapter, you will learn:

- About basics of SCSI technology and components
- How SCSI hard drives compare to IDE drives
- How to install a SCSI device
- Troubleshooting tips for SCSI

In Chapter 8, you learned about IDE hard drives. This chapter covers another technology, SCSI, which provides better performance and greater expansion capabilities for many internal and external devices, including hard drives, CD-ROM drives, DVD drives, and scanners. SCSI devices tend to be faster, more expensive, and more difficult to install than similar IDE devices. Because they are more expensive and more difficult to install, they are mostly used in corporate settings and are seldom seen in the small office or used on home PCs. This chapter discusses how SCSI technology works, as well as advantages and disadvantages of SCSI.

SCSI Basics

A+
CORE
1.7

SCSI (pronounced "scuzzy") stands for **Small Computer System Interface** and is a standard for communication between a subsystem of peripheral devices and the system bus. The SCSI bus can contain, and be used by, up to seven or 15 devices, depending on the SCSI standard. The SCSI bus controller can be an expansion card called a host adapter or can be embedded on the motherboard. Notebook computers that support SCSI can use a PC Card (PCMCIA) host adapter, or the host adapter can be an internal card using the Mini PCI standard or some other proprietary standard. Chapter 20 gives more information about PC Cards and Mini PCI adapters. In this section, you will learn how a SCSI subsystem is structured, how it works, and what variations of SCSI there are.

The SCSI Subsystem

✔ **A+ EXAM TIP**

The A+ Core exam expects you to know that a SCSI host adapter on a portable system can be an insertable PC Card or it can be an internal adapter.

If a motherboard does not have an embedded SCSI controller, the gateway from the SCSI bus to the system bus is the host adapter, a card inserted into an expansion slot on the motherboard. The adapter card, called the **host adapter**, is responsible for managing all devices on the SCSI bus. A host adapter can support both internal and external SCSI devices, using one connector on the card for a ribbon cable or round cable to connect to internal devices, and an external port that supports external devices (see Figure 22-1). All the devices and the host adapter form a single daisy chain. In Figure 22-1 this daisy chain has two internal devices and two external devices, with the SCSI host adapter in the middle of the chain.

When a device on the SCSI bus must communicate with the system bus, the data passes through the host adapter. The host adapter keeps up with the interchange between the devices on the SCSI bus and the system bus. SCSI technology has the added advantage of letting two devices on the SCSI bus pass data between them without going through the CPU. This method of data transmission provides a convenient way to back up a SCSI hard drive to a tape drive on the same SCSI subsystem, without involving the CPU.

Figure 22-2 compares IDE and SCSI bus communication. With an IDE drive (on the left in Figure 22-2), the CPU communicates with the hard drive controller, which is contained in the hard drive case, through the system bus. Recall from Chapter 8 that the hard drive controller communicates directly with the system bus. With a SCSI hard drive (on the right in the figure), the CPU communicates over the system bus to the SCSI host adapter, which communicates over the SCSI bus to the SCSI interface controller in the hard drive case. This SCSI interface controller communicates with the hard drive controller, which, in turn, communicates with the hard drive.

A+
CORE
1.7

Termination here

SCSI hard drive

SCSI hard drive

Two external SCSI devices

SCSI ribbon cable

Host adapter
with internal
and external
connections

SCSI
scanner

SCSI
CD-ROM
drive

Terminator
installed

SCSI cable

Figure 22-1   Using a SCSI bus, a SCSI host adapter can support internal and external SCSI devices

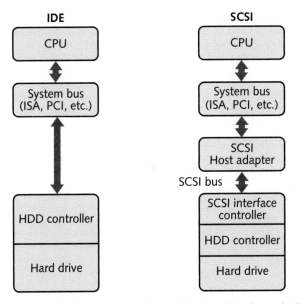

IDE

CPU

System bus
(ISA, PCI, etc.)

HDD controller

Hard drive

SCSI

CPU

System bus
(ISA, PCI, etc.)

SCSI
Host adapter

SCSI bus

SCSI interface
controller

HDD controller

Hard drive

Figure 22-2   SCSI hard drives communicate with the CPU through the SCSI host adapter, but IDE drives
communicate directly on the system bus

22

Many SCSI standards have evolved over several years. The maximum number of devices the SCSI bus can support depends on the type of SCSI being used. Some SCSI buses can link up to seven devices, others up to 15. Each device on the bus is assigned a number from 0 to 15 called the **SCSI ID,** by means of DIP switches, dials on the device, or software settings. The host adapter is generally assigned a number larger than all other devices, either 7 or 15; some come factory-set to the highest SCSI ID. Cables connect the devices physically in a daisy chain, sometimes called a straight chain. The devices can be either internal or external, and the host adapter can be at either end of the chain or somewhere in the middle. The SCSI ID identifies the physical device, which can have several logical devices embedded in it. For example, a CD-ROM jukebox–a CD-ROM changer with trays for multiple CDs–might have seven trays. Each tray is considered a logical device and is assigned a **Logical Unit Number (LUN)** to identify it, such as 1 through 7 or 0 through 6. The ID and LUN are written as two numbers separated by a colon. For instance, if the SCSI ID is 5, the fourth tray in the jukebox is device 5:4.

The technology of a SCSI device can be the same as the technology of a similar device that is not SCSI, with the added ability to use the SCSI bus and communicate with the host adapter. A device is a SCSI device not because of its technology, but because of the bus it uses.

Just like an IDE drive, a SCSI drive has its controller mounted inside the drive housing and can have a variable number of sectors per track. Low-level formatting of a SCSI drive is sometimes possible, and even recommended by the manufacturer, because the SCSI controller is likely to contain the firmware to do the job. (See the drive's documentation.) In theory, a SCSI drive can simply be an IDE drive with one more chip on the controller card in the drive housing and a different kind of data connection designed to fit the SCSI standard. In practice, however, SCSI drives are of higher quality, having higher rotational speeds and lower seek times than IDE drives. The SCSI chip within the drive housing that controls data transfer over the SCSI bus is called the **SBAC (SCSI bus adapter chip).**

To reduce the amount of electrical "noise," or interference, on a SCSI cable, each end of the SCSI chain has a **terminating resistor.** The terminating resistor can be a hardware device plugged into the last device on each end of the chain, or the chain can have software-controlled termination resistance, which makes installation simpler.

Now that you've learned the basic structure and function of a SCSI subsystem, let's look closely at two of its important components: host adapters and device drivers.

Host Adapters

An important issue when you install a SCSI bus system for the first time is the sophistication of the host adapter. More expensive host adapters are often easier to install because the installation software does more of the work for the installer and offers more help than does less expensive adapter software. This section discusses issues to consider when selecting a host adapter.

BIOS

A SCSI host adapter controller has BIOS that uses memory addresses on the PC and controls the operation of the SCSI bus. This SCSI controller uses a DMA channel, IRQ, and I/O addresses. You must install a SCSI device carefully to avoid resource conflicts with devices that are not on the SCSI subsystem. When you are looking for a host adapter, look for one that is Plug and Play compatible and has a configuration utility built into its ROM to make the setup process easier. Check also for software that configures termination automatically and assigns system resources. Working with this software is easier than setting jumpers or DIP switches on the card, because it allows you to make a change without opening the case. Also, look for a host adapter whose BIOS can configure SCSI devices using the bus controlled by the adapter. Finally, see how many devices the BIOS supports; for today's systems and SCSI devices, using a host adapter that supports up to 15 peripherals is best.

Expansion Slot

The host adapter must fit the expansion slot you plan to use. For a Pentium motherboard, you probably can choose either a 16-bit ISA host adapter or a PCI host adapter. Choose the 32-bit PCI bus for faster data transfer rate, instead of the 16-bit ISA bus. The newest host adapters are using the latest 64-bit PCI-X buses.

Bus Mastering

Choose a host adapter that uses bus mastering, discussed in Chapter 10, if your system bus supports it. Remember that a bus master attached to the PCI bus can access memory and other devices without accessing the CPU. For PCI buses that do support bus mastering, you have the added advantage that when bus mastering is used, the SCSI host adapter does not require a DMA channel.

SCAM-Compliant

SCAM (**SCSI Configuration AutoMatically** or SCSI Configuration AutoMagically, depending on the literature you're reading) is a method by which SCSI devices and the host adapter can be Plug and Play compliant. SCAM-compliant host adapters and devices can assign SCSI IDs dynamically at startup. Many SCSI devices currently in use are not SCAM-compliant, and you will need to set the unique ID on the device, using jumpers, rotary dials, or other methods. Newer SCSI host adapters use software that comes with the card to configure the SCSI BIOS. With the software, you can set the SCSI IDs, SCSI parity checking, termination, and system resources used by the card.

There are two levels of SCAM. Level 1 requires that the devices, but not the host adapter, be assigned an ID at startup by software. Level 2 requires that the host adapter, as well as the devices, be assigned an ID at startup by software. SCSI devices must be SCAM-compliant to carry the logo "Designed for Windows." Some older host adapters that are not SCAM-compliant are configured by jumpers.

Table 22-1 lists vendors for SCSI host adapters.

22

Vendor	Web Site
Adaptec	www.adaptec.com
ACARD Technology	www.acard.com
Intel	www.intel.com
LSI Logic	www.lsilogic.com
SCSI Stuff	www.scsistuff.com
Promise Technology	www.promise.com

Table 22-1   Vendors for SCSI host adapters

SCSI Device Drivers

SCSI device drivers are needed to enable an operating system to communicate with a host adapter. Many computers have some SCSI interface software in their system BIOS–enough, in fact, to allow a SCSI hard drive to be the boot device of the system. The system BIOS can access the SCSI drive, execute the load program in the drive's Master Boot Record, and load the SCSI device drivers stored on the hard drive into memory. If a system has two hard drives, one IDE and one SCSI, the IDE drive must be the boot device, unless system BIOS can support booting from a SCSI drive even when an IDE drive is present. This is because the motherboard BIOS takes precedence over the BIOS on the SCSI host adapter, which generally includes driver support for hard drives.

For most SCSI devices, support is not built into the host adapter BIOS or the system BIOS, and separate drivers are required. Although many drivers are available, using the drivers recommended or provided by the device vendor is best. Two popular driver types are **Advanced SCSI Programming Interface (ASPI)** and **Common Access Method (CAM)**. Both of these device driver standards describe the way the host adapter communicates with the SCSI device driver. ASPI, the more popular of the two, was originally developed by Adaptec and then licensed to other makers of SCSI devices. With CAM, a single driver can control several host adapters.

The manufacturer of the host adapter usually provides the SCSI driver on floppy disk or CD-ROM. Windows NT/2000/XP and Windows 9x/Me have built-in support for many SCSI devices. These OSs also provide SCSI drivers for a SCSI CD-ROM drive on their rescue disks, such as the Windows 9x/Me startup disk, so that you can have access to the SCSI CD-ROM drive when troubleshooting a failed boot.

Variations in SCSI

Just as with IDE/ATA standards, SCSI standards have improved over the years and use different names. SCSI standards are developed by the SCSI T10 Technical Committee (*www.t10.org*) and sent to ANSI, which publishes and maintains the official versions of the standards. The SCSI Trade Association, which promotes SCSI devices and standards, can also be accessed at *www.t10.org*. In addition to varying standards, SCSI also uses different types of cabling and different bus widths. This section covers variations within SCSI technology.

Bus Width

The two general categories of all SCSI standards used on PCs have to do with the width in bits of the SCSI data bus, either 8 bits (**narrow SCSI**) or 16 bits (**wide SCSI**). In almost every case, if the SCSI standard is 16 bits, then the word *wide* is in the name for the standard. In most cases, the word *narrow* is not mentioned in names for 8-bit standards. Narrow SCSI uses a cable with a 50-pin connector (also called an A cable), and wide SCSI uses a cable with a 68-pin connector (also called a P cable).

NOTE
The wide SCSI specification allows for a data path of 32 bits, although this is not broadly implemented in PCs. When you see a SCSI device referred to as wide, you can generally assume 16 bits.

Signaling Methods Used on SCSI Cables

A SCSI cable can be built in two different ways, depending on the method by which the electrical signal is placed on the cable: single-ended and differential. Both types of cables send a signal on a pair of twisted wires. In **single-ended (SE) cables**, one of the wires carries voltage and the other is a ground; in **differential cables**, both wires carry voltage and the signal is calculated to be the difference between the two voltages (see Figure 22-3). A single-ended cable is less expensive than a differential cable, but the maximum cable length cannot be as long because data integrity is not as great. With differential cabling, signal accuracy is better; noise on the line and electromagnetic interference are less likely to affect signaling because the reading is the difference between the two signals rather than the amplitude of one signal. Differential signaling also sends an extra verifying signal for each bit, providing greater reliability and reducing the chance of data errors.

When differential signaling was first introduced, the difference in voltage between the two wires was high (called **High Voltage Differential**, or HVD). This required a large amount of power and circuitry and made it impossible to mix differential and single-ended devices on a system without burning out the hardware. HVD became obsolete with the introduction of the SCSI-3 standard. The introduction of **Low Voltage Differential** (LVD) signaling and termination made it possible to develop less

22

expensive, low-voltage interfaces on the device, host adapter, cables, and terminators. As its name implies, LVD signaling uses lower voltages on the two-wire pair. It provides for cable lengths up to 12 meters (about 39.4 feet) and is required with Ultra SCSI standards. There is a type of LVD signaling called LVD/SE multimode that can work with SE devices and cables. If an LVD/SE device is used on a bus with SE devices, it uses the SE signaling method, which is slower and cannot accommodate longer cable lengths. Table 22-2 lists and describes the four types of cables.

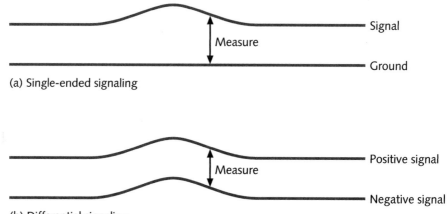

(a) Single-ended signaling

(b) Differential signaling

Figure 22-3 A SCSI pair of wires can carry a signal using (a) ground and a signal, or (b) a positive and negative signal, but differential signaling is less likely to be affected by noise on the line

CAUTION

Never use an HVD device on a bus with SE or LVD devices, because the high voltage put on the cable by the HVD device can destroy the low-voltage devices.

Cables for both narrow SCSI and wide SCSI can be either single-ended or differential. Single-ended, HVD, and LVD cables look the same, so you must make sure that you use the correct cable. It's important to know that you cannot look at a cable, the cable connector, or the connector on a device and know what type of signaling it uses. Connecting an HVD device to a SCSI bus using SE or LVD devices could burn the SE or LVD devices with the high voltage from the HVD device. Look at the device documentation to learn what type of signaling a device uses, or look for a symbol on the device that indicates the signaling method. Figure 22-4 shows the different symbols used on devices and cables to show what kind of signaling they use.

SCSI Cable	Maximum Length (meters and feet)	Maximum Speed	Transfer Rate	Description
Single-ended (SE)	3 M (10 ft.) for wide or 6 M (20 ft.) for narrow SCSI	20 MHz	40 Mbps	One wire in the pair is ground.
High voltage differential (HVD)	25 M (82 ft.)	20 or 40 MHz	40 Mbps	Both wires in the pair have high voltage.
Low voltage differential (LVD)	12 M (40 ft.) for 15 devices or 25 M (80 ft.) for 7 devices	320 MHz	80 Mbps	Both wires in the pair have low voltage.
LVD/SE multimode				If one SE device is on the bus, the smaller length and speed apply.

Table 22-2   SCSI cables

SE SCSI

Single-ended SCSI

DIFF SCSI

High voltage differential SCSI
(obsolete beginning with SCSI-3)

LVD SCSI

Low voltage differential SCSI

LVD/SE SCSI

SCSI devices that can work in LVD or SE mode

Figure 22-4   These symbols tell what type of signaling a device or cable uses

22

Adapters are available for mixing single-ended and differential devices and cables, but using them is not recommended. Mixing single-ended and differential signaling types is not a good idea because of the different ways they transmit data. Even with adapters, incompatible connections between single-ended and differential signals can damage both the host adapter and the devices connected to it. An exception to this principle is LVD/SE devices designed to work with either LVD or SE and revert to SE mode whenever the two are connected. Even then, however, know that the device is running at a slower speed than it could run if connected to an all-LVD signaling system, and that all cables in the system must meet the shorter SE standard lengths.

Connectors Used with SCSI Cables

The connector type or the number of pins on a SCSI cable connector is not affected by the signaling method used. Within each signaling method, the number of pins can vary. Figure 22-5 shows just a few of the many types of SCSI connectors. Although there are two main types of SCSI connectors, 50-pin (A cable) and 68-pin (P cable), there are other, less common types as well, such as the 80-pin SCA (Single Connector Attachment) connector used with some hot-swapping drives. Only 80-pin connectors supply power to the device in the connector; other devices require separate power connections. A SCSI bus can support more than one type of connector, and you can use connector adapters in order to plug a cable with one type of connector into a port using another type of connector.

NOTE

If you select a host adapter that supports both 50-pin connections and 68-pin connections, you can add a variety of devices to your system without purchasing a second host adapter.

For each type of connector, there can be variations in shape and pin density. Different companies and device manufacturers can make different connector types. For example, in an attempt to trim the size of the connector, a 25-pin SCSI connector was designed for narrow SCSI. The problem was that this connector looked like a parallel port connector. Never plug a SCSI connector into a parallel port or vice versa; you can damage equipment, because the signals work completely differently.

The good news in all this variety is that adapters are generally available to connect one type of connector to another, meaning that you can mix wide and narrow SCSI devices that use different connector variations. If you have any wide devices on your system at all, the cable from the host adapter must have a 68-pin connector, and you will need to use converters to attach 50-pin narrow devices.

Figure 22-5   The most popular SCSI connectors are 50-pin, A cable connectors for narrow SCSI and 68-pin, P cable connectors for wide SCSI

NOTE

When constructing an external SCSI chain, attach wide devices first (closest to the host adapter), and finish the chain with your narrow devices.

Most recent SCSI devices and buses use D-shaped 50-pin or 68-pin connectors that cannot be plugged in incorrectly. Older 50-pin connectors did not have this shape and could be oriented incorrectly. To line up a 50-pin connector to an internal SCSI device, look for a red or blue stripe on one side of the cable; this stripe lines up with pin 1 on the connector. Look also for a tab on one edge of the connector and a corresponding notch where you are to insert it.

The SCSI bus inside a computer is a ribbon or round cable, and the device connectors for internal devices are plugs at different positions on the cable. Having multiple connectors on the SCSI bus (see Figure 22-6) enables you to connect multiple internal devices easily. One end of the bus attaches to the host adapter, and for best results, you should always plug a device into the last connector on the cable.

22

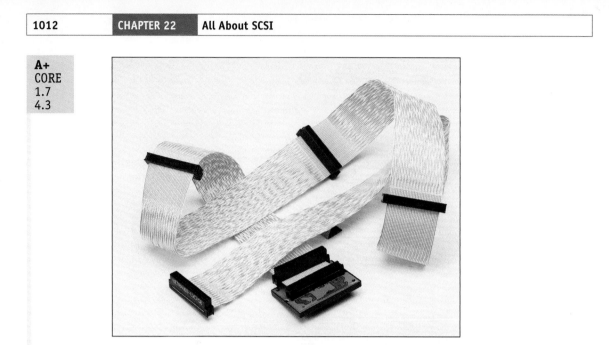

Figure 22-6   Internal SCSI cables can be ribbon cables or round cables and can support several devices. This 68-pin ribbon cable by Adaptec supports single-ended and LVD connections.

For external SCSI chains, there are two connectors on each device; both can send or receive information. That means it doesn't matter which connector on one device is linked to which connector on the next. A cable goes from the host adapter to a connector on the first device, then another cable goes from the second connector on the first device to a connector on the second device, and so on. The last connector on the last device must be filled with a terminator, unless that device provides software termination. External SCSI chains work like some Christmas lights: if one goes out, they all go out. Therefore, when connecting devices in an external SCSI chain, you should make sure to snap in the retaining clips or wires to complete the connection.

Termination

Termination prevents an echo effect from electrical noise and reflected data at the end of the SCSI daisy chain, which can cause interference with data transmission. Each end of a SCSI chain must be terminated, and there are several ways to do that:

- The host adapter can have a switch setting that activates or deactivates a terminating resistor on the card, depending on whether or not the adapter is at one end of the chain.
- A device can have either a single SCSI connection requiring that the device be placed at the end of the chain, or the device can have two connections. When a device has two connections, the second connection can be used to connect another device or to terminate the chain by placing an external terminator on

the connection. This external terminator serves as the terminating resistor (see Figure 22-7).

Figure 22-7   External SCSI terminator

- The device at the end of the chain can also be terminated by a resistor physically mounted on that device in a specially designated socket.
- Some devices have built-in terminators (internal terminators) that you can turn on or off with a jumper setting on the device.
- Termination can be controlled by software. Sometimes this software uses automatic termination that does not require your intervention.

Figure 22-1 shows the terminators needed at the end of both internal and external SCSI chains. In the figure, there is no terminator on the host adapter, which has both internal and external devices attached to it. Only when you have both types of devices attached to a host adapter do you remove termination from the host adapter.

There are several types of terminators:

- **Passive terminators,** the least reliable type, are used with SCSI-1 devices that operate at low speed and at short distances. They use simple resistors only and are rarely used today, as they are not sufficient for today's faster SCSI devices and longer cabling distances. Passive termination should only be used with narrow SCSI.
- **Active terminators** include voltage regulators in addition to the simple resistors used with passive termination. Most of today's single-ended SCSI cables use active termination, which was recommended with SCSI-2. Active termination is used with wide SCSI and is required with fast SCSI. It also works better over longer distances than passive termination.
- **Forced perfect terminators (FPTs)** are a more advanced version of active terminators and include a mechanism to force signal termination to the correct voltage, eliminating most signal echoes and interference. FPTs are more expensive and more reliable than passive and active terminators.

22

A+
CORE
1.7
4.3

Passive terminators, active terminators, and FPTs are all used with single-ended SCSI cables. Differential cables use either HVD or LVD terminators.

SCSI-1, SCSI-2, and SCSI-3

The three major versions of SCSI are SCSI-1, SCSI-2, and SCSI-3, commonly known as Regular SCSI, Fast SCSI, and Ultra SCSI. SCSI-1 was the original version of the SCSI standard. It covered the design of wiring on the SCSI bus but did not include a common command set. Therefore, there were still a lot of incompatibilities between SCSI-1 devices. With SCSI-1, only an 8-bit data bus was used, and there could be only seven devices besides the host adapter.

SCSI-2 improved the standard by developing a common command set so that devices could communicate with each other more easily. It also introduced wide SCSI, which expanded the width of the data bus to 16 bits and the number of possible devices to 15. SCSI-2 also made parity checking of the data bus mandatory.

SCSI-3, which has grown to be a set of standards rather than a single standard, supports both parallel and serial data transmission, supports FireWire connections, and increases the possible rate of data transfer to 320 MB/sec and higher. The **SPI (SCSI Parallel Interface)** standard is part of SCSI-3 and specifies how SCSI devices are connected. There have been three versions of SPI; the latest is Ultra 320 SCSI. Beginning with Ultra SCSI (SCSI-3), the SCSI standard supports SCAM, which you learned about earlier in the chapter. SCSI-3 uses an 8-, 16-, or 32-bit data bus and supports up to 32 devices on a system.

NOTE Because SCSI can be so difficult to configure, a growing trend in the industry is to replace SCSI with FireWire (IEEE 1394), especially since some newer high-end motherboards provide FireWire support. Another contender to replace SCSI is FCAL (Fiber Channel Arbitrated Loop), which uses fiberoptic cabling. Both FireWire and FCAL use serial data transmission. FCAL is used on higher-end systems than FireWire.

✔ **A+ EXAM TIP**

The A+ Core exam expects you to know about these SCSI standards and interface types: narrow, fast, wide, ultra-wide, LVD, and HVD.

Because SCSI standards vary, when you buy a new SCSI device, you must be sure that it is compatible with the SCSI bus you already have, taking into consideration that some SCSI standards are backward-compatible. If the new SCSI device is not compatible, you cannot use the same SCSI bus, and you must buy a new host adapter to build a second SCSI bus system, increasing the overall cost of adding the new device.

Table 22-3 summarizes characteristics of the different SCSI standards. Other names used in the industry for these standards are also listed in the table. Note that both Fast SCSI (SCSI-2) and Ultra SCSI (SCSI-3) have narrow and wide versions.

A+
CORE
1.7
4.3

Standard Name	Standard Number	Bus Width (Narrow = 8 bits, Wide = 16 bits)	Transfer Rate (MB/sec)	Maximum Number of Devices
Regular SCSI	SCSI-1	Narrow	5	8
Fast SCSI or Fast Narrow	SCSI-2	Narrow	10	8
Fast Wide SCSI or Wide SCSI	SCSI-2	Wide	20	16
Ultra SCSI, Ultra Narrow, or Fast-20 SCSI	SCSI-3	Narrow	20	8
Wide Ultra SCSI or Fast Wide 20	SCSI-3	Wide	40	16
Ultra2 SCSI or SPI-2	SCSI-3	Narrow	40	8
Wide Ultra2 SCSI	SCSI-3	Wide	80	16
Ultra3 SCSI or SPI-3	SCSI-3	Narrow	80	8
Wide Ultra3 SCSI or Ultra 160 SCSI	SCSI-3	Wide	160	16
Ultra 320 SCSI (Ultra4 SCSI or SPI-4)	SCSI-3	Wide	320*	16

*SPI-4 is expected to soon be rated at 640 MBps and then 1280 MBps.

Table 22-3   Summary of SCSI standards

The latest SCSI standard, serial SCSI, also called serial attached SCSI (SAS), is expected to be readily available about the time this book is in print. Serial SCSI will allow for more than 15 devices on a single SCSI chain, use smaller, longer, round cables, and use smaller hard drive form factors that can support larger capacities. Serial SCSI is compatible with serial ATA drives in the same system, and claims to be more reliable and better performing than serial ATA. For more information on serial SCSI, see the SCSI Trade Association's Web site at *www.serialattachedscsi.com.*

Table 22-4 summarizes cable specifications for the SCSI standards listed in Table 22-3. Note that 8-bit narrow SCSI uses a 50-pin cable and 16-bit wide SCSI uses a 68-pin cable.

22

A+
CORE
1.7
4.3

SCSI Standard Name	Maximum Length of Single-Ended Cable (Meters)	Maximum Length of Differential Cable (Meters)	Cable Type
Regular SCSI	6	25	50-pin
Fast SCSI or Fast Narrow	3	25	50-pin
Fast Wide SCSI or Wide SCSI	3	25	68-pin
Ultra SCSI, Ultra Narrow, or Fast-20 SCSI	1.5	25	50-pin
Wide Ultra SCSI or Fast Wide 20	1.5	25	68-pin
Ultra2 SCSI or SPI-2		12 LVD	50-pin
Wide Ultra2 SCSI			68-pin
Ultra3 SCSI or SPI-3		12 LVD	50-pin
Wide Ultra3 SCSI or Ultra 160 SCSI		12 LVD	68-pin
Ultra 320 SCSI (Ultra4 SCSI or SPI-4)		12 LVD	68-pin

Table 22-4   SCSI standard cable specifications

Comparing IDE and SCSI

Before we move on to how to install SCSI devices, let's compare SCSI to IDE technology. When selecting hard drives and other devices, you need to know which technology they use and the advantages and disadvantages of each. When you use a single disk drive with an operating system such as Windows 98 or Windows Me, you may actually find that an IDE drive provides better performance than a comparable SCSI drive. Features of SCSI drives that are improvements over IDE increase performance mainly where a heavy load is placed on a system and on its components–for example, when multiple hard drives are installed on a high-end server. Also, some operating systems, such as Windows 2000 and XP, include increased support for SCSI features and can take better advantage of them.

Consider the following issues when choosing between an IDE hard drive and a SCSI hard drive:

- Parallel ATA/IDE can support up to four internal drives. Serial ATA combined with parallel ATA/IDE can support up to six internal and external drives, and SCSI can support up to 15 internal and external drives. For more than six drives in a system, use SCSI.
- SCSI drives perform better in a RAID array than IDE drives.
- SCSI devices are generally higher quality than IDE devices and more expensive.
- IDE devices require a separate IRQ for each IDE channel; SCSI requires only one for the entire chain.
- Both IDE and SCSI are generally backward-compatible, in that most fast hardware can work with slower devices.
- A SCSI hard drive with its supporting host adapter and cable costs more than an IDE hard drive.
- A SCSI subsystem provides faster data transfer than an IDE drive, although the SCSI bus is the source of the performance rather than the hard drive technology.
- SCSI generally provides better performance than IDE and is often used on high-demand servers.
- A good SCSI host adapter allows you to connect other SCSI devices to it, such as a printer, scanner, or tape drive.
- Without SCSI technology, if you have two IDE drives on the same IDE channel, only one of them can be busy at any one time. For instance, without SCSI, if one of your IDE devices is a CD-ROM, the hard drive must wait for the CD-ROM to complete a task before it can work again. With SCSI, two or more devices can operate simultaneously. If you plan to transfer a lot of data from CD-ROM to hard drive, this is a good reason to choose SCSI.

In summary, SCSI is more expensive than IDE but gives you better performance.

NOTE It is possible, but not recommended, to mix SCSI and IDE devices on a system. Both types of devices will try to monopolize system resources, and you might experience conflicts as a result.

Installing SCSI Devices

A+ CORE 1.2 1.7

As you learned, there are many different types of SCSI and many variations within the components of a SCSI subsystem. Although the installation of a SCSI system may sound complicated and requires many decisions about what components to buy, the installation instructions for SCSI devices and host adapters are usually very thorough and well written. If you carefully follow all instructions, SCSI installations can be smooth and problem free. This section covers how to install SCSI devices, beginning with a host adapter and then moving on to a scanner and a hard drive as examples.

22

**A+
CORE
1.2
1.7**

First, let's look at some basic steps for SCSI installation:

1. Set any jumpers or switches on the host adapter, install it in the correct expansion slot on your motherboard, and install the host adapter drivers.

2. For each device that has them, use jumpers or switches to assign the SCSI ID.

3. Attach cabling to the host adapter and then to each device.

4. Verify that both ends of the SCSI chain are terminated.

5. Power up one device. After you verify that it works, power up the next device. Continue until you verify that all devices work.

6. Install drivers and software required to interface between the SCSI subsystem and the operating system.

Installing a Host Adapter Card

APPLYING CONCEPTS

For a Plug and Play system using Windows 2000/XP or Windows 9x/Me, follow these general steps to install a host adapter:

1. Install the card in an expansion slot.

2. In most cases, default settings for the host adapter are correct, but you can change or verify these settings using the setup program. For example, to use a setup program that comes on a floppy disk bundled with the adapter, boot the PC from the floppy disk. The disk boots the system (using DOS) and automatically executes the SCSI setup program. In this example of one setup program, the two options on the opening menu are SCSI Disk Utilities (for installing a SCSI hard drive) and Configure the Host Adapter. Select **Configure the Host Adapter**. You see the host adapter configuration screen (see Figure 22-8).

3. Verify the settings. Under the Advanced Configuration Options in Figure 22-8, you see two settings: enable or disable Plug and Play, and enable or disable SCAM support. Both are normally set to enable. Note in Figure 22-8 that the SCSI ID for the host adapter is 7 and that parity checking is enabled. After verifying settings, exit the setup program, remove the floppy disk, and reboot.

4. When Windows loads, it senses a new hardware device and automatically launches the Add New Hardware Wizard. Because Windows supports the host adapter, it loads the device drivers automatically and installs the host adapter.

5. To verify that the host adapter is correctly installed, open **Device Manager**. Double-click **SCSI controllers**. The Adaptec host adapter should appear, as shown in

Figure 22-9 for Windows 98. Select the host adapter and click **Properties** to display the host adapter Properties dialog box, also shown in Figure 22-9. Click the **Resources** tab to note the resources assigned to the card by Plug and Play. (For Windows 2000/XP Device Manager, you can view a device's properties by right-clicking the device and selecting **Properties** on the shortcut menu.)

Figure 22-8 Setup software included with a SCSI host adapter is used to change SC SI BIOS settings on the card

Figure 22-9 Device Manager displays the newly installed host adapter

22

A+
CORE
1.2
1.7

NOTE Notice the broken diamond symbol in Figure 22-9, which you saw earlier in Figure 22-4. The symbol for single-ended SCSI devices is sometimes used to symbolize SCSI in general.

✔ **A+ EXAM TIP**

The A+ Core exam expects you to know how to install a SCSI host adapter.

After you install the host adapter, you are ready to install the external SCSI device. For example, if the device is a SCSI scanner, follow these directions:

1. Install the software to run the scanner, which includes the scanner driver.
2. Plug the SCSI cable into the host adapter port.
3. Plug the other end of the cable into the scanner.
4. Set the SCSI ID on the scanner and install a terminator on the scanner.
5. Connect the scanner's power cord to a wall outlet, and turn on the scanner.
6. Restart your PC and test the scanner.

Setting Device IDs During Installation

A+
CORE
1.2
1.7

If your SCSI subsystem is SCAM-compliant, SCSI IDs are assigned automatically. However, SCAM does not work unless your OS, devices, and host adapter all support the SCAM standard. Without SCAM compliance, you must set device SCSI IDs manually. Remember that each ID must be unique; no two devices on the same SCSI channel can have the same ID number. (If you have more than one SCSI adapter on a system, you can reuse IDs.) For narrow SCSI, the IDs are 0–7, and for wide SCSI, the IDs are 0–15. Generally, you can assign almost any ID number to any device. However, the host adapter usually has the ID 7 or 15, and some devices may come from the manufacturer with their IDs already set. Many SCSI hard drives, for example, are automatically set to SCSI ID 6.

✔ **A+ EXAM TIP**

The A+ Core exam expects you to know how to set SCSI jumpers using binary equivalents.

To set IDs for external devices, you use either a push-button selector or rotary selector, as shown in Figure 22-10. The push-button selector has buttons to increase and decrease the number, and the rotary selector works like a radio dial that you turn to the number you want. Some ID selectors for external devices are designed to be adjusted with a screwdriver, so that you cannot accidentally change the ID by bumping the device.

To set IDs for internal devices, you use a set of jumpers on the device. Most new devices use a binary code to set IDs, with three pin pairs for narrow SCSI and four pin pairs for wide SCSI. Figure 22-11 shows the jumper settings for wide SCSI IDs.

A+
CORE
1.2
1.7

Figure 22-10   This rotary dial on the rear of a SCSI scanner is used to set the SCSI ID, which is now set to 6

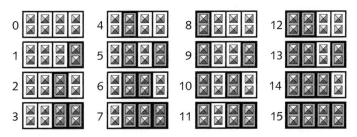

Figure 22-11   Wide SCSI ID binary jumper settings for internal devices

Installing a SCSI Hard Drive

When you install a SCSI hard drive, make sure that your host adapter and the cables you use are compatible with the SCSI drive. Figure 22-12 shows the different connectors on SCSI hard drives. A 40-pin IDE connector is included for comparison. When matching SCSI standards and interfaces, the vendor can help you.

When preparing for the installation, read the documentation for both the SCSI host adapter and the hard drive before beginning; most SCSI documentation is well written and thorough. In addition to the procedure already discussed in Chapter 8 for IDE hard drives, a SCSI installation requires that you configure the SCSI host adapter and the SCSI hard drive so that they can communicate with each other.

22

A+
CORE
1.2
1.7

40-pin IDE connector with power connector

50-pin SCSI connector with power connector

68-pin SCSI connector with power connector

80-pin SCSI SCA connector

Figure 22-12   Connector types for SCSI hard drives

This is done as follows:

1. *Set SCSI IDs.* Set the ID for each device on the SCSI bus. The host adapter documentation probably explains that the host adapter must be set to ID 7 or 15. If the hard drive is to be the boot device for the system, its ID is likely to be 0. The second hard drive ID is usually 1. These ID settings might be set by jumpers or DIP switches on the drive.

2. *Disable or enable disk drive and hard drive controllers.* If the host adapter has a built-in disk drive controller that you are not using, it might be necessary to disable the controller with jumpers or DIP switches, or from the SCSI software setup program. The host adapter documentation explains how to do this. Incidentally, if you are not using a SCSI hard drive or disk drive controller on your motherboard, you must disable these controllers by setting jumpers or DIP

A+
CORE
1.2
1.7

switches on the motherboard or by changing settings in CMOS setup. See the documentation for your motherboard. Sometimes CMOS setup gives you the option of booting from the SCSI hard drive even if an IDE hard drive is installed.

3. *Check terminating resistors.* Devices on both ends of the bus must have terminating resistors. Check the documentation for the two devices on each end of the SCSI chain to see how the termination is done.

4. *Run CMOS setup for a SCSI system.* After you physically install the SCSI host and drive, tell setup that the SCSI system is present. Remember that for SCSI devices, the computer does not communicate with the hard drive directly but interfaces with the SCSI host adapter. To use a SCSI hard drive, some computers require that you tell setup that no hard drive is present. The SCSI host provides that information to the computer during startup. Sometimes, the computer setup lets you choose a SCSI hard drive type. That's all it needs to know; the SCSI host adapter takes over from there. To recognize a SCSI drive, some computers require that the drive type be set to 1 in CMOS setup.

5. *Load SCSI device drivers.* Windows operating systems offer their own SCSI drivers, although if the host adapter documentation recommends that you use the adapter's driver instead, then do so. After you physically install the drive and change CMOS setup, the next step in any hard drive installation is to boot from a floppy disk. The hard drive package will include a bootable disk or CD that loads the device driver to access the SCSI system.

Troubleshooting SCSI Devices

A+
CORE
1.7
2.1

When you use a variety of SCSI devices, installation and configuration can get complicated. To make this process as easy as possible, keep these general tips in mind:

- As always, keep detailed notes on device installation and configuration for use in troubleshooting and backtracking, and always read all documentation for devices you are trying to add to and use with your system. Record all switch and jumper settings for your SCSI devices. Record all system resources and addresses used by the host adapter.
- If you are adding several SCSI devices to your system, add them one at a time rather than all at once. First install the host adapter and, if you are using one, the SCSI hard drive, and make sure they work before you try to install additional peripherals.
- Use components of good quality. Do not sacrifice quality just to pay a little less. For example, higher-quality cables usually experience less degradation of data and less interference, and higher-quality active terminators generally do a better job than cheaper passive ones, even if you have some devices that are not Fast SCSI.

22

A+
CORE
1.7
2.1

■ Limit cable length whenever possible to improve performance and reduce the chance that data will become corrupted.

Here are some things to check if you have problems with installing SCSI devices:

■ SCSI drivers will look for their devices when the computer boots, so make sure to turn on all external SCSI devices before you turn on the computer.
■ Check the connections of all SCSI cables, power connections, and adapters. Sometimes moving and reattaching them can clear up connection problems.
■ Many problems with SCSI devices are caused by incorrect termination. Remember that both ends of a SCSI chain must be terminated and that termination should be disabled at all other points in the chain. If the host adapter is at one end of the chain, it must have termination enabled; if it is in the middle of the chain, it must have termination disabled.
■ Check with your motherboard's manufacturer to make sure you have the most updated BIOS, so that PCI slots operate correctly. Also check to make sure you have up-to-date drivers for your SCSI devices.
■ Install a PCI host adapter in a PCI bus that supports bus mastering–not all PCI slots on older motherboards do. Try removing the host adapter and reseating it in another PCI slot.

✔ **A+ EXAM TIP**

The A+ Core exam expects you to be able to troubleshoot SCSI installations.

After you install SCSI devices, if you also have IDE devices, your system attempts to boot from the IDE drive first. To cause it to boot from a SCSI drive, you must either change the boot order or remove the non-SCSI drives to cause it to boot from a SCSI drive. If your system has only SCSI drives installed and still will not boot, check these things:

■ The BIOS setup drive configuration for your computer should be set to "No Drives Installed." Most BIOSs only support IDE drives. If you tell the system that no drives are installed, it attempts to boot from another device, such as a SCSI drive.
■ Verify that the SCSI drive that you want to boot from is partitioned, that it has a primary partition, and that the boot partition is set as active.
■ If nothing else works, back up the SCSI hard drive and then do a low-level format on it. A Format utility is included with the host adapter for this purpose.

CHAPTER SUMMARY

▸ The SCSI bus requires a controller embedded on the motherboard or on a host adapter inserted into an expansion slot. If the motherboard has a SCSI controller, a SCSI port or connector will be somewhere on the board. The host adapter is the more common way of supporting SCSI.

▸ The term *SCSI hard drive* refers more to the bus used by the drive than to the technology of the drive. Internally, SCSI and IDE drives work in basically the same way.

▸ There are several variations of SCSI buses and devices, including SCSI-1, SCSI-2, SCSI-3, Wide SCSI, Ultra SCSI, and Ultra Wide SCSI.

▸ Every SCSI bus subsystem requires a SCSI controller and unique SCSI IDs assigned to each device, including the host adapter.

▸ The SCSI host adapter should generally be set to ID 7 or 15, since these IDs have the highest priority.

▸ The narrow SCSI bus has an 8-bit data path, and the wide SCSI bus has a 16-bit data path.

▸ Each end of the SCSI bus must have a terminating resistor, which can be controlled by hardware or software.

▸ Narrow SCSI uses a 25-pin or 50-pin connector (also called an A cable), and wide SCSI uses a 68-pin connector (also called a P cable).

▸ The two types of SCSI cabling are single-ended and differential.

▸ There are three types of termination for single-ended cabling: passive, active, and forced perfect.

▸ There are two types of signaling for differential SCSI cabling: HVD and LVD. HVD became obsolete with the introduction of SCSI-3. HVD uses a higher voltage than LVD signaling does.

▸ When selecting a SCSI host adapter, consider the SCSI standards the adapter supports, the bus slot the adapter will use, the device driver standard used by the host adapter, the issue of single-ended versus differential SCSI, SCAM compliance, and whether or not the host offers bus mastering.

▸ Each device on a SCSI bus is assigned a number from 0 to 15, called the SCSI ID. Logical devices within a physical device, such as trays within a CD changer, are assigned a separate number called a LUN.

▸ The two main types of SCSI device drivers are ASPI and CAM. When selecting a host adapter, you should pick one that supports either ASPI or CAM.

▸ You can limit the chance of data becoming corrupted by buying high-quality cables, limiting cable length, and using high-end terminators.

22

▶ If you have an IDE hard drive and a SCSI hard drive installed on the same system, the system attempts to boot from the IDE hard drive first. If you want to boot from a SCSI drive, you must change the boot order in Setup or remove the non-SCSI drives.

▶ One of the most common causes for problems with the SCSI subsystem is incorrect termination.

KEY TERMS

For explanations of key terms, see the Glossary near the end of the book.

active terminator
Advanced SCSI Programming
   Interface (ASPI)
Common Access Method (CAM)
differential cable
forced perfect terminator (FPT)
High Voltage Differential (HVD)

host adapter
Logical Unit Number (LUN)
Low Voltage Differential (LVD)
narrow SCSI
passive terminator
SBAC (SCSI bus adapter chip)
SCAM (SCSI Configuration
   AutoMatically)

SCSI (Small Computer System
   Interface)
SCSI ID
single-ended (SE) cable
SPI (SCSI Parallel Interface)
terminating resistor
termination
wide SCSI

REVIEWING THE BASICS

1. What is the difference between narrow SCSI and wide SCSI?

2. Name at least three advantages of using SCSI over IDE.

3. Can you mix single-ended and differential devices on a SCSI subsystem? Why or why not?

4. What is SCAM, and how does it make device installation easier?

5. To what SCSI ID number should the host adapter be set for narrow SCSI?

6. How many devices can wide SCSI support, not including the host adapter?

7. What are the two most common standards for SCSI device drivers?

8. With what type of device would you use a 25-pin connector? A 50-pin? A 68-pin? An 80-pin?

9. What are the two basic types of cabling for SCSI? How are they similar and how are they different?

10. Why was the 25-pin SCSI connector developed? What is the problem with its use?

11. If you have any wide SCSI devices on your system, the cable from the host adapter must have a(n) _____-pin connector.

12. What types of termination are used for single-ended cables? For differential?

13. How does active termination improve upon passive termination?

14. Why is it more expensive to add peripheral devices to a SCSI subsystem than with IDE?

15. How do you set SCSI device IDs if your host adapter is not SCAM-compliant?

16. What might happen if a SCSI bus is not properly terminated?

17. What problems might you experience with low-quality SCSI cabling?

18. If you have an IDE hard drive and a SCSI hard drive on the same system, from which drive will your system attempt to boot first?

19. How is the LUN related to the SCSI ID?

20. How is a SCSI hard drive similar to an IDE hard drive? How is it different?

THINKING CRITICALLY

1. When installing a SCSI hard drive, when should you set your system BIOS to "No Drives Installed"?

   a. When the system BIOS supports booting from a SCSI device

   b. When the system BIOS does not support booting from a SCSI device

   c. Always

   d. Never

2. What would be different about performing a hard-drive-to-tape backup with IDE devices and with SCSI devices? What are the advantages of using SCSI devices over IDE devices for backups?

3. How would three jumpers be set to indicate SCSI ID 6?

22

HANDS-ON PROJECTS

PROJECT 22-1: Investigating SCSI Standards

Research the Web sites of manufacturers of host adapters and other SCSI products, and answer the following questions. Print Web pages to support your answers.

1. Give an example of a host adapter that uses LVD signaling. What is the price of the host adapter?

2. Suppose this LVD host adapter is to be used with external devices that use 68-pin connectors. Give an example of a terminator that can be used with one of these devices. What is the price of the terminator?

3. What is the price of a 10-foot or longer SCSI cable that can be used with LVD signaling and has 68-pin connectors at both ends?

4. Give an example of a SCSI hard drive that is 137 GB or larger. What is the price of the drive?

5. What type of connector does the hard drive in Question 4 have? What type of termination does it use? How is the SCSI ID set?

PROJECT 22-2: Setting SCSI IDs

Investigate and answer the following questions about setting SCSI IDs:

1. You are installing an internal SCSI hard drive that you want to set to SCSI ID 14. There are four jumpers on the drive. How do you set the jumpers?

2. You are installing an internal SCSI hard drive that you want to be the boot device. How do you determine what SCSI ID to give the drive?

PROJECT 22-3: Investigating SCSI Technologies

Adaptec (*www.adaptec.com*) is a leader in manufacturing SCSI devices. It has a standard called SpeedFlex. Using the Adaptec Web site as your source, write a short paper (about one page) explaining what SpeedFlex technology does.

PROJECT 22-4: Comparing SCSI and IDE

Visit a computer store and compare SCSI and IDE hard drives. Answer the following questions:

1. How many different models of SCSI drives and IDE drives does the store keep in stock? How many manufacturers are represented?

2. What are some typical sizes, speeds, and prices of SCSI drives and IDE drives?

3. Based on your observations, does it seem that SCSI or IDE drives are the higher-end drives?

4. Based on the number of drives of each type in stock, which is more popular, SCSI or IDE?

5. Which type of drive is the better buy based on size? Based on performance?

PROJECT 22-5: Pricing a SCSI System

Price a complete SCSI system for a power-user workstation, including a host adapter, internal ribbon cable, internal hard drive, and internal CD-ROM drive. Try to keep the cost as reasonable as possible without sacrificing quality. List the products and their cost, and include printouts of the Web pages describing each product. What is the total cost of the SCSI system?

22

Purchasing a PC or Building Your Own

This chapter presents guidelines for purchasing a new PC and detailed, step-by-step procedures for building a PC from parts. If you need a computer for your own personal use, consider assembling it yourself, not necessarily to save money but to benefit in other ways. If you don't want to build a PC, you must choose between purchasing a brand-name PC or a clone.

After-sales service and support are probably the most important criteria to consider when purchasing a PC. In general, a brand-name PC (such as Dell or Gateway) might cost more, but generally you will get better service and support than you will for a PC built with parts from companies whose names you don't recognize. Important reasons to build your own PC are the knowledge you gain and complete control over every part you purchase, which allows you to make a customized, integrated system.

Selecting a Personal Computer to Meet Your Needs

So far, this book has been full of information concerning which computers, peripheral devices, operating systems, and software to buy, and how to manage and maintain them once they are yours. However, hardware and software change daily, and it's important to stay informed if you make buying decisions or give purchasing advice on an ongoing basis. When you need more computing power or additional options, consider upgrading the current PC or buying a new one.

Upgrading a PC

**A+
CORE
1.9
1.10**

Sometimes it is appropriate to upgrade an existing PC rather than purchase a new one. Consider adding more memory, upgrading the CPU or adding a second CPU, adding a second hard drive, upgrading the video card, upgrading the motherboard, and adding more fans for cooling. Generally, an upgrade is appropriate if its cost does not exceed half the value of the current system, and if the resulting system does not contain legacy components that prevent the upgraded system from performing well. Don't upgrade a computer system that is more than five years old, as the cost of the upgrade will probably exceed the value of the current system. In this case, a new PC is your best option.

Here are some important points to keep in mind when upgrading:

✔ **A+ EXAM TIP**

The A+ Core exam expects you to be able to make decisions about upgrading components on a PC when given an upgrading scenario.

- Before upgrading the OS, verify that you can get drivers for each device in the system. Some legacy devices might not have the latest OS drivers available.
- Match the motherboard bus types to the expansion cards and consider the number of expansion slots available on the motherboard. There are several types of AGP slots, and your video card must match the AGP standards your motherboard supports. In addition, PCI Express is faster but costs more. It's probably not a good idea to use every expansion slot on the motherboard. Overheating can become an issue, and some motherboards are made so that if you use certain connectors on the board (such as a wireless connector), the last PCI slot is disabled.
- When upgrading the processor, keep in mind the voltage requirements and the possible need for an extra ATX12V 4-pin connector on the motherboard to support the processor. You might need to install a voltage regulator module, as described in Chapter 5. Check the motherboard documentation for the processor speeds and types the board supports and how they are supported.
- When making a decision to upgrade the motherboard, know that you might also have to buy new memory modules and a new processor that the new board supports. Verify that all components that connect to the current motherboard are compatible with the new board.

**A+
CORE
1.9
1.10**

- When adding a second processor to the system, verify that your OS supports dual processing. Also, check the motherboard documentation to ensure that you are using two processors that work together on this board.
- When upgrading memory, follow the guidelines in Chapter 6 to match memory modules to what the motherboard supports and what is already installed.
- When making major upgrades of the motherboard, processor, or peripheral devices, verify that your hard drive has enough available space to support the extra needs of these devices. You might need to upgrade the hard drive or add a second drive.
- When upgrading or adding a new hard drive, match the ATA/IDE or SCSI standards your motherboard or controller card supports to the new drive.
- If you think you might need to flash BIOS before installing a new peripheral, do so and verify that the motherboard and existing peripherals are working before you invest in the new device. Also, install the latest updates and patches to your OS.

Buying a New PC

You can choose one of three alternatives when selecting a PC: buy a brand-name PC, buy a clone, or buy parts and assemble a PC yourself–which, in effect, results in your own personally designed clone.

A brand-name PC, sometimes called an **IBM-compatible PC,** is a PC manufactured by a company with a widely recognized name such as Hewlett-Packard, Packard Bell, Dell, Gateway, or IBM. A **clone** is generally understood to mean a PC assembled by a local company with parts manufactured by several companies. There are advantages and disadvantages to purchasing both brand-name and clone PCs, in the areas of warranties, service contracts, and ease of obtaining replacement and additional parts. For instance, while it may seem an advantage that brand-name PCs and most clones come with some software already installed, the software is not necessarily standard, brand-name software. The preinstalled software can be any variety of shareware, unknown software, and so forth, and the documentation and original installation disks for the software may not be included in the total package.

When selecting a computer system that will include both hardware and software, begin by taking an overall view of the decisions you must make. Start by answering these questions:

- How will the computer be used now and in the future?
- What functionality do you want the computer to have (within its intended use)?
- What hardware and software do you need to meet this functionality?
- What is your budget?
- If you determine that a clone meets your needs, do you want to assemble it yourself?

23

To make the best possible decision, consider the first question to be the most important, the second question the next most important, and so on. For example, if you intend to use the computer for multimedia presentations and accessing the Internet, the functionality required is considerably different from that of a computer used for software development.

After you identify the intended purpose of the computer, list the functionality required to meet the needs of the intended purpose. For example, if the computer is to be used for playing games, some required functionality might be:

- Ability of the hardware to support game software
- Excellent video and sound
- Sophisticated input methods, such as a joystick or controller

If the computer is to be used for software development, required functionality might include:

- The ability to support the standard hardware and software environment that most customers using the developed software might have
- The ability to run software development tools and hardware to support the software
- A high-quality monitor and a comfortable keyboard and mouse for long work hours
- A removable, high-capacity storage device for easy transfer and storage of developed software
- Reliable warranty and service to guarantee minimal downtime (A three-year parts warranty is the minimum you should buy.)

After the required functionality is defined, the next step, defining what hardware and software are needed, is much easier. For example, if a comfortable keyboard designed for long work hours is required, begin by researching the different types of keyboards available, and try out a few in stores if necessary. It would be a mistake to purchase the cheapest keyboard in the store for this intended purpose. However, for game playing, an expensive, comfortable keyboard is probably not needed because most games use other input devices. Spending your resources on a sophisticated joystick probably makes more sense.

As noted above, the least possible amount of downtime is a requirement for software development. This is also true for many business-use computers, and it is the most important reason that businesses choose brand-name computers over clones.

Purchasing a Brand-Name PC vs. a Clone

As you have most likely noticed, brand-name PCs generally cost more than clone PCs with similar features. One reason is that you pay extra money for after-sales service. For example, some PCs come with a three-year warranty, a 24-hour-service help line with a toll-free number, and delivery of parts to your place of business. Know how the service agreement works. Does the agreement require you to take the PC to the store or ship it to the manufacturer, or is onsite service provided? A clone manufacturer might also give good service, but this may be due to the personalities of a few employees rather than to company policies. Most likely, company policies for clone PCs are not as liberal and all-encompassing as those of a brand-name manufacturer. Most brand-name manufacturers provide additional support generally not provided by companies that build clone PCs, such as functional Web sites, updated drivers and utilities, and online troubleshooting or user manuals.

On the other hand, many brand-name manufacturers use nonstandard parts with their hardware and nonstandard approaches to setting up their systems, making their computers more proprietary than clones. One of the most common ways for a brand-name manufacturer to make its computer more proprietary is to put components, such as support for video, directly on the motherboard rather than use more generic expansion cards.

Additionally, rather than being updated by a setup program in BIOS, the CMOS setup program might be stored on the hard drive. The shape and size of the computer case might be such that a standard motherboard does not fit; only the brandname board will do. These practices can make upgrading and repairing brand-name PCs more difficult, because you are forced to use the brand-name parts and service. Also, in some areas of the country, it may be difficult to find authorized dealers and service centers for brand-name PCs.

Selecting Software

Your decisions about software selection are driven by the functionality requirements for the PC, as identified in the previous sections. Choose the operating system first. For Windows, you will probably want to select the latest OS supported by your system. Currently, that is Windows XP Professional or Windows XP Home Edition. For the corporate market, where security and remote access are important, choose Windows XP Professional. When choosing software, consider these questions:

- What do you want the software to do? (This will be defined by your answers to the functionality questions listed earlier.)
- Is compatibility with other software or data required? Consider compatibility with your existing system as well as with office systems if you telecommute.
- Is training available if you do not already have the skills needed to use the software?
- How good is the software's documentation?
- What are the company's upgrade policies?
- How well known or popular is the software? (The more popular it is, the more likely you'll find good training materials, trained people, technical support, and other compatible software and hardware.)

Caution is in order if you are buying a brand-name or clone computer that has pre-installed software with which you are not familiar. The software may not provide the functionality you need and may not have good documentation, reliable upgrades, or support. Unless you feel that you have the skill to manage this software, you're probably better off staying with mainstream-market software. One way to identify which brand of software is the most prevalent in the industry is to browse the computer

23

books section of a local bookstore, looking for the software that has the most "how to" books written about it. Also see trade magazines, the Internet, and your local retailer.

> A good resource for reviews of hardware and software components, plus free trial downloads of many software programs, is *www.cnet.com* by CNET Networks, Inc.

Selecting Hardware

The two most important criteria to consider when selecting hardware are compatibility and functionality. Begin by considering the motherboard. (See Chapter 5 for more information about how to select one.) Here are other topics you should consider:

- If you intend to use the PC for multimedia applications, including games, you want a high-speed CPU, a high-quality video card, and plenty of memory.
- If you plan to use the PC for heavy network use, buy a PC with plenty of processing power.
- If you connect to the Internet using a modem, buy a high-quality one.
- When selecting a computer case, keep in mind that tower cases generally offer more room than desktop units and are easier to work with when adding new devices. Make sure the case has a reset button and, if security is an issue, a key lock to limit access to the inside of the case. Some cases even have a lock on the floppy drive to prevent unauthorized booting from a floppy disk.
- Select a power supply that will supply enough power for your components. (Refer to Chapter 4 for help on calculating the total power needs of your system.)
- The documentation for a component should be easy to read and comprehensive, and the manufacturer's Web site should offer easy-to-find technical support and the latest drivers.
- A device should have a warranty and be compatible with all hardware and software in your system.

Internal devices are usually less expensive than external devices, because external devices have the additional expenses of their own power supply and case. Internal devices also offer the advantage of not requiring desk space, and their cables and cords are neatly tucked away. Some advantages of external devices are that they can be moved easily from one computer to another, and they can be reset or disabled by powering down and back up without having to reboot the entire system.

If you've ever shopped for a peripheral device, such as a printer or a sound card, you know what a large variety of features and prices are in today's market. Research pays. In general, when selecting a device for an existing system or building a new system, you should know the following about your computer system:

- Which CPU, system bus, and local bus you have
- How much memory you have

- What size hard drive your system has
- Which OS you are using and what version it is (for example, Windows 2000 Professional or Windows XP Home Edition)
- How much space is available on your hard drive
- For internal devices, how many drives, bays, or expansion slots and what kinds of slots are free in your computer

NOTE

When buying a device and other components that the device will use, such as an expansion card or cable, they are more likely to be compatible if you buy everything from the same source.

Selecting a Total Package

When selecting a complete computer package, including hardware and software, consider these points:

- What hardware and software are included? Are the hardware and software compatible with those found on the general market? (For example, if you want to upgrade your video card or word processor, how difficult would that be?)
- What is the warranty and return or exchange policy? Is there a restocking fee?
- What onsite or local service is available? Do you know anyone who has used this service, and was it satisfactory?
- Is the system ACPI- and Energy Star-compliant? (For information about ACPI and Energy Star, see Chapter 4.)
- What software comes preinstalled?
- What documentation or manuals come with the system?
- Does the manufacturer maintain a Web site with useful support features, utilities, and updates?
- Does the motherboard allow for expansion of RAM?
- What expansion slots are not being used? (Always allow some room to grow.)
- Can features such as video on the motherboard be disabled if necessary? (Refer to Chapter 5 for other guidelines on selecting motherboards.)
- How much does the system cost?

When considering price, keep in mind that high-priced to middle-range-priced PCs are most likely to be network compatible and easily expandable; they offer a broader range of support and have had extensive testing of vendor products for reliability and compatibility. Low-priced PCs may not have been tested for network compatibility; also, they offer a limited range of support, and the quality of components may not be as high.

When considering preinstalled software, remember that sometimes unneeded software is more of a hindrance than a help, needlessly taking up space. For example, it is not uncommon for a brand-name computer to come with three or four applications for Internet access (for example, America Online, CompuServe, and Microsoft Network) because of licensing agreements that distributors have with online

23

providers. Typically, only one application is needed. Sometimes having more than one on your computer causes problems.

NOTE

Beware of pirated software installed on preassembled PCs. Vendors sometimes sell counterfeit software by installing unauthorized software on computers. This practice is called **hard-disk loading**. Vendors have even been known to counterfeit disk labels and Certificates of Authenticity. Look for these warning signs that software purchased from vendors is pirated: it has no end-user license, mail-in product registration card, documentation, or original CDs; documentation is photocopied; or disks have handwritten labels. Accept nothing less than the original installation CDs for all installed software.

Preparing to Build Your Own PC

Assembling your own PC takes time, skill, and research, but it can be a great learning experience. You might even want to consider it your "rite of passage" toward being a PC technician. All the skills needed to be a PC technician are tested: research, knowledge of user needs and the computer market, planning, organization, patience, confidence, problem solving, and extensive knowledge of both hardware and software. If you intend to become a corporate-level technician, you most certainly should put together at least one whole PC before starting your first job, and set up a small home network as well.

However, don't build your PC to save money, because you probably won't. The total price of all parts usually about equals the price of a comparable clone PC that is prebuilt. Here are a few good reasons to assemble your own PC:

- The whole process can be quite fun.
- Knowledge is power. The knowledge and experience gained in researching the parts to buy, studying the documentation, and finally assembling the PC cannot be overemphasized.
- When you buy all the parts and software for a PC individually, you also get the documentation for each hardware component. This is most likely not the case when you buy a preassembled PC. If you plan to upgrade your PC later, having this documentation can be very valuable.
- Many prebuilt PCs come with preloaded software. You may not receive the original CDs or disks or the documentation for these programs. That can be a problem when you try to maintain your system, and most likely indicates that the software is distributed illegally. (Don't accept preinstalled software unless it also includes the installation disks and documentation.) When you buy each software package individually, you are assured that the distribution is legal, and you have the installation disks, CDs, and documentation.
- When you purchase each computer part individually, you are more likely to understand exactly what you are buying, and you can be more particular about

the selection of each component. You have control over the brand and features of each component in the PC.

Here are a few reasons why you might not want to build your own PC:

- If you are in a rush to get a PC up and running, assembling your own is probably not a good idea, especially if you are a first-time builder. The process takes time and requires patience, and the first time you do it, you most likely will make a few mistakes that will need to be resolved.
- Individual parts may be warrantied, but if you build your own PC, there is no overall warranty on the PC. If a warranty or a service agreement is important, then look for a ready-built PC with these services included.
- Clone PCs have been tested to ensure that individual components are compatible. When building your own PC, you might select incompatible components. For this reason, buy high-quality mainstream components to best ensure compatibility.
- Don't plan to assemble a PC for the first time unless you have access to an experienced technician or a technical service center you can consult if you encounter a problem you cannot resolve. For example, you might buy all the parts from a store that has a service center. The store might offer to assemble the PC for you for a charge ($50 to $75 is about right). If you find you cannot resolve a problem, you can always go back to the store for this service.
- Remember, you probably won't save money assembling the PC.

Getting Ready for Assembly: Selecting Parts

If you have decided to buy parts and assemble a PC, expect the process to take some time. The motherboard and expansion cards are full of connections, ports, and perhaps jumpers, and you must read the documentation carefully to determine just how to configure the motherboard and all components to work together. Technicians in service centers can assemble a PC in less than an hour, but they have already assembled the same group of parts many times!

Planning the assembly of a PC is like packing for a camping trip to a remote location. You must plan for everything you need before you begin. As you select and purchase each part, two things are important: functionality and compatibility with other parts.

Almost every computer needs these essentials: motherboard, CPU, RAM, hard drive, CD-ROM drive (or you can substitute a DVD drive or CD-RW drive for added functionality), floppy drive, case, power supply, video card, monitor, keyboard, and mouse. And, most likely, you also want a sound card and modem. Make careful and informed decisions about every part you buy. Selecting each component requires reviewing your functionality, compatibility, and budget needs and determining what parts meet your criteria. Select the motherboard first, and then select the other parts around this most important component.

23

When selecting parts, including the motherboard, carefully examine the documentation. Look for good documentation that you can understand without struggling. When buying parts for your first assembly, you should probably not use mail order. Buy from a reputable local dealer who allows you to examine a part and look at its documentation, and who is willing and able to answer any technical questions you may have. Know the store's return policy and the manufacturer's warranty for each part.

If you can buy the motherboard, CPU, and memory from the same dealer, who can help you determine that all three are compatible, do so to avoid problems later with compatibility. The documentation for the motherboard is quite valuable. Make sure it's readable and complete. If it's not, look on the manufacturer's Web site for additional documentation before making the purchase. Does the motherboard support USB, FireWire, or SCSI? The CPU needs at least one fan or cooler and the case needs at least one exhaust fan. Does the entire system need additional fans? Ask the dealer for recommendations, and read the documentation for the CPU. A dealer often sells a motherboard with the CPU and fan already installed and jumpers on the motherboard set correctly.

After you select the motherboard, CPU, and RAM, select the case and accompanying power supply. Remember the two rules: The case must meet your predetermined functionality requirements, and it must be compatible with other parts (especially the motherboard). Next, select the hard drive and other drives.

If the video logic is not included on the motherboard (for clone motherboards it probably is not), select the video card next, and make sure that you have a PCI Express slot or an AGP slot to accommodate it. There are several types of AGP slots. Match your AGP video card to the type your motherboard provides. Finally, select other peripherals, including a mouse, keyboard, and monitor.

Getting Ready for Assembly: Final Preparations

When all parts are purchased, prepare well for the assembly. Prepare a work area that is well lit and uncluttered. Before you start, read all documentation and plan the assembly through, from beginning to end. If you have questions or are unsure how to proceed, find answers to your concerns before you begin. For example, if you're not sure how to set the jumpers on the motherboard, even after you read the documentation, take the documentation to your technical support source (a dealer, a service center, a knowledgeable friend), and ask for help in interpreting the settings in the documentation before you start the work. Often you can find a detailed diagram of the motherboard on the manufacturer's Web site, complete with proper settings for specific CPUs.

NOTE

While working, don't get careless about protecting yourself and your equipment against static electricity. (Review the safety precautions in Chapter 4.) Always use the ground strap on your wrist.

Building a Personal Computer, Step by Step

This section is a step-by-step, detailed description of building a simple Pentium 4 PC that includes a hard drive, a floppy drive, and a CD-RW drive. Depending on what you decide you want your computer for and what functionality and budget you are operating with, you may choose to build a different PC, with a different CPU and different parts. Documentation and manufacturer Web sites are, as always, good resources for installation procedures and general information on specific parts. While we do not have the space to provide instructions on the assembly of many different PCs, the examples we give will provide you with background and guidance and demonstrate how to approach the task at hand.

The text describes some problems actually encountered during an assembly. I wish I could invite you to work beside me, reading the documentation for a jumper setting, deciding just which card should go in which slot for the best overall fit, and enjoying the pleasure of turning on the PC and seeing it boot up for the first time. However, the best I can do is introduce you to the experience through this book. My hope is that you will have the opportunity to experience it yourself one day.

Overview of the Assembly Process

After the research is done and the parts purchased, organize everything you need to assemble the PC. Have the parts with their accompanying documentation and software available, together with your PC tools. You'll need a safe place to work, with a ground mat and ground strap. Be careful to follow all safety rules and precautions discussed in this and previous chapters. Work methodically and keep things organized. If you find yourself getting frustrated, take a break. Remember, you want the entire experience to be fun!

The general process for putting together a computer is as follows:

1. Verify that you have all parts you plan to install.

2. Prepare the computer case by installing the case fans and I/O shield, removing the plates that cover the drive bays, and installing the spacers.

3. Install the drives.

4. Determine proper configuration settings for the motherboard, and set any jumpers or switches on the motherboard.

5. Install the CPU and CPU fan.

6. Install RAM in the appropriate slots on the motherboard.

7. Install the motherboard and attach cabling.

23

8. Install the video card.

9. Install the modem card (or wait until Step 12 to install it).

10. Plug the computer into a power source, and attach the monitor, keyboard, and mouse.

11. Boot the computer, check the CMOS settings, and make sure that everything is configured and working properly before replacing the computer case. At this point you are ready to install the OS.

12. Install any peripheral devices you need, such as a modem card or printer, and any applications such as Microsoft Office.

Step 1: Verify That You Have All the Parts

For the PC we are building in this chapter, the parts purchased before beginning the assembly are listed. The parts to be installed inside the case and some tools are shown in Figure 23-1.

Figure 23-1   Components needed to assemble a PC

- ATX mid-tower case with power supply (a 300-watt, ATX12V-compliant power supply is required for this motherboard, because the Pentium 4 requires a supplemental power connector)

- Motherboard (Asus P4P800 Deluxe with FireWire)
- Pentium 4 CPU that runs at 2.4 GHz
- RAM (Two 256-MB DDR DIMMs)
- Video card (ATI Radeon 8500, 62-MB AGP with DVI)
- Hard drive (Seagate Barracuda 80-GB, 7200–RPM, 6-MB buffer with serial ATA)
- Floppy drive
- CD-RW drive (Samsung 52 × 24 × 52 CD-RW)
- Monitor, mouse, and keyboard
- Modem card (Lucent 56K V.92 PCI)
- Cables, cords, drivers, and documentation

Before you begin installation, make sure you have everything you need to complete it, including tools, documentation, and all components. As discussed in earlier chapters, it is a good idea to have a notebook for all product documentation, lists of the components and settings for your PC, and detailed installation and troubleshooting notes.

Step 2: Prepare the Computer Case

Before you can install components in a computer case, you must prepare the case. Figure 23-2 shows the empty computer case before any components are installed in it. The first step to prepare the case is to install an exhaust fan. (Refer back to Figure 4-19 in Chapter 4.) In addition to the power supply fan and the CPU fan, an exhaust fan over the vent underneath the power supply helps keep the temperature inside the case at a level that will not damage the CPU. Position the fan in place over the vent, and secure it with four screws.

As you learned in Chapter 5, the next thing to do is to install the spacers (see Figure 23-3) in the holes on the bottom of the case, to keep the motherboard from touching the case and possibly shorting. When you install the motherboard, the holes on the motherboard will line up with the spacers, as shown in Figure 23-3. Hold the motherboard over the case so you can see where the holes in the board and case line up, and install a spacer in every hole in the case that lines up with a hole in the motherboard, so that all the holes in the motherboard can have screws. You should use at least four spacers, and will probably use six. Regardless of how many you use, you will end up with some holes in the case that you don't use. The other holes allow the case to accommodate more than one motherboard form factor.

23

Wide drive bays
Narrow drive bays

Front vent
Power supply

Faceplate punched out

Faceplates cover holes for back of expansion cards
I/O shield
Vent for rear exhaust fan

Figure 23-2 The empty computer case with I/O shield installed

Spacer installed

Spacer not installed

Hole in motherboard for screw to attach board to spacer

Figure 23-3 The spacers line up with the holes on the motherboard and keep it from touching the case

The next step to prepare the case is to install an I/O shield. Recall that in Chapter 5 you learned how to install an I/O shield in a computer case to help protect ports coming off the motherboard. If the case comes with several shields, as it probably will, select the one that correctly fits the ports on your motherboard. Figure 23-2 shows the I/O shield installed.

Step 3: Install Drives

A+
CORE
1.2
1.6
2.1

The next step is to install drives in the case. Some technicians prefer to install the motherboard first, but we are installing the drives first; if the motherboard is already in the case before the drives are installed, there is the risk of dropping a drive on the motherboard and damaging it. Also, once the drives are installed, we will not attach power cords until after the motherboard is in place. This ensures that the cords will not be in the way when we install the motherboard.

Looking back at Figure 23-2, you can see that the case has a group of wide bays in which we will install the CD-RW drive, and a narrow removable bay in which we will install the floppy drive and hard drive.

 NOTE When installing drives, be sure to use short screws that will not protrude too deeply into the drive and damage it.

Configure Jumpers on Each IDE Drive in the System

Recall from Chapter 8, when using parallel ATA, there can be up to two IDE controllers on a motherboard, the primary and secondary IDE controllers. Each controller can support up to two drives, a master and a slave, for a total of up to four IDE drives in a system. However, this motherboard supports serial ATA and parallel ATA, thus supporting up to six IDE devices. The following rules apply:

- CMOS setup recognizes four IDE controllers: primary IDE (master and slave using parallel ATA), secondary IDE (master and slave using parallel ATA), third IDE (master using serial ATA), and fourth IDE (master using serial ATA).
- Using Windows 2000/XP, there can be up to six IDE devices in a system: up to four parallel ATA drives and up to two serial ATA hard drives.
- Using Windows 98/Me or Windows NT, there can be up to four drives in a system: one or two parallel ATA drives using a single IDE channel and one or two serial ATA hard drives using the two serial ATA channels.
- Using Windows 98/Me or Windows NT, serial ATA can be disabled in CMOS setup and the system can then have up to four parallel ATA drives.
- In CMOS setup, if Windows 2000/XP is installed, set the IDE operating mode to Enhanced Mode, which supports up to six devices. If Windows 98/Me or Windows NT is installed, set the IDE operating mode to Compatible Mode, which supports up to four devices.

In this installation, we are using two IDE devices, a hard drive using a serial ATA cable connected to a serial ATA connection and a CD-RW drive using a 40-pin IDE ribbon cable connected to the primary IDE channel. A serial ATA cable and connection support only a single serial ATA hard drive, which is assumed to be the master device on the controller and, therefore, does not have any jumpers to set. We set the CD-RW drive jumpers for the drive to be the single drive on the IDE channel.

23

Later, when we first boot up the system, we will enter CMOS setup and verify that serial ATA is enabled and that the IDE operating mode is set to Enhanced Mode, because we will be installing Windows XP.

Install the CD-RW Drive

We decided to install the CD-RW drive in the top wide bay to keep it up out of the way. Follow these steps and be sure you are wearing your ground bracelet as you work:

- This bay has a clipping system to secure the drive, rather than using screws as some bays do (see Figure 23-4). Using two fingers, squeeze the two clips on each side of the bay together to release them and pull them forward. Remove the faceplate from the front of the bay.
- Install the CD-RW drive in the bay (see Figure 23-5). To see how far to push the drive into the bay, align it with the front of the case, as shown in Figure 23-6. (After the motherboard is installed, we'll also install the CD-RW data cable, power cord, and audio cord.)

Faceplate removed

Bracing clips

Figure 23-4   To prepare a large bay for the CD-RW drive, punch out the faceplate and pull the bracing clips forward

A+
CORE
1.2
1.6
2.1

Figure 23-5   Slide the CD-RW drive into the bay

Figure 23-6   To judge how far to insert the CD-RW drive in the bay, align it with the front of the case

23

A+
CORE
1.2
1.6
2.1

Install the Hard Drive

This case has a removable bay for small drives. The bay is secured with three screws on the front of the case and a clipping mechanism on the side of the bay. Remove the screws and then remove the bay. Position the hard drive flush with the front of the bay and secure the drive with four screws, two on each side of the drive (see Figure 23-7).

Install the Floppy Drive

Remove a faceplate on the front of the bay for the floppy drive and position the floppy drive in the bay, so that it will align later with the front of the case. Secure the floppy drive to the bay with four screws, two on each side of the bay. Slide the bay into the case. You will hear the clipping mechanism clip into place when the bay is all the way in. Secure the bay to the case with three screws. You can see two of these screw holes in Figure 23-8. The third one is on top of the bay.

Figure 23-7   Use four screws to secure each drive to the bay

A+
CORE
1.2
1.6
2.1

Clipping mechanism pops
into position when the bay
is all the way in

Screw holes to secure the
bay to the case

Figure 23-8   Slide the bay into the case as far as it will go

Step 4: Set Jumpers or Switches on the Motherboard

A+
CORE
1.2
1.3

We are installing the Asus P4P800 Deluxe motherboard shown in Figure 23-9 with the processor installed. All connections used in this installation are labeled in the figure. When working with the motherboard or other circuit boards, be particularly concerned about the possibility of ESD damage. Make sure you are properly grounded at all times. Also, try not to touch edge connectors or other sensitive portions of components.

> ✔ **A+ EXAM TIP**
>
> The A+ Core exam expects you to understand the importance of correctly setting jumpers on the motherboard during an installation.

Figure 1-9 in Chapter 1 shows the ports on the back of this motherboard. There are ports for the mouse and the keyboard, an RJ-45 network port, 1394 (FireWire) port, four USB ports, a serial port, three regular sound ports, and one S/PDIF digital sound port. Note that this motherboard has embedded support for sound and Ethernet, eliminating the need for separate expansion cards to add these features.

The first things to do when preparing a motherboard to go into the case are to study the motherboard's documentation, determine what jumpers or DIP switches are on the board, and determine how to set them. This board has several jumper groups to consider:

23

Audio connector
to CD drive

CPU auxiliary
power connector

Power connector
for CPU fan

Extra USB connectors

Serial ATA connector for HDD

Exhaust fan power

IDE connector for CD-RW drive

ATX power connector

Floppy drive connector

Group of pins for
LED connectors

Figure 23-9 Asus P4P800 Deluxe motherboard with all connections used in this installation labeled

- A three-pin jumper group to clear CMOS RAM (also known as RTC RAM or real-time clock RAM). Figure 23-10 shows the documentation for how to set these jumpers. The default position is not to clear CMOS RAM.
- A three-pin jumper group to control the keyboard wake-up feature, and a three-pin jumper group for each USB connection to control if a USB device can wake up the system. The default position for each group is to disable the feature.
- A six-pin jumper group to control SMBus support to PCI slots. The SMBus (System Management Bus) standard supports the ACPI standard and can be used by an SMBus-enabled NIC to communicate information about installed hardware and overheating errors. The default position is to disable this feature.

Leave all jumpers in their default positions. Figure 23-11 shows the clear CMOS RAM and SMBus support jumper groups. Also notice in this photograph the group of connector pins to the right of the jumpers. These pins are for extra USB connectors on the front of the case. The coin cell battery to power CMOS RAM is also showing behind the jumpers. To compare this photograph with the diagram in Figure 23-10, rotate the diagram 180 degrees.

A+
CORE
1.2
1.3

Figure 23-10   The motherboard documentation shows how to set each jumper group. This figure shows how to find and set the jumpers to control clearing CMOS RAM.

Three-pin jumper group set at normal position to *not* clear CMOS RAM

Six-pin jumper group set to default position to *disable* SMBus support to PCI slots

Figure 23-11   Two jumper groups with jumpers set to default positions

Step 5: Install the CPU and CPU Fan

Next, we will install the CPU and the CPU fan on the motherboard. Following the detailed instructions in Chapter 5, install the CPU into the 478-pin ZIF socket on the motherboard and place a small amount of thermal compound on top of the processor, to conduct heat from the CPU to the heat sink. Line up the clip assembly with the retention mechanism already installed on the motherboard, and press lightly on all four corners until it snaps in place (see Figure 23-12). Once the cooler assembly is in place, push down the two clip levers on top of the assembly (refer back to Figure 5-37 in Chapter 5). Different coolers use different types of clipping mechanisms, so follow the directions that come with the cooler.

23

Figure 23-12   Carefully push the cooler assembly clips into the retention mechanism on the motherboard until they snap into position

Connect the power cord from the CPU fan to the power connection on the mother-board next to the cooler (see Figure 23-13).

Step 6: Install RAM on the Motherboard

From discussions in Chapter 6, you know how to select the right kind and right amount of RAM for your motherboard, and you know that you should be careful to match size, manufacturer, production batch, and mode. Our motherboard has four DIMM slots that can support 64-MB, 128-MB, 512-MB, and 1-GB DDR DIMMs. We will be installing two DIMMs, each with 256 MB of memory. For optimum per-formance, the motherboard documentation suggests to install two DIMMs in the two blue sockets, which are sockets one and three (see Figure 23-14).

NOTE

Motherboard manufacturers tend to make some sockets blue, to indicate you should use them first when there is more than one socket from which to choose.

Figure 23-13 Connect the CPU fan power cord to the motherboard power connector

Figure 23-14 Install the two DIMMs in the two blue RAM sockets

Before inserting each module in its socket, pull the supporting arms on the sides of the socket outward. Notches on the edge of each module will help you orient it

A+
CORE
1.2
1.3

correctly in the socket. Insert the module straight down in the socket; when it is fully inserted, the supporting arms should pop back into place.

Step 7: Install the Motherboard and Attach Cabling

Let's review what we've done so far. We've prepared the case by installing the exhaust fan and the spacers, installed drives, and attached the processor, cooling assembly, and memory modules to the motherboard. The next steps are to install the motherboard itself into the case and attach the cabling and power connections.

- Place the motherboard into the case so that the holes on the motherboard align with the holes on the spacers. Attach the motherboard to the case, using the spacers to receive the screws (see Figure 23-15). Be careful not to use excessive force when moving the motherboard into place and attaching it to the case; that could warp the board and damage the circuits on it.
- Connect the power cord from the exhaust fan to the auxiliary fan power connection on the motherboard. Note that sometimes a motherboard will not have this connection. In that situation, connect the exhaust fan power cord to a power cord from the power supply.

Figure 23-15   Use screws to attach the motherboard to the case via the spacers

A+
CORE
1.2
1.3

- Connect the 4-pin auxiliary power cord coming from the power supply to the motherboard, as shown in Figure 23-16. This cord supplies the supplemental power required for a Pentium 4 processor.
- Connect the 20-pin ATX P1 power cord from the power supply to the motherboard, as shown in Figure 23-17.
- Connect a regular 4-pin power cord to the CD-RW drive and connect a miniature 4-pin power cord to the floppy drive.

Figure 23-16   The auxiliary 4-pin power cord provides power to the Pentium 4 processor

23

A+
CORE
1.2
1.3

Figure 23-17   The 20-pin connector supplies power to the motherboard

A+ EXAM TIP

The A+ Core exam expects you to be able to install a serial ATA hard drive.

■ A serial ATA hard drive uses a special power cord shown in Figure 23-18. Connect one end to a regular 4-pin power cord from the power supply and connect the other end to the hard drive (see Figure 23-19).

A+
CORE
1.2
1.3

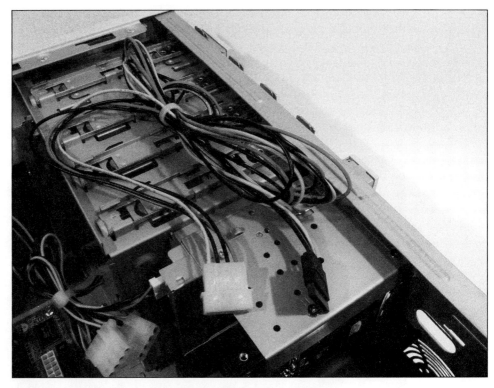

Figure 23-18   A serial ATA hard drive uses a special power cord

Bottom of hard drive

Figure 23-19   Connect the special serial ATA power cord to the power connector on the serial ATA hard drive

- After the power cords are connected, locate and connect the front leads to the switches, speaker, and lights on the front of the case (see Figure 23-20). Note

23

that each front lead is labeled, although in the figure you can see that the one on the left is difficult to read. (It's the speaker lead.) Sometimes there will be corresponding screen-printed labels on the board to tell you which lead goes on which pins. If the pins are not labeled on the board, as with this motherboard, check your documentation. The motherboard might come with a sticker that goes inside the case and shows a diagram of the motherboard with labels for the front leads. If the motherboard documentation is not clear, you can also check the motherboard manufacturer's Web site for additional documentation. Figure 23-21 shows this motherboard's documentation, which describes the connectors for each of the leads.

Figure 23-20   Locate the lead wires coming from the case that connect to the pins on the motherboard to control the LEDs and buttons on the front of the case

- This case has two extra USB ports on the front and the motherboard has extra USB connectors for them. Connect the cable coming from the ports on the case to the first USB connector on the motherboard (see Figure 23-22).

Figure 23-21   Connector group for front panel leads

- Normally the CD audio cord connects from the CD-RW drive to the sound card, in order to play music CDs. Because sound support is embedded on the motherboard, look at the motherboard documentation to determine where to connect the CD audio cord to the board. Connect the CD audio cord to the CD-RW drive and the other end to the connector on the motherboard, as shown in Figure 23-23.
- Next, install the data cables to each drive. Install the floppy drive cable with the twist between the motherboard and the drive, making this drive A in the final configuration. Connect the 40-pin IDE cable to the CD-RW drive and the primary IDE connector on the motherboard. This motherboard has IDE connectors that will only allow the IDE cable to connect in the correct orientation.

23

Two USB ports on
the front of the case

Figure 23-22   Connect the cable coming from the USB ports on the front of the case to one of the two U
SB connectors on the motherboard

Figure 23-23   The audio cable connected to the audio connector on the motherboard. The other end of t
he cable is connected to the CD-RW drive.

- The motherboard has two serial ATA connectors labeled SATA1 and SATA2.
  Connect the serial ATA cable to the hard drive and the other end to the first of
  the two serial ATA connectors (see Figure 23-24).

A+
CORE
1.2
1.3

Two serial
ATA connectors

Figure 23-24   Connect the serial ATA connector to the serial ATA hard drive and the first serial ATA connector on the motherboard

Step 8: Install the Video Card

A+
CORE
1.2
1.8

The next step is to install the video card. The AGP 8X slot on this motherboard supports +1.5V AGP cards. There are several different types of AGP slots. Be sure you match the right AGP video card to the AGP slot on your motherboard. The video card we are installing, shown in Figure 23-25, fits into an AGP 8X slot and includes a registration tab that allows the card to fit into an AGP Pro slot.

Registration tab

Figure 23-25   The video card, with a tab that allows it to be used in an AGP Pro slot

23

A+
CORE
1.2

In general, when installing an expansion card, first read the documentation for the card and set any jumper switches or DIP switches on it. Like most cards today, the video card we are installing is Plug and Play-compatible and has no jumpers.

✔ A+ EXAM TIP

The A+ Core exam expects you to know how to install a video card.

The AGP slot has a retention mechanism around it that helps hold the card securely in the slot. Some motherboards require that you install this retention mechanism on the slot before you install the card, as shown in Figure 23-26.

NOTE

Some motherboards have an AGP retention mechanism that installs over the AGP slot to help stabilize the video card. This board has a built-in extender that does not require installing.

Figure 23-26   Some motherboard installations require you to install a retention mechanism around the A GP slot before installing the video card

For this installation, remove the faceplate for the slot from the computer case, and slide back the retention mechanism on the slot. Insert the card in the slot and slide the retention mechanism back in position. The retention mechanism slides over the registration tab at the end of the AGP slot to secure the card in the slot. Use a single screw to secure the card to the computer case (see Figure 23-27).

Step 9: Install the Modem Card

A+
CORE
1.2

The modem card is not considered an essential device, so you might decide to install it after you have tested the system and installed the operating system. If you choose to install the card now, install it in a PCI slot. Remove the faceplate, insert the card, and use a screw to secure it.

Figure 23-27   Secure the video card to the case with a single screw

Step 10: Plug In the Computer and Attach External Devices

A+ CORE 2.1

The installation of devices inside the case is now complete. Before you plug in the computer, make sure that no cords are obstructing the fans. Figure 23-28 shows the case with all internal components installed. Notice that some cables are coiled and tied with plastic ties. (Don't use rubber bands for this task because they can deteriorate over time, break, and drop into the case.) Tying up cords makes the inside of the case less cluttered and prevents cords from obstructing airflow and fans. You do not do this, however, until after you test the system to make sure everything works.

Attach the monitor and keyboard, and plug in the computer. You can also attach the mouse at this point, or you can leave it off and attach it after you test the system. It is unlikely that the mouse will cause problems during the initial startup process, but you won't really need it; also, it is a good idea to start up using only the components you absolutely need, especially when first constructing a system.

23

Figure 23-28 The case with all the internal components installed

Step 11: Boot the Computer, Check Settings, and Verify Operation

It is a good idea to test the system before replacing the case cover, to make changes easier if something goes wrong. However, because some systems require the cover to be on to achieve proper airflow, do not run the system for any length of time without the cover on. Also, some server cases have cover switch latches that do not allow you to power up the system unless the case cover is in place. The boot process and CMOS settings were covered in Chapter 3 and reviewed in the general installation process in Chapter 5, which we followed in this chapter. Boot the system and enter CMOS setup. Refer back to Chapter 5 for the list of CMOS settings you need to check. If you plan to boot from a Windows setup CD to install an OS, verify that the boot sequence includes the CD drive.

When you exit CMOS, the computer will reboot. Observe POST and verify that no errors occur. If there are no errors, congratulations! You have put your system together correctly. (If there are errors, see your motherboard documentation or Appendix A in this book for explanations.) Turn off the computer and slide the case cover back in place, as shown in Figure 23-29. The front cover snaps into position (see Figure 23-30). Now you are ready to prepare the hard drive for the OS (see Chapter 8) and install the operating system.

Figure 23-29   Slide the case cover back on once you know the system is working

Step 12: Install Peripheral Devices and Applications

Finally, install any peripheral devices you need, such as a modem card or printer, and any applications such as Microsoft Office.

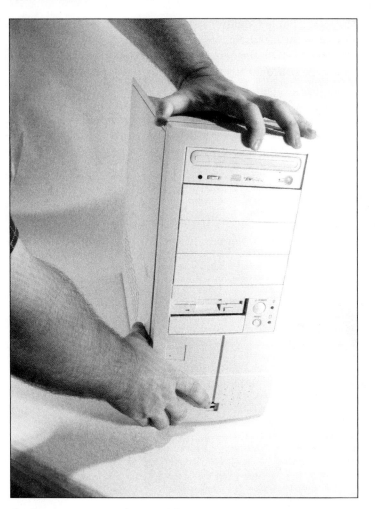

Figure 23-30 The front cover snaps into position

CHAPTER SUMMARY

▶ The most important reason to buy a brand-name PC rather than a clone is after-sales service.

▶ The proprietary designs of many brand-name PCs force you to use only their parts and service when upgrading or maintaining the PC.

▶ Middle-range PCs offer more network capability, expandability, support, and prior testing than low-end PCs.

▶ Some reasons to build your own PC are the knowledge you will gain, the control you will have over the choice of individual parts, the availability of documentation and original software disks, and the satisfaction of having built the PC yourself.

▶ When choosing to build your own PC, be aware that the process will take time, that you will likely encounter problems along the way, that there will be no warranty on the assembled product, and that you probably will not save money.

▶ Plan the project of assembling a PC well. Get answers to any questions you may have on the details before you begin. Keep things organized as you work. Expect the project to be fun.

▶ When assembling a PC, follow this general plan: (1) verify that you have all parts you plan to install, (2) prepare the computer case, (3) install drives, (4) determine and set jumpers and DIP switches for the motherboard, (5) install the CPU and CPU fan, (6) install RAM on the motherboard, (7) install the motherboard in the case, and attach all cables and power cords, (8) install the video card and any other expansion cards, (9) install the modem card, (10) plug in the computer, and connect the mouse, keyboard, and monitor, (11) boot the computer, verify that settings are correct and that no errors occur, and replace the computer case, and (12) install any peripherals and other software you need on your system.

KEY TERMS

For explanations of key terms, see the Glossary near the end of the book.

clone   hard-disk loading   IBM-compatible PC

REVIEWING THE BASICS

1. What are the advantages of buying a well-known, brand-name computer?

2. What are the advantages of buying a less-expensive PC clone?

3. When purchasing a computer system that has preinstalled software, what else should you be certain to obtain from the vendor with this software?

4. List three reasons why it may be wise to build your own PC. List three reasons, other than fear, why you may not want to build your own PC.

5. When is it most likely best to buy a new system rather than upgrade an old or

6. Why is it necessary to match your AGP video card to your motherboard AGP slot?

7. What is one reason to install drives before installing the motherboard?

8. When using serial ATA, which operating systems support up to six IDE drives?

9. What is the purpose of the thermal compound placed on top of the processor?

10. In what type of configuration is one end of the audio cord connected to the CD drive and the other end connected to the motherboard?

11. Why is it a good idea not to put the case cover back on right after you've installed all the internal components?

12. What is the purpose of installing spacers in a computer case?

13. Name three possible sources of information for connecting the front leads.

14. Which drive cable has a twist in it, and why?

15. Give one advantage of not installing drive cables until after the motherboard is installed in the case.

16. Why should you use short screws when securing drives?

17. What is the purpose of tying power cords and cables together before closing the computer case?

18. What is the purpose of the registration tab on the video card in this chapter's example installation?

19. Name the component that fits around the AGP slot and helps to stabilize the video card.

20. Why should you not run a system for a long time with the case cover removed?

THINKING CRITICALLY

1. Assume that you are shopping for a new personal computer. Answer the following questions to help in making the best buying decision.

   a. What is the intended purpose or purposes of the computer?

   b. What functions must the computer have to satisfy each intended purpose?

   c. What hardware and software components are needed to perform each function?

   d. For each hardware and software component, what is one question that you want answered about the component before you make your decision?

2. List one or more features of the motherboard used in this chapter that might make it difficult to upgrade.

3. What would have happened if you had attempted to install regular DIMMs on the motherboard in this chapter rather than the DDR DIMMs the board supports?

   a. The motherboard would have been damaged when it was first turned on.

   b. No damage would have occurred, but the system would not have booted correctly.

   c. Regular DIMMs are notched differently than DDR DIMMs, so you would not have been able to put the DIMMs in the RAM slots.

   d. Regular DIMMs are shorter than DDR DIMMs, so you would have recognized they would not fit on this motherboard when you tried to install them.

4. Suppose you want to test a motherboard used in an installation before you proceed too far into the installation. From the devices listed below, select the minimum devices that you must install before you can boot the system to confirm that the motherboard BIOS starts POST:

   a. Mouse

   b. Computer case and power supply

   c. Monitor

   d. Hard drive

   e. Keyboard

   f. Floppy drive

   g. CD-RW drive

   h. Motherboard

   i. Video card

   j. Modem card

   k. Processor

   l. RAM

5. Describe how you could test the motherboard in Question 4 with the least amount of time invested in the installation.

6. What device should be uninstalled before you proceed with the entire installation, to protect this device from damage?

23

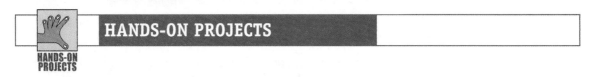

HANDS-ON PROJECTS

PROJECT 23-1: Practicing Computer Assembly Skills

Work with a partner. With your partner not watching, carefully diagram where every wire and cable inside your computer is connected. Disconnect all cable connections: power, drives, and LED indicators. Have your partner replace each connection without your help. Work together with your partner to inspect the connections carefully, using your diagram as an aid. Reboot and test the computer.

PROJECT 23-2: Planning an Upgrade

Using a motherboard manual other than the one you may have used in this chapter, write down what configuration settings must be changed to upgrade a CPU or to change the system bus speed.

PROJECT 23-3: Planning to Buy Parts for a PC

Using the list of components in this chapter and resources on the Internet, find prices for the components and determine what it would cost to assemble this system. (If a component is no longer available, substitute a similar component.) Come up with a total price for building the system, and explain how you arrived at your calculation.

Finally, assume that you are a graphic artist, a software developer, or a serious computer game player. What components would you add to this system, and why? How much would it cost to add them? Would you buy different components from the ones in the list for the basic system built in this chapter, such as more memory, a faster processor, or a larger hard drive? Why or why not?

PROJECT 23-4: Comparing Motherboards

Go to the Asus Web site at *www.asus.com*, and locate the documentation for the Asus P4P800 Deluxe motherboard shown in this chapter or a similar motherboard. List the key features of this motherboard as advertised on the Web site. Then go to the Intel Web site at *www.intel.com*. Find a motherboard that has the same or similar features. Print the Web page advertising this Intel board. Which board did you select? Using a price comparison Web site such as *www.nextag.com*, compare the prices of the two boards. Which is the better buy?

Troubleshooting and Maintenance Fundamentals

In this chapter, you will learn:

- About your role as a PC technician in troubleshooting and maintenance, and tools available to help you in those roles

- How to approach a troubleshooting problem

- How to develop a preventive maintenance plan and what to include in it

This chapter gives you some common-sense guidelines to solving computer problems. When trying to solve a computer problem, you want to avoid making the situation worse by damaging the equipment, software, or data, or by placing undue stress on the user. When approaching a computer problem, follow the important safety precautions that you have learned in other chapters as well as the ones you will learn in this chapter.

Troubleshooting Perspectives and Tools

As a PC troubleshooter, you might have to solve a problem on your own PC or for someone else. As a PC technician, you might fulfill four different job functions:

- *PC support technician.* A PC support technician works on-site, closely interacting with users, and is responsible for ongoing PC maintenance. Of the four technicians listed here, a PC support technician is the only one responsible for the PC before trouble occurs, and therefore is able to prepare for a problem by keeping good records and maintaining backups (or teaching users how to do so).
- *PC service technician.* A PC service technician goes to a customer site in response to a service call and, if possible, repairs a PC on-site. PC service technicians are usually not responsible for ongoing PC maintenance but do usually interact with users.
- *Bench technician.* A bench technician works in a lab environment, might not interact with users of the PCs being repaired, and is not permanently responsible for them. Bench technicians probably don't work at the site where the PC is kept. They may be able to interview the user to get information about the problem, or they may simply receive a PC to repair without being able to talk to the user.
- *Help-desk technician.* A help-desk technician provides telephone or online support. Help-desk technicians, who do not have physical access to the PC, are at the greatest disadvantage of the four types of technicians. They can only interact with users over the phone and must obviously use different tools and approaches than technicians at the PC.

This chapter emphasizes the job of the on-site PC support technician. However, the special needs and perspectives of the service technician, bench technician, and help-desk technician are also addressed.

Troubleshooting Tools

Several hardware and software tools can help you diagnose and repair computer problems. The tools you choose depend on the amount of money you can spend and the level of PC support you provide.

Essential tools for PC troubleshooting are listed here. All but the bootable rescue disk can easily be purchased in one handy PC toolkit:

- Bootable rescue disks for any OS you might work on (you may need several different ones)
- Ground bracelet and/or ground mat
- Flat-head screwdriver
- Phillips-head or cross-head screwdriver

- Torx screwdriver set, particularly size T15
- Tweezers, preferably insulated ones, for picking pieces of paper out of printers or dropped screws out of tight places
- Chip extractor to remove chips (to pry up the chip; a simple screwdriver is usually more effective, however)
- Extractor, a spring-loaded device that looks like a hypodermic needle (When you push down on the top, three wire prongs come out that can be used to pick up a screw that has fallen into a place where hands and fingers can't reach.)

The following tools might not be essential, but they are very convenient:

- Multimeter to check the power supply output (see Appendix E)
- Needle-nose pliers for removing jumpers and for holding objects in place while you screw them in (especially those pesky nuts on cable connectors)
- Flashlight to see inside the PC case
- AC outlet ground tester
- Small cups or bags to help keep screws organized as you work
- Antistatic bags (a type of Farady Cage) to store unused parts
- Pen and paper for taking notes
- Diagnostic cards
- Utility software, virus detection software, and diagnostic software on floppy disks or CD

Keep your tools in a toolbox designated for PC troubleshooting. If you put disks and hardware tools in the same box, don't include a magnetized screwdriver, and be sure to keep the disks inside a hard plastic case to protect them from scratches and dents. Make sure the diagnostic and utility software you use is recommended for the hardware and software you are troubleshooting.

Bootable Rescue Disk

Recall from Chapter 3 that an essential tool for PC troubleshooting is a bootable rescue disk. Not only can it boot the PC even when the hard drive fails, but you are ensured of the cleanest boot possible. By *clean boot* we mean that the boot does not load any extraneous software, drivers, or other memory-resident programs (TSRs) that might be loaded from startup routines on the hard drive.

POST Diagnostic Cards

Although not essential, many hardware and software tools can help you diagnose a PC problem. Before purchasing these tools, read the documentation about what they can and cannot do, and, if possible, read some product reviews. The Internet is a good source of information. One hardware diagnostic tool, a diagnostic card, is discussed in this section. In the next section, we will look at several diagnostic software applications.

Diagnostic cards are designed to discover and report computer errors and conflicts at POST. If you have a problem that prevents the PC from booting, you can install

24

the diagnostic card in an expansion slot on the motherboard and then attempt to boot. The card monitors the boot process and reports errors, usually as coded numbers on a small LED panel on the card. You then look up the number in the documentation that accompanies the card to get more information about the error and its source.

Examples of these cards are:

- Amber Debug Card by Phoenix Technologies (*www.phoenix.com*)
- PCI Error Testing/Debug Card by Trigen Industries (*www.computex.com*)
- POSTcard V3 by Unicore Software, Inc. (*www.unicore.com*)
- Post Code Master by MSD, Inc. (*www.msd.com*)
- POSTmortem Diagnostics Card by System Optimization, Inc. (*www.sysopt.com*)

Diagnostic Software

Diagnostic software is generally used to identify hardware problems. Although many utility and diagnostic software programs are available, here we look at only a few. If the software rates itself as professional-level, it generally assumes greater technical expertise and provides more features than end-user or novice-level software. The most effective diagnostic software does not run from the Windows OS, because Windows might sometimes mask a hardware problem. Here are a few examples of diagnostic software.

- *PC-Technician by Windsor Technologies, Inc.* This professional-level or industry-standard PC diagnostic software loads and operates without using the PC's installed operating system, because it has its own proprietary OS built in. Results are thus unaltered by any errors in the PC's OS. PC-Technician can relocate itself during testing and successfully test all of main memory. The ability to relocate is important, since software that tests memory cannot test the portion where it is currently loaded. PC-Technician bypasses standard ROM BIOS when translation mode is used by the system, so that the diagnostic software communicates directly with the hard drive controller. PC-Technician comes with test plugs (called loop-back plugs) that test parallel and serial ports by looping data out of and back to the port. These loop-back tests (also called wrap tests) determine that hardware ports are working. There is a downloadable version of this software called TuffTEST-Pro. For more information, see the company's Web site, *www.windsortech.com.*
- *PC-Diagnosys by Windsor Technologies, Inc.* This software is designed for less-experienced PC technicians and end users; it is smaller, easier to use, and less expensive than PC-Technician. See *www.windsortech.com.*
- *Data Lifeguard Tools by Western Digital.* This free software gives detailed information about the hard drives installed on a system. It reports errors and can fix some types of hard drive errors. See *support.wdc.com/dlg.* In addition, most major hard drive manufacturers provide their own diagnostic software on their Web sites to be used to support their drives. For example, Maxtor offers PowerMax and Gateway offers Gwscan.exe.

- Some programs that test memory are Memtest86 by Chris Brady (*www.memtest86.com*), Windows Memory Diagnostic by Microsoft (*oca.microsoft.com/en/windiag.asp*), and DocMemory by CST Inc. (*www.docmemory.com*).

General-Purpose Utility Software

Utility software can be designed to diagnose problems, repair and maintain the software on a PC, recover corrupted or deleted data on the hard drive or floppy disks, provide security, monitor system performance, and download software updates from the Internet. The utility software might use the installed operating system or might provide its own. Use the software to diagnose and solve problems, but don't run it continuously in the background because it can slow down a system. Some useful utilities for solving hardware and software problems are outlined in Table 24-1.

NOTE

It's a good idea to stay informed about new utility software as it becomes available because you might run into a situation where one could save you time. A good source of information about utility software is PC Magazine. Go to *www.pcmag.com* and search for utilities.

Software	Manufacturer's Web Site	Description
Norton Utilities by Symantec	*www.symantec.com*	Norton Utilities by Symantec is general-purpose, user-friendly, utility software that provides a variety of functions, including the ability to recover lost or damaged data from a hard drive.
CheckIt Suite by Smith Micro Software	*www.checkit.com*	CheckIt by Smith Micro is a general-purpose software and hardware utility product that includes hard drive testing, performance testing, port testing (loop-back plugs included), and setup for resource conflicts.
PartitionMagic by PowerQuest	*www.powerquest.com/ partitionmagic*	PartitionMagic lets you create, resize, and merge partitions on a hard drive without losing data. You can use the software to easily run multiple operating systems, convert file system types, and fix partition table errors.
SpinRite by Gibson Research	*www.grc.com*	SpinRite scans a hard drive for errors and can perform a low-level format without losing the data (called a non-destructive format), and can sometimes recover lost data.

Table 24-1 (continued)

24

Software	Manufacturer's Web Site	Description
Administrator's Pak by Winternals	www.winternals.com	Several utilities in this software suite can be used to boot a system from CD (each has its own operating system on the CD) and can be used to repair a dead OS, recover data, change forgotten passwords, repair system files, repair partition tables, and rewrite the MBR program.
SiSoftware Sandra 2004 by SiSoftware	www.sisoftware.co.uk	SiSoftware Sandra is benchmarking, diagnostic, and tune-up software that can be used to solve hardware and software problems.
Spybot Search & Destroy by PepiMK Software	www.safer-networking.org	This privacy protection software searches out and removes installed programs that track Internet activity or display pop-up ads.

Table 24-1   Utility software used to solve PC problems

NOTE

In addition to general-purpose utility software, you should have antivirus software available to scan for viruses when you are diagnosing a PC problem and use the software regularly to prevent viruses from attacking your system. See Chapter 9 for a list of antivirus software.

Some PC technicians find it useful to make their own personal tech CD that contains several favorite utilities, diagnostic software, and antivirus software. For example, you could burn a CD with these software utilities: SpinRite, Windows Memory Diagnostic, and Data Lifeguard Tools. You would also want antivirus software on the CD. An example of antivirus software that can be run from a CD is Trend Micro Damage Cleanup Service by Trend Micro (*www.trendmicro.com/download/dcs.asp*).

Your Approach to Troubleshooting

A+ CORE 2.2

When a computer doesn't work and you're responsible for fixing it, you should generally approach the problem first as an investigator and discoverer, always being careful not to compound the problem through your own actions. If the problem seems difficult, see it as an opportunity to learn something new. Ask questions until you understand the source of the problem. Once you understand it, you're almost done, because most likely the solution will be evident. Take the attitude that you can understand the problem and solve it, no matter how deeply you have to dig, and you probably will. In this section we look at how to approach a troubleshooting problem, including how to interact with the user and how to handle an emergency.

Fundamental Rules

A+
CORE
2.2

Here are a few fundamental rules for PC troubleshooting that I've found work for me. Always keep in mind that you don't want to make things worse, so you should use the least destructive solution.

✔ **A+ EXAM TIP**

The A+ Core exam expects you to be able to decide what to do next when given a trouble shooting scenario. The rules listed in this section will help prepare you to become a good troubleshooter.

Make backups before making changes   Whether you are working on hardware or software, always back up essential programs and data before working on a computer.

Approach the problem systematically   Start at the beginning and walk through the situation in a thorough, careful way. This one rule is invaluable. Remember it and apply it every time. If you don't find the explanation to the problem after one systematic walk-through, then repeat the entire process. Check and double-check to find the step you overlooked the first time. Most problems with computers are simple, such as a loose cable or circuit board. Computers are logical through and through. Whatever the problem, it's also very logical. First, try to reproduce the problem, and then try to figure out whether it is a hardware or software problem.

Divide and conquer   This rule is the most powerful. Isolate the problem. In the overall system, remove one hardware or software component after another, until the problem is isolated to a small part of the whole system. Here are a few examples of applying this rule:

- Remove any memory-resident programs (TSRs) to eliminate them as the problem.
- Boot from a disk to eliminate the OS and startup files on the hard drive as the problem.
- Remove any unnecessary hardware devices, such as a scanner card, internal modem, and even the hard drive. Once down to the essentials, start exchanging components you know are good for those you suspect are bad, until the problem goes away.

Don't overlook the obvious   Ask simple questions. Is the computer plugged in? Is it turned on? Is the monitor plugged in? Most problems are so simple that we overlook them because we expect the problem to be difficult. Don't let the complexity of computers fool you. Most problems are easy to fix. Really, they are!

Check simple things first   It is more effective to first check the components that are easiest to replace. For example, if the video does not work, the problem may be with the monitor or the video card. When faced with the decision of which one to exchange first, choose the easy route: Exchange the monitor before the video card.

Make no assumptions   This rule is the hardest to follow, because there is a tendency to trust anything in writing and assume that people are telling you exactly what happened. But documentation is sometimes wrong, and people don't always describe events as they occurred, so do your own investigating. For example, if the

24

user tells you that the system boots up with no error messages, but that the software still doesn't work, boot for yourself. You never know what the user might have overlooked.

Become a researcher   Following this rule is the most fun. When a computer problem arises that you can't easily solve, be as tenacious as a bulldog. Read, make phone calls, ask questions, then read more, make more calls, and ask more questions. Take advantage of every available resource, including online help, the Internet, documentation, technical support, and books such as this one. Learn to use a good search engine on the Web such as *www.google.com*. What you learn will be yours to take to the next problem. This is the real joy of computer troubleshooting. If you're good at it, you're always learning something new.

Write things down   Keep good notes as you're working. They'll help you think more clearly. Draw diagrams. Make lists. Clearly and precisely write down what you're learning. Later, when the entire problem gets "cold," these notes will be invaluable.

Reboot and start over   This is an important rule. Fresh starts are good for us and uncover events or steps that we might have overlooked. Take a break; get away from the problem. Begin again.

Establish your priorities   This rule can help make for a satisfied customer. Decide what your first priority is. For example, it might be to recover lost data, or to get the PC back up and running as soon as possible. Consult the user or customer for advice when practical.

Keep your cool and don't rush   In an emergency, protect the data and software by carefully considering your options before acting and by taking practical precautions to protect software and OS files. When a computer stops working, if unsaved data is still in memory or if data or software on the hard drive has not been backed up, look and think carefully before you leap! A wrong move can be costly. The best advice is not to hurry. Carefully plan your moves. Read the documentation if you're not sure what to do, and don't hesitate to ask for help. Don't simply try something, hoping it will work, unless you've run out of more intelligent alternatives!

Don't assume the worst   When it's an emergency and your only copy of data is on a hard drive that is not working, don't assume that the data is lost. Much can be done to recover data. Recall that if you want to recover lost data on a hard drive, don't write anything to the drive; you might write on top of lost data, eliminating all chances of recovery.

Know your starting point   Before trying to solve a computer problem, know for certain that the problem is what the user says it is. If the computer does not boot, carefully note where in the boot process it fails. If the computer does boot to an OS, before changing anything or taking anything apart, verify what does and what doesn't work, preferably in the presence of the user.

Gathering Information

A+
CORE
2.2

When you are trying to solve a computer problem, the rules just explained will pre-pare you for a successful course of action. Before you take corrective action, however, you need to gather as much information about the situation as possible. This section covers ways to gather information on a computer problem you are troubleshooting.

Interacting with the User

✔ **A+ EXAM TIP**

The A+ Core exam expects you to know how to inter-act with a user and know what question to ask given a troubleshooting scenario.

Ask the user to explain exactly what happened when the computer stopped working. What procedure was taking place at the time? What had just happened? What recent changes did the user make? When did the computer last work? What has happened in the mean-time? What error messages did the user see? Ask the user to listen while you repeat the problem to make sure you understand it cor-rectly. Re-create the circumstances that existed when the computer stopped in as much detail as you can. Make no assumptions. All users make simple mistakes and then overlook them. If you realize that the problem was caused by the user's mistake, take the time to explain the proper procedures, so that the user understands what went wrong and what to do next time.

Use diplomacy and good manners when you work with a user to solve a problem. For example, if you suspect that the user dropped the PC, don't ask, "Did you drop the PC?" Put the question in a less accusatory manner: "Could the PC have been dropped?" If the user is sitting in front of the PC, don't assume you can take over the keyboard or mouse without permission. Also, if the user is present, ask permission before you make a software or hardware change, even if the user has just given you permission to interact with the PC.

When working at the user's desk, consider yourself a guest and follow these gen-eral guidelines:

- Don't talk down to or patronize the user.
- Don't take over the mouse or keyboard from the user without permission.
- Don't use the phone without permission.
- Don't pile your belongings and tools on top of the user's papers, books, etc.
- Accept personal inconvenience to accommodate the user's urgent business needs. For example, if the user gets an important call while you are working, delay your work until the call is over.

Whether or not you are at the user's desk, you should follow these guidelines when working with the user:

- Don't take drastic action such as formatting the hard drive before you ask the user about important data that may not be backed up.
- Provide users with alternatives where appropriate before making decisions for them.

- Protect the confidentiality of data on the PC, such as business financial information.
- Don't disparage the user's choice of computer hardware or software.
- If you make a mistake or must pass the problem on to someone with more expertise, be honest.

In some PC support situations, it is appropriate to consider yourself as a support to the user as well as to the PC. Your goals may include educating the user as well as repairing the computer. If you want users to learn something from a problem they caused, explain how to fix the problem, and walk them through the process if necessary. Don't fix the problem yourself unless they ask you to. It takes a little longer to train the user, but it is more productive in the end because the user learns more and is less likely to repeat the mistake.

Ask the user questions to learn as much as you can about the problem. Refer to Chapter 4 for several sample questions, the most important being, "Can you show me how to reproduce the problem?"

Investigating the Problem on the Computer

VIDEO

Troubleshooting
a Boot
Problem—1

After you interview the user, the next step in troubleshooting is to gather as much information as you can about the problem by examining the computer. Find out these things:

- What operating system is installed?
- What physical components are installed? What processor, expansion cards, drives, and peripheral devices are installed? Is the PC connected to a network?
- What is the nature of the problem? Does the problem occur before or after the boot? Does an error message appear? Does the system hang at certain times? Start from a cold boot, and do whatever you must do to cause the problem to occur. What specific steps did you take to duplicate the problem?
- Can you duplicate the problem? Does the problem occur every time you do the above steps, or is the problem intermittent? Intermittent problems are generally more difficult to solve than problems that occur consistently.

Isolating the Problem

The next step in problem solving is to isolate the source of the problem by doing the following.

Consider the possibilities   Given what you've learned by interviewing the user, examining the computer, and duplicating the problem, consider what might be the source of the problem, which might or might not be obvious at this point. For example, if a user complains that his Word documents are getting corrupted, possible sources of the problem might be that the user does not know how to save documents properly, the software or the OS might be corrupted, the PC might have a virus, or the hard drive might be intermittently failing.

Eliminate simple things first   In our example of the problem with corrupted Word documents, the most obvious or simplest source of the problem is that the user is not saving documents properly. Eliminate that possibility as the source of the problem before you look at the software or the hard drive. Another example is a CD-ROM drive that does not work. The problem might be that the CD is scratched or cracked. Check that first.

Eliminate the unnecessary   This rule can be applied in many ways—for example, when the PC does not boot successfully. In this case, it is often unclear if the problem is with the hardware or software. When using Windows 2000/XP or Windows 9x/ Me, you can boot into Safe Mode and eliminate much of the OS customized configuration. But if you still have problems, you may be able to boot from your bootable rescue disk(s).

Boot from a floppy disk that you know is good or boot from the OS setup CD. If the problem goes away, you have narrowed down the problem to the hard drive. You can deduce that the problem is with (1) the OS or applications installed on the hard drive or (2) the hard drive and/or its subsystem that is used as the boot device.

If you suspect the problem is caused by faulty hardware, eliminate any unnecessary hardware devices. If the PC still boots with errors, disconnect the network card, the CD-ROM drive, the mouse, and maybe even the hard drive. You don't need to remove the CD-ROM or hard drive from the bays inside the case. Simply disconnect the data cable and the power cable. Remove the network card from its expansion slot. Remember to place it on an antistatic bag or ground mat, not on top of the power supply or case. If the problem goes away, you know that one or more of these devices is causing the problem. Replace them one at a time until the problem returns. Remember that the problem might be a resource conflict. If the network card worked well until the CD-ROM drive was reconnected and now neither works, try the CD-ROM drive without the network card. If the CD-ROM drive works, you most likely have a resource conflict.

Trade good for suspected bad   When diagnosing hardware problems, this method works well if you can draw from a group of parts that you know work correctly. Suppose the monitor does not work; it appears dead. The parts of the video subsystem are the video card, the power cord to the monitor, the cord from the monitor to the PC case, and the monitor itself. Also, don't forget that the video card is inserted into an expansion slot on the motherboard, and the monitor depends on electrical power. Suspect each of these five components to be bad; try them one at a time. Trade the monitor for one that you know works. Trade the power cord, trade the cord to the PC video port, move the video card to a new slot, and trade the video card. When you're trading a good component for a suspected bad one, work methodically by eliminating one component at a time. Don't trade the video card and the monitor and then turn on the PC to determine if they work. It's possible that both the card and the monitor are bad, but assume that only one component is bad before you consider whether multiple components need trading.

In this situation, suppose you keep trading components in the video subsystem until you have no more variations. Next, take the entire subsystem—video card, cords, and monitor—to a PC that you know works, and plug each of them in. If they

24

A+
CORE
2.2

work, you have isolated the problem to the PC, not the video. Now turn your attention back to the PC: the motherboard, the software settings within the OS, the video driver, and other devices. Knowing that the video subsystem works on the good PC gives you a valuable tool. Compare the video driver on the good PC to the one on the bad PC. Make certain the CMOS settings, software settings, and other settings are the same.

VIDEO

Troubleshooting
a Dial-Up
Problem

Trade suspected bad for good An alternate approach works well in certain situations. If you have a working PC that is configured similarly to the one you are troubleshooting (a common situation in many corporate or educational environments), rather than trading good for suspected bad, you can trade suspected bad for good. Take each component that you suspect is bad and install it in the working PC. If the component works on the good PC, then you have eliminated it as a suspect. If the working PC breaks down, then you have probably identified the bad component.

Intermittent Problems

Intermittent problems can make troubleshooting challenging. The trick in diagnosing problems that come and go is to look for patterns or clues as to when the problems occur. If you or the user can't reproduce the problem at will, ask the user to keep a log of when the problems occur and exactly what messages appear. Tell the user that intermittent problems are the hardest to solve and might take some time, but that you won't give up. Show the user how to get a printed screen of the error messages when they appear. Here's the method:

- For simple DOS systems, the Print Screen key directs the displayed screen to the printer.
- In Windows, the Print Screen key copies the displayed screen to the Clipboard.
- Launch the Paint software accessory program and paste the contents of the Clipboard into the document. You might need to use the Zoom Out command on the document first. You can then print the document with the displayed screen, using Paint. You can also paste the contents of the Clipboard into a document created by a word-processing application such as Word.

Preventive Maintenance

A+
CORE
3.1

So far we have mainly discussed how to troubleshoot problems that have already occurred. In this section, we will discuss some steps you can take to prevent certain computer problems from occurring in the first place. The more preventive maintenance work you do initially, the fewer problems you are likely to have later, and the less troubleshooting and repair you will have to do.

If you are responsible for the PCs in an organization, make and implement a preventive maintenance plan to help prevent failures and reduce repair costs and downtime. In addition, you need a disaster recovery plan to manage failures when they occur. PC failures are caused by many different environmental and human

A+
CORE
3.1

factors, including heat, dust, magnetism, power supply problems, static electricity, human error (such as spilled liquids or an accidental change of setup and software configurations), and viruses. The goals of preventive maintenance are to reduce the likelihood that the events that cause PC failures will occur and to lessen the damage if they do.

When designing a preventive maintenance plan, consider what you can do to help prevent each cause of PC failure, and write into the plan the preventive actions you can take. Think through the situation caused by each problem. What would happen to the PC, the software, the data, the user's productivity, and so on, if a failure occurred? What would you do and what materials would you like to have in that situation? What can you do ahead of time to help make the situation less disastrous? Your answers to those questions will lead you to create effective preventive maintenance and disaster recovery plans. This section focuses on the preventive maintenance plan.

For example, consider the problem caused by a user accidentally changing the CMOS setup. What can you do to prevent that from occurring? Consider setting a supervisor password to CMOS. If CMOS does get accidentally changed, how can you solve the problem? What can you do now to prepare for that event? By answering these three questions, you might arrive at these preventive maintenance and recovery procedures: (1) Make a backup copy of setup on floppy disk, (2) label the disk and keep it in a safe place, (3) educate the user about the importance of not changing setup, and (4) keep a maintenance record of this PC, including the last time setup was backed up.

When a PC Is Your Permanent Responsibility

When you are the person responsible for a PC, either as the user or as the ongoing support person for the PC and the user, prepare for future troubleshooting situations. This section describes tasks and procedures for doing this.

Organize the Hard Drive Root Directory

In the root directory, keep only startup files for your system and necessary initialization files for the software. Software applications or files containing data don't belong in the root directory, although these applications sometimes put initialization files in the root directory to be used when they first load. Keep application software files and their data in separate directories.

Filenames and extensions can help identify files that application software puts in the root directory to initialize itself. For example, Prodigy.bat is a DOS batch file that the Prodigy software uses to execute. Other software packages often use .bat files for this same purpose. Other file extensions to look for as initialization files are .ini, .bin, and .dat. If you are not sure of the purpose of one of these files, leave it in the root directory. Some software packages might not work if their file isn't in the root directory.

24

**A+
CORE
3.1**

Create Rescue Disks

After you clean up the root directory, make a set of rescue disks for the OS, and test your disks to make sure that they work; label them with the computer model, date, and OS version; and keep them available at the PC. If you have problems with the hard drive, you can use these disks to boot the PC. Use utility software to back up the hard drive partition table to floppy disk.

Document All Setup Changes, Problems, and Solutions

When you first set up a new computer, start a record book about this computer, using either a file on disk or a notebook dedicated to this machine. In this notebook or file, record any changes in setup data as well as any problems you experience or maintenance that you do on this computer. Be diligent in keeping this notebook up to date, because it will be invaluable in diagnosing problems and upgrading equipment. Keep a printed or handwritten record of all changes to setup data for this machine, and store the record with the hardware and software documentation.

> **NOTE** You can also keep a record of all troubleshooting you do on a computer in a word-processing document that lists all the problems you have encountered and the solutions you used. This will help you save time in troubleshooting problems you have encountered before. Store the document file on a floppy disk that you keep with the computer's documentation.

If you are not the primary user of the computer, you might want to keep the hardware documentation separate from the computer itself. Label the documentation so that you can easily identify that it belongs to this computer. Some support people tape a large envelope inside the computer case, containing important documentation and records specific to that computer. Keep the software reference manuals in a location that is convenient for users.

Record Setup Data

Keep a record of CMOS, showing hard drive type, drive configuration, and so on. Use a CMOS save program, or use Norton Utilities or similar third-party utility software to save the setup data on a floppy disk. This information should be stored on a floppy disk along with the software necessary to use it. Label the disk with the PC type, date, and any information needed to use the disk. Put the disk in a safe place.

If you don't have access to software to save setup data, use the Print Screen key to print the setup screens. If the Print Screen key does not work while you view setup on the PC, carefully copy down on paper all settings that you changed from the default settings. CMOS can lose these settings, and you will want to be able to reconstruct them when necessary. To do that, you would restore default settings and then use your written record to change the ones that you set manually. Also keep a record of DIP switch settings and jumper settings on the motherboard. You can record these settings the first time you remove the cover of the machine. At the very least, record the settings before you change them! Keep all this information in your notebook.

When installing an expansion card, write information about the card in your notebook, and keep the documentation that came with it in your notebook. If you must change jumper settings or DIP switches on the card, be certain to write down the original settings before you change anything. When the card is configured correctly, write down the correct settings in your notebook or on the documentation for the card. It is unlikely that a user will accidentally change these settings and then ask you to fix them, but you never know!

Take Practical Precautions to Protect Software and Data

If software files become corrupted, the most thorough approach is to restore the software from backups or to reinstall the software. To simplify both of these time-consuming tasks, here are a few suggestions:

- Before you install a new software package, back up the Windows 2000/XP system state. For Windows XP, create a Restore Point.
- For Windows 9x/Me, because many software packages overwrite files in the \Windows\System directory during installation, back up this entire directory before you begin an installation if you have the hard drive space.
- Don't compress your hard drive, because compressed drives are more likely to become corrupted than those that are not compressed.
- Don't store data files in the same directory as the software, so that there will be less chance of accidentally deleting or overwriting a software file.
- Using Windows Explorer, enable "Do not show hidden files and folders" and "Hide protected operating system files." Users cannot accidentally delete what they can't see.

Back up original software   According to copyright laws, you have the right to make a backup of the installation CD or floppy disks in case the CD or disks fail. The copyright most likely does not allow you to distribute these backup copies to friends, but you can keep your copy in a safe place in the event that something happens to the original.

Back up data on the hard drive   Don't expect the worst but prepare for it! If important data is kept on the hard drive, back up that data on a regular basis on tape (using utility software designed for that purpose), on removable hard drives, on floppy disks, or on a company file server. Don't keep important data on only one medium.

A Preventive Maintenance Plan

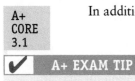

A+
CORE
3.1

✔ A+ EXAM TIP

The A+ Core exam expects you to know how to clean internal and external components, maintain a hard drive, and verify a UPS or surge suppressor as part of a regular preventive maintenance plan.

In addition to the guidelines given in the previous sections, it is important to develop an overall preventive maintenance plan. If your company has established written guidelines for PC preventive maintenance, read them and follow the procedures necessary to make them work. If your company has no established plan, make your own. A preventive maintenance plan tends to evolve from a history or pattern of malfunctions within an organization. For example, dusty environments can mean more maintenance, whereas a clean environment can mean less maintenance. Table 24-2 lists some guidelines for developing a preventive maintenance plan that may work for you.

The general idea of preventive maintenance is to do what you can to make a PC last longer and cause as little trouble as possible. You may also be responsible for ensuring that data is secure and backed up, that software copyrights are not violated, and that users are supported. As with any plan, when designing your preventive maintenance plan, first define your overall goals, and then design the plan accordingly. The guidelines listed in Table 24-2 primarily address the problems that prevent a PC from lasting long and from performing well.

VIDEO

Preventative
Maintenance

Component	Maintenance	How Often
Inside the case	• Make sure air vents are clear. • Use compressed air to blow the dust out of the case, or use a vacuum to clean vents, power supply, and fan. • Ensure that chips and expansion cards are firmly seated.	Yearly
CMOS setup	• Keep a backup record of setup (for example, using Norton Utilities or CMOS Save).	Whenever changes are made
Floppy drive	• Only clean the floppy drive when the drive does not work.	When the drive fails
Hard drive	• Perform regular backups.	At least weekly

Table 24-2 (continued)

A+
CORE
3.1

Component	Maintenance	How Often
	• Automatically execute a virus scan program at startup.	At least daily
	• Update antivirus software signature files (virus definitions)	Weekly
	• Defragment the drive and recover lost clusters regularly.	Monthly
	• Don't allow smoking around the PC.	Always
	• Place the PC where it will not be jarred, kicked, or bumped.	Always
	• Position the PC so air can circulate around it and into the front air vents	Always
	• Back up the partition table to floppy disk	Whenver changes are made
Keyboard	• Keep the keyboard clean.	Monthly
	• Keep the keyboard away from liquids.	Always
Mouse	• Clean the mouse rollers and ball.	Monthly
Monitor	• Clean the screen with a soft cloth.	At least monthly
	• Make sure air vents are clear.	Always
Printers	• Clean out the dust and bits of paper, using compressed air and	At least monthly or as

Table 24-2 (continued)

24

Component	Maintenance	How Often
	a vacuum. Small pieces of paper can be removed with tweezers, preferably insulated ones. • Clean the paper and ribbon paths with a soft, lint-free cloth. • Don't re-ink ribbons or use recharged toner cartridges. • If the printer uses an ozone filter, replace it as recommended by the manufacturer. • Replace other components as recommended by the manufacturer.	recommended by the manufacturer
UPS/ Suppressors	• Run weak battery test. • Run diagnostic test.	As recommended by manufacturer
Software	• If directed by your employer, check that only authorized software is present. • Regularly delete files from the Recycle Bin and \Temp directories.	At least monthly
Written record	• Keep a record of all software, including version numbers and the OS installed on the PC. • Keep a record of all hardware components installed, including hardware settings. • Record when and what preventive maintenance is performed. • Record any repairs done to the PC.	Whenever changes are made

Table 24-2   Guidelines for developing a PC preventive maintenance plan

NOTE

Dust is not good for a PC because it insulates PC parts like a blanket, which can cause them to overheat; therefore, ridding the PC of dust is an important part of preventive maintenance. Some PC technicians don't like to use a vacuum inside a PC because they're concerned that the vacuum might produce ESD. Use compressed air to blow the dust out of the chassis, power supply, and fan, or use a special antistatic vacuum designed to be used around sensitive equipment.

Moving Equipment

When shipping a PC, remember that rough handling can cause damage, as can exposure to water, heat, and cold. The PC can also be misplaced, lost, or stolen. When you are preparing a PC for shipping, take extra precautions to protect it and its data. Follow these general guidelines when preparing to ship a PC:

- Back up the hard drive onto a tape cartridge or other backup medium separate from your computer. If you don't have access to a medium that can back up the entire drive, back up important system and configuration files to a floppy disk or other media. Whatever you do, don't ship a PC that has the only copy of important data on the hard drive, or data that should be secured from unauthorized access.
- Remove any removable disks, tape cartridges, or CDs from the drives. Make sure that the tapes or disks holding the backup data are secured and protected during transit. Consider shipping them separately.
- Turn off power to the PC and all other devices.
- Disconnect power cords from the electrical outlet and the devices. Disconnect all external devices from the computer.
- If you think someone might have trouble later identifying which cord or cable belongs to which device or connection, label the cable connections with white tape or white labels.
- Coil all external cords and secure them with plastic ties or rubber bands.
- Pack the computer, monitor, and all devices in their original shipping cartons or similar boxes with enough packing material to protect them.
- Purchase insurance on the shipment. Postal insurance is not expensive and can save you a lot of money if materials are damaged in transit.

Disposing of Used Equipment

✔ A+ EXAM TIP

The A+ Core exam expects you to know how to follow environmental guidelines to dispose of batteries, CRTs, chemical solvents, and cans. If you're not certain how to dispose of a product, see its MSDS document.

As a PC technician, it will often be your responsibility to dispose of used equipment and consumables, including batteries, printer toner cartridges, and monitors. Table 24-3 lists such items and how to dispose of them. Manufacturer documentation and local environmental regulators can also provide disposal instructions or guidance. Monitors and power supplies can contain a charge even after the devices are unplugged. To discharge the capacitors in either type of device, place a screwdriver across a hot prong and the ground prong of the electrical connections, as shown in Figure 24-1. To discharge the actual CRT in a monitor, the monitor must be opened. Ask a technician trained to fix monitors to do this for you.

A **material safety data sheet (MSDS)** explains how to properly handle substances such as chemical solvents. An MSDS includes information such as physical data, toxicity, health effects, first aid, storage, disposal,

A+
CORE
3.1
3.3

and spill procedures. It comes packaged with the chemical, or you can order one from the manufacturer, or find one on the Internet (see *www.ilpi.com/msds*).

Figure 24-1   Discharge the capacitors in a monitor before disposal

Part	How to Dispose
Alkaline batteries including AAA, AA, A, C, D, and 9 volt	Dispose of these batteries in the regular trash. First check to see if there are recycling facilities in your area.
Button batteries used in digital cameras, Flash Path, and other small equipment Battery packs used in notebooks	These batteries can contain silver oxide, mercury, lithium, or cadmium and are considered hazardous waste. Dispose of them by returning them to the original dealer or by taking them to a recycling center. To recycle, pack them separately from other items. If you don't have a recycling center nearby, contact your county for local regulations for disposal.
Laser printer toner cartridges	Return these to the manufacturer or dealer to be recycled.
Ink-jet printer cartridges Computers Monitors Chemical solvents and cans	Check with local county or environmental officials for laws and regulations in your area for proper disposal of these items. The county might have a recycling center that will receive them. Discharge a monitor before disposing of it.

Table 24-3   Computer parts and how to dispose of them

Fire Extinguishers

A+
CORE
3.1

No discussion of preventive maintenance would be complete without mentioning the importance of having a fire extinguisher handy that is rated to handle fires ignited by electricity. The National Fire Protection Association (NFPA), an organization that creates standards for fire safety, says a fire has one of three ratings:

- *Class A.* A fire that is fueled by ordinary combustible materials such as wood, trash, or clothes
- *Class B.* A fire that is fueled by flammable liquids such as oil, gasoline, kerosene, propane gas, and some plastics
- *Class C.* A fire that is ignited and heated by electricity

It's the Class C fire that we are concerned about in this discussion. For a fire to be rated as a Class C fire, regardless of what is burning, the fire must have been ignited by electricity and must keep burning because electrical energy is providing heat. If you take away the electrical current, then the fire becomes a Class A or Class B fire. Mount a fire extinguisher rated for Class C fires near your workbench but not directly over your work area. If equipment were to catch on fire, you wouldn't want to have to reach over it to get to the fire extinguisher. Know how to use the extinguisher.

CHAPTER SUMMARY

- ▶ Tools for solving computer problems include a repair kit, bootable disk, and diagnostic hardware and software.

- ▶ Two important rules when troubleshooting are to eliminate unnecessary hardware and software and to trade components you know are good for those you suspect may be bad.

- ▶ Learn to ask the user questions (using good manners and diplomacy) that help you understand the history behind the problem.

- ▶ One reliable method of solving intermittent problems is to keep a log of when they occur.

- ▶ Problems with computers can be divided into two general groups: those that prevent the computer from booting successfully and those that occur after the computer boots.

- ▶ Diagnostic cards give error codes based on POST errors.

24

▸ Diagnostic software performs many tests on a PC. Some of these software programs use their own proprietary operating systems.

▸ Utility software can update and repair device drivers and applications. Some utility software downloads these updates from the Internet.

▸ Keep bootable disk(s) specific to the operating system installed on PCs you support.

▸ Keep backups of hard drive data and software.

▸ Back up the hard drive partition table to floppy drive. Keep a written record of CMOS setup changes, or save CMOS setup on disk.

▸ PC failures are caused by many environmental and human factors, including heat, dust, magnetism, power supply problems, static electricity, spilled liquids, viruses, and human error.

▸ The goals of preventive maintenance are to make PCs last longer and work better, protect data and software, and reduce repair costs.

▸ A PC preventive maintenance plan includes blowing dust from the inside of the computer case, keeping a record of setup data, backing up the hard drive, and cleaning the mouse, monitor, and keyboard.

▸ Protecting software and hardware documentation is an important preventive maintenance chore.

▸ Never ship a PC when the only copy of important data is on its hard drive.

▸ A Class C fire extinguisher is rated to put out a fire ignited and kept burning by electricity.

KEY TERMS

For explanations of key terms, see the Glossary near the end of the book.

diagnostic cards   diagnostic software   material safety data sheet (MSDS)

REVIEWING THE BASICS

1. Name four jobs that can all be categorized as a PC technician.

2. Of the four jobs in Question 1, which one job might never include interacting with the PC's primary user?

3. Using the rule "trade good for suspected bad," describe how to easily trouble-shoot a video problem.

4. Give five possible questions that should be asked of a user who is experiencing computer problems.

5. What is the best way to document intermittent problems?

6. Using Windows, list the steps to print a screen that shows an error message.

7. List one or two preventive maintenance measures that help protect each of the following: computer case, CMOS setup, floppy drive, hard drive, keyboard, mouse, printer, and software.

8. List at least three tasks you should complete before moving or shipping a computer.

9. How do you properly dispose of a battery pack from a notebook computer? A broken monitor? A toner cartridge from a laser printer?

10. What class of fire extinguisher is used for electrical fires?

THINKING CRITICALLY

1. As a help-desk technician, list some good detective questions to ask if the user calls to say, "My PC won't boot."

2. Starting with the easiest procedures, list five things to check if your PC does not boot.

3. Someone calls saying he has attempted to install a modem, but the modem does not work. List the first four questions you ask.

HANDS-ON PROJECTS

PROJECT 24-1: Interacting with the User

Rob, a PC service technician, has been called on-site to repair a PC. He has not spoken directly with the user, Lisa, but he knows the floor of the building where she works, and can look for her name on her cubicle. The following is a description of his actions. Create a table with two columns. List in one column the mistakes he made and in the next column the correct action he should have taken.

24

Rob's company promised that a service technician would come some time during the next business day after the call was received. Rob was given the name and address of the user and the problem, which was stated as "PC will not boot." Rob arrived the following day at about 10 A.M. He found Lisa's cubicle, but she was not present. Since Lisa was not present, Rob decided not to disturb the papers all over her desk, so he laid his notebooks and tools on top of her work.

Rob tried to boot the PC, and it gave errors indicating a corrupted FAT on the hard drive. He successfully booted from a disk and was able to access a C prompt. A DIR command returned a mostly unreadable list of files and subdirectories in the root directory. Next Rob used Norton Utilities to try to recover the files and directories but was unable to do so. He began to suspect that a virus had caused the problem, so he ran a virus scan program that did not find the suspected virus.

He made a call to his technical support to ask for suggestions. Technical support suggested that he try partitioning and formatting the hard drive to remove any possible viruses and recover the hard drive. Rob partitioned and formatted the hard drive and was on the phone with technical support, in the process of reloading Windows XP from the company's file server, when Lisa arrived.

Lisa took one look at her PC and gasped. She caught her breath and asked where her data was. Rob replied, "A virus destroyed your hard drive. I had to reformat."

Lisa tried to explain the importance of the destroyed data. Rob replied, "Guess you'll learn to make backups now." Lisa left to find her manager.

PROJECT 24-2: Developing Help-Desk Skills

Work with a partner who will play the role of the user. Sit with your back to the user, who is in front of the PC. Troubleshoot the problem and talk the user through to a solution. Abide by these rules:

1. A third person created an error so that the PC does not boot successfully. Neither you nor your partner knows what the third person did.

2. The user pretends not to have technical insight but to be good at following directions and willing to answer any nontechnical questions.

3. Don't turn around to look at the screen.

4. Practice professional mannerisms and speech.

5. As you work, keep a log of the "phone call to the help desk," recording in the log the major steps toward diagnosing and correcting the problem.

6. When the problem is resolved, have the third person create a different problem that causes the PC not to boot correctly, and exchange roles with your partner.

PROJECT 24-3: ## Saving CMOS Setup Using Freeware

Research the Internet for freeware to save CMOS setup data on a floppy disk. Print the Web page of the product. Download the program and use it to save the setup data to disk. When you run the software, print the main menu of the software. Try these Web sites when looking for software: *www.zdnet.com*, *www.cnet.com* and *www.download.com*.

PROJECT 24-4: ## Creating a Preventive Maintenance and Disaster Recovery Plan

Assume that you are a PC technician responsible for all 30 to 35 PCs of a small organization. The PCs are networked to a file server that is backed up each evening. No PC has power protection or line conditioning. Although some users make back-ups of data on their PCs to tape drives or a Zip drive, the company does not have a procedure to back up data or software. Your supervisor asked you to submit a preventive maintenance and disaster recovery plan for these PCs and to estimate the amount of time you will spend on preventive maintenance each month for the next 12 months. She also asked you to submit a suggested PC data backup plan for all users to follow, which will become a company policy. Do the following to create these plans and estimate your time:

1. List the possible causes of PC failures.

2. Using the list you created in Step 1, list what you can do to prevent these problems. Divide the list into two categories: what you plan to do one time for each PC or user and what you plan to do on a routine or as-needed basis.

3. For each PC, estimate the amount of time you need to implement the one-time-only plan and the amount of time you need each year for ongoing maintenance.

4. Based on your answers to Question 3, how much time do you plan to spend on preventive maintenance, on average, each month for the next 12 months?

5. In response to the request for a recommended company policy to back up all PC data, write a policy for users to follow to back up data on their PCs. Since all PCs are networked to the file server, suggest that company policy require data on a PC to be backed up to the file server, where it will be backed up nightly in case of a file server failure. Write the backup policy and instructions on how to implement it.

24

PROJECT 24-5: Researching Disposal Rules

Research the laws and regulations in your community concerning the disposal of batteries and old computer parts. Answer these questions regarding your community:

1. How do you properly dispose of a monitor?

2. How do you properly dispose of a battery pack used by a notebook computer?

3. How do you properly dispose of a large box of assorted computer parts, including hard drives, floppy drives, computer cases, and circuit boards?

PROJECT 24-6: Researching PC Support

A PC support technician is expected to stay abreast of new technologies, and the Internet is an excellent source of information to do that. Access each of the Web sites listed below, and print one Web page from each site that shows information that might be useful for a support technician.

Organization	Web Site
BYTE Magazine	www.byte.com
CNET, Inc.	www.cnet.com
COOK Network Consultants (Internet glossary)	www.cookreport.com
F_Secure Corp	www.f-secure.com
How Stuff Works	www.howstuffworks.com
internet.com Network	www.pcwebopedia.com
Kingston Technology (information about memory)	www.kingston.com
Microsoft Technical Resources	support.microsoft.com
MK Data	www.karbosguide.com
The PC Guide	www.pcguide.com
PC Today Online	www.pctoday.com
PC World	www.pcworld.com
TechTarget	www.techtarget.com
Tom's Hardware Guide	www.tomshardware.com
ZDNet (publishes several technical magazines)	www.zdnet.com
Zoom Telephonics, Inc.	www.modems.com

Error Messages and Their Meanings

A+
OS
3.1
CORE
2.1

Table A-1 lists error messages and their meanings. This table can help you when you are diagnosing computer problems. For other error messages, consult your motherboard or computer documentation or use a good search engine to search for the error message on the Internet.

Error Message	Meaning of the Error Message
Invalid partition table Error loading operating system Missing operating system Invalid boot disk Inaccessible boot device	The Master Boot program at the beginning of the hard drive displays these messages when it cannot find the active partition on the hard drive or the boot record on that partition. Use Diskpart or Fdisk to examine the drive for errors. Check the hard drive manufacturer's Web site for other diagnostic software.
Bad sector writing or reading to drive	Sector markings on the disk may be fading. Try ScanDisk or reformat the disk.
Beeps during POST	Before the video is checked, during POST, the ROM BIOS communicates error messages with a series of beeps. Each BIOS manufacturer has its own beep codes, but the following are examples of some BIOS codes. For specific beep codes for your motherboard, see the Web site of the motherboard or BIOS manufacturer.
One beep followed by three, four, or five beeps	Motherboard problems, possibly with DMA, CMOS setup chip, timer, or system bus.
Two beeps	The POST numeric code is displayed on the monitor.
Two beeps followed by three, four, or five beeps	First 64K of RAM has errors.
Three beeps followed by three, four, or five beeps	Keyboard controller failed or video controller failed.

Table A-1 (continued)

A+
OS
3.1
CORE
2.1

Error Message	Meaning of the Error Message
Four beeps followed by two, three, or four beeps	Problem with serial or parallel ports, system timer, or time of day.
Continuous beeps	Problem with power supply.
Configuration/CMOS error	Setup information does not agree with the actual hardware the computer found during boot. May be caused by a bad or weak battery or by changing hardware without changing setup. Check setup for errors.
Hard drive not found	The OS cannot locate the hard drive, or the controller card is not responding.
Fixed disk error	The PC cannot find the hard drive that setup told it to expect. Check cables, connections, power supply, and setup information.
Invalid drive specification	The PC is unable to find a hard drive or a floppy drive that setup tells it to expect. Look for errors in setup, or for a corrupted partition table on the hard drive.
No boot device available	The hard drive is not formatted, or the format is corrupted, and there is no disk in drive A. Boot from a bootable floppy and examine your hard drive for corruption.
Non-system disk or disk error Bad or missing Command.com No operating system found	The disk in drive A is not bootable. Remove the disk in drive A and boot from the hard drive. Command.com on drive C might have been erased, or the path could not be found. For Windows 9x/Me or DOS, use the Sys command to restore system files.
Not ready reading drive A: Abort, Retry, Fail?	The disk in drive A is missing, is not formatted, or is corrupted. Try another disk or remove the disk to boot from the hard drive.
Numeric codes during POST	Sometimes numeric codes are used to communicate errors at POST. Some examples for IBM XT/AT error codes include:
Code in the 100 range	Motherboard errors
Code in the 200 range	RAM errors
Code in the 300 range	Keyboard errors
Code in the 500 range	Video controller errors
Code in the 600 range	Floppy drive errors
Code in the 700 range	Coprocessor errors
Code in the 900 range	Parallel port errors
Code in the 1100–1200 range	Async (communications adapter) errors
Code in the 1300 range	Game controller or joystick errors
Code in the 1700 range	Hard drive errors
Code in the 6000 range	SCSI device or network card errors

Table A-1 (continued)

Error Message	Meaning of the Error Message
Code in the 7300 range	Floppy drive errors
Track 0 bad, disk not usable	This usually occurs when you attempt to format a floppy disk using the wrong format type. Check the disk type and compare it with the type specified in the format command.
Missing operating system, error loading operating system	The MBR is unable to locate or read the OS boot sector on the active partition, or there is a translation problem on large drives. Boot from a bootable floppy and examine the hard drive file system for corruption.
Unknown error at POST	See the Web site of the system BIOS manufacturer: • AMI BIOS: *www.ami.com* • Award BIOS and Phoenix BIOS: *www.phoenix.com* • Compaq or HP: *www.hp.com* • Dell: *www.dell.com* • IBM: *www.ibm.com* • Gateway: *www.gateway.com*
Invalid directory	A command issued in the Autoexec.bat file references a working directory that does not exist. Check the Autoexec.bat file for errors.
Bad command or file not found	The OS command just executed cannot be interpreted, or the OS cannot find the program file specified in the command line. Check the spelling of the filename. When working with DOS or from a Windows startup disk, check that the path to the program file has been given to the OS in Autoexec.bat.
Insufficient memory	This error happens during or after the boot under Windows when too many applications are open. Close some applications. A reboot might help.
Incorrect DOS version	When you execute a DOS external command, the OS looks for a program file with the same name as the command. It finds that this file belongs to a different version of the OS than the one that is now running. Use the Setver command in Autoexec.bat.
Write-protect error writing drive A:	Let the computer write to the disk by setting the switch on a 3½-inch disk or removing the tape from a 5¼-inch disk.
Error in Config.sys line xx	There is a problem loading a device driver or with the syntax of a command line. Check the command line for errors. Verify that the driver files are in the right directory. Reinstall the driver files.

Table A-1 (continued)

A+
OS
3.1
CORE
2.1

Error Message	Meaning of the Error Message
Himem.sys not loaded, missing or corrupt Himem.sys	Himem.sys is corrupted, not in the right directory, or not the right version for the currently loaded OS. Verify Himem.sys.
Device not found	Errors in System.ini, Win.ini, or the registry. Look for references to devices or attempts to load device drivers. Use Device Manager to delete a device or edit System.ini or Win.ini.
Device/Service has failed to start	A hardware device or driver necessary to run the device or critical software utility is causing problems. This type of problem is best handled using OS troubleshooting methods and tools.

Table A-1   Error Messages and Their Meanings

ASCII Character Set and Ansi.sys

A SCII (American Standard Code for Information Interchange) is a coding system used by personal computers to store character data, such as letters of the alphabet, numerals, some symbols, and certain control characters. There are 128 characters defined by the standard ASCII character set. Each ASCII character is assigned an 8-bit code that converts to a decimal number from 0 to 127, although in the standard set, the first bit is always 0. The first 31 values, which are nonprintable codes, are for control characters used to send commands to printers or other peripheral devices. Files that store data as ASCII characters are sometimes called ASCII files, ASCII text files, or simply text files. ASCII can be read by most text editors and word processors and is considered the universal file format for personal computers. Autoexec.bat is one example of an ASCII file.

In addition to the standard ASCII character set, some manufacturers use an extended ASCII character set that is specific to their equipment and is not necessarily compatible with other computers. The extended ASCII character sets use the codes 128 through 255.

The American National Standards Institute (ANSI), an organization responsible for many computer standards, developed an extended character set using codes 128 through 255 that includes special characters such as letters in an international alphabet and accents, currency symbols, and fractions. ANSI has also defined a series of control codes that can be used to control monitors. For example, a sequence of control codes can clear a monitor, cause characters to be displayed upside down, or put color on a DOS screen. Ansi.sys is a device driver that, when loaded in a DOS environment, provides these monitor and keyboard functions. Ansi.sys is loaded from the Config.sys file with this command:

```
Device=C:\DOS\Ansi.sys
```

Some DOS programs need Ansi.sys loaded in order to interpret the extended character set entered from the keyboard, display these characters on the screen, and control the monitor in other ways.

Table B-1 lists the standard ASCII character set. Note that items 2 through 32, the control characters, and the extended ASCII character set are not included.

Item Number	Symbol	Meaning	ASCII in Decimal Representation	ASCII in Binary Representation	ASCII in Hex Representation
1	.	Null	0	0000 0000	0
33	b/	Space	32	0010 0000	20
34	!	Exclamation point	33	0010 0001	21
35	"	Quotation mark	34	0010 0010	22
36	#	Number sign	35	0010 0011	23
37	$	Dollar sign	36	0010 0100	24
38	%	Percent sign	37	0010 0101	25
39	&	Ampersand	38	0010 0110	26
40	'	Apostrophe, prime sign	39	0010 0111	27
41	(	Opening parenthesis	40	0010 1000	28
42	)	Closing parenthesis	41	0010 1001	29
43	*	Asterisk	42	0010 1010	2A
44	+	Plus sign	43	0010 1011	2B
45	,	Comma	44	0010 1100	2C
46	-	Hyphen, minus sign	45	0010 1101	2D
47	.	Period, decimal point	46	0010 1110	2E
48	/	Slant	47	0010 1111	2F
49	0		48	0011 0000	30
50	1		49	0011 0001	31
51	2		50	0011 0010	32
52	3		51	0011 0011	33
53	4		52	0011 0100	34
54	5		53	0011 0101	35

Table B-1 (continued)

Item Number	Symbol	Meaning	ASCII in Decimal Representation	ASCII in Binary Representation	ASCII in Hex Representation
55	6		54	0011 0110	36
56	7		55	0011 0111	37
57	8		56	0011 1000	38
58	9		57	0011 1001	39
59	:	Colon	58	0011 1010	3A
60	;	Semicolon	59	0011 1011	3B
61	<	Less than sign	60	0011 1100	3C
62	=	Equals sign	61	0011 1101	3D
63	>	Greater than sign	62	0011 1110	3E
64	?	Question mark	63	0011 1111	3F
65	@	Commercial at sign	64	0100 0000	40
66	A		65	0100 0001	41
67	B		66	0100 0010	42
68	C		67	0100 0011	43
69	D		68	0100 0100	44
70	E		69	0100 0101	45
71	F		70	0100 0110	46
72	G		71	0100 0111	47
73	H		72	0100 1000	48
74	I		73	0100 1001	49
75	J		74	0100 1010	4A
76	K		75	0100 1011	4B
77	L		76	0100 1100	4C
78	M		77	0100 1101	4D
79	N		78	0100 1110	4E
80	O		79	0100 1111	4F

Table B-1 (continued)

Item Number	Symbol	Meaning	ASCII in Decimal Representation	ASCII in Binary Representation	ASCII in Hex Representation
81	P		80	0101 0000	50
82	Q		81	0101 0001	51
83	R		82	0101 0010	52
84	S		83	0101 0011	53
85	T		84	0101 0100	54
86	U		85	0101 0101	55
87	V		86	0101 0110	56
88	W		87	0101 0111	57
89	X		88	0101 1000	58
90	Y		89	0101 1001	59
91	Z		90	0101 1010	5A
92	[	Opening bracket	91	0101 1011	5B
93	\	Reverse slant	92	0101 1100	5C
94	]	Closing bracket	93	0101 1101	5D
95	^	Caret	94	0101 1110	5E
96	_	Underscore	95	0101 1111	5F
97	`	Acute accent	96	0110 0000	60
98	a		97	0110 0001	61
99	b		98	0110 0010	62
100	c		99	0110 0011	63
101	d		100	0110 0100	64
102	e		101	0110 0101	65
103	f		102	0110 0110	66
104	g		103	0110 0111	67
105	h		104	0110 1000	68
106	i		105	0110 1001	69

Table B-1 (continued)

Item Number	Symbol	Meaning	ASCII in Decimal Representation	ASCII in Binary Representation	ASCII in Hex Representation
107	j		106	0110 1010	6A
108	k		107	0110 1011	6B
109	l		108	0110 1100	6C
110	m		109	0110 1101	6D
111	n		110	0110 1110	6E
112	o		111	0110 1111	6F
113	p		112	0111 0000	70
114	q		113	0111 0001	71
115	r		114	0111 0010	72
116	s		115	0111 0011	73
117	t		116	0111 0100	74
118	u		117	0111 0101	75
119	v		118	0111 0110	76
120	w		119	0111 0111	77
121	x		120	0111 1000	78
122	y		121	0111 1001	79
123	z		122	0111 1010	7A
124	{	Opening brace	123	0111 1011	7B
125			Split vertical bar	124	0111 1100	7C
126	}	Closing brace	125	0111 1101	7D
127	~	Tilde	126	0111 1110	7E
128	Δ	Small triangle	127	0111 1111	7F

Table B-1   Standard ASCII character set

The Hexadecimal Number System and Memory Addressing

U nderstanding the number system and the coding system that computers use to store data and communicate with each other is fundamental to understanding how computers work. Early attempts to invent an electronic computing device met with disappointing results as long as inventors tried to use the decimal number system, with the digits 0–9. Then John Atanasoff proposed using a coding system that expressed everything in terms of different sequences of only two numerals: one represented by the presence of a charge and one represented by the absence of a charge. The numbering system that can be supported by the expression of only two numerals is called base 2, or binary; it was invented by Ada Lovelace many years before, using the numerals 0 and 1. Under Atanasoff's design, all numbers and other characters would be converted to this binary number system, and all storage, comparisons, and arithmetic would be done using it. Even today, this is one of the basic principles of computers. Every character or number entered into a computer is first converted into a series of 0s and 1s. Many coding schemes and techniques have been invented to manipulate these 0s and 1s, called **bits** for **bi**nary dig**its**.

The most widespread binary coding scheme for microcomputers, which is recognized as the microcomputer standard, is called ASCII (American Standard Code for Information Interchange). (Appendix B lists the binary code for the basic 127-character set.) In ASCII, each character is assigned an 8-bit code called a **byte**. The byte has become the universal single unit of data storage in computers everywhere. Table C-1 lists common terms used in the discussion of how numbers are stored in computers.

Term	Definition
Bit	A numeral in the binary number system: a 0 or a 1.
Byte	8 bits.
Kilobyte	1024 bytes, which is 2 to the 10th power, often rounded to 1000 bytes.
Megabyte	Either 1024 kilobytes or 1000 kilobytes, depending on what has come to be standard practice in different situations. For example, when calculating floppy disk capacities, 1 megabyte = 1000 kilobytes; when calculating hard drive capacity, traditionally, 1 megabyte = 1024 kilobytes.

Table C-1 (continued)

Term	Definition
Gigabyte	1000 megabytes or 1024 megabytes, depending on what has come to be standard practice in different situations.
ASCII	American Standard Code for Information Interchange coding scheme used for microcomputers, which assigns a 7- or 8-bit code to all characters and symbols. See Appendix B for more information.
Hex	Short for hexadecimal. A number system based on 16 values (called base 16), which is explained in this appendix. Uses the 16 numerals 0, 1, 2, 3, 4, 5, 6, 7, 8, 9, A, B, C, D, E, and F. Hex numbers are often followed by a lowercase h to indicate they are in hex (example: 78h).

Table C-1   Computer terminology

Computers convert binary data into the hexadecimal (hex) number system because it is much less complex than converting data into decimal numbers, and it is much easier for human beings to read hex numbers than to read binary numbers. This way, even though the actual processing and inner workings of computers use the binary system, they often display information using the hex system.

Learning to "Think Hex"

One skill a knowledgeable computer support person must have is the ability to read hex numbers and convert hex to decimal and decimal to hex. Once you understand one numbering system (decimal), you can understand any numbering system (including binary and hexadecimal), because they all operate on the same basic principle: place value. So we begin there.

Place Value

A key to understanding place value is to think of a number system as a method of grouping multiple small units together until there are enough of them to be packed into a single larger group, then grouping multiple larger groups together until there are enough of them to form an even larger group, and so on. In our (decimal) number system, once there are 10 units of any group, that group becomes a single unit of the next larger group. So, groups of 10 units are packed into groups of tens; groups of 10 tens are packed into groups of hundreds; groups of 10 hundreds are packed into groups of thousands, and so forth.

An easy way to understand number systems is to think of the numbers as being packaged for shipping, into boxes, cartons, crates, truckloads, and so on. For the decimal numbering system, consider packing widgets (units) into boxes (tens), which are packed into cartons (100s), which are packed into crates (1000s), and so forth. The same analogy works for binary, hexadecimal, and all other number systems.

Our friend Joe, in Figure C-1, is a widget packer in the shipping department of the ACE Widget Co. Joe can ship single widgets, or he can pack them in boxes, cartons, crates, and truckloads. He can fit three, and only three, widgets to a box; only three boxes into one carton ($3 \times 3 = 9$ widgets); only three cartons into one crate ($3 \times 9 = 27$ widgets); and only three crates into one truck ($3 \times 27 = 81$ widgets). He is not allowed to pack more widgets into boxes, cartons, crates, or truckloads than those specified. Neither is he allowed to send out a box, carton, crate, or truckload that is not completely filled.

1 truckload
holds 3 crates
(81 widgets)

1 crate
holds 3 cartons
(27 widgets)

1 carton
holds 3 boxes
(9 widgets)

1 box
holds 3
widgets

single
widgets

Figure C-1   Joe in the shipping department groups widgets in singles, boxes, cartons, crates, and truc kloads all in groups of three

Joe receives an order to ship out 197 widgets. How does he ship them? The answer is shown in Figure C-2. Joe sends out 197 widgets grouped into 2 truckloads ($2 \times 81 = 162$ widgets), 1 crate (27 widgets), no cartons, 2 boxes ($2 \times 3 = 6$ widgets), and 2 single widgets. We can write this grouping of widgets as 21022, where the "place values" from left to right are truckloads, crates, cartons, boxes, and units, which in this case are (in decimal) 162 widgets, 27 widgets, 0 widgets, 6 widgets, and 2 widgets. Notice that each "place value" in our widget-packing system is a multiple of 3, because the widgets are grouped into three before they are packed into boxes; the boxes are grouped into three before they are packed into cartons, and so on. By grouping the widgets into groups of 3s in this manner, we converted the decimal number (base 10) 197 into the ternary number (base 3) 21022. Joe's widget-packing method is a base three, or ternary, system. The numerals in the ternary number system are 0, 1, and 2. When you get to the next value after 2, instead of counting on up to 3, you move one place value to the left and begin again with 1 in that position, which represents 3. So, counting in base 3 goes like this: 0, 1, 2, 10, 11, 12, 20, 21, 22, 100, 101, and so on. This is the same as Joe's never shipping out three of any one group unless they are packed together into one larger group. For example, Joe wouldn't ship three individual boxes, he would ship one carton.

| 2 trucks | 1 crate | 0 cartons | 2 boxes | 2 singles |

Figure C-2   Joe's shipment of 197 widgets: 2 truckloads, 1 crate, 0 cartons, 2 boxes, and a group of 2 singles

You can easily apply the widget-packing analogy to another base. If Joe used 10 instead of three, he would be using base 10 (decimal) rules. So, numbering systems differ by the different numbers of units they group together. In the hex number system, we group by 16. So, if Joe were shipping in groups of 16, as in Figure C-3, single widgets could be shipped out up to 15, but 16 widgets would make one box. Sixteen boxes would make one carton, which would contain 16 × 16, or 256, widgets. Sixteen cartons would make one crate, which would contain 16 × 256, or 4096, widgets.

Suppose Joe receives an order for 197 widgets to be packed in groups of 16. He will not be able to fill a carton (256 widgets), so he ships out 12 boxes (16 widgets each) and five single widgets:

12 × 16 = 192, and 192 + 5 = 197

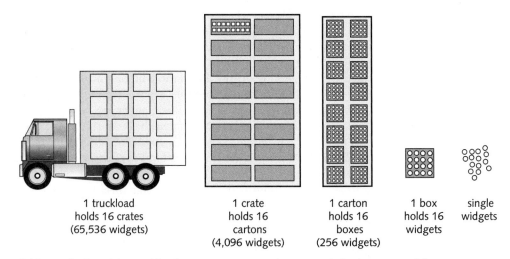

| 1 truckload
holds 16 crates
(65,536 widgets) | 1 crate
holds 16
cartons
(4,096 widgets) | 1 carton
holds 16
boxes
(256 widgets) | 1 box
holds 16
widgets | single
widgets |

Figure C-3   Widgets displayed in truckloads, crates, cartons, boxes, and singles grouped in 16s

You approach an obstacle if you attempt to write the number in hex. How are you going to express 12 boxes and 5 singles? In hex, you need single numerals to represent the numbers 10, 11, 12, 13, 14, and 15 in decimal. Hex uses the letters A through F for the numbers 10 through 15. Table C-2 shows values expressed in the decimal, hex, and binary numbering systems. In the second column in Table C-2, you are counting in the hex number system. For example, 12 is represented with a C. So you say that Joe packs C boxes and 5 singles. The hex number for decimal 197 is C5 (see Figure C-4).

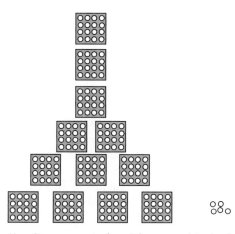

Figure C-4   Hex C5 represented as C boxes and 5 singles = 197 decimal

Decimal	Hex	Binary	Decimal	Hex	Binary	Decimal	Hex	Binary
0	0	0	14	E	1110	28	1C	11100
1	1	1	15	F	1111	29	1D	11101
2	2	10	16	10	10000	30	1E	11110
3	3	11	17	11	10001	31	1F	11111
4	4	100	18	12	10010	32	20	100000
5	5	101	19	13	10011	33	21	100001
6	6	110	20	14	10100	34	22	100010
7	7	111	21	15	10101	35	23	100011
8	8	1000	22	16	10110	36	24	100100
9	9	1001	23	17	10111	37	25	100101
10	A	1010	24	18	11000	38	26	100110
11	B	1011	25	19	11001	39	27	100111

Table C-2 (continued)

Decimal	Hex	Binary	Decimal	Hex	Binary	Decimal	Hex	Binary
12	C	1100	26	1A	11010	40	28	101000
13	D	1101	27	1B	11011			

Table C-2   Decimal, hex, and binary values

For a little practice, calculate the hex values of the decimal values 14, 259, 75, and 1024 and the decimal values of FFh and A11h.

How Exponents Are Used to Express Place Value

If you are comfortable with using exponents, you know that writing numbers raised to a power is the same as multiplying that number by itself the power number of times. For example, $3^4 = 3 \times 3 \times 3 \times 3 = 81$. Using exponents in expressing numbers can also help us easily see place value, because the place value for each place is really the base number multiplied by itself a number of times, based on the place value position. For instance, look back at Figure C-1. A truckload is really $3 \times 3 \times 3 \times 3$, or 81, units, which can be written as 3^4. A crate is really $3 \times 3 \times 3$, or 27, units. The numbers in Figure C-1 can therefore be written like this:

Truckload = 3^4 Crate = 3^3 Carton = 3^2 Box = 3^1 Single = 3^0

(Any number raised to the 0 power equals 1.) Therefore, we can express the numbers in Figure C-2 as multiples of truckloads, crates, cartons, boxes, and singles like this:

	Truckloads	Crates	Cartons	Boxes	Singles
21022 (base 3)	2×3^4	1×3^3	0×3^2	2×3^1	2×3^0
Decimal equivalent	162	27	0	6	2

When we sum up the numbers in the last row above, we get 197. We just converted a base 3 number (21022) to a base 10 number (197).

Binary Number System

It was stated earlier that it is easier for computers to convert from binary to hex or from hex to binary than to convert between binary and decimal. Let,s see just how easy. Recall that the binary number system only has two numerals, or bits: 0 and 1. If our friend Joe in shipping operated a "binary" shipping system, he would pack like this: 2 widgets in a box, 2 boxes in one carton (4 widgets), two cartons in one crate (8 widgets), and two crates in one truckload (16 widgets). In Figure C-5, Joe is asked to pack 13 widgets. He packs 1 crate (8 widgets), 1 carton (4 widgets), no boxes, and 1 single. The number 13 in binary is 1101:

$$(1 \times 2^3) + (1 \times 2^2) + (0 \times 2^1) + (1 \times 2^0) = 8 + 4 + 0 + 1$$
$$= 13$$

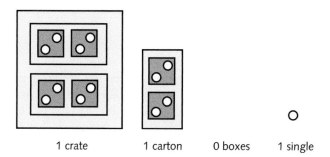

    1 crate   1 carton   0 boxes   1 single

Figure C-5   Binary 1101 = 13 displayed as crates, cartons, boxes, and singles

Now let's see how to convert binary to hex and back again. The largest 4-bit number in binary is 1111. This number in decimal and hex is:

```
binary 1111 = 1 group of 8 = 8
              1 group of 4 = 4
              1 group of 2 = 2
                  1 single = 1
                     TOTAL = 15 (decimal)
    Therefore, 1111 (binary) = 15 (decimal) = F (hex)
```

This last calculation is very important when working with computers: F is the largest numeral in the hex number system and it only takes 4 bits to write this largest hex numeral: F (hex) = 1111 (binary). So, every hex numeral (0, 1, 2, 3, 4, 5, 6, 7, 8, 9, A, B, C, D, E, and F) can be converted into a 4-bit binary number. Look back at the first 16 entries in Table C-2 for these binary values. Add leading zeroes to the binary numbers as necessary.

When converting from hex to binary, take each hex numeral and convert it to a 4-bit binary number, and string all the 4-bit groups together. Fortunately, when working with computers, you will almost never work with more than two hex numerals at a time. Here are some examples:

1. To convert hex F8 to binary, do the following: F = 1111, and 8 = 1000. Therefore, F8 = 11111000 (usually written 1111 1000).

2. To convert hex 9A to binary, do the following: 9 = 1001, and A = 1010. Therefore, 9A = 1001 1010.

Now try converting from binary to hex:

1. To convert binary 101110 to hex, first group the bits in groups of 4, starting at the right and moving left, adding leading zeros as necessary: 0010 1110.

2. Then convert each group of 4 bits in binary to a single hex numeral: 0010 = 2, and 1110 = E. The hex number is 2E.

Writing Conventions

Sometimes when you are dealing with hex, binary, and decimal numbers, it is not always clear which number system is being used. If you see a letter in the number, you know the number is a hex number. Binary numbers are usually written in groups of four bits. Sometimes a hex number is preceded by 0x, as in 0xFF. This book follows the convention of placing a lowercase h after a hex number, like this: 2Eh.

Memory Addressing

Computers often display memory addresses in the hex number system. You must either "think in hex" or convert to decimal. It's really easier, with a little practice, to think in hex. Here's the way it works:

Memory addresses are displayed as two hex numbers. An example is C800:5.

The part to the left of the colon (C800) is called the *segment address*, and the part to the right of the colon (5) is called the *offset*. The offset value can have as many as four hex digits. The actual memory address is calculated by adding a zero to the right of the segment address and adding the offset value, like this: C800:5 = C8000 + 5 = C8005.

The first 640K of Windows 9x or DOS memory is called conventional memory. Look at how that memory is addressed, first in decimal and then in hex (assuming 1 kilobyte = 1024 bytes):

640K = 640 × 1024 = 655,360

There are 655,360 memory addresses in conventional memory, where each memory address can hold 1 byte, or 8 bits, of either data or program instructions. The decimal value 655,360 converted to hex is A0000 (10 × 16⁴). So, conventional memory addresses begin with 00000h and end with A0000h minus 1h or 9FFFFh. Written in segment-and-offset form, conventional memory addresses range from 0000:0 to 9FFF:F.

Recall that upper memory is defined as the memory addresses from 640K to 1024K. The next address after 9FFF:F is the first address of upper memory, which is A0000, and the last address is FFFFF. Written in segment-and-offset terms, upper memory addresses range from A000:0 to FFFF:F.

Here is one way to organize the conversion of a large hex value such as FFFFF to decimal (remember F in hex equals 15 in decimal).

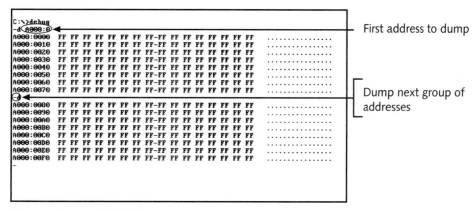

FFFFF converted to decimal:

$$15 \times 16^0 = 15 \times 1 = 15$$
$$15 \times 16^1 = 15 \times 16 = 240$$
$$15 \times 16^2 = 15 \times 256 = 3,840$$
$$15 \times 16^3 = 15 \times 4096 = 61,440$$
$$15 \times 16^4 = 15 \times 65,536 = 983,040$$
$$\text{TOTAL} = 1,048,575$$

Remember that FFFFF is the last memory address in upper memory. The very next memory address is the first address of extended memory, which is defined as memory above 1 MB. If you add 1 to the number above, you get 1,048,576, which is equal to 1024 × 1024, which is the definition of 1 megabyte.

Displaying Memory with DOS DEBUG

In Figure C-6 you see the results of the beginning of upper memory displayed. The DOS DEBUG command displays the contents of memory. Memory addresses are displayed in hex segment-and-offset values. To enter DEBUG, type the following command at the C prompt and press Enter:

```
C:\> DEBUG
```

First address to dump

Dump next group of addresses

Figure C-6   Memory dump: -d A000:0

You create a memory "dump" when you tell the system to record the contents of memory to a file or display it on screen; a dump can be useful when troubleshooting. Type the following dump command to display the beginning of upper memory (the hyphen in the command is the DEBUG command prompt) and press Enter:

```
-d A000:0
```

Memory is displayed showing 16 bytes on each line. The A area of memory (the beginning of upper memory) is not used unless the computer is using a monochrome monitor or this area is being used as an upper memory block. In Figure C-6, the area contains nothing but continuous 1s in binary or Fs in hex. The ASCII interpretation is on the right side. To view the next group of memory addresses, you can type *d* at the hyphen and press Enter. DEBUG displays the next 128 addresses.

The A and B ranges of upper memory addresses (upper memory addresses that begin with A or B when written in hex) are used for monochrome monitors. The C range contains the video BIOS for a color monitor. Figure C-7 shows the dump of the beginning of the C range.

There is more than one way—in fact there are many ways—to identify the same segment-and-offset value. Try these commands to display the same upper memory addresses:

```
-d C000:0
-d BFF1:00F0
-d BFFF:0010
-d BEEE:1120
```

First address to dump

Figure C-7   Memory dump: -d C000:0

In summary, reading and understanding binary and hex numbers are essential skills for managing computers. All data is stored in binary in a computer and is often displayed in hex. Memory addresses are often displayed in hex segment-and-offset terms. An address in memory can be written in a variety of segment-and-offset values. The actual memory address is calculated by placing one zero to the right side of the segment address and adding the resulting value to the offset value. To exit DEBUG, type *q* for quit and press Enter at the hyphen prompt.

FAT Details

This appendix gives you the details of the FAT file system. The FAT file system for a floppy disk or HDD logical drive uses a boot record, FAT, and root directory table. The layout of each of these items is described, as well as how they work together.

OS Boot Record

An OS boot record at the beginning of a floppy disk or volume (logical drive) is used during the boot process to inform the OS how the disk or volume is organized. If the disk or volume is the boot device, the boot program at the end of the boot record loads the first Windows hidden file, Io.sys, or Ntldr. Table D-1 shows the complete layout for the boot record.

The eleventh item in Table D-1 is the number of heads, which is the number of surfaces allocated for the volume. The top and bottom of each disk equal two surfaces or heads. For a floppy disk, the number of heads is always two. The medium descriptor byte tells the OS what type of disk this is. Table D-2 gives the values of this descriptor byte.

Description	Number of Bytes
Machine code	11
Bytes per sector	2
Sectors per cluster	1
Reserved	2
Number of FATs	1
Number of root directory entries	2
Number of logical sectors	2
Medium descriptor byte	1

Table D-1 (continued)

Description	Number of Bytes
Sectors per FAT	2
Sectors per track	2
Heads	2
Number of hidden sectors	2
Total sectors in logical volume	4
Physical drive number	1
Reserved	1
Extended boot signature record	1
32-bit binary volume ID	4
Volume label	11
Type of file system (FAT12, FAT16, or FAT32)	8
Program to load operating system (bootstrap loader)	Remainder of the sector

Table D-1   Layout of the boot record on each logical drive or floppy disk

Disk Type	Description Bytes
3½-inch double-density floppy disk, 720K	F9
3½-inch high-density floppy disk, 1.44 MB	F0
Hard disk	F8

Table D-2   Disk type and descriptor byte

Root Directory Table

The root directory contains information about each file and subdirectory stored in it. Each directory entry is 32 bytes long, although only 22 bytes are used. Table D-3 lists how the 22 bytes are used. Although earlier versions of Windows did limit the number of entries in the root directory for a hard drive, Windows 98 and later Windows OSs do not. Note, however, that Microsoft recommends that you keep only about 150 entries in any one directory. Having any more entries slows access to the directory. A 3½-inch high-density floppy disk can have up to 224 entries in the root directory.

Root Directory Bytes	Usage
8	Name of file
3	File extension
1	Attribute byte (special meaning for each bit)
10	Not used
2	Time of creation or last update
2	Date of creation or last update
2	Starting cluster number in binary
4	Size of file in binary

Table D-3 Root directory information for each file

Note that the root directory has no provision for the period (often referred to as "dot") that we normally see between the filename and the file extension in OS command lines. The period is not stored in directories but is only used in OS command lines to indicate where the filename ends and the file extension begins.

File attributes are used for various purposes. One file attribute byte is broken into bits, and each bit has a specific meaning. The first two bits are not used. Table D-4 lists the meanings of the other six bits, beginning with the leftmost bit in the byte and moving to the right. Several of these bits can be changed using the Attrib command or Windows Explorer.

Bit	Description	Bit = 0	Bit = 1
1, 2	Not used		
3	Archive bit	Not to be archived	To be archived
4	Directory status	File	Subdirectory
5	Volume label	Not volume label	Is volume label
6	System file	Not system file	Is system file
7	Hidden file	Not hidden	Hidden
8	Read-only file	Read/write	Read-only

Table D-4 Meaning of each bit in the directory attribute byte for each file (reading from left to right across the byte)

> Bit 3, the archive bit, is a switch used to indicate whether the file has changed since the last backup and should be backed up next time a backup is made.

NOTE

How the OS Uses the FAT and Directory Table

Notice that the root directory contains only the starting cluster number. To find out what other clusters store the file, look in the file allocation table. For example, suppose a file named Mydata.txt begins at cluster 5 and requires three clusters to hold the file. The OS takes the following steps to read the file. (The first three are numbered in Figure D-1.)

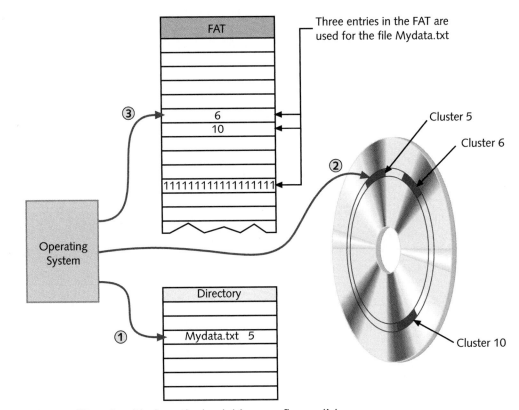

Figure D-1   How an OS reads a file from the hard drive or a floppy disk

1. The OS goes to the root directory and reads the name of the file (Mydata.txt) and the first cluster number (5).

2. The OS retrieves the contents of cluster 5 on the floppy disk, which is the first segment of the file.

3. The OS turns to the FAT, looks at the fifth position in the FAT, and reads 6, which says the next segment of the file is in cluster 6.

4. It retrieves the second segment of the file from cluster 6 on the floppy disk.

5. The OS turns to the sixth position in the FAT and reads 10, which says the next segment of the file is in cluster 10.

6. It retrieves the third segment of the file from cluster 10 on the floppy disk.

7. The OS turns to the tenth position in the FAT and reads all 1s in the FAT entry, which says this is the last cluster in the file. (If the FAT is FAT16, then an entry of 16 ones is written in the FAT. If it is FAT32, then an entry of 28 ones is written.)

NOTE

By dividing the size of a file by the number of bytes per cluster and rounding up to the nearest whole number, you can determine how many clusters the file occupies.

The root directory and all subdirectories contain the same information about each file. Only the root directory has a limitation on the number of entries. Subdirectories can have as many entries as disk space allows. Because long filenames require more room in a directory than short filenames, assigning long filenames reduces the number of files that can be stored in the root directory.

Electricity and Multimeters

This appendix gives you a general introduction to what electricity is and how it is measured. In addition, you will learn to use a multimeter to measure the voltage output of a power supply.

Electricity: A Basic Introduction

To most people, volts, ohms, watts, and amps are vague words that have to do with electricity. If these terms are mysterious to you, they will become clear in this section, which discusses electricity in nontechnical language and uses simple analogies.

Electricity is energy and water is matter, but the two have enough in common to make some comparisons. Consider Figure E-1. The water system shown in the top part of the figure is closed– that is, the amount of water in the system remains the same because no water enters and no water leaves the system. The electrical system in the lower part of the figure is similar in several respects. Think of electricity as a stream of tiny charged particles (electrons) that flow like water along the path of least resistance.

Just as water flows down because of the force of gravity, electricity flows from negative to positive because of the force of like charges repelling one another. The water pump produces water pressure in the system by lifting the water, and a battery produces electrical pressure in the system by creating a buildup of negative charges (in the form of electrons) in one location, which are driven to move. This difference in charge, which is similar to water pressure in a water system, is called potential difference. Water seeks a place of rest, moving from a high to a low elevation, and electrons seek a place of rest by moving from a negatively charged location (sometimes called "hot") to a positively charged location (sometimes called "ground"). In the figure, as water flows through the closed system, the water wheel harnesses some of its force and converts it to a form of energy, motion. Also in the figure, as the electrons flow in the closed electrical system called a circuit, the light bulb harnesses some of the force of the moving electrons and converts it to another form of energy, light. When the water returns to the pool, water pressure decreases and the water is at rest. When the electrons arrive at the positive side of the battery, electrical potential difference decreases, and the system is at rest.

(a) Water system

(b) Electrical system

Figure E-1   Two closed systems: (a) water system with pump, wheel, and pool;(b) electrical system with battery and light bulb

Electron flow goes from the hot point, or negative terminal, to the ground, or positive terminal. Because early theories of electricity assumed that electricity flowed from positive to negative, most electronics books show the current flowing from positive to negative. This theory is called conventional current flow; if it were used in Figure E-1, the figure would show reversed positive and negative symbols.

Electrical energy has properties that you can measure in various ways. Table E-1 defines four properties of electricity, how they can be measured, and some examples of each. These properties are explained in detail in the following sections.

Unit	Definition	Computer Example
Volt (measures potential difference)	Abbreviated as V (for example, 110 V). Volts are measured by finding the potential difference between the electrical charges on either side of an electrical device in an electrical system.	An AT power supply provides four separate voltages: +12 V, -12 V, +5 V, and -5 V. An ATX power supply provides these voltages and +3.3 V as well.
Amp or ampere (measures electrical current)	Abbreviated as A (for example, 1.5 A). Amps are measured by placing an ammeter in the flow of current and measuring that current.	A 17-inch monitor requires less than 2 A to operate. A small laser printer uses about 2 A. A CD-ROM drive uses about 1 A.
Ohm (measures resistance)	Abbreviated with the symbol Ω (for example, 20 Ω). Devices are rated according to how much resistance to electrical current they offer. The ohm rating of a resistor or other electrical device is often written somewhere on the device. The resistance of a device is measured when the device is not connected to an electrical system.	Current can flow in typical computer cables and wires with a resistance of near zero Ω.
Watt (measures power)	Abbreviated W (for example, 20 W). Watts are calculated by multiplying volts by amps.	A computer power supply is rated at 200 to 600 W.

Table E-1   Measures of electricity

Voltage

The first measure of electricity listed in Table E-1 is potential difference. First, consider how to measure the water pressure in Figure E-1. If you measure the pressure of the water directly above the water wheel and then measure the pressure just as the water lands in the pool, you find that the water pressure above the wheel is greater than the water pressure below it.

Now consider the electrical system. If you measure the electrical charge on one side of the light bulb and compare it with the electrical charge on the other side of the bulb, you see a difference in charge. The potential difference in charge creates an electrical force called **voltage**, which drives the electrons through the system between two points. Voltage is measured in units called **volts (V)**.

In Figure E-2, the leads of a **voltmeter**, a device for measuring electrical voltage, are placed on either side of a light bulb that consumes some electrical power. The potential difference between the two points on either side of the device is the voltage in the closed system. Voltage is measured when the power is on.

12 volts

Figure E-2   A voltmeter measuring the voltage across a bulb and a battery

Amps

The volume of electrons (or electricity) flowing through an electrical system is called current. Look back at Figure E-1. The volume or amount of water flowing through the water system does not change, although the water pressure changes at different points in the system. To measure that volume, you pick one point in the system and measure the volume of water passing through that point over a period of time. The electrical system is similar. If you measure the number of electrons, or electrical current, at any point in this system, you find the same value as at any other point, because the current is constant throughout the system. (This assumes that the entire closed water or electrical system has only a single pipe or a single wire.) Electrical current is measured in **amperes** (**A**), abbreviated **amps**. Figure E-3 shows an **ammeter**, a device that measures electrical current in amps. You place the ammeter in the path of the electrical flow so that the electrons must flow through the ammeter. The measurement, which you take with the power on, might not be completely accurate because the ammeter can influence the circuit.

12 volts

Figure E-3 Battery and bulb circuit with ammeter in line

Because the current flows through an ammeter, check the rating of the ammeter before measuring amps to make sure it can handle the flow of electricity. More flow than the ammeter is designed to handle can blow the meter's fuse.

NOTE

Relationship Between Voltage and Current

Refer again to the water system in Figure E-1. To increase the volume of water flowing through the system, you increase the difference in water pressure between the low and high points (which is called the pressure differential). As the pressure differential increases, the water flow (or current) increases, and as the water pressure differential decreases, the water flow (or current) decreases. Another way of saying this is: There is a direct relationship between pressure differential and current. An electrical system works the same way. As the electrical potential difference (or voltage) increases, the electrical current increases; as the voltage decreases, the current decreases. There is a direct relationship between voltage and current.

Ohms

Suppose you are working your water pump to full capacity. If you still want to increase the overall power of your water system–so the wheel turns faster to produce more mechanical energy–you could decrease the resistance to water flow, allowing more water to flow to push the wheel faster. You might use a larger pipe or a lighter water wheel, or, if the system has a partially open water valve, you could open the valve more; these alternatives all would lower resistance to water flow. As resistance decreases, current increases. As resistance increases (smaller pipes, heavier wheel, partially closed valve), current decreases.

Similarly, **resistance** in an electrical system is a property that opposes the flow of electricity. As electrical resistance increases, the flow of electrons decreases. As resistance decreases, the electricity increases. (A condition of low resistance that allows current to flow in a completed circuit is called **continuity**). When too much electricity flows through a wire, it creates heat energy (similar to friction) in the wire. This heat energy can cause the wire to melt or burn, which can result in an electrical fire, just as too much water current can cause a pipe to burst. Reducing the size of a wire reduces the amount of electricity that can safely flow through it. Electrical resistance is measured in **ohms (Ω)**.

Resistors are devices used in electrical circuits to resist the flow of electricity. These devices control the flow of electricity in a circuit, much as partially closed valves control the flow of water.

Relationships of Resistance to Current and Voltage

Voltage and current have a direct relationship. This means that when voltage increases, current increases. Resistance has an inverse relationship with current and a direct relationship with voltage. This means that as resistance increases, current decreases if voltage remains constant, such as when you use a dimmer switch to dim a light. As a general rule, the more voltage you expect in an electrical system, in order for current to remain constant, the more resistance you must add in the form of a larger-capacity resistor. This last statement is known as Ohm's Law. A similar statement defines the relationship among the units of measure: volts, amps, and ohms. One volt drives a current of one amp through a resistance of one ohm.

Wattage

Wattage is the total amount of power needed to operate an electrical device. When thinking of the water system, you recognize that the amount of water power used to turn the water wheel is not just a measure of the water pressure that forces current through the system. The amount of power also depends on the amount of water available to flow. For a given water pressure, you have more power with more water flow and less power with less water flow. A lot of power results when you have a lot of pressure and a lot of current.

As with the water system, electrical power increases as both voltage and current increase. Wattage, measured in **watts (W)**, is calculated by multiplying volts by amps in a system ($W = V \times A$). For example, 120 volts times 5 amps is 600 watts. Note that while volts and amps are measured to determine their value, watts are calculated from those values.

We now turn our attention to how to use a multimeter to measure voltage output of a computer's power supply.

Measure the Voltage of a Power Supply

If you suspect a problem with a power supply, the simplest and preferred solution is to replace it with a new one. However, in some situations, you might want to measure the voltage output. When a power supply works properly, voltages all fall within an acceptable range (plus or minus 10 percent). However, be aware that even if measured voltage falls within the appropriate range, a power supply can still cause problems. This is because problems with power supplies are intermittent–in other words, they come and go. Therefore, if the voltages are correct, you should still suspect the power supply is the problem when certain symptoms are present. To learn for certain whether the power supply is the problem, replace it with a unit you know is good.

Using a Multimeter

A voltmeter measures the difference in electrical potential between two points, in volts, and an ammeter measures electrical current in amps. Figure E-4 shows a multimeter, which can be used as either a voltmeter or an ammeter or can measure resistance or continuity (the presence of a complete circuit with no resistance to current), depending on a dial or function switch setting.

Figure E-4   A digital multimeter

Less expensive multimeters commonly measure voltage, resistance, and continuity, but not amps. Measure voltage and amps while the electricity is on. Measure resistance and continuity while the electricity is off. For the specific details of how to use your multimeter, consult the manual, which explains what you can measure with the multimeter and how to use it.

Multimeters are sometimes small, portable, battery-powered units. Larger ones are designed to sit on a countertop and are powered by a wall outlet. A multimeter can provide either a digital or an analog display. A digital display shows the readings as digits on an LCD (liquid crystal display) panel. A digital multimeter is sometimes called a DMM (digital multimeter) or a DVM (digital voltage meter). An analog display shows the readings as a needle moving across a scale of values.

Before you begin to use a multimeter, you must tell it three things: (1) what you want it to measure (voltage, current, or resistance), (2) whether the current is AC or DC, and (3) what range of values it should expect. If you are measuring the voltage output from a wall outlet (110–120 V), the range should be much higher than when you are measuring the voltage output of a computer power supply (3–12 V). Setting the range high assures you that the meter can handle a large input without pegging the needle (exceeding the highest value the meter is designed to measure) or damaging the meter. However, if you set the range too high, you might not see the voltage register at all. Set the range low enough to ensure that the measure is as accurate as you need but not lower than the expected voltage. When you set the range too low on some digital multimeters, the meter reads OL on the display.

For example, to measure the voltage of house current, if you expect the voltage to be 115 volts, set the voltage range from 0 to somewhere between 120 and 130 volts. You want the high end of the range to be slightly higher than the expected voltage. To protect themselves, most meters do not allow a very large voltage or current into the meter when the range is set low. Some multimeters are autorange meters, which sense the quantity of input and set the range accordingly.

A meter comes with two test probes. One is usually red and the other black. Install the red probe at the positive (+) jack on the meter and the black probe at the negative (-) jack.

How to Measure Voltage

To measure voltage, place the other end of the black probe at the ground point and the other end of the red probe at the hot point, without disconnecting anything in the circuit and with the power on. For example, to measure voltage using the multimeter in Figure E-4, turn the function switch dial to DCV for DC voltage measurement. This meter is autoranging, so that's all that needs to be set. With the power on, place the two probes in position and read the voltage from the LCD panel. The DATA-H (data hold) switch allows you to freeze the displayed reading.

When using a multimeter to measure voltage, current, or resistance, be careful not to touch a chip with the probes.

How to Measure Current

In most troubleshooting situations, you will measure voltage, not current. However, you should know how to measure current. To measure current in amps, the multimeter itself must be part of the circuit. Disconnect the circuit at some point so that you can connect the multimeter in line to find a measure in amps. Not all multimeters can measure amps.

How to Measure Continuity

You can also use a multimeter to measure continuity. If there is little or no resistance (less than 20 ohms gives continuity in a PC) in a wire or a closed connection between two points, the path for electricity between the two points is unhindered or "continuous." This measurement is taken with no electricity present in the circuit.

For example, if you want to know that pin 2 on one end of a serial cable is connected to pin 3 on the other end of the cable, set the multimeter to measure continuity, and work without connecting the cable to anything. Put one probe on pin 2 at one end of the cable and the other probe on pin 3 at the other end. If the two pins connect, the multimeter shows a reading on the LCD panel, or a buzzer sounds (see the multimeter documentation). In this situation, you might find that the probe is too large to extend into the pinhole of the female connection of the cable. A straightened small paper clip works well here to extend the probe. However, be very careful not to use a paper clip that is too thick and might widen the size of the pinhole, because this can later prevent the pinhole from making a good connection.

One way to determine if a fuse is good is to measure continuity. Set a multimeter to measure continuity, and place its probes on each end of the fuse. If the fuse has continuity, then it is good. If the multimeter has no continuity setting, set it to measure resistance. If the reading in ohms is approximately zero, there is no resistance and the fuse is good. If the reading is infinity, resistance is infinite; the fuse is blown and should not be used.

How to Measure the Voltage of a Power Supply

To determine whether a power supply is working properly, measure the voltage of each circuit the power supply supports. First, open the computer case and identify all power cords coming from the power supply. Look for the cords from the power supply to the motherboard and other power cords to the drives (see Figure E-5).

Figure E-5   Multimeter measuring voltage on an AT motherboard

The computer must be turned on to test the power supply output. Be very careful not to touch any chips or disturb any circuit boards as you work. The voltage output from the power supply is no more than 14 volts, not enough to seriously hurt you if you accidentally touch a hot probe. However, you can damage the computer if you are not careful.

You can hurt yourself if you accidentally create a short circuit from the power supply to ground through the probe. If you touch the probe to the hot circuit and to ground, you divert current from the computer circuit and through the probe to ground. This short might be enough to cause a spark or to melt the probe, which can happen if you allow the two probes to touch while one of them is attached to the hot circuit and the other is attached to ground. Make sure the probes only touch one metal object, preferably only a single power pin on a connector, or you could cause a short.

Because of the danger of touching a hot probe to a ground probe, you might prefer not to put the black probe into a ground lead too close to the hot probe. Instead, when the directions say to place the black probe on a lead very close to the hot probe, you can use a black wire lead on an unused power supply connection meant for a hard drive. The idea is that the black probe should always be placed on a ground or black lead.

All ground leads are considered at ground, no matter what number they are assigned. Therefore, you can consider all black leads to be equal. For an AT motherboard, the ground leads for P8 and P9 are the four black center leads 5, 6, 7, and 8. For an ATX motherboard, the ground leads are seven black leads in center positions on the ATX P1 power connector. The ground leads for a hard drive power connection are the two black center leads, 2 and 3.

The following sections first discuss how to measure the power output for AT and ATX motherboards and then discuss the procedure for a secondary storage device.

Measuring Voltage Output to an AT Motherboard

1. Remove the cover of the computer. The voltage range for each connection is often written on the top of the power supply. The two power connections to the motherboard are often labeled P8 and P9. Figure E-6 shows a close-up of the two connections, P8 and P9, coming from the power supply to the motherboard. Each connection has six leads, for a total of 12 leads. Of these 12, four are ground connections and lead 1 is a "power good" pin, used to indicate that the motherboard is receiving power. Table E-2 lists the purposes of these 12 leads.

Figure E-6   AT power supply connections

Connection	Lead	Description	Acceptable Range
P8	1	"Power Good"	
	2	Not used or +5 volts	+4.4 to +5.2 volts
	3	+12 volts	+10.8 to +13.2 volts
	4	-12 volts	-10.8 to -13.2 volts
	5	Black ground	
	6	Black ground	
P9	7	Black ground	
	8	Black ground	
	9	-5 volts	-4.5 to -5.5 volts
	10	+5 volts	+4.5 to +5.5 volts
	11	+5 volts	+4.5 to +5.5 volts
	12	+5 volts	+4.5 to +5.5 volts

Table E-2 Twelve leads to the AT motherboard from the AT power supply

2. Set the multimeter to measure voltage ins a range of 20 volts, and set the AC/DC switch to DC. Insert the black probe into the negative (-) jack and the red probe into the positive (+) jack of the meter.

CAUTION

Be certain the multimeter is set to measure voltage and not current (amps). If the multimeter is set to measure current, you might damage the power supply or motherboard or both.

3. Turn on the multimeter and turn on the computer.

4. To measure the +12-volt circuit and all four ground leads:

   a. Place the red probe on lead 3. The probe is shaped like a needle. (Alligator clips don't work too well here.) Insert the needle down into the lead housing as far as you can. Place the black probe on lead 5. The acceptable range is +10.8 to +13.2 volts.

   b. Place the red probe on lead 3, and place the black probe on lead 6. The acceptable range is +10.8 to +13.2 volts.

    c. Place the red probe on lead 3, and place the black probe on lead 7. The acceptable range is +10.8 to +13.2 volts.

    d. Place the red probe on lead 3, and place the black probe on lead 8. The acceptable range is +10.8 to +13.2 volts.

5. To measure the -12-volt circuit, place the red probe on lead 4, and place the black probe on any ground lead or on the computer case, which is also grounded. The acceptable range is -10.8 to -13.2 volts.

6. To measure the -5-volt circuit, place the red probe on lead 9, and place the black probe on any ground. The acceptable range is -4.5 to -5.5 volts.

7. To measure the three +5-volt circuits:

    a. Place the red probe on lead 10, and place the black probe on any ground. The acceptable range is +4.5 to +5.5 volts.

    b. Place the red probe on lead 11, and place the black probe on any ground. The acceptable range is +4.5 to +5.5 volts.

    c. Place the red probe on lead 12, and place the black probe on any ground. The acceptable range is +4.5 to +5.5 volts.

8. Turn off the PC and replace the cover.

Measuring Voltage Output to an ATX Motherboard

To measure the output to the ATX motherboard, follow the procedure just described for the AT motherboard. Recall that the ATX board uses 3.3, 5, and 12 volts coming from the power supply. Figure E-7 shows the power output of each pin on the connector. Looking at Figure E-7, you can see the distinguishing shape of each side of the connector. Notice the different hole shapes (square or rounded) on each side of the connector, ensuring that the plug from the power supply is oriented correctly in the connector. Also notice the notch on the connector and on the pinout diagram on the right side of the figure. This notch helps orient you as you read the pinouts. You can also use the color of the wires coming from the power supply to each pin on the P1 connector to help orient the connector. Table E-3 lists the leads to the motherboard and their acceptable voltage ranges.

Figure E-7   Power connection on an ATX motherboard

Unnotched Side			Notched Side		
Lead	Description	Acceptable Range (Volts)	Lead	Description	Acceptable Range (Volts)
1	+3.3 volts	+3.1 to +3.5V	11	+3.3 volts	+3.1 to +3.5V
2	+3.3 volts	+3.1 to +3.5V	12	-12 volts	-10.8 to -13.2V
3	Black ground		13	Black ground	
4	+5 volts	+4.5 to +5.5V	14	Power supply on	
5	Black ground		15	Black ground	
6	+5 volts	+4.5 to +5.5V	16	Black ground	
7	Black ground		17	Black ground	
8	Power Good		18	-5 volts	-4.5 to -5.5V
9	+5 volts standby	+4.5 to +5.5V	19	+5 volts	+4.5 to +5.5V
10	+12 volts	+10.8 to +13.2V	20	+5 volts	+4.5 to +5.5V

Table E-3   Twenty leads to the ATX motherboard from the ATX power supply

NOTE Dell ATX power supplies and motherboards made after 1998 might not use the standard P1 pin-outs for ATX, although the power connectors look the same. For this reason, *never* use a Dell power supply with a non-Dell motherboard, or a Dell motherboard with a non-Dell power supply, without first verifying that the power connector pinouts match; otherwise, you might destroy the power supply, the motherboard, or both. End PC Noise (*www.endpcnoise.com*) sells a pinout converter to convert the P1 connector of a Dell power supply or motherboard to standard ATX. Also, PC Power and Cooling (*www.pcpowerandcooling.com*) makes a power supply modified to work with a Dell motherboard.

E

Testing the Power Output to a Floppy or Hard Drive

The power cords to the hard drive, CD-ROM drive, floppy drive, and other drives all supply the same voltage: one +5-volt circuit and one +12-volt circuit. These connectors use four leads; the two outside connections are hot, and the two inside connections are ground (see Figure E-6). The power connection to a 3.5-inch floppy disk drive is usually a miniature connection, slightly smaller than other drive connections, but still with four pins. Follow these steps to measure the voltage to any drive:

1. With the drive plugged in, turn on the computer.

2. Set the multimeter to measure voltage, as described earlier.

3. Place the red probe on lead 1, shown in the drive connection callout in Figure E-6, and place the black probe on lead 2 or 3 (ground). The acceptable range is +10.8 to +13.2 volts.

4. Place the red probe on lead 4, and place the black probe on lead 2 or 3 (ground). The acceptable range is +4.5 to +5.5 volts.

You may choose to alter the method you use to ground the black probe. In Step 4, the red probe and black probe are very close to each other. You may choose to keep them farther apart by placing the black probe in a ground lead of an unused hard drive connection.

Practicing Measuring the Output of Your Power Supply

To practice, measure the power output to your motherboard and to the hard drive. Fill in the following charts. Note that red and black leads refer to the color of the probes.

AT Motherboard

Red Lead	Black Lead	Voltage Measure
3	5	
3	6	
3	7	
3	8	
4	Ground	
9	Ground	
10	Ground	
11	Ground	
12	Ground	

ATX Motherboard

Red Lead	Black Lead	Voltage Measure
10	7	
10	5	
10	3	
10	17	
10	16	
10	15	
10	13	
9	Ground	
6	Ground	
4	Ground	
2	Ground	
1	Ground	
20	Ground	
19	Ground	
18	Ground	

(continued)

Red Lead	Black Lead	Voltage Measure
12	Ground	
11	Ground	

Hard Drive

Red Lead	Black Lead	Voltage Measure
1	3	
4	2	

The Professional PC Technician

A s a professional PC technician, you can manage your career by staying abreast of new technology and striving for top professional certifications. In addition, you should maintain excellent customer relationships, behave with professionalism, and seek opportunities for joining professional organizations. As you know, PC technicians provide service to customers over the phone or online, in person on-site, and sometimes in a shop where they have little customer contact. While each setting poses specific challenges, almost all of the recommendations in this appendix apply across the board.

What Customers Want: Beyond Technical Know-How

Probably the most significant indication that a PC technician is doing a good job is that customers are consistently satisfied. You should provide excellent service and treat customers as you would want to be treated in a similar situation. One of the most important ways to achieve customer satisfaction is to do your best by being prepared, both technically and nontechnically. Being prepared includes knowing what customers want, what they don't like, and what they expect from a PC technician.

Your customers can be "internal" (you both work for the same company) or "external" (your customers come to you or your company for service). Customers can be highly technical or technically naive, represent a large company or simply own a home PC, be prompt or slow at paying their bills, want only the best (and be willing to pay for it) or be searching for bargain service, be friendly and easy to work with or demanding and condescending. In each situation, the key to success is always the same: Don't allow circumstances or personalities to affect your commitment to excellence.

The following traits distinguish one competent technician from another in the eyes of the customer:

- *Have a positive and helpful attitude.* This helps to establish good customer relationships.
- *Own the problem.* Taking ownership of the customer's problem builds trust and loyalty, because the customer knows you can be counted on.
- *Be dependable.* Customers appreciate those who do as they say. If you promise to be back at 10:00 the next morning, be back at 10:00 the next morning.

If you cannot keep your appointment, never ignore your promise. Call, apologize, let the customer know what happened, and reschedule your appointment.

- *Be customer-focused.* When you're working with or talking to a customer, focus on him or her. Make it your job to satisfy this person, not just your organization, your boss, your bank account, or the customer's boss.
- *Be credible.* Convey confidence to your customers. Being credible means being technically competent and knowing how to do your job well, but credible technicians also know when the job is beyond their expertise and when to ask for help.
- *Maintain integrity and honesty.* Don't try to hide your mistakes from your customer or your boss. Everyone makes mistakes, but don't compound them by a lack of integrity. Accept responsibility and do what you can to correct the error.
- *Know the law with respect to your work.* For instance, observe the laws concerning the use of software. Don't use or install pirated software.
- *Act professionally.* Customers want a technician to look and behave professionally. Dress appropriately for the environment. Consider yourself a guest at the customer's site.
- *Perform your work in a professional manner.* If a customer is angry, allow the customer to vent, keeping your own professional distance. (You do, however, have the right to expect a customer not to talk to you in an abusive way.)

Support Calls: Providing Good Service

Customers want good service. Even though each customer is different and might expect different results, the following characteristics constitute good service in the eyes of most customers:

- The technician responds and completes the work within a reasonable time.
- For on-site visits, the technician is prepared for the service call.
- The work is done right the first time.
- The price for the work is reasonable and competitive.
- The technician exhibits good interpersonal skills.
- If the work extends beyond a brief on-site visit or phone call, the technician keeps the customer informed about the progress of the work.

Planning for Good Service

Whether you support PCs on the phone or online, on-site, or in a shop, you need a plan to follow when you approach a service call. This section surveys the entire service situation, from the first contact with the customer to closing the call. Follow these general guidelines when supporting computers and their users:

- Almost every support project starts with a phone call. Follow company policies to obtain the specific information you should take when answering an initial call.
- Don't assume that an on-site visit is necessary until you have asked questions to identify the problem and asked the caller to check and try some simple things while on the phone with you. For example, the customer can check cable connections, power, and monitor settings, and can look for POST error messages.
- Be familiar with your company's customer service policies. You might need to refer questions about warranties, licenses, documentation, or procedures to other support personnel or customer relations personnel. Your organization might not want you to answer some questions, such as questions about upcoming releases of software or new products, or questions about your personal or company experience with supporting particular hardware or software.
- After reviewing your company's service policies, begin troubleshooting. Take notes, and then interview the customer about the problem so you understand it thoroughly. Have the customer reproduce the problem, and carefully note each step taken and its results. This process gives you clues about the problem and about the customer's technical proficiency, which helps you know how to communicate with the customer.
- Search for answers. If the answers to specific questions or problems are not evident, become a researcher. Learn to use online documentation, expert systems, and other resources that your company provides.
- Use your troubleshooting skills. Isolate the problem. Check for user errors. What works and what doesn't work? What has changed since the system last worked? Reduce the system to its essentials. Check the simple things first. Use the troubleshooting guidelines throughout this book to help you think of approaches to test and try.
- If you have given the problem your best, but still haven't solved it, ask for help. You learn when to ask for help from experience. Once you have made a reasonable effort to help, and it seems clear that you are unlikely to be successful, don't waste a customer's time.
- After a call, create a written record to build your own knowledge base. Record the initial symptoms of the problem, the source of the problem you actually discovered, how you made that discovery, and how the problem was finally solved. File your documentation according to symptoms or according to solutions.

F

Making an On-Site Service Call

When a technician makes an on-site service call, customers expect him or her to have both technical and interpersonal skills. Prepare for a service call by reviewing information given you by whoever took the call. Know the problem you are going to address, the urgency of the situation, and what computer, software, and hardware need servicing. Arrive with a complete set of equipment appropriate to the visit, which might include a tool kit, flashlight, multimeter, grounding strap and mat, and bootable disks that have been scanned for viruses.

Set a realistic time for the appointment (one that you can expect to keep) and arrive on time. When you arrive at the customer's site, greet the customer in a friendly manner. Use Mr. or Ms. and last names rather than first names when addressing the customer, unless you are certain that the customer expects you to use first names. The first thing you should do is listen; save the paperwork for later.

As you work, be as unobtrusive as possible. Don't make a big mess. Keep your tools and papers out of the customer's way. Don't use the phone or sit in the customer's desk chair without permission. If the customer needs to work while you are present, do whatever is necessary to accommodate that.

Keep the customer informed. Once you have collected enough information, explain the problem and what you must do to fix it, giving as many details as the customer wants. When a customer must make a choice, state the options in a way that does not unfairly favor the solution that makes the most money for you as the technician or for your company.

After you have solved the problem:

- Allow the customer time to be fully satisfied that all is working before you close the call. Does the printer work? Print a test page. Does the network connection work? Can the customer log on to the network and access data on it?
- If you changed anything on the PC after you booted it, reboot one more time to make sure that you have not caused a problem with the boot.
- Review the service call with the customer. Summarize the instructions and explanations you have given during the call. This is an appropriate time to fill out your paperwork and explain to the customer what you have written.
- Explain preventive maintenance to the customer (such as deleting temporary files from the hard drive or cleaning the mouse). Most customers don't have preventive maintenance contracts for their PCs and appreciate the time you take to show them how they can take better care of their computers.

Phone Support

When someone calls asking for support, you must control the call, especially at the beginning. Follow these steps at the beginning of a service call:

- Identify yourself and your organization. (Follow the guidelines of your employer as to what to say.)
- Ask for and write down the name and phone number of the caller. Ask for spelling if necessary. If your help desk supports businesses, get the name of the business that the caller represents.
- Your company might require that you obtain a licensing or warranty number to determine if the customer is entitled to receive your support free of charge, or that you obtain a credit card number, if the customer is paying by the call. Get whatever information you need at this point to determine that you should be the one to provide service, before you start to address the problem.
- Open up the conversation for the caller to describe the problem.

Phone support requires more interaction with customers than any other type of PC support. To give clear instructions, you must be able to visualize what the customer sees at his or her PC. Patience is required if the customer must be told each key to press or command button to click. Help-desk support requires excellent communication skills, good phone manners, and lots of patience. As your help-desk skills improve, you will learn to think through the process as though you were sitting in front of the PC yourself. Drawing diagrams and taking notes as you talk can be very helpful.

If you spend many hours on the phone at a help desk, use a headset instead of a regular phone to reduce strain on your ears and neck. If your call is accidentally disconnected, call back immediately. Don't eat or drink while on the phone. If you must put callers on hold, tell them how long it will be before you get back to them. Don't complain about your job, your company, or other companies or products to your customers. A little small talk is okay and is sometimes beneficial in easing a tense situation, but keep it upbeat and positive. As with on-site service calls, let the user make sure that all is working before you close the phone call. If you end the call too soon and the problem is not completely resolved, the customer can be frustrated, especially if it is difficult to contact you again.

When the Customer Is Not Knowledgeable

A help-desk call is the most difficult situation to handle when a customer is not knowledgeable about how to use a computer. When on-site, you can put a PC in good repair without depending on a customer to help you, but when you are trying to solve a problem over the phone, with a customer as your only eyes, ears, and hands, a computer-illiterate user can present a challenge. Here are some tips for handling this situation:

- Don't use computer jargon while talking. For example, instead of saying, "Open Windows Explorer," say, "Using your mouse, right-click the Start button and select Explore from the menu."
- Don't ask the customer to do something that might destroy settings or files without first having the customer back them up carefully. If you think the customer can't handle your request, then ask for some on-site help.
- Frequently ask the customer what the screen displays to help you track the keystrokes and action.
- Follow along at your own PC. It's easier to direct the customer, keystroke by keystroke, if you are doing the same things.
- Give the customer plenty of opportunity to ask questions.
- Compliment the customer whenever you can, to help the customer gain confidence.
- If you determine that the customer cannot help you solve the problem without a lot of coaching, you may need to tactfully request that the caller have someone with more experience call you.

NOTE

When solving computer problems in an organization other than your own, check with technical support instead of working only with the PC user. The user may not be aware of policies that have been set on the PC to prevent changes to the OS, hardware, or applications.

When the Customer Is Overly Confident

Sometimes customers are proud of their computer knowledge. Such customers may want to give advice, take charge of a call, with hold information they think you don't need to know, or execute commands at the computer without letting you know, so that you don't have enough information to follow along. A situation like this must be handled with tact and respect for the customer. Here are a few tips:

- When you can, compliment the customer's knowledge, experience, or insight.
- Ask the customer's advice. Say something like, "What do you think the problem is?" (However, don't ask this question of customers who are not confident, because they most likely don't have the answer and might lose confidence in you.)
- Slow the conversation down. You can say, "Please slow down. You're moving too fast for me to follow. Help me understand."
- Don't back off from using problem-solving skills. You must still have the customer check the simple things, but direct the conversation with tact. For example, you can say, "I know you've probably already gone over these simple things, but could we just do them again together?"

- Be careful not to accuse the customer of making a mistake.
- Use technical language in a way that conveys that you expect the customer to understand you.

When the Customer Complains

When you are on-site or on the phone, a customer might complain to you about your organization, products, or service, or the service and product of another company. Consider the complaint to be helpful feedback that can lead to a better product or service and better customer relationships. Here are a few suggestions on how to handle complaints and customer anger:

- Be an active listener, and let customers know that they are not being ignored. Look for the underlying problem. Don't take the complaint or the anger personally.
- Give the customer a little time to vent, and apologize when you can. Then start the conversation from the beginning, asking questions, taking notes, and solving problems. If this helps, don't spend a lot of time finding out exactly whom the customer dealt with and what happened to upset the customer.
- Don't be defensive. It's better to leave the customer with the impression that you and your company are listening and willing to admit mistakes.
- If the customer is complaining about a product or service that is not from your company, don't start off by saying, "That's not our problem." Instead, listen to the customer complain. Don't appear as though you don't care.
- If the complaint is against you or your product, identify the underlying problem if you can. Ask questions and take notes. Then pass these notes on to people in your organization who need to know.
- Sometimes simply making progress or reducing the problem to a manageable state reduces the customer's anxiety. As you are talking to a customer, summarize what you have both agreed on or observed so far in the conversation.
- Point out ways that you think communication could be improved. For example, you might say, "I'm sorry, but I'm having trouble understanding what you want. Could you please slow down, and let's take this one step at a time."

When the Customer Does Not Want to End a Phone Call

Some customers like to talk and don't want to end a phone call. In this situation, when you have finished the work and are ready to hang up, you can ease the caller into the end of the call. Ask if anything needs more explanation. Briefly summarize the main points of the call, and then say something like, "That about does it. Call if you need more help." Be silent about new issues. Answer only with "yes" or "no." Don't take the bait by engaging in a new topic. Don't get frustrated. As a last resort, you can say, "I'm sorry, but I must go now."

When You Can't Solve the Problem

You are not going to solve every computer problem you encounter. Knowing how to escalate a problem to those higher in the support chain is one of the first things you should learn on a new job. When escalation involves the customer, generally follow these guidelines:

- Before you escalate, first ask knowledgeable coworkers for suggestions for solving the problem, which might save you and your customer the time and effort it takes to escalate it.
- Know your company's policy for escalation. What documents do you fill out? Who gets them? Do you remain the responsible "support" party, or does the person now addressing the problem become the new contact? Are you expected to keep in touch with the customer and the problem, or are you totally out of the picture?
- Document the escalation. It's very important to include the detailed steps necessary to reproduce the problem, which can save the next support person lots of time.
- Pass the problem on according to the proper channels of your organization. This might mean a phone call, an online entry in a database, or an e-mail message.
- Tell the customer that you are passing the problem on to someone who is more experienced and has access to more extensive resources. In most cases, the person who receives the escalation will immediately contact the customer and assume responsibility for the problem. However, you should follow through, at least to confirm that the new person and the customer have made contact.
- If you check back with the customer only to find out that the other support person has not called or followed through to the customer's satisfaction, don't lay blame or point fingers. Just do whatever you can to help within your company guidelines. Your call to the customer will go a long way toward helping the situation.

Recordkeeping and Information Tools

If you work for a service organization, it will probably have most of the tools you need to do your job, including forms, online recordkeeping, procedures, and manuals. In some cases, help-desk support personnel may have software to help them do their jobs, such as programs that support the remote control of customers' PCs (one example is pcAnywhere), an online help utility, or a problem-solving tool developed specifically for their help desk.

Several types of resources, records, and information tools can help you support PCs, such as the following:

- Specific software or hardware that you support must be available to you to test, observe, and study, and to use to re-create a customer's problem whenever possible.
- You should have a copy of–and be familiar with–the same documentation that the user sees.
- Hardware and software products generally have more technical documentation than just a user manual. A company should make this technical documentation available to you when you support its product.
- Online help targeted to field technicians and helpdesk technicians is often available for a product. This online help will probably include a search engine that searches by topics, words, error messages, and the like.
- Expert systems software is designed and written to help solve problems. It uses databases of known facts and rules to simulate human experts' reasoning and decision-making. Expert systems for PC technicians work by posing questions about a problem, to be answered either by the technician or the customer. The response to each question triggers another question from the software, until the expert system arrives at a possible solution or solutions. Many expert systems are "intelligent," meaning that the system will record your input and use it in subsequent sessions to select more questions to ask and approaches to try.
- Call tracking can be done online or on paper. Most organizations have a call-tracking system that tracks (1) the date, time, and length of help-desk or on-site calls, (2) causes of and solutions to problems already addressed, (3) who did what, and when, and (4) how each call was officially resolved. Call-tracking software or documents can also help to escalate calls when necessary and track the escalation.

Professional Organizations and Certifications

The work done by PC technicians has been viewed as a profession only within the past few years. The most significant certifying organization for PC technicians is the Computing Technology Industry Association (CompTIA, pronounced "comp-TEE-a"). CompTIA sponsors the A+ Certification Program, and manages the A+ Service Technician Certification Examination, which measures the knowledge of job tasks and behavior expected of entry-level technicians. To become certified, you must pass two test modules: the A+ Core Hardware exam and the A+ Operating System Technologies exam. A+ Certification has industry recognition, so it should be your first choice for certification as a PC technician. As evidence of this industry recognition, these companies now include A+ Certification in their requirements for employment:

- ENTEX Information Services requires that all service employees have A+ Certification.
- GE Capital Services requires that all service employees have A+ Certification one year after hire.
- Okidata requires that all field service technicians have A+ Certification.
- Packard Bell requires all employees to be A+ certified within 90 days of hire.

Some other organizations for which A+ Certification is mandatory are Aetna U.S. Healthcare; BancTec, Inc.; Computer Data, Inc.; Computer Sciences Corp.; Delta Airlines; Dow Jones & Company; the FBI; the U.S. Department of Justice; Gateway; Tandy Corporation; TSS IBM; US Airways; and Wang.

CompTIA has over 13,000 members from every major company that manufactures, distributes, or publishes computer-related products and services. For more information about CompTIA and A+ Certification, see the CompTIA Web site at *www.comptia.org.*

Other certifications are more vendor-specific. For example, Microsoft, Novell, and Cisco offer certifications to use and support their products. These are excellent choices for additional certifications when your career plan is to focus on these products.

Why Certification?

Many people work as PC technicians without any formal classroom training or certification. However, by having certification or an advanced technical degree, you prove to yourself, your customers, and your employers that you are prepared to do the work and are committed to being educated in your chosen profession. Certification and advanced degrees serve as recognized proof of competence and achievement, improve your job opportunities, create a higher level of customer confidence, and often qualify you for other training or degrees.

In addition to becoming certified and seeking advanced degrees, the professional PC technician should also stay abreast of new technology. Helpful resources include on-the-job training, books, magazines, the Internet, trade shows, interaction with colleagues, seminars, and workshops. Probably the best-known trade show is COMDEX and Windows World, where you can view the latest technology, hear industry leaders speak, and network with vast numbers of organizations and people. For more information about COMDEX and Windows World, see the Web site *www.comdex.com.*

Protecting Software Copyrights

As a computer support technician, you will be faced with the legal issues and practices surrounding the distribution of software. When someone purchases software from a software vendor, that person has only purchased a license for the software, which is the right to use it. The buyer does not legally *own* the software, and therefore does not have the right to distribute it. The right to copy the work, called a copyright, belongs to the creator of the work or others to whom the creator transfers this right.

As a PC technician you will be called upon to install, upgrade, and customize software. You need to know your responsibilities in upholding the law, especially as it applies to software copyrights. Copyrights are intended to legally protect the intellectual property rights of organizations or individuals to creative works, which include books, images, and software. While the originator of a creative work is the original owner of a copyright, the copyright can be transferred from one entity to another.

The Federal Copyright Act of 1976 was designed in part to protect software copyrights by requiring that only legally obtained copies of software be used; the law also allows for one backup copy of software to be made. Making unauthorized copies of original software violates the Federal Copyright Act of 1976, and is called software piracy, or more officially, software copyright infringement. Making a copy of software and then selling it or giving it away is a violation of the law. Because it is so easy to do, and because so many people do it, many people don't realize that it's illegal. Normally, only the person who violated the copyright law is liable for infringement; however, in some cases, an employer or supervisor is also held responsible, even when the copies were made without the employer's knowledge. The Business Software Alliance (a membership organization of software manufacturers and vendors) has estimated that 26 percent of the business software in the United States is obtained illegally.

Site licensing, whereby a company can purchase the right to use multiple copies of software, is a popular way for companies to provide software to employees. With this type of license, companies can distribute software to PCs from network servers or execute software directly off the server. Read the licensing agreement of any software to determine the terms of distribution.

One of two associations committed to the prevention of software piracy is the Software Information Industry Association, a nonprofit organization that educates the public and enforces copyright laws. Its Web address is *www.siia.net*, and its anti-piracy hotline is 1-800-388-7478. Another organization is the Business Software Alliance, which manages the BSA Anti-Piracy Hotline at 1-888-NOPIRACY. The BSA can also be reached at its e-mail address: *software@bsa.org*. Its Web site is *www.bsa.org*. These associations are made up of hundreds of software manufacturers and publishers in North and Latin America, Europe, and Asia. They promote software raids on large and small companies; in the United States, they receive the cooperation of the U.S. government to prosecute offenders.

F

What Does the Law Say?

The Federal Copyright Act of 1976 protects the exclusive rights of copyright holders. It gives legal users of software the right to make one backup copy. Other rights are based on what the copyright holder allows. In 1990, the U.S. Congress passed the Software Rental Amendment Act, which prevents the renting, leasing, lending, or sharing of software without the express written permission of the copyright holder. In 1992, Congress instituted criminal penalties for software copyright infringement, which include imprisonment for up to five years and/or fines of up to $250,000 for the unlawful reproduction or distribution of 10 or more copies of software.

What Are Your Responsibilities Under the Law?

Your first responsibility as an individual user is to use only software that has been purchased or licensed for your use. As an employee of a company that has a site license to use multiple copies of the software, your responsibility is to comply with the license agreement. It is also your responsibility to purchase only legitimate software. Purchasers of counterfeit or copied software face the risk of corrupted files, virus-infected disks, inadequate documentation, and lack of technical support and upgrades, as well as the legal penalties for using pirated software.

Introducing Linux

U nix is a popular OS used to control networks and to support applications used on the Internet. A variation of Unix is Linux (pronounced "Lih-nucks"), an OS created by Linus Torvalds when he was a student at the University of Helsinki in Finland. Basic versions of this OS are available for free, and all the underlying programming instructions (called source code) are also freely distributed. Like Unix, Linux is distributed by several different companies, whose versions of Linux are sometimes called distributions. Popular distributions of Linux are shown in Table G-1. Linux can be used both as a server platform and a desktop platform, but its greatest popularity has come in the server market. Hardware requirements for Linux vary widely, depending on the distribution and version installed.

For more information on Linux, see *www.linux.org* as well as the Web sites of the different Linux distributors.

Name	Comments	Web site
Red Hat Linux	The most widely used distribution in the world, from Red Hat Software.	*www.redhat.com*
OpenLinux	Produced by The SCO Group (formerly Caldera International). Aimed at business users.	*www.sco.com*
UnitedLinux	A Linux distribution created by multiple Linux vendors as a common base product on which numerous Linux applications can be designed to run.	*www.unitedlinux.com*
TurboLinux	Focused on providing high-end, specialized server software to businesses.	*www.turbolinux.com*
Mandrake	Built on Red Hat Linux with many additional packages. Popular at retail outlets.	*www.mandrakelinux.com*
Stampede	A distribution optimized for speed.	*www.stampede.org*

Table G-1 (continued)

Name	Comments	Web site
Debian	A noncommercial Linux distribution targeted specifically to free software enthusiasts. Debian does not have a company behind it. It is created and maintained by developers of free software.	www.debian.org
SuSE	The leading German distribution. Increasingly popular in the United States.	www.novell.com/linux/suse
Yellow Dog Linux	A version of Linux for Macintosh computers, written for the PowerPC processor.	www.yellowdoglinux.com

Table G-1　Popular Linux distributions

Some of the advantages and disadvantages of Linux are:

- Linux rarely crashes.
- Basic versions can be downloaded and installed free of charge.
- Linux distributions that include technical support and software packages are available at a lower cost than other operating systems.
- Linux has strong features for handling network connections.
- Source code is available to users, enabling customization of the development environment.
- Linux on an inexpensive PC is an excellent training tool for learning Unix.
- Linux can be difficult to install, particularly for users who are not familiar with Unix commands.
- Most distributions of Linux run from a command line, which can be difficult for casual users to operate.
- Documentation can be spotty.
- Optimizing a Linux system can take a significant investment of time and research.
- Not as many desktop applications are available for Linux as for Windows, though a Windows-like office suite (Star Office) can be installed.

Network services such as a Web server or e-mail server often are provided by a computer running the Linux operating system. Linux is well suited to support various types of servers. Because Linux is very reliable and does not require a lot of computing power, it is sometimes used as a desktop OS, although it is not as popular for this purpose because it is not easy to use.

As a PC support technician, you should know a little about Linux, including a few basic commands, which are covered in this appendix. You will learn about root and user accounts, file structure, some common commands, and how to use the vi editor. The material in this section is meant as a general introduction to the OS. The organization of files and folders, the desktop's appearance, and the way each command works might be slightly different with the distribution and version of Linux you are using.

Root Account and User Accounts

Recall that an operating system is composed of a kernel, which interacts with the hardware and other software, and a shell, which interacts with the user and the kernel. Linux is a Unix-like operating system, and can use more than one shell, just as with other versions of Unix. The default shell for Linux is the Bash shell. The name stands for "Bourne Again Shell" and takes the best features from two previous shells, the Bourne and the Korn shells.

For a Linux or Unix server, the system administrator is the person who installs updates to the OS (called patches), manages backup processes, supports the installation of software and hardware, sets up user accounts, resets passwords, and generally supports users. The system administrator has root privileges, which means that he or she can access all the functions of the OS; the principal user account is called the root account. The administrator protects the password to the root account because this password gives full access to the system. When logged on, the administrator is logged on as the user root. You can use the *who* command to show a list of all users currently logged on to the system. In the following example, typing *who* shows that three users are currently logged on: the root user, James, and Susan.

```
who
root tty1 Oct 12 07:56
james tty1 Oct 12 08:35
susan tty1 Oct 12 10:05
```

NOTE

The Linux command prompt for the root user is different from the command prompt for ordinary users. The root command prompt is #, and other users have the $ command prompt.

Directory and File Layout

The main directory in Unix and Linux is the root directory and is indicated with a forward slash. (In Unix and Linux, directories in a path are separated with forward slashes, in contrast to the backward slashes used by DOS and Windows.) Use the *ls* command, which is similar to the DOS Dir command, to list the contents of the root directory. The command (*ls -l /*) and its results are shown in Figure G-1. Notice that the *-l* parameter is added to the command, which displays the results using the long format, and that there are spaces included before and after the parameters of the command. Also notice in the figure the format used to display the directory contents. The *d* at the beginning of each entry indicates that the entry is a directory, not a file. The other letters in this first column have to do with the read and write privileges assigned to the directory and the right to execute programs in the directory. The name of the directory is in the last column. The rights assigned the directory can apply to the owner of the directory, to other users, or to an entire group of users.

```
root@localhost.localdomain: /root

File   Edit   Settings   Help

[root@localhost /root]# ls -l /
total 149
drwxr-xr-x    2 root    root      4096 Sep 14 09:05 bin
drwxr-xr-x    3 root    root      1024 Jan 15 17:02 boot
drwxr-xr-x   14 root    root     81920 Jan 15 17:03 dev
drwxr-xr-x    2 root    root      4096 Jan  4 09:55 Dload
drwxr-xr-x   41 root    root      4096 Jan 15 17:03 etc
drwxr-xr-x    4 root    root      4096 Dec 20 12:15 home
drwxr-xr-x    6 root    root      4096 Sep 14 09:22 lib
drwxr-xr-x    2 root    root     16384 Sep 14 08:57 lost+found
drwxr-xr-x    2 root    root         0 Jan 15 17:03 misc
drwxr-xr-x    4 root    root      4096 Dec  4 13:43 mnt
drwxr-xr-x    2 root    root      4096 Aug 23  1999 opt
dr-xr-xr-x   59 root    root         0 Jan 15 12:02 proc
drwxr-x---   16 root    root      4096 Jan 15 17:03 root
drwxr-xr-x    2 root    root      4096 Sep 14 09:23 sbin
drwxrwxrwt    8 root    root      4096 Jan 15 17:03 tmp
drwxr-xr-x   16 root    root      4096 Sep 14 09:18 usr
drwxr-xr-x   17 root    root      4096 Sep 14 09:22 var
[root@localhost /root]# []
```

Figure G-1   A directory listing using the ls command

Table G-2 lists directories that are created in the root directory during a typical Linux installation. The actual list of directories for a Linux computer that you work with may be a little different, because the directories created in the root directory depend on what programs have been installed.

Directory	Description
/bin	Contains programs and commands necessary to boot the system and perform other system tasks not reserved for the administrator, such as shutdown and reboot.
/boot	Consists of components needed for the boot process, such as boot loaders.
/dev	Holds device names, which consist of the type of device and a number identifying the device. Actual device drivers are located in the /lib/ modules /[kernel version]/ directory.
/etc	Contains system configuration data, including configuration files and settings and their subdirectories. These files are used for tasks such as configuring a user account, changing system settings, and configuring a domain name resolution service.
/home	Contains user data. Every user on the system has a directory in the /home directory, such as /home/jean or /home/scott, and when a user logs on, that directory becomes the current working directory.
/lib	Stores common libraries used by applications so that more than one application can use the same library at one time. An example is the library of C programming code, without which only the kernel of the Linux system could run.

Table G-2 (continued)

Directory	Description
/lost+found	Stores data that is lost when files are truncated or when an attempt to fix system errors is unsuccessful.
/opt	Contains installations of third-party applications such as Web browsers that do not come with the Linux OS distribution.
/root	The home directory for the root user; contains only files specific to the root user. Do not confuse this directory with the root directory, which contains all the directories listed in this table.
/sbin	Stores commands required for system administration.
/tmp	Stores temporary files, such as the ones that applications use during installation and operation.
/usr	Constitutes the major section of the Linux file system and contains read-only data.
/var	Holds variable data such as e-mail, news, print spools, and administrative files.

Table G-2   Directories in a typical Linux root directory

Linux Commands

This section describes some basic Linux and Unix commands, together with simple examples of how some are used. As you read along, be aware that all commands entered in Linux or Unix are case sensitive, meaning that uppercase and lowercase matter. Table G-3 shows some common commands for Linux and Unix. This is not meant to be a comprehensive list of commands, but simply a list you might find useful in working with files, directories, network connections, and system configuration. In the rest of the section, you will learn how to use a few common commands. For all of these procedures, assume that you are in your home directory (which would be /home/*<yourname>*/).

Command	Description
cat	Lets you view the contents of a file. Many Linux commands can use the redirection symbol > to redirect the output of the command. For example, use the redirection symbol with the cat command to copy a file: `cat /etc/shells > newfile` The contents of the shells file are written to newfile.
cd	Changes the directory. For example, `cd/etc` changes the directory to /etc.

Table G-3 (continued)

Command	Description
chmod	This command changes the attributes assigned to a file and is similar to the DOS Attrib command. For example, to grant read permission to the file myfile: `chmod+r myfile`
clear	Clears the screen. This command is useful when the screen has become cluttered with commands and data that you no longer need to view.
cp	Used to copy a file: `cp <source> <destination>`
date	Entered alone, this command displays the current system date setting. Entered in the format `date <mmddhhmmyy>`, this command sets the system date. For example, to set the date to Dec 25, 2003 at 11:59 in the evening: `date 1225235903`
echo	Displays information on the screen. For example, to display which shell is currently being used, enter this command: `echo $SHELL`
fdisk	Creates or makes changes to a hard drive partition table: `fdisk <hard drive>`
grep	Searches for a specific pattern in a file or in multiple files: `grep <pattern> <file>`
hostname	Displays a server's FQDN: `hostname`
ifconfig	Used to troubleshoot problems with network connections under TCP/IP. This command can disable and enable network cards and release and renew the IP addresses assigned to these cards. For example, to show all configuration information: `ifconfig -a` To release the given IP address for a TCP/IP connection named eth0 (the first Ethernet connection of the system): `ifconfig eth0 -168.92.1.1`
kill	Kills a process instead of waiting for the process to terminate: `kill <process ID>`
ls	The ls command is similar to the DOS Dir command, which displays a list of directories and files. For example, to list all files in the /etc directory, using the long parameter for a complete listing: `ls -l /etc`
man	Displays the online help manual, called man pages. For example, to get information about the echo command: `man echo` The manual program displays information about the command. To exit the manual program, type q.
mkdir	This command makes a new directory: `mkdir <directory>`
|more	Appended to a command to display the results of the command on the screen one page at a time. For example, to page the ls command: `ls |more`
mv	Moves a file or renames it, if the source and destination are the same directory: `mv <source> <destination>`

Table G-3 (continued)

Command	Description
netstat	Shows statistics and status information for network connections and routing tables: `netstat`
nslookup	Queries domain name servers to look up domain names: `nslookup`
ping	Used to test network connections by sending a request packet to a host. If a connection is successful, the host will return a response packet: `ping <host>`
ps	Displays the process table so that you can identify process IDs for currently running processes (once you know the process ID, you can use the kill command to terminate a process): `ps`
pwd	Shows the name of the present working directory: `pwd`
reboot	Reboots the system: `reboot`
rm	Removes the file or files that are specified: `rm <file>`
rmdir	This command removes a directory: `rmdir <directory>`
route	Entered alone, this command shows the current configuration of the IP routing table. Entered in the format `route[options]`, it configures the IP routing table.
traceroute	Shows the route of IP packets; used for debugging connections on a network: `traceroute <host>`
useradd	Adds a user to a system: `useradd [option] <user>`
userdel	Removes a user from a system: `userdel <user>`
vi	Launches a full-screen editor that can be used to enter text and commands: `vi <file>`
whatis	Displays a brief overview of a command. For example, to get quick information about the echo command: `what is echo`
who	Displays a list of users currently logged in: `who`

Table G-3   Some common Linux and Unix commands

Editing Commands

When you add options and file or directory names to a command, it can get quite long, and if you make a mistake while typing the command, you will want to edit it. Also, once the command has been entered, you can retrieve it, edit it, and press Enter to reissue the command. Some shells allow you to use the arrow, Backspace, Insert, and Delete keys to edit command lines, but other shells do not. Instead, use the following keystrokes to edit a command line:

- Alt+D   Delete a word
- Ctrl+K   Delete from the current position to the end of the line
- Ctrl+A   Move the cursor to the beginning of the command line

- Alt+B   Move the cursor left one word
- Alt+F   Move the cursor right one word

For example, follow these steps to edit a command line:

1. Type **who is this** but DO NOT press Enter.

2. To move one word to the left, press **Alt+B** so that your cursor is positioned on the word "is."

3. To delete the word "is," press **Alt+D.**

4. To delete the portion of the command line that follows the current cursor position, press **Ctrl+K.**

5. To move the cursor to the beginning of the command line, press **Ctrl+A.**

Viewing the Shells File

The shells file in the /etc directory contains a list of available shells to use on a Linux system. Each shell incorporates slightly different support for programming and scripting languages. Additionally, different Linux shells may use keystrokes other than the ones you just learned in supporting command line editing; the keystrokes in the procedure in the last section work in Bash, the default Linux shell. To determine whether you are using the Bash shell, type echo $shell and press Enter. If you see the output /bin/bash, you are using the Bash shell. If you are not using the Bash shell, type bash and press Enter to change to the Bash shell.

To view a list of available shells:

1. Type **cat /etc/shells,** and then press **Enter.**

2. A list of available shells appears. This list may include the entries /bin/bash, /bin/bsh, /bin/csh, /bin/sh, /bin/tcsh, and /bin/zsh. Notice that all these shells are stored in the /bin directory. Type **clear,** and then press **Enter** to clear the screen.

3. Type **cat –n /etc/shells,** and then press **Enter.** Notice that this time, the same list of shells is displayed with a number before each line because you used the –n option. (See Figure G-2.) Notice in the figure that the current user is root.

Figure G-2   Use the Cat command to display a list of shells

Redirecting Output

When you entered the command cat /etc/shells in the preceding procedure, the list of available shells, which is the output of that command, was sent to the screen. What if you wanted to save that list? You would use the **redirection symbol**, which is the greater-than (>) sign, to direct the output to a file, perhaps with the name available_shells. Use these steps:

1. Go to the root directory by typing **cd /** and pressing **Enter**.

2. Type **cat /etc/shells > available_shells**, and then press **Enter**.

3. Notice that no command output appears on the screen, because the output has been saved to the new file available_shells (the file is created when the command is entered). To view the contents of the file, type **cat available_shells**, and then press **Enter**.

The file was created in the current directory, which is the root directory.

Creating a Directory

It is not a good idea to store data files in the root directory, so let's create a directory to which to move the new file available_shells:

1. Type **mkdir myfiles**, and then press **Enter**. This creates a directory named myfiles under the current directory, which is root.

2. Type **cd myfiles** to change from the current directory to the new directory.

3. Type **mv /available_shells .** and then press **Enter** (don't overlook the period at the end of the command line; type it, too). This moves the file from the root

directory to the current directory, which is /myfiles. The source directory is the root and the destination directory is /myfiles. The period in a command line means the current directory.

4. Type **ls** to see the contents of the myfiles directory. The available_shells file is listed. (See Figure G-3.)

```
root@localhost.localdomain: /myfiles                          _ □ ×

 File   Edit   Settings   Help

[root@localhost /root]# cd /
[root@localhost /]# cat -n /etc/shells > available_shells
[root@localhost /]# mkdir myfiles
[root@localhost /]# cd myfiles
[root@localhost /myfiles]# mv /available_shells .
[root@localhost /myfiles]# ls
available_shells
[root@localhost /myfiles]# []
```

Figure G-3   Creating and moving files to a directory

Using the vi Editor

You were introduced to the vi command in Table G-3 earlier in the appendix. This command launches the vi editor, which got its name because it is a visual editor; at one time, vi was the most popular Unix text editor. It is still used with shells that don't allow the use of the arrow, Delete, or Backspace keys. You can use the editor in insert mode, in which you can enter text, or command mode, which allows you to enter commands to perform editing tasks to move through the file. In this section, you will learn how to create and use commands on a text file in the vi editor. All of these commands are case sensitive.

Let's create and work with a file called mymemo.

1. To open the vi editor and create a file at the same time, type the command followed by the filename, as follows: **vi mymemo**.

2. The vi editor screen is shown in Figure G-4. Notice that the filename is shown at the bottom of the screen and that the cursor is at the top of the screen.

3. When you first open the vi editor, you are in command mode, which means that anything you type will be interpreted as a command by the vi editor. Type **i** to switch to insert mode. You will not see the command on the screen, and

you do not need to press Enter to execute it. The command automatically switches you to insert mode. When you are in insert mode, the word INSERT is shown at the bottom of the screen.

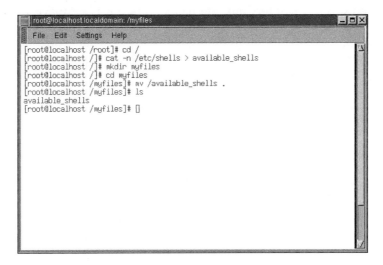

Figure G-4   The vi text editor

4. Type the first two sentences of Step 3 as the text for your memo. If your shell supports it, practice using the arrow keys to move the cursor through the text, up, down, left, and right, one character at a time. You will see the keystrokes used to perform the same movements in Table G-4; they can be used if the arrow keys are not supported.

5. To switch back to command mode, press the **Esc** key. Now you are ready to enter commands to manipulate your text. Type **H** to move the cursor to the upper-left corner of the screen. You must use an uppercase H, because all these commands are case sensitive.

6. Type **W** repeatedly until you reach the beginning of the word "first."

7. Type **dw** to delete the word "first." To delete one character at a time, you would use x; to delete an entire line, you would use dd.

8. To save the file and exit the vi editor, type **:x** and press **Enter**. This will save the file and close the editor.

Table G-4 lists the vi editor commands to move the cursor. There are many more commands to manipulate text, set options, cancel, or temporarily leave a vi editor session. For a more complete list of vi editor commands, see a reference dedicated to Linux.

Window Managers

Because many users prefer a Windows-style desktop, several applications have been written to provide a GUI for Unix and Linux. These GUIs are called window managers. One popular desktop environment application is GNU Network Object Model Environment (GNOME). GNOME (pronounced "guh-nome") provides a desktop that looks and feels like Windows 98, but is free software designed to use a Linux kernel. The major components of a GNOME window are shown in Figure G-5. For more information about GNOME, see the organization's Web site at *www.gnome.org.* Another popular Linux window manager is the KDE Desktop (*www.kde.org*).

Figure G-5   GNOME is popular desktop environment software used on Linux systems

Command	Alternate	Description
Ctrl+B	Pg up	Back one screen
Ctrl+F	Pg down	Forward one screen
Ctrl+U	--	Up half a screen
Ctrl+D	--	Down half a screen
k	Up arrow	Up one line
j	Down arrow	Down one line
h	Left arrow	Left one character

Table G-4 (continued)

Command	Alternate	Description
l	Right arrow	Right one character
W	--	Forward one word
B	--	Back one word
0 (zero)	--	Beginning of the current line
$	--	End of current line
NG	--	Line specified by number *n*
H	--	Upper-left corner of screen
L	--	Last line on the screen

Table G-4   vi editor commands

G

Supporting Notebooks

R ecent statistics show that more than half of personal computers purchased in 2003 were notebook computers, and 26 percent of personal computers in use today are notebooks. As notebooks become more and more popular, PC service technicians will need to know how to support them. This appendix focuses on the special skills and considerations required to support notebooks, showing you how to disassemble, trouble-shoot, and maintain them.

Special Considerations when Supporting Notebooks

In many situations, the task of troubleshooting, upgrading, and maintaining a notebook computer requires the same skills, knowledge, and procedures as when servicing a desktop computer. However, special considerations when supporting notebooks include warranty issues, service manuals, software diagnostic tools provided by the manufacturer, special tools for disassembling the notebook, special requirements of the operating system, and some differences in troubleshooting approaches. When you think of all the new notebooks sold this past year or so, learning all these skills can position you for some great career opportunities supporting notebooks!

Warranty Concerns

Whereas a desktop computer is often assembled from parts made by a variety of manufacturers, notebook computers are almost always sold by a vendor that either manufactured the notebook or had it manufactured as a consolidated system. Most manufacturers or retailers offer at least a one-year warranty and the option to purchase an extended warranty. Therefore, when problems arise while the notebook is under warranty, you are dealing with a single manufacturer or retailer to get support or parts. After the notebook is out of warranty, this manufacturer or retailer can still be your one-stop shop for support and parts.

The warranty often applies to all components in the system, but it can be voided if someone other than an authorized service center services the notebook. Therefore, you as a service technician must be very careful not to void a warranty that the customer has purchased. Warranties can be voided by opening the case, removing part labels, installing other-vendor parts, upgrading the OS, or disassembling the system unless directly instructed to do so by the service center help desk personnel.

Before you begin troubleshooting, to avoid problems with a warranty, always ask the customer, "Is the notebook under warranty?" If the notebook is under warranty, look at the documentation to find out how to get technical support. Options are phone numbers, chat rooms on the Web, and e-mail. Use the most appropriate option. Before you contact technical support, have the notebook model and serial number ready (see Figure H-1). You'll also need the name, phone number, and address of the person or company that made the purchase.

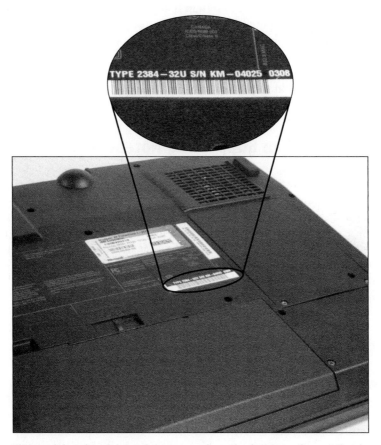

Figure H-1   The model and serial number stamped on the bottom of a notebook are used to identify the notebook to service desk personnel

Based on the type of warranty purchased by the notebook's owner, the manufacturer might send an on-site service technician, ask you to ship or take the notebook to an authorized service center, or help you solve the problem over the phone.

Service Manuals and Other Sources of Information

Desktop computer cases tend to be similar to one another, and components in desktop systems tend to be interchangeable among manufacturers. Not so with notebooks. Notebook manufacturers tend to take great liberty in creating their own unique computer cases, buses, cables, connectors, drives, circuit boards, fans, and even screws, all of which are likely to be proprietary in design.

Every notebook model has a unique case. Components are installed in unique ways and opening the case for each notebook model is done differently. Because of these differences, servicing notebooks can be very complicated and time consuming. For example, a hard drive on one notebook is accessed by popping open a side panel and sliding the drive out of its bay. However, to access the hard drive on another model notebook, you must remove the keyboard, video card, memory modules, internal antennae, and even the LCD panel. If you are not familiar with a particular notebook model, you can do damage to the case as you pry and push trying to open it. Trial and error is likely to damage a case. Even though you might successfully replace a broken component, the damaged case can result in an unhappy customer.

Fortunately, a notebook service manual can save you much time and effort—if you can locate one (see Figure H-2). Two notebook vendors, IBM and Dell, provide their service manuals online free of charge (see Figure H-3). In addition, Compaq offers detailed information on its Web site to help you service its notebooks (see Figure H-4). For all notebook manufacturers, check the FAQ pages of their Web sites for help in tasks such as opening a case without damaging it and locating and replacing a component.

Figure H-2   A notebook service manual tells you how to use diagnostic tools, troubleshoot a notebook, and replace components

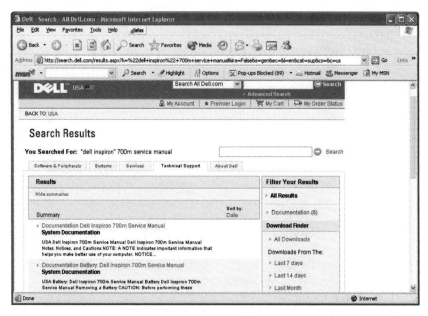

Figure H-3   For Dell notebooks, download the service manual from the Dell Web site at *www.dell.com*

Figure H-4   The Compaq Web site (*www.hp.com*) provides detailed instructions for troubleshooting and replacing components

Sometimes, you can find service manuals on the Web. One useful and very interesting Web site that contains service manuals for several different brands of notebooks as well as service manuals for lots of other electronic devices is *www.eserviceinfo.com*. It is published out of Bulgaria. Some of these service manuals are presented as files with a .rar file extension. An RAR file is a compressed file similar to a ZIP file, except a very large file can be broken into two or more RAR files. You can download a trial version of the software to manage RAR files from RARLAB at *www.rarlab.com*.

Of course, do not forget about the user manuals. They may contain directions for upgrading and replacing components that do not require disassembling the case. User manuals also include troubleshooting tips and procedures.

For more information, you can also use a Web search engine (for example, Google at *www. google.com*) to perform a search on the computer model and component that is giving you the problem. Collect all possible information and technical resources. Remember, notebooks can be damaged much more easily than desktop systems and require a higher level of patience and expertise to service them. Become a researcher and use trial and error only as a last resort. To aid you in your research, Table H-1 lists notebook manufacturers, their Web sites, and their market share.

H

NOTE

When you purchase a replacement part for a notebook from the notebook's manufacturer, most often the manufacturer also sends you detailed instructions for exchanging the part.

Manufacturer	Web Site	Market Share*
Dell Computer	www.dell.com	27%
Compaq and HP	www.hp.com	20%
Toshiba	www.csd.toshiba.com	12%
IBM	www.ibm.com	9%
Apple	www.apple.com	5%
Sony (VAIO)	www.sonystyle.com	5%
Gateway	www.gateway.com	4%
Fujitsu/Fuji	www.fujitsu.com	1%
Acer America	global.acer.com	1%
eMachines by Gateway	www.emachines.com	.8%
Others	N/A	15.2%

Table H-1   Notebook manufacturers (source: IDC WW Quarterly PC Tracker, 2004)

NOTE   Searching the Web for information about notebooks can yield some interesting results. For example, here is a personal Web site where an individual posted documentation about his HP Omnibook notebook: *http://24.237.160.4/files/omnibook/*.

Diagnostic Tools Provided by Manufacturers

Most notebook manufacturers provide diagnostic software that can help you test components to determine which component needs replacing. As one of the first steps when servicing a notebook, check the user manual, service manual, or manufacturer Web site to determine if diagnostic software exists and how to obtain it and use it. Use the software to pinpoint the problem component, which can then be replaced.

For older notebooks, the software is usually contained on a floppy disk and run from the disk. This test disk might come with the notebook or can be purchased from the manufacturer as a separate item. Check the manufacturer Web site for test software that can be downloaded for a particular model notebook. For newer notebooks, the software is stored on the hard drive and accessed by pressing certain keys during the boot process.

An example of diagnostic software is PC-Doctor, which is used by several IBM ThinkPad models. The test software is stored on a floppy disk, CD, or hard drive. If stored on a floppy disk or CD, you can boot from the device to run the tests. If the software is stored on the hard drive, you can run it from the Windows Start menu or by pressing a function key at startup before Windows loads. Either way, PC-Doctor can run tests on the keyboard, video, speakers, mouse, joystick, floppy disk drive, CD drive, DVD drive, wireless LAN, motherboard, processor, serial and parallel ports, hard drive, ZIP drive, and memory. To learn how to use the software, see the notebook's service manual or user manual.

Operating System Upgrades

Notebook computers are sold with an operating system preinstalled at the factory. The OS load is tailored by the manufacturer to satisfy the specific needs of the notebook. Drivers installed are also specific to proprietary devices installed in the notebook. Diagnostic software is often written specifically for a notebook and its installed OS. For all these reasons, use caution when deciding to upgrade to a new OS.

For desktop systems, upgrading the operating system is usually a good thing to do if the desktop system has the power and hard drive space to support the new OS. Not so with notebooks. Generally, the operating system preinstalled on the notebook should last the life of the notebook unless there is a good reason to upgrade. For example, if you need to improve security on a notebook, you might want to upgrade from Windows 98 to Windows 2000 or Windows XP. Windows 2000 might be the appropriate choice if the notebook manufacturer has a Windows 2000 build for this particular model notebook, but does not have a Windows XP build for it. Purchase the OS and supporting device drivers specific to your notebook from the notebook manufacturer and follow their specific instructions for the installation.

If you decide to upgrade the OS using an off-the-shelf version of Windows 2000 or Windows XP, just as with a desktop system, first determine that all components in the system are compatible with the upgrade. Be certain to have available all the device drivers you need for the new OS before you upgrade. Download the drivers from the notebook manufacturer's Web site and store them in a folder on the hard drive. After you upgrade the OS, install the drivers from this folder. The notebook manufacturer might also suggest you first flash the BIOS before you perform the upgrade.

Most notebook computers come with one or more support CDs provided by the manufacturer. This CD might or might not contain an installable version of the OS preinstalled on the notebook. If you need to install the OS again such as when you are replacing a faulty hard drive, you might have to request that the notebook manufacturer provide you with a CD for the OS installation. (Most likely there is a small charge for this service.) Some notebooks come with the files needed to install a new copy of the OS stored on the hard drive in a separate partition. See the user reference manual for how to access these files. Of course, this won't work if your hard drive is broken, and you're replacing it with a new drive. The support CD should definitely contain all the device drivers you need for the currently installed OS and might contain device drivers for another OS. For example, if Windows 98 is installed on a system, the support CD most likely contains device drivers for Windows 98 and Windows 2000.

One interesting situation occurred when I attempted to upgrade a notebook computer from Windows 98 to Windows 2000. The support CD that came with the notebook claimed to have on it device drivers for the internal modem and network cards for both OSs. I performed the OS upgrade and then attempted to use this support CD to install the Windows 2000 modem and network drivers. They would not install. I discovered the drivers on the CD were not the correct drivers for this system. However, without the modem or network ports working, I could not connect to the Internet to download good drivers. The solution was to download the drivers onto another computer and burn a CD with the drivers. Then, I used that CD on the notebook to install the drivers.

Replace or Substitute a Component

As you'll see later in this appendix, replacing components on notebooks can be time consuming and require a lot of patience and know-how. Sometimes, it's wiser to simply avoid opening the case and working inside it. Instead, you could simply use CMOS setup to disable an internal component and then use an external device in its place. For example, if a keyboard fails, you can use a wireless keyboard with an access point connected to the USB port. Also, if an internal modem fails, the simplest solution might be to disable the internal modem and replace it with a PC Card modem card.

H

NOTE

Before making the decision to replace an internal part, ask the question, "Can an external device or PC Card substitute?" Many customers appreciate these solutions, as most often they are much less labor-intensive and less costly.

To disable an internal device, enter CMOS setup when the notebook is booting. Table H-2 lists how to access CMOS setup for different notebook computers.

Notebook Model	To Run CMOS Setup
IBM ThinkPad models series 240, 390, 570, iSeries 1200, 1300, 1400, 1500, 172x, A20, A21, A22, A30, A31, R30, R31, R32, S30, S31, T20, T21, T22, T23, T30, X20, X21, X23, X24, X30, X31	Press F1 when the ThinkPad logo appears during the boot.
IBM ThinkPad R40, R40e, T40	During startup, press the Access IBM button. Then select Start setup utility.
IBM ThinkPad 510, 300350500	Put the system in MS-DOS mode (not a DOS box under Windows) and then press Ctrl+Alt+F3 at a DOS prompt.
IBM ThinkPad 310, 315310E	Press F2 when the ThinkPad logo appears during booting.
IBM ThinkPad 365C, CS365CD, CSD365, ED	Put the system in MS-DOS mode (not a DOS box under Windows) and then press Ctrl+Alt+F11 at a DOS prompt.
IBM ThinkPad 365X, 365XD	During booting, press and hold down the F1 key until the Setup screen appears.
IBM ThinkPad 360, 355, 380, 385, 560, 600, 701x, 76x, 770	During booting, press and hold down the F1 key until the Setup screen appears. Also, for the 701 notebook, you can access CMOS setup at any time by pressing the Fn and F1 keys.
IBM ThinkPad 700x, 720x	During booting, press Ctrl+Alt+Ins right after the memory count.
IBM ThinkPad 710T, 730T	During booting, press and hold down the suspend/resume switch.
Toshiba Satellite models 16xx, 17xx, 30xx, 100x, 19xx, 1000, 1200, 1100x	Turn the system off. Press the power button and then press and hold down F2 until the CMOS Setup screen appears.

Table H-2 (Continued)

Notebook Model	To Run CMOS Setup
Toshiba Satellite models 500x, 510x, 520x	A CMOS Setup program is not included in the motherboard ROM. To access setup, after Windows is loaded, open Control Panel and double-click the HWSetup program.
Toshiba all Libretto, all Portege, and other Satellite models not listed above	Three ways to access setup: ■ In Windows, double-click HWSetup in Control Panel. ■ Power off and on the system. During the boot, when you see the message to press F1, press it. ■ In MS-DOS mode (not a DOS box inside Windows), run the TSETUP program, which can be downloaded from the Toshiba Web site.
Compaq Presario models	During booting, press F2 when the logo screen appears.
Compaq Evo models	During booting, when the message "F10 = ROM Based Setup" appears, press F10.
Compaq Prosignia models	During booting, while the cursor is blinking, press F10.
Dell, Gateway, Sony, Acer, and most other notebooks	During booting, press F2 when the logo appears.

Table H-2   How to access CMOS setup for different notebooks

Protecting the Notebook and Its Data

Because a notebook computer is smaller and lighter than a desktop system and is carried out into public places, it is more susceptible to being stolen. In addition, many times the most valuable thing in the notebook is the data. For these reasons, it is important for a PC support technician to know about ways to protect the notebook and its data.

Security Devices

According to the Safeware Insurance Group, the owner of a notebook computer has a 1 in 14 chance of it being stolen. Some commonsense rules can help protect your notebook. When traveling, always know where your notebook is. If you're standing at an airport counter, tuck your notebook case securely between your ankles. When flying, never check in your notebook as baggage, and don't store it in airplane overhead bins; keep it at your feet. Never leave a notebook in an unlocked car or hotel room and, when you're using it, always log off the network before you walk away from it. When leaving work, lock your notebook in a secure place or use a notebook cable lock to secure it to your desk. Figure H-5 shows a cable lock system. Most notebooks have a security slot on the case to connect the cable lock.

Figure H-5   Use a cable lock system to secure a notebook computer to a desk to help prevent it from being stolen (courtesy of Kensington Technology Group)

Another security device you can use is a theft-prevention plate that includes a label identifying the notebook, which is permanently engraved into your notebook case. The identifying numbers or bar code identify you, the owner, and can also clearly establish to police that the notebook has been stolen. Two sources of theft-prevention plates and cable locks are Computer Security Products, Inc. (*www.computersecurity.com*) and Flexguard Security System (*www.flexguard.com*).

Passwords

Passwords can be effective ways to secure valuable data. Here are four types of passwords that can be used on notebooks:

- *Power-on password (POP)*. This password, sometimes called a BIOS password, is set in CMOS setup. The password must be entered before the operating system will load. The problem with power-on passwords is they can easily be cleared by opening the case and removing the backup battery that powers CMOS RAM.
- *Supervisor password (SVP)*. A supervisor password is also set in CMOS setup. After a supervisor password is set, CMOS setup cannot be accessed without

entering the password. It prevents unauthorized changes to the notebook's configuration; system administrators find it useful when managing multiple notebooks for users. The password is stored on a special security chip on the motherboard that is not part of CMOS RAM, and, therefore, cannot be cleared by removing the CMOS RAM battery. If it is forgotten, it cannot be reset.

- *Hard drive password (HDP).* This password resides on the hard drive, and data on the hard drive cannot be changed without entering this password. The advantage of using a hard drive password over a power-on password or supervisor password is that if the hard drive is removed and installed in another notebook, it still protects the hard drive's data. Just as with the power-on password, the hard drive password is requested by the system when it is powering up.

When you purchase a used notebook computer, be certain to have the seller remove any power-on, supervisor, or hard drive passwords. If these passwords are set and you don't know them, you will not be able to change CMOS setup or access the data on the hard drive.

If you need to access hard drive data or CMOS setup on an IBM ThinkPad when you have forgotten the hard drive password or supervisor password, one service you can use is Nortek Computers (*www.nortek.on.ca*), which also offers a data recovery service for notebook hard drives.

- *Windows passwords.* Windows operating systems offer passwords designed to prevent unauthorized access to the system or to the data managed by the system. These Windows passwords were discussed earlier in the book as each Windows OS was covered. Also covered were various data encryption techniques that can also be used to protect data. All these techniques and passwords work on desktop and notebook computers.

Data Backups

As discussed earlier in the book, if you can't get along without the data, back it up. Don't trust your hard drive with data you can't do without; back it up to another media. Backing up data was covered earlier in the book.

One problem with backups on notebook computers is that standard backup techniques often rely on company file servers, CD burners, or other media that are not always available when traveling with your notebook. If you need to back up data or have access to this backed-up data while traveling, one solution is an online backup service such as @Backup (*www.backup.com*) or Computer Security Products, Inc. (*www.computersecurity.com*).

Preventive Maintenance

Notebook computers tend to not last as long as desktop computers because they are portable and, therefore, subjected to more wear and tear. Some things you can do to keep a notebook working longer are as follows:

- Don't bump, knock, or move the notebook when it's running. When it is not running, don't drop it, not even a few inches.
- Don't place heavy objects on top of the notebook case.
- Keep your notebook at a controlled temperature. For example, never leave it in a car overnight when it is cold, and don't leave it in a car during the day when it's hot.
- Don't leave the notebook in a dusty or smoke-filled area.
- Don't power it up and down unnecessarily.
- Protect the notebook from overheating by not running it when it's still inside the case or partially covered with a blanket or anything else that would prevent proper air circulation around it.
- Don't pick up the notebook by the LCD panel. Pick it up from the base.
- Don't connect a modem in a notebook to a private branch exchange (PBX) or other digital telephone service such as that used in some hotels because these private telephone systems often carry too much voltage on the phone line, which can damage the modem.
- If a notebook has just come indoors from the cold, don't turn it on until it reaches room temperature. In some cases, condensation on the hard drive platters can cause problems. Some manufacturers recommend that when you receive a new notebook shipped to you during the winter, leave it in its shipping carton for several hours before you open the carton to prevent subjecting the notebook to a temperature shock.
- Protect a notebook against ESD. If you have just come in from the cold on a low-humidity day when there is the possibility that you are carrying ESD, don't touch the notebook until you have grounded yourself.
- Protect a notebook against EMI. Keep it away from ham radio equipment, strong electric fans, or other devices that emit strong EMI.
- Before placing a notebook in a carrying case for travel, remove any CDs, DVDs, or PC Cards and put them in protective covers. Verify that the system is powered down and not in suspend or standby mode.
- Notebook manufacturers recommend you only use a soft dry cloth to clean your LCD panel.
- Keep backups current and occasionally verify that your recovery procedure works by restoring some data from backup.
- Occasionally empty the Recycle Bin, delete temporary files, scan the hard drive for errors, backup the system state, and defragment files.
- Keep OS updates and antivirus software current. Run antivirus software in the background to scan e-mail for viruses. If your antivirus software has the feature, enable automatic download of updates.
- Never, ever connect to the Internet using a public wireless connection or ISP without first turning on a software firewall.
- Never, ever open e-mail attachments unless you trust the sender and have scanned for viruses.

A well-used notebook, especially one that is used in dusty or dirty areas, needs cleaning occasionally. Here are some cleaning tips:

- It is not necessary to disassemble a notebook for routine cleaning. In fact, you can clean the LCD panel, battery connections, keyboard, touch pad, or even memory contacts as needed without opening the notebook case.
- Clean the LCD panel with a soft dry cloth. If the panel is very dirty, you can dampen the cloth with water. Even though some books advise using a mixture of isopropyl alcohol and water to clean an LCD panel, notebook manufacturers say not to.
- Use a can of compressed air meant to be used around computer equipment to blow dust and small particles out of the keyboard, track ball, and touch pad. Turn the notebook at an angle and direct the air into the sides of the keyboard. Then use a soft, damp cloth to clean key caps and touch pad.
- If keys are sticking, remove the keyboard so you can better spray under the key with compressed air. If you can remove the key cap, remove it and clean the key contact area with contact cleaner. One example of a contact cleaner you can use for this purpose is Stabilant 22 (*www.stabilant.com*). Reinstall the keyboard and test it. If the key still sticks, replace the keyboard.
- Remove the battery and clean the battery connections with a contact cleaner. You might also consider removing the memory modules and cleaning these contacts.

Disassembling and Reassembling Notebooks

Working on notebooks requires special tools and extra patience. Most of today's notebooks are designed so that commonly replaced components, such as the memory, the backup battery, and the hard drive, are easy to get to without opening the computer case. Also remember that sometimes it's less costly to simply substitute an external component for one inside the case. In this section, you'll learn how to replace easy-to-get-to components and how to do a full disassemble of a notebook.

Special Tools for Disassembling a Notebook

Just as when you are working with desktop systems, before opening the case of a notebook or touching sensitive components, you should always use a ground strap to protect the system against ESD. You can attach the alligator clip end of the ground strap to an unpainted metallic surface on the notebook. This surface could be, for instance, a port on the back of the notebook (see Figure H-6). If a ground strap is not available, ground yourself by touching a metallic unpainted part of the notebook such as a port on the back before you touch a component inside the case.

Figure H-6   To ground yourself, attach the alligator clip of a ground strap to an I/O port on the back of the notebook

Screws and nuts on a notebook are smaller than a desktop system and require smaller tools. You will need the following tools to disassemble a notebook, although you can get by without several of them. See Figure H-7 for a display of some of these tools:

- Antistatic ground strap
- Small flat-head screwdriver
- Number 1 Phillips-head screwdriver
- Dental pick (useful for prying without damaging plastic cases, connectors, and screw covers)
- Torx screwdriver set, particularly size T5
- Something such as a pill box to keep screws and small parts organized
- Notebook for note taking or digital camera (optional)
- Shroud gauge (also called a case cracker; used to pry open cases; optional)
- Flashlight (optional)
- Three-prong extractor to pick up tiny screws (optional)

Notebooks contain many small screws of various sizes and lengths. When reassembling, put screws back where they came from so that when you reassemble the system, you won't use screws that are too long and that can protrude into a sensitive component and damage it. As you remove a screw, store or label it so you know where it goes when reassembling. One way to do that is to place screws in a pill box with each cell labeled. Another way is to place screws on a soft padded work surface and use white labeling tape to label each set of screws. A third way to organize screws is to put them on notebook paper and write beside them where the screw belongs (see Figure H-8). Whatever method you use, work methodically to keep screws and components organized so you know what goes where when reassembling.

Figure H-7   Tools for disassembling a notebook computer

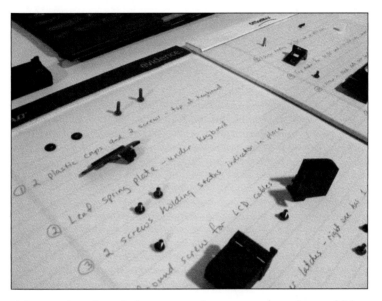

Figure H-8   Using a notepad can help you organize screws so you know which screw goes where when reassembling

As you disassemble the computer, if you are not following directions from a service manual, keep notes as you work to help you reassemble later. Draw diagrams and label things carefully. Include in your drawings cable orientations and screw locations. You might consider using a digital camera. Take photos as you work and use the photos to guide you through the reassemble process.

Some notebook manufacturers suggest you use a shroud gauge, also called a case cracker, to pry open a case. A small flat-head screwdriver will also do the job. Compaq offers a notebook tool repair kit that includes a shroud gauge, loop-back port testers, pick, and various sizes torx, flat-head, and Phillips screwdrivers.

Preparation for Servicing a Notebook

Before attempting to replace or upgrade a component installed in a notebook, always do the following:

- If the computer is working, have the user back up any important data stored on the notebook.
- Ground yourself by using an antistatic ground strap. If no ground strap is available, periodically touch the port to discharge any static electricity on your body.
- Turn off any attached devices such as a printer and then shut down the notebook.
- Disconnect the AC adapter from the computer and from the electrical outlet.
- If the notebook is attached to a port replicator or docking station, release it to undock the computer.
- Remove the battery pack.
- Remove any PC Cards.

You are now ready to follow specific instructions for your particular notebook model to replace or upgrade an internal component. Some components can easily be accessed by either removing a panel to expose the component or by removing a screw or two and then sliding the component out the side of the case. When a component can be accessed this easily, most users can do the job if given detailed instructions. However, some components, such as the LCD panel or motherboard, are not so easily accessed. To get to these components requires opening the case and disassembling the notebook. This section first looks at components that are easily accessed and then looks at a full disassemble of a system.

Components that Are Easy to Get To

Components installed on notebook computers that are easily installed or replaced without disassembling the computer include memory, hard drives, optical drives, floppy drives, batteries, and PC Cards. The following sections provide examples of easy replacements.

Replacing a Hard Drive

Older notebook computers required that you disassemble the computer to replace the hard drive. With newer notebooks, you can easily replace a drive. For example, to remove the IBM ThinkPad X20 hard drive, first power down the system and remove the battery pack. Then remove a coin screw that holds the drive in place (see Figure H-9). Pull the drive out of its bay, and replace it with a new drive. Next replace the screw and power up the system.

Figure H-9   Replacing the hard drive in an IBM ThinkPad X20

When the system boots up, if CMOS setup is set to autodetect hard drives, BIOS recognizes the new drive and searches for an operating system. If the drive is new, boot from a Windows startup CD and install the OS.

Upgrading Memory

Primary memory on notebook computers can be stored on credit card memory modules, SO-DIMMs, SO-RIMMs, and proprietary memory modules. Some examples are shown in Figure H-10.

Figure H-10   Sample notebook memory modules

Most notebooks are designed for easier access to memory. For example, for the notebook shown in Figure H-11, to replace a memory module, turn the notebook upside down. Remove the screws and the panel cover to expose the modules. Fortunately, replacing memory on most newer notebooks is as easy as this.

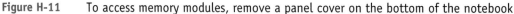

Figure H-11   To access memory modules, remove a panel cover on the bottom of the notebook

Full Disassemble of a Notebook

If you enjoy putting together a thousand-piece jigsaw puzzle, you'll probably enjoy working on notebook computers. With desktop systems, replacing a component is not a time-consuming task, but with notebooks, the job could take several hours. This section gives you some tips and procedures to help make your work easier.

If you take the time to carefully examine the notebook's case before attempting to open it, you will probably find markings provided by the manufacturer to assist you in locating components that are commonly upgraded. If you have a service manual, your work will be much easier than without one. However, after a little practice, you'll see that notebook assemblies have some things in common and disassembling one gets easier with experience.

The best way to learn to disassemble a notebook is to practice on an old one that you can afford to break. Find an old Dell or IBM ThinkPad for which you can download the service manual from the Dell or IBM Web site. Then carefully and patiently follow the disassemble instructions and then reassemble it. When done, you can congratulate yourself and move on to newer notebooks. One advantage of starting out this way is that the older notebooks are often more difficult to disassemble than the newer ones. By starting with an older one, you learn skills that will make disassembling a new notebook much easier. One caution is worth repeating: Always make sure the notebook you are disassembling is not under warranty. You don't want to void that warranty.

When disassembling a notebook, consider the following tips:

- Take your time. Patience is needed to keep from scratching or marring plastic screw covers, hinges, and the case.
- As you work, don't force anything. If you find yourself forcing something, you're likely to break it.
- Always wear a ground strap or use other protection against ESD.
- When removing cables, know that sometimes cable connectors are ZIF connectors. To disconnect a cable from a ZIF connector, first pull up on the connector and then remove the cable (see Figure H-12).
- Use a dental pick or very small screwdriver to pry up the plastic cover hiding a screw (see Figure H-13). Screws around the LCD panel and keyboard are often hidden beneath plastic circles pasted on top of the screw. This plastic can easily be damaged or lost.

Figure H-12   To disconnect a ZIF connector, first push up on the connector, release the latch, and then remove the cable

Figure H-13   Use a small screwdriver or dental pick to pry up the plastic cover hiding a screw

Disassembling an Older ThinkPad

As a general rule, the older the notebook is, the more difficult it will be to disassemble, and the ThinkPad is no exception. Fortunately, though, the older IBM ThinkPad 755c notebook, which uses a 486 processor, uses some disassemble procedures that are typical to several older notebooks. Those notebooks are displayed in the figures in the following step sequence.

1. The easy-to-get-to drives and battery pack are hidden under the keyboard. Release the spring latches on both sides of the keyboard and raise it. You can then use a ribbon or handle connected to the battery, hard drive, and floppy drive to remove each (see Figure H-14).

Figure H-14   Raise the keyboard as a lid, which exposes drives and the battery inside the case

2. To remove the keyboard, pry up the black plastic covers near the keyboard hinges, and remove the screws under these covers, which allows you to then remove the keyboard hinges. Next remove the plastic cover at the top of the keyboard, which exposes the three cable connectors for the keyboard (see Figure H-15). Disconnect these three ZIF connectors by first using a small screwdriver or dental pick to raise the sides of the connector, which releases pressure on the cable. Then remove the cable.

Figure H-15   Three ZIF connectors hold the three keyboard cables in place

3. This notebook uses a DRAM credit card memory module. The module is removed by sliding it out of its motherboard slot (see Figure H-16).

Figure H-16   Remove the DRAM memory module

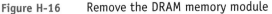

4. To remove the modem card, audio card, or DC controller card, you must first remove a speaker shield located just under the top half of the keyboard (see Figure H-17). The shield is secured with 10 screws. Remove the screws and then the shield. Take care to record where each screw goes as they are not all the same size.

Figure H-17   A speaker shield separates the keyboard from the audio card underneath

5. The audio card is now exposed. Lift it up, gently disconnecting it from its slot on the motherboard (see Figure H-18). Then disconnect the audio cable.

Figure H-18   Remove the audio card and then disconnect the audio cable

6. If you need to remove the DC controller, first remove the LCD panel assembly, which is rather tedious as the LCD panel is connected to the motherboard by several small wires and cables. After they are removed, the DC controller is exposed and can be removed by first removing two screws and a bracket that hold it in place.

7. Next, the backup and standby batteries can be removed and then the motherboard. (These batteries are covered in the next section.) The motherboard comes out of the case with the rear panel assembly still connected (see Figure H-19). The PCMCIA slot assembly is then exposed and can be removed.

Ports connected to rear of motherboard

H

Figure H-19   The motherboard is removed from the case with the rear panel assembly connected, which can then be removed

This notebook is one of the more difficult to disassemble. Figure H-20 shows all parts ready to be reassembled in reverse order.

Figure H-20   Notebook parts disassembled

NOTE After assembling a notebook, before powering it up, turn the notebook upside down a couple of times and listen for any rattles that might indicate a loose screw, spring, or other small part. If you hear any rattles, disassemble the notebook and correct the problem.

Disassembling a Newer Dell Notebook

In this next example, we'll disassemble a Pentium II notebook, the Dell Latitude CPi. This notebook is more typical of newer notebooks because there are not so many small brackets and screws.

NOTE If you plan to disassemble a Dell Latitude computer, download the entire service manual from the Dell Web site so that you will have the complete details of the procedures. In this appendix, to conserve space, some details have been omitted.

1. Back up data, turn the system off, and remove the battery pack. Put on a ground strap to protect the system against ESD.
2. Remove the hard drive by turning the computer over and removing two screws on the bottom near the hard drive door. Then pull the drive out of the case (see Figure H-21).

Figure H-21   Remove the hard drive by first removing two screws that hold the drive in place

3. Another easy-to-get-to component is the memory card. First remove the plate on the bottom of the computer. Then gently push the two clips outward on each side of the memory card. Rotate it up and out of the slot (see Figure H-22).

Figure H-22   Remove the memory module card by first releasing clips on both sides of the card

4. You can now open the case. Figure H-23 shows the order of components to be removed. First on the bottom of the computer, remove six screws that hold the keyboard to the case.

Figure H-23   Exploded view of Dell Latitude notebook

5. Next push the latches on the palm rest assembly outward to release the assembly from the keyboard.
6. Then insert a small screwdriver under the edge of the blank key on the right edge of the keyboard and push up on the keyboard (see Figure H-24). Lift the keyboard up and out.

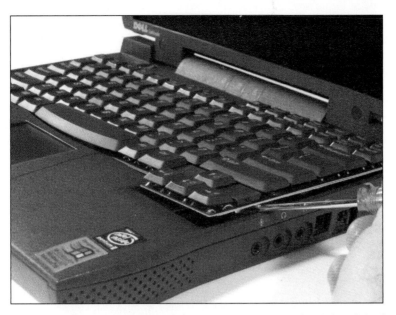

Figure H-24   Pry up the keyboard using the edge of a blank key on the right of the keyboard

7. The rear assembly is removed next. To do that, remove the 12 screws on each side of a port and on the right and left sides of the back cover. The back cover can then be removed (see Figure H-25).

Figure H-25   Twelve screws hold the back cover in place

8. The palm rest assembly is removed next by first disconnecting the touch pad cable from the ZIF connector, removing six screws that hold the assembly in place, and then removing the assembly itself.

9. The display assembly is removed next. Its components are shown in Figure H-26. First remove the grounding screw from the LCD interface cable and disconnect the interface cable from the connector on the motherboard. Close the display.

Display assembly bezel

Display assembly top cover

Figure H-26   Exploded LCD panel assembly

10. Remove the four hinge screws, two on each side, and lift the display assembly from the case.

11. To disassemble the LCD panel assembly, first remove the four screws along the top of the assembly and the two screws on the bottom (refer to Figure H-26). Be certain to keep track of which screw goes where;they are not all the same size.

12. Separate the front bezelfrom the LCD panel by first prying them apart slightly. You can then see hidden snaps holding them together. Release the hidden snaps and remove the bezel.

CAUTION

As you work, be careful to not put pressure on the LCD panel. If it breaks so that fluid gets on your skin or in your eyes, run water over your skin or eyes for at least 15 minutes.

13. Next remove the audio card (see Figure H-27). To do that, remove the screw holding the speaker shield in place and then remove the shield. Next disconnect the audio wires and microphone wires from the audio board, and lift the audio board from the case.

5-mm screw

Speaker shield

Audio board

Speaker wires

Figure H-27   To remove the audio board, first remove the speaker shield

14. The motherboard is removed next (see Figure H-28). First remove the two screws holding the thermal cooling assembly in place and then remove the assembly, which is on top of the processor. Then remove the air flow duct.

Figure H-28   Exploded motherboard assembly

15. Remove the left rear foot on the base of the computer and then remove the two screws holding the motherboard in place. Then lift it out of the case.

Solving Common Problems with Notebooks

This section contains some general troubleshooting steps to follow when solving problems with notebooks. Problems with software and hardware are covered.

When troubleshooting notebook problems, as a first consideration, always remember to protect the user's data and to find out what warranty the notebook might be covered by.

Protecting and Retrieving Data

VIDEO

Recovering
Data on a
Laptop

Sometimes, the most important component in a notebook computer is the user data. If data is not backed up but the hard drive is not physically damaged, before you begin servicing the system, you can download the data to a hard drive in a desktop system. After the data is safe on another computer, the user can relax and you can focus on getting the notebook working. Follow these steps:

1. Obtain a notebook IDE adapter kit such as the one purchased from PC Cables (*www.pccables.com*, see Figure H-29), used to install a notebook hard drive in a desktop system.

H

Figure H-29   Use an IDE adapter kit to install a notebook hard drive into a desktop system

2. Remove the notebook hard drive from the notebook and, using the adapter kit, install the drive in the desktop.
3. Copy the data onto a hard drive in the desktop system.
4. If appropriate, you can then put the notebook hard drive back in the notebook to help you troubleshoot the system.

If you must replace the notebook hard drive, you can use the converter kit to install the drive in the desktop system and copy the data from the desktop system onto the new drive, before or after you have installed the OS on the drive.

Slow Systems, Pop-Up Ads, and Viruses

A slow, sluggish system that is slow to boot or hangs at odd times is likely to contain a worm or virus. Also pop-up ads are an annoyance most users want to avoid. In most cases, the solution is to first clean the system using antivirus software, spyware blockers, ad blockers, and other utility tools. After the system is clean, install antivirus software and a firewall to protect the system in the future. Consider the following general guidelines:

- It's impossible to give a step-by-step solution to clean every system. A utility tool that will work on one virus, OS, or worm might not work in another situation. You need to know about several tools that might help and try first one and then the next until the system is clean.
- As a last resort, you can back up the data, format the hard drive, reinstall the OS and applications, and then restore the data. Obviously, you'll want to avoid this if possible because it is so time consuming.
- Protecting against spyware, worms, ads, and viruses is like shooting at a moving target. What works today might not work tomorrow. Continue to educate yourself about new utilities and techniques to fight the never-ending battle against these predators.
- When cleaning a system, try the simple, less dangerous tools first before you move on to the more dangerous ones. For example, run a search and destroy utility in default mode that is less invasive before you attempt to remove a virus by manually editing the registry. In this way, you're less likely to do damage as you work.
- The following are some good tools to start with that have proven to be reliable, are fairly harmless to a system, and are also very effective:

  - Use good antivirus software such as Norton AntiVirus by Symantec (*www.symantec.com*), McAfee VirusScan by McAfee Associates, Inc. (*www.mcafee.com*), or F-Prot by Frisk Software International (*www.f-prot.com*).
  - To clean up unwanted ads, Trojans, browser hijackers, and tracking, try Ad-Aware by Lavasoft (*www.lavasoftusa.com*).
  - If that doesn't do the job, next try SpyBot Search & Destroy by PepiMK Software (*www.safer-networking.org*). Try the default mode first, which is the least invasive.

Problems with the Power System

A notebook computer can be powered by an AC adapter connected to an electrical outlet, a DC adapter connected to an outlet in a vehicle, or an installed battery pack. In servicing notebooks, problems you might encounter that do not require opening the notebook case are a faulty battery pack and a faulty AC or DC adapter. Components inside the notebook case that are considered field replaceable units (FRUs) and might cause problems include the DC controller board (see Figure H-30), the backup battery, and the standby battery (see Figure H-31). Not all notebooks use a standby battery, which is used to temporarily hold the system in suspend mode while you are exchanging a battery pack or connecting an AC adapter.

Figure H-30   The DC controller board, sometimes called the DC-DC card, controls voltage to internal components

Battery pack

Backup battery
Standby battery

Figure H-31   Notebooks can use a battery pack, a backup battery to power CMOS setup, and a suspend battery (optional)

To extend the life of the battery pack, consider these tips:

- A battery pack's life expectancy depends on the number of times the battery pack is charged. Therefore, to extend its life, don't keep it in the notebook when an AC or DC adapter is powering the system unless you want to charge the battery pack.
- When using the battery pack, to reduce power consumption, remove any PC Cards you are not using.
- Optical drives use a lot of power. Therefore, whenever possible, connect the notebook to an electrical outlet to play a movie on DVD or use a CD.
- Use standby or hibernate mode whenever you are not using the notebook.

Here are some guidelines when troubleshooting problems with the power system:

- Check the power light. For many notebooks, a blinking light indicates the notebook has power and is in standby mode. If the power light is steady, the system has power. If the light is off, press the power button.
- The battery charge might be depleted. Connect the AC adapter.
- The AC adapter might not be solidly connected at both ends. Also check the connectors at the adapter unit, as shown in Figure H-32.

Check
connections
at these points

Figure H-32   When troubleshooting an AC adapter, check connections at all points

- Eliminate power strips or other devices that might cause problems. Connect the AC adapter directly to an electrical outlet.
- Note that the memory modules might be defective or loose. Try reseating them.
- If the system fails only when the AC adapter is connected, it might be defective. Try a new AC adapter, or, if you have a multimeter, use it to verify the voltage output of the adapter. Do the following for an adapter with a single center pin connector:

  - Unplug the AC adapter from the computer, but leave it plugged into the electrical outlet.
  - Using a multimeter set to measure voltage in the 1 to 20 V DC range, place the red probe of the multimeter in the center of the DC connector that would normally plug into the DC outlet on the notebook. Place the black probe on the outside cylinder of the DC connector (see Figure H-33).

Figure H-33   To use a multimeter to test this AC adapter, place the red probe (which, in the image, is in the person's left hand) in the center connector and the black probe on the outside

- The voltage range should be plus or minus 5 percent of the accepted voltage. For example, if a notebook is designed to use 16V, the voltage should measure somewhere between 15.5 and 17V DC.
- If you boot the notebook and discover CMOS setup has lost configuration information or the date and time are wrong, most likely the small battery inside the case that powers CMOS RAM needs replacing. Notebook manufacturers sometimes call this battery the backup battery or reserve battery. Notebook service manuals will provide instructions to exchange the battery. If you don't have a service manual, and you order the battery from the notebook manufacturer, most likely they will send you the battery along with detailed instructions as to how to install it. Before you decide to replace the battery, if you have a multimeter, look on the battery for the voltage output and use the multimeter to determine if the voltage is correct. If not, replace the battery. If backup batteries need replacing often, replace the motherboard.
- Sometimes the backup battery is easy to get to, and sometimes it isn't. Figure H-34 shows an example of one IBM ThinkPad in which the backup battery is easily accessed by removing a plate on the bottom of the notebook.

Figure H-34 For this notebook, access the backup battery by removing a plate on the bottom of the notebook

A backup battery is often a lithium battery, which can explode if not treated correctly. Dispose of a used battery by taking it to a recycle center or following other county regulations for disposing of hazardous waste.

- With some notebooks, the backup battery is more difficult to get to. For example, to access the backup battery in an older notebook (see Figure H-35), you must first remove the keyboard and then the floppy drive to expose the black battery cover shown in the figure. A screw holds the cover in place. Remove the screw and then the cover. Unplug the battery from the motherboard and then remove it. Notice in the figure the standby battery is nearby.

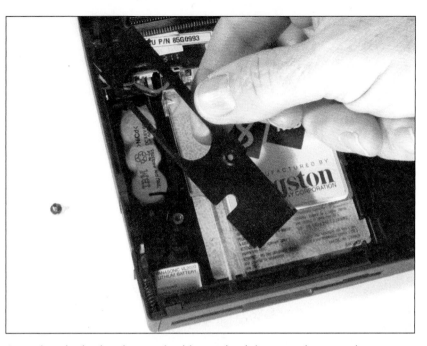

Figure H-35   Accessing the backup battery in this notebook is a complex procedure

- If suspend mode or standby mode does not work, the problem might be a faulty battery, DC controller, or motherboard. Eliminate the battery as the problem by trying suspend mode or standby mode while connected to an electrical outlet. If the problem still persists, first replace the DC controller and then replace the motherboard.
- Some notebooks can hold suspend mode for a short time while you exchange a battery pack or install an AC adapter after the battery pack is discharged. These systems use a standby battery. If the standby battery does not work, first try replacing the standby battery, then the DC controller. If this doesn't work and the situation merits having the standby battery function, replace the motherboard.

Problems with Video

Problems with the video system can be caused by display settings, the power system, or a faulty LCD panel or inverter board. Use Table H-3 as a starting point to troubleshoot video.

Problem	What to Do
Display is blank	■ The problem might be caused by lack of power. Check the power light. Check the battery. Try another electrical outlet. Check the AC adapter. Check the power properties for incorrect settings. ■ Possibly a loose connection. Try reseating the LCD connector inside the notebook. ■ The LCD panel or inverter board might be broken. Try connecting a regular monitor to the system using the video port on the back of the notebook. If the monitor works, consider replacing the LCD assembly. Is the system under warranty?
Display is hard to read	■ The LCD panel might be set to dim so it's hard to read. Try adjusting the brightness level. See the user manual to learn how. ■ Consider electrical devices that might give interference, such as a powerful speaker system, stereo systems, fans, or halogen or fluorescent lights. ■ Is the notebook in direct sunlight? Try eliminating glare. ■ Try restoring the refresh rate and other Windows display settings to default values.
Bright dots, dark dots, bright or dark vertical or horizontal lines, discoloration, dents, or bubbles appear on the LCD panel	■ All these symptoms indicate a damaged LCD panel. A few defective dots on a LCD panel (for example, less than 11 dots) is considered a cosmetic problem, and notebook manufacturers generally will not replace the LCD panel under warranty. If the problems are disruptive, replace the LCD panel.
Screen flickers	■ Most likely, display settings need adjusting and the LCD panel is not the problem.
LCD contrast and brightness cannot be adjusted	■ Try reseating the LCD connector inside the notebook. ■ Replace the LCD assembly.
LCD panel is unreadable, characters are missing, or incorrect characters display	■ Try reseating the LCD connector inside the notebook. ■ Replace the LCD assembly.

Table H-3   Problems with video and what to do about them

If you must replace the LCD panel or inverter board, be certain you purchase the same LCD assembly installed in the notebook. Variations in LCD panels are that some are monochrome, some are color, some have contrast and brightness adjustments, and some don't. In most cases, putting a different LCD assembly in a notebook than the one it is designed to support will not work.

Sometimes, a notebook LCD panel including the entire cover and hinges are considered a single field replaceable unit, and sometimes components within the LCD assembly are considered an FRU. For example, the field replaceable units for the display panel in Figure H-36 are the LCD front bezel, the hinges, the LCD panel, the inverter card, the LCD interface cables, the LCD USB cover, and the rear cover. In most cases, you would replace only the LCD panel and perhaps the inverter card.

Figure H-36   Components in an LCD assembly

The following are some general directions to replace an LCD panel:

- Remove the battery pack.
- For many notebooks, to remove the LCD top cover, you must first remove the keyboard assembly.
- Sometimes, you must also remove screws in the back of the notebook to release the hinge assembly.
- Remove the hinge covers; be careful not to break these plastic covers.
- After you remove the hinge screws, you should then be able to lift the cover off the notebook case (see Figure H-37).

Remove screws

Push back hinges

Remove LCD cover from base

Figure H-37 Remove the top LCD cover by first removing hinge screws and disconnecting the hinges; then lift off the cover

- The LCD panel might connect to the notebook case by way of wires running through the hinge assembly, cables, or a pin connector. Cables might be connected to the motherboard using ZIF connectors. As you remove the LCD top cover, be careful to watch for how the panel is connected. Don't pull on wires or cables as you remove the cover, but first carefully disconnect them.
- Next remove screws that hold the top cover and LCD panel together. Sometimes, these screws are covered with black plastic circles. First use a dental pick or small screwdriver to pick off these covers. You should then be able to remove the front bezel and separate the rear cover from the LCD panel.
- For notebooks that provide a USB connection on the top cover, the cable system might be complex. Carefully remove all connections (see Figure H-38).

Figure H-38   Removing the cable system from the rear of an LCD panel

A Notebook Gets Wet

To prevent a shock, if a notebook gets wet and is connected to an electrical outlet, turn off the electricity at the circuit breaker before touching the notebook or any cables connected to it. Then do the following:

- Turn off the computer and disconnect the AC adapter from the computer and from the electrical outlet.
- Turn off any attached devices such as a printer and disconnect them from the power source.

- Ground yourself by touching a metal unpainted part of the notebook such as a serial or parallel port on the back of the notebook.
- Remove any PC Cards or removable drives.
- Remove the battery pack.
- Remove the hard drive and memory modules.
- Open the notebook up and set it across two bricks or books so that air can circulate around it.
- Allow the notebook and all components to dry for at least 24 hours at room temperature. Don't use a hair dryer or fan to speed up the drying. Don't reassemble the components until you are sure all are dry. Then reinstall the hard drive and memory modules. Connect the notebook to the AC adapter and turn it on. Verify that the notebook is working and then install the battery pack, removable drives, and PC Cards. If the notebook does not work, begin the troubleshooting process as described earlier in the appendix.

The Notebook Is Dropped

If the notebook is dropped, do the following:

- If the system is still running, save your work and close any open files or applications. Shut down the computer.
- Disconnect the AC adapter from the notebook and from the electrical outlet.
- Turn off and disconnect any external devices such as a printer and remove the battery pack.
- Reinstall the battery pack or the AC adapter and turn on the notebook.
- If the notebook does not work correctly, begin troubleshooting the system that is not working.

General OS or Application Problems

Face problems such as applications crashing, programs not responding, and OS errors just as you would for a desktop system. Just as with desktop systems, follow these general guidelines:

- Begin by closing the problem application or, for OS problems, by rebooting the system. If you cannot use the Start menu or Task Manager to perform a normal restart, then you can turn off the notebook using the power button. If the power button does not work, most notebooks have a reset hole. Push an open paper clip into the hole to force a system restart. If the computer doesn't have a reset hole, as a last resort, you can disconnect the power supply (either the AC adapter or the battery pack).
- For OS problems, restart the system and begin troubleshooting using the general guidelines presented earlier in the book for each OS.

- For application problems, restart the application. A full restart of the system might help. Consider that the application data file might be corrupted; try another file. Try searching the Web for error messages and downloading patches from the software manufacturer Web site.
- Scan for viruses.

Problems Connecting to the Network

Here are some general guidelines for solving network problems:

- Check the network cable to be sure it is firmly connected at both ends.
- Check the network lights near the network jack on the back of the notebook. A green light indicates the network is active. For some systems, an amber light indicates the OS recognizes that a network is present.
- Try rebooting the computer and logging on to the network. If the problem still persists, treat it as you would a network problem with a desktop system. Check the network configuration. Verify other computers can access the network. Try a different network wall jack. Try reinstalling the network card device drivers.

Problems with the Hard Drive or Other Drives

Treat these problems as you would similar problems on a desktop system:

- Enter CMOS setup and verify that BIOS recognizes the hard drive correctly.
- Try reseating the drive and reconnecting cables to the drive.
- For the hard drive, run Windows 9x/Me ScanDisk or Windows 2000/XP Error checking. For a DVD drive, reinstall the drivers. Try a different CD or DVD.

More Errors and What to Do About Them

Table H-4 contains a list of common and not-so-common error messages and what to do about them. In addition to this list, error messages given throughout the book that apply to desktop systems also might apply to notebooks. If you receive an error message that is not in the list or you are not familiar with, first check the Web site of the notebook manufacturer or the notebook service manual. Search on the error message to find out what to do. If this doesn't give results, do a general Web search using a search engine.

H

Error Message	What to Do
Operating system not found	■ Remove any bootable devices, such as a floppy disk or CD, and try a reboot. ■ Suspect damaged system files on the hard drive. For Windows 2000/XP, try booting to the Advanced Options menu by pressing F8 during the boot. ■ Try booting from a support CD or rescue disk for the OS and examine the hard drive for errors. ■ Go to CMOS setup and verify that the hard drive is correctly identified. ■ Reseat the hard drive. ■ Troubleshoot the operating system installed on the hard drive. ■ Reinstall the operating system. ■ Replace the motherboard.
Insert bootable media	The OS is trying to boot from a CD or floppy disk that is not bootable. Replace the disk or CD and try booting again or try booting from the hard drive.
Nonsystem disk error	Remove the floppy disk and reboot.
Device address conflicts Allocation error for device I/O device IRQ conflict	■ Try loading default values in CMOS setup. ■ Replace the backup battery. ■ Replace the motherboard.
Invalid system configuration data	■ Reseat and then replace RAM. ■ Replace the motherboard.
Auxiliary device failure	■ The touch pad or mouse has failed. Try rebooting. ■ Does an external mouse work using a USB port? If so, you might not want to go to the expense and trouble of exchanging the touch pad.
Bad command or filename	■ Look in the Autoexec.bat file or Config.sys file for errors. Try booting without these files.
Cache disabled due to failure	■ The processor's cache memory failed. Most often, this means replacing the processor or the entire motherboard with an embedded processor.
Gate A20 error	■ Try reseating memory modules. ■ Replace memory. ■ Replace the motherboard.

Table H-4 (Continued)

Error Message	What to Do
Data error	<ul><li>Run Scandisk or error checking.</li><li>Consider backing up all data and reformatting the hard drive. Then reinstall the OS and restore data from backup.</li><li>Sometimes, you can do a low level format. Check the hard drive or notebook manufacturer Web site for software to do the job.</li></ul>
Hard disk controller error	<ul><li>Try rebooting.</li><li>Verify the hard drive is recognized correctly in CMOS setup.</li><li>Replace the hard drive.</li><li>Replace the motherboard, but first verify the system works when there is no hard drive installed. Try booting from a CD or floppy disk.</li></ul>
Memory count at POST or available memory under Windows is decreasing	<ul><li>Suspect a faulty memory module. First try reseating the modules and then replace them.</li></ul>
Error reading PC Card	<ul><li>Try reseating the card and rebooting.</li><li>Reinstall the drivers for the PC Card.</li></ul>
Keyboard controller error	<ul><li>Try reseating the internal keyboard cable.</li><li>Try an external keyboard, disabling the internal keyboard.</li><li>Replace the keyboard.</li></ul>
One beep and the LCD panel is blank	<ul><li>Reseat the LCD connectors.</li><li>Replace the LCD panel.</li><li>Replace the motherboard.</li></ul>
Intermittent problems	<ul><li>Intermittent problems might or might not have to do with hardware. Run diagnostic software. If a hardware component fails the diagnostic test, replace it. Then rerun the test.</li><li>Keep detailed records of what happened just before intermittent problems occur. Watch for patterns that might uncover the source of the problem.</li></ul>
Modem is not working	<ul><li>Use diagnostic software to test the modem.</li><li>Reseat the modem connectors.</li></ul>

Table H-4 (Continued)

Error Message	What to Do
	■ Reinstall the modem drivers. ■ Consider using a PC Card modem and disable the internal modem. ■ Replace the modem card. ■ Replace the motherboard.
The system does not detect a PC Card	■ Try a different PC Card. ■ Reinstall the PCMCIA drivers. ■ Consider using a USB port for external devices rather than depending on the PC Card slot. ■ Replace the PCMCIA assembly. ■ Replace the motherboard.
Sound does not work	■ Check speaker volume, both with the OS and the notebook volume controls. ■ Use diagnostic software to test audio. ■ Replace the speaker. ■ Replace the audio card.
Forgotten passwords	■ The power-on password can be reset by entering the supervisor password and then making the change in CMOS setup. ■ If the supervisor password is not set, then reset the power-on password by removing the backup battery to clear CMOS RAM. ■ If the supervisor password or hard drive password is forgotten, you're in for it! Try a data recovery service such as Nortek Computers (*www.nortek.on.ca*).

Table H-4 Error messages and what to do about them

NOTE

Newsgroups can be an interesting source of information when repairing notebooks. Check out the Yahoo newsgroup "laptoprepair" at *groups.yahoo.com/group/Laptop_Repair/*.

Windows XP Service Pack 2

A service pack is an accumulated downloadable assortment of all fixes and patches to an operating system or application. This appendix covers Windows XP Service Pack 2 (SP2). Specifically, you learn about what is included in Service Pack 2, how to use its new features, and how to install it.

Service Pack 2 Fixes and Features

In the Microsoft Knowledge Base Article 811113, Microsoft lists more than 800 articles containing detailed explanations of problems with Windows XP that were fixed with SP2. Most of these fixes involved security problems. The major changes included in SP2 are as follows:

- It provides improved security features, including the ability to block harmful email attachments, spyware, downloads from Web sites, and Internet Explorer pop-up ads. Windows Firewall is improved and automatically applied to an Internet connection. Note that before SP2, Windows Firewall was called Internet Connection Firewall (ICF).
- The new Windows Security Center, accessed from the Control Panel, is designed to conveniently show you how security is applied to your system and makes recommendations for adjustments. You can use this window to configure security settings.
- With SP2, Outlook Express can better protect email addresses and has improved protection from spam and harmful email attachments.
- Automated updates for Windows are now easier to implement.
- Internet Explorer has better control over add-ons.
- With SP2, you now have access to various fixes for the basic operating system functions, wired and wireless networking, Windows setup, and video support.

Using Service Pack 2 Features

Most of the SP2 changes to Windows XP are not visible to the user; they work behind the scenes to plug up security holes and make the OS work better. However, important SP2 features that are visible to the user are the Windows Security Center, Windows Firewall, and several enhancements to Internet Explorer. All these new features are discussed in this section.

Windows Security Center

The addition of Windows Security Center to Windows XP is evidence that security is a huge concern now, more than ever, for Microsoft and its customers. Antivirus software and firewalls that were once considered optional are now considered essential to all computer users who access the Internet.

When you first boot up Windows XP with SP2, the first new thing you notice is the Windows Security Alert icon in the Windows taskbar (see Figure I-1). The balloon from this icon informs you of potential problems with security on your PC. If you click the balloon, the Windows Security Center window appears (see Figure I-2). You can also access this window from the Control Panel (see Figure I-3).

Figure I-1   The Windows Security Alert icon is new to Windows XP Service Pack 2

Figure I-2   The Windows Security Center tracks security settings and features installed on the OS

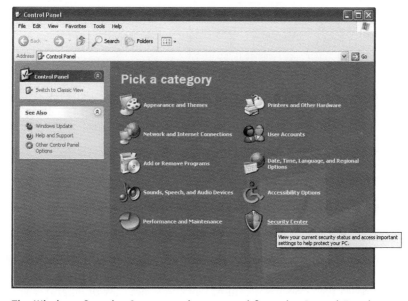

Figure I-3   The Windows Security Center can be accessed from the Control Panel

The Windows Security Center tracks information about Windows Firewall, antivirus software installed and running, and automatic updates for the OS. Notice in Figure I-2 that the user is told the firewall and automatic updates features are set correctly, but antivirus software is not installed. If you click on the Recommendations button, the window in Figure I-4 appears suggesting that you get antivirus software. Click the How? button and you are linked to the Microsoft Web site for advice. This site recommends you install antivirus software from one of the following companies:

- Computer Associates at *www.ca.com*
- F-Secure at *www.fsecure.com*
- McAfee at *www.mcafee.com*
- Panda Software at *www.pandasoftware.com*
- Symantec at *www.symantec.com*
- TrendMicro at *www.trendmicro.com*

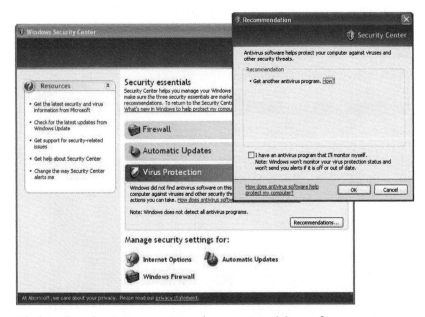

Figure I-4   Windows Security Center recommends you get antivirus software

You can also use the Windows Security Center to adjust settings for Windows automatic updates. To do so, click Automatic Updates (as shown in Figure I-2). The window in Figure I-5 then appears. From it, you can select how often and when to download and install updates to Windows XP. Updates are important for security purposes to fix holes in Windows security as they become known.

Figure I-5   Manage Automatic Updates from the Windows Security Center

Windows Firewall

Recall that before SP2, Internet Connection Firewall was accessed from the Network Connections window by right-clicking on a network icon and selecting Properties from the shortcut tab. You then clicked the Advanced tab, and from the window that appeared, you could turn the firewall on or off and control the type of services allowed to access the system.

With SP2, Internet Connection Firewall is now named Windows Firewall and has several new settings that you can adjust to make the firewall more effective. You can access it from the Network Connections window or the new Windows Security Center. From the Windows Security Center, click Windows Firewall to open the Windows Firewall window (see Figure I-6). You can turn the firewall off and on and control exceptions where remote activity is allowed in.

To control exceptions, you can click the Exceptions tab (see Figure I-7). Exceptions listed are File and Printer Sharing, MSN Messenger 6.2, Remote Assistance, Remote Desktop, and UPnP Framework (Universal Plug-and-Play Framework). (UPnP is a network protocol intended to be used by small wireless devices such as MP3 players to connect wirelessly to a PC.) Allowing these programs access through the firewall solves the problem caused by Internet Connection Firewall blocking normal activity on a local network. In addition, using firewall exceptions also solved the security risk of having to drop the firewall when using Remote Assistance or Remote Desktop.

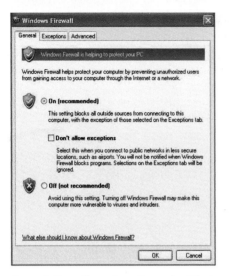

Figure I-6   Control firewall settings from the Windows Firewall window

Figure I-7   Use the Exceptions tab to control what programs and hosts are allowed past the firewall

You can click Add Program to see a list of programs (for example, Internet Hearts) that can also be allowed to communicate with the PC as an exception. Click Add Port to open a port that normally would be blocked by the firewall, and click Edit to control the IP addresses of those computers allowed to use these open ports.

Using these new features of Windows Firewall, you have much more control over who is allowed to communicate with your PC so that it is no longer necessary to entirely drop the firewall in order to allow certain types of communication in.

NOTE   Even with all the new and stronger security features of Windows Firewall, Microsoft still recommends that you use a hardware firewall to protect your system from attack. Software firewalls are better than no firewall at all, but a hardware firewall offers greater protection.

Better Security with Internet Explorer

Several features of SP2 offer better security for Internet Explorer. These features include:

- For convenience, the Internet Options window can be accessed from the Windows Security Center.
- Pop-up windows are often used as a malicious way to tempt you to download spyware and adware. Service Pack 2 Pop-up Blocker is automatically set to block most pop-ups and inform you that it has done so. To change these Pop-up Blocker settings, open Internet Explorer, click Tools, point to Pop-up Blocker, and then click Pop-up Blocker Settings, as shown in Figure I-8. From the Pop-up Blocker Settings window that appears, you can create a list of Web sites that are allowed to present pop-ups and control how Pop-up Blocker informs you when it blocks a pop-up. From the IE Tools menu, you can also temporarily turn off Pop-up Blocker.

File Edit View Favorites	Tools	Help
Mail and News ▶		
Pop-up Blocker ▶	Turn Off Pop-up Blocker	
Manage Add-ons...	Pop-up Blocker Settings...	
Synchronize...		
Windows Update		
Windows Messenger		
Sun Java Console		
Internet Options...		

Figure I-8   Internet Explorer Pop-up Blocker can be turned on or off and you can adjust its settings

NOTE   If pop-ups appear on your desktop even though Pop-up Blocker is turned on, it is possible you have already been infected with spyware or adware. Try cleaning your system using Ad-Aware by Lavasoft (*www.lavasoftusa.com*) or SpyBot Search & Destroy by PepiMK Software (*www.safer-networking.org*).

- Add-ons to Internet Explorer are also controlled from the Tools menu. To see a list of add-ons already installed, click Tools, and then click Manage Add-ons. From the Manage Add-ons window that appears, you can update, disable, and enable add-ons.
- Just below the IE toolbar, the IE Information Bar appears when it needs to display a notice that a Web site has attempted to download a file or install an add-on without your permission. When a message appears in the Information Bar, click on the bar and then IE will ask you what action to take.

Installing Service Pack 2

This section covers how to install Service Pack 2. If you are responsible for a Windows XP computer, keep it current with all updates and service packs as part of your strategy to maintain the highest security level possible. If you purchase Windows XP today, the setup CD contains Windows XP with Service Pack 2, so it is not necessary to install the service pack. If you are using an older version of Windows XP that doesn't have SP2 installed, the only reason you would *not* want to install it is you don't have the resources on your computer to handle it. SP2 requires at least a 233 MHz processor, 64 MB of RAM, and 1.8 GB of free space on the hard drive during the installation.

If you don't have Windows XP SP2 and do have the minimum computer resources, install SP2 using one of these three methods:

- Connect to the Internet and download and install the service pack.
- If you cannot connect to the Internet or have a very slow connection, you can order the service pack on CD free of charge from Microsoft. To do so, go to *update.microsoft.com*, and click the link "What to know before you install Windows XP Service Pack 2." By following this link, you will be given the opportunity to order the CD.
- In a corporate setting, a network administrator installs the service pack from a remote location. How to perform a network installation of a service pack is not covered in this appendix.

Here are the general steps to download and install SP2 when you are connected to the Internet:

1. Using software discussed earlier in the book, scan your system for viruses and remove any unwanted spyware or adware.
2. If you are using a notebook computer or a brand-name desktop computer, check the computer manufacturer Web site. It might offer a customized version of SP2 specific to your computer or give you specific instructions as to how to download and install the service pack from the Microsoft Web site.
3. If you are using a notebook, use the AC adapter for power rather than the battery pack to be sure that power does not fail during the installation.
4. Log off all users to the computer and log yourself on as an Administrator.

5. Back up any important data files on your computer. This is always a good practice before installing new software or service packs. Close all open applications.

6. Using Internet Explorer, go to the Microsoft Web site at *update.micrsoft.com*. (You can also click **Start, All Programs, Windows Update**.) Then click **Express Install (Recommended)**. The Web site scans your computer for needed updates and displays the list.

7. If it lists Service Pack 2 as an available update, then your system is ready for it. If it does not list it, then you need to download and install other updates in preparation for installing SP2. Click **Install**.

8. The download and installation process is automatic (see Figure I-9). It requires some time, so be patient. When finished, it will ask you to restart your computer. Click **Restart now**.

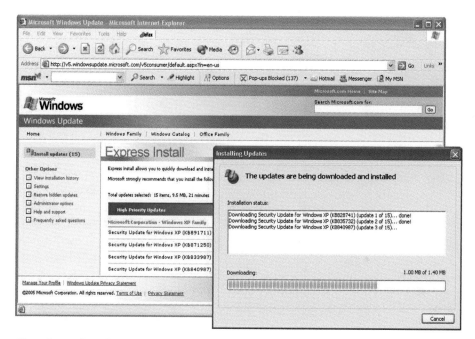

Figure I-9   The Microsoft Web site lists available updates for this computer and automatically downloads and installs them

9. After you reboot, access the Microsoft Web site again. Click **Express Install (Recommended)**. It should now list Service Pack 2 as the single available update. Click **Install**.

10. When the download is completed, the Welcome to Windows XP Service Pack 2 Setup Wizard appears. Click **Next**. The service pack now installs.

11. Restart your computer. Open Control Panel and then open the Windows Security Center applet. Verify that security settings are as you want them to be.

Glossary

This glossary defines the key terms listed at the end of each chapter and other terms related to managing and maintaining a personal computer.

100BaseT — An Ethernet standard that operates at 100 Mbps and uses STP cabling. Also called Fast Ethernet. Variations of 100BaseT are 100BaseTX and 100BaseFX.

10Base2 — An Ethernet standard that operates at 10 Mbps and uses small coaxial cable up to 200 meters long. Also called ThinNet.

10Base5 — An Ethernet standard that operates at 10 Mbps and uses thick coaxial cable up to 500 meters long. Also called ThickNet.

32-bit flat memory mode — A protected processing mode used by Windows NT/2000/XP to process programs written in 32-bit code early in the boot process.

3-D RAM — Special video RAM designed to improve 3-D graphics simulation.

80 conductor IDE cable — An IDE cable that has 40 pins but uses 80 wires, 40 of which are ground wires designed to reduce crosstalk on the cable. The cable is used by ATA/66, ATA/100, and ATA/133 IDE drives.

802.11a/b/g — *See* IEEE 802.11a/b/g.

access point (AP) — A device connected to a LAN that provides wireless communication so that computers, printers, and other wireless devices can communicate with devices on the LAN.

ACPI (Advanced Configuration and Power Interface) — Specification developed by Intel, Compaq, Phoenix, Microsoft, and Toshiba to control power on notebooks and other devices. Windows 98 and Windows 2000/XP support ACPI.

active backplane — A type of backplane system in which there is some circuitry, including bus connectors, buffers, and driver circuits, on the backplane.

Active Directory — A Windows 2000 and Windows 2003 directory database and service that allows for a single point of administration for all shared resources on a network, including files, peripheral devices, databases, Web sites, users, and services.

active matrix — A type of video display that amplifies the signal at every intersection in the grid of electrodes, which enhances the pixel quality over that of a dual-scan passive matrix display.

active partition — The primary partition on the hard drive that boots the OS. Windows NT/2000/XP calls the active partition the system partition.

active terminator — A type of terminator for single-ended SCSI cables that includes voltage regulators in addition to the simple resistors used with passive termination.

adapter address — *See* MAC address.

adapter card — A small circuit board inserted in an expansion slot and used to communicate between the system bus and a peripheral device. Also called an interface card.

administrator account — In Windows NT/ 2000/ XP, an account that grants to the administrator(s) rights and permissions to all hardware and software resources, such as the right to add, delete, and change accounts and to change hardware configurations.

Advanced Options menu — A Windows 2000/XP menu that appears when you press F8 when Windows starts. The menu can be used to troubleshoot problems when loading Windows 2000/XP.

Advanced SCSI Programming Interface (ASPI) — A popular device driver that enables operating systems to communicate with a SCSI host adapter. (The "A" originally stood for Adaptec.)

Advanced Transfer Cache (ATC) — A type of L2 cache contained within the Pentium processor housing that is embedded on the same core processor die as the CPU itself.

AirPort — The term Apple computers use to describe the IEEE 802.11b standard.

alternating current (AC) — Current that cycles back and forth rather than traveling in only one direction. In the United States, the AC voltage from a standard wall outlet is normally between 110 and 115 V. In Europe, the standard AC voltage from a wall outlet is 220 V.

ammeter — A meter that measures electrical current in amps.

ampere or **amp (A)** — A unit of measurement for electrical current. One volt across a resistance of one ohm will produce a flow of one amp.

amplifier repeater — A repeater that does not distinguish between noise and signal; it amplifies both.

ANSI (American National Standards Institute) — A nonprofit organization dedicated to creating trade and communications standards.

answer file — A text file that contains information that Windows NT/2000/XP requires in order to do an unattended installation.

antivirus (AV) software — Utility programs that prevent infection or scan a system to detect and remove viruses. McAfee Associates' VirusScan and Norton AntiVirus are two popular AV packages.

application program interface (API) call — A request from software to the OS to access hardware or other software using a previously defined procedure that both the software and the OS understand.

ARP (Address Resolution Protocol) — A protocol that TCP/IP uses to translate IP addresses into physical network addresses (MAC addresses).

ASCII (American Standard Code for Information Interchange) — A popular standard for writing letters and other characters in binary code. Originally, ASCII characters were seven bits, so there were 127 possible values. ASCII has been expanded to an 8-bit version, allowing 128 additional values.

asynchronous SRAM — Static RAM that does not work in step with the CPU clock and is, therefore, slower than synchronous SRAM.

AT — A form factor, generally no longer produced, in which the motherboard requires a full-size case. Because of their dimensions and configuration, AT systems are difficult to install, service, and upgrade. Also called full AT.

AT command set — A set of commands that a PC uses to control a modem and that a user can enter to troubleshoot the modem.

ATAPI (Advanced Technology Attachment Packet Interface) — An interface standard, part of the IDE/ATA standards, that allows tape drives, CD-ROM drives, and other drives to be treated like an IDE hard drive by the system.

attenuation — Signal degeneration over distance. Attenuation is solved on a network by adding repeaters to the network.

ATX — The most common form factor for PC systems presently in use, originally introduced by Intel in 1995. ATX motherboards and cases make better use of space and resources than did the AT form factor.

audio/modem riser (AMR) — A specification for a small slot on a motherboard to accommodate an audio or modem riser card. A controller on the motherboard contains some of the logic for the audio or modem functionality.

autodetection — A feature on newer system BIOS and hard drives that automatically identifies and configures a new drive in the CMOS setup.

Autoexec.bat — A startup text file once used by DOS and used by Windows to provide backward-compatibility. It executes commands automatically during the boot process and is used to create a16-bit environment.

Automated System Recovery (ASR) — The Windows XP process that allows you to restore an entire hard drive volume or logical drive to its state at the time the backup of the volume was made.

Automatic Private IP Address (APIPA) — An IP address in the address range 169.254.x.x, used by a computer when it cannot successfully lease an IP address from a DHCP server.

autorange meter — A multimeter that senses the quantity of input and sets the range accordingly.

Baby AT — An improved and more flexible version of the AT form factor. Baby AT was the industry standard from approximately 1993 to 1997 and can fit into some ATX cases.

back side bus — The bus between the CPU and the L2 cache inside the CPU housing.

backplane system — A form factor in which there is no true motherboard. Instead, motherboard components are included on an adapter card plugged into a slot on a board called the backplane.

backup — An extra copy of a file, used in the event that the original becomes damaged or destroyed.

backup domain controller (BDC) — In Windows NT, a computer on a network that holds a read-only copy of the SAM (security accounts manager) database.

Backup Operator — A Windows 2000/XP user account that can back up and restore any files on the system regardless of its having access to these files.

bandwidth — In relation to analog communication, the range of frequencies that a communications channel or cable can carry. In general use, the term refers to the volume of data that can travel on a bus or over a cable stated in bits per second (bps), kilobits per second (Kbps), or megabits per second (Mbps). Also called data throughput or line speed.

bank — An area on the motherboard that contains slots for memory modules (typically labeled bank 0, 1, 2, and 3).

baseline — The level of performance expected from a system, which can be compared to current measurements to determine what needs upgrading or tuning.

basic disk — A way to partition a hard drive, used by DOS and all versions of Windows, that stores information about the drive in a partition table at the beginning of the drive. Compare to dynamic disk.

batch file — A text file containing a series of OS commands. Autoexec.bat is a batch file.

baud rate — A measure of line speed between two devices such as a computer and a printer or a modem. This speed is measured in the number of times a signal changes in one second. *See also* bits per second (bps).

beam detect mirror — Detects the initial presence of a laser printer's laser beam by reflecting the beam to an optical fiber.

best-effort protocol — *See* connectionless protocol.

binary number system — The number system used by computers; it has only two numbers, 0 and 1, called binary digits, or bits.

binding — The process by which a protocol is associated with a network card or a modem card.

BIOS (basic input/output system) — Firmware that can control much of a computer's input/ output functions, such as communication with the floppy drive and the monitor. Also called ROM BIOS.

bit (binary digit) — A0or1used by the binary number system.

bits per second (bps) — A measure of data transmission speed. For example, a common modem speed is 56,000 bps, or 56 Kbps.

block mode — A method of data transfer between hard drive and memory that allows multiple data transfers on a single software interrupt.

blue screen — A Windows NT/2000/XP error that displays against a blue screen and causes the system to halt. Also called a stop error.

Bluetooth — A standard for wireless communication and data synchronization between devices, developed by a group of electronics manufacturers and overseen by the Bluetooth Special Interest Group.

Bluetooth uses the same frequency range as 802.11b, but does not have as wide a range.

BNC connector — A connector used with thin coaxial cable. Some BNC connectors are T-shaped and called T-connectors. One end of the T connects to the NIC, and the two other ends can connect to cables or end a bus formation with a terminator.

boot loader menu — A startup menu that gives the user the choice of which operating system to load such as Windows 98 or Windows XP which are both installed on the same system, creating a dual boot.

boot partition — The hard drive partition where the Windows NT/2000/XP OS is stored. The system partition and the boot partition may be different partitions.

boot record — The first sector of a floppy disk or logical drive in a partition; it contains information about the disk or logical drive. On a hard drive, if the boot record is in the active partition, then it is used to boot the OS. Also called boot sector.

boot sector — *See* boot record.

boot sector virus — An infectious program that can replace the boot program with a modified, infected version of the boot command utilities, often causing boot and data retrieval problems.

Boot.ini — A Windows NT/2000/XP hidden text file that contains information needed to build the boot loader menu.

bootable disk — For DOS and Windows, a floppy disk that can upload the OS files necessary for computer startup. For DOS or Windows 9x/Me, it must contain the files Io.sys, Msdos.sys, and Command.com.

bootstrap loader — A small program at the end of the boot record that can be used to boot an OS from the disk or logical drive.

bridge — A device used to connect two or more network segments. It can make decisions about allowing a packet to pass based on the packet's destination MAC address.

bridging protocol — *See* line protocol.

Briefcase — A system folder in Windows 9x/Me that is used to synchronize files between two computers.

broadband — A transmission technique that carries more than one type of transmission on the same medium, such as cable modem or DSL.

broadcast — Process by which a message is sent from a single host to all hosts on the network, without regard to the kind of data being sent or the destination of the data.

brouter — A device that functions as both a bridge and a router. A brouter acts as a router when handling packets using routable protocols such as TCP/IP and IPX/SPX. It acts as a bridge when handling packets using nonroutable protocols such as NetBEUI.

brownouts — Temporary reductions in voltage, which can sometimes cause data loss. *Also called* sags.

BTX (Balanced Technology Extended) — The latest form factor expected to replace ATX. It has higher quality fans, is designed for better air flow, and has improved structural support for the motherboard.

buffer — A temporary memory area where data is kept before being written to a hard drive or sent to a printer, thus reducing the number of writes to the devices.

built-in user account — An administrator account and a guest account that are set up when Windows NT/2000/XP is first installed.

burst EDO (BEDO) — A refined version of EDO memory that significantly improved access time over EDO. BEDO was not widely used because Intel chose not to support it. BEDO memory is stored on 168-pin DIMM modules.

burst SRAM — Memory that is more expensive and slightly faster than pipelined burst SRAM. Data is sent in a two-step process; the data address is sent, and then the data itself is sent without interruption.

bus — The paths, or lines, on the motherboard on which data, instructions, and electrical power move from component to component.

bus mouse — A mouse that plugs into a bus adapter card and has a round, 9-pin mini-DIN connector.

bus riser — *See* riser card.

bus speed — The speed, or frequency, at which the data on the motherboard is moving.

bus topology — A LAN architecture in which all the devices are connected to a bus, or one communication line. Bus topology does not have a central connection point.

byte — A collection of eight bits that is equivalent to a single character. When referring to system memory, an additional error-checking bit might be added, making the total nine bits.

cabinet file — A file with a .cab extension that contains one or more compressed files and is often used to distribute software on disk. The Extract command is used to extract files from the cabinet file.

cable modem — A technology that uses cable TV lines for data transmission requiring a modem at each end. From the modem, a network cable connects to a NIC in the user's PC.

CAM (Common Access Method) — A standard adapter driver used by SCSI.

capacitor — An electronic device that can maintain an electrical charge for a period of time and is used to smooth out the flow of electrical current. Capacitors are often found in computer power supplies.

CardBus — The latest PCMCIA specification. It improves I/O speed, increases the bus width to 32 bits, and supports lower-voltage PC Cards, while maintaining backward compatibility with earlier standards.

cards — Adapter boards or interface cards placed into expansion slots to expand the functions of a computer, allowing it to communicate with external devices such as monitors or speakers.

carrier — A signal used to activate a phone line to confirm a continuous frequency; used to indicate that two computers are ready to receive or transmit data via modems.

CAS Latency (CL) — A feature of memory that reflects the number of clock cycles that pass while data is written to memory.

CAU (Controlled-Access Unit) — *See* MAU.

CCITT (Comité Consultatif International Télégraphique et Téléphonique) — An international organization that was responsible for developing standards for international communications. This organization has been incorporated into the ITU. *See also* ITU.

CD (change directory) command — A command given at the command prompt that changes the default directory, for example CD \Windows.

CDFS (Compact Disc File System) — The 32-bit file system for CD discs and some CD-R and CD-RW discs that replaced the older 16-bit mscdex file system used by DOS. *See also* Universal Disk Format (UDF).

CD-R (CD-recordable) — A CD drive that can record or write data to a CD. The drive may or may not be multisession, but the data cannot be erased once it is written.

CD-RW (CD-rewritable) — A CD drive that can record or write data to a CD. The data can be erased and overwritten. The drive may or may not be multisession.

central processing unit (CPU) — Also called a microprocessor or processor. The heart and brain of the computer, which receives data input, processes information, and executes instructions.

chain — A group of clusters used to hold a single file.

checksum — A method of error checking transmitted data, whereby the digits are added and their sum compared to an expected sum.

child directory — *See* subdirectory.

child, parent, grandparent backup method — A plan for backing up and reusing tapes or removable disks by rotating them each day (child), week (parent), and month (grandparent).

chip creep — A condition in which chips loosen because of thermal changes.

chip set — A group of chips on the motherboard that controls the timing and flow of data and instructions to and from the CPU.

CHS (cylinder, head, sector) mode — The traditional method by which BIOS reads from and writes to hard drives by addressing the correct cylinder, head, and sector. Also called normal mode.

circuit board — A computer component, such as the main motherboard or an adapter board, that has electronic circuits and chips.

CISC (complex instruction set computing) — Earlier CPU type of instruction set.

clamping voltage — The maximum voltage allowed through a surge suppressor, such as 175 or 330 volts.

clean install — Installing an OS on a new hard drive or on a hard drive that has a previous OS installed, but without carrying forward any settings kept by the old OS, including information about hardware, software, or user preferences. A fresh installation.

client/server — A computer concept whereby one computer (the client) requests information from another computer (the server).

client/server application — An application that has two components. The client software requests data from the server software on the same or another computer.

clock speed — The speed, or frequency, expressed in MHz, that controls activity on the motherboard and is generated by a crystal or oscillator located somewhere on the motherboard.

clone — A computer that is a no-name Intel- and Microsoft-compatible PC.

cluster — One or more sectors that constitute the smallest unit of space on a disk for storing data (also referred to as a file allocation unit). Files are written to a disk as groups of whole clusters.

CMOS (complementary metal-oxide semiconductor) — The technology used to manufacture microchips. CMOS chips require less electricity, hold data longer after the electricity is turned off, are slower, and produce less heat than earlier technologies. The configuration, or setup, chip is a CMOS chip.

CMOS configuration chip — A chip on the motherboard that contains a very small amount of memory, or RAM — enough to hold configuration, or setup, information about the computer The chip is powered by a battery when the PC is turned off. Also called CMOS setup chip or CMOS RAM chip.

CMOS setup — (1) The CMOS configuration chip. (2) The program in system BIOS that can change the values in the CMOS RAM.

CMOS setup chip — *See* CMOS configuration chip.

COAST (cache on a stick) — Memory modules that hold memory used as a memory cache. *See* memory cache.

coaxial cable — Networking cable used with10-Mbps Ethernet ThinNet or ThickNet.

cold boot — *See* hard boot.

combo card — An Ethernet card that contains more than one transceiver, each with a different port on the back of the card, in order to accommodate different cabling media.

Command.com — Along with Msdos.sys and Io.sys, one of the three files that are the core components of the real-mode portion of Windows 9x/Me. Command.com provides a command prompt and interprets commands.

comment — A line or part of a line in a program that is intended as a remark or comment and is ignored when the program runs. A semicolon or an REM is often used to mark a line as a comment.

communication and networking riser (CNR) — A specification for a small expansion slot on a motherboard that accommodates a small audio, modem, or network riser card.

compact case — A type of case used in low-end desktop systems. Compact cases, also called low-profile or slimline cases, follow either the NLX, LPX, or Mini LPX form factor. They are likely to have fewer drive bays, but they generally still provide for some expansion.

Compatibility Mode utility — A Windows XP utility that provides an application with the older Microsoft OS environment it was designed to operate in.

compressed drive — A drive whose format has been reorganized in order to store more data. A compressed drive is really not a drive at all; it's actually a type of file, typically with a host drive called H.

computer name — Character-based host name or NetBIOS name assigned to a computer.

Config.sys — A text file used by DOS and supported by Windows 9x/Me that lists device drivers to be loaded at startup. It can also set system variables to be used by DOS and Windows.

Configuration Manager — A component of Windows Plug and Play that controls the configuration process of all devices and communicates these configurations to the devices.

connectionless protocol — A protocol such as UDP that does not require a connection before sending a packet and does not guarantee delivery. An example of a UDP transmission is streaming video over the Web. Also called a best-effort protocol.

connection-oriented protocol — In networking, a protocol that confirms that a good connection has been made before transmitting data to the other end. An example of a connection-oriented protocol is TCP.

console — A centralized location from which to execute commonly used tools.

constant angular velocity (CAV) — A technology used by hard drives and newer CD-ROM drives whereby the disk rotates at a constant speed.

constant linear velocity (CLV) — A CD-ROM format in which the spacing of data is consistent on the CD, but the speed of the disc varies depending on whether the data being read near the center or the edge of the disc.

continuity — A continuous, unbroken path for the flow of electricity. A continuity test can determine whether or not internal wiring is still intact, or whether a fuse is good or bad.

control blade — A laser printer component that prevents too much toner from sticking to the cylinder surface.

conventional memory — Memory addresses between 0 and 640K. Also called base memory.

cooler — A combination cooling fan and heat sink mounted on the top or side of a processor to keep it cool.

CRC (cyclical redundancy check) — A process in which calculations are performed on bytes of data before and after they are transmitted to check for corruption during transmission.

credit card memory — A type of memory used on older notebooks that could upgrade existing memory by way of a specialized memory slot.

C-RIMM (Continuity RIMM) — A placeholder RIMM module that provides continuity so that every RIMM slot is filled.

cross-linked clusters — Errors caused when more than one file points to a cluster, and the files appear to share the same disk space, according to the file allocation table.

crossover cable — A cable used to connect two PCs into the simplest network possible. Also used to connect two hubs.

CVF (compressed volume file) — The file on the host drive of a compressed drive that holds all compressed data.

data bus — The lines on the system bus that the CPU uses to send and receive data.

data cartridge — A type of tape medium typically used for backups. Full-sized data cartridges are 4 × 6 2⅝ inches in size. A minicartridge is only 3¼ × 2½ 2⅝ inches in size.

data line protector — A surge protector designed to work with the telephone line to a modem.

data path size — The number of lines on a bus that can hold data, for example, 8, 16, 32, and 64 lines, which can accommodate 8, 16, 32, and 64 bits at a time.

data throughput — *See* bandwidth.

datagram — *See* packet.

DC controller — A card inside a notebook that converts voltage to CPU voltage. Some notebook manufacturers consider the card to be an FRU.

DCE (Data Communications Equipment) — The hardware, usually a dial-up modem, that provides the connection between a data terminal and a communications line. *See also* DTE.

DDR SDRAM — *See* Double Data Rate SDRAM.

DDR2 SDRAM — A version of SDRAM that is faster than DDR and uses less power.

default gateway — The gateway a computer on a network will use to access another network unless it knows to specifically use another gateway for quicker access to that network.

default printer — The printer Windows prints to unless another printer is selected.

defragment — To "optimize" or rewrite a file to a disk in one contiguous chain of clusters, thus speeding up data retrieval.

demodulation — The process by which digital data that has been converted to analog data is converted back to digital data. *See* modulation.

desktop — The initial screen that is displayed when an OS has a GUI interface loaded.

device driver — A program stored on the hard drive that tells the computer how to communicate with an input/output device such as a printer or modem.

DHCP (Dynamic Host Configuration Protocol) server — A service that assigns dynamic IP addresses to computers on a network when they first access the network.

diagnostic cards — Adapter cards designed to discover and report computer errors and conflicts at POST time (before the computer boots up), often by displaying a number on the card.

diagnostic software — Utility programs that help troubleshoot computer systems. Some Windows diagnostic utilities are CHKDSK and SCANDISK. PC-Technician is an example of a third-party diagnostic program.

dial-up networking — A Windows 9x/Me and Windows NT/2000/XP utility that uses a modem and telephone line to connect to a network.

differential backup — Backup method that backs up only files that have changed or have been created since the last full backup. When recovering data, only two backups are needed: the full backup and the last differential backup.

differential cable — A SCSI cable in which a signal is carried on two wires, each carrying voltage, and the signal is the difference between the two. Differential signaling provides for error checking and greater data integrity. Compare to single-ended cable.

digital certificate — A code used to authenticate the source of a file or document or to identify and authenticate a person or organization sending data over the Internet. The code is assigned by a certificate authority such as VeriSign and includes a public key for encryption. Also called *digital ID* or *digital signature*.

digital ID — *See* digital certificate.

digital signature — *See* digital certificate.

DIMM (dual inline memory module) — A miniature circuit board used in newer computers to hold memory. DIMMs can hold up to 2 GB of RAM on a single module.

diode — An electronic device that allows electricity to flow in only one direction. Used in a rectifier circuit.

DIP (dual inline package) switch — A switch on a circuit board or other device that can be set on or off to hold configuration or setup information.

direct current (DC) — Current that travels in only one direction (the type of electricity provided by batteries). Computer power supplies transform AC to low DC.

Direct Rambus DRAM — A memory technology by Rambus and Intel that uses a narrow, very fast network-type system bus. Memory is stored on a RIMM module. Also called RDRAM or Direct RDRAM.

Direct RDRAM — *See* Direct Rambus DRAM.

directory table — An OS table that contains file information such as the name, size, time and date of last modification, and cluster number of the file's beginning location.

discrete L2 cache — A type of L2 cache contained within the Pentium processor housing, but on a different die, with a cache bus between the processor and the cache.

disk cache — A method whereby recently retrieved data and adjacent data are read into memory in advance, anticipating the next CPU request.

disk cloning — *See* drive imaging.

disk compression — Compressing data on a hard drive to allow more data to be written to the drive.

disk imaging — *See* drive imaging.

Disk Management — A Windows 2000/XP utility used to display, create, and format partitions on basic disks and volumes on dynamic disks.

disk quota — A limit placed on the amount of disk space that is available to users. Requires a Windows 2000/XP NTFS volume.

disk thrashing — A condition that results when the hard drive is excessively used for virtual memory because RAM is full. It dramatically slows down processing and can cause premature hard drive failure.

Display Power Management Signaling (DPMS) — Energy Star standard specifications that allow for the video card and monitor to go into sleep mode simultaneously. *See also* Energy Star.

distribution server — A file server holding Windows setup files used to install Windows on computers networked to the server.

DMA (direct memory access) channel — A number identifying a channel whereby a device can pass data to memory without involving the CPU. Think of a DMA channel as a shortcut for data moving to/from the device and memory.

DMA transfer mode — A transfer mode used by devices, including the hard drive, to transfer data to memory without involving the CPU.

DNS (domain name service or **domain name system)** — A distributed pool of information (called the name space) that keeps track of assigned domain names and their corresponding IP addresses, and the system that allows a host to locate information in the pool. Compare to WINS.

DNS server — A computer that can find an IP address for another computer when only the domain name is known.

docking station — A device that receives a notebook computer and provides additional secondary storage and easy connection to peripheral devices.

domain — In Windows NT/2000/XP, a logical group of networked computers, such as those on a college campus, that share a centralized directory database of user account information and security for the entire domain.

domain controller — A Windows NT/2000 computer which holds and controls a database of (1) user accounts, (2) group accounts, and (3) computer accounts used to manage access to the network.

domain name — A unique, text-based name that identifies a network.

DOS box — A command window.

Dosstart.bat — A type of Autoexec.bat file that is executed by Windows 9x/Me in two situations: when you select Restart the computer in MS-DOS mode from the shutdown menu or you run a program in MS-DOS mode.

dot pitch — The distance between the dots that the electronic beam hits on a monitor screen.

Double Data Rate SDRAM (DDR SDRAM) — A type of memory technology used on DIMMs that runs at twice the speed of the system clock.

doze time — The time before an Energy Star or "Green" system will reduce 80 percent of its activity.

Dr. Watson — A Windows utility that can record detailed information about the system, errors that occur, and the programs that caused them in a log file. Windows 9x/Me names the log file \Windows\Drwatson\WatsonXX.wlg, where XX is an incrementing number. Windows 2000 names the file \Documents and Settings\user\Documents\DrWatson\Drwtsn32.log. Windows XP calls the file Drwatson.log.

drive imaging — Making an exact image of a hard drive, including partition information, boot sectors, operating system installation, and application software to replicate the hard drive on another system or recover from a hard drive crash. Also called *disk cloning* and *disk imaging*.

DriveSpace — A Windows 9x/Me utility that compresses files so that they take up less space on a disk drive, creating a single large file on the disk to hold all the compressed files.

drop height — The height from which a manufacturer states that its drive can be dropped without making the drive unusable.

DSL (Digital Subscriber Line) — A telephone line that carries digital data from end to end, and can be leased from the telephone company for individual use. DSL lines are rated at 5 Mbps, about 50 times faster than regular telephone lines.

DTE (Data Terminal Equipment) — Both the computer and a remote terminal or other computer to which it is attached. *See also* DCE.

dual boot — The ability to boot using either of two different OSs, such as Windows 98 and Windows XP.

dual channel — A motherboard feature that improves memory performance by providing two 64-bit channels between memory and the chipset. DDR and DDR2 memory can use dual channels.

dual-scan passive matrix — A type of video display that is less expensive than an active-matrix display and does not provide as high-quality an image. With dual-scan display, two columns of electrodes are activated at the same time.

dual-voltage CPU — A CPU that requires two different voltages, one for internal processing and the other for I/O processing.

dump file — A file that contains information captured from memory at the time a stop error occurred.

DVD (digital video disc or digital versatile disk) — A faster, larger CD format that can read older CDs, store over 8 GB of data, and hold full-length motion picture videos.

dye-sublimation printer — A type of printer with photo-lab-quality results that uses transparent dyed film. The film is heated, which causes the dye to vaporize onto glossy paper.

dynamic disk — A way to partition one or more hard drives, introduced with Windows 2000, in which information about the drive is stored in a database at the end of the drive. Compare to basic disk.

dynamic IP address — An assigned IP address that is used for the current session only. When the session is terminated, the IP address is returned to the list of available addresses.

dynamic RAM (DRAM) — The most common type of system memory, it requires refreshing every few milliseconds.

dynamic volume — A volume type used with dynamic disks for which you can change the size of the volume after you have created it.

dynamic VxD — A VxD that is loaded and unloaded from memory as needed.

ECC (error-correcting code) — A chip set feature on a motherboard that checks the integrity of data stored on DIMMs or RIMMs and can correct single-bit errors in a byte. More advanced ECC

schemas can detect, but not correct, double-bit errors in a byte.

ECHS (extended CHS) mode — *See* large mode.

ECP (Extended Capabilities Port) — A bidirectional parallel port mode that uses a DMA channel to speed up data flow.

EDO (extended data out) — A type of RAM that may be 10–20 percent faster than conventional RAM because it eliminates the delay before it issues the next memory address.

EEPROM (electrically erasable programmable ROM) — A type of chip in which higher voltage may be applied to one of the pins to erase its previous memory before a new instruction set is electronically written.

EIDE (Enhanced IDE) — A standard for managing the interface between secondary storage devices and a computer system. A system can support up to six serial ATA and parallel ATA IDE devices or up to four parallel ATA IDE devices such as hard drives, CD-ROM drives, and Zip drives.

electromagnetic interference (EMI) — A magnetic field produced as a side effect from the flow of electricity. EMI can cause corrupted data in data lines that are not properly shielded.

electrostatic discharge (ESD) — Another name for static electricity, which can damage chips and destroy motherboards, even though it might not be felt or seen with the naked eye.

Emergency Repair Disk (ERD) — A Windows NT record of critical information about your system that can be used to fix a problem with the OS. The ERD enables restoration of the Windows NT registry on your hard drive.

Emergency Repair Process — A Windows 2000 process that restores the OS to its state at the completion of a successful installation.

emergency startup disk (ESD) — *See* rescue disk.

Emm386.exe — A DOS and Windows 9x/Me utility that provides access to upper memory for 16-bit device drivers and other software.

Encrypted File System (EFS) — A way to use a key to encode a file or folder on an NTFS volume to protect sensitive data. Because it is an integrated system service, EFS is transparent to users and applications and is difficult to attack.

encrypting virus — A type of virus that transforms itself into a nonreplicating program in order to avoid detection. It transforms itself back into a replicating program in order to spread.

encryption — The process of putting readable data into an encoded form that can only be decoded (or decrypted) through use of a key.

Energy Star — "Green" systems that satisfy the EPA requirements to decrease the overall consumption of electricity. *See also* Green Standards.

enhanced BIOS — A system BIOS that has been written to accommodate large-capacity drives (over 504 MB, usually in the gigabyte range).

EPIC (explicitly parallel instruction computing) — The CPU architecture used by the Intel Itanium chip that bundles programming instructions with instructions on how to use multiprocessing abilities to do two instructions in parallel.

EPP (Enhanced Parallel Port) — A parallel port that allows data to flow in both directions (bidirectional port) and is faster than original parallel ports on PCs that allowed communication only in one direction.

EPROM (erasable programmable ROM) — A type of chip with a special window that allows the current memory contents to be erased with special ultraviolet light so that the chip can be reprogrammed. Many BIOS chips are EPROMs.

error correction — The ability of a modem to identify transmission errors and then automatically request another transmission.

Ethernet — The most popular LAN architecture that can run at 10 Mbps (ThinNet or ThickNet), 100 Mbps (Fast Ethernet), or 1 Gbps (Gigabit Ethernet).

Execution Trace Cache — A type of Level 1 cache used by some CPUs to hold decoded operations waiting to be executed.

executive services — In Windows NT/2000/XP, a group of components running in kernel mode that interfaces between the subsystems in user mode and the HAL.

expansion bus — A bus that does not run in sync with the system clock.

expansion card — A circuit board inserted into a slot on the motherboard to enhance the capability of the computer.

expansion slot — A narrow slot on the motherboard where an expansion card can be inserted. Expansion slots connect to a bus on the motherboard.

extended memory — Memory above 1024K used in a DOS or Windows 9x/Me system.

extended partition — The only partition on a hard drive that can contain more than one logical drive.

external cache — Static cache memory, stored on the motherboard or inside the CPU housing, that is not part of the CPU (also called L2 or L3 cache).

external command — Commands that have their own program files.

faceplate — A metal plate that comes with the motherboard and fits over the ports to create a well-fitted enclosure around them.

Fast Ethernet — *See* 100BaseT.

FAT (file allocation table) — A table on a hard drive or floppy disk that tracks the clusters used to contain a file.

FAT12 — The 12-bit wide, one-column file allocation table for a floppy disk, containing information about how each cluster or file allocation unit on the disk is currently used.

fault tolerance — The degree to which a system can tolerate failures. Adding redundant components, such as disk mirroring or disk duplexing, is a way to build in fault tolerance.

Fiber Distributed Data Interface (FDDI) — A ring-based network that does not require a centralized hub and can transfer data at a rate of 100 Mbps.

field replaceable unit (FRU) — A component in a computer or device that can be replaced with a new component without sending the computer or device back to the manufacturer. Examples: power supply, DIMM, motherboard, floppy disk drive.

file allocation unit — *See* cluster.

file extension — A three-character portion of the name of a file that is used to identify the file type. In command lines, the file extension follows the filename and is separated from it by a period. For example, Msd.exe, where exe is the file extension.

file system — The overall structure that an OS uses to name, store, and organize files on a disk. Examples of file systems are FAT32 and NTFS.

file virus — A virus that inserts virus code into an executable program file and can spread whenever that program is executed.

filename — The first part of the name assigned to a file. In DOS, the filename can be no more than eight characters long and is followed by the file extension. In Windows, a filename can be up to 255 characters.

firewall — Hardware or software that protects a computer or network from unauthorized access.

FireWire — See IEEE 1394.

firmware — Software that is permanently stored in a chip. The BIOS on a motherboard is an example of firmware.

flash ROM — ROM that can be reprogrammed or changed without replacing chips.

flat panel monitor — A desktop monitor that uses an LCD panel.

FlexATX — A version of the ATX form factor that allows for maximum flexibility in the size and shape of cases and motherboards. FlexATX is ideal for custom systems.

flow control — When using modems, a method of controlling the flow of data to adjust for problems with data transmission. Xon/Xoff is an example of a flow control protocol.

folder — See subdirectory.

folder redirection — A Windows XP feature that allows a user to point to a folder that can be on the local PC or somewhere on the network, and its location can be transparent to the user.

forced perfect terminator (FPT) — A type of SCSI active terminator that includes a mechanism to force signal termination to the correct voltage, eliminating most signal echoes and interference.

forgotten password floppy disk — A Windows XP disk created to be used in the event the user forgets the user account password to the system.

form factor — A set of specifications on the size, shape, and configuration of a computer hardware component such as a case, power supply, or motherboard.

formatting — Preparing a hard drive volume or floppy disk for use by placing tracks and sectors on its surface to store information (for example, FORMAT A:).

FPM (fast page mode) — A memory mode used before the introduction of EDO memory. FPM improved on earlier memory types by sending the row address just once for many accesses to memory near that row.

fragmentation — The distribution of data files on a hard drive or floppy disk such that they are stored in noncontiguous clusters.

fragmented file — A file that has been written to different portions of the disk so that it is not in contiguous clusters.

frame — The header and trailer information added to data to form a data packet to be sent over a network.

front-side bus (FSB) — See system bus.

FTP (File Transfer Protocol) — The protocol used to transfer files over a TCP/IP network such that the file does not need to be converted to ASCII format before transferring it.

full AT — See AT.

full backup — A complete backup, whereby all of the files on the hard drive are backed up each time the backup procedure is performed. It is the safest backup method, but it takes the most time.

full-duplex — Communication that happens in two directions at the same time.

fully qualified domain name (FQDN) — A host name and a domain name such as jsmith.amazon.com. Sometimes loosely referred to as a domain name.

gateway — A computer or other device that connects networks.

GDI (Graphics Device Interface) — A Windows 9x/Me component that controls screens, graphics, and printing.

General Protection Fault (GPF) — A Windows error that occurs when a program attempts to access a memory address that is not available or is no longer assigned to it.

Gigabit Ethernet — The newest version of Ethernet. Gigabit Ethernet supports rates of data transfer up to 1 gigabit per second but is not yet widely used.

gigahertz (GHz) — One thousand MHz, or one billion cycles per second.

global user account — Sometimes called a domain user account, the account is used at the domain level, created by an administrator, and stored in the SAM (security accounts manager) database on a Windows 2000 or Windows 2003 domain controller.

graphics accelerator — A type of video card that has an on-board processor that can substantially increase speed and boost graphical and video performance.

graphics DDR (G-DDR), graphics DDR2, graphics DDR3 — Types of DDR, DDR2, and DDR3 memory specifically designed to be used in graphics cards.

Green Standards — A computer or device that conforms to these standards can go into sleep or doze mode when not in use, thus saving energy and helping the environment. Devices that carry the Green Star or Energy Star comply with these standards.

ground bracelet — A strap you wear around your wrist that is attached to the computer case, ground mat, or another ground so that ESD is discharged from your body before you touch sensitive components inside a computer. Also called static strap, ground strap, ESD bracelet.

group profile — A group of user profiles. All profiles in the group can be changed by changing the group profile.

guard tone — A tone that an answering modem sends when it first answers the phone, to tell the calling modem that a modem is on the other end of the line.

Guest user — A user who has limited permissions on a system and cannot make changes to it. Guest user accounts are intended for one-time or infrequent users of a workstation.

HAL (hardware abstraction layer) — The low-level part of Windows NT/2000/XP, written specifically for each CPU technology, so that only the HAL must change when platform components change.

half life — The time it takes for a medium storing data to weaken to half of its strength. Magnetic media, including traditional hard drives and floppy disks, have a half-life of five to seven years.

half-duplex — Communication between two devices whereby transmission takes place in only one direction at a time.

handshaking — When two modems begin to communicate, the initial agreement made as to how to send and receive data.

hard boot — Restart the computer by turning off the power or by pressing the Reset button. Also called a cold boot.

hard copy — Output from a printer to paper.

hard drive — The main secondary storage device of a PC, a small case that contains magnetic coated platters that rotate at high speed.

hard drive controller — The firmware that controls access to a hard drive contained on a circuit board mounted on or inside the hard drive housing. Older hard drives used firmware on a controller card that connected to the drive by way of two cables, one for data and one for control.

hard drive standby time — The amount of time before a hard drive will shut down to conserve energy.

hard-disk loading — The illegal practice of installing unauthorized software on computers for sale. Hard-disk loading can typically be identified by the absence of original software disks in the original system's shipment.

hardware — The physical components that constitute the computer system, such as the monitor, the keyboard, the motherboard, and the printer.

hardware address — *See* MAC address.

hardware cache — A disk cache that is contained in RAM chips built right on the disk controller. Also called a buffer.

hardware interrupt — An event caused by a hardware device signaling the CPU that it requires service.

hardware profile — A set of hardware configuration information that Windows keeps in the registry. Windows can maintain more than one hardware profile for the same PC.

HCL (hardware compatibility list) — The list of all computers and peripheral devices that have been tested and are officially supported by Windows NT/2000/XP (see *www.microsoft.com/whdc/hcl/default.mspx*).

head — The top or bottom surface of one platter on a hard drive. Each platter has two heads.

heat sink — A piece of metal, with cooling fins, that can be attached to or mounted on an integrated chip (such as the CPU) to dissipate heat.

hertz (Hz) — Unit of measurement for frequency, calculated in terms of vibrations, or cycles per second. For example, for 16-bit stereo sound, a frequency of 44,000 Hz is used. *See also* megahertz.

hexadecimal notation (hex) — A numbering system that uses 16 digits, the numerals 0–9, and the letters A–F. Hexadecimal notation is often used to display memory addresses.

hibernation — A notebook OS feature that conserves power by using a small trickle of electricity. Before the notebook begins to hibernate, everything currently stored in memory is saved to the hard drive. When the notebook is brought out of hibernation, open applications and their data are returned to the state before hibernation.

hidden file — A file that is not displayed in a directory list. Whether to hide or display a file is one of the file's attributes kept by the OS.

high memory area (HMA) — The first 64K of extended memory.

High Voltage Differential (HVD) — A type of SCSI differential signaling requiring more expensive hardware to handle the higher voltage. HVD became obsolete with the introduction of SCSI-3.

high-level formatting — Formatting performed by means of the DOS or Windows Format program (for example, FORMAT C:/S creates the boot record, FAT, and root directory on drive C and makes the drive bootable). Also called OS formatting.

Himem.sys — The DOS and Windows 9x/Me memory manager extension that allowed access to memory addresses above 1 MB.

hive — Physical segment of the Windows NT/ 2000/ XP registry that is stored in a file.

hop count — *See* time to live (TTL).

host — Any computer or other device on a network that has been assigned an IP address. Also called node.

host adapter — The circuit board that controls a SCSI bus supporting as many as seven or fifteen separate devices. The host adapter controls communication between the SCSI bus and the PC.

host bus — *See* memory bus or system bus.

host drive — Typically drive H on a compressed drive. *See* compressed drive.

host name — A name that identifies a computer, printer, or other device on a network.

hot-pluggable — *See* hot-swappable.

hot-swappable — A device that can be plugged into a computer while it is turned on and the computer will sense the device and configure it without rebooting, or the device can be removed without an OS error. Also called hot-pluggable.

HTML (HyperText Markup Language) — A markup language used for hypertext documents on the World Wide Web. This language uses tags to format the document, create hyperlinks, and mark locations for graphics.

HTTP (HyperText Transfer Protocol) — The protocol used by the World Wide Web.

HTTPS (HTTP secure) — A version of the HTTP protocol that includes data encryption for security.

hub — A network device or box that provides a central location to connect cables.

hypertext — Text that contains links to remote points in the document or to other files, documents, or graphics. Hypertext is created using HTML and is commonly distributed from Web sites.

i.Link — *See* IEEE 1394.

IBM Data Connector – *See* IDC.

IDC (IBM Data Connector) — A connector used with STP cable on a Token Ring network. Also called a *UDC (Universal Data Connector)*.

I/O addresses — Numbers that are used by devices and the CPU to manage communication between them. Also called ports or port addresses.

I/O controller card — An older card that can contain serial, parallel, and game ports and floppy drive and IDE connectors.

IBM-compatible PC — A computer that uses an Intel (or compatible) processor and can run DOS and Windows.

ICMP (Internet Control Message Protocol) — Part of the IP layer that is used to transmit error messages and other control messages to hosts and routers.

IDE (Integrated Drive Electronics or Integrated Device Electronics) — A hard drive whose disk controller is integrated into the drive, eliminating the need for a controller cable and thus increasing speed, as well as reducing price. *See also* EIDE.

IEEE 1284 — A standard for parallel ports and cables developed by the Institute for Electrical and Electronics Engineers and supported by many hardware manufacturers.

IEEE 1394 — Standards for an expansion bus that can also be configured to work as a local bus. It is expected to replace the SCSI bus, providing an easy method to install and configure fast I/O devices. Also called FireWire and i.Link.

IEEE 1394.3 — A standard, developed by the 1394 Trade Association, that is designed for peer-to-peer data transmission and allows imaging devices to send images and photos directly to printers without involving a computer.

IEEE 802.11a/b/g — IEEE specifications for wireless communication and data synchronization. Also known as Wi-Fi. Apple Computer's versions of 802.11b/g are called AirPort and AirPort Extreme.

IMAP4 (Internet Message Access Protocol version 4) — Version 4 of the IMAP protocol, which is an e-mail protocol that has more functionality than its predecessor, POP. IMAP can archive messages in folders on the e-mail server and can allow the user to choose not to download attachments to messages.

incremental backup — A time-saving backup method that only backs up files changed or newly created since the last full or incremental backup. Multiple incremental backups might be required when recovering lost data.

infestation — Any unwanted program that is transmitted to a computer without the user's knowledge and that is designed to do varying degrees of damage to data and software. There are a number of different types of infestations, including viruses, Trojan horses, worms, and logic bombs.

information (.inf) file — Text file with an .inf file extension, such as Msbatch.inf, that contains information about a hardware or software installation.

infrared transceiver — A wireless transceiver that uses infrared technology to support some wireless devices such as keyboards, mice, and printers. A motherboard might have an embedded infrared transceiver, or the transceiver might plug into a USB or serial port. The technology is defined by the Infrared Data Association (IrDA). Also called an *IrDA transceiver* or *infrared port*.

initialization files — Configuration information files for Windows. System.ini is one of the most important Windows 9x/Me initialization files.

inkjet printer — A type of ink dispersion printer that uses cartridges of ink. The ink is heated to a boiling point and then ejected onto the paper through tiny nozzles.

Institute of Electrical and Electronics Engineers (IEEE) — A nonprofit organization that develops standards for the computer and electronics industries.

instruction set — The set of instructions, on the CPU chip, that the computer can perform directly (such as ADD and MOVE).

intelligent UPS — A UPS connected to a computer by way of a USB or serial cable so that software on the computer can monitor and control the UPS. Also called *smart UPS*.

interlaced — A type of display in which the electronic beam of a monitor draws every other line with each pass, which lessens the overall effect of a lower refresh rate.

internal bus — The bus inside the CPU that is used for communication between the CPU's internal components.

internal cache — Memory cache that is faster than external cache, and is contained inside CPU chips (also referred to as primary, Level 1, or L1 cache).

internal command — Commands that are embedded in the Command.com file.

Internet Connection Firewall (ICF) — Windows XP software designed to protect a PC from unauthorized access from the Internet.

Internet Connection Sharing (ICS) — A Windows 98 and Windows XP utility that uses NAT and acts as a proxy server to manage two or more computers connected to the Internet.

Internet service provider (ISP) — A commercial group that provides Internet access for a monthly fee. AOL, Earthlink, and CompuServe are large ISPs.

intranet — A private network that uses the TCP/IP protocols.

Io.sys — Along with Msdos.sys and Command.com, one of the three files that are the core components of the real mode portion of Windows 9x/Me. It is the first program file of the OS.

IP (Internet Protocol) — The rules of communication in the TCP/IP stack that control segmenting data into packets, routing those packets across networks, and then reassembling the packets once they reach their destination.

IP address — A 32-bit address consisting of four numbers separated by periods, used to uniquely identify a device on a network that uses TCP/IP protocols. The first numbers identify the network; the last numbers identify a host. An example of an IP address is 206.96.103.114.

IPX/SPX (Internetwork Packet Exchange/ Sequenced Packet Exchange) — A networking protocol suite first used by Novell NetWare, and which corresponds to the TCP/IP protocols.

IrDA transceiver — *See* infrared transceiver.

IRQ (interrupt request) line — A line on a bus that is assigned to a device and is used to signal the CPU for servicing. These lines are assigned a reference number (for example, the normal IRQ for a printer is IRQ 7).

ISA (Industry Standard Architecture) slot — An older slot on the motherboard used for slower I/O devices, which can support an 8-bit or a 16-bit data path. ISA slots are mostly replaced by PCI slots.

ISDN (Integrated Services Digital Network) — A digital telephone line that can carry data at about five times the speed of regular telephone lines. Two channels (telephone numbers) share a single pair of wires.

isochronous data transfer — A method used by IEEE 1394 to transfer data continuously without breaks.

ITU (International Telecommunications Union) — The international organization responsible for developing international standards of communication. Formerly CCITT.

JPEG (Joint Photographic Experts Group) — A graphical compression scheme that allows the user to control the amount of data that is averaged and sacrificed as file size is reduced. It is a common Internet file format. Most JPEG files have a .jpg extension.

jumper — Two wires that stick up side by side on the motherboard and are used to hold configuration information. The jumper is considered closed if a cover is over the wires, and open if the cover is missing.

kernel — The portion of an OS that is responsible for interacting with the hardware.

kernel mode — A Windows NT/2000/XP "privileged" processing mode that has access to hardware components.

key — (1) In encryption, a secret number or code used to encode and decode data. (2) In Windows, a section name of the Windows registry.

keyboard — A common input device through which data and instructions may be typed into computer memory.

LAN (local area network) — A computer network that covers only a small area, usually within one building.

lands — Microscopic flat areas on the surface of a CD or DVD that separate pits. Lands and pits are used to represent data on the disk.

laptop computer — *See* notebook.

large mode — A mode of addressing information on hard drives that range from 504 MB to 8.4 GB, addressing information on a hard drive by translating cylinder, head, and sector information in order to break the 528-MB hard drive barrier. Also called ECHS mode.

large-capacity drive — A hard drive larger than 504 MB.

laser printer — A type of printer that uses a laser beam to control how toner is placed on the page and then uses heat to fuse the toner to the page.

Last Known Good configuration — In Windows NT/2000/XP, registry settings and device drivers that were in effect when the computer last booted successfully. These settings can be restored during the startup process to recover from errors during the last boot.

LBA (logical block addressing) mode — A mode of addressing information on hard drives in which the BIOS and operating system view the drive as one long linear list of LBAs or addressable sectors, permitting drives to be larger than 8.4 GB (LBA 0 is cylinder 0, head 0, and sector 1).

Level 1 (L1) cache — *See* internal cache.

Level 2 (L2) cache — *See* external cache.

Level 3 (L3) cache — *See* external cache.

Limited user — Windows XP user accounts known as Users in Windows NT/2000, which have read-write access only on their own folders, read-only access to most system folders, and no access to other users' data.

line conditioner — A device that regulates, or conditions, power, providing continuous voltage during brownouts and spikes.

line protocol — A protocol used to send data packets destined for a network over telephone lines. PPP and SLIP are examples of line protocols.

line speed — *See* bandwidth.

line-interactive UPS — A variation of a standby UPS that shortens switching time by always keeping the inverter that converts AC to DC working, so that there is no charge-up time for the inverter.

LMHosts — A text file located in the Windows folder that contains NetBIOS names and their associated IP addresses. This file is used for name resolution for a NetBEUI network.

local bus — A bus that operates at a speed synchronized with the CPU frequency. The system bus is a local bus.

local I/O bus — A local bus that provides I/O devices with fast access to the CPU. The PCI bus is a local I/O bus.

local printer — A printer connected to a computer by way of a port on the computer. Compare to network printer.

local profile — User profile that is stored on a local computer and cannot be accessed from another computer on the network.

local user account — A user account that applies only to a local computer and cannot be used to access resources from other computers on the network.

logic bomb — Dormant code added to software that is triggered by a predetermined time or event.

logical drive — A portion or all of a hard drive partition that is treated by the operating system as though it were a physical drive. Each logical drive is assigned a drive letter, such as drive C, and contains a file system. Also called a volume.

logical geometry — The number of heads, tracks, and sectors that the BIOS on the hard drive controller presents to the system BIOS and the OS. The logical geometry does not consist of the same values as the physical geometry, although calculations of drive capacity yield the same results.

Logical Unit Number (LUN) — A number assigned to a logical device (such as a tray in a CD changer) that is part of a physical SCSI device, which is assigned a SCSI ID.

lost allocation units — *See* lost clusters.

lost clusters — File fragments that, according to the file allocation table, contain data that does not belong to any file. The command CHKDSK/F can free these fragments. Also called lost allocation units.

low insertion force (LIF) socket — A socket that requires the installer to manually apply an even force over the microchip when inserting the chip into the socket.

Low Voltage Differential (LVD) — A type of differential signaling that uses lower voltage than does HVD, is less expensive, and can be compatible with single-ended signaling on the same SCSI bus.

low-level formatting — A process (usually performed at the factory) that electronically creates the hard drive tracks and sectors and tests for bad spots on the disk surface.

low-profile case — *See* compact case.

LPX — A form factor in which expansion cards are mounted on a riser card that plugs into a motherboard. The expansion cards in LPX systems are mounted parallel to the motherboard, rather than perpendicular to it as in AT and ATX systems.

MAC (Media Access Control) address — A 6-byte hexadecimal hardware address unique to each NIC card and assigned by the manufacturer. The address is often printed on the adapter. An example is 00 00 0C 08 2F 35. Also called a physical address, an adapter address, or a hardware address.

macro — A small sequence of commands, contained within a document, that can be automatically executed when the document is loaded, or executed later by using a predetermined keystroke.

macro virus — A virus that can hide in the macros of a document file.

main board — *See* motherboard.

mandatory user profile — A roaming user profile that applies to all users in a user group, and individual users cannot change that profile.

Master Boot Record (MBR) — The first sector on a hard drive, which contains the partition table and a program the BIOS uses to boot an OS from the drive.

master file table (MFT) — The database used by the NTFS file system to track the contents of a logical drive.

material safety data sheet (MSDS) — A document that explains how to properly handle substances such as chemical solvents; it includes information such as physical data, toxicity, health effects, first aid, storage, disposal, and spill procedures.

megahertz (MHz) — One million Hz, or one million cycles per second. *See* hertz (Hz).

memory — Physical microchips that can hold data and programming, located on the motherboard or expansion cards.

memory address — A number assigned to each byte in memory. The CPU can use memory addresses to track where information is stored in RAM. Memory addresses are usually displayed as hexadecimal numbers in segment/offset form.

memory bus — *See* system bus.

memory cache — A small amount of faster RAM that stores recently retrieved data, in anticipation of what the CPU will request next, thus speeding up access. *See also* system bus.

memory dump — The contents of memory saved to a file at the time an event halted the system. Support technicians can analyze the dump file to help understand the source of the problem.

memory extender — For DOS and Windows 9x/Me, a device driver named Himem.sys that manages RAM, giving access to memory addresses above 1 MB.

memory paging — In Windows, swapping blocks of RAM memory to an area of the hard drive to serve as virtual memory when RAM is low.

memory-resident virus — A virus that can stay lurking in memory even after its host program is terminated.

microATX — A recent version of the ATX form factor. MicroATX addresses some new technologies that have been developed since the original introduction of ATX.

MicroDIMM — A type of memory module used on sub-notebooks that has 144 pins and uses a 64-bit data path.

microprocessor — *See* central processing unit (CPU).

Microsoft Management Console (MMC) — A utility to build customized consoles. These consoles can be saved to a file with an .msc file extension.

Mini PCI — The PCI industry standard for desktop computer expansion cards, applied to a much smaller form factor for notebook expansion cards.

Mini-ATX — A smaller ATX board that can be used with regular ATX cases and power supplies.

minicartridge — A tape drive cartridge that is only 3¼ × 2½ × ⅜inches. It is small enough to allow two drives to fit into a standard 5½ -inch drive bay of a PC case.

minifile system — In Windows NT/2000/XP, a simplified file system that is started so that Ntldr (NT Loader) can read files from any file system the OS supports.

Mini-LPX — A smaller version of the LPX motherboard.

mixed mode — A Windows 2000 mode for domain controllers used when there is at least one Windows NT domain controller on the network.

MMX (Multimedia Extensions) — Multimedia instructions built into Intel processors to add functionality such as better processing of multimedia, SIMD support, and increased cache.

modem — From MOdulate/DEModulate. A device that modulates digital data from a computer to an analog format that can be sent over telephone lines, then demodulates it back into digital form.

modem eliminator — *See* null modem cable.

modem riser card — A small modem card that uses an AMR or CNR slot. Part of the modem logic is contained in a controller on the motherboard.

modem speed — The speed at which a modem can transmit data along a phone line, measured in bits per second (bps). Also called line speed.

modulation — Converting binary or digital data into an analog signal that can be sent over standard telephone lines.

monitor — The most commonly used output device for displaying text and graphics on a computer.

motherboard — The main board in the computer, also called the system board. The CPU, ROM chips, SIMMs, DIMMs, RIMMs, and interface cards are plugged into the motherboard.

motherboard bus — *See* system bus.

motherboard mouse — *See* PS/2-compatible mouse.

mouse — A pointing and input device that allows the user to move a cursor around a screen and select programs with the click of a button.

MP3 — A method to compress audio files that uses MPEG level 1. It can reduce sound files as low as a 1:24 ratio without losing much sound quality.

MPEG (Moving Pictures Experts Group) — A processing-intensive standard for data compression for motion pictures that tracks movement from one frame to the next and only stores the data that has changed.

Msdos.sys — In Windows 9x/Me, a text file that contains settings used by Io.sys during booting. In DOS, the Msdos.sys file was a program file that contained part of the DOS core.

MultiBank DRAM (MDRAM) — A type of video memory that is faster than VRAM and WRAM, but can be more economical because it can be installed on a video card in smaller increments.

multicasting — A process in which a message is sent by one host to multiple hosts, such as when a video conference is broadcast to several hosts on the Internet.

multimeter — A device used to measure the various components of an electrical circuit. The most common measurements are voltage, current, and resistance.

multipartite virus — A combination of a boot sector virus and a file virus. It can hide in either type of program.

multiplier — The factor by which the bus speed or frequency is multiplied to get the CPU clock speed.

multiscan monitor — A monitor that can work within a range of frequencies and thus can work with different standards and video cards. It offers a variety of refresh rates.

multisession — A feature that allows data to be read from or written to a CD during more than one session. This is important if the disk was only partially filled during the first write.

Multistation Access Unit (MSAU or MAU) — A centralized hub used in Token Ring networks to connect stations. Also called CAU.

multitasking — Doing more than one thing at a time. A true multitasking system requires two or more CPUs, each processing a different thread at the same time. Compare to cooperative multitasking and preemptive multitasking.

multithreading — The ability to pass more than one function (thread) to the OS kernel at the same time, such as when one thread is performing a print job while another reads a file.

name resolution — The process of associating a NetBIOS name or host name to an IP address.

narrow SCSI — One of the two main SCSI specifications. Narrow SCSI has an 8-bit data bus. The word "narrow" is not usually included in the names of narrow SCSI devices.

NAT (Network Address Translation) — A process that converts private IP addresses on a LAN to the proxy server's IP address before a data packet is sent over the Internet.

native mode — A Windows 2000 mode used by domain controllers when there are no Windows NT domain controllers present on the network.

NetBEUI (NetBIOS Extended User Interface) — A fast, proprietary Microsoft networking protocol used only by Windows-based systems, and limited to LANs because it does not support routing.

NetBIOS (Network Basic Input/Output System) — An API protocol used by some applications to communicate over a NetBEUI network. NetBIOS has largely been replaced by Windows Sockets over a TCP/IP network.

network adapter — *See* network interface card.

network drive map — Mounting a drive to a computer, such as drive E, that is actually hard drive space on another host computer on the network.

network interface card (NIC) — An expansion card that plugs into a computer's motherboard and provides a port on the back of the card to connect a PC to a network. Also called a network adapter.

network operating system (NOS) — An operating system that resides on the controlling computer in the network. The NOS controls what software, data, and devices a user on the network can access. Examples of an NOS are Novell Netware and Windows 2000 Server.

network printer — A printer that any user on the network can access, through its own network card and connection to the network, through a connection to a standalone print server, or through a connection to a computer as a local printer, which is shared on the network.

NLX — A low-end form factor that is similar to LPX but provides greater support for current and emerging processor technologies. NLX was designed for flexibility and efficiency of space.

NNTP (Network News Transfer Protocol) — The protocol used by newsgroup server and client software.

node — *See* host

noise — An extraneous, unwanted signal, often over an analog phone line, that can cause communication interference or transmission errors. Possible sources are fluorescent lighting, radios, TVs, lightning, or bad wiring.

noninterlaced — A type of display in which the electronic beam of a monitor draws every line on the screen with each pass.

non-memory-resident virus — A virus that is terminated when the host program is closed. Compare to memory-resident virus.

nonparity memory — Eight-bit memory without error checking. A SIMM part number with a 32 in it (4 × 8 bits) is nonparity.

nonvolatile — Refers to a kind of RAM that is stable and can hold data as long as electricity is powering the memory.

normal mode — *See* CHS mode.

North Bridge — That portion of the chip set hub that connects faster I/O buses (for example, AGP bus) to the system bus. Compare to South Bridge.

notebook — A portable computer that is designed for travel and mobility. Notebooks use the same technology as desktop PCs, with modifications for conserving voltage, taking up less space, and operating while on the move. Also called a laptop computer.

NTFS (NT file system) — The file system for the Windows NT/2000/XP operating systems. NTFS cannot be accessed by other operating systems such as DOS. It provides increased reliability and security in comparison to other methods of organizing and accessing files. There are several versions of NTFS that might or might not be compatible.

Ntldr (NT Loader) — In Windows NT/2000/XP, the OS loader used on Intel systems.

NTVDM (NT virtual DOS machine) — An emulated environment in which a 16-bit DOS application resides within Windows NT/2000/XP with its own memory space or WOW (Win16 on Win32).

null modem cable — A cable that allows two data terminal equipment (DTE) devices to communicate in which the transmit and receive wires are cross-connected and no modems are necessary.

octet — Term for each of the four 8-bit numbers that make up an IP address. For example, the IP address 206.96.103.114 has four octets.

ohm (Ω) — The standard unit of measurement for electrical resistance. Resistors are rated in ohms.

on-board ports — Ports that are directly on the motherboard, such as a built-in keyboard port or on-board serial port.

operating system (OS) — Software that controls a computer. An OS controls how system resources are used and provides a user interface, a way of managing hardware and software, and ways to work with files.

operating system formatting — *See* high-level formatting.

P1 connector — Power connection on an ATX motherboard.

P8 connector — One of two power connectors on an AT motherboard.

P9 connector — One of two power connectors on an AT motherboard.

packet — Segment of network data that also includes header, destination address, and trailer information that is sent as a unit. Also called data packet or datagram.

page fault — An OS interrupt that occurs when the OS is forced to access the hard drive to satisfy the demands for virtual memory.

page file — *See* swap file.

Pagefile.sys — The Windows NT/2000/XP swap file.

page-in — The process in which the memory manager goes to the hard drive to return the data from a swap file to RAM.

page-out — The process in which, when RAM is full, the memory manager takes a page and moves it to the swap file.

pages — 4K segments in which Windows NT/2000/XP allocates memory.

parallel ATA (PATA) — An older IDE cabling method that uses a 40-pin flat data cable or an 80-conductor cable and a 40-pin IDE connector. *See also* serial ATA.

parallel port — A female 25-pin port on a computer that can transmit data in parallel, 8 bits at a time, and is usually used with a printer. The names for parallel ports are LPT1 and LPT2.

parity — An error-checking scheme in which a ninth, or "parity," bit is added. The value of the parity bit is set to either 0 or 1 to provide an even number of ones for even parity and an odd number of ones for odd parity.

parity error — An error that occurs when the number of 1s in the byte is not in agreement with the expected number.

parity memory — Nine-bit memory in which the ninth bit is used for error checking. A SIMM part number with a 36 in it (4 × 9 bits) is parity. Older PCs almost always use parity chips.

partition — A division of a hard drive that can be used to hold logical drives.

partition table — A table at the beginning of the hard drive that contains information about each partition on the drive. The partition table is contained in the Master Boot Record.

passive backplane — A type of backplane system in which the backplane contains no circuitry at all. Passive backplanes locate all circuitry on a mothercard plugged into a backplane.

passive terminator — A type of terminator for single-ended SCSI cables. Simple resistors are used to provide termination of a signal. Passive termination is not reliable over long distances and should only be used with narrow SCSI.

patch — An update to software that corrects an error, adds a feature, or addresses security issues. Also called an update or service pack.

patch cable — A network cable that is used to connect a PC to a hub.

path — (1) A drive and list of directories pointing to a file such as C:\Windows\command. (2) The OS command to provide a list of paths to the system for finding program files to execute.

PC Card — A credit-card-sized adapter card that can be slid into a slot in the side of many notebook computers and is used for connecting to modems, networks, and CD-ROM drives. Also called PCMCIA Card.

PC Card slot — An expansion slot on a notebook computer, into which a PC Card is inserted. Also called a PCMCIA Card slot.

PCI (Peripheral Component Interconnect) bus — A bus common on Pentium computers that runs at speeds of up to 33 MHz or 66 MHz, with a 32-bit-wide or 64-bit-wide data path. PCI-X, released in September 1999, enables PCI to run at 133 MHz. For some chip sets, it serves as the middle layer between the memory bus and expansion buses.

PCMCIA (Personal Computer Memory Card International Association) Card — See PC Card.

PCMCIA Card slot — See PC Card slot.

PDA (Personal Digital Assistant) — A small, hand-held computer that has its own operating system and applications.

peer-to-peer network — A network of computers that are all equals, or peers. Each computer has the same amount of authority, and each can act as a server to the other computers.

peripheral devices — Devices that communicate with the CPU but are not located directly on the motherboard, such as the monitor, floppy drive, printer, and mouse.

physical address — See MAC address.

physical geometry — The actual layout of heads, tracks, and sectors on a hard drive. Refer also to logical geometry.

PIF (program information file) — A file used by Windows to describe the environment for a DOS program to use.

pin grid array (PGA) — A feature of a CPU socket whereby the pins are aligned in uniform rows around the socket.

Ping (Packet Internet Groper) — A Windows and Unix command used to troubleshoot network connections. It verifies that the host can communicate with another host on the network.

pinout — A description of how each pin on a bus, connection, plug, slot, or socket is used.

PIO (Programmed I/O) transfer mode — A transfer mode that uses the CPU to transfer data from the hard drive to memory. PIO mode is slower than DMA mode.

pipelined burst SRAM — A less expensive SRAM that uses more clock cycles per transfer than non-pipelined burst but does not significantly slow down the process.

pits — Recessed areas on the surface of a CD or DVD, separating lands, or flat areas. Lands and pits are used to represent data on a disc.

pixel — A small spot on a fine horizontal scan line. Pixels are illuminated to create an image on the monitor.

Plug and Play (PnP) — A standard designed to make the installation of new hardware devices easier by automatically configuring devices to eliminate system resource conflicts (such as IRQ or I/O address conflicts). PnP is supported by Windows 9x/Me, Windows 2000, and Windows XP.

polling — A process by which the CPU checks the status of connected devices to determine if they are ready to send or receive data.

polymorphic virus — A type of virus that changes its distinguishing characteristics as it replicates itself. Mutating in this way makes it more difficult for AV software to recognize the presence of the virus.

POP (Post Office Protocol) — The protocol that an e-mail server and client use when the client requests the downloading of e-mail messages. The most recent version is POP3. POP is being replaced by IMAP.

port — (1) As applied to services running on a computer, a number assigned to a process on a computer so that the process can be found by TCP/IP. Also called a port address or port number. (2) Another name for an I/O address. *See also* I/O address. (3) A physical connector, usually at the back of a computer, that allows a cable from a peripheral device, such as a printer, mouse, or modem, to be attached.

port address — *See* I/O address.

port number — *See* port.

port replicator — A device designed to connect to a notebook computer in order to make it easy to connect the notebook to peripheral devices.

port settings — The configuration parameters of communications devices such as COM1, COM2, or COM3, including IRQ settings.

port speed — The communication speed between a DTE (computer) and a DCE (modem). As a general rule, the port speed should be at least four times as fast as the modem speed.

POST (power-on self test) — A self-diagnostic program used to perform a simple test of the CPU, RAM, and various I/O devices. The POST is performed by startup BIOS when the computer is first turned on, and is stored in ROM-BIOS.

power conditioner — A line conditioner that regulates, or conditions, power, providing continuous voltage during brownouts.

power scheme — A feature of Windows XP support for notebooks that allows the user to create groups of power settings for specific sets of conditions.

power supply — A box inside the computer case that supplies power to the motherboard and other installed devices. Power supplies provide 3.3, 5, and 12 volts DC.

power-on password — A password that a computer uses to control access during the boot process.

PPP (Point-to-Point Protocol) — A protocol that governs the methods for communicating via modems and dial-up telephone lines. The Windows Dial-up Networking utility uses PPP.

PPPoE (Point-to-Point Protocol over Ethernet) — The protocol that describes how a PC is to interact with a broadband converter box, such as cable modem, when the two are connected by an Ethernet cable, connected to a NIC in a PC.

preemptive multitasking — A type of pseudo-multitasking whereby the CPU allows an application a specified period of time and then preempts the processing to give time to another application.

primary cache — *See* internal cache.

primary domain controller (PDC) — In a Windows NT network, the computer that controls the directory database of user accounts, group accounts, and computer accounts on a domain. *See also* backup domain controller.

primary partition — A hard disk partition that can contain only one logical drive.

primary storage — Temporary storage on the motherboard used by the CPU to process data and instructions. Memory is considered primary storage.

printer — A peripheral output device that produces printed output to paper. Different types include dot matrix, ink-jet, and laser printers.

printer maintenance kit — A kit purchased from a printer manufacturer that contains the parts, tools, and instructions needed to perform routine printer maintenance.

private IP address — An IP address that is used on a private TCP/IP network that is isolated from the Internet.

process — An executing instance of a program together with the program resources. There can be more than one process running for a program at the same time. One process for a program happens each time the program is loaded into memory or executed.

processor — *See* central processing unit (CPU).

processor speed — The speed, or frequency, at which the CPU operates. Usually expressed in GHz.

product activation — The process that Microsoft uses to prevent software piracy. For example, once Windows XP is activated for a particular computer, it cannot be installed on another computer.

program — A set of step-by-step instructions to a computer. Some are burned directly into chips, while others are stored as program files. Programs are written in languages such as BASIC and C++.

program file — A file that contains instructions designed to be executed by the CPU.

protected mode — An operating mode that supports preemptive multitasking, the OS manages memory and other hardware devices, and programs can use a 32-bit data path. Also called 32-bit mode.

protocol — A set of rules and standards that two entities use for communication.

Protocol.ini — A Windows initialization file that contains network configuration information.

proxy server — A server that acts as an intermediary between another computer and the Internet. The proxy server substitutes its own IP address for the IP address of the computer on the network making a request, so that all traffic over the Internet appears to be coming from only the IP address of the proxy server.

PS/2-compatible mouse — A mouse that plugs into a round mouse PS/2 port on the motherboard. Sometimes called a motherboard mouse.

public IP address — An IP address available to the Internet.

QIC (Quarter-Inch Committee or **quarter-inch cartridge)** — A name of a standardized method used to write data to tape. These backup files have a .qic extension.

RAID (redundant array of inexpensive disks or **redundant array of independent disks)** — Several methods of configuring multiple hard drives to store data to increase logical volume size and improve performance, or to ensure that if one

hard drive fails, the data is still available from another hard drive.

RAM (random access memory) — Memory modules on the motherboard containing microchips used to temporarily hold data and programs while the CPU processes both. Information in RAM is lost when the PC is turned off.

RAM drive — An area of memory that is treated as though it were a hard drive, but works much faster than a hard drive. The Windows 9x/Me startup disk uses a RAM drive. Compare to virtual memory.

RARP (Reverse Address Resolution Protocol) — A protocol used to translate the unique hardware NIC addresses (MAC addresses) into IP addresses (the reverse of ARP).

RDRAM — *See* Direct Rambus DRAM.

read/write head — A sealed, magnetic coil device that moves across the surface of a disk either reading data from or writing data to the disk.

real mode — A single-tasking operating mode whereby a program has 1024K of memory addresses, has direct access to RAM, and uses a 16-bit data path. Using a memory extender (Himem.sys) a program in real mode can access memory above 1024K. Also called 16-bit mode.

Recovery Console — A Windows 2000/XP command interface utility and OS that can be used to solve problems when Windows cannot load from the hard drive.

rectifier — An electrical device that converts AC to DC. A PC power supply contains a rectifier.

refresh — The process of periodically rewriting data, such as on dynamic RAM.

refresh rate — As applied to monitors, the number of times in one second an electronic beam can fill the screen with lines from top to bottom. Also called vertical scan rate.

registry — A database that Windows uses to store hardware and software configuration information, user preferences, and setup information.

re-marked chips — Chips that have been used and returned to the factory, marked again, and resold. The surface of the chips may be dull or scratched.

Remote Assistance — A Windows XP feature that allows a support technician at a remote location to have full access to the Windows XP desktop.

repeater — A device that amplifies signals on a network so they can be transmitted further down the line.

rescue disk — A floppy disk that can be used to start up a computer when the hard drive fails to boot. Also called emergency startup disk (ESD) or startup disk.

resistance — The degree to which a device opposes or resists the flow of electricity. As the electrical resistance increases, the current decreases. *See* ohm and resistor.

resistor — An electronic device that resists or opposes the flow of electricity. A resistor can be used to reduce the amount of electricity being supplied to an electronic component.

resolution — The number of pixels on a monitor screen that are addressable by software (example: 1024×768 pixels).

restore point — A snapshot of the Windows Me/XP system state, usually made before installation of new hardware or applications.

REt (Resolution Enhancement technology) — The term used by Hewlett-Packard to describe the way a laser printer varies the size of the dots used to create an image. This technology partly accounts for the sharp, clear image created by a laser printer.

RIMM — A type of memory module developed by Rambus, Inc.

ring topology — A network topology in which the nodes in a network form a ring. Each node is connected only to two other nodes, and a centralized hub is not required.

RISC (Reduced Instruction Set Computing) chips — Chips that incorporate only the most frequently used instructions, so that the computer operates faster (for example, the PowerPC uses RISC chips).

riser card — A card that plugs into a motherboard and allows for expansion cards to be mounted parallel to the motherboard. Expansion cards are plugged into slots on the riser card.

RJ-11 — A phone line connection found on modems, telephones, and house phone outlets.

RJ-45 connector — A connector used with twisted-pair cable that connects the cable to the NIC.

roaming user profile — A user profile for a roaming user. Roaming user profiles are stored on a server so that the user can access the profile from anywhere on the network.

ROM (read-only memory) — Chips that contain programming code and cannot be erased.

ROM BIOS — *See* BIOS.

root directory — The main directory created when a hard drive or disk is first formatted. In Linux, it's indicated by a forward slash. In DOS and Windows, it's indicated by a backward slash.

routable protocol — A protocol that can be routed to interconnected networks on the basis of a network address. TCP/IP is a routable protocol, but NetBEUI is not.

router — A device that connects networks and makes decisions as to the best routes to use when forwarding packets.

sags — *See* brownouts.

sampling rate — The rate of samples taken of an analog signal over a period of time, usually expressed as samples per second, or hertz.

SBAC (SCSI bus adapter chip) — The SCSI chip within a device housing that controls data transfer over the SCSI bus.

SCAM (SCSI Configuration AutoMatically) — A method of configuring SCSI device settings that follows the Plug and Play standard. SCAM makes installation of SCSI devices much easier, provided that the devices are SCAM-compliant.

scanning mirror — A component of a laser printer consisting of an octagonal mirror that can be directed in a sweeping motion to cover the entire length of a laser printer drum.

SCSI (Small Computer System Interface) — A fast interface between a host adapter and the CPU that can daisy chain as many as 7 or 15 devices on a single bus.

SCSI ID — A number from 0 to 15 assigned to each SCSI device attached to the daisy chain.

SDRAM II — *See* Double Data Rate SDRAM (DDR SDRAM).

secondary storage — Storage that is remote to the CPU and permanently holds data, even when the PC is turned off, such as a hard drive.

sector — On a disk surface one segment of a track, which almost always contains 512 bytes of data.

security accounts manager (SAM) — A portion of the Windows NT/2000/XP registry that manages the account database that contains accounts, policies, and other pertinent information about local accounts.

sequential access — A method of data access used by tape drives, whereby data is written or read sequentially from the beginning to the end of the tape or until the desired data is found.

serial ATA (SATA) — An ATAPI cabling method that uses a narrower and more reliable cable than the 80-conductor cable. *See also* parallel ATA.

serial ATA cable — An IDE cable that is narrower and has fewer pins than the parallel IDE 80-conductor cable.

serial mouse — A mouse that uses a serial port and has a female 9-pin DB-9 connector.

serial port — A male 9-pin or 25-pin port on a computer system used by slower I/O devices such as a mouse or modem. Data travels serially, one bit at a time, through the port. Serial ports are sometimes configured as COM1, COM2, COM3, or COM4.

service pack — *See* patch.

session — An established communication link between two software programs. On the Internet, a session is created by TCP.

SFC (System File Checker) — A Windows tool that checks to make sure Windows is using the correct versions of system files.

SGRAM (synchronous graphics RAM) — Memory designed especially for video card processing that can synchronize itself with the CPU bus clock.

shadow RAM or **shadowing ROM** — ROM programming code copied into RAM to speed up the system operation, because of the faster access speed of RAM.

shell — The portion of an OS that relates to the user and to applications.

shielded twisted-pair (STP) cable — A cable that is made of one or more twisted pairs of wires and is surrounded by a metal shield.

shortcut — An icon on the desktop that points to a program that can be executed or to a file or folder.

signal-regenerating repeater — A repeater that is able to distinguish between noise and signal. It reads the signal and retransmits it without the accompanying noise.

Sigverif.exe — A Windows 2000/XP utility that allows you to search for digital signatures.

SIMD (single instruction, multiple data) — A process that allows the CPU to execute a single instruction simultaneously on multiple pieces of data, rather than by repetitive looping.

SIMM (single inline memory module) — A miniature circuit board used in older computers to hold RAM. SIMMs hold 8, 16, 32, or 64 MB on a single module.

simple volume — A type of dynamic volume used on a single hard drive that corresponds to a primary partition on a basic disk.

single-ended (SE) cable — A type of SCSI cable in which two wires are used to carry a signal, one of which carries the signal itself; the other is a ground for the signal.

single-voltage CPU — A CPU that requires one voltage for both internal and I/O operations.

slack — Wasted space on a hard drive caused by not using all available space at the end of clusters.

sleep mode — A mode used in many "Green" systems that allows them to be configured through CMOS to suspend the monitor or even the drive, if the keyboard and/or CPU have been inactive for a set number of minutes. *See also* Green Standards.

slimline case — *See* compact case.

SLIP (Serial Line Internet Protocol) — A line protocol used by regular telephone lines that has largely been replaced by PPP.

Smart Multistation Access Unit (SMAU) — *See* MAU.

smart UPS – *See* intelligent UPS.

SMARTDrive — A hard drive cache program that came with Windows 3.x and DOS and can be executed as a TSR from the Autoexec.bat file (for example, Device=Smartdrv.sys 2048).

SMTP (Simple Mail Transfer Protocol) — The protocol used by e-mail clients and servers to send e-mail messages over the Internet. *See* POP and IMAP.

snap-ins — Components added to a console using the Microsoft Management Console.

SNMP (Simple Network Management Protocol) — A protocol used to monitor and manage network traffic on a workstation. SNMP works with TCP/IP and IPX/SPX networks.

socket — *See* session.

SO-DIMM (small outline DIMM) — A type of memory module used in notebook computers that uses DIMM technology and can have either 72 pins or 144 pins.

soft boot — To restart a PC without turning off the power, for example, in Windows XP, by clicking Start, Turn Off Computer, and Restart. Also called warm boot.

soft power — *See* soft switch.

soft switch — A feature on an ATX system that allows an OS to power down the system and allows for activity such as a keystroke or network activity to power up the system. Also called soft power.

software — Computer programs, or instructions to perform a specific task. Software may be BIOS, OSs, or applications software such as a word-processing or spreadsheet program.

software cache — Cache controlled by software whereby the cache is stored in RAM.

solid ink printer — A type of printer that uses sticks or blocks of solid ink. The ink is melted and then jetted onto the paper as the paper passes by on a drum.

SO-RIMM (small outline RIMM) — A 160-pin memory module used in notebooks that uses Rambus technology.

South Bridge — That portion of the chip set hub that connects slower I/O buses (for example, an ISA bus) to the system bus. Compare to North Bridge.

spacers — *See* standoffs.

spanned volume — A type of dynamic volume used on two or more hard drives that fills up the space allotted on one physical disk before moving to the next.

SPI (SCSI Parallel Interface) — The part of the SCSI-3 standard that specifies how SCSI devices are connected.

spikes — Temporary surges in voltage, which can damage electrical components. Also called swells.

spooling — Placing print jobs in a print queue so that an application can be released from the printing process before printing is completed. Spooling is an acronym for simultaneous peripheral operations online.

SSE (Streaming SIMD Extension) — A technology used by the Intel Pentium III and later CPUs and designed to improve performance of multimedia software.

SSL (secure socket layer) — A secure protocol developed by Netscape that uses a digital certificate including a public key to encrypt and decrypt data.

staggered pin grid array (SPGA) — A feature of a CPU socket whereby the pins are staggered over the socket in order to squeeze more pins into a small space.

standby time — The time before a "Green" system will reduce 92 percent of its activity. *See also* Green Standards.

standoffs — Round plastic or metal pegs that separate the motherboard from the case, so that components on the back of the motherboard do not touch the case.

star bus topology — A LAN that uses a logical bus design, but with all devices connected to a central hub, making a physical star.

star ring topology — A topology that is physically arranged in a star formation but is logically a ring because of the way information travels on it. Token Ring is the primary example.

star topology — A LAN in which all the devices are connected to a central hub.

start bits — Bits that are used to signal the approach of data.

startup BIOS — Part of system BIOS that is responsible for controlling the PC when it is first turned on. Startup BIOS gives control over to the OS once it is loaded.

startup disk — *See* rescue disk.

startup password — *See* power-on password.

stateless — Term for a device or process that manages data or some activity without regard to all the details of the data or activity.

static electricity — *See* ESD.

static IP address — An IP address permanently assigned to a workstation.

static RAM (SRAM) — RAM chips that retain information without the need for refreshing, as long as the computer's power is on. They are more expensive than traditional DRAM.

static VxD — A VxD that is loaded into memory at startup and remains there for the entire OS session.

stealth virus — A virus that actively conceals itself by temporarily removing itself from an infected file that is about to be examined, and then hiding a copy of itself elsewhere on the drive.

stop error — An error severe enough to cause the operating system to stop all processes.

streaming audio — Downloading audio data from the Internet in a continuous stream of data without first downloading an entire audio file.

striped volume — A type of dynamic volume used for two or more hard drives that writes to the disks evenly rather than filling up allotted space on one and then moving on to the next. Compare to spanned volume.

subdirectory — A directory or folder contained in another directory or folder. Also called a child directory or folder.

subnet mask — A subnet mask is a group of four numbers (dotted decimal numbers) that tell TCP/IP if a remote computer is on the same or a different network.

subsystems — The different modules into which the Windows NT/2000/XP user mode is divided.

surge suppressor or **surge protector** — A device or power strip designed to protect electronic equipment from power surges and spikes.

suspend time — The time before a "Green" system will reduce 99 percent of its activity. After this time, the system needs a warm-up time so that the CPU, monitor, and hard drive can reach full activity.

swap file — A file on the hard drive that is used by the OS for virtual memory. Also called a page file.

swells — *See* spikes.

switch — A device used to segment a network. It can decide which network segment is to receive a packet, on the basis of the packet's destination MAC address.

synchronization — The process by which files and programs are transferred between PDAs and PCs.

synchronous DRAM (SDRAM) — A type of memory stored on DIMMs that runs in sync with the system clock, running at the same speed as the motherboard.

synchronous SRAM — SRAM that is faster and more expensive than asynchronous SRAM. It requires a clock signal to validate its control signals, enabling the cache to run in step with the CPU.

SyncLink DRAM (SLDRAM) — A type of DRAM developed by a consortium of 12 DRAM manufacturers. It improved on regular SDRAM but is now obsolete.

Sysedit — The Windows System Configuration Editor, a text editor generally used to edit system files.

system BIOS — BIOS located on the motherboard.

system board — *See* motherboard.

system bus — The bus between the CPU and memory on the motherboard. The bus frequency in documentation is called the system speed, such as 400 MHz. Also called the memory bus, front-side bus, local bus, or host bus.

system clock — A line on a bus that is dedicated to timing the activities of components connected to it. The system clock provides a continuous pulse that other devices use to time themselves.

system disk — Windows terminology for a bootable disk.

system partition — The active partition of the hard drive containing the boot record and the specific files required to load Windows NT/2000/XP.

system resource — A channel, line, or address on the motherboard that can be used by the CPU or a device for communication. The four system resources are IRQ, I/O address, DMA channel, and memory address.

System Restore — A Windows Me/XP utility, similar to the ScanReg tool in earlier versions of Windows, that is used to restore the system to a restore point. Unlike ScanReg, System Restore cannot be executed from a command prompt.

system state data — In Windows 2000/XP, files that are necessary for a successful load of the operating system.

System Tray — An area to the right of the taskbar that holds the icons of small applets launched at startup.

System.ini — A text configuration file used by Windows 3.x and supported by Windows 9x/Me for backward-compatibility.

TAPI (Telephony Application Programming Interface) — A standard developed by Intel and Microsoft that can be used by 32-bit Windows communications programs for communicating over phone lines.

TCP (Transmission Control Protocol) — Part of the TCP/IP protocol suite. TCP guarantees delivery of data for application protocols and establishes a session before it begins transmitting data.

TCP/IP (Transmission Control Protocol/ Internet Protocol) — The suite of protocols that supports communication on the Internet. TCP is responsible for error checking, and IP is responsible for routing.

telephony — A term describing the technology of converting sound to signals that can travel over telephone lines.

terminating resistor — The resistor added at the end of a SCSI chain to dampen the voltage at the end of the chain.

termination — A process necessary to prevent an echo effect of power at the end of a SCSI chain, resulting in interference with the data transmission.

thermal printer — A type of line printer that uses wax-based ink, which is heated by heat pins that melt the ink onto paper.

ThickNet — *See* 10Base5 Ethernet.

ThinNet — *See* 10Base2 Ethernet.

thread — Each process that the CPU is aware of; a single task that is part of a longer task or program.

TIFF (Tagged Image File Format) — A bitmapped file format used to hold photographs, graphics, and screen captures. TIFF files can be rather large, and have a .tif file extension.

time to live (TTL) — Number of routers a network packet can pass through on its way to its destination before it is dropped. Also called hop count.

TLS (Transport Layer Security) — A protocol used to secure data sent over the Internet. It is an improved version of SSL.

token ring — An older LAN technology developed by IBM that transmits data at 4 Mbps or 16 Mbps.

top-level domain — The highest level of domain names, indicated by a suffix that tells something about the host. For example, .com is for commercial use and .edu is for educational institutions.

touch screen — An input device that uses a monitor or LCD panel as a backdrop for user options. Touch screens can be embedded in a monitor or LCD panel or installed as an add-on device.

tower case — The largest type of personal computer case. Tower cases stand vertically and can be as high as two feet tall. They have more drive bays and are a good choice for computer users who anticipate making significant upgrades.

trace — A wire on a circuit board that connects two components or devices.

track — One of many concentric circles on the surface of a hard drive or floppy disk.

training — *See* handshaking.

transceiver — The component on a NIC that is responsible for signal conversion. Combines the words transmitter and receiver.

transformer — A device that changes the ratio of current to voltage. A computer power supply is basically a transformer and a rectifier.

transistor — An electronic device that can regulate electricity and act as a logical gate or switch for an electrical signal.

translation — A technique used by system BIOS and hard drive controller BIOS to break the 504-MB hard drive barrier, whereby a different set of drive parameters are communicated to the OS and other software than that used by the hard drive controller BIOS.

Travan standards — A popular and improved group of standards for tape drives based on the QIC standards and developed by 3M.

Trojan horse — A type of infestation that hides or disguises itself as a useful program, yet is designed to cause damage at a later time.

TSR (terminate-and-stay-resident) — A program that is loaded into memory and remains dormant until called on, such as a screen saver or a memory-resident antivirus program.

UART (universal asynchronous receiver-transmitter) chip — A chip that controls serial ports. It sets protocol and converts parallel data bits received from the system bus into serial bits.

UDC (Universal Data Connector) — *See* IDC (IBM Data Connector).

UDP (User Datagram Protocol) — A connectionless protocol that does not require a connection to send a packet and does not guarantee that the packet arrives at its destination. UDP is faster than TCP because TCP takes the time to make a connection and guarantee delivery.

unattended installation — A Windows NT/ 2000/ XP installation that is done by storing the answers to installation questions in a text file or script that Windows NT/2000/XP calls an answer file so that the answers do not have to be typed in during the installation.

Universal Disk Format (UDF) file system — A file system for optical media used by all DVD discs and some CD-R and CD-RW discs.

unshielded twisted-pair (UTP) cable — A cable that is made of one or more twisted pairs of wires and is not surrounded by a metal shield.

upgrade install — The installation of an OS on a hard drive that already has an OS installed in such a way that settings kept by the old OS are carried forward into the upgrade, including information about hardware, software, and user preferences.

upper memory — In DOS and Windows 9x/Me, the memory addresses from 640K up to 1024K, originally reserved for BIOS, device drivers, and TSRs.

upper memory block (UMB) — In DOS and Windows 9x/Me, a group of consecutive memory addresses in RAM from 640K to 1MB that can be used by 16-bit device drivers and TSRs.

UPS (uninterruptible power supply) — A device designed to provide a backup power supply during a power failure. Basically, a UPS is a battery backup system with an ultrafast sensing device.

URL (Uniform Resource Locator) — An address for a resource on the Internet. A URL can contain the protocol used by the resource, the name of the computer and its network, and the path and name of a file on the computer.

USB (universal serial bus) port — A type of port designed to make installation and configuration of I/O devices easy, providing room for as many as 127 devices daisy-chained together.

USB host controller — Manages the USB bus. If the motherboard contains on-board USB ports, the USB host controller is part of the chipset. The USB uses only a single set of resources for all devices on the bus.

user account — The information, stored in the SAM database, that defines a Windows NT/ 2000/XP user, including username, password, memberships, and rights.

user component — A Windows 9x/Me component that controls the mouse, keyboard, ports, and desktop.

user mode — In Windows NT/2000/XP, a mode that provides an interface between an application and the OS, and only has access to hardware resources through the code running in kernel mode.

user profile — A personal profile about a user that enables the user's desktop settings and other operating parameters to be retained from one session to another.

User State Migration Tool (USMT) — A Windows XP utility that helps you migrate user files and preferences from one computer to another in order to help a user makes a smooth transition from one computer to another.

V.92 — The latest standard for data transmission over phone lines that can attain a speed of 56 Kbps.

value data — In Windows, the name and value of a setting in the registry.

VCACHE — A built-in Windows 9x/Me 32-bit software cache that doesn't take up conventional memory space or upper memory space as SMARTDrive did.

VESA (Video Electronics Standards Association) VL bus — An outdated local bus used on 80486 computers for connecting 32-bit adapters directly to the local processor bus.

VFAT (virtual file allocation table) — A variation of the original DOS 16-bit FAT that allows for long filenames and 32-bit disk access.

video card — An interface card installed in the computer to control visual output on a monitor. Also called display adapter.

virtual device driver (VxD or VDD) — A Windows device driver that may or may not have direct access to a device. It might depend on a Windows component to communicate with the device itself.

virtual machine — One or more logical machines created within one physical machine by Windows, allowing applications to make serious errors within one logical machine without disturbing other programs and parts of the system.

virtual memory — A method whereby the OS uses the hard drive as though it were RAM. Compare to RAM drive.

virtual real mode — An operating mode that works similarly to real mode provided by a 32-bit OS for a 16-bit program to work.

virus — A program that often has an incubation period, is infectious, and is intended to cause damage. A virus program might destroy data and programs or damage a disk drive's boot sector.

virus signature — A set of distinguishing characteristics of a virus used by antivirus software to identify the virus.

VMM (Virtual Machine Manager) — A Windows 9x/Me program that controls virtual machines and the resources they use including memory. The VMM manages the page table used to access memory.

volatile — Refers to a kind of RAM that is temporary, cannot hold data very long, and must be frequently refreshed.

volt (V) — A measure of potential difference in an electrical circuit. A computer ATX power supply usually provides five separate voltages: +12V, –12V, +5V, –5V, and +3.3V.

voltage — Electrical differential that causes current to flow, measured in volts. *See* volt.

voltage regulator module (VRM) — A device embedded or installed on the motherboard that regulates voltage to the processor.

voltmeter — A device for measuring electrical AC or DC voltage.

volume — *See* logical drive.

VRAM (video RAM) — RAM on video cards that holds the data that is being passed from the computer to the monitor and can be accessed by two devices simultaneously. Higher resolutions often require more video memory.

VxD — *See* virtual device driver.

wait state — A clock tick in which nothing happens, used to ensure that the microprocessor isn't getting ahead of slower components. A 0-wait state is preferable to a 1-wait state. Too many wait states can slow down a system.

WAN (wide area network) — A network or group of networks that span a large geographical area.

warm boot — *See* soft boot.

watt (W) — The unit used to measure power. A typical computer may use a power supply that provides 200W.

wattage — Electrical power measured in watts.

WDM (Win32 Driver Model) — The only Windows 9x/Me Plug and Play component that is found in Windows 98 but not Windows 95. WDM is the component responsible for managing device drivers that work under a driver model new to Windows 98.

WFP (Windows File Protection) — A Windows 2000/XP tool that protects system files from modification.

wide SCSI — One of the two main SCSI specifications. Wide SCSI has a 16-bit data bus. *See also* narrow SCSI.

Wi-Fi — *See* IEEE 802.11b.

wildcard — A * or ? character used in a command line that represents a character or group of characters in a filename or extension.

Win.ini — The Windows initialization file that contains program configuration information needed for running the Windows operating environment. Its functions were replaced by the registry beginning with Windows 9x/Me, which still supports it for backward compatibility with Windows 3.x.

Win16 on Win32 (WOW) — A group of programs provided by Windows NT/2000/XP to create a virtual DOS environment that emulates a 16-bit Windows environment, protecting the rest of the OS from 16-bit applications.

Win386.swp — The name of the Windows 9x/Me swap file. Its default location is C:\Windows.

WINS (Windows Internet Naming Service) — A Microsoft resolution service with a distributed database that tracks relationships between NetBIOS names and IP addresses. Compare to DNS.

WinSock (Windows Sockets) — A part of the TCP/IP utility software that manages API calls from applications to other computers on a TCP/IP network.

wireless LAN (WLAN) — A type of LAN that does not use wires or cables to create connections, but instead transmits data over radio or infrared waves.

workgroup — In Windows, a logical group of computers and users in which administration, resources, and security are distributed throughout the network, without centralized management or security.

worm — An infestation designed to copy itself repeatedly to memory, on drive space or on a network, until little memory or disk space remains.

WRAM (window RAM) — Dual-ported video RAM that is faster and less expensive than VRAM. It has its own internal bus on the chip, with a data path that is 256 bits wide.

zero insertion force (ZIF) socket — A socket that uses a small lever to apply even force when you install the microchip into the socket.

zone bit recording — A method of storing data on a hard drive whereby the drive can have more sectors per track near the outside of the platter.

Index

THOMSON
COURSE TECHNOLOGY™

A+ PC Repair
Total Solution

COURSE TECHNOLOGY PROVIDES THE TOTAL SOLUTION FOR CERTIFICATION AND SUCCESS!